# Encyclopedia of Data Science and Machine Learning

John Wang
*Montclair State University, USA*

## Volume II

Published in the United States of America by
    IGI Global
    Engineering Science Reference (an imprint of IGI Global)
    701 E. Chocolate Avenue
    Hershey PA, USA 17033
    Tel: 717-533-8845
    Fax: 717-533-8661
    E-mail: cust@igi-global.com
    Web site: http://www.igi-global.com

Library of Congress Cataloging-in-Publication Data

Names: Wang, John, 1955- editor.
Title: Encyclopedia of data science and machine learning / John Wang,
  editor.
Description: Hershey, PA : Engineering Science Reference, an imprint of IGI
  Global, [2023] | Includes bibliographical references and index. |
  Summary: "This book examines current, state-of-the-art research in the
  areas of data science, machine learning, data mining, optimization,
  artificial intelligence, statistics, and the interactions, linkages, and
  applications of knowledge-based business with information systems"--
  Provided by publisher.
Identifiers: LCCN 2021027689 (print) | LCCN 2021027690 (ebook) | ISBN
  9781799892205 (h/c) | ISBN 9781799892212 (ebook)
Subjects: LCSH: Big data. | Data mining. | Machine learning.
Classification: LCC QA76.9.B45 E54 2022 (print) | LCC QA76.9.B45 (ebook)
  | DDC 005.7--dc23
LC record available at https://lccn.loc.gov/2021027689
LC ebook record available at https://lccn.loc.gov/2021027690

British Cataloguing in Publication Data
A Cataloguing in Publication record for this book is available from the British Library.

All work contributed to this book is new, previously-unpublished material. The views expressed in this book are those of the authors, but not necessarily of the publisher.

For electronic access to this publication, please contact: eresources@igi-global.com.

# Editorial Advisory Board

# List of Contributors

# Alphabetical Table of Contents

*Volume I: 1-618; Volume II: 619-1246; Volume III: 1247-1870; Volume IV: 1871-2498; Volume V: 2499-3143*

# Table of Contents by Category

## Volume I

## Section: Accounting Analytics

    *Wikil Kwak, University of Nebraska at Omaha, USA*
    *Xiaoyan Cheng, University of Nebraska at Omaha, USA*
    *Yong Shi, University of Nebraska at Omaha, USA*
    *Fangyao Liu, Southwest Minzu University, China*
    *Kevin Kwak, University of Nebraska at Omaha, USA*

    *Toshifumi Takada, National Chung Cheng University, Taiwan*

## Section: Approximation Methods

    *Jean-Éric Pelet, LARGEPA, Panthéon-Assas University, Paris, France*
    *Santiago Belda, Universidad de Alicante, Spain*
    *Dounia Arezki, Computer Science Faculty, Science and Technology University of Oran, Algeria*

## Section: Autonomous Learning Systems

    *Indraneel Dabhade, O Automation, India*

# Section: Big Data Applications

## Section: Big Data as a Service

## Section: Big Data Systems and Tools

## Section: Business Intelligence

## Volume II

## Section: Causal Analysis

## Section: Chaos Control, Modeling, and Engineering

## Section: Cloud Infrastructure

## Section: Cognitive Science

## Section: Computational Intelligence

## Section: Computational Statistics

## Section: Computer Vision

## Section: Customer Analytics

## Section: Data Processing, Data Pipeline, and Data Engineering

# Volume III

## Section: Data Visualization and Visual Mining

## Section: Decision, Support System

## Section: Deep Neural Network (DNN) of Deep Learning

## Section: E-Learning Technologies and Tools

## Section: Emerging Technologies, Applications, and Related Issues

# Section: Information Extraction

    *Fabian N. Murrieta-Rico, Universidad Politécnica de Baja California, Mexico*
    *Moisés Rivas-López, Universidad Politécnica de Baja California, Mexico*
    *Oleg Sergiyenko, Universidad Autónoma de Baja California, Mexico*
    *Vitalii Petranovskii, Universidad Nacional Autónoma de México, Mexico*
    *Joel Antúnez-García, Universidad Nacional Autónoma de México, Mexico*
    *Julio C. Rodríguez-Quiñonez, Universidad Autónoma de Baja California, Mexico*
    *Wendy Flores-Fuentes, Universidad Autónoma de Baja California, Mexico*
    *Abelardo Mercado Herrera, Universidad Politécnica de Baja California, Mexico*
    *Araceli Gárate García, Universidad Politécnica de Baja California, Mexico*

# Section: Internet of Things

    *Shivlal Mewada, Government Holkar Science College, India*

    *Matthew J. Drake, Duquesne University, USA*

# Section: Malware Analysis

    *Thomas Alan Woolman, On Target Technologies, Inc., USA*
    *Philip Lunsford, East Carolina University, USA*

# Section: Management Analytics

    *Maximiliano Emanuel Korstanje, University of Palermo, Argentina*
    *Martha Omara Robert Beatón, University of Havana, Cuba*
    *Maite Echarri Chávez, University of Havana, Cuba*
    *Massiel Martínez Carballo, University of Havana, Cuba*
    *Victor Martinez Robert, University of Havana, Cuba*

    *Jorge Gomes, Universidade Lusófona das Humanidades e Tecnologias, Portugal*
    *Mário Romão, ISEG, Universidade de Lisboa, Portugal*

# Section: Marketing Analytics

    *Tasnia Fatin, Putra Business School, Universiti Putra Malaysia, Malaysia*
    *Mahmud Ullah, Department of Marketing, University of Dhaka, Bangladesh*
    *Nayem Rahman, School of Business and Information Technology, Purdue University Global, USA*

## Section: Object Detection

## Section: Performance Metrics

## Section: Predictive Analytics

## Section: Pricing Analytics

## Section: Qualitative Research

## Section: Recommender Systems

*Mustapha Kamal Benramdane, CNAM, France*
*Samia Bouzefrane, CNAM, France*
*Soumya Banerjee, MUST, France*
*Hubert Maupas, MUST, France*
*Elena Kornyshova, CNAM, France*

## Section: Reinforcement Learning

## Section: Simulation and Modeling

## Section: Smart City

## Section: Social Media Analytics

## Section: Supply Chain Analytics and Management

## Section: Symbolic Learning

## Section: Time Series Analysis

## Section: Transfer Learning

## Section: Transport Analytics

## Section: Unsupervised and Supervised Learning

# Foreword

There has been tremendous progress made in Data Science and Machine Learning over the last 10 – 15 years, leading to the Data Science becoming the major driving force of the Fourth Industrial Revolution and a significant factor in the current cycle of economic expansion. The need for data scientists is growing exponentially and machine learning has become one of the "hottest" professions in the labor market.

The field of Data Science is expanding both in-depth and in-breadth. In particular, we have witnessed widespread adoption of data science methods across a broad class of industries and functional areas, including health sciences and pharmaceuticals, finance, accounting, marketing, human resource management, operations and supply chains. Data-driven approaches have been deployed in such diverse set of applications as drug discovery, analysis of medical data and decision support tools for physicians, financial applications, including robo-advising, predictive maintenance of equipment and defect detection, Internet of Things (IoT), precision agriculture, physics and chemistry, to name a few. All these industries and applications enjoy adoption of a wide range of machine learning methods, the scope of which grew significantly over the last 10 – 15 years. In addition to the evolutionary growth and expansion of classical machine learning techniques, the last decade has witnessed revolutionary breakthroughs in such areas as Deep Learning, scalable machine learning methods capable of handling Big Data, the size of which grows exponentially over time in many applications, and the analysis of unstructured data, such as text using NLP-based methods, images and videos using Computer Vision techniques, and voice using Speech Recognition methods.

Given all this progress in Machine Learning and Data Science, it is high time to aggregate all this new knowledge "under one roof," and this Encyclopedia of Data Science and Machine Learning serves this purpose. It covers 188 different topics across the whole spectrum of the field written by leading academic scholars and industry practitioners describing the progress made in the respective areas over the last 10 – 15 years and reflecting the State-of-the-Art for each topic.

Since data science and machine learning are evolving rapidly, the authors also describe the challenges and present promising future research directions in their respective areas, delineating interesting work that lies ahead for the scholars to address these challenges. Therefore, this Encyclopedia remains what it is – a milestone on a long and exciting road that lies ahead of us in Data Science and Machine Learning.

*Alexander Tuzhilin*
*New York University, USA*
*May 2022*

# Preface

Big Data and Machine Learning (BDML) are driving and harnessing the power of the Fourth Industrial Revolution, also referred to as Industry 4.0 or 4IR, which revolutionizes the way companies, organizations, and institutions operate and develop. With the age of Big Data upon us, we risk drowning in a flood of digital data. Big Data has now become a critical part of the business world and daily life, as the synthesis and synergy of Machine Learning (ML) and Big Data (BD) have enormous potential.

BDML not only deals with descriptive and predictive analytics but also focuses on prescriptive analytics through digital technology and interconnectivity. It has continuously explored its "depth" and expanded its "breadth". BDML will remain to maximize the citizens' "wealth" while promoting society's "health".

The *Encyclopedia of Data Science and Machine Learning* examines current, state-of-the-art research in the areas of data science, ML, data mining (DM), optimization, artificial intelligence (AI), statistics, and the interactions, linkages, and applications of knowledge-based business with information systems. It provides an international forum for practitioners, educators, and researchers to advance the knowledge and practice of all facets of BDML, emphasizing emerging theories, principles, models, processes, and applications to inspire and circulate cutting-edge findings into research, business, and communities (Wang, 2022).

How can a manager get out of a data-flooded "mire"? How can a confused decision-maker navigate through a "maze"? How can an over-burdened problem solver clean up a "mess"? How can an exhausted scientist bypass a "myth"? The answer to all of the above is to employ BDML.

As Roy et al. (2022) point out, data has become the center point for almost every organization. For quite a long time, we are familiar with Descriptive Analytics (what happened in the past) and Diagnostic Analytics (why something happened in the past), as well as Predictive Analytics (what is most likely to happen in the future). However, BDML could go much above and beyond them with Prescriptive Analytics (what should be done now), which recommends actions companies, and organizations can take to affect those outcomes. The digital transformation, the horizontal and vertical integration of these production systems, as well as the exploitation via optimization models, can make a gigantic jump with this giant digital leverage.

BDML can turn *Data* into *value*; Transform *information* into *intelligence;* Change *patterns* into *profit;* Convert *relationships* into *resources*. Companies and organizations can make *Faster* (real-time or near real-time), *Frequent*, and *Fact-based* decisions. In an ever-evolving market, 4IR with a set of technologies can stimulate innovations and rapid responses. Knowledge workers can proactively take action before an unfriendly event occurs (Wang, 2008).

Having been penetrated and integrated into almost every aspect of our work and life, as well as our society itself, AI and related cutting-edge technologies will enhance human capacities, improve efficiencies, and optimize people's lives. AI would not replace human intelligence, rather than amplify it. As *AI evolves* and *humans* adapt, AI and humans go forward together in the long run because AI and people both bring different capabilities to society.

According to Klaus Schwab, the World Economic Forum Founder and Executive Chairman, 4IR intellectualizes precipitous change to industrial and societal prototypes and processes in the 21st century due to increasing interconnectivity and smart automation and finally blurs the lines among the physical, digital, and biological worlds. Part of the 4IR is the manner in which all types of machines and devices interact, correspond, and cooperate with each other. Even though there will be obvious job losses due to the replacement of tasks that humans have conducted for years by autonomous machines and/or software. On the contrary, there could be new business opportunities and plenty of new jobs for controlling "the new electricity" (Philbeck & Davis, 2018; Moll, 2022).

There are 207 qualified full chapters among 271 accepted proposals. Finally, the encyclopedia contains a collection of 187 high-quality chapters, which were written by an international team of more than 370 experts representing leading scientists and talented young scholars from more than 45 countries and regions, including Algeria, Argentina, Austria, Bangladesh, Brazil, Canada, Chile, China, Colombia, Cuba, Denmark, Egypt, El Salvador, Finland, France, Germany, Ghana, Greece, Hong Kong, Hungary, Indonesia, Iraq, Japan, Lebanon, Macau, Malaysia, Mexico, Netherland, New Zealand, Poland, Portugal, Saudi Arabia, Serbia, Singapore, South Africa, Sweden, Switzerland, Syria, Taiwan, Tunisia, Turkey, UK, USA, Venezuela, Vietnam, etc.

They have contributed great effort to create a source of solid, practical information, informed by the sound underlying theory that should become a resource for all people involved in this dynamic new field. Let's take a peek at a few of them:

Jaydip Sen has published around 300 articles in reputed international journals and referred conference proceedings (IEEE Xplore, ACM Digital Library, Springer LNCS, etc.), and 18 book chapters in books published by internationally renowned publishing houses. He is a Senior Member of ACM, USA a Member of IEEE, USA. He has been listed among the top 2% scientists in the globe as per studies conducted by Stanford University for the last consecutive three years 2019 - 2021. In his contributed chapter Prof. Sen and his co-author, Dutta have evaluated the performance of two risk-based portfolio design algorithms.

Leung - who has authored more than 300 refereed publications on the topics of data science, ML, BDM and analytics, and visual analytics (including those in ACM TODS, IEEE ICDE, and IEEE ICDM) - presents two encyclopedia articles. One of them presents up-to-date definitions in BDM and analytics in the high-performance computing environment and focuses on mining frequent patterns with the MapReduce programming model. Another one provides the latest comprehensive coverage on key concepts and applications for BD visualization; it focuses on visualizing BD, frequent patterns, and association rules.

Lorenzo Magnani is Editor-in-Chief of the Series Sapere, Springer. Thanks to his logico-epistemological and cognitive studies on the problem of abductive cognition (that regards all kinds of reasoning to hypotheses) explained in this chapter both virtues and limitations of some DL applications, taking advantage of the analysis of the famous AlphaGo/AlphaZero program and the concepts of locked and unlocked strategies. Furthermore, he is the author of many important articles and books on epistemology, logic, cognitive science, and the relationships between ethics, technology, and violence.

The chapter 'AI is transforming insurance with five emerging business models' is the culmination of three years of research into how AI is disrupting insurance. Zarifis has recently won a 'best paper award' at a leading conference and Cheng has recently been published in MIS Quarterly for related work. AI is disrupting many distinct parts of our life, but insurance is particularly interesting as some issues like risk and privacy concerns are more important. After several case studies, this chapter identifies that there are five emerging models in insurance that are optimal for AI.

In "Artificial Intelligence, Consumers, and the Experience Economy," Chang and Mukherjee's excellent synthesis of AI and consumers in the modern economy provides a much-needed knowledge base for stakeholders tasked to deploy AI. In "Using Machine Learning Methods to Extract Behavioral Insights from Consumer Data," they present a comprehensive discussion of new data sources and state-of-the-art techniques for researchers and practitioners in computational social science. The chapters are built on their projects supported by the Ministry of Education, Singapore, under its Academic Research Fund (AcRF) Tier 2 Grant No. MOE2019-T2-1-183 and Grant No. MOE2018-T2-1-181, respectively.

Based on many years of application development by CY Pang and S. Pang's cognitive data analysis of many industrial projects, this chapter proposes a programming paradigm specific to BD processing. Pang was the lead architect of a $1.6 billion enterprise software project and was awarded a special architectural design trophy. He has received awards of $20,000 and $5,000 for outstanding innovation from a company he previously worked for. By the way, CY Pang was awarded a Prestige Scholarship from Peter House, Cambridge to complete his Ph.D. at the University of Cambridge, UK.

Vitor provides an excellent overview of multidimensional search methods for optimization and the potential these methods have to solve optimization problems more quickly. With almost ten years of industry experience, Vitor is an expert in optimization methods and the modeling of complex systems using operations research and data analytics techniques. He is also a recipient of the Nebraska EPSCoR FIRST Award, supported by the National Science Foundation to advance the research of early-career tenure-track faculty.

Lee's chapter on evidence-based data-driven pain management bears multi-facet importance. Nearly 40 million anesthetics are administered each year in the United States. And over 10.7% of Americans use prescription pain medication on a regular basis. The findings highlight the optimal safe dose and delivery mechanism to achieve the best outcome. The study showcases the persistence of overprescription of opioid-type drugs, as it finds that the use of fentanyl has little effect on the outcome and should be avoided.

Auditors must evaluate the volatility and uncertainty of the client company at the initial stage of the audit contract because it directly influences the audit risk. Takada contributes to auditing research and accounting education for 40 years. He has been awarded for his research and contributions to his excellent papers and accounting education by the *Chinese Auditing Association* and by the *Japanese Auditing Association*.

Nguyen and Quinn propose an optimal approach to tackle the well-known issue of the imbalance in bankruptcy prediction. Their approach has been evaluated through a rigorous computation including the most popular current methods in the literature. They have also made other main contributions in the area of imbalanced classification by winning the 2020 Literati Awards for Outstanding Author Contribution.

Rodríguez is the Bioethics of Displacement pioneer, a field that merges futurism, belongingness, and life. He has also published analytic papers and fieldwork on crises and big social changes such as pandemics, Anthropocene, AI takeover, cyborgs, digital securitization and terrorist attacks. As a chair, the author leads the research on the first decolonized corruption index. Torres shares his more than 15 years of wealth of experience in Predictive Maintenance management as a speaker at global summits such as Scalable and PMM Tech Dates. The author leads the first non-taxonomic error mode proponent of AI implementation.

Kurpicz-Briki, Glauser, and Schmid are using unique API technologies to measure the impact of online search behavior using several different online channels. Their method allows the identification of the specific channels, where keywords have been searched, and a restriction of regions, using the domains. Such technologies provide a major benefit for different application domains, including public health. In times such as a pandemic crisis, it is highly relevant for different stakeholders to identify the impact of their communications on the user community as well as the well-being of the population. Using the method proposed by the authors, this can be done while fully respecting the privacy of the users.

Sensors sense the environment and process large sets of data. Monitoring the data to detect malicious content is one of the biggest challenges. The previous work used mean variation to ease the surveillance of information. Ambika's proposal minimizes the effort by classifying the streamed data into three subsets. It uses the k-nearest neighbor procedure to accomplish the same. The work conserves 10.77% of energy and tracks 27.58% of more packets. Map-reduce methodology manages large amounts of data to a certain extent. Ambika's other proposal aims to increase processing speed by 29.6% using a hashing methodology.

In today's world, text-based sentiment analysis brings the attention of all. By looking at the people requirement, Tripathy and Sharaff propose a hybridized Genetic Algorithm (GA)-based feature selection method to achieve a better model performance. In the current study, they have customized the GA by using the SVM to evaluate the fitness value of the solutions. The proposed idea is essential as the technique reduces the computational cost by reducing sufficient features without affecting the performance. The proposed model can be implemented in any field to filter out the sentiment from the user's review.

Alberg and Hadad present the novel Interval Gradient Prediction Tree ML Algorithm that can process incoming mean-variance aggregated multivariate temporal data and make stable interval predictions of a target numerical variable. Empirical evaluations of multi-sensor aircraft datasets have demonstrated that this algorithm provides better readability and similar performance compared to other ML regression tree algorithms.

The environmental, societal, and cultural imperatives press for innovative, prompt, and practical solutions for grave humanitarian problems we face in the 21st century. The climate crisis is felt everywhere; natural disasters are rampant. Can technology provide reasonable means to humanitarian supply chains? What potential uses can AI offer in establishing sustainable humanitarian logistics (SHL)? Ülkü, an award-winning professor and the director of CRSSCA-Centre for Research in Sustainable Supply Chain Analytics, and his research associate Oguntola of Dalhousie University - Canada review the latest research on the applications of AI technology on SHL.

Aguiar-Pérez, the leading author of this chapter, provides the audience an insight into what ML is and its relation with AI or DL. He has an extended experience in the field of ML, DL, BD, and IoT in various sectors (automotive, smart roads, agriculture, livestock, heritage, etc.), including collaboration with companies, EU-funded research projects, publications, and postgraduate teaching experience. The rest of the authors work with him in the Data Engineering Research Unit of the University of Valladolid.

Bagui, a highly accomplished author of several books on databases and Oracle, presents a very timely chapter on the improvements made in Oracle 19c's multitenant container architecture and shows how these improvements aid in the management of Big Data from the perspective of application development. The added functionality that comes with the integration of Big Data platforms, alongside the flexibility and improvement that comes with a container and pluggable databases, has allowed Oracle to be in the forefront in the handling of Big Data.

As an internationally renowned interdisciplinary information and data professional, Koltay's chapter on Research Data Management (RDM) is of interest not only for both professionals of DS and ML but is related to any research activity. He is also a widely published author in these fields. In 2021, his contribution to IGI Global books included an entry on information overload. His book, titled Research Data Management and Data Literacy (Chandos, 2021) contains a more detailed explanation of the subjects, contained in this chapter.

Zhao is a DS professional with experience in industry, teaching, and research. He is a leading BD expert in the IR BD & AI Lab in New Jersey, USA. He provides multiple chapters to the book by covering a broad range of BD applications in vast perspectives of urgent demands in DS research objectives, such as DSS, DL, computer vision, BD architecture designs, and applied BD analytics in Covid-19 research. As such, he did excellent work in those chapters and made significant contributions to the book.

Based on their discovery of action rules and meta-actions from client datasets, Duan and Ras propose a strategy for improving the number of promoters and decreasing the number of detractors among customers. Moreover, the improved/enhanced action rules can be utilized in developing actionable strategies for decision makers to reduce customer churn, which will contribute to the overall customer churn study in the business field. The authors target the domain represented by many clients, each one involved with customers in the same type of business. Clients are heavy equipment repair shops, and customers are owners of such equipment.

The A2E Process Model for Data Analytics is simple without being simplistic and comprehensive without being complicated. It balances technology with humanity and theories with practices. This model reflects Jay Wang's decades-long multi-disciplinary training and experience in STEM, Behavioral Science, and Management Science. While existing process models such as CRISP-DM, SEMMA, and KDD were developed for technical professionals with limitations and low adoption rates, the A2E Model is more approachable to subject matter experts, business analysts, and social scientists. The A2E Model will elevate the analytics profession by fostering interdisciplinary collaborations of all stakeholders and increasing the effectiveness and impacts of analytics efforts.

Turuk explores Audio and video-based Emotion Recognition using the Backpropagation Algorithm, which is the backbone of ML and DL architectures. This chapter analyses everyday human emotions such as Happy, Sad, Neutral, and Angry using audio-visual cues. The audio features such as Energy & MFCC and video features using the Gabor filter are extracted. Mutual information is computed using video features. The readers will benefit and motivated to conduct further research in this domain. The application may be extended to a lie detector using Emotions.

Stojanović and Marković-Petrović focus on continuous cyber security risk assessment in Industrial Internet of Things (IIoT) networks, and particularly on possibilities of DL approaches to achieve the goal. The authors successfully complement their previous work regarding the cyber security of industrial control systems. They concisely review the theoretical background and provide an excellent framework for the continuous risk assessment process in the IIoT environment. DL can be integrated into edge-computing-based systems and used for feature extraction and risk classification from massive raw data. The chapter ends with a list of proposals for further studies.

Climate change is a very important issue and each person on our planet must have a culture of keeping it clean. Pollution increased yearly due to the increased consumption of fossil fuels. Alsultanny has many research papers in climate change and renewable energy. He led a UNDP team for writing reports on energy consumption in Bahrain. Alsultanny did an innovative method in his chapter, by utilizing the pollution gases data, these data currently are BD, because they are registered yearly in every minute, and from many monitoring pollutions stations.

Deliyska and Ivanova conducted timely research and practical work representing an important contribution to data modeling in sustainable science. Applying ontological engineering and a coevolutionary approach, a unique metamodel of sustainable development is created containing structured knowledge and mutual links between environmental, social, and economic dimensions in this interdisciplinary area. Specialists in different fields can use the proposed metamodel as a tool for terminology clarification, knowledge extraction, and interchange and for the structuring of ML models of sustainable development processes.

Hedayati and Schniederjans provide a broad spectrum of issues that come into play when using digital technologies to benefit healthcare. This is even more important where the pandemic has forced healthcare models to rapidly adjust towards compliance with local, regional, and national policy. The dissemination and creation of knowledge become paramount when considering the benefits and drawbacks of the rapid changes in technology applications worldwide. The authors consider several insights from the American Hospital Association Compliance to provide some questions researchers and practitioners may consider when addressing knowledge management via digital technology implementation in healthcare settings.

Pratihar and Kundu apply the theory of fuzzy logic to develop a classification and authentication system for beverages. It emphasizes the versatility of fuzzy logic to deal with the higher dimensional and highly non-linear sensor data obtained from e-tongue for different beverage samples. Commonly used mapping techniques (for dimension reduction of a data set) and clustering techniques (for classification) were also briefly discussed. This study provides a perspective on developing a fuzzy logic-based classifier/authenticator system in the future for beverages, foods, and others and their quality control and monitoring.

Drake discusses the use of IoT technology to improve SCM. As firms look to improve their supply chain resilience in response to the COVID-19 pandemic and other disruptions, IoT data increases visibility, traceability, and can help firms to mitigate risks through added agility and responsiveness. The improved decision-making made possible by IoT data creates a competitive advantage in the market.

Today, high-dimensional data (multi-omics data) are widely used. The high dimensionality of the data creates problems (time, cost, diagnosis, and treatment) in studies. Ipekten et al. introduce the existing solutions to these problems and commonly used methods. Also, the authors present the advantages of the methods over each other and enlighten the researchers that using suitable methods in terms of performance can increase the reliability and accuracy of the studies. Finally, the authors advise on what can be done in the future.

Learning analytics (LA), a promising field of study that started more than a decade ago but has blossomed in recent years, addresses the challenges of LA specifically in education, integrating it as a fundamental element of the Smart Classroom. Ifenthaler and Siemens among others discuss the primary features, the benefits, and some experiences. In addition, the team of authors of the chapter has contributed more than twelve publications on this topic in the last 3 years in leading journals and publishers.

Current advances in AI and ML in particular have raised several concerns regarding the trustworthiness and explainability of deployed AI systems. Knowledge-Based approaches based on symbolic representations and reasoning mechanisms can be used to deploy AI systems that are explainable and compliant with corresponding ethical and legal guidelines, thus complementing purely data-driven approaches.

Batsakis and Matsatsinis, both having vast theoretical backgrounds and experience in this research area, offer an overview of knowledge-based AI methods for the interested AI practitioner.

Noteboom and Zeng provide a comprehensive review of applications of AI and ML and data analytics techniques in clinical decision support systems (CDSSs) and make contributions including, 1) the current status of data-driven CDSSs, 2) identification and quantification of the extent to which theories and frameworks have guided the research, 3) understanding the synergy between AI/ML algorithms and modes of data analytics, 4) directions for advancing data-driven CDSSs to realize their potential in healthcare.

Fisogni investigates the emotional environment which is grounded in any human/machine interaction. Through the lenses of metaphysics and system thinking the author sketches a highly valuable insight, for sure an unprecedented challenge for DSs. In fact, only a philosophical foundation of the big issues of this realm can bring about a change in the quality of understanding an increasingly melted environment humans/machines in the Onlife era.

In "Hedonic Hunger and Obesity", Demirok and Uysal touch upon a remarkable topic and explain ways of identification for people with hedonic nutrition and the conditions that are effective in the states that trigger hunger state in humans. In addition, in this text, the authors ensample hormones that suppress and trigger hunger.

Yen and her coauthors contributed a chapter on how ML creates the virtual singer industry. Virtual singers have great market potential and even advantages over their human counterparts. Despite the bright future of virtual singers, the chapter has discussed difficulties virtual singers face, especially their copyright protection by legislation. Literature on the technical aspects of virtual singers is also reviewed, and a list of additional readings is provided for readers interested in the ML algorithms behind virtual singers.

Rastogi is working on Biofeedback therapy and its effect on Diabetes diseases, a currently very active healthcare domain. He brings back the glory of Indian Ancient Vedic Sciences of Jap, Pranayama, Healing techniques, and the effect of Yajna and Mantra science on Diseases and pollution control. Also, He has developed some interesting mathematical models with algorithms on Swarm Intelligence approaches like PSO, ACO BCO, etc. for better human life via Spiritual Index and higher consciousness.

Isikhan presents a comparison of a new proposal for the modeling of Ceiling and Floor Effect dependent variables and classical methods. It has been noticed that there are very few publications evaluating the regression modeling of ceiling and floor effect observations in recent years. The modeling method with regression-based imputation, which clinicians can use as an alternative to classical models for ceiling and floor effective observations, is explained in detail. The performances of the newly proposed imputation-based regression and other classical methods were validated based on both real clinical data, synthetic data, as well as a 500 replicated cross-validation method.

Drignei has extensive experience with time series modeling and analysis. Prior to this work, he addressed statistical modeling aspects of space-time data, such as temperatures recorded over space and time. His research has been published in leading statistics journals. The current work deals with seasonal times series recorded at a large number of time points. Such data sets will become more common in the future, in areas such as business, industry, and science. Therefore, this chapter is timely and important because it sheds new light on modeling aspects of this type of data sets.

Data visualization plays a key role in the decision-making process. Visualization allows for data to be consumable. If data is not consumable, there is a tendency to ignore the facts and rely more on biases. Researchers have found that cognitive biases do exist within data visualizations and can affect decision-making abilities. Anderson and Hardin provide background on cognitive biases related to data visualizations, with a particular interest in visual analytics in BD environments. A review of recent studies related to mitigating cognitive biases is presented. Recommendations for mitigating biases in visualizations are provided to practitioners.

Puzzanghera explores the impact of AI on administrative law. He combines IT systems with administrative activity and researches the processors that prepare content and the implications that arise. He analyzes the European Commission's proposal in regard to the legislation of AI in Europe and the importance of safeguarding human rights in the introduction of AI in administrative activity.

How ML impacts the catering industry? Liu et al. provide a comprehensive vision to readers with real-life examples and academic research. Researchers at business schools may have their attention drawn to the impact of ML on operations, management, and marketing, while scholars with solid ML backgrounds may become aware of industry issues, identify new research questions, and link their expertise to practical problems through reading the chapter.

Di Wang's research interests include 4D printing technology, robot control, remanufactured industry, and energy schedule in the smart city. Combinatorial optimization is a widely applied field at the forefront of combinatorics and theoretical computer science. With BD challenges, deep reinforcement learning opens new doors to solve complex combinatorial optimization problems with overwhelming advantages over traditional methods.

Firmansyah and Harsanto focus on exploring BD and Islamic finance. The utilization of BD in Islamic financial institutions (IFIs) has been perceived as a source of competitive advantage in today's era. Many IFIs have been more dependent on BD technologies than ever before in order to keep up with the changing customers' demands, lifestyles, and preferences.

With his experience of working in both industry and academic research, Indraneel highlights progress made in integrating AI with industry and helps bridge the reality and challenges faced while summarizing the state of Industry 4.0. The author engages audiences from different sectors without overburdening the reader with incoherent technical details. A practitioner in the fields of DS and cybersecurity, the author brings experience interacting with clients and customers from different fields, including manufacturing, legal, and product developers.

Yang, Wu, & Forrest examine the textual aspects of consumer reviews. As a critical source of information for online shoppers, researchers have spent considerable time examining the potential impact of consumer reviews on purchasing behavior. The authors contribute to the existing body of knowledge by proposing a conceptual framework for capturing the internal relationships between major textual features discovered in prior research.

Kara and Gonce Koçken are researchers studying mathematical programming problems in fuzzy environments. In the study, a novel fuzzy solution approach to multi-objective solid transportation problems is developed by using different membership functions, which can help the studies in transportation systems.

Millham demonstrates the various spheres of the emerging 4IR and how they interrelate with the application, opportunities, expectations, and challenges of a smart city. Because many of these smart city applications are very complex and interact with each other using various technologies, several nature-inspired algorithms are introduced as a way to provide intelligent and coordinated management of these entities.

The development of novel measurement and detection techniques is a rapidly growing area, where the generation of vast amounts of information requires novel methods for analysis. Murrieta-Rico explores a new direction of his research by combing the know-how for generating a big dataset from a digital frequency measurement, with the application of the principal component analysis (PCA). As a result, a powerful methodology for data analysis is presented. In addition, these results can be used for extending the capabilities of ML systems based on sensors.

Coimbra, Chimenti, and Nogueira contribute to the debate related to human-machine interaction in social media. The work helped to understand the mechanisms and motivators of this relationship. In addition, the article presented a historical evolution of the debate on the interaction between machines and men in decision-making, distributing the result of the literature review in three historical cycles. The research was carried out through a survey of YouTube users to understand the interaction mechanism along with its motivators.

As a transformational general-purpose technology, AI is impacting marketing as a function, and marketing managers' activities, capabilities, and performance. Oberoi emphasizes how the job of a marketing manager will be evolving into understanding which kind of AI can and should be applied to which kind of marketing actions for better performance. Marketing managers will have to go through a learning curve and acquire new skills.

Singh and Dev have discussed the concepts of data warehouse and OLAP technology to deal with real-life applications efficiently. The topic is useful in the modern digital era as businesses are dealing with data from heterogeneous sources. The chapter presents the case study of the tourism industry as it deals with multidimensional data like tourist, hospitality, and tourist products. This chapter will be helpful in understanding how to generate multi-dimensional reports that will show the information according to the needs of policymakers.

Ramos has made many contributions to the potential of Business Intelligence tools, combined with DM algorithms methods to produce insights about the tourism business, highlighting an aspect of the investment potential of tourism organizations in this type of system, from those related to accommodation, management of tourist destinations, to tourist transport, restaurants, among other businesses complementary to the tourist activity, with a view to innovation and increasing financial performance, which includes examples ranging from the application of OLAP techniques to the application of ML methods.

Balsam depicts the meaning and role of metamodels in defining the abstract syntax of the language by which developers communicate, design, and implement systems including the selection of the design, implementation methods, and techniques for increasingly complex systems to satisfy customers' needs, particularly if the system has to be delivered in a considerably fleeting time. The author highlights different aspects of meta-models standards, categories, the process of creating the metamodel, and challenges in the research of metamodeling.

Dharmapala contributes a novel method to the field of research in 'Classification of employee categories in allocating a reward, with input features from survey responses.' In the past, researchers conducted qualitative and quantitative analyses on this subject as it is an important topic to any organization that strives to boost the morale of its employees. The author opened a new direction in future research on the subject by using ML algorithms, and the results obtained were promising.

Mudrakola identifies the gap and future scope for Breast cancer applications like the impact of chemical therapy, prognosis analysis among various treatment types and stages, etc. From basic to the latest trends, the author's extensive literature survey will direct the root to aspects needed to analyze work on medical applications specific to Breast cancer.

Rani et al. highlight the venues of user-generated content (UGC) in Industry 4.0. This chapter's contribution is highly interesting for any digital content creator and non-paid professionals. The importance of UGC on consumer behavior in the era of Industry 4.0 will be explained, allowing stakeholders to assess their efficacy in Internet communication and enhancing the digital process required for modern marketing. The chapter aims to link existing ideas and provide a holistic picture of UGC by concentrating on future research.

Ibrahim et al. seek to provide an understanding of the relationship between member support exchange behavior and self-disclosure intention in online health support communities using a data-driven literature review. Seeking or providing support in online communities may be useful but having to disclose personal information publicly online is a critical privacy risk – intention counts.

Rusko introduces the main perspectives of industrial revolutions. He found interesting backgrounding details for the chapter about the disruptions of the industrial revolutions. Kosonen updates the paper with the effects of Covid-19 and contemporary digitizing development.

I would like to highlight a number of authors who have received special stunning honors: Eva K Lee has published over 220 research articles, and fifty government and state reports, and has received patents on innovative medical systems and devices. She is frequently tapped by a variety of health and security policymakers in Washington for her expertise in personalized medicine, chronic diseases, healthcare quality, modeling and decision support, vaccine research and national security, pandemic, and medical preparedness. Lee has received multiple prestigious analytics and practice excellence awards including INFORMS Franz Edelman award, Daniel H Wagner prize, and the Caterpillar and Innovative Applications in Analytics Award for novel cancer therapeutics, bioterrorism emergency response, and mass casualty mitigation, personalized disease management, ML for best practice discovery, transforming clinical workflow and patient care, vaccine immunity prediction, and reducing hospital-acquired infections. She is an INFORMS Fellow. She is also inducted into the American Institute for Medical and Biological Engineering (AIMBE) College of Fellows, the first IE/OR engineer to be nominated and elected for this honor. Her work has been funded by CDC, HHS, NIH, NSF, and DTRA. Lee was an NSF CAREER Young Investigator and Whitaker Foundation Young Investigator recipient.

Petry and Yager are both internationally known for their research in computational intelligence, in the area of fuzzy set theory and applications, and are both IEEE Fellows and have received prestigious awards from the IEEE. They have collaborated here as it represents extensions of their previous research on this topic. Hierarchical concept generalization is one important approach to dealing with the complex issues involving BD. This chapter provides insights on how to extend hierarchical generalization to data with interval and intuitionistic forms of uncertainty.

The globalization of the software development industry continues to experience significant growth. The increasing trend of globalization brings new challenges and increases the scope of the core functions of the software development process. Pal introduces a distributed software development knowledge management architecture. Kamalendu has published research articles in the software development community in the ACM SIGMIS Database, Expert Systems with Applications, DSSs, and conferences. Kamalendu was awarded the best research paper on data analytic work at a recent international conference. He is a member of the British Computer Society, the IET, and the IEEE Computer Society.

Badia's research has been funded by the National Science Foundation (including a prestigious CAREER Award) and has resulted in over 50 publications in scientific journals and conferences. His chapter demonstrates how to use SQL in order to prepare data that resides in database tables for analysis. The reader is guided through steps for Exploratory Data Analysis (EDA), data cleaning (including dealing with missing data, outliers, and duplicates), and other tasks that are an integral part of the Data Scientist day-to-day. The references provide a guide for further study.

Srinivasan explains the three components of graph analytics and provides illustrative examples as well as code for implementation. His chapter is one of the few primers of graph DS/analytics that covers a variety of topics in the discipline. The author does active research in graph analytics methods and applications in healthcare, ML explainability, and DL and regularly publishes in top journals and conferences in information systems, healthcare, and computer science. He received best paper awards in INFORMS Workshop on Data Science (2021) and the 6th International Conference on Digital Health (2016), respectively.

Knowledge explosion pushes BDML, a multidisciplinary subject, to ever-expanding regions. Inclusion, omission, emphasis, evolution, and even revolution are part of our professional life. In spite of our efforts to be careful, should you find any ambiguities of perceived inaccuracies, please contact me at prof.johnwang@gmail.com.

*John Wang*
*Montclair State University, USA*

## REFERENCES

Moll, I. (2022). The Fourth Industrial Revolution: A new ideology. *tripleC: Communication, Capitalism & Critique*, 20(1), 45–61.

Philbeck, T., & Davis, N. (2018). The Fourth Industrial Revolution: Shaping a new era. *Journal of International Affairs*, 72(1), 17–22.

Roy, D., Srivastava, R., Jat, M., & Karaca, M. S. (2022). A complete overview of analytics techniques: Descriptive, predictive, and prescriptive. *Decision Intelligence Analytics and the Implementation of Strategic Business Management*, 15-30.

Wang, J. (Ed.). (2008). *Data Warehousing and Mining: Concepts, Methodologies, Tools, and Applications* (Vols. 1–6). IGI Global. doi:10.4018/978-1-59904-951-9

Wang, J. (Ed.). (2022). *Encyclopedia of Data Science and Machine Learning*. IGI Global. https://www.igi-global.com/book/encyclopedia-data-science-machine-learning/276507

# Acknowledgment

The editor would like to thank all authors for their insights and excellent contributions to this major volume. I also want to thank the many anonymous reviewers who assisted me in the peer-reviewing process and provided comprehensive and indispensable inputs that improved our book significantly. In particular, the Editorial Advisory Board members, including Xueqi Cheng (Chinese Academy of Science), Verena Kantere (University of Ottawa, Canada), Srikanta Patnaik (SOA University, India), Hongming Wang (Harvard University), and Yanchang Zhao (CSIRO, Australia), have all made immense contributions in terms of advice and assistance, enhancing the quality of this volume. My sincere appreciation also goes to Prof. Alexander Tuzhilin (New York University). Despite his busy schedule, he has written three forewords for my consecutive encyclopaedias, over an 18-year span, in this expanding and exploring area.

In addition, the editor wishes to acknowledge the help of all involved in the development process of this book, without whose support the project could not have been satisfactorily completed. I owe my thanks to the staff at IGI Global, whose support and contributions have been invaluable throughout the entire process, from inception to final publication. Special thanks go to Gianna Walker, Angelina Olivas, Katelyn McLoughlin, and Melissa Wagner, who continuously prodded me via email to keep the project on schedule, and to Jan Travers and Lindsay Wertman, whose enthusiasm motivated me to accept their invitation to take on this project.

I would also like to extend my thanks to my brothers Zhengxian, Shubert (an artist, https://portraitartist.com/detail/6467), and sister Joyce Mu, who stood solidly behind me and contributed in their own unique ways. We are thankful for the scholarships which we have been provided, without which it would not have been possible for all of us to come and study in the U.S.

Finally, I want to thank my family: my parents for supporting me spiritually throughout my life and providing endless encouragement; my wife Hongyu for taking care of two active and rebellious teenagers, conducting all family chores, and not complaining to me too much.

This book was special due to the stresses and difficulties posed by the Covid-19 pandemic. We thank and salute the authors who had to overcome numerous challenges to help make this volume a reality. Our authors had to persevere through unprecedented circumstances to enable this masterful encyclopedia. Now, it is time to celebrate and reap the fruits of our demanding work! Cheese and cheers!

# Interactive Workbook on Science Communication

**Gilbert Ahamer**

https://orcid.org/0000-0003-2140-7654

*Austrian Academy of Sciences, Austria*

## BACKGROUND

The *organisations* involved in the following cases include secondary schools, universities, university clusters, transnational university partnerships, international environmental NGOs, and the European Union's external policy. These organisations range from public to private and from idealistic to pragmatic. All of them plan to "change the world" and for that target they undertake to *exchange views and perspectives* among the stakeholders concerned. This paper approaches to find answers to the specific set of questions through cases of international collaborative educational projects.

In this article, the term *"workbook"* means a written text that is used for a series of (online) workshops during which the authentic opinion and value systems of the partners are formed into an *administrative guideline* and into *practical suggestions* for concrete future work.

The goal and justification of the chapter consists in drawing attention to data scientists inhowfar their research findings can be conveyed to a larger public, thus justifying received research grants.

## 1. INTRODUCTION

### 1.1 Setting the Frame

This article proposes a structured set of draft "Guidelines on science communication" that were elaborated by the author in the framework of Component 4 within the European Union (EU) Twinning project entitled "Supporting inter-sectoral collaboration possibilities between Research and Industry" (GE 18 ENI OT 02 19) during the years 2020-2021 in a dialogic process between Twinning beneficiary (the Shota Rustaveli National Science Foundation of Georgia SRNSFG) and the Twinning team comprised of several science-related EU member state organisations[1].

According to the Terms of Reference (ToR, 2020), "the overall objective of the project is to help Georgian Institutions to strengthen Georgia's Science, Technology and Innovation (STI) system. This should be achieved by identifying and addressing the main priorities and challenges the system is confronted with and the best ways of approaching these challenges with the aim of ensuring an interdisciplinary approach, collaborative research and promoting evidence-based policy implementation in line with the EU-Georgia Association Agreement (AA)."

DOI: 10.4018/978-1-7998-9220-5.ch037

## 1.2 Key Procedural Decisions

The following seven fundamental decisions were made by the author as a grand orientation for dialogic cooperation on science communication:

1. Procedurally and didactically, the intention of this workbook is to place its user (reader) into an *active role* which practically means to fill in the empty boxes (shown in the following figures).
2. In practice, the addressee (or client, in this case SRNSFG) will prepare their actual authentic science communication program based on *own initiative* and own responsibility, while the present workbook facilitates this task by preparing the structure, format, and logic model.
3. This workbook may be adapted further along the dialogic process described in section 21.
4. This is a concrete work plan and work strategy. It should help SRNSFG staff to produce their own strategic program on science communication (SC).
5. The underlying reason for science communication is to inform the public about the achievements and chances provided by the science sector for society. Such information should be most effectively transported to the various stakeholder groups within society, which are graphically represented by the logo on the cover page.
6. Science is seen as a key agent for societal innovation and progress, thus promoting Georgia's development on all cultural, societal, political and economic levels.
7. The economic need for science communication arises from the need for effectively making use of those funds which society invests into society. The resulting role of science as innovator and generator of workplaces should be facilitated by allowing the broad public to take proactive roles, e.g., as founders of start-ups and SMEs (Small and Medium Enterprises). Such communication therefore triggers new action – in case it is successful.

## 1.3 The Dialogic Procedure

The following procedures lead to the development of the guidelines:

- "Science communication guidelines" are *no standard product* in science administration, for which a clear definition or clear requirements would exist, nor are there striking examples in other national science administrations. SC guidelines have to be freshly invented anyhow.
- Based on the literature analyses performed for this project, and based on earlier science communication workshops, the involved stakeholders cooperatively develop a mindset for "science communication guidelines". Because of inexistant standards or norms, **this product is converted into a process**.
- After completion of draft guidelines until July 2021, such a *dialogic process* was started in autumn 2021 by which the draft guidelines were further discussed, adapted and reshaped for the needs of the Georgian beneficiaries.

According to Figure 1, the dialogic procedure includes bi-weekly micro-workshops (meaning 2-hour online working meetings with one partner from each side, EU and Georgia) and mainly serves for the inculturation of the guidelines and the explanation of its dialogic-procedural spirit into a formerly hierarchical "command-and-control" work atmosphere.

As preparation for every micro-workshop, a section of the draft guidelines is sent to the beneficiary.

*Figure 1. The dynamic communicative and dialogic procedure which takes the place of an undefinable static product, namely "science communication guidelines"*

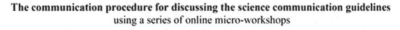

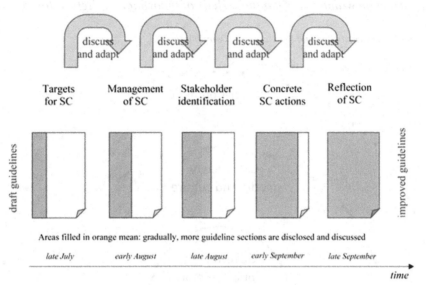

## 2. ELEMENTS IN SCIENCE COMMUNICATION

There is vast literature on supporting best practice examples (Brubaker, 2021; Youth Stem, 2021; Bowers, 2021; Könneker, C.,2021; Hargittai et al., 2018; IIASA, 2021; Schäfer, 2020; Research International, 2021; EC, 2021; Artur, 2021; Brownell et al., 2013; Loroño-Leturiondo & Davies, 2018; The Blue Reporters, 2017; Bultitude, 2011; Kuehne et al., 2014; Cooke et al., 2017; Ahamer & Schrei, 2004; Ahamer, 2008, 2013a, b, 2020; Ahamer & Mayer, 2013) which may be used for further reading.

### 2.1 The Quintuple Helix Model

A very useful logic model is the "quintuple helix model" presented in literature as adapted from Carayannis et al. (2012, 2019), Carayannis et al. (2012), Carayannis and Campbell (2014), Lindberg et al. (2014), Farinha et al. (2016), and based on the initial idea by Etzkowitz (2008).

Each group within society deserves a different and well-targeted style of science communication. The best is to look at a recent model how society innovation works.

Starting from an earlier "triple helix model", the updated quintuple helix model includes (see logo):

- **Research & University**,
- **Civil Society & NGOs**,
- **Industry & Enterprises**,
- **Governance & Administration**,
- **Media**.

Individuals from each of these 5 stakeholder groups have messages for the other groups.

Which processes steer innovation, and how to support them? Figure 2 suggests a relative ordering scheme within the "quintuple helix model".

*Figure 2. Detailed structure within the "Quintuple Helix of Innovation". Slightly different names might occur*
*Image design source: RTA Inese Gavarāne and the Georgian Twinning team*

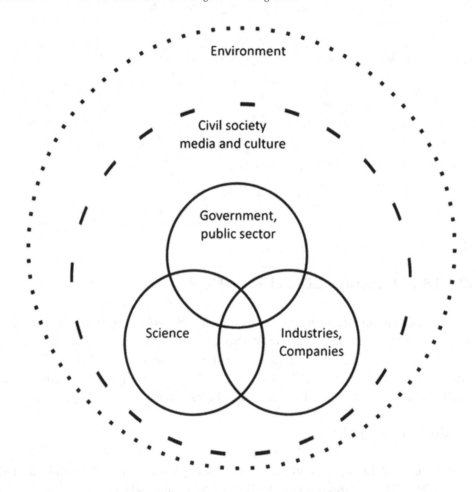

## 2.2 Key Elements in the Procedures of Science Communication

As the SC guidelines are a workbook (by literary genre), we are starting out with very clear and structured steps in the following proposed work sequence, which is sketched in the general oversight graphics of Figure 3.

With many business development models (Borrmann et al., 2020; Bulkeley et al., 2016; Steiner and Hartmann, 2006; Aldin et al., 2004; Motała et al., 2008), the selected sequence of actioning is essential. The leftmost step in Figure 3 is to identify the right audience. Therefore, let us take 2 pre-steps.

In the following text, the reader is addressed by the word "you" in order to convey the atmosphere of imminent action on the side of the reader who acts in self-starting and self-responsible manner when generating an administrative document via dialogue with all involved stakeholders.

*Figure 3. The proposed sequence of action in the workbook on science communication*
*Image source: Imaginis (2020)*

**Pre-step 1:** to whom will you speak?

Therefore, resulting work steps are to identify the targeted addressees of communication. You may wish to use Table 1, in order to create a preliminary concretisation of your wishes. Before embarking on the entire structured process, you can narrow down your vision to selected groups.

*Table 1. As a quick first orientation, note down to whom actually you wish to speak during implementation of this activity (to be filled in by experts)*

| Stakeholder group | Included: yes/no | Examples for addressees |
|---|---|---|
| Research & University | | |
| Civil Society & NGOs | | |
| Industry & Enterprises. | | |
| Governance & Administration | | |
| Media | | |

Now that you know your target group preliminarily, start to conceive the gist, the meta-message.

**Pre-step 2:** what is your dream, actually?

*Figure 4. The dream is the strongest force impacting future reality*
*(Marquis & Wilber, 2008. Wilber, 1993, 1997, 2000, 2005; Seiler, 2017, Chopra, 2019).*

Write down your ultimate (individual or corporate) dream (i.e., mental concept) for your work here:

---
*My personal dream for this work is …*

---

## 3. COMMUNICATION MEDIUM, LANGUAGE, DESIGN AND STRUCTURE

---
- Which SC targets does Georgia need?
  o …
- Which types and tools of SC does Georgia need?
  o …
  o …
  o …

---

With your preliminary definitions on "with whom you will speak" and "what your key message is", TT

The next stages allow you to actively contribute to a national science fund's development and to the science system.

Principally, practical encouragement to communicate science to a wider pubic is provided especially by Brown University (2014) and furthermore by vast literature (Newcastle University, 2021; Eise, 2021; Nature Career Brief, 2021; ASCB, 2021; Fischhoff, 2019) and had been conveyed in a preparatory workshop on 19-20 November 2020 to our Georgian partner institution (Ahamer 2020). Therein, elements for a "cookbook" on science communication are shown in Figure 5, representing fast-to-use practical recommendations.

*Figure 5. Elements of a "cookbook" on science communication, as contained in workshop slides to support national staff working in science funds*
Image source: Screenshot of the original in (Ahamer, 2020).

Looking at Figure 5 allows to compare the various methodologies presented. As a common denominator, the basic sequence of decisions was provided by Figure 3.

Your reflection of these various slides presenting practical tips: Write down what you can need best in your case. If desired, write what you would add to these methodical steps.

My improved methodology includes moreover ...

In your view, **what is needed** and **what are the targets** for science communication (SC) for Georgia?

---

*Needed is:*
- ...
- ...

*The most important 5 items from an initial perspective:*
o ...
o ...
o ...
o ...
o ...

*What are the targets for science communication (SC)?*
o ...
o ...
o ...

---

# 3. STARTING TO DRAFT SCIENCE COMMUNICATION ACTIVITIES

## 3.1 A Draft SWOT Analysis

The very current abbreviation SWOT (Investopedia, 2021, Mindtools, 2021) stands for **S**trengths, **W**eaknesses, **O**pportunities, and **T**hreats.

As an orientation, enter into Figure 6 the typical Strengths, Weaknesses, Opportunities, and Threats of present-day science communication in your country (4 items each). This will provide you a starting diagnosis.

## 3.2 A Draft Collection of Activities

A first rough collection and sequence of planned activities:

Before thinking about stakeholders (in ch. 4), the following planning of a preliminary sequence of activities is helpful:

---

*I preliminarily think of the following activities within science communication ...*
1. ...
2. ...
3. ...
4. ...
5. ...
6. ...

*Starting from the results provided earlier, how can these targets be achieved by 5 idealised measures for Science Communication?*
1. ...
2. ...
3. ...
4. ...
5. ...

---

*Figure 6. The fundamental and preliminary SWOT analysis to be filled in by the national expert, in order to quickly map all existing experts*

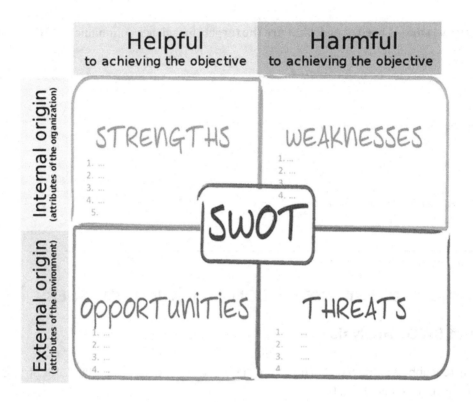

**Some first ideas** for SC performed by individual research groups (based on a series of nationally funded projects) for what SRNSFG could finance in a dedicated program (FWF, 2020a):

1. Popularisation of the results of projects financed by SRNSFG
2. YouTube channels with regular videos about finished SRNSFG-funded research, made by youth for youth
3. A biochemical laboratory for schools in collaborative manner (not only in presentation mode) where pupils can cooperate in everyday-compatible biochemistry experiments, e.g. immunobiology and house dust allergies
4. Scientific robot building for teachers and students: from the idea to the product – including image processing, social and ethical aspects
5. Pupils prepare scientific experiments within the frame of an "academy" under mentoring (FWF, 2020b)[2]
6. Cooking and tattooing in medieval times, mediated through videos[3]
7. Mountain lakes as geological archives
8. Virtual experiments on the gravitational effects of a quantum system[4]
9. Brain research hands-on: for youth and families to cooperate[5]
10. Astronomy to go: for children[6]
11. 'War of Pictures'. Press Photography in Austria 1945-1955[7]
12. Verbal aggression and social variables Gender - age - social status[8]

13. Breaking The Wall - Playful interfaces for audience participation and artistic expression in musical live performances: 3 Music Participation Days[9]
14. Grrrls! Making Art, Making Media, Making Change Camp[10]
15. Dance and Migration[11]
16. The virtual sand pit: industrial production technologies[12]
17. Sounds of Matter: Material physics and oscillations[13]
18. Human Sensors: Urban Emotions, Participatory Planning, Human Sensing, Social Media, Wearable Sensing, Science Communication
19. A new drive for wheelchairs[14]

---

*Explain which of the above ideas are suitable for your country and which not?*
- *...*

---

## 3.3 A Draft Management Cycle

A suggestion for a management procedure in SRNSFG in order to create and manage activities in science communication in shown in Figure 7.

In order to implement Georgian science communication in reality, what can be done to care for the following idealised steps in a cyclic (annual) management procedure? The following is suggested:

1. SRNSFG head legitimises the generation of ideas for science communication (SC) within SRNSFG and defines financial resources
2. The persons (or the department, in case it exists) responsible for SC create concrete and operational suggestions for action
3. Persons responsible for SC discuss these actions inside SRNSFG and includes improvements
4. Persons responsible for SC discuss actions with outside stakeholders, and include improvements
5. Persons responsible for SC implement concrete actions – while monitoring the success – and reports results to SRNSFG Director General, who triggers next, improved round of action; and to the Ministry.

As a next step, let us identify concrete stakeholders for a concrete "stakeholder process" on SC in Georgia, that enhances self-responsible work according to the pedagogic strategy of "scaffolding" (Naidu et al., 2003).

## 4. IDENTIFYING THE STAKEHOLDERS FOR SCIENCE COMMUNICATION ACTIVITIES

A concrete guide according to the "quintuple helix" model described earlier includes institutions and individual names. These will depend on the activity types, therefore start with the next planned type (Table 2).

*Figure 7. A suggestion for a management procedure in SRNSFG in order to create and manage activities in science communication*
*Source: own deliberation*

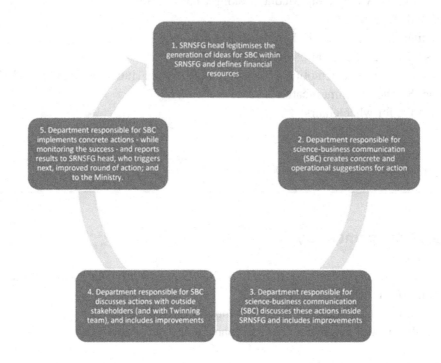

*Table 2. Detailed stakeholder selection process: how to identify cooperation partners*

| Stakeholder group | Where to find: some examples | Examples for concrete persons |
|---|---|---|
| Research & University | University list, ordered according to ranking<br>List of research institutions | Department leaders in charge for science communication and members of these departments, vice-deans.<br>Professors in pedagogy with dedicated interest<br>Your concrete names: … |
| Civil Society & NGOs | List of private and public schools<br>Educational NGOs<br>Educational, school children's and parents' initiatives<br>National UNESCO branches<br>Formal parent associations | NGOs already contacted for SC<br>Authors of educational books and brochures<br>Founders of societal initiatives<br>Actors within museums<br>Your concrete names: … |
| Industry & Enterprises | Heads of departments of proactive industry and commence<br>Founders of start-ups<br>Chamber of Commerce – international and communication departments | List of mentioned industry partners according to earlier EU projects in Georgia<br>Experienced clients of national innovation agencies and other cooperation programs to date<br>Your concrete names: … |
| Governance & Administration | Ministries responsible for science – and for economy<br>Ministries responsible for media<br>State agencies in science communication<br>Innovation agencies and similar actors | Developers of science communication plans during the last years<br>Department leaders<br>Conversation partners for earlier studies<br>Your concrete names: … |
| Media | Journalists in public and private media responsible for science<br>Young media founders<br>Georgia offices of international media channels such as YouTube, Wikipedia etc. | Radio and TV channels' journalists with a science leaning<br>Book authors<br>Authors of brochures on science<br>Your concrete names: … |

These personalities can be invited by an email, which is followed by a telephone call the next day. According to your plans, define a regular communication process with these stakeholders.

## 4.1 First Ideas for Concrete Actions: Prototyping SC

*Figure 8. Concrete actions*

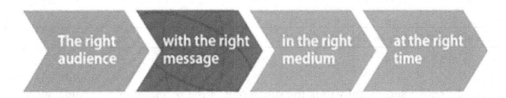

For the **targets** defined in the 1st workshop by SRNSFG, namely

1. attracting investors,
2. jointly working corporations,
3. for the aim of "Georgia needs development: social, cultural, economic, and in all direction",
4. and the needed SC types of "Knowledge, learning, personal & professional development" the following **questions** are asked and answered (see *Figure 3* on page 5, and above):
   - Who is the right audience? …
   - What is the right message? ...
   - What is the right medium? …
   - What is the right time? ...

**Identifying Georgian science stakeholders:** Whom do we know so far? the most important institutions within the five stakeholder groups are:

1. Research & University: …
2. Governance & Administration: …
3. Civil Society & NGOs: …
4. Media: …
5. Industry & Enterprises: ...

## 5. CONCRETE ACTION: COMMUNICATION MEDIUM, LANGUAGE, DESIGN AND STRUCTURE

### 5.1 Now We Proceed According to The Top 9 Tips For "Science Communication" Skills (Figure 5 Above):

Make sure you understand what your audience is interested in and adapt your communication.

**Step 1. Understand your audience.** *Put yourself in their shoes.* How your research affects their lives.

> *My audience wants to hear and see now this key message: …*
> *…*
> *… and this factual content: …*
> *… and this emotional message: …*

**Step 2. Build your message**. *What single idea should they leave the room with?* What do you want to achieve?

> *This single idea will stick in listeners' mind after the message: …*

Until now, the reader successfully took the standpoint of the *recipient* of communication.

**Step 3. Connect with the public**. *Why should they care about my work?* Convey emotion, make them laugh

Added to the content-related interest comes now the *emotional* level of the message, which is most crucial for any communicative success. What will make your communication *successful*?

> *The listeners care and are attracted about my message because …*

Until here, you are sure about all levels of communication from the side of the *recipient*.

At this stage, you might wish to take a step back and reflect on your project: Where do you find positive examples ("best practice" models) for successful communication? If it is attractive to you, find some in the web, or look at the selection on slide 61ff in the workshop ppt (Ahamer, 2020). Practical examples can inspire you for your next steps.

**Step 4. Tell your public a story**. *Storytelling humanises scientists* – they can be felt like "real, normal humans like you and me". Share a personal or professional anecdote to establish an individual *link of understanding* with your public.

**Step 5. Talk to journalists**. Start by understanding why they care about your research.

> *Convert your intended message into a story; this includes an evolving drama and narrative …*

It's a public service.

Journalists, when first hearing about your message, can be able to facilitate your conversion into a drama. They know that "communication" is a <u>service</u> of the author to the public.

> *After contact with a professional, I understand my concrete message and drama looks like this:*
> *…*

**Step 6. Make your science understandable**. We usually *overestimate* how familiar audience is with the topic. No jargon.

Use clear and short sentences. Subject + predicate + object. Streamline complex thoughts into simple language. Just as if you met your friend in the bus and tell them your everyday story among friends.

> *Look what I experienced – retell your **story** (not science) in brief, simple sentences*
> - ...
> - ...
> - ...

**Step 7. Deal with controversial topics**. Expect your public's preconceived ideas. Respect their opinion.

Just in case your story is politically or culturally sensitive, manage those sections and convert into non-hurting language.

> *Sensible text is here adapted to multiple convictions of readers, to optimise acceptance ...*
> - ...

**Step 8. Embrace uncertainty**. What is true today may not be as accurate tomorrow. *Uncertainty excites.*

Play with the imagination of your public in order to engage their phantasy and induce them to ponder on the theme further, and to mix it with their own dreams and expectations for a better future

*Why this message really starts to work within the readers'mind and phantasy ...*

Until here, you optimised your text through steps 4-8. Your initial story might persist, or might have been modify. Reflect on the past steps of improvement, and reconsider how this will help your idea.

**Step 9. Mix communication channels**. Articles, conference talks, press, social media, blogs, videos.

Now that the story is identified and optimised, we are now coming back to a main theme of chapter 3, namely "choose the suitable medium", and at the same time to the third of four blue arrows, namely "in the right medium".

## 5.2 Developing Concrete SC Projects for Georgia

1. <u>**Workshops**</u> with customers (.
2. <u>**Training**</u> for the foundation staff in <u>successful communication</u> with <u>business stakeholders</u> on <u>how to raise the interest</u>.
3. <u>**Green Deal**</u>: For awareness raising, popular <u>public lectures </u>for target groups.
4. Promotional materials and links to public information tools

5. Workshops / action for Horizon Europe project development (2-4 short workshops, for different target groups)

## 5.3 Planning of Concrete SC Projects for Georgia Could Have the Following Structure

Title of a selected measure

Scientific researchers with participation of school students
<u>Strategy and goals</u>: (up to 1 page)

The aim of the measure/call is to improve the quality of education of students of general education institutions, to bring education and research closer, to integrate research into the learning process; To interest schoolchildren in science through the popularization of research; Promoting the development of research skills among students; Increase teacher motivation to engage in student research; Increasing the interest of scientists, including young scientists (masters and doctoral students) in participating in the school process; Introducing innovations in the learning process that will help increase the efficiency of the work of general education institutions will help the student to understand the importance of this or that subject, which will increase his interest in science.

## 6. RECOMMENDATIONS FOR STAKEHOLDERS

First, perceive the "stakeholder landscape" in which you are situated Figure 8, and identify which relationship you have to each of them, and how you can optimise its efficiency.

*Figure 9. Stakeholder landscape for science communication: scientists, science journalists, PR officers*

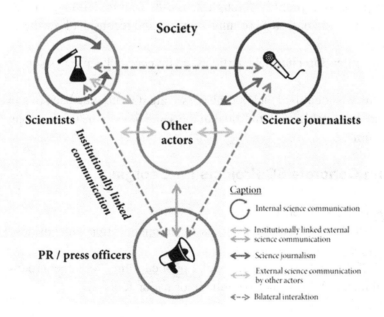

In this section, practical advice includes:

- Optimise search engine optimization (SEO) – and use one of the numerous tools available for free in the Internet, or ask a professional to do this for you
- Think of additional platforms, such as ResearchGate, LinkedIn etc.
- Find good examples on YouTube, such as Science Communication: It's No Joke!_and the other ones on slide 67 in the ppt
- Use The EU Guide to Science Communication
- Apply the supporting tips from Figure 9

And thus further improve your product, including showing it to your friends, family, schoolmates from decades ago, and colleagues – just in order to receive authentic reactions.

*Figure 10. Stakeholder landscape for science communication: scientists, science journalists, PR officers. Image Source: The EU Guide to Science Communication.*

After having viewed this and other publicly available material, define here the plans on how to promote and present science communication activities, and tick off what is already finished:

---

*Concrete actions of <u>promoting</u> and presenting science communication:*
1. Know your audience. ...
2. Identify the goals of communication. ...
3. Start with the most important information. ...
4. Avoid jargon. ...
5. Be relatable. ...
6. Provide visuals. ...
7. Stick to three points. ...
8. Talk about the scientific process.

---

## 7. A LIST OF SUGGESTED SCIENCE COMMUNICATION CHECKS AND QUALITY CRITERIA

If you need more inspiration, you may use a table to structure your science communication:

A.  **Ensure good management**
    1.  Have *resources* been allocated (time and money)?
    2.  Are *professional* communicators involved?
    3.  Is continuity ensured?
B.  **Define your goals and objectives**
    1.  Are there any goals and objectives?
    2.  Are your goals and objectives neither too ambitious nor too weak?
C.  **Pick your audience**
    1.  Is your audience well *defined*?
    2.  Does it include all relevant target groups?
D.  **Choose your message**
    1.  Is it news?
    2.  Are you connecting to what your audience wants to know?
        See through your audience's eyes
    3.  Are you connecting to your own communication objectives?
E.  **Use the right medium and means**
    1.  Do they reach the audience?
    2.  Do they go beyond the obvious?
F.  **Evaluate your efforts**

## CONCLUSION

This article proposes a dialogic procedure for creating "science communication guidelines" for a national science fund in countries of the European Neighbourhood.

Given the fact that no norm exists as to how such guidelines look like, a stepwise process of mutually agreeing on targets was embarked on, and these steps were documented by means of the present workbook.

From such workbook, a more formal text can be established in accordance with prevailing administrative frames.

## ACKNOWLEDGMENT

The author thanks for great collaboration within the EU Twinning Project to Georgia entitled "Supporting inter-sectoral collaboration possibilities between Research and Industry" (GE 18 ENI OT 02 19, within a part of this work was performed) and especially the Resident Twinning Advisor (RTA) Inese Gavarāne from the side of the EU Member States and the responsible for science communication Maka Kajaia from the side of the Twinning beneficiary, namely the Shota Rustaveli National Science Foundation of Georgia (SRNSFG).

# REFERENCES

Ahamer, G. (2008). Virtual Structures for mutual review promote understanding of opposed standpoints. *The Turkish Online Journal of Distance Education*, *9*(1), 17-43. https://tojde.anadolu.edu.tr/

Ahamer, G. (2013a). Quality assurance in transnational education management – the developmental "Global Studies" curriculum. In Handbook of Research on Transnational Higher Education Management. IGI Global. doi:10.4018/978-1-4666-4458-8.ch015

Ahamer, G. (2013b), GISS and GISP facilitate higher education and cooperative learning design. In Handbook of Research on Transnational Higher Education Management. IGI Global. doi:10.4018/978-1-4666-4458-8.ch001

Ahamer, G. (2020). *Workshop on science communication, in the frame of the science -business communication Twinning defined in ToR*. Available at https://www.researchgate.net/publication/345671729_Training_Insights_Design_of_science_communication_activities

Ahamer, G., & Mayer, J. (2013). Forward looking: Structural change and institutions in highest-income countries and globally. *Campus-Wide Information Systems*, *30*(5), 386–403. doi:10.1108/CWIS-08-2013-0034

Ahamer, G., & Schrei, C. (2004). Exercise 'Technology Assessment' through a gaming procedure. *Journal of Desert Research*, *5*(2), 224–252.

Aldin, N., Brehmer, P., & Johansson, A. (2004). Business development with electronic commerce: Refinement and repositioning. *Business Process Management Journal*, *10*(1), 44–62. doi:10.1108/14637150410518329

Artur, S. (2021). *How to communicate science without 'dumbing it down'*. American Association for the Advancement of Science AAAS. Available at https://www.aaas.org/programs/center-public-engagement-science-and-technology/reflections/how-communicate-science

ASCB. (2021). *Best Practices in Science Communication*. Available at.https://www.ascb.org/science-policy-public-outreach/science-outreach/communication-toolkits/best-practices-in-effective-science-communication/

Borrmann, M., Lindner, S., Hofer-Fischanger, K., Rehb, R., Pechstädt, K., Wiedenhofer, R., . . . Roller-Wirnsberger, R. E. (2020). Strategy for deployment of integrated healthy aging regions based upon an evidence-based regional Ecosystem—The styria model. *Frontiers in Medicine, 7*. doi:10.3389/fmed.2020.510475

Bowers, J. (2021). *Communicating science and inspiring audiences of different ages. La Fête de la Science*. Available at.https://www.hindawi.com/post/communicating-science-and-inspiring-audiences-different-ages/

Brown University. (2014) *Quick Guide to Science Communication*. Brown University Science Center. https://www.brown.edu/academics/science-center/sites/brown.edu.academics.science-center/files/uploads/Quick_Guide_to_Science_Communication_0.pdf

Brownell, S., Price, J. V., & Steinman, L. (2013). Science Communication to the General Public: Why We Need to Teach Undergraduate and Graduate Students this Skill as Part of Their Formal Scientific Training. *Journal of Undergraduate Neuroscience Education, 12*(1), E6–E10. https://www.researchgate.net/publication/259249951_Science_Communication_to_the_General_Public_Why_We_Need_to_Teach_Undergraduate_and_Graduate_Students_this_Skill_as_Part_of_Their_Formal_Scientific_Training PMID:24319399

Brubaker, A. (2021) *The impressionables: Science communication to engage children and teens.* DCSWA. https://dcswa.org/professional-development-day-2017/the-impressionables-science-communication-to-engage-children-and-teens/

Bulkeley, H., Coenen, L., Frantzeskaki, N., Hartmann, C., Kronsell, A., Mai, L., ... Voytenko Palgan, Y. (2016). Urban living labs: Governing urban sustainability transitions. *Current Opinion in Environmental Sustainability, 22*, 13–17. doi:10.1016/j.cosust.2017.02.003

Bultitude, K. (2011). The Why and How of Science Communication. In P. Rosulek (Ed.), *Science Communication*. European Commission. https://www.scifode-foundation.org/attachments/article/38/Karen_Bultitude_-_Science_Communication_Why_and_How.pdf

Carayannis, E. G., Acikdilli, G., & Ziemnowicz, C. (2019). Creative Destruction in International Trade: Insights from the Quadruple and Quintuple Innovation Helix Models. *Journal of the Knowledge Economy*. Advance online publication. doi:10.100713132-019-00599-z

Carayannis, E. G., Barth, T. D., & Campbell, D. F. J. (2012). The Quintuple Helix innovation model: global warming as a challenge and driver for innovation. *Economics, Journal of Innovation and Entrepreneurship, 1*(2). https://innovation-entrepreneurship.springeropen.com/articles/10.1186/2192-5372-1-2 doi:10.1186/2192-5372-1-2

Carayannis, E. G., & Campbell, D. F. J. (2014). *Developed Democracies versus Emerging*. https://www.amazon.com/Smart-Quintuple-Helix-Innovation-Systems/dp/3030015165

Chopra, D. (2019). *Metahuman: Unleashing Your Infinite Potential*. Harmony Books.

Cooke, S. J., Gallagher, A. J., Sopinka, N. M., Nguyen, V. M., Skubel, R. A., Hammerschlag, N., Boon, S., Young, N., & Danylchuk, A. J. (n.d.). Considerations for effective science communication. *FACETS, 2*, 233-248. https://www.facetsjournal.com/doi/10.1139/facets-2016-0055 doi:10.1139/facets-2016-0055

EC. (2021). *Science Communication*. https://ec.europa.eu/research/participants/documents/downloadPublic?documentIds=080166e5ccaa3072&appId=PPGMS

Eise, J. (2021). *What institutions can do to improve science communication*. https://www.nature.com/articles/d41586-019-03869-7

Etzkowitz, H. (2008), *The Triple Helix: University-Industry-Government Innovation in Action*. Routledge. https://www.amazon.com/Triple-Helix-University-Industry-Government-Innovation-Action/dp/0415964512

Farinha, L., Ferreira, J., & Gouveia, B. (2016). Networks of Innovation and Competitiveness: A Triple Helix Case Study. *Journal of the Knowledge Economy, 7*(1), 259–275. doi:10.100713132-014-0218-3

Fischhoff, B. (2019, April). Evaluating science communication. *Proceedings of the National Academy of Sciences of the United States of America, 116*(16), 7670–7675. doi:10.1073/pnas.1805863115 PMID:30478063

FWF. (2020a). *Science communication for selected funded projects.* Austrian Science Fund. https://www.fwf.ac.at/de/forschungsfoerderung/antragstellung/wisskomm

FWF. (2020b). *Science communication for selected funded projects.* Austrian Science Fund. https://pf.fwf.ac.at/de/wissenschaft-konkret/project_pdfs/pdf_abstracts/wkp14d.pdf

Hargittai, E., Füchslin, T., & Schäfer, M. S. (2018). How Do Young Adults Engage With Science and Research on Social Media? Some Preliminary Findings and an Agenda for Future Research. *Social Media + Society, 4*(3). Advance online publication. doi:10.1177/2056305118797720

IIASA. (2021). *Science Communication Fellowship.* https://iiasa.ac.at/web/home/about/workingatiiasa/Science_Communication_Fellowship.html

Imaginis. (2020). *B2B marketing.* https://www.imaginisbd.com/step-1-of-b2b-marketing-catch-the-attention-of-the-right-people/

Investopedia. (2021). *SWOT analysis.* https://www.investopedia.com/terms/s/swot.asp

Könneker, C. (2021). *Young Researchers and Science Communication: Results of an Extensive Survey.* Lindau Nobel Laureate Meeting. https://www.lindau-nobel.org/de/blog-young-researchers-and-science-communication/

Kuehne, L. M., Twardochlieb, L. A., Fritschie, K. J., Mims, M. C., Lawrence, D. J., Gibson, P. P., Stewart-Koster, B., & Olden, J. D. (2014). Practical Science Communication Strategies for Graduate Students. *Conservation Biology, 28*(5), 1225–1235. doi:10.1111/cobi.12305 PMID:24762116

Lindberg, M., Lindgren, M., & Packendorff, J. (2014). Quadruple Helix as a Way to Bridge the Gender Gap in Entrepreneurship: The Case of an Innovation System Project in the Baltic Sea Region. *Journal of the Knowledge Economy, 5*(1), 94–113. doi:10.100713132-012-0098-3

Loroño-Leturiondo, M., & Davies, S. R. (2018). Responsibility and science communication: Scientists' experiences of and perspectives on public communication activities. *Journal of Responsible Innovation, 5*(2), 170–185. doi:10.1080/23299460.2018.1434739

Marquis, A., & Wilber, K. (2008). Unification beyond eclecticism and integration: Integral psychotherapy. *Journal of Psychotherapy Integration, 18*(3), 350–358. doi:10.1037/a0013560

Mindtools. (2021). *SWOT analysis.* https://www.mindtools.com/pages/article/newTMC_05.htm

Motała, D., Pawłowski, E., Pawłowski, K., & Tzcieliński, S. (2008). Designing an effective management system for enterprises: Concepts and verification. *Human Factors and Ergonomics in Manufacturing, 18*(5), 525–547. doi:10.1002/hfm.20123

Naidu, S., Ip, A., & Linser, R. (2003). *Dynamic Goal-Based Role-Play Simulation on the Web: A Case Study.* Univ. of Melbourne. https://www.roleplaysim.org/papers/Naidu_etal.html

Nature Career Brief. (2021). *Toolkit: How to work in science communication.* https://www.nature.com/articles/d41586-019-01359-4

Newcastle University. (2021). *Science Communication. Support for communicating your research to a range of audiences, and identifying communication routes.* Available at https://libguides.ncl.ac.uk/sciencecommunication

Research International. (2021). *Science and the Public: Mapping Science Communication Activities.* Available at https://assets.publishing.service.gov.uk/government/uploads/system/uploads/attachment_data/file/260650/science-and-public-mapping-science-communication-activities.pdf

Schäfer, M. (2020). *The science of science communication: Why it matters.* https://www.hindawi.com/post/science-science-communication-why-it-matters

Seiler, L. M. (2021). *Mögest du glücklich sein.* Komplett Medien GmbH.

Steiner, M., & Hartmann, C. (2006). Organizational learning in clusters: A case study on material and immaterial dimensions of cooperation. *Regional Studies, 40*(5), 493–506. doi:10.1080/00343400600757494

The Blue Reporters. (2017). *A study shows: Public is interested in science.* http://www.thebluereporters.com/2017/06/public-science-communication-2/

ToR. (2020). *Terms of Reference of the Twinning Project entitled "Supporting inter-sectoral collaboration possibilities between Research and Industry"* (GE 18 ENI OT 02 19). https://um.fi/documents/385176/0/Twinning+fiche+GE+18+ENI+OT+02+19.pdf/ba9da89b-06a1-1c05-4787-74f3224f9d85?t=1566808809072

Wilber, K. (1993). The great chain of being. *Journal of Humanistic Psychology, 33*(3), 52–65. doi:10.1177/00221678930333006

Wilber, K. (1997). An integral theory of consciousness. *Journal of Consciousness Studies, 4*(1), 71–92.

Wilber, K. (2000). Waves, streams, states and self: Further considerations for an integral theory of consciousness. *Journal of Consciousness Studies, 7*(11-12), 145–176.

Wilber, K. (2005). Toward A comprehensive theory of subtle energies. *Explore (New York, N.Y.), 1*(4), 252–270. doi:10.1016/j.explore.2005.04.016 PMID:16781546

Youth Stem. (2021). *Guidance for Science Communication Articles.* Youth Stem Matters. Available at https://www.youthstem2030.org/ysm-submit/science-communication-article

## ENDNOTES

[1] Including Joanneum Research (JR), Austria, the Austrian Science Fund (FWF), Austria, the Austria Research Promotion Agency (FFG), Austria, German Aerospace Center (DLR) Project Management Agency, Germany, and Daugavpils University (DU), Latvia.

[2] see https://pf.fwf.ac.at/de/wissenschaft-konkret/project_pdfs/pdf_abstracts/wkp14d.pdf

[3] See https://pf.fwf.ac.at/de/wissenschaft-konkret/project_pdfs/pdf_abstracts/wkp115d.pdf

[4] See https://pf.fwf.ac.at/de/wissenschaft-konkret/project_pdfs/pdf_abstracts/wkp143d.pdf

[5] See https://pf.fwf.ac.at/de/wissenschaft-konkret/project_pdfs/pdf_abstracts/wkp87d.pdf

[6] See https://pf.fwf.ac.at/de/wissenschaft-konkret/project_pdfs/pdf_abstracts/wkp80d.pdf

[7] See https://pf.fwf.ac.at/de/wissenschaft-konkret/project_pdfs/pdf_abstracts/wkp43d.pdf

[8] See https://pf.fwf.ac.at/de/wissenschaft-konkret/project_pdfs/pdf_abstracts/wkp98d.pdf
[9] See https://pf.fwf.ac.at/de/wissenschaft-konkret/project_pdfs/pdf_abstracts/wkp126d.pdf
[10] See https://pf.fwf.ac.at/de/wissenschaft-konkret/project_pdfs/pdf_abstracts/wkp10d.pdf
[11] See https://pf.fwf.ac.at/de/wissenschaft-konkret/project_pdfs/pdf_abstracts/wkp32d.pdf
[12] See https://pf.fwf.ac.at/de/wissenschaft-konkret/project_pdfs/pdf_abstracts/wkp67d.pdf
[13] See https://pf.fwf.ac.at/de/wissenschaft-konkret/project_pdfs/pdf_abstracts/wkp84d.pdf
[14] See https://pf.fwf.ac.at/de/wissenschaft-konkret/project_pdfs/pdf_abstracts/wkp130d.pdf

# International Trade, Economic Growth, and Turkey

**Aytaç Gökmen**
*Çankaya University, Turkey*

## BACKGROUND OF THE STUDY

The debate over whether international trade spur economic development or economic development spur international trade has long been on the agenda of economists. The existence of exports as an instigator of economic growth dates back to the times of mercantilism which accentuates the conformity of international trade. Since then, numerous authors have in a similar manner emphasized the importance of international trade for the development of a country. For example, the classical economists manifested that trade instigates growth in essentially bilateral ways. On the one hand, the increase in exports accommodate for more optimal distribution of sources and afterwards enhance productivity. Moreover, the classicals believed that by means of international trade, a state may acquire the necessary raw materials and equipment which it is not able to manufacture by itself. This transfer of materials serves a profound means of economic development. Identically, in his theory of exports of surplus, Adam Smith denoted that by managing to export the commodities of excess capacity or simply widening the market, the productivity of a country could increase, thereby concluding in an increase in the wealth of a nation. Consequently, Ricardo postulated that exports would enable specialization as a state shall manufacture and trade in those commodities in which it has got a competitive advantage. A widening scale of production should be probable and thereby, economies of scale would be comprised. Nonetheless, one may identify five ways in which a country's international trade could favorably impact on the economy with the; revenue effect, capital accumulation effect, substitution affect, income distribution affect and weighted elements effect. When aggregated altogether, these effects of exports reinforce the economic development gradually. Additionally, rising export earnings should lead to the ease of constraints on growth by improving the capacity of trading fundamental inputs in the form of intermediate and capital goods. Therefore, one could conclude that an increase in the volume of exports foster capital accumulation and economic growth consequently (Sannassee et al., 2014).

## INTRODUCTION

International trade can be postulated as a potential stimulator of a country's economic growth. The value and volume of commerce fostering economic growth has been ascribed to several factors involving more efficient utilization of sources, employing economies of scale and labor training, fostered technological change and moving investments towards more productive sectors and businesses. While, the export-leg growth (ELG) hypothesis indicates that exports necessarily promote economic growth, the import-led growth (ILG) hypothesis stands for economic growth would be stimulated by growth in imports. Imports do not only cause to long-run economic growth by catering endogenous businesses with access to the

DOI: 10.4018/978-1-7998-9220-5.ch038

necessary inputs and foreign technology, but also act as a medium for transfer of growth-developing foreign research and development (R&D) knowledge from developed to developing states (Bastola & Sapkota, 2015).

The correlation among international trade, commercial openness and economic growth have been debated over the years. Commerce enables the integration with the resources of innovation and developed gains from foreign direct investment. By rising the size of the market, international trade enables economies better utilize the possible benefits of increasing returns to scale and economies of specialization. Trade openness enhances the transfer of new technologies, lead to technological progress and productivity development as well as these advantages rest on the degree of openness. Foreign trade and economic growth are based on the premise that trade constitutes economic incentives which fosters productivity by two dynamics; in the short-run, trade diminishes resource misallocation and; in the long-run, it enables the transfer of technological improvement. Commercial development could also cause governments to commit reform programs under the pressure of international rivalry, thus achieve economic development. Nevertheless, commercial development policies act as an important role in accomplishing higher growth as well as human development. Commercial improvement in in developing countries has thus been implemented with the expectation of growth promotion. Moreover, macroeconomic stability and advantageous investment environment shall supplement to trade development (Egbetunde & Obamuyi, 2018).

The correlation between openness of an economy and economic growth are two considerable issues for development of a country. While on the one hand, one can state that a nation's openness can attract more investment and improve its commercial potential, on the other hand, international trade causes faster growth and increase income per capita. Henceforth, more opened and outward-oriented economies consistently outperform states restrictive commercial policies and foreign investment regimes (Cieslik & Tarselewsak, 2011). Moreover, the aim of this paper first to analyze the importance and correlation of international trade and economic growth also involving the foreign investments and their impact on the commercial development, then scrutinize the international trade and economic growth issues in particular of Turkey.

## 1. INTERNATIONAL TRADE, ECONOMIC GROWTH & THEIR CORRELATION: A THEORETICAL APPRAISAL

The accomplishment of sustainable economic growth is one of the most important priority of any country, especially the developing ones. Recently, international trade has been noticed as one of the significant factors which designates economic growth in the world. Institutions such as the World Trade Organization (WTO), International Monetary Fund (IMF), United Nations (UN) and Organization for Economic Cooperation and Development (OECD) consistently promote countries, especially the developing ones to emphasize growth sequences by means of trade liberalization in order to assure expected growth at increasing rates. Foreign trade is a significant factor of the gross domestic product (GDP) especially in developed and emerging countries, that enhances the economic growth of a state. One can state that international trade contributes positively to the economic growth of a country by means of benefits from economies of scale particularly in small and developing countries; promotes competition through efficiency; and fosters the transfer of knowledge. International trade is a necessary source of foreign exchange that is needed for the importation of intermediate and capital items needed for domestic production. International trade also ensures access to new technology, different varieties of consumer goods as well as increases capacity to enhance productivity, employment and economic growth. The increasing volume of exportation is beneficial for a country and desirable. Yet, the debate on import is two-fold. On the contrary to exports, too much of importation worsens foreign exchange volume of a country and commercial balance, which causes lower economic growth. Besides, in some instances, importation is considered as a growth-promoting factor, especially to acquire capital items, technology and knowledge. Therefore, international trade facilitates the goods, services and factors move across the frontiers and emerge as a considerable factor of economic growth and development (Safiyanu & Chua, 2020; Cieslik & Tarselewsak, 2011).

None of the countries in the globe is able to manufacture everything by itself, because, the nature has not gifted each and every country with the same productive sources. Therefore, each and every country are supposed to be based on international trade to meet the necessities of its citizens. International trade is the exportation and importation of goods, services and technology among countries in the world. Exportation and importation have an indispensable role in the growth of an economy. Increasing volume of exports assists countries to widen the scale of production to acquire economies of scale, to manufacture qualitative and quantitative products as well as help economies to obtain foreign exchange reserves which in turn help importation of technology, capital and rare raw materials which enhances international competitiveness and fostering bargaining power. ELG approach and the idea behind the ELG is that increasing volume of exports instigates the investment and production capacity which later fortifies the productivity and causes effective and efficient utilization of resources and instigates international competitiveness. While exports are important for a country, on the other hand, importation may have positive results. By means of importing commodities which are costlier to manufacture in home country, countries do not only save financial resources, but also save the necessary time that is essential to produce goods and services to be used in the exportation process (Kumari, 2014).

International trade plays a significant role in the development of both developing and developed countries. Entire states in the world are interdependent because of different distribution of resources. International trade is not only indispensable, but also cater for the improvement of the economic situations of countries. Therefore, international trade and especially export promotion are beneficial in various aspects such as (Afzal, 2006):

- Better capacity utilization, improvement in economies of scale and greater technical improvement.
- Spill-over effects due to better utilization of labor, knowledge and technology.
- Positive reflections on the balance of payments deficits and foreign exchange shortages especially in developing countries.
- International trade widens the markets, enhances the division of labor, fosters technical innovation and thus countries enjoy better returns on scale.

Export markets are almost boundless and do not have limitations on growth with respect to the demand side. Henceforth, exports could be regarded as an important medium of development in income and as a factor of aggregate demand. Moreover, the impact from the demand side could also be considered as an increase in exports and may finally influence growth by means of the provision of foreign exchange that causes for the increase in imports of capital goods. Additionally, an increase in the importation of capital goods conclude in improving capital formation and, in turn, lead to the promotion of output and production growth. The importation of capital goods from technologically more advanced states may improve the volume of outputs and, thus, overall economic growth, such as imported machinery and equipment involve technology and knowledge and thereby transferred by means of international trade.

Nevertheless, there is a positive impact of exports on GDP growth rate resulting from technology diffusion and augmentation in the efficiency of factors of production to a higher extent, stemming from exports producing industry to non-exporting industries (Ali & Li, 2018).

Export growth and export expansion could be hypothesized to make several fundamental contributions to economic growth. These could be termed as (Zang & Baimbridge, 2012):

- First, higher volume of exports could lead to decreasing the exchange constraint and higher volume of the importation of capital and intermediate goods could be acquired.
- Second, the home country would be able to concentrate investments in the sectors in which it enjoys comparative advantage.
- Third, having access to international markets could lead to economies of scale in the export sector.
- Forth, export growth could be an indicator of an increase in the demand for a country's output and thereby, serves to enhance real output by procuring a means which a country could enjoy new technologies and new ideas.
- Eventually, export growth shall instigate greater savings and investment volume which prompts overall economic growth.

As one could postulate that economic growth could cause the improvement of the capabilities and technology which constitutes a comparative advantage and thus, enables an increase in exports, while higher output growth shall prompt higher investment, that is a part which can be a reason for the increase in the export capacity. Output growth which is induced by export growth may stimulate productivity growth and this shall make goods more competitive and gives impetus to export growth. Besides, when an economy acquires a growth advantage, it would be inclined to keep it, thereby enhancing its overall economic potential (Zang & Baimbridge, 2012). First part of the study is focused on the issue of international trade and its dichotomy of exports and imports comprehensively. Next section is on the correlation of international trade with foreign investments and finance.

## 2. EXPORTS, IMPORTS, FOREIGN DIRECT INVESTMENTS & FINANCE

Foreign direct investment (FDI) inflows have generally a favorable impact on host countries' economic affairs and development initiatives by means of inflow of valuable technology and know-how which along with the efforts of local businesses can help the economy obtain momentum. Nevertheless, international trade also acts as a catalyst of economic growth by inducing more efficient production of goods and services, along with offshoring production to countries which enjoy comparative advantage in manufacturing them. Resting on specific factors like the level of human capital, domestic investment, infrastructural development of the host country, macroeconomic stability as well as commercial and institutional policies introduced by the government of the host country impact on the inflow of FDI inflow and trade on the economic growth of the host countries. Nevertheless, since a host country receives more capital, knowledge, know-how, contemporary technology and etc. by means of FDI, it would be favorable to benefit from such resources for the development of the commercial potential (Bhattacharya, 20110).

The new theory of growth has indicated that the role of exports in growth processes might cause economies of scale. Developing countries which previously applied to import substitution, industrialization have enjoyed rapid growth by turning their focus on ELG. FDI has both direct and indirect effect on exports. Multinational businesses could be one of the sources to enhance exports at least in the short-run, especially for domestic businesses lacking basic capabilities. Multinational businesses could help to keep businesses up-to-date with respect to consumer demand international safety requirements and distribution standards. Identically, vertical integration through intra-business as well as deals between foreign and local businesses increase the volume of FDI and exports of local businesses. The direct correlation between FDI and exports includes the effect of FDI on competitiveness of domestic businesses by modern technology. Since multinational businesses enjoy specific advantage of consumer choice, market information and government support, they could instigate the efficiency of host country businesses through new means of production and processing. The export volume of domestic businesses would increase when multinational businesses purchase more inputs from the endogenous markets. Furthermore, FDI could be regarded as the fundamental source of technology spillovers, quality production and enhanced exports from domestic businesses (Ahmad et al. 2018).

FDI and exports contribute to economic growth by numerous channels. Both, the neoclassical and endogenous approaches stimulate the positive impact of FDI on economic growth. The impact of FDI on export could be twofold. First, FDI prompts the integration of new inputs and modern technologies through capital accumulation in host countries. Second, by means of knowledge transfers, FDI instigates the available stock of human capital by training, skill acquisition and developments in managerial capacities. FDI could influence long-run development by generating cumulative income in production with spillover effects. Similarly, domestic businesses can benefit from the technological advantage of multinational businesses by means of learning-by-doing. This would eventually increase rivalry in domestic markets and enables human capital movement, thereby, augmenting the output volume and sustain a greater growth in host countries. Especially for developing countries, with limited industrial infrastructure, FDI has the potential to access export markets and to enable to import of the intermediary and capital goods which ultimately increases the exports level and economic growth. In turn, the growth-led FDI hypothesis emphasizes the availability of efficient growing markets, skilled human capital as well as enhanced political, social and industrial infrastructure to attract a great deal of foreign inflows. Fast economic growth increases the volume of aggregate production, market depth and aggregate demand which instigates the inflows of capital involving FDI in the host country (Ahmad et al. 2018; Cieslik & Tarselewsak, 2011).

The world has experienced an unprecedented period of international trade and FDI liberalization as well as may international development organizations agree that external openness would cause an augmented volume of economic growth. According to IMF, the policies towards free trade are among the more significant elements instigating economic growth and convergence in developing economies. On the other hand, OECD reports that more open and out-ward oriented economies consistently outperform states with restraining commerce and foreign investment regimes. Identically, the World Bank states that international trade unleashes unprecedented opportunity for growth and development. Eventually, the UN reports that FDI contributes towards financing sustained economic growth in the long-run (Cieslik & Tarselewsak, 2011).

The impact of financial markets on economic growth has attracted substantial attention, especially with reads to comprehensive development strategies. Effective contributions on the finance-growth nexus denote financial development as a significant precondition in the long-run economic growth, meaning that financial sector development is a crucial means of economic policy. Financial markets ensure an economy with vital services involving, for instance, the management of risk and formation as well as pooling and mobilization of savings. More comprehensive and efficient deeper financial systems provide the real sector more effectively with financial services. Linkages between financial and economic development could take different forms. On the one hand, the financial sector could impact on the economic growth by means of the accumulation channel or allocational channel. This capital accumulation could lead to increasing savings and become a source for international trade activities. Moreover, the accumulation of channel implies the finance-induced economic growth effect of physical and human capital accumulation. The allocation channel orients on the financed-induces efficiency gains in resource allocation which improve economic growth. On the other hand, financial development could also be instigated by economic growth. For example, in a growing economy, the private sector shall demand new financial instruments and a developed access to external finance. Financial operations then simply expand the step with general economic improvement positioning which could be termed as demand-following hypothesis. The real sector could reassure the financial system with the funds necessary to manage financial deepening, finally allowing for a capitalization on financial economies of scale which in turn facilitates economic development (Gries et al., 2011; Rahman et al., 2015).

A possible relationship between finance and trade opens up a further channel by means of which financial systems and real sectors might interact. On the one hand, better financial systems could generate a comparative advantage for industrial sectors which heavily rely on external financing. Countries with developed financial systems are expected to present commercial structures linked to finance-dependent industry sectors. On the other hand, increased trade openness might instigate demand for new financial sectors, for instance, with respect to risk diversification, trade insurance or financing in the face of international trade and international competition. States with better financial systems present higher trade shares in industries which are based on external finance, as a result, finance is a fundamental determinant of international trade. The interaction between finance and trade openness also enables for more sophisticated ways to economic development. If finance stimulates trade openness, it might subsequently instigate economic growth when openness is found to be an economic growth factor. For example, economic openness might stimulate economic growth by improving a country's level of specialization. On the other hand, economic development could also prompt trade openness, for instance, by means of shifts in production and demand patterns as well as increased levels of international integration accompanying with industrialization experiences (Gries et al., 2011; Rahman et al., 2015).

## 3. INTERNATIONAL TRADE, ECONOMIC GROWTH & TURKEY: A CONTEMPORARY ANALYSIS

The issue of economic growth has always been on the agenda of both developed and developing countries. Since Adam Smith's economic theory, international trade has been regarded as a fundamental contributor to the growth of the global economy and even more important role in developing and emerging economies. The main factor lying under the ELG paradigm was the exception for growth in national output parallel to quick export growth. If this situation is evaluated with respect to Turkey, in 1980s, Turkey had adjusted international trade regime of its economy into export-led economic growth policy. Since then, international trade extension, especially exports, have lead the economy through alleviating balance of payments constraints, restoring the confidence of the international financial institutions and external creditors as well as instigating efficient economic growth. After the 1980s, improving international trade, and declining foreign trade deficit, by especially increasing exports, utilizing permanent devaluation strategy and extensive export promotions, became the priority of economic policies. Nonetheless, in post-1980s era, an increase in exports were acquired for a short time and then a fluctuating trend dominated the growth of exports (Bahramian & Saliminezhad, 2020; Güvercin, 2020).

*Table 1. Main economic indicators for the Republic of Turkey (billion USDs)*

| | 2009 | 2010 | 2011 | 2012 | 2013 | 2014 | 2015 | 2016 | 2017 | 2018 | 2019 | 2020 |
|---|---|---|---|---|---|---|---|---|---|---|---|---|
| **GDP¹** | 647 | 772 | 775 | 789 | 823 | 799 | 718 | 863 | 852 | 714 | 784,8 | 706,3 |
| **GDP per Capita (thousand)** | 8890 | 10560 | 11205 | 11588 | 12480 | 12112 | 11019 | 10883 | 10602 | 9632 | 9,117 | 9042 |
| **CPI²ᵂ** | 6,5 | 6,4 | 10,5 | 6,2 | 7,4 | 8,2 | 8,8 | 8,5 | 11,9 | 20,3 | 11,84 | 11,89 |
| **WPI³ᵂ** | 5,9 | 8,9 | 13,3 | 2,5 | 7,0 | 6,4 | 5,7 | 9,9 | 15,5 | 33,6 | 7,36 | 14,33 |
| **Unemployment Rate %** | 13,1 | 11,1 | 9,1 | 8,4 | 9,0 | 9,9 | 10,3 | 10,9 | 10,9 | 11,0 | 13,7 | 13,4 |
| **Export** | 102,1 | 113,9 | 134,9 | 152,5 | 151,8 | 157,6 | 143,8 | 142,5 | 157,1 | 168 | 132,7 | 118,3 |
| **Import** | 140,9 | 185,5 | 240,8 | 236,5 | 251,7 | 242,2 | 207,2 | 198,6 | 233,8 | 223,0 | 153,8 | 156,1 |
| **Foreign Trade Balance** | -38,8 | -71,7 | -105,9 | -84,1 | -99,9 | -84,6 | -63,4 | -56,1 | -76,7 | -55,0 | -21,1 | -37,3 |
| **Current Account Balance** | -11,4 | -44,6 | ,74,4 | -48,0 | -63,6 | -43,6 | -32,1 | -32,6 | -47,1 | -27,8 | -25,1 | -29,7 |
| **FDI⁴** | 8,6 | 9,1 | 16,2 | 13,6 | 12,9 | 12,8 | 17,6 | 14,0 | 11,5 | 13,0 | 12,4 | 8,06 |
| **Foreign Debt Stock** | 268,7 | 291,6 | 303,7 | 339,5 | 339,8 | 401,9 | 396,1 | 404,2 | 453,2 | 444,9 | 436,9 | 435,8 |

**Source**: Turkish Statistical Institute, Central Bank of the Republic of Turkey, Ministry of Finance and Treasury and Ministry of Commerce.

Table 1 reflects the situation with respect to the Turkish economy. The GDP has been increasing since 2009 but it began to decline after 2016. Moreover, the GDP per capita had considerably declined after 2017. Both wholesale price index and consumer price index have two digit numbers which cannot be accepted as a healthy economy. Unemployment rates are in two digits and 1 in every 4 young citizens are unemployed. All among, two of the most important figures are export and import figures. The volume of export has been rising for almost a decade. Yet, when the situation is evaluated with respect to imports, the volume of imports accedes beyond exports which lead to a foreign trade deficit. As one can view in Table 1, the negative balance between exports and imports is considerable. Financing this negative trade balance is a question mark. One source to finance this this negative trade balance could be attracting more foreign direct investment and/or foreign debt. However, the FDI volume which is received is far from covering the trade deficit and the volume of international debt stock is substantial. Therefore, Turkey has got to develop industries which it can enjoy specialization and focus on core competence in developed industries. Thus, one can state that international trade volume of Turkey is not good enough to cover its negative trade balance and its foreign debt stock. Exports makes up the opportunity for nations which enjoy negative trade balance to go further than the restricted home markets and to infiltrate over the economies of scale. It also facilitates foreign exchange inflow and improves output development by increasing capital formation by means of expanded imports of intermediate goods. Also, due to intense competition in the global market, the development of exports improved efficient resource allocation and capacity utilization. Furthermore, the growth exports contribute to enhancing the transfer of know-how by interacting with foreign businesses (Bahramian & Saliminezhad, 2020). In the case of Turkey, a considerable part of the imports within the total international trade volume are intermediate and capital goods which cannot be produced in Turkey. Therefore, by importing the intermediate and capital goods, it is very difficult for Turkey have access to new technologies and know-how, which in turn may give

Turkey a competitive advantage in the global markets. Also, since there is a negative trade balance, an increase in the foreign exchange volume and capital formation shall not be expected.

With economic growth, the level of social welfare would increase fast and in a stable manner. Most of the studies in scientific literature indicate that international trade, especially exports, is a determining factor of economic growth. In most of the studies made, the growth of an economy is from exports to economic growth. However, it is difficult to state this for Turkey. It is evident in Table 1 that export volume is behind the import volume substantially which contradicts with the export-led economic growth hypothesis. On the other hand, whether the imports trigger the exports by means of indispensable inputs is another issue of debate. Moreover, in order to stabilize the sequence of exporting as well as increase both the volume and diversity of export commodities, export markets and exported goods and services shall be diversified. Nonetheless, for the diversification of exports within the total international trade volume and diversification of commodities are indicators of sustainability. Along with the diversification of export commodities, the diversification of export markets is also important. When the export destinations are diversified, countries would preserve the stability in their export income. Moreover, the diversification of exports shall instigate economic growth and income per capita. However, in the case of Turkey, exports are far behind the imports. The main destination of exports is the European Union (EU) which applies strict rules for receiving imported commodities from Turkey. Thus, commodities falling short of these standards cannot realize the expected export-led growth hypothesis. Yet, the diversity of the Turkish products is significant. The main export products manufactured by Turkey are automotive, chemical components, textiles, steel, electronics, other metals, machine and components, and furniture[5]. The diversity of exportation is significant with respect to the sustainability of the economic growth for both developed and developing countries. Therefore, these countries shall not disregard the diversification of exports within the overall commercial volume. The diversification of exportation stimulates economic growth and then economic growth induces social welfare (Erbay & Aktuna, 2019; Altun & Benli, 2021). Therefore, the increase in the volume of both volume and diversification of exports have positive impact on economic growth. However, when Table 1 is considered, there is a trade deficit and GDP volume declines. With respect to these figures, it is possible to state that the Turkish economy is prone to external shocks.

Exportation could facilitate the optimal distribution of national resources to more effectively within the framework of international trade. Accordingly, the optimal distribution of resources by means of exporting would facilitate states to obtain comparative advantage over themselves. By all means, increasing competition and economies of scale would lead to effectiveness and efficiency in production. Foreign exchange obtained by exportation would facilitate the importation of intermediate and capital goods which cannot be produced domestically and GDP volume may increase. Nonetheless, there is decline in the volume of overall GDP from 2017 to 2020. The sequence keeps decline along with GDP per capita. In this vein, whether there will be an increase in the foreign exchange savings is a question mark. Moreover, the foreign exchange stock in the Central Bank diminishes[6]. An increase in exportation instigates the demand for its output as well as causes an increase in GDP and consumption. Nevertheless, exportation entails exporting countries acquire or manufacture the necessary technology that is indispensable for increasing international trade volume. Therefore, international trade and especially exportation are essential for a country to develop (Yapraklı, 2007; Güvercin, 2020). In this vein, the Republic of Turkey does its best to enhance its commercial potential. Yet, whether it does good-enough is a question mark. As Table 1 is viewed, some figures are good enough and some figures shall be developed. However, since Turkey is one of the twenty largest economy in the world, it will do its best to achieve a substantial trade volume, acquire competitive advantage, obtain foreign exchange reserves, diversify commercial goods and improve overall GDP.

## FUTURE RESEARCH DIRECTIONS

This is an eclectic article which deals on foreign trade, economics and relation to the economic growth in Turkey. International trade is quite important for Turkey since, many of the goods and services cannot be produced in Turkey. However, there is a grave situation with regards to this issue. The Republic of Turkey has always had a negative trade balance, meaning that this deficit shall be compensated with other financial sources, namely foreign direct investment (FDI). Yet, the inflow FDI in Turkey is not enough. Therefore, the future direction and research of a new paper could be the issue of FDI inflow and economic growth in Turkey.

## CONCLUSION

The Republic of Turkey is at the threshold of Eurasia converging east with the west and north with south as well as one of the twenty largest economies in the world. Turkey is at the crossroads of various trade routes. Therefore, the Turkish economy is one of the sound ones in Europe, Eurasia and the Middle East. However, none of the economies in the world, whether developed or developing, is free from commercial and economic issues as well as self-sufficient. International trade is beneficial for a country with respect to diversifying commercial commodities, saving of foreign exchange, obtainment of technology and know-how as well as obtainment of capital and intermediary goods which cannot be manufactured alone with domestic resources. When the situation is evaluated with respect to Turkey, it has an increasing GDP rate that over the years, yet it has been in decline in the recent years. This is also true for its GDP per capita. Moreover, Turkey enjoys has a commercial volume in which imports exceed exports. This means that the difficultly earned currency is spent on imported products. Whether the imported products (capital + intermediate goods) improve the technology and know-how is a question mark. On the other hand, since there is negative trade balance as a result of imports exceeding exports, the desired economic growth level may not be acquired. Therefore, one can state that instead of following an export led-growth strategy, Turkey might be following an import-led economic growth strategy. However, these assumptions are controversial and shall be the subject of another study.

## REFERENCES

Afzal, M. (2006). Causality between Exports, World Income and Economic Growth in Pakistan. *International Economic Journal*, *20*(1), 63–77. doi:10.1080/10168730500515399

Ahmad, F., Draz, M. U., & Yang, S.-C. (2018). Causality nexus of exports, FDI and economic growth of the ASEAN5 economies: Evidence from panel data analysis. *The Journal of International Trade & Economic Development*, *27*(6), 685–700. doi:10.1080/09638199.2018.1426035

Ali, G., & Li, Z. (2018). Exports-led growth or growth-led exports in the case of China and Pakistan: An empirical investigation from the ARDL and Granger causality approach. *The International Trade Journal*, *32*(3), 293–314. doi:10.1080/08853908.2017.1379449

Altun, M., & Benli, M. (2021). Export Product Diversification and Growth Performance of Turkey. *Dumlupınar University Journal of Social Sciences*, *67*, 138–158.

Bahramian, P., & Saliminezhad, A. (2020). On the relationship between export and economic growth: A nonparametric causality-in-quantiles approach for Turkey. *The Journal of International Trade & Economic Development*, *29*(1), 131–145. doi:10.1080/09638199.2019.1648537

Bastola, U., & Sapkoata, P. (2015). Causality between trade and economic growth in a least developed country: Evidence from Nepal. *Journal of Developing Areas*, *49*(4), 197–213. doi:10.1353/jda.2015.0138

Bhattacharya, M. (2010). Causal nexus between trade, FDI and economic growth – evidence from India. *Paradigm*, *14*(1), 12–23.

Cieslik, A., & Tarselewska, M. (2011). External Openness and Economic Growth in Developing Countries. Review of growth in the world. *Economies*, *15*(4), 729–744.

Egbetunde, T., & Obamuyi, T. M. (2018). Foreign Trade and Economic Growth: A Study of Nigeria and India. *Acta Universitatis Danubius*, *14*(7), 72–87.

Erbay, E. R., & Aktuna, A. (2019). Economic Growth and The Importance of Exportation in International Trade. *Balkan and Near Eastern Journal of Social Sciences*, *5*(3), 90–95.

Gries, T., Kraft, M., & Meierrieks, D. (2011). Financial deepening, trade openness and economic growth in Latin America and the Caribbean. *Applied Economics*, *43*(30), 4729–4739. doi:10.1080/00036846.2010.498352

Güvercin, D. (2020). Boundaries on Turkish export-oriented industrialization. *Journal of Economic Structures*, *9*(46), 2–115.

Kumari, J. (2014). Export, Import and Economic Growth in India: A Study. *International Journal of Global Management*, *5*(1), 38–43. doi:10.1177/0019466220140307

Rahman, M. F., Shahbaz, M., & Farroq, A. (2015). Financial Development, International Trade and Economic Growth in Australia: New Evidence From Multivariate Framework Analysis. *Journal of Asia-Pacific Business*, *16*(1), 21–43. doi:10.1080/10599231.2015.997625

Safiyanu, S. S., & Chua, S. Y. (2020). Foreign Trade & Economic Growth in sub-Saharan African Countries: Dynamic Common Corelated Effects Estimator (CS-ARDL). *Pertanika Journal of Social Science & Humanities*, *28*(2), 1143–1161.

Sannassee, R. V., Seetanatah, B., & Jugessur, J. (2014). Export-Led Growth Hypothesis: A Meta-Analsis. *Journal of Developing Areas*, *48*(1), 361–385. doi:10.1353/jda.2014.0018

Yapraklı, S. (2007). The causality between exports and economic growth: An econometric analysis on Turkey. *METU Development Journal*, *34*, 97–112.

Zang, W., & Baimbridge, M. (2012). Exports, imports and economic growth in South Korea and Japan: A tale of two economies. *Applied Economics*, *44*(3), 361–372. doi:10.1080/00036846.2010.508722

## ADDITIONAL READING

Appleyard, D., & Field, A. (2017). *International Economics*. Pearson.

Boyes, W., & Melwin, M. (2005). *Economics*. Houghton Mifflin Company.

Gerber, J. (2014). *International Economics. Pearson*. United Sates of America.

Hill, C., & Hult, T. (2019). *International Business, McGraw-Hill Education*. United Sates of America.

## KEY TERMS AND DEFINITIONS

**Economic Growth:** Economic growth is an increase in the production of economic goods and services, compared from one period of time to another.

**Export-Leg Growth:** ELG hypothesis indicates that exports necessarily promote economic growth.

**Foreign Direct Investment (FDI):** A foreign direct investment (FDI) is a purchase of an interest in a company by a company or an investor located outside its borders.

**Gross Domestic Product (GDP):** GDP is the total value of goods and services sold in the course over the course a year.

**Import-Led Growth:** ILG hypothesis stands for economic growth would be stimulated by growth in imports.

**Inflation:** A steady increase in the price level of the economy of a country.

**International Trade:** International trade is the exchange of goods and services among countries. International trade allows countries to expand their markets and access goods and services that otherwise may not have been available domestically.

## ENDNOTES

[1] Gross Domestic Product.

[2] Consumer price index.

[3] Wholesale price index.

[4] Foreign direct investment.

[5] www.tim.org.tr

[6] Central Bank of the Republic of Turkey, Ministry of Finance and Treasury, and Ministry of Commerce.

# Machine Learning and Exploratory Data Analysis in Cross–Sell Insurance

**Anand Jha**
*Rustamji Institute of Technology, BSF Academy, Tekanpur, India*

**Brajkishore Prajapati**
*Rustamji Institute of Technology, BSF Academy, Tekanpur, India*

## INTRODUCTION

A financial shield against a risk or threat is insurance. A business corporation that sells such financial shield and an entity that buys such financial shield are called insurer and insured respectively. A written agreement between insurer and the insured defines this financial shield and called *policy document* or *insurance policy*. But this financial shield is given to insured in lieu of monetary payment called premium (Aswani et al., 2020).

The insurance policies can be of several kinds according to the different kinds of risks. Some popular types of insurance are Life Insurance, Health Insurance, Vehicle Insurance, Travel Insurance and Property Insurance (Bacry et al., 2020). This basic idea of risk or monetary risk reduction is the reason to run entire industry (Batra et al., 2021).

Insurance industry access to volume of data generated with the advent of technologies has tremendously increased (Accenture, 2018). It can be said that more data have been created, collected in the past couple of years than the human society has ever produced due to irresistible explosion in data from a host of sources, like telematics, Internet usage, social media bustle, voice analytics, connected sensors and wearable devices.

Big data can be unstructured, semi-structured and structured (Chakraborty & Kar, 2017; Kar, 2016). It is well known fact that *actuarial formulas* are still in use by several insurance businesses, but now data science and analytics can be utilized to excerpt hidden information that can help for improved strategic as well as administrative decision making than the conventional techniques. (Chowdhury et al., 2020; Karhade et al., 2019). Use of data technologies can have a serious role in different facets of the insurance business like risk assessment, claim analysis, underwriting analysis, customer profiling and fraud detection etc. (Das et al., 2020; Das et al., 2021).

Together with various data analysis and visualization techniques, Machine Learning (ML) as a subdomain of artificial intelligence (AI) come as a rescue to Insurance Industry to facilitate such datasets. Machine learning teaches computers to think in a similar way as humans, thus learning and improving upon past experiences. Practically almost all tasks that can be accomplished with a data-defined pattern or set of rules can be automated with machine learning (Accenture, 2018). Machine learning (ML) techniques can be effectively used across Structured, Semi Structured or Unstructured datasets (Burri et al., 2019), (Chakraborty & Kar, 2017; Kar, 2016). But most insurers are struggling to maximise the benefits of machine learning and thus not able to unearth analytical insights hidden into datasets. Since machine learning is in use during last few decades, it is not a novel technology. *Supervised learning, Unsupervised Learning and Reinforcement Learning* are three core classes of machine learning. Majority

DOI: 10.4018/978-1-7998-9220-5.ch039

of insurers are working with supervised learning for risk assessment by means of identified parameters to obtain preferred outcome. But during last few decades, unsupervised learning is also gaining popularity among present age insurers.

Thus we can say that state of affairs in insurance industry is witnessing a slow but steady change due to an environment characterised by increased competition, elastic marketplaces, complex claims, risk appetite and premium leakage, expense administration, subrogation, new business, new product development, policy servicing, distribution fraud behaviour, sales, customer experience and tighter regulation. This changing scenario also forcing insurers to explore new ways to use predictive modelling and machine learning to retain their competitive edge, boost business operations and enhance customer satisfaction. Most insurers process and analyse a small percentage of data they have access to. They process mostly structured data since it is obtainable from their traditional databases. This worsens to unravel worth not only from their structured data, but also ignoring the valuable insights hidden in their unstructured data. Emergent data analytical techniques can reap benefits from this unstructured data by effectively mining it to get business insights.

This chapter discusses relevance of machine learning and application of data visualization techniques for making better strategic decisions in insurance industry, especially for cross-sell insurance through a dataset.

## BACKGROUND

Insurance companies have been gradual to embrace technological change compared to other industries because insurance is among one of the old and extensively regulated industry in the world with marine insurance was the first kind of insurance (Rawat et al., 2021). Insurance Industry is still soaked in paper-based processes that are slow, manual and require human intervention. Even in this digital era, customers are asked to go for a time-consuming paperwork when getting a claim reimbursed or signing up for a new insurance policy. In this process customers may be paying more for insurance policies since policies are not custom-made according to their exclusive needs. In a digital era, this may end up with an unhappy customer experience.

One of the buzzword of digital decade is Artificial Intelligence and this means the use of machines to pretend human intelligence (Kose et al., 2015; Kraus et al., 2020). AI or ML can help in practically all domains of insurance business beginning from pricing strategies (Larson & Sinclair, 2021; Maehashi & Shintani, 2020), risk selection, personalization of policies to document underwriting etc. (McGlade & Scott-Hayward, 2019; Mita et al.,2021).

Some of the potential use cases (Burri et al., 2019; Accenture, 2018; Shroff R., 2019) of machine learning in health insurance are:

**Insurance Advice:** Machine learning can take a noteworthy role in customer service, from the initial interaction to helping a customer requires to select most relevant and cost effective health insurance policy. Recent surveys show that customers are happy to receive computer-generated insurance advice because they are looking for personalised solutions as made promising by machine learning algorithms that review their profiles and recommend tailor-made insurance policies. Other than using machine learning in back end, insurers are also using artificial intelligence by using chat-bots on messaging apps to resolve claims queries and answer simple questions. (Khan et al., 2014; Knighton et al., 2020) focused on the great scope of betterment in conventionally used methods in insurance business for policy advice and enrolment.

**M**

**Claim Processing:** Insurers are deploying machine learning beginning from claims registration to claims settlement in order to advance operational efficiency, enhancing the customer experience, reducing the claims settlement time, cut claim costs and better case management. (Khan et al., 2014; Knighton et al., 2020) discussed improved methods can be used for claim settlement of insurance business.

**Fraud Detection:** fraud in insurance sector is a 40-million USD industry per year (Rawat et al., 2021) Machine learning is helping insurers to identify potential fraudulent claims since machine learning algorithms are superior to traditional predictive models because they can knock into unstructured, semi structured data as well as structured data to find perceptions on customer behaviour.

**Risk Management:** As compared to humans, machine learning can deliver more applicable premium prediction, prediction on policy losses, predictions on coverage changes and thus manage risk more effectually.

Figure 1 demonstrates the growth of the machine learning marketplace in different continents over the period of 2017-2024. It displays the hastening acceptance and serious significance of machine learning. (Accenture, 2018; NASSCOM, 2020).

*Figure 1. Growth of machine learning marketplace in different continents from 2017 to 2024*

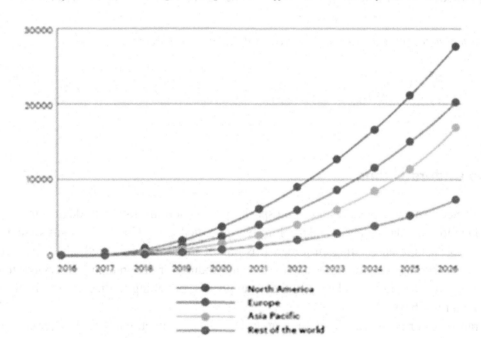

## MACHINE LEARNING FRAMEWORK FOR CROSS-SELL INSURANCE ANALYSIS

Realization of machine learning and data science techniques requires a well-defined process. The outlining framework of machine learning used in this analysis is shown in Figure 2. This approach is based on Yufeng Guo's 7 Steps of Machine Learning but adapted according to (Nguyen et al., 2019)

1. *Business Understanding*: It is generally conceptualized from the provided business mission explanations and data description.
2. *Data Collection & Understating*: Preparing a representation of data, this may involve taking pre-collected datasets from Kaggle, UCI etc. and then contemplative provided data and its documentation.
3. *Data Preparation*: Consists of data transformations such as data type conversions, correcting errors, dealing with missing values, removing duplicates, randomize data, eliminating duplicates, performing exploratory data analysis (EDA) i.e. visualizing data from different angles to decipher pertinent relationships among collected features (variables), feature engineering i.e. features extraction and feature selection, dimensionality reductions and splitting data into training and validation collections.
4. *Training and Modelling*: Different machine learning algorithms are considered and trained with different set of parameters. This phase may time consuming and compute-intensive since this involves train-test-evaluate cycle repetitively.
5. *Model evaluation*: the selected model can be executed using some metrics against validation data and/or unseen data to choose the best model that stratify the objective performance of the task.
6. *Model deployment*: This means using trained and tuned model for implementation of functionalities like prediction, classification, making business decisions in real business domain.

*Figure 2. Machine learning framework for cross-sell insurance analysis*

## Business Understanding

We have selected insurance business domain especially cross-sell insurance for demonstrating the importance of exploratory data analysis and machine learning modelling. Cross sell means selling a related or matching products to an existing customer. It is one of most operative methods of marketing. An example of cross-selling is selling different investment products or tax preparation services to existing clients who have taken retirement plans. Another example may be selling credit cards to a bank customer who has a loan form bank.

In insurance sector cross-sell means selling an insurance product, e.g. health insurance policy to existing customers of financial service company or even selling health insurance to existing customers of vehicle insurance. The reason for this cross-sell is that an insurer of different domain or a financial company may plan to reap opportunities in an emerging insurance sector like health insurance sector.

## Dataset Collection and Understanding

We have taken dataset from Kaggle (Gupta S., 2021) for presenting the role of exploratory data analysis in cross sell insurance as well as to build some machine learning models for predicting customers' response to proposed cross sell policies.

In machine learning, the quality of data used for data analysis and to train predictive models is equally important as the collection of data (Accenture, 2018). The dataset needs to be representative and

*Table 1. Dataset description*

| S. No. | Feature Name | Feature Definition |
|---|---|---|
| 1 | ID | Unique Identifier for a row /record |
| 2 | City_Code | Code for the City of the customers |
| 3 | Region_Code | Code for the Region of the customers |
| 4 | Accomodation_Type | Tell whether Customer Owns or Rents the house |
| 5 | Reco_Insurance_Type | Joint or Individual type for the recommended insurance |
| 6 | Upper_Age | Maximum age of the customer |
| 7 | Lower_Age | Minimum age of the customer |
| 8 | Is_Spouse | Whether the customers are married to each other (in case of joint insurance) |
| 9 | Health_Indicator | Encoded values for health of the customer |
| 10 | Holding_Policy_Duration | Duration (in years) of holding policy (a policy that customer has already subscribed to with the company) |
| 11 | Holding_Policy_Type | Type of holding policy |
| 12 | Reco_Policy_Cat | Encoded value for recommended health insurance |
| 13 | Reco_Policy_Premium | Annual Premium (INR) for the recommended health insurance |
| 14 | Response (Target Feature) | 0: Customer did not show interest in the recommended policy, 1: Customer showed interest in the recommended policy |

balanced so that it can give a better picture and avoid any bias. Generally, insurers struggle to provide such relevant datasets that makes exploratory data analysis as well as training of models more difficult.

The dataset used in our analysis has 14 features as mentioned in Table 1.

The dataset has 50882 customers profile with varying demographics expressed using 14 features (including target variable).

Although we have used dataset from Kaggle (Gupta, 2021) but there are other ways also to get required dataset like using an internally available dataset or gathering data using a survey as shown in figure 3.

*Figure 3. Procedure for data collection for cross-sell insurance*

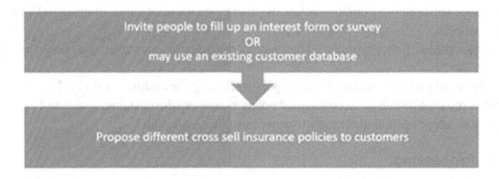

## Data Preparation

The primary data preparation methods e.g. data transformation, exploratory data analysis (EDA), feature engineering can be categorized into sub-categories like under-sampling, oversampling, feature encoding, feature transformation, data augmentation, and dimensionality reduction. Some of them can further be categorized, for example dimensionality reduction can be done by feature selection or feature extraction. Similarly, over-fitting can be dealt with regularization, threshold setting, pruning and dropout. (Bachniak et al., 2017; Rawat et al., 2021)

In cross sell insurance, exploratory data analysis (EDA) is equally as important as building a machine learning model for prediction and classification. This is due to fact that only exploratory data analysis (EDA) can help in finding answers to queries related to improving marketing strategies, creating a business model and better decision making because EDA can help in answering questions by creating various visualization diagrams that discover hidden relationships among different features of data that cannot be observed by simply looking at dataset (Rawat et al., 2021Bourke D, 2019). EDA can answer miscellaneous queries like:

- What question(s) are we trying to solve (or prove wrong)?
- What kind of data do we have and how do we treat different types?
- What's missing from the data and how do we deal with it?
- Where are the outliers and why should we care about them?
- How can you add, change or remove features to get more out of data?

In this chapter, the selected dataset is analysed to answer the following queries for cross-sell of health insurance product by means of EDA.

1. Are customers who owns a house more likely to show interest in the proposed health insurance policy, leading to acceptance of the same.
2. Are married customers more inclined towards a proposed health insurance policy, leading to acceptance of the same than the single customers?
3. Are customers with low health indicators more expected to show interest in the recommended health insurance policy?
4. How does holding policy duration affect the interest in and acceptance of proposed health insurance policy?
5. How does holding policy type impact the customer's choice of accepting the proposed health insurance policy?
6. Is category of proposed health insurance policy affecting the customer's choice?
7. What is the relationship of recommended policy premium with customer's interest?
8. How does upper age and lower age influence customer's decision?

## Data Pre-Processing

With predictive modelling projects, machine learning algorithms learn a mapping from input variables to a target variable using structured data or tabular data where rows depict the actual data whereas columns depict the features, this data characterize the problem under consideration. Thus machine learning models cannot be trained and evaluated on raw data, we must transform the data to meet the require-

**M**

ments of individual machine learning models because qualitative data is necessary for such models to function efficiently. Further we must choose a representation for the data that best exposes the unknown underlying structure of the prediction problem to the machine learning algorithms in order to get the best performance. Here we have done (1) variable type identification and type casting and (2) missing value analysis with our dataset as a part of data pre-processing step, other possible prepossessing task include Synthetic Minority Over-Sampling Technique (SMOTE) that is required for an imbalance dataset, encoding data values in dataset.

## VARIABLE IDENTIFICATION AND TYPE CASTING

Dataset used here has 6 variables of type *"int64"*, 2 variables of type *"float64"* and 6 variables of type *"object"* as shown in figure 4.

*Figure 4. Data type identification of features (variables) in dataset*

```
<class 'pandas.core.frame.DataFrame'>
RangeIndex: 50882 entries, 0 to 50881
Data columns (total 14 columns):
 #   Column                   Non-Null Count   Dtype
---  ------                   --------------   -----
 0   ID                       50882 non-null   int64
 1   City_Code                50882 non-null   object
 2   Region_Code              50882 non-null   int64
 3   Accomodation_Type        50882 non-null   object
 4   Reco_Insurance_Type      50882 non-null   object
 5   Upper_Age                50882 non-null   int64
 6   Lower_Age                50882 non-null   int64
 7   Is_Spouse                50882 non-null   object
 8   Health Indicator         39191 non-null   object
 9   Holding_Policy_Duration  30631 non-null   object
 10  Holding_Policy_Type      30631 non-null   float64
 11  Reco_Policy_Cat          50882 non-null   int64
 12  Reco_Policy_Premium      50882 non-null   float64
 13  Response                 50882 non-null   int64
dtypes: float64(2), int64(6), object(6)
memory usage: 5.4+ MB
```

Below are some observations about dataset features:

- *Upper_Age, Lower_Age, Holding_Policy_Duration, Reco_Policy_Cat, Reco_Policy_Premium* are numerical features.
- *City_Code, Region_Code, Accomodation_Type, Reco_Insurance_Type, Is_Spouse, Health Indicator, Holding_Policy_Type, Response* (target variable) are categorical Features. *Holding_ Policy_Type* is in fact an Ordinal feature.
- *ID* feature is neither a numeric nor a categorical feature. In fact, it is not a feature but it is a unique Id for the customer.

- Holding_Policy_Duration is a numerical feature, but its data type is given as Object, so it must have converted to float type before building any model.
- *Region_Code and Holding_Policy_Type* are categorical features, but the data type given are int64 and float64 respectively. So convert it into object type.
- *Response* (target variable) is a categorical feature.

It is clear that some of the features require data type conversion before they can be used for exploratory data analysis as well as to build any machine learning model. After data type conversion, the data types are shown in figure 5.

*Figure 5. Variables of dataset after required type conversion*

```
<class 'pandas.core.frame.DataFrame'>
RangeIndex: 50882 entries, 0 to 50881
Data columns (total 14 columns):
 #   Column                  Non-Null Count  Dtype
---  ------                  --------------  -----
 0   ID                      50882 non-null  int64
 1   City_Code               50882 non-null  object
 2   Region_Code             50882 non-null  object
 3   Accomodation_Type       50882 non-null  object
 4   Reco_Insurance_Type     50882 non-null  object
 5   Upper_Age               50882 non-null  int64
 6   Lower_Age               50882 non-null  int64
 7   Is_Spouse               50882 non-null  object
 8   Health Indicator        39191 non-null  object
 9   Holding_Policy_Duration 30631 non-null  object
 10  Holding_Policy_Type     30631 non-null  object
 11  Reco_Policy_Cat         50882 non-null  int64
 12  Reco_Policy_Premium     50882 non-null  float64
 13  Response                50882 non-null  object
dtypes: float64(1), int64(4), object(9)
memory usage: 5.4+ MB
```

## MISSING VALUES ANALYSIS

Result of missing values analysis is shown in Table 2 below. A heat-map in figure 6 is also depicting the same information as in Table 2.

It can be inferred from Table 2 and Figure 6 that there are 23%, 40%, 40% values are missing in "Health_Indicator", "Holding_Policy_Duration", "Holding_Policy_Type" features respectively. We cannot drop missing values since the percentage is very high otherwise we miss some important information. Thus KNN imputation method used for missing values because it is a predictive method which takes count of every feature of data and predicts missing values (Obadia Y., 2017)

*Table 2. Missing values analysis of dataset*

| S. No. | Feature Name | Count of Missing Values |
|--------|--------------|------------------------|
| 1 | ID | 0 |
| 2 | City_Code | 0 |
| 3 | Region_Code | 0 |
| 4 | Accomodation_Type | 0 |
| 5 | Reco_Insurance_Type | 0 |
| 6 | Upper_Age | 0 |
| 7 | Lower_Age | 0 |
| 8 | Is_Spouse | 0 |
| 9 | Health Indicator | 11691 |
| 10 | Holding_Policy_Duration | 20251 |
| 11 | Holding_Policy_Type | 20251 |
| 12 | Reco_Policy_Cat | 0 |
| 13 | Reco_Policy_Premium | 0 |
| 14 | Response | 0 |

*Figure 6. Heat-map showing which features are having missing values in dataset*

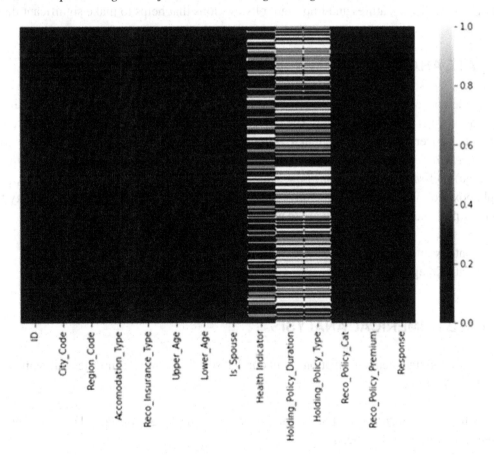

## EXPLORATORY DATA ANALYSIS

Exploratory Data Analysis (EDA) means preliminary analysis of dataset, to find important measures, metrics, features and relationship between measures so that we can gain an insight into trends, patterns, detect outliers, detect anomalies of the dataset. EDA is done with the help of statistics and data visualization to understand various features of data which is not easily thinkable by simply observing the dataset. Therefore, EDA is necessary to be done before creating any machine learning model. The main objectives of EDA are (1) data description and understanding, (2) to ensure results produced by data scientists are valid and applicable to any desired business outcomes and (3) model formulation. EDA can be classified into following categories:

1.    Univariate Analysis
2.    Bivariate Analysis
3.    Multivariate Analysis

Each of them can be further divided into graphical and non-graphical methods. Graphical methods involve *visualization* that establishes a kind of communication with the data When we look at the data, it is only a file in a spreadsheet, it does not have any interpretation within it, but when we visualize data, we gain insights into it. To explain the process, we have conducted exploratory data analysis of chosen dataset using histogram, 2d scatter plot, count plot and correlation matrix (heat map) etc. to find the relationship between features and important observations that helps to make significant decisions.

## UNIVARIATE ANALYSIS

*Uni* means one and *variate* means variable, so univariate analysis involves single variable i.e. it does not find relationships between variables. The objective of univariate analysis is to derive the data, summarize it and discover pattern(s) present in it. Some patterns that can be easily identified with univariate analysis are *central tendency* (mean, mode and median), *dispersion* (range, variance), *quartiles* (inter-quartile range) and *standard deviation*. Few examples of univariate analysis are bar-graph, pie-chart, line-graph, box plot, whisker plot, cumulative distributive function (CDF), probability density function (PDF), violin plot and histogram. Univariate analysis can be of two types:

1.    Univariate Numerical Analysis
2.    Univariate Categorical Analysis

## UNIVARIATE NUMERICAL ANALYSIS

Table 3 shows some statistical information about our dataset. Table 3 communicates following statistical insights into our dataset:

- The count for all features is 50882 which is equal to the length of data. Therefore, no missing values are present in these features.

- The mean and 50%-median of *"Upper_Age", "Lower_Age" and "Reco_Policy_cat"* features are very close. So these features may have a *normal distribution curve.*
- There is a much difference in the 75%-median and max value of *"Upper_Age", "Lower_Age" and "Reco_Policy_Premium"* features, so *some outliers may be present* in these features.

*Table 3. Statistical Insights into data by Univariate Numerical Analysis*

|          | ID            | Upper_Age     | Lower_Age     | Reco_Policy_Cat | Reco_Policy_Premium |
|----------|---------------|---------------|---------------|-----------------|---------------------|
| **count**    | 50882.000000  | 50882.000000  | 50882.000000  | 50882.000000    | 50882.000000        |
| **mean**     | 25441.500000  | 44.856275     | 42.738866     | 15.115188       | 14183.950069        |
| **Std. Dev.**| 14688.512535  | 17.310271     | 17.319375     | 6.340663        | 6590.074873         |
| **min**      | 1.000000      | 18.000000     | 16.000000     | 1.000000        | 2280.000000         |
| **25%**      | 12721.250000  | 28.000000     | 27.000000     | 12.000000       | 9248.000000         |
| **50%**      | 25441.500000  | 44.000000     | 40.000000     | 17.000000       | 13178.000000        |
| **75%**      | 38161.750000  | 59.000000     | 57.000000     | 20.000000       | 18096.000000        |
| **max**      | 50882.000000  | 75.000000     | 75.000000     | 22.000000       | 43350.400000        |

The figure 7 shows another type of univariate analysis called *density plots* applied on our dataset. Following observations can be deduced from figure 7:

1. The mean and median almost same for both *"Upper_Age"* and *"Lower_Age"* features but the distribution doesn't look like *Gaussian* distribution.
2. 68% of the customer's *"Upper_Age"* lies in the range of [27.55 - 67.17] and *"Lower_Age"* lies in the range of [25.26 - 60.06]
3. *Skewness is acceptable* to 0.5. So we conclude that the *"Lower_Age"* and *"Upper_Age"* features are not skewed. *Skewness is a measure of a dataset's lack of symmetry.* It measures the degree of distortion from normal distribution. A skewness value of zero represents a symmetrical dataset i.e. dataset having normal distribution (SPC, 2018). Generally, if the skewness is between -0.5 and 0.5, the data are fairly symmetrical, if the skewness is between -1 and – 0.5 or between 0.5 and 1, the data are moderately skewed and if the skewness is less than -1 or greater than 1, the data are highly skewed.

The kurtosis parameter is a measure of the combined weight of the tails relative to the rest of the distribution. Kurtosis is the degree of peaked-ness (flatness) of a distribution

4. *"Reco_Policy_Cat"* and *"Reco_Policy_Premium"* features have a left and right skewed distribution respectively.
5. 68% of the values of *"Reco_Policy_Cat"* lies in the range [8.77-21.46] and *"Reco_Policy_Premium"* lies in the range of [7593.88 - 20774.02]
6. Density plot clearly shows that *some outliers present* in *"Reco_Policy _Premium."*

*Figure 7. Density plots (Univariate Analysis)*

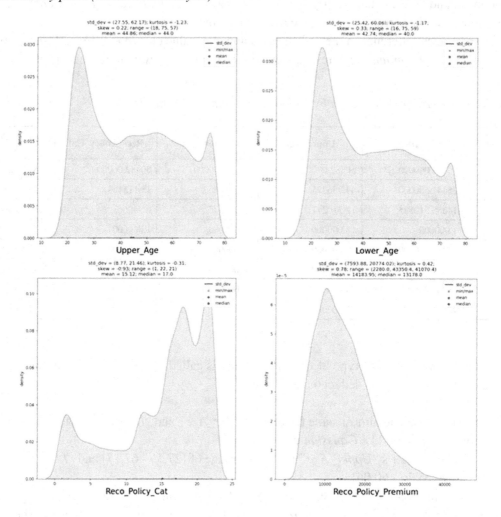

*Figure 8. Box plot of "Upper_Age" and "Lower_Age" features*

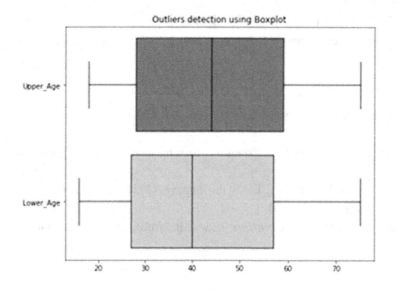

*Figure 9. Box plot of "Reco_Policy_Cat" feature*

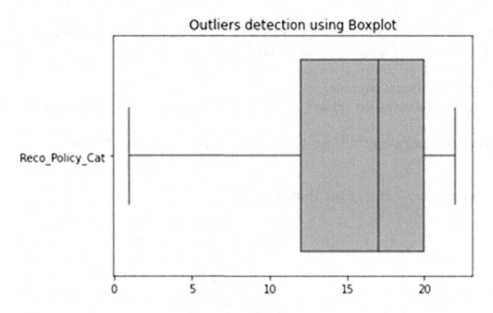

*Figure 10. Box plot of "Reco_Policy_Premium" features*

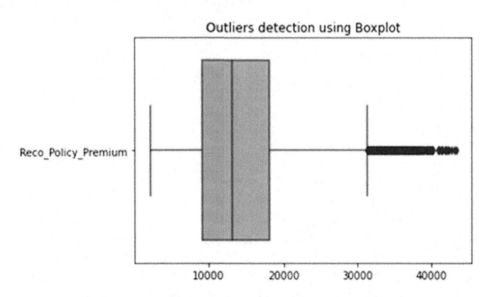

Another type of univariate analysis is box plotting that can be used for finding outliers in features of the dataset. A boxplot analysis as shown in figure 8, 9, 10 clearly indicates that *"Reco_Policy_Premium"* feature contains some outliers.

## UNIVARIATE CATEGORICAL ANALYSIS

Categorical analysis of "*City_Code*" feature with the help of a count plot is shown in figure 11. Following Observations can be deduced form Figure 11:

1. There are 36 different city code.
2. 17% of the total customers belongs to "C1" city, 15% belongs to "C2" city while 9% belongs to city "C3".
3. Customers belong to city "C1" are 4 times the customers belong to "C9" city.

*Figure 11. Count plot for "City_Code" feature*

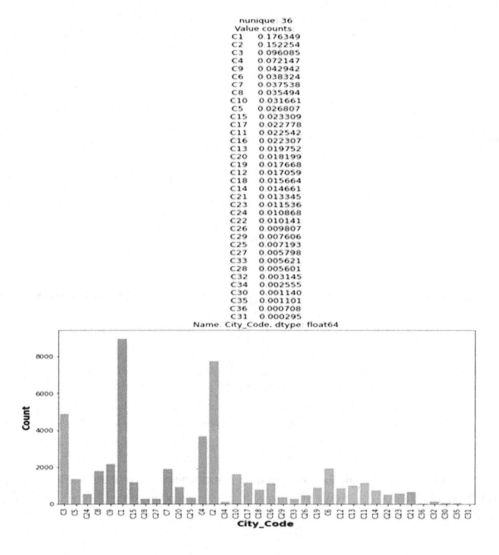

Following Observations can be deduced form Figure 12 i.e. count plot for feature "*Accomodation_Type*":

1. There are 2 unique accommodation types i.e. rented and owned.

2.  54% of customers live in their own house, while 45% customers live in rented house.
3.  The above visualization also hints at *new hypothesis*: are customers who own a house show more interest in proposed health policies.

*Figure 12. Count plot for "Accomodation_Type" feature*

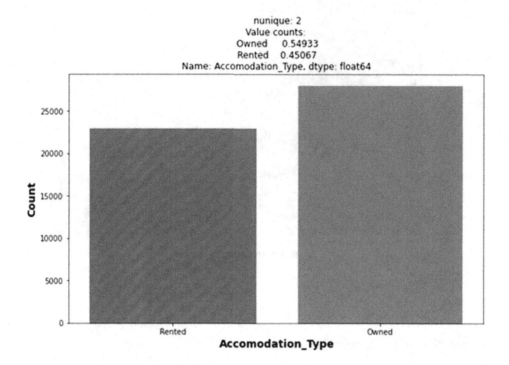

Data visualization in Figure 13 shows univariate categorical analysis of *"Reco_Insurance_Type"* feature and advises that almost 80% customers show interest in individual insurance, while 20% interested in joint insurance.

Data visualization in Figure 14 depicts the univariate categorical analysis of *"Is_Spouse"* feature and conveys that 16% customers are married among whom showing interest.

Univariate categorical analysis of *"Health_Indicator"* feature is shown in figure 15 conveys 33% customers have "X1" health Indicator, while 26% customers have "X2".

Figure 16 depicts the count plot of *"Holding_Policy_Duration"* communicates followings:

- As policy period increases, customer decreases.
- 14% customers have policies with a period of 14+ years.
- Customers with 1-year policy period is more than 4 times of customers with 8-years period.
- A new hypothesis that are the customers with policy period of 1-2 years more likely to show interest in the proposed health policy.

Univariate categorical analysis of *"Holding_Policy_Type"* feature is depicted in figure 17 but it is almost impossible to get any insight about data from this visualization.

*Figure 13. Count Plot for "Reco_Insurance_Type" feature*

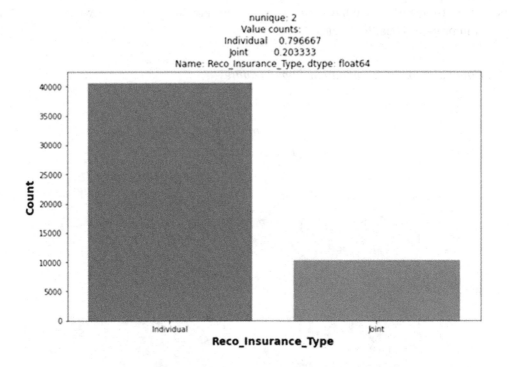

*Figure 14. Count Plot for "Is_Spouse" feature*

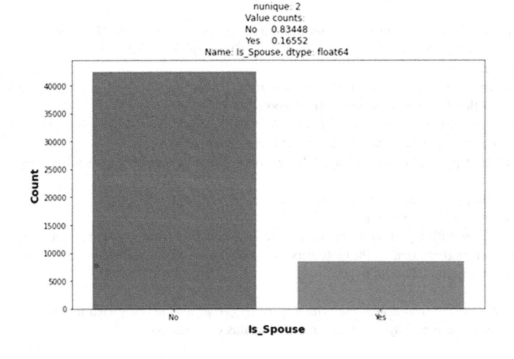

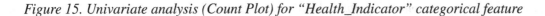

*Figure 15. Univariate analysis (Count Plot) for "Health_Indicator" categorical feature*

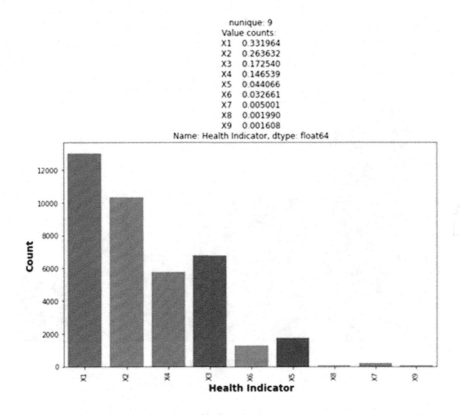

*Figure 16. Univariate analysis (Count Plot) for "Holding_Policy_Duration" categorical feature*

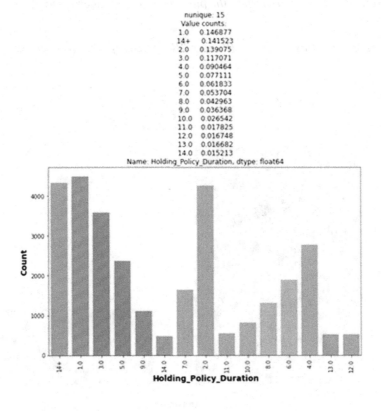

*Figure 17. Univariate analysis (Count Plot) for "Holding_Policy_Type" categorical feature*

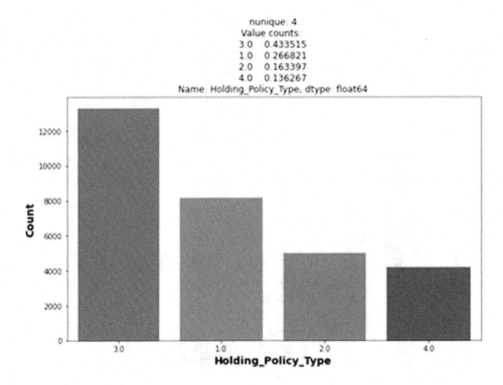

Figure 18 shows univariate categorical analysis of "Response" feature (target variable). It conveys that 76% customers are not showing interest in proposed cross sell health policies while 23% customers are interested. Therefore, it *hints at improving the business strategy* for cross sell health insurance policy.

*Figure 18. Univariate analysis using Count Plot for "Response" feature (Target Variable)*

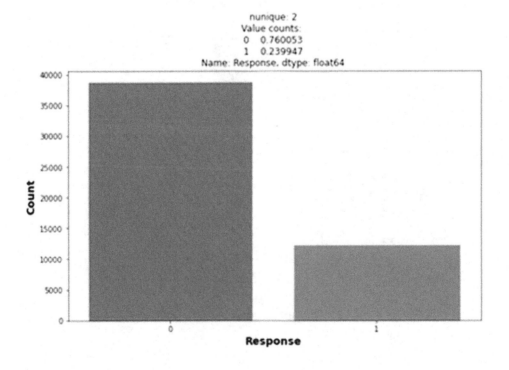

# BIVARIATE ANALYSIS

*Bi* means two and *variate* means variable. Bivariate analysis discovers relationships between two variables (dependent or independent). Bivariate analysis can be used to find the relationship between a feature (variable) in dataset and target feature (variable). One example of bivariate analysis can be establishing relation between age and result of students of a class. Here age is independent variable and result is dependent variable. Bivariate analysis is really helpful in testing hypotheses of association. It is a kind of analysis that is helpful in predicting a value for one variable (called a *dependent variable*) if the value of the other variable (called *independent variable*) is already known. Scatter plot, regression plot, violin plot, correlation coefficients, Chi-square test and T-test are some of the frequently used visualization techniques to do the bivariate analysis. Bivariate analysis can be of following types:

1. Numerical – Numerical Bivariate Analysis, both variables are numerical.
2. Categorical – Categorical Bivariate Analysis, both variables are categorical.
3. Numerical – Categorical Bivariate Analysis, one variable is numerical and other is categorical.

## NUMERICAL – NUMERICAL BIVARIATE ANALYSIS

Correlation analysis and pair plotting of our dataset are done to showcase example of numerical-numerical bivariate analysis.

### Correlation Analysis

Both *Pearson and Spearman correlation* are applied on dataset. Results are depicted in Table 4, Table 5 and in Figure 19.

*Table 4. Numerical-numerical bivariate analysis through Pearson correlation*

| Correlation matrix using Pearson correlation | | | |
|---|---|---|---|
| Feature/variable | Upper_Age | Lower_Age | Reco_Policy_Cat | Reco_Policy_Premium |
| Upper_Age | 1.000000 | 0.921392 | 0.025257 | 0.792689 |
| Lower_Age | 0.921392 | 1.000000 | 0.021163 | 0.615739 |
| Reco_Policy_Cat | 0.025257 | 0.021163 | 1.000000 | 0.060989 |
| Reco_Policy_Premium | 0.792689 | 0.615739 | 0.060989 | 1.000000 |

*Table 5. Numerical-numerical bivariate analysis through Spearman correlation*

| Correlation matrix using Spearman correlation | | | |
|---|---|---|---|
| Feature/variable | Upper_Age | Lower_Age | Reco_Policy_Cat | Reco_Policy_Premium |
| Upper_Age | 1.000000 | 0.909629 | 0.024441 | 0.835294 |
| Lower_Age | 0.909629 | 1.000000 | 0.021338 | 0.669743 |
| Reco_Policy_Cat | 0.024441 | 0.021338 | 1.000000 | 0.061397 |
| Reco_Policy_Premium | 0.835294 | 0.669743 | 0.061397 | 1.000000 |

*Figure 19. Numerical-numerical bivariate analysis via Pearson & Spearman correlation*

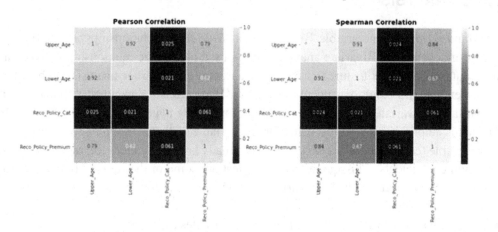

From Table 4, Table 5 and figure 19, two conclusions can be drawn: (1) in both Pearson and Spearman correlation features *"Upper_Age" and "Lower_Age" are highly correlated* with each other. Therefor we may *drop one of them*, so that our model does not have any bias. (2) *"Reco_Policy_Premium" is also having linear positive relationship* with *"Upper_Age" and "Lower_Age"*.

## Pair Plotting

We have done pair plotting of *"Upper_Age", "Lower_Age", "Reco_Policy_Cat", "Reco_Policy_Premium"* features. It can be inferred from figure 20 that *"Upper_Age",* and *"Lower_Age"* looks like a symmetric upper triangle and lower triangle. We can make use of this in feature engineering.

## NUMERICAL – CATEGORICAL BIVARIATE ANALYSIS

This analysis is done to assess hypothesis concerning customers' interest in proposed cross sell health insurance product, like:

- What impact do features *"Upper_Age"* and *"Lower_Age"* have on customers' interest?
- Does recommended policy category i.e. feature *"Reco_Policy_Cat"* affect the customers' interest?
- What is the relationship of feature *"Reco_Policy_Premium"* to customers' interest?

Hypothesis testing is an essential technique in statistics which evaluates two mutually exclusive proclamations, to determine which statement is sustained by the data (Agrawal, 2019). Generally, hypothesis testing is done through:

1. T-Test
2. Z-Test
3. Chi-Square Test
4. ANOVA Test

*Figure 20. Pair Plotting of "Upper_Age", "Lower_Age", "Reco_Policy_Cat"," Reco_Policy_Premium"*

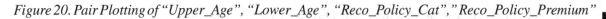

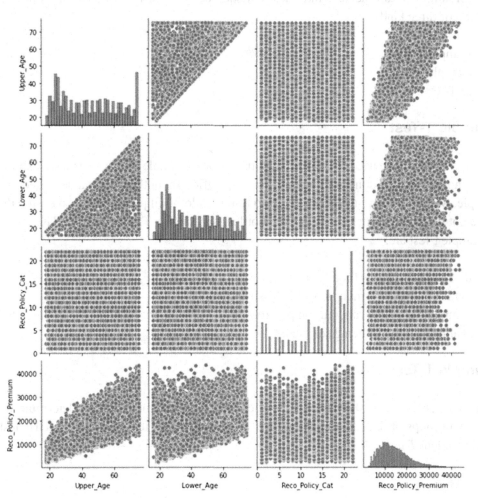

The general steps for hypothesis testing are:

1. Set hypothesis
2. Set significance Level, criteria for a decision
3. Compute test statistics
4. Make a decision

## T- Test

T-test allows testing of a hypothesis applicable to a population. It does so by calculating the means of two data groups. T-test can be used when:

1. We do not know the population variance and
2. Sample size is small, n < 30.

For larger sample sizes, other tests like z-test, chi-square test or f-test will produce more accurate results. T-test are of three kinds:

1. One-sample T-test
2. Two-sample T-test
3. Paired T-test

## One Sample T-Test

One-sample T–test can be used to test null hypothesis. The variable used in this test is known as "*Test Variable*" and its mean is compared against a pre-specified (hypothesized) value called "*test value*". For example, when a factory supervisor wants to test a random sample of bottles to ensure that the machines are not under-filling or over-filling the bottles, one sample T-test can help. The assumptions of the one-sample t-test are:

1. The data are continuous (not discrete).
2. The data follow the normal probability distribution.
3. The sample is a simple random sample from its population i.e. each sample in the population has an equal probability of being selected.

## Two Sample T-Test

This type of t-test compares the means of two separate independent groups to determine whether the means of two groups of data significantly differ from each other. It is also a parametric test and also called Independent *T-test*.

## Paired T-Test

It is also called dependent sample T-test. It is a univariate test that tests for a significant difference between two variables. When we need to survey a group of people twice with same parameters, paired T-test can be used to determine whether mean (average) has changed between the first and second survey. For example, if blood pressure for an individual before and after some treatment or specific condition are collected, the paired sample T-test is the right choice.

## Z-Test

Z-Test is statistical way of testing a hypothesis. Z-test is used when:

- Sample size is large, n $^3$ 30
- Data points should be independent from each other.
- Data should have a normal distribution.
- Your data should be randomly selected from a population, where each item has an equal chance of being selected.
- Sample sizes should be equal if at all possible.

**M**

There are two kinds of Z-test:

- *One-Sample Z test:* We perform the One-Sample Z-test when we want to compare a sample mean with the population mean. The one-sample z-test assumes that the data are a simple random sample from a population of normally distributed. This assumption denotes that the data are continuous and distribution is symmetric.
- *Two-Sample Z test:* Two independent data groups are tested to determine whether mean of two samples is equal or not.

Result of Z-test is a number called z-score or z-statistic.

## P-Value and Critical Value

In hypothesis testing, test statistic used to decide whether to accept or reject the null hypothesis. This *decision is taken based on a number, called a p-value.* P-value is the probability value that measures the chance of getting results at least as extreme as the results actually observed during the test, if the null hypothesis is correct. A p-value is associated with *critical value.* Since the p-value is just a value, we need to compare it with the critical value ($\alpha$):

1. P-value > $\alpha$ (Critical value): Fail to reject the null hypothesis of the statistical test.
2. P-value £ $\alpha$ (Critical value): Reject the null hypothesis of the statistical test.

Figure 21 and figure 22 depicts calculation of p-value using T-test and Z-test for features *"Upper_Age"* and *"Lower_Age"* respectively. Following observations can be drawn based on these figures:

- There is no significant difference in the upper age and lower age of the customers on the basis of showing interest in the recommended health policy. Therefore *"Upper_Age"* and *"Lower_Age"* features *do not affect customer interest* in the recommended health policy.
- No outliers present in" Upper_*Age"* and *"Lower_Age"* features.

*Figure 21. P-value calculation using T-test and Z-test for feature "Upper_Age"*

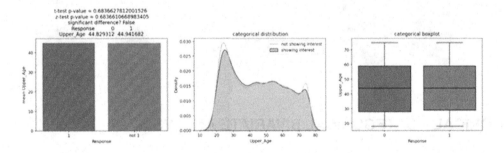

Figure 23 shows the calculation of p-value using T-test and Z-test for *"Reco_Polcy_Cat"* feature, from this figure it can be deduced that the recommended policy cat i.e. *"Reco_Policy_Cat"* feature significantly influences the customers' interest in the proposed health policy.

*Figure 22. P-value calculation using T-test and Z-test for feature "Lower_Age"*

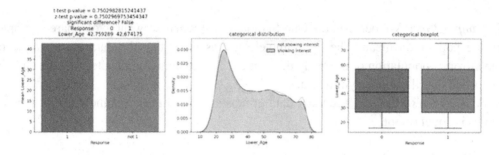

*Figure 23. p-value calculation using T-test and Z-test for feature "Reco_Policy_Cat"*

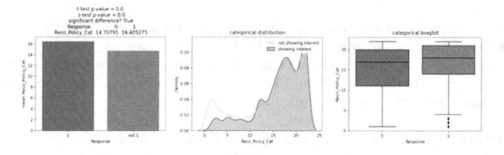

Similarly figure 24 shows the calculation of p-value using T-test and Z-test for *"Reco_Polcy_Premium"* feature. From figure 24, it can be inferred that there is no significant difference in the recommended policy premium. Therefore, *"Reco_Policy_Premium"* feature *will not affect the customers' response* (acceptance or rejection) to the proposed cross sell health insurance policy.

*Figure 24. p-value calculation using T-test and Z-test for feature "Reco_Policy_Premium"*

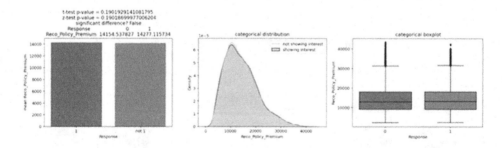

## CATEGORICAL – CATEGORICAL BIVARIATE ANALYSIS

We have done Categorical-Categorical bivariate analysis using grouped count plot for categorical features taking Response as our target feature and Chi-square test.

We performed categorical-categorical bivariate analysis using grouped count plot and chi-square test for the following hypothesis:

- Are the customers owning a house are more likely to show interest in the proposed health insurance policy?
- Are customers married to each-other more likely to show interest in the proposed health insurance policy?
- Are the customers with low health more likely to show interest in the proposed health insurance policy?
- What is the impact of policy period on customers' response to the health insurance policy?
- Does holding policy type i.e. *"Holding_Policy_Cat"* affect customers' interest in the proposed health insurance policy?
- Does recommended policy category i.e. *"Recommend_Policy_Cat"* affect customers' interest in the proposed health insurance policy?

## Chi-Square Test

A chi-square statistic is a way to show a relationship between two categorical variables. It is a kind of statistical filter method that can be used to assess the correlation between different features using their frequency distribution. The chi-squared statistic is a single number that tells us, how much difference exists between observed counts and expected counts (in case of no relationship at all in the population). It is calculated based on the difference between expected frequencies and the observed frequencies in one or more categories of the frequency table

The formula for calculating chi-square test is:

$$x^2 = \sum \frac{(0-E)^2}{E}$$

Where O is observed cell value, E is expected cell value and å is the sum of all cells.
We can interpret chi-square test results as follows:

- If there is a large difference between the observed and expected values, then the value of chi-square statistic ($x^2$) will be small and null hypothesis proves true.
- If there is a small difference between the observed and expected values, then the value of chi-square statistic ($x^2$) will be large and null hypothesis proves false.

The null hypothesis for a chi-square independence test is that two categorical variables are independent in some population. Independence means that the relative frequencies of one variable are identical over all levels of some other variable.

A p-value may be calculated for a chi-square test statistic. The p-value will tell us if our test results are significant or not. For this, following information needed:

1. Degrees of freedom. It is *the number of categories minus 1*. It can be calculated as: *degrees of freedom = (number of rows – 1) x (number of columns – 1)*
2. The alpha level (α). This is chosen by analyst. *The usual alpha level is 0.05 (5%), but could also have other levels like 0.01 or 0.10.*

*Figure 25. Bivariate analysis of feature "City_Code" and "Response" using Chi-square test*

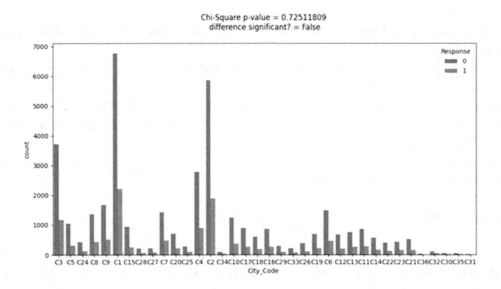

*Figure 26. Bivariate analysis of feature "Accomodation_Type" and "Response" using Chi-square test*

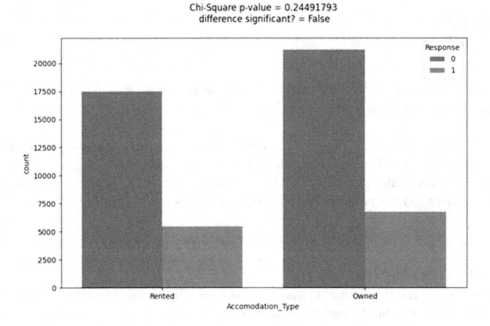

*Figure 27. Bivariate analysis of feature "Reco_Insurance_Type" and "Response" using Chi-square test*

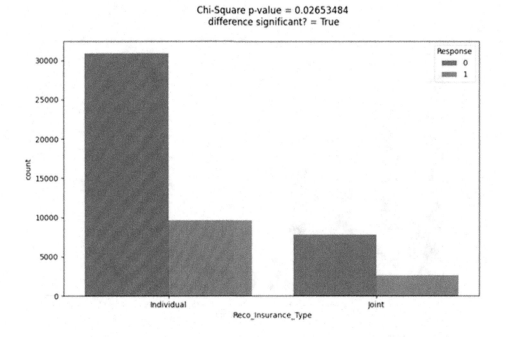

*Figure 28. Bivariate analysis of feature "Is_Spouse" and "Response" using Chi-square test*

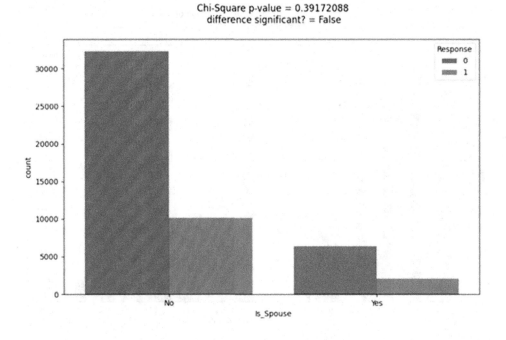

*Figure 29. Bivariate analysis of feature "Health_Indicator" and "Response" using Chi-square test*

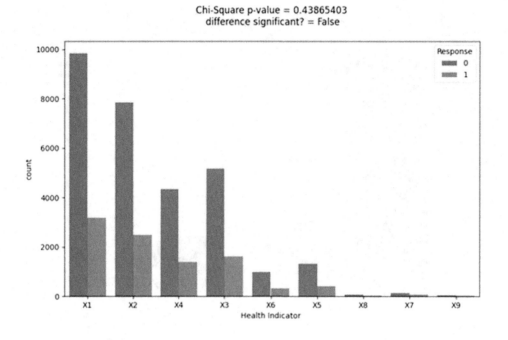

*Figure 30. Bivariate analysis of feature "Holding_Policy_Duration" and "Response" using Chi-square test*

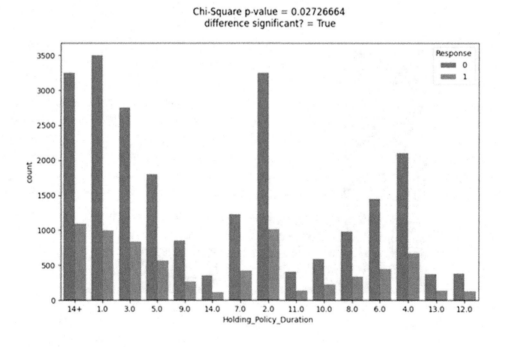

*Figure 31. Bivariate analysis of feature "Holding_Policy_Type" and "Response" using Chi-square test*

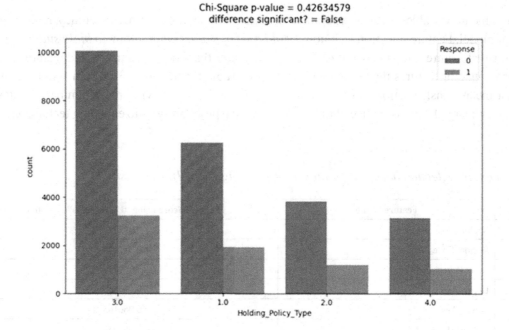

Figure 25 to 31 demonstrates the categorical-categorical bivariate analysis by taking response as one categorical feature. We can infer form these figures that features *"Reco_Insurance_Type"* and *"Holding_Policy_Duration"* affect customer's response towards proposed health policy.

## FEATURE ENGINEERING

Feature *engineering is the significant* step of *data preparation*. During feature engineering: (1) *new features are created* exploiting the knowledge gained during EDA as well as domain knowledge of dataset and (2) *encoding techniques* like stage, label, dummy (one hot), frequency and target encoding are applied on dataset. New features can be generated using ratio of, applying any scientific or statistical formula on, and doing any mathematical transformation of existing features (Rawat et al., 2021). We have done feature engineering as follows:

- New features are generated by *mean transformation* over *"Reco_Policy_Premium"* feature.
- Applying *frequency encoding* on features having more than two categories like *"City_Code"*, *"Region_Code"," Health_Indicator", "Holding_Policy_Duration"," Holding_Policy_Type"*
- Applying *target encoding* on features that are ordinal like *"Reco_Policy_Cat", "Holding_Policy_Duration", "Health_Indicator", "Holding_Policy_Type"*.
- We have also performed *label encoding* on categorical features which have two possible values like" Accomodation_*Type", "Reco_Insurance_Type", "Is_Spouse"*.

## FEATURE SELECTION

Use of redundant variables reduces generality, increases complexity, decreases accuracy, reduces performance of model. Feature selection techniques, *find a set of features that allows to build suitable models.* We performed feature selection using *Extra Trees classifier* that does has a tree based feature selection. The importance of features thus obtained is shown in Table 6 and figure 32. From figure 32, we can infer that mean transformation of the nominal categorical features having more number of categories helps in increasing the performance of the model while the probability ratio encoding techniques do not.

*Table 6. Feature selection based on feature score as using Extra Trees classifier*

| S. No. | Feature Name | Feature Score using "Extra Trees" classifier |
|---|---|---|
| 1 | Region_Code_mean | 0.072597 |
| 2 | Region_Code_freq | 0.072042 |
| 3 | Reco_Policy_Premium | 0.070953 |
| 4 | Upper_Age | 0.066659 |
| 5 | Lower_Age | 0.066165 |
| 6 | Holding_Policy_Duration_freq | 0.053080 |
| 7 | Holding_Policy_Duration_mean | 0.052708 |
| 8 | Health_Indicator_mean | 0.046114 |
| 9 | Health Indicator_freq | 0.045978 |
| 10 | Reco_Policy_Cat | 0.045281 |
| 11 | Health Indicator | 0.041663 |
| 12 | Holding_Policy_Type_freq | 0.038584 |
| 13 | Holding_Policy_Type_mean | 0.038021 |
| 14 | Holding_Policy_Duration | 0.034755 |
| 15 | Reco_Policy_Cat_freq | 0.029903 |
| 16 | Reco_Policy_Cat_mean | 0.027457 |
| 17 | Holding_Policy_Type | 0.022521 |
| 18 | Accomodation_Type | 0.020698 |
| 19 | City_Code_freq | 0.016574 |
| 20 | City_Code_mean | 0.016261 |

## FUTURE RESEARCH DIRECTIONS

Our future work aims working with a different insurance dataset that allows us to explore *Dimensionality Reduction* techniques. Feature engineering and dimensionality reduction both are part of data preparation and done before model creation. We have already explored feature engineering for decision support in this chapter. Dimensionality reduction can be approached in two ways: (1) Feature Selection and (2) Feature Extraction. Feature selection can further be conducted using (1) Chi-Square test, (2) Recursive Feature Elimination (RFE) and (3) Tree Based Feature Selection.

*Figure 32. Feature Selection using "Extra Trees Classifier"*

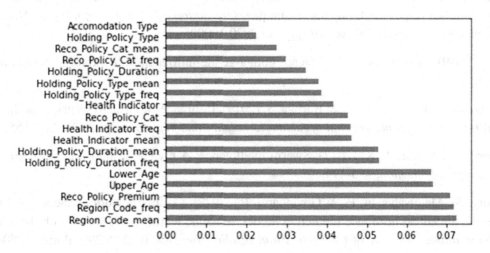

## CONCLUSION

The emergence of recent technologies is terrifically reshaping the insurance landscape. Statistical tools are intrinsic part of insurance industry and thus it is not surprising that insurers are trying to embrace machine learning to remain competitive, customer centric, drive operational brilliance and boosting growth. Insurance industry have requisite domain knowledge, actuaries, claims supervisors, financiers to support use of machine learning and data visualization techniques with help of data scientist. This chapter presented exploratory data analysis for decision support in insurance industry.

## REFERENCES

Accenture. (2018). https://www.accenture.com/_acnmedia/pdf-84/accenture-machine-leaning-insurance.pdf

Agrawal Y. (2019). https://towardsdatascience.com/hypothesis-testing-in-machine-learning-using-python-a0dc89e169ce

Aswani, R., Ghrera, S. P., Chandra, S., & Kar, A. K. (2021). A hybrid evolutionary approach for identifying spam websites for search engine marketing. *Evolutionary Intelligence*, *14*(4), 1803–1815. doi:10.100712065-020-00461-1

Bachniak, D., Rauch, L., Król, D., Liput, J., Słota, R., Kitowski, J., & Pietrzyk, M. (2017). Sensitivity analysis on HPC systems with Scalarm platform. *concurrency and Computation. Practice and Experience*, *29*(9), e4025. doi:10.1002/cpe.4025

Bacry, E., Gaiffas, S., Leroy, F., Morel, M., Nguyen, D. P., Sebiat, Y., & Sun, D. (2020). SCALPEL3: A scalable open-source library for healthcare claims databases. *International Journal of Medical Informatics*, *141*, 104203. doi:10.1016/j.ijmedinf.2020.104203 PMID:32485553

Batra, J., Jain, R., Tikkiwal, V. A., & Chakraborty, A. (2021). A comprehensive study of spam detection in e-mails using bio-inspired optimization techniques. *International Journal of Information Management Data Insights*, *1*(1), 100006. doi:10.1016/j.jjimei.2020.100006

BourkeD. (2019). https://towardsdatascience.com/a-gentle-introduction-to-exploratory-data-analysis-f11d843b8184

Burri, R. D., Burri, R., Bojja, R. R., & Buruga, S. (2019). Insurance claim analysis using machine learning algorithms. *International Journal of Advanced Science and Technology*, *127*(1), 147–155.

Chakraborty, A., & Kar, A. K. (2017). Swarm intelligence: A review of algorithms. *Nature-inspired computing and optimization*, 475-494.

Chowdhury, S., Mayilvahanan, P., & Govindaraj, R. (2022). Optimal feature extraction and classification-oriented medical insurance prediction model: Machine learning integrated with the internet of things. *International Journal of Computers and Applications*, *44*(3), 278–290. doi:10.1080/120621 2X.2020.1733307

Das, D., Chakraborty, C., & Banerjee, S. (2020). A framework development on big data analytics for terahertz healthcare. In *Terahertz biomedical and healthcare technologies* (pp. 127–143). Elsevier. doi:10.1016/B978-0-12-818556-8.00007-0

Das, S., Datta, S., Zubaidi, H. A., & Obaid, I. A. (2021). Applying interpretable machine learning to classify tree and utility pole related crash injury types. *IATSS Research*, *45*(3), 310–316. doi:10.1016/j.iatssr.2021.01.001

GuptaS. (2021). https://www.kaggle.com/imsparsh/imsparsh

Kar, A. K. (2016). Bio inspired computing–a review of algorithms and scope of applications. *Expert Systems with Applications*, *59*, 20–32. doi:10.1016/j.eswa.2016.04.018

Karhade, A. V., Ogink, P. T., Thio, Q. C., Broekman, M. L., Cha, T. D., Hershman, S. H., Mao, J., Peul, W. C., Schoenfeld, A. J., Bono, C. M., & Schwab, J. H. (2019). Machine learning for prediction of sustained opioid prescription after anterior cervical discectomy and fusion. *The Spine Journal*, *19*(6), 976–983. doi:10.1016/j.spinee.2019.01.009 PMID:30710731

Khan, F. H., Bashir, S., & Qamar, U. (2014). TOM: Twitter opinion mining framework using hybrid classification scheme. *Decision Support Systems*, *57*, 245–257. doi:10.1016/j.dss.2013.09.004

Knighton, J., Buchanan, B., Guzman, C., Elliott, R., White, E., & Rahm, B. (2020). Predicting flood insurance claims with hydrologic and socioeconomic demographics via machine learning: Exploring the roles of topography, minority populations, and political dissimilarity. *Journal of Environmental Management*, *272*, 111051. doi:10.1016/j.jenvman.2020.111051 PMID:32677622

Kose, I., Gokturk, M., & Kilic, K. (2015). An interactive machine-learning-based electronic fraud and abuse detection system in healthcare insurance. *Applied Soft Computing*, *36*, 283–299. doi:10.1016/j.asoc.2015.07.018

Kraus, M., Feuerriegel, S., & Oztekin, A. (2020). Deep learning in business analytics and operations research: Models, applications and managerial implications. *European Journal of Operational Research*, *281*(3), 628–641. doi:10.1016/j.ejor.2019.09.018

Larson, W. D., & Sinclair, T. M. (2022). Nowcasting unemployment insurance claims in the time of COVID-19. *International Journal of Forecasting*, 38(2), 635–647. doi:10.1016/j.ijforecast.2021.01.001 PMID:35185232

Maehashi, K., & Shintani, M. (2020). Macroeconomic forecasting using factor models and machine learning: An application to Japan. *Journal of the Japanese and International Economies*, 58, 101104. doi:10.1016/j.jjie.2020.101104

McGlade, D., & Scott-Hayward, S. (2019). ML-based cyber incident detection for Electronic Medical Record (EMR) systems. *Smart Health (Amsterdam, Netherlands)*, 12, 3–23. doi:10.1016/j.smhl.2018.05.001

Mita, Y., Inose, R., Goto, R., Kusama, Y., Koizumi, R., Yamasaki, D., Ishikane, M., Tanabe, M., Ohmagari, N., & Muraki, Y. (2021). An alternative index for evaluating AMU and anti-methicillin-resistant Staphylococcus aureus agent use: A study based on the National Database of Health Insurance Claims and Specific Health Checkups data of Japan. *Journal of Infection and Chemotherapy*, 27(7), 972–976. doi:10.1016/j.jiac.2021.02.009 PMID:33618976

NASSCOM. (2020). https://nasscom.in/knowledge-center/publications/unravelling-ai-healthcare-india

Nguyen, G., Dlugolinsky, S., Bobák, M., Tran, V., Lopez Garcia, A., Heredia, I., Malík, P., & Hluchý, L. (2019). Machine learning and deep learning frameworks and libraries for large-scale data mining: A survey. *Artificial Intelligence Review*, 52(1), 77–124. doi:10.100710462-018-09679-z

ObadiaY. (2017). https://towardsdatascience.com/the-use-of-knn-for-missing-values-cf33d935c637

Rawat, S., Rawat, A., Kumar, D., & Sabitha, A. S. (2021). Application of machine learning and data visualization techniques for decision support in the insurance sector. *International Journal of Information Management Data Insights*, 1(2), 100012. doi:10.1016/j.jjimei.2021.100012

ShroffR. (2019). https://towardsdatascience.com/how-are-insurance-companies-implementing-artificial-intelligence-ai-aaf845fce6a7

SPC. (2018). https://www.spcforexcel.com/knowledge/basic-statistics/are-skewness-and-kurtosis-useful-statistics

## ADDITIONAL READING

Alloghani, M., Al-Jumeily, D., Mustafina, J., Hussain, A., & Aljaaf, A. J. (2020). A systematic review on supervised and unsupervised machine learning algorithms for data science. *Supervised and unsupervised learning for data science*, 3-21.

Cox, V. (2017). Exploratory data analysis. In *Translating Statistics to Make Decisions* (pp. 47–74). Apress. doi:10.1007/978-1-4842-2256-0_3

Franke, T. M., Ho, T., & Christie, C. A. (2012). The chi-square test: Often used and more often misinterpreted. *The American Journal of Evaluation*, 33(3), 448–458. doi:10.1177/1098214011426594

Gentleman, R., & Carey, V. J. (2008). Unsupervised machine learning. In *Bioconductor case studies* (pp. 137–157). Springer. doi:10.1007/978-0-387-77240-0_10

Jiang, T., Gradus, J. L., & Rosellini, A. J. (2020). Supervised machine learning: A brief primer. *Behavior Therapy*, *51*(5), 675–687. doi:10.1016/j.beth.2020.05.002 PMID:32800297

Kassambara, A. (2017). *Practical guide to cluster analysis in R: Unsupervised machine learning* (Vol. 1). Sthda.

Kim, T. K. (2015). T test as a parametric statistic. *Korean Journal of Anesthesiology*, *68*(6), 540–546. doi:10.4097/kjae.2015.68.6.540 PMID:26634076

Kotsiantis, S. B., Zaharakis, I., & Pintelas, P. (2007). Supervised machine learning: A review of classification techniques. *Emerging artificial intelligence applications in computer engineering, 160*(1), 3-24.

McHugh, M. L. (2013). The chi-square test of independence. *Biochemia Medica*, *23*(2), 143–149. doi:10.11613/BM.2013.018 PMID:23894860

Nasteski, V. (2017). An overview of the supervised machine learning methods. *Horizons. b, 4*, 51-62.

Sharpe, D. (2015). Chi-square test is statistically significant: Now what? *Practical Assessment, Research & Evaluation*, *20*(1), 8.

Statistics, L. (2013). *Hypothesis testing*. The Null and Alternative Hypothesis.

Zaykin, D. V. (2011). Optimally weighted Z-test is a powerful method for combining probabilities in meta-analysis. *Journal of Evolutionary Biology*, *24*(8), 1836–1841. doi:10.1111/j.1420-9101.2011.02297.x PMID:21605215

Zou, K. H., Fielding, J. R., Silverman, S. G., & Tempany, C. M. (2003). Hypothesis testing, I: Proportions. *Radiology*, *226*(3), 609–613. doi:10.1148/radiol.2263011500 PMID:12601204

## KEY TERMS AND DEFINITIONS

**Bivariate Analysis:** *Bi* means two and *variate* means variable. Bivariate analysis discovers relationships between two variables/features. Bivariate analysis can be used to find the relationship between a feature in dataset and target feature (variable).

**Chi-Square Test:** Chi-square statistic is a kind of statistical filter method that can be used to assess the correlation between different features using their frequency distribution. It is a number that tells us, how much difference exists between observed counts and expected counts (in case of no relationship at all in the population).

**Critical Value:** P-value is the probability value that measures the chance of getting results at least as extreme as the results actually observed during the test, if the null hypothesis is correct. Since the p-value is just a value, we need to compare it with the critical value ($\alpha$): P-value > $\alpha$ (Critical value): Fail to reject the null hypothesis of the statistical test.P-value £ $\alpha$ (Critical value): Reject the null hypothesis of the statistical test.

**Exploratory Data Analysis (EDA):** Preliminary analysis of dataset in order to find important measures, metrics, features and relationship between measures so that we can gain an insight into trends, patterns, detect outliers in the dataset.

**M**

**Feature Engineering:** Feature engineering means creating new features exploiting the knowledge gained during exploratory data analysis as well as domain knowledge of dataset and application of encoding techniques like stage, label, dummy (one hot), frequency, target encoding.

**Machine Learning:** Machine Learning makes computers to learn something. It uses massive data and learning algorithms. The algorithms train themselves using this data in order to learn without being specifically programmed.

**P-Value:** In hypothesis testing, test statistic used to decide whether to accept or reject the null hypothesis. This decision is taken based on a number, called P-value. P-value is the probability value that measures the chance of getting results at least as extreme as the results actually observed during the test, if the null hypothesis is correct.

**Reinforcement Learning:** Reinforcement learning established on interaction with the environment. In this type of learning, machine learns to react to an environment on their own. Reinforcement learning is useful in the field of Robotics, Gaming, etc.

**Supervised Learning:** When the machine learns under supervision, it is called supervised learning. It uses a labelled dataset. Labelled dataset means that it contains the answer or solution to each problem dataset. For example, a labelled animal dataset may contain images with labels like elephant, cat, etc. Machine learning model, trained with the labelled dataset can predict the animal whenever a new animal image fed to the model by comparing that image with the labelled dataset.

**T-Test:** T-test allows testing of a hypothesis applicable to a population. It does so by calculating the means of two data groups. Z-test is used when sample size is small, $n < 30$.

**Univariate Analysis:** The objective of univariate analysis is to derive the data, summarize it and discover pattern(s) present in it. *Uni* means one and *variate* means variable, so univariate analysis involves single variable, i.e., it does not find relationships between variables.

**Unsupervised Learning:** In unsupervised learning, machine learns itself without any supervision. No labelled dataset is available in unsupervised learning. Unsupervised learning is a kind of self-organized learning. Objective of unsupervised learning to discover the underlying patterns.

**Z-Test:** Z-Test is statistical way of testing a hypothesis. Z-test is used when sample size is large, $n^3 30$.

# Tracking Buying Behavior by Analyzing Electronic Word of Mouth

**Mubina Khondkar**
*University of Dhaka, Bangladesh*

## INTRODUCTION

Word of mouth (WOM) is an informal communication tool to spread information about companies, brands, and buying experiences. In today's web 3.0 era, the internet is playing an important role in peoples' daily life and the web is providing the opportunity for electronic word of mouth (eWOM) communication through virtual media such as online discussion forums, electronic bulletin boards, newsgroups, blogs, review sites, and social networking sites (Goldsmith, 2006; Chu and Kim, 2011). Consumers are empowered to collect information from a vast geographically dispersed group of consumers, rather than from a few of them, who have experience with relevant products or services (Ratchford et al., 2001). Online shopping has become an everyday reality and consumers can express their opinions easily on the websites about the quality, price, style of the products, the service quality aspects including delivery time, different service attributes, and return policy (Filieri et al., 2021).

This research shows that the potential consumers search for others' opinions and recommendations when they are about to shop which is consistent with existing literature (Gani et al., 2021). Consumers are turning to online reviews to make purchase decisions ranging from where to travel, eat and stay, to the choice of doctors and consultants. Even in the case of recreation such as watching movies people check the reviews. Through eWOM, online retailers can influence consumers and can find their shortcomings and defects at all stages of their business operations relatively easily, to take corrective measures to improve their services. eWOM is getting more popular than traditional advertising and any other market-generated information because of the pervasive virtual media. It has become an unavoidable issue for managers and marketers to pay attention to because of the phenomenal growth of (Bickart and Schindler, 2001). In 2014, the total unique monthly visitors of Facebook was 0.9 billion; Twitter was 0.31 billion; LinkedIn was 0.255 billion; Pinterest was 0.250 billion; Yelp was 0.135 billion and Google was 0.120 billion (Fusion 360, 2015). As of November 2021, Google had 2.98 billion unique visitors, YouTube had 1.7 billion, Facebook had 1.53 billion and Wikipedia had 1.39 billion (Statista, 2022). The increasing popularity and increased number of digital platforms have created a challenging context. It has now become difficult to manage eWOM, as it might have both positive and negative impacts and thus, it can be stringent for the reputation of the business. Within minutes, a company or a product can be branded positively or impacted negatively in the consumers' minds. Consumers are interested in checking the reviews because of information availability, but sometimes they are demotivated to check the reviews because of misleading information and information overload.

There has been substantial growth in eWOM communities, but there are limited publications on the impacts of eWOM on the purchase behavior of consumers in Bangladesh. This research looks at the impacts that online reviews have on consumers' purchase decisions - taking into consideration of the motivating factors, reviewers' characteristics, website characteristics, and problems associated with eWOM. A dearth of related literature exists that focuses on the impacts of eWOM on consumer

DOI: 10.4018/978-1-7998-9220-5.ch040

purchase behavior in Bangladesh. This research aims to address this dearth. The insights would inform e-commerce site owners to understand the broader aspects of eWOM on consumers' purchase intention and inspire researchers to conduct further research in this area. The findings of this research will also help marketers to make an informed decision about eWOM management.

## BACKGROUND

### Statement of the Problem

There exists a dearth of literature regarding how eWOM influences consumers' purchase intention in Bangladesh. Therefore, understanding the realities around this phenomenon is imperative to capitalize on the pervasive digital technology and the impressive growth of mobile phones and the internet. The following research question is derived from this context.

*How does eWOM influence consumer purchase intention in Bangladesh?*

### Overview of eWOM

WOM can be considered as a free form of advertisement or promotion which is shared by consumers and triggered by an event that the customer has experienced (Khondkar, 2018; Mosley, 2022). This event could be something beyond expectation such as negative publicity which can destroy the image of the company, products, and services. It is an organic way of spreading information or informal communication between various parties. 92% of customers believe suggestions or recommendations from friends and family than advertising (Nielson, 2017). A related term known as buzz marketing refers to the promotion of a company or its products or services through predetermined objectives designed to get consumers and the media talking positively about the company, products, and services (Sırma, 2009). eWOM is also connected to another concept called viral marketing which can be compared to viruses as it tries to create an infectious diffusion and the messages, like viruses, are subjected to rapid multiplication and reach millions of consumers at a time.

Electronic peer-to-peer communication can be referred to as eWOM and described as "any positive or negative statement made by potential, actual, or former customers about a product or company, which is made available to a multitude of people and institutions via the Internet." (Hennig-Thurau et al., 2004:39). eWOM can be thought of as exchanging opinions, posting comments, reviews, and critiques on any digital platform. The advent of the Internet has provided consumers with an opportunity for gathering unbiased product-related information from consumers and they are capable enough to offer their consumption-related advice through eWOM. It is found that eWOM can be shared on various online platforms such as discussion forums, news blogs, vlogs, boycotts websites, review websites, and social media including Facebook, Twitter, Instagram, Snapchat, and LinkedIn (Thurau et al., 2004; Kauffman et al., 2021). eWOM and/or published statements on the web can reach far beyond the local community and personal connections within a short time (Rabben and Larsen, 2017). While traditional WOM is made orally, eWOM is available in written form and interested people can observe and access the information for an indefinite period until removed for public access (Park et al., 2007).

WOM marketing can be described as consumer-to-consumer marketing in which information is generated and distributed by consumers. Such information communicated through the Internet is called eWOM, and it has a profound influence on consumer behavior (Babić Rosario et al., 2016; Verma and Yadav, 2021). eWOM refers to any attempt by a former, potential, or actual consumer to highlight the positive or negative attributes of a product or company on an online platform (Hennig-Thurau et al., 2004). Consumers work as both the sender and receiver of eWOM whereas marketers usually search for that eWOM to strategize and manage their activities (Babić Rosario et al., 2020). Some experts have identified three steps in the eWOM process – the creation of eWOM, exposure of eWOM, and evaluation of eWOM (ibid). It is now being used to understand consumer insights with the help of text and hashtag analytics, sentiment, and different machine learning tools (Verma and Yadav, 2021). As a result, nowadays most companies are allocating larger portions of their marketing budgets to generate and manage the eWOM process to gauge the positive effect (Moorman, 2015).

## Research Objective

Tracking buying behavior based on the impact of one particular factor like eWOM is a daunting and difficult task, if not impossible, but an important one too, because of the close connection between these two issues as explored by reviewing and evident from the existing literature as stated in the overview of the eWOM section. Country or component-specific buying behavior tracking technologies are yet to be sophisticated enough to display precise performances in this regard.

In this context, initiating a discourse to identify the eWOM-related factors that can influence the purchase intentions of the consumers in the emerging economy of Bangladesh, and the probability of using these eWOM factors to develop applications to track factor specific buying behavior seems to be worth helping business people run their business more effectively by tracking the buying behavior of their customers based on eWOM.

Such research may also be replicated in different countries of the world to develop country-specific applications to track any single factor-based buying behavior.

## FOCUS OF THE STUDY

### Consumer Buying Process and eWOM

The consumer buying process includes everything that a consumer does at the time of purchasing. Usually, consumers follow a five-step process when making a purchase decision and these include need identification, information search, evaluation of alternatives, purchase decision making, and post-purchase evaluation (Solomon et al., 2011). The need recognition stage is not highly related to eWOM, but even at this stage, there is a possibility of consumers discovering a latent need when exposed to eWOM. At the information search stage, eWOM plays the most important role (Lee and Youn, 2009).

Online reviews help consumers to make purchase decisions. Nowadays, consumers are exposed to unlimited options of offerings. Online reviews can help consumers choose among a wide range of alternatives. With the increasingly widespread acceptance of social media, social media influencers have also been working as valued sources of eWOM that considerably influence buying process (Zhou et al., 2021). Most consumers are risk-averse, and their purchase decision is often influenced by negative reviews. Consumers trust other consumers' opinions or experiences more than advertisements (Bickart and Schindler, 2001; Muzareba, 2007; Chu and Kim, 2011).

Therefore, eWOM plays an important role in consumers' overall decision-making process mostly in the case of evaluation of the alternative options, gathering information about available options, and post-purchase evaluation. Identifying and understanding the motives that induce consumers to seek information is pivotal to figuring out related consumer behavior and the appropriateness of eWOM for meeting the needs (Assael, 1998).

## Impacts of eWOM on Purchase Intention

The Impacts of eWOM on purchase behavior have generated significant academic interest. The first inconclusive area involves eWOM metrics that include volume, valence, variance, mere existence, and specific content which have a profound influence on consumer purchase intention (reach, preference, consumer agreement). Many researchers find that the number of online reviews or volume has a more profound influence on purchase intention than any other metrics and that it can predict sales (Liu, 2006; Duan et al., 2008; Whinston 2008; Gu et al., 2012; Ho-Dac et al., 2013; Xiong and Bharadwaj, 2014). Contrary to this agreement, some researchers conclude that valence is more effective than volume while influencing purchase intention (Dellarocas et al., 2007; Chintagunta et al., 2010). Others (Sun, 2012) posit that variance, mere existence (Davis and Khazanchi, 2008), and specific content (Onishi and Manchanda, 2012) can influence consumers' purchase intention.

There exist differing opinions among researchers regarding the impact of negative eWOM on purchase behavior. Some studies have shown that consumers are more influenced by negative eWOM and it can lead to a reduction in sales (Chevalier and Mayzlin, 2006; Sun, 2012); conversely, other studies have identified that the presence of negative eWOM makes consumers aware and increases product evaluations by creating interest among consumers. (Doh and Hwang, 2009; Hiura et al., 2010; Kikumori and Ono, 2013). These varying propositions pose difficulties in the case of the development of a systematic insight that can assist marketers to make informed decisions about eWOM management (Babić Rosario et al., 2016). Bae and Lee (2011) claimed that different genders react differently toward online reviews. According to them, males are more influenced by positive online reviews than females. In addition, females are more influenced by negative reviews than males are. They also found that females perceive online shopping as riskier, and they are hesitant to adopt it.

Fan and Miao (2012) opined similarly, and they incorporated the Elaboration Likelihood Model with a wider perspective and argued that perception of the credibility of eWOM communication content, its acceptance, and ultimately the consumer buying intention depend on gender.

Product characteristics, competition, and platform characteristics can influence the effectiveness of eWOM on purchase intention (Babić Rosario et al., 2016). The influence of eWOM is more effective in the case of low-triable products than high-triable products because the experience of other consumers can reduce the perceived risk regarding quality (ibid). They find that the eWOM is greater for the industry in which few competitors are existing because high competition can lead to choosing overload. They also claim that the eWOM generated from community-based sites is more effective than any other platforms such as blogs and online product review sites. eWOM generated by these platforms encourages participants to reveal their identity and develop interconnected networks of relationships which is more valuable to recipients than eWOM which originates from platforms in which users' identities are anonymous and relationships are not fostered (Babić Rosario et al., 2016).

Sussman and Siegel (2003) argue that people seek and adopt necessary information posted on computer-mediated communication platforms which eventually shape their purchase decision making. Information adoption model supported analyses show that argument quality works as the central influence while source credibility is the peripheral influence (ibid). The effects of review quality and quantity vary with the level of involvement. Low involvement consumers accept what other consumers recommend because they are less motivated whereas high involvement consumers seek more useful information and high-quality reviews which are logical and persuasive (Sharifpour et al., 2016).

People can have different motives to write an online review, that are hidden from the public eye and make it harder for consumers to distinguish between effective and irrelevant reviews (Metzger, 2007). In traditional WOM settings, consumers rely on social cues such as personal relations, facial expressions, and personality traits, but the anonymous nature of eWOM prevents consumers from gaining such knowledge and they face difficulties in case of evaluating information (Lee and Youn, 2009).

Experts argue that review works as a crucial factor that considerably affects buying decisions (Liu et. al., 2008). A score index algorithm, assisted with a sentence-weight classification scheme to classify all the sentences in consumer reviews, also evidenced the efficacy of reviews in assisting consumers to make purchase decisions (Hu and Wu, 2009). Cheung and Thadani (2010) identified four factors - stimulus, communicator, response, and receiver – that can reveal the effects of eWOM at an individual level. It is found that consumers adopt online reviews to reduce perceived risks of the negative consequences of online buying (Bae and Lee, 2011). This correlation is pivotal as these negative consequences can influence their attitude towards a certain product and ultimately their buying decision. A recent study has developed a broader picture of the eWOM ecosystem and has found that quality of argument, valence, the usefulness of eWOM, and trust work as the most effective factors in shaping consumers' purchase intentions, whereas source credibility and volume of eWOM work as the least effective factors (Ismagilova et al., 2020). In addition to these, the credibility of eWOM, emotional trust, and attitude toward websites can also work as the other effective factors in this regard (ibid).

## Integrated Conceptual Framework

In light of the interacting factors found in the consumer buying process, their purchase intention, and eWOM by reviewing the existing literature as stated above, the following integrated conceptual framework (Figure 1) is developed to show how eWOM is connected to the concerned factors and purchase behavior.

## RESEARCH METHODOLOGY

In this study, a conclusive research design is used because the aim is to test specific hypotheses and examine specific relationships. The sampling frame consists of the consumers living in Dhaka and buying online from several e-commerce sites in Bangladesh including daraz.com.bd, priyoshop.com, akhoni.com, bikroy.com, and rokomari.com. These sites sell different sorts of products including preowned ones and thereby are representative of e-commerce business in the country. Respondents are selected from Dhaka only because most of the e-commerce has been operating to its full potential in this city.

The respondents are involved both in checking and providing opinions online. The effective sample size is 120 and they belong to four age groups - 16 to 25, 26 to 35, 36 to 50, and above 50. Initially, 75 male and 75 female potential respondents were approached considering the population gender ratio but only 120 respondents responded. As the e-commerce population size is unknown to the researcher, it is difficult to do probability sampling. So non-probability judgmental sampling technique has been used for this research. Both primary and secondary data are used for this research. Primary data was collected

*Figure 1. Conceptual framework (research team's construct*

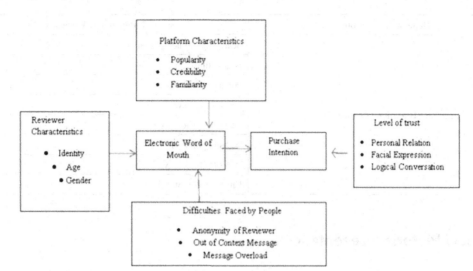

using a questionnaire whereas secondary data was collected from books, journal articles, reports, blogs, and other scholarly publications.

The questionnaire was sent to the respondents mostly through the Facebook platform with the help of the professional networks of the author. In addition to personal Facebook accounts, several Facebook user groups were used to reach out to the respondents. Some respondents were connected through email only as they did not have their Facebook accounts or did not want to get involved through their Facebook accounts. As most e-commerce sites allow consumers to shop using either an email account or a Facebook account, this approach to get connected to the respondents was useful. Analysis of primary data was supported by SPSS software.

## RESEARCH HYPOTHESES

The following hypotheses are developed based on the research question - how does eWOM influence consumer purchase intention in Bangladesh? Based on the question the hypotheses are:

Null hypothesis ($H_0$): There is no impact of eWOM on consumer purchase intention.

Alternative hypothesis ($H_a$): There is an impact of eWOM on consumer purchase intention.

The following dependent variable and independent variables (Table 1) are identified to support the analyses of the results of the hypotheses tests. Frequency distribution and a one-sample t-test will be used to identify the relationships among these variables.

## DATA ANALYSIS AND RESEARCH FINDINGS

In this section, findings are presented pictorially and analyzed with the help of descriptive statistics. Results of the hypotheses testing are also depicted along with interpretations. Sources of all the figures showing the graphical presentations, and the tables showing the descriptive statistics are the research team's construct.

*Table 1. Dependent and independent variables related to eWOM (research team's construct)*

| Dependent Variable | Independent Variables |
|---|---|
| **Purchase Intention of Consumers** | Searching online opinion |
| | High rating |
| | Positive review |
| | Negative review |
| | Acquiring information |
| | Website popularity |
| | Website credibility |
| | Unfamiliarity of website |

## Graphical / Pictorial Presentations

Figure 2 above shows that among 120 respondents, 65 respondents or 54% of the total respondents are female whereas 55 respondents or 46% are males. This implies that compared to female, the male is more interested to participate as respondents in research projects, given an equal number of male and female were approached. Figure 2 also shows the frequency distribution of the respondents' age groups. 77 (64%) of total respondents fall in 16 to 25, 34 (28%) fall in 26 to 35, 8 (7%) fall in 36-50, and 1 (1%) fall in age group of 50 and above. This implies that youth are more interested to take part in an online survey.

Figure 3 shows that most of the respondents are highly educated. Among 120 respondents, 73 (61%) have an honors degree and 38 (32%) have a master's degree.

Figure 4 shows that among 120 respondents, 108 (90%) read online reviews carefully and 12 (10%) do not read online reviews. Exposure to online reviews is therefore overwhelmingly high.

Figure 5 shows that majority of the respondents are students which implies that having a job might not be the most crucial factor for consumers to purchase online. This might also mean that students have either a consistent source of funds or involvement in informal income-generating activities. Among the 120 respondents, 69 (58%) are students and 41 (34%) are jobholders. The rest of the respondents are housewives, businesspeople, and other professionals.

Figure 6 shows that among the 120 respondents, 40 (33%) have no income of their own and are dependent on family income, 36 (30%) respondents have an income ranging from BDT1,000 to BDT15,000, and 29 (24%) of them have more than BDT30,000 to less than or equal to BDT45,000 income. Only 6 (5%) respondents have income within BDT15,000 to BDT30,000 range and 9 (8%) respondents have

*Figure 2. Gender and age distribution*

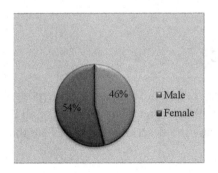 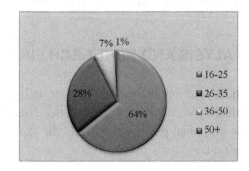

*Figure 3. Educational profile*

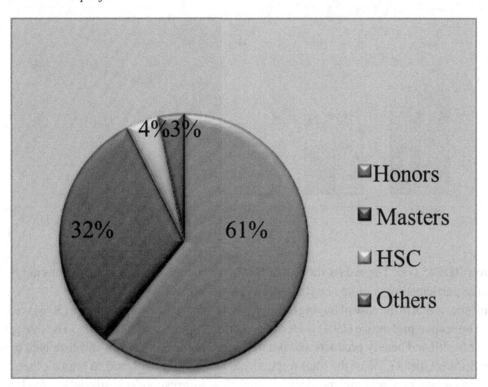

*Figure 4. Exposure to online reviews*

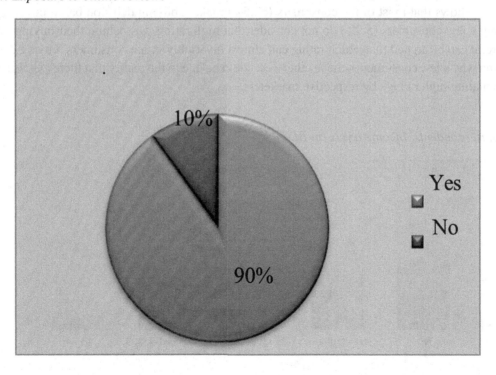

*Figure 5. Respondents' occupational profiles*

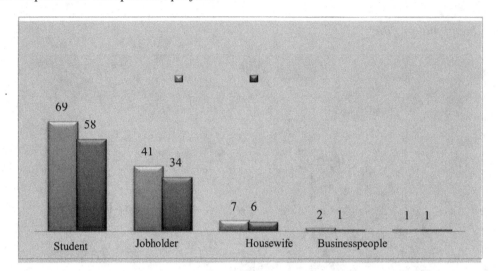

income over BDT45,000. These data show that the higher income of an individual does not necessarily indicate high participation in online buying and/or related involvements.

Figure 7 shows that in the case of buying through e-commerce, the first preference (30%) is for clothing products. The second preference (19%) is for both electronic goods and food items. The third preference (16%) is for health and beauty products and the fourth preference (8%) is for travel-related products.

Figure 8 shows that 47.5% of the total respondents agreed that they tend to search others' opinions before making a new product purchase decision, and 33.8% of respondents strongly agreed that. These evidence the strong influence of online reviews on online purchasing. Only 3.3% of respondents disagreed, 8% strongly disagreed, and 10% were neutral on this matter. Therefore, it can be concluded that eWOM has a considerable impact on purchase intention.

Figure 9 shows that most of the consumers (82.5%) make a buying decision based on high ratings while only a few consumers (5.9%) do not consider that high rating was behind their buying decision. Therefore, it can be argued that a high rating can almost invariably shape consumers' buying decisions. The reason why a few consumers believe otherwise could be due to the reality that there exist allegations of manipulating high ratings by respective marketers.

*Figure 6. Respondents' income levels (in BDT)*

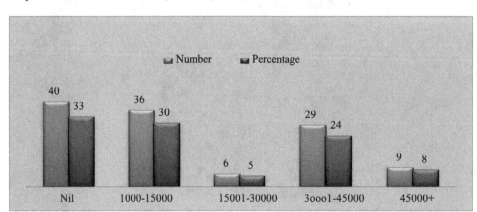

*Figure 7. Frequently purchased product*

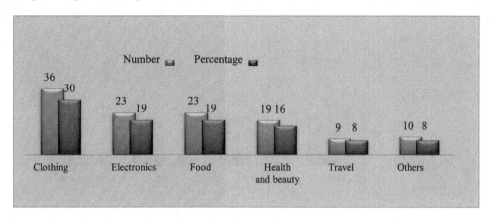

*Figure 8. New product purchase and others' opinions*

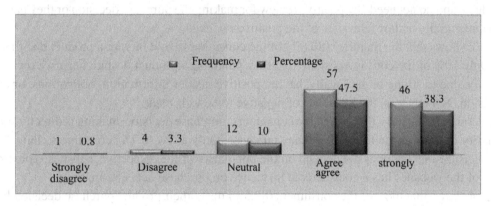

Figure 10 shows that a considerable number of consumers (31.7%) use online sources to collect product-related information, but their intention is not to purchase. Marketers should understand why they collect information and try to transform them into consumers. However, most of the consumers (39.2%) collect online information for making a buying decision. Therefore, the collection of product-related information from online sources is strongly related to making a buying decision.

Figure 11 shows that almost all (85%) consumers make purchase decisions when they find positive reviews of their respective products. Only a few (2.5%) consumers deny the impact of product-related

*Figure 9. Influence of high ratings on purchase decision*

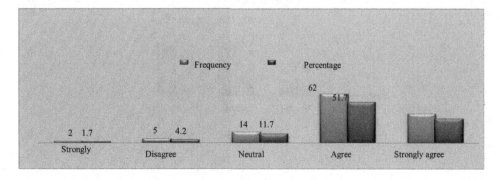

*Figure 10. Information collection and purchase intention*

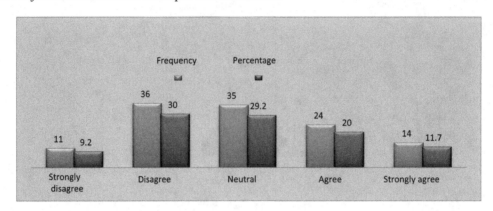

positive reviews on their purchase decision-making. This might implicate either they are strongly loyal to the products and do not need any positive review for making the purchase decision or they have doubts about the authenticity and/or relevance of the positive reviews.

Figure 12 shows that the majority (80.8%) of the consumers avoid buying a product due to negative reviews. Only 10% of the consumers share that they purchase a product despite negative reviews of it. This could be due to strong brand loyalty, having positive insider information, obligations, or any kind of compulsion. Nonetheless, the influence of negative reviews is clear.

Figure 13 shows that most (74.2%) of the consumers' purchase decision-making is directly shaped by the popularity of the website from where they purchase. Only a few (6.7%) consumers claim that their purchase decision-making does not depend on the popularity of the respective websites. Therefore, the popularity of the websites has a considerable influence on purchase decision-making.

Figure 14 shows that most of the consumers (82.5%) make their product purchase decision based on the credibility of the respective websites. Only 5.8% of the consumers claim that their purchase decisions do not depend on the credibility of the respective websites. Therefore, the credibility of the website has considerable influence over consumers' purchase decision-making.

Figure 15 shows that most of the consumers (41.7%) consider familiarity with the website while considering the reviews on those respective sites to shape their purchase decision-making. However, a considerable portion of the consumers (31.7%) also claim that they are equally happy to purchase from

*Figure 11. Impacts of positive reviews on purchase decision*

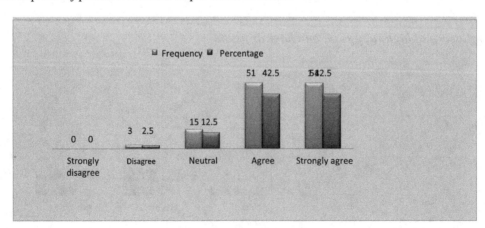

websites that are unfamiliar to them. Further research can identify insights on this matter which particularly might help new website owners to sell products through those.

*Figure 12. Negative reviews and purchase decisions*

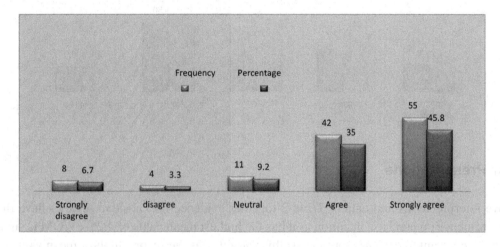

*Figure 13. Purchase and popularity of the website*

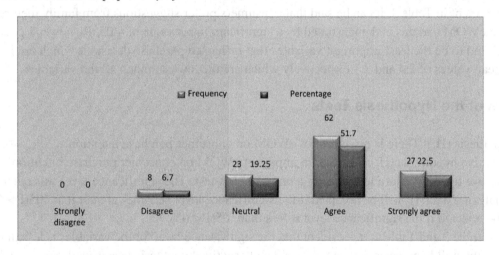

*Figure 14. Credibility of the website and purchase decision*

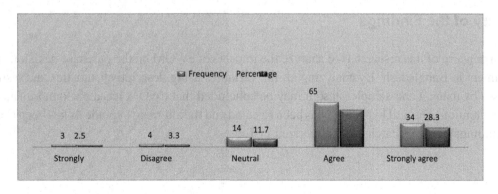

*Figure 15. Familiarity of the website and purchase decision*

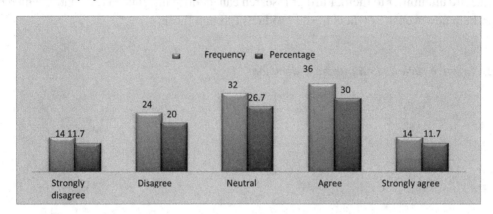

## Tabular Presentations

The above interpretations and data in Table 2 together evidence that positive reviews have the most profound influence on purchase intention as it has the highest mean value of 4.25. eWOM is significant when consumers want to try a new product as this variable has the second highest mean value of 4.19. High ratings of the product and credibility of the website also have profound influences on purchase intentions as the mean values are 4.05 and 4.02 respectively.

As is evident in Table 2, it can be said that consumers prefer suggestions from family members and friends to eWOM and this is demonstrated by a significant mean value of 4.05. Reviewers' gender and age are found to be the least important variables that influence purchase decisions which are indicated by the mean values of 2.4 and 2.7 respectively which are the lowest among all the variables.

## Results of the Hypothesis Tests

Null hypothesis ($H_0$): There is no impact of eWOM on consumer purchase intention.

Alternative hypothesis ($H_a$): There is an impact of eWOM on consumer purchase intention.

The above hypotheses are tested using a one-sample t-test. The significance level was taken as 5% while analyzing data. $H_0$ will be accepted if the significance level becomes greater than .05($P > .05$) but $H_0$ will be rejected if the significance level is less than .05($P < .05$).

As per Table 3 and Table 4, it is evident that the significance level for the variables is less than 0.05. Therefore, the null hypothesis is rejected, and the alternative hypothesis is accepted. So, it can be said that eWOM has an impact on purchase intention.

## Summary of the Findings

The main concern of this research is to analyze the impacts of eWOM on the purchase decision-making of consumers in Bangladesh. By analyzing all the variables using descriptive statistics and testing the hypotheses by using a one-sample t-test, it may be concluded that eWOM has a profound influence on purchase intention. The null hypothesis has been rejected and the alternate hypothesis has been accepted. All the findings of the research are summarized in Table 5.

*Table 2. Statistical insights*

| Items | N | Range | Minimum | Maximum | Mean | Std. Deviation |
|---|---|---|---|---|---|---|
| Search for others' opinions online | 120 | 4.0 | 1.0 | 5.0 | 4.192 | .8127 |
| Received high ratings | 120 | 4.0 | 1.0 | 5.0 | 4.058 | .8628 |
| Positive reviews | 120 | 3.0 | 2.0 | 5.0 | 4.250 | .7697 |
| Negative reviews | 120 | 4.0 | 1.0 | 5.0 | 4.100 | 1.1332 |
| Gather information only | 120 | 4.0 | 1.0 | 5.0 | 2.950 | 1.1585 |
| Popularity of the website | 120 | 3.0 | 2.0 | 5.0 | 3.900 | .8240 |
| Credibility of the website | 120 | 4.0 | 1.0 | 5.0 | 4.025 | .8741 |
| Unfamiliar website | 120 | 4.0 | 1.0 | 5.0 | 3.100 | 1.1980 |
| Gender of the reviewer | 120 | 4.0 | 1.0 | 5.0 | 2.400 | 1.1768 |
| Reviewer's age | 120 | 4.0 | 1.0 | 5.0 | 2.733 | 1.0980 |
| Occupation or level of education | 120 | 4.0 | 1.0 | 5.0 | 3.075 | 1.2310 |
| Online review is risky | 120 | 4.0 | 1.0 | 5.0 | 3.142 | 1.0556 |
| Difficult to find relevant information | 120 | 4.0 | 1.0 | 5.0 | 3.508 | .9258 |
| Privacy of personal information | 120 | 4.0 | 1.0 | 5.0 | 3.825 | 1.1051 |
| Biased and misleading | 120 | 4.0 | 1.0 | 5.0 | 3.175 | .9136 |
| Prefer suggestions from family | 120 | 3.0 | 2.0 | 5.0 | 4.058 | .8628 |
| Worried about decision | 120 | 4.0 | 1.0 | 5.0 | 3.375 | .9354 |
| Trust other customers opinions | 120 | 4.0 | 1.0 | 5.0 | 3.408 | 1.1189 |
| Information availability | 120 | 4.0 | 1.0 | 5.0 | 3.875 | .8941 |
| Valid N (listwise) | 120 | | | | | |

# FUTURE RESEARCH DIRECTIONS

This research produced an important contribution to the existing literature on the emerging and rapidly changing field of the digital world, focusing specifically on the impacts of eWOM on consumers in Bangladesh. A few very useful managerial implications for online retailers and managers have been extracted from the research findings, which will certainly lead to some further research in this field.

*Table 3. One-sample statistics*

| Variable | N | Mean | Std. Deviation | Std. Error Mean |
|---|---|---|---|---|
| Searching for others' opinions online | 120 | 4.192 | .8127 | .0742 |
| Received high ratings | 120 | 4.058 | .8628 | .0788 |
| Gather information only | 120 | 2.950 | 1.1585 | .1058 |
| Positive reviews | 120 | 4.250 | .7697 | .0703 |
| Negative reviews | 120 | 4.100 | 1.1332 | .1034 |
| Popularity of the website | 120 | 3.900 | .8240 | .0752 |
| Credibility of the website | 120 | 4.025 | .8741 | .0798 |
| New and unfamiliar website | 120 | 3.100 | 1.1980 | .1094 |

*Table 4. One-sample test*

| Variable | Test Value = 0 | | | | | |
| --- | --- | --- | --- | --- | --- | --- |
| | t | df | Sig. (2-tailed) | Mean Difference | 95% Confidence Interval of the Difference | |
| | | | | | Lower | Upper |
| Searching online opinions | 56.502 | 119 | .000 | 4.1917 | 4.045 | 4.339 |
| Received high ratings | 51.525 | 119 | .000 | 4.0583 | 3.902 | 4.214 |
| Gathering information only | 27.895 | 119 | .000 | 2.9500 | 2.741 | 3.159 |
| Positive reviews | 60.487 | 119 | .000 | 4.2500 | 4.111 | 4.389 |
| Negative reviews | 39.636 | 119 | .000 | 4.1000 | 3.895 | 4.305 |
| Popularity of the website | 51.847 | 119 | .000 | 3.9000 | 3.751 | 4.049 |
| Credibility of the website | 50.442 | 119 | .000 | 4.0250 | 3.867 | 4.183 |
| Unfamiliar website | 28.345 | 119 | .000 | 3.1000 | 2.883 | 3.317 |

## Managerial Implications and Recommendations

- Consumers often think that information available on websites is biased and misleading. So, website operators should not exaggerate information and they should provide authentic information regarding the quality and price of the products and services. The questions asked by the consumers should be answered quickly and accurately.

*Table 5. Summary of the findings*

| Serial | Result | Supporting Evidence |
| --- | --- | --- |
| 1 | Education is highly related to the impact of eWOM. The online consumers who are giving and receiving online opinions have a high educational background. | • Among 120 respondents 61% have Honors and 32% have master's degrees. |
| 2 | Income is not so important. Even the consumers who are not earning money and are dependent on others are regular users of online purchases and are influenced by online reviews. | • 33% of respondents have no income of their own. |
| 3 | eWOM is more effective in case of buying a new product than an existing product as consumers are more curious about new product benefits and costs. | • The higher mean value 4.19 for online search for new products. |
| 4 | Positive reviews and the credibility of the websites are the most important variables which can influence the purchase intention. | The highest mean value was 4.25 for positive reviews. The mean value for credibility is 4.02. |
| 5 | The gender of the reviewer is the least important variable. The second least important variable is the age of the reviewers. Both variables have no impact on purchase intention. | • The lowest mean value was 2.4 for gender and 2.7 for age. 30.8% of respondents strongly disagree in the case of gender, and 31.7% disagree about age. |
| 6 | Consumers are concerned about the privacy of their personal information in case of providing reviews on social networking sites. | • The higher mean value is 3.85 for this variable. 37.5% agree, and 30.8% strongly agree regarding the issue of privacy. |
| 7 | Though consumers are influenced by eWOM they are worried about their decisions because of the questionable credibility of such reviews. | • 49.2% agree and 6% strongly agree that they worry about decisions due to the credibility of reviews. |

- Globally, most of the target customers who are involved in online shopping and use eWOM communication are the younger generation. However, in Bangladesh, other age groups also use online shopping. Therefore, the online sellers should expand the customer base and involve other age groups by taking related initiatives.
- Many consumers find it difficult to find relevant information because of information overload. Providing too much information should be avoided. Information regarding the products and services should be concise, and unnecessary comments should be managed effectively by the website owners.
- Many consumers are concerned about the privacy of their personal information when sharing their opinions or experiences on any social networking site. Online marketers should develop appropriate mechanisms to restrict undue access to personal information and ensure privacy.

## Probable Future Research Projects and Areas

Based on the recommendations made above for the online retailers and managers, further research may be conducted on the following areas.

- Measuring promptness of online business owners to react to the comments made about their products and services on different websites frequently followed by the customers of the concerned business.
- Understanding the online browsing habit and buying behavioral patterns of different age groups in developing countries.
- Identifying the ways consumers understand related information or online content to deal with the eWOM in a more specific, concise, and focused manner.
- Identifying the ways to improve security aspects of the websites by collecting data regularly on the information leakage issues to keep customers' personal and private information safe and secure in the best possible ways by inventing & using the latest technologies.

In addition, as per the findings of this research, a considerable portion of the consumers (31.7%) claim that they are equally happy to purchase from websites that are unfamiliar to them. Further research can identify insights on this matter which particularly might help new website owners or new marketers to sell products through their web platforms. Future research is also needed to understand the dynamics of internet readiness, culture, and the economic situation regarding the impacts of eWOM on purchase decision-making in the context of developing countries.

## CONCLUSION

This research reveals that online comments or reviews are important factors that influence Bangladeshi consumers' purchase decisions. More than 80% of the participants claim that they read online reviews before making an online purchase. Higher ratings, positive reviews, popularity, and credibility of the websites are important variables that influence consumers to make purchase decisions. Consumers are more interested in checking the online reviews and asking more questions about a new brand.

The research reveals that clothing, food, and electronics are the most frequently purchased online products by consumers. Some consumers check online reviews and ask questions to get information only but purchase from physical stores. They are interested in reading online reviews and sharing their experiences because of information availability and accessibility. However, many consumers are concerned about the privacy of personal information while providing any comment on social networking sites.

Some consumers prefer traditional WOM to eWOM because they trust recommendations from friends and family members than the opinions provided by unknown people. They believe that the opinions available on the websites are biased and misleading. eWOM should be correct, unbiased, and relevant because it is not always possible for consumers to observe and reach out to the product in person before purchasing. Thus, sellers and consumers should be careful and remain honest while talking about a brand.

## ACKNOWLEDGMENT

This paper is an outcome of the extended and extensive research effort exerted by the author. The author genuinely acknowledges respondents' valued contributions to this research in the form of information they provided.

## REFERENCES

Assael, H. (1998). *Consumer Behavior and Marketing Action*. Thomson.

Babić Rosario, A., de Valck, K., & Sotgiu, F. (2020). Conceptualizing the electronic word-of-mouth process: What we know and need to know about eWOM creation, exposure, and evaluation. *Journal of the Academy of Marketing Science*, *48*(3), 422–448. doi:10.100711747-019-00706-1

Babić Rosario, A., Sotgiu, F., De Valck, K., & Bijmolt, T. H. (2016). The effect of electronic word of mouth on sales: A meta-analytic review of platform, product, and metric factors. *JMR, Journal of Marketing Research*, *53*(3), 297–318. doi:10.1509/jmr.14.0380

Bae, S., & Lee, T. (2011). Gender differences in consumers' perception of online consumer reviews. *Electronic Commerce Research*, *11*(2), 201–214. doi:10.100710660-010-9072-y

Bickart, B., & Schindler, R. M. (2001). Internet forums as influential sources of consumer information. *Journal of Interactive Marketing*, *15*(3), 31–40. doi:10.1002/dir.1014

Cheung, C. M., & Thadani, D. R. (2010). The Effectiveness of Electronic Word-of-Mouth Communication: A Literature Analysis. *Bled eConference, 23*, 329-345.

Chintagunta, P. K., Gopinath, S., & Venkataraman, S. (2010). The effects of online user reviews on movie box office performance: Accounting for sequential rollout and aggregation across local markets. *Marketing Science*, *29*(5), 944–957. doi:10.1287/mksc.1100.0572

Chu, S. C., & Kim, Y. (2011). Determinants of consumer engagement in electronic word-of-mouth (eWOM) in social networking sites. *International Journal of Advertising*, *30*(1), 47–75. doi:10.2501/IJA-30-1-047-075

Davis, A., & Khazanchi, D. (2008). An empirical study of online word of mouth as a predictor for multi-product category e-commerce sales. *Electronic Markets*, *18*(2), 130–141. doi:10.1080/10196780802044776

Dellarocas, C., Zhang, X. M., & Awad, N. F. (2007). Exploring the value of online product reviews in forecasting sales: The case of motion pictures. *Journal of Interactive Marketing*, *21*(4), 23–45. doi:10.1002/dir.20087

Doh, S. J., & Hwang, J. S. (2009). How consumers evaluate eWOM (electronic word-of-mouth) messages. *Cyberpsychology & Behavior*, *12*(2), 193–197. doi:10.1089/cpb.2008.0109 PMID:19072076

Duan, W., Bin, G., & Andrew, B. W. (2008). The dynamics of online word-of-mouth and product sales: An empirical investigation of the movie industry. *Journal of Retailing*, *84*(2), 233–242. doi:10.1016/j.jretai.2008.04.005

Fan, Y. W., & Miao, Y. F. (2012). Effect of electronic word-of-mouth on consumer purchase intention: The perspective of gender differences. *International Journal of Electronic Business Management*, *10*(3), 175–181.

Filieri, R., Galati, F., & Raguseo, E. (2021). The impact of service attributes and category on eWOM helpfulness: An investigation of extremely negative and positive ratings using latent semantic analytics and regression analysis. *Computers in Human Behavior*, *114*, 106527. doi:10.1016/j.chb.2020.106527

Fusion 360. (2015). *3 Less Popular Social Media Platforms Worth Tapping Into for Overall Brand Success*. Fusion 360. Available at: https://fusion360agency.com/3-less-popular-social-media-platforms-worth-tapping-into-for-overall-brand-success/

Gani, M. O., Faroque, A. R., Muzareba, A. M., Amin, S., & Rahman, M. (2021). An integrated model to decipher online food delivery app adoption behavior in the COVID-19 pandemic. *Journal of Foodservice Business Research*, 1–41. doi:10.1080/15378020.2021.2006040

Goldsmith, R. E. (2006). Electronic word-of-mouth. In M. Khosrow-Pour (Ed.), *Encyclopedia of E-Commerce, E-Government and Mobile Commerce*. Idea Group Publishing. doi:10.4018/978-1-59140-799-7.ch067

Gu, B., Park, J., & Konana, P. (2012). Research note—The impact of external word-of-mouth sources on retailer sales of high-involvement products. *Information Systems Research*, *23*(1), 182–196. doi:10.1287/isre.1100.0343

Hennig-Thurau, T., Gwinner, K. P., Walsh, G., & Gremler, D. D. (2004). Electronic word-of-mouth via consumer-opinion platforms: What motivates consumers to articulate themselves on the internet? *Journal of Interactive Marketing*, *18*(1), 38–52. doi:10.1002/dir.10073

Ho-Dac, N. N., Carson, S. J., & Moore, W. L. (2013). The effects of positive and negative online customer reviews: Do brand strength and category maturity matter? *Journal of Marketing*, *77*(6), 37–53. doi:10.1509/jm.11.0011

Hu, X., & Wu, B. (2009, September). Classification and summarization of pros and cons for customer reviews. *2009 IEEE/WIC/ACM International Joint Conference on Web Intelligence and Intelligent Agent Technology*, *3*, 73-76. 10.1109/WI-IAT.2009.234

Ismagilova, E., Slade, E. L., Rana, N. P., & Dwivedi, Y. K. (2020). The effect of electronic word of mouth communications on intention to buy: A meta-analysis. *Information Systems Frontiers*, *22*(5), 1203–1226. doi:10.100710796-019-09924-y

Kauffman, L., Weisberg, E. M., & Fishman, E. K. (2021). Not only for career networking: Can LinkedIn be used for radiology education? *Current Problems in Diagnostic Radiology*. PMID:34210558

Khondkar, M. (2018). A case on the traditional bangladeshi cuisine brand-haji biryani. *International Journal of Research in Business Management.*, *6*(5), 59–68.

Kikumori, M., & Ono, A. (2013). *Paradoxical relationship between the amount of negative eWOM messages and positive consumer attitude*. Working Paper, Keio University.

Lee, M., & Youn, S. (2009). Electronic word of mouth (eWOM). *International Journal of Advertising*, *28*(3), 473–499. doi:10.2501/S0265048709200709

Liu, Y. (2006). Word of mouth for movies: Its dynamics and impact on box office revenue. *Journal of Marketing*, *70*(3), 74–89. doi:10.1509/jmkg.70.3.074

Liu, Y., Huang, X., An, A., & Yu, X. (2008, December). Modeling and predicting the helpfulness of online reviews. In *2008 Eighth IEEE International Conference on Data Mining* (pp. 443-452). IEEE. 10.1109/ICDM.2008.94

Metzger, M. J. (2007). Making sense of credibility on the Web: Models for evaluating online information and recommendations for future research. *Journal of the American Society for Information Science and Technology*, *58*(13), 2078–2091. doi:10.1002/asi.20672

Moorman, C. (2015). *The CMO Survey Highlights and Insights, August 2013*. Academic Press.

Mosley, M. (2022). Word-of-Mouth Marketing: Why It's Incredibly Important [Blog]. *Referralrock*. Available at: https://referralrock.com/blog/Word-of-mouth-marketing/

Muzareba, A. M. (2007). Conventional approach to celebrity endorsement might not create success stories for business. *D.U. Journal of Marketing*, *10*, 1–31.

Nielsen. (2017). *Millennials on millennials: A look at viewing behavior, distraction and social media stars*. Available at: https://www.nielsen.com/us/en/insights/news/2017/millennials-on-millennials-a-look-atviewing-behavior-distraction-social-media-stars.html

Onishi, H., & Manchanda, P. (2012). Marketing activity, blogging and sales. *International Journal of Research in Marketing*, *29*(3), 221–234. doi:10.1016/j.ijresmar.2011.11.003

Ratchford, B. T., Talukdar, D., & Lee, M. S. (2001). A model of consumer choice of the Internet as an information source. *International Journal of Electronic Commerce*, *5*(3), 7–22. doi:10.1080/1086441 5.2001.11044217

Sharifpour, Y., Sukati, I., & Alikhan, M. N. A. B. (2016). The influence of electronic word-of-mouth on consumers' purchase intentions in Iranian telecommunication industry. *American Journal of Business, Economics and Management*, *4*(1), 1–6.

Sırma, E. (2009). *Word-of-mouth marketing from a global perspective* (Doctoral dissertation).

Statista. (2022). *Global top websites by monthly visits 2020*. Statista. Available at: https://www.statista.com/statistics/1201880/most-visited-websites-worldwide/

Sun, M. (2012). How does the variance of product ratings matter? *Management Science*, *58*(4), 696–707. doi:10.1287/mnsc.1110.1458

Sussman, S. W., & Siegal, W. S. (2003). Informational influence in organizations: An integrated approach to knowledge adoption. *Information Systems Research*, *14*(1), 47–65. doi:10.1287/isre.14.1.47.14767

Verma, S., & Yadav, N. (2021). Past, present, and future of electronic word of mouth (EWOM). *Journal of Interactive Marketing*, *53*, 111–128. doi:10.1016/j.intmar.2020.07.001

Zhou, S., Barnes, L., McCormick, H., & Cano, M. B. (2021). Social media influencers' narrative strategies to create eWOM: A theoretical contribution. *International Journal of Information Management*, *59*, 102293. doi:10.1016/j.ijinfomgt.2020.102293

## ADDITIONAL READING

Cheung, C. M., & Lee, M. K. (2012). What drives consumers to spread electronic word of mouth in online consumer-opinion platforms. *Decision Support Systems*, *53*(1), 218–225. doi:10.1016/j.dss.2012.01.015

Cheung, C. M., Lee, M. K., & Rabjohn, N. (2008). The impact of electronic word-of-mouth: The adoption of online opinions in online customer communities. *Internet Research*, *18*(3), 229–247. doi:10.1108/10662240810883290

Hennig-Thurau, T., Walsh, G., & Walsh, G. (2003). Electronic word-of-mouth: Motives for and consequences of reading customer articulations on the Internet. *International Journal of Electronic Commerce*, *8*(2), 51–74. doi:10.1080/10864415.2003.11044293

Hsieh, J. K., Hsieh, Y. C., & Tang, Y. C. (2012). Exploring the disseminating behaviors of eWOM marketing: Persuasion in online video. *Electronic Commerce Research*, *12*(2), 201–224. doi:10.100710660-012-9091-y

Ismagilova, E., Dwivedi, Y. K., Slade, E., & Williams, M. D. (2017). *Electronic word of mouth (eWOM) in the marketing context: A state of the art analysis and future directions*. Springer International Publishing. doi:10.1007/978-3-319-52459-7

Jansen, B. J., Zhang, M., Sobel, K., & Chowdury, A. (2009). Twitter power: Tweets as electronic word of mouth. *Journal of the American Society for Information Science and Technology*, *60*(11), 2169–2188. doi:10.1002/asi.21149

Litvin, S. W., Goldsmith, R. E., & Pan, B. (2008). Electronic word-of-mouth in hospitality and tourism management. *Tourism Management*, *29*(3), 458–468. doi:10.1016/j.tourman.2007.05.011

Phelps, J. E., Lewis, R., Mobilio, L., Perry, D., & Raman, N. (2004). Viral marketing or electronic word-of-mouth advertising: Examining consumer responses and motivations to pass along email. *Journal of Advertising Research*, *44*(4), 333–348. doi:10.1017/S0021849904040371

Vilpponen, A., Winter, S., & Sundqvist, S. (2006). Electronic word-of-mouth in online environments: Exploring referral networks structure and adoption behavior. *Journal of Interactive Advertising*, *6*(2), 8–77. doi:10.1080/15252019.2006.10722120

## KEY TERMS AND DEFINITIONS

**Behavior:** Any activity which is done or demonstrated by people or other creatures as an inevitable outcome of the interactions among the inherent driving forces with the external forces around in each situation or setting.

**Buying Intention:** Any wishful thinking or real thinking to have something under one's ownership in exchange for a settled price as per the existing exchange system operating in any locality, region, or country.

**Discussion Forum:** An actual or virtual gathering of a group of people engaged in or involved with the same or similar issues, to share their ideas, thoughts, and knowledge on that specific issue or topic in the process of answering the queries of the other members in the group to resolve different problems or just to have fun.

**Trust:** The assured feelings of comfort, safety, and security of a person, party, or a living entity on another person(s), the party(ies), or living entities regarding any sorts of activities they intend or plan to do together.

**Word of Mouth:** Uncensored and uncontrolled talks of people on some challenging, entertaining, hot, or interesting current issues, which spread very rapidly having a huge impact on the participating community.

# Web Service in Knowledge Management for Global Software Development

**Kamalendu Pal**

https://orcid.org/0000-0001-7158-6481

*City, University of London, UK*

## INTRODUCTION

Software system development has transitioned from a solo activity of designing standalone development activities to a distributed and collaborative production that needs a team-based software developer's contribution. Many software project staff now contribute to multiple projects. Due to this work practice, project boundaries blur, not just in terms of their work and how they design and develop software but also their communication channels and knowledge management practice. This way, software development is a knowledge-intensive practice. For example, people work in software development teams to bundle the man-powers and use the systematic approach to share system design knowledge. This collaborative knowledge sharing mechanism is known as *'knowledge management'* in software industries.

Modern software systems play a vital role in shaping significant social challenges (Jansen et al., 2009) (Pal, 2019). Software is an essential value-adding component of most consumer products (e.g., mobile phones, digital music systems, automobiles). Moreover, software systems are also heavily used in the aerospace industry, industrial business process automation, and control systems (Pal, 2020) (Pal & Karakostas, 2020). In these software applications, malfunction or error can cause loss of life or injury, and error-free software is crucial to the safety and wellbeing of people and businesses. Hence, there is an increasing requirement for applying strict engineering discipline to the development of software systems (Pal, 2021a) (Pal, 2021b); and requirements are context sensitive in which the system need-to-be operate (Sawyer et al., 2010) (Sharp et el., 1999).

Consequently, software products must be verified against their requirements throughout the development process like any engineering product. Different software development process models (e.g., Waterfall, Spiral, V-Model) have evolved over the decades to accommodate challenges in software development practice. This way, software development process models play a crucial role to provide a systematic and organized approach to software development (Sommerville, 2019). According to Kevin Roebuck (2012), a traditional Software Development Life Cycle (SDLC) provides the framework for planning and controlling the development or modification of software products, along with the methodologies and process models used for software development.

The design and development of software is a complex process consisting of many interdependent activities that involve many stages such as inception, initial design, detailed design and development, implementation and testing, operation, maintenance, and retirement. This includes requirements analysis, technical development, project management, quality assurance, and customer support activities. In addition, requirement analysis has always been with any human act of design, so it may seem strange

DOI: 10.4018/978-1-7998-9220-5.ch041

that they have been singled out for study in computer science and created a subject area known as requirement engineering.

Requirement engineering is a term used to describe the business processes involved in eliciting, documenting, and maintaining requirements for a software system. It is about discovering what the users need the system to do for them. For example, one can define a requirement as "a specification of what should be implemented". There are two types of requirements: (i) functional requirements – what behaviour the system should offer; and (ii) non-functional requirements – a specific property related to quality assurance, time, or cost of development related issues. They are a statement of *what* the software system should do and not *how* it should.

When making software requirements elicitation and specification, requirement engineers share their experiences; these experiences (i.e., knowledge) need to be used in the software development process. In addition, knowledge in software development results from perception, realization, rational thinking, experience, or innate reasoning ability. Knowledge is intuitive and exists within people, part of human reasoning and decision making. Therefore, knowledge is hard to capture in words or understand entirely logically. Knowledge is a framework for "evaluating and incorporating new experiences and information". It is the basis for the process, which continues along time (Davenport & Prusak, 1998).

It is vital to have a digital infrastructure to manage software development knowledge, which will help the software development team effectively do their work. This chapter will focus on software requirement engineering (SRE) related knowledge management issues. In addition, there are several research works (Wouters, Deridder & Van Paesschen, 2000) (Mayank, Kositsyna & Austin, 2004) (Lasheras et al., 2009) (Kaiya & Saeki, 2006) published in recent years that relates to knowledge management in software requirement engineering.

Requirement engineering business activities typically involve people from at least two distinct fields: (1) business consulting area (e.g., clients and other stakeholders); and (2) software development area (e.g., business engineers, system architects, software project managers). These diverse groups of people often produce information flows and knowledge exchange that need to be captured in an automated way by which global participants can interact with this newly formed system. This automated system needs to accommodate the different UML (Unified Modelling Language) models of proposed software development and to critique these models at different business meetings. In other words, this automated environment will help gather, analyze, and document software requirements. In addition, it will help the global software development actors manage collaboratively and share their knowledge through this global digital platform.

This global software platform will use the Internet, Intranet, or any other computer network to connect with the different stakeholders for software development purposes. Its central constituent part is web service-based technology, and web service can strengthen communication and information exchange within a community. Different web service-based 'web portal' infrastructures appeared to provide an open and effective communication forum for their members. A web portal collects and presents relevant information for the community in a simplistic sense, and users can publish and access events or information to the community.

This new semantic enhanced web service is known as semantic web. Ontologies are the backbone technology for the Semantic Web and, more generally – for managing formalized knowledge in the context of distributed systems. In an ontology-based system, information is made better understandable for the computer application, thus assisting end-users to search, extract, interpret and process information efficiently. Therefore, semantic web technologies can improve the information sharing process by overcoming the problems of standard web portals. Finally, this chapter presents the key features of an ontology-based web portal framework, known as CKIA (Collaborative Knowledge Integration Architecture), for integrating distributed business information systems in a global software development project.

The rest of the chapter is organized as follows. Section 2 outlines background information on the current software industry. The next session highlights some related research works. It includes what software requirements are and why they are needed in the system development process. Section 4 presents the use of ontologies in the software requirement engineering domain. Section 5 explains some knowledge management issues in software development and highlights its use in this domain. Section 6 illustrates the main constituent parts of the CKIA framework through a business scenario related to a web portal-based application to a virtual software project in the domain of enterprise resource planning (ERP). Section 7 describes the future research directions. Finally, Section 8 concludes the chapter with concluding remarks.

## BACKGROUND INFORMATION OF CURRENT SOFTWARE INDUSTRY

Recent decades have observed the effects of globalization in different industries (e.g., software development, hardware manufacturing). This way, globally distributed collaborations and virtual teams have become increasingly common in many work practices, particularly in software system design and development (Kotlarsky & Oshri, 2005) (Krishna et al., 2004). Additionally, ongoing evolutions in information and communication technologies (ICTs) have made it possible to collaborate effectively in a distributed working environment. Moreover, from small projects enabled by ICTs, business organizations now embark on major complex software development projects across multiple locations.

For example, many organizations in developed countries are outsourcing parts of their information technology (IT) services and developing business processes to developing nations (Carmel & Agarwal, 2002), which results in strategic projects on a bigger scale and with a longer lifespan. Examples include DuPont, the US-based global company, that in 2006 signed a sourcing contract with the computer service centre (CSC) and Accenture to design and develop SAP-based ERP application software systems globally across more than 20 locations at a cost exceeding one billion US dollar.

This way, global software development communities offer a real-time platform for collaboration and knowledge sharing to almost anyone on the globe. Collaboration and team performance depend on the socialization of the dispersed team members (Andres, 2002). Socialization refers to how individuals acquire the behaviours, attitudes, and knowledge necessary for participation in an organization (Ahuja & Galvin, 2003) (Goodman & Wilson, 2000). It is also stated that through socialization, the norms, identity, and cohesion between team members develop, enabling team members to effectively communicate and perform (Ahuja & Galvin, 2003) (Hinds & Weisband, 2003). However, the existing research on socialization is based on co-located teams. In non-co-located teams, further research has highlighted the adequate conditions under which socialization can be supported effectively. For example, digital communication technologies can enhance the socialization of a newcomer in a virtual team (Ahuja & Galvin, 2003).

Nonetheless, non-co-located teams may vary in their degree of virtuality (Crowston et al., 2005), the length of the project, and the number of remotely distributed counterparts involved. The key objective of this research is to understand how globally distributed teams support the re-acquisition of norms and attitudes over time. Data were drawn from several globally distributed software development projects at SAP, LeCroy and Baan organizational levels. Moreover, the case analyses suggest that various activities were carried out before, during, and after face-to-face meetings to support socialization between remote counterparts. In conclusion, the lifecycle of socialization in globally distributed teams (GDTs) is described, and suggestions to managers and further research are made. Following this introduction, the next section provides reviews of the literature relating to global software development.

## RELATED RESEARCH WORKS

Several researchers have tried to address different issues of global software development. A detailed account of the issues/problems being faced by global software development and their solutions proposed by different researchers is discussed in this section. Sangwan and Ros (Sangwan & Ros, 2008) stress that communication, coordination, and control mechanisms are significant issues in global software development.

Korkala and fellow researchers (Korkala et al., 2010) applied traditional and agile methods in global software development. The study's findings show that agile methods provide better results in global software development. However, the study suffers from the limitation that the data was collected from only one group, and other teams were ignored.

Grechanik and colleagues (Grechanik et al., 2010) discussed communication and coordination challenges among developers and testers and their impacts on the overall project. The research identifies many issues that can arise due to poor communication and coordination between testers and developers and highlight their impact on the project. However, a fitting framework or model must communicate and coordinate between developers and testers to resolve these issues. Rammasubbu and Balan (Rammasubbu & Balan, 2008) point out specific research directions to enhance the governance scheme for Distributed Software Development projects.

Software engineering (SE) knowledge is dynamic and evolves with technology, organizational culture, and the changing needs of an organization's software development practices. Kess and Haapasalo (Kess & Haapasalo, 2002) argue that software processes are knowledge processes structured within a KM framework. Aurum et al. (Aurum et al., 2003) point out that software development can be improved by recognizing related knowledge content and structure and appropriate knowledge and engaging in planning activities. For example, Basili and fellow researchers (Basili et al., 1994) (Basili et al., 2001) acknowledge that for an organization to implement the 'Experience Factory' (EF) approach for KM, several potential barriers to success must be overcome. First, they argue that while the EF aims to institute a learning organization, it requires a significant investment of time and effort. Second, they stress the need to leverage alternate approaches to distribute knowledge quickly. Third, the 'Answer Garden' approach is depicted as a short-term solution to questions that may not require extended responses.

Johansson and other researchers (Johansson et al., 1999) apply an 'Experience Engine' approach to KM in SE as a subset of the EF. They list problems identified with the EF approach, such as its experimental nature, the organizational restructuring it prompts, and its reliance upon an experience base containing a vast amount of written documentation. Further, they assert that experience is best transferred when the receiver is "actually doing something related to the experience being transferred" (Johansson et al., 1999). Finally, the researchers claim that written documentation is not referred to when problems occur and emphasize the short life span of software engineering knowledge.

Kess and Haapasalo (Kess & Haapasalo, 2002) advocated using project reviews to improve software quality. The results of a case study into a telecommunications organization are disclosed, revealing the centrality of knowledge creation, and sharing to improve the software development process. It is argued that project reviews enable both tacit and explicit knowledge to be managed effectively. Inspection metrics are portrayed as integral to brainstorming sessions, which deliver feedback to various phases in the software development process.

A research group (Dingsøyr et al., 2001) provides insight into small to medium organizations' problems in addressing KM in SE. They consider postmortem reviews and experience reports as two approaches suitable for collecting software development knowledge. They conclude that lightweight postmortem reviews reveal more about software development practices, while experience reports are more suited to client relationships and interaction.

Rus and Lindvall (Rus & Lindyall, 2002) declare that organizations must facilitate formal and informal knowledge sharing between software developers. They assert that KM complements existing approaches to software process improvement rather than seeking to replace them. KM activities designed to support SE are grouped into three categories: the purpose of outputs, the scope of inputs and the effort required to process inputs. Several options for implementing and using KM systems for SE are advanced, such as expert identification, creating KM champions, document management, and predictive modelling to direct decision-making.

Moreover, in every software development project, the software engineers must understand the proposed system specifications and development tools (e.g., case tools, programming languages, database development software) and the company's guidelines and in-house practice policies. Accordingly, software development is a very knowledge-intensive process. To this end, more complex cognitive structures are required. These are denoted as "knowledge". In order to organize the knowledge, knowledge management becomes a vital task. The final product is software, and every step leading there can be realized through a computer. Hence, everything is digital. This aspect makes it particularly interesting to study computer-based knowledge management in software development.

## KNOWLEDGE MANAGEMENT IN REQUIREMENT ENGINEERING

Most global software companies agree that knowledge is an essential asset for success and survival in an increasingly competitive and global market (Pal, 2022a).

### Knowledge Management Processes

Alavi and Leidner (2001) describe the knowledge management processes of a company, based on what they call a knowledge system, the individuals and groups that share their knowledge in a company, as shown in Figure 1. In this knowledge system, the authors elaborate on the different activities related to knowledge management. This whole web of knowledge management activities is constructed on top of the modes of knowledge creation outlined by Nonaka (1994). On an individual level, every person has tacit and explicit knowledge. The knowledge is being transferred back and forth through externalization and internalization within the individual or through combination and socialization between individuals. However, similarly to tacit and explicit knowledge of individuals, every group (e.g., team members) has two types of memory: Episodic and semantic.

A group's semantic memory represents the available explicated knowledge, for example, a document on a file server. The explicit knowledge of an individual can be made available for the rest of the group by transferring it to the semantic memory of the group. Also, an individual can increase their explicit knowledge by accessing the group's semantic memory. For this learning from the group's semantic memory, the group's episodic memory is critical.

Episodic memory represents the collection of shared experiences of the group. Every individual contributes with parts of their tacit knowledge to it. Beyond the interaction of people is the utilization of knowledge. The knowledge application is always based on an individual's tacit knowledge. At the same time, when applying knowledge, the individual learns from that, which feeds back to the individual's tacit knowledge.

Additionally, the application of knowledge can also be based on the semantic memory directly, which feeds back to the group's episodic memory. This system of knowledge sharing among individuals in a group occurs in different areas of a company. Each of these groups then shares their knowledge via a group dialogue. The process of managing knowledge involves the following actions:

- Knowledge gathering - acquisition and collection of the knowledge to be managed.
- Knowledge organization and structuring -imposing a structure on the knowledge acquired to manage it effectively.
- Knowledge refinement - correcting, updating, adding, defining knowledge, in short, maintaining knowledge.
- Knowledge distribution - bringing the knowledge to the professionals who need it.

## Relevance of Knowledge Management in Software Development

As software development is an abstract engineering discipline, knowledge management is essential. When developing software, a high degree of coordination (Kraut and Streeter, 1995) and management (Sommerville, 2001) (Pressman, 2000) become vital tasks. Because the focus is to solve specific problems, the organization of software projects often differs enormously from one to the other (Mockus et al., 2002). For example, Sveiby (1997) points out that most business organizations face similar problems administrating their intellectual capital. Hence, knowledge management for software development companies is a vast field with various approaches (Aurum et al., 2008).

Rus and Lindvall (2002) describe three aspects of software development supported by knowledge management: Core software engineering activities, product & project memory, and learning & improvement. The core activities of software engineering contain the management of documents or competencies and software reuse.

With product and project memory, the authors refer to the evolution of software, e.g., with the help of systems for version control, change management or design documentation. Finally, the learning and improvement include a recording of results and experiences. The reason is to learn from that and improve future decisions or activities. The desire to improve in these three areas of concern motivates knowledge management in software development.

In order to conduct knowledge management successfully, many different approaches are possible and documented. For example, Liebowitz and Megbolugbe (2003) propose a framework for implementing knowledge management, which combines an activity cycle of knowledge management levels and the resulting knowledge objects. The different knowledge management levels are essential: conceptualization, reflection, acting, and review. Each lead to the four knowledge objects: Goals, risks, constraints, or measures. The diversity of dimensions illustrates the complexity of knowledge management.

Information systems that are applied to manage a company's knowledge or support managing a company's knowledge are referred to as knowledge management systems. For example, Alavi and Leidner (2001) conducted a literature review and illustrated different perspectives on knowledge with their implications (see Table 1).

This chapter presents a knowledge management approach grounded to research on knowledge engineering and semantic web technology. During the past few decades, knowledge engineering has been a field that has been concerned with capturing, analyzing, organizing, structuring, representing, manipulating, and maintaining knowledge to obtain intelligent solutions for industrial problems. It is, therefore, no surprise that knowledge engineering techniques (e.g., rule-based reasoning, case-based reasoning) can be of high value for knowledge management, which is precisely concerned with the issues for global software development.

*Table 1. Knowledge perspectives and their implications*

| Perspectives | | Implications for Knowledge Management (KM) | Implications for Knowledge Management Systems (KMS) |
|---|---|---|---|
| Knowledge (data and information) | Data is facts, raw numbers. Information is processed / interpreted data. Knowledge is personalized information. | KM focuses on exposing individuals to potentially helpful information and facilitating the assimilation of information. | KMS will not appear radically different from the existing information system (IS) but will be extended towards helping users assimilate information. |
| State of mind | Knowledge is the state of knowing and understanding. | KM involves enhancing an individual's learning and understanding through the provision of information. | Information technology (IT) is to provide access to sources of knowledge rather than knowledge itself. |
| Object | Knowledge is an object to be stored and manipulated. | Key KM issue is building and managing knowledge stocks. | The role of IT involves gathering, storing, and transferring knowledge. |
| Process | Knowledge is a process of applying expertise. | KM focuses on knowledge flows and the process of creation, sharing, and distributing knowledge. | The role of IT is to provide a link among sources of knowledge to create wider breadth and depth of knowledge flows. |
| Access to Information | Knowledge is a condition of access to information. | KM focuses on organized access to and retrieval of content. | The role of IT is to provide effective search and retrieval mechanisms for locating relevant information. |
| Capability | Knowledge is the potential to influence action. | KM is about building core competencies and understanding strategic expertise. | The role of IT is to enhance intellectual capital by supporting the development of individual and organizational competencies. |

This chapter approaches knowledge management is based on ontologies and makes knowledge assets intelligently accessible to people in global software development companies. The following sections describe an approach to intelligent knowledge management that explicitly uses ontology and semantic web-based portal technology. The proof of concept is given by a prototype development involving knowledge management of a virtual organization.

## OVERVIEW OF WEB SERVICE AND MOTIVATION

Web services have become the popular choice for implementing service delivery systems that are distributed and interoperable. These services are built by core technologies that cater to services' communication, description, and discovery. The standards that provide these functionalities are Simple Object Access Protocol (SOAP), Web Services Description Language (WSDL), and Universal Description, Discovery, and Integration (UDDI) (OASIS, 2004). These XML-based standards use common Internet Protocols to exchange service requests and responses. (Extensible Markup Language, XML, is a standard platform-independent data format across the enterprise) Figure 1A shows the relationship of these technologies as a standard stack for web services, and Figure 1B briefly describes service publishing, service requesting and service finding mechanisms using a simple diagrammatic representation.

In this way, web services aim to use the web as a worldwide infrastructure for distributed computation to conduct seamless business processes. However, as the set of available web services increases, it becomes crucial to have automated service discovery mechanisms to help find services that match a requester's requirement.

*Figure 1. Diagrammatic representation of web service technologies: (A) Web service standards stack and (B) Web service relationships diagram*

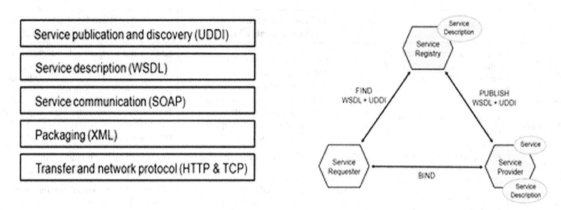

Finding appropriate web services depends on the facilities available for service providers to describe the capabilities of their services and for service requesters to describe their needs in an unambiguous form that is ideally machine-readable. For example, ordinary web service descriptions need to be enriched using domain ontology (or semantic markup) to achieve this objective. The following section introduces the concept of semantic annotation mechanisms of web services.

## Semantic Web Service and Ontology

Semantic web service is an emerging information technology (IT) paradigm in which the main goal is to realize the development of distributed applications in a heterogeneous business environment. The underlying technology is extended with rich semantic representations developed in the Semantic Web and automatic reasoning developed in artificial intelligence. For example, consider two databases that refer to '*jacket*' and '*coat*' respectively; a program that compares or combines information across the two databases must know that these two terms are being used to mean the same thing. Ideally, the programs must have a way to discover such common meanings for whatever databases it encounters. A solution to this problem is provided using collections of information called *ontologies* (Gruber, 1993) (Pal, 2018).

## Ontology: Meaning, Usage, and Representation

Ontologies may vary not only in their content but also in their structure and implementation. An ontology could be used for describing simple lexicons or controlled vocabularies to categorically organize thesauri and taxonomies where terms are given distinguishing properties, to full-blown ontologies where these properties can define new concepts and where concepts have named relationships. Ontologies also differ concerning the scope and purpose of their content. However, in the last few decades, the Web Ontology Language (OWL) has become the de-facto standard for the knowledge representation in the Semantic Web. It is based on a logic thought to be especially computable, known as Description Logics (DLs) (Baader & Nutt, 2003). It is a fragment of First-Order Logic.

## Web Service Description of a Business Scenario

Varied materials need to be procured for garment manufacturing supply chain management purposes in the inventory management system. Material attribute ontology design can be viewed from higher perspectives, such as semantic meanings or logical reasoning. However, this chapter focuses on one pragmatic perspective: a definition of concepts (or taxonomies) in the domain and related relations. In order to illustrate the functionalities of domain ontologies, a simple business scenario has been used to demonstrate the activities.

## An Example of Business Case for Matchmaking Algorithm

A simple 'retail sales scenario' describes the implemented system functionalities. It envisions an application running on a mobile computer that allows its user to purchase Jackets from an online business. This example considers how a request is matched with the service advertised for jacket selling. An algorithm tries to perform semantic matching for relevant Jersey. The algorithm is shown in ALGORITHM 1, and it takes two ontological concepts, the root node (root) and the concepts graph (G), as input and computes a semantic similarity between the concepts as output. The part of the ontology hierarchy used in this example is shown in Figure 4. Each node of this hierarchy represents a concept. In the experimental comparison, semantic similarity among Jersey, Waistcoat, Sweater, Vest, Cardigan, Pullover, and Jumper are considered.

## Semantic Web Services and Case-Based Reasoning

Semantic web service initiatives define information systems infrastructure, which enriches the human-readable data with machine-readable annotations. In order to achieve these objectives, one main issue would be the *markup* of web services to make them computer interpretable. Powerful tools should be facilitated across the *web service lifecycle* (Papazoglou, 2012).

At the same time, the research community has intensively been working on similarity-based *retrieval* and *adoption* of past solutions to match recent problems: two main aspects in the working semantic web service applications. Case-Based Reasoning (CBR) is one thriving applied computing community that programs the idea of finding a solution to a problem based on experience of similar types of problems. CBR systems are analogical reasoning systems (Liang & Konsynski, 1993) (Pal & Palmer, 1999). CBR system aims to infer a solution for a problem at hand from solutions of a set of previously solved similar problems. In recent years, *ontologies, and descriptive logics* (DLs) have become systems of interest for the CBR community (Watson, 1997) (Pal & Campbell, 1997). Moreover, some the real-world CBR applications are taking advantage of the descriptive logics (DLs) reasoning mechanisms for the processes involved in the CBR cycle.

In CKIA, efforts of the semantic web services lifecycle management and CBR cycle are trying to find synergies between both. Given a certain requirement describing the user goals, automatic web service discovery typically uses a dedicated inference mechanism to answer queries conforming to the logic formalism and the terms defined in the ontology.

## PROPOSED SYSTEM FRAMEWORK

This section briefly presents the overall architecture of the CKIA system and illustrates the interplay of the different components. The computational framework of CKIA is shown in Figure 2. It uses a relational similarity assessment measure between implicitly stated concepts. Finally, the proposed framework accepts the service consumer request, consisting of new service requirements (e.g., input, output, precondition). Next, the user requirement information is parsed for further processing; and final semantically ranked web services are presented to the service consumer.

The dynamics of CKIA are as follows:

- Initially, the service repository is populated with semantically enriched web service descriptions for specific application areas with software requirement engineering related issues.
- The service requester inputs the service requirements using CKIA's interface.
- The service matchmaking module takes the retrieved cases and the annotation of problem description from the semantic description generator module (with the system framework), run them through a matchmaking algorithm and forward the closest match web service to the requester.

*Figure 2. Diagrammatic representation of the CKIA*

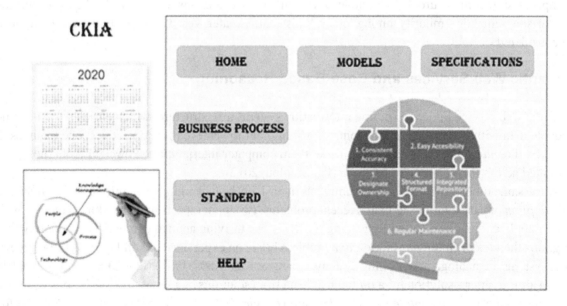

The ontologically enhanced web service descriptions are manually encoded in the CKIA service repository. In the processing of ontological concept matching, when dealing with the similarity between concepts, it considers inheritance (i.e., the relationship between supper-class and subclass) relations and considers the distance relationship between concepts. For example, a concept similarity matching method based on semantic distance has been used in CKIA to consider the inheritance relations and semantic distance between concepts carefully. The CKIA uses structural case-based reasoning (S-CBR) for services and the relevant ontological concepts storage purpose, and it uses rule-based reasoning (RBR) for service similarity assessment. As shown in Figure 3, the algorithm is used to discover semantic web services advertised within CKIA.

In CKIA, the similarity between concepts $C_i$, $C_j$ can be expressed by a number, and its values can fall somewhere between 0 and 1. It may be viewed as a one-directional relation, and its larger values imply a higher similarity between the concepts. The concept similarity is described as follows:

*Concept Similarity:* An ontological concept (C) similarity $(\partial)$ is considered as a *relation*, and it can be defined as $\partial$: C x C → [0, 1]. In simple, it is a function from a pair of concepts to a real number between *zero* and *one* expressing the degree of similarity between two concepts such that:

1. $\forall C_1 \in G, \quad \partial(C_1, C_1) = 1$
2. $\forall C_1, C_2 \in G, \quad 0 \le \partial(C_1, C_2) \le 1$
3. $\forall C_1, C_2, C_3 \cdot G, \quad \text{IF } Sim_d(C_1, C_2) > Sim_d(C_1, C_3) \quad \text{THEN } \partial(C_1, C_2) < \partial(C_1, C_3)$

The above properties provide the range of semantic similarity function $\partial(C_j, C_j)$. For exactly similar concepts, the similarity is $\partial(C_1, C_1) = 1$ ; when two concepts have nothing in common, their similarity is $\partial(C_1, C_2) = 0$ . In this way, the output of the similarity function should be in closed interval [0, 1]. Here $Sim_d$ represents the semantic distance and $(C_1, C_2, C_3)$ represent three concepts of graph G. In CKIA, the following semantic similarity $(\partial)$ function has been used for computation purpose:

$$\partial(C_1, C_2) = \frac{1}{\text{deg}* Sim_d(C_1, C_2) + 1}$$

$C_1$ and $C_2$ represent two concepts and 'deg' represent the impact degree of semantic distance on semantic similarity, and it should be between $0 < \text{deg} \le 1$. A weight allocation function is used, as shown below, to compute the semantic similarity between concepts:

$$w(C_m, C_n) = [\max(depth(C_m)) + \frac{OrderNumber(C_n)}{TNodes(G) + 1} + 1]^{-1}$$

Where, $C_m$ and $C_n$ represent two nodes directly connected, $\max(depth(C_m))$ represents the maximum depth of the node $C_m$ (the depth of the root node is equal to 0 and 1 for the nodes directly connected to the root node and so on), TNodes(G) and OrderNumber($C_n$) represent the total number of nodes in concept graph G and the order number of the node ($C_n$) between their siblings.

In Table 2, (a) is the result of synonymy similarity (Giunchiglia et al, 2004), (b) tabulates the results of Jian and Conrath similarity (Jiang & Conrath, 1997) results, (c) tabulates the results of path similarity (Varelas et al, 2005), and (d) tabulates the results of the proposed Algorithm-I used in CKIA. In this experiment, a suitable value for *deg* parameter is considered.

*Algorithm 1. Algorithm for semantic similarity computation*

---

Algorithm 1

---

input: two concepts ($C_1,C_2$), root node (root), concepts graph (G)
output: semantic similarity value between two concepts
1:  begin
2:  if $C_1$ and $C_2$ are same concept then $Sim_d = 0$
3:  else
4:      if $C_1$ and $C_2$ are directly connected then $Sim_d = w(C_1, C_2)$
5:      else
6:          if idirect path connection exist then
7:              $S_{path01} = $ ShortestPath $(G, C_1, Root_N)$
8:              $S_{path02} = $ ShortestPath $(G, C_2, Root_N)$
9:              $Sim_d = w(S_{path01}) + w(S_{path02}) - 2*w(CSPath]$
10:         end if
11:             $\partial(C_1, C_2) = \dfrac{1}{deg \cdot Sim_d + 1}$
12:     end if
13: end if
14: return $\partial$
15: end

---

*Figure 3. The hierarchical concept relationships*

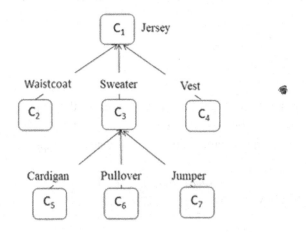

As shown in Table 2, the synonymy similarity measure can only find similarities between the same concepts, and Jian and Conrath' similarity measure is better than the synonymy similarity measure. The path similarity measure and CKIA's used method are better than the above two methods. The path similarity measure can find the semantic similarity between concepts, but the similarity score is low. The CIA's similarity method can also get the semantic similarity between concepts, and the similarity score is high.

*Table 2. The results of various similarity measures*

|       | $C_1$ | $C_2$ | $C_3$ | $C_4$ | $C_5$ |
|-------|-------|-------|-------|-------|-------|
| $C_1$ | 1.00  | 0.00  | 0.00  | 0.00  | 0.00  |
| $C_2$ | 0.00  | 1.00  | 0.00  | 0.00  | 0.00  |
| $C_3$ | 0.00  | 0.00  | 1.00  | 0.00  | 0.00  |
| $C_4$ | 0.00  | 0.00  | 0.00  | 1.00  | 0.00  |
| $C_5$ | 0.00  | 0.00  | 0.00  | 0.00  | 1.00  |

(a) Synonymy similarity

|       | $C_1$ | $C_1$ | $C_1$ | $C_1$ | $C_1$ |
|-------|-------|-------|-------|-------|-------|
| $C_1$ | 1.00  | 0.60  | 0.41  | 0.97  | 0.52  |
| $C_2$ | 0.42  | 1.00  | 0.81  | 0.60  | 0.36  |
| $C_3$ | 0.97  | 0.81  | 1.00  | 0.68  | 0.44  |
| $C_4$ | 0.60  | 0.60  | 0.68  | 1.00  | 0.53  |
| $C_5$ | 0.52  | 0.36  | 0.44  | 0.53  | 1.00  |

(b) James & Conrath similarity

|       | $C_1$ | $C_2$ | $C_3$ | $C_4$ | $C_5$ |
|-------|-------|-------|-------|-------|-------|
| $C_1$ | 1.00  | 0.25  | 0.50  | 0.20  | 0.20  |
| $C_2$ | 0.25  | 1.00  | 0.50  | 0.33  | 0.16  |
| $C_3$ | 0.50  | 0.50  | 1.00  | 0.25  | 0.16  |
| $C_4$ | 0.20  | 0.33  | 0.25  | 1.00  | 0.20  |
| $C_5$ | 0.20  | 0.16  | 0.16  | 0.20  | 1.00  |

(c) Path similarity

|       | $C_1$ | $C_2$ | $C_3$ | $C_4$ | $C_5$ |
|-------|-------|-------|-------|-------|-------|
| $C_1$ | 1.00  | 0.48  | 0.65  | 0.51  | 0.38  |
| $C_2$ | 0.48  | 1.00  | 0.65  | 0.51  | 0.38  |
| $C_3$ | 0.65  | 0.65  | 1.00  | 0.71  | 0.48  |
| $C_4$ | 0.51  | 0.51  | 0.71  | 1.00  | 0.59  |
| $C_5$ | 0.38  | 0.38  | 0.48  | 0.59  | 1.00  |

(d) The proposed algorithm

## FUTURE RESEARCH DIRECTIONS

Considering the novelty of the semantic features provided by unique semantic web technologies in this chapter, the work done constitutes only the starting point of a more-wide research initiative. For example, semantic web technologies are appropriately exploited, providing enhanced capabilities concerning standard web portals, such as improved information creation, maintenance, and access. The ontology concepts are very well integrated into creating, maintaining, and accessing steps, guiding, and supporting the user in these tasks. The usability and general assessment of the portal need to be evaluated. The portal also lacks community features to support and improve communication between community members. Indeed, many improvements and open points need to be solved. Further development of successful semantic web portals should focus on the above criteria, international standards, and global software project management legal issues.

## CONCLUSION

This chapter reviews some of the business and technology challenges that companies face today in software design and development business activities for information sharing between business partners and describes how several of these difficulties could be overcome using semantic web service. In addition, knowledge management evolved into a service management discipline that aims to integrate the existing management approach into orchestration.

In this chapter, a software development information sharing architecture between business partners is described using a semantic web service framework. The architecture is based on a hybrid knowledge-based service matchmaking framework, which uses structural case-based reasoning (S-CBR) and rule-based reasoning (RBR). It uses ontology enhanced web service descriptions, object-oriented S-CBR knowledge representation, description logic (DL) for service formalization, and an algorithm to measure ontological concept similarity based on semantic distance. This algorithm considers the inheritance relation between concepts and the level of concepts in ontology hierarchy; an experimental evaluation of the proposed algorithm is presented. In this architecture, ontological concepts play an essential role in developing the semantic web to define shared terms in web resources in global software development.

## REFERENCES

Ahuja, M. K., & Galvin, J. E. (2003). Socialization in virtual groups. *Journal of Management, 29*(2), 161–185. doi:10.1177/014920630302900203

Akkiraju, R., Farrell, J., Miller, J., Nagarajan, M., Schmidt, M., Sheth, A., & Verma, K. (2005). *Web Service Semantics - WSDL-S*. A joint UGA-IBM Technical Note, version 1.0. http://lsdis.cs.uga.edu/projects/METEOR-S/WSDL-S

Andres, H. P. (2002). A Comparison of face-to-face and virtual software development teams. *Team Performance Management, 8*(1/2), 39–48. doi:10.1108/13527590210425077

Antoniou, G., & Harmelen, F. V. (2008). *A Semantic Web Primer*. The MIT Press.

Aurum, A., Daneshgar, F., & Ward, J. (2008, May). Investigating Knowledge Management practices in software development organizations An Australian experience. *Information and Software Technology, 50*(6), 511–533. doi:10.1016/j.infsof.2007.05.005

Aurum, A., Jeffery, R., Wohlin, C., & Handzic, M. (2003). *Managing Software Engineering Knowledge*. Springer. doi:10.1007/978-3-662-05129-0

Baader, F., & Nutt, W. (2003). *Basic Description Logics, The description logic handbook*. Cambridge University Press.

Basili, V., Costa, P., Lindvall, M., Mendonca, M., & Seaman, C. (2001). An Experience Management System for a Software Engineering Research Organisation. *Proceedings of 26th Annual NASA Goddard Software Engineering Workshop*, 29-35. 10.1109/SEW.2001.992652

Basili, V. R., Caldiera, G., & Rombach, H. D. (1994). Experience Factory. In J. J. Marciniak (Ed.), *Encyclopedia of Software Engineering*. John Wiley and Sons.

Bergmann, R., & Schaaf, M. (2003). Structural Case-Based Reasoning and Ontology-Based Knowledge Management: A Perfect Match? *Journal of Universal Computer Science, UCS, 9*(7), 608–626.

Berners-Lee, T., Hendler, J., & Lassila, O. (2001). The Semantic Web. *Scientific American, 284*(May), 34–43. doi:10.1038cientificamerican0501-34 PMID:11323639

Bianchini, D., Antonellis, V. A., Melchiori, M., & Salvi, D. (2006). Semantic Enriched Service Discovery. *International Conference in Data Engineering Workshop*, 38.

Cai, M., Zhang, W. Y., Zhang, K., & Li, S. T. (2010). SWMRD: A Semantic Web-based manufacturing resource discovery system for cross-enterprise collaboration. *International Journal of Production Research*, *48*(120), 3445–3460. doi:10.1080/00207540902814330

Cardoso, J. (2006). Discovering Semantic Web Services with and without a Common Ontology Commitment. *IEEE Service Computing Workshop*, 183-190.

Cardoso, J., & Sheth, A. (2003). Semantic e-Workflow Composition. *Journal of Intelligent Information Systems*, *21*(3), 191–225. doi:10.1023/A:1025542915514

Carmel, E., & Agarwal, R. (2002). The Maturation of Offshore Sourcing of Information Technology Work. *MIS Quarterly Executive*, *1*(2), 65–77.

Cassar, G., Barnaghi, P., & Moessner, K. (2014). Probabilistic matchmaking methods for automated service discovery. *IEEE Transactions on Services Computing*, *7*(4), 654–666. doi:10.1109/TSC.2013.28

Copacino, W., & Anderson, D. (2003). Connecting with the Bottom Line: A Global Study of Supply Chain Leadership and its Contribution to the High-Performance Business. *Accenture, 1*.

Crowston, K., Howison, J., Masango, C., & Eseryel, U. Y. (2005). *Self-organization of teams for free/libre open-source software development*. In Academy of Management Conference, Honolulu, HI.

Dingsøyr, T., Brede Moe, N., & Nytro, O. (2001). Augmenting Experience reports with Lightweight Postmortem Reviews. *Third International Conference on Product-Focused Software Process Improvement, PROFES 2001*.

Domingue, J., Cabral, L., Galizia, S., Tanasescu, V., Gugliotta, A., Norton, B., & Pedrinaci, C. (2008). IRS-III: A Broker-based Approach to Semantic Web Service. *Journal of Web Semantics*, *6*(2), 109–132. doi:10.1016/j.websem.2008.01.001

Farrag, T. A., Saleh, A. I., & Ali, H. A. (2013). Toward SWSS discovery: Mapping from WSDL to OWL-S based on ontology search and standardization engine. *IEEE Transactions on Knowledge and Data Engineering*, *25*(3), 1135–1147. doi:10.1109/TKDE.2012.25

Fensel, D., & Busslcr, C. (2002). The Web Service Modeling Framework WSMF. *Electronic Commerce Research and Applications*, *1*(2), 113–137. doi:10.1016/S1567-4223(02)00015-7

Fugate, B., Sahin, F., & Mentzer, J. T. (2006). Supply Chain Management Coordination Mechanisms. *Journal of Business Logistics*, *27*(2), 129–161. doi:10.1002/j.2158-1592.2006.tb00220.x

Ganeshan, R., & Harrison, T. P. (1995). *An introduction to supply chain management*. Supply Chain Management, Version 1. Available from http://silmaril.smeal.psu.edu/misc/supply_chain_intro.html

Gibbs, W. (1994, September). Software's chronic crisis. *Scientific American*, *271*(3), 72–81.

Giunchiglia, F., Shvaiko, P., & Yatskevich, M. (2004). S-Match: an algorithm and an implementation of semantic matching. *Proceedings of 1st European Semantic Web Symposium (ESWS)*, 3053, 61-75. 10.1007/978-3-540-25956-5_5

Goodman, P. S., & Wilson, J. M. (2000). Research in Groups and Teams. *JAI Press*.

Grechanik, M., Jones, J. A., Orso, A., & van der Hoek, A. (2010). Bridging Gaps between Developers and Testers in Globally, Distributed Software Development. *Proceedings of the FSE/SDP Workshop on Future of Software Engineering Research*, 149-154.

Grimm, S., Monk, B., & Preist, C. (2006). Matching Semantic Service Descriptions with Local Closed-World Reasoning. *European Semantic Web Conference*, 575-589. 10.1007/11762256_42

Gruber, T. R. (1993). *A Translation Approach to Portable Ontology Specifications*. Stanford University, Computer Science Department, Knowledge Systems Laboratory, Technical Report KSL 92-71.

Guarino, N., & Giaretta, P. (1995). *Ontologies and Knowledge Base: Towards a Terminological Classification Toward Very Large Knowledge Base: Knowledge Building and Knowledge Sharing*. IOS Press.

Hinds, P., & Weisband, S. (2003). Creating Conditions for Effective Virtual Teams. *Jossey-Bass*.

Jansen, S., Finkelstein, A., & Brinkkemper, S. (2009). A Sense of Community: A Research Agenda for Software Ecosystems. *International Conference on Software Engineering - Companion, ICSE, Companion Software Engineering-Companion Volume*, 187-190.

Jansen, S., Finkelstein, A., & Brinkkemper, S. (2009). A Sense of Community: A Research Agenda for Software Ecosystems. *First International Workshop on Software Ecosystems (IWSECO-2009)*, 34-48.

Jiang, J. J., & Conrath, D. W. (1997). Semantic similarity based on Corpus Statistics and Lexical Taxonomy. *Proceedings of International Conference Research on Computational Linguistics*.

Johansson, C., Hall, P., & Coquard, M. (1999). Talk to Paula and Peter – They are Experienced. *Proceedings of the Workshop of Learning Software Organizations*, 69-76.

Kaiya, H., & Sacki, M. (2006). Using Domain Ontology as Domain Knowledge for Requirement Elicitation. *Proceedings of the 14th IEEE International Requirements Engineering Conference*, 189-198.

Kalakota, R., & Whiston, A. (1997). *Electronic commerce: a manager's guide*. Addison Wesley.

Kaufer, F., & Klusch, M. (2006). WSMO-MX: A Logic Programming Based Hybrid Service Matchmaker. *European Conference on Web Services*, 161-170. 10.1109/ECOWS.2006.39

Kess, P., & Haapasalo, H. (2002). Knowledge creation through a project review process in software production. *International Journal of Production Economics*, *80*(1), 49–55.

Kess, P., & Haapasalo, H. (2002). Knowledge creation through a project review process in software production. *International Journal of Production Economics*, *80*(1), 49–55.

Kiefer, C., & Bernstein, A. (2008). The Creation and Evaluation of iSPARQL Strategies for Matchmaking. *European Semantic Web Conference*, 463-477. 10.1007/978-3-540-68234-9_35

Klusch, M., Fries, B., & Sycara, K. (2008). OWLS-MX: A Hybrid Semantic Web Service Matchmaker for OWL-S Services. *Journal of Web Semantics*.

Korkala, M., Pikkarainen, M., & Conboy, K. (2010). A Case Study of Customer Communication in Globally Distributed Software Product Development. *Proceedings of the 11th International Conference on Product-Focused Software*, 43-46.

**W**

Kotlarsky, J., & Oshri, I. (2005). Social Ties, Knowledge Sharing and Successful Collaboration in Globally Distributed System Development Projects. *European Journal of Information Systems, 14*(1), 37–48.

Krishna, S., Sahay, S., & Walsham, G. (2004). Managing cross-cultural issues in global software outsourcing. *Communications of the ACM, 47*(4), 62–66.

Lajmi, S., Ghedira, C., & Ghedira, K. (2006a). How to apply CBR method in web service composition. In *Second International Conference on Signal-Image Technology and Internet-Based Systems (SITI'2006)*. Springer Verlag.

Lajmi, S., Ghedira, C., Ghedira, K., & Benslimane, D. (2006b). Web_CBR: How to compose web service via case-based reasoning. *IEEE International Symposium on Service-Oriented Applications, Integration and Collaboration held with the IEEE International Conference on eBusiness Engineering (ICEBE 2006)*.

Laliwala, Z., Khosla, R., Majumdar, P., & Chaudhary, S. (2006). Semantic and Rule-Based Event-Driven Dynamic Web Service Composition for Automation of Business Processes. *Proceedings of the IEEE Service Computing Workshop (SCW06)*.

Lambert, D. M., & Cooper, M. C. (2000). Issues in Supply Chain Management. *Industrial Marketing Management, 29*(1), 65–83. doi:10.1016/S0019-8501(99)00113-3

Lasheras, J., Valencia-Garcia, R., Fernandez-Breis, J. T., & Toval, A. (2009). Modeling Reusable Security Requirements Based on Ontology Framework. *Journal of Research and Practice in Information Technology, 4*(2), 119–133.

Li, J., Sikora, R., Shaw, M. J., & Woo Tan, G. A. (2006). Strategic analysis of inter-organizational information sharing. *Decision Support Systems, 42*(1), 251–266. doi:10.1016/j.dss.2004.12.003

Li, L., & Horrocks, I. (2003). A Software Framework for Matchmaking Based on Semantic Web Technology. *International Conference in World Wide Web*, 331-339. 10.1145/775152.775199

Li, M., Yu, B., Rana, O. F., & Wang, Z. (2008). Grid Service Discovery with Rough Sets. *IEEE Transactions on Knowledge and Data Engineering, 20*(6), 851–862. doi:10.1109/TKDE.2007.190744

Li, S. H. (2002). *An Integrated Model for Supply Chain Management Practice, Performance and Competitive Advantage* [PhD Dissertation]. University of Toledo, Toledo, OH.

Liang, T., & Konsynski, B. R. (1993). Modeling by analogy: Use of analogical reasoning in model management systems. *Decision Support Systems, 9*(1), 113–125. doi:10.1016/0167-9236(93)90026-Y

Liebowitz, J., & Megbolugbe, I. (2003, April). A set of frameworks to aid the project manager in conceptualizing and implementing knowledge management initiatives. *International Journal of Project Management, 21*(3), 189–198. doi:10.1016/S0263-7863(02)00093-5

Martin, D., Burstein, M., Mcdermott, D., Mcilraith, S., Paolucci, M., Sycara, K., Mcguinness, D. L., Sirin, E., & Srinivasan, N. (2007). Bringing Semantics to Web Services with OWL-S. *World Wide Web (Bussum), 10*(3), 243–277. doi:10.100711280-007-0033-x

Martin, D., Paolucci, M., McIlraith, S., Burstein, M., McDermott, D., McGunness, D., Barsia, B., Payne, T., Sabou, M., Solanki, M., Srinivasan, N., & Sycara, K. (2004). Bringing Semantics to Web Services: The OWL-S Approach. *Proceeding of First International Workshop Semantic Web Services and Web Process Composition.*

Maryam, A., & Dorothy, E. L. (2002). Review: Knowledge Management and Knowledge Management Systems: Conceptual Foundations and Research Issues. *Management Information Systems Quarterly, 25*(1), 107–136.

Matskin, M., Maigre, R., & Tyugu, E. (2007). Computational logical semantics for business process language. In *Proceedings of second international conference on Internet and Web applications and services (ICIW 2007)*. IEEE Computer Society.

Mayank, V., Kositsyna, N., & Austin, M. (2004). *Requirements Engineering and Semantic Web, Part II. Representation, Management, and Validation of Requirements and System-Level Architectures, ISR Technical Report*. University of Maryland.

McIlraith, S., & Martin, D. (2003). Bringing Semantics to Web Services. *IEEE Intelligent Systems, 18*(1), 90–93. doi:10.1109/MIS.2003.1179199

Mockus, A., Fielding, R. T., & Herbsleb, J. D. (2002, July). Two Case Studies of Open-Source Software Development: Apache and Mozilla. *ACM Transactions on Software Engineering and Methodology, 11*(3), 309–346. doi:10.1145/567793.567795

Nonaka, I. (1994). A Dynamic Theory of Organizational Knowledge Creation. *Organization Science, 5*(1), 14–37. doi:10.1287/orsc.5.1.14

OASIS. (2004). *Introduction to UDDI: Important Features and Functional Concepts*. Organization for the Advancement of Structured Information Standards.

OMG. (2009). *Business Process Model and Notation*. https://www.omg.org/spec/BPMN/1.2/(2009)

Pal, K. (2018). Ontology-Based Web Service Architecture for Retail Supply Chain Management. *Procedia Computer Science*, 985 - 990.

Pal, K. (2019). Markov Decision Theory-Based Crowdsourcing Software Process Model. In Crowdsourcing and Probabilistic Decision-Making in Software Engineering: Emerging Research and Opportunities. IGI Global.

Pal, K. (2020). Framework for Reusable Test Case Generation in Software System Testing. In Software Engineering for Agile Application Development. IGI Global.

Pal, K. (2021a). Customers Role in Software Development under Agile. In eXtreme Programming Projects, in Contemporary Challenges for Agile Project Management. IGI Global.

Pal, K. (2021b). A Case Study of Knowledge Management and Organizational Culture in an Undergraduate Software Development Team Project. In Contemporary Challenges for Agile Project Management. IGI Global.

Pal, K. & Campbell, J. A. (1997). An Application of Rule-Based and Case-Based Reasoning within a Single Legal Knowledge-Based System. *ACM SIGMIS Database: the DATABASE for Advances in Information Systems, 28*(4), 48-63.

Pal, K., & Karakostas, B. (2020). Software Testing Under Agile, Scrum, and DevOps. In Agile Scrum Implementation and Its Long-Term Impact on Organizations. IGI Global.

Pal, K., & Palmer, O. (2000). A decision-support system for business acquisition. *Decision Support Systems, 27*(4), 411–429. doi:10.1016/S0167-9236(99)00083-4

Paliwal, A. V., Shafiq, B., Vaidya, J., Xiong, H., & Adam, N. (2012). Semantics-based automated service discovery. *IEEE Transactions on Services Computing, 5*(2), 260–275. doi:10.1109/TSC.2011.19

Papazoglou, M. (2012). *Web Services and SOA: Principles and Technology*. Pearson.

Pathak, J., Koul, N., Caragea, D., & Honavar, V. G. (2005). A Framework for Semantic Web Services Discovery. *ACM International Workshop on Web Information and Data Management*, 45-50. 10.1145/1097047.1097057

Patil, A., Oundhaka, S., Sheth, A., & Verma, K. (2004). METEOR-S Web service Annotation Framework. *Proceedings of the Thirteenth International World Wide Web Conference*, 553-562.

Pressman, R. S. (2000). *Software engineering: A Practitioner's Approach (European Adaption)* (5th ed.). McGraw-Hill International.

Rammasubbu, N., & Balan, R. K. (2008). Towards Governance Scheme for Distributed Software Development Projects. *Proceedings of the 1st International Workshop on Software Development Governance*, 11-14.

Roman, D., Keller, U., Lausen, H., de Bruijn, J., Lara, R., Stollberg, M., Polleres, A., Feier, C., Bussler, C., & Fensel, D. (2005). Web service modeling ontology. *Applied Ontology, 1*(1), 77–106.

Roman, D., Kopecky, J., Vitvar, T., Domingue, J., & Fensel, D. (2015). WSMO-Lite and hRESTS: Lightweight semantic annotations for Web services and RESTful APIs. *Journal of Web Semantics, 31*, 39–58. doi:10.1016/j.websem.2014.11.006

Rus, I., & Lindvall, M. (2002, June). Knowledge Management in Software Engineering. *IEEE Software, 19*(3), 26–38. doi:10.1109/MS.2002.1003450

Rus, I., & Lindvall, M. (2002). Knowledge Management in Software Engineering. *IEEE Software, 19*(3), 26–38.

Sangwan, R. S., & Ros, J. (2008). Architectural Leadership and Management in Globally Distributed Software Development. *Proceedings of the 1st International Workshop on Leadership and Management in Software Architecture*, 17-22.

Sawyer, P., Bencomo, N., Whittle, J., Letier, E., & Finkelstein, A. (2010). Requirements-aware Systems: A Research Agenda for RE for Self-adaption Systems. *18th IEEE International Requirements Engineering Conference*, 95-103. 10.1109/RE.2010.21

Sharp, H., Finkelstein, A., & Gala, G. (1999). Stakeholder Identification in the Requirements Engineering Process. *Proceeding of the 10th International Workshop on Database and Expert Systems Applications*, 387-391.

Shingo, S. (1988). *Non-Stock Production*. Productivity Press.

Skoutas, D., Simitsis, A., & Sellis, T. (2007). A Ranking Mechanism for Semantic Web Service Discovery. *IEEE Congress on Services*, 41-48.

Sommerville, I. (2019). *Software Engineering*. Addison-Wesley.

Studer, R., Benjamins, V. R., & Fensel, D. (1998). Knowledge engineering: Principles and methods. *Data & Knowledge Engineering*, 25(1-2), 161–197. doi:10.1016/S0169-023X(97)00056-6

Sveiby, E. K. (1997). *The New Organizational Wealth: Managing & Measuring Knowledge-Based Assets*. Berrett-Koehler Publishers, Inc.

Sycara, K., Widoff, S., Klusch, M., & Lu, J. (2002). LARKS: Dynamic Matching Among Heterogeneous Software Agents in Cyberspace. *Autonomous Agents and Multi-Agent Systems*, 5(2), 173–203. doi:10.1023/A:1014897210525

Sycara, K. P., Paolucci, M., Ankolekar, A., & Srinivasan, N. (2003). Automated Discovery, Interaction and Computation of Semantic Web Services. *Journal of Web Semantics*, 1(1), 27–46. doi:10.1016/j.websem.2003.07.002

Varelas, G., Voutsakis, E., Raftopoulou, P., Petrakis, E. G. M., & Milios, E. (2005). Semantic Similarity methods in WordNet and their application to information retrieval on the Web. *Proceedings of the 7th annual ACM international workshop on web information and data management*.

Verma, K., Sivashanmugam, K., Sheth, A., Patil, A., Oundhakar, S., & Miller, J. (2005). METEOR-S WSDI: A Scalable P2P Infrastructure of Registries for Semantic Publication and Discovery of Web Services. *Information Technology and Management*, 6(1), 17–39.

Vrijhoef, R., & Koskela, L. (1999). Role of supply chain management in construction. *Proceedings of the Seventh Annual Conference of the International Group for Lean Construction*, 133-146.

Wang, L., & Cao, J. (2007). Web Services Semantic Searching Enhanced by Case-Based Reasoning. *18th International Workshop on Database and Expert Systems Applications*.

Wang, P., Jin, Z., Liu, L., & Cai, G. (2008). Building Toward Capability Specifications of Web Services Based on an Environment Ontology. *IEEE Transactions on Knowledge and Data Engineering*, 20(4), 547–561.

Watson, I. (1997). *Applying Case-Based Reasoning: Techniques for Enterprise Systems*. Morgan Kaufman.

Wouters, B., Deridder, D., & Van Paesschen, E. (2000). The Use of Ontologies as a Backbone for Use Case Management. *Proceedings of the European Conference on Object Object-Oriented Programming ECOOP, Workshop: Object and Classifications, a Natural Convergence*.

WSDL-S. (2005). http://www.w3.org/Submission/WSDL-S/

Zhang, W. Y., Cai, M., Qiu, J., & Yin, J. W. (2009). Managing distributed manufacturing knowledge through multi-perspective modelling for Semantic Web applications. *International Journal of Production Research*, 47(23), 6525–6542.

## ADDITIONAL READING

Acampora, G., Gaeta, M., & Loia, V. (2011, May). Combining multi-agent paradigm and memetic computing for personalized and adaptive learning experiences. *Computational Intelligence*, *27*(2), 141–165. doi:10.1111/j.1467-8640.2010.00367.x

Acampora, G., Loia, V., & Gaeta, M. (2010, May). Exploring e-learning knowledge through ontological memetic agents. *IEEE Computational Intelligence Magazine*, *5*(2), 66–77. doi:10.1109/MCI.2010.936306

Aggarwal, C. C., Gates, S. G., & Yu, P. S. (2004, February). On using partial supervision for text categorization. *IEEE Transactions on Knowledge and Data Engineering*, *16*(2), 245–255. doi:10.1109/TKDE.2004.1269601

Ballan, L., Bertini, M., Del Bimbo, A., & Serra, G. (2010, October–December). Video annotation and retrieval using ontologies and rule learning. *IEEE MultiMedia*, *17*(4), 80–88. doi:10.1109/MMUL.2010.4

Besana, P., & Robertson, D. (2008). Probabilistic dialogue models for dynamic ontology mapping. *Lecture Notes in Computer Science*, *5327*, 41–51. doi:10.1007/978-3-540-89765-1_3

Bhowmick, P. K., Roy, D., Sarkar, S., & Basu, A. (2010). A framework for manual ontology engineering for management of learning material repository. *Int. J. Comput. Sci. Appl.*, *7*(2), 30–51.

Bittencourt, I. I., Costa, E., Silva, M., & Soares, E. (2009, May). A computational model for developing semantic Web-based educational systems. *Knowledge-Based Systems*, *22*(4), 302–315. doi:10.1016/j.knosys.2009.02.012

## KEY TERMS AND DEFINITIONS

**Case-Based Reasoning:** Case-based reasoning (CBR) is one of the useful mechanisms for both modeling human reasoning and building intelligent software application systems. The basic principle of case-based reasoning systems is that of solving problems by adapting the solution of similar problems solved in the past. A CBR system consists of a *case base*, which is the set of all cases that are known to the system. The case base can be thought of as a specific kind of knowledge base that contains only cases. When a new case is presented to the system, it checks the case base for similar cases that are most relevant to the case in hand, in a *selection process*. If a similar case is found, then the system retrieves that particular case and attempts to modify it (if necessary) to produce a potential solution for the new case. The process is known as *adaption*.

**Description Logic:** Knowledge-based software system relies on its stored knowledge and decision-making mechanisms. At the time of knowledge-based system design and development stages, software engineers use different knowledge representation techniques; and one of the techniques is symbolic logic-based representation. Different symbolic logic representation is used for knowledge presentation purpose. Description Logics (DLs) are a family of knowledge representation languages that can be used to represent the knowledge of an application domain in a structured way.

**Ontology:** Information sharing among supply chain business partners using information system is an important enabler for supply chain management. There are different types of data to be shared across supply chain, namely – order, demand, inventory, shipment, and customer service. Consequently, information about these issues needs to be shared in order to achieve efficiency and effectiveness in supply chain management. In this way, information-sharing activities require that human and/or machine agents agree on common and explicit business-related concepts (the shared conceptualizations among hardware/ software agents, customers, and service providers) are known as explicit ontologies; and these help to exchange data and derived knowledge out of the data to achieve collaborative goals of business operations.

**Rule-Based Reasoning:** In conventional rule-based reasoning, both common sense knowledge and domain specific domain expertise are represented in the forms of plausible rules (e.g., **IF** *<precondition(s)>* **THEN** *<conclusion(s)>*). For example, an instance of a particular rule: IF {(*Sam has a driving license*) AND (*Sam is drunk*) AND (*Sam is driving a logistic distribution track*) AND (*Sam is stopped by police*)} THEN {(*Sam's driving license will be revoked by the transport authority*)}. Moreover, rule-based reasoning requires an exact match on the precondition(s) to predict the conclusion(s). This is very restrictive, as real-world situations are often fuzzy and do not match exactly with rule preconditions. Thus, there are some extensions to the basic approach that can accommodate partial degrees of matching in rule preconditions.

**Semantic Web Service:** The advantages of integrating and coordinating supply chain business partners' information service applications, which are loosely distributed among participants with a wide range of hardware and software capabilities, are immensely important issue from operation of global supply chain. Web service is an information technology-based solution for system interoperability; and in this technology business services are described in a standard web service description language (WSDL). Establishing the compatibility of services is an important prerequisite to service provision in web service operation. Web service has embraced the concepts of enriching distributed information systems with machine-understandable semantic metadata (known as ontology); and these new breed of web services are known as semantic web service. In this way, semantic web service provides a common framework for web-based services, which allows data to be shared and reuse across application, enterprise, and extended community boundaries.

**Software Development Knowledge Management:** As software development is an abstract engineering discipline, knowledge management is essential. When developing software, a high degree of coordination and management of distributed knowledge become vital tasks.

# Section 8
# Causal Analysis

# Hedonic Hunger and Obesity

**Ceren Ural**
*Tekirdag Namık Kemal University, Turkey*

**Nazan Tokatli Demirok**
iD https://orcid.org/0000-0003-1936-9337
*Tekirdag Namık Kemal University, Turkey*

## INTRODUCTION

One of the most basic needs in human life is nutrition. Today, people no longer consume nutrients only when they are needed physiologically (Berthoud, 2011). Now people want to consume food because of the pleasure of eating the food itself, rather than hunger and energy needs. This situation is explained by hedonism. According to hedonism, the meaning of life lies in pleasure. The pleasure that occurs when a person consumes the food they enjoy increases their eating behavior (Lowe & Levine, 2005).

Hedonic hunger obstructs homeostatic pathways when energy in the body is higher than normal, increasing the person's desire to eat food with good flavor (Lutter & Nestler, 2009). Homeostatic hunger is a condition in which the pleasure from eating increases, regardless of the taste of food, in order to eliminate energy deficits as a result of the negative energy balance that occurs after the person's energy stores are depleted (Aliasghari et al., 2019).

Enjoying food can stimulate "non-homoeostatic" eating and therefore potentially contribute to obesity (Mela, 2006). Obesity involves genetic and environmental interactions. It is also a serious and chronic disease. It can lead to various serious disorders, especially for the cardiovascular and endocrine systems. The increasing prevalence of obesity globally is reportedly associated with increased eating behavior and pleasure from eating. In addition to the interactions between hunger and taste, the response to perceived pleasure and nutrient cues also affects which food an individual chooses. This indirectly regulates appetite control (Lowe & Butryn, 2007). These changes in energy balance cause differentiation of the weight of the individual. With these differences in energy intake, the availability of high-energy foods in all areas, abnormally large portions and abundance leads to the emergence of hedonic factors and naturally hedonic hunger. These obstruct internal homeostatic systems causing a person's body weight balance to deteriorate (Mela, 2006).

The aim of this review is to explain the concepts of hedonic and homeostatic hunger, to address the formation of feelings of hunger and satiety in humans, and to examine the relationship between these conditions with obesity, which is a major health problem in the modern age.

DOI: 10.4018/978-1-7998-9220-5.ch042

## BACKGROUND

### Formation of Hunger and Satiety Sensations

Hunger and appetite are different concepts. While hunger is a physiological condition that occurs when the individual does not get the nutrients they need, appetite is a psychological condition (Carola et al., 1990). Ghrelin, identified in studies conducted by Kojima and colleagues in the stomach of mice in 1999, is located in the oxyntic mucosa of the stomach. It also contains 28 amino acids (Kojima et al., 1999).

The feeling of satiety is the occurrence of signals indicating intake of the amount of nutrients the individual needs, and then the end of the nutrient intake. Satiety and fullness are two important concepts that should not be confused with each other. Fullness means a complete cessation of food intake, while satiety describes the time from the end of nutrient intake to the occurrence of a feeling of hunger that manifests itself sometime later (Carola et al., 1990).

### Peptides Regulating Food Taking

Peptides that regulate food intake are divided into orexigenic and anorexigenic peptides according to their effects on human eating behavior (Hagan et al., 2000). When the feeling of hunger manifests itself in a person, orexigenic peptides come into play and stimulate food intake. Anorexigenic peptides are peptides that stop food intake when the person does not need energy, i.e. when the feeling of satiation occurs (Li et al., 2003).

### Peptides That Inhibit Food Consumption

#### Leptin

Leptin contains 167 amino acids. Leptin is a structured hormone (Zhang et al., 1994). It is responsible for controlling the amount of body fat in humans. It is also a protein that controls the homeostasis of energy expenditure. Leptin is synthesized in the main adipose tissue in the body (Wilding et al., 2002).

Leptin can be found freely in the blood and is dependent on a protein. In various studies, it was observed that leptin in serum of obese individuals is largely in free form (Brabant et al., 2000).

#### Corticotropin Releasing Factor (CRF)

CRF is a hypothalamic neuropeptide with destructive properties. CRF also plays an important role in energy balance (Hagan et al., 2000).

CRF acts on the sympathetic nervous system and increases its effect. Thus, it stimulates energy expenditure and lipolysis by providing body heat from fat (Gultekin et al., 2004).

#### α - melanocyte stimulating hormone (α-MSH)

The melanocortin hormone receptor is expressed in many regions of the hypothalamus. Appetite suppression is also provided through MC3 and MC4 receptors. Due to excess expression, deficiency in the MC4 receptor or any changes (mutations) that may occur in the receptor result in obesity (Parker, 2010).

## Cocaine and Amphetamine Regulated Transcript (CART)

CART is an anorexigenic with 102 amino acids that occurs as a result of the breakdown of precursor proteins. While the central administration of CART significantly reduces food intake, anti-CART antibodies were observed to stimulate nutrition (Lambert et al., 1998).

## Bombesin

This is an intestinal hormone. It was observed that Bombesin and GRP reduce the intake of food in humans and animals. Studies reported that fat individuals are less susceptible to the feeling of satiety caused by the bombesin than underweight individuals (Halford & Blundell, 2000).

## Serotonin

Serotonin stimulates satiation through the 5-HT2C receptor. Various obesity drugs increase the synaptic effect of serotonin and stimulate serotonergic pathways, reducing a person's nutrient intake and body weight (Gultekin et al., 2004).

The condition of eating is under the control of neural mechanisms. This is effective in the release of serotonin when the person exhibits eating behavior. Insulin release due to carbohydrate inflow into the body and the elevation in plasma tryptophan increase serotonin release (Wurtman & Wurtman, 1995).

## Dopamine

It has a serotonin-like effect. Activation reduces nutrient intake. It is claimed that D1 receptors help this effect (Halford & Blundell, 2000).

## Histamine

In many studies, it was observed that histamine suppresses appetite. This effect is caused by stimulating H1 receptors. It is also suggested that histamine, in some cases with the NPY, plays a role in the occurrence of loss of appetite (Gultekin et al., 2004).

## Cholecystokinin (CCK)

It is a peptide-structured hormone secreted from the duodenum. CCK is defined as a satiety agent in humans. This is due to the fact that it has a similar effect to satiety in the person and causes an unpleasant sense of smell and anxiety (Halford & Blundell, 2000). It also oscillates in the central nervous system besides the digestive system. Cholecystokinin is one of the hormones that is effective in the formation of satiation. After food intake, it quickly enters circulation in different forms and there is no change in levels for about 5 hours (Crawley & Corwin, 1994).

## Insulin

Insulin is a hormone secreted by the β cells of the Langerhans islets of the pancreas. It has an important role in the regulation of nutrition and on metabolism. Changes in insulin release and sensitivity are risk factors for obesity (Li et al., 2003).

The effect of insulin was detected using experimental animals. As a result, it was observed that insulin reduces energy intake when applied by the central route. However, this effect does not occur in animals with leptin deficiency. For this reason, it was suggested that insulin and leptin together are effective in regulating energy metabolism (Wilding, 2002).

## Peptides That Stimulate Food Intake

### Neuropeptide Y (NPY)

This is a polypeptide abundant in the peripheral nervous system containing 36 amino acids (Parker, 2010). It has an important role in regulating the body weight of the individual. In cases such as hunger, rigorous and prolonged exercise, breastfeeding and glucose, the NPY-ergic pathway in the AN and PVN is stimulated. Thus, appetite increases and energy expenditure is suppressed. This increases energy storage.

Plasma levels of NPY vary in some cases. These situations include: stress, pheochromocytoma, neuroblastoma, lymphoblastoma, leukemia, malignant hypertension (Gultekin et al., 2004; Kokot & Ficek, 1999).

### Ghrelin

Ghrelin is a hormone that is effective in the onset of the eating action and is produced in small amount in the pancreas, although the majority of its production is from the stomach. Ghrelin production in the pancreas occurs mostly at the fetal stage and when the concentration is examined, it turns out that it is 6-7 times higher than in the stomach (Cortelazzi et al., 2003).

The intestinal parts of the duodenum, jejunum, ileum and colon also produce ghrelin, but the density of ghrelin decreases as it progresses from the duodenum to the colon. The level of ghrelin in plasma is controlled by food intake and diurnal rhythm. Ghrelin levels in the body are high during the daytime. Leptin, like ghrelin, is high in the morning. In the evening, the level of ghrelin is low in the body. (Tschöp et al., 2011).

The task of ghrelin is not just to start the act of eating it also plays a role in glucose metabolism. Ghrelin levels are regulated and decreased by food-borne signals such as energy consumed as a result of nutrition and glucose in the bloodstream. For this purpose, a study with mice showed that ghrelin release increases with hunger, and ghrelin release decreases as a result of carbohydrate intake (Cummings et al., 2001).

### Nitric Oxide (NO)

Nitric oxide regulates appetite in a person. Preventing the production of nitric oxide from the central pathway reduces nutrient intake. At the same time, the administration of nitric oxide donors (l-arginine) increases nutrient intake (Morley & Flood, 1991).

## Glucose, Tryptophan, L-arginine and Fatty Acids

These nutrients have large roles in regulating an individual's appetite. The anterior hypothalamus contains nerve cells sensitive to glucose, some of which were suggested to be sensitive to insulin. The state of hunger is one of the characteristics of hypoglycemia. As a result of hypoglycemia, a feeling of hunger occurs and small changes in blood glucose levels were observed. Fatty acids also play a role in regulating appetite. Leptin, on the other hand, was suggested to be effective in regulating fatty acids in some cases (Wilding, 2002).

Tryptophan and L-arginine amino acids play roles in regulating appetite. Its physiological effects are not clearly defined (Morley & Flood, 1991).

## Factors Affecting Taste

There are many factors that affect the choice of nutrients. Individual differences play an important role in taste perception. However, many factors such as obesity, age, genetic characteristics, diseases, gender, drugs used, smoking, alcohol, etc. can be listed (Mela, 2001).

## Age

With aging, there is a decrease in taste sensitivity (Methven et al., 2012). Detecting emotional eating behavior at an early age is of great importance in preventing weight gain and preventing future eating behavior disorders (Goosens et al., 2009).

## Gender

A study was conducted including men and women of different ages and with different daily activities. Women were more sensitive to bitter tastes than men, while men were more sensitive to sweet, sour and salty tastes than women (Köse & Şanlıer, 2015).

## Drug Use

Many drugs can lead to misconceptions in the perception of taste in the person and impaired taste function. The use of illegally supplied drugs/substances may also cause loss of appetite (Beers et al., 2003).

## Diseases

Events that cause taste changes in the person can be listed as infections, diseases, depression and similar psychological disorders, some medications and emotional stress (Abetz & Savage, 2009).

## FOCUS OF THE ARTICLE

### Homeostatic Hunger and Hedonic Hunger

### Hunger

The word hunger is a term used to describe the situation that occurs biologically as a natural consequence of energy needs from the past to the present (Lowe & Butryn, 2007). Today, however, this phenomenon is explained as homeostatic hunger which increases the behavior of eating in the person when their energy stores are empty. This stabilizes energy (Lutter & Nestler, 2009).

With the decrease of blood glucose level in a person, the level of free fatty acids in the blood increases. This creates a feeling of hunger. Hunger is a situation in which the need for energy in metabolism is obtained from intra-body stores. In case of hunger, the body's glucose needs are strongly regulated. This regulation is provided by glucose, glycogenolysis (destruction of glycogen stores in the liver) and gluconeogenesis (glucose synthesis from lipids and proteins) (Moffett et al.,1993).

### Homeostatic Hunger

The most important step in maintaining homeostatic control of food intake is the regulation of energy balance (Lutter & Nestler, 2009). The hypothalamus is a part of the brain that has important tasks such as controlling nutrient intake and regulating energy balance (Berthoud et al., 2017).

### Hedonism

Hedonic systems are defined as pleasure signals and can encourage the person to eat when they do not need nutrients physiologically. The presence of loved foods, smelly foods, and catering can create appetite in the person. Mood is also highly effective in the hedonic system, but the same mood may not affect appetite in different people in the same way. In cases of sadness or anxiety, there are people who eat more than usual, while there are also individuals who reduce their food consumption considerably. Social and environmental factors can also both reduce and increase appetite (Berthoud, 2011).

When a person who has finished lunch and left the table is offered their favorite food, their refusal is considered hedonic hunger. Hedonic hunger obstructs homeostatic pathways when there is a lot of energy in the body. This leads to increased desire for the consumption of delicious food (Lutter & Nestler, 2009).

### Hedonic Hunger

Today people tend to eat based on the presence or idea of delicious foods, not usually due to a physiological need for energy. Behaviors that lead the person to consume nutrients are not directed only by physiological needs. This is also associated with responses to nutritional cues. Many factors affect the food consumption of individuals in daily life. Especially "snacks", which are defined as foods consumed outside of the main meal times, reflect their optional food choices. This is more affected by environmental nutrient cues (Lowe & Levine, 2005).

Individual sensitivity, which causes weight gain in the person, can lead to increased motivation to eat without metabolic need. According to the results obtained from functional magnetic resonance imaging (fMRI) studies, hypersensitivity to nutrient cues is reported to cause an increase in body weight and body fat, but also reduce the success of weight loss programs and hedonic hunger causes weight gain in the person (Lipsky et al., 2016).

Today, eating usually occurs in the absence of hunger. This condition is called "non-homeostatic" or "hedonic" eating. These terms refer to nutrient intake associated with cognitive, rewarding and emotional factors that are not regulated by metabolic feedback (Lee & Dixon, 2017). Hedonic hunger refers to the strong promotion of nutrient intake in an environment where extremely tasty nutrients are ubiquitous and also contributes significantly to the growth of the obesity problem (Monteleone et al., 2012).

Eating is of great importance in order for the individual to survive. At the same time, nutrient intake is associated with pleasure and reward control. The pleasure-reward system is encoded in the cortico-limbic section of the brain (Berthoud & Morrison, 2008). Nucleus accumbens and caudate nucleus are dopaminergic reward pathways responsible for the management of expectation and motivation. Amygdala and hippocampus are centers of learning; anterior insula controls sensory activity; orbitofrontal cortex is involves in reward evaluation-control and decision-making process; and the corticolimbic system is responsible for activities such as energy balance, memory, learning and emotional regulation (Lee & Dixon, 2017).

Homeostatic and hedonic pathways interact with each other at all times. Structures that regulate homeostatic energy such as leptin, insulin and ghrelin affect the activity of the corticolimbic system. At the same time, signals generated by the corticolimbic system, that processes sensory, cognitive and reward information, can similarly affect the homeostatic system related to the regulation of the energy balance (Berthoud, 2011). In hedonic nutrient intake, dopamine, endocannabinoids and opioids are released, which cause the suppression of satiety mediators together with the permanent stimulation of hypothalamic signals for foods that are quite tasty. This causes the brain's reward circuits to act. In this case, energy intake is maintained only due to the properties of rewarding and delicious nutrients, and consumption occurs. Ghrelin and orexigenic local mediators, which are orexigenic peptides, are said to play roles in mediating the reward process of endocannabinoids (Monteleone et al., 2012).

The evaluation of hedonic hunger is a very important and difficult issue. It is stated that the optimal time frame for evaluating hedonic hunger is 2-3 hours after nutrient intake. This is intended to ensure that answers about nutrients are hedonic (Lowe & Butryn, 2007).

## Factors Affecting Hedonic Hunger

### Individual Differences

In addition to psychological, social and cultural factors, physiological conditions of the individual also affect food intake. According to the results of a study on this subject, there were also differences in the appetite levels of individuals belonging to different populations (Gregersen et al., 2011).

### Stress

Fluctuations in appetite level can lead to eating much more than necessary, or emotional eating, as well as bulimia or anorexia nervosa. Stress can also affect the types of food selected for eating. When under stress, people choose sweets and fatty foods with more calories, and there is a decrease in the consumption of fruits and vegetables (Zellner et al., 2006; De & Mithieux, 2015).

## Age

When the individual enters the aging process, all functions decrease. Sensory losses also occur. With aging, decreased taste sensitivity and taste threshold, odor functions, etc. are observed. It was suggested that older male individuals experience less hunger compared to young male individuals (Gregersen et al., 2011).

## Gender

There was no difference in the rating of appetite in men and women. However, it was found that women were more satiated than men. The reason for this condition is thought to be changes in the concentration of hormones such as estradiol, which are responsible for eating behavior, and areas in the hypothalamus regulating appetite. It is suggested that high estradiol concentrations in women may be partially responsible for lower hunger and higher satiety (Gregersen et al., 2011).

## Happiness

It is known from studies that the mood of the individual has an effect on eating behavior. In their study, Turner et al. (2010) found that the number of individuals with nutritional control consuming chocolate snacks decreased considerably during positive moods. In individuals who were completely free in their eating habits, they showed more chocolate snack eating behaviors, as opposed to the group capable of control.

## Eating Habits

Habits are of great importance in human life. Hedonic hunger is said to be an important determinant of unhealthy eating habits (Verhoeven et al., 2012).

In a study examining individual regulation of unhealthy eating habits on their own, there was a positive relationship between consumption of sugary foods, habits and hedonic hunger. But individuals who maintained self-control were observed to consume less sugary nutrients (Naughton et al., 2015).

## Cigarette Smoking

It was observed that individuals with smoking habit experience satiety for longer. At the same time, they had less nutrient consumption compared to non-smokers. Nicotine in cigarettes suppresses hunger, increases satiation and reduces energy intake. Understanding about the cause of decreased appetite in smokers is still limited. However, recent research suggests that both POMC receptors and gastric ejaculation are stimulated (Gregersen et al., 2011).

## Physical Activity Level

The levels of physical activity of individuals vary in terms of hunger status. In individuals who exercise at hard/moderate levels, lower satiety duration and higher hunger and nutrient intake were observed compared to individuals who exercised lightly or not at all. However, this contradicts the finding that acute exercise reduces leptin and insulin levels 24 hours a day and increases PYY levels, which should show a positive correlation between exercise and satiety. In this case, there may be significant individual differences between exercise intensity and appetite response which should be accounted for (Cooper et al., 2011).

## Menstrual Cycle

In women, the state of hunger varies according to the menstrual cycle. This is due to the change in estradiol concentrations during the menstruation cycle (Del Parigi et al., 2002).

## Sensitivity to Food Cues and Body Weight

There are many visual nutrient cues on television, on the computer, and in environments where people eat. Sensitivity to visual nutrient cues was found to cause activation of reward-related pathways in response to nutrients. At the same time, it was suggested that they increase hedonic hunger and are positively related to BMI (Thomas et al., 2013).

The body weight and hedonic hunger of the individual can interact with the obesogenic environment to convince them of their nutrient intake. A study found that increased delicious nutrients in the environment played an important role in increasing the eating behavior of slightly fat individuals (Thomas et al., 2011).

## Dietary Practice and Restrictive Dietary Behaviors

Restrictive behaviors of the individual are one of the factors that can affect the state of hedonic hunger. Studies suggested that individuals who exhibit restrictive dietary behaviors to avoid excessive nutrient intake will exhibit more hedonic hunger than those who do not exhibit restrictive nutritional behavior while hungry (Lowe & Butryn, 2007).

It was reported that people who exhibit chronically restrictive dietary behaviors but have also been on a diet for a long time are highly susceptible to consuming foods prohibited by the diet (Herman & Polivy, 1975).

Another study investigated hedonic hunger changes in individuals after the implementation of a commercial weight loss program for twelve weeks, the hedonic hunger status of individuals was examined. With the increase in behaviors about weight control in the individual, hedonic hunger decreased. This was associated with greater body weight loss (O'Neil et al., 2012).

A behavioral weight loss program applied to adult individuals examined behavioral differences and the hedonic hunger relationship to weight loss. It was reported that behaviors about weight control decreased at high hedonic hunger levels. With this program, the behavioral conditions for weight control improved and hedonic hunger decreased. At the same time, these changes were reported to be associated with greater body weight loss. This suggests that behaviors in favor of weight control and improvements in hedonic hunger are significantly related (Theim et al., 2013).

## SOLUTIONS AND RECOMMENDATIONS

### Hedonic Hunger and Obesity

Obesity is a major problem seen in developed countries and developing countries (Schwartz et al., 2000). It is one of the most important causes of preventable diseases and premature deaths in Western societies. This health problem is a disease that involves the interactions of many factors (Hruby et al., 2016).

Today, the prevalence of obesity is increasing. The underlying reasons for this are the increased amount of energy and lack of physical activity. The addition of fats and sugars, which give a high amount of flavor to food, is one of the important reasons for this situation. The high amount of fat and sugar added to food significantly increases the flavor of the product. But foods that are delicious and increase pleasure are also known to increase hedonic hunger (Salbe et al., 2004). Individuals who are genetically susceptible to obesity become more vulnerable when they become obese and there is an energy imbalance. In this case, both the food environment and delicious food contribute greatly to the development of obesity (Egecioglu et al., 2011).

Many researchers around the world attribute the reason for weight gain in children to the increase in the consumption of harmful foods. In addition, the abundance of these foods on children's menus accelerates this increase (Parker et al., 2010). Rapid socio-economic developments, genetic predisposition, decreased physical activity with urbanization, ease of obtaining energy-intensive and delicious foods, chronic diseases due to obesity and obesity are increasing globally all over the world (Cheung et al., 2018). This is thought to be due to pleasure, not need (Lowe & Butryn, 2007).

Hedonic hunger is the desire to eat because of the flavor rewards. This occurs through the mesolimbic dopamine system. Obesity is encountered due to some defects in the homeostatic signals or excessive or inappropriate reactions to the hedonic aspects of food in motivating excessive consumption or nutrient intake. Hedonic hunger is thought to be one of the reasons for the rapid rise of obesity and mild obesity worldwide (Aliasghari et al., 2019).

The food consumed in the case of hedonic hunger was found to be associated with the frequency and severity of the loss of control over eating, regardless of the state of hunger. This is also associated with short-term weight gain (Feig et al., 2018).

Homeostatic regulation mechanisms are emphasized in the food preferences of obese people. This revealed that the reward value of food is key (Ziauddeen et al., 2015). In one study, people with a high body mass index had greater striatal and ventromedial prefrontal cortex activation as well as weaker hypothalamic activation. In the same study, people's preferences between healthy and unhealthy foods were more pronounced when they were hungry, and that hunger increased the reward value of foods with high energy content (Harding et al., 2018).

In a study evaluating the hedonic hunger status of patients who had gastric band surgery, obese patients who had undergone surgery and a control group who did not undergo interventions were compared and the results of individuals who underwent surgery were found to be lower (Ullrich et al., 2013). A study of university students suggested that hunger is not only a feature of obese individuals, but also an important factor in the risk of developing obesity (Ribeiro et al., 2018).

In a study about the consumption of foods that contain different amounts of fat, foods rich in fat content were found to cause high pleasure in obese individuals (Blundell & Finlayson, 2004).

The study, which identified the nutrient intakes of identical twins, found that obese people were more likely to consume fatty foods than those who were underweight. Compared to fatty food preferences, people who were defined as underweight had 17% preference for fatty foods and obese people had 52%.

However, when it comes to sugary foods, the situation changed. While 39% of obese people preferred sugary food, 30% of underweight individuals preferred it (Rissanen et al., 2002).

General operations performed for weight loss in obesity are gastric band and gastric bypass methods. As a result of a comparison study on these two methods, both pathways caused a decrease in the hunger level of individuals. However, after gastric bypass operation, hedonic response to food was low and glucagon-like peptides, peptides and bile acid levels in the blood were high. It was noted that the preferred gastric bypass method was more successful for weight loss (Scholtz et al., 2014). It was reported that ghrelin levels decreased significantly after gastric bypass operation (P < *0.005*), but other mechanisms such as glucagon-like peptide and PYY were much more effective in terms of nutrient intake and body weight reduction than decreased ghrelin concentration (Carrasco et al., 2012).

In the study of a population of obese adults, there was an interaction between hedonic hunger and physiological hunger. At the same time, it was observed that people who are hungry experience a stronger desire to consume nutrients and that their confidence in their ability to control eating behavior decreases. This was also shown to be evident among people with high hedonic hunger (Rejeski et al., 2012).

In a study in which individuals were classified as obesity-sensitive and resistant to obesity, people's hedonic hunger status and nutritional tendencies were examined. As a result of the study, people in the group that were susceptible to obesity have higher hedonic hunger levels than people in the obesity-resistant group (P=0.035), although they were not obese. This resulted in an increase in the tendency towards delicious foods, even in cases where there is no need for energy. People susceptible to obesity exposed themselves to more conditioning and restrictions when eating. This made them more susceptible to nutrient cues and led individuals to positive energy balance and energy intake over time (Thomas et al., 2013).

It is important to distinguish between delicious foods to be consumed when there is no need for energy, and the true amount of delicious food consumed in such a situation (Lowe & Butryn, 2007).

Uzun Akkaya et al. (2022) studied with 174 healthy university students and teprted that there was a weak positive correlation between hedonic hunger and depression.

Ribeiro et al., (2018) used PFS (Power of Food Scale) to measure hedonic hunger in a cross-sectional study. They reported that hedonic hunger levels are associated with obesity status with the being obese increase in the PFS Food Available score (scores differed significantly).

Aliasghari et al. (2021) studied with 372 healthy overweight/obese and found that the polymorphism of ANKK1 (rs1800497) and polymorphism of the DRD2 gene (rs1799732) showed significant associations with BMI and hedonic hunger and the frequencies of T and Del alleles were greater.

## FUTURE RESEARCH DIRECTIONS

More studies are needed to fully understand the mechanism in the relationship between hedonic hunger and obesity. Hedonic hunger should be evaluated for all reasons. The Guidance and Counseling can prevent the hedonism lifestyle of people. Obesity can be prevented by increasing the awareness of people about healthy diet.

# CONCLUSION

Today, many people are not hungry, but they eat because of their pleasure in consuming that delicious food. When these foods contain high levels of fat, sugar and salt, weight gain is inevitable.

Studies in this review show that higher consumption of high-energy nutrients rather than healthy food alternatives causes the obesity epidemic. For this reason, it is of great importance that the individual makes appropriate and healthy choices instead of unhealthy food preferences.

Articles describing the relationship between hedonic hunger and obesity are limited. More studies are needed to fully understand the mechanisms underlying these events.

# REFERENCES

Abetz, L. M., & Savage, N. W. (2009). Burning mouth syndrome and psychological disorders. *Australian Dental Journal*, *54*(2), 84–93. doi:10.1111/j.1834-7819.2009.01099.x PMID:19473148

Aliasghari, F., Nazm, S. A., Yasari, S., Mahdavi, R., & Bonyadi, M. (2021). Associations of the ANKK1 and DRD2 gene polymorphisms with overweight, obesity and hedonic hunger among women from the Northwest of Iran. *Eating and Weight Disorders*, *26*(1), 305–312. doi:10.100740519-020-00851-5 PMID:32020513

Aliasghari, F., Yaghin, N. L., & Mahdavi, R. (2019). Relationship between hedonic hunger and serum levels of insulin, leptin and BDNF in the Iranian population. *Physiology & Behavior*, *199*, 84–87. doi:10.1016/j.physbeh.2018.11.013 PMID:30445066

Beers, M. H., Fletcher, A., Jones, T. V., Porter, R., Berkwits, M., & Kaplan, J. L. (2003). The Merck Manual of Medical Information. New York: Pocket Books.

Berthoud, H. R. (2011). Metabolic and hedonic drives in the neural control of appetite: Who is the boss? *Current Opinion in Neurobiology*, *21*(6), 888–896. doi:10.1016/j.conb.2011.09.004 PMID:21981809

Berthoud, H.-R., & Morrison, C. (2008). The Brain, Appetite, and Obesity. *Annual Review of Psychology*, *59*(1), 55–92. doi:10.1146/annurev.psych.59.103006.093551 PMID:18154499

Berthoud, H. R., Münzberg, H., & Morrison, C. D. (2017). Blaming the Brain for Obesity: Integration of Hedonic and Homeostatic Mechanisms. *Gastroenterology*, *152*(7), 1728–1738. doi:10.1053/j.gastro.2016.12.050 PMID:28192106

Blundell, J. E., & Finlayson, G. (2004). Is susceptibility to weight gain characterized by homeostatic or hedonic risk factors for overconsumption? *Physiology & Behavior*, *82*(1), 21–25. doi:10.1016/j.physbeh.2004.04.021 PMID:15234585

Brabant, G., Horn, R., Von Zur Mühlen, A., Mayr, B., Wurster, U., Heidenreich, F., Schnabel, D., Grüters-Kieslich, A., Zimmermann-Belsing, T., & Feldt-Rasmussen, U. (2000). Free and protein bound leptin are distinct and independently controlled factors in energy regulation. *Diabetologia*, *43*(4), 438–442. doi:10.1007001250051326 PMID:10819236

Carola, R., Harley, J. P., Charles, R., & Naback, P. (1990). *Functions of the liver. Human Anatomy and Physiology*. McGraw-Hill Publishing Company.

Carrasco, F., Rojas, P., Csendes, A., Codoceo, J., Inostroza, J., Basfi-fer, K., Papapietro, K., Watkins, G., Rojas, J., & Ruz, M. (2012). Changes in ghrelin concentrations one year after resective and non-resective gastric bypass: Associations with weight loss and energy and macronutrient intakes. *Nutrition (Burbank, Los Angeles County, Calif.)*, 28(7–8), 757–761. doi:10.1016/j.nut.2011.11.004 PMID:22305536

Cooper, J. A., Watras, A. C., Paton, C. M., Wegner, F. H., Adams, A. K., & Schoeller, D. A. (2011). Impact of exercise and dietary fatty acid composition from a high-fat diet on markers of hunger and satiety. *Appetite*, 56(1), 171–178. doi:10.1016/j.appet.2010.10.009 PMID:21035513

Cortelazzi, D., Cappiello, V., Morpurgo, P. S., Ronzoni, S., De Santis, M. N., Cetin, I., ... Spada, A. (2003). Circulating levels of ghrelin in human fetuses. *European Journal of Endocrinology*, 149(2), 111–116. doi:10.1530/eje.0.1490111 PMID:12887287

Crawley, J. N., & Corwin, R. L. (1994). Biological actions of cholecystokinin. *Peptides*, 15(4), 731–755. doi:10.1016/0196-9781(94)90104-X PMID:7937354

Cummings, D. E., Purnell, J. Q., Frayo, R. S., Schmidova, K., Wisse, B. E., & Weigle, D. S. (2001). A preprandial rise in plasma ghrelin levels suggests a role in meal initiation in humans. *Diabetes*, 50(8), 1714–1719. doi:10.2337/diabetes.50.8.1714 PMID:11473029

De, F. V., & Mithieux, G. (2015). Glucose homeostasis and gut-brain connection. *Medecine Sciences. Ms*, 31(2), 168–173. PMID:25744263

Del Parigi, A., Chen, K., Gautier, J. F., Salbe, A. D., Pratley, R. E., Ravussin, E., Reiman, E. M., & Tataranni, P. A. (2002). Sex differences in the human brain's response to hunger and satiation. *The American Journal of Clinical Nutrition*, 75(6), 1017–1022. doi:10.1093/ajcn/75.6.1017 PMID:12036808

Egecioglu, E., Skibicka, K. P., Hansson, C., Alvarez-Crespo, M., Anders Friberg, P., Jerlhag, E., ... Dickson, S. L. (2011). Hedonic and incentive signals for body weight control. *Reviews in Endocrine & Metabolic Disorders*, 12(3), 141–151. doi:10.100711154-011-9166-4 PMID:21340584

Feig, E. H., Piers, A. D., Kral, T. V. E., & Lowe, M. R. (2018). Eating in the absence of hunger is related to loss-of-control eating, hedonic hunger, and short-term weight gain in normal-weight women. *Appetite*, 123, 317–324. doi:10.1016/j.appet.2018.01.013 PMID:29331366

Goosens, L., Braet, C., Vlierberghe, L. V., & Mels, S. (2009). Loss of control over eating in overweight youngsters: The role of anxiety, depression and emotional eating. *European Eating Disorders Review*, 17(1), 68–78. doi:10.1002/erv.892 PMID:18729132

Gregersen, N. T., Møller, B. K., Raben, A., Kristensen, S. T., Holm, L., Flint, A., & Astrup, A. (2011). Determinants of appetite ratings: The role of age, gender, BMI, physical activity, smoking habits, and diet/weight concern. *Food & Nutrition Research*, 55(1), 7028. doi:10.3402/fnr.v55i0.7028 PMID:21866221

Gültekin, H., Şahin, S., & Budak, N. (2004). Feeding Behaviour: Pharmacological Target Molecules. *Journal of Health Science*, 13.

Hagan, M. M., Rushing, P. A., Pritchard, L. M., Schwartz, M. W., Strack, A. M., Van Der Ploeg, L. H. T., ... Seeley, R. J. (2000). Long-term orexigenic effects of AgRP-(83-132) involve mechanisms other than melanocortin receptor blockade. *American Journal of Physiology - Regulatory Integrative and Comparative Physiology, 279*(1).

Halford, J. C. G., & Blundell, J. E. (2000). Pharmacology of appetite suppression. *Progress in Drug Research*, 25–58. PMID:10857385

Harding, I. H., Andrews, Z. B., Mata, F., Orlandea, S., Martínez-Zalacaín, I., Soriano-Mas, C., Stice, E., & Verdejo-Garcia, A. (2018). Brain substrates of unhealthy versus healthy food choices: Influence of homeostatic status and body mass index. *International Journal of Obesity*, *42*(3), 448–454. doi:10.1038/ijo.2017.237 PMID:29064475

Herman, C. P., & Polivy, J. (1975). Anxiety, restraint, and eating behavior. *Journal of Abnormal Psychology*, *84*(6), 666–672. doi:10.1037/0021-843X.84.6.666 PMID:1194527

Hruby, A., Manson, J. A. E., Qi, L., Malik, V. S., Rimm, E. B., Sun, Q., Willett, W. C., & Hu, F. B. (2016). Determinants and consequences of obesity. *American Journal of Public Health*, *106*(9), 1656–1662. doi:10.2105/AJPH.2016.303326 PMID:27459460

Kojima, M., Hosoda, H., Date, Y., Nakazato, M., Matsuo, H., & Kangawa, K. (1999). Ghrelin is a growth-hormone-releasing acylated peptide from stomach. *Nature*, *402*(6762), 656–660. doi:10.1038/45230 PMID:10604470

Kokot, F., & Ficek, R. (1999). Effects of Neuropeptide Y on Appetite. *Mineral and Electrolyte Metabolism*, *25*(4–6), 303–305. doi:10.1159/000057464 PMID:10681656

Köse, S., & Şanlier, N.KÖSE. (2015). Hedonic Hunger and Obesity [Review]. *Turkiye Klinikleri Journal of Endocrinology*, *10*(1), 16–23. doi:10.5336/endocrin.2014-41443

Lambert, P. D., Couceyro, P. R., Mcgirr, K. M., Dall Vechia, S. E., Smith, Y., & Kuhar, M. J. (1998). CART peptides in the central control of feeding and interactions with neuropeptide Y. *Synapse (New York, N.Y.)*, *29*(4), 293–298. doi:10.1002/(SICI)1098-2396(199808)29:4<293::AID-SYN1>3.0.CO;2-0 PMID:9661247

Lee, P. C., & Dixon, J. B. (2017). 1 Aralık). Food for Thought: Reward Mechanisms and Hedonic Overeating in Obesity. *Current Obesity Reports*, *6*(4), 353–361. doi:10.100713679-017-0280-9 PMID:29052153

Li, G., Mobbs, C. V., & Scarpace, P. J. (2003). Central pro-opiomelanocortin gene delivery results in hypophagia, reduced visceral adiposity, and improved insulin sensitivity in genetically obese Zucker rats. *Diabetes*, *52*(8), 1951–1957. doi:10.2337/diabetes.52.8.1951 PMID:12882910

Lipsky, L. M., Nansel, T. R., Haynie, D. L., Liu, D., Eisenberg, M. H., & Simons-Morton, B. (2016). Power of Food Scale in association with weight outcomes and dieting in a nationally representative cohort of U.S. young adults. *Appetite*, *105*, 385–391. doi:10.1016/j.appet.2016.06.012 PMID:27298083

Lowe, M. R., & Butryn, M. L. (2007). Hedonic hunger: A new dimension of appetite? *Physiology & Behavior*, *91*(4), 432–439. doi:10.1016/j.physbeh.2007.04.006 PMID:17531274

Lowe, M. R., & Levine, A. S. (2005). Eating motives and the controversy over dieting: Eating less than needed versus less than wanted. *Obesity Research*, *13*(5), 797–806. doi:10.1038/oby.2005.90 PMID:15919830

Lutter, M., & Nestler, E. J. (2009). Homeostatic and Hedonic Signals Interact in the Regulation of Food Intake. *The Journal of Nutrition*, *139*(3), 629–632. doi:10.3945/jn.108.097618 PMID:19176746

Mela, D. J. (2001). Determinants of Food Choice: Relationships with Obesity and Weight Control. *Obesity Research, 9*(11), 249–255. doi:10.1038/oby.2001.127 PMID:11707550

Mela, D. J. (2006). Eating for pleasure or just wanting to eat? Reconsidering sensory hedonic responses as a driver of obesity. *Appetite, 47*(1), 10–17. doi:10.1016/j.appet.2006.02.006 PMID:16647788

Methven, L., Allen, V. J., Withers, C. A., & Gosney, M. A. (2012). Ageing and taste. *The Proceedings of the Nutrition Society, 71*(4), 556–565. doi:10.1017/S0029665112000742 PMID:22883349

Moffett, D. F., Moffett, S. B., & Schauf, C. L. (1993). *Human physiology : foundations & frontiers.* Mosby.

Monteleone, P., Piscitelli, F., Scognamiglio, P., Monteleone, A. M., Canestrelli, B., Di Marzo, V., & Maj, M. (2012). Hedonic eating is associated with increased peripheral levels of ghrelin and the endocannabinoid 2-arachidonoyl-glycerol in healthy humans: A pilot study. *The Journal of Clinical Endocrinology and Metabolism, 97*(6), E917–E924. doi:10.1210/jc.2011-3018 PMID:22442280

Morley, J. E., & Flood, J. F. (1991). Evidence that nitric oxide modulates food intake in mice. *Life Sciences, 49*(10), 707–711. doi:10.1016/0024-3205(91)90102-H PMID:1875780

Naughton, P., McCarthy, M., & McCarthy, S. (2015). Acting to self-regulate unhealthy eating habits. An investigation into the effects of habit, hedonic hunger and self-regulation on sugar consumption from confectionery foods. *Food Quality and Preference, 46*, 173–183. doi:10.1016/j.foodqual.2015.08.001

O'Neil, P. M., Theim, K. R., Boeka, A., Johnson, G., & Miller-Kovach, K. (2012). Changes in weight control behaviors and hedonic hunger during a 12-week commercial weight loss program. *Eating Behaviors, 13*(4), 354–360. doi:10.1016/j.eatbeh.2012.06.002 PMID:23121787

Parker, K., Salas, M., & Nwosu, V. C. (2010). High fructose corn syrup: Production, uses and public health concerns. *Biotechnology and Molecular Biology Reviews, 5*(5), 71–78.

Rejeski, W. J., Burdette, J., Burns, M., Morgan, A. R., Hayasaka, S., Norris, J., Williamson, D. A., & Laurienti, P. J. (2012). Power of food moderates food craving, perceived control, and brain networks following a short-term post-absorptive state in older adults. *Appetite, 58*(3), 806–813. doi:10.1016/j.appet.2012.01.025 PMID:22329987

Ribeiro, G., Camacho, M., Santos, O., Pontes, C., Torres, S., & Oliveira-Maia, A. J. (2018). Association between hedonic hunger and body-mass index versus obesity status. *Scientific Reports, 8*(1), 5857. doi:10.103841598-018-23988-x PMID:29643337

Rissanen, A., Hakala, P., Lissner, L., Mattlar, C. E., Koskenvuo, M., & Rönnemaa, M. (2002). Acquired preference especially for dietary fat and obesity: A study of weight-discordant monozygotic twin pairs. *International Journal of Obesity, 26*(7), 973–977. doi:10.1038j.ijo.0802014 PMID:12080452

Salbe, A. D., DelParigi, A., Pratley, R. E., Drewnowski, A., & Tataranni, P. A. (2004). Taste preferences and body weight changes in an obesity-prone population. *The American Journal of Clinical Nutrition, 79*(3), 372–378. doi:10.1093/ajcn/79.3.372 PMID:14985209

**H**

Scholtz, S., Miras, A. D., Chhina, N., Prechtl, C. G., Sleeth, M. L., Daud, N. M., Ismail, N. A., Durighel, G., Ahmed, A. R., Olbers, T., Vincent, R. P., Alaghband-Zadeh, J., Ghatei, M. A., Waldman, A. D., Frost, G. S., Bell, J. D., le Roux, C. W., & Goldstone, A. P. (2014). Obese patients after gastric bypass surgery have lower brain-hedonic responses to food than after gastric banding. *Gut, 63*(6), 891–902. doi:10.1136/gutjnl-2013-305008 PMID:23964100

Schwartz, M. W., Woods, S. C., Porte, D., Seeley, R. J. & Baskin, D. G. (2000). Central nervous system control of food intake. *Nature.* . doi:10.1038/35007534

Theim, K. R., Brown, J. D., Juarascio, A. S., Malcolm, R. R., & O'Neil, P. M. (2013). Relations of Hedonic Hunger and Behavioral Change to Weight Loss Among Adults in a Behavioral Weight Loss Program Utilizing Meal-Replacement Products. *Behavior Modification, 37*(6), 790–805. doi:10.1177/0145445513501319 PMID:24013101

Thomas, E. A., Bechtell, J. L., Vestal, B. E., Johnson, S. L., Bessesen, D. H., Tregellas, J. R., & Cornier, M. A. (2013). Eating-related behaviors and appetite during energy imbalance in obese-prone and obese-resistant individuals. *Appetite, 65*, 96–102. doi:10.1016/j.appet.2013.01.015 PMID:23402714

Thomas, J. G., Doshi, S., Crosby, R. D., & Lowe, M. R. (2011). Ecological momentary assessment of obesogenic eating behavior: Combining person-specific and environmental predictors. *Obesity (Silver Spring, Md.), 19*(8), 1574–1579. doi:10.1038/oby.2010.335 PMID:21273995

Tschöp, M., Wawarta, R., Riepl, R. L., Friedrich, S., Bidlingmaier, M., Landgraf, R., & Folwaczny, C. (2011). Post-prandial decrease of circulating human ghrelin levels. *Journal of Endocrinological Investigation, 24*(6), RC19–RC21. doi:10.1007/BF03351037 PMID:11434675

Turner, S. A., Luszczynska, A., Warner, L., & Schwarzer, R. (2010). Emotional and uncontrolled eating styles and chocolate chip cookie consumption. A controlled trial of the effects of positive mood enhancement. *Appetite, 54*(1), 143–149. doi:10.1016/j.appet.2009.09.020 PMID:19815044

Ullrich, J., Ernst, B., Wilms, B., Thurnheer, M., Hallschmid, M., & Schultes, B. (2013). The hedonic drive to consume palatable foods appears to be lower in gastric band carriers than in severely obese patients who have not undergone a bariatric surgery. *Obesity Surgery, 23*(4), 474–479. doi:10.100711695-012-0818-6 PMID:23179243

Uzun Akkaya, K., Uslu, B., & Ateş Özcan, B. (2022). The Relationship of Hedonic Hunger With Depression and Physical Activity in Students of Faculty of Health Sciences. *Topics in Clinical Nutrition, 37*(1), 33–40. doi:10.1097/TIN.0000000000000267

Verhoeven, A. A. C., Adriaanse, M. A., Evers, C., & De Ridder, D. T. D. (2012). The power of habits: Unhealthy snacking behaviour is primarily predicted by habit strength. *British Journal of Health Psychology, 17*(4), 758–770. doi:10.1111/j.2044-8287.2012.02070.x PMID:22385098

Wilding, J. P. H. (2002). Neuropeptides and appetite control. *Diabetic Medicine, 19*(8), 619–627. doi:10.1046/j.1464-5491.2002.00790.x PMID:12147141

Wurtman, R. J., & Wurtman, J. J. (1995). Brain serotonin, carbohydrate-craving, obesity and depression. *Obesity Research, 3*(S4), 477S–480S. doi:10.1002/j.1550-8528.1995.tb00215.x PMID:8697046

Zellner, D. A., Loaiza, S., Gonzalez, Z., Pita, J., Morales, J., Pecora, D., & Wolf, A. (2006). Food selection changes under stress. *Physiology & Behavior*, 87(4), 789–793. doi:10.1016/j.physbeh.2006.01.014 PMID:16519909

Zhang, Y., Proenca, R., Maffei, M., Barone, M., Leopold, L., & Friedman, J. M. (1994). Positional cloning of the mouse obese gene and its human homologue. *Nature*, 372(6505), 425–432. doi:10.1038/372425a0 PMID:7984236

Ziauddeen, H., Alonso-Alonso, M., Hill, J. O., Kelley, M., & Khan, N. A. (2015). Obesity and the Neurocognitive Basis of Food Reward and the Control of Intake. *Advances in Nutrition*, 6(4), 474–486. doi:10.3945/an.115.008268 PMID:26178031

## ADDITIONAL READING

Chmurzynska, A., Mlodzik-Czyzewska, M. A., Radziejewska, A., & Wiebe, D. J. (2021). Hedonic hunger is associated with intake of certain high-fat food types and BMI in 20-to 40-year-old adults. *The Journal of Nutrition*, 151(4), 820–825. doi:10.1093/jn/nxaa434 PMID:33693662

Fox, C. K., Northrop, E. F., Rudser, K. D., Ryder, J. R., Kelly, A. S., Bensignor, M. O., Bomberg, E. M., Bramante, C. T., & Gross, A. C. (2021). Contribution of Hedonic Hunger and Binge Eating to Childhood Obesity. *Childhood Obesity*, 17(4), 257–262. doi:10.1089/chi.2020.0177 PMID:34061621

Kaur, K., & Jensen, C. D. (2021). Does hedonic hunger predict eating behavior and body mass in adolescents with overweight or obesity? *Children's Health Care*, 1–15.

Manasse, S. M., Espel, H. M., Forman, E. M., Ruocco, A. C., Juarascio, A. S., Butryn, M. L., Zhang, F., & Lowe, M. R. (2015). The independent and interacting effects of hedonic hunger and executive function on binge eating. *Appetite*, 89, 16–21. doi:10.1016/j.appet.2015.01.013 PMID:25613129

Mead, B. R., Boyland, E. J., Christiansen, P., Halford, J. C., Jebb, S. A., & Ahern, A. L. (2021). Associations between hedonic hunger and BMI during a two-year behavioural weight loss trial. *PLoS One*, 16(6), e0252110. doi:10.1371/journal.pone.0252110 PMID:34106941

O'Neil, P. M., Theim, K. R., Boeka, A., Johnson, G., & Miller-Kovach, K. (2012). Changes in weight control behaviors and hedonic hunger during a 12-week commercial weight loss program. *Eating Behaviors*, 13(4), 354–360. doi:10.1016/j.eatbeh.2012.06.002 PMID:23121787

Schultes, B., Ernst, B., Wilms, B., Thurnheer, M., & Hallschmid, M. (2010). Hedonic hunger is increased in severely obese patients and is reduced after gastric bypass surgery. *The American Journal of Clinical Nutrition*, 92(2), 277–283. doi:10.3945/ajcn.2009.29007 PMID:20519559

Witt, A. A., & Lowe, M. R. (2014). Hedonic hunger and binge eating among women with eating disorders. *International Journal of Eating Disorders*, 47(3), 273–280. doi:10.1002/eat.22171 PMID:24014479

## KEY TERMS AND DEFINITIONS

**H**

**Food Cue:** Food cues include situations associated with food-related memories or viewing of food stimuli, advertisements.

**Hedonic Hunger:** Person preoccupation with and desire to consume foods for the purposes of pleasure and in the absence of physical hunger.

**Homeostatic Pathways:** Pathways involved in the maintenance of the internal environment of an organism, the stability of normal body states and the feedback regulatory mechanisms that control them.

**Obesity:** A person who's very overweight, with a lot of body fat.

**Power of Food Scale (PFS):** Measures individual reactions to the presence of food in the environment.

**Restrictive Diet:** A diet that limits foods.

**Satiety Sensations:** Term is a sense of fullness after eating.

# Section 9
# Chaos Control, Modeling, and Engineering

# Vapor Compression Refrigeration System Data–Based Comprehensive Model

**Jesús-Antonio Hernández-Riveros**
*Universidad Nacional de Colombia, Colombia*

**Gerardo José Amador Soto**
*Universidad Nacional de Colombia, Colombia*

## INTRODUCTION

VCRS are the most used cold production method worldwide. Approximately 30% of the energy is consumed in applications related to air conditioning (Jahangeer et al., 2011). VCRS integrate elements from multiple energy domains using the reverse Rankine cycle to subtract heat from a lower temperature tank to a higher temperature tank, figure 1. Much energy is required for such tasks. Energy comes from the power injection of an external source of electromechanical work (Wcomp) to compress and circulate a refrigerant, which undergoes phase changes as it absorbs and delivers heat. The refrigeration cycle to obtain the desired temperature inside a chamber begins when the refrigerant enters the compressor as saturated vapor (state 1) to be isentropically compressed until reaching a certain pressure and temperature in the superheated region (state 2). The compressed refrigerant enters the condenser to transfer heat (Qs) to the environment. The refrigerant leaves the condenser as saturated liquid (state 3). To low the refrigerant temperature, an expansion valve applies adiabatic throttling. in state 4, so it absorbs heat (Qe) in the evaporator space. The refrigerant is heated to recover its saturated vapor state repeating the cycle. Figure 1 represents the heat transfer in case of reversible processes. The area under the curve for process 4-1 represents the heat absorbed (Qe) by the refrigerant in the evaporator and the area under the curve for process 2-3 represents the heat rejected (Qs) in the condenser.

*Figure 1. Temperature-entropy for the thermal cycle of a VCSR*

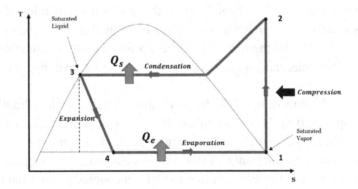

DOI: 10.4018/978-1-7998-9220-5.ch043

There is a growing interest in improving the energy efficiency of VCRS. Refrigerators accounts for a substantial portion of the annual energy consumption in the average home. The report (United Nations Environment Programme, 2018) on potentials to improve energy efficiency of refrigeration, air conditioning and heat pumps, highlights among the main measures with the greatest impact on energy saving: 1.- minimize the load of cooling, 2.- minimize temperature rise, 3.- consider variable operating conditions, 4.- select the most efficient refrigeration cycle and components, and, 5.- design effective control systems and verify operational performance correcting faults in existing systems. Given the need to improve the design, operation and use of energy in cold production, are necessary models that characterize in the most approximate way the real behavior of the installation (Belman Flores, 2008). A VCRS is a machine that from the electrical domain (motor) makes a conversion to the rotational mechanical domain (torque and RPM) acting on the hydraulic domain (pressure and flow) to finally reach the thermal domain, figure 2.

*Figure 2. a) Diagram of a VCRS, b) Elements in a domestic fridge*

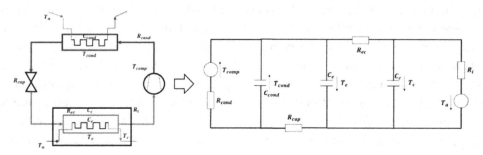

This chapter illustrates the multidomain modeling of a VCRS to offer a holistic and unified representation that facilitates energy saving strategies and behaviors characterization of its components. The VCRS modeling starts from experimental data in the thermal domain on a commercial fridge (Schné et al., 2015) and is complemented with catalog data from other domains. This VCRS multi-domain model is not limited to the current state but includes recent advances in variable-speed compressors and adjustable-expansion valves. This approach allows exploring into the impact the new technologies that are projected as future solutions in intelligent control that affect the dynamics of the VCRS process. There are difficulties in achieving *a priori* a comprehensive visualization of the coupled behavior of a multidomain system. In VCRS, the thermal part has been studied in-depth but if the aim is to increase energy efficiency, the electromechanical excitation that drives the internal dynamics of the compressor must be considered.

The VCRS holistic model is made up of electrical, rotational mechanical, hydraulic, and thermal submodels. The Bond Graph (BG) method was applied. BG is based on the exchange and preservation of energy among elements; it applies equally to any energy domain. BG represents in a unified way with a minimum number of symbols the different elements of a system and their energetic interactions as well as the cause-effect relationships. The BG resulting model is a coupled differential equations system in state variables corresponding to the existing energy domains. In this chapter, the dynamic relationships among the various variables of each energy domain that make up the VCRS are modeled. The VCRS holistic model serves to identify the potential for energy savings in different behavior routes resulting from the intervention within the dynamics of the system. In the thermal dynamics, a model found experimentally (Schné et al., 2015) from a commercial fridge with a mixed topology circuit approach with thermal resistors and capacitances is used. The parameters of the electrical, rotational mechanical and hydraulic sub-models were taken from technical information of the same refrigerator. The VCRS holistic model arises from the union of the experimental-based thermal sub-model with the theoretical sub-models supported by catalog data of the electrical motor and the compressor driving the thermal circuit.

The empirical thermal model assumes as known the compressor action in the production of cold. In a real VCRS, pressure and flow generation by the compressor depend on the mechanical action of an electrical motor. VCRS energy efficiency studies are limited in a thermal model to the COP calculation, and their effectiveness can only be known *a posteriori* through *in situ* measurements. With a VCRS holistic model is possible to know *a priori* the energy consumption at the electrical power source, as well as the energy efficiency of each component and of the total system.

The resulting behaviors from the VCRS holistic model are very close to the experimental measurements since the sub-models in each energy domain correspond to the topology and parameters of the physical installation. Due to the unified representation of the power flows and the modular nature of BG, integrating an experimental model with a theoretical model is not a problem. The approach applied in this chapter allows finding integral solutions without transforming the VCRS model to disciplinary representations that reduce the behavior space of the system; it respects the dynamics of the problem physics and the dynamics of the control system, as well as those of its interconnection. A holistic model of a VCRS is a felt lack in the scientific literature. The objective of this chapter is to present a comprehensive model of a VCRS. A model that includes the electrical, rotational mechanical and hydraulic components interacting with the thermal component, as found in the reality of refrigeration systems.

## BACKGROUND ON ENERGY-BASED MODELING

Modeling the whole dynamics of a VCRS is not an easy task due to the high complexity in representing the simultaneous interaction of different forms of energy. The refrigerant phase changes during the reverse Rankine cycle usually limiting VCRS models to the thermal domain, leaving aside the electromechanical and hydraulic effects. On the other hand, due to the discontinuity generated by the traditional on-off valve, there are few studies on the dynamics of the complete system. The most notable VCRS operating characteristics must be considered: high thermal inertia, multiple energy domains, high coupling among components, strong non-linearities, uncertainty, disturbances, dead times, etc. The common approach to capture these considerations is building a monodisciplinary model for each physical domain and then assembling sub-models in a numerical environment. Each monodisciplinary representation is limited to a specialized design and analysis (van Beek, van den Ham, and Rooda, 2002). This procedure also leads to a global model but can add more complexity to the problem and lose actual intra-extra component physical correspondence.

A representation of a multidomain system can be built in the same way from unified theories, with the difference that a global and integrating model is generated from the beginning, resulting in a naturally coupled equations for the total and partial dynamics of the system. It is convenient to select a unified theory to model a VCRS to visualize the behavior of the complete system without losing physical correspondence and without needing subsequent fixes. If energy efficiency is of interest, the model must provide information related to energy consumption for the entire system. A unified way to approach this problem is by using a common language (energy) to comprehensively model the components of different energy domains. Those theories are based on analogies among the fields of physics and obtain a global model of an entire system.

This approach has enormous advantages by delivering both the dynamic relationships and the energy consumption of both the total system and its components, allowing greater energy knowledge in subsequent stages of system modeling (design, implementation, operation, control). A global and integrating model is generated from the power source, that is, the beginning of the process, to the variable of interest, that is, the output, resulting coupled differential equations system constructed to describe the complete problem. Some benefits of using these techniques are greater modeling and numerical simulation efficiency; facilitate the modeling of complex problems with clear rules of interconnection and preserving its physical structure; establish an energy characterization of the whole system or its individual components regardless of the domain; reusable, modular and incremental models; each object is determined by constitutive relationships, allowing top-down and bottom-up modeling. By applying a systematic procedure, the dynamic relations, the energy relations, and the point values in energy of the total system and/or of its specific components can be easily obtained.

Two main lines of unified theories for modeling multidomain systems are:

1.  Graphical: based on the analogies between energy domains, figure 3, represent the system as a set of interconnected components.
2.  Mathematical: based on energy conservation principles apply the first principles to describe the dynamics of each component.

*Figure 3. A multidomain system under the approach of unified theories based on energy*

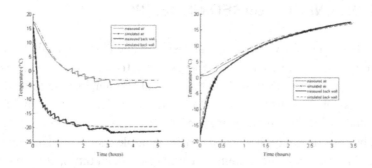

The most common techniques in unified modeling (Borutzky, 2015) are: BG, Linear Graph, Virtual Plant Principle, Hamiltonian formalism. Except for BG, which is applied interchangeably to all energy domains and their combinations, the other techniques have only been successful in electromechanical problems.

## Modeling by BG

An engineering system is composed of elements interacting with each other, exchanging energy and information, thus determining the dynamics of the system. Energy is the fundamental quantity exchanged between the elements of a system. Potential energy establishes the effort variable in the system, while kinetic energy establishes the flow variable. Power is defined as the product of effort and flow. In translational mechanics, power is the product of force and speed; in electrical systems, the product of voltage and current; in hydraulic systems, the product of pressure and volumetric flow; in the magnetic domain, the product of the magnetomotive force and the flux rate; and in the thermal domain the product of the temperature and the entropic flow gives the power. Thus, in any system, be it mechanical, electrical, acoustic, chemical, hydraulic, or thermal, we can define a generalized effort variable, e(t), and a generalized flow variable, f(t), whose product, equation (1), delivers the power exchanged between elements.

$$P(t) = e(t)*f(t) \tag{1}$$

In BG representation, the flow of energy exchange (power) between elements is represented by bonds. Through this link, an element exchanges effort and flow with the rest of the system. Due to its graphical nature of visualizing the power exchange, which includes storage, dissipation and transformation, BG methodology allows the integrated modeling of behavior regardless of the physical nature of the studied system. BG can be used for structural and causal analysis, both essential to design control and monitoring systems, allowing the development of robust systems in fault detection; in (Sellami, Aridhi, Mzoughi, Mami, 2018) and (Ghiaus, 1999) the advantage of diagnosing a failure without any prior knowledge of possible failures in VCRS devices is highlighted. A BG model can be refined by adding more elements, such as thermal losses, inertia, and storage effects. The causal properties of the BG language allow the modeler to solve the modeling even before the detailed equations have been derived. The independent graphical notation capturing the distribution and flow of power/energy within a dynamic system (Kypuros, 2013) reveals the analogies between domains more than as simple equations that are analogous, as physical concepts applied that are analogues (Broenink, 1999), Table 1. BG modeling can be considered as an integrated computer-aided tool in the field of engineering and a method of mathematical modeling of complex systems.

*Table 1. Generalized power variables, analogies for energy domains*

| Energetic Domain | Power Variables | |
|---|---|---|
| Generalized | Generalized Effort | Generalized Flux |
| Electric | Voltage (u) [V] | Current (i) [A] |
| Translational Mechanic | Force (F) [N] | Velocity (v) [m/s] |
| Rotational Mechanic | Torque ($\tau$) [N.m] | Angular Velocity ($\omega$) [Rad/s] |
| Hydraulic | Pressure (p) [Pa] | Volumetric Flow Rate ($\dot{V}$) [$m^3/s$][] |
| Thermal | Temperature (T) [°C] | Entropic Flow Rate ($\dot{S}$) [J/ (K.s)] |
| Chemical Transformation | Chemical Potential ($\mu$) [J/Mol] | Molar Flow Rate ($\dot{\xi}$) [Mol/s] |
| Kinetic Chemistry | Chemical Affinity (A) [J/Mol] | Reaction Rate ($\dot{n}$) [Mol/s] |
| Economy | Unit Price (Pu) [$/unit] | Order Flow Rate (fc) [Unit/Period] |

## Bonds and Ports

The connection between two elements or two sub-models is called a power link or Bond Graph; it is drawn as a single line (figure 4). This link denotes an ideal energy flow between two connected sub-models. Energy entering the bond at one end immediately leaves the bond at the other end (power continuity).

*Figure 4. Representation of information and causal assignment using BG*

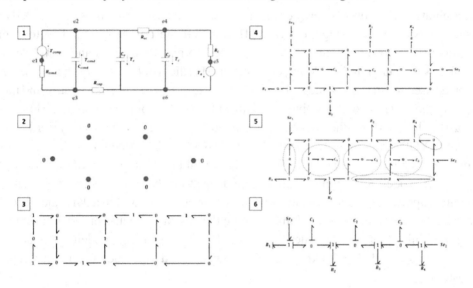

The flow of energy along a bond has the physical dimension of power, this being the product of two variables: effort and flow. In every physical domain, there is such a combination of variables. These pairs of variables are called conjugate variables and if in one end enters effort at the other end leaves flow in the opposite direction and vice versa. To understand the connection established by a bond, this bond can be interpreted in two different ways:

1. As an energy interaction: the connected subsystems form a load with each other through their energy exchange. A power bond represents a connection in which a physical quantity is exchanged.
2. As a bilateral signal flow: the connection is interpreted as two signals, an effort and a flow, flowing in the opposite direction to each other, thus determining the computational direction of the bond variables. For one of the connected sub-models, the effort is the input and the flow the output, while, for the other sub-model, the input and the output are of course set by the flow and the effort, respectively.

These two ways of conceiving a bond are essential in BG modeling. Modeling begins by indicating the physical structure (topology) of the system. The bonds are first interpreted as energy interactions, and then the bonds are given computational direction, interpreting the bonds as bilateral signal flows. During modeling, it is not yet necessary to decide what the computational direction of the variables is. Determining the computational direction during modeling restricts the reuse of the sub-model. However, it is necessary to derive the mathematical model (set of differential equations) from the graph.

The process of determining the computational direction of the bond variables is called causal analysis. The result is indicated in the graph by the so-called causal trace, which indicates the direction of the effort, and is called bond causality (figure 4). The analogies between different systems are shown in Table 2. Thus, from a unified base, different systems can be represented by the same set of differential equations. These analogies have a physical basis: the underlying physical concepts are analogous, and consequently the resulting differential equations are analogous. Physical concepts are based on energy and energy exchange.

*Table 2. Generalized energy variables, analogies for energy domains*

| Energetic Domain | Energy Variables | |
|---|---|---|
| | Generalized Momentum | Generalized Displacement |
| Generalized | | |
| Electric | Linked Mag. Flux ($\lambda$) [Vs] | Charge (q) [C] |
| Translational Mechanic | Inertia Momentum (p) [N.s] | Displacement (x) [m] |
| Rotational Mechanic | Angular Momentum (L) [N.m.s] | Angular Displacement ($\theta$) [Rad] |
| Hydraulic | Hydraulic Momentum (ph) [Pa. s] | Volume ($V$) [$m^3$] |
| Thermal | - | - |
| Chemical Transformation | - | - |
| Economy | Economic Momentum (pe) | Order Flow Rate (qe) |

In the representation of dynamic systems, energy variables are associated with state variables. Two types of energy variables are used: generalized moment p(t) and generalized displacement q(t). These are obtained by integrating the power variables with respect to time, as can be seen in equations (2) and (3).

$$p\left(t\right) = \int_{-\infty}^{t} e\left(\tau\right) d\tau = p_0 + \int_{t0}^{t} e\left(\tau\right) d\tau \tag{2}$$

$$q\left(t\right) = \int_{-\infty}^{t} f\left(\tau\right) d\tau = q_0 + \int_{t0}^{t} f\left(\tau\right) d\tau \tag{3}$$

Rewritten in differential form we have equations (4) and (5).

$$\frac{dp\left(t\right)}{dt} = e(\tau) \tag{4}$$

$$\frac{dq\left(t\right)}{dt} = f\left(\tau\right) \tag{5}$$

The behavior with respect to energy is independent of the domain. It is the same in all disciplines of engineering, as can be concluded by comparing an RLC circuit with a spring-mass-damper system. This leads to identical BG, as will be seen later.

## Elements

The basic elements in BG can be categorized and represented mathematically based on how they use, store, and convert energy. They are sources of power, storage elements, dissipative elements, unions of interconnection, and scale or domain changers.

Power Sources: There are two basic elements of 1 port: the effort source and the flow source. They are used for idealized representations of elements such as voltage or current sources, external forces, pressure sources, etc. (figure 5). As the names suggest, an effort source specifies an effort into the system (the presence of potential energy) and a flow source specifies a flow into the system (the presence of kinetic energy).

*Figure 5. Examples of effort and flow sources: (a) voltage source, (b) current source, (c) external force input, and (d) external velocity input*

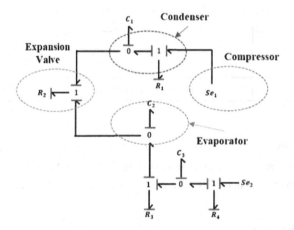

Energy Storage Elements: There are two types of storage elements: generalized capacitance, or C elements; generalized inductance, or I elements. The generalized variables of displacement (q) and moment (p) are the state variables of the system because of a process of accumulation (or integration). C elements are basic elements that store potential energy (figure 6). They are characterized by a constitutive relationship that directly relates the effort to the generalized displacement, equation (6). If the element is linear, the generalized capacitance, C, is defined by the equation (7).

$$q = \Phi c(e) \tag{6}$$

$$C = \frac{q}{e} \tag{7}$$

*Figure 6. Examples of C and I elements, respectively: (a) spring, mass (b) torsion shaft, steering wheel (c) electrical capacitor, inductance and (d) hydraulic accumulator, pipeline*

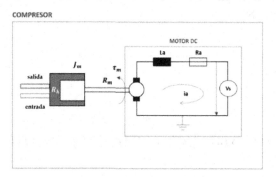

I elements are basic elements that store kinetic energy (figure 6). They are characterized by a constitutive relationship that directly relates impulse to flow, Equation (8). If element I is modeled by a linear constitutive relationship, the generalized inertia I is defined as Equation (9):

$$p = \Phi_I(f) \tag{8}$$

$$I = \frac{p}{f} \tag{9}$$

<u>Dissipative elements</u>: In general, for resistive elements, with a linear constitutive relationship, the generalized resistance of the element, R, is defined as in Equation (10). See figure 7.

$$R = \frac{e}{f} \tag{10}$$

*Figure 7. Examples of single-port R elements (a) mechanical damper, (b) roller bearing, (c) electrical resistance, and (d) hydraulic valve*

<u>Transformers and Gyrators</u>: Ideal transformers, *TF*, are characterized by a constitutive relationship that directly relates the effort in the first port (e1), with the effort in the second port (e2), and the flux in the second port (f2), with the flow on the first port (f1). The constitutive relationships of an ideal linear

transformer are in Equations (11) and (12). Where $n$ is called the modulus of the transformer and indicates the proportional relationship between the effort and the fluxes on each side. Examples of transformers for different domains in figure 8.

$$e_1 = n \bullet e_2 \tag{11}$$

$$f_2 = n \bullet f_1 \tag{12}$$

*Figure 8. Examples of TF elements (a) rigid lever, (b) pair of gears, (c) electrical transformer, and (d) hydraulic piston*

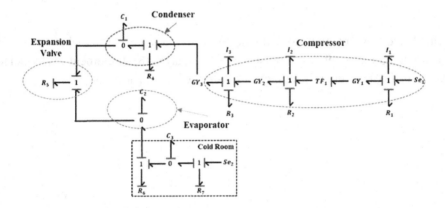

The second two-port item is the Gyrator, GY. Like the transformer, the gyrator transmits energy (figure 9). However, the direct relationship is between the effort on one side and the flow on the other side. The constitutive relations of an ideal linear gyrator are in equations (13) and (14). See figure 9.

$$e_1 = r \bullet f_2 \tag{13}$$

$$e_2 = r \bullet f_1 \tag{14}$$

*Figure 9. Examples of GY elements (a) ideal electric motor and (b) ideal centrifugal pump*

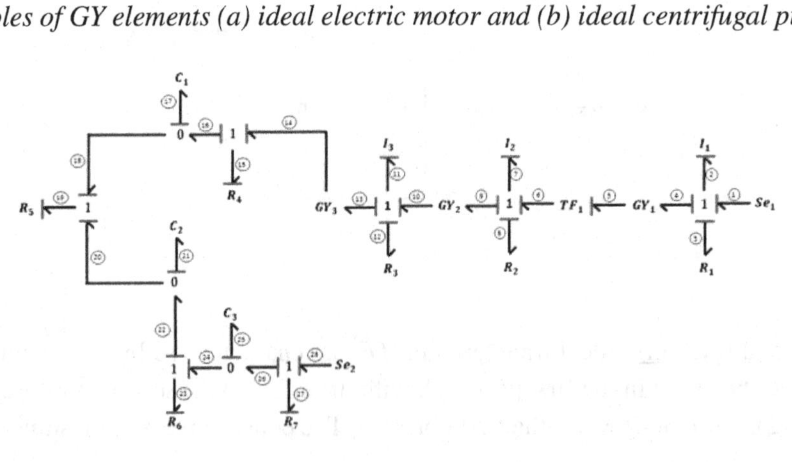

Junctions: Junctions are used to interconnect the basic elements. They serve to represent the interaction of the constitutive relationships associated with the 1 and 2 port elements, figure 10. As with basic 2-port elements, junctions conserve energy. Junctions, in general, can have many ports connected (that is, two or more ports). Because energy is conserved in a junction, the energy going in must equal the energy going out, Equations (15) and (16).

$$P_{in} = P_{out} \tag{15}$$

which can be rewritten as:

$$P_{in} - P_{out} = 0 \tag{16}$$

For a union with j = 1,2,3, ..., n ports, this expression can generally be written as Equation (17):

$$\sum_{j=1}^{n} P_j = \sum_{j=1}^{n} e_j \bullet f_j = 0 \tag{17}$$

For a -0- joint, of common effort, the main condition dictates Equation (18)

$$e_1 = e_2 = e_n \tag{18}$$

The sum of the flows for a -0- junction arises from substituting Equation (18) in equation (17), resulting in the expression (19).

$$\sum_{j=1}^{n} P_j = \sum_{j=1}^{n} e_j \bullet f_j = e_j \sum_{j=1}^{n} f_j = 0 \Rightarrow \sum_{j=1}^{n} f_j = 0 \tag{19}$$

For a common flow, -1- junction, the main condition dictates Equation (20):

$$f_1 = f_2 = f_n \tag{20}$$

The sum of the efforts for a junction -1- arises from substituting Equation (20) in Equation (17), resulting in the expression (21).

$$\sum_{j=1}^{n} P_j = \sum_{j=1}^{n} e_j \bullet f_j = f_j \sum_{j=1}^{n} e_j = 0 \Rightarrow \sum_{j=1}^{n} e_j = 0 \tag{21}$$

## COMPREHENSIVE MODEL OF THE WHOLE VCRS

The comprehensive model of the VCRS has been developed by applying the BG unified energy-based modeling technique. This process starts from using an experimental-based model (Schné et al., 2015) that only describes the dynamics of a thermal cycle, without exploring into the effects that the compressor imposes on the rest of the system and the respective restrictions of the electrical motor. To overcome this obstacle, hereby it is proposed to represent the refrigeration cycle using a unified energy-based modeling technique that allows us to integrate the internal dynamics of the motor-compressor group without losing the real physical correspondence of the complete system and without the need to redefine the initial experimental model. The base model for the thermal cycle is detailed below, followed by a description of the modeling process of the complete system using the technique of power links from BG.

Base Model of the Thermal Cycle: The base thermal model used in this chapter was proposed by (Schné et al., 2015). This thermal model, figure 10, was developed based on an experiment on a commercial fridge. The dynamical behaviors generated by this model correspond to the empirically measured performances. Temperatures, thermal resistances, fluxes, and heat storage capacities are addressed analogously to an electrical circuit as voltages, resistors, currents, and capacitors, respectively (figure 10).

*Figure 10. Basic diagram of the thermal part of a VCRS and its analogous electrical diagram*

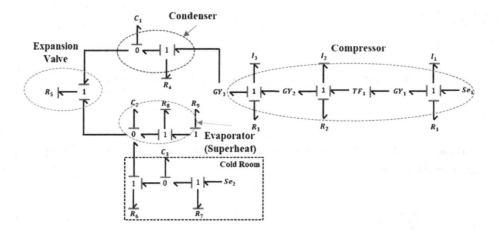

To represent the dynamics of the heat exchangers, accumulator elements of type C are used for the evaporator (Ce), condenser (Ccond) as well as for the cold chamber (Cc). Type R elements are used to model the heat convection between the refrigerant and the inner pipe wall in the different sections of the thermal circuit. For the section between the compressor and the condenser, Rcond is used, and between the evaporator and the cold chamber, Rec is used. Another aspect of this system that can be represented by a type R element is the thermal insulation inside the inner compartment, (Ri), in relation to the ambient temperature outside (Ta). The expansion device for this model is seen as a mechanical restriction (a choke valve) of the refrigerant fluid represented by Rcap. For the identification of the model parameters, real measurement data was collected from different operating conditions. Figure 11 shows the behavior curves for the cooling and heating stages, both for the temperature in the evaporator and in the cold chamber. The curves that come from a direct measurement and the curves originating from the proposed theoretical model are compared.

It should be made clear that although the dynamics produced by this thermal model (Schné et al., 2015) coincide with the experimental observations, the model does not include superheating. Superheating is important because it gives an indication of whether the amount of refrigerant flowing into the evaporator is appropriated for the load. The complete model of the VCRS (electrical+mechanical +hydraulic+thermal) will first be developed without superheating in the thermal part to demonstrate its construction from the experimental data. Subsequently, the complexity of the thermal part will be increased by adding the superheating circuit and thus generating a comprehensive model of the VCRS.

*Figure 11. Cooling and heating phase for the temperature in the cold room and evaporator. Reproduced from (Schné et al., 2015)*

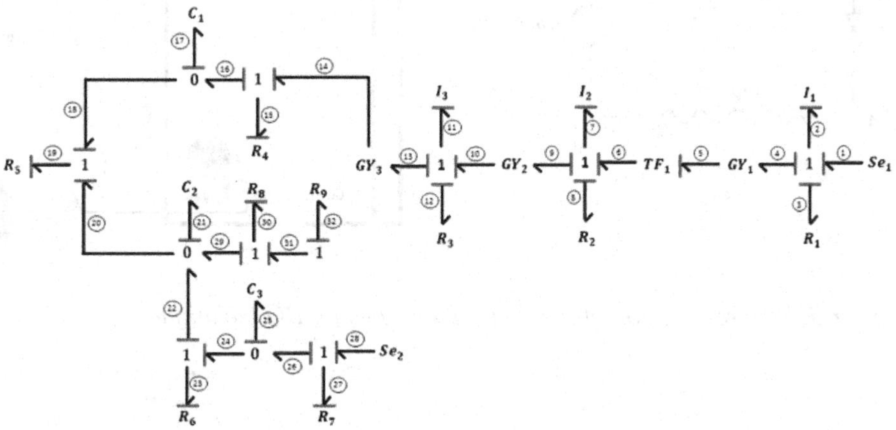

This model represents the thermal operation of the fridge with sufficient precision to allow intelligent control, but without the need to model every little detail of the operation, although the possibility of increasing in order of complexity if required is not excluded. In the technical literature, there are detailed and precise models (Hermes & Melo, 2008), (Bejarano, 2017), but in most occasions, it is too complex to implement them in real life. In the case modeled in this chapter, the phenomenological precision that they provide is not required. The general dynamics of the thermal cycle model is not only non-linear, but also exhibits strong couplings between inputs, or sources of excitation, and the state variables. In the following section, the procedure to model the thermal cycle using the unified technique BG will be discussed- Later, the dynamics of the electric motor-compressor group is integrated.

## Thermal Cycle Modeling Using BG Technique

The procedure to obtain the graphic model of the thermal cycle of the refrigeration system using the BG technique (figure 12) is next.

1.  Identify efforts and assign them a -0- junction.
2.  Identify all the differences in effort required to connect the ports of all the elements. Use a junction -1- and draw them as such on the BG.
3.  Identify elements and connect them to the respective unions.
4.  Simplify the Bond Graph by applying the corresponding simplification rules (Hroncová & Gmiterko, 2013).

Finally, in figure 13 is the BG model of the experimental thermal model.

*Figure 12. Systematic procedure to obtain the BG model of the thermal cycle*

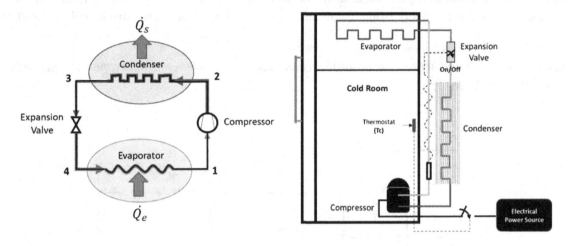

*Figure 13. Power link representation of the thermal cycle using BG technique*

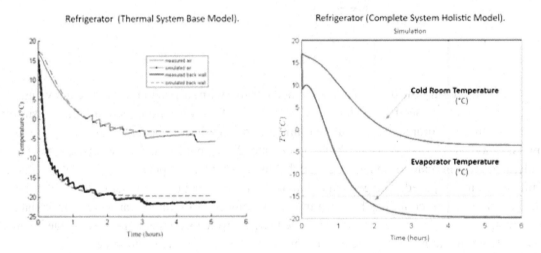

## Compressor Modeling

From the experimental base thermal model, described above, arises the need to detail the action of the compressor with greater precision (simplified in the experimental base model only by its temperature Tcomp) and thus have a holistic vision of the complete refrigeration system. For the compressor model, a DC motor was used, with a series connection, whose electrical power injection source, Vs, feeds the rest of the system. An AC motor with a variable speed drive would have the same effect on the VCRS, its operation can disturb the quality of energy in the power source, which is not the subject of this chapter. The selection of a DC motor was made with the purpose of facilitating the simulation of the VCRS acting with variable speed. The rotor of the motor is composed of a rotating coil that is made of a copper winding with resistance Ra and inductance La. Thus, for the electrical part, there is a circuit with a source of voltage, resistance and inductance connected in series, figure 14.

*Figure 14. Schematic of an electromechanical system*

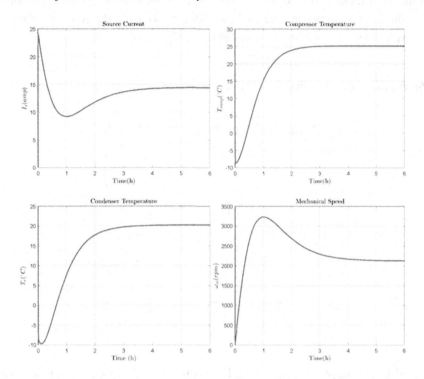

For the mechanical part, there is rotational inertia, Jm, and mechanical friction resistance, Rm. The electrical and mechanical components of the system are coupled by an ideal gyrator, GYm, which represents the electromechanical coupling between both sides. This element relates the torque generated on the mechanical part with the current conducted through the electrical part. Furthermore, it relates the electromotive force (voltage drop on the electrical side due to the generation of torque on the mechanical side) with the angular velocity of the rotating shaft. Finally, the effects due to compression are included, such as friction losses, Rh, and the accumulation of inertial energy in the walls of the pipe, Jh, which connects with the thermal cycle. See figure 15.

*Figure 15. Representation by BG for the compressor*

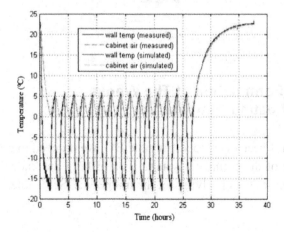

The modular union of these two subsystems (one experimental in the thermal domain and the other theoretical adding the electrical-mechanical-hydraulic domains) using the BG technique allows obtaining a comprehensive model of a refrigeration system. See figure 16.

*Figure 16. Modular union of the thermal cycle and the motor-compressor group using BG technique*

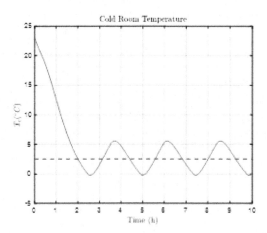

The fully labeled Bond Graph is in figure 17. From this unified graphical representation, the mathematical model of the VCRS is derived directly and systematically applying the steps below.

*Figure 17. Assignment of flows and efforts for each power bond*

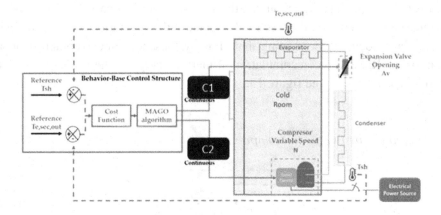

## State Variable Model Formulation of The Whole VCRS Without Superheating Temperature

Once the graphical model has been developed from the BG, we proceed to obtain the differential equations defining the behavior of the complete system. Establishing the known values, the relationships among the elements of the system and solving for the unknowns. See Table 3.

*Table 3. Procedure to obtain the mathematical model of the complete system using the Bond Graph*

| Initial Known Values | Relations/Unions | | |
|---|---|---|---|
| **Efforts** | **Efforts** | | **Fluxes** |
| $e_1 = Se_1$ | $e_1 = e_2 + e_3 + e_4$ | $e_3 = R_1{}^*f_3$ | $f_{16} = f_{17} + f_{18}$ |
| $e_{17} = q_{C1}/C_1$ | $e_6 = e_7 + e_8 + e_9$ | $e_8 = R_2{}^*f_8$ | $f_{22} = f_{21} + f_{20}$ |
| $e_{21} = q_{C2}/C_2$ | $e_{10} = e_{11} + e_{12} + e_{13}$ | $e_{12} = R_3{}^*f_{12}$ | $f_{26} = f_{25} + f_{24}$ |
| $e_{25} = q_{C3}/C_3$ | $e_{14} = e_{15} + e_{16}$ | $e_{15} = R_4{}^*f_{15}$ | $f_1 = f_2 = f_3 = f_4$ |
| $e_{28} = Se_3$ | $e_{19} = e_{18} + e_{20}$ | $e_{19} = R_5{}^*f_{19}$ | $f_6 = f_7 = f_8 = f_9$ |
| | $e_{24} = e_{23} + e_{22}$ | $e_{23} = R_6{}^*f_{23}$ | $f_{10} = f_{11} = f_{12} = f_{13}$ |
| **Fluxes** | $e_{28} = e_{27} + e_{26}$ | $e_{27} = R_7{}^*f_{27}$ | $f_{14} = f_{15} = f_{16}$ |
| $f_2 = p_{I1}/I_1$ | $e_{16} = e_{17} = e_{18}$ | $e_4 = k_1{}^*f_5$ | $f_{18} = f_{19} = f_{20}$ |
| $f_7 = p_{I2}/I_2$ | $e_{20} = e_{21} = e_{22}$ | $e_9 = k_2{}^*f_{10}$ | $f_{22} = f_{23} = f_{24}$ |
| $f_{11} = p_{I3}/I_3$ | $e_{24} = e_{25} = e_{26}$ | $e_{13} = k_3{}^*f_{14}$ | $f_{26} = f_{27} = f_{28}$ |
| Summary of Efforts and Fluxes | | | |

$$e_1 = Se_1$$
$$f_1 = \left(\frac{1}{I_1}\right)^* p_{I1}$$

$$e_2 = Se_1 - \left(\frac{R_1}{I_1}\right)^* p_{I1} - \left(\frac{k_1}{I_2{}^*tf}\right)^* p_{I2}$$
$$f_2 = \left(\frac{1}{I_1}\right)^* p_{I1}$$

$$e_3 = \left(\frac{R_1}{I_1}\right)^* p_{I1}$$
$$f_3 = \left(\frac{1}{I_1}\right)^* p_{I1}$$

$$e_4 = \left(\frac{k_1}{I_2{}^*tf}\right)^* p_{I2}$$
$$f_4 = \left(\frac{1}{I_1}\right)^* p_{I1}$$

$$e_5 = \left(\frac{k_1}{I_1}\right)^* p_{I1}$$
$$f_5 = \left(\frac{1}{I_2{}^*tf}\right)^* p_{I2}$$

$$e_6 = \left(\frac{k_1}{I_1{}^*tf}\right)^* p_{I1}$$
$$f_6 = \left(\frac{1}{I_2}\right)^* p_{I2}$$

$$e_7 = \left(\frac{k_1}{I_1{}^*tf}\right)^* p_{I1} - \left(\frac{R_2}{I_2}\right)^* p_{I2} - \left(\frac{k_2}{I_3}\right)^* p_{I3}$$
$$f_7 = \left(\frac{1}{I_2}\right)^* p_{I2}$$

$$e_8 = \left(\frac{R_2}{I_2}\right)^* p_{I2}$$
$$f_8 = \left(\frac{1}{I_2}\right)^* p_{I2}$$

$$e_9 = \left(\frac{k_2}{I_3}\right)^* p_{I3}$$
$$f_9 = \left(\frac{1}{I_2}\right)^* p_{I2}$$

*continues on following page*

*Table 3. Continued*

| | |
|---|---|
| $e_{10} = \left(\dfrac{k_2}{I_2}\right)*p_{I2}$ | $f_{10} = \left(\dfrac{1}{I_3}\right)*p_{I3}$ |
| $e_{11} = \left(\dfrac{k_2}{I_2}\right)*p_{I2} - \left(\dfrac{R_3}{I_3}\right)*p_{I3} - \left(\dfrac{k_3{}^2}{R_4*I_3}\right)*p_{I3} - \left(\dfrac{k_3}{R_4*C_1}\right)*q_{C1}$ | $f_{11} = \left(\dfrac{1}{I_3}\right)*p_{I3}$ |
| $e_{12} = \left(\dfrac{R_3}{I_3}\right)*p_{I3}$ | $f_{12} = \left(\dfrac{1}{I_3}\right)*p_{I3}$ |
| $e_{13} = \left(\dfrac{k_3{}^2}{R_4*I_3}\right)*p_{I3} - \left(\dfrac{k_3}{R_4*C_1}\right)*q_{C1}$ | $f_{13} = \left(\dfrac{1}{I_3}\right)*p_{I3}$ |
| $e_{14} = \left(\dfrac{k_3}{I_3}\right)*p_{I3}$ | $f_{14} = \left(\dfrac{k_3}{R_4*I_3}\right)*p_{I3} - \left(\dfrac{1}{R_4*C_1}\right)*q_{C1}$ |
| $e_{15} = \left(\dfrac{k_3}{I_3}\right)*p_{I3} - \left(\dfrac{1}{C_1}\right)*q_{C1}$ | $f_{15} = \left(\dfrac{k_3}{R_4*I_3}\right)*p_{I3} - \left(\dfrac{1}{R_4*C_1}\right)*q_{C1}$ |
| $e_{16} = \left(\dfrac{1}{C_1}\right)*q_{C1}$ | $f_{16} = \left(\dfrac{k_3}{R_4*I_3}\right)*p_{I3} - \left(\dfrac{1}{R_4*C_1}\right)*q_{C1}$ |
| $e_{17} = \left(\dfrac{1}{C_1}\right)*q_{C1}$ | $f_{17} = \left(\dfrac{k_3}{R_4*I_3}\right)*p_{I3} - \left(\dfrac{1}{R_4*C_1}\right)*q_{C1} - \left(\dfrac{1}{R_5*C_1}\right)*q_{C1} + \left(\dfrac{1}{R_5*C_2}\right)*q_{C2}$ |
| $e_{18} = \left(\dfrac{1}{C_1}\right)*q_{C1}$ | $f_{18} = \left(\dfrac{1}{R_5*C_1}\right)*q_{C1} + \left(\dfrac{1}{R_5*C_2}\right)*q_{C2}$ |
| $e_{19} = \left(\dfrac{1}{C_1}\right)*q_{C1} + \left(\dfrac{1}{C_2}\right)*q_{C2}$ | $f_{19} = \left(\dfrac{1}{R_5*C_1}\right)*q_{C1} + \left(\dfrac{1}{R_5*C_2}\right)*q_{C2}$ |
| $e_{20} = \left(\dfrac{1}{C_2}\right)*q_{C2}$ | $f_{20} = \left(\dfrac{1}{R_5*C_1}\right)*q_{C1} + \left(\dfrac{1}{R_5*C_2}\right)*q_{C2}$ |
| $e_{21} = \left(\dfrac{1}{C_2}\right)*q_{C2}$ | $f_{21} = \left(\dfrac{1}{R_6*C_3}\right)*q_{C3} - \left(\dfrac{1}{C_2}\right)\left(\dfrac{1}{R_6} + \dfrac{1}{R_5}\right)*q_{C2} - \left(\dfrac{1}{R_5*C_1}\right)*q_{C1}$ |
| $e_{22} = \left(\dfrac{1}{C_2}\right)*q_{C2}$ | $f_{22} = \left(\dfrac{1}{R_6*C_3}\right)*q_{C3} - \left(\dfrac{1}{C_2*R_6}\right)*q_{C2}$ |

*continues on following page*

*Table 3. Continued*

| | |
|---|---|
| $e_{23} = \left(\dfrac{1}{C_3}\right) * q_{C3} - \left(\dfrac{1}{C_2}\right) * q_{C2}$ | $f_{23} = \left(\dfrac{1}{R_6 * C_3}\right) * q_{C3} - \left(\dfrac{1}{C_2 * R_6}\right) * q_{C2}$ |
| $e_{24} = \left(\dfrac{1}{C_3}\right) * q_{C3}$ | $f_{24} = \left(\dfrac{1}{R_6 * C_3}\right) * q_{C3} - \left(\dfrac{1}{C_2 * R_6}\right) * q_{C2}$ |
| $e_{25} = \left(\dfrac{1}{C_3}\right) * q_{C3}$ | $f_{25} = \left(\dfrac{1}{R_7}\right) * Se_3 - \left(\dfrac{1}{C_3}\right)\left(\dfrac{1}{R_7} + \dfrac{1}{R_6}\right) * q_{C3} + \left(\dfrac{1}{C_2 * R_6}\right) * q_{C2}$ |
| $e_{26} = \left(\dfrac{1}{C_3}\right) * q_{C3}$ | $f_{26} = \left(\dfrac{1}{R_7}\right) * Se_3 - \left(\dfrac{1}{C_3 * R_7}\right) * q_{C3}$ |
| $e_{27} = Se_3 - \left(\dfrac{1}{C_3}\right) * q_{C3}$ | $f_{27} = \left(\dfrac{1}{R_7}\right) * Se_3 - \left(\dfrac{1}{C_3 * R_7}\right) * q_{C3}$ |
| $e_{28} = Se_3$ | $f_{28} = \left(\dfrac{1}{R_7}\right) * Se_3 - \left(\dfrac{1}{C_3 * R_7}\right) * q_{C3}$ |

In Table 4, a system of six first-order differential equations whose structure defines the complete dynamics of the VCRS is shown.

*Table 4. Set of differential equations of the complete VCRS without superheating*

| In terms of momentum and general displacement |
|---|
| $e_2 = \dfrac{dp_{I1}}{dt} = Se_1 - \left(\dfrac{R_1}{I_1}\right) * p_{I1} - \left(\dfrac{k_1}{tf * I_2}\right) * p_{I2}$ |
| $e_7 = \dfrac{dp_{I2}}{dt} = \left(\dfrac{k_1}{tf * I_1}\right) * p_{I1} - \left(\dfrac{R_2}{I_2}\right) * p_{I2} - \left(\dfrac{k_2}{I_3}\right) * p_{I3}$ |
| $e_{11} = \dfrac{dp_{I3}}{dt} = \left(\dfrac{k_2}{I_2}\right) * p_{I2} - \dfrac{1}{I_3}\left(\dfrac{k_3^{\,2}}{R_4} + R_3\right) * p_{I3} + \left(\dfrac{k_3}{C_1 * R_4}\right) * q_{C1}$ |
| $f_{17} = \dfrac{dq_{C1}}{dt} = \left(\dfrac{k_3}{I_3 * R_4}\right) * p_{I3} - \dfrac{1}{C_1}\left(\dfrac{1}{R_4} + \dfrac{1}{R_5}\right) * q_{C1} - \left(\dfrac{1}{C_2 * R_5}\right) * q_{C2}$ |

*continues on following page*

*Table 4. Continued*

$$f_{21} = \frac{dq_{C2}}{dt} = -\left(\frac{1}{C_1 * R_5}\right) * q_{C1} - \frac{1}{C_2}\left(\frac{1}{R_6} + \frac{1}{R_5}\right) * q_{C2} + \left(\frac{1}{C_3 * R_6}\right) * q_{C3}$$

$$f_{25} = \frac{dq_{C3}}{dt} = \left(\frac{1}{R_7}\right) * Se_3 + \left(\frac{1}{C_2 * R_6}\right) * q_{C2} - \frac{1}{C_3}\left(\frac{1}{R_7} + \frac{1}{R_6}\right) * q_{C3}$$

**In terms of generalized flow and effort**

$$\frac{df_{I1}}{dt} = \left(\frac{1}{I_1}\right) * Se_1 - \left(\frac{R_1}{I_1}\right) * f_{I1} - \left(\frac{k_1}{I_1 * tf}\right) * f_{I2}$$

$$\frac{df_{I2}}{dt} = \left(\frac{k_1}{tf * I_2}\right) * f_{I1} - \left(\frac{R_2}{I_2}\right) * f_{I2} - \left(\frac{k_2}{I_2}\right) * f_{I3}$$

$$\frac{df_{I3}}{dt} = \left(\frac{k_2}{I_3}\right) * f_{I2} - \frac{1}{I_3}\left(\frac{k_3^2}{R_4} - R_3\right) * f_{I3} - \left(\frac{k_3}{I_3 * R_4}\right) * e_{C1}$$

$$\frac{de_{C1}}{dt} = \left(\frac{k_3}{C_1 * R_4}\right) * f_{I3} - \frac{1}{C_1}\left(\frac{1}{R_4} + \frac{1}{R_5}\right) * e_{C1} - \left(\frac{1}{C_1 * R_5}\right) * e_{C2}$$

$$\frac{de_{C2}}{dt} = -\left(\frac{1}{C_2 * R_5}\right) * e_{C1} - \frac{1}{C_2}\left(\frac{1}{R_6} + \frac{1}{R_5}\right) * e_{C2} + \left(\frac{1}{C_2 * R_6}\right) * e_{C3}$$

$$\frac{de_{C3}}{dt} = \left(\frac{1}{C_3 * R_7}\right) * Se_2 + \left(\frac{1}{C_3 * R_6}\right) * e_{C2} - \frac{1}{C_3}\left(\frac{1}{R_7} + \frac{1}{R_6}\right) * e_{C3}$$

Table 5 shows the equivalence between the BG variables and the physical variables.

*Table 5. Variables of the comprehensive VCRS energy-based model (first version)*

| BG Nomenclature | | Multidomain Energy System Nomenclature | |
|---|---|---|---|
| **Sources** | | | |
| $Se_1$ | Generalized effort source | $V_s$ | Voltage source |
| $Se_2$ | Generalized effort source | $T_a$ | Room temperature |
| **Resistances** | | | |
| $R_1$ | Generalized resistance | $R_a$ | Electric resistance |
| $R_2$ | Generalized resistance | $R_m$ | Mechanical friction |
| $R_3$ | Generalized resistance | $R_h$ | Hydraulic friction |
| $R_4$ | Generalized resistance | $R_{cond}$ | Compressor-condenser thermal resistance |
| $R_5$ | Generalized resistance | $R_{cap}$ | Mechanical restriction expansion valve |

*continues on following page*

*Table 5. Continued*

| BG Nomenclature | | Multidomain Energy System Nomenclature | |
|---|---|---|---|
| $R_6$ | Generalized resistance | $R_{ec}$ | Evaporator cold room thermal resistance |
| $R_7$ | Generalized resistance | $R_i$ | Exterior interior thermal resistance |
| $R_8$ | Generalized resistance | $R_{sh}$ | Superheat thermal resistance |
| $R_9$ | Generalized resistance | $R_s$ | Thermal loss |
| **Potential Energy Storage Capacities** | | | |
| $C_1$ | Generalized capacitance | $C_{cond}$ | Condenser heat storage capacity |
| $C_2$ | Generalized capacitance | $C_e$ | Evaporator heat storage capacity |
| $C_3$ | Generalized capacitance | $C_c$ | Cold room heat storage capacity |
| **Kinetic Energy Storage Capacities** | | | |
| $I_1$ | Generalized inertia | $L_a$ | Electrical inductance |
| $I_2$ | Generalized inertia | $J_m$ | Mechanical rotational inertia |
| $I_3$ | Generalized inertia | $J_h$ | Hydraulic inertia |
| **Gyrator** | | | |
| $k_1$ | Domain ratio | $r_m$ | Electric mechanical domain change |
| $k_2$ | Domain ratio | $r_h$ | Mechanical hydraulic domain change |
| $k_3$ | Domain ratio | $r_t$ | Hydraulic thermal domain change |
| tf | Transformation ratio | tf | Converting revolutions per minute |

Table 6 describes the system of differential equations for the complete VCRS model using the physical system notation.

*Table 6. Differential equations of the complete VCRS without superheating*

| BG nomenclature | Energy system nomenclature |
|---|---|
| $$\frac{df_{I1}}{dt} = -\left( \frac{R_1*f_{I1} + \frac{k_1}{tf}*f_{I2} - Se_1}{I_1} \right)$$ | $$\frac{di_a}{dt} = -\left( \frac{R_a*i_a + \frac{r_m}{tf}*\omega_m - V_s}{L_a} \right)$$ |
| $$\frac{df_{I2}}{dt} = -\left( \frac{-\frac{k_1}{tf}*f_{I1} + R_2*f_{I2} + k_2*f_{I3}}{I_2} \right)$$ | $$\frac{d\omega_m}{dt} = -\left( \frac{-\frac{r_m}{tf}*i_a + R_m*\omega_m + r_h*Q_h}{J_m} \right)$$ |
| $$\frac{df_{I3}}{dt} = -\left( \frac{k_2*f_{I2} - R_3*f_{I3} + \frac{k_3\left(e_{C1} - k_3*f_{I3}\right)}{R_4}}{I_3} \right)$$ | $$\frac{dQ_h}{dt} = -\left( \frac{r_h*\omega_m - R_h*Q_h + \frac{r_t\left(T_{Cond} - r_t*Q_h\right)}{R_{cond}}}{J_h} \right)$$ |

*continues on following page*

*Table 6. Continued*

| BG nomenclature | Energy system nomenclature |
|---|---|
| $$\frac{de_{C1}}{dt} = -\left(\frac{\dfrac{e_{C1} - k_3 {}^* f_{I3}}{R_4} + \dfrac{e_{C1} + e_{C2}}{R_5}}{C_1}\right)$$ | $$\frac{dT_{Cond}}{dt} = -\left(\frac{\dfrac{T_{Cond} - r_t {}^* Q_h}{R_{cond}} + \dfrac{T_{Cond} + T_e}{R_{cap}}}{C_{cond}}\right)$$ |
| $$\frac{de_{C2}}{dt} = \frac{\dfrac{e_{C3} - e_{C2}}{R_6} - \dfrac{e_{C1} + e_{C2}}{R_5}}{C_2}$$ | $$\frac{dT_e}{dt} = \frac{\dfrac{T_C - T_e}{R_{ec}} - \dfrac{T_{Cond} + T_e}{R_{cap}}}{C_e}$$ |
| $$\frac{de_{C3}}{dt} = -\left(\frac{\dfrac{e_{C3} - e_{C2}}{R_6} + \dfrac{e_{C3} - Se_2}{R_7}}{C_3}\right)$$ | $$\frac{dT_c}{dt} = -\left(\frac{\dfrac{T_C - T_e}{R_{ec}} + \dfrac{T_C - T_a}{R_i}}{C_C}\right)$$ |

The differential model in Table 6 reproduces the thermal dynamics observed experimentally (Schné et al., 2015). Originally, those dynamics were reproduced exclusively by thermal actions. From the differential model in Table 6, these dynamics are now produced considering the effects corresponding to the electrical motor, the mechanical load, and the result of the compressor, all acting on thermal circuit.

## State Variable Model Formulation of The Whole VCRS With Superheating Temperature

The thermal circuit including the superheating temperature is in figure 18.

*Figure 18. Representation by BG of the thermal circuit including the superheating*

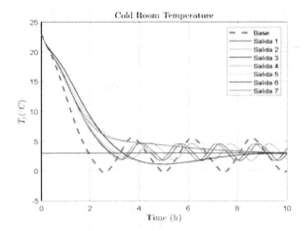

The fully labeled BG of the comprehensive VCRS model is in figure 19. This model includes all the elements composing a VCRS, i.e., electrical motor, rotational load, compressor, and thermal circuit with superheating.

*Figure 19. Modular union of the complete thermal cycle and the motor-compressor group using BG, with assignment of flows and efforts for each power bond*

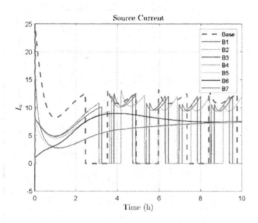
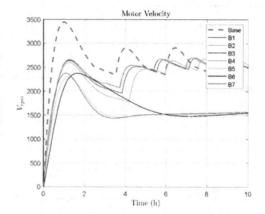

As done before, from the unified graphical representation in figure 19, it is possible to derive directly and systematically the comprehensive mathematical model of a VCRS which corresponds to experimental data in (Schné et al., 2015), see Table 7.

*Table 7. Differential equation system of the comprehensive VCRS (with superheating)*

| BG nomenclature | Energy system nomenclature |
|---|---|
| $$\frac{df_{I1}}{dt} = -\left(\frac{R_1 * f_{I1} + \frac{k_1}{tf} * f_{I2} - Se_1}{I_1}\right)$$ | $$\frac{di_a}{dt} = -\left(\frac{R_a * i_a + \frac{r_m}{tf} * \omega_m - V_s}{L_a}\right)$$ |
| $$\frac{df_{I2}}{dt} = -\left(\frac{-\frac{k_1}{tf} * f_{I1} + R_2 * f_{I2} + k_2 * f_{I3}}{I_2}\right)$$ | $$\frac{d\omega_m}{dt} = -\left(\frac{-\frac{r_m}{tf} * i_a + R_m * \omega_m + r_h * Q_h}{J_m}\right)$$ |
| $$\frac{df_{I3}}{dt} = -\left(\frac{k_2 * f_{I2} - R_3 * f_{I3} + \frac{k_3\left(e_{C1} - k_3 * f_{I3}\right)}{R_4}}{I_3}\right)$$ | $$\frac{dQ_h}{dt} = -\left(\frac{r_h * \omega_m - R_h * Q_h + \frac{r_t\left(T_{Cond} - r_t * Q_h\right)}{R_{cond}}}{J_h}\right)$$ |

*continues on following page*

*Table 7. Continued*

| BG nomenclature | Energy system nomenclature |
|---|---|
| $$\frac{de_{C1}}{dt} = -\left(\frac{\dfrac{e_{C1} - k_3 * f_{I3}}{R_4} + \dfrac{e_{C1} + e_{C2}}{R_5}}{C_1}\right)$$ | $$\frac{dT_{Cond}}{dt} = -\left(\frac{\dfrac{T_{Cond} - r_t * Q_h}{R_{cond}} + \dfrac{T_{Cond} + T_e}{R_{cap}}}{C_{cond}}\right)$$ |
| $$\frac{de_{C2}}{dt} = -\left(\frac{\dfrac{e_{C1} + e_{C2}}{R_5} - \dfrac{e_{C3} - e_{C2}}{R_6} + \dfrac{e_{C2}}{R_8 * \left(\dfrac{R_9}{R_8} + 1\right)}}{C_2}\right)$$ | $$\frac{dT_e}{dt} = -\left(\frac{\dfrac{T_{Cond} + T_e}{R_{cap}} - \dfrac{T_C - T_e}{R_{ec}} + \dfrac{T_e}{R_{sh} * \left(\dfrac{R_s}{R_{sh}} + 1\right)}}{C_e}\right)$$ |
| $$\frac{de_{C3}}{dt} = -\left(\frac{\dfrac{e_{C3} - e_{C2}}{R_6} + \dfrac{e_{C3} - Se_2}{R_7}}{C_3}\right)$$ | $$\frac{dT_c}{dt} = -\left(\frac{\dfrac{T_C - T_e}{R_{ec}} + \dfrac{T_C - T_a}{R_i}}{C_C}\right)$$ |

## BEHAVIORAL ANALYSIS OF THE VCRS

The comprehensive model of the VCRS was built by joining the experimental thermal model with the theoretical electromechanical-hydraulic model. Parameters on Table 8 were used for the simulation of this model. The values of the thermal model come from the experimental process of systems identification applied in a commercial domestic fridge working with R404a as a refrigerant fluid. The parameters of the proposed models in the electrical, mechanical, and hydraulic domains were taken from technical manuals of both the original refrigerator and commercial components.

*Table 8. Parameters of the comprehensive model of the VCRS*

| | | | | |
|---|---|---|---|---|
| $V_s = 220\ v$ | $R_h = 1e-5\ Pa.s/m^3$ | $R_{ec} = 0.325°C/W$ | $C_{cond} = 0.6\ J$ | $r_m = 0.4042$ |
| $L_a = 0.0185\ H$ | $J_h = 0.00018\ N.s/m^2$ | $R_i = 0.475°C/W$ | $C_e = 0.64\ J$ | $r_h = 1.7988$ |
| $R_a = 9.01\ \Omega$ | $T_a = 20°C$ | $R_{sh} = 8.5°C/W$ | $C_c = 3.2\ J$ | $r_t = 76.7397$ |
| $R_m = 1e-5\ N.m.s/rad$ | $R_{cond} = 0.099°C/W$ | $R_s = 2.5°C/W$ | | $tf = 9.549$ |
| $J_m = 0.00015\ kg.m^2$ | $R_{cap} = 0.01°C/W$ | | | |

Figure 20 shows the verification by the VCRS holistic model of the original experimental behavior for the two state variables: Temperature in the Cold Chamber and Temperature in the Evaporator. Now, other state variables of the VCRS can be observed through the holistic model, figure 21.

*Figure 20. Comparison of the temperature in the evaporator and in the cold chamber for the experimental thermal model vs the comprehensive VCRS model*

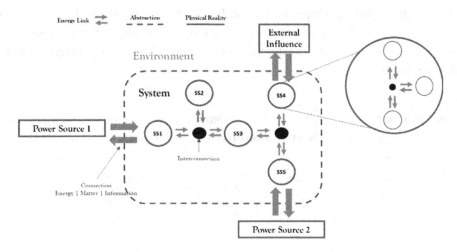

*Figure 21. Other state variables (internal dynamics) from the comprehensive model of the VCRS*

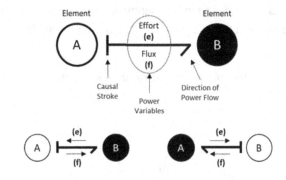

The comprehensive model of the whole VCRS allows a holistic view of the system, achieving identify forms of intervention that facilitate minimizing the consumption of the input power (electrical energy) while ensuring desired operating conditions. General energy consumption is calculated by integrating power for a defined period of observation. In the BG model, this calculation is immediate due to the knowledge of the effort and flow variables at all moments, equation (22).

$$E(t) = \int P(t)\,dt = \int e(t) {}^* f(t)\,dt \qquad (22)$$

From equation (22) it is possible to know the real impact on energy due to a direct intervention in the dynamics of the process. By always having the effort and flow variables available, for the entire system and for any of its components, the power information can be expressed. In this way, an energy analysis is established, initially based on the traditional "On-Off" control commonly used in domestic refrigerators. Subsequently, an energy analysis will be carried out with the new continuous control technologies.

## Operation by Traditional On-Off Control

Conventionally, when the indoor temperature is high and exceeds the desired value, the compressor turns on; otherwise, it turns off. The on/off operation not only consumes a large amount of energy, but also causes large variations in the indoor temperature. Figure 22 shows the original on-off behavior experimentally measured.

*Figure 22. Simulation of the real behavior vs the thermal experimental model. Temperature in the cold chamber (blue) and temperature in the evaporator (red). Taken from (Schné et al., 2015)*

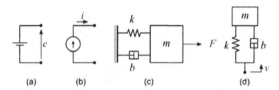

On the other hand, figure 23 shows the reproduction of this on-off behavior achieved with the comprehensive model of the VCRS. The change in frequency depends on the on-off valve setting used. In the holistic simulation, the extremes and the mean oscillation are the same obtained in the experimentation.

*Figure 23. Simulation of the experimental behavior of the temperature in the cold room using the comprehensive model of the VCRS*

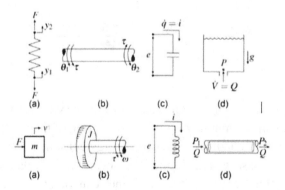

The total energy consumed by the VCRS is that in the electrical power input source. Its calculation results from the multiplication of the effort variable, *e1*, by the flow variable, *f1*, from figure 19. Energy is the integration of this product, as in equation (23). The calculation of the total energy consumption of the VCRS under the traditional on-off control dynamics, during a working period of 25 hours is .

$$E_{source} = \int P_{source}(t)\,dt = \int V_s(t) * i_a(t)\,dt \tag{23}$$

Recently, modern refrigeration systems have started incorporating variable-speed compressors to improve energy efficiency and cooling performance. However, these actuators should be adequately controlled by feedback, or the system may exhibit a poorer performance than conventional machines (Lin & Yeh, 2007). For this reason, two controllers were designed for the VCRS to manage the temperature of the cold chamber from a variable-speed compressor which is projected as part of the new technologies that it wants to implement in these systems.

The design of each controller for the VCRS is model independent, in the sense that their tuning is data driven. It is carried out by an evolutionary learning of trajectories method, which has been used in other complex cases such as a Split Range control (Soto. & Hernandez-Riveros., 2019) and the tuning of the IFAC Benchmark PID (Soto et al., 2018). A description of the controller design method is in figure 24. In this case, the comprehensive model for the VCRS is used only as data generator for tuning the controllers.

*Figure 24. Illustration of the controller design using the comprehensive model of the VCRS*

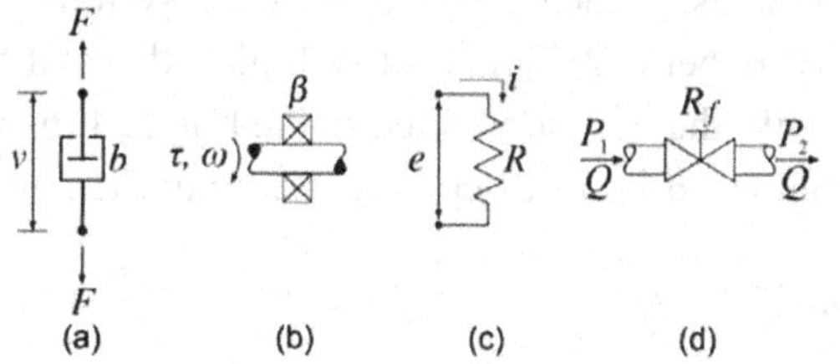

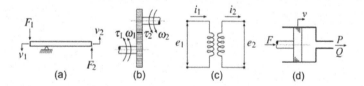

Figure 25 and figure 26 illustrate the set of behavioral trajectories due to direct intervention within the process. Outputs 1, 2, 3 and 4 correspond to the discrete control strategy. Outputs 5, 6 and 7 correspond to the continuous control strategy. The comprehensive model makes it possible to observe all the state variables simultaneously and calculate the energy consumption of the entire system as well as its individual components, while the desired reference is accomplished. The six strategies were applied to meet the operating condition of 3 °C in the cold chamber together with the decrease in the total energy consumption of the VCRS. The results on energy consumption of the entire VCRS are in Table 9.

*Figure 25. Output temperature behavior trajectories applying the intervention strategies in the VCRS*

*Figure 26. Trajectories of behavior of electric current and motor speed applying intervention strategies in the VCRS*

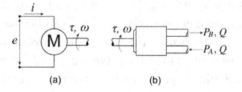

*Table 9. Energy Consumption of the electric Source by the VCRS for a reference of 3 °C in the cold*

| Experimental Base = 3.748e+04 J | |
|---|---|
| Discrete control | Continuous control |
| O1=1.354e+04 J | O5=1.274e+04 J |
| O2=1.415e+04 J | O6=1.549e+04 J |
| O3=1.332e+04 J | O7=1.323e+04 J |
| O4=1.331e+04 J | |

## FUTURE RESEARCH DIRECTIONS

To measure the efficiency of refrigeration systems, the Coefficient of Performance (COP) is commonly used. COP is the ratio between the useful heat subtracted by the system and the work supplied to carry out this action, equation (24). A higher COP equates to a higher thermal cycle performance. Using the BG model, we can directly identify the heat subtracted in the bond 21, as well as the mechanical power by multiplying both power variables of bond 14 corresponding to the compressor output.

$$COP_{VCRS} = \frac{Cooling\ Power}{Compressor's\ Power} = \frac{Q_e}{W_c} = \frac{f_{21}}{e_{14}*f_{14}} = \frac{112.339}{25.000*49.504} = 9.077\% \tag{24}$$

The COP usually exceeds 1, because a VCRS instead of just converting work to heat (which, if 100% efficient, would be a COP of 1), it pumps additional heat from a heat source to where the heat is required.

The COP is applied only to the thermal circuit, it does not represent de efficiency of the whole refrigeration system. Taking advantage of the comprehensive model of the VCRS now is also possible to calculate the efficiency of the complete system, equation (25). From this model is possible to determine the value of the electrical power source that drives the process by multiplying both power variables of the bond 1. Total efficiency of the VCRS is easier to verify experimentally.

$$Efficiency_{VCRS} = \frac{Output\ Power}{Input\ Power} = \frac{Q_e}{V_S*I_a} = \frac{f_{21}}{e_1*f_1} = \frac{112.339}{220*14.452} = 3.533\% \tag{25}$$

## CONCLUSION

In this chapter, the development of a comprehensive model of a VCRS based on power flows was presented. The construction of the model starts from the empirical identification of the thermal part of a commercial refrigerator, which is complemented with theoretical models based on catalog data of the electrical, rotational mechanical and hydraulic parts.

Usually, the global analysis of a VCRS is difficult due to its heterogeneity and multidomain nature. The power flow approach of a system emphasizes the couplings between elements of different physical fields. The unified formalism provided by the BG method was used to illustrate the dynamics of each component of the VCRS, as well as their total dynamics and the energy transfers in the system. The presented methodology combining experimental and theoretical data offers interesting solutions in terms of complex systems analysis; it is possible to observe both the dynamics of the manifest variables, as well as the dynamics of the latent variables, as well as the energy consumption at any point in the VCRS. This comprehensive model allows for realistic simulations and control options, without reducing the observation problem to a linear input-output case. As the refrigeration by vapor compression is a system that mechanically forces the circulation of a fluid in a closed circuit, creating zones of high and low pressure so that the fluid absorbs heat in one place and dissipates it in another, achieving the desired value of temperature in the cold chamber means great effects on the pressure and flow of the refrigerant. These effects depend on the torque and speed that an electrical motor applies to the compressor, with the consequent changes in the electrical variables of such motor. With the comprehensive VCRS model that was developed in this chapter, observing all these phenomena simultaneously is now possible.

The importance and interest of a unifying methodology such as BG should be emphasized, which facilitates the homogeneous modeling of multidomain systems such as VCRS, integrating experimental and theoretical data. This formalism allows without great complications add modules to each domain, such as the heat emitted by the electric motor, or to detail each sub-model at the desired level or even to change it for another, for example, a switched moving-boundary approach to heat exchangers.

This chapter fills a gap in the scientific literature by presenting, for the first time, a comprehensive model of the VCRS. This model, based on experimental data, can be used as a benchmarking for studies of energy activity indicators, controller effectiveness and impact of incorporating new technologies in VCRS.

## REFERENCES

Bejarano, G. (2017). *Optimization and multivariable control of refrigeration systems*. https://idus.us.es/xmlui/handle/11441/63847

Belman Flores, J. M. (2008). *Desarrollo de un modelo físico para una instalación de producción de frío por compresión de vapor utilizando el refrigerante R134a. Validación experimental y aplicación para la simulación energética.* http://hdl.handle.net/10803/384550

Borutzky, W. (2015). *Bond graph model-based fault diagnosis of hybrid systems.* https://doi.org/doi:10.1007/978-3-319-11860-4

Broenink, J. F. (1999). *Introduction to physical systems modelling with bond graphs.* https://www.cs.mcgill.ca/~hv/articles/PhysicalModelling/BondGraphsV2.pdf

Ghiaus, C. (1999). *Fault diagnosis of air conditioning systems based on qualitative bond graph.* Energy and Buildings. doi:10.1016/S0378-7788(98)00070-X

Hermes, C. J. L., & Melo, C. (2008). *A first-principles simulation model for the start-up and cycling transients of household refrigerators.* https://doi.org/doi:10.1016/j.ijrefrig.2008.04.003

Hroncová, D., & Gmiterko, A. (2013). *Bond graphs of the electrical RLC circuit.* https://doi.org/. http://www.sciepub.com/AJME/abstract/1075 doi:10.12691/AJME-1-7-33

Jahangeer, K. A., Tay, A. A. O., & Raisul Islam, M. (2011). *Numerical investigation of transfer coefficients of an evaporatively-cooled condenser.* https://doi.org/doi:10.1016/j.applthermaleng.2011.02.007

Kypuros, J. A. (2013). *System dynamics and control with bond graph modeling.* https://doi.org/doi:10.1201/b14676

Schné, T., Jaskó, S., & Simon, G. (2015). *Dynamic models of a home refrigerator.* https://doi.org/. https://www.researchgate.net/publication/324929106_Dynamic_Models_of_a_Home_Refrigerator doi:10.1515/macro-2015-0010

Sellami, A., Aridhi, E., Mzoughi, D., & Mami, A. (2018). *Performance of the bond graph approach for the detection and localization of faults of a refrigerator compartment containing an ice quantity.* https://doi.org/ doi:10.1142/S2010132518500281

Soto, G. J. A., López, J. M. G., & Hernández-Riveros, J. A. (2018). *Coupled evolutionary tuning of PID controllers for the benchmark on vapor compression refrigeration.* https://doi.org/ doi:10.1016/j.ifacol.2018.06.146

Soto, G. J. A., & Hernandez-Riveros, J.-A. (2019). *Evolutionary split range controller for a refrigeration system.* https://doi.org/ doi:10.5220/0007930803410351

United Nations Environment Programme. (2018). The Importance of Energy Efficiency in the Refrigeration and Heat Pump Sectors. *Environment Programme, Briefing Note A.* https://ozone.unep.org/sites/default/files/2019-08/briefingnote-a_importance-of-energy-efficiency-in-the-refrigeration-air-conditioning-and-heat-pump-sectors.pdf

van Beek, D. A., van den Ham, A., & Rooda, J. E. (2002). *Modelling and control of process industry batch production systems.* https://doi.org/ doi:10.3182/20020721-6-ES-1901.00555

## ADDITIONAL READING

Ahmed, R., Mahadzir, S., Erniza Mohammad Rozali, N., Biswas, K., Matovu, F., & Ahmed, K. (2021). Artificial intelligence techniques in refrigeration system modelling and optimization: A multi-disciplinary review. *Sustainable Energy Technologies and Assessments.* Advance online publication. doi:10.1016/j.seta.2021.101488

Kim, J. G., Han, C. H., & Jeong, S. K. (2020). Disturbance observer-based robust control against model uncertainty and disturbance for a variable speed refrigeration system. *International Journal of Refrigeration.* Advance online publication. doi:10.1016/j.ijrefrig.2020.03.019

Kong, D., Yin, X., Ding, X., Fang, N., & Duan, P. (2021). Global optimization of a vapor compression refrigeration system with a self-adaptive differential evolution algorithm. *Applied Thermal Engineering.* Advance online publication. doi:10.1016/j.applthermaleng.2021.117427

Li, G., Han, Y., Li, M., Luo, X., Xu, Y., Wang, Y., & Zhang, Y. (2021). Study on matching characteristics of photovoltaic disturbance and refrigeration compressor in solar photovoltaic direct-drive air conditioning system. *Renewable Energy.* https://doi.org/https://doi.org/10.1016/j.renene.2021.03.110

Lin, J. L., & Yeh, T. J. (2007). *Modeling, identification and control of air-conditioning systems.* https://doi.org/ doi:10.1016/j.ijrefrig.2006.08.009

Luyben, W. L. (2019). Control of compression refrigeration processes with superheat or saturated boiling. *Chemical Engineering and Processing.* Advance online publication. doi:10.1016/j.cep.2019.03.005

Nikhil Babu, P., Mohankumar, D., Manoj Kumar, P., Makeshkumar, M., Gokulnath, M., Gurubalaji, K., Harrish, G., & Ashok, M. (2021). Energy efficient refrigeration system with simultaneous heating and cooling. https://doi.org/ doi:10.1016/j.matpr.2021.03.072

Omer, A. M. (2022). *Performance, modelling, measurement and simulation of energy efficiency for heat exchanger, refrigeration and air conditioning BT - Sustainable Energy Development and Innovation: Selected Papers from the World Renewable Energy Congress (WREC) 2020.* https://doi.org/10.1007/978-3-030-76221-6_23

## KEY TERMS AND DEFINITIONS

**Bond Graph:** A graphical representation of a physical dynamic system which is regarded as composed of components with a port transferring energy among them by flow and potential variables.

**Data Catalog:** A data set, created by the manufacturer, summarizing the performance and other characteristics of a machine or component in sufficient detail that allows a user, installation technician or design engineer to understand the behavior of a specific product.

**Empirical Modeling:** Process of building a mathematical representation that reflects the behavior of a system observed on data from a specific experiment made on that system.

**Energy Efficiency:** The process of using less energy to get the same job done. Efficient energy use results in energy bills and pollution reducing.

**Evolutionary Algorithms:** Heuristic search methods inspired by evolution and living organisms to solving problems that cannot be easily work out in polynomial time.

**Multidomain Modeling:** A model characterized by having components belonging to different engineering disciplines assembled into a larger simulation system.

**Vapor Compression Refrigeration:** A system which circulates a liquid refrigerant alternately compressing and expanding it, changing it from liquid to vapor. As this change happens, heat is either absorbed or expelled by the system, resulting in a change in temperature of the surrounding air.

# Section 10
# Cloud Infrastructure

C

# Cryptic Algorithms:
## Hiding Sensitive Information in Cloud Computing

**Shivlal Mewada**

https://orcid.org/0000-0001-5543-8622

*Government Holkar Science College, India*

## INTRODUCTION

### An Overview

In today's digital world, there is an immense growth of data which is difficult for the users to store and share it locally. Due to this, a greater number of users switch to cloud storing facilities. But somehow, the data stored in the cloud might be manipulated or lost due to the unavoidable software bugs, hardware flaws and human inaccuracy in the cloud. In order to check whether the data is stored accurately in the cloud storage, many remote data integrity auditing schemes have been implemented.

The data stored in the cloud storages is frequently shared across multiple users in other cloud storage applications, such as Google Drive, Dropbox and iCloud. Data sharing in cloud storage allows a number of users to share their data with others. However, shared data in the cloud platforms might contain some tactful or sensitive information. For example, the Health Records, Bank Transactions, Confidential information etc. stored and shared in the cloud usually contains tactful or sensitive information. If these documents are directly uploaded to the cloud to be shared for research purposes, the sensitive information of data owner will be inevitably released to the cloud and the researchers. Thus, it is important to achieve remote data integrity auditing on the terms that the sensitive information of shared data is protected. A typical method of solving this problem is to encrypt the whole shared file before sending it to the cloud storages, and then verify the integrity of this encrypted file. This method provides the sensitive information hiding since only the data owner can decrypt this file. But, the whole shared file will be will not be available others. For example, encrypting the Health Records of infectious disease to patients can protect the privacy of patient and hospital, but this encrypted Health Record cannot be efficiently used by researchers for further findings any more. Distributing the decryption method to the researchers seems to be a possible solution to the above problem. However, it is impractical to accept this method in real scenarios due to the following reasons.

Firstly, distributing decryption method needs secure sources of communication, which is difficult to be implemented for each researcher in some instances. Further, it seems very hard for a user to know which researchers will use his/her Health Records in the near future when he/she uploads the Health Records to the cloud. As a conclusion, it is impractical to hide sensitive information by encrypting the whole shared file. Thus, how to execute data storing and sharing simultaneously with sensitive information hiding in remote data integrity auditing is very dominant and valuable.

DOI: 10.4018/978-1-7998-9220-5.ch044

## Related Work

In process to check the integrity of the data blocks stored in the cloud storage, many remote data integrity auditing schemes have been proposed. To reduce the computation burden on user, a Third-Party Auditor (TPA) is introduced to ensure the integrity of the data stored in cloud for user. (K. Ren, 2012, G. Ateniese, 2007) here author, proposed a notation of Provable Data Possession (PDP) to ensure the data possession on the unreliable cloud storage. In their scheme, homomorphic authenticators and random sampling strategies are used to achieve block less verification and reduce hardware costs. In order to protect the data privacy, Wang et al. (C. Wang, 2013) proposed a privacy-preserving remote data integrity auditing scheme with the employment of a random masking technique. Solomon et al. (S. G. Worku, 2014) utilized a different random masking technique to further construct a remote data integrity auditing scheme supporting data privacy protection. Wang et al. (Y. Zhang, 2011) proposed another remote data integrity auditing scheme supporting full data dynamics by utilizing Merkle Hash Tree. In (B. Wang, 2012) authors designed a privacy-preserving shared data integrity auditing scheme by modifying the ring signature for secure cloud storage. With the employment of the Shamir secret sharing technique, Luo et al. (Y. Luo, 2015) constructed a shared data integrity auditing scheme supporting user revocation. The aforementioned schemes all rely on Public Key Infrastructure (PKI), which incurs the considerable overheads from the complicated certificate management. To simplify certificate management, Yu et al. (H. Wang, 2015) constructed a remote data integrity auditing scheme with perfect data privacy preserving in identity-based cryptosystems. Wang et al. (H. Wang, 2016) proposed an identity-based data integrity auditing scheme satisfying unconditional anonymity and incentive. Zhang et al. (Y. Zhang, 2018) proposed an identity-based remote data integrity auditing scheme for shared data supporting real efficient user revocation. Other aspects, such as privacy-preserving authenticators (W. Shen, 2017) and data deduplication (J. Li, 2016, S. Gonth, 2020, S. Mewada, 2013, Vivek R., 2013, Mewada, 2011, 2015, 2016, 2020, 2021) in remote data integrity auditing have also been explored. However, all of existing remote data integrity auditing schemes cannot support data sharing with sensitive information hiding. In this paper, we explore how to achieve data sharing with sensitive information hiding in identity-based integrity auditing for secure cloud Storage.

## SYSTEM METHODOLOGY

### A) Process

STEP 1: Firstly, data owner generates a private key using his/her unique contact number.

STEP 2: Then the owner himself blinds the original file i.e., hides sensitive/personal information and passes the blinded file to the sanitizer module in the system.

STEP 3: Sanitizer module sanitizes the blinded file i.e., per-forms the 2nd step of hiding sensitive/personal information of the data owner. After the sanitization process, sanitized file is stored into the cloud storage.

STEP 4: At any point if the data owner needs a confirmation that the file stored in the cloud is completely sanitized then he delegates a Third-Party Auditor (TPA) Module to check the file stored in cloud.

STEP 5: Third Party Auditor (TPA) Module sends a auditing challenge to the cloud and in return cloud system responds with an auditing proof.

STEP 6:    TPA sends the mail to user with attachment that file store in the cloud. Lastly TPA verifies the proof and passes the result to the data owner.

## B) Algorithms Used

1.  **Setup Algorithm-** This algorithm is run by the PKG. This algorithm also set up the system for further process. It takes as input a security parameter. It outputs the master secret key and the system public parameters.

2.  **Extraction Algorithm-** This is an algorithm run by the PKG. It takes as input the system public parameters, the master secret key, and a user's contact number. It outputs the user's private key. The user can verify the correctness of private key and accept it as his private key only if it passes the verification.

3.  **Sanitization Algorithm-** Sanitization Algorithm is a sensitive information sanitization algorithm run by the sanitizer module. It takes as input the blinded file. It outputs the sanitized file.

4.  **Proof Generation Algorithm-** This algorithm is run by the cloud. It takes as input the sanitized file, the corresponding signature set and the auditing challenge. It out-puts an auditing proof that is used to demonstrate the cloud truly possesses this sanitized file.

5.  **Proof Verification Algorithm-** This is a proof verification algorithm run by the TPA. It takes as input the auditing challenge, system public parameters and the auditing proof P. The TPA can verify the correctness of proof.

## C) Cryptographic Algorithms

*Figure 1. AES encryption*

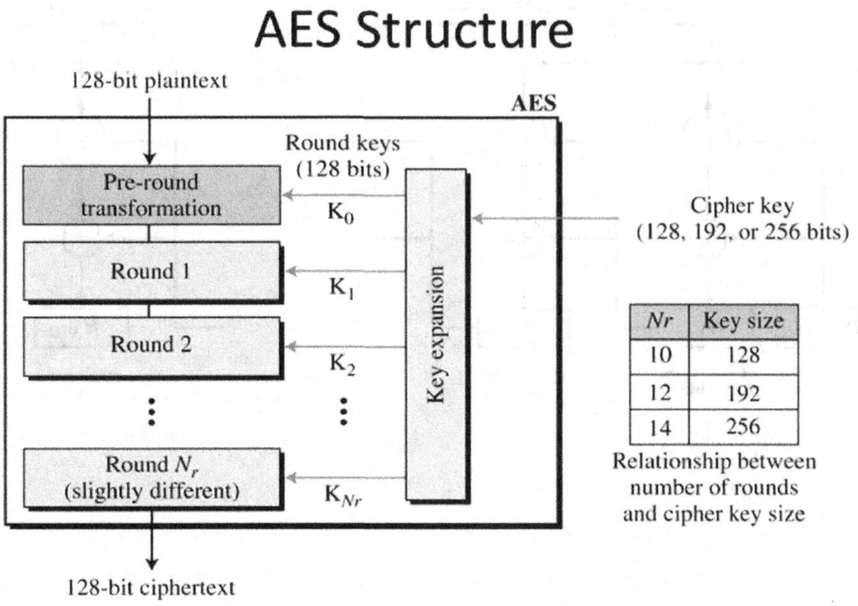

## AES Algorithm

AES-128 uses a 128-bit key length to encrypt and decrypt a block of messages, while AES-192 uses a 192-bit key length and AES-256 a 256-bit key length to encrypt and decrypt messages. Each cipher encrypts and decrypts data in blocks of 128 bits using cryptographic keys of 128, 192 and 256 bits, respectively.

## SHA Algorithm

$$T1 = h+Ch(e, f, g) + (512\sum 1e) + Wt + KtT2$$
$$= (512\sum 0a) + M\ aj(a, b, c)$$

Where, T1, T2 – Variables

    h - Hash code (Initialization Vector)

    Ch - Conditional Function

    Wt- Word Generating

    Kt- Constant

*Figure 2. SHA*

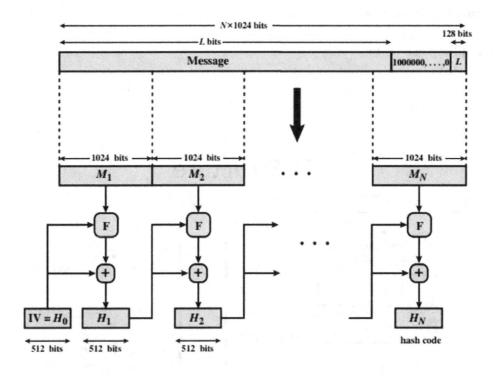

## MD5 Algorithm

A = b+ ((a+g(b, c, d) +X[k] +T[i])<<< s)

Where, a, b, c, d – Buffers
  g - Primitive Functions
  ¡¡¡s - Circular Left Shift
  X[k] - 32 bit word
  T[i] - 32 bit word in matrix

*Figure 3. MD5*

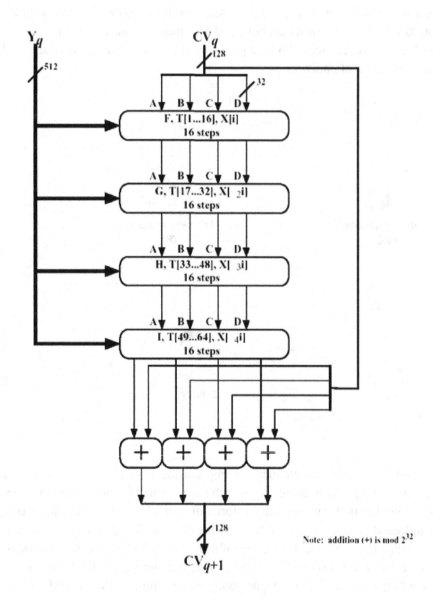

Note: addition (+) is mod $2^{32}$

## SYSTEM MODELING AND ANALYSIS

The system model involves five different modules: the cloud storage services, the data owner, the sanitizer, the Private Key Generator (PKG) and the Third Party Auditor (TPA), as shown below figure.

(1)　Cloud Storage services: The cloud provides enormous data storage space to the data owner. Through the cloud storage service, data owner can upload their data to the cloud and share their data with others.

(2)　Data owner: The data owner is a member of an organization or an individual, who has large number of files or data blocks to be stored in the cloud storage.

(3)　Sanitizer: The sanitizer is responsible for sanitizing the sensitive data corresponding to the personal sensitive information or the organization's sensitive information in the file and uploading the sanitized file to the cloud storage.

(4)　PKG: The Private Key Generator (PKG) is trusted by other modules. It is responsible for generating the private key for the data owner according to his unique Contact number.

(5)　TPA: The Third Party Auditor (TPA) is a public verifier. It is in charge of verifying the data stored in the cloud on behalf of data owners.

*Figure 4. Data hiding*

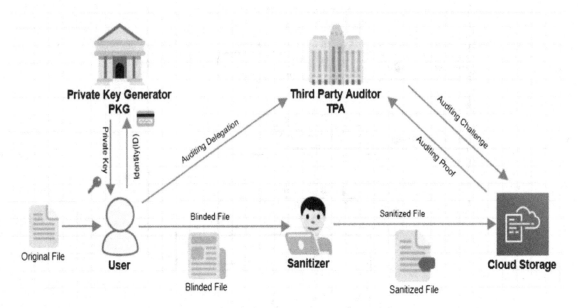

Here, we give an illustrative example in above Fig.4, in this example; Data owner has files that need to be stored in cloud storages for sharing or research usage. This file may contain the owner's or organizations sensitive information. This sensitive information should be replaced with encoded texts when the records are uploaded to cloud for research or sharing purpose. So, the data owner (user) firstly blinds the data corresponding to the personal sensitive information of the file that needs to be stored in cloud. Then the user sends this blinded file to the sanitizer. The sanitizer can be illustrated as the administrator of the whole record information system. The personal sensitive information should not be revealed to the sanitizer or any other modules of the system. After receiving the file from the user, the sanitizer sanitizes these blinded data corresponding to the personal or organization's sensitive information.

Finally, the sanitizer sends this sanitized file to the cloud storage. When the User wants to verify the integrity of the sanitized file stored in the cloud, he sends an auditing delegation to Third Party Auditor (TPA). Then the TPA sends an auditing challenge to the cloud. To which, the cloud responds with an auditing proof of data possession. Then, the TPA checks the integrity of the sanitized file by checking whether this auditing proof is correct or not. Finally, he reports the results to the data owner via Email Verification System.

The other end of this system is that if the outsiders or Researchers try to access the file from the public cloud storage then they can access only the sanitized file which is a secure step for data owner as his personal information or organizations sensitive information is hidden.

## RESULT AND DISCUSSION

All these experiments use Java programming language with the javax-crypto Library. In our experiments, we set the base field size to be 128 bits, the size of data file to be 20MB composed by 1,000,000 blocks, and the length of user unique contact id to be 10 digits.

In this experiment, the number of challenged data blocks varies from 0 to 1,000. The computation overheads of challenge proof verification and generation on the TPA it linearly increases along with the number of challenged data blocks. The computation overhead of proof verification varies from 0.317s to 11.505s. In Comparison with the time of proof verification, the time of challenge generation increases slowly, just varying from 0.013s to 0461s. We have the observation the computation overhead of proof generation on the cloud side varies from 0.021s to 3.981s. So we can conclude that, with the more challenged data blocks, both the TPA and the cloud will spend the more computation overheads.

## CONCLUSION

In this system, we implement an identity-based data integrity auditing scheme for secure cloud storage, which supports data sharing with sensitive information hiding. This system works on a unique privacy-preserving mechanism that endorses an accessible examining of sensitive shared data stored in the cloud that is information that cannot be fetched by the others. The users/clients can efficiently accumulate their sensitive data in the cloud. The file reserved in the cloud can be shared and utilized by others on the condition that the confidential data of the recorded file is to be protected. The proof of the file stored in the cloud is sent to the user through E-mail. The security proof and the experimental analysis demonstrates that the implemented scheme achieves desirable security and efficiency. The records which are reserved in the cloud can be gotten to by others relying on the prerequisite that the intricate data of the document is secured. The storage of data in the cloud might be corrupted or lost due to some different factors, and each possesses a unique problem for data recovery. Loss of data is caused by unavoidable defective software, their bugs, hardware failure and human errors in the cloud. So, to confirm whether the information is reserved effectively in the cloud, a multitude of remote information respectability examining procedures have been done to store the information in the cloud. The proposed plan accomplishes security and more efficiency. This implemented program accomplishes desirable security and efficiency. This System further can be inherited and improved for batch auditing.

# REFERENCES

Ateniese, G., Burns, R., Curtmola, R., Herring, J., Kissner, L., Peterson, Z., & Song, D. (2007, October). Provable data possession at untrusted stores. In *Proceedings of the 14th ACM conference on Computer and communications security* (pp. 598-609). ACM.

Bedi, P., Mewada, S., Vatti, R. A., Singh, C., Dhindsa, K. S., Ponnusamy, M., & Sikarwar, R. (2021). Detection of attacks in IoT sensors networks using machine learning algorithm. *Microprocessors and Microsystems*, 82, 103814. doi:10.1016/j.micpro.2020.103814

Chopra, U., Thakur, N., & Sharma, L. (2019). Cloud Computing: Elementary Threats and Embellishing Countermeasures for Data security. *Globe, 1*(2), 10-25.

Gonthireddy, S., & Pasupuleti, S. K. (2020). Secure Big Data Deduplication with Dynamic Ownership Management in Cloud Computing. In *Advanced Computing and Intelligent Engineering* (pp. 249–263). Springer. doi:10.1007/978-981-15-1483-8_22

Li, J., Li, J., Xie, D., & Cai, Z. (2015). Secure auditing and deduplicating data in cloud. *IEEE Transactions on Computers*, 65(8), 2386–2396. doi:10.1109/TC.2015.2389960

Luo, Y., Xu, M., Fu, S., Wang, D., & Deng, J. (2015, August). *Efficient integrity auditing for shared data in the cloud with secure user revocation. In 2015 IEEE Trustcom/BigDataSE/ISPA* (Vol. 1). IEEE.

Mewada, S. (2021). Data mining-based privacy preservation technique for medical dataset over horizontal partitioned. *International Journal of E-Health and Medical Communications*, 12(5), 50–66. doi:10.4018/IJEHMC.20210901.oa4

Mewada, S., Gautam, S. S., & Sharma, P. (2020). Artificial bee colony-based approach for privacy preservation of medical data. *International Journal of Information System Modeling and Design*, 11(3), 22–39. doi:10.4018/IJISMD.2020070102

Mewada, S., Sharma, P., & Gautam, S. S. (2016, March). Exploration of efficient symmetric AES algorithm. In *2016 Symposium on Colossal Data Analysis and Networking (CDAN)* (pp. 1-5). IEEE.

Mewada, S., Sharma, P., & Gautam, S. S. (2016, March). Exploration of efficient symmetric algorithms. In *2016 3rd International Conference on Computing for Sustainable Global Development (INDIACom)* (pp. 663-666). IEEE. 10.1109/CDAN.2016.7570921

Mewada, S., Shrivastava, A., Sharma, P., Purohit, N., & Gautam, S. S. (2015). Performance analysis of encryption algorithm in cloud computing. *International Journal on Computer Science and Engineering*, 3, 83–89.

Mewada, S., Singh, U. K., & Sharma, P. (2011). Security Based Model for Cloud Computing. *IRACST-International Journal of Computer Networks and Wireless Communications*, 1(1), 13–19.

Ni, J., Zhang, K., Yu, Y., Lin, X., & Shen, X. S. (2018). Providing task allocation and secure deduplication for mobile crowdsensing via fog computing. *IEEE Transactions on Dependable and Secure Computing*, 17(3), 581–594. doi:10.1109/TDSC.2018.2791432

Raich, V., Sharma, P., Mewada, S., & Kumbhkar, M. (2013). Performance Improvement of Software as a Service and Platform as a Service in Cloud Computing Solution. *ISROSET-International Journal of Scientific Research in Computer Science and Engineering*, 1, 13–16.

Ren, K., Wang, C., & Wang, Q. (2012). Security challenges for the public cloud. *IEEE Internet Computing*, *16*(1), 69–73. doi:10.1109/MIC.2012.14

Shen, W., Yang, G., Yu, J., Zhang, H., Kong, F., & Hao, R. (2017). Remote data possession checking with privacy-preserving authenticators for cloud storage. *Future Generation Computer Systems*, *76*, 136–145. doi:10.1016/j.future.2017.04.029

Wang, B., Li, H., & Li, M. (2013, June). Privacy-preserving public auditing for shared cloud data supporting group dynamics. In *2013 IEEE International Conference on Communications (ICC)* (pp. 1946-1950). IEEE. 10.1109/ICC.2013.6654808

Wang, C., Chow, S. S., Wang, Q., Ren, K., & Lou, W. (2011). Privacy-preserving public auditing for secure cloud storage. *IEEE Transactions on Computers*, *62*(2), 362–375. doi:10.1109/TC.2011.245

Wang, H. (2014). Identity-based distributed provable data possession in multicloud storage. *IEEE Transactions on Services Computing*, *8*(2), 328–340. doi:10.1109/TSC.2014.1

Wang, H., He, D., Yu, J., & Wang, Z. (2016). Incentive and unconditionally anonymous identity-based public provable data possession. *IEEE Transactions on Services Computing*, *12*(5), 824–835. doi:10.1109/TSC.2016.2633260

Wang, Q., Wang, C., Ren, K., Lou, W., & Li, J. (2010). Enabling public auditability and data dynamics for storage security in cloud computing. *IEEE Transactions on Parallel and Distributed Systems*, *22*(5), 847–859. doi:10.1109/TPDS.2010.183

Worku, S. G., Xu, C., Zhao, J., & He, X. (2014). Secure and efficient privacy-preserving public auditing scheme for cloud storage. *Computers & Electrical Engineering*, *40*(5), 1703–1713. doi:10.1016/j.compeleceng.2013.10.004

# Review on Reliability and Energy-Efficiency Issues in Cloud Computing

**Chitra A. Dhawale**

*P. R. Pote College of Engineering and Management, India*

**Kritika A. Dhawale**

*SkyLark Drones, Banglore, India*

## INTRODUCTION

Cloud computing is an ongoing revolution in ICT that employs virtualization technologies to deliver a powerful and flexible computing environment.

Gartner predicts Public Cloud Services Market will reach $397.4B by 2022 (Columbus, 2021). Because of the size and complexity of cloud data centers, dependability and energy efficiency are two major concerns that must be addressed. Cloud computing system (CCS) reliability can be defined in terms of security or in terms of resource and service failures.

On the other hand, the energy required to operate the cloud infrastructure is also increasing in proportion to the operational costs. According to Gartner, the electricity consumption by cloud-based data centers has increased to 1012.02 Billion kwh by 2020 (Columbus, 2021).

Each year, data centers in the United States release 100 million metric tonnes of carbon dioxide, which will rise to 1034 metric tones by 2020 (Cook & Horn, 2011). Researchers are under pressure to find innovative strategies to reduce energy usage since huge computing infrastructures' energy consumption, heat output, and carbon footprint have increased. Researchers and designers have spent the previous few decades focusing on improving the system's performance in terms of speed, space, and efficiency. However, the main concern should be energy use.

Amazon announced the construction of a 150 MW wind farm in January 2015, which will generate approximately 500,000 MW of wind energy. The energy generated by the wind farm will be utilized to power AWS (Amazon Web Services) data centers, both existing and future.

Google, IBM, and other cloud vendors are also attempting to make cloud services and data centers more energy-efficient and environmentally friendly.

## CLASSIFICATION OF FAILURES

The occurrence-based classification is related to the sequence among the failures i.e whether the occurrence of one failure leads to the occurrence of another or not in the system. **Occurrence-based failures** are again categorized into **independent and correlated failures**. Independent failures occur discretely. This type of occurrence is hypothetical because the literature has demonstrated that there is a correlation between failures (Fu & Xu, 2007) [4] (Yigitbasi et al., 2010) [6]. **In correlated failures**, the occurrence

DOI: 10.4018/978-1-7998-9220-5.ch045

*Figure 1. Classification of failures*

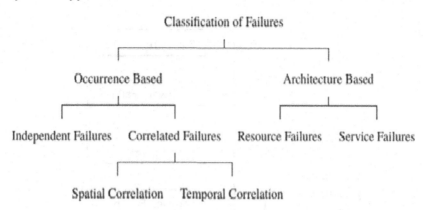

of a subsequent failure is correlated to each other. The correlated failures could be a spatial correlation and temporal correlation.

The failures are further separated into two types in the architecture-based classification: Resource Failure and Service Failure. Resource failure, as the name implies, is caused by the loss of certain physical resources, such as a system failure, a network or power outage, or a software error. The majority of the literature on failure tolerance has focused on resource failures (Fu, 2010) [8] (Vishwanath & Nagappan, 2010).

## CAUSES OF FAILURES

It is important to identify the causes of failures in Cloud Computing Services (CCS) to make them more reliable and available at all times. Various causes of cloud computing problems are depicted in Fig. 2.

### Software Failure

Failure in software causes much loss in business and revenue. In October 2013, Knight Capital's[7] suffer from a loss of $440 million due to 45 min of software downtime. Another major service outage had seen in January 2015 for 20 min, in which Yahoo Inc. and Microsoft's search engine, Bing, went down during the code update.

### Hardware Failure

Hardware failure accounts for around 4% of all failures in cloud-based data centers. Hard disc drives account for 78 percent of all hardware failures/replacements (Vishwanath & Nagappan, 2010). In 2007, the two most popular hardware components delivered to Google for repair were hard disc drives and memory modules (Barroso et al., 2013).

*Figure 2. Classification of causes of failure*

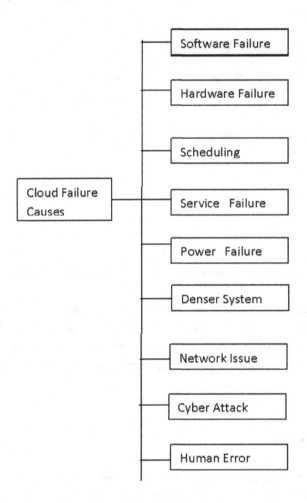

## Scheduling

Scheduling refers to the allocation of resources to incoming In the case of a large number of incoming requests and the restricted size of the queue, some requests may not get service which causes the overflow. Failure prediction (Salfner et al., 2010) plays a vital role in identifying system resources that are prone to failure. Schedulers can then avoid placing tasks on those resources that are less reliable.

## Service Failure

As per Dai et.al (Dai et al., 2010), during peak time, due to a large number of requests, although resources are under operation but cannot satisfy the increasing demand. This results in in-service failure. At the execution, stage requests are handover to physical resources.

## Power Failure

In 2011, the massive tsunami in Japan put the whole country in a power crisis for a long time, and all the consumer services were affected. It is estimated that natural disasters contribute around 22% in cloud computing service outages. **Recently On March 3, 2020,** **Microsoft Azure** services in Microsoft's East U.S. data center region encountered more than six hours of outage. **IBM Cloud** suffered a multi-zone, four-hour interruption of services on **June 10, 2020,** that affected IBM cloud customers in Washington, D.C., Dallas, London, Frankfurt, and Sydney.

## Denser System

As a result of the high device density, heat release increases, and as a result, it affects the normal working of devices. Facebook has revealed that by packing the machines densely, the electrical current began to overheat and melt Ethernet sockets and other crucial components. In 2013 data centers, Microsoft faced a severe outage that affected its cloud services including Outlook, Hotmail, SkyDrive, and Micro- soft's image sharing service due to overheating issues.

## Network Infrastructure

In the case of the real-time application over the cloud, the performance of the network plays an important role. A small increment in the network delay can be termed as an SLA (Service Level Agreements) violation which will be considered as a service failure. Around 3% of the service failures happened due to the loss of network connectivity (Institute, 2016).

## Cyberattacks

IBM's report on cyber security intelligence has argued that 55% of cybercrimes or threats were from people having access to an organization's systems, such that employees. Recently a major Ransome attack occurred in various regions of the world and causes much loss in the economy, the major in 2021 are listed in a report (Cloudian, n.d.)

## Human Errors

Along with cyber-attacks, human errors also has a big weight (22%) for the causes of failures in CCS with an average cost of $489 per incident.

## RELIABLE CLOUD COMPUTING SERVICES

Reliability in cloud computing is how consistently a cloud computing system can provide its services without interruption and failure. According to the definition provided in (Quality Excellence for Suppliers of Telecommunications Forum (QuEST Forum), 2010), the reliability is defined as:

*The ability of an item to perform a required function under stated conditions for a stated time period.*

Based on the service type, cloud models can be used as Software as a Service (SaaS), Platform as a Service (PaaS), and Infrastructure as a Service (IaaS). Mike et al. from Microsoft Corporation in (Mike et al., 2014) proposed three different design principles approaches mainly design with resilience, design with data integrity and design with recoverability.

## Service Failure Management in Cloud Computing

To provide reliable services in cloud computing, one needs to manage service failures. All the proposed architectures and techniques designed for a well-behaved cloud environment have to be redesigned for a failure-prone cloud environment. All the failure management techniques are categorized into two groups i.e **Reactive and Proactive Failure Management.**

### Reactive Failure Management

In this case, corrective measures are taken after the occurrence of failure. Just like in networking domain the reactive routing protocols donot maintain o routing tables. All the routes are created on demand. In the same way, whenever failures have occurred in cloud services, the required measures will be taken by restarting the services from the last execution instance recorded earlier using checkpointing or logging.

Sharma et. Al in (Sharma et al., 2015) threw light on Reactive failure management techniques which work in a similar way to reactive routing strategies in networks

### i. Checkpointing

As per the name, this technique saves the current state of a executing process on some backup resources and on the occurrence of failure, the process will be restarted or rolled back by using the last saved state. Checkpointing can random or periodic in nature. Various cloud management software suits such as UniCloud by Oracle, Intels Data Center Manager (DCM) are incorporated with the checkpointing mechanism to provide uninterruptable cloud computing services (Sharma et al., 2015). It has been argued that in the large-scale systems like clouds, checkpointing mechanisms could create large overheads as well, if performed frequently

### ii. Replication

Replicationis another reactive method to provide fault tolerance in which the backup resources are used to run replicas of the running processes. Replication can be Primary Backup (Passive) replication or Active replication. Various cloud computing providers use replication mechanism to provide fault tolerance at various levels. Microsofts Azure uses virtual machine replication to provide fault tolerance at the cloud level. In the case of the failure of a virtual machine, Azure always keeps replicated VMs to take charge of the failed VM. At Infrastructure as a Service level, OpenStack, an open-source cloud computing platform uses data replication to store data by writing the _les and objects at multiple disks spread throughout the servers in the data centers. There are many more examples where the replication is in use like DFS replication, Apache Hadoop, Amazon EBS etc. A complete survey of replication mechanisms has been done by Rachid Guerraoui et al. (Guerraoui & Schiper, 1996). The biggest challenge to run the replicas of a process is to maintain the consistency between the replicas and propagation of update messages.

### iii. Logging

Logging means storing information at some safe place. During the entire lifecycle of process from creation to termination, the intermediate states are saved and re-saved to current state at some stable location on storage device as a log file. This log file is used to recover the process in case of system crashes or failure (Guerraoui & Schiper, 1996). All the logged messages are evaluated in the same order in which they were generated. Once the new process has created after a crash, the state of the new process should be consistent with other running processes. If the state of the process remains inconsistent then the process will be known as orphan process. For the smooth running of system, checkpoint and logging work with hands and hands together. Process of logging can be Orphan process based and Storage based.

## Proactive Failure Management

In proactive failure management deals with the preventive measures which are to be taken before the occurrence of failure. FuandXu in 2007 (Fu & Xu, 2007) and Islam et al.,2012 (Islam et al., 2012) worked on preventive measures. **Migration** is the method that is used to provide fault tolerance by incorporating failure prediction methods. Migration may be related to a **processor with a virtual machine.** Considering the dynamic nature of cloud infrastructure, Virtual Machine Migration is studied well.

## Pre-copy and Post copy

Shribman et.al and Hines et.al in (Shribman & Hudzia, 2013) (Hines et al., 2009) presented study on VM migration approaches. They include study for two different cases i.e **The pre-copy and Post-Copy Migration.**

**Pre-Copy** consists of two phases: The warm-up Phase and the top-and-copy Phase. In warm up phase, hypervisor copies the state of the running VMs such as CPU state, memory state, and state of other devices from a faulty server to the destination server. As the warm-up phase completes, the virtual machine stops at the source machine and stop and copy phase initiates. The stop and copy phase copies the remaining things like files and pages in the memory that gets modified called dirty pages during the warm-up phase. After the transfer of all the pages the virtual machine resumes its execution over the destination machine. Many of the hypervisors such as VMware, Xen, KVM are using pre-copy migration approach (Hines et al., 2009).

## Post-Copy Approach

**In the Post Copy** method, the virtual machine pauses at the source machine after the warm-up phase is finished, and the stop and copy phase begins. Running virtual machines are suspended at the source nodes and moved to the destination nodes with incomplete execution state attributes such as CPU state. In parallel the source machine also stay active serving the migrated VMs. Whenever a VM do not get page in its local memory, it generates a page fault (network fault). On the generation of a network fault or page fault, destination machine redirects the page request to the source machine which in-turn responds with the faulted page.

## ENERGY MANAGEMENT IN CLOUD COMPUTING

Cloud service providers are concerned about the energy consumption of the underlying complex infrastructure that provides cloud services, in addition to the reliability of cloud computing services. Cutting energy usage will make it even more profitable by lowering operational expenditures, just as enhancing cloud service reliability makes it profitable by attracting more users or clients.

## Static Power Management

Static Power Management is done in an offline way at the system level at design time. Energy consumption is managed at the CPU and System level. As per the published work by Valentini et al., (Valentini et al., 2013), CPU contributes approximately 35-50% of power/energy consumption. System components such as memory components, network facilities, and software systems consume less power as compared to the CPU (Valentini et al., 2013). System-level power optimization includes the geographical distribution of machines (Tiwana et al., 2010), component compatibility, and network topologies that reduce power consumption.

## Dynamic Power Management

Dynamic power management (DPM) deals with the regulation of energy consumption by using software-based policies. As previously stated, the CPU consumes the most power, followed by the memory units. As a result, in the vast majority of cases, DPM approaches rely on two components for power/energy regulation: the CPU and memory. As per work published by Kim and Rotem (Kim & Rotem, 2012), the mechanical activities of disc storage systems are anticipated to consume about one-third of the total electricity provided to data centers.

## ENERGY EFFICIENCY TECHNIQUES IN CLOUD COMPUTING

In this section, an overview of different energy efficiency techniques is taken. This may help the reader understanding significant comparisons of different approaches.

The technique proposed by Rodero et al., (Rodero et al., 2012) is primarily a thermal-aware energy management scheme that actually allocates the VMs based on the application characteristics accordingly. Beloglazov and Buyya (Beloglazov & Buyya, 2010a) [32]. Resource-level virtualization has been implemented by the techniques Liao et al. (Liao et al., 2012), and Paya and Marinescu (Paya & Marinescu, 2013).

The techniques Beloglazov and Buyya (Beloglazov et al., 2011) [34] involve switching off unused nodes to reduce the energy consumption and implement full virtualization methodology. Deore et al. (Deore et al., 2012) involves running of multiple virtual OSs over a fully functioning host OS, whereas Kim et al. (Kim et al., 2011) implement hardware virtualization, which consists of running multiple guest OSs directly on top of base hardware. This technique also uses power aware DVFS scaling for energy management.

## EQUILIBRIUM BETWEEN RELIABILITY AND ENERGY EFFICIENCY IN CLOUD COMPUTING

As mentioned in earlier sections it has been observed that much research has done separately either on service reliability or energy efficiency in cloud computing. Existing approaches, as examined, provide

*Table 1. Survey of energy efficiency techniques in CCS*

| Publication | Implementation | Performance |
|---|---|---|
| Kusic et al. (Kusic et al., 2009) | A setup of heterogeneous Dell PowerEdge servers, VMware's ESX Server 3.0 Enterprise Edition running Linux RedHat 2.4 kernel, and SUSE Enterprise Linux Server Edition 10 OS per virtual machine | This LLC-based technique saves up to 26% energy with 1.6% of total service request's SLA violations. |
| Ahmad and Vijaykumar (Ahmad & Vijaykumar, 2010) | The proposed method has been tested in a 40×12 inch data center consisting of 1,120 blade servers arranged in four rows. Every single row has seven 40U racks. It uses AirPAK, a computational fluid dynamics simulator for experiencing cooling mock-up in a data center. | Powerade has been compared with spatial subsetting and inverse temperature. The following observations have been made: Powerade and spatial subsetting acquire free power; however, both alleviate the response period dilapidation The power savings for the Powerade scheme vary with load levels: • For loads ranging from 30% to 70%: Powerade-d attains considerable power cutback up to 22%–36% • At 80% loading: PowerTrade scheme performs better than PowerTrade- PowerTrade–SurgeGuard duo lower power. |
| Feller et al. (Feller et al., 2011) | Implemented in a Java-based simulation toolkit developed by the authors and operates on homogeneous hosts, each having 24 cores, 50GB RAM, 1TB storing capability, and 10GBit/sec net connectivity | ACO metaheuristic algorithm has been compared with the adaptive edition of first-fit decreasing approach. —Based on the comparison, the ACO-based approach utilizes a lesser number of host machines and offers higher resource utilization and energy profits. —Normally, 4.7% of hosts and 4.1% of power is saved. |
| Rodero et al. (Rodero et al., 2012) | A C++ event-driven simulator named Kento-perf simulator | 8%–25% of energy savings |
| Shi et al. (Shi et al., 2011) | CloudSim Cloud simulator | In the case of implementing pure MQMPM, some delay in the predicted sequence is observed, whereas with the implementation of LTPM and MQMPM, the number of violations due to delayed utilization trends is reduced. —In a continuous increasing period, the combined algorithm is better. —During flat and smooth periods, the use of FPRRM helps to reduce unnecessary high resource reservations. |
| Beloglazov and Buyya (Beloglazov et al., 2012; Beloglazov & Buyya, 2010a; Beloglazov & Buyya, 2010b; Beloglazov et al., 2011) | CloudSim Toolkit 2.0 | Consumes approximately the same level of energy but ensures almost less than 1% SLA violations and a lesser number of VM migrations compared with other algorithms such as DVFS and non-power-aware policy |
| Liao et al. (Liao et al., 2012) | The development environment consists of Ubuntu-11.10-server-AMD 64 and qemu-KVM-0.14.1 as the hypervisor with 10 heterogeneous physical machines. OpenStack acts as the cloud platform | Requires a lesser number of physical machines to balance the workload as compared to the Round-Robin (RR) scheduling scheme —Consumes less energy compared with RR scheduling algorithm and Random |
| Deore et al. (Deore et al., 2012) | VirtualBox 3.1 Cloud Environment | Involves a lesser number of VMs compared with the bully approach, hybrid algorithm, and RR scheduling algorithm Conserves approximately 21% of energy, more than that conserved by the bully, RR, and hybrid algorithms |

*continued on following page*

*Table 1. Continued*

| Publication | Implementation | Performance |
|---|---|---|
| Beloglazov and Buyya (Kim et al., 2011) | CloudSim Toolkit | When thresholds are between 30% and 70%: Minimum migration policy results in power cutback by 66%, 83%, and 23% compared with dynamic-voltage frequency scaling, non-power-aware, and ST schemes, respectively —When thresholds are between 50%–90%: MM policy offers 87%, 74%, and 43% energy savings |
| Paya and Marinescu (Paya & Marinescu, 2013) | Implemented on clusters with variable sizes, namely, 20, 40, 60, 80, and 100 cluster nodes | Approximately 70% of servers operate in the optimal region, and only 5% of them are in the two undesirable regions and 25% run in the two suboptimal regions in a cluster of 20–100 servers |
| Kliazovich et al. (Kliazovich et al., 2013) and Kocaoglu et al. (Kocaoglu et al., 2012) | GreenCloud simulator<br>• DVFS and Dynamic Power<br>• Management (DPM) scaling<br>• approaches | DENs technique is compared with RR and green scheduler<br>• DENs methodology leaves a lesser number of servers idle compared with the green scheduler<br>• RR is the least energy efficient |

cloud computing service reliability and have proven to be very efficient and optimized (L'Ecuyer & Malenfant, 1988).

Cloud computing service providers say, on the one hand, that their cloud services are more than 99 percent available in terms of uptime, with only 80 hours of downtime per year on average, by employing these approaches. However, all the given methods require extra back-up and storage resources to store logs and checkpoints to allow last state system recovery in the case of failure or interruption. Adding extra resources to the infrastructure increases the energy on consumption at a greater rate than reliability gains and has a direct impact on the profit margins of the service providers and users and negatively impacts natural environment.

System energy consumption is reduced through energy management methods that regulate system performance and hardware resources. Running resources at a low power scaling level or turning off inactive resources such as backups are two significant approaches for reducing energy usage. However, these techniques impair system reliability.

For example if a machine breaks due to hardware or software failure before completing the tasks and there is no scope for recovery of resources, then all virtual machines with their respective processes need to restart. This will result in a significant increase in overhead costs, such as energy use. This will dramatically increase overheads such as energy consumption and resource utilization. Service providers will lose a lot of revenue in terms of penalties for SLA violations and most importantly, trust of the users.

System energy consumption is reduced through energy management methods that regulate system performance and hardware resources. Running the resources at a low power scaling level or shutting off idle resources such as backup are two major approaches for lowering energy consumption and lowering the system's re- responsibility.

# CURRENT STATUS OF COMBINED APPROACH FOR RELIABILITY AND ENERGY EFFICIENCY MECHANISMS IN CLOUD COMPUTING

Hamid Reza Faragardi et al. (Faragardi et al., 2013) established a mathematical model based on Integer Linear Programming (ILP) to regulate the reliability and energy consumption in Cloud Computing by considering service quality in terms of service deadlines.

Faragardi developed a Poisson process-based failure model to induce failures into the systems, which provides continuous and independent failures. Along with the failure model, an energy model based on CPU utilization has also been presented. A single ILP-based cost function has been utilized to balance both energy and reliability utilizing the equations for reliability and energy consumption. In comparison to a hybrid genetic algorithm, the proposed solution enhanced energy utilization and system dependability by 17 percent and 9 percent, respectively.

Ifeanyi P. Egwutuoha et al., (Egwutuoha et al., 2013) have proposed a generic proactive energy e cient fault tolerance model for CCS executing high-performance computing (HPC) applications that is independent of redundant resources.

By multiplying the LM-sensor readings of all system components, a mathematical model has been built to evaluate the weight of the current condition. Following the calculation of the current weight, the critical state threshold value was compared. Decisions about the provisioning of additional resources, the relinquishment of flawed ones, and the movement of processes have all been made based on the comparative results. To keep the method cost-effective and energy-efficient, no additional resources are allocated to provide fault tolerance at first.

Peter Garraghan et al. (Garraghan et al., 2014). have done an empirical analysis by using google traces to analyze the failure-related energy waste in cloud computing environments. This analysis highlights the impact of failures at the task level (software level) and server level (hardware failures). All the terminal events taken from Google cluster traces are divided into three categories: Kill, Evict and Task fail. SpecPower2008 benchmark (Benchmarks,) has been used to calculate the energy consumption per failure event. In the study, it has been noted that Kill and Evict contribute to more energy wastage (48% and 39% respectively) than task failures (13%).

Zhang et al., (Zhang et al., 2015) proposed three algorithms to solve the challenge of maximizing reliability while maintaining energy conservation for precedence constraint jobs in heterogeneous clusters. The algorithms are RHFT (Reliability-aware Heterogeneous Earliest Finish Time), RCPOP (Reliability-aware Critical-Path-On-a-Processor), and RMEC (Reliability Maximization with Energy Constraint).

## CONCLUSION

Despite the fact that cloud computing technologies are already widely used, there is much scope for investigations in many respects. In this chapter, we've looked at a variety of failures, along with a variety of methods aimed at increasing the reliability of CCS. Clouds are becoming larger and more complex, resulting in massive energy usage and massive carbon footprints. This chapter also provided an overview of major energy management approaches employed in CCS. From the analysis we came to know that, there is an urgent need to explore the essential trade-off between service reliability and energy use. We also included the current status of combined approaches for reliability and energy efficiency techniques used in CCS. This Chapter can help the upcoming researchers for further avenues of research in CCS.

# REFERENCES

Ahmad, F., & Vijaykumar, T. N. (2010, March). Joint optimization of idle and cooling power in data centers while maintaining response time. *ACM SIGPLAN Notices*, *45*(3), 243–256. doi:10.1145/1735971.1736048

Barroso, L. A., Clidaras, J., & Hölzle, U. (2013). The data center as a computer: An introduction to the design of warehouse-scale machines. *Synth. Lect. Comput. Archit.*, *8*(3), 1–154.

Beloglazov, A., Abawajy, J., & Buyya, R. (2012). Energy-aware resource allocation heuristics for efficient management of data centers for Cloud computing. *Future Generation Computer Systems*, *28*(5), 755–768. doi:10.1016/j.future.2011.04.017

Beloglazov, & Buyya. (2010a). Adaptive threshold-based approach for energy-efficient consolidation of virtual machines in cloud data centers. In *Proceedings of the 8th International Workshop on Middleware for Grids, Clouds and e-Science*. ACM. DOI:10.1145/1890799.1890803

Beloglazov, & Buyya. (2010b). Energy efficient allocation of virtual machines in cloud data centers. *10th IEEE/ACM International Conference on Cluster, Cloud and Grid Computing (CCGrid'10)*, 577–578. 10.1109/CCGRID.2010.45

Beloglazov, A., Buyya, R., Lee, Y. C., & Zomaya, A. (2011). A taxonomy and survey of energy-efficient data centers and cloud computing systems. *Advances in Computers*, *82*(2), 47–111. doi:10.1016/B978-0-12-385512-1.00003-7

*Benchmarks*. (2000). Standard Performance Evaluation Corporation.

Cloudian. (n.d.). https://cloudian.com/ransomware-attack-list-and-alerts/

Columbus, L. (2021). *Business Community*. https://www.business2community.com/cloud-computing/gartner-predicts-public-cloud-services-market-will-reach-397-4b-by-2022-02405076

Cook, G., & Horn, J.V. (2011). *How Dirty is Your Data? A Look at the Energy Choices that Power Cloud Computing*. Academic Press.

Dai, Y.-S., Yang, B., Dongara, J., & Zhang, G. (2010). *Cloud Service Reliability: Modeling and Analysis*. Academic Press.

Deore, S. S., Patil, A. N., & Bhargava, R. (2012, October). Energy-efficient scheduling scheme for virtual machines in cloud computing. *International Journal of Computers and Applications*, *56*, 10. doi:10.5120/8275-1877

Egwutuoha, I., Chen, S., Levy, D., Selic, B., & Calvo, R. (2013). Energy efficient fault tolerance for High-Performance Computing (HPC) in 53 the cloud. *Sixth International Conference on Cloud Computing (CLOUD)*, 762-769. 10.1109/CLOUD.2013.69

Faragardi, H. R., Rajabi, A., Shojaee, R., & Nolte, T. (2013). Towards energyaware resource scheduling to maximize reliability in cloud computing systems. *10th International Conference on High Performance Computing and Communications (HPCC)*, 1469-1479.

Feller, E., Rilling, L., & Morin, C. (2011). Energy-aware ant colony based workload placement in clouds. In *Proceedings of IEEE/ACM 12th International Conference on Grid Computing*. IEEE. 10.1109/Grid.2011.13

Fu, S. (2010). Failure-aware resource management for high-availability computing clusters with distributed virtual machines. *Journal of Parallel and Distributed Computing*, *70*(4), 384–393. doi:10.1016/j.jpdc.2010.01.002

Fu, S., & Xu, C.-Z. (2007). Exploring event correlation for failure prediction in coalitions of clusters. In *Proceedings of the Conference on Supercomputing (SC'07)*. ACM/IEEE. 10.1145/1362622.1362678

Gallet, M., Yigitbasi, N., Javadi, B., Kondo, D., Iosup, A., & Epema, D. (2010). Amodelfor space-correlated failures in large-scale distribute dsystems. In *Euro-Par2010- Parallel Processing* (pp. 88–100). Springer. doi:10.1007/978-3-642-15277-1_10

Garraghan, P., Moreno, I. S., Townend, P., & Xu, J. (2014). An analysis of failure related energy waste in a large-scale cloud environment. *IEEE Transactions on Emerging Topics in Computing*, *2*(2), 166–180. doi:10.1109/TETC.2014.2304500

Guerraoui, R., & Schiper, A. (1996). Fault-tolerance by replication in distributed systems. In *Proceedings of Reliable Software Technologies-Ada-Europe'96* (pp. 38–57). Springer. doi:10.1007/BFb0013477

Hines, M. R., Deshpande, U., & Gopalan, K. (2009). Post-copy live migration of virtual machines. *ACM SIGOPS Oper.Syst.Rev.*, *43*(3), 14–26. doi:10.1145/1618525.1618528

Institute, P. (2016). Cost of Data Center Outages. Academic Press.

Islam, S., Keung, J., Lee, K., & Liu, A. (2012). Empirical prediction models for adaptive resource provisioning in the cloud. *Future Generation Computer Systems*, *28*(1), 155–162. doi:10.1016/j.future.2011.05.027

Kim, J., & Rotem, D. (2012). FREP: Energy proportionality for disk storage using re- plication. *Journal of Parallel and Distributed Computing*, *72*(8), 960–974. doi:10.1016/j.jpdc.2012.03.010

Kim, K. H., Beloglazov, A., & Buyya, R. (2011). Power-aware provisioning of virtual machines for real-time Cloud services. *Concurrency and Computation*, *23*(13), 1491–1505. doi:10.1002/cpe.1712

Kliazovich, Bouvry, & Khan. (2013). DENS: Data center energy-efficient networkaware scheduling. *Cluster Computing*, *16*(1), 65–75. doi:10.1007/s10586-011-0177-4

Kocaoglu, M., Malak, D., & Akan, O. B. (2012). Fundamentals of green communications and computing: Modeling and simulation. *Computer*, *45*(9), 40–46. doi:10.1109/MC.2012.248

Kusic, Kephart, Hanson, Kandasamy, & Jiang. (2009). Power and performance management of virtualized computing environments via lookahead control. *Cluster Computing*, *12*(1), 1–15. doi:10.1007/s10586-008-0070

L'Ecuyer & Malenfant. (1988). Computing optimal checkpointing strategies for rollback and recovery systems. *IEEE Transactions on Computers*, *37*(4), 491-496.

Liao, Chang, Hsu, Zhang, Lai, & Hsu. (2012). Energy-efficient resource provisioning with SLA consideration on cloud computing. *41st International Conference on Parallel Processing Workshops (ICPPW'12)*, 206–211. 10.1109/ICPPW.2012.31

Mike, A., Shannon, B., David, B., Sean, F., Margaret, L., Tim, R., Michael, R., Dan, R., Frank, S., Sian, S., & Jason, W. (2014). *An introduction to designing reliable cloud services*. Academic Press.

Paya & Marinescu. (2013). *Energy-Aware Application Scaling On a Cloud*. arXiv:1307.3306

Philp, I. (2005). Software failures and the road to a petaflop machine. *Proceedings of the 11th International Symposium on High Performance Computer Architecture (HPCA-11)*, 125–128.

*Quality Excellence for Suppliers of Telecommunications Forum (QuEST Forum).* (2010). Academic Press.

Rodero, I., Viswanathan, H., Lee, E. K., Gamell, M., Pompili, D., & Parashar, M. (2012). Energy-efficient thermal-aware autonomic management of virtualized HPC cloud infrastructure. *Journal of Grid Computing, 10*(3), 447–473. doi:10.100710723-012-9219-2

Salfner, F., Lenk, M., & Malek, M. (2010). A survey of online failure prediction methods. *ACM Computing Surveys, 42*(3), 10. doi:10.1145/1670679.1670680

Schroeder, B., & Gibson, G. (2010). A large-scale study of failures in high-performance computing systems. *IEEE Trans. Dependable Secur. Comput., 7*(4), 337–350.

Sharma, Y., Javadi, B., & Si, W. (2015). On the reliability and energy efficiency in cloud computing. *Proceedings of the 13th Australian Symposium on Parallel and Distributed Computing (AusPDC 2015), 37*, 111–114.

Shi, Y., Jiang, X., & Ye, K. 2011. An energy-efficient scheme for cloud resource provisioning based on CloudSim. *International Conference on Cluster Computing (CLUSTER'11)*, 595–599. 10.1109/CLUSTER.2011.63

Shribman, A., & Hudzia, B. (2013). Pre-copy andpost-copy vmlive migration for memory intensive applications. In *Euro-Par2012: Parallel Processing Workshops* (pp. 539–547). Springer.

Tiwana, B., Balakrishnan, M., Aguilera, M. K., Ballani, H., & Mao, Z. M. (2010). Location, location, location!: modeling data proximity in the cloud. In *Proceedings of the 9th ACM SIGCOMM Workshop on Hot Topics in Networks*. ACM. 10.1145/1868447.1868462

Valentini, G. L., Lassonde, W., Khan, S. U., Min-Allah, N., Madani, S. A., Li, J., Zhang, L., Wang, L., Ghani, N., Kolodziej, J., Li, H., Zomaya, A. Y., Xu, C.-Z., Balaji, P., Vishnu, A., Pinel, F., Pecero, J. E., Kliazovich, D., & Bouvry, P. (2013). An overview of energy efficiency techniques in cluster computing systems. *Cluster Computing, 16*(1), 3–15. doi:10.100710586-011-0171-x

Vishwanath, K. V., & Nagappan, N. (2010). Characterizing cloud computing hardware reliability. In *Proceedings of the 1ˢᵗ ACM symposium on Cloud computing*. ACM. 10.1145/1807128.1807161

Yigitbasi, N., Gallet, M., Kondo, D., Iosup, A., & Epema, D. (2010). Analysis and modeling of time-correlated failures in large-scale distributed systems. In *Proceedings of the 11ᵗʰ International Conference on Grid Computing (GRID)*. IEEE/ACM.

Zhang, L., Li, K., Xu, Y., Mei, J., Zhang, F., & Li, K. (2015). Maximizing reliability with energy conservation for parallel task scheduling in a heterogeneous cluster. *Inf. Sci., 319*, 113–131. doi:10.1016/j.ins.2015.02.023

# Section 11
# Cognitive Science

# Abductive Strategies in Human Cognition and in Deep Learning Machines

**Lorenzo Magnani**

*University of Pavia, Italy*

## INTRODUCTION

On a full-size 19x19 board, in 2015, Google DeepMind's program AlphaGo (capable of playing the famous Go game) defeated Fan Hui, the European Go champion and a 2 dan (out of 9 dan) professional, five times out of five with no handicap. In March 2016, Google also defeated Lee Sedol, a 9 dan player widely regarded as the world's finest champion. In four of the five games, the DeepMind software beat Lee. The program was extremely innovative, with many novel moves and a good capacity to replicate human behavior. It learned from a variety of human-played games using a technique known as "reinforcement learning". The program's more current version, in turn, plays against itself to improve the efficiency of its deep neural networks: AlphaZero is a more modern richer version of AlphaGo, as detailed fully and suitably in https://en.wikipedia.org/wiki/AlphaZero.

We can say that heuristics are used to arrive at a specific target thanks to their organization in strategies. We can consider computational strategies as a compound of heuristic processes, that is, processes composed of good choices of the subsequent state of a cognitive routine – according to some opportunely chosen criteria. In game theory, however, the definition of strategy is broader, encompassing everything from how agents interact with one another to a wide range of interwoven or collective cognitive operations. In turn, ecological thinking (or ecological rationality) (Gigerenzer and Selten, 2002; Raab and Gigerenzer, 2005; Gigerenzer and Brighton, 2009) sees strategies as processes that exploit a large amount of data and knowledge, requiring a lot of computational effort; heuristics, on the other hand, perform simple and effective moves, even if they are less rigorous. Cognitive heuristics are simply described as "rules of thumb" in various parts of computer and cognitive science studies. I'll take the widely held AI viewpoint that sees strategies as a collection of successively selected acceptable heuristics.

I believe that we can evaluate what I just called strategic cognition in the context of Magnani's (2009) studies on abductive cognition, emphasizing the contrast be-tween what I called locked and unlocked strategies (see also Magnani (2019, 2020). I also used these ideas as components of the framework of an altogether new dynamic approach to the nature of computation in my recent book (Magnani, 2022b). In this theory, I emphasize the importance of unconventional computing as a continuous and fantastic process of cognitive domestication of ignorant entities.

Deep learning machines (and thus AlphaGo/AlphaZero programs) are assumed to work with locked strategies, a fact that has a big impact on the type of creativity they may produce. I have extensively explained in my studies that the various sorts of human, animal, and computational hypothetical cognition can be accounted for using the crucial idea of abduction. Selective abduction (Magnani, 2001) – for example, in medical diagnosis (where we must "choose" from a "repository" of al-ready accessible hypotheses) – and creative abduction (Magnani, 2001) – were introduced (abduction that provides new

DOI: 10.4018/978-1-7998-9220-5.ch046

hypotheses).[1] Not only, I have always emphasized that abduction is not only sentential, in the sense that it is carried out using human language resources (oral or written, or artificially constructed using symbols, as in mathematics and logic), but also "model-based" and "manipulative". Model-based abduction is concerned with the exploitation of internal cognitive acts that use models such as simulations, visualizations, and images; manipulative abduction is concerned with the exploitation of the so-called external character of human cognition, in which what I have dubbed the "eco-cognitive" character of cognition is central, because we must consider all those cognitive processes (embodied, embedded, situated, and enacted) in which the function of external models (for example, artifacts) is important. In this situation, manipulative action can provide new data – previously unavailable – and new heuristics capable of improving the methods agents use to solve challenges that necessitate the creative production (or just the selection) of relevant hypotheses. I argued that manipulative abduction is a type of "thinking via doing" and not only about doing in a pragmatic sense (cf. Magnani 2009). It is patent that we face cases of manipulative abduction in the case of deep learning machines (and in the case of the games we are considering in this article): the cognitive processes are intrinsically linked to the manipulation of the stones, and several cognitive embodied moments are at stake, along with the required visualization of the entire external context, the competitor, and so on.

## BACKGROUND

It is commonly known that abduction research has advanced our understanding of creative cognition, even in the simple situation of a play in a Go game. The two main concepts I recently introduced during my investigations on abduction, knowledge-enhancing abduction and eco-cognitive openness, explained in (Magnani, 2017), are an excellent resource for delving into the locked and unlocked abductive strategies I mentioned earlier. Locked and unlocked strategies are important conceptual tools for analyzing the central cognitive features of deep learning machines. These strategies are present in human cognition, but they are currently impossible to locate in machines: yes, they yield creative outputs, but they are sadly endowed with varying degrees of creativity, and the presence of locked strategies in computing machines jeopardizes high level creativity. These considerations become obvious in the case of deep learning programs like AlphaGo, which try to automate various sorts of abductive reasoning.

I do believe that these programs exhibit what I call locked abductive strategies, which exhibit weak (even if amazing) types of hypothetical creative cognition because they are constrained in what I call eco-cognitive openness, which is more typical of human cognitive processes dealing with abductive creative reasoning: cognitive strategies are unlocked in this last human case. The fact that these programs are not based on logic, and that the main intellectual tradition associated to a formalization of abduction was in fact based on logic, does not pose an issue for the arguments I have illustrated in (Magnani, 2019). Indeed, abduction can occur at a sub-symbolic level in both humans and machines, so it is no surprise that deep learning machines can produce abductive results in this way. Not only, we have to remember that abduction is also characterized by multimodality (for example, it can be performed exploiting diagrams), as I have described in (Magnani, 2009 and 2017). Indeed, we must emphasize that humans frequently guess abductive hypotheses not only as a result of manipulating the external world, which is appropriately filled with cognitive representations and appropriate artifacts but also as a result of embodied and unconscious capacities (which also characterize some aspects of cognition in higher mammals, that surely do not take advantage of symbolic syntactic language). AI has always presented a variety of methodologies, formalisms, and algorithms that can be used to build programs that execute abductive tasks. What distinguishes the abductive performance seen in AlphaGo, a deep learning AI program?

## COMPUTATIONAL, NATURAL, AND ARTIFICIAL GAMES

### Strategies in Natural and Artificial Environments: Locked and Unlocked

AlphaGo is an autonomous computational deep learning program that plays Go and can compete with people. Go is a game played by human agents, and AlphaGo is an artificial computational deep learning software that also plays Go and can compete with humans.[2] Because it was created by human actors who established rules, a specific board, and other material items, such as stones, we can call Go "artificial." AlphaGo/AlphaZero is, so to speak, much more artificial, the result of technological innovation, an engineered product derived from the cognitive abilities of a tiny group of people. There are also "natural cognitive games," such as the pre-linguistic cognitive "natural game" between humans and their surroundings, in which "unlocked" strategies (which I will describe shortly) are at play, as exemplified by the Husserlian phenomenological tradition (Husserl, 1931), a kind of "natural game" encompassing embodied aspects and distributed cognitions, as well as visual, kinesthetic, and motor sensations, as described in more detail in (Magnani, 2018). There are no limitations and no local constraints in this "natural" game. There are no pre-set backdrops. To summarize, humans are not obliged to play a game that is confined, for example, by a certain (unchangeable in structure) Go board, which effectively *locks* cognitive strategies. The situation is heavily limited by a defined board, and determined stones and rules.

### As an Abductive Engine, Reading Ahead

Reading ahead, as Go players say, is the culmination of a cluster of anticipations aimed at being extremely strong and dependable (both deeply-minded or intuitive). They consist of 1. groups of prospective moves to be chosen and their outcomes. A current scenario at a given time, as represented by the board, "adumbrates" – Husserlian concept! – a later possible more productive scenario at another time, which is the result of an expected smart abduction, which will be followed by another abduction regarding the action that leads to a new move; 2. possible countermoves to each move; 3. further possibilities after each of those countermoves. Even in enormously intricate circumstances, it appears that some of the strongest Go competitors can read up to 40 moves ahead.

Global influence, interaction between distant stones, keeping the entire board in mind during local skirmishes, and other difficulties involving the overall game are some of the various techniques used by human players in the game Go; also allowing a tactical loss when it yields a strategic benefit is a possible strategy. All of these techniques, no matter how numerous and varied, are "locked": the entities of each scenario remain the same throughout the game. The only changes that are permitted are those that affect the number of available stones in play and their placement on the board in a finite and fixed environment (no novel rules, no novel entities, no novel boards, etc.) These strategies are unable to use information other than that which is offered in the limited scenario.

Of course, the "human" player can use internal sources not inextricably linked to previous time spent playing Go, but other kinds of skills from other variegated fields of cognition to enhance and strengthen his strategies, but this does not negate the fact that he is working in a locked situation: this kind of mental openness of the human simply refers to the fact that, even if the strategies in this human

Go player's case are locked strategies, he is still working in a locked situation. Hence, human strategies are locked in relation to the external fixed scenario, but more open in relation to mental references to other available extended strategic endowments; in AphaGo and deep learning programs, the strategic storage cannot – at least for the time being – take advantage of that mental "openness" and versatility typical of humans: the reservoir of strategies is merely generated/learned to play the game by checking data from thousands of games (played by humans).[3]

## THE MAXIMIZATION OF ECO-COGNITIVE OPENNESS IS JEOPARDIZED BY LOCKING ABDUCTIVE STRATEGIES

Magnani (2017), as I previously stated, a typical outcome of good abductive reasoning is the ability to enhance knowledge in a more or less creative way, ranging from medical diagnosis (in which we at least learn something new about a patient) to new knowledge generated, for example, in the case of scientific discovery. We have already mentioned that an autonomous game player like AlphaGo uses a variety of learned effective cognitive procedures to accomplish knowledge-enhancing abductions.

What I am adamant about is that we can only achieve exceptional selective or creative optimal abductive results thanks to an "openness" of the cognitive environment, that is, we need what I call (Magnani, 2017) *optimization of eco-cognitive situatedness*, in which eco-cognitive openness is fundamental. In a recent book (Magnani, 2022b), I have also underlined that, in general, a form of "ecology" of the cognitive settings available to human beings making abductions – and thus occasionally guessing new hypotheses – must be adopted to favor discoverability and defend human creativity. To obtain good creative and selective abduction cognitive strategies, they must not be "locked" in an external fixed eco-cognitive environment, that is, in a scenario marked by rigid and finite definitory rules, as well as finite material entities, which would rigidly work as cognitive mediators capable of governing agents' reasoning, as described by (Hintikka, 2007).

In (Magnani, 2015; 2016; 2017) I stressed the need, in the case of aiming at getting good abductive cognition in science of what I called maximization of eco-cognitive openness and situatedness. For example, the "situatedness" of related cognitive activities in scientific reasoning is undoubtedly linked to what I refer to as eco-cognitive features, which are associated with situations in which knowledge is freely "traveling" and where the richness and maximization of available information is guaranteed. In this case the maximization refers to the optimization of situatedness that can only be accomplished by maximizing the changeability of the starting data that characterizes abductive cognitive processes: inputs must be maximally expanded, reconstructed, or changed, and the same must be done with respect to the knowledge enforced during the hypothetical reasoning process. Analogously in general abductive cognition, we need a good "cognitive environment" in which information is intelligently organized, even if not necessarily maximized. In general, abductive strategies to hypotheses are particularly information-sensitive and deal with a constant stream of facts and information that must be promoted and updated as needed – for example, in science or in other disciplines.

## THE CRUCIALITY OF ABDUCTIVE ERRORS

Uncertainty, doubt, surprise, and incomplete information characterize human abductive inferential processes, in which new perspectives are constantly adopted, which are either opportunely – consciously

– directed or random, also allowing "fuzziness in the initial conditions, the starting assumptions of our traveling in the memory space (our archive of certainties) (Vitiello, 2012, pp. 335-336). Minati and Vitiello (2006) define what they call the "dissipative brain" as an unpredictable brain in which the uniqueness of its identity and the unrepeatability of the emergent cognitive processes are guaranteed. "It is a primary hypothesis underlying all abduction that the human mind is akin to the truth in the sense that in a finite number of guesses it will light upon the correct hypothesis" (Peirce, 7.220, 1866–1913): this means that human abductive cognition is "akin to the truth" but not without defects; making mistakes is a feature of human hypothetical abductive cognition. The dissipative model of the brain emphasizes that the incoming flux of information that arrives at the brain through perceptions cannot be discontinued, we cannot switch off a mammal human brain as we can do in the case of a laptop. It is the dissipative brain's quality that allows for the birth of wholly new cognitive views while also allowing for the emergence of the new most highly creative ones when information flux is not severely impeded (for example, due to social and political dysfunction).

Turing machines are not allowed to make mistakes, but in the case of the dissipative brain, errors are intrinsic to the system dynamics, so errors are not related to those made, for example, by an observer when measuring a quantity as a "deviation from accuracy," or as a "system-observer relational feature." Unpredictability has an impact on the dissipative brain's quantum fluctuations processes. As (Minati and Vitiello, 2006, p. 71) point out, unpredictability is inextricably tied to errors:

*Sometimes mistakes are useful to introduce or observe unexpected behaviors or results. Testing a newly designed machine has in general the meaning of detecting erratic behaviors to be avoided in an improved design of the tested machine. When mistakes are not rejected, they constitute additions to or extensions of the observer knowledge. Examples are in production processes and discoveries made by chance. In these cases, the term by chance means indeed by mistake (with respect to what was expected). In some sense, the term discovery is equivalent to the term mistake (the discovery is always by chance, otherwise it is not a discovery).[ . . . ] Inside a given context, the unpredictable behavior is not a "negation", is not a "deviance" with respect to any possible behavior. It is a novelty.*

## BIG DATA IS MASSIVE, BUT IT IS LOCKED

I quoted an interesting piece about the so-called dissipative brain from Vitiello in subsection in the previous section. "The process of symmetry breaking is triggered by some external input; the 'choice' of the specific symmetry pattern which is actually realized is, on the contrary, 'internal' to the system. Therefore, one speaks of self-organizing dynamics: ordering is an inner (spontaneous, indeed) dynamical process. [...] in the brain, contrary to the computer case, ordering is not imported from the outside, it is the outgrowth of an 'internal' dynamical process of the system (Vitiello, 2012, pp. 316-317).

If we assume that, unlike computers, ordering in the brain is the result of an "internal" dynamical process of the system, a question emerges. What happens when you combine machine learning (and deep learning) with massive data, which is now almost always available in digital form? In light of the arguments I made in this chapter, we must acknowledge that when it comes to the computational exploitation of huge data, we still have to deal with an "ordering" process that is imported into the machine from the outside. This order is defined by the related software, but it is heavily influenced by the data that humans provide to the system. These data, such as in the instance of AlphaGo/AlphaZero, are part of a constrained field in which we can see the availability of a massive avalanche of data, albeit coming from limited and specific sources. Even in the case of AlphaZero, which uses data that it has previously generated, we are dealing with data manipulations involving a large number of Go games, games, and games. When we say that ordering is not imported from the outside, it is the outgrowth of an 'internal' dynamical process of the system" we are simply referring to the fact that the internal computational ordering processes are unable to "cleave" the locked – in the sense I have attributed to this adjective in section 1 above – character of the informational scenario that feeds the system asking for more openness in the reservoir of information.

Researchers studying the epistemological, cognitive, legal, and ethical issues surrounding big data in general, as well as the relationship between big data and machine learning (and deep learning), have emphasized the need to de-contextualize facts from their original context in order to improve the quality of their eventual computational manipulation. To give you an example, consider biological data. Researchers studying the epistemological, cognitive, legal, and ethical issues surrounding big data in general, as well as the relationship between big data and machine learning (and deep learning), have emphasized the need to de-contextualize facts from their original context in order to improve the quality of their eventual computational manipulation. To give you an example, consider biological data. "One of the main tasks of database curators is to decontextualise the data that are included in their resources, so that they can travel outside of their original production context and become available for integration with other datasets (thus forming a big data collection) [...] Despite constant advances, it is still impossible to automate the de-contextualisation of most types of biological data" (Leonelli, 2014, p. 4). In other words, using the lexicon I have introduced in this chapter, "unlocking" the data set remains a difficult – extra-computational – "human" task that involves both cognitive, institutional, and ethical issues related to the problem of "fitting standards" of epistemological decency in the subsequent computational treatment of big data: "Researchers who wish to submit their data to a database need to make sure that the format that they use, and the metadata that they provide, fit existing standards – which in turn means acquiring updated knowledge on what the standards are and how they can be implemented, if at all; and taking time out of experiments and grantwriting (Leonelli, 2014, p. 4).[4]

To summarize, big data must be "unlocked" according to different policies in order to pursue satisfactory epistemological virtues, not only from the well-known (and still to be deepened and clarified) legal and ethical points of view, but also because they must be "curated" in order to favor, for example in biology, excellent abductive processes of scientific discovery across biological subareas. These policies regarding eco-cognitive openness cannot be carried out by computers; only humans are capable of carrying them out. The various computational tools, and especially the ones based on machine learning (and deep learning), used to deal with big data are often opaque in the perspective of their functions and in their basic cognitive suppositions, and often seem to reach results that are unreliable in the perspective of scientific rationality. As Leonelli sums up: "This increases the worry that big data science may be grounded upon, and ultimately supporting, the process of making human ingenuity hostage to an alien, artificial and ultimately unintelligible intelligence" Leonelli (2020).[5] Calude and Longo (2017) argue that the exploitation of big databases favors the production of spurious correlations, which are not good creative abductions, and base their arguments on deep classical insights from ergodic theory, Ramsey theory, and algorithmic information theory.[6]

## CREATIVITY IS HAMPERED BY LOCKING STRATEGIES

As we saw before, optimizing situatedness is linked to unlocked strategies. Instead, locked techniques, such as those seen in the Go game, AlphaGo/AlphaZero, and deep learning systems, limit originality. As I mentioned in part 2.2, a bad scenario tends to reduce eco-cognitive openness. As I previously stated, the stones, board, and rules in the game of Go are fixed and predefined. We should also mention that, in general, the presence of inflexible and unchanging situations in the natural and artificial world, even though clearly tied to the presence of stabilities, which in turn give rise to habits of conduct, tends to stifle human creativity. As knowledge derived from physics informs us, the creative brain is nourished by a free stream of information originating from an open and expanded informational environment, perceiving human brains as constitutively open dissipative systems.

It is not feasible to play Chess or adopt a different rule or another unusual cognitive process during a Go game, thereby confirming that the bizarre element of the game is still dependable and appropriate to the game you committed to playing. In the case of scientific discovery, on the other hand, the scientist [or a group of scientists] frequently consults a variety of external models and freely modifies his reasoning strategies, for example, to reach new analogies or to favor other unexpected cognitively fruitful cognitive processes (prediction, simplification, confirmation, falsification, and so on) in order to improve and enrich the abductive creative process.

In conclusion:

1. in contrast to high-level "human" creative abductive inferences, the position of artificial games (and their deep learning computational partners) in terms of the non-strategic information that is used is quite poor;

2. in Go (and similar games) and deep learning systems like AlphaGo/AlphaZero, where strategies and heuristics are "locked," this is the only component of the game that can be improved: strategies and related heuristics can be exploited in novel ways, and new ones can be invented. Other sorts of knowledge will not be altered, and all other features will remain unchanged. Of course, the essence of Go, Chess, and other games is the dominance of strategy, which explains the impressiveness of the more intelligent movements of human champions (and, of course, AlphaGo/AphaZero). Unfortunately, this strategy dominance is also the quality that makes the creativity at risk even less than it is in the most intricate situations of human selective abduction (medical diagnosis, for example). At the same time, this flaw explains the ease with which[7]

Many executives are using and planning to use deep learning programs to help scientists address relevant real-world challenges in healthcare, as well as other sectors like scientific reasoning. Many business applications are presently underway as a result of the commercialization of deep learning AI systems. The Wikipedia entry DeepMind (https://en.wikipedia.org/wiki/DeepMind), date of access 30 December 2021[8], clearly reports the contested case concerning the so-called "NHS data-sharing controversy." However, it appears that, despite the epistemological and cognitive ambiguities I've discussed in this essay, as well as the constraints of so-called locked strategies, deep learning systems can provide opportunities for business and market integration.

Epistemologists, logicians, and cognitive scientists, in my opinion, must keep an eye on how these AI gadgets are used: good AI software, which is a huge new possibility in terms of data analytics, can easily be turned into a tool that does not meet rigorous epistemological and/or ethical requirements. Even though I do not intend to address this topic in this post, I can mention some recent discoveries concerning the current computational exploitation of huge data, which can lead to computer-discovered correlations that are tainted by epistemic specks. Unfortunately, according to Calude and Longo (2017, p. 595), certain "correlations appear only due to the size, not the nature, of data. In 'randomly' generated, large enough databases too much information tends to behave like very little information". Even if obtained through complicated manufactured artifacts, some misleading correlations as outcomes of deep learning that are claimed to be "creative abductions" can just be straightforward generalizations. I am unable to go into greater detail about the issues surrounding the effects of deep learning computational programs on ethics and society; instead, in this chapter, I focused on some basic cognitive, logical, and epistemological issues in order to emphasize the differences between locked and unlocked strategies in the case of human and computational intelligence.

## FUTURE RESEARCH DIRECTIONS

I used the concepts of locked and unlocked strategies, abduction, and optimization of eco-cognitive openness as examples of key concepts capable of highlighting the fundamental epistemological and cognitive differences between deep learning computational cognitive performances (I used the program Alphago/AlphaZero as an example) and human ones. My research on abduction, which emphasized the relevance of the idea of eco-cognitive openness, contributed to demonstrating how this openness is lacking in deep learning systems but not in high-level human inferential creative and diagnostic inferences. Deep learning programs like AlphaGo/AlphaZero use locked abductive methods, putting eco-cognitive openness in jeopardy. Un-locked abductive strategies, on the other hand, represent the high-level sorts of abductive creative and diagnostic reasoning that are unique to human cognition and respect what eco-cognitive openness requires. I also quoted an important physics-based perspective that sees human brains as "open" and "dissipative systems": brains are always open and coupled with their surroundings in an ongoing endeavor to reach equilibrium with them: the cruciality of errors typical of abduction is in tune with this physical perspective.

## CONCLUSION

I used the concepts of locked and unlocked strategies, abduction, and optimization of eco-cognitive openness as examples of key concepts capable of highlighting the fundamental epistemological and cognitive differences between deep learning computational cognitive performances (I used the program Alphago/AlphaZero as an example) and human ones. My research on abduction, which emphasized the relevance of the idea of eco-cognitive openness, contributed to demonstrating how this openness is lacking in deep learning systems but not in high-level human inferential creative and diagnostic inferences. Deep learning programs like AlphaGo/AlphaZero use locked abductive methods, putting eco-cognitive openness in jeopardy. Un-locked abductive strategies, on the other hand, represent the high-level sorts of abductive creative and diagnostic reasoning that are unique to human cognition and respect what eco-cognitive openness requires. I also quoted an important physics-based perspective that sees human brains as "open" and "dissipative systems": brains are always open and coupled with their surroundings in an ongoing endeavor to reach equilibrium with them: the cruciality of errors typical of abduction is in tune with this physical perspective.

## ACKNOWLEDGMENT

Some of the concepts in this paper have been covered previously in my book *Eco-Cognitive Computationalism. Cognitive Domestication of Ignorant Entities*, Springer, Cham, Switzerland, 2022. I owe a debt of gratitude to John Woods, Atocha Aliseda, Woosuk Park, Giuseppe Longo, Gordana Dodig-Crnkovic, Luís Moniz Pereira, Paul Thagard, Joseph Brenner, the two reviewers, and my collaborators Selene Arfini and Alger Sans Pinillos for their insightful critiques and interesting exchanges that helped me enrich my analysis of the issues addressed in this chapter.

This research was supported by PRIN 2017 Research [Grant Number 20173YP4N3]—MIUR, Ministry of University and Research, Rome, Italy.

## REFERENCES

Aliseda, A. (2006). *Abductive Reasoning. Logical Investigations into Discovery and Explanation*. Springer.

Binder, W. (2021). AlphaGo's deep play: Technological breakthrough as social drama. In J. Roberge & M. Castelle (Eds.), *The Cultural Life of Machine Learning*. Palgrave Macmillan. doi:10.1007/978-3-030-56286-1_6

Calude, C. S., & Longo, G. (2017). The deluge of spurious correlations in big data. *Foundations of Science*, 22(3), 1595–1612. doi:10.100710699-016-9489-4

Curran, N. M., Sun, J., & Hong, J. W. (2020). Anthropomorphizing AlphaGo: A content analysis of the framing of Google DeepMind's AlphaGo in the Chinese and American press. *AI & Society*, 35(3), 727–735. doi:10.100700146-019-00908-9

Gabbay, D. M., & Woods, J. (2005). *The Reach of Abduction*. North-Holland.

Gigerenzer, G., & Brighton, H. (2009). Homo heuristicus: Why biased minds make better inferences. *Topics in Cognitive Science*, 1(1), 107–143. doi:10.1111/j.1756-8765.2008.01006.x PMID:25164802

Gigerenzer, G., & Selten, R. (2002). *Bounded Rationality. The Adaptive Toolbox*. The MIT Press. doi:10.7551/mitpress/1654.001.0001

Grant, T. D., & Wischik, D. J. (2020). From Holmes to AlphaGo. In *On the path to AI*. Palgrave Macmillan. doi:10.1007/978-3-030-43582-0_9

Hintikka, J. (2007). *Socratic Epistemology. Explorations of Knowledge-Seeking by Questioning*. Cambridge University Press. doi:10.1017/CBO9780511619298

Husserl, E. (1931). *Ideas. General Introduction to Pure Phenomenology* (W. R. Boyce Gibson, Trans.). Northwestern University Press.

Hutchins, E. (2005). Material anchors for conceptual blends. *Journal of Pragmatics*, 37(10), 1555–1577. doi:10.1016/j.pragma.2004.06.008

Josephson, J. R., & Josephson, S. G. (Eds.). (1994). *Abductive Inference. Computation, Philosophy, Technology*. Cambridge University Press. doi:10.1017/CBO9780511530128

Kawamleh, S. (2021). Can machines learn how clouds work? The epistemic implications of machine learning methods in climate science. *Philosophy of Science*, 88(5), 1008–1020. doi:10.1086/714877

Leonelli, S. (2014). What difference does quantity make? On the epistemology of Big Data in biology. *Big Data & Society*, 1(1). Advance online publication. doi:10.1177/2053951714534395 PMID:25729586

Leonelli, S. (2020). Scientific research and big data. In The Stanford Encyclopedia of Philosophy. Metaphysics Research Lab, Stanford University.

Magnani, L. (2001). *Abduction, Reason, and Science. Processes of Discovery and Explanation*. Kluwer Academic/Plenum Publishers. doi:10.1007/978-1-4419-8562-0

Magnani, L. (2002). Epistemic mediators and model-based discovery in science. In L. Magnani & N. J. Nersessian (Eds.), *Model-Based Reasoning: Science, Technology, Values* (pp. 305–329). Kluwer Academic/Plenum Publishers. doi:10.1007/978-1-4615-0605-8_18

Magnani, L. (2009). *Abductive Cognition. The Epistemological and Eco-Cognitive Dimensions of Hypothetical Reasoning*. Springer. doi:10.1007/978-3-642-03631-6

Magnani, L. (2015). The eco-cognitive model of abduction. 'Apagwgh¿ now: Naturalizing the logic of abduction. *Journal of Applied Logic, 13*(3), 285–315. doi:10.1016/j.jal.2015.04.003

Magnani, L. (2016). The eco-cognitive model of abduction. Irrelevance and implausibility exculpated. *Journal of Applied Logic, 15*, 94–129. doi:10.1016/j.jal.2016.02.001

Magnani, L. (2017). *The Abductive Structure of Scientific Creativity. An Essay on the Ecology of Cognition*. Springer. doi:10.1007/978-3-319-59256-5

Magnani, L. (2018). Playing with anticipations as abductions. strategic reasoning in an eco-cognitive perspective. *Journal of Applied Logic – IfColog Journal of Logics and their Applications, 5*(5), 1061–1092.

Magnani, L. (2019). AlphaGo, locked strategies, and eco-cognitive openness. *Philosophies, 4*(1), 8. doi:10.3390/philosophies4010008

Magnani, L. (2020). Anticipations as abductions in human and machine cognition. Deep learning: Locked and unlocked capacities. *Postmodern Openings, 11*(4), 230–247. doi:10.18662/po/11.4/232

Magnani, L. (2022a). *Discoverability. The Urgent Need of an Ecology of Human Creativity*. Springer. doi:10.1007/978-3-030-93329-6

Magnani, L. (2022b). *Eco-Cognitive Computationalism. Cognitive Domestication of Ignorant Entities*. Springer. doi:10.1007/978-3-030-81447-2

Magnani, L., & Bertolotti, T. (Eds.). (2017). *Handbook of Model-Based Science*. Springer. doi:10.1007/978-3-319-30526-4

Minati, G., & Vitiello, G. (2006). Mistake making machines. In G. Minari, E. Pessa, & M. Abram (Eds.), *Systemics of Emergence: Research and Development* (pp. 67–78). Springer. doi:10.1007/0-387-28898-8_4

Peirce, C. S. (1866–1913). Collected Papers of Charles Sanders Peirce. Harvard University Press.

Prigogine, I., & Stengers, I. (1984). *Order out of Chaos. Man's New Dialogue with Nature*. Bantam.

Raab, M., & Gigerenzer, G. (2005). Intelligence as smart heuristics. In R. J. Sternberg & J. E. Prets (Eds.), *Cognition and Intelligence. Identifying the Mechanisms of the Mind* (pp. 188–207). Cambridge University Press.

Vallverdú, J. (2020). Approximate and situated causality in deep learning. *Philosophies, 5*(1), 2–10. doi:10.3390/philosophies5010002

Vitiello, G. (2012). The dissipative brain. In G. Globus, K. H. Pribram, & G. Vitiello (Eds.), *Brain and Being. At the boundary between science, philosophy, language and arts* (pp. 317–338). John Benjamins.

## ADDITIONAL READING

Binder, W. (2021). AlphaGo's deep play: Technological breakthrough as social drama. In J. Roberge & M. Castelle (Eds.), *The Cultural Life of Machine Learning*. Palgrave Macmillan. doi:10.1007/978-3-030-56286-1_6

Calude, C. S., & Longo, G. (2017). The deluge of spurious correlations in big data. *Foundations of Science*, *22*(3), 595–612. doi:10.100710699-016-9489-4

Curran, N. M., Sun, J., & Hong, J. W. (2020). Anthropomorphizing AlphaGo: A content analysis of the framing of Google DeepMind's AlphaGo in the Chinese and American press. *AI & Society*, *35*(3), 727–735. doi:10.100700146-019-00908-9

Grant, T. D., & Wischik, D. J. (2020). From Holmes to AlphaGo. In *On the path to AI*. Palgrave Macmillan. doi:10.1007/978-3-030-43582-0_9

Magnani, L. (2009). *Abductive Cognition. The Epistemological and Eco-Cognitive Dimensions of Hypothetical Reasoning*. Springer. doi:10.1007/978-3-642-03631-6

Magnani, L. (2019). AlphaGo, locked strategies, and eco-cognitive openness. *Philosophies*, *4*(1), 8. doi:10.3390/philosophies4010008

Magnani, L. (2022). *Discoverability. The Urgent Need of an Ecology of Human Creativity*. Springer. doi:10.1007/978-3-030-93329-6

## KEY TERMS AND DEFINITIONS

**Abduction:** Reasoning to hypotheses.

**AlphaGo:** Computation AI program capable to automatically play Go game.

**Big Data:** Big data is a field that deals with methods for analyzing and methodically extracting information from, or otherwise dealing with data volumes that are too large or complicated for typical data-processing application software to handle.

**Dissipative Brain:** A model of human brain based on quantum physics.

**Go:** Famous game based on a blackboard and two players.

**Locked Strategies:** Based on a rigid and fixed scenario.

**Unlocked Strategies:** Based on an unlimited source of evidence.

## ENDNOTES

[1] Other classical works on abductive cognition that have to be quoted are (Josephson & Josephson, 1994, Gabbay & Woods 2005, & Aliseda 2006).

2    Recent studies on AlphaGo touch various interesting aspects: (Curran, Sun & Hong, 2021) illustrate a mixed-method content analysis of Chinese and American news media coverage of the program performaces; (Grant & Wischik, 2020) cover the relationship between induction and reinforcement learning in the framework of a comparison with legal doctrine as derived from contested judicial decisions; (Binder, 2021) actualizes Victor Turner's concept of "social drama" in order to examine the case of AlphaGo as a technological breakthrough in AI research, thanks to an analysis of the games of AlphaGo and the discourses surrounding them.

3    I have to note that my notion of locked strategy is not related to the standard nomenclature of the game theory, for more synthetic information see, for example, Wikipedia entry Go (game) https://en.wikipedia.org/wiki/Go_(game).

4    More information can be found in (Leonelli, 2020).

5    See my recent book (Magnani, 2022) for more on the overall topic of discoverability and its ramifications, which includes the current issue of big data curation.

6    See (Kawamleh, 2021) for a recent intriguing discussion regarding the limits of using machine learning in climate change prediction, which deals with scientists' replacement of physically grounded parameterizations with neural networks that do not directly or indirectly represent physical processes. Vallverdù (2020) provides a justification of deep learning and machine learning achievements in terms of their ability to produce approximation causation through the discovery of correlations between indirect components. Finally, readers interested in a comprehensive and in-depth examination of the current epistemological, social, and political issues surrounding big data, algorithms, machine learning, artificial intelligence, and social networks should consult (Numerico, 2021), which emphasizes the fact that more or less reliable predictions generated by computational systems can become de facto "prescriptions" capable of subtly altering human behavior.

7    Some information about the history of AI's so-called automated scientific discovery is presented in (Magnani, 2009, chapter two).

8    DeepMind is a British artificial intelligence company founded in September 2010 and taken over by Google in 2014, the company also created the AlphaGo program.

# Humanities, Digitizing, and Economics

**Torben Larsen**

(iD) https://orcid.org/0000-0002-5704-7753

*University of Southern Denmark, Denmark*

## INTRODUCTION

2020 mankind is in the middle of a technological revolution by the creative class that will fundamentally alter the way people live, work, and relate to each other. The scale, scope, and complexity of this transformation is unlike anything humankind has experienced before. In order to unfold it. This 'Fourth Industrial Revolution' was announced by the World Economic Forum (Schwab, 2017).

The First Industrial Revolution as previewed by Adam Smith in his 1776 'Inquiry into the Growth of Nations' was simply to mechanize production. This industrial breakthrough was characterized by novel inventions such as the 'Spinning Jenny' and the 'Power loom' that enabled increasing production with fewer man-hours. However, in a broader sense the new mechanical machines followed from the development of new energy sources such as coal, the steam engine and petroleum for use in combustion-engines.

The Second Phase of Industrialization in the 19th Century established Industrialization in Europe and North America. It was based on electric power to create mass production factories with highly specialized employees and far more complex products.

After World War II, a Third Phase of Industrialization arose from increased collaboration between industry and science and departments in private companies specialized in R&D. This collaboration invented electronics and information technology to automate production, pharmaceuticals, and chemicals as Plastics.

The Fourth Industrial Phase arises from the Third. It is symbolized by the Internet invented by Berner Lee in 1983. It fuses technologies that blurs the lines between the physical, digital, and biological spheres. There are three reasons why today's transformations driven by the creative class represent not merely a prolongation of the third industrial phase but rather the arrival of a Fourth and distinct one regarding *velocity*, *scope*, and *systems impact*. The speed of current breakthroughs has no historical precedent. When compared with previous industrial revolutions, the Fourth is evolving at an exponential rather than a linear pace. It disrupts almost every industry in every country. The breadth and depth of these changes herald the transformation of entire systems of production, management, and governance.

The possibilities of billions of people connected by mobile devices, with unprecedented processing power, storage capacity, and access to knowledge, are unlimited. These possibilities will be multiplied by emerging technology breakthroughs in fields such as artificial intelligence, robotics, the Internet of Things, autonomous vehicles, 3D printing, nanotechnology, biotechnology, materials science, energy storage, and quantum computing. These gains are in all that astonishing compared to the living conditions of ordinary simple peasants before the Industrial Revolutions that this Chapter aims to interpret the whole process in a broad socioeconomic context.

DOI: 10.4018/978-1-7998-9220-5.ch047

# BACKGROUND

This series of Industrial Revolutions have been that successful that it challenges the whole Ecosystem which implies a deep crisis in Economics, too:

- An intra-disciplinary polarization between the Chicago School of Economics aiming to restrict interference in the market forces to monetary policy (Interest rate and amount of money) versus the Austrian School of Economics aiming to strengthen psychological knowledge among economists (Menger, 1971)
- A contemporary representative of the Austrian School is the psychologist Kahneman (2011) who was awarded the Nobel prize of Economics 2002
- An International Student Initiative for Pluralism in Economics is formalized (ISIPE, 2014)

To understand the present crisis of Economics it is necessary to recognize the background in British Empiricism where philosophers as Bacon, Locke and Hume in the 18th Century claimed that the classical philosophy was biased by four types of prejudices:

- Conservatism

Human nature resists changes. Many cases show that when persons are offered either a cheaper or better service then are only a third immediately ready to adopt it (Heijden, 2019)

- Anchoring

Humans understand situations in a holistic way wherefore the core of the situation has a lot of impact even if it is irrelevant to the outcome. An important example is modern advertising where association of any product with a well known brand enhances sales (Erk et., 2002)

- Temper

People differ on the optimist-pessimist scale which affects their decision- making pattern. Optimists get easily engaged in new ideas/projects, while pessimists preview all the difficulties. For instance, reinforces the loss aversion of pessimists the amplitude of business cycles as advanced in the prospect theory (Kahneman & Tversky, 1979)

- Incomplete Knowledge

In the private sector specialist knowledge is recognized, while in collective affairs (politics) the moral standard is still supposed to be decisive in the democratic world. However, in the modern complex societies top qualifications are as important as in the private sector

Empirical science aims to prevent prejudices by empirical verification (falsification) of subjective theories, before they eventually are accepted as knowledge. This guides Economics as the field of pragmatism, too (James, 1907). The original intention of empiricism was to guide ordinary people towards a truthful life. However, it has primarily given a quantum leap to natural sciences such as physics, chemistry and medicine. By entrepreneurial ingenuity, positivist science is implemented in the complex products and services benefiting the population of the industrialized world. This modern dichotomy between the natural sciences and the Humanities is already described by Snow in "The Two Cultures" (1959). In order to clarify the strategic conditions of sustainable development in this background, the advanced use of digitizing in brain science, especially brain scanners, frames an interdisciplinary approach to Economics termed Neuroeconomics. As a veritable "Mind reading" technology, Neuroeconomics is the substantial base of this Chapter.

## FOCUS OF THE ARTICLE

The root of our democratic culture is the Antique Greece (5th Century BC) where it was an exclusive Constitution for the Top of society. With the French Revolution 1789, democracy became for all with emphasis on representative elections and a tripartite societal power between 1) Parliament, 2) Government and 3) The Judicial system. So, the cultural spirit of democracy arises from the Humanities and Arts. Interdisciplinary economics is in this background presented as a dialogue with the Humanities represented by the German Artist and PhD Hiltrud Schinzel contributing with a series of paintings. In reply to the Humanities, Larsen explains the classical liberal growth model, political economy and economic psychology. The dialogue on the Humanities and Economics develops in four scenes:

1    The Humanities and Economic Growth
2    Alienation and Neuroeconomic Psychology
3    Economics of the Green-house Effect
4    Human Resource Development (HRD)

## SOLUTIONS AND RECOMMENDATIONS

### Scene 1. The Humanities and Economic Growth

The historical root of Democracy, originating modern economic growth from the midst of the 18th Century, is a hybrid of

- Antique Greek invention of the natural sciences by Aristotle in the 5. Century BC matured in British Empiricism in the 17. Century by philosophers as Bacon and Hume
- Christianity as matured with Protestantism 1536

Schinzel illustrates the aspirations of the Humanities as that of a positive psychology in accordance with Goldberg (1993):

In the Younger Stone Age about 10.000 years ago, man began to mold the earth with more sophisticated tools to improve productivity in the `Mesopotamian Half Moon` as Plowing with a Yoke of Cattle that earlier exclusively were subject to hunting. In a few generations Agriculture made the global population rise from 3 to 100 million. Agriculture initiated, too, a change of human relations from *sharing to privatization* as persons farming a particular piece of land were allowed to keep the outcome for themselves. Thus, the first stage of Economics is that of giving gifts as those with the better outcome of farming could give better gifts at social celebrations. This implied about 3.000 B.C. the invention of money as

*Figure 1. Doctor and Patient*

indicators of value for *trade* and facilitating *hoarding* or storing of wealth as basics of monetary economics. The change from sharing to privatization of goods appears as the strongest cultural change so far.

In modern times, a Scottish university teacher observed the market-based economic growth by mechanics as the `Spinning Jenny` and `Steam Engines` (Smith, 1776). Figure 1 explains the general mechanism of economic growth as exemplified by the plow increasing the outcome of agriculture. Before the plow, man could choose between producing 5 units of corn or 20 fish. With an optimal combination corresponding to E1. With the plow, man could redouble his harvest of corn to 10 units and reach the optimal product combination E2 with a far better overall level of satisfaction (from Utility level U2 to U3). This improves human survival to an extent that increased world population many fold and enabled construction of the Egyptian pyramids. All that economic growth requires from ordinary consumers is the ability to maximize utility from a set of options which explains the extraordinary success. The level of economic growth is quantified as the Gross Domestic Product (GDP) per capita.

Today, the middle class disposes of more than double of what is needed to satisfy basal physiological and social needs as illustrated in Figure 3. This forms a growing split between `Consumerism` and `Simple Living` for health, ecology with economies on household spending. An obvious choice for a growing share of households as technological progress materializes only as lower and lower marginal consumer improvements by digitizing.

"Simple Living" can express itself by at least 5 different ways:

- A classical alternative to short-term consumption is savings eventually with active investment
- Focus on unfolding of individual interests/talents as elaborated in scene 2

- Engagement in works for the "Common Good", for instance Charity
- Minimization of the personal contribution to $CO_2$-emission and waste of materials.

However, large changes require inclusive political action as elaborated in Scene 3

*Figure 2. Axioms of market-driven growth*

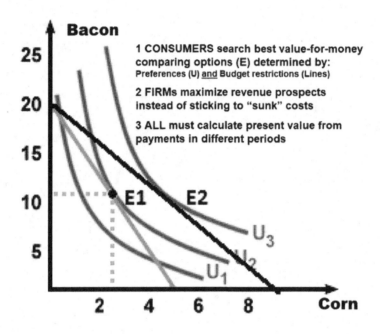

*Figure 3. The existential consumer choice*

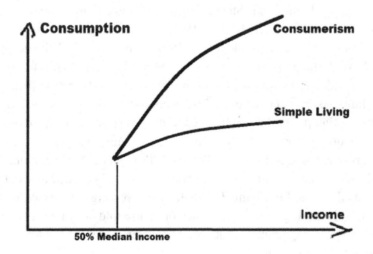

- Recognition of the stress load related to modern business life motivates many people in the workforce to prioritize health and life-expectancy as elaborated in Scene 4

## Scene 2. Alienation and Creative Man

The term `Alienation` arises in modern time from the German term `Entfremdung` referring to the Hegelian dialectic system (1821). Hegel claimed that his synthetic level of history (Ding-an-sich) represented real life (Ding-fùr-uns). However, the historical legacy from Kant (1781) says that the only human reality is `Ding-fùr-uns`, that is what we perceive. This schism between the subjective reality (Ding-fùr-uns) and the objective reality (Ding-an-sich) gave rise to a broad human feeling of alienation as artistically expressed, for instance in the novel "The Process" (Kafka, 1925), and reinterpreted in connection with industrialization. Schinzel illustrates alienation as related to the machine culture in HS2.

*Figure 4. The Machine*

Alienation is considered the first state of what today is characterized by WHO as epidemic job-related stress as indicated by the frequency of Depression diagnoses (Marcus et al., 2912). Depression is 2020 the second leading cause of world disability; by 2030 Depression is expected to be the largest contributor to the burden of disease.

A modern alternative to alienation is the "Rise of the Creative Class" claimed on the basis of statistical analysis of changes in the US Job-structure 1970-2000 (Florida, 2012). The rise of the creative class in some countries from 10% of the workforce in 1970 to +40% in 2010 (Andersen and Lorentzen, 2005) constitutes the base of a Fifth Industrial Revolution that changes the focus of Economics from consumption (GDP per capita) to unfoldment of creativity facilitated by long-term decline in the marginal utility of consumption (Figure 3).

*Figure 5. Marginal utility and the industrial revolutions*

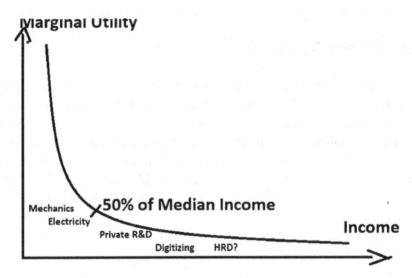

The low marginal utility of individual consumption is complemented by social welfare systems that further reduces the individual risk of risk-taking:

1. The most cost-effective finance of collective needs for healthcare, social service and education is that of public finance as supported by Social statistics regarding OECD
2. The most simple, comprehensible and effective political intervention for counteracting economic inequality related to globalization (Francese and Mulas-Granados (2015; Piketty 2014) is according to a series of Nobel Laureates in Economics that of Universal Basic Income (UBI). UBI at a level of 50% of median income can be financed by 1) Pay-off in existing cash subsidies, 2) Cancellation of bottom deductions, 3) Savings on compulsory activation programs for social clients and 4) Simplification of personal subsidies an deductions
3. Systematic public accountant with multinational companies (MNC) is no longer an exception but the main rule due to the monopolization by globalization

A complementary aspect of globalization, to the hegemony of MNC, is an increasing demand for creative skills in all aspects of digitizing and the derived options for far more individuals. A study comparing the relative efficacy of entrepreneurs compared with other, Academic educated business managers (Laurie-Martinez et al., 2005), demonstrates the broad effect on quality. The specific psychological profile of an entrepreneur is identified as a `Pilot-in-the-plane`, see Figure 4 (Saraswathy et al., 2005). A Pilot must 1) Assure at least finance of his business activity by an alternative budget on his `Affordable Loss`, 2) Be sensible enough to prioritize "Bird-in-hand" for "10 Birds on the roof", 3) Diversified in his management style as a "Crazy Quilt" that unites the broadest possible spectrum of skills relevant to his project and 4) Optimistic to turn obstacles around to assets, for instance making a sour citrus sweet by adding sugar.

Before industrialization people got their identity from their special ethnic culture. During industrialization, professional life plays a larger and larger role to ordinary people. Now we have got a prototype of a creative man to guide a good professional career. The transition from an ethnic identity to that of

*Figure 6. Pilot-in-the-plane entrepreneurship*

a creative professional is a deep mental transition for most people. On this background Scene 4 of this dialogue focuses on using digitizing, especially in brain research, to constitute a new phase of economic development that deserve the characteristic of Fifth Industrial Revolution on Human Resource Development (HRD) as previewed in Figure 3. However, before dealing with such intra-human topics, it's necessary to deal with the global threat from the Greenhouse effect.

## Scene 3. Economics of the Green-House Effect

Schinzel and Larsen agree that the Green-house effect, as illustrated in Figure 5, is an issue that deserves Global Top priority in the economic policy of nations. The central intervention towards the Greenhouse effect is according to economics a CO2 Tax (ET) that includes social cost in market prices (Making the polluter pay) (Pigou, 1920). ET is alone 70% of the road to Carbon Neutrality because it gives `Free Enterprise` a strong incentive to develop carbon neutral technology. The major part of the social burden for low incomes / small businesses can be compensated by the revenue of ET. The remaining part of the ET revenue must be used to subsidize the development of new carbon neutral technology in critical sectors as 1) Agriculture and 2) Transport by air and sea.

Already, the classical Humanities has previewed a human development relevant to the broader scope on Economics required that of being with a Janus Head with the special capability to look around 360° as illustrated by Schinzel in HS3.

In contemporary economic behavior, a specific domain demanding a wider Janus-outlook is that of political economy as illustrated in Figure 6. The different economic-political ideologies in modern democracies constitute a continual spectrum of positions from Neoliberalism holding entrepreneurial freedom as crucial to economic growth with Communism as the opposite position claiming a central management of business life to protect the weakest segment of the population. A model of democratic development is `Inclusive Democracy` (Barry-Jones 2001; Gare 2003). As historical experiences reject both poles of economic-political ideology:

*Figure 7. Reinforcing global heating*

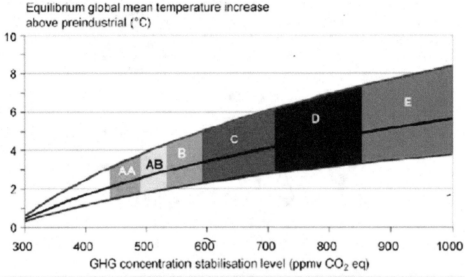

Equilibrium global mean temperature increase above preindustrial (°C)

GHG concentration stabilisation level (ppmv $CO_2$ eq)

**Legend on *Critical Climatic Tipping Points:***
Melting of Arctic and Antarctic ice-sheets raising global sea levels and reducing reflection
Melting Permafrost in The Tundra releases Methane with 20-fold stronger Green-house effect
Dieback of Amazonas Rain Forest reducing absorption of $CO_2$ from the atmosphere
Disruption of the Gulf Stream transporting warm water from Equator to the Northern Hemisphere

*Figure 8. The Janus Head*

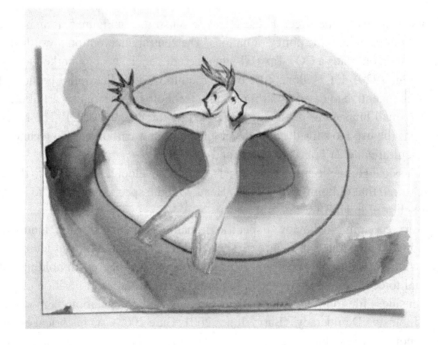

- The Greenhouse effect rejects Neoliberalism
- The large scale social experiment with centrally planned economy in Eastern Europe 1917-89 is demonstrated as ineffective (Maddison, 2003)

`Inclusive Democracy` can be implemented as democratic economic-political coalitions across-the-center that combine free entrepreneurial ingenuity with protection of the economic weaker segments of the population. Already, center-oriented economic-political ideologies as social liberalism and social democracy are strong democratic players:

Note: Extremist ideologies (Communism and Neoliberalism) are either ineffective or catastrophic. However, already center-oriented ideologies such as `Social Liberalism` and `Social Democrats` do have a long history.

*Figure 9. Inclusive democracy*

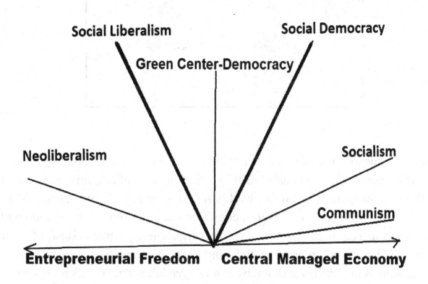

The target assumption on economic agents in general and particularly the moderation by center-orientation supports the development of an inclusive economic-political thinking with a broader population base than the 50-50% fighting of the democratic wings originated in the 19th Century by the formation of socialist/communist alternatives to liberalism. The share of center-profiles grows over time due to stimulation of creativity both in the upbringing of offspring, demands on the labor market and political experiences.

## Scene 4. Future Research Directions

From the point of view of the Humanities a basal quality of human relations is the transparency of decision-making as illustrated by H. Schinzel in HS4.

The option to develop a transparent psychology arises from modern brain scanners which enables enough resolution to identify subtle human emotions as well as cognitive processes. This quality is combined with specific problem solving in functional magnetic resonance imaging (fMRI) in the inter-disciplinary field Neuroeconomics. This raises a scenario of far more effective technological facilities

*Figure 10. Transparency*

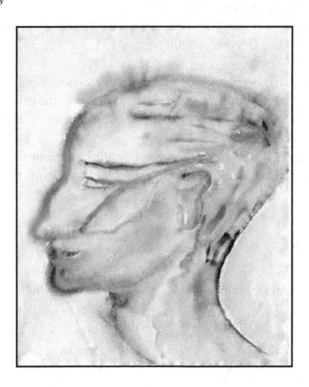

for Human Resource Development (HRD). A review of Neuroeconomics advances a neuroeconomic model of economic decision- making (Larsen, 2017). The dynamics of cognitive integration arises from the Pro Reptile Brain Stem as passion. At the level of the Mammal MidBrain fear modulates passion to our animal emotions. At the Neocortical level of cognition our emotions are integrated with experience by our ability to Analysis (Cortical Asymmetry). This tripartite dynamics constitutes our Temper as illustrated in Figure 7. The X-axis represents the Autonomic Nervous System (ANS) which is an ambivalent state of passion as internally inhibited by fear (Amygdala). The Y-axis represents "Analysis" or screening as indicated by Hemispheric asymmetry in the EEG. The overall state of integration of "Fear" and "Analysis" is the typical baseline position on the integration curve (Circle) that indicates individual Temper or `Risk-aversion`. Neuroeconomic trials on Complex (Intertemporal) respective Explorative choices show that the best cognitive integration is accomplished for both moderate arousal Analysis. In this way moderate risk-willingness (Temper) appears as a basic economic decision-making quality.

`Willingness to take risks in general` is operated on a scale from 0 through 10 in a representative survey on 'risk attitudes' with 20,000 respondents (Dohmen et al., 2012). The correlation on important life domains are: 1) Car driving (r=0.49), 2) Financial matters (r=0.50), 3) Careers (r=0.61), 4) Sports/leisure (r=0.56), and 5) Health (r=0.48). The Dohmen-scale has an average of 4.4 with SD=2.25. More factors affect the 'General risk willingness', however, the single far most important factor is gender as females are moderately more risk-averse than males (Average: Male=5 and Female=4). The wiring of the brain shows gender differences where males have strong Frontal-Posterior connections which promote stringent logical thinking while females have better interhemispheric connections promoting collaborative and balanced thinking.

The relation between 'Risk Willingness' and the 'Big Five' is investigated in a correlation study (Becker et al., 2012). The overall conclusion is a positive correlation between risk willingness and personality traits as extraversion and open-mindedness and on the other side a negative correlation between risk-willingness and personality traits as agreeable/ conscientious and risk-avert. Neuroeconomic Psychology has five different behavioral profiles as illustrated in Figure 7. The most flexible center-profile is the Open-minded due to a unique ability to interpret novel impressions in a context of well-known experiences (Gountas & Corciari 2012 and Kern et al. 2019).

The Big5, identified by statistical correlation analysis, differs from the 4 classical Tempers identified by cognitive empathy in the Greek Antique (Sanguine, Phlegmatic, Melancholic and Choleric). The difference is that Open-minded is a modern Temper inspiring Agreeables to extraversion due to liberal modern manners of rising offspring, more intense formal education in science and a rising demand for creativity in business life. In this way, the share of Open-minded people can rise relatively quickly as claimed by Florida (2012). In contrast to the Agreeables, extreme Tempers as Extraverts and Risk-averse are rooted in genetics and therefore far more difficult to change by culture and education.

*Figure 11. Economic psychology*

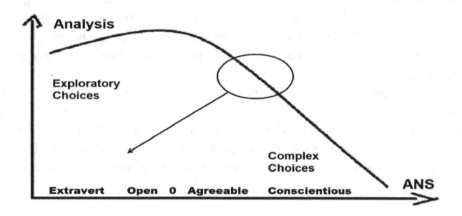

The social validity of the `Big Five Taxonomy` is demonstrated in a study of students in different Academic Majors using the `Big Five` Taxonomy (Vedel, 2016). The psychological differences across Majors are often moderate (about 0.5 standard deviation), but especially open-mindedness differentiates strongly among Majors. Relevant findings are:

- Students of political science score high on both Open-mindedness and Extraversion
- Students of economics, law and medicine score high on Extraversion
- Students of science (including engineering) score high on Agreeable
- Students of psychology/arts/humanities score high on Open-mindedness and Risk-aversion

Students of economics are more extraverted than students of other majors. A later study elaborates the characteristics of students of Economics/Business as more infected by the `Dark Triad` (Narcissism, Psychopathy and Machiavellianism) in contrast to students of psychology (Vedel & Thomsen, 2017).

Figure 7 frames too cognitive training the Fifth Industrial Revolution shifting the economic focus from consumption to unfolding of creative potentials:

**1.** Figure 7 can be used for individual training of the psychological sensitivity to the Temper of other persons. A Norwegian population interview study (N=1000) on risk-attitude and behavior confirms both the positive (Extraverts and Open-minded) and negative (Agreeable and Conscientious) cross correlations of Becker et al. 2012 (Breivika et al., 2020). Also, this study confirms that males are more willing to take economic risks than females. Finally, the Norwegian study does not include the Neurotic trait, because it's a diagnosis that should not be applied among normal persons. For sensitivity training, simply ask yourself and other:

- Are you willing to take a chance or risk-averse?
- Do you make decisions fast or rather slow?

Regarding other persons you may compare their answer with your expectation and experience that you step by step improve your sensitivity to the 4 Tempers in Figure 7.

**2.** The individual Temper is subject to change by somatic, cognitive and sensory inputs. On this background the primary neurological advice for better mental health is self-control or *stamina* based on physical fitness (Oaten & Cheng, 2006).

**3.** The action-mechanism of classical Indo-European meditation procedures is an extraordinary in-depth relaxation, illustrated in Figure 7 as a movement from the circle towards Origo, that relaxes repressed fear-responses to the benefit of improved cognitive integration (Larsen, 2017). This opens a scenario of better stress-management by meditative in-depth-relaxation as documented in a meta-analysis (Manzoni et al., 2008). An impartial monitoring of this type of mental training is as simple as a galvanic skin resistance meter.

**4.** The individual cognitive integration can be improved by adopting falsification for self-criticism recollecting long-term memories (LTM). A model of LTM is illustrated in Figure 8 (Baddeley, 2010). The center of recollection (Analysis) is the Dorsolateral Prefrontal Cortex (dlPFC). Can you ask yourself questions without biasing the answer? Do you remember to open your questions with an `Else`, too? Do you use your imagination recollecting both similarities and differences? Is your vocabulary large enough to verbalize your experiences?

*Figure 12. Baddeley's Model of long-term memorization (LTM)*

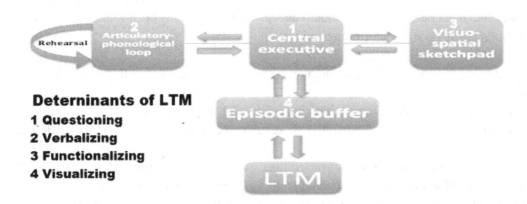

**5.** A number of simple medical instruments for personal biofeedback enables in practice laymen to verify the model of economic psychology advanced in Figure 7:

- The position on the X-axis during resting is indicated by the "Heart rate variability". This parameter can be measured by App`s that can be free downloaded to smartphones
- The Position on the Y-axis during resting is indicated by the degree of asymmetry of hemispheres That can be measured by simple instruments for electroencephalography (EEG)
- The effectiveness of meditative in-depth relaxation (The Arrow-effect) can be measured by simple instruments for galvanic skin resistance (GSR)
- A crucial long-term health benefit from regular meditation is indicated by the diastolic blood pressure as measured on cheap blood pressure meters.

## CONCLUSION

This study integrates the Humanities and Economics in four scenes. The outcome is a pragmatic humanity where:

1.  The market-based growth meets humanistic aspirations of positive human relations
2.  The humanistic criticism of alienation of classical human relations in market economies is counteracted by the advancement of:
    a.  A research-based model of creative man referring to Saraswathy`s model of Pilot-in-the-plane entrepreneurship
    b.  Explanation of the substantial economic freedom for a broad middle class in the industrialized world
    c.  Explanation of the social welfare state based on Universal Basic Income (UBI) and free public services for collective needs as healthcare, education and social security
3.  The Humanities and the profession of economics both recognize the Greenhouse effect as a serious threat towards the present human civilization. The basic means of economics for transition to a carbon neutral economy is a $CO_2$ Tariff at the source of emission. Such $CO_2$ Tariff changes the price structure in a way that mobilizes private entrepreneurial ingenuity to develop carbon neutral products
4.  Inspired by the classical symbol of a Janus head, modern scanner-based neuroeconomic research identifies psychological open-mindedness as the practical implementation of the ability to pluralist analysis. A crucial field test on pluralist thinking is the ability to form economic-political coalitions across-the-center. The digital revolution can facilitate the development of open-mindedness by a series training facilities that in all may constitute a Fifth Industrial Revolution

One of the founders of Economics had a vision of Economics as a positivist alternative to belief systems (Marshall, 1890). The principles constituting an interdisciplinary framework for Economics is implemented in a new Textbook (Larsen, 2021).

## ACKNOWLEDGMENT

In order to assure the interdisciplinary validity, the Author is thankful to sparring with and contributions from the following specialists in related disciplines:

- The development of a specific heuristic on sensitivity to the Big Five is complemented by PhD (Psych) Anna Vedel
- Stress Management by Meditative In-depth-relaxation is complemented by by Professor Emeritus (MD) Are Holen
- Author Ole D. Nielsen has summarized the state of the `Simple Living`- movement
- As mentioned above two economists from the Danish Climate Council, Ulla Blatt Bendtsen and Luis Birk Stewart, have advised on the calculation of a CO2 Emission Tariff
- The direct regular sparring partners are PhD Erik Frandsen on scientific method, economist Leif Justesen on business economics and organization, Anne-Stine Larsen on humanistic communication and Professor Emeritus Terkel Christiansen on public welfare policy

# REFERENCES

Andersen & Lorentzen. (2005). *The Geography of the Danish Creative Class – A Mapping and Analysis Danish part of "Technology, Talent and Tolerance in European Cities: A comparative analysis"*. CBS.

Baddeley, A. (2010). Working Memory. *Current Biology, 20*(4), 136–140. doi:10.1016/j.cub.2009.12.014 PMID:20178752

Barry-Jones, R. J. (Ed.). (2001). Inclusive Democracy. In Encyclopedia of International Political Economy. Routledge.

Becker, A., Decker, T., & Dohmen, T. (2012). The Relationship between Economic Preferences and Psychological Personality Measures. *Annual Review of Economics, 4*(1), 453–478. doi:10.1146/annurev-economics-080511-110922

Breivika, G., Sanda, T. S., & Sookermany, A. M. (2020). *Risk-taking attitudes and behaviors in the Norwegian population: the influence of personality and background factors*. Routledge.

Climate Change. (2021). *The Physical Science Base. Summary for Policymakers*. IPCC.

Dohmen, T., & Falk, A. (2012). *Individual Risk Attitudes: Measurement, Determinants and Behavior*. JEEA.

Erk, S., Spitzer, M., Wunderlich, A. P., Galley, L., & Walter, H. (2002). Cultural Objects modulate reward circuitry. *Neureport, 13*(18), 2499–2503. doi:10.1097/00001756-200212200-00024 PMID:12499856

Florida, R. (2012). *The Rise of the Creative Class-Revisited:10th Anniversary Edition*. Basic Books.

Francese, M., & Mulas-Granados, C. (2015). *Functional Income Distribution and Its Role in Explaining Inequality*. IMF. doi:10.5089/9781513549828.001

Gare, A. (2003). Beyond Social Democracy? Takis Fotopoulos' Vision of an Inclusive Democracy as a New Liberatory Project. *Democracy & Nature, 9*(3), 345–358. doi:10.1080/1085566032000159982

Goldberg, L. R. (1993). The structure of phenotypic personality traits. *The American Psychologist, 48*(1), 26–34. doi:10.1037/0003-066X.48.1.26 PMID:8427480

Gountas J, Corciari J (2010). Inside the Minds of Trendsetters. *Aus Magazine Sci/Tech*, 14-17.

Hegel, C. W. F. (1821). *The Science of Logic*. Academic Press.

Heijden, J. (2019). *Urban climate governance informed by behavioral insights: A commentary and research agenda School of Government*. Victoria University of Wellington.

ISIPE. (2014). *An international student call for pluralism in economics. Open Letter in The Guardian*. Author.

James, J. (1907). *Pragmatism's Conception of Truth. Lecture 6 in Pragmatism. A New Name for Some Old Ways of Thinking*. Longman Green and Co. doi:10.1037/10851-000

Kafka, F. (1925). *Der Process*. Verlag Die Schmiede.

Kahneman, D. (2011). *Thinking, Fast and Slow*. Farrar, Straus & Giroux.

Kahneman, D., & Tversky, A. (1979). Prospect Theory: An Analysis of Decision under Risk. *Econometrica, 47*(2), 263–292. doi:10.2307/1914185

Kern, M. L., McCarthy, P. X., Chakrabarty, D., & Rizoiu, M.-A. (2019). Social media-predicted personality traits and values can help match people to their ideal jobs. *Proceedings of the National Academy of Sciences of the United States of America, 116*(52), 26459–26464. doi:10.1073/pnas.1917942116 PMID:31843929

Larsen, T. (2017). Homo Neuroeconomicus – a Neuroeconomic Review of Functional Magnetic Resonance Imaging of Economic Choice. *IJUHD, 7*(1), 44–57.

Larsen, T. (2019). Neuroeconomic Psychology - 3 Cognitive Training Modules for End-users. *IJPCE, 9*(1), 1–22.

Larsen, T. (2021). *Applied Doughnut Economics by Neuroeconomics for Business and Politics*. IGI. doi:10.4018/978-1-7998-6424-0

Laurie-Martinez, D., & Canessa, N. (2005). Frontopolar Decision-making Efficiency: Comparing effectiveness of experts with different educational backgrounds during an exploration-exploitation task. *Frontiers in Human Neuroscience, 7*, 1–10.

Luhr. (1997). *The Simple Living Guide: A Sourcebook for Less Stress and More Joyful Living*. Harmony.

Maddison, A. (2003). *The World Economy: Historical Statistics*. OECD.

Manzoni, G. M., Pagnini, F., Castelnuovo, G., & Molinari, E. (2008). Relaxation training for anxiety: A ten-years systematic review with meta-analysis. *BMC Psychiatry, 8*(1), 41. doi:10.1186/1471-244X-8-41 PMID:18518981

Markus, M., Yasami, M. T., & Ommeren, M. (2012). *DEPRESSION–A Global Public Health Concern*. WHO. doi:10.1037/e517532013-004

Marshall, A. (1890). *Principles of Economics*. Great Minds Series.

Menger, C. (1871). *Principles of Economics*. University of Vienna.

Oaten, M., & Cheng, K. (2006). Longitudinal gains in self-regulation from regular physical exercise. *British Journal of Health Psychology, 11*(4), 717–733. doi:10.1348/135910706X96481 PMID:17032494

Pigou, A. C. (1920). *The Economics of Welfare*.

Piketty, T. (2014). *Capital in the Twenty-First Century*. Belknap/Harvard University Press. doi:10.4159/9780674369542

Popper, K. R. (1959). *The Logic of Scientific Discovery*. Routledge.

Raworth, K. (2017). *Doughnut Economics*. Chelsea Publishing.

Saraswathy, S., & Read, S. (2001). *Effectual Entrepreneurship*. Routledge.

Schmith, A. (1776). *Inquiry into the Growth of Nations*. Academic Press.

Schwab, K. (2017). *The Fourth Industrial Revolution*. Penguin Random Books.

Snow, E. (1959). *The Two Cultures. The Rede Lecture*. Cambridge University Press.

Vedel, A. (2016). The Personality of Academic Majors. *American Scientist*.

Vedel, A., & Thomsen, D. K. (2017). The Dark Triad among academic majors. *Personality and Individual Differences*, *116*, 81–105. doi:10.1016/j.paid.2017.04.030

## KEY TERMS AND DEFINITIONS

**Behavioral Economics:** The study of the effects of psychological, cognitive, emotional, cultural, and social factors on economic decisions of individuals and institutions and how those decisions vary from those implied by classical theory.

**Big 5:** Statistical correlation identifies five basic personality traits: extravert, open-minded, agreeable, conscientious, and neurotic.

**Economic Psychology:** A comprehensive model for prediction of economic behavior.

**Entrepreneurial Ingenuity:** The special set of qualities of founders of successful firms as specified in the Pilot-in-the-plane model of Saraswathy.

**Macroeconomics:** The study of key factors in aggregate economy, e.g., multiplicators, to guide politicians.

**Market Economy:** The interaction of consumers and suppliers on production and distribution of scarce (pecuniary) goods and services. Consumers are expected to maximize utility by comparing choices within their budget limit. Suppliers are expected to maximize their return-of-investment (ROI) supplying the most competitive goods and services to consumers.

**Neuroeconomics:** An interdisciplinary approach to behavioral science between economics, neurology, and psychology.

**Pigou Tax:** Tax on negative third-party effects, e.g., pollution, corresponding to the costs of the society.

**Risk-Preference:** Value function of economic agents formed by reward-seeking, cognitive activity, and fear. Correlation studies with personality traits shows it is parted in negative and positive wings:

**Risk-Aversion:** Correlates with personality traits as neuroticism, conscientious and agreeable.

**Risk-Willingness:** Correlates with personality traits as extravert and open-minded.

**Stress-Management:** User-driven healthcare to improve mental health e.g. physical exercise, diet and deep relaxation (meditation).

**Third Party Effects:** Positive or negative effects of economic transactions on persons that are not directly involved. Classical economics considers third-party effects as a political issue. Modern economics outlined in this chapter considers third-party effects as originated by the economic system, wherefore it must be internalized in the discipline of economics.

**UBI:** Basic non-conditioned subsidy to all adult citizens corresponding to 50% of net median income. It gives social security to low incomes, a net benefit to middle incomes and is mostly paid by high incomes.

# The Social Impact of Artificial Intelligence

**Zeinab Arees**

(iD) https://orcid.org/0000-0002-1799-3243

*Tishreen University, Syria*

## INTRODUCTION

World is witnessing many developments that enter into the social life, thus societies are affected by the new elements that entering them, such as Artificial Intelligence (AI). It entered societies and developed to become, within several decades, the center of modern life. It is widely agreed that the computer scientists John McCarthy, Marvin Minsky, Nathaniel Rochester and Claude Shannon are the first who coined the term "Artificial Intelligence" in 1955. They use the term to describe the capability of machines to "use language, form abstractions and concepts, to solve kinds of problems now reserved for humans" (Liu, 2020, 3). Artificial Intelligence is increasingly embedded in our everyday interactions, starting from repetitive mechanized actions (Karnouskos, 2017, 23). This chapter reviews the social importance of AI, in addition to the fields that using it in the society sectors, as well as the requirements that AI achieves in society, by reviewing the effect of AI on society since the beginning to the present day, and reviewing its effect on different age groups, by shedding the light from a social point of view on the most prominent advantages and disadvantages of AI. This chapter also reviews the prominent challenges that the application of AI in the social field faces, and the expected future achievements by AI in society.

## BACKGROUND

The authors will explore the impact of AI in society by reviewing its social impact in the societal sectors, in addition to explore the Importance of AI in both of developed and developing societies. AI also has an effect from its beginning to the present especially, by developing AI tools to achieve sustainable development in society. Generally, Artificial Intelligence is concerned with developing techniques that allow computers to act in a manner that seems like an intelligent organism, such as a human. (Raynor, 1999, 13). While on the other hand, Social impact refers both to the impact as experienced and provided by individuals, but also that of the organization as an organization, independently of any single member (Onyx, 2014, 5). Furthermore, Artificial Intelligence (AI) is best understood as a "Technosocial system," from an anthropological view, meaning that the technical aspects of AI are intrinsically and intimately connected to its social aspects. Social values and assumptions shape how we perceive, design, and use AI, as well as inform our perceptions, hopes, and fears of these technologies (Hagerty; Rubinov, 2019, 4). In addition, AI in the recent time leading to future discussions about the existence of Artificial Intelligence in the world. The idea of creating AI is aimed at making human life easier (Shabbir; Anwer, 2015, 7). The authors will discuss the Advantages & Disadvantages of AI uses in different societies such as facilitating life matters of society members, accuracy of the processes in dealing with AI de-

DOI: 10.4018/978-1-7998-9220-5.ch048

vices, while on the other hand some of AI Disadvantages appear in the lack of human interaction among society members, as AI has replaced humans in several fields. Then the authors will also examine the social challenges that are facing AI, such as the robots interacting with the elders. Although AI robots perform human functions, but they are programmed to provide services for the elders according to AI systems, so these robots are lacked to the emotional reaction, which may be needed by elders in certain situations and circumstances. This section will demonstrate the future perspective of AI by discussing the future vision of its social impact, thus many possibilities are rising in mind, such as the society future for reaching a better life to human societies in the AI age. Unfortunately, the reality of war, destruction, famine, diseases and poverty, especially in developing countries, how AI could mitigate these problems and contribute in humanity well-being in the future? Moreover, to these possibilities there are expectations about achieving sustainable development, that AI may provide better life for future generations. Accordingly, an important question arises: Is this future vision revolve about a possibility of the greatest benefit will be only prevailed in developed countries?

## MAIN FOCUS OF THE CHAPTER

### Issues, Controversies, Problems

There is existing research on Social Impact of Artificial Intelligence (Ertel, 2019; Hagerty & Rubinov, 2019; Holt, 2018; Liu, 2020; Majumdar & Chattopadhyay, 2020; Nadikattu, 2016; Naidu, 2019; Tai, 2020; Trappl, 1987). Although there are many studies that show the social impact of artificial intelligence, but the social aspect was chosen deliberately by authors in order to confirm its importance especially because of the change in social communication in society after the entry of social media, where the form of social communication has changed to be through screens and smart phones, which reduced of face-to-face social communication that eventually caused the social-media silence phenomenon. Most of literatures in AI highlighted on the Social Impact in societal sectors. Nevertheless, there is a little attention on studying the aspect of AI robots that are dealing with humans. The authors argue that these issues might face problems with the creation of emotions for robots that are dealing with people. On a similar note, there are relevant researches concerning in the Impact of AI on youth (Hasse, Cortesi, Lombana-Bermudez, & Gasser, 2019; Howley III, 2019; Penn, 2020; United Nations Children's Fund (UNICEF), 2012), but their results were before the spread of Covid 19 and imposing preventive measures by social distancing, thus during this period, social communication became virtual, which requires to research again and comparing the results if they will be the same or will have new results.

### Chapter Lists

1. **The Importance of Artificial Intelligence in Society (IAIS):**
   a.  The Importance of AI in developed societies:

It is important to highlight on the importance of the privacy and safety issues of AI systems, so these issues have become even more important in the context of telecommunications and service provider networks, given their impact on society and the potential for harm to users (FCC's Technological Advisory Council, 2021, 19). The examples of the contribution of AI in the growth Global South are two areas: (1) supporting new businesses and innovation, (2) optimizing economic building blocks such as financial service (Smith & Neupane, 2018, 51). The strategic importance of AI is evaluated according to its importance to society members who use its technologies, so the social can be considered a direct consequence of the strategic importance of AI in the development of advanced technologies. However, this does not mean that any type or degree of technological growth whatsoever is socially acceptable (Arbib et al, 1987, 86).

b.    The Importance of AI in developing societies:

The absence of the AI development in developing countries that the world is witnessing in makes its importance not evident fully in these countries. A few areas, which are particularly relevant to developing countries, such as Health Care in developing countries, which are endemically short of medical workers. Primary care in particular involves many routine procedural tasks, which makes up a significant part of the work of doctors. Even starting from here could be a huge win for developing countries. (Oxford Government Review, 2018, 25). In Industry, and Innovation AI is a frontier technology by nature. Adaption of AI will generally bring innovative ways of production and enhance productivity. In Agriculture for example, recent advances in image recognition allowed researchers to help identify crop diseases at sites using smartphones (United Nations, 2017, 6). In Education, AI systems designed to support teachers in delivering better content. Like all humans, no teacher is perfect, AI system is harder to create than the educational AI described above, but it would be valuable. (Oxford Government Review, 2018, 25). Presently with the onset of the COVID-19 pandemic, the method of distance-education has been completely relied upon due to the imposition of safety measures and the prevention of gatherings during last past two years. However, some developing countries are considering the entry of AI into them is kind of luxury, because they have more important priorities than AI techniques, from their point of view, and these priorities are about less developed matters, but these countries couldn't achieve these priorities yet. Artificial Intelligence has a key role to play in the world of technology of developing nations like Nigeria, where almost everything is done manually there, despite the fact that we now live in the time where a lot of works are taken over by machines (Artificial Intelligence) (Robinson, 2018, 38).

2.    **Artificial Intelligence's Fields in Society (AIFS):**
    a.    Economics and Labor Market:

AI is important in economic development, where AI can increase productivity by creating new specialized competencies through improving automation processes. A 2017 PwC report estimated that "AI could contribute up to $15.7 trillion to the global economy in 2030, more than the current output of China and India combined", stemming from productivity gains through businesses automating processes and augmenting their existing labor force with AI technologies (Smith & Neupane, 2018, 51). The low cost of producing AI tools is an essential reason that makes AI production is increasing over time rapidly. A phenomenal drop in computing costs has led to an explosion in installed computing power and storage capacity. Simple smartphones today are significantly more powerful than the computer that brought the first man to the moon. The costs for producing an iPhone 7, for instance, currently stands at around US$220; in the 1980s it would have been around US$1.2 million (Naidu, 2019, 4). Besides, a range of factors play a role in shaping the impact of AI on employment, including political, economic, and cultural elements, as well as the capabilities and technical features of AI technologies. Using the best available research evidence from across disciplines can help develop policies that share across society the benefits of these technology-enabled changes (The G7 Science Academies, 2019, 3). Therefore, there is a high competitiveness among manufacturers of AI tools in the labor markets in order to raise their profit rates. Nevertheless, the resulting disparity may fall disproportionately along lines of race, class, and gender; research anticipating the economic and societal impact of such disparity could be useful (Russell; Dewey; Tegmark, 2015, 106).

   b.   Industry and Agriculture:

   Artificial intelligence programs have an essential role in manufacturing process and in many industries, as they are programmed effectively to carry out many tasks efficiently with the speed in productivity. Thus AI programs save time and effort with this high productivity that also save production cost which increase financial profits. The industry has to arrive at a consensus on these guidelines to enable policy makers to devise accurate legislations (Walch, 2020, 73). Therefore, there is a necessity requires setting clear guidelines and legislations that are related to using AI tools, especially legislations that are related to user privacy, as these legislations are punishing whom violate them. There is a need for appropriate law and control mechanisms for AI because in the upcoming future, there will be an increase in the use of AI (Nigerian Communications Commission, 2020, 26). In many countries in the Global South, agriculture is an important component of the economy, and much of the population relies on farming as a source of food. However, healthy crops and successful harvests can fall prey to disease, insects, and drought. Moreover, countries in the Global South are still depending mostly on traditional agriculture, despite of the development in agricultural methods, but farmers are depending on manual labor methods instead of modern agricultural methods (Smith & Neupane, 2018, 42). Improving accuracy of cognitive computing technologies such as image recognition is changing agriculture. Traditionally, agriculture has relied on the eyes and hands of experienced farmers to identify the right crops to pick. Thus, the entry of AI into the agricultural has brought a quantum leap by increasing the productivity of agricultural crops, as AI facilitates the farmers' task of by the entry of robots. "Harvesting" robots equipped with AI technologies and data from cameras and sensors can now make this decision in real time. This type of robot can increasingly perform tasks that previously required human labor and knowledge (OECD, 2019, 52).

   c.   Education and Innovation:

   The role of AI systems appears in educating process by distance learning, so that AI-fueled curriculum plans built on the foundations of AI systems, which provide a systematic, structured form of education. AI-fueled curriculum plans, often referred to as "curriculum playlists," and intelligent tutoring systems, offer personalized learning experiences for youth, adapting instruction and feedback to students' capabilities and needs. Whereas the system curates for each student through daily-individualized learning activities based on a curriculum, and the latter through one-to-one tutoring that aims to mimic human tutoring (Hasse, 2019, 9). High school graduation is associated with relatively higher overall lifetime earnings and life expectancy, and lower rates of unemployment and incarceration. However, there are some specializations of college graduates may not find opportunities in the labor market, so this problem requires of AI systems creating a balance by collecting data of students by giving them the advice for studying a specific university majors that have job opportunities in the labor market. These systems are able to create a balance between different academic disciplines, in addition to their ability to link education inputs and outputs to meet the requirements of the labor market. Interventions can help those falling behind in their educational goals, but given limited resources, such programs must focus on the right students at the right time and with the right message. Over the past several years, several school districts around the US have been collaborating with universities to develop AI based systems to help them identify at risk students who are unlikely to finish high school on time (Hager et al, 2017, 12). Some AI programs have high efficiency as speed in performance, which make them outperform more than human performance. Despite the ability of the human workforce to do the same tasks, but sometimes humans may not have the same speed or in case the employees accomplish tasks at the same duration, they may not have done them as same quality as smart machines in big factories. In addition, artificially intelligent technology (robots) involves smart machines that process a large amount of data that a human being cannot be in position to perform. By so robotics are assuming repetitive duties that require creativity and knowledge base (Shabbir; Anwer, 2015, 2). To be successful, AI innovations will need to overcome understandable human fears of being marginalized. There are concerns related to the extent of the skill of smart machines that they may cause high rates of unemployment due to the preference of using them instead of human labor in many factories. As well as several companies employed robots who have taken administrative positions that were occupied by human staff previously. AI will likely replace tasks rather than jobs in the near term, and will also create new kinds of jobs. (Holt, 2018, 43).

    d.    Health Care and Environment:

AI offers significant potential benefits in the systems that support decision-making in health and care. Structural problems in this field can lead to diagnostic errors, possible failure of expertise and inefficient communication of information among researches, engineering and clinical worlds. Many AI medical devices can detect and diagnose diseases accurately more than traditional medical examinations that rely on asking about the patient's symptoms to diagnose the disease case, while modern AI devices can detect many emerging diseases, in addition to diagnose of the patient's condition accurately. AI can help assess huge amounts of research publications, spot unlikely, weak correlations in huge data sets, analyze images, and other data produced by the healthcare systems and develop new technologies (The G7 Science Academies, 2019, 4). AI applications in healthcare and pharmaceuticals can help detect health conditions early, deliver preventative services, optimise clinical decision-making, and discover new treatments and medications. AI applications not only provide accurate diagnosis for diseased cases, but also provide the appropriate prescriptions. They can facilitate personalised healthcare and precision medicine, while powering self-monitoring tools, applications and trackers. AI in healthcare offers potential benefits for quality and cost of care (OECD, 2019, 61). The entry of AI into the environmental field helped in providing precautionary and preventive measures to face during environmental disasters such as hurricanes and forest fires, beside how to act in such situations. Artificial Intelligence has been applied to environmental management problems as, for example, in using expert systems advising emergency response teams about how to deal with industrial accidents, in using expert systems to assist in granting hazardous waste site permits, in modeling water quality, fish stock prediction, and many other environmental engineering applications (Cortés, Sànchez-Marrè, Ceccaroni, Rodríguez-Roda, & Poch, 2000, 78-79). Artificial intelligence provides tools for the meaningful manipulation of qualitative knowledge like ecological relationships into a computer-friendly quantitative form, which can be used to arrive at a qualitative decision. AI applications help environmental researchers by their delving into the environmental science and trying to control it. The limits of artificial intelligence are not discovered yet in the development of ecology, as the application is premature, and is expected to be exposed in the coming decade (Naidu, 2019, 5).

3. **Requirements of Artificial Intelligence in Society (RAIS):**
   a. Technical Requirements of AI:

There are several requirements that must be met in artificial intelligence systems, including technical requirements that have been developed based on foundations that meet the needs of society. Technical Requirements For human-centered AI based systems a. Interpretability. b. Explainability. c. Fairness/ equality/Unbiasedness. d. Transparency and Trustworthiness. e. Safety/Security. f. Ethics (Fagbola; Thakur, 2019, 201-202). Modern AI tools are produced to meet community needs and requirements. So people expect of AI to make many daily tasks easier for them by using smart applications for instance to pay bills by cellphone apps, that had changed after AI apps for paying which required going to several places and waiting in queues for paying bills monthly. Takes into account the context of use of the technology by looking at both technology capability and non-technical requirements such as business requirements, regulatory and policy requirements, application domain needs, and ethical and societal concerns (Diab, 2020, 11).

   b. Requirements of AI in developing societies:

One of problems that developing countries may face is the lack of experience in using AI applications, which may be high cost for developing countries. AI applications in medical care have the potential to fill gaps in developing countries. Sometimes developing countries lack experienced teachers or qualified doctors who need to keep abreast of the latest medical developments and receive the training on modern medical devices. UNESCO study shows that 27.3 million primary school teachers will need to be recruited worldwide, and remarked that trained teachers are in short supply in many countries. Energy is a cornerstone for sustainable development in the region. AI-powered automation may replace some repetitive jobs and create new types of AI or IT related jobs. AI is a frontier technology by nature. Adaption of AI will generally bring innovative ways of production and enhance productivity. AI has immense potential for developing countries is in increasing agricultural efficiency (United Nations, 2017, 6-7). In May 2019, the UN System Chief Executives Board for Coordination (CEB) adopted a UN system-wide strategic approach and roadmap for supporting capacity development on AI. It outlines an internal plan to support capacity development efforts related to AI technologies, especially for developing countries, with a particular emphasis on the 'bottom billion', in the context of achieving the SDGs. Many international organizations seek to enhance and support the effectiveness of policies that are related to AI by developing plans for developing countries, as these plans take into account the social specificity within some developing countries that marginalize the role of women, while these plans target is the empowerment of women and girls in those countries. Furthermore, it has a specific commitment to maintain strong ethical and human rights guardrails, ensuring that AI developments do not exceed the capacity to protect society, particularly marginalized, vulnerable and the poorest populations, including women and girls (United Nations, 2021, 9).

4. **The Effect of Artificial Intelligence on Society (EAIS):**
   a. The Effect of AI on Society since the beginning to the present day:

The historical starting point was in the 50s of the last century in the work of the logician and mathematician Alan Turing, who asked in his research whether a machine could think? Can a machine perform same functions that humans are doing? For example, Turing has famous experiment, which is considered a reference in the Artificial Intelligence Test, where two human persons and a computer are placed in a closed room, with hidden identities of the two persons from each other and from the computer. If these persons cannot distinguish the verbal or written speech between the computer and the human person, which means that this computer is intelligent (Gamoura; Muhammed; Crouch, 2018, 6). The middle of the twentieth century, with its particular technological, cultural, and intellectual climate, gave birth to a new scientific discipline: artificial intelligence (AI). The development of AI technologies has taken a place relatively rapidly, for example, the development of producing new generations of smart phones. Thus, the newborn is growing relatively rapidly compared to other scientific disciplines, and is already approaching adolescence (Arbib et al, 1987, 89). The link between AI term and society is clearly visible. As of today, AI is a word that is highly relevant socially as in industries and businesses. The technology of AI is a crucial lynchpin concerning in digitization or digital transformation taking over things today. Some companies position themselves in such a way that they can capitalize on the ever-increasing data amounts being collected and generated (Nadikattu, 2016, 909). Even though some people believe intelligent machines could one day replace humans, having intelligent robots in the workplace would create safer and more efficient work environments, which complement humans instead of completely replacing them. There are some concerns about the possibility of relying completely on doing jobs by robots, which are considered as coming to take away their jobs from humans. On the other hand relying on doing jobs by robots refer to provide an integrated manner of work in achieving tasks by either robots or human employees, according to the kind of tasks. Currently people use artificial intelligence to make intelligent machines to help those in need (Holt, 2018, 3).

   b.    The Effect of AI on different age groups:

   AI will not only influence how youth work, but also how they play. Social technologies that collect large amounts of user data and video games that incorporate AI-powered characters are popular with youth (social media platforms, such as Facebook and Twitter, and video games such as Rocket League or No Man's Sky). AI applications are very popular, especially among young generation, these trends necessitate an understanding of how young people's data is being used — in the context of play/leisure, education, and other domains — and how youth can effectively navigate privacy and safety concerns surrounding AI-driven technologies (Hasse, 2019, 15). Today, children are fluent in using smartphones at early age, and they are experiencing distance learning through artificial intelligence applications due to the emerging epidemic of the Covid-19 virus. Despite the importance and advantages of AI applications, the current health circumstances have reduced their social communication with peers by playing outdoors instead of playing through game applications, which have a negative effect on children's social intelligence. Many children today grow up surrounded by AI-powered voice assistants that sound or act human. The concern is that it is unknown how this interaction will influence children's wellbeing? Research done by MIT shows early evidence that interactions between children and AI devices may alter children's perception of their own intelligence (Howley, 2019, 16). Many of adolescents expressed awareness that companies sell data to third parties and that as a result, companies should also shoulder responsibility for the safe use of their AI-powered products (United Nations Children's Fund (UNICEF), 2021, 15). Many teenagers use game applications that asked to insert some personal information for completing the registration, so that they give personal information to start using these games without giving awareness if these games are safe and trusted. Policy makers, in partnership with youth, can reduce the strong influence of technological... just as time limits on the working day have led to greater productivity and satisfaction at work, the exercise of limits on advanced digital technologies will improve life for the next generation (Penn, 2020, 3). The young are the most affected on social media by disinformation (fake news or life) when browsing photos on social media that may not be real or even exist, but its negative impact on teenagers is still exist through their tries to imitate what they see on social media. Many teenagers are affected by certain fashion trends, especially teenage girls are tending to become fashionistas, so their interest is limited inside smartphone screens to get large number likes for their photos and large number views for their videos in order to be famous by attracting the largest number of followers on social media.

5. **Advantages & Disadvantages of Artificial Intelligence on Society (ADAIS):**
   a.   Advantages of AI in the sectors of society:

In principle, algorithms and domain-specific AIs bring many advantages. Algorithms are important in developing AI systems, whose advantages are increasing with the continuous developing of systems by creating better versions of previous ones with every new update of AI systems. They have influenced our lives for the better and are expected to keep doing so at an ever-increasing rate in the future, provided that the necessary precautions are taken (Mannino et al, 2015, 4). AI will dramatically improve the efficiency of the workplace and maybe augment the work done by humans. One of AI advantage when it entered the field of jobs was the competition within the work environment between human employees and AI systems by demonstrating efficiency in their performance comparing to the efficiency in performance by AI systems, which accompanied by increased productivity rates for these businesses. As AI is taking over dangerous and repetitive tasks, it frees up the manual labor involved so that people can apply the same rigor in other jobs that are better for them, such as tasks involving empathy and creativity. People should work in more engaging posts, which will increase job satisfaction and happiness (Nadikattu, 2016, 909).

   b.   Disadvantages of AI in the sectors of society:

The use of artificial intelligence by replacing human subjects, it brings general problem of putting people out of work. Companies, which make use of artificial intelligence, rely on reducing the number of human subjects with whom they are involved. The idea of replacing employees with AI systems is a possibility in many cases, as it is considered a problem that causes losing of jobs to some employees. On one hand the lack of an alternative solution after employees are laid off from work. On the other hand, the available opportunities to do the same jobs companies are also employing AI systems instead of these laid-off employees. The case, therefore, brings in some major problems given the fact that it reduces the number of people who have the chance of benefiting from the different employment opportunities that could be put across by such companies (Nadimpalli, 2017, 4). A huge social change that disrupts the way of living in the human community will occur. Humankind has to be industrious to make their living, but with the service of AI, we can just program the machine to do a thing for us without even lifting a tool. Human closeness will be gradually diminishing, as AI will replace the need for people to meet face to face for idea exchange. AI will stand in between people, as the personal gathering will no longer be needed for communication" (Tai, 2021, 340). One of disadvantages that is produced by AI systems in society was social-media silence phenomenon, which associated with the absence of realistic face-to-face social interaction. Moreover, this phenomenon is observed frequently in many public places, where several people are sitting together but they are busy with their smartphones and talking to each other by social media or chatting virtually with other people. It is not only exist at public places as cafes, but also at homes when family members are sitting together in the same room, but they are not talking to each other, but talking to other people by social media. Thus, as social media made the world as a small village, but on the other hand, it makes a distance among people who are actually close in distance sharing the same house or even sharing the same room. Although some articles have addressed the relationship between the social and the technical, they have rarely moved beyond identifying problems in each area. Thus, the efforts have not added up to a holistic and comprehensive solution. In our view, this results from a selective perception of what algorithmic (UN) fairness is: some researchers see it as a technical phenomenon and seek solutions in technology (Dolata; Feuerriegel; & Schwabe, 2021, 20).

## 6.    Challenges facing Artificial Intelligence in Society (CAIS):

AI can analyze different collected information of various nature. This has brought in greatest concerns over data protection, cyber security as well as data privacy (Majumdar; Chattopadhyay, 2020, 307). One of challenges that facing AI is the issue of privacy penetration and customer's concerns about the privacy and the protection of their personal data. The growth of AI across sectors, societies, and economies brings complex, inter-connected challenges can be bucketed together under four AI 'topics' that are at the forefront of APAC policy-makers' discussions as they define and frame national approaches to AI: Infrastructure, Access to data, Skills and human capital, Trust and partnerships and Ecosystem and entrepreneurship (International Institute of Communications, 2020, 9-11). The AI capabilities demonstrated by the Stanford study give a glimpse into how AI can threaten privacy: both through the rampant collection of data and the capacity for de-anonymizing subjects. In conclusion, these concerns have recently been documented in a report by human rights organizations Article 19 and Privacy International, which notes "AI-driven consumer products . . . are frequently equipped with sensors that generate and collect vast amounts of data without the knowledge or consent of those in its proximity (Latonero, 2018, 14). In addition to high efficiency and quality in performance that characterize artificial intelligence systems, unlike humans, for example computers are able to share entire content of their memory – and thus their complete knowledge – in seconds with other computers. Thus with AI learning can be distributed (Ertel, 2019, 21). AI-driven technologies have a pattern of entrenching social divides and exacerbating social inequality, particularly among historically marginalized groups (Hagerty; Rubinov, 2019, 2). This marginalization appears clearly between developed countries and developing countries that are lacking capability to produce AI tools or even buy them. The data that AI technology is using to train and learn mostly does not cover all the aspect of human behaviour. Intelligence comes from learning, whether you are human or machine. Systems usually have a training phase in which they "learn" to detect the right patterns and act according to their input (Hussein; Halimu; Siddique, 2020, 18). There is a challenge facing AI systems by inability to predict the social behavior of humans, due to be programmed according to specific system with static solutions. While in many cases, the behavior of individuals or customers' needs dynamic solution or behaviour, while robot is dealing with humans in same way regardless of their unexpected reactions. There is often a disconnect between the design and application stages of an AI project. This is especially critical if the system is to be applied in humanitarian contexts. The tools may be designed without adequate contextual knowledge; often they are developed to be suitable for business and marketing decision-making rather than for humanitarian aid in the developing world (Pizzi; Romanoff; Engelhard, 2020, 155).

### 7. The Future Perspective of Artificial Intelligence in Society (FPAIS):

Questions tend around the future of work frame and crop up in discussions on AI. By future of work, mean the effect of AI on the supply of and demand for human labor. With the technology still rising and smart intelligent robots have been developed, we may see a future where individuals are being paid just for being citizens which will be important in helping to combat the job-stealing automation (Hussein; Halimu; Siddique, 2020, 17). The key focus of anxiety in this space is the extent to which advances in AI enable artificial agents to do tasks cheaply and there by replace human agents who earn income by doing those tasks (Osoba; Welser, 2017, 8). There are concerns about future perceptions of AI systems is the possibility of finding effective alternative solutions for unemployment and privacy protection issues. While data protection, transparency, and accountability mechanisms go far toward mitigating human rights abuses in the use of AI, they do not solve all of the foreseeable problems. For instance, in the future, AI systems may substantially affect economic opportunities or facilitate war or conflict globally (Andersen, 2018, 35). AI will have all the advantages of colonize the world without the help of human beings. In the near future, self-replicating AI could be made where human colonies beyond the earth will never have potentials to fight in the free space with critical terms. The future Artificial Intelligence in various regions in the world may be because of various investigation technologies such as stellar travel (Shabbir; Anwer, 2015, 7). The achievements of AI do not stop at a certain point; it also aspires to develop for reaching more broadly far places in outer space, where humans always aspired to live on other planets, which AI systems are seeking to achieve in the future in order to provide sustainable development, that is one of the most important topics about the future of humanity by securing and providing sustainable resources for future generations, which requiring developed plans by AI systems because of their ability to store and process huge data for planning in the process of sustainable development. (The International Development Innovation Alliance (IDIA), 2019, 7).

## SOLUTIONS AND RECOMMENDATIONS

In the final analysis, social impact is shown clearly that Artificial Intelligence is gradually reducing of face-to-face social communication and the notable example about this is (social-media silence phenomenon) by daily overuse of social media.

The interest in the delivery of Artificial Intelligence tools to developing countries is only theoretical perceptions issue.

The future researches have to search deeply about the social impact of Artificial Intelligence on young people because they are always influenced easily by new trends especially the teenagers.

## FUTURE RESEARCH DIRECTIONS

The future trends of Artificial Intelligence promise in a better life, where the main dependence will be on Artificial Intelligence, so that humans will enjoy their lives while robots are doing jobs and services for society.

## CONCLUSION

In conclusion, Artificial Intelligence achieves many benefits in: society, economic, educational, industrial, and agricultural and health...etc. On the other hand, AI faces some crises that are resulted of the usage of Artificial Intelligence, such as unemployment. In addition to the fact that developing countries need developed of Artificial Intelligence tools, where the majority of these countries still doing works manually, despite of the technical development in the world. As for Artificial Intelligence devices, there are a large proportion of flaws in their applications in the social field, such as the use of social media that allows anyone to post posts easily, but these posts may contain disinformation and fake news or sometimes these posts are just a personal opinion about something that may be wrong and not related to the truth at all. On the other hand, if AIs will replace humans so many questions arise; can mechanical translation become perfect that it will take the human translator's role in the future? Is it possible to reach the desired location by providing the exact and the shortest-distance directions by map applications easily? Will the weather forecast app be able to give a more punctual about weather? Will robots be able to give expressions of sympathy and feeling?

## ACKNOWLEDGMENT

This research received no specific grant from any funding agency in the public, commercial, or not-for-profit sectors.

## REFERENCES

Arbib, M.A., & ... (1987). *Impacts of Artificial Intelligence Scientific, Technological, Military, Economic, Societal, Cultural, and Political*. Elsevier Science Publishing Company.

Cortés, U., Sànchez-Marrè, M., Ceccaroni, L., R-Roda, I., & Poch, M. (2000). Artificial Intelligence and Environmental Decision Support Systems. *Applied Intelligence*, *13*(1), 77–91. doi:10.1023/A:1008331413864

Diab, W. (2020). *Artificial Intelligence*. SC 42 Overview, ITU Workshop on AI and Data Commons, Switzerland.

Dolata, M., Feuerriegel, S., & Schwabe, G. (2021). A Sociotechnical View of Algorithmic Fairness. *Information Systems Journal*. Retrieved from https://arxiv.org/ftp/arxiv/papers/2110/2110.09253.pdf

Ertel, W. (2019). *Artificial Intelligence and Society*. Retrieved from https://www.researchgate.net/publication/342110375

Fagbola, T.M., & Thakur, S.C. (2019). *Towards the Development of Artificial Intelligence-based Systems: Human-Centered Functional Requirements and Open Problems*. Artificial Intelligent, Robotics, and Human-Computer Interaction, China.

FCC's Technological Advisory Council. (2021). *The Importance of Artificial Intelligence and Data for the Telecommunications Industry and the FCC*. Working Group on Artificial Intelligence and Computing. Retrieved from https://www.fcc.gov/sites/default/files/fcc_aiwg_2020_whitepaper_final.pdf

Gamoura, S.C., Muhammed, B., & Crouch, H. (2018, November). *Artificial Intelligence Between Reality And Hope: A Technical and Field Study*. International Forum "Artificial Intelligence: A New Challenge to Law?", Algeria.

Hager, G.D. (2017). *Artificial Intelligence for Social Good*. Computing Community Consortium, Washington.

Hagerty, A., & Rubinov, I. (2019). *Global AI Ethics: A Review of the Social Impacts and Ethical Implications of Artificial Intelligence*. Retrieved from https://arxiv.org/ftp/arxiv/papers/1907/1907.07892.pdf

Hasse, A., Cortesi, S., Lombana-Bermudez, A., & Gasser, U. (2019). Youth and Artificial Intelligence: Where We Stand. Berkman Klein Center for Internet & Society at Harvard University.

Holt, M. (2018). *Artificial Intelligence in Modern Society*. Murray State University. Retrieved from https://digitalcommons.murraystate.edu/cgi/viewcontent.cgi?article=1148&context=bis437

Howley III, R.J. (2019). *The Effects of Artificial Intelligence on the Youth* [Master's Thesis]. Utica College.

Hussein, B.R., Halimu, C., & Siddique, M.T. (2020, November). The Future of Artificial Intelligence and its Social. *Economic and Ethical Consequences. International Conference on Advances in Computing and Technology: Virtual.*

Karnouskos, S. (2017). *The Interplay of Law, Robots and Society, in an Artificial Intelligence Era* [Master's Thesis]. Umeå University.

Latonero, M. (2018). *Governing Artificial Intelligence: Upholding Human Rights & Dignity. Data & Society.* Retrieved from https://datasociety.net/wp-content/uploads/2018/10/DataSociety_Governing_Artificial_Intelligence_Upholding_Human_Rights.pdf

Liu, Z. (2021). *Sociological perspectives on artificial intelligence: A typological reading.* John Wiley & Sons Ltd. Retrieved from https://onlinelibrary.wiley.com/doi/epdf/10.1111/soc4.12851

Majumdar, D., & Chattopadhyay, H.K. (2020, October). Artificial intelligence and its impacts on the society. *International Journal of Law*, *6*(5), 306–310.

Mannino, A. (2015). *Artificial Intelligence: Opportunities and Risks*. Policy Paper. The Effective Altruism Foundation.

Nadikattu, R.R. (2016, September). The Emerging Role of Artificial Intelligence in Modern Society. *International Journal of Creative Research Thoughts*, *4*(4), 906–911. https://www.researchgate.net/publication/343179789

Nadimpalli, M. (2017, June). Artificial Intelligence Risks and Benefits. *International Journal of Innovative Research in Science, Engineering and Technology*, *6*(6). https://www.researchgate.net/publication/319321806

Naidu, A. (2019). *Review: Impact of Artificial Intelligence on Society*. Working Paper Series. Centre for Society and Policy, India.

Nigerian Communications Commission. (2020). *Ethical and Societal Impact Of Artificial Intelligence (AI)*. Retrieved from https://www.ncc.gov.ng/docman-main/research-development/919-ethical-and-societal-impact-of-artificial-intelligence-ai/file

OECD. (2019). *Artificial Intelligence in Society*. OECD Publishing. doi:10.1787/eedfee77-

Onyx, J. (2014, May). A Theoretical Model of Social Impact. *Cosmopolitan Civil Societies Journal, 6*(1), 1-18. Retrieved from https://www.researchgate.net/profile/Jenny-Onyx/publication/272731688_Social_Impact_a_Theoretical_Model/links/566f51cb08aecdcd235625d4/Social-Impact-a-Theoretical-Model.pdf?origin=publication_detail

Osoba, O.A., & Welser, IV, W. (2017). *The Risks of Artificial Intelligence to Security and the Future of Work*. RAND Corporation.

Oxford Government Review. (2018). *How AI Could Transform Developing Countries*. Retrieved from https://pathwayscommission.bsg.ox.ac.uk/sites/default/files/inline-files/How%20AI%20could%20trans-form%20developing%20countries_0.pdf

Penn, J. (2020, October). *AI and Youth 2020: Win the Battle, Lose the War?* Youth Knowledge Forum, 'New Times, New Methods' Exploring youth research methods in the context of COVID-19, European Union–Council.

Pizzi, M., Romanoff, M., & Engelhardt, T. (2021). AI for humanitarian action: Human rights and ethics. *International Review of the Red Cross, 102*(913), 145–180.

Robinson, R.N. (2018, December). Artificial Intelligence: Its Importance, Challenges and Applications in Nigeria. *Direct Research Journal of Engineering and Information Technology, 5*(5), 36–41.

Russell, S., Dewey, D., & Tegmark, M. (2015). *Research Priorities for Robust and Beneficial Artificial Intelligence*. Association for the Advancement of Artificial Intelligence.

Shabbir, J., & Anwer, T. (2015, August). Artificial Intelligence and its Role in Near Future. *Journal of Latex Class Files, 14*(8), 1–11. https://arxiv.org/pdf/1804.01396

Smith, M.L., & Neupane, S. (2018). *Artificial Intelligence And Human Development*. International Development Research Centre.

Tai, M. C.-T. (2020, August). The impact of artificial intelligence on human society and bioethics. *Tzu-Chi Medical Journal, 32*(4), 339–343. doi:10.4103/tcmj.tcmj_71_20 PMID:33163378

The G7 Science Academies. (2020). *Artificial Intelligence and Society*. Summit of the G7 Science Academies Artificial Intelligence and Society, France.

The International Development Innovation Alliance (IDIA). (2019). *Artificial Intelligence and International Development: An Introduction*. The AI & Development Working Group of (IDIA). Retrieved from https://static1.squarespace.com/static/5b156e3bf2e6b10bb0788609/t/5e1f0a37e723f0468c1a77c8/1579092542334/AI+and+international+Development_FNL.pdf

Trappl, R. (1987). Impacts of Artificial Intelligence: Scientific, Technological, Military, Economic, Societal, Cultural, And Political. Elsevier Science Publishers B.V.

United Nations. (2017). Artificial Intelligence in Asia and the Pacific. Economic and Social Commission for Asia and the Pacific (ESCAP).

United Nations. (2021). *Resource Guide On Artificial Intelligence (AI) Strategies*. United Nations Office of the Secretary-General's Envoy on Technology.

United Nations Children's Fund (UNICEF). (2021). *Adolescent Perspectives on Artificial Intelligence: A Report on Consultations with Adolescents across the World.* Office of Global Insight and Policy.

Wright, J., & Atkinson, D. (2019, August). *The impact of artificial intelligence within the recruitment industry: Defining a new way of recruiting. WEI International Academic Conference on Business, Economics, Management and Finance.*

## ADDITIONAL READING

Andersen, L. (2018). *Human Rights in the Age of Artificial Intelligence.* Retrieved from https://www.accessnow.org/cms/assets/uploads/2018/11/AI-and-Human-Rights.pdf

Jha, S., & Topol, E. J. (2018, February). Information and Artificial Intelligence. *Journal of the American College of Radiology, 15*(3), 509–511. doi:10.1016/j.jacr.2017.12.025 PMID:29398501

Marwala, L., & Nkomfe, M. (2016). *The Fourth Industrial revolution and the case for equitable distribution of income.* Retrieved from https://ujcontent.uj.ac.za/vital/access/services/Download/uj:41922/SOURCE1

Raynor, W.J. (1999). *The International Dictionary of Artificial Intelligence.* Glenlake Publishing Company.

The International Institue of Communications. (2020). *Artificial Intelligence in the Asia-Pacific Region: Examining policies and strategies to maximise AI readiness and adoption.* The International Institute of Communications.

## KEY TERMS AND DEFINITIONS

**Developing Countries:** They are countries, some of them have the resources and some other lack to the resources, but they share facing great difficulties and obstacles to develop these resources.

**Development:** It is a process based on improving and developing the resources available to individuals.

**Inequality:** It is the lack of equality between individuals or countries.

**Privacy:** It is the personal information and data of individuals that no one has the right to know about without the permission of the concerned person him/herself.

**Productivity:** It is a result of planned work that plays role in determining whether the productivity is high or low.

**Robots:** They are Artificial Intelligence Devices that are equipped with programs that reflect the image as a person automatically.

**Safety of Artificial Intelligence Systems:** It is a system based on high protection of personal data for customers, and users of artificial intelligence applications

**Sustainable-Development:** A process aims to preserve available resources and rationalize consumption in order to ensure the survival for future generations.

**Unemployment:** Is a state of individuals are not doing a job despite their ability to do it.

# Section 12
# Computational Intelligence

**A**

# AI-Based Emotion Recognition

**Mousami Prashant Turuk**

(iD) https://orcid.org/0000-0002-0103-9789

*Pune Institute of Computer Technology, India*

**Sreemathy R.**

*Pune Institute of Computer Technology, India*

**Shardul Sandeep Khandekar**

*Pune Institute of Computer Technology, India*

**Soumya Sanjay Khurana**

(iD) https://orcid.org/0000-0001-7336-1382

*Pune Institute of Computer Technology, India*

## INTRODUCTION

Due to the recent advancements in technology, humans can interact with computers in ways that were previously unimaginable. Human-computer interaction is a multi-disciplinary field that focuses on designing computer technology to ease the interaction between computers and humans. New modalities such as voice and gestures are used to interact with computers that extend the traditional methods confined to keyboard and mouse. For human-to-human communication, voice and vision play a significant role. Thus, it is desirable for computers to comprehend the environment from visual as well as audio cues. This desire is supported by the growth in computer vision, natural language processing and the era of machine learning and deep learning which has helped to model the real world. Machine learning has provided a means for machines to extract useful information from images as well as speech. Various machine learning applications like image classification, image segmentation, object detection, text understanding and pattern recognition are being used on a day-to-day basis. Even with such advancements in the field, machines still fail to understand the 'emotion' of the person and this might lead to a failure in understanding the context provided entirely. In the current era of Industry 4.0, due to the availability of huge amounts of data, industries in every field are using artificial intelligence to tackle the problem of pattern recognition. Emotion is a mental or psychological state which is mainly associated with feelings, thought process and behavior of humans. Emotional state of a person conveys not only his mood but also his personality. Humans are able to exchange information through multiple domains like speech, text and visual images. In verbal communication, the same word expressed in different emotions can convey different meanings. Identification of emotional states using only audio cues is hence inadequate and needs to be in fusion with visual cues. This chapter aims to analyze and present a unified approach for audio-visual emotion recognition based on back propagation algorithm.

Emotion is a concept involving three components:

DOI: 10.4018/978-1-7998-9220-5.ch049

- Subjective experience.
- Expressions (audio-visual: face, gesture, posture, voice intonation, breathing noise).
- Biological arousal (heart rate, respiration frequency/intensity, perspiration, temperature, muscle tension, brain wave).

After recognizing universality within emotions despite the cultural differences, (Ekman et al., 1978). classified six emotional expressions to be universal: happiness, sadness, anger, disgust, surprise and fear.

Computer vision techniques have enabled the computer to understand the environment. Interacting with computers in voice and gesture modalities is much more natural for people, and the progression is towards the kind of interaction between humans. Despite these advances, one necessary ingredient for natural interaction is still missing, that is emotions. Emotions play an important role in human-to-human communication and interaction, allowing people to express them beyond the verbal domain. The ability to understand human emotions is desirable for the computer in some applications such as improving driver safety, medical conditions and lie detection. This chapter recognizes human emotions based on audio-visual cues.

Prosodic features in the audio and facial emotions exhibited on the face can help the computer make some inferences about the user's emotional state. The emotional frontier is the next obstacle to be surmounted in understanding humans. Facial expressions can be considered not only as the most natural form of displaying human emotions but also as a key non-verbal communication technique. If efficient methods can be brought about to automatically recognize these facial expressions, striking improvements can be achieved in the area of human computer interaction. Research in facial emotion recognition has been carried out in hope of attaining these enhancements. Moreover, there are other applications which can benefit from automatic facial emotion recognition. Artificial Intelligence has long relied on the area of facial emotion recognition to gain intelligence on how to model human emotions convincingly in robots. Recent improvements in this area have encouraged the researchers to extend the applicability of facial emotion recognition to areas like chat room avatars, video conferencing avatars, lie detection etc. The ability to recognize emotions can be valuable in face recognition applications. Suspect detection systems and intelligence improvement systems meant for children with brain development disorders are some other beneficiaries.

The area of human-computer interaction (HCI) will be much more effective if a computer is able to recognize the emotional state of human beings. Emotional states have a greater effect on the face which can predict the mood of the person. Faces are accessible windows into the mechanisms which governs emotional and social lives. About 70% of human communication is based on non-verbal communication such as facial expressions and body movements.

Despite the many theories, it is evident that people display these expressions to various degrees. One frequently studied task is the judgment of emotions—how well can human observers tell the emotional expressions of others, in the voice, on the face, etc.? Related questions are: Do these represent their true emotions? Can they be convincingly portrayed? How well can people conceal their emotions? In such tasks, researchers often use two different methods to describe the emotions.

One approach is to label the emotions in discrete categories, that is, human judges must choose from a prescribed list of word labels, such as joy, fear, love, surprise, sadness, etc. One problem with this approach is that the stimuli may contain blended emotions.

Also, the choice of words may be too restrictive, or culturally dependent. Another way is to have multiple dimensions or scales to describe emotions. Instead of choosing discrete labels, observers can indicate their impression of each stimulus on several continuous scales, like pleasant–unpleasant, atten-

*Figure 1. (a). Emotion model (Courtesy of Yang et al. (2008)), (b) Block Diagram of the proposed method, (c) Energy graphs for different emotions*

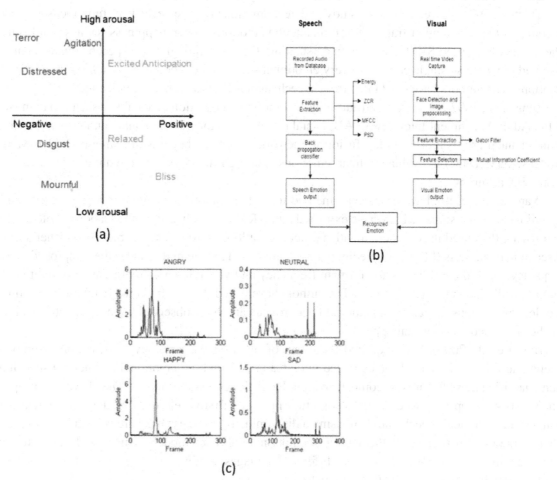

tion–rejection, simple–complicated, etc. Two common scales are valence and arousal. Valence describes the pleasantness of the stimuli, with positive (or pleasant) on one end, and negative (or unpleasant) on the other. Ideally, happiness has a positive valence, while disgust has a negative valence. The other dimension is arousal or activation. Sadness has low arousal, whereas surprise has high arousal level as shown in Figure 1(a).

Many machine-learning based methods have been proposed for handling emotion recognition problems. Audio recognition by (Alonso et. al., 2015; Dai et. al., 2015)., physiological by (Zheng et al., 2015; Chanel et al., 2015; Jatupaiboon et al., 2015). and visual signals have been explored for emotion recognition.

## BACKGROUND

In recent years, recognizing human emotions from facial expression and speech has exponentially increased attraction in the field of artificial intelligence due to its usage in human-computer interaction. Researchers have presented different methodologies to recognize human emotions through single and dual modalities such as affective speech or facial expression. A brief survey has been presented in this section to get the overview of the work accomplished by the researchers.

(Yu et al., 2001). have proposed a study to detect emotions from speech. The study focuses on short utterances of speech demonstrating four fundamental emotions: anger, happiness, sadness, and neutral. The authors have used SVM given the understanding that even though most speech signals cannot be assigned to a precise single category, every emotional state can be recognized as a mixture of multiple emotions. The authors have used pitch from speech signals as a fundamental voice feature.

(Zeng et al., 2007). have explored audio-visual emotion recognition in a realistic scenario in the form of the Adult Attachment Interview (AAI). Facial texture from the visual channel and prosody from the audio channel are then used with a fusion framework called Adaboost Multi-stream Hidden Markov Model (AdaMHMM) to evaluate human emotions. Through this approach the authors have achieved about 80% accuracy.

(Wang et al., 2008). have proposed a method for human emotion recognition using a combination of audio and visual signals. They have extracted audio features such as d by the Gabor wavelets. These features are then used in conjunction with a proposed multi-classifier scheme, based on Fisher's Linear Discriminant analysis (FLDA) to predict human emotions. This method reduces the dimprosodic, Mel-frequency cepstral coefficients and formant frequency and visual features representeensionality of the features while having better accuracy. The authors have tested this method on a database consisting of people from various language and cultural backgrounds and have observed the accuracy to be highest for the combined audio-visual approach.

(Busso et al., 2009). have explored the effect of pitch on the accuracy of detection of emotions through audio signals. They have extracted pitch features from both emotional and neutral speech and then quantified these features by comparing nested logistic regression models. They have also proposed a new two-step approach to emotion recognition in which firstly, reference models are trained using neutral and emotional speech and then, using a discriminator, a fitness measure is calculated to predict whether the input was closer to the neutral or emotional reference models. This model was tested on a database with over 20 emotions in three different languages, getting an accuracy of about 77% which was higher than previous conventional models

(Wu et al., 2010). have explored speech emotion recognition based on two main classifiers, the first based on acoustic-prosodic (AP) information and another one based on semantic labels (SL). They have used GMMs, SVMs, MLPs as three base classifier types in conjunction with a Meta Decision Tree (MDT) for the purpose of classifier fusion for AP and an existing knowledge base called HowNet to extract emotion association rules (EARs) for SL. The authors have tested the proposed methodology for four emotion states. The accuracy for the combination algorithm is higher as compared to the individual accuracies of the AP and SL based algorithms.

(Lajevardi et al., 2012). introduced a tensor perceptual color framework (TPCF) for facial expression recognition (FER), which is based on information contained in color facial images. The TPCF provides multilinear image analysis in different color spaces. Features are extracted using Log-Gabor filters. The mutual information quotient method is used for feature selection. These features are further classified using a multiclass linear discriminant analysis (LDA).

(Zhang et al., 2012). have investigated the performance of audio-visual emotion recognition against the respective individual performances of audio and visual emotion recognition. They have used local binary pattern (LBP) for facial expression recognition and typical acoustic features such as prosody, voice quality and MFCC for speech emotion recognition. These two modalities are then combined at a feature level and classified using an SVM. The authors have tested their algorithm on the eNTERFACE database and claim to get an accuracy of 66.51% which is higher than the individual accuracy of audio and visual recognition algorithms.

(Samantaray et al., 2015). have proposed a novel approach for the recognition of human emotions by combining prosody features (pitch, energy and zero crossing rate), quality features (Formant Frequencies, Spectral features), derived features (MFCC, LPCC) and dynamic features (Mel-Energy spectrum dynamic Coefficients). The features in conjunction with a multilevel SVM classifier have been used for the detection of seven discrete emotions (including anger, disgust, fear, happiness, sadness, neutral and surprise) in five native Assamese languages with an accuracy of more than 80%.

(Wei et al., 2016). proposed a facial emotion recognition method based on weighted features which is driven by the fact that emotion can be described by facial expression and each facial expression feature has a distinct impact on recognition results. The facial expression image is divided into uniform subregions to get the weighted feature of the Gaussian kernel. Support Vector Machine (SVM based classifier is used to differentiate Emotions). The authors have evaluated their algorithm on the Cohn-Kanade dataset with significantly higher precision of 93% when compared to SVM having a precision of 83%.

(Zheng et al., 2016). handled the issue of recognizing facial expression across domains. They have combined the source domain labeled facial image set with the target domain unlabeled auxiliary image set and applied the transductive transfer regularized least squares regression (TTRLSR) model. Based on the learned TTRLSR model, predictions of class labels are done for the auxiliary facial image set. SVM classifier is used to predict facial emotion using color-based facial features

(ELLaban et al., 2017). have proposed a real-time system to recognize 8 emotions confined to an E-learning environment. The authors have used the Viola-Jones algorithm to detect faces, gabor filters to extract the information for the detected region of interest, Principal Component Analysis to select the features. The authors have used k-NN and SVM classifiers to recognize emotions.

(Deshmukh et al., 2019). have explored two methods of emotion detection from audio signals using features, such as pitch, short term energy (STE) and Mel-frequency cepstral coefficients (MFCC). Once the features are extracted, they are passed to a classifier model which was trained on the North American English act and natural speech corpus. The authors also used regional databases in Hindi and Marathi to train and test their custom classifier on three different emotions. They have tested their model using a two and three feature extraction method to obtain accuracies of 61.5% and 79.5% respectively.

A majority of studies have been carried out in the field of human recognition focusing on either speech or facial expression alone. When one modality alone is not good enough to accurately determine an emotion, the performance or accuracy of recognition can be improved by taking into consideration the other modality. In some cases, similar facial expressions may have different vocal characteristics, and vocal emotions having similar properties may have distinct facial behaviors. Although these two modalities do not couple strongly in time, they seem to complement each other.

Most of the research works in the domain of speech emotion recognition are carried out of preprocessed databases that have audio cues stored as phrases in isolated forms. The machines are trained to recognize the speech emotion in isolated phrases or sentences. This limits the applications of speech emotion recognition. Also, the literature claims that even with both audio and video modalities being combined to achieve a high accuracy, it is still a challenge. Hence, it is crucial to develop a system with lower computational power using minimum features that function in real-time and possess the ability to model the emotional state of the user from continuous video and speech with high accuracy. The proposed method demonstrates the use of audio and video cues to determine the emotion of the person in real-time with high accuracy.

## SOLUTIONS AND RECOMMENDATIONS

The audio-visual based emotion recognition is elaborated in Figure 1(b). From the audio samples, the most prominent features like energy and MFCC are calculated. Texture based features from the Gabor filter with different orientations are extracted from the video samples and mutual information of the test images with respect to the reference images is calculated. Both audio and video features are then given to the neural classifier to accurately predict the universal human emotions like Happy, Anger, Sad and Neutral.

### Audio

Prominent features like energy, Mel Frequency Cepstrum Coefficients (MFCC), Zero Crossing Rate (ZCR), Power Spectral Density (PSD) and Discrete Cosine Transform (DCT) are extracted from the recorded audio signals.

### Energy

The energy associated with speech is time varying in nature and is subjected to variations of voice intensity. Hence, the interest for any automatic speech processing method is to detect the energy variations with time. It also gives energy to the short-term region of speech. By the nature of production, the speech signal consists of voiced, unvoiced or silent regions. Further the energy associated with voiced region is large compared to unvoiced or silence region will have least or negligible energy. Energy plays a vital role in classifying emotions as it gives the measure of intensity as described by (Lee et al., 2005). The energy of the speech signal is calculated using equation 1.

$$energy = \sum_{k=0}^{\infty} x(m)^2 . h\left(n - m\right) \tag{1}$$

where, $h(n) = w(n)^2$

Figure 1(c) shows the relationship between different emotions and their corresponding energy levels.

### Mel Frequency Cepstrum Coefficients (MFCC)

In sound processing, the Mel-Frequency Cepstrum (MFC) is a representation of the short-term power spectrum of a sound, based on a linear cosine transform of a log power spectrum on a nonlinear Mel scale of frequency. Mel-frequency Cepstral coefficients (MFCCs) are coefficients that collectively form the Mel Frequency Cepstrum (MFC). They are derived from a type of Cepstral representation of the audio clip (a nonlinear "spectrum-of-a-spectrum"). The difference between the Cepstrum and the Mel-frequency Cepstrum is that in the MFC, the frequency bands are equally spaced on the Mel scale, which approximates the human auditory system's response more closely than the linearly-spaced frequency bands used in the normal Cepstrum as mentioned by (Kuang et al., 2013). This frequency warping can

*Figure 2. (a). Block Diagram for MFCC, (b). Graphs of MFCC for different emotions, (c). Graphs of PSD output for various Emotions*

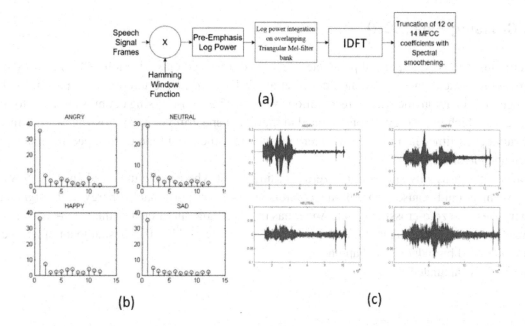

(a)

(b)                                                    (c)

allow for better representation of sound. Majority of the researchers claimed that MFCC is a distinct feature for audio-based emotion recognition. MFCCs are commonly derived as presented in Figure 2(a).

The computation steps in the MFCC are as follows

1.    Apply FFT to the windowed Speech signal. Calculate the Power Spectrum or the squared magnitude of the signal
2.    As Human ear has unequal sensitivity at different frequencies, pre-emphasis is carried out to equal the sensitivity.
3.    The auditory system is modeled as a mel filter bank which is triangular in nature.
4.    The Power Spectrum and overlapping critical triangular filter banks are integrated.
5.    To achieve spectral magnitude compression, the log power spectrum is computed.
6.    IDFT of the Log Power Spectrum gives MFCC.
7.    The spectrum is truncated by using the first twelve or fourteen coefficients.

Figure 2(b) represents the MFCC coefficients for four different emotions namely ANGRY, NEUTRAL, HAPPY and SAD recorded by a single speaker. The MFCC coefficients have been measured using the above steps in MATLAB. The first twelve coefficients have been plotted for the four different emotions. From the plot it is observed that Neutral emotion MFCC values are lesser than the other emotions.

## Power Spectral Density (PSD)

The Welch Method is used to plot the PSD of the signal. To make the signal speech, a stationary window of 10ms is used. (Saini, 2015). has elaborated the significance of PSD for speech analysis. It represents the strength of energy variation over frequency. The results are depicted in Figure 2(c). The Neutral has the least energy variations. The Angry and Happy emotions have maximum variations. The results are depicted in Figure 2(c).

## Zero Crossing Rate (ZCR)

Zero-crossing rate is an important parameter for voiced/unvoiced classification as well as for emotion classification as mentioned by (Ramdinmawii et al., 2017). It is also often used as a part of the front-end processing in automatic speech recognition systems. The zero-crossing count is an indicator of the frequency at which the energy is concentrated in the signal spectrum or Zero-crossing rate is a measure of the number of times in a given time interval/frame that the amplitude of the speech signals passes through a value of zero.

Voiced speech usually shows a low zero-crossing count whereas the unvoiced speech shows high zero-crossing count because zero-crossing count is inversely proportional to energy of the signal, more the energy less the zero-crossing count. Anger has the most amount of energy thus zero-crossing count for anger is very less as compared to other emotions, where neutral has the most amount of zero- crossing rate preceded by sadness and happiness.

The ZCR is calculated using equation 2.

$$Z_n = \sum_{m=-\infty}^{\infty} \frac{1}{2} \mid \mathrm{sgn}[x(m] - \mathrm{sgn}[x(m+1)] \mid w(n-m)$$

(2)

where, $\mathrm{sgn}(x[n]) = 1\, \mathrm{sgn}(x[n]) = -1$

## Classifier

Different audio emotions are classified using supervised learning. Supervised learning is the machine learning task of inferring a function from labeled training data. The training data consist of a set of training examples. In supervised learning, each example is a pair consisting of an input object (typically a vector) and a desired output value (also called the supervisory signal). A supervised learning algorithm analyzes the training data and produces an inferred function, which can be used for mapping new examples. An optimal scenario will allow for the algorithm to correctly determine the class labels for unseen instances. This requires the learning algorithm to generalize from the training data to unseen situations in a "reasonable" way.

## Back Propagation Algorithm

The back propagation algorithm is generally used with multi-layer feed forward networks, also called Back Propagation networks (BPN's). These networks usually consist of processing elements with continuous differentiable activation functions. This algorithm changes the weights of a BPN to correctly classify a given input from a set of predefined input-output training pairs as explained by Deepa, S. N., & Sivanandam, S. N. (2011). This is a method in which the error is propagated to the hidden unit by simply using the gradient descent method similar to the one used in a simple perceptron network with differentiable units.

The aim of the network is to train the network to achieve a balance between its ability to respond (memorization) and its ability to respond in a similar but not identical manner as demonstrated dur-

*Figure 3. (a). Architecture of Back-Propagation network, (b). Output of Gabor filter, (c). Output of Gabor filter when compared to reference test image (Courtesy of Dhall et al. (2012), Dhall et al. (2014)), (d). Comparison of audio, video and audio-video modalities*

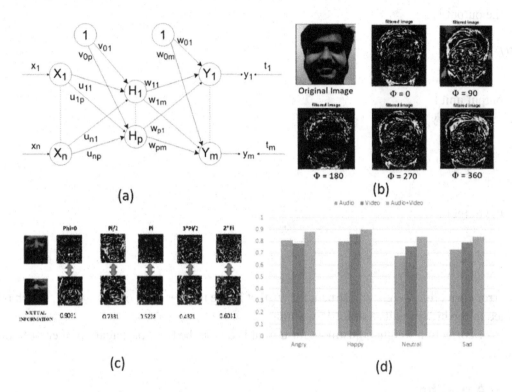

ing training (generalization). This algorithm is different in the process by which the updation of the weights of the hidden layers takes place during the training of the network as described by Deepa, S. N., & Sivanandam, S. N.(2011). The training occurs in three stages, the feed-forward of the input training pattern, the calculation and back-propagation of the error and updation of weights. The testing of the BPN involves the computation of the feed-forward phase only.

BPN's usually are multi-layer as shown in Figure 3(a), consisting of an input layer, a hidden layer and an output layer. The neurons in the output and hidden layers have biases, which also act as weights. These biases are the connections from nodes that have their activation set to 1.

The terminologies used in the algorithm below are as follows:

- x = input training vector (x1, x2, x3..., xn)
- t = target output vector (t1, t2, t3..., tn)
- $\alpha$ = learning rate parameter
- xi = input unit i
- u0j = bias on jth hidden unit
- w0k = bias on kth output unit
- hj = hidden unit j.

The net input to $h_{inj}$ is

$$h_{inj} = u_{0j} + \sum_{i=1}^{n} x_i u_{ij} \tag{3}$$

And the output is

$$h_j = f(h_{inj}) \tag{4}$$

$y_k$ = output unit k
The net input to $y_k$ is

$$y_{ink} = w_{0k} + \sum_{j=1}^{p} h_j w_{jk} \tag{5}$$

And the output is

$$y_k = f(y_{ink}) \tag{6}$$

$\delta_k$ = error correction weight adjustment for $w_{jk}$ that is due to an error at output unit $y_k$, which is back-propagated to the hidden units that feed into unit $y_{k.s}$

$\delta_j$ = error correction weight adjustment for $u_{ij}$ that is due to the back-propagation of error to the hidden unit $h_j$.

## Training Algorithm

The training algorithm is explained using equations (7) to (21).

Step 0: Initialize weights and learning rate
Step 1: Perform Steps 2-9 when stopping condition is False
Step 2: Perform Steps 3-8 for each training pair

(Phase 1: Feed-forward phase)

Step 3: Apply input xi to each input unit which in-turn sends it to the hidden unit (i = 1 to n).
Step 4: The weighted input signals are summed up at the hidden unit $h_j$ (j = 1 to n) to calculate the net input, using the formula:

$$h_{inj} = u_{0j} + \sum_{i=1}^{n} x_i u_{ij} \tag{7}$$

Calculate output of the hidden unit by applying its activation functions over $h_{inj}$ (bipolar or binary sigmoidal activation function) and send the output signal from the hidden unit to the input of output layer units.

$$h_{inj} = u_{0j} + \sum_{i=1}^{n} x_i u_{ij}$$

$$h_j = f(h_{inj})$$
(8)

**A**

Step 5: For each output unit $y_k$ (k = 1 to m), calculate the net input:

$$y_{ink} = w_{0k} + \sum_{j=1}^{p} h_j w_{jk}$$
(9)

And apply the activation function to compute output signal

$$y_k = f(y_{ink})$$
(10)

(Phase 2: Back-propagation of error)

Step 6: Each output unit $y_k$ (k = 1 to m) receives a target pattern corresponding to the input training pattern and computes the error correction term:

$$\delta_k = \left(t_k - y_k\right) f'\left(y_{ink}\right)$$
(11)

On the basis of the calculated error correction term, update the change in weights and bias:

$$\Delta W_{jk} = \alpha \delta_k h_j$$
(12)

$$\Delta W_{0k} = \alpha \delta_k$$
(13)

Also, send $\delta_k$ to the hidden layer backwards.

Step 7: Each hidden unit $h_j$ (j = 1 to p) sums its delta inputs from the output units:

$$\delta inj = \sum_{k=1}^{m} \delta_k w_{jk}$$
(14)

The term $\delta_{inj}$ gets multiplied with the derivative of $f(h_{inj})$ to calculate the error term:

$$\delta_i = \delta_{inj} f'\left(h_{inj}\right)$$
(15)

On the basis of the calculated $\delta_j$, update the change in weights and bias:

$$\Delta u_{ij} = \alpha \delta_j x_i$$
(16)

$$\Delta u_{0j} = \alpha \delta_j$$
(17)

(Phase 3: Weight and bias updation)

Step 8: Each output unit yk (k = 1 to m) updates the bias and weights:

$$W_{jk}(new) = W_{jk}(old) + \Delta w_{jk} \tag{18}$$

$$w_{0k}(new) = w_{ij}(old) + \Delta w_{0k} \tag{19}$$

Each hidden unit hj (j = 1 to p) updates its bias and weights:

$$u_{ij}(new) = u_{ij}(old) + \Delta u_{ij} \tag{20}$$

$$u_{0j}(new) = u_{0j}(old) + \Delta u_{0j} \tag{21}$$

Step 9: Check for stopping conditions, which may be a certain number of epochs or when the actual output equals the target output.

## Testing Algorithm

The testing algorithm is explained using equations (22) to (25).

Step 0: Initialize the weights, which are taken from the training algorithm.
Step 1: Perform Steps 2-4 for each input vector.
Step 2: Set the activation of the input unit for $x_i$ (i = 1 to n).
Step 3: Calculate the net input to the hidden unit x and its output for j = 1 to p.

$$h_{ink} = u_{0j} + \sum_{i=1}^{n} x_i u_{ij} \tag{22}$$

$$h_j = f(h_{inj}) \tag{23}$$

Step 4: Now compute the output of the output layer unit for k = 1 to m.

$$y_{ink} = w_{0k} + \sum_{i=1}^{n} h_j w_{jk} \tag{24}$$

$$y_k = f(y_{ink}) \tag{25}$$

## Video

Real time video frames are captured using a webcam and a haar-cascade face detector is used to detect faces. Image pre-processing operations like conversion from RGB to gray to get prominent features using a gabor filter, noise removal is done on the image. Gabor filter features are extracted from the detected face for various orientations like 0, pi/2, pi, 3*pi/2, 2*pi. The features extracted and features of the reference images are compared by finding out the mutual information between them. The result for which mutual information is highest is the detected human emotion.

## Feature Extraction

For feature extraction, a gabor filter is used which provides contours or texture of an image. Gabor filter is a linear filter which is popular for detecting edges. Frequency and orientation representations of Gabor filters are similar to those of the human visual system as mentioned by (Khan et al, 2017). and they have been found to be particularly appropriate for texture representation and discrimination by (Xia et al., 2018). Gabor filters are a traditional choice for obtaining localized frequency information as there is no variance to illumination, rotation, scale and translation. They offer the best simultaneous localization of spatial and frequency information. Orthogonal directions are represented in the gabor filter using real and imaginary components which can be used as an individual entity. The Gabor filter bank is generated using gabor filters with different orientations and scales.

Gabor filter is a Gaussian kernel function modulated by a sinusoidal plane wave. The filter consists of a real and an imaginary component which represents the orthogonal directions. The two components are formed by complex numbers or can be used individually.

$$g\left(x, y; \lambda, \phi, \psi, \sigma, \gamma\right) = \exp(-\frac{x'^2 + \gamma^2 y'^2}{2\sigma^2}) \cos(2\pi \frac{x'}{\lambda} + \psi) \qquad (26)$$

$$g\left(x, y; \lambda, \phi, \psi, \sigma, \gamma\right) = \exp(-\frac{x'^2 + \gamma^2 y'^2}{2\sigma^2}) \sin(2\pi \frac{x'}{\lambda} + \psi) \qquad (27)$$

Where,

$$x' = x \cos \phi + y \sin \phi$$

$$y' = -x \sin \phi + y \cos \phi$$

$\lambda$ represents the wavelength of the sinusoidal factor, $\phi$ represents the orientation of a Gabor function, $\psi$ is the phase offset, $\sigma$ is the sigma of the Gaussian envelope and $\gamma$ gives the spatial aspect ratio, and specifies the ellipticity of the support of the Gabor function. The filter bank with several filters is mainly used to extract multi-orientation and multi-scale features from the given face image. This filter bank generally consists of Gabor filters of 5 different scales and 8 orientations (Kyrki et al., 2004).

The steps for gabor based extraction from gray scale images are as follows:

- At first each filter in the gabor filter bank is convoluted with the gray scale image.
- The resulting filtered images are down-sampled to reduce the repetitive information
- Feature vector is obtained from each down-sampled image
- Normalization of each feature vector is carried out with zero mean and unit variance.
- The normalized feature vectors are combined to get the resultant feature vector of an image.

The output of the gabor filter for various orientations is shown in Figure 3(b).

Orientations used are $\phi = 0,90,180,270,360$. Feature vectors obtained are further utilized for computing the mutual information.

## Feature Selection

To classify various emotions, mutual information (MI) values are used as it gives the most prominent results. MI is the feature selection module that helps to improve the performance of learning models by removing most irrelevant and redundant features from the feature space. It is based on the Maximum relevance and Minimum Redundancy algorithm. According to MI feature selection criteria, if a feature vector has expressions randomly or uniformly distributed in different classes, its MI with these classes is zero. If a feature vector is strongly different from other features for different classes, it will have a large MI.

## Mathematical Equation for Mutual Information

Figure 3(c) represents the mutual information calculated for various emotions and tested for a reference emotion from the dataset. Gabor filter output for each reference image for all five orientations is obtained. The emotion having fidelity with the reference image has the highest MI coefficient.

$$MI\left(x,y\right) = \sum_{i,j}^{m,n} p\left(x_i, y_j\right) loglog(\frac{p\left(x_i, y_j\right)}{p\left(x_i\right)p\left(y_j\right)}) \tag{28}$$

Experimentation is carried out on 50 audio and video samples of the following utterance: "Are you seriously doing that?" in four different emotions. The same utterance has been recorded in the following emotions: Anger, Happy, Sad and neutral.

The result of energy measured from the speech signal of six speakers from 200 samples is recorded in Table 1. The energy of the "angry" emotion is found to be higher than the other emotions. Energy values for specific emotions are confined to a particular range. Ideally the value of energy is high for "anger" emotion and low for "sad" and "neutral" emotion. To enhance the accuracy for recognition and classification energy is used in conjunction with MFCC. The corresponding MFCC features extracted for different speakers showcasing different emotions are shown in Table 2.

Video emotion recognition is carried out using a Gabor Filter to get the texture features.Gabor filter output for 5 orientations 0, pi/2, pi, 3*pi/2, 2*pi are computed for one input image and reference images for all 4 emotions. Mutual information (MI) is computed between 5 gabor filter outputs of an input image and a Gabor filter output of 20 reference images (angry, happy, sad, and neutral). Table 3 shows the calculated MI values between input images and different reference images with various Gabor filter orientation. The extracted MI coefficients are used to train the classifier by using the back-propagation algorithm. The predicted emotion corresponds to the highest MI value.

The proposed method is also tested on the most popular dataset for visual emotion dataset provided by (Dhall et al., 2012; Dhall et al., 2014). and the results are encouraging. The experimentation has been carried out on more than 50 audio recordings and 50 video samples per class for emotion classification.

# Audio Results

Energy: (same sentence, different emotions, different speakers)

Sentence said: "Are you seriously doing that?"

Table 1 shows the result of energy features and table 1 clearly shows the angry emotion has the highest energy. The measured energy for five out of the six speakers for the ANGRY emotion is the highest. Similarly for the HAPPY emotion five out of six speakers have the second highest energy measured. All the six speakers for the SAD emotion have an energy level lesser than Angry and Happy emotion. All the six speakers have less energy for Neutral Emotion. From the table we can clearly conclude the energy feature provides a clear indication of the Uttered emotion in the majority of the speakers.

*Table 1. Result of energy feature*

| Speaker no. | Angry | Happy | Neutral | Sad |
|:---:|:---:|:---:|:---:|:---:|
| 1 | 90.272 | 65.132 | 22.498 | 5.124 |
| 2 | 223.273 | 65.132 | 22.498 | 7.124 |
| 3 | 390.780 | 96.827 | 19.563 | 9.807 |
| 4 | 120.860 | 300.381 | 54.833 | 36.920 |
| 5 | 153.830 | 62.414 | 47.030 | 28.349 |
| 6 | 45.440 | 52.907 | 10.667 | 8.534 |

MFCC: (same sentence, different emotions, different speakers)

Sentence said: "Are you seriously doing that?"

The below table shows various values of MFCC for 3 speakers for 4 emotions.

Table 2 shows the first five MFCC coefficients of three speakers with four different emotions. Table clearly shows the MFCC coefficients are least for the Neutral Emotion followed by SAD emotion for majority of the cases. The distinction between Angry and Happy are not distinct using MFCC coefficients in some of the cases. There is fluctuation in the MFCC coefficients for various emotions as the recording environment is not ideal. Hence, to improvise the performance of the system the energy and MFCC.

# Mutual Information

Table 3 depicts the calculated Mutual Information between the test image and 20 reference images as shown in Figure 3(c). The Table 3 shows the Emotion predicted based on mutual information is Happy as the values are observed maximum for various fi angles for HAPPY emotion

The experimental results are given in Table 4 and depicted in Figure 3(d). As shown in Table 4, the performance of audio-visual emotion recognition is better than the individual audio and video modalities. This indicates the fusion of audio and video cues at the feature level achieves better performance than facial expression and affective speech. The results of the approach are shown in Table 4.

*Table 2. Result of MFCC feature*

| Emotion | MFCC 1 | MFCC 2 | MFCC 3 | MFCC 4 | MFCC 5 |
|---|---|---|---|---|---|
| Speaker 1 | | | | | |
| **Angry** | 10.624 | 7.658 | 2.712 | 2.589 | 1.453 |
| **Happy** | 4.440 | 2.759 | 0.512 | 1.632 | 0.807 |
| **Sad** | 9.595 | 6.932 | 2.540 | 2.513 | 1.607 |
| **Neutral** | 9.961 | 7.069 | 2.569 | 2.763 | 1.514 |
| Speaker 2 | | | | | |
| **Angry** | 11.164 | 6.582 | 3.315 | 1.823 | 1.776 |
| **Happy** | 11.697 | 6.845 | 3.303 | 1.992 | 2.139 |
| **Sad** | 10.594 | 6.256 | 3.234 | 1.775 | 1.718 |
| **Neutral** | 10.296 | 6.026 | 3.064 | 1.695 | 1.628 |
| Speaker 3 | | | | | |
| **Angry** | 10.169 | 7.320 | 2.632 | 2.471 | 1.292 |
| **Happy** | 10.759 | 7.746 | 2.623 | 2.543 | 1.494 |
| **Sad** | 10.040 | 7.251 | 2.578 | 2.494 | 1.413 |
| **Neutral** | 9.150 | 6.507 | 2.159 | 2.254 | 1.159 |

*Table 3. Mutual Information between the input image and 20 reference images*

| Emotion | $\Phi = 0$ | $\Phi = \pi/2$ | $\Phi = \pi$ | $\Phi = 3\pi/2$ | $\Phi = 2\pi$ |
|---|---|---|---|---|---|
| Angry | 0.8718 | 1.2380 | 0.7026 | 0.8818 | 1.0845 |
| Sad | 0.6974 | 1.1042 | 0.5811 | 0.7380 | 0.9796 |
| Happy | 0.8957 | 1.2407 | 0.7096 | 0.8998 | 1.0957 |
| Neutral | 0.6731 | 1.1256 | 0.5563 | 0.7581 | 0.9205 |

*Table 4. Comparison of audio, video and audio-video results*

| Methods | Face-expression | Audio Expression | Audio-Visual Expression |
|---|---|---|---|
| Accuracy | 79.75% | 75.5% | 85.75% |

In recent years due the advancements in neural networks many researchers have implemented deep learning-based approaches for emotion recognition using audio-visual cues (Cornejo et al., 2019; Ma et al., 2019, Tripathi et al., 2019; Kwon et al., 2020). In deep learning approaches even though there is a significant improvement in feature extraction capabilities, enhancement in the model complexity to cope up with huge datasets still a prominent improvement in accuracy remains a challenge and hence the scope of the research. Our future work aims to design deep learning-based approaches for audio-video emotion recognition to gain a higher accuracy.

A

# FUTURE RESEARCH DIRECTIONS

The research nay be extended using deep learning architectures with different features for emotion recognition. Multimodal automatic emotion recognition systems have a great potential in various fields like Human Computer Interaction, Healthcare and Behavioral modelling. Developing ubiquitous, fast and accurate wearable technology using complex ML models for the reliable emotion recognition is the need of the era.

# CONCLUSION

This chapter provides the advancements in the field of video modality, audio modality and a combination of audio-visual modalities for emotion recognition. The chapter presents audio-visual based emotion recognition using the most prominent features like MFCC and energy from audio samples. The texture-based features use the gabor filter in different orientations from the video samples and have been used to calculate the mutual information of the test images with respect to reference images. The mutual information is computed from the video images and is used to accurately predict human emotions using a back propagation classifier. The experimentation has been carried out independently with the audio features and video features. Finally, the experimentation has been carried out combinedly with the audio and video features. State-of-the-art methods use many features to detect the emotions, based on audio-visual cues, increasing the algorithmic computational complexity. The devised method showcases high accuracy with the use of a few but prominent features to detect the four emotions, happy, sad, anger and neutral. The proposed technique is very promising as accuracy obtained using only audio cues is 75.5%, using only video cues is 79.75% and combined audio-visual cues gives an accuracy of 85.75% which is higher as compared to any machine learning-based algorithm.

# REFERENCES

Ab, H. (2017). A real-time system for facial expression recognition using support vector machines and k-nearest neighbor classifier. *International Journal of Computers and Applications, 159*(8), 23–29. doi:10.5120/ijca2017913009

Alonso, J. B., Cabrera, J., Medina, M., & Travieso, C. M. (2015). New approach in quantification of emotional intensity from the speech signal: Emotional temperature. *Expert Systems with Applications, 42*(24), 9554–9564. doi:10.1016/j.eswa.2015.07.062

Breiman, L. (2001). Random forests. *Machine Learning, 45*(1), 5–32. doi:10.1023/A:1010933404324

Burges, C. J. (1998). A tutorial on support vector machines for pattern recognition. *Data Mining and Knowledge Discovery, 2*(2), 121–167. doi:10.1023/A:1009715923555

Busso, C., Lee, S., & Narayanan, S. (2009). Analysis of emotionally salient aspects of fundamental frequency for emotion detection. *IEEE Transactions on Audio, Speech, and Language Processing, 17*(4), 582–596. doi:10.1109/TASL.2008.2009578

Caruana, R. (1997). Multitask learning. *Machine Learning, 28*(1), 41–75. doi:10.1023/A:1007379606734

Chanel, G., & Mühl, C. (2015). Connecting brains and bodies: Applying physiological computing to support social interaction. *Interacting with Computers*, 27(5), 534–550. doi:10.1093/iwc/iwv013

Cornejo, J., & Pedrini, H. (2019, December). Bimodal emotion recognition based on audio and facial parts using deep convolutional neural networks. *2019 18th IEEE International Conference On Machine Learning And Applications (ICMLA)*, 111-117. 10.1109/ICMLA.2019.00026

Dai, W., Han, D., Dai, Y., & Xu, D. (2015). Emotion recognition and affective computing on vocal social media. *Information & Management*, 52(7), 777–788. doi:10.1016/j.im.2015.02.003

Daugman, J. G. (1985). Uncertainty relation for resolution in space, spatial frequency, and orientation optimized by two-dimensional visual cortical filters. *Journal of the Optical Society of America. A, Optics and Image Science*, 2(7), 1160–1169. doi:10.1364/JOSAA.2.001160 PMID:4020513

Deshmukh, G., Gaonkar, A., Golwalkar, G., & Kulkarni, S. (2019). Speech based emotion recognition using machine learning. *2019 3rd International Conference on Computing Methodologies and Communication (ICCMC)*, 812-817. 10.1109/ICCMC.2019.8819858

Dhall, A., Goecke, R., Joshi, J., Sikka, K., & Gedeon, T. (2014). Emotion recognition in the wild challenge 2014: Baseline, data and protocol. *Proceedings of the 16th international conference on multimodal interaction*, 461-466. 10.1145/2663204.2666275

Dhall, A., Goecke, R., Lucey, S., & Gedeon, T. (2012). Collecting large, richly annotated facial-expression databases from movies. *IEEE MultiMedia*, 19(03), 34–41. doi:10.1109/MMUL.2012.26

Ekman, P., & Friesen, W. V. (1978). *Facial action coding systems*. Consulting Psychologists Press. doi:10.1037/t27734-000

Haghighat, M., Zonouz, S., & Abdel-Mottaleb, M. (2013). Identification using encrypted biometrics. *International Conference on Computer Analysis of Images and Patterns*, 440-448. 10.1007/978-3-642-40246-3_55

Haq, S., Jackson, P. J., & Edge, J. (2009). Speaker-dependent audio-visual emotion recognition. AVSP, 53-58.

Itti, L., Koch, C., & Niebur, E. (1998). A model of saliency-based visual attention for rapid scene analysis. *IEEE Transactions on Pattern Analysis and Machine Intelligence*, 20(11), 1254–1259. doi:10.1109/34.730558

Jatupaiboon, N., Pan-Ngum, S., & Israsena, P. (2015). Subject-dependent and subject-independent emotion classification using unimodal and multimodal physiological signals. *Journal of Medical Imaging and Health Informatics*, 5(5), 1020–1027. doi:10.1166/jmihi.2015.1490

Khan, S., Hussain, M., Aboalsamh, H., & Bebis, G. (2017). A comparison of different Gabor feature extraction approaches for mass classification in mammography. *Multimedia Tools and Applications*, 76(1), 33–57. doi:10.100711042-015-3017-3

Kuang, Y., & Li, L. (2013). Speech emotion recognition of decision fusion based on DS evidence theory. *2013 IEEE 4th International Conference on Software Engineering and Service Science*, 795-798. 10.1109/ICSESS.2013.6615425

Kwon, S. (2020). A CNN-assisted enhanced audio signal processing for speech emotion recognition. *Sensors (Basel)*, *20*(1), 183. doi:10.339020010183 PMID:31905692

Kyrki, V., Kamarainen, J. K., & Kälviäinen, H. (2004). Simple Gabor feature space for invariant object recognition. *Pattern Recognition Letters*, *25*(3), 311–318. doi:10.1016/j.patrec.2003.10.008

Lajevardi, S. M., & Wu, H. R. (2012). Facial expression recognition in perceptual color space. *IEEE Transactions on Image Processing*, *21*(8), 3721–3733. doi:10.1109/TIP.2012.2197628 PMID:22575677

Lee, C. M., & Narayanan, S. S. (2005). Toward detecting emotions in spoken dialogs. *IEEE Transactions on Speech and Audio Processing*, *13*(2), 293–303. doi:10.1109/TSA.2004.838534

Ma, Y., Hao, Y., Chen, M., Chen, J., Lu, P., & Košir, A. (2019). Audio-visual emotion fusion (AVEF): A deep efficient weighted approach. *Information Fusion*, *46*, 184–192. doi:10.1016/j.inffus.2018.06.003

Mistry, K., Zhang, L., Neoh, S. C., Lim, C. P., & Fielding, B. (2016). A micro-GA embedded PSO feature selection approach to intelligent facial emotion recognition. *IEEE Transactions on Cybernetics*, *47*(6), 1496–1509. doi:10.1109/TCYB.2016.2549639 PMID:28113688

Olshausen, B. A., & Field, D. J. (1996). Emergence of simple-cell receptive field properties by learning a sparse code for natural images. *Nature*, *381*(6583), 607–609. doi:10.1038/381607a0 PMID:8637596

Ramdinmawii, E., Mohanta, A., & Mittal, V. K. (2017). Emotion recognition from speech signal. TEN-CON 2017-2017 IEEE Region 10 Conference, 1562-1567. doi:10.1109/TENCON.2017.8228105

Saini, J., & Mehra, D. (2015). Power Spectral Density Analysis of Speech Signal using Window Techniques. *International Journal of Computers and Applications*, *131*(14), 33–36. doi:10.5120/ijca2015907549

Samantaray, A. K., Mahapatra, K., Kabi, B., & Routray, A. (2015). A novel approach of speech emotion recognition with prosody, quality and derived features using SVM classifier for a class of North-Eastern Languages. *2015 IEEE 2nd International Conference on Recent Trends in Information Systems (ReTIS)*, 372-377. 10.1109/ReTIS.2015.7232907

Seng, K. P., Ang, L. M., & Ooi, C. S. (2016). A combined rule-based & machine learning audio visual emotion recognition approach. *IEEE Transactions on Affective Computing*, *9*(1), 3–13. doi:10.1109/TAFFC.2016.2588488

Sivanandam, S. N., & Deepa, S. N. (2011). *Principles of soft computing*. John Wiley & Sons.

Tripathi, S., Kumar, A., Ramesh, A., Singh, C., & Yenigalla, P. (2019). *Deep learning based emotion recognition system using speech features and transcriptions*. doi:10.48550/arXiv.1906.05681

Wang, Y., & Guan, L. (2008). Recognizing human emotional state from audiovisual signals. *IEEE Transactions on Multimedia*, *10*(5), 936–946. doi:10.1109/TMM.2008.927665

Wei, W., & Jia, Q. (2016). Weighted feature Gaussian kernel SVM for emotion recognition. *Computational Intelligence and Neuroscience*, *2016*, 1–7. Advance online publication. doi:10.1155/2016/7696035 PMID:27807443

Wu, C. H., & Liang, W. B. (2010). Emotion recognition of affective speech based on multiple classifiers using acoustic-prosodic information and semantic labels. *IEEE Transactions on Affective Computing*, *2*(1), 10–21. doi:10.1109/T-AFFC.2010.16

Xia, Z., Lv, R., & Sun, X. (2018). Rotation-invariant Weber pattern and Gabor feature for fingerprint liveness detection. *Multimedia Tools and Applications*, 77(14), 18187–18200. doi:10.100711042-017-5517-9

Yang, Y. H., Lin, Y. C., Su, Y. F., & Chen, H. H. (2008). A regression approach to music emotion recognition. *IEEE Transactions on Audio, Speech, and Language Processing*, 16(2), 448–457. doi:10.1109/TASL.2007.911513

Yu, Chang, Xu, & Shum. (2001). *Emotion Detection from Speech to Enrich Multimedia Content.* . doi:10.1007/3-540-45453-5_71

Zeng, Z., Hu, Y., Roisman, G. I., Wen, Z., Fu, Y., & Huang, T. S. (2007). Audio-visual spontaneous emotion recognition. *Artificial Intelligence for Human Computing*, 72-90. doi:10.1007/978-3-540-72348-6_4

Zhang, S., Li, L., & Zhao, Z. (2012, December). Audio-visual emotion recognition based on facial expression and affective speech. *International Conference on Multimedia and Signal Processing*, 46-52. 10.1007/978-3-642-35286-7_7

Zheng, W., Zong, Y., Zhou, X., & Xin, M. (2016). Cross-domain color facial expression recognition using transductive transfer subspace learning. *IEEE Transactions on Affective Computing*, 9(1), 21–37. doi:10.1109/TAFFC.2016.2563432

## ADDITIONAL READING

Ganchev, T., Fakotakis, N., & Kokkinakis, G. (2005, October). Comparative evaluation of various MFCC implementations on the speaker verification task. *Proceedings of the SPECOM*, 1, 191-194.

Gouyon, F., Pachet, F., & Delerue, O. (2000, December). On the use of zero-crossing rate for an application of classification of percussive sounds. *Proceedings of the COST G-6 conference on Digital Audio Effects (DAFX-00)*.

Hecht-Nielsen, R. (1992). Theory of the backpropagation neural network. In *Neural networks for perception* (pp. 65–93). Academic Press. doi:10.1016/B978-0-12-741252-8.50010-8

Jones, J. P., & Palmer, L. A. (1987). An evaluation of the two-dimensional Gabor filter model of simple receptive fields in cat striate cortex. *Journal of Neurophysiology*, 58(6), 1233–1258. doi:10.1152/jn.1987.58.6.1233 PMID:3437332

McCaffrey, J. (2012). Neural Network Back-Propagation for Programmers. *MSDN Magazine*.

Nielsen, M. A. (2015). *Neural networks and deep learning, 25*. Determination press.

Rojas, R. (2013). *Neural networks: a systematic introduction*. Springer Science & Business Media.

Sahidullah, M., & Saha, G. (2012). Design, analysis and experimental evaluation of block based transformation in MFCC computation for speaker recognition. *Speech Communication*, 54(4), 543–565. doi:10.1016/j.specom.2011.11.004

## KEY TERMS AND DEFINITIONS

**A**

**Back-Propagation:** Backpropagation is an algorithm to fine-tune weights and biases to improve the accuracy and reduce error for the artificial neural network outputs.

**FFT:** The Fast Fourier Transform (FFT) is obtained by decomposing a sequence of values into components of different frequencies.

**HCI:** Human-computer interaction (HCI) is a multidisciplinary field of study that focuses on the design of computer technology and the interaction between humans and computers.

**MFCC:** Mel-Frequency Cepstrum (MFC) is a representation of the short-term power spectrum of a sound, based on a linear cosine transform of a log power spectrum on a nonlinear Mel scale of frequency.

**MI:** The mutual information (MI) of two random variables is a measure of the mutual dependence between the two variables.

**PSD:** The power spectral density (PSD) of the signal describes the power present in the signal as a function of frequency, per unit frequency.

**ZCR:** The zero-crossing rate (ZCR) is the rate at which a signal changes from positive to zero to negative or from negative to zero to positive.

# An Intelligent Virtual Medical Assistant for Healthcare Prediction

**Jeya Mala D.**

ⓘ https://orcid.org/0000-0002-2100-8218

*Vellore Institute of Technology, Chennai, India*

**Pradeep Reynold A.**

*InduTch Composites Pvt. Ltc., India*

## INTRODUCTION

In city life, healthcare is an essential and significant part of every citizen to lead a healthy life. A typical healthcare system has to include the needs of patients, physicians, lab technicians, specialists etc. It needs to keep track of various stages of healthcare including monitoring, diagnostics, treatments, reports etc. Due to the increase of population density with steady increase of old age population along with the rise of pandemic diseases, challenges such as high demand of hospitals; personal medical care and administration of medical resources have been posed on traditional healthcare systems.

Traditional healthcare applications can no longer be trusted or completely relying upon due to the rapid spread of dangerous diseases worldwide. Hence, the medical practitioners, healthcare industries etc., are now focusing on developing smart healthcare solutions to tackle the challenges in delivering smart solutions especially during this pandemic era (Sumayya, 2020).

Smart healthcare is generally the combination of healthcare practices with information technology such as IoT, cloud computing, mobile communications, big data analytics and Artificial Intelligence (AI) / Machine Learning (ML) techniques. They act as an alternative of conventional medical service systems and manual or human based health management systems.

The IoT enabled healthcare systems are playing a crucial role in smart city applications. These kinds of applications can be used as assistants to detect the transmissible diseases, monitoring of treatments and further healthcare management activities. Apart from these, the application of AI in the area of smart healthcare has gained huge impact on providing more efficient, cost effective and personalized solutions.

Nowadays, machine learning techniques embedded in automated healthcare solutions have impact on providing robust and reliable solutions in smart healthcare. Also, management activities related to customer healthcare information management, customer insurance management, Laboratory equipments management, Doctors' prescriptions management etc. have been equipped with intelligent methods to improve the efficiency in storing, retrieving and processing of data from the repositories and to take intelligent decision making.

The current research works explore the application of AI and ML in smart healthcare systems and their allied areas. It is essential to trace the patients' historical data in crucial life saving situations and to prescribe immediate medications to rescue the patient's health are accomplished nowadays by intelligent solutions.

DOI: 10.4018/978-1-7998-9220-5.ch050

A

In this connection, several research works are carried out to apply Machine Learning (ML) and Artificial Intelligence (AI) to get greater impact on healthcare domain and its administration activities. The healthcare industries are now in need of a better independent solution to help the people by applying AI integrated medical solutions. Many industries and individual researchers are nowadays developing several applications using current programming languages such as Python (Admin, 2020).

It is predicted that, by 2025, there shall be at most 50% of increase in the automated, smart healthcare devices shall occupy the healthcare industry. The information technology organizations help achieve these kinds of personalized, automated healthcare services by significantly reducing the need for human assistants by means of AI based solutions (Sundaravadivel, Kougianos, Mohanty &Ganapathiraju, 2018).

Some of the significant advantages of AI based healthcare systems include (i) cost reduction and improved quality; (ii) more efficient healthcare products (iii) robust solution to the patients and their caretakers (iv) enhanced internal functionality.

In this connection, several smart applications such as AI powered Chatbots, Robots, Virtual nurse with AR etc. are developed to assist the patients, old-age people etc (Dodhia, Jha, Anudeep & Sarmah P, 2017).

This chapter discusses on the related work in this area of research, virtual medical assistant development, application of ML in virtual assistants' decision making process etc.

## LITERATURE REVIEW

Manne &Kantheti (2021) have analyzed the use of AI in healthcare in various sectors. They have concluded that, organizations involved in healthcare research are more interested in applying AI based research. Also, they have exhibited the challenges involved in the application of AI in domains such as Radiology, Drug design etc.

Davahli (2021) has proposed safety guidelines for implementing AI black box models in order to reduce the unexpected accidents and other unwanted incidents. They have developed a multi-attribute value model approach by extracting the corresponding attributes and their scale values. Their proposed system can detect AI based risks and how to prevent incidents before their occurrence etc.

Balaha, Balaha & Ha (2021) have assessed the importance of automatic diagnosis of COVID-19 infection discovery as it has emerged as a pandemic and a contagious disease. Their study suggested a hybrid COVID-19 framework based on Deep Learning (DL), Genetic Algorithm (GA), and Weighted Sum (WS) etc. They have employed pre-trained models and CNN based analysis. The hybrid CNN framework proposed by them has used learning, classification and parameters optimization. Their extensive work targeted towards the applicability verification and generalization of their proposed solution.

Richardson, Smith, & Curtis (2021) have conducted a survey on patient's view on the use of technologies in healthcare. Their results indicated the patients' concern over security, safety and costs in using such AI based smart healthcare systems.

Parashar, Chaudhary & Rana (2021) have conducted their research in the area of applying ML in healthcare. From their study, they have identified that most of the smart healthcare applications are related to life threatening diseases such as cancer and epilepsy. They have also identified the application of explainable AI and Interpretable AI is gaining their importance in smart healthcare solutions.

Waring, Lindvall &Umeton(2020) have provided a review of the existing literature in applying automated machine learning (AutoML) to assist healthcare workers with limited data science experience in effectively utilizing machine learning models. They have also discussed about the potential benefits and drawbacks of utilizing AutoML in healthcare, as well as existing AutoML applications in healthcare.

Holm (2020), has provided an insight on the need for patient-centric approach. They have elaborated the application of explainable AI in AI based diagnostics.

Coronato, Naeem, Pietro & Paragliola(2020) have analyzed the application of Reinforcement Learning (RL) in medical applications and how it can be used for personalized treatments. They have exhibited the future contributions in this area and the potential limitations in the existing works.

A smart healthcare system was developed in the research work (Islam, Rahaman &Islam, 2020) was equipped with five sensors: heart rate sensor and body temperature sensor (LM35) for patient condition monitoring and room temperature sensor (DHT11), CO sensor (MQ-9), and CO2 sensor (MQ-135)) for monitoring the living environment condition. The processing unit is ESP32 which gets the signals and are transferred to a web server for further processing and taking efficient decisions.

Rong, Mendez, Assi,Zhao&Sawan(2020) have summarized the latest development of applications of AI in biomedical operations based research. Their review report has provided a detailed analysis on tremendous applications of AI in healthcare to AI based researchers. Also, their study helped to analyze the frontier and scope of AI based research in healthcare.

Asan,Bayrak&Choudhury(2020) have analyzed the impact of human trust on AI technology especially in healthcare applications. They have focused on clinicians who are the primary users of healthcare systems and presented the various factors that can shape the trust between such end users and AI based clinical systems.

Nguyen (2019) in his paper presented the development of more than one AI function that can be used to build a diagrammatic conceptual model using AI which is running on Blockchain technology. They have proposed an assistant that helps in effective communication between patients and doctors. Their medical assistant helps in assigning appointment time to patients when the doctor is free and also send reminder to the doctors on the upcoming appointment or surgery or any other medical oriented work tasks. They have also suggested the use of deep learning to analyze the patient's healthcare record and provide possible solutions after the patient's treatment is completed.

Chan, Estève, Fourniols, Escriba & Campo (2012) have provided an extensible report on the R&D done in the area of Smart Wearable Systems (SWS) for health monitoring. Their work is influenced by the application of nano-technologies; sensor technology, smart fabrics etc. and they gave a report on how this AI based wearable computing helps allowing individual patient management and monitoring of his/her status. Their objective was to examine the current research in wearable to serve as references for researchers and provide perspectives for future research.

## BACKGROUND

One of the most significant contributions in healthcare industry is the development of virtual nursing or medical assistant (Ahmed &Ahmed, 2006). This has helped the reduction of pressure on frontline workers and the problem of staff shortage in patients' care especially during the pandemic situations.

AI equipped medical assistants have tremendously helped all the stakeholders by providing assistance in terms of voice recognition, integrated solution in monitoring the health condition in terms of pulse rate, body temperature, and pressure and so on. Several healthcare industries have developed such artificial virtual assistants to help healthcare sector.

A

## AI Embedded Chatbots for Healthcare

The Chatbots embedded with AI can act as health assistants for personal healthcare. Especially, during the pandemic period of huge spread of diseases, people expect home care based solutions instead of directly going to the hospitals to enquire about their illness.

A UK based start-up company has developed a Chatbot that acts as a personal assistant to provide early prevention and diagnosis of diseases. When a person gives the symptom to this Chatbot, it will search its knowledge base to identify the disease and also asks more questions to the user to get more insights about the disease. If needed, the Chatbot then provides appropriate advises and the actions to be taken based on the analysis.

Chatbots are also developed with AI to clarify some essential basic communications between the patients and the doctors before they are starting up their treatment. This can significantly reduce the cost and time spent by the patients in the healthcare sector. These AI powered Chatbots can also help physicians to get recommendations and actions to be taken based on a series of questions.

## Robots in Healthcare

The task of the Robots in the medical laboratories are not only on guiding the elderly and physically challenged people but also in getting the lab results and convey them to the doctors and physicians on behalf of the patients. Based on the embedded knowledge base, the Robots are able to interpret the results and they themselves can add more tests on need basis.

They can also provide suggestions in the patient's regional language itself to help him to understand the results. The physicians can use the help of these Robots to make critical decisions. Also, complex surgeries are nowadays taken care by the Robots as they are strictly following the procedures embedded in the knowledge base. Using ML and Data Analytics, the Robots can able to identify the best practices followed by the physicians during the surgeries.

As everything is based on the programmed logic and on the ML algorithms embedded to take critical decisions, it certainly reduces the inefficiencies in terms of failures of surgeries. Due to this, negative results of some of the failed surgeries are avoided as the Robots are developed with high precision.

## AI and ML assisted Medical Image Processing

The complex part of medical applications is image processing of scanned images. It is really difficult due to the voluminous amount of information present in these images and so it becomes essential to automate those using ML and AI algorithms for automatic analysis and result reporting.

Also, the future medical imaging applications include, the patients to take photos of the ailments they have in any remote places using their mobile camera and having algorithms to parse these images to at least identify the basic information about the patients.

Then by using the Chatbots, it becomes possible to get more detailed information from the patients by having interactive questions with them. IBM has come up with several tools to assist the healthcare in terms of IBM Watson Studio to develop AI powered systems for healthcare.

## AI and ML based Healthcare Assistants

Wearable computing is helping healthcare monitoring in an improved manner. When AI is embedded in wearable computing, the devices are able to send insights on the current status of the patients for further processing and take necessary actions. Especially, when they are provided with elders and patients' with critical illnesses, they can independently send the information to the associated stakeholders to help them in an efficient manner.

Even for healthy individuals, to monitor their current level of calories burning state and the habits of the patient to improve their current status, these AI embedded healthcare monitoring systems will help. In some critical cases of cardiac arrests during heavy workouts can also be monitored before they became catastrophic by the way of using them as life saving measures.

Nowadays, with much more innovations the healthcare industry is providing better solutions to secure the patients' health and also the associated healthcare data. By adopting and adapting to the current scenarios, the healthcare domain can provide more reliable, available and scalable solutions to meet the current needs.

AI can provide its support to decision support systems to aid early diagnosis of patient's status, and to perform data analysis on the generic and specific information got from these devices to give more accurate information about the patients to the doctors in order to take necessary steps to help the patients.

## PROPOSED INTELLIGENT MEDICAL ASSISTANT FRAMEWORK

The proposed solution is an intelligent assistant that has ML embedded in the device or application.

*Figure 1. Intelligent medical assistant with ML*

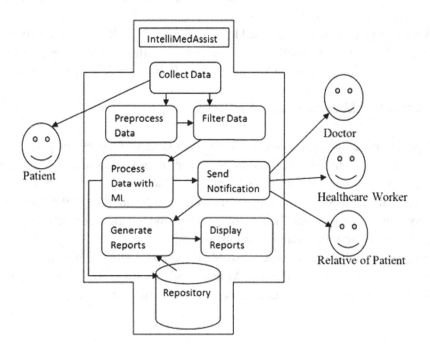

A

The proposed solution has various modules to do the processing of healthcare data in order to decide the appropriate next action to be taken. The agent takes the patient's data from the wearable devices or from the monitoring devices.

The collected data will be the raw, unprocessed data and cannot be directly taken for decision making and processing. Hence, it has to be preprocessed to get only the relevant data from the entire data collected. Also, it may contain noisy data too. The discrepancies present in the data will be monitored and those data are preprocessed to get only the relevant information. These preprocessed data need to be analyzed and categorized to filter only the needed information based on the problem. Say, for instance if data is needed to check the current status of pressure or sugar level or his ECG rate, the Filter module will filter the relevant data.

Then in the Processing module, the filtered data will be processed and the appropriate result will be notified. However, if this module is not equipped with ML algorithm, then it can't do any existing data based analysis as for some patients to take effective decision making, this historic data analysis is the most important aspect.

Hence, in the above proposed framework, the Process module is equipped with ML algorithm. Then this processed data with appropriate outcome is notified to the persons associated with the patient. And also it is stored in the repository for further processing.

If needed, the reports are generated as visual models and textual reports to be used for later purposes.

## Healthcare Prediction using ML

There are several ML models applied for healthcare data analysis. Some of them are listed here

1. Logistic Regression
2. K-Nearest Neighbor (KNN)
3. Support Vector Machine (SVM)
4. Gaussian Naive Bayes
5. Decision Tree
6. Random Forest
7. Gradient Boost

Each of these algorithms / models are applied for different purposes. Here, a brief outline of each of these models is given.

## Logistic Regression Model

This regression model is a supervised ML algorithm that applies classification for predicting the results from a dataset. It is a statistical model to build the ML models where the dependent variable is binary. It is used to provide the relationship between one dependent and one or more independent variables. These independent variables can be of type nominal, ordinal or interval.

It builds a regression model to predict the outcome of analysis that falls under either 1 or 0 category. However, here this 1 or 0 value can be represented in other categories too.

## Using the K-Nearest Neighbor method (KNN Algorithm)

This algorithm is one of the very simple ML algorithm which works under supervised learning category. This algorithm assumes the similarity between the available data and the new data and places the new data into a particular category that is most similar to the available ones. The algorithm stores the available data and then based on the similarity it classifies it into the relevant category.

It can be used for both regression and classification. It is a non-parametric algorithm and so no assumptions are made on underlying data. During training phase, the algorithm stores the dataset and whenever a new data comes in, it classifies it into the corresponding category based on its similarity.

## SVM, or the Support Vector Machine

This ML algorithm comes under Supervised learning algorithm and is used for both classification and regression. It is used to create the decision boundary that can create classes from the n-dimensional space. Now, when a new data comes, it will find the appropriate class and places it in that class. This boundary that helps to take decision is called hyperplane. Hence, the objective of SVM is to find a hyper plane in this n-dimensional space to uniquely classify the data points.

## Naive Bayes (Gaussian)

This model follows Gaussian normal distribution and it supports the classification of data streams that comes in a continuous manner. Generally, Naïve Bayes is a group of supervised learning algorithms that works based on Naives theorem. It is highly applied to the problems where dimensionality of the inputs is very high. Hence, it is applied for high complex real world problems.

It has an assumption that, the value of a particular feature is independent of the value of any other feature. The training of Naïve Bayes classifiers can be done more efficiently. With a small training data, it is able to estimate the parameters needed for classification.

For continuous data, the model takes an assumption that, these continuous values which are associated with each class are distributed based on Gaussian distribution. And also, there is an assumption that there is no co-variance between dimensions.

## Decision Tree Based Classification

The Decision trees are coming under Supervised learning algorithm in which the data is split up continuously with respect to a particular parameter. The tree has two important entities namely decision nodes and leaves. The leaves represent the final outcomes. The decision nodes represent the points of split to take further decision making and outcome generation.

## Random Forest Method

This ML algorithm comes under supervised learning and it can be used for both regression and classification. It works based on ensemble learning in which multiple classifiers are combined to solve a complex problem and hence helps to improve the performance of the model.

Based on the various subsets present in the given dataset, a number of decision trees are generated and the average is taken to improve the accuracy of that dataset.

## Gradient Boost Algorithm

It is most powerful prediction model used to take many crucial decisions. In this model, Boosting method is applied to transform weak learners to strong learners. Here, each new tree identified is placed in a modified version of the original dataset. This Gradient Boosting algorithm follows the Ada Boost algorithm in which the first tree's value is increased based on the observations and the second tree is developed based on this weighted data.

The idea is to improve the predictions of the first tree by combining tree1 with tree2. Then classification is done by identifying the error in it and then a third tree is derived to predict the revised individuals. This process is repeated for a certain number of iterations to get higher accuracy outcome.

Among these algorithms, in this chapter thebasic 'Logistic Regression' ML algorithm is applied as it is going to be placed in the Virtual Medical Assistant to predict the heart disease of a patient based on the collected values from his/her history. Hence, there is no need for high complex algorithms which otherwise will make the process being getting delayed to take quick decisions.

## LogisticRegression Model

Among the many different ML algorithms, the Logistic Regression is a most popular supervised machine learning algorithm which comes under classification algorithms of ML. It is used to provide a discrete set of classes to the observed set of input data (Pant, 2019). For this chapter, to understand the application of ML in virtual medical assistants, this algorithm is applied. However, the readers can apply any of the other ML algorithms to compare their efficiency for their research publications.

Some typical examples of Logistic Regression Model applied in real world domains are: Classification of E-Mails, Fraudulent transactions identification, Tumor identification etc. The model gets the observations as data set and transforms it to the output as probability value of 0 or 1 or as multi-linear functions that fits a particular class by applying logistic sigmoid function.

It is a predictive analysis algorithm that works based on the probability theory (Pant, 2019).

This model uses a complex cost function using 'Sigmoid' function which is also called as 'Logistic' function. In order to map the predicted values into probability values, the Logistic Regression model applies the Sigmoid Function. It helps to map the real value to probability value in the range of 0 to 1 (Pant, 2019).

*Figure 2. Sigmoid function in logistic regression model*

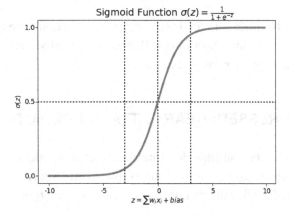

Now, the cost function is defined in Eqn. (1) as given below:

$$Cost\ (h_\theta(x),\ y) = \begin{cases} -log\left(h_\theta(x)\right) & \text{if } y = 1 \\ -log\left(1 - h_\theta(x)\right) & \text{if } y = 0 \end{cases} \tag{1}$$

The combination of these two functions is given as a single function given in Eqn.(2) as given below:

$$J(\theta) = -1/m \sum y^{(i)} log\left(h\theta(x)\right) + (1 - y^{(i)})\ log(1\text{-}h_\theta(x))] \tag{2}$$

Now, to minimize the cost value, the Gradient Descent is applied. It is given in Eqn. (3) as given below:

$$\theta j := \theta j - \alpha \frac{\delta}{\delta\theta j} J(\theta) \tag{3}$$

To get the minimization of cost function, repeat the same calculation as given in the below equation Eqn. (4):

$Min_\theta\ J(\theta)$:

Repeat

$$\{$$
$$\theta j := \theta j - \sum h\theta(x^i) - y^i)xj^{(i)} \tag{4}$$
$$\}$$

In this chapter, this ML algorithm is applied to showcase how an intelligent medical assistant can take efficient decisions based on the predictions given by the model.

## SAMPLE - ML EMBEDDED INTELLIGENT MEDICAL ASSISTANT FOR HEART DISEASE PREDICTION

The sample dataset taken is from Kaggle for Heart Disease Prediction based on Logistic Regression Model based Classification Algorithm. This Logistic Regression based ML classification algorithm uses data of the patients such as age, gender, lab test results.

## PROBLEM TO BE ADDRESSED: HEART ATTACK PREDICTION

One of the significant reasons for choosing this Heart attack prediction problem, is heart disease has become a very crucial and highly a deadly disease among adults. Based on a survey, it was identified that, 30% of deathcases per year reported are due to heart diseases. Hence, several researchers are performing their research on the prediction of such deadly disease before it occurs using innovative solutions. One such significant move is to apply machine learning algorithm in IoT devices to generate fruitful predictions.

## Predicting the Heart Attack Using Dataset

To demonstrate the working of the ML algorithm in heart disease prediction, a dataset is selected from Kaggle which is given by Greg (2020).

For demonstration purpose, this chapter takes only 16 attributes for analytics. Based on the 'target' parameter value, the heart disease prediction can be done.

## Dataset Taken for Learning Purpose

../input/heart-disease-prediction-using-logistic-regression/framingham.csv (Greg, 2020)

## Attribute Information

Personal Data

- Sex: male or female(Nominal)
- Age: Age of the patient;(Continuous - Although the recorded ages have been truncated to whole numbers, the concept of age is continuous)
- Current Smoker: whether or not the patient is a current smoker (Nominal)
- Cigs Per Day: the number of cigarettes that the person smoked on average in one day.(can be considered continuous as one can have any number of cigarettes, even half a cigarette.)

Medical(history)

- BP Meds: whether or not the patient was on blood pressure medication (Nominal)
- Prevalent Stroke: whether or not the patient had previously had a stroke (Nominal)
- Prevalent Hyp: whether or not the patient was hypertensive (Nominal)
- Diabetes: whether or not the patient had diabetes (Nominal)

Medical(Current)

- Tot Chol: total cholesterol level (Continuous)
- Sys BP: systolic blood pressure (Continuous)
- Dia BP: diastolic blood pressure (Continuous)
- BMI: Body Mass Index (Continuous)
- Heart Rate: heart rate (Continuous - In medical research, variables such as heart rate though in fact discrete, yet are considered continuous because of large number of possible values.)
- Glucose: glucose level (Continuous)

Predict Variable (desired target)

- 10 year risk of coronary heart disease CHD (binary: "1", means "Yes", "0" means "No")

## Sample Python Code for Logistic Regression Model to Predict Heart Disease

This chapter gives the exact outcomes of Greg (2020) to help the researchers to understand the application of Logical Regression Model in Machine Learning for prediction in an accurate manner.

The following Python code gives the analysis results as given by Greg (2020) in Kaggle.

```
df <- read.csv("../input/heart-disease-prediction-using-logistic-regression/
framingham.csv")
In [3]:
head(df)
```

It gives the attributes of the Data set as given in table 1.

*Table 1. A data.frame: 6 × 16*

| | Sex | age | education | CurrentSmoker | cigsPerDay | BPMeds | PrevalentStroke | prevalentHyp | diabetes | totChol | sysBP | diaBP | BMI | heartRate | glucose | TenYearCHD |
|---|---|---|---|---|---|---|---|---|---|---|---|---|---|---|---|---|
| | \<int\> | \<int\> | \<int\> | \<int\> | \<int\> | \<int\> | \<int\> | \<int\> | \<int\> | \<int\> | \<dbl\> | \<dbl\> | \<dbl\> | \<int\> | \<int\> | \<int\> |
| 1 | 1 | 39 | 4 | 0 | 0 | 0 | 0 | 0 | 0 | 195 | 106.0 | 70 | 26.97 | 80 | 77 | 0 |
| 2 | 0 | 46 | 2 | 0 | 0 | 0 | 0 | 0 | 0 | 250 | 121.0 | 81 | 28.73 | 95 | 76 | 0 |
| 3 | 1 | 48 | 1 | 1 | 20 | 0 | 0 | 0 | 0 | 245 | 127.5 | 80 | 25.34 | 75 | 70 | 0 |
| 4 | 0 | 61 | 3 | 1 | 30 | 0 | 0 | 1 | 0 | 225 | 150.0 | 95 | 28.58 | 65 | 103 | 1 |
| 5 | 0 | 46 | 3 | 1 | 23 | 0 | 0 | 0 | 0 | 285 | 130.0 | 84 | 23.10 | 85 | 85 | 0 |
| 6 | 0 | 43 | 2 | 0 | 0 | 0 | 0 | 1 | 0 | 228 | 180.0 | 110 | 30.30 | 77 | 99 | 0 |

```
# Convert binary variables to characters for better visualization
df <- df %>%
mutate(sex= as.character(sex),
currentSmoker= as.character(currentSmoker),
prevalentHyp= as.character(prevalentHyp),
        diabetes = as.character(diabetes),
TenYearCHD= as.character(TenYearCHD))
In [9]:
linkcode
x <- ggplot(data = df, mapping =aes(x = as.factor(TenYearCHD), y = age, fill
=TenYearCHD)) +
geom_boxplot()
y <- ggplot(data = df, mapping =aes(x = as.factor(TenYearCHD), y =totChol,
color =TenYearCHD)) +
geom_boxplot()
p <-plot_grid(x, y)
```

```
title <-ggdraw() +draw_label("1. Relationship between TenYearCHD and Age / To-
tCHOL", fontface='bold')
plot_grid(title, p, ncol=1, rel_heights=c(0.1, 1))
# Convert binary variables to characters for better visualization
df <- df %>%
  mutate(male = as.character(male),
currentSmoker= as.character(currentSmoker),
prevalentHyp= as.character(prevalentHyp),
        diabetes = as.character(diabetes),
TenYearCHD= as.character(TenYearCHD))
In [9]:
x <- ggplot(data = df, mapping =aes(x = as.factor(TenYearCHD), y = age, fill
=TenYearCHD)) +
geom_boxplot()
y <- ggplot(data = df, mapping =aes(x = as.factor(TenYearCHD), y =totChol,
color =TenYearCHD)) +
geom_boxplot()
p <-plot_grid(x, y)
title <-ggdraw() +draw_label("1. Relationship between TenYearCHD and Age / To-
tCHOL", fontface='bold')
plot_grid(title, p, ncol=1, rel_heights=c(0.1, 1))
```

In Figure3, the relationship between the age of a person and the impact of it on Heart attack is analyzed. It is found that, for elder age group people, the possibility of heart attack is very high.

*Figure 3. Relationship graph*

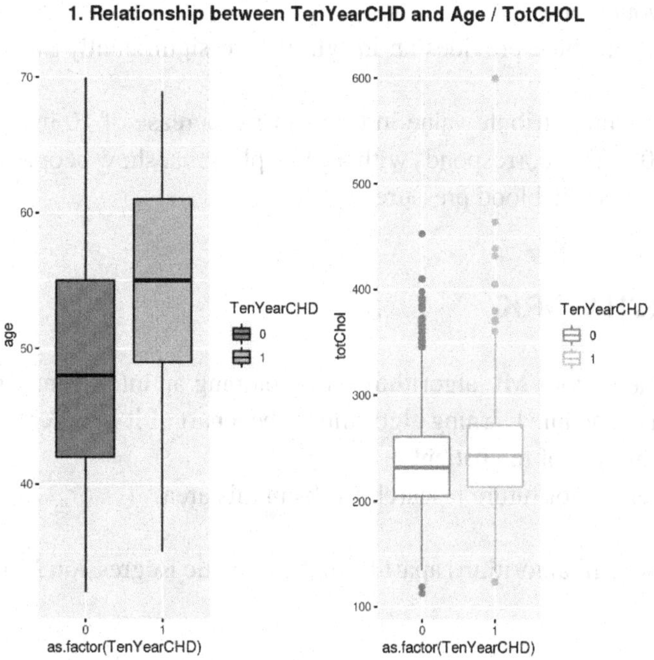

881

*Figure 4. Specificity Vs. Sensitivity*

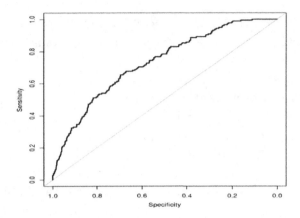

The figure 4 indicates area under the curve is 0.7277 which indicates the prediction that, the possibility of heart attack is much in people who are in the elder group and those who have regular smoking habit.

## Prediction Results

The outcome of the training and testing of the given data set is 0.73 and 0.74 respectively and it indicates that, the Logistic Regression Model is able to predict the heart disease. The significant attributes are the sex of the patient, age, cigarettes per day, systolic blood pressure, and glucose levels.

The effects of these attributes are as follows:

(i)  The attribute 'Sex' of the patient has huge impact on the result. Especially, for Male the heart disease prediction is higher when compared to Female.

(ii)  Age attribute has most common impact on the heart disease. The high impact is on old age people compared to the young ones.

(iii)  Cigarettes Per Day attribute provides an insight that, it significantly increases the heart disease occurrence by 10%.

(iv)  Systolic Blood Pressure attribute value in terms of its increase of 10 units increases the odds of heart disease by 20%. This corresponds with the box plots that show people with heart disease have much higher mean systolic blood pressure.

## FUTURE RESEARCH WORK

This chapter analyses the various ML algorithms in developing an intelligent virtual medical assistant which is equipped with a machine learning algorithm to be a part of it in order to take crucial decisions based on the current condition of the patient.

There are several avenues for future research works in this area:

•  Application of other ML algorithms apart from the Logistic Regression Model to have predictions in the agent.

**A**

- As the analysis of historical data may take more time, the application of cloud based solution to get immediate results based on the data can be considered.
- The application of Edge Analytics in the case of IoT based virtual assistants can also be a future research direction by the researchers.
- Comparison of accuracy and efficiency of different ML algorithms embedded in the virtual assistant can be done as one of the future works.
- The constraints and limitations of applying AI and ML in healthcare can also be a future research work to help the other researchers to understand the downsides and to provide improvement heuristics.

## CONCLUSION

From the collected data and the analysis is done on the data using ML algorithms, we can understand how far the healthcare of a patient can be easily and effectively getting analyzed and monitored. The future of medical world is solely relying on such virtual medical assistants due to reasons such as age and pandemic situations. Hence, if a virtual healthcare assistant is equipped with ML as part of it, the results diagnostics will be effective and faster.

## REFERENCES

Admin, J. (2020). *How to create your AI virtual assistant using Python*. https:// www. analyticsvidhya. com / blog/2020/09/ai-virtual-assistant-using-python/

Ahmed, S. I., & Ahmed, S. (2006). Design And Implementation Of A Virtual Assistant For Healthcare Professionals Using Pervasive Computing Technologies. *E&I Elektrotechnik und Informationstechnik, 123*(4), 112–120. doi:10.100700502-006-0335

Asan, O., Bayrak, A. E., & Choudhury, A. (2020). Artificial Intelligence And Human Trust In Healthcare: Focus On Clinicians. *Journal of Medical Internet Research, 22*(6), e15154. doi:10.2196/15154 PMID:32558657

Balaha, H. M., Balaha, M. H., & Ha, A. (2021). Hybrid COVID-19 Segmentation And Recognition Framework (HMB-HCF) Using Deep Learning And Genetic Algorithms. *Artificial Intelligence in Medicine, 119*, 102156. doi:10.1016/j.artmed.2021.102156 PMID:34531015

Chan, M., Estève, D., Fourniols, J. Y., Escriba, C., & Campo, E. (2012). Smart Wearable Systems: Current Status And Future Challenges. *Artificial Intelligence in Medicine, 56*(3), 137–156. doi:10.1016/j.artmed.2012.09.003 PMID:23122689

Coronato, A., Naeem, M., Pietro, D. G., & Paragliola, G. (2020). Reinforcement Learning For Intelligent Healthcare Applications: A Survey. *Artificial Intelligence in Medicine, 109*, 101964. doi:10.1016/j.artmed.2020.101964 PMID:34756216

Davahli, M. R., Karwowski, W., Fiok, K., Wan, T., & Parsaei, H. R. (2021). Controlling Safety Of Artificial Intelligence Based Systems In Healthcare. *Symmetry, 13*(1), 102. doi:10.3390ym13010102

Dodhia, M., & Jha, R.K., & Anudeep, S. P. (2017). Virtual Healthcare Assistant. *International Journal of Advance Research and Innovative Ideas in Education*, *3*(5), 1–15. 16.0415/IJARIIE-6638

Greg. (2020). *Logistic regression to predict heart disease*. https:// www.kaggle.com /dileep070/heart-disease-prediction-using-logistic-regression

Islam, M. M., Rahaman, A., & Islam, M. R. (2020). Development of Smart Healthcare Monitoring System in IoT Environment. *SN. Computer Science*, *1*(3), 1–11. doi:10.100742979-020-00195-y PMID:33063046

Manne, R., & Kantheti, S. C. (2021). Application of Artificial Intelligence in Healthcare: Chances And Challenges. *Current Journal of Applied Science and Technology*, *40*(6), 78–89. doi:10.9734/cjast/2021/v40i631320

Nguyen, T. L. (2018). Blockchain in healthcare: A new technology benefit for both patients and doctors. *2018 Portland International Conference on Management of Engineering and Technology (PICMET) proceedings*, 1-6. 10.23919/PICMET.2018.8481969

Pant, A. (2019). *Introduction to logistic regression*. https:// towardsdatascience.com /introduction-to-logistic-regression-66248243c148

Parashar, G., Chaudhary, A., & Rana, A. (2021). Systematic Mapping Study Of AI/Machine Learning In Healthcare And Future Directions. *SN. Computer Science*, *2*(6), 461. doi:10.100742979-021-00848-6 PMID:34549197

Ploug, T., & Holm, S. (2020). The Four Dimensions Of Contestable AI Diagnostics - A Patient-Centric Approach To Explainable AI. *Artificial Intelligence in Medicine*, *107*, 101901. doi:10.1016/j.artmed.2020.101901 PMID:32828448

Richardson, J. P., Smith, C., Curtis, S., Watson, S., Zhu, X., Barry, B., & Sharp, R. R. (2021). Patient Apprehensions About The Use Of Artificial Intelligence In Healthcare. *NPJ Digital Medicine*, *4*(1), 140. doi:10.103841746-021-00509-1 PMID:34548621

Rong, G., Mendez, A., Assi, E. B., Zhao, B., & Sawan, M. (2020). Artificial Intelligence In Healthcare: Review And Prediction Case Studies. *Engineering*, *6*(3), 291–301. doi:10.1016/j.eng.2019.08.015

Sumayya. (2020). *10 Healthcare technology trends to improve your well-being*. https:// learn.g2.com/ Healthcare-Technology-Trends

Sundaravadivel, P., Kougianos, E., Mohanty, S. P., & Ganapathiraju, M. K. (2018). Everything You Wanted To Know About Smart Health Care: Evaluating The Different Technologies And Components Of The Internet Of Things For Better Health. *IEEE Consumer Electronics Magazine*, *7*(1), 18–28. doi:10.1109/MCE.2017.2755378

Waring, J., Lindvall, C., & Umeton, R. (2020). Automated Machine Learning: Review of the State-Of-The-Art And Opportunities For Healthcare. *Artificial Intelligence in Medicine*, *104*, 101822. Advance online publication. doi:10.1016/j.artmed.2020.101822 PMID:32499001

# ADDITIONAL READING

Chui, K. T., Lytras, M. D., & Vasant, P. (2020). Combined generative adversarial network and fuzzy C-means clustering for multi-class voice disorder detection with an imbalanced dataset. *Applied Sciences (Basel, Switzerland)*, *10*(13), 4571. doi:10.3390/app10134571

Davenport, T., & Kalakota, R. (2019). The potential for artificial intelligence in healthcare. *Future Healthcare Journal*, *6*(2), 94–98. doi:10.7861/futurehosp.6-2-94 PMID:31363513

Grewal, A., Kaur, M., & Park, J. H. (2019). A unified framework for behaviour monitoring and abnormality detection for smart home. *Wireless Communications and Mobile Computing*, *2019*, 1–16. doi:10.1155/2019/1734615

Khedher, L., Ramírez, J., Górriz, J. M., Brahim, A., & Segovia, F. (2015). Early diagnosis of Alzheimer's disease based on partial least squares, principal component analysis and support vector machine using segmented MRI images. *Neurocomputing*, *151*, 139–150. doi:10.1016/j.neucom.2014.09.072

Kumar, G. (2016). A survey on machine learning techniques in health care industry. *International Journal of Recent Research Aspects*, *3*(2), 128–132.

Secinaro, S., Calandra, D., Secinaro, A., Muthurangu, V., & Biancone, P. (2021). The role of artificial intelligence in healthcare: A structured literature review. *BMC Medical Informatics and Decision Making*, *21*(1), 125. doi:10.118612911-021-01488-9 PMID:33836752

Sweilam, N. H., Tharwat, A. A., & Moniem, N. K. A. (2010). Support vector machine for diagnosis Cancer disease: A comparative study. *Egyptian Informatics Journal*, *11*(2), 81–92. doi:10.1016/j.eij.2010.10.005

Zhao, H., Chen, J., & Lin, Y. (2021). Intelligent recognition of hospital image based on deep learning: The relationship between adaptive behavior and family function in children with ADHD. *Journal of Healthcare Engineering*, *2021*, 1–11. doi:10.1155/2021/4874545 PMID:34188788

# KEY TERMS AND DEFINITIONS

**Artificial Intelligence (AI):** As per the father of AI, McCarthy, "AI is the science and engineering of making the Machine to be intelligent". It helps to make a computer system, a robot or a device to be programmed in such a way that, it mimics the activities of a human by providing a set of rules in the form of a knowledge base and an inference engine to take appropriate decisions automatically.

**Automated Image Diagnostics:** It applies computer assisted mechanism to get the results of medical images taken for a patient to derive results by applying systematic procedures which are provided in the form of software.

**AutoML:** Automated Machine Learning (AutoML) helps non-machine learning experts to apply the different ML algorithms to get the efficiency level in applying them for a particular domain.

**Chatbots:** They are software applications that acts as an agent to perform a particular activity. It uses AI and Natural Language Processing (NLP) to interact with the users based on their needs and it guides the users to get the desired outcome. Example: Siri, Sales Assistants in E-Commerce Sites, etc.

**Data Analytics:** It is the science of applying algorithms to analyze the unprocessed raw data to get some fruitful conclusions. Several techniques are applied to the data analytics process. Statistical analytics is one of the ways of getting insight on the data that is derived from an application domain such as Finance, Share Markets, Manufacturing departments, etc.

**Machine Learning (ML):** It is the subset of Artificial Intelligence which helps the system to learn from the dataset without having any specific programs.

**Predictive Analytics:** It is the branch of data analytics to get predictions on the future by using historical data with current conditions by means of applying statistical algorithms, machine learning algorithms etc. Example: Sales forecasting, Share market price forecasting, Weather forecasting, etc.

**Smart Healthcare:** It is a semi/fully automated service that apply computer technology such as IoT, Internet Notifications, Wearable Devices, Mobile networks, Cloud services with Artificial Intelligence and Machine Learning to provide an efficient healthcare solution.

**Virtual Medical Assistant:** Generally this assistant can be a human or a robot or a device that acts as a medical professional and sits with the patient to help the patient, medical practitioners and relatives of the patients by performing daily recurrent activities. It is generally a remote employee that works in a remote location to give the regular updates of the patient and taking care of the patients based on the current diagnostics results.

**Wearable Computing:** It is the study and application of sensory and computational devices as wearable in order to get the person's current body condition attributes such as temperature, pressure, oxygen level etc. Typical examples are: Smart Watches, Smart Clothing, etc.

A

# Artificial Intelligence–Based Behavioral Biometrics

**Muskan Gupta**
*Vellore Institute of Technology, Vellore, India*

**B. K. Tripathy**
*Vellore Institute of Technology, Vellore, India*

## INTRODUCTION

The traditional authentication methods are based on passwords or PINs, which are not suited to the kind of interaction a user has with more and more portable devices. The problem arises as these authentication methods are based on point-of-entry, where they check a user once before he starts a session, and keep you logged in until a user exits that session (Clarke and Furnell, 2007). This leads to several vulnerabilities to the systems, where a person may target a post-login session.

With the advancements of technology, we have turned towards the usage of biometric security (Gorman, 2003). Biometric security ("Something you are") is a reliable solution that is much preferred over a password ("Something you know") or a token ("Something you have"). Biometric characteristics, being inherently individual are difficult to mimic or change. Studies suggest that biometrics recognition has the potential to support distinctive personality traits, can associate itself with the current system, and become an essential part of the present validation system.

Now, depending on the number of traits that are used for validation a biometric system can be divided into two systems: Uni-modal biometric system and Multimodal biometric system. The Uni-model systems use one biometric trait that can be an aid in the process of recognition. But the use of a single trait has proved to have many drawbacks such as restricted degree of freedom, spoofing and presence of noise in sensed data (A. Buriro,2016), (Kresimir and Mislav, 2004). On the other hand, we have a multi-modal biometric system that uses multiple traits for verification.

Based on this, in this chapter, we are trying to understand the two systems, in one of the emerging fields in this sector, Behavioral Biometrics which proposes a system of continuous authentication which is also non-intrusive in the workflow of the user. In general, they are particularly well equipped for verification of people who make use of laptops, smartphones, smart cars, or points of sale terminals. As the amount of digital appliances used in our surroundings is increasing exponentially (De et al, 2020), so does the prospects for utilization of this up-and-coming technology. It also provides numerous benefits over traditional biometric technologies. Collection of data for behavioral biometric verification often does not require any peculiar hardware and is also cost-efficient and can be cumulated non-obtrusively or without even the awareness of the patron. While most behavioral biometrics are not adequately distinctive to support trustworthy human identification, they have been manifested to yield rapturous accuracy for identity verification. So to explore this field more we did a comprehensive review in the paper is done

DOI: 10.4018/978-1-7998-9220-5.ch051

by comparing different parameters for verification of behavioral biometric approaches, and addressing the evolution of study and applications of behavioral biometrics (Fairhurst et al, 2017).

## BIOMETRIC AND ITS TYPES

Let's, first understand the term "biometrics", it is extracted from the Greek words 'bio' which infers life and 'metric' means to measure. So in simple words, Biometrics refers to the study of metrics or traits associated with life, and interestingly it is used in the field of computer science as a technique to identify individuals.

Biometric identifiers can be seen as differentiating, quantifiable traits which are manipulated to label and characterize an individual.

Biometric is broadly segmented into two parts: physiological versus behavioral characteristics.

### Physiological Biometric

Physiological characteristics are linked to the static traits of an organism that are not prone to variation over time. Some implementation of physiological traits is face recognition (Tripathy and Sasikumar, 2012), (Debgupta et al, 2020), hand geometry, fingerprint (Tripathy et al, 2012), iris recognition, DNA, retina and many more. A useful face identification technique with masks is given in (Surya et al, 2021).

### Behavioral Biometric

The behavioral avenue of biometrics is restricted to the behavioral traits of an organism that is related to the personal behaviour of an individual such as voice recognition, signature recognition, gait and keystroke dynamics and based on the number of features or metrics it is segmented as uni and multimodal.

### Physiological Versus Behavioral Biometric

If we use physical biometric techniques to authenticate users in an online platform it can be considered that the use of a single physical biometric data point for authentication at the time of login, is the same as entering a static second password – as it can never be changed (due to human constraints) if compromised. Thus the major issue with physiological biometrics is that it can be compromised or leaked. For instance, a fingerprint– the use of such a physical biometric attribute is the same as saving a list of passwords in your laptop, but instead of it being just on their laptop, they simply leave a copy on everything they touch to be a cup they pick up or a chewing gum they discard.

So as a solution we have a more secure, user-friendly technique that makes use of the signals generated by how a person interacts with their surroundings. When these behavioral signals are accumulated they are highly effective at authenticating as they are not only self enrolling but also tolerant to change in the behavioral pattern of the users. Unlike physiological biometrics, behavioral biometrics data points cannot be duplicated or stolen thus is of no use to a malicious user and even if there is a case of high fidelity copy of legitimate user interaction, the attempt to recreate a previous interaction would be considered as an anomaly.

Now, as the prominence of behavioral over physiological biometrics is clear let's delve deep into the domain of behavioral biometrics. The classification of behavioral biometrics is detailed in Figure 1.

*Figure 1. Types of behavioral biometrics*

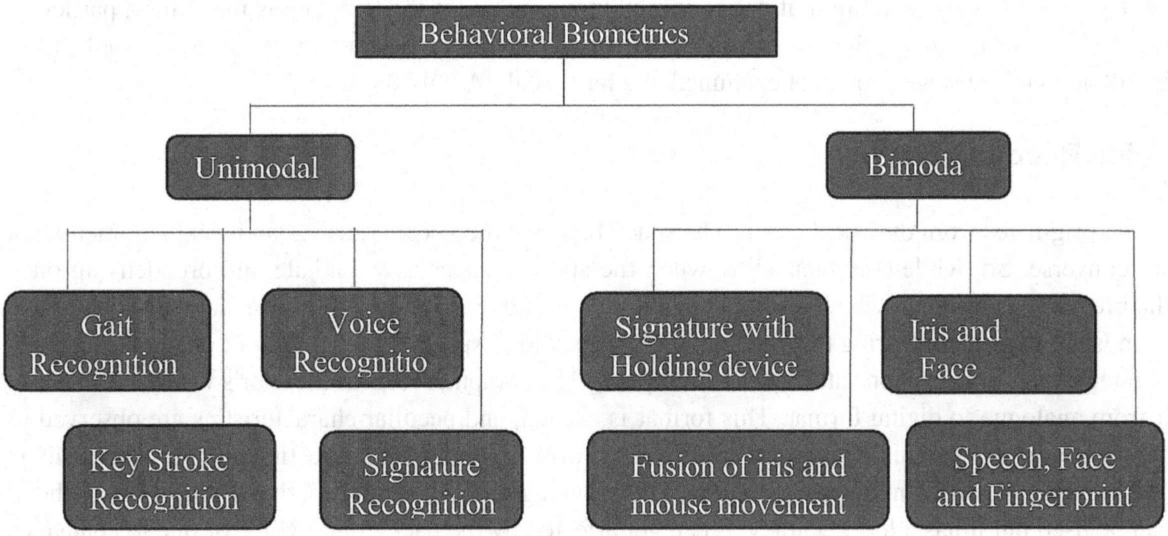

## UNI-MODAL BEHAVIORAL BIOMETRICS

Biometric identification systems that are dependent on one trait (biometric) of a user for recognition and verification is known as uni-modal systems.

## Gait Recognition

People often perceive that they can recognize an individual from a distance easily by identifying the style of how one walks. This wonted experience, accompanied with neoteric development in biometrics, has led to the instigation of gait recognition as a kind of biometric recognition. So, in other words, it is one of the biometrics that is based on the idiosyncratic manner of how an individual walks. This technique truly justifies the credibility as it can be attained without the approbation of the individual being observed one of the positive aspects of gait is that it can be done using normal surveillance cameras from a distance at a low cost. But there are numerous factors, for example, physical changes because of pregnancy, injury, weight gain or weight loss, a person's mood or drugs and alcohol which may make a person unbalanced that can adversely affect this mode of biometric. Moreover, it can also be feigned and can get affected by the surroundings or clothes that one wear. (Alsadi, 2015), (Derawi et al, 2010).

## Keystroke Recognition

Every individual has his typing style. Typing styles are the most effective way of collecting the data between user and system. They become a useful tool to acquire the level of authentication when it is adequately sampled and analyzed.

This technique recognizes a person on various styles of typing skills that one can have. To implement this in real time a keyboard is required, which is coupled to a computer. During verification the user is told to type a set of words in a particular time interval, if a misprint occurs, one has to start all over again. The criteria for verification includes cumulative typing speed, elapsed time between consecutive strokes, the way of typing, time of holding each key and whether the user let off the shift key or the letter key first. The main benefit of this system is that it is software-based and can be collaborated with other modes of technique. In addition, it needs nominal training and if the template is made for a particular word and it is vandalized, then the word can be substituted, and a new template can be devised. But it is still at an initial stage and is not examined at a large scale(Antal,2014).

## Voice Recognition

Voice originates from the vocal cords. The space between the vocal cords expands and contract when we converse. So, while communicating when the space reduces as we inhale and broadens up once the breath goes through, which results in distinctive sound. So, we can say as this happens distinctive sounds are generated. During this method, the user is told to speak in the vicinity of characters or a list of integers, on a microphone attached to a computer. The computer records the user's voice and converts it from analogue to digital format. This format is cached, and peculiar characteristics are observed to create a template. Various samples are taken and a profile is created by contrasting numerous recordings and intuiting the different iterating patterns. The advantages of this model are that a simple microphone can be used but it has a low accuracy as can get affected by the background voice or due to change of voice of an individual due to ageing, illness and other factors. (Bansal et al, 2015), (Markowitz, 2000))

## Signature

Signature Recognition tests the behavioral aspects within which one tend to sign his/her name. This method relies on behavioral characteristics like modification in temporal arrangement, pressure, speed, overall size and numerous directions of strokes throughout the course of the signing. The supposing copying of signatures looks straightforward visually, but it's difficult to replicate the activities associated with it. The device consists of a pen (stylus) and a writing tablet that is associated with a local system. The user needs to sign on the tablet with a pen. Then all the information about the peculiar characteristics of the user has been analyzed to forms a template, which is then cached in a database. The user must sign many times to ensure an accurate template is retrieved and stored. The benefit of this method is that it is a non-invasive technique that is recognized at a large scale and is difficult to forge. But the drawback is that the signature shouldn't belong or be short because if it's long then it will contain a high number of dynamic information and thus create an issue for the system to spot the consistent and distinctive data points. On the other hand, if it is too short, there may not be enough data for the system to create a peculiar template. Moreover, it should be made sure that the enrollment process of the signature is done under the same environmental condition like the user should be sitting, or resting one's arm. (Fang and Wu, 2018)

## MULTI-MODAL BEHAVIORAL BIOMETRICS

Biometric identification systems that utilize or is using a mixture of two or more biometric traits to recognize a person/organism is known as multimodal biometric systems. The essential factor for making use of multimodal biometric systems is to enhance the recognition rate. The latest technology with audiovisual features and Deep Neural Nets is given in (Bose and Tripathy, 2020).

## Signature while Holding the Device

This authentication method is to be used for portable devices such as mobile phones. This system considers the micro-movements of the device and the movement of the finger of the user as he is writing on the screen. But it does not consider the final image of the signature; rather it takes into account only the movements and the pattern of the finger movement. This technique has been implemented on several commercially available devices as it does not require the usage of any additional hardware to work. Multiple sensors are used in tandem to record the data. The sensors start working when the user first touches the screen and do not stop until he removes his finger signalling the end of the input. The negative aspect of this model includes intraclass variability, variations in signatures of the same user. It also includes similarity between signatures of different users and takes a long time than physiological biometric (approx. 3 sec) .in Addition two-handed usage is supported. But on the other hand, it also provides average power consumption is low, Signature-based authentication is already used in other modes and Signature is easier to remember compared to a passcode. (Buriro et al, 2016)

## Fusion of Iris and Mouse Movement

This is an authentication method that is to be used for desktops or laptops. Since each of these methods individually has many disadvantages, we use a fusion of these to reduce the error rate. The systems which already use iris scanning can be easy modified using software to create a multi-modal approach for iris with mouse tracking. The advantages of this method are that it reduces identification time, applies differences in space using dynamic time warping for extraction of features from the eye. Moreover, the mouse dynamics can be done in a single instance which is short and convenient for the user, but the error rate could be 5% to 10% and many factors could decrease the accuracy of recognition especially for iris. (Kasprowski and Katarzyna, 2018)

## Iris and Face Recognition

This authentication methodology is utilized as a combination of face recognition and Iris recognition. Besides enhancing the identification performance, the fusion of each of the biometrics has many alternative benefits like increasing user population coverage and decreasing enrollment failure.

Two different strategies can be used for achieving this multimodal technique. The primary technique is to calculate either an unweighted or weighted sum of the two similar distances and contrast the distances to a threshold. The second technique is to treat the similar distances of face and iris classifiers as a two-dimensional feature vector and use a classifier such as the Fisher's discriminant analysis or a neural network with radial basis function (RBFNN) to classify the vector as being real or a fraud. An operational iris authentication system would not consider bad quality pictures. The system conjointly shows that fusion could be a way to reduce the enrollment failure rate. At an equivalent time, a bigger range of subjects was misclassified by the complete face verification system, which may be classified simply with the combined system however it needs IR light and detector. What is more actinic radiation should be reduced for the highest accuracy needed for search and conjointly troubles with pictures size and quality (Jain and Wang, 2003).

## Speech, Face and Fingerprint

This multimodal biometric system uses face and finger images and voice signals for the event of the projected system. Feature from every biometric document has been extracted and consolidated on the idea of score level fusion to cut back feature dimension. After extraction of the features from completely different samples these features are consolidated using the feature-level fusion approach that has been used for fusing of all the feature values. These features are consolidated on the idea of various parts and magnitudes. After fusion, these options are held on in a dataset file so can be used for the recognition method. Within the method of recognition completely different testing samples are loaded to the system and these samples are used for extraction of features mistreatment extraction approaches Computation speed increases because of reduction in feature dimension of consolidated options. This proposed system provides an accuracy of ninety-eight per cent. This provides better security than an alternative biometric system as a result of the illegal availability of all the traits of a single person who isn't on the market to match and perform any illegal operation. (Kaur and Kaur, 2018)

## COMPARISON

In Table 1, we provide a comparative analysis of different methods of multimodal behavioral biometrics and in Table 2 we provide a similar comparison for the uni-modal behavioral biometrics.

The different techniques in the above tables are factored based on Reliability, ease of use, error, cost, hardware requirements, stability, intrusive and accuracy parameters. If we talk about the usability of these technologies the primary parameters to consider include reliability and accuracy. So when [Table1] is compared to [Table 2], it can be observed that for multimodal behavioral biometrics these parameters are high for all methods while for unimodal the methods can not be trusted blindly with an exception to iris recognition. But in terms of cost and ease of use, the unimodal are better.

*Table 1. Multimodal Behavioral Biometrics*

| Method | References | Reliability | Ease of Use | Errors | Cost | Hardware required | Long term stability | Intrusive | Accuracy |
|---|---|---|---|---|---|---|---|---|---|
| **Signature + Motion Sensing** | (A. Buriro, B. Crispo, F. Delfrari and K. Wrona, 2016) | High (95% True Acceptance Rate) | High (Trainin g Time: 3.5 - 9.3s) | Hand Injury, tiredness | Medium | Sensors already present in smartphones | High (68.33% SUS Score) | Low (Sign In time: 3.7-3.8s) | High (when person is close to stationary), Low (When person is in motion) |
| **Iris + Mouse Movement** | (Kasprowski Pawel, Katarzyna Harezlak, 2018) | High (Iris is highly secure) | Medium (Iris requires decent lighting conditio ns) | Hand injury | High | Special (Infrared Iris Scanner) | Medium (Accuracy improves over time) | Medium (Requires waiting for iris scan) | High (92.9%) |
| **Iris + Facial Recognition** | (Jain Anil K, Wang Yunhong, Tan Tieniu, 2003) | Very High (2-9.8% Error Rate at 15-75% threshold) | Medium (Iris requires decent lighting conditio ns) | Lighting conditions | High | Special (Infrared Iris Scanner) | High (Using neural network, accuracy improves) | Medium (Proper lighting and eyes wide open required) | High (Very Low error rate, around 2%) |
| **Voice + Face + Fingerprint** | (Kaur Ravdeep, Kaur Baldip, 2018) | Very High (98.7 Genuine Acceptance Rate) | Low () | Cold, dryness of finger | Medium | Sensors already present in Smartphones | Medium (System improves over time) | Medium (Fingerprint becomes intrusive) | Very High (98.7%) |

*Table 2. Unimodal Behavioral Biometrics*

| Method | References | Reliability | Ease of Use | Errors | Cost | Hardware required | Stability | Intrusive | Accuracy |
|---|---|---|---|---|---|---|---|---|---|
| **Facial Recognition** | (Kaur Ravdeep, Kaur Baldip, 2018) | Medium | High | Lighting, glasses | Low | Common | Medium | Low | Low |
| **Signature Recognition** | (J. Fang, 2018) | Low | High | Changing signature, rushed writing | Low | Common | Medium | Low | Medium |
| **Keystroke Dynamics** | (Antal,2014) | Low | High | Hand injury, tiredness | Low | Common | Low | Low | Low |
| **Voice Recognition** | (Shweta Bansal, Alok Kushwala, S.S. Agrawal, 2015), (Markowitz, J. A.,000) | Low | Medium | Noise, cold | Low | Common | Medium | Medium | Medium |
| **Mouse Movement** | (D. A. Schulz, 2006) | Low | High | Hand injury, tiredness | Low | Common | Low | Low | Low |
| **Motion Sensing (Handheld)** | (A. Buriro, B. Crispo, F. Delfrari and K. Wrona, 2016) | Low | High | Any physical activity | Medium | Somewhat common | Low | Low | Low |
| **Iris Recognition** | (Hugo Proença, Luís A. Alexandre, 2012) | High | Medium | Poor lighting, direct sunlight | High | Special | High | Medium | High |
| **Gait** | (Alsaadi Israa,2015),(M. O. Derawi, C. Nickel, P. Bours and C. Busch, 2010) | Medium | High | Tiredness | Low | Common | Low | Low | Low |

So there is scope for a lot of improvement as all the multimodal behavioral technologies are not very user friendly and cost-effective.

## USE CASES OF BEHAVIORAL BIOMETRICS

To date, behavioral biometrics technology has been deployed in four distinct types of applications: Continuous Authentication, Risk-Based Authentication and Fraud Detection and Prevention.

## Continuous Authentication

Continuous authentication can be seen as a verification process aimed at providing permanent identity verification and cybersecurity protection. This process estimates the probability that a discrete network user is whom you are talking about throughout the session. However, the continuous authentication method is quite new.

Behavioral biometrics enables persistent authentication due to its nature of passive data collection. Continuous authentication provides proof of a user's identity over some time.

Although trust in that authentication may naturally vary, the ability that behavioral biometrics provides to perform continuous authentication bridges an important gap that's common in many current security programs.

## Fraud Detection and Prevention

One of the primary use cases for behavioral biometrics is fraud detection and prevention. It is majorly used in financial, enterprise and government applications. For example, a financial services provider may use a behavioral biometrics application to examine months' worth of historical user data to better identify

(1)    what circumstances are flagged as potential fraud events, and
(2)    to validate the fidelity and utility of those alerts.

## Risk-Based Authentication

Risk-based authentication (RBA) uses ratings to determine if someone can take action on the platform. This can be a login or transaction, among other things.

The ratings are calculated primarily based totally on threat regulations that examine numerous factors.

There are two main objectives for risk-based authentication. It includes blocking suspicious users and allowing legitimate users to access online platforms without irrelevant hindrances. Web visitors classified as dangerous must be asked for additional credentials such as a passphrase, 2FA code, or additional identification.

Behavioral biometrics is also used to prevent risk-based authentication for transactions conducted via online platforms. Specifically, a range of behavioral data generated by an individual using a device is analyzed in conjunction with the completion of a legacy single-transaction authentication method.

## AI AND BEHAVIORAL BIOMETRICS

The role of AI in behavioral biometrics is peculiar. It is not like other applications like image recognition and speech processing, here the AI is executing a task that no human can do because the signals in which the user's behavioral data is encoded is not in a form that can be comprehended by humans. Even a narrow AI give better accuracy than the most experienced human. (Krishna, 2021)

Typically, behavioral biometrics involved extraction of key signal characteristics— such as the length of stride, speed of typing, or characteristic user flows through a graphic user interface—which are further modelled for each user. This ultimately builds the characterization of all users and allows them to distinguish one individual from another. Recent developments in deep learning made this procedure more specific to each user, allowing the AI to recognize and model those characteristics of each user's behavior that sets them apart— which helps to distinguish them from all the other users—which ultimately results in increasing the efficiency and performance.

## FUTURE OF BIOMETRICS WITH AI

All the above-discussed methods are implemented by using AI in which the AI analysis of factors like accuracy, speed and so on, makes for a system that is enduring recently and is rarely subjected to false positives and negatives, i.e. saving both time and other liquid assists. Systems that execute AI technology can also be utilized for the steady monitoring of different traits. For instance, in a notably secure destination where an individual regularly works on documentation, artificial intelligence can persistently monitor the typing behaviour of the worker to keep a check on data tampering is occurrences and the identity of the person editing the document. AI systems can also be used in combination with more traditional forms of biometric verification such as iris and retinal scans.

Advancement in artificial intelligence can also be advantageous to these old but efficient methods of biometric verification. For instance, machine vision has shown impressive accuracy and can aid some other techniques that were previously seen as unwanted to be faster, and more efficient for the users. But artificial intelligence to biometrically recognize Homo sapiens is not the final note in biometric advancements. Recent technological modifications bring out a new issue–which we must accurately identify.

These days we are regularly making use of robots, androids, AI, virtual avatars, and other similar entities in our lives. As Yampolskiy and Gavrilova explain in their paper (De et al, 2020) a cost-efficient, dependable, and decentralized method is required to recognize the agents as they regularly work with humans in both our physical and digital world.

## CONCLUSION

Combining different biometric techniques has proven to be an extremely reliable approach in experiments and real-life biometric recognition applications. Multimodal biometric systems can conquer various constraints that we face in identical systems. For instance, the solution to the issue of non-globalization can be ensured by using multiple characteristic biometrics for the optimal segment of the population. It also increases the complexity for a hacker or attacker to deceive multiple biometric properties of an authorized user at once. The fusion of different biometric data is the key to multimodal biometrics. But, the application is not restricted to security, recently it has been proposed that the future for marketers is in biometrics with vision AI behind can help get insights over the subconscious recollection of how customers interact with advertisements in real life. So, we can say that the application and innovation in the field of biometric and artificial intelligence have just begun.

## REFERENCES

Antal, M., & Szabo, L. (2014). *László & Izabella*. Keystroke Dynamics on Android Platform.

Bansal, S., Kushwala, A., & Agrawal, S.S. (2015). An overview on Speaker Identification Technologies. *IRJASET, 3*(6), 179-186.

Bhatt, S., & Santhanam, T. (2013). Keystroke dynamics for biometric authentication — A survey. *2013 International Conference on Pattern Recognition, Informatics and Mobile Engineering*, 17-23. 10.1109/ICPRIME.2013.6496441

Bose, A., & Tripathy, B. K. (2020). Deep Learning for Audio Signal Classification. De Gruyter Publications.

Burino, A., Crispo, B., Delfrari, F., & Wrona, K. (2016). *Hold and Sign: A Novel Behavioral Biometrics for Smartphone User Authentication. In 2016 IEEE Security and Privacy Workshops.* SPW.

Clarke, N., & Furnell, S. M. (2007). Advanced user authentication for mobile devices. *Computers & Security, 26*(2), 109–119. doi:10.1016/j.cose.2006.08.008

De, R., Pandey, N., & Pal, A. (2020). *Impact of digital surge during Covid-19 pandemic: A viewpoint on research and practice.* doi:10.1016/j.ijinfomgt.2020.102171

Debgupta, R., Chaudhuri, B. B., & Tripathy, B. K. (2020). A Wide ResNet-Based Approach for Age and gender Estimation in Face Images. *International Conference on Innovative Computing and Communications, Advances in Intelligent Systems and Computing, 1087,* 517-530. 10.1007/978-981-15-1286-5_44

Delac & Grgic. (2004). A survey of biometric recognition methods. *46th International Symposium Electronics in Marine, ELMAR-2004.*

Derawi, M. O., Nickel, C., Bours, P., & Busch, C. (2010). Unobtrusive User-Authentication on Mobile Phones Using Biometric Gait Recognition. *2010 Sixth International Conference on Intelligent Information Hiding and Multimedia Signal Processing,* 306-311. 10.1109/IIHMSP.2010.83

Fairhurst, M., Li, C., & Da Costa-Abreu, M. (2017). Predictive biometrics: A review and analysis of predicting personal characteristics from biometric data. *Biometrics IET, 6*(6), 369–378. doi:10.1049/iet-bmt.2016.0169

Fang, J., & Wu, W. (2018). Research on Signature Verification Method Based on Discrete Fréchet Distance. *IOP Conference Series: Materials Science and Engineering,* 359. 10.1088/1757-899X/359/1/012003

Gorman, L. O. (2003). Comparing passwords, tokens, and biometrics for user authentication. *Proceedings of the IEEE, 91*(12), 2019–2040. doi:10.1109/JPROC.2003.819605

Israa, A. (2015). Physiological Biometric Authentication Systems, Advantages, Disadvantages And Future Development: A Review. *International Journal of Scientific & Technology Research, 4,* 285–289.

Jain Anil, K., Wang, Y., & Tan, T. (2003). Combining Face and Iris Biometrics for Identity Verification. *Lecture Notes in Computer Science, 2688.*

Markowitz, J. A. (2000). Voice biometrics. *Communications of the ACM, 43*(9), 66–73. doi:10.1145/348941.348995

Menzefricke, K. (2021). *AI- and ML-driven Behavioural Biometrics Emerge as a Key Advantage in Multifactor Authentication.* https://www.frost.com/news/press-releases/ai-and-ml-driven-behavioural-biometrics-emerge-as-a-key-advantage-in-multifactor-authentication/

Pawel, K., & Harezlak, K. (2018). Fusion of eye movement and mouse dynamics for reliable behavioral biometrics. *Pattern Analysis & Applications, 21*(1), 91–103. doi:10.100710044-016-0568-5

Prabhakar, S., Pankanti, S., & Jain, A. K. (2003). Biometric Recognition: Security & Privacy Concerns. *IEEE Security and Privacy Magazine, 1*(2), 33–42. doi:10.1109/MSECP.2003.1193209

Proença, H., & Alexandre, L. A. (2012). Introduction to the Special Issue on the Recognition of Visible Wavelength Iris Images Captured At-a-distance and On-the-move. *Pattern Recognition Letters, 33*(8), 963–964. doi:10.1016/j.patrec.2012.03.003

Ravdeep, K., & Baldip, K. (2018). Secure Multimodal Biometric Recognition Based on Speech, Face and Fingerprint Using Feature Level Fusion Approach. *International Advanced Research Journal in Science, Engineering and Technology, 5*(8), 95–100. doi:10.17148/IARJSET.2018.58511

Saevanee, H., Clarke, N., & Furnell, S. M. (2012). *Multi-modal Behavioural Biometric Authentication for Mobile Devices. In Advances in Information and Communication Technology* (Vol. 376). Springer.

Schulz, D. A. (2006). Mouse Curve Biometrics. *2006 Biometrics Symposium: Special Session on Research at the Biometric Consortium Conference*, 1-6.

Shen, P. (2013). A Survey of Keystroke Dynamics Biometrics. The Scientific World Journal.

Tripathy, B. K., Chandramoulli, P. V. S. S. R., & Ranajit, B. (2012, May). A New Approach for Fingerprint recognition using Earth Mover's Distance. *International Journal of Advanced Research in Computer Science, 3*(3), 223.

Tripathy, B. K., & Sasikumar, G. (2012). Design and Implementation of Face Recognition System in Mat lab Using the Features of Lips. *Int. Jour. of Intelligent Systems and Applications, 8.* https://www.ibia.org/download/datasets/3839/Behavioral%20Biometrics%20white%20paper.pdf

Yagna Sai Surya, Geetha Rani, & Tripathy, B.K. (2021). Social Distance Monitoring and Face Mask Detection Using Deep Learning. *ICCIDM 2021.*

Yampolskiy, R. V., & Gavrilova, M. L. (2012). Biometrics for Artificial Entities. *IEEE Robotics & Automation Magazine, 19*(4), 48–58. doi:10.1109/MRA.2012.2201574

## ADDITIONAL READING

Abdulrahman, S. A., & Alhayani, B. (2021). A comprehensive survey on the biometric systems based on physiological and behavioural characteristics. *Materials Today: Proceedings.* Advance online publication. doi:10.1016/j.matpr.2021.07.005

Berghoff, C., Neu, M., & von Twickel, A. (2021). The Interplay of AI and Biometrics: Challenges and Opportunities. *Computer, 54*(09), 80–85. doi:10.1109/MC.2021.3084656

Bolle, R. M., Connell, J. H., Pankanti, S., Ratha, N. K., & Senior, A. W. (2013). *Guide to biometrics.* Springer Science & Business Media.

Carlaw, S. (2020). Impact on biometrics of Covid-19. *Biometric Technology Today, 2020*(4), 8–9. doi:10.1016/S0969-4765(20)30050-3

Gavrilova, M. L., & Monwar, M. (2013). *Multimodal biometrics and intelligent image processing for security systems.* IGI Global. doi:10.4018/978-1-4666-3646-0

Jain, A. K., Flynn, P., & Ross, A. A. (Eds.). (2007). *Handbook of biometrics.* Springer Science & Business Media.

Kairinos, N. (2019). The integration of biometrics and AI. *Biometric Technology Today*, *2019*(5), 8–10. doi:10.1016/S0969-4765(19)30069-4

Modi, S. K. (2011). *Biometrics in identity management: Concepts to applications*. Artech House.

Rane, S., Wang, Y., Draper, S. C., & Ishwar, P. (2013). Secure biometrics: Concepts, authentication architectures, and challenges. *IEEE Signal Processing Magazine*, *30*(5), 51–64. doi:10.1109/MSP.2013.2261691

Rodgers, W., Yeung, F., Odindo, C., & Degbey, W. Y. (2021). Artificial intelligence-driven music biometrics influencing customers' retail buying behavior. *Journal of Business Research*, *126*, 401–414. doi:10.1016/j.jbusres.2020.12.039

van Esch, P., Stewart Black, J., Franklin, D., & Harder, M. (2020). Al-enabled biometrics in recruiting: Insights from marketers for managers. *Australasian Marketing Journal*.

## KEY TERMS AND DEFINITIONS

**AI:** Artificial intelligence is intelligence equipped by machines.

**Authentication:** It is the process to identify if the claim made is valid or not.

**Behavioral:** It refers to the intrinsic quality of how an individual behaves.

**Biometric:** Bio means life and metrics infer measurements. So the study of categorization of someone based on their life characteristics that can be measured is called biometrics.

**Multi-Modal:** Biometric identification systems that are dependent on more than one trait (biometric) of a user for recognition and verification is known as uni-modal systems.

**Security:** It is a sense of protection provided to an individual with regard to something that is considered sensitive or confidential.

**Uni-Modal:** Biometric identification systems that are dependent on one trait (biometric) of a user for recognition and verification is known as uni-modal systems.

A

# Artificial Neural Networks and Data Science

**Trevor Bihl**

*Air Force Research Laboratory, USA*

**William A. Young II**

*Ohio University, USA*

**Adam Moyer**

*Ohio University, USA*

**Steven Frimel**

*Air Force Research Laboratory, USA*

## INTRODUCTION

Artificial neural networks (ANNs) provide an ability to identify known and obvious patterns in the data as well as Knowledge Discovery in Datasets (KDD). KDD, the process of finding non-obvious patterns or trends in complicated systems or datasets (Mannila, 1996), is critical to providing useful algorithmic processes. ANNs leverage biologically-inspired computational pattern recognition methods to predict, describe, classify, group, categorize and identify information from data sources (Jain, Duin, & Mao, 2000). One advantage of ANNs is that they are able to learn nonlinear patterns in data in an efficient manner. The non-linear patterns in data and the complex algorithms result in ANNs, and resultant ANN models, being complex and opaque to many users (Weckman, et al., 2009). While ANNs have been applied in many business applications, these applications have been tempered and approached with some hesitation due to a lack of understanding and misconceptions of what is occurring because of the 'black-box' nature of ANNs (Dewdney, 1997).

ANNs methods consist of interconnected networks of weights and nodes, in which the weights are trained on patterns in data through statistical learning methods (Jain, Duin, & Mao, 2000). Although ANNs are computationally complex, inherently ANNs are statistical in nature and epistemologically similar in function to Bayesian methods (Beck, King, & Zeng, 2004), using conditional probability and likelihood methods (Verikas & Bacauskiene, 2002). Various software packages are now available for practitioners, including NeuroDimensions (2005), Matlab (2010), JMP (Sall, Lehman, Stephens, & Creighton, 2012), Python (Vasilev, Slater, Spacagna, Roelants, & Zocca, 2019), and R (2008). Many of these software packages are open-source in nature, e.g., R and Python. The objective of this chapter is to provide readers with a general background of ANNs, ANN business applications, and developing quality ANN models. The target audience is intended to be readers who may not be familiar with this form of mathematical modeling and application but may want to pursue and investigate ANN techniques for their business needs.

DOI: 10.4018/978-1-7998-9220-5.ch052

In Bihl, Young, and Weckman (2018), the authors provided a brief overview of ANNs and their applications in business with an example end-to-end analysis of business data using ANNs with the JMP13 Pro platform. Herein, the authors expand upon this discussion with a concise background of the ANNs, considerations for deep learning, proper methods to developing and deploying repeatable ANNs, and the processes needed to support the development through the deployment of ANNs to support business applications.

## BACKGROUND

Computational ANNs are based on the biological neuron models consisting of multiple interconnected nodes termed "neurons." However, unlike biologic neurons, ANNs employ statistical methods to learn patterns between inputs and outputs (Jain, Duin, & Mao, 2000). A conceptualization showing the ANN interconnected neurons is presented in Figure 1. Through organizational and iterative principles, connection weights between neurons, inputs, and outputs are computed to learn a nonlinear input-output relationship (Jain, Duin, & Mao, 2000).

Inputs to ANNs, such as Figure 1, are in data form and are analogous to biological axons from other neurons feeding into a neuron's dendrites (Bihl, Young II, & Weckman, 2018). In biologic neurons, the cell processes the inputs, this is represented through hidden nodes in an artificial neuron whereby a transfer and activation function process the input data and an output signal is created. The outputs are then analogous as axons in biology and probabilities in ANNs (Bihl, Young II, & Weckman, 2018). However, biological neurons are currently understood to communicate in a complex manner through molecular, electrical, cellular, systems, and behavioral means (Sweatt, 2016) (Kandel, Siegelbaum, Mack, & Koester, 2021); thus, artificial neurons are a considerable simplification of the system using only the electrical aspect of transmission.

*Figure 1. Basic conceptualization of an ANN*

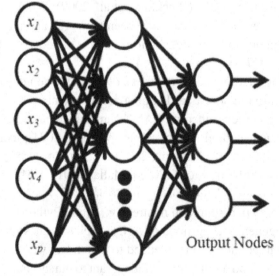

When artificial neurons are assembled as seen in Figure 2, the end result is an ANN which has a mapping between independent inputs ($X_1$, $X_2$, $X_3$, and $X_p$), connection weights ($W_1$, $W_2$, $W_3$, and $W_p$), and bias (B), and a dependent variable/output (Y) (Bihl, Young II, & Weckman, 2018). The weights (W1.. Wn) represent the strength of the association between independent and dependent variables (positive, negative, or zero). These weights are determined through statistical methods (Bihl, Young II, & Weckman, 2018). In several cases, the statistical methods are referred as to iterative training approaches in which known inputs and outputs are used to set the weights. The inputs are provided to the ANNs and the weights are adjusted until the input produces the correct output.

ANNs differ from the biological neurons based on the paradigm/generation they follow, as conceptualized in Figure 3. The inspiration of biology in ANNs has yielded multiple generations of meta-architectural approaches. First generation ANNs began with McCulloch and Pitts (McCulloch & Pitts, 1943) who developed the earliest known artificial neuron model which is conceptualized in the leftmost column of Figure 3. The McCulloch and Pitts (MP) model, or perceptron, produced a binary/digital step function for the output of the neuron if a signal achieved a threshold (Wang, Lin, & Dang, 2020). The MP perceptron neuron model led to further developments resulting in multi-layer networks, termed threshold circuits, Hopfield networks, and Boltzmann machines (Maass, 1997). Notably, MP perceptrons are further universal approximators for digital computations and thus any Boolean function can be computed by a multilayer perceptron with a single hidden layer (Maass, 1997).

*Figure 2. Biological Neuron with biologically inspired Artificial Neuron*

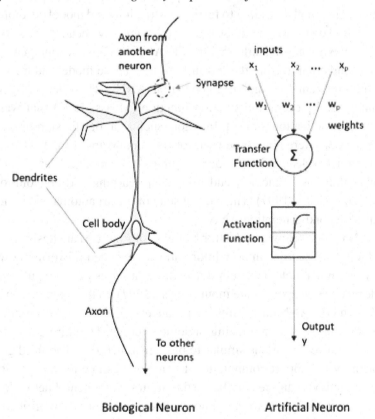

*Figure 3. Conceptualization ANN generations with analogs to biology, adapted and extended from (Wang, Lin, & Dang, 2020)*

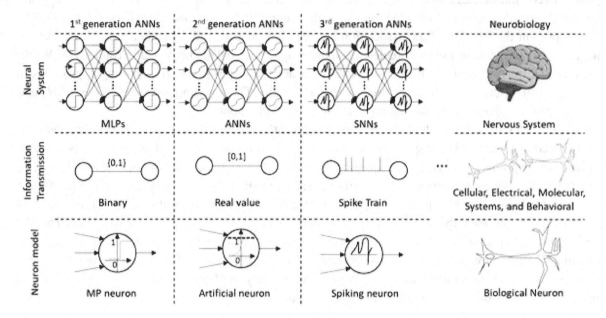

Despite the benefits of the MP model, there are multiple difficulties in the implementation due to the non-differentiable nature of the model, leading to further abstractions and model developments. The step function of early ANNs based on the MP model was difficult to employ because of its non-differentiable nature and difficulty/complexity in efficiently training the ANN weights. Second generation ANNs are conceptualized in the second column from the left in Figure 3. These models addressed many known limitations and shortcomings found in the first generation ANNs. These second generation ANNs implemented a continuous and piecewise activation function (Maass, 1997) that was differentiable. By including a differentiable activation, or cost, function, such as a logistic sigmoid, gradient descent methods, e.g. backpropagation, were able to be used for training (Wang, Lin, & Dang, 2020) (Maass, 1997). Second generation networks can handle analog inputs and outputs (Maass, 1997) and include feedforward, recurrent, radial basis function, and most deep learning and convolutional approaches (Wang, Lin, & Dang, 2020) (Maass, 1997). The current state of the art automated artificial intelligence applications employ these second generation ANNs.

Third generation ANN models (shown in the third column of Figure 3) are designed to form a closer approximation to the biological neurons in how information is encoded mirroring how information is transmitted electrically through a biological neural network as a series of spike pulses/delta functions, which fire when a node receives an appropriate input (Maass, 1997). In third generation ANNs information is encoded as spikes and the ANN only "fires" or produces spikes when the stimulus is present and does not continuously transmit signals mimicking biologic neurons. The third generation neurons are highly energy efficient in sparse operations similar to biological neurons. The third generation ANNs also suffer from an inability to support computational complexities due to the sparsity of operations and that gradient descent methods can't readily be used to train spiking neural networks. Notably, third generation ANNs are still not equivalent to the biological neuron as many simplifications are used. It is feasible that there are additional ANN models/generations that will exist between the current third generation models and neurobiology seen in the rightmost column in Figure 3. The current theoretical state of the art in ANNs is within this third generation.

In the future, one goal will be to develop not only ANNs comprised of neurons but to form these systems into artificial nervous systems mimicking biological systems. In biology, when multiple neurons are combined with the groupings of neurons form a nervous system that enables information to be processed and transferred between the various neurons. Leveraging further neuroscience understandings would involve applying similar approaches to ANNs, wherein multiple neurons are brought together into a neural cognitive architecture that creates a portion of an artificial nervous system. Unlike biological neurons, ANNs are trained on an individual model so to mimic a nervous systems, multiple ANNs trained on separate models or data sources need to be combined together to form an artificial nervous system that will mimic a nervous system that can combine multiple pieces of information together to develop a solution. This would effectively fuse the information together to form a decision.

## ANN Properties

In operation, ANNs generally consist of three types of layers: input, hidden, and output with each layer consisting of computational neurons that have various connections to the other layers. The input layers connect the real-world data to the input of the ANN. Typically, there is one neuron for each input data feed. Layers between the input and output layers are typically termed 'hidden' because they act as 'black-box' transformations where the mechanism for prediction is not transparent to users (Olden & Jackson, 2002). Similarly, the output layer consists of interconnections between the various hidden layers and the output of the ANN. The number of output neurons is dependent and equal to the number of unique outputs for the ANN. The most utilized ANN architecture in practice is the multilayer perceptron (MLP) model as seen in the neural interpretation diagram (NID) of Figure 4 (Özesmi & Özesmi, 1999).

*Figure 4. Multi-Layered ANN, adapted from (Young, Holland, & Weckman, 2008)*

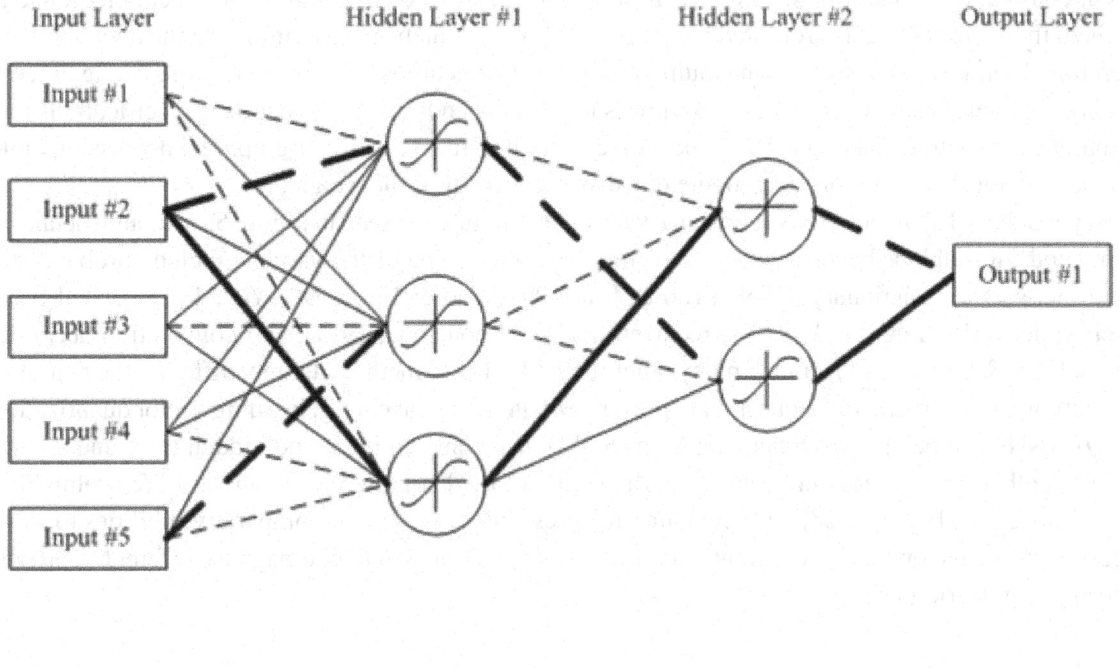

The four layer MLP ANN in Figure 4 uses hyperbolic tangent activation functions and, moving from left to right, one sees that the first layer (or input layer) is connected to the first hidden layer, with the output of the first hidden layer then feeding into any subsequent hidden layers, with the results passed to the output layer. In this diagram, solid lines represent excitation signals (or positive weights), dashed lines represent inhibitory signals (or negative weights), and line thickness reflect the magnitude of the weight.

The number of layers associated with a network design and the number of neurons in each hidden layer is ongoing areas of research. The design of the network, the number of layers, and how they are connected is part of the art of the design of the neural network. There is not an empirical set of functions that are used to define the number of layers and how the neurons are connected between each layer/level. The number of neurons associated with the input and output layers and a function of the number of input and output sources. The number of hidden levels and the number of neurons at each level is an iterative solution space based on the training data and the system specifications. If too few layers and neurons, the results will not meet the specifications for the system. This is an underdefined network. To prevent not meeting the specifications, in many cases, the designers will use more layers and neurons than needed to meet the specification results and reduce the number of design iterations. The resulting network is over-defined and results in a larger ANN than necessary and requires additional training time, iterations, and data but does not negatively impact the results of the network. Many of the network designers feel that this is an adequate trade provided there is enough measured or measured and synthetic data to train the resulting ANN to achieve the desired operating specifications. Currently, many of the operating networks could be reduced in size and have lower training times and training data sets since they are over-defined.

Similar to the design of the network, the training of the network and setting the internal weights between the neurons at each level is an iterative process that requires time and data. For second generation neural networks, a backpropagation technique is used along with supervised training approaches to set the weights. In supervised backpropagation, a data set is provided to the network and the output is determined. The output is compared to the known response. If the answer is the weights are maintained and the next example is provided to the network. If the results are incorrect, the system adjusts the weights, and a new data set is provided to the system. This process continues at each level until the output can accurately identify the targets within a given set of specifications. When the target range is reached, the various weights are stored in a reference file that can be used to initialize the network in an operational setting, assuming the same number of levels and neurons. This is a time-consuming process that has been automated but still may take hours to days depending on the accuracy specifications and the number of training data sets. This process has benefited from the use of graphical processing units and mathematical accelerators to compute the answers and adjust the weights.

Beyond the MLP model, ANNs come in a variety of structures as seen in Figure 5. Although detailing all methods available is beyond the scope of this overview, some of the variants include probabilistic neural networks, evolutionary ANNs (Yao & Liu, 1997; Yao & Liu, 1998; Yao, 1999), radial basis function networks (Looney C., 1997), recurrent ANNs (Looney C., 1997), and convolution networks (Duda, Hart, & Stork, 2001), among many other methods. These methods largely differ by the nature of connections (feedforward or feedback), the presence of an output layer (e.g. learning vector quantization (LVQ) ANNs, a type of Self-Organizing Map (SOM), have only an input and hidden layer and are applicable in this structure for clustering), and the nature of the learning rules (Jain, Mao, & Mohiuddin, 1996; Looney C., 1997, p. 368). Different architectures exists due to their comparative abilities to solve different problems, operate in different data dimensions, and/or provide homage to different neuroscience and engineering principles.

*Figure 5. General Taxonomy of ANN Architectures, taken from (Bihl T. J., 2015) and adapted from (Jain, Mao, & Mohiuddin, 1996) using the ANN families of (Looney C., 1997)*

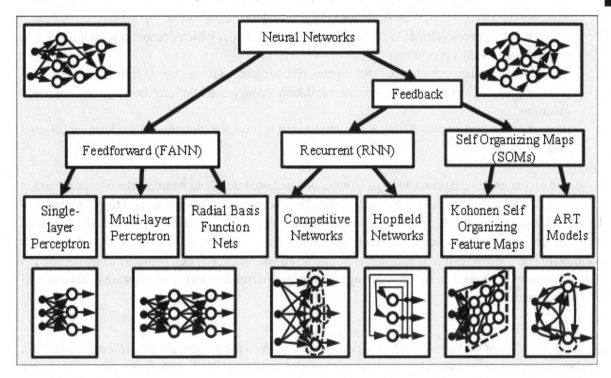

Generally, guidance on determining architecture-based settings, referred to as hyperparameters, has been ad hoc or heuristic in nature (Gao, Chen, & Qin, 2010) that involves both science and art. As mentioned in Mendenhall (Mendenhall, 2006), there are "no hard-and-fast rules" in ANN architecture determination. As seen in Figure 5, a wide variety of basic ANN architectures exist and thus selecting one depends on the general appropriateness for the task at hand as well as familiarity with the algorithm and availability of the code. This often involves comparing algorithm performance benchmark results to select high-performing algorithms for similar tasks.

## Deep Learning

Deep Learning is a multi-level ANN, typically containing 4 or more hidden layers. Due to a large amount of interconnected nonlinear functions, deep learning provides intrinsic automated feature selection abilities which have led to revolutionary, versus evolutionary, gains in computer vision, speech recognition, and other areas between the 2000s-2010s (Ball, Anderson, & Chan Sr, 2017). Deep learning extends the second generation of neural networks whereby combined feature extraction/filtering classification is learned to characterize patterns in data. These hidden layers' connectivity varies depending on the ANN architecture employed (the number of interconnected layers and the number of neurons at any given layer) and the accuracy specification. Deep learning architectures are an extension of ANN architectures, and the variants were developed and differ based on application. There are four primary architectures used in practice which have revolutionized computer vision and speech recognition (Ball, Anderson, & Chan Sr, 2017) (Hori, Cho, & Watanabe, 2018), among other areas. The four types of architectures are shown in figure 6.

These are the:

1.  Autoencoder (AE), which is an ANN for unsupervised data exploration
2.  Deep Belief Network (DBM), a probabilistic graphical model which combines probabilities and graph theory for data processing
3.  Convolutional neural network (CNN), a primarily computer vision approach that leverages concepts from biology to mimic visual data exploitation through convolutions, pooling, and nonlinear functions
4.  Recurrent neural network (RNN), a temporal based approach with connections forming directed cycles.

Based on the multiple layers, and large number of associated weighted neurons, the user is not aware of how the ANN makes decisions. Several studies have been started leading to additional research to be able to explain how the AI/ANN came to a particular result. In Explainable AI and ANN structures steps are programmed into the ANN structure to provide explanations and information to the user. In addition to being able to explain the result, explainable AI has also developed metrics that can be used to determine how the network is learning during training by determining which weights are being changed and by how much.

*Figure 6. Example of the four mainstream deep learning architectural approaches: a) autoencoder (AE), b) deep belief network (DBM), c) convolutional neural network (CNN), and d) recurrent NN (RNN), adapted from (Ball, Anderson, & Chan Sr, 2017)*

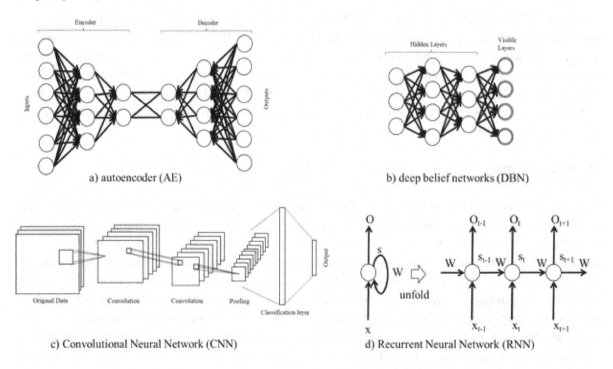

## Third Generation ANNs

The current theoretical state of the art in ANNs (third column in Figure 3) are referred to as Spiking Neural Networks (SNNs) based on the individual neurons producing a spike response when an appropriate input has been provided. SNNs are designed to be closer to biological neurons by employing a Dirac or delta function or spiking behavior (Maass, 1997). In comparison to traditional ANNs, which will hold a constant value, an SNN will only generate a spike if trained to do so (Maass, 1997). In addition, the SNN does not hold a constant output but produces an output when the stimulus is first detected. The SNN returns to a null output after the initial detection. If the stimulus should be reobserved or changes, the SNN will refire. The result is a sparser operation than a traditional ANN and, due to the temporal aspects of the SNN algorithmic model, SNNs are naturally applied to time sampled problems (Farr, Jones, Bihl, Boubin, & DeMange, 2020) (Zhang, Rong, Neri, & Pérez-Jiménez, 2014). SNNs have been seen to be more efficient in high-speed continuous monitoring functions (Blouw, Choo, Hunsberger, & Eliasmith, 2018). Furthermore, the biological inspiration and sparsity yields efficiency in the neurons operations in energy usage and in speed. The spiking short term neuron or node response when an appropriate signal is present followed by the node returning to 0 results in a corresponding reduction in power consumption over traditional ANNs (Blouw, Choo, Hunsberger, & Eliasmith, 2018). However, limitations and a complex trade space exists in SNNs. One issue with SNNs is that they are not easy or straightforward to train in a given software or in hardware applications. In addition, the hardware versions of SNNs are highly specialized and are typically prototypical in nature such that they are not commercially available for wide scale operations and applications.

## DESIGN DECISIONS IN DEVELOPING ANNS

A variety of design decisions exist in developing ANNs. The design decisions will be based on a combination of the type/generation of the ANNs/neuron models that are to be used, the purpose of the network, and the specifications for the ANNs output. The decisions include the underlying architecture and ANN paradigm, determining an appropriate training/testing split for the data, and hyperparameter selection. Discussions on many such issues can be found in (Bihl, Young II, & Weckman, 2018). Due to the myriad of possible decisions, ANNs are often criticized as providing irreproducible results and being opaque in nature (Potember, 2017). Potember (2017) described these problems as a lack of addressing the "ilities" in algorithm use, e.g.: the reliability, repeatability, replicability, trust-ability, and explain-ability of the algorithms. To reduce the uncertainty and provide for repeatability and consistency in design and results, the ANN system design should be approached in a systematic fashion. The design issues can be thought of as relating to the typical questions users of automation ask (Woods, 1996):

- What is it doing?
- Why is it doing that?
- What will it do next?

As laid out in (Bihl, Schoenbeck, Steeneck, & Jordan, 2020), approaching AI and ANN algorithm development in a systematic manner can help answer these questions, alleviate issues with the "ilities", and further facilitate easier development of algorithmic solutions.

## Recommended Systematic ANN Development to Deployment Procedure

CRISP-DM (CRoss-Industry Standard Process for Data Mining) is a general end-to-end (business concept to deployment) processes which exist to develop and deploy algorithmic solutions (Shearer, 2000). The work in (Bihl, Schoenbeck, Steeneck, & Jordan, 2020) extended CRISP-DM to include addressing algorithmic development questions directly related to the "ilities" by documenting the 1) selection of a dataset, 2) selection of an AI algorithm from literature or a library, and then 3) automatically determining workable hyperparameter settings without expert algorithmic knowledge. The extended CRISP-DM+ process is presented in Figure 7 and further described in (Bihl, Schoenbeck, Steeneck, & Jordan, 2020). The CRISP-DM+ approach is recommended for ANN development to addresses multiple issues with AI "ilities," including the repeatability and replicability of results through automating the various hyperparameter selection issues of ANNs. The CRISP-DM+ process includes additional steps of: A) preprocessing: data wrangling and algorithm architecture selection, B) initial training and hyperparameter optimization, and C) evaluating results. With the addition of these steps, the CRISP-DM+ process begins with an understanding of the problem to be solve and yields a deployed ANN solution.

*Figure 7. CRISP-DM+ Model where the CRISP-DM approach is overlaid with general steps (A, B, C) to develop ML solutions (Bihl, Schoenbeck, Steeneck, & Jordan, 2020)*

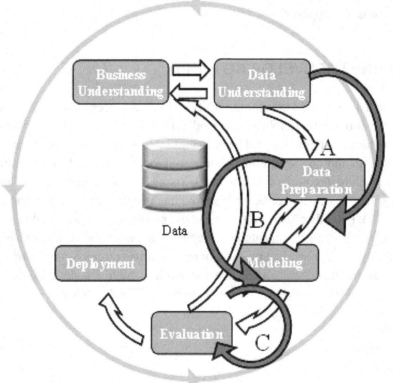

A1.  Data Wrangling
A2.  Select ML Architecture
B1.  Train ML Model Using Default Weights
B2.  Optimize Hyperparameters
C.  Test & Compare Optimized Models

## Hyperparameter Determination

A hyperparameter is a tunable variable that can be optimized as part of the training and evaluation process. As part of the training process, individual hyperparameters are collected and evaluated to determine how well the ANN is functioning and identify how the network weights are changed. A conceptual example of the problem in determining hyperparameters and yielding usable results is presented in Figure 8 and adapted from (Bihl, Schoenbeck, Steeneck, & Jordan, 2020) (Duda, Hart, & Stork, 2001). This example shows the primary goal of optimizing one architecture parameter, the learning rate $\varepsilon$ which is the rate at which an algorithm converges to a good solution (w*). Ideally, finding the optimal rate, $\varepsilon = \varepsilon_{opt}$ in Figure 8a, is desirable; however, this is often impossible to find for any meaningful solution due to the existence of multiple local optima. In addition, it may not be possible to optimize all hyperparameters simultaneously resulting in optimal performance for one parameter at the expense/critical sub-optimal performance for a different parameter. Slower, sub-optimal, Figure 8b, can yield good results but take a considerable amount of training time; in general, since optimal is difficult to find, searching for near-optimal, Figure 8c, is often the best whereby convergence is relatively quick and performance is stable. However, the importance of hyperparameter tuning can be seen in Figures 8d and 8e which have overly larger learning rates and yield highly oscillatory behaviors. Notably, the real behaviors are much more complex than this simple example.

*Figure 8. Conceptualization of a general hyperparameter problem, taken from (Bihl, Schoenbeck, Steeneck, & Jordan, 2020), adapted from (Duda, Hart, & Stork, 2001, pp. 312-313)*

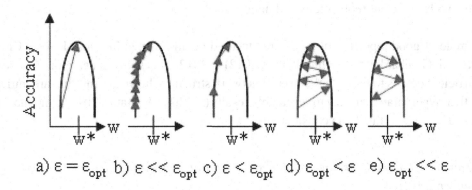

Finding the 'right' hyperparameters to identify and then optimize for an ANN is important for robustness. Approaches for finding hyperparameters are either model-free or model-based in nature (Bihl, Schoenbeck, Steeneck, & Jordan, 2020). Model-free approaches generally fall into one of four camps: 1) scientific, e.g. grid searches or design of experiments-based (Chiu, Cook, Pignatiello, & Whittaker, 1997), 2) haphazard, e.g. a coder experientially finding settings that "just work," 3) procedural based searches, described further in (Young W., 2010), or 4) random searches which use random seeds (notably a competitive method and a good baseline). Model-based approaches employ what can be considered as a wrapper that optimizes the underlying ANN as a function. Model-based methods systematically determine settings for an ANN through their own approaches. Examples of model-based approaches include evolutionary algorithms (Lorenzo, Nalepa, Kawulok, Ramos, & Pastor, 2017) and Bayesian optimization (Snoek, Larochelle, & Adams, 2012). Currently, while not the absolute state of the art,

Bayesian optimization is one of the most competitive hyperparameter optimization methods for ANNs (Snoek, Larochelle, & Adams, 2012). Despite recent advances have demonstrated alternative methods which outperform Bayesian optimization, c.f. (Li, Jamieson, DeSalvo, Rostamizadeh, & Talwalkar, 2017) (Ozaki, Yano, & Onishi, 2017). However, Bayesian optimization is a valuable tool since it is readily available, reliable, and well known (Bihl, Schoenbeck, Steeneck, & Jordan, 2020).

## Documentation and Repeatability

One issue with ANNs is the variability in the results and the inability to repeat results which have precluded the widespread use, adoption, and trust (Zhang G., 2007). When using an ANN, or any other machine learning method, one needs to provide sufficient details on the algorithm, the data, and experimental conditions (Zhang G., 2007). For example, merely reporting that an ANN was used to develop the model based on the given data is insufficient to be repeatable as one is not privy to all the hyperparameter settings and training details (Bihl, Schoenbeck, Steeneck, & Jordan, 2020). One of the issues is that if the training information is provided in a different order, the ANN hyperparameters may be optimized differently resulting in different weights and in some cases different results. However, with a complicated ANN, reporting these details could be very lengthy and largely impossible; thus, the authors (Bihl, Schoenbeck, Steeneck, & Jordan, 2020) proposed that what is needed is not all of the settings, but rather:

1. The architecture, algorithms, and software
2. The data and data splitting methods
3. The hyperparameter determination method, e.g., Bayesian Optimization, and initialization settings
4. Results with sufficient replications and intervals.

An example of good reporting of ANN architectural details is seen in Table 1, from Cireşan et al. (Ciresan, Giusti, Gambardella, & Schmidhuber, 2012) in 2012. This shows a network of some complexity with sufficient details to recreate the overall network structure; however, missing are initial learning rates and other hyperparameters key to repeatable results (Mishkin & Matas, 2015). And including them would expand the size of this table considerably.

*Table 1. Example of a Deep Learning architecture and parameters from (Ciresan, Giusti, Gambardella, & Schmidhuber, 2012)*

| Layer | Type | | Kern. Size |
|---|---|---|---|
| 0 | Input | 1 map of 95x95 neurons | |
| 1 | Convolutional | 48 maps of 92x92 neurons | 4x4 |
| 2 | Max pooling | 48 maps of 46x46 neurons | 2x2 |
| 3 | Convolutional | 48 maps of 42x42 neurons | 5x5 |
| 4 | Max pooling | 48 maps of 21x21 neurons | 2x2 |
| 5 | Convolutional | 48 maps of 18x18 neurons | 4x4 |
| 6 | Max pooling | 48 maps of 9x9 neurons | 2x2 |
| 7 | Convolutional | 48 maps of 6x6 neurons | 4x4 |
| 8 | Max pooling | 48 maps of 3x3 neurons | 2x2 |
| 9 | Fully connect. | 200 neurons | 1x1 |
| 10 | Fully connect. | 2 neurons | 1x1 |

For larger-and-larger neural networks, a table like Table 1 can become cumbersome and take considerable space. One solution is that presented by Cireşan et al. in 2012 (Cireşan, Meier, & Schmidhuber, 2012) and extended in (Bihl, Schoenbeck, Steeneck, & Jordan, 2020). Here, the network is expressed by a simple expression, which can be decoded using a brief and largely straightforward handbook as presented in Table 2. The notation in Table 2 notably includes the same details as seen in Table 1 but can enable one to write very large networks as an equation.

*Table 2. Brief handbook from (Bihl, Schoenbeck, Steeneck, & Jordan, 2020) of Cireşan-style notation for neural networks, extended from (Cireşan, Meier, & Schmidhuber, 2012)*

| Notation | Meaning | Example |
|---|---|---|
| $y \times z$ | Input size is of dimensionality $y \times z$ | 48x48 |
| $xCy$ | Convolutional layer with $x$ maps and filters of $y \times y$ weights | 8C3 |
| MPy_p | Max pooling layer with $y \times y$ pooling and $p$ stride | MP2_2 |
| APy | Average pooling layer of | AP2 |
| ReLu | rectified linear units layer of size $y \times y$ | ReLu |
| SM | Softmax layer | SM |
| BN | Batch normalization Layer | BN |
| Dox | Drop out layer with x nodes | DO25 |
| xN | Fully connected layer of $x$ neurons | 100N |
| CL | Classification layer of $x$ neurons | CL10 |

For example, using the notation in Table 2, we can decompose LeNet-4 (LeCun, et al., 1995), a seminal network that largely started the Deep Learning domain in 1995. Using Table 2, LeNet-4 can be represented as:

32x32-4C5-AP2-16C5-AP2-120N-10N-SM-CL　　　　　　　　　　　　　　　　(1)

From here, one would need to describe their data and data splitting methods, hyperparameter determination method, and results. For this, one could state the repeatable details concisely. For example, "The network in equation (1), was deployed on MNIST using the pre-divided training and testing sets with Bayesian Optimization, using the Bayesopt library (Martinez-Cantin, 2014), used to find best settings from a search region that included the initial search region bounds in Table 3, after xyz replications the results were…" Thus, one would be able to independently verify the stated performance.

## APPLICATIONS OF ANNs

A variety of applications employ ANNs as the authors noted and listed in (Bihl, Young II, & Weckman, 2018). Beyond such business applications, ANNs are pervasively used in computer vision (Ball, Anderson, & Chan Sr, 2017), science and experimentation (Abiodun, et al., 2018), computational neuroscience (Amunts, et al., 2019), pattern recognition (Duda, Hart, & Stork, 2001), and many other areas. Depending on the application, other concerns might be warranted in developing and deploying ANNs.

*Table 3. General Hyperparameters for Deep Learning, with Initial Search Region, from (Bihl, Schoenbeck, Steeneck, & Jordan, 2020)*

| Param. | Meaning | Initial Search Interval |
|---|---|---|
| *lr* | Learning Rate - update speed at each training step | [0.0001, 0.01] |
| *mep* | Number of Epochs - An epoch is one time through the entire training data | [5, 8] |
| *lrdf* | Learn Rate Drop Factor - Percentage of the Learn Rate to retain after a specified period | [0.75, 0.9] |
| *lrdp* | Learn Rate Drop Period - The epoch at which the Learn Rate Drop Factor is employed | [3, 7] |
| *mom* | Momentum - the carryover of the Learning Rate from one epoch to the next | [0.95, 1.0] |
| *mbs* | The Batch Size - the number of training samples to consider at one time | [128, 256] |
| *dn* | Number of Dense Nodes - The size of the fully connected classifier layer | [1/2•NC, 10•NC] |

## Dedicated Hardware for Deploying ANNs

While many publications in ANN involve creating the best algorithm to solve a problem, the key end result of an ANN should always focus on the application, i.e., what and where will the final model be employed and for what purpose will the ANN be used? Beyond training ANNs, employing trained computational inference algorithms is still often computationally expensive (Thórisson & Helgasson, 2012). Thus, one must inherently consider final hardware constraints, *i.e.* Size, Weight, and Power (SWaP), on which the trained model will be used (Bihl & Talbert, Analytics for Autonomous C4ISR within e-Government: a Research Agenda, 2020). While high-SWaP capacity, *e.g.* web-based search engines, can use dedicated on-demand supercomputer time, other applications, *e.g.* edge-based processing on smart phones or single CPU computers, have SWaP constraints that may limit what algorithms can be used. For example, a deep network might require a graphics processing unit (GPU) in order to run, but not all edge-based systems have such hardware. Thus, computation comes at a cost both monetarily as well as with SWAP.

In addition to such general concerns, some ANN solutions are optimally deployed on appropriate "AI Accelerator" hardware (Gudivada, Irfan, Fathi, & Rao, 2016). Such systems are advanced electronics that are used to get around CPU-based Moore's Law bottlenecks on computation abilities. AI accelerator approaches include technologies and capabilities such as current parallel computing, GPUs (highly optimal for deep learning), and neuromorphic chips (highly optimal for spiking ANNs) (Bihl & Talbert, Analytics for Autonomous C4ISR within e-Government: a Research Agenda, 2020). Again, there are situations where it is not practical or feasible to implement these solutions from a monetary costs, SWAP or technology risk.

## Big Data Implications

Training of an ANN is computational demanding; however, once trained, the underlying ANN model is not necessarily computationally costly to use. When analyzing 'Big Data,' many challenges exist as documented by the authors in (Bihl, Young, & Weckman, 2015). As a strategy, developing ANNs on a subset of the data and then retraining the model as needed would be beneficial. Additionally, many large datasets contain more features than necessary and non-salient features can degrade performance; thus, feature selection and dimensionality reduction analysis (DRA) before training are often needed to make quality ANNs. DRA methods include input reduction methods (sensitivity, correlation studies, etc.) (Young W., Weckman, Thompson, & Brown, 2008; Hernandez, Nesic, Weckman, & Ghai, 2006; Bihl, Bauer, & Temple, 2016), and ANN-based feature screening methods (Bauer, Alsing, & Greene, 2000; Verikas & Bacauskiene, 2002), to find a finite select core of key features.

## Small Data Implications

Limited, or scarce, data is also a serious problem that often impedes the development of efficient ANNs. ANN training procedures typically require the partitioning of data into subsets to prevent over-fitting (Porter, et al., 2001). In some cases, there is not enough available sample data to properly train and test the ANN. Since a cross-validation dataset act as an additional testing set, some researchers who do not have enough or cannot afford to hold out a separate independent testing set data (Lendassea, Simonb, Wertzc, & Verleysen, 2005). Based on these training and data partitioning philosophies utilized within the application of ANN design, larger datasets are at times more ideal than smaller ones. However, issues exist when small datasets or imbalanced datasets are analyzed. To overcome these limitations, some methods do exist such as under-sampling, over-sampling, and artificial sampling methods. Over-sampling, or boosting, is a simple or naïve strategy that simply reproduces sampled data to improve the predictive accuracy of ANN when sample sizes are small (Seiffert & et al., 2008). Under-sampling involves making the training data groups as equal as possible to avoid biasing (Seiffert & et al., 2008). Artificial sampling provides uses real sample information to create additional synthetic samples to increase the sample size for training (Bui, 2004). While all strategies have been utilized successfully in practice, 1) more research is needed for robust comparisons and 2) simpler methods, such as under-sampling, perform very well in practice when compared to more complicated methods (Seiffert & et al., 2008; Long & Servedio, 2010). The user must be aware of the implications and the shortcomings of employing these techniques in how the ANNs results will be affected and how this may limit the application of the ANN.

## Knowledge Extraction

Practitioners employ the KDD process for a variety of reasons; one being to understand complex systems better (Browne, et al., 2003). Knowledge Extraction (KE) techniques are often applied to mathematical models to gain insight. ANNs, though powerful in their prediction and applicability, are still viewed today as a black-box model (Lek & Guegan, 1999). To eliminate the black-box mentality, three classification approaches are used to extract knowledge from an ANN. These methods include decomposition, pedagogical, and eclectic methods.

Decomposition methods use the internal structure of the ANN architecture to derive a primitive form of KE. One technique used to inspect a network's activity visually is the NID, as seen in Figure 4 (Özesmi & Özesmi, 1999). Decomposition can become cumbersome and difficult as the number of levels within an ANN increase in Deep Learning applications for instance. Pedagogical methods do not use the internal structure to derive or extract knowledge from a network. Instead, pedagogical methods use the network's map of input to output relationships and reformulate the relationships via another representation, e.g. decision trees (Schmitz, Aldrich, & Gouws, 1999; Young W., Weckman, Hari, Whiting II, & Snow, 2012). This can be thought of as a refined black box in which the transfer function results for the various types of data inputs are mapped and displayed in another form that allows easier interpretation. The results are simplified over the complex relationships inside the ANN.

The pedagogical method can result in an easier depiction of the ANN actions than the decomposition method but may lack understanding of what is occurring within the network. This can assist the user in understanding the results but may not provide insight or explainability. Finally, eclectic methods utilize a collection of decomposition and pedagogical methods, as seen in Validity Interval Analysis (VIA) method (Thrun, 1995). This method combines the techniques from both the other methods to provide an understanding of the ANN while capturing the mapping of inputs to outputs. These methods may not provide sufficient detail or information to support the ANN explainability and may result in complex diagrams that are difficult to interpret.

## FUTURE RESEARCH DIRECTIONS

As mentioned above, the current theoretical state of the art in ANNs involves SNNs. SNNs aim to be closer to biology by exhibiting a spiking behavior with byproducts being increased power efficiencies (Farr, Jones, Bihl, Boubin, & DeMange, 2020) (Blouw, Choo, Hunsberger, & Eliasmith, 2018). However, limitations and a complex trade space exist in SNNs and addressing developmental issues and finding novel applications is one area of increasing research in ANNs. These approaches further highlight a complex hardware and software solution to increase efficiencies and the versatility of ANN solutions.

A further domain of ANNs with increasing interest due to their low computational demands are quaternion ANNs (Bill, Champagne, Cox, & Bihl, 2021). Quaternion ANNs model data and the ANN structures as 4-dimensional quaternions, thereby an intrinsic dimensionality reduction is at work (Bill, Champagne, Cox, & Bihl, 2021). However, one difficulty with Quaternion ANNs is that their algorithmic model is non-differentiable, and thus standard ANN learning processes are not directly applicable. Current work has developed heuristic-based approaches for Quaternion ANN training (Bill, Champagne, Cox, & Bihl, 2021); however, these have shown considerable reductions in size when compared to traditional ANNs, they are still prototypical in nature and need further development before wide-spread adoption.

Further questions on the ability to transfer what was learned in one domain and apply it to another domain are of increasing interest. Transfer learning is an AI technique that leverages the concept in biology that knowledge and skills applied in one domain are transferrable to a new domain (Torrey & Shavlik, 2010). In ANNs, transfer learning became of prime interest in extending the use of the feature extraction layers from a deep neural network for a slightly different problem. Conceptually, this could be an image recognition task where you later collect data for a new class. It is more efficient to use the already developed feature extraction process, but one needs to train a classifier to recognize the originally known classes plus the new class. Transfer learning approaches in which the network can apply and add additional classes become beneficial if there are few observations and collected data associated with the new classes. Figure 9 presents the general transfer learning concept as posed by (Mari, Bromley, Izaac, Schuld, & Killoran, 2020). Here, an ANN, $A$, is trained on the original data and classes, $D_1$. The ANN A consists of two separable parts, a detector ANN followed by a classifier which could either be an ANN or a support vector machine. The output of the detector and classifier yields the results, $R_A$. When new, but similar, data, $D_2$, with new classes is presented one either has to repeat the whole process of training the ANN that yielded the model $A'$, or one can remove the feature extraction part of the ANN and then use this as an input to a new classifier, $B$. The new classifier could be an ANN or, as often is the practice, an alternative and quickly trained classifier, such as a support vector machine (Marcelino, 2018).

Finally, considerable research in addressing the "ilities" associated with AI, and ANNs in particular, are of growing research interest (Bihl, Schoenbeck, Steeneck, & Jordan, 2020) (Potember, 2017). This is particularly seen in endeavors to better explain the inner workings of algorithms and provide an understanding of why decisions are made and what occurred to create these decisions (Samek, Montavon,

Lapuschkin, Anders, & Müller, 2021). While the current directions are in the eXplainable AI (XAI) domain, this field extends considerable prior work in rule extraction approaches (Thrun, 1995).

*Figure 9. General concept of transfer learning, adapted and extended from (Mari, Bromley, Izaac, Schuld, & Killoran, 2020)*

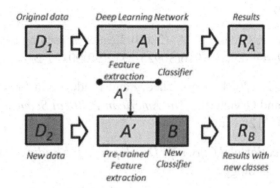

## CONCLUSION

The authors presented a brief primer on ANNs, which summarizes issues related to ANN background, architecture selection, model building, and applications. Since publishing earlier versions of this paper (Young, Bihl, & Weckman, 2014) (Bihl, Young II, & Weckman, 2018), ANNs have increased in applications, but are still not as well-received as simpler methods, c.f. (Dewdney, 1997) (Nenni, Giustiniano, & Pirolo, 2013) (Toh, Dondelinger, & Wang, 2019). Another emerging direction is the use of deep learning; however, issues with deep learning show that it is not a solution to all problems. It should be noted that additional reading has been provided in (Bihl, Young II, & Weckman, 2018) which provides a brief summary listing of business disciplines. Additionally, readers are directed to summary papers by Li (1994), Wong et al. (1997), Vellido et al. (1999), Smith and Gupta (Smith & Gupta, 2000), Haikmpoor et al. (2011), and Tkáč and Verner (2016), as extended reviews of ANN applications in business.

## ACKNOWLEDGMENT

This work was cleared for public release under case AFRL-2022-1434, the views in this work are the view of the authors only and do not represent any position of the US Government, Department of Defense, US Air Force, or Air Force Research Laboratory.

## REFERENCES

Abiodun, O., Jantan, A., Omolara, A., Dada, K., Mohamed, N., & Arshad, H. (2018). State-of-the-art in artificial neural network applications: A survey. *Heliyon*, *4*(11), e00938. doi:10.1016/j.heliyon.2018. e00938 PMID:30519653

Amunts, K., Knoll, A., Lippert, T., Pennartz, C., Ryvlin, P., Destexhe, A., Jirsa, V. K., D'Angelo, E., & Bjaalie, J. (2019). The Human Brain Project—Synergy between neuroscience, computing, informatics, and brain-inspired technologies. *PLoS Biology*, *17*(7), e3000344. doi:10.1371/journal.pbio.3000344 PMID:31260438

Ball, J., Anderson, D., & Chan, C. Sr. (2017). Comprehensive survey of deep learning in remote sensing: Theories, tools, and challenges for the community. *Journal of Applied Remote Sensing*, *11*(4), 1. doi:10.1117/1.JRS.11.042609

Bauer, K. W. Jr, Alsing, S. G., & Greene, K. A. (2000). Feature screening using signal-to-noise ratios. *Neurocomputing*, *31*(1-4), 29–44. doi:10.1016/S0925-2312(99)00147-2

Beck, N., King, G., & Zeng, L. (2004, May). Theory and Evidence in International Conflict: A Response to de Marchi, Gelpi, and Grynaviski. *The American Political Science Review*, *98*(2), 379–389. doi:10.1017/S0003055404001212

Bihl, T. J. (2015). *Feature Selection and Classifier Development for Radio Frequency Device Identification*. Air Froce Institute of Technology.

Bihl, T. J., Bauer, K., & Temple, M. A. (2016). A Comparison of Feature Selection Methods for RF-DNA Fingerprinting Using ZigBee Device Emissions. *IEEE Transactions on Information Forensics and Security*. Advance online publication. doi:10.1109/TIFS.2016.2561902

Bihl, T. J., Young, W. A. II, & Weckman, G. R. (2015). Defining, Understanding and Addressing Big Data. *International Journal of Business Analytics*, *3*(2), 1–32. doi:10.4018/IJBAN.2016040101

Bihl, T., & Talbert, M. (2020). Analytics for Autonomous C4ISR within e-Government: a Research Agenda. *Proceedings of the 53rd Hawaii International Conference on System Sciences*, 2218-2227. 10.24251/HICSS.2020.271

Bihl, T., Schoenbeck, J., Steeneck, D., & Jordan, J. (2020). Easy and Efficient Hyperparameter Optimization to Address Some Artificial Intelligence "ilities". *Proceedings of the 53rd Hawaii International Conference on System Sciences*, 943-952. 10.24251/HICSS.2020.118

Bihl, T., Young, I. I. W., & Weckman, G. (2018). Artificial neural networks and their applications in business. Encyclopedia of Information Science and Technology, Fourth Edition, 6642-6657.

Bill, J., Champagne, L., Cox, B., & Bihl, T. (2021). Meta-Heuristic Optimization Methods for Quaternion-Valued Neural Networks. *Mathematics*, *9*(9), 938. doi:10.3390/math9090938

Blouw, P., Choo, X., Hunsberger, E., & Eliasmith, C. (2018). *Benchmarking Keyword Spotting Efficiency on Neuromorphic Hardware*. arXiv preprint arXiv:1812.01739.

Browne, A., Hudson, B., Whitley, D., Ford, M., Picton, P., & Kazemian, H. (2003). Knowledge extraction from neural networks. *Proceedings of the 29th Annual Conference of the IEEE Industrial Electronics Society*, 1909-1913.

Bui, T. D. (2004). *Neural network analysis of sparse datasets: An application to the fracture system in folds of the Lisburne formation, Northeastern Alaska* [Ph.D. Dissertation]. Texas A&M University, Department of Petroleum Engineering, College Station, TX.

Chiu, C.-C., Cook, D. F., Pignatiello, J. P., & Whittaker, A. D. (1997). Design of a radial basis function neural network with a radius-modification algorithm using response surface methodology. *Journal of Intelligent Manufacturing, 8*(2), 117–124. doi:10.1023/A:1018504704266

Ciresan, D., Giusti, A., Gambardella, L., & Schmidhuber, J. (2012). Deep neural networks segment neuronal membranes in electron microscopy images. *Advances in Neural Information Processing Systems*, 2843–2851.

Cireşan, D., Meier, U., & Schmidhuber, J. (2012). *Multi-column deep neural networks for image classification.* arXiv preprint arXiv:1202.2745. doi:10.1109/CVPR.2012.6248110

Dewdney, A. K. (1997). The Apprentice Builds a Brain: Misled by Metaphors. In *Yes, We Have No Neutrons*. John Wiley & Sons.

Duda, R. O., Hart, P. E., & Stork, D. G. (2001). *Pattern Classification* (2nd ed.). John Wiley & Sons.

Farr, P., Jones, A., Bihl, T., Boubin, J., & DeMange, A. (2020). 2020, April. Waveform Design Implemented on Neuromorphic Hardware. *IEEE International Radar Conference (RADAR)*, 934-939.

Gao, P., Chen, C., & Qin, S. (2010). An optimization method of hidden nodes for neural network. *International Workshop on Education Technology and Computer Science (ETCS)*, 53-56. 10.1109/ETCS.2010.300

Gudivada, V., Irfan, M., Fathi, E., & Rao, D. (2016). Cognitive analytics: Going beyond big data analytics and machine learning. Handbook of Statistics, 35, 169-205.

Hakimpoor, H., Bin Arshad, K. A., Tat, H. H., Khani, N., & Rahmandoust, M. (2011). Artificial neural networks' applications in management. *World Applied Sciences Journal, 14*(7), 1008–1019.

Hernandez, S., Nesic, S., Weckman, G., & Ghai, V. (2006). Use of Artificial Neural Networks for Predicting Crude Oil Effect on $CO_2$ Corrosion of Carbon Steels. *Corrosion Journal, 62*(6).

Hori, T., Cho, J., & Watanabe, S. (2018). End-to-end speech recognition with word-based RNN language models. *IEEE Spoken Language Technology Workshop (SLT)*, 389-896. 10.1109/SLT.2018.8639693

Jain, A. K., Duin, R. P., & Mao, J. (2000, January). Statistical Pattern Recognition: A Review. *IEEE Transactions on Pattern Analysis and Machine Intelligence, 22*(1), 4–37. doi:10.1109/34.824819

Jain, A. K., Mao, J., & Mohiuddin, K. M. (1996). Artificial neural networks: A tutorial. *Computer, 29*(3), 31–44. doi:10.1109/2.485891

Kandel, E., Siegelbaum, S., Mack, S., & Koester, J. (2021). *Principles of Neural Science* (6th ed.). McGraw-Hill Education/Medical.

LeCun, Y., Jackel, L., Bottou, L., Cortes, C., Denker, J., Drucker, H., . . . Vapnik, V. (1995). Learning algorithms for classification: A comparison on handwritten digit recognition. *Neural networks: The statistical mechanics perspective*.

Lek, S., & Guegan, J. (1999). Artificial neural networks as a tool in ecological modeling, an introduction. *Ecological Modelling, 120*(2-3), 65–73. doi:10.1016/S0304-3800(99)00092-7

Lendassea, A., Simonb, G., Wertzc, V., & Verleysen, M. (2005). Fast bootstrap methodology for regression model selection. *Neurocomputing, 64*, 161–181. doi:10.1016/j.neucom.2004.11.017

Li, E. Y. (1994). Artificial neural networks and their business applications. *Information & Management*, *27*(5), 303–313. doi:10.1016/0378-7206(94)90024-8

Li, L., Jamieson, K., DeSalvo, G., Rostamizadeh, A., & Talwalkar, A. (2017). Hyperband: A novel bandit-based approach to hyperparameter optimization. *Journal of Machine Learning Research*, *18*(1), 6765–6816.

Long, P. M., & Servedio, R. A. (2010). Random classification noise defeats all convex potential boosters. *Machine Learning*, *78*(3), 287–304. doi:10.100710994-009-5165-z

Looney, C. (1997). *Pattern Recognition Using Neural Networks*. Oxford University Press.

Looney, C. G. (1997). *Pattern Recognition Using Neural Networks*. Oxford University Press.

Lorenzo, P., Nalepa, J., Kawulok, M., Ramos, L., & Pastor, J. (2017). Particle swarm optimization for hyper-parameter selection in deep neural networks. *Proceedings of the Genetic and Evolutionary Computation Conference*, 481-488. 10.1145/3071178.3071208

Maass, W. (1997). Networks of spiking neurons: The third generation of neural network models. *Neural Networks*, *10*(9), 1659–1671. doi:10.1016/S0893-6080(97)00011-7

Mannila, H. (1996). Data mining: machine learning, statistics, and databases. *Eight International Conference on Scientific and Statistical Database Management*, 1-8.

Marcelino, P. (2018, Oct. 23). *Transfer learning from pre-trained models*. Retrieved from Towards Data Science: https://towardsdatascience.com/transfer-learning-from-pre-trained-models-f2393f124751

Mari, A., Bromley, T., Izaac, J., Schuld, M., & Killoran, N. (2020). *Transfer learning in hybrid classical-quantum neural networks*. Quantum. doi:10.22331/q-2020-10-09-340

Martinez-Cantin, R. (2014). Bayesopt: A bayesian optimization library for nonlinear optimization, experimental design and bandits. *Journal of Machine Learning Research*, *15*(1), 3735–3739.

MATLAB. (2010). *MATLAB version 7.10.0 (R2010a)*. MathWorks Inc.

McCulloch, W., & Pitts, W. (1943). A Logical Calculus of the Ideas Immanent in Nervous Activity. *The Bulletin of Mathematical Biophysics*, *5*(4), 115–133. doi:10.1007/BF02478259

Mendenhall, M. J. (2006). *A Neural Relevance Model for Feature Extraction from Hyperspectral Images, and its Application in the Wavelet Domain* [PhD Dissertation]. Rice University.

Mishkin, D., & Matas, J. (2015). *All you need is a good init*. arXiv preprint arXiv:1511.06422.

Nenni, M. E., Giustiniano, L., & Pirolo, L. (2013). Demand forecasting in the fashion industry: A review. *International Journal of Engineering Business Management*, *5*, 1–6. doi:10.5772/56840

NeuroDimensions. (2005, Dec). *Newsletters*. Retrieved 2009, from NeuroDimensions: http://www.neurosolutions.com/newsletters.html

Olden, J. D., & Jackson, D. A. (2002). Illuminating the "black box": A randomization approach for understanding variable contributions in artificial neural networks. *Ecological Modelling*, *154*(1-2), 135–150. doi:10.1016/S0304-3800(02)00064-9

Ozaki, Y., Yano, M., & Onishi, M. (2017). Effective hyperparameter optimization using Nelder-Mead method in deep learning. *IPSJ Transactions on Computer Vision and Applications, 9*(1).

Özesmi, S., & Özesmi, U. (1999). An artificial neural network approach to spatial habitat modeling with interspecific interaction. *Ecological Modelling, 116*(1), 15–31. doi:10.1016/S0304-3800(98)00149-5

Porter, C., O'Donnell, C., Crawford, E., Gamito, E., Errejon, A., Genega, E., Sotelo, T., & Tewari, A. (2001). Artificial Neural Network Model To Predict Biochemical Failure After Radical Prostatectomy. *Molecular Urology, 5*(4), 159–162. doi:10.1089/10915360152745830 PMID:11790277

Potember, R. (2017). *Perspectives on research in artificial intelligence and artificial general intelligence relevant to DoD*. MITRE Corporation.

Sall, J., Lehman, A., Stephens, M., & Creighton, L. (2012). *JMP start statistics: a guide to statistics and data analysis using JMP*. SAS Institute.

Samek, W., Montavon, G., Lapuschkin, S., Anders, C., & Müller, K. (2021). Explaining deep neural networks and beyond: A review of methods and applications. *Proceedings of the IEEE, 109*(3), 247–278. doi:10.1109/JPROC.2021.3060483

Schmitz, G., Aldrich, C., & Gouws, F. (1999). ANN-DT: An algorithm for extraction of decision trees from artiˉcial neural networks. *IEEE Transactions on Neural Networks, 10*(6), 1392–1401. doi:10.1109/72.809084 PMID:18252640

Seiffert, C. (2008). A comparative study of data sampling and cost sensitive learning. *IEEE International Conference on Data Mining Workshops*, 46-52. 10.1109/ICDMW.2008.119

Shearer, C. (2000). The CRISP-DM model: The new blueprint for data mining. *Journal of Data Warehousing, 5*(4), 13–22.

Smith, K. A., & Gupta, J. N. (2000). Neural networks in business: Techniques and applications for the operations researcher. *Computers & Operations Research, 27*(11), 1023–1044. doi:10.1016/S0305-0548(99)00141-0

Snoek, J., Larochelle, H., & Adams, R. (2012). Practical Bayesian optimization of machine learning algorithms. *Advances in Neural Information Processing Systems*, 2951–2959.

Sweatt, J. D. (2016). Neural plasticity and behavior—Sixty years of conceptual advances. *Journal of Neurochemistry, 139*(2), 179–199. doi:10.1111/jnc.13580 PMID:26875778

Team, R. D. (2008). *R: A Language and Environment for Statistical Computing*. R Foundation for Statistical Computing.

Thórisson, K., & Helgasson, H. (2012). Cognitive architectures and autonomy: A comparative review. *Journal of Artificial General Intelligence, 3*(2), 1–30. doi:10.2478/v10229-011-0015-3

Thrun, S. (1995). Extracting rules from articial neural networks with distributed representations. In G. Tesauro, D. Touretzky, & T. Leen (Eds.), Advances in Neural Information Processing Systems (Vol. 7). MIT Press.

Tkáč, M., & Verner, R. (2016). Artificial neural networks in business: Two decades of research. *Applied Soft Computing, 38*, 788–804. doi:10.1016/j.asoc.2015.09.040

Toh, T., Dondelinger, F., & Wang, D. (2019). Looking beyond the hype: Applied AI and machine learning in translational medicine. *EBioMedicine*, *47*, 607–615. doi:10.1016/j.ebiom.2019.08.027 PMID:31466916

Torrey, L., & Shavlik, J. (2010). Transfer learning. In *Handbook of research on machine learning applications and trends: algorithms, methods, and techniques* (pp. 242–264). IGI Global. doi:10.4018/978-1-60566-766-9.ch011

Vasilev, I., Slater, D., Spacagna, G., Roelants, P., & Zocca, V. (2019). *Python Deep Learning: Exploring deep learning techniques and neural network architectures with Pytorch, Keras, and TensorFlow*. Packt Publishing Ltd.

Vellido, A., Lisboa, P. J., & Vaughan, J. (1999). Neural networks in business: A survey of applications. *Expert Systems with Applications*, *17*(1), 51–70. doi:10.1016/S0957-4174(99)00016-0

Verikas, A., & Bacauskiene, M. (2002). Feature selection with neural networks. *Pattern Recognition Letters*, *23*(11), 1323–1335. doi:10.1016/S0167-8655(02)00081-8

Wang, X., Lin, X., & Dang, X. (2020). Supervised learning in spiking neural networks: A review of algorithms and evaluations. *Neural Networks*, *125*, 258–280. doi:10.1016/j.neunet.2020.02.011 PMID:32146356

Weckman, G., Millie, D., Ganduri, C., Rangwala, M., Young, W., Rinder, M., & Fahnenstiel, G. (2009). Knowledge Extraction from the Black Box in Ecological Monitoring. *Journal of Industrial and Systems Engineering*, *3*(1), 38–55.

Wong, B. K., Bodnovich, T. A., & Selvi, Y. (1997). Neural network applications in business: A review and analysis of the literature (1988-1995). *Decision Support Systems*, *19*(4), 301–320. doi:10.1016/S0167-9236(96)00070-X

Woods, D. (1996). Decomposing automation: Apparent simplicity, real complexity. *Automation and human performance: Theory and applications*, 3-17.

Yao, X. (1999). Evolving artificial neural networks. *Proceedings of the IEEE*, *87*(9), 1423–1447. doi:10.1109/5.784219

Yao, X., & Liu, Y. (1997). A New Evolutionary System for Evolving Artificial Neural Networks. *IEEE Transactions on Neural Networks*, *8*(3), 694–713. doi:10.1109/72.572107 PMID:18255671

Yao, X., & Liu, Y. (1998). Towards designing artificial neural networks by evolution. *Applied Mathematics and Computation*, *91*(1), 83–90. doi:10.1016/S0096-3003(97)10005-4

Young, W. (2010). *A Team-Compatibility Decision Support System to Model the NFL Knapsack Problem: An Introduction to HEART* [PhD Dissertation]. Ohio University.

Young, W. A., Bihl, T. J., & Weckman, G. R. (2014). Artificial Neural Networks for Business Analytics. In Encyclopedia of Business Analytics and Optimization (pp. 193-208). doi:10.4018/978-1-4666-5202-6.ch019

Young, W., Holland, W., & Weckman, G. (2008). Determining Hall of Fame Status for Major league Baseball Using an Artificial Neural Network. *Journal of Quantitative Analysis in Sports*, *4*(4). Advance online publication. doi:10.2202/1559-0410.1131

Young, W. II, Weckman, G., Hari, V., Whiting, I. I. H. II, & Snow, A. (2012). Using artificial neural networks to enhance CART. *Neural Computing & Applications, 21*(7), 1477–1489. doi:10.100700521-012-0887-4

Young, W., Weckman, G., Thompson, J., & Brown, M. (2008). Artificial Neural Networks for Knowledge Extraction of Concrete Shear Strength Prediction. *International Journal of Industrial Engineering - Theory, Applications, and Practice, 15*(1).

Zhang, G. (2007). Avoiding pitfalls in neural network research. *IEEE Transactions on Systems, Man and Cybernetics. Part C, Applications and Reviews, 37*(1), 3–16. doi:10.1109/TSMCC.2006.876059

Zhang, G., Rong, H., Neri, F., & Pérez-Jiménez, M. (2014). An optimization spiking neural P system for approximately solving combinatorial optimization problems. *International Journal of Neural Systems, 24*(5), 1440006-1 - 1440006-16.

## KEY TERMS AND DEFINITIONS

**Back-Propagation:** A supervised learning method used to determine the weights of an ANN, where the difference between the desired and the model's output is minimized.

**Epoch:** The representation of an entire training set of sample data through the learning algorithm so that an ANN's weights can be determined.

**Knowledge Extraction:** The process of discovering how input attributes are used within an ANN to formulate the output such that one can validate functional relationships within the model.

**Neuron:** An individual building block of an ANN in which weighted input values are transformed via a transfer function into an output, which is typically passed to other portions of the network.

**Over-Fitting:** Occurs when a mathematical model describes random error or noise instead of the real underlying relationships within a dataset, which artificially produces desirable goodness of fit metrics for training data, but produces poor metrics for testing data.

**Post-Processing:** A process of utilizing a trained mathematical model in order to improve the understanding of the database that has been modeled.

**Pre-Processing:** A process of preparing a dataset in order to develop a mathematical model.

**Supervised Learning:** A learning strategy in which the desired output, or dependent attribute, is known.

**Unsupervised Learning:** A learning strategy in which the desired output, or dependent attribute, is unknown.

# Machine Learning Algorithms in Human Gait Analysis

**Aditi A. Bhoir**
*Sardar Patel College of Engineering, India*

**Tanish A. Mishra**
*Sardar Patel College of Engineering, India*

**Jyotindra Narayan**
https://orcid.org/0000-0002-2499-6039
*Indian Institute of Technology, Guwahati, India*

**Santosha K. Dwivedy**
https://orcid.org/0000-0001-6534-8989
*Indian Institute of Technology, Guwahati, India*

## INTRODUCTION

Gait Analysis (GA) is the quantitative description of walking in terms of its mechanical aspects (Whittle, 2014). An illustration of various phases of the human gait can be seen in Figure 1. It is also defined as a synchronized movement of lower-limbs passing through various phases while maintaining a postural balance. If the coordinated movement of the human legs disturbs, the gait trajectory is considered as deviated one and called as abnormal gait. Therefore, the practical significance of the clinical gait analysis is known for the assessment of neurological, neuromuscular, and neurodegenerative disorders within different age groups. Moreover, the clinical data of abnormal gait helps medical professionals to understand the onset of any disease after neural impairment. Research into this topic has made steady progress over the past fifteen years through the proliferation of AI/ML-driven techniques into the field.

GA is carried out based on kinematics and kinetics, the former being concerned with the description of movement without considering forces that cause said movement and the latter doing the opposite. Kinematic approaches rely on joint angles, segment angles, and related angular velocities and accelerations. In contrast, kinetic approaches use ground reaction forces (GRFs), plantar forces, joint reaction forces, and torques. These are equally important to a comprehensive and valuable analysis of the pathological gait. Nowadays, exploiting healthy gait data, researchers have designed, developed, and controlled various lower-limb rehabilitation devices for motion assistance and gait rehabilitation of patients suffering from neural disorders (Kalita et al., 2021).

DOI: 10.4018/978-1-7998-9220-5.ch053

*Figure 1. Human gait cycle*

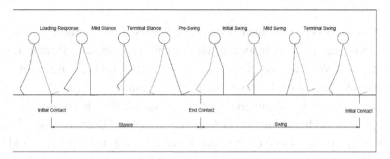

## BACKGROUND

The gait data acquisition is often carried out through relational mapping of optometric and inertial sensor readings with supervised or unsupervised learning. Various approaches for tackling gait analysis through AI/ML methodologies have been documented over time. Choi et al. (2013) presented a 13-26-3 layered input-hidden-output ANN (Artificial Neural Network) used to estimate GRFs along three axes. Oh et al. (2013), through a different approach involving a smaller FFNN (Feed Forward Neural Network) of 14-3-6, managed to attain not only the reaction forces but moments along the three axes. Some of the said limitations of this approach were addressed by Ardestani et al. (2015) and successfully obtained the standard and rehabilitation gait patterns. A TDNN (Time Delay Neural Network) was utilized with genetic algorithms to get these results.

Further, it is essential to note that aside from the methodology used for the analysis, specifics of data collection methods can also strongly impact the efficacy. Positioning of the sensors can strongly affect the quality of data and results. The sensor position also affects data compatibility, making it challenging to address the potency of analysis methods that use different sensor positions. This was discussed by Mu et al. (2020) in their attempt to develop a supervised model that could transfer from sensors mounted in one position corresponding to a labeled phase space to another that does not have labels. The applications of these GA methods are vast and expansive, finding use in gender identification by Guffanti et al. (2020); Parkinson's Disease by Mu et al. (2017); Cerebral Palsy based on research by Choisne et al. (2020) and in simple gait event detection in several different studies. Recently, Narayan and Kumar Dwivedy (2021) proposed a low-cost gait rehabilitation device where clinical gait analysis is used as a reference trajectory for the gait correction of Cerebral Palsy subjects.

Although significant developments are being carried out in gait analysis using machine learning techniques, the comprehensive reviews on such techniques are very limited in the literature. The motivation behind this research lies in the possibility of quick, inexpensive, and accurate monitoring and analysis of pathological gait to understand root causes before the prescription of remedial treatments. Therefore, in this work, a mini yet systematic review is carried out to understand related technological contributions, which are as follows:

- Details of data acquisition methods and their classifications and types of data used in human gait analysis.
- In-depth exploration of four categories of relevant and effective ML techniques, i.e., Supervised, Unsupervised, Probabilistic, and Hybrid learning for gait analysis
- Discussions and future inferences for available gait data in the literature.

## DATA ACQUISITION METHODS

Data relevant to gait analysis is usually measured indirectly through wearable or non-wearable sensors. The latter, however, often requires sophisticated equipment and specialized facilities, making the process tedious and expensive. With the use of wearable optometric and inertial sensors, these costs can be brought down significantly and allow for continuous gait monitoring leading to better health outcomes. The relation between gait kinetic and kinematic data and sensor data is complex and non-linear; however, this complexity can be addressed using AI/ML techniques and deep learning. In a few gait analysis procedures, wearable sensors are placed on the human body, such as the hips, feet, and knees, to measure different properties of the human gait (Tao et al., 2012, Abdul Razak et al., 2012). The sensor selection depends on the maximum allowable pressure, the range of pressure it offers, sensitivity, and linear movement. Piezoelectric, capacitive, and resistive sensors are the most commonly used pressure sensors.

### Non-Wearable Sensors

*Image Processing-* This is the most widely used method in the literature. In this method, cameras are used to acquire the data related to the human gait cycle in videos and images. Image processing techniques such as segmentation extract the gait from those images and videos. In the clinical field, Arias-Enriquez et al. (2012) developed a fuzzy system to interpret the kinetic analysis of the knee and thigh. In a recent study, Viswakumar et al. (2019) presented a cost-effective method for gait analysis using a mobile phone camera and a 2D pose estimation system. Nagymáté and Kiss (2019) developed an affordable system for gait analysis using augmented reality markers.

- Stereoscopic Vision- This method helps determine the depth of points in various images using a stereo camera system. Liu et al. (2010) presented a 3D approach for gait recognition using images captured by stereoscopic vision.
- Structured Light- In this method, the projection of a light sequence is used under geometric calibration on the object under the study. Narayan et al. (2020) presented the Kinect-LabVIEW experimental setup to capture the gait motion of healthy young adults (males and females) in the sagittal plane.
- Infrared Thermography (IRT)- It is the process of producing visual images based on surface temperatures. Xue et al. (2010) applied this method to recognize human gait parameters and found 78% to 91% accuracy.

*Floor sensors-* Floor sensors depend on the ground reaction forces. The sensors are placed on the "force platforms" (Muro-De-La-Herran et al., 2014). The sensors can also be located on the walkways where gait data is measured. Two types of floor sensors are used, i.e., pressure measurement systems and force platforms. Although both quantify pressure, force platforms do not directly measure the force exerted. Liu et al. (2012) developed a floor sensors method to estimate step length and foot angles.

The main advantage of the non-wearable sensors is that several gait-related parameters can be collected from a heavy set of modalities with minimal power constraints. However, limited space is present for working, and the sensors are often costly. Also, these types of systems are not applicable for outdoor applications.

# Wearable Sensors

In the case of wearable sensors, the sensors are located at different human body positions to measure the gait cycle parameters. Extensometers, gyroscopes, force sensors, inclinometers, and accelerometers can be used in this approach.

*Inertial Sensors-*These are the electronic devices used for measuring and reporting the object's speed, acceleration, randomness, orientation, and different forces acting on the object. Inertial sensors use a combination of accelerometers and gyroscopes. Inertial Measurement Units (IMU) is one of the most used sensor technology in gait analysis. Bastas et al. (2018) compared the step demarcation algorithms based on the IMU technique for the gait analysis in lower limb prosthesis users. In another work, Sant'Anna et al. (2012) designed a system using inertial sensors to quantify gait normality and symmetry. The system was evaluated in the lab against 3D kinematic measurements.

*Force Sensors-* Force sensors are mainly used to measure the GRF under the foot, and then they return a voltage or current, which is in proportion with the force applied. Pressure sensors, a class of force sensors, measure the exerted forces on the sensor without considering the magnitude of axial components. Capacitive, resistive and piezoelectric sensors are the most popular sensors of this type. The sensor selection depends on the maximum allowable pressure, the range of pressure it offers, sensitivity, and linear movement. Lou et al. (2017) developed a graphene-based flexible pressure sensor to measure plantar pressure in gait analysis.

*Goniometers Sensors-* Angles of different joints, i.e., hips, ankles, and knees, can be measured using these sensors. Resistance is the critical factor in strain gauge-based goniometers; the value of the resistance changes according to the flexed value of the sensor. Domínguez et al. (2013) used mechanical or inductive goniometers to develop a digital system using encoders to measure the knee joint position. Roy et al. (2018) developed a technique for recording joint coordinates of the human's lower limb using a camera and goniometer sensors.

*Ultrasonic Sensors-*Ultrasonic sensors are used to record the measurements like separation distance between feet, stride length, and short step. Ultrasonic sensors use a method to detect an object in which by knowing the speed of the sound traveling through the air, a sensor can measure the time the wave is taking to reflect from the object. The range of the measurement is between 1.7 cm to 450 cm. Ashhar et al. (2018) designed a Doppler-tolerant ultrasonic system with multiple access localization to analyze gait parameters.

*Electromyography (EMG)-* EMG is an electrical expression of the contracting muscle; the muscle can be voluntary or involuntary. The EMG signal is acquired using non-invasive surface electrodes or invasive wire or needle electrodes. Studies have shown that surface electromyography (sEMG) has been highly beneficial in the non-invasive assessment of pathophysiological mechanisms which block the gait function. These hindering can be related to paresis, loss of motor selectivity, and passive muscle-tendon properties (Frigo and Crenna, 2009). Wentink et al. (2014) determined gait initiation using the EMG at a prosthetic leg in another work.

The advantages of wearable sensors lie in analyzing the gait cycle for a longer duration. These systems are not necessarily costly. Unlike non-wearable sensors, these sensors are suitable for outdoor applications. Various parts of the human body can be studied using these sensors. However, only a limited amount of power can be consumed by such sensors. These devices are not easily portable, and the external environment affects the working of these sensors.

Invoking wearable and non-wearable sensors, four data types can be measured during gait analysis: anthropometric, spatiotemporal, kinematic, and kinetic data. *Anthropometric data* consist of physical measurements of the humans such as height, weight, body mass index (BMI), body circumference (arm, waist, hip, and calf), and elbow amplitude. *Spatiotemporal data* are related to both space and time. It consists of stance and swing times, stride and step lengths, and walking speed. Data pertaining to spatiotemporal gait characteristics for various age ranges are given in Table 1, compiled from (Mills and Barrett, 2001, Begg and Sparrow, 2006, Sutherland, 1997). *Kinematic data* include the displacements of body segments, joint angular positions and rates, and angular range of the motion. *Kinetic data* consists of ground reaction forces (GRFs), torques, mechanical joints and powers, and potential kinetic energy. A summary of wearable and non-wearable data acquisition methods discussed in the paper is given in Table 2.

*Table 1. Spatiotemporal gait characteristics for various age ranges*

| Age group (years) | Stance phase (s) | Swing phase (s) | Stride length (m) | Step length (m) | Walking speed (m/s) |
|---|---|---|---|---|---|
| **Young (1-7)** | 0.32-0.54 | 0.19-0.27 | 0.23-0.57 | 0.20-0.32 | 0.64-1.14 |
| **Adult (8-65)** | 0.62-0.70 | 0.36-0.40 | 1.68-1.72 | 0.68-0.85 | 1.30-1.46 |
| **Elderly (> 65)** | 0.68-0.72 | 0.42-0.44 | 1.66-1.70 | 0.44-0.60 | Declines 15% per decade |

*Table 2. Classification of data acquisition methods*

| | Reference | Sensor Used | Type of Data | Application |
|---|---|---|---|---|
| **Non-Wearable** | Arias-Enriquez et al. (2012) | Camera | Spatiotemporal, Kinematic | Interpretation of Kinetic Analysis |
| | Viswakumar et al. (2019) | Camera | Spatiotemporal, Kinematic | Gait Analysis |
| | Nagymáté and Kiss (2019) | Camera | Spatiotemporal, Kinematic | Cost-effective Gait Analysis |
| | Liu et al. (2012) | Floor Sensor | Kinetic, Spatiotemporal | Step length and foot angle estimation |
| **Wearable** | Bastas et al. (2018) | Inertial | Kinetic | Gait Analysis of lower limb prosthesis users |
| | Sant'Anna et al. (2012) | Inertial | Kinetic | Gait normality and symmetry quantification |
| | Lou et al. (2017) | Force | Kinetic | Plantar Pressure Measurement |
| | Domínguez et al. (2013) | Goniometer | Kinematic | Knee Joint Position Measurement |
| | Roy et al. (2018) | Goniometer, Camera | Kinematic, Spatiotemporal | Lower Limb Joint Coordinate documentation |
| | Ashhar et al. (2018) | Ultrasonic | Spatiotemporal | Analysis of gait parameters |
| | Wentink et al. (2014) | Electromyography | Spatiotemporal | Prediction of Gait Initiation |

## MACHINE LEARNING IN GAIT ANALYSIS

The kinematic and kinetic factors that characterize gait, like flex angles of various joints, the angular velocities, and the ground reaction forces and moments, are either difficult or downright impossible to measure in inexpensive, convenient ways. Therefore, these must be obtained through indirect means using electronic sensors like inertial and optometric sensors. The relationship between these measured and objective variables is often non-linear and complex. For this reason, the relational mapping between the two is a problem that's uniquely and particularly suited to being solved by machine learning and, more specifically, deep learning. The logic structure of a general machine learning algorithm can be seen in Figure 2.

Machine learning may either be supervised or unsupervised. Supervised learning uses a feature vector with a set of labeled data. The objective is to establish a functional relation that best maps the input feature vector to the corresponding label. In unsupervised learning, no labels are provided to the algorithm, and instead, a relationship between various inputs is devised by the algorithm itself to obtain an output. Supervised learning tends to be more prevalent in the context of gait analysis; since accurate definitions of learning objectives for conducting unsupervised learning are difficult to select (Best and Begg, 2006). In addition to the supervised and unsupervised learning methods, there are also other specific categories pertinent in gait analysis that are worth elaborating on, namely probabilistic learning and hybrid techniques. The probabilistic learning methods rely on the mathematical aspects of probability theory while the hybrid ones encompasses the amalgamation of different supervised and unsupervised learning methods. It is relevant to mention that these two categories are not mutually exclusive with supervised and unsupervised learning. Nowadays, hybrid learning approaches are quite famous in the assessment of clinical gait analysis.

*Figure 2. Schematic workflow representation of ML algorithms in gait analysis*

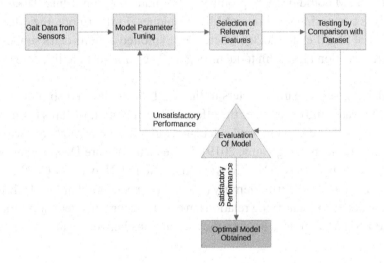

## Supervised Learning

Various supervised learning algorithms are applicable in gait analysis, such as Support Vector Machines (SVM), Neural Networks (NN), Random Forest (RF), k-nearest neighbor (kNN), and decision trees (Khera and Kumar (2020)). A schematic flow of the method can be seen in Figure 3 below.

According to Costilla-Reyes et al. (2020), a training algorithm may be either of shallow learning type or deep learning type. Shallow learning refers to those types that require predefined relations between the outputs and inputs. As mentioned earlier, examples are the SVM, k-Nearest Neighbors, random forests, and fuzzy logic. In a work by Guffanti et al. (2020), SVM has been exploited successfully to

*Figure 3. Schematic flow of Supervised Learning*

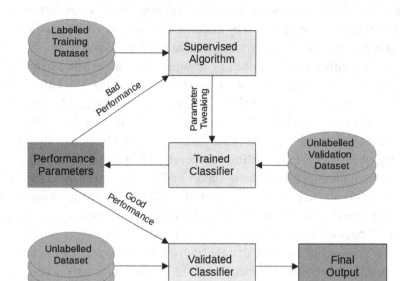

identify gender using gait data from depth cameras, and achieved an accuracy over 96%. Caramia et al. (2018) suggested that SVM could be more promising technique for identifying Parkinson's Disease using IMU sensors while comparing six different ML techniques. Furthermore, the effectiveness of SVM is evident in the work of Sharif et al. (2020), where they exploited a multi-class support vector machine (MSVM) in a feature selection algorithm to identify gait. The complete architecture of the algorithm is given in Figure 4.

The adjective 'deep' in deep learning refers to the depth of the layered structure, modeled through weights and biases, activates and deactivates the effects of certain input features to create a function that minimizes the error between the expected and calculated output. A neural network with more than three layers is often considered 'deep' (Sugiyama, 2019). Some examples are Deep Belief Networks (DBN), Generative Adversarial Networks (GAN), Convolutional Neural Networks (CNN), Recurrent Neural Networks (RNN), and Long-Short Term Memory (LSTM) (a special kind of RNN) (Bastas et al., 2018). LSTM techniques are potent at identifying relations in events occurring over short time intervals. Liu et al. (2016) have used LSTM techniques to learn the associations between gait features using gait trajec-

*Figure 4. Flow diagram of the proposed method (Sharif et al., 2020)*

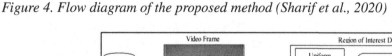

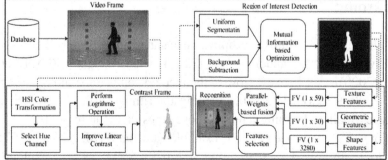

tories, validated by healthy participants imitating knee injuries to help design a lower limb exoskeleton for patient rehabilitation purposes. Mu et al. (2020) have used Bilateral LSTM and Multi-Source Domain Adversarial Neural Network to address the incompatibility of gait analysis frameworks based on sensor positioning. Wu et al. (2016) employed a deep CNN for human identification by analyzing cross-view gait. A substantial increase in performance was observed, at 94.2% against the 65% of handmade feature engineering on identical datasets. In very recent work, Narayan and Dwivedy (2021) proposed a Bayesian regularisation (BR)-based back propagation multi-layer perceptron neural network (BPMLPNN) to estimate the biomechanical joint angles of the lower limb over a gait cycle. They carried out the training process in two stages, i.e., stance and swing. The proposed model was tested for 19 and 50 years old participants. Finally, the results for healthy subjects are compared with unhealthy subjects of a similar age group. The BR-BPMLPNN technique is found to be promising with less dataset.

## Unsupervised Learning

Unsupervised learning is carried out using clustering techniques that recognize the difference in the value of feature vectors and the cluster centroid to classify the data into specific subgroups. With its characteristic of not requiring labeled datasets, this learning technique can recognize gait patterns in specific and distinct conditions. A schematic of this technique can be seen in Figure 5 below. A few examples of this type of learning are k-means clustering, Hidden Markov models (HMM), Principal Component Analysis (PCA), Rapid Centroid Estimation (RCE), and Expectation-Maximisation (EM) Clustering.

K-means and self-organizing maps (SOM) are used by Choisne et al. (2020) to help identify children with cerebral palsy (CP) with an accuracy of 100%. It is worth noting that the study was limited in scope in terms of the number and variety of participants making their results somewhat inconclusive. Chakraborty and Nandy (2020) detected the gait phase with an accuracy of 96.92% using the Microsoft Kinect sensor and classical k-Means learning algorithm. Mu et al. (2017) were able to identify four main clusters for detecting subtypes of Parkinson's disease using k-Means. Jatesiktat et al. (2018) were able to apply an entirely novel unsupervised learning architecture to extract gait phase rather than specific gait events to circumvent the need for handcrafted features altogether. The two-phase method uses consecutive pairs of time series data to prevent the network from considering sequences moving backward in time. A special cost function is used to force the neural network to learn the concept of phase.

*Figure 5. Schematic Diagram for Unsupervised Learning*

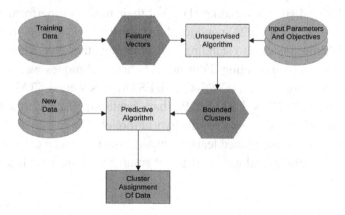

## Probabilistic Learning

Probabilistic learning employs probability distribution functions over various output classes to categorize the set of input feature vectors. Instead, this technique returns a distribution function over the output classes rather than mapping the inputs to a single most probable output. Some examples are the Naive Bayesian technique, Gaussian Process Regression, and HMM, which may also be categorized in unsupervised learning as mentioned in Section 3.2. Ma et al. (2019) were able to obtain an accuracy of 95.8% for the detection of contact between the foot and the ground using an adaptive weighted Naive Bayes model. In other work by Mileti et al. (2017), scalar continuous Hidden Markov Model (cHMM) was used for successful gait phase partition in patients affected by Parkinson's disease experiencing motor fluctuations. Bei et al (2018) also used a Bayesian classifier for movement disorder detection and outperformed kNN and SVM with an accuracy of around 94%. Probabilistic graphical models exploit the complex multivariate probability distributions and have most applications in machine learning, image procession, and computer vision. Formulating any problem with the probabilistic approach provides a natural means for forming a hierarchical structure (Lan et al., 2012). Deep neural networks can get compelling results on the individual activity recognition tasks if combined with probabilistic graphical models.

## Hybrid Techniques

As the name suggests, hybrid techniques employ features from one or more ML methodologies. Mixed techniques are used in combination and increase the performance and accuracy to minimize the restrictions of any one method when applied in isolation. Chen et al (2020) implemented a combination of LSTM and SVM for describing the gait of osteoarthiritis patients, quantitatively. Deng et al. (2015) used a message passing neural network (MPNN) and CNN for group activity recognition and obtained 76.5-80.6% accuracy. These semi-supervised models can be exercised using limited labeled data for better goals. This is particularly useful when labeled information is scarce; however, it is not non-existent. If used correctly, it can enhance the model's versatility by avoiding overfitting the labeled data. In other work by Prasad et al. (2016), the fuzzy logic approach has been combined with a plethora of 'vanilla' ML techniques to create hybrids like Fuzzy SVMs used for clinical gait analysis through a gait monitoring platform. Further, Phu et al. (2018) were able to apply the fuzzy c-mean algorithm for gait filtering with an accuracy of 98.14%

A combination of ELM (Extreme Learning Machine) along with PCA for feature reduction was used by Gupta and Semwal (2020) to classify 9 types of gait (walking at natural speed (N), walking very slow (XS), walking slow (S), walking medium (M), walking fast (L), walking on toes (T), walking on heels (H), stair ascending (U), and stair descending (D)) and their model outperformed SVM and kNN. In another recent paper, Semwal et al (2021) conducted a study with 50 subjects to classify the following 7 walking activities: (i) natural walk, (ii) standing, (iii) climbing stairs, (iv) knees bending (crouching) (v) jogging, (vi) running, and (vii) cycling. Four novel hybrid techniques were used by them, namely CNN–LSTM, CNN–gated recurrent unit (CNN–GRU), LSTM–CNN and LSTM–GRU and achieved the maximum accuracy of 99.34%. CNN, LSTM, GRU have achieved 97.26%, 90.67%, 77.38% accuracy on their own, establishing clear superiority for the hybrid models.

Conclusively, the four above-mentioned learning algorithms have been exploited to classify, detect, and visualize healthy and pathological gait. A detailed summary of such studies involving these algorithms is given in Table 3.

*Table 3. Machine learning classification in human gait analysis*

| Machine learning technique | Learning type | Application | Reference |
|---|---|---|---|
| SVM, Naïve Bayesian, DT | Supervised | Disorder Detection | Caramia et al. (2018) |
| LSTM, ANN | Supervised | Data transformation | Mu et al. (2020) |
| SVM | Supervised | Gait Identification | Guffanti et al. (2020) |
| CNN | Supervised | Human identification | Wu et al. (2016) |
| LSTM | Supervised | Gait trajectory prediction | Liu et al. (2016) |
| BRBPNN | Supervised | Gait trajectory prediction | Narayan and Dwivedy (2021) |
| MSVM | Supervised | Gait Identification | Sharif et al. (2020) |
| K-means | Unsupervised | Disorder Subtype detection | Mu et al. (2017) |
| K-mean, SOM | Unsupervised | Disorder detection | Choisne et al. (2020) |
| Microsoft Kinect k-Means | Unsupervised | Gait phase detection | Chakraborty and Nandy (2020) |
| cHMM | Probabilistic | Disorder Detection | Mileti et al. (2017) |
| Bayesian Filter | Hybrid | Disorder Detection | Bei et al. (2018) |
| Adaptive Weighted Naïve Bayesian | Probabilistic | Ground Contact Detection | Ma et al. (2019) |
| LSTM, SVM | Hybrid | Disorder Detection | Chen et al. (2020) |
| CNN, MPNN | Hybrid | Group activity recognition | Deng et al. (2015) |
| Fuzzy SVMs | Hybrid | Clinical gait analysis | Prasad et al. (2016) |
| Fuzzy c-Mean | Hybrid | Gait Filtering | Phu et al. (2018) |
| GRU, LSTM, CNN | Hybrid | Gait type detection | Semwal et al (2021) |
| PCA, SVM, ELM, kNN | Hybrid | Gait type detection | Gupta and Semwal (2020) |

## DISCUSSION AND FUTURE DIRECTIONS

This paper presents recent developments and advancements in the research of human gait analysis. Many articles and research papers published in highly reputed journals are considered for writing this comprehensive review. Despite the thorough work that has been carried out in this field, there are still some limitations and challenges. The current methods used for data acquisition are more accurate; however, these methods cannot collect actual human gait cycle patterns. The cause for these limitations is hardware and one-direction viewpoints. A 3D space of viewpoints is needed to capture the real data and patterns related to the human gait cycle.

Medical engineering and machine learning have been practiced jointly to identify and detect behavior, events, disruptions, and system control. As per Devanne et al. (2016), the methodological reliability approaches should be implemented. Another area requiring more research is the correlation between the external factors that influence the human gait cycle. It is seen that the typical walking pattern of humans is affected by the physical, environmental, psychological, extrinsic, and intrinsic factors. Researchers are still not able to find the correlation between these factors. Today, computational techniques are widely used and applied in human gait research. As gait data is not homogeneous, multidimensional, and time-varying, it is difficult to proceed with this data further. However, the solution for this problem is deep learning architecture, as abnormality in the data can be detected by this technique. If this technique is used, there is no requirement of the engineering hand (LeCun et al., 2015). Gait analysis is a complex phenomenon due to its transitory behavior. The recent development is in pathology, which requires high force because of diversity in the participants. Therefore, the biomechanics need to be precisely estimated, and the inclusion of attribute analysis methods is necessary. However, deep learning techniques provide a solution for the replicated involved process, and thus the methodology for decision making is understood without any interruptions.

Real-time tests are needed in offline analytic techniques for more efficient and intelligent appliances. A generalized gait model can be widely adopted for different environments, diversity levels, and transfer learning. Therefore, the gait data from one subject can be considered for other participants with similar diseases using the machine learning strategies (Lonini et al., 2016). Artificial intelligence and machine learning are effective in short-term implementations of human gait research such as disease for casting and detection, disease magnification, recovery speed, and natural human working that govern rehabilitation devices. However, technological advancements and improvements would be more beneficial by fabricating sensor-dependent techniques with a minimum cost solution, constant governing, and easy portability. Such methods are developed to include processing of long-term parameters, management, and systematic storage of data.

The absence of variety, highly long recording times, and artificial walking atmospheres involved in the gait analysis can be reduced with the help of sensor-based technologies. The difficulty is collaborating computational intelligence methods with these techniques onboard the hardware, providing a solution for real-time implementation. Accelerometers and gyroscopes appear to be indispensable measurement instruments in nearly all the studies mentioned and are highly effective and inexpensive for gait classification and disorder identification. Microsoft Kinect also seems to be gaining traction as a cheap and effective alternative to the plethora of sensors needed otherwise. Scope for investigating the effectiveness of different types and positions of sensors on the same data set and using the same methods seems to exist.

Based on the data presented, it is clear that the scope for further research is substantial. The field has made steady progress over the years, and techniques have been honed to obtain exceptional results. Accuracies higher than 95% for gait disorder detection are expected and found to outperform traditional methods, despite various techniques being used significantly. LSTM and SVM have been used most commonly in the supervised domain due to their high effectiveness and versatility, whereas K-Means Clustering is particularly pervasive in the unsupervised domain.

## CONCLUSION

The main contribution of this paper is to provide a brief yet systematic review of the role of machine learning techniques in human gait analysis. In this work, machine learning in various gait studies during the last ten years has been reviewed, followed by the gait data acquisition methods. The ML algorithms have been primarily categorized and presented in supervised and unsupervised ones with special mentions for probabilistic and hybrid techniques. Machine learning techniques have been found beneficial because they can provide an accurate and fast prediction or classification of healthy and unhealthy gait data despite the highly non-linear nature of the involved functions. The future directions and opportunities for young researchers working in clinical gait analysis have been briefly discussed. Moreover, this paper will provide a convenient starting point for young and enthusiastic researchers to contribute with minimal issues.

## REFERENCES

Abdul Razak, A. H., Zayegh, A., Begg, R. K., & Wahab, Y. (2012). Foot plantar pressure measurement system: A review. *Sensors (Basel)*, *12*(7), 9884–9912. doi:10.3390120709884 PMID:23012576

Ardestani, M. M., Moazen, M., & Jin, Z. (2015). Sensitivity analysis of human lower extremity joint moments due to changes in joint kinematics. *Medical Engineering & Physics*, *37*(2), 165–174. doi:10.1016/j.medengphy.2014.11.012 PMID:25553962

Arias-Enriquez, O., Chacon-Murguia, M. I., & Sandoval-Rodriguez, R. (2012, August). Kinematic analysis of gait cycle using a fuzzy system for medical diagnosis. In *2012 Annual Meeting of the North American Fuzzy Information Processing Society (NAFIPS)* (pp. 1-6). IEEE. 10.1109/NAFIPS.2012.6291049

Ashhar, K., Khyam, M. O., Soh, C. B., & Kong, K. H. (2018). A Doppler-tolerant ultrasonic multiple access localization system for human gait analysis. *Sensors (Basel)*, *18*(8), 2447. doi:10.339018082447 PMID:30060515

Bastas, G., Fleck, J. J., Peters, R. A., & Zelik, K. E. (2018). IMU-based gait analysis in lower limb prosthesis users: Comparison of step demarcation algorithms. *Gait & Posture*, *64*, 30–37. doi:10.1016/j.gaitpost.2018.05.025 PMID:29807270

Bei, S., Zhen, Z., Xing, Z., Taocheng, L., & Qin, L. (2018). Movement disorder detection via adaptively fused gait analysis based on kinect sensors. *IEEE Sensors Journal*, *18*(17), 7305–7314. doi:10.1109/JSEN.2018.2839732

Begg, R. K., & Sparrow, W. A. (2006). Ageing effects on knee and ankle joint angles at key events and phases of the gait cycle. *Journal of Medical Engineering & Technology*, *30*(6), 382–389. doi:10.1080/03091900500445353 PMID:17060166

Best, R., & Begg, R. (2006). Overview of movement analysis and gait features. In *Computational intelligence for movement sciences: neural networks and other emerging techniques* (pp. 1–69). IGI Global. doi:10.4018/978-1-59140-836-9.ch001

Caramia, C., Torricelli, D., Schmid, M., Munoz-Gonzalez, A., Gonzalez-Vargas, J., Grandas, F., & Pons, J. L. (2018). IMU-based classification of Parkinson's disease from gait: A sensitivity analysis on sensor location and feature selection. *IEEE Journal of Biomedical and Health Informatics*, *22*(6), 1765–1774. doi:10.1109/JBHI.2018.2865218 PMID:30106745

Chakraborty, S., & Nandy, A. (2020, February). An Unsupervised Approach For Gait Phase Detection. In *2020 4th International Conference on Computational Intelligence and Networks (CINE)* (pp. 1-5). IEEE. 10.1109/CINE48825.2020.234396

Chen, F., Cui, X., Zhao, Z., Zhang, D., Ma, C., Zhang, X., & Liao, H. (2020). Gait acquisition and analysis system for osteoarthritis based on hybrid prediction model. *Computerized Medical Imaging and Graphics*, *85*, 101782. doi:10.1016/j.compmedimag.2020.101782 PMID:32919311

Choi, A., Lee, J. M., & Mun, J. H. (2013). Ground reaction forces predicted by using artificial neural network during asymmetric movements. *International Journal of Precision Engineering and Manufacturing*, *14*(3), 475–483. doi:10.100712541-013-0064-4

Choisne, J., Fourrier, N., Handsfield, G., Signal, N., Taylor, D., Wilson, N., Stott, S., & Besier, T. F. (2020). An unsupervised data-driven model to classify gait patterns in children with cerebral palsy. *Journal of Clinical Medicine*, *9*(5), 1432. doi:10.3390/jcm9051432 PMID:32408489

Costilla-Reyes, O., Vera-Rodriguez, R., Alharthi, A. S., Yunas, S. U., & Ozanyan, K. B. (2020). Deep learning in gait analysis for security and healthcare. In *Deep Learning: Algorithms and Applications* (pp. 299–334). Springer. doi:10.1007/978-3-030-31760-7_10

Phu, D. X., Huy, T. D., & Ha, T. H. (2018). An Implementation of Neuro-Fuzzy System for Gait Analysis in a Smart Insole of Exoskeleton. *2018 4th International Conference on Green Technology and Sustainable Development (GTSD),* 611-614. 10.1109/GTSD.2018.8595659

Deng, Z., Zhai, M., Chen, L., Liu, Y., Muralidharan, S., Roshtkhari, M. J., & Mori, G. (2015). *Deep structured models for group activity recognition.* doi:10.5244/C.29.179

Devanne, M., Wannous, H., Daoudi, M., Berretti, S., Del Bimbo, A., & Pala, P. (2016, December). Learning shape variations of motion trajectories for gait analysis. In *2016 23rd International Conference on Pattern Recognition (ICPR)* (pp. 895-900). IEEE. 10.1109/ICPR.2016.7899749

Domínguez, G., Cardiel, E., Arias, S., & Rogeli, P. (2013, August). A digital goniometer based on encoders for measuring knee-joint position in an orthosis. In *2013 World Congress on Nature and Biologically Inspired Computing* (pp. 1-4). IEEE. 10.1109/NaBIC.2013.6617835

Frigo, C., & Crenna, P. (2009). Multichannel SEMG in clinical gait analysis: A review and state-of-the-art. *Clinical Biomechanics (Bristol, Avon), 24*(3), 236–245. doi:10.1016/j.clinbiomech.2008.07.012 PMID:18995937

Guffanti, D., Brunete, A., & Hernando, M. (2020). Non-invasive multi-camera gait analysis system and its application to gender classification. *IEEE Access: Practical Innovations, Open Solutions, 8,* 95734–95746. doi:10.1109/ACCESS.2020.2995474

Gupta, A., & Semwal, V. B. (2020). Multiple task human gait analysis and identification: ensemble learning approach. In *Emotion and information processing* (pp. 185–197). Springer. doi:10.1007/978-3-030-48849-9_12

Jatesiktat, P., Anopas, D., & Ang, W. T. (2018, July). Unsupervised phase learning and extraction from repetitive movements. In *2018 40th Annual International Conference of the IEEE Engineering in Medicine and Biology Society (EMBC)* (pp. 227-230). IEEE. 10.1109/EMBC.2018.8512196

Kalita, B., Narayan, J., & Dwivedy, S. K. (2021). Development of active lower limb robotic-based orthosis and exoskeleton devices: A systematic review. *International Journal of Social Robotics, 13*(4), 775–793. doi:10.100712369-020-00662-9

Khera, P., & Kumar, N. (2020). Role of machine learning in gait analysis: A review. *Journal of Medical Engineering & Technology, 44*(8), 441–467. doi:10.1080/03091902.2020.1822940 PMID:33078988

Lan, T., Sigal, L., & Mori, G. (2012, June). Social roles in hierarchical models for human activity recognition. In *2012 IEEE Conference on Computer Vision and Pattern Recognition* (pp. 1354-1361). IEEE. 10.1109/CVPR.2012.6247821

LeCun, Y., Bengio, Y., & Hinton, G. (2015). Deep learning. *Nature, 521*(7553), 436-444.

Liu, D. X., Du, W., Wu, X., Wang, C., & Qiao, Y. (2016, December). Deep rehabilitation gait learning for modeling knee joints of lower-limb exoskeleton. In *2016 IEEE International Conference on Robotics and Biomimetics (ROBIO)* (pp. 1058-1063). IEEE. 10.1109/ROBIO.2016.7866465

Liu, H., Cao, Y., & Wang, Z. (2010, May). Automatic gait recognition from a distance. In *2010 Chinese Control and Decision Conference* (pp. 2777-2782). IEEE. 10.1109/CCDC.2010.5498729

**M**

Liu, Y., Zhang, J., Wang, C., & Wang, L. (2012, November). Multiple HOG templates for gait recognition. In *Proceedings of the 21st International Conference on Pattern Recognition (ICPR2012)* (pp. 2930-2933). IEEE.

Lonini, L., Gupta, A., Kording, K., & Jayaraman, A. (2016, August). Activity recognition in patients with lower limb impairments: do we need training data from each patient? In *2016 38th Annual International Conference of the IEEE Engineering in Medicine and Biology Society (EMBC)* (pp. 3265-3268). IEEE.

Lou, C., Wang, S., Liang, T., Pang, C., Huang, L., Run, M., & Liu, X. (2017). A graphene-based flexible pressure sensor with applications to plantar pressure measurement and gait analysis. *Materials (Basel)*, *10*(9), 1068. doi:10.3390/ma10091068 PMID:28891991

Ma, H., Yan, W., Yang, Z., & Liu, H. (2019). Real-time foot-ground contact detection for inertial motion capture based on an adaptive weighted naive bayes model. *IEEE Access: Practical Innovations, Open Solutions*, *7*, 130312–130326. doi:10.1109/ACCESS.2019.2939839

Mileti, I., Germanotta, M., Alcaro, S., Pacilli, A., Imbimbo, I., Petracca, M., Erra, C., Di Sipio, E., Aprile, I., Rossi, S., Bentivoglio, A. R., Padua, L., & Palermo, E. (2017, May). Gait partitioning methods in Parkinson's disease patients with motor fluctuations: A comparative analysis. In *2017 IEEE International Symposium on Medical Measurements and Applications (MeMeA)* (pp. 402-407). IEEE. 10.1109/MeMeA.2017.7985910

Mills, P. M., & Barrett, R. S. (2001). Swing phase mechanics of healthy young and elderly men. *Human Movement Science*, *20*(4-5), 427–446. doi:10.1016/S0167-9457(01)00061-6 PMID:11750671

Mu, F., Gu, X., Guo, Y., & Lo, B. (2020, October). Unsupervised Domain Adaptation for Position-Independent IMU Based Gait Analysis. In *2020 IEEE Sensors* (pp. 1-4). IEEE.

Mu, J., Chaudhuri, K. R., Bielza, C., de Pedro-Cuesta, J., Larrañaga, P., & Martinez-Martin, P. (2017). Parkinson's disease subtypes identified from cluster analysis of motor and non-motor symptoms. *Frontiers in Aging Neuroscience*, *9*, 301. doi:10.3389/fnagi.2017.00301 PMID:28979203

Muro-De-La-Herran, A., Garcia-Zapirain, B., & Mendez-Zorrilla, A. (2014). Gait analysis methods: An overview of wearable and non-wearable systems, highlighting clinical applications. *Sensors (Basel)*, *14*(2), 3362–3394. doi:10.3390140203362 PMID:24556672

Nagymáté, G., & Kiss, R. M. (2019). Affordable gait analysis using augmented reality markers. *PLoS One*, *14*(2), e0212319. doi:10.1371/journal.pone.0212319 PMID:30763399

Narayan, J., & Dwivedy, S. K. (2021). Biomechanical Study and Prediction of Lower Extremity Joint Movements Using Bayesian Regularization-Based Backpropagation Neural Network. *Journal of Computing and Information Science in Engineering*, *22*(1), 014503. doi:10.1115/1.4051599

Narayan, J., & Kumar Dwivedy, S. (2021). Preliminary design and development of a low-cost lower-limb exoskeleton system for paediatric rehabilitation. *Proceedings of the Institution of Mechanical Engineers. Part H, Journal of Engineering in Medicine*, *235*(5), 530–545. doi:10.1177/0954411921994940 PMID:33588634

Narayan, J., Pardasani, A., & Dwivedy, S. K. (2020, July). Comparative gait analysis of healthy young male and female adults using Kinect-Labview setup. In *2020 International Conference on Computational Performance Evaluation (ComPE)* (pp. 688-693). IEEE. 10.1109/ComPE49325.2020.9200155

Oh, S. E., Choi, A., & Mun, J. H. (2013). Prediction of ground reaction forces during gait based on kinematics and a neural network model. *Journal of Biomechanics*, *46*(14), 2372–2380. doi:10.1016/j.jbiomech.2013.07.036 PMID:23962528

Prasad, R., Babu, S., Siddaiah, N., & Rao, K. (2016). A review on techniques for diagnosing and monitoring patients with Parkinson's disease. *Journal of Biosensors & Bioelectronics*, *7*(203), 2.

Roy, G., Bhuiya, A., Mukherjee, A., & Bhaumik, S. (2018). Kinect camera-based gait data recording and analysis for assistive robotics-an alternative to goniometer based measurement technique. *Procedia Computer Science*, *133*, 763–771. doi:10.1016/j.procs.2018.07.121

Sant'Anna, A., Wickström, N., Eklund, H., Zügner, R., & Tranberg, R. (2012, February). Assessment of gait symmetry and gait normality using inertial sensors: in-lab and in-situ evaluation. In *International Joint Conference on Biomedical Engineering Systems and Technologies* (pp. 239-254). Springer.

Semwal, V. B., Gupta, A., & Lalwani, P. (2021). An optimized hybrid deep learning model using ensemble learning approach for human walking activities recognition. *The Journal of Supercomputing*, *77*(11), 12256–12279. doi:10.100711227-021-03768-7

Sharif, M., Attique, M., Tahir, M. Z., Yasmim, M., Saba, T., & Tanik, U. J. (2020). A machine learning method with threshold-based parallel feature fusion and feature selection for automated gait recognition. *Journal of Organizational and End User Computing*, *32*(2), 67–92. doi:10.4018/JOEUC.2020040104

Sugiyama, S. (2019). *Human behavior and another kind in consciousness*. IGI Global. doi:10.4018/978-1-5225-8217-5

Sutherland, D. (1997). The development of mature gait. *Gait & Posture*, *6*(2), 163–170. doi:10.1016/S0966-6362(97)00029-5

Tao, W., Liu, T., Zheng, R., & Feng, H. (2012). Gait analysis using wearable sensors. *Sensors (Basel)*, *12*(2), 2255–2283. doi:10.3390120202255 PMID:22438763

Viswakumar, A., Rajagopalan, V., Ray, T., & Parimi, C. (2019, November). Human gait analysis using OpenPose. In *2019 Fifth International Conference on Image Information Processing (ICIIP)* (pp. 310-314). IEEE. 10.1109/ICIIP47207.2019.8985781

Wentink, E. C., Schut, V. G. H., Prinsen, E. C., Rietman, J. S., & Veltink, P. H. (2014). Detection of the onset of gait initiation using kinematic sensors and EMG in transfemoral amputees. *Gait & Posture*, *39*(1), 391–396. doi:10.1016/j.gaitpost.2013.08.008 PMID:24001871

Whittle, M. W. (2014). *Gait analysis: an introduction*. Butterworth-Heinemann.

Wu, Z., Huang, Y., Wang, L., Wang, X., & Tan, T. (2016). A comprehensive study on cross-view gait based human identification with deep cnns. *IEEE Transactions on Pattern Analysis and Machine Intelligence*, *39*(2), 209–226. doi:10.1109/TPAMI.2016.2545669 PMID:27019478

Xue, Z., Ming, D., Song, W., Wan, B., & Jin, S. (2010). Infrared gait recognition based on wavelet transform and support vector machine. *Pattern Recognition*, *43*(8), 2904–2910. doi:10.1016/j.patcog.2010.03.011

## ADDITIONAL READING

Begg, R. (2008). Artificial intelligence techniques in medicine and health care. In Intelligent Information Technologies: Concepts, Methodologies, Tools, and Applications (pp. 1750-1757). IGI Global. doi:10.4018/978-1-59904-941-0.ch098

Gonzalez, F. A., & Romero, E. (Eds.). (2009). *Biomedical image analysis and machine learning technologies: Applications and techniques: Applications and techniques*. IGI Global.

Prakash, C., Kumar, R., & Mittal, N. (2018). Recent developments in human gait research: Parameters, approaches, applications, machine learning techniques, datasets and challenges. *Artificial Intelligence Review*, *49*(1), 1–40. doi:10.100710462-016-9514-6

Shetty, S., & Rao, Y. S. (2016, August). SVM based machine learning approach to identify Parkinson's disease using gait analysis. In *2016 International Conference on Inventive Computation Technologies (ICICT)* (Vol. 2, pp. 1-5). IEEE. 10.1109/INVENTIVE.2016.7824836

Specht, D. F. (1991). A general regression neural network. *IEEE Transactions on Neural Networks*, *2*(6), 568–576. doi:10.1109/72.97934 PMID:18282872

Suzuki, K. (Ed.). (2012). *Machine learning in computer-aided diagnosis: Medical imaging intelligence and analysis: Medical imaging intelligence and analysis*. IGI Global.

Vieira, J., Dias, F. M., & Mota, A. (2004, March). Neuro-fuzzy systems: a survey. In *5th WSEAS NNA international conference on neural networks and applications, Udine, Italia* (pp. 87-92). WSEAS.

Wang, L., Cheng, L., & Zhao, G. (Eds.). (2009). *Machine Learning for Human Motion Analysis: Theory and Practice: Theory and Practice*. IGI Global.

## KEY TERMS AND DEFINITIONS

**Data Acquisition:** Data acquisition methods are used to acquire different types of data related to human gait parameters.

**Gait Analysis:** A quantitative description of walking in terms of its mechanical aspects.

**Hybrid Learning:** When several different types of machine learning techniques are used in sequence or in parallel, the approach is termed as hybrid.

**Machine Learning:** The creation and utilisation of computer algorithms that identify patterns in data without explicit instructions through the use of statistical and optimisation methods.

**Non-Wearable Sensors:** This type of sensors do not have interference to person's routine.

**Probabilistic Learning:** A machine learning technique that tries to infer probability distribution functions over the possible outputs by using either supervised or unsupervised approach.

**Supervised Learning:** A sub-category of machine learning that uses labelled data to infer relationships between the input and output.

**Unsupervised Learning:** A sub-category of machine learning that creates data clusters used for categorisation by using a rough learning objective, no. of clusters, etc. as input along with the dataset.

**Wearable Sensors:** This type of sensors are placed on human's body to measure different gait parameters and they enable person's status monitoring.

# Machine Learning Algorithms:
## Features and Applications

**Hamed Taherdoost**

https://orcid.org/0000-0002-6503-6739

*University Canada West, Canada*

## INTRODUCTION

Human has developed machines to accimplish tasks that are not easily processed and analyzed by human brain. Intellignet tools and machines lead businesses to be more creative and procuctive through creating competittve advantage for businesses. The initial concept of intelligent machines was shaped in the mid-twentieth century when Alan Mathison Turing first thought about the possibility of employing machines to process data. Then, Artificial Intelligence that is considered as a branch of computer science was developed at a rapid pace. Machine Learning that its learning capacitiy is not dependent on programming was initially based on the simulation of human intelligence. Today, ML that is generally defined as learning from different levels and classes of data (Amornsamankul, Pimpunchat et al. 2019) through employing different algorithms to make accurate predictions (Das and Behera, 2017) is broadly used in various fields ranging from biomedical science and spacecraft to biological science (El Naqa and Murphy, 2015) aiming to solve problems that are mainly based on big datasets. ML can solve complex projects through processing complicated and big data inputs to predict potential threats and profitable opportunities for businesses that are widely reliant on data to proceed. This review discusses and compares popu;ar and commnly used Supervised Learning, Unsupervised Learning, Semi-Supervised Learning, Reinforcement Learning, Neural Network Learning, and Instance-Based Learning methods and algorithms.

## MACHINE LEARNING

Since ML employs diffremt types of models and algoritms based on AI to proceed with the learning phase from data (Sze, Chen et al. 2017).

It is almost believed that the difference between ML and AI is very slight which leads to being used interchangeably in many cases. However, ML is mainly defined as one of the most important subsets of AI. On the other hand, AI has a close association with computers or machines to make decisions based on datasets (Osarogiagbon, Udeze et al. 2015). ML applies various types of algorithms or models based on an AI to proceed with the learning phase from data (Sze, Chen et al. 2017).

The modern definition of ML is incorporated with a psychologist scientist from Cornell University Frank Rosenblatt who created a procedure that was capable of recognizing the alphabet by inspiration from the human nervous system called "perception". It becomes the prototype of a modern Artificial Neural Network (Fradkov, 2020). In 1967, the first algorithm Nearest Neighbor algorithm was first de-

DOI: 10.4018/978-1-7998-9220-5.ch054

veloped and became the basic pattern recognition (Cover and Hart, 1967). There are various algorithms and classes of Machine Learning, but no one is free from limitations and deficiencies. The main reason for many developments has been the necessity of providing a simple and clear equation or solution that is easy to understand and solve problems. Although researchers believe that the employment of ML for many real-life issues and challenges is difficult, many extraordinary developments have happened in this area. In this review, the most practical and popular algorithms of Machine Learning and modifications which happen to make them more reliable, accurate, and user-friendly have been studied.

## MACHINE LEARNING ALGORITHMS

The development of a Machine Learning application relies on using an appropriate ML algorithm. Since the appealing concept of ML has been an interesting topic for researchers, they have categorized ML algorithms innovatively. ML algorithms are generally categorized into four main classes including Supervised, Unsupervised, Semi-supervised, and Reinforcement learning. However, in this chapter, algorithms are discussed in more detailed categories based on their specifications. An overview of the subjects covered in this review is shown in Figure. 1.

### Supervised Learning

Supervised Learning is known as the subset of ML and AI. The procedure of this algorithm is based on learning from labeled data for predicting the result more accurately. This algorithm is called Supervised since its learning process takes place through observation of variables. The process of learning will be continued till an acceptable level of accuracy is achieved. This type of learning is based on training data to make decisions, minimizes errors, compares and calculates desired outcomes. However, labeling large amounts of input and output big data in the training and testing phases can be a laborious task that consumes a considerable amount of time (Lee & Shin, 2020).

This algorithm is mostly used in bioinformatics, database marketing, spam detection, speech recognition, and many other fields. Supervised Machine Learning algorithm refers to methods that need assistance to perform, and starts its operation by classifying input data into two classes: a) Train, and b) Test.

The output of the training class contains variables to be classified. This can happen by learning the pattern from training data and applying them for predicting or classifying (Kotsiantis, 2007).

Some of the most popular Supervised Machine Learning algorithms that are discussed here are Decision Tree, Naïve Bayes, Support Vector Machine (SVM), Logistic Regression, and Random Forest.

### Decision Tree

Decision Tree was first developed in 1959, by William Belson, a British researcher (Belson, 1959). This algorithm is defined as an alternating result from different series of decisions. One of the most popular areas to employ decision trees are planning and defining strategies. One of the advantages of a decision tree that makes it preferable to employ is its simplicity. There are different types and modifications of Decision Trees. The main difference between these algorithms is the mathematical model chosen to split attributes in extracting the Decision Tree rules. Decision Tree employs different algorithms to classify input data. For instance, CART, ID3, and C4.5 are popular algorithms in this regard (Richter and Khoshgoftaar, 2018).

*Figure 1. Different algorithms of machine learning*

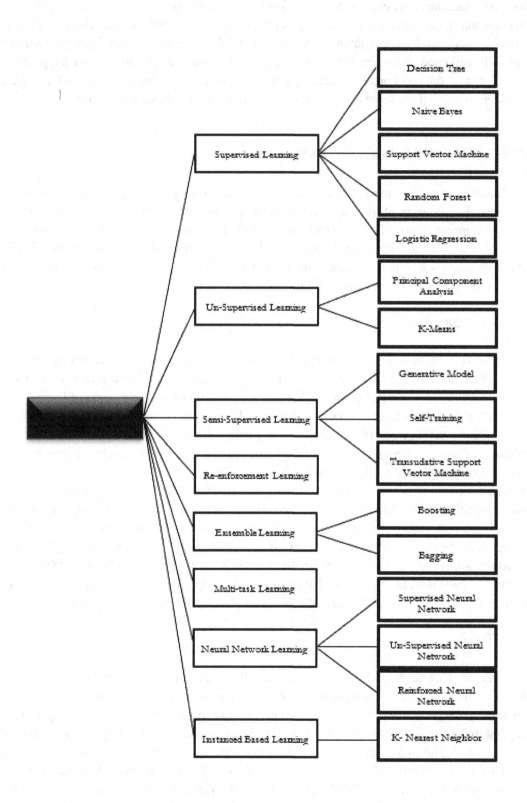

The process of classifying data in a Decision Tree is based on categorizing the input by their values. The most frequent function of Decision Tree is categorizing and classifying purposes. A decision tree draws a tree-like model with branches and nodes. The nodes and branches are responsible for attributes and nude values respectively (Kotsiantis, 2007).

## Naïve Bayes

Thomas Bayes, a British scientist (1701-1761), developed the Bayes theorem which is the basis of Naive Bayes Classifier (Raschka, 2014). The theory became popular after he was dead. He was born in Hertfordshire and studied logic and theology at the University of Edinburgh from 1719 to 1722. Naïve Bayes is the simplest classifier that is based on the theory that the probability of each attribute is independent from the others. The probability is calculated based on the probability of each class with the highest probability (Belavagi and Muniyal, 2016). Bayes rule determines the output of a probability (Etaiwi, Biltawi et al. 2017). The NB method is a practical and accurate method to be used in big data.

The main function of Naïve Bayes is classifying texts in industry. This method is highly efficient in clustering and classifying. Naïve Bayes or Bayesian networks work on the basis of conditional probability.

## Support Vector Machine (SVM)

SVM is a popular and practical technique that originally was defined and formulated by three scientists in 1963 (Hapsari, Utoyo et al. 2020). In 1992, Bernhard Boser, Isabelle Guyon, and Vladimir Vapnik worked on a classification system that was non-linear and was performed by using kernel tricks. Kernel trick is capable of maximizing the margin hyperplanes. The main idea of creating SVM was classifying datasets and working on margin calculation. The processing data contains putting margins between different classes of data, and to minimize the classification error, SVM maximizes the difference of margin and data classes. SVM works on statistical theory and structural risk minimization. The hyperplane is the key factor of classification in SVM which employs training data with maximum margin (the total distance of hyperplane and closest training data). In data processing by SVM, those hyperplanes which are capable of highest margin are known as the most proper candidate (Belavagi and Muniyal, 2016, Lynch, Abdollahi et al. 2017).

## Logistic Regression

This method is based on the concept of logistic function and meanwhile is an efficient method to develop a regression model (Zekic-Susac, Sarlija et al. 2016). Logistic Regression analyzes the relation between a single or multiple predictor (Reed and Wu, 2013). If data needs multiple classifications, this algorithm would be the best choice to process. The basic rule of processing data in this method is the chance of occurrence to fitting data with a logistics function. The logistic selects the likelihood value through processing data, which has a value of 0 and 1 (Belavagi and Muniyal, 2016). The outcome of Logistic Regression is the basic material to create a prediction method.

## Random Forest

Random Forest (Breiman, 2001) is the result of combining prediction trees when each tree poses the two following conditions:

a) Each tree is based on a vector selected randomly,
b) The distribution is equal in all trees,

This method was created and developed in 2001, for classification and regression (Fawagreh, Gaber *et al.* 2014). RF is a method created by combining tree predictors. This method has two popular characteristics:

a) The more trees in numbers lead to induction error coverage,
b) Sometimes it is not sustainable for overfitted data (Omary and Mtenzi, 2010).

Some of the ML algorithms are complex to process data and generate accurate results; however, they are precise. Meanwhile, others are easier to employ in practice but may pose some deficiencies during data processing. Decision Tree algorithm results are simple, clear, quick, and also understandable. Deficiencies such as increasing substantially with too much data, lead to lower accuracy rate and unreliable final output (Omary and Mtenzi 2010, Kourou, Exarchos *et al.* 2015, William, Ware *et al.* 2018).

## Unsupervised Learning

An Unsupervised Learning algorithm is not much dependent on data as the processing data contains learning from the dataset. Therefore, it can be employed to realize relationship between input data and in cases that there is no information about output data.

Normally, unsupervised Learning refers to the previous patterns learned from data and applies them to the newly fed data as input. Unsupervised Learning algorithms try to find similarities in input data and categorize them to make insights about data set. The most known applications of this algorithm are for clustering or feature reduction in a dataset.

Some of the most popular Supervised Machine Learning algorithms that are discussed here are K-Means Clustering and Principal Component Analysis (PCA).

### K-Means Clustering

This algorithm is one of the subsets of Unsupervised Learning algorithms developed by two scientists from Yale University (Hartigan and Wong 1979). This algorithm is capable of organizing clusters from a large amount of data, and then classifying them into related groups. As the name indicates, this method is able to detect and form clusters and determine the average value as the core of the cluster (Shwartz, Singer et al. 2007). A clustered data is represented in Figure 2.

To exemplify K-Means Clustering in real-world, consider searching for Apple in the Google. The search engine will provide you with all search results about Apple including iPad, iPhone, Mac, TV, and Watch. However, applying K-means algorithm helps to cluster web pages based on similar device types. Apple Watch pages in one group and iPhone web pages in another group (T.K, Annavarapu, & Bablani, 2021).

### Principal Component Analysis (PCA)

In 1901, another current popular algorithm was created that called PCA (Pearson, 1901). The main goal of PCA is to decrease the dataset size to facilitate the computing process. For comprehending the data

*Figure 2. Principal Component Analysis(PCA)*
*Source; Dey (2016)*

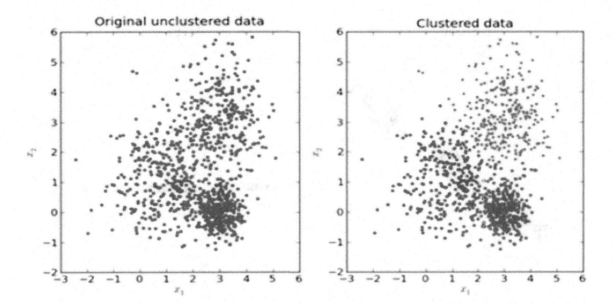

processing with this algorithm, Dey (2016) explained it through an example which demonstrated that a 2D dataset turns to 1D by the means of PCA as shown in Figure 3.

## Semi-Supervised Learning

The fundamental idea of creating this method was the combination of both features of Supervised and Unsupervised Learning. Semi-Supervised has a better performance where the datasets are unlabeled and achieving labeled data is time-consuming and costly (Zhu and Goldberg, 2009) since it operates through a two-stage or multistage process.

In addition, in cases that available labeled data is limited because of different constraints, the available labeled data can be employed to create rules for classification purposes through supervised machine learning, and at the same time, these rules can be used to label the remained data through unsupervised machine learning. In the end, all data is labeled that can be used in the training phase through supervised machine learning algorithms (Lee & Shin, 2020).

Semi-Supervised Learning has sub-categories including Generative Model, Self-Training, and Transudative Support Vector Machine (TSVM) which are discussed in the following.

### Generative Model

Generative Model is among the popular and applicable methods and is based on the mathematical formulation as below:

p(x,y) = p(y)p(x|y) where p(x|y).

The most frequent application of this method is recognizing mixed components in an unlabeled dataset.

*Figure 3. Clustered Data*
Source; Dey (2016)

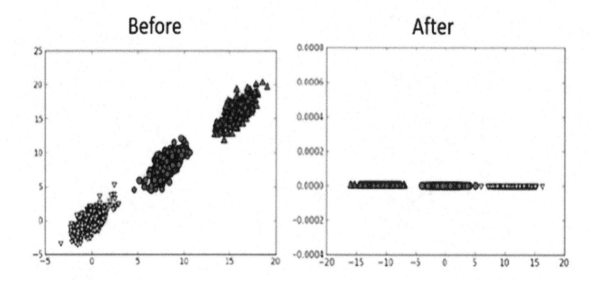

## Self-Training

The second method in this category is Self-Training, which is a classifier model with a portion of labeled data. The process of this algorithm contains feeding unlabeled datasets to the system and finally creating a mixture of prediction and labeled data. The mentioned process is capable of repeating afterward. As the process of classification starts to learn automatically, this method has been called the Self-training method.

## Transudative Support Vector Machine (TSVM)

TSVM is a modified and extended format of SVM (Kasabov and Pang, 2004). In the TSVM method, both labeled and unlabeled data are considered for processing. This method is famous for its capability of maximizing the margin value of both labeled and unlabeled data. It is worth mentioning that TSVM has difficulties detecting an accurate and exact solution to an NP-hard problem.

## Reinforcement Learning

The next learning algorithm can make final decisions by using the most positive results. Reinforcement Learning is one of the most controversial research topics and it is getting even more popular by researchers. Reinforcement Learning employs environmental feedback and the mechanisms of reward for training. Unlike supervised machine learning algorithms that use input and output data sets for training, various actions will be tested through Reinforcement Learning to realize actions that bring along the most reward (Lee & Shin, 2020).

In this method, the learner has no background or information on the processing procedure unless it introduces the desired situation. The process selected by the learner affects future data processing. This method is highly dependent on the two below factors:

A.   Trial and error searching process
B.   Delayed output (Sutton, 1992).

A real-life application of Reinforcement Learning is summarizing long texts. Salesforce.com has employed an algorithm that runs to generate summaries of the model and then compares the outcome summary with the ground truth to realize if it fully covers the reality and scores, it accordingly. If the summary is good, the models will be updated to generate such exact summaries in the future; otherwise, the model should be penalized and make changes in the generation of summaries (Paulus, Xiong, & Socher, 2017).

Some reinforcement learning algorithms that are most popular in the application are policy-gradient, temporal-difference learning (TD), and Q-learning algorithms.

## Q-Learning

Q-learning is not much dependent on current policies and moves beyond the random actions to find actions that are not necessarily defined in the current policy; however, maximize the overall future rewards. That is the reason why this algorithm is commonly regarded as off-policy. The letter Q in the title of the algorithm stands for quality to represent the effectiveness of actions that gain maximum rewards to influence current actions in the decision-making process. A real-world example of Q-learning is policies in automatic parking. Q-learning helps to avoid collision and maintain a steady speed based on changing lane and overtaking actions (Fan, Wang, Xie, & Yang, 2020).

## Policy-Gradient

Policy gradient methods are popular and useful since they can be employed in both continuous and discrete spaces to model the dominant policy directly. Policy gradient methods directly learn from the policy unlike Q-learning and reach convergence faster. This leads to being much faster in environments with small spaces and work effectively in continuous and discrete spaces despite of guarantying convergence to local maxima (Cobbe, Hilton, Klimov, & Schulman, 2021).

## Temporal-Difference Learning

TD methods are one step or multi-step algorithms that help to predict a quantity that originally is dependent on future values. The learning process develops by differences and changes that may happen each time of running in different steps. Predictions constantly get updates in each step to make them closer to the prediction of similar quantity that will be considered in the next time of running (Seymour et al., 2004).

## Multitask Learning

Multitask Learning has been created as an assistant to help other learners to perform efficiently. After applying multitask learning algorithms to an issue, this algorithm can recall the previous patterns of finding the solution to the problem and the process of achieving a specific result. This algorithm still employs the learned pattern to solve similar problems. This situation in which two algorithms cooperate is known as the inductive transfer mechanism. The rapidity in this learning algorithm is higher than an individual as the systems start to learn concurrently (Caruana, 1997).

## Ensemble Learning

Ensemble Learning is defined as a situation when the combination of various independent learners, forms a unison learner. The components of this combination can be different algorithms. This learning algorithm has been a popular topic since the 1990s. Observations demonstrated that this combinational form of data processing can perform better and more efficiently in comparison to a single learner (Maclin and Opitz, 1999) since it reduces the likelihood of noise, bias, or variance considerably.

Two of the most popular Ensemble Learning techniques are Boosting and Bagging.

## Boosting

Boosting is defined as a method to reduce the bias rate in data processing in both discrete and continuous spaces. This method employs a combination of weak learners (which is defined as an improper classifier) and makes a unison and strong one out of them. A strong learner is capable of cooperating closely with accurate classification. The main idea of this method is to make strong learners out of weak learners through a range of a sequential iterations.

## Bagging

In a situation where the precision of ML is not desirable, Bagging (Bootstrap), is a very useful method. This algorithm is designed to classify data with high accuracy and regression. Another application of Bagging is providing a platform to overcome overfitting and reducing the variance rate (Dey, 2016). Bagging can be used in both continuous and discrete spaces likewise Boosting.

## Neural Network Learning (ANN)

ANN is inspired based on the notion of the human nervous system. Warren McCullough and Walter Pitts introduced Neural Network in 1944 (Arbib, 2000). To understand how ANN works, it is essential to obtain a background knowledge of data processing in a neuron cell where Dendrites are responsible for receiving electrical signals. Then, data is sent to Dendrite terminals by the means of another section called Axon. Neural Network is recognized as the core and heart of electrical signals which move through the brain.

ANN processes the input dataset similar to a neuron cell. The data processing through ANN includes three major steps (Dey, 2016):

a)    The first step is responsible for receiving the input dataset
b)    Then, the second step processes data,
c)    And finally, as the next step, the final result will be computed.

Since ANN emulates the same process as a neuron cell and changes the information by the means of an electrical signal, it is called Neural Network Learning (Amato, Lopez et al. 2013).

M

## Supervised Neural Network

This algorithm predicts the output beforehand and then it is compared to the actual output generated by the dataset. For achieving the desired result, the parameters can be alternated and again processed using the algorithm. The most well-known application of this algorithm is in Feed-Forward Neural Network.

## Unsupervised Neural Network

This method has no foregoing hypothesis on the final result. This method can organize and classifying data based on their likelihood. The data processing happens through detecting the correlation between data and finally classifying it in proper clusters.

## Reinforced Neural Network

The basic idea of this algorithm is to imitate human behavior with the environment (Hiregoudar, 2014). The responses from the environment will determine if the final decision made by the method is properly correct or not. If the output is detected as the proper answer, the patterns that generated the decision to see whether it is strengthened or not, the strands are weakened. This method has also no prior background of the final result (Hiregoudar et al., 2014).

### Instance-Based Learning

This method contains some basic patterns. Through processing data, the system applies the defined patterns to the fed data as input. That is the reason why this method is called Instance-based Learning. Another well-known name of this method is Lazy Learner which indicates that the system starts performing when test data is fed into it. By increasing the data dimension, the complexity increases as well.

## K Nearest Neighbor (K-NN)

K-NN has been developed by two scientists in 1951 and was expanded later by Thomas Cover (Firouz, Alireza et al. 2021). KNN, which is a classifier without demanding any parameters, needs well-labeled training data as the main input for the learner. After introducing the data, it compares both data and decides which one is the most correlated one (Dey, 2016).

## MACHINE LEARNING ALGORITHMS APPLICATIONS IN DIFFERENT FIELDS

The art of ML applies to many various types of issues from industry to medicine. It is predicted that investment in ML and AI will go beyond $77.6 billion till 2022 IDC (2018). The seriousness about the potential of ML reveals since pioneer enterprises are constantly recruiting professionals in ML.

The results obtained through ML are highly reliable for taking the next step or planning a schedule for businesses or medical approaches (Sokolova and Lapalme, 2007). ML has many different applications. Three major types of ML algorithms including Clustering, Classification, and Prediction are commonly used in enterprises for different purposes.

## Clustering

Clustering is an unsupervised ML algorithm that groups different sets of objectives based on their similar features in a space that is multidimensional. Objects in different clusters are basically different in features in comparison to those in the same clusters. Clustering algorithms can be used in enterprises to divide customers into different segments and customize services and products. For instance, clustering can help to increase customer satisfaction through receiving comments from customers in similar clusters. A prominent enterprise in this regard is Netflix that has used ML and Clustering algorithms widely (Najafabadi, Mahrin, Chuprat, & Sarkan, 2017). Netflix has divided its more than 130 million global users into 1,000 classifications and has realized their tastes and preferences in watching movies to recommend them. Besides, Clustering can be employed for layout and location purposes based on purchasing behavior of similar customers. As an instance, clustering techniques have been used by Macy's to recognize cluster membership in its different stores to consequently decide on locations for its stores that lead to the maximum sales based on the cross-sectional data (Carr, 2013). The same algorithm was also used by AutoZone for to segment stores with similar products (SAS, 2011).

## Classification

Classification algorithms help to identify classes and categories as they are observed. The difference between classification and clustering is that classes are already realized to be employed for training and testing purposes. To exemplify classification in the real world is to assign a loan applicant in a class that is worthy to receive a credit or not. For doing so, historical data about payments of loan applicants will be used for training the dataset and consequently serving customers more efficiently in banking industry. One of the successful cases of employing classification algorithms in banking sector is JPMorgan Chase that is the largest American bank. JPMorgan Chase used customers' historical data, market status and financial background to distinguish customers that are worthy for future equity offerings (Chase, 2017).

Classification algorithms have also demonstrated to work efficiently in retail industry, classification can be employed to classify customers' reviews on different products ranging from very positive to very negative and provide customized services for customers. Walmart also employs classification algorithms to categorize fresh vegetables and fruit by gathering information about specifications and standards of products and combines this information with images from vegetables and fruit products. This helps Walmart to decide on the priority of selling perishable products in all branches (Musani, 2018).

Classification can be also used to categorize in cases that there are large numbers of documents. State Street uses classification algorithms to categorize news publications and deliver accurate newsfeeds to its clients based on their preferences out of large amounts of English-language news publications (Street, 2018).

## Prediction

One of the most common applications of ML is finding patterns in data to make predictions about future events. Prediction differs from classification since classification algorithms make categories based on current conditions of data; however, prediction algorithms used data to realize what may happen in the future. A real-life example of prediction algorithms is using data to realize marketing trends that may affect the business.

Prediction algorithms work efficiently in the banking sector for choosing the most appropriate investment strategies. JPMorgan employs historical data in prediction algorithms to realize the best possible trade orders to execute (McDowell, 2018).

Machine learning is also useful for preventive maintenance purposes. Manufactories like General Electric Company (GE) use data that is generated by machines to predict the time that machines need maintenance and the likelihood of any type of anomaly in machines (Forbes, 2017) .Deere & Company that is a leading company in production of agricultural equipment has also employed prediction algorithm to realize plants that may need fertilizers, pesticides, and chemicals in future and the optimal amount based on demand (Grosch, 2018).

In a broader view, ML has many other different applications. For instance, predicting student performance by using algorithms like ANN and Decision Tree result in more accurate and reliable outputs (Shahiri, Husain et al. 2015). Another application of ML is designing an automated consulting system for offering the best-matched course for students who intend to enroll in a college or university. These kinds of researches aim to predict the most suitable educational path for increasing future success. Decision tree (c4.5) and k-Means clustering were applied to study the most accurate results (MohamedAly, Hegazy et al. 2013). On the other hand, and in the industry sector, ANN, DT (C4.5), and Neural Decision Tree were applied to predict the production of petroleum (Li, Chan et al. 2013) although SVM is applied for prediction oil usage. Results demonstrated that SVM is the most suitable method to forecast oil usage and has higher performance and accuracy among Back Propagation Neural Network (BPNN) and Auto-Regressive Integrated Moving Average (ARIMA) (Xie, Yu et al. 2006).

Machine Learning algorithms have been used in Agriculture sector too. Logistic regression was applied to predict grain loss during harvest which showed high accuracy in 86.25% of cases (Huang, Li et al. 2017). Besides, SVM and ANN were used to classify sugar beets based on image data and showed a 92.92% accuracy rate (Bakhshipour and Jafari, 2018).

Besides industry and education sectors, ML applied in banking and finance sectors too. For instance, Decision Tree, Random Forest, and Logistics Regression were applied to sample credit card data and to classify them into two categories including bad account and good account. Results demonstrated that decision trees and random forests performed more efficiently than logistic regression (Butaru, Chen et al. 2016).

## MACHINE LEARNING ALGORITHMS IN A GLANCE

Tables in this section, compare major ML algorithms and provide an overview on advantages and disadvantages of ML algorithms.

*Table 1. Comparison between Supervised and Unsupervised Learning*

| Parameter | Supervised Learning | Unsupervised Learning |
|---|---|---|
| *Input data* | It works based on labeled data | It works based on unlabeled data |
| *Computational complexity* | It is simple | It contains complicated processing |
| *Accuracy* | It is highly accurate | It is not very accurate |

*Table 2. Advantages and Disadvantages of Supervised, Un-Supervised, Semi-Supervised and Reinforcement Learning*

| Algorithm | Advantages | Disadvantages |
|---|---|---|
| *Supervised Learning* | -It is based on reusable training data unless features change | -Classes may not match spectral classes<br>-High differences in consistency<br>-Cost and time are determinant in selecting data |
| *Un-Supervised Learning* | -Previous knowledge of the image area is required<br>-Human error is minimized<br>-It produces unique spectral classes | -It works regardless to spatial among data<br>-It can take time to interpret the spectral classes |
| *Semi-Supervised Learning* | -Easy to understand<br>-Very stable<br>-Simple<br>-Highly efficient | -Iteration results are not stable<br>-It does not apply to network-level data<br>-Low accuracy |
| *Reinforcement Learning* | Applicable to complex problems<br>Proper for long-term results with high difficulty in processing data<br>Very similar to the human learning process with high perfection in result | High chance of overloading of states leads to diminishing output<br>Not proper for simple issues<br>Too much calculation and computation |

*Table 3. Pros and Cons of Supervised Learning*

| Algorithm | Pros | Cons |
|---|---|---|
| *SVM* | § It provides better performance with high domination data<br>§ It provides better performance with different classes of data | § It is time-consuming<br>§ It performs poorly with overlapped classes<br>§ It requires appropriate hyperparameters selection |
| *Decision Trees* | § It normalizes unnecessary data<br>§ It handles missing values<br>§ It is easy to understand<br>§ It can automatically select feature selection | § It is sensitive to overfitting<br>§ It is sensitive to data that needs more time to train decision trees |
| *Naive Bayes* | § It is time-saving<br>§ It can work best with large datasets<br>§ It is not sensitive to irrelevant features<br>§ It works best with multiclass prediction | § It is a bad estimator |
| *Logistic Regression* | § It is simply applicable<br>§ It is effective<br>§ It does not need feature scaling<br>§ It does not need to turn hyperparameters | § Not proper for non-linear data<br>§ Not proper for highly correlated features<br>§ Not a very powerful algorithm |
| *Random Forest* | § It minimizes errors<br>§ It is highly efficient on imbalanced datasets<br>§ It is applicable for large data<br>§ It is applicable for missing data<br>§ It minimizes effects on outliers<br>§ It is fine with overfitting | § It is dependent on predictive factors<br>§ It works based on uncorrelated predictions |

*Table 4. Pros and Cons of Un-Supervised Learning*

| Algorithm | Pros | Cons |
|---|---|---|
| *K- Means Clustering* | It performs as a clustering model to detect the highest value for the iteration | It is slow in learning<br>It is not very accurate |
| *Principal Component Analysis* | It detects the highest value for every iteration | It does not classify data in a proper arrangement |

# ALGORITHM SELECTION

It is challenging for business owners to choose among different machine learning algorithms. There is no one-size-fits-all machine learning algorithm that works in different cases (Kotthoff, 2014). A range of different factors including the velocity of data, variety, volume, and the case may influence the performance of machine learning algorithms. However, the main challenge in choosing among algorithms is to manage the trade-off between two interpretability and accuracy variables (Operskalski & Barbey, 2016). If the algorithm performs well in practice, it is accurate. If it is possible to explain to users how a decision was made using an algorithm, then, the algorithm is interpretable (Valdes et al., 2016).

Choosing the best machine-learning set of rules for collection of related data is critical for every machine-training program. There is no problem-solving procedure to be named as the best; however, paying attention to some points will help throwing away problems. For instance, working problems should be well translated in the first place. As shown in Figure 4, the way managers can select a suitable machine –training algorithm for collection of related data and be equally flawless and translatable (Lee & Shin, 2019).

*Figure 4. Algorithm selection process*

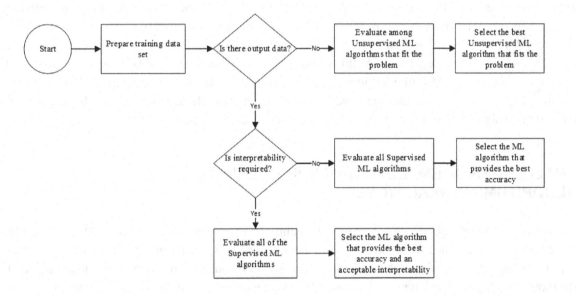

Supervised training data are employed to develop a forecasting model where the training collection of data has at least one output variable corresponding to the input variables like market and economic as input factors and stock price as an example of the output variable.

Unsupervised Learning algorithms are used when the training data does not have an output variable. Such algorithms can be used for Clustering for instance, where customer demographic data are available; however, customers have not been divided into different groups.

Choosing the right algorithm for your business depends on the type of information and exactness. Therefore, when a bank decides to start an automatic virtual assistant for customers with a huge amount of customer personal and financial data as an input variable to be fed into a chatbot, the important factor is the accuracy of responses that the chatbot gives to customers rather than giving explanations so the company should choose a supervised training algorithm with the highest accuracy of responses as output variable.

Because the output variable (a refinancing recommendation) depends on the input variables (various financial and economic parameters), supervised learning is suitable for this application. As the bank needs to be able to explain its recommendations, the machine-learning application should be interpretable. Therefore, the bank should decide not to bother evaluating black-box machine-learning algorithms, such as random forests or DNNs. The bank should instead evaluate logistic regression and a decision tree for supervised learning, and it may then find the decision-tree model to be highly interpretable and more accurate than the logistic regression. As this scenario shows, the selection process can proceed iteratively, in parallel, and flexibly. Man- agers should ideally evaluate multiple machine-learning algorithms in parallel to determine the highest achievable accuracy, and they should use the information generated from this testing as a benchmark in selecting the most interpretable al- algorithm available. This benchmark can then serve as a target accuracy level for that algorithm.

Also, If the same bank decides to develop a machine training program for suggesting refinancing its clients to reach the goal of empowering a business by loans with lower interest rates and reducing financial cost a large set of data including financial factors and re decisions and is needed to train the machine by using a supervised learning model in which the input variables (various financial and economic parameters), refinancing suggestion as output variable is used and there is no need for examining hidden machine-learning data, such as random forests or DNNs for the machine training program to be comprehensible. The bank should instead evaluate prior data value prediction and a decision tree for supervised learning, and it may then find the decision-tree model to be highly interpretable and more accurate than the logistic regression. As this scenario shows, the selection process can proceed iteratively, in parallel, and flexibly. Machine-learning algorithms evaluation and determining the highest achievable accuracy should be done by managers and obtained information should be used in selecting the most interpretable algorithm that serves as a target accuracy level for that algorithm.

## CHALLENGES OF EMPLOYING MACHINE LEARNING ALGORITHMS IN REAL-WORLD

The main concern in using machine learning algorithms is data governance challenges (Jordan & Mitchell, 2015). Likewise, other inventions may encounter several issues regarding privacy, accessibility, and sharing of information. We emphasize four technical and managerial problem areas quite differently: the moral, shortage of machine learning professionals, the shortage of data quality, and the cost-benefit.

### Moral Issues

Lack of understanding to employ machine learning algorithms morally may lead to unwanted impacts on the entire society (Mittelstadt, Allo, Taddeo, Wachter, & Floridi, 2016). Moral issues can occur at any time during machine training deployment. Therefore, a company should care to adapt itself to regulations related to confidentiality of information (for instance personal data of patients).

The hidden error might occur later due to learning based on stereotypes such as gender, race, age and discriminations existed in machine training algorithms which should be avoided so users find it equally available. Nowadays, moral issues in a business can be detected by unprecedented levels of complexity, intense competition, pressure from stakeholders, and social obligations (Stedham, Yamamura, & Beekun, 2007).

In black-box algorithms that process between input and output are narrow prejudice in financial decisions suggested by machine learning programs, it is difficult to detect. Therefore, bank managers under severe work pressure might tend to use these applications even though their investment suggestions are biased. Otherwise, in the case of selecting job applicants, machine learning programs may imitate biased human preferences if not adequately trained (Turilli, 2007).

For deploying an ethical machine-learning program, cooperation between researchers, developers, and policymakers will be required to be matched with the moral standards of the organization, governments have started to regulate machine learning and automation. An example of this is the SELF DRIVE Act and the AV START Act passed by US Congress to address the safety of driverless vehicles, and the FUTURE of Artificial Intelligence Act to address AI concerns. For the benefit of people and society Facebook, Google, Microsoft, and IBM have mentioned moral problems regarding artificial intelligence and improving common knowledge of AI through partnership (Wright & Schultz, 2018).

Goodness will be used as a model in ethical decision-making, moral design, and AI usage. Besides, these initiatives in the public and private sectors are paying attention to ethical standards in artificial intelligence. While using application managers must develop corporate ethical standards and practices for reducing biased training information and ensure compliance with ethical standards (Neubert & Montañez, 2020).

## Shortage of Machine Learning Professionals

Due to more job positions in computer engineers and machine learning, the demand for AI-related jobs is growing twice as it was before by 119% in recent years (Culbertson, 2018). In 2017, reports of social media showed machine-learning engineering turned up as a top job resulting in skills gap be widened but only 3% of surveyed companies had a plan to increase their budget for reskilling programs in the next three years (LinkedIn, 2017).

Universities have expanded their machine training and AI-related syllabus but meeting manufactural needs for a talented workforce in this area still seems so far away. In such a case, retraining staff is important. Developing online games that teach machine learning by GE global company is an example of this, and it has held a conference where scientists get familiar with new roles. Many of its employees received their certification in data analytics. To have a staff that is skilled in machine-learning engineers inside a company, special revision is needed for the current career development program (Woyke, 2017).

## Shortage of Data Quality

The success of ML algorithms in the real world is highly reliant on the quality of data. In ML, data is qualified in case that it fits well for a specific purpose. Data quality not only is important in training data but also is significant during using the algorithm in operation. Unqualified data, on the contrary, can lead to making inappropriate decisions. As an example, if sensors in medical monitoring provide incorrect data with errors, fatal consequences in decision-making will be generated in the application of the algorithm.

The quality of data will be declined in case that data is gathered from various sources and is unstructured in different forms ranging from text to voice and image data (Lee, 2017). Since a considerable amount of data is commonly unstructured data, companies should establish a process to develop quality data through collecting and evaluating data and eliminating inaccurate data to be fed to the application of ML for operational purposes.

## Cost-Benefit

Since ML can benefit different businesses, investment in this area seems to be rewarding for stakeholders. However, there may be a delay between investment in ML and reward. Therefore, managers should obtain a clear understanding of the costs and benefits of investment in ML and consequently make a wise decision. Besides, managers need to justify to stakeholders if an ML project can be beneficial for the business since there is also a high risk of project failure in such cases (Lee & Lee, 2015). This gets even more difficult to justify stakeholders to invest in ML algorithm in cases that tangible costs of the project are remarkably higher than tangible outcomes of the project even if intangible benefits are considerable.

## CONCLUSION

ML is an art of mathematical and statistical science which assures the fed dataset finds the appropriate and suitable pattern to have an accurate and reliable output. ML procedure is based on a whole new system of computer science that is highly capable to perform accurately, and rapidly (Ayoub, 2020). Machine Learning Algorithms differ broadly in applications and methods based on their variables and datasets. Well-known methods of ML are mostly subsets of supervised, Unsupervised, Reinforcement, Semi-supervised, Multi-Task, Ensemble, Neural Network, and Instanced Based Learning, each one with its specific advantages and disadvantages.

As the models become more functional and developed, they also become more advanced. From the performance perspective, it is believed that neural networks are one of the best models since they are relatively recent and advanced. Although each model has its efficiency for different datasets, some models such as Naive Bayes will perform sufficiently with highly independent data. If the dataset is medium-sized and not very complicated, SVM will be a promising model. In a case that datasets consist of the linear relationship between dependent and independent variables, then linear regression, logistic regression, and SVM are more assuring. If the dataset is small and the relationship between the dependent and independent variable is not clear, k-NN will be a smart choice. Therefore, before deciding on which ML algorithm to use, there should be enough information about the data sets.

To select the most appropriate algorithm to process data, many factors need to be considered. Items like the complexity of the model, time, accuracy, nature of data, and other factors are determining in final results. For example, in comparison to linear regression and NN, linear regression is easier to apply but on the other hand, it is not very accurate and applicable when the relationship between input and output to be learned is not linear.

Results gained by Logistic Regression are very clear and understandable because they are simple, clear, and straightforward. Logistic regression is a practical algorithm for uncomplicated, small, and simple data since large data will cause complexity and the parameter estimation procedure of logistic regression can lead to inaccurate estimates of parameters (Omary and Mtenzi, 2010, Reed and Wu, 2013).

SVM is known as a very accurate and applicable model. This method is capable of handling overfitting but poses deficiencies in processing large data. The Naive Bayes process contains simple computations of probability, and the negative point of this method is that the attributes or variables must be statistically independent. Further, ANN is based on a bioelectric network in the human brain. It is a very complex method with a complicated procedure but is very applicable and sufficient for missing data, large data, and complicated problems (Kourou, Exarchos et al. 2015)

From aforementioned samples and articles discussed in this chapter, it can be concluded that although Machine Learning is a helpful part of modern scientific research, there is no particular approach or algorithm to be used in different types of data and for creating a prediction model through Machine Learning in many types of research, more than one forecasting model is used to find the fittest model. Each one has its advantages and disadvantages, and it might need some modifications as new classes of data and issues become the topic of research. Though many scientists constantly work on this interesting subject, still more investigation and research seem inevitable.

## REFERENCES

Ahmad, M. W., Mourshed, M., & Rezgui, Y. (2017). Trees vs Neurons: Comparison between random forest and ANN for high-resolution prediction of building energy consumption. *Energy and Building*, *147*, 77–89. doi:10.1016/j.enbuild.2017.04.038

Amato, F., López, A., Peña-Méndez, E. M., Vaňhara, P., Hampl, A., & Havel, J. (2013). Artificial neural networks in medical diagnosis. *Journal of Applied Biomedicine*, *11*(2), 47–58. doi:10.2478/v10136-012-0031-x

Amornsamankul, S. (2019). A Comparison of Machine Learning Algorithms and Their Applications. *International Journal of Simulation: Systems, Science & Technology, 8*, 1-17.

Arbib, M. (2000). Warren McCulloch's search for the Logic of the Nervous System. *Perspectives in Biology and Medicine*, *43*(2), 193–216. doi:10.1353/pbm.2000.0001 PMID:10804585

Ayoub, M. (2020). A review on machine learning algorithms to predict daylighting inside buildings. *Solar Energy*, *202*, 249–275. doi:10.1016/j.solener.2020.03.104

Azadeh, A., Saberi, M., & Seraj, O. (2010). An integrated fuzzy regression algorithm for energy consumption estimation with non-stationary data: A case study of Iran. *Energy*, *35*(6), 2351–2366. doi:10.1016/j.energy.2009.12.023

Bakhshipour, A., & Jafari, A. (2018). Evaluation of support vector machines and artificial neural networks in weed detection using shape features. *Computers and Electronics in Agriculture*, *145*, 153–160. doi:10.1016/j.compag.2017.12.032

Belavagi, M. C., & Muniyal, B. (2016). Performance Evaluation of Supervised Machine Learning Algorithms for Intrusion Detection. *Procedia Computer Science*, *89*, 117–123. doi:10.1016/j.procs.2016.06.016

Belson, W. A. (1959). Matching and Prediction on the Principle of Biological Classification. *Journal of the Royal Statistical Society. Series C, Applied Statistics*, *8*(2), 65–75.

Breiman, L. (2001). Random Forests. *Machine Learning*, *45*(1), 5–32. doi:10.1023/A:1010933404324

Butaru, F., Chen, Q., Clark, B., Das, S., Lo, A. W., & Siddique, A. (2016). Risk and risk management in the credit card industry. *Journal of Banking & Finance*, *72*, 218–239. doi:10.1016/j.jbankfin.2016.07.015

Carr, J. (2013). *A simple approach to retail clustering*. Wilson Perumal and Company.

Caruana, R. (1997). Multitask Learning. *Machine Learning, 28*(1), 41–75. doi:10.1023/A:1007379606734

Chang, P.-C., Fan, C.-Y., & Lin, J.-J. (2011). Monthly electricity demand forecasting based on a weighted evolving fuzzy neural network approach. *International Journal of Electrical Power & Energy Systems, 33*(1), 17–27. doi:10.1016/j.ijepes.2010.08.008

Chase, J. M. (2017). *Innovations in finance with machine learning, big data, and artificial intelligence: Summary of the latest research and trends.* Academic Press.

Chou, J.-S., & Bui, D.-K. (2014). Modeling heating and cooling loads by artificial intelligence for energy-efficient building design. *Energy and Building, 82*, 437–446. doi:10.1016/j.enbuild.2014.07.036

Cover, T., & Hart, P. (1967). Nearest neighbor pattern classification. *IEEE Transactions on Information Theory, 13*(1), 21–27. doi:10.1109/TIT.1967.1053964

Culbertson, D. (2018). *Demand for AI talent on the rise.* Retrieved from https://www.hiringlab.org/2018/03/01/demand-ai-talent-rise/

Das & Behera. (2017). A Survey on Machine Learning: Concept, Algorithms and Applications. *International Journal of Innovative Research in Computer and Communication Engineering, 5.*

Dey, A. (2016). Machine Learning Algorithms: A Review. *International Journal of Computer Science and Information Technologies, 7*, 1174–1179.

Edwards, R. E., New, J., & Parker, L. E. (2012). Predicting future hourly residential electrical consumption: A machine learning case study. *Energy and Building, 49*, 591–603. doi:10.1016/j.enbuild.2012.03.010

El Naqa, I., & Murphy, M. J. (2015). *What Is Machine Learning? In Machine Learning in Radiation Oncology: Theory and Applications.* Springer International Publishing. doi:10.1007/978-3-319-18305-3

Enayatifar, R., Sadaei, H. J., Abdullah, A. H., & Gani, A. (2013). Imperialist competitive algorithm combined with refined high-order weighted fuzzy time series (RHWFTS–ICA) for short term load forecasting. *Energy Conversion and Management, 76*, 1104–1116. doi:10.1016/j.enconman.2013.08.039

Etaiwi, W., Biltawi, M., & Naymat, G. (2017). Evaluation of classification algorithms for banking customer's behavior under Apache Spark Data Processing System. *Procedia Computer Science, 113*, 559–564. doi:10.1016/j.procs.2017.08.280

Fan, C., Xiao, F., & Zhao, Y. (2017). A short-term building cooling load prediction method using deep learning algorithms. *Applied Energy, 195*, 222–233. doi:10.1016/j.apenergy.2017.03.064

Fawagreh, K., Gaber, M. M., & Elyan, E. (2014). Random forests: From early developments to recent advancements. *Systems Science & Control Engineering, 2*(1), 602–609. doi:10.1080/21642583.2014.956265

Forbes. (2017). *How AI and machine learning are helping drive the GE digital transformation.* Retrieved from https://www.forbes.com/sites/ciocentral/2017/06/07/how-ai-and-machine-learning-are-helping-drive-the-gedigital-transformation/#4f3464321686

Fradkov, A. L. (2020). Early History of Machine Learning. *IFAC-PapersOnLine, 53*(2), 1385–1390. doi:10.1016/j.ifacol.2020.12.1888

Grosch, K. (2018). *John Deere: Bringing AI to agriculture.* Digital Initiative.

Hapsari, D. P., Utoyo, I., & Purnami, S. W. (2020). Text Categorization with Fractional Gradient Descent Support Vector Machine. *Journal of Physics: Conference Series, 1477*(2), 022038. doi:10.1088/1742-6596/1477/2/022038

Hartigan, J. A., & Wong, M. A. (1979). Algorithm AS 136: A K-Means Clustering Algorithm. *Journal of the Royal Statistical Society. Series C, Applied Statistics, 28*(1), 100–108.

He, B., Shi, Y., Wan, Q., & Zhao, X. (2014). Prediction of Customer Attrition of Commercial Banks based on SVM Model. *Procedia Computer Science, 31*, 423–430. doi:10.1016/j.procs.2014.05.286

Hiregoudar, B. S. (2014). A survey: Research summary on neural networks. *International Journal of Research in Engineering and Technology, 3*(15), 385–389. doi:10.15623/ijret.2014.0315076

Huang, T., Li, B., Shen, D., Cao, J., & Mao, B. (2017). Analysis of the grain loss in harvest based on logistic regression. *Procedia Computer Science, 122*, 698–705. doi:10.1016/j.procs.2017.11.426

Jordan, M. I., & Mitchell, T. M. (2015). Machine learning: Trends, perspectives, and prospects. *Science, 349*(6245), 255–260. doi:10.1126cience.aaa8415 PMID:26185243

Kasabov & Pang. (2004). *Transductive support vector machines and applications in bioinformatics for promoter recognition.* Academic Press.

Kavousi-Fard, A., Samet, H., & Marzbani, F. (2014). A new hybrid Modified Firefly Algorithm and Support Vector Regression model for accurate Short Term Load Forecasting. *Expert Systems with Applications, 41*(13), 6047–6056. doi:10.1016/j.eswa.2014.03.053

Kotsiantis, S. (2007). Supervised Machine Learning: A Review of Classification Techniques. *Informatica (Slovenia), 31*, 249–268.

Kotthoff, L. (2014). Algorithm Selection for Combinatorial Search Problems: A Survey. *Association for the Advancement of Artificial Intelligence., 35*(3), 48–60. doi:10.1609/aimag.v35i3.2460

Kourou, K., Exarchos, T. P., Exarchos, K. P., Karamouzis, M. V., & Fotiadis, D. I. (2015). Machine learning applications in cancer prognosis and prediction. *Computational and Structural Biotechnology Journal, 13*, 8–17. doi:10.1016/j.csbj.2014.11.005 PMID:25750696

Kyung-Bin, S. (2005). Short-term load forecasting for the holidays using fuzzy linear regression method. *IEEE Transactions on Power Systems, 20*(1), 96–101. doi:10.1109/TPWRS.2004.835632

Lee, I., & Lee, K. (2015). The Internet of Things (IoT): Applications, investments, and challenges for enterprises. *Business Horizons, 58*(4), 431–440. doi:10.1016/j.bushor.2015.03.008

Lee, I., & Shin, Y. J. (2019). Machine learning for enterprises: Applications, algorithm selection, and challenges. *Business Horizons, 63*(2), 157–170. doi:10.1016/j.bushor.2019.10.005

Lee, I., & Shin, Y. J. (2020). Machine learning for enterprises: Applications, algorithm selection, and challenges. *Business Horizons, 63*(2), 157–170. doi:10.1016/j.bushor.2019.10.005

Li, K., Su, H., & Chu, J. (2011). Forecasting building energy consumption using neural networks and hybrid neuro-fuzzy system: A comparative study. *Energy and Building, 43*(10), 2893–2899. doi:10.1016/j.enbuild.2011.07.010

Li, X., Chan, C. W., & Nguyen, H. H. (2013). Application of the Neural Decision Tree approach for prediction of petroleum production. *Journal of Petroleum Science Engineering*, *104*, 11–16. doi:10.1016/j.petrol.2013.03.018

LinkedIn. (2017). *LinkedIn's 2017 U.S. emerging jobs report*. Retrieved from https://economicgraph.linkedin.com/research/LinkedIns-2017-US-Emerging-Jobs-Report

Lynch, C. M., Abdollahi, B., Fuqua, J. D., de Carlo, A. R., Bartholomai, J. A., Balgemann, R. N., van Berkel, V. H., & Frieboes, H. B. (2017). Prediction of lung cancer patient survival via supervised machine learning classification techniques. *International Journal of Medical Informatics*, *108*, 1–8. doi:10.1016/j.ijmedinf.2017.09.013 PMID:29132615

Maclin & Opitz. (1999). *Popular Ensemble Methods: An Empirical Study*. Academic Press.

McDowell, H. (2018). JP Morgan trading team develops machine learning model for equity desk. *The Trade*. Retrieved from https://www.thetradenews.com/jp-morgans-trading-team-develop-machine-learning-model-equity-desk/

Mittelstadt, B. D., Allo, P., Taddeo, M., Wachter, S., & Floridi, L. (2016). The ethics of algorithms: Mapping the debate. *Big Data & Society*, *3*(21), 1–21. doi:10.1177/2053951716679679

Mocanu, E., Nguyen, P. H., Gibescu, M., & Kling, W. L. (2016). Deep learning for estimating building energy consumption. *Sustainable Energy, Grids and Networks*, *6*, 91–99. doi:10.1016/j.segan.2016.02.005

MohamedAly, W., Fathy Hegazy, O., & Mohmmed Nagy Rashad, H. (2013). Automated Student Advisory using Machine Learning. *International Journal of Computers and Applications*, *81*(19), 19–24. doi:10.5120/14271-2341

Mohammed, M. (2016). *Machine Learning: Algorithms and Applications*. Academic Press.

Musani, P. (2018). *Eden: The tech that's bringing fresher groceries to you*. Retrieved from https://corporate.walmart.com/newsroom/community/20180301/eden-the-tech-thats-bringing-fresher-groceries-to-you

Najafabadi, M. K., Mahrin, M. N., Chuprat, S., & Sarkan, H. M. (2017). Improving the accuracy of collaborative filtering recommendations using clustering and association rules mining on implicit data. *Computers in Human Behavior*, *67*, 113–128. doi:10.1016/j.chb.2016.11.010

Neubert, M. J., & Montañez, G. D. (2020). Virtue as a framework for the design and use of artificial intelligence. *Business Horizons*, *63*(2), 195–204. doi:10.1016/j.bushor.2019.11.001

Omary & Mtenzi. (2010). Machine Learning Approach to Identifying the Dataset Threshold for the Performance Estimators in Supervised Learning. *International Journal for Infonomics, 3*.

Operskalski, J. T., & Barbey, A. K. (2016). Risk literacy in medical decision-making. *Science*, *352*(6284), 413–414. doi:10.1126cience.aaf7966 PMID:27102467

Osarogiagbon, A. U. (2015). Modeling Petrophysical Property Variations in Reservoir Sand Bodies Using Artificial Neural Network and Object-Based Techniques. *SPE Nigeria Annual International Conference and Exhibition*. 10.2118/178278-MS

Paulus, R., Xiong, C., & Socher, R. (2017). *A Deep Reinforced Model for Abstractive Summarization*. Academic Press.

Pearson, K. (1901). LIII. On lines and planes of closest fit to systems of points in space. *The London, Edinburgh and Dublin Philosophical Magazine and Journal of Science*, 2(11), 559–572. doi:10.1080/14786440109462720

Penya, Y. K. (2011). Short-term load forecasting in non-residential Buildings. *IEEE Africon '11.*

Rahman, A., Srikumar, V., & Smith, A. D. (2018). Predicting electricity consumption for commercial and residential buildings using deep recurrent neural networks. *Applied Energy*, 212, 372–385. doi:10.1016/j.apenergy.2017.12.051

Raschka, S. (2014). *Naive Bayes and Text Classification I - Introduction and Theory*. https://arxiv.org/pdf/1410.5329.pdf

Reed, P., & Wu, Y. (2013). Logistic regression for risk factor modeling in stuttering research. *Journal of Fluency Disorders*, 38(2), 88–101. doi:10.1016/j.jfludis.2012.09.003 PMID:23773663

Richter, A. N., & Khoshgoftaar, T. M. (2018). A review of statistical and machine learning methods for modeling cancer risk using structured clinical data. *Artificial Intelligence in Medicine*, 90, 1–14. doi:10.1016/j.artmed.2018.06.002 PMID:30017512

SAS. (2011). *After market service: 2011 auto industry leadership forum*. Retrieved from http://www.sas.com/images/landingpage/docs/AftermarketService-AutoForum.pdf

Shahiri, A., Husain, W., & Rashid, N. A. (2015). A Review on Predicting Student's Performance Using Data Mining Techniques. *Procedia Computer Science*, 72, 414–422. doi:10.1016/j.procs.2015.12.157

Shwartz, S. S. (2007). Pegasos: Primal Estimated sub - Gradient Solver for SVM. *Proceedings of the 24th International Conference on Machine Learning*. 10.1145/1273496.1273598

Sokolova, M., & Lapalme, G. (2007). *Performance Measures in Classification of Human Communications. In Advances in Artificial Intelligence*. Springer Berlin Heidelberg.

Stedham, Y., Yamamura, J. H., & Beekun, R. I. (2007). Gender differences in business ethics: Justice and relativist perspectives. *Business Ethics (Oxford, England)*, 16(2), 163–174. doi:10.1111/j.1467-8608.2007.00486.x

Street, S. (2018). *State Street Verus: FAQ*. Retrieved from https://www.statestreet.com/content/dam/statestreet/documents/SSGX/18-33087_Verus_FAQ.pdf

Sutton, R. S. (1992). Introduction: The Challenge of Reinforcement Learning. *Machine Learning*, 8(3), 225–227. doi:10.1007/BF00992695

Sze, V., Chen, Y.-H., Yang, T.-J., & Emer, J. S. (2017). Efficient Processing of Deep Neural Networks: A Tutorial and Survey. *Proceedings of the IEEE*, 105(12), 2295–2329. doi:10.1109/JPROC.2017.2761740

T R, P. (2015). A Comparative Study on Decision Tree and Random Forest Using R Tool. *IJARCCE*, 196-199.

T.K., B., Annavarapu, C. S. R., & Bablani, A. (2021). Machine learning algorithms for social media analysis: A survey. *Computer Science Review*, 40, 100395. doi:10.1016/j.cosrev.2021.100395

Turilli, M. (2007). Ethical protocols design. *Ethics and Information Technology*, 9(1), 49–62. doi:10.100710676-006-9128-9

Valdes, G., Luna, J. M., Eaton, E., Simone, C. B. II, Ungar, L. H., & Solberg, T. D. (2016). MediBoost: A Patient Stratification Tool for Interpretable Decision Making in the Era of Precision Medicine. *Scientific Reports, 6*(1), 37854. doi:10.1038rep37854 PMID:27901055

Wai, R. (2012). Intelligent daily load forecasting with fuzzy neural network and particle swarm optimization. *IEEE International Conference on Fuzzy Systems*. 10.1109/FUZZ-IEEE.2012.6250819

Wang, Y., Niu, D., & Ma, X. (2010). Optimizing of SVM with Hybrid PSO and Genetic Algorithm in Power Load Forecasting. *JNW, 5*(10), 1192–1200. doi:10.4304/jnw.5.10.1192-1200

Wi, Y.-M., Joo, S.-K., & Song, K.-B. (2012). Holiday Load Forecasting Using Fuzzy Polynomial Regression with Weather Feature Selection and Adjustment. *IEEE Transactions on Power Systems, 27*(2), 596–603. doi:10.1109/TPWRS.2011.2174659

William, W., Ware, A., Basaza-Ejiri, A. H., & Obungoloch, J. (2018). A review of image analysis and machine learning techniques for automated cervical cancer screening from pap-smear images. *Computer Methods and Programs in Biomedicine, 164*, 15–22. doi:10.1016/j.cmpb.2018.05.034 PMID:30195423

Woyke, E. (2017). *General Electric builds an AI workforce*. Retrieved from https://www.technologyreview.com/s/607962/general-electric-buildsan-ai-workforce/

Wright, S. A., & Schultz, A. E. (2018). The rising tide of artificial intelligence and business automation: Developing an ethical framework. *Business Horizons, 61*(6), 823–832. doi:10.1016/j.bushor.2018.07.001

Xie, W. (2006). *A New Method for Crude Oil Price Forecasting Based on Support Vector Machines. In Computational Science – ICCS 2006*. Springer Berlin Heidelberg.

Xuemei, L. (2009). Building cooling load forecasting model based on LS-SVM. *Information Processing, Asia-Pacific Conference on,* 55-58. 10.1109/APCIP.2009.22

Yang, H., & Huang, C. (1998). A new short-term load forecasting approach using self-organizing fuzzy ARMAX models. *IEEE Transactions on Power Systems, 13*(1), 217–225. doi:10.1109/59.651639

Yun, K., Luck, R., Mago, P. J., & Cho, H. (2012). Building hourly thermal load prediction using an indexed ARX model. *Energy and Building, 54*, 225–233. doi:10.1016/j.enbuild.2012.08.007

Zekic-Susac, M., Šarlija, N., Has, A., & Bilandžić, A. (2016). Predicting company growth using logistic regression and neural networks. *Croatian Operational Research Review, 7*(2), 229–248. doi:10.17535/crorr.2016.0016

Zhu, X., & Goldberg, A. B. (2009). Introduction to Semi-Supervised Learning. *Synthesis Lectures on Artificial Intelligence and Machine Learning, 3*(1), 1–13. doi:10.1007/978-3-031-01548-9

M

# Machine Learning and Emotions

**Primavera Fisogni**
*La Provincia di Como Daily Newspaper, Italy*

## INTRODUCTION

Emotions play a primary role in shaping human intelligence in virtue of the continuous and mutual sensitive/cognitive exchange with the environment. On the other side, for machines, it is impossible to have forms of knowledge that are not programmed, managed, or piloted by humans. Furthermore, for humans the process of learning is deeply interwoven with the emotional ground of the living condition. And for machines? We could not improve the attitude of learning, in digital devices, without enhancing their capacity of sensing. There is a wide consensus among scholars that smart devices can learn emotions at different degrees, however, the rising of the emotional wave in digital devices has not yet been explored. Thus, also machines sense in a specific way. Any effort to highlight this extreme, although limited ability, could enhance fruitful interactions of machines with humans and develop strategies in deep learning techniques (Guo, 2022).

## BACKGROUND

Philosophy can feel the gap by investigating whether machine sense and how. The aim of this paper is to indicate a zero degree of emotional power in smart devices: this ability does not exist *per se* but in the interaction with humans. The Onlife world, where the real and the digital are melted together, provides machines with an environment that makes possible the existence of an enlarged sensitivity. Through the lenses of metaphysics and system thinking an unprecedented challenge for data sciences is given. In fact, only a philosophical foundation of the big issues of this realm can bring about a change in the quality of understanding a more and more melted environment human/machines in the Onlife era.

### The Environment of Emotions and The Act of Sensing

To give machines skills of emotional intelligence is one of the most challenging tasks in the domain of human-centered computing (Turing, 1950), especially since the very idea of 'affective computing' was coined by Picard (1997). Nevertheless, the implementation of artificial intelligence applied to smart robots (Kugel, 2002) has shown the necessity of including cognitive models able to respond to emotional interactions with the offline world for enhancing the quality of their interrelations with humans (Franzoni, 2019; Brezeal, 2003; Fellous, 2004).

The increasing anthropological frame applied to Machine learning and humanoid-robots domain invites philosophy to take part in the debate, by offering theoretical tools that might integrate the computational point of view. This paper is aimed at introducing an anthropological issue in the discussion about the 'emotional side' of machines, a still under-researched environment.

DOI: 10.4018/978-1-7998-9220-5.ch055

As a point of departure, we should interrogate about the stuff of emotions, whose role is perceived as 'strategic' (Frank, 1991) in the making of consciousness (Damasio, 1994, 1999), although the discussion whether emotions are independent of cognition or not is disputed (Leventhal & Scherer, 1987; Lazarus, 1982). The most intrinsic nature of emotion is understood from the question:

*How does a living substratum give rise to an emotion?*

Despite its simplicity, this question marks a veritable turn for the discussion about an AI that feels, because it moves the focus of the problem from learned emotions, which are piloted and managed by humans to a minimum degree of self-sensing for smart devices. What lies beneath an emotion, for a human, is the capacity of *sensing*. In philosophical anthropology, the term refers to the capacity to grasp something essential of things (De Monticelli, 2005): it's an act that provides both sensitive and cognitive contents (Czerwinski, 2021).

It was philosopher and theologian Thomas Aquinas in the 13th Century to focus on the moral stuff of emotions, arguing that the inclination to the world of life orients the agent to what is primarily good, the *positum* or *datum*: only when this original positive is willed by the person, it becomes properly (moral) good. According to the *Quaestio 15* formulated in the Ia IIae Pars of the *Summa Theologiae*, the Aquinas' masterpiece, the philosopher could argue that sensing is an essential component of the will in virtue of two main movements: it orients action to the end and provides the will with a 'taste' of the object itself. In modern times phenomenology deeply investigated sensing as a sensitive act (*fühlen*) at the junction between human beings and the world of life.

Recently philosophy has relaunched the role of sensing in ethical conduct, for being the primary source of values and, since the early infancy, the original approach to what is good or bad (Fisogni, 2015). The physical substratum of consciousness is, nevertheless, an increasingly relevant topic also for neurosciences (Tononi, Boly, Massimini & Koch, 2016). We can briefly summarize the essential traits of sensing, before moving into the core of the investigation.

- Sensing is an original experience of human beings and it is deeply related to the human condition of being-in-the-world as a primarily source of thinking (Zajonic, 1986).
- Sensing is the source of emotions.
- Sensing plays a role in human conduct (Brock, 1992) not only because it picks up values, but primarily because it moves will towards the good, from the 'zero degree' of being something more than nothing (*positivum / datum*) to the highest level of a positive content that is willed for itself (the moral good). For Gendling what derives from sensitive approach to the environment – felt meaning – is a veritable power that shapes one's act. He assumes that «generally we act with such a "feel" of the action to guide us». (Gendlin, 1997: 68-69).
- Sensing also drives attention (a cognitive act) to the world of life from the inside, moving from emotions (Westerink & al., 2011).
- Sensing reveals the existence of other subjects/objects and provides the transcendental conditions for interpersonal relations.

The attitude of sensing, which the humans experience at the highest degree, for the cognitive and moral implications that it provides, is a common feature for all animated beings. Although animals are not persons, for some extent they hold a minimum degree of personal profile, at least some species like mammals. This capacity is properly rooted in sensing and consists of *being aware of themselves*. The feeling to be-in-a-body is possession of oneself noted phenomenologist Stein (2005) relaunching the insight of biologist and philosopher Conrad-Martius for whom animals too are dominated and possessed by the ego (1921). Hence, non-human animals make at least two related experiences of sensing: 1) they feel to be in a body 2) and they are aware to interact with other animated beings/objects.

Plants are able to feel the external stimuli throughout their protective layer: they react to light, to external attacks, to severe environmental conditions, and respond adaptively. Many experiments bring into light a sophisticated capacity to communicate with other plants, in which a certain degree of awareness is recognized. However, it is hard to conclude about consciousness in plants because of the absence of a central neuronal system and the consequent incapacity to feel part of a body. If we consider intelligence the capacity to solve problems, then also a green leaf could be said 'intelligent' (Mancuso, 2015).

### *How Does a Machine Sense?*

Although only a few traits have been sketched before, we should conclude that sensing is an *A-class* experience of awareness that allows 1) humans to emotionally, intellectually, ethically grasp what is felt and 2) let other animated individuals be acquainted with the sensitive domain, more (animal) or less (plants). This consideration makes clearer why emotions are recognized as 'intelligent' or, to say it differently, why emotional contents are a kind of thinking (Minsky, 2006) «aimed at summarizing, focusing and prioritizing cognitive tasks» (Franzoni, 2019: 2). In animated beings any emotion takes a part in understanding and transforming the environment. If we turn to non-animated beings like machines, we should reformulate the crucial question – do they have emotions? - into – *how do they sense?* Although emotions belong *per se* only to living individuals, its zero degrees or capacity of *sensing*, also pertains to machines.

It's a fact that machines are not endowed with a sensitive body as humans, animals, and plants. However, touch technology is for smart devices the substitute for skin and sensitive tissues (Yohanan & MacLean, 2012). Hence, it can be said that *digital devices sense*, at least in a very superficial way, at the level of their skin-like surface. What makes a sharp distinction between the way a machine or a person senses is the capacity to have a moral experience. In the domain of machines, the recognition of good/bad inputs is possible only in virtue of specific algorithms (Hossain, M. S. & G. Muhammad, 2019). Although machines can be said 'intelligent', they cannot act freely.

All their outputs, also the most brilliant responses to the environment are always programmed and managed by human agents. Indeed, digital devices have a limited degree of sensitivity which should be taken highly into consideration in the discourse about emotions in machines and specifically in Machine learning processes, as it will be shown in the next paragraph, through the lenses of systemic thinking.

## Enlarged Sensitivity in The Onlife Environment

Interactive emotions between humans and machines are at the core of the interconnected world, where the real and the digital are melted together. It is properly through this interplay that devices share with humans the felt sensory experience which belongs to persons: a result that might enhance the emotional processes. Moving from this premise, it could be argued that *a new sensitive platform is originated in the Onlife interaction*. It cannot be reduced to the integration of the two different subsystems (humans/machines). It is properly an emergence.

Through the lenses of systemic thinking (Bertalannfy, 1967; Minati, 2019; Urbani Ulivi, 2019) emergences are phenomena that emerge with completely novel and unexpected characters. According to this theoretical perspective (Urbani Ulivi, 2019), objects and events are considered open systems; they are not mere aggregations or sums of parts, but primarily dynamic units, to which pertain qualities that depend upon many interactions and processes, internal or external to the system, within the frame of continuous exchanges with the environment that gives rise to systemic properties (or II type systemic properties).

Onlife interactions belong to this domain.

A term coined by Italian philosopher and Oxford scholar Floridi (2014, 2015), the hybrid environment between offline and online recalls the mangrove society, brings about a radical change in the way we perceive what reality is.

Location and presence, in the Onlife domain, are no more the «two inseparable sides of the same human condition» as it happened in «an exclusively analog world» as Floridi assumed (2017: 124). The blurring borders of the hyperconnected world give rise to fluid phenomena, through the transition from the analog to the digital, from the offline to the online. If, as Russo assumes «arguably the biggest transformation provoked by the digital revolution is the creation of a hybrid dimension between online and offline» (2018: 663), emergent properties and entities are generated by the systemic processes of the Onlife environment.

It is important to underline that these new entities belong to a proper level of reality: being connected, for example, cannot be reduced to the use of digital devices (smartphone, Pc, etc), but should be seen as a proper way of existence which comes from the convergence of the digital tools and human activity.

The conceptualization of the Onlife domain made a step forward hybridization. According to this frame, phenomena like the sensitive interaction between humans and machines cannot be reduced to a coexistence that gives rise to interferences (González, 2013b: 13-14). Such an interpretation would be not only imprecise but incomplete and even misleading. Otherwise, it should be better, more appropriate to speak of *enlarged emotional interaction* or *enlarged sensitivity*. Let's move into the core of this investigation.

Within the emotional interplay between humans (offline) and digital devices (online), two macro-systems are given. Persons have a felt sensory experience that results from a conscious approach to themselves and to the environment: it always postulates a sensitive/conscious/willing agent. For machines is simply impossible to make such a complex experience, except in digital interactions. The digital, in fact, can be activated by a human subject in virtue of the human touch. The machine is programmed to recognize the skin's pressure, the first step for an *enlarged sensitivity*. Many other aspects of the agent's emotional stuff can be recognized through the detection of the touch. In other words, when the sensing platform of the machine is activated by the human skin, a sophisticated process of learning starts. Machine cognitive capacity or 'digital intelligence' is stimulated to interpret, recognize, organize the emotional input of the agent. On the other side, the human subject orients his/her action towards the responses of the machine, assuming at the same time some feature of the device itself: the agent learns to regulate the touch in order to enhance the interaction; the agent enters into the digital domain and grasp, in an intuitive way, the dynamics of this realm. Processes that are not comparable with the ones of the offline world. Sensing is not transformed but enlarged, for including both characters of the real and the digital. The very power of the digital, as Floridi (2017) noticed, lies in the act of cut and paste, two related steps in which consists also the starting point of the enlarged sensitivity. The human skin becomes a *unicum* with the digital surface of the device, which brings the user into the processes of the machine.

Each touch, by becoming a prolonged extension of the person, gives rise to a number of emotional inputs and outputs. Differently from programmed emotional frames, which enable a machine to recognize some feelings of the consumer, in the exchange of human/smart-devices the screen stimulates and orients the emotional responses of the user. Through the interaction the digital environment becomes, properly speaking, a *subject:* it activates the response of an intelligent individual.

This is a very relevant goal for Machine learning, whose consequences are not yet fully understood. What is important to highlight is that a new environment is created in the interaction human/smart machine: only if we assume that such a change has taken place, it is possible to imbue technology with emotional intelligence. In the Onlife perspective, as Floridi underlines (2017) within the melted domain we do not need coupling but de-coupling. What does it mean?

For Machine learning it could mean that enhancing emotional intelligence in devices should not translate into new o more complex technological artifacts: emotional robots, so to speak, belong to this area. To couple is to add sensitive skills to machines, so that they can better operate with humans from the very first touch. To de-couple is to orient research goals to the melted platform where the interconnection begins. As location and presence are inseparable sides, also human and machine senses are interrelated. Enlarged sensitivity has a relevant anthropological consequence, as it will be sketched in the next paragraph.

## A Zero Degree of Moral Sense In The Machines Through Enlarged Sensitivity

We all know that machines cannot be said moral agents because they do not act freely. However, a moral minimum can be noticed as a result of the processes of interaction in the Onlife domain. The argumentation moves from the phenomenological results achieved before: in the interconnected world, humans and machines share a common sensing platform, which enables both of them *to feel* and *to learn.* In philosophical terms, such a consideration means to look at devices as quasi-personal subjects whose cognitive/sensitive abilities are not simply the consequence of machines imbued with emotional inputs but emergences resulting from a melted digital/real environment (human+devices).

What is needed now is to search for *a zero degree of moral sense* in the machine according to the offline/online interaction.

Thomas Aquinas called *vis aestimativa* – internal sense faculty or the ability of adaptation to the environment, by learning what is good or bad in instinctual terms. In the light of these premises, I argue that we do not have to talk about the rationality of the machines, but more properly, to focus on a certain degree of axiological skill of human-interacting devices.

*A criticism could be moved at this point. Are machines 'moral' subjects?*

No, they are not *per se*, but they can enter into the moral interplay with the person by stimulating responses, behavior, acts, in positive or negative terms: digital connection is the first step for an enlarged sensing platform could be given.

A set of consequences are expected from the capacity of sensing-together. The very first step goes in the direction of the adaptation, by the machine, of what a human feels to a wide range of situations (Westerink & al., 2011): the coffee machine starts working when the computer feels that the user need a break; computing «can be a powerful tool in enabling people to be more productive, healthier, emotionally resilient» (Czerwinski & al., 2021).

A step forward is about human agency, where machines are influencing everyday life according to the enlarged sensitivity. I'll briefly sketch two cases-study. A smart machine can activate the moral responses of the agent. Recent studies in the realm of cyber terrorism (Fisogni, 2019, 2020) evidence that the lone actor gets easier and faster to his *goal* not primarily because, as linear thinking suggests, «the internet accelerates the process of radicalization» (von Behr, Reding, Edwards & Gribbon, 2013, p. xiii) but in virtue of a more limited decision-making process if compared to the multiple decision-making clusters of a complex terror system. The Onlife environment plays, in the process from the 'possible' to the 'effective' attack, the key role of a *moral enabler*. As a double interactive platform, it is neutral per se: it can either facilitate or make more difficult for something to happen. In the case of the lone terrorist actors, it creates the conditions for a fertile ground for taking a decision, for moving someone to act. stimulates responses, behaviors, acts.

A promising field of studies in the interrelation of humans and digital machines refers to the orientation of lifestyle and behaviors. Recent investigations on the hikikomori syndrome or severe social withdrawal highlight the possibility of coming back to social life according to the digital interaction (Fisogni and Fisogni, 2020). The lack of contact with the 'real' world, accompanied by the loss of temporal frame is compensated with the immersive approach to the digital environment. As Tateno, Kato, Skoukaukas, and Guerrero reported (2016), a patient affected by the syndrome started going out, leaving his room, after downloading Nintendo's smartphone game Pokémon Go.

## FUTURE RESEARCH DIRECTIONS

Despite its limits, this philosophical investigation strives to focus on the blurring borders of the interrelation between the user (human) and digital devices, in order to provide valuable theoretical tools for an emerging issue both in AI literature and metaphysics. As Rasetti assumes: «Indeed, besides human/human we have machine/machine interactions and human/machine interactions, namely augmented phase spaces of cognitive functions, more complex classification of behaviors, a novel role of mind (in the deep sense of self-consciousness) and of the living vs. inert quality of the physical support. For sure an unprecedented challenge for data science» (Rasetti, 2021: 154-155).

## CONCLUSION

Philosophy can enhance the understanding of 'emotional computing' by exploring the emotional interactions of humans and smart devices (Spezialetti & al., 2020). The author argues that this step is not only possible but deeply related to any discourse about human-robot interaction (Breazeal, 2003; Fellous, 2004) because digital machines work only in virtue of the human touch. Within the Onlife domain, a huge number of human operations are managed in a melted environment where the real and the digital are interconnected.

These interactions generate veritable processes that cannot be reduced to one (human) or the other system (machine). They simply emerge as novel phenomena. According to this frame also a digital device, for some limited aspects could be recognized as a 'sensitive subject' and an 'enlarged sensitivity' might open paths, for human-robot interaction, which are not limited to the application of emotional design to machines.

To highlight the melted environment human/machine, the aim of this investigation is nevertheless important to strengthen the idea of what intelligence is for a machine as well as for a human. We should move away from reasoning in terms of cause and effect in order to grasp a more complex conceptualization (Urbani Ulivi and Fisogni, 2021) where emotions are tools with which human intelligence shows itself. This work aims to introduce new concepts and ideas in the Machine learning debate: the author is are aware that their proposal will greatly benefit from any suggestion, addition and correction introduced in the debate.

## REFERENCES

Agazzi, E. (2019). Systemic Thinking: An Introduction. In L. Urbani Ulivi (Ed.), *The Systemic Turn in Human and Natural Sciences. A Rock in The Pond* (pp. xi–xvii). Springer. doi:10.1007/978-3-030-00725-6

Aquinas, T. (1985). Somma teologica. Bologna: Edizioni Studio Domenicano.

Baia, A. E., Biondi, G., Franzoni, V., Milani, A., & Poggioni, V. (2022). Lie to me: Shield Your Emotions from Prying Software. *Sensors (Basel)*, *22*(3), 967. doi:10.339022030967 PMID:35161713

Balamurani, R., Lall, P. B., Taneja, K., & Krishna, G. (2022). Detecting Human Emotions Through Physiological Signals Using Machine Learning. In R. R. Raje, F. Hussain, & R. J. Kannan (Eds.), *Artificial Intelligence and Technology* (pp. 587–602). Springer. doi:10.1007/978-981-16-6448-9_57

Breazeal, C. (2003). Emotion and sociable humanoid robots. *International Journal of Human-Computer Studies*, *59*(1–2), 119–155. doi:10.1016/S1071-5819(03)00018-1

Chen, M., Zhang, Y., Qiu, M., Guizani, N., & Hao, Y. (2018). SPHA: Smart personal health advisor based on deep analytics. *IEEE Communications Magazine*, *56*(3), 164–169. doi:10.1109/MCOM.2018.1700274

Conrad-Martius, E. (1921). *Metaphysische Gespräche*. Verlag Max Niemeyer.

Czerwinski, M., Hernandez, J., & McDuff, D. (2021). Building an AI That Feels: AI systems with emotional intelligence could learn faster and be more helpful. *IEEE Spectrum*, *58*(5), 32–38. doi:10.1109/MSPEC.2021.9423818

Damasio, A. R. (1994). *Descartes's Error. Emotion, Reason and the Human Brain*. A. Grosset-Putnam Books.

Damasio, A. R. (1999). *The Feeling of What Happens: Body and Emotion in the Making of Consciousness*. Hartcourt, Brace & Company.

De Monticelli, R. (2005). *L'anima e il sentire. In L'anima. Annuario di filosofia*. Mondadori.

Doctor, F., Karyotis, C., Iqbal, R., & James, A. (2016). An intelligent framework for emotion aware e-healthcare support systems. *IEEE Symposium Series on Computational Intelligence*, 1-8. 10.1109/SSCI.2016.7850044

Fellous, J.-M. (2004). From Human Emotions to Robot Emotions. *2004 AAAI Spring Symp. Archit. Model. Emot. Cross-Disciplinary Found*. Retrieved from: https://www.aaai.org/Papers/Symposia/Spring/2004/SS-04-02/SS04-02-008.pdf

Fisogni, P. (2015). The Origins of the Moral Sense and the Role of Caring in Early Infancy. *Encyclopaideia*, *14*(4), 83–101. doi:10.6092/issn.1825-8670/5037

Fisogni, P. (2019). Cyber Terrorism and Self-Radicalization - Emergent Phenomena of Onlife Age: An Essay Through the General System Theory. *International Journal of Cyber Warfare & Terrorism*, *9*(3), 21–35. doi:10.4018/IJCWT.2019070102

Fisogni, P., & Fisogni, A. (2020). The Experience of Void within Derealization and Disconnection. *Journal of Psychiatry and Psychology Research*, *4*(2), 231–235.

Floridi, L. (2014). *The Fourth Revolution – How the Infosphere is reshaping Human Reality*. Oxford University Press.

Floridi, L. (Ed.). (2015). *The Onlife Manifesto. Being Human in a Hyperconnected Era*. Springer Open.

Floridi, L. (2017). Infraethics-on the Condition of Possibility of Morality. *Philosophy & Technology*, *30*(4), 391–394. doi:10.100713347-017-0291-1

Frank, R. H. (1991). *Passions within reason: The strategic role of the emotions*. W. W. Norton.

Franzoni, V., Milani, A., Nardi, D., & Valleverdù, J. (2019). Emotional Machines: The Next Revolution. *Web Intelligence*, *17*(1), 1–7. doi:10.3233/WEB-190395

Gendlin, E. (1997). *Experiencing and the Creation of Meaning. A Philosophical and Psychological Approach to the Subjective*. Northwestern University Press.

Guo, J. (2022). Deep learning approach to text analysis for human emotion detection from big data. *Journal of Intelligent Systems*, *31*(1), 113–126. doi:10.1515/jisys-2022-0001

Harley, J. M., Lajoie, S. P., Frasson, C., & Hall, N. C. (2015). An Integrated Emotion-Aware Framework for Intelligent Tutoring Systems. In Artificial Intelligence in Education. AIED 2015. Lecture Notes in Computer Science (vol. 9112, pp. 616-619). Springer. doi:10.1007/978-3-319-19773-9_75

Hossain, M. S., & Muhammad, G. (2019). Emotion Recognition Using Deep Learning Approach from Audio-Visual Emotional Big Data. *Information Fusion*, *49*, 69–78. doi:10.1016/j.inffus.2018.09.008

Isen, A. M. (2001). An Influence of Positive Affect on Decision Making in Complex Situations: Theoretical Issues with Practical Implications. *Journal of Consumer Psychology*, *11*(2), 75–85. doi:10.1207/S15327663JCP1102_01

Kugel, P. (2002). Computing machines can't be intelligent (... and Turing said so). *Minds and Machines*, *12*(4), 563–579. doi:10.1023/A:1021150928258

La Brock, S. (1992). *Action and Conduct. A Thomistic Study*. Romae, Athenaeum Sanctae Crucis.

Lazarus, R. S. (1982). Thoughts on the Relations Between Emotion and Cognition. *The American Psychologist*, *37*(9), 1019–1010. doi:10.1037/0003-066X.37.9.1019

Leventhal, H., & Scherer, K. (1987). The Relationship of Emotions to Cognition: A Functional Approach to a Semantic Controversy. *Cognition and Emotion*, *1*(I), 3–28. doi:10.1080/02699938708408361

Lin, K., Xia, F., Wang, W., Tian, D., & Song, J. (2016). System Design for Big Data Application in Emotion-Aware Healthcare. *IEEE Access: Practical Innovations, Open Solutions*, *4*, 6901–6909. doi:10.1109/ACCESS.2016.2616643

**M**

Mancuso, S., & Viola, A. (2015). *Brilliant Green: The Surprising History of Science and Plant Intelligence*. Island Press.

Minati, G. (2019). Phenomenological Structural Dynamics of Emergence. An Overview of How Emergence Emerges. In L. Urbani Ulivi (Ed.), *The Systemic Turn in Human and Natural Sciences. A Rock in The Pond* (pp. 1–39). Springer. doi:10.1007/978-3-030-00725-6_1

Picard, R. (1997). Affective Computing. *M.I.T. Media Laboratory Perceptual Computing Section Technical Report, 321*, 1-16. Retrieved from: https://affect.media.mit.edu/pdfs/95.picard.pdf

Rasetti, M. (2021). Representing Behavior, Consciousness, Learning: Will a Purely Classical Artificial Intelligence Be Enough? In G. Minati (Ed.), *Multiplicity and Interdisciplinarity. Essays in Honor of Eliano Pessa* (pp. 135–157). Springer. doi:10.1007/978-3-030-71877-0_10

Spezialetti, M., Placidi, G., & Rossi, S. (2020). *Frontiers in Robotics and AI, 21*(December). https://www.frontiersin.org/articles/10.3389/frobt.2020.532279/full

Stein, E. (2005). *Potenz und Akt: Studien zu einer Philosophie des Seins*. Herder.

Tononi, G., Boly, M., Massimini, M., & Koch, C. (2016). Integrated information theory: From consciousness to its physical substrate. *Nature Reviews. Neuroscience, 17*(7), 450–461. doi:10.1038/nrn.2016.44 PMID:27225071

Turing, A. M. (1950). Computing machinery and intelligence. *Mind, 59*(236), 433–460. doi:10.1093/mind/LIX.236.433

Urbani Ulivi, L., & Fisogni, P. (2021). Reasoning About Reason: Why Philosophy Should Now Abandon Monism in Favour of Pluralism. In G. Minati (Ed.), *Multiplicity and Interdisciplinarity. Essays in Honor of Eliano Pessa* (pp. 189–206). Springer. doi:10.1007/978-3-030-71877-0_13

Von Bertalanffy, L. (1967). *General System Theory. Foundations, Development, Applications*. Braziller.

Westerink, J., Krans, M., & Ouwerkerk, M. (Eds.). (2011). *Sensing Emotions. The Impact of Context on Experience Measurements*. doi:10.1007/978-90-481-3258-4

Yohanan, S., & MacLean, K. E. (2012). The role of affective touch in human–robot interaction: Human intent and expectations in touching the haptic creature. *International Journal of Social Robotics, 4*(2), 163–180. doi:10.100712369-011-0126-7

Zajonc, R. B. (1980). Feeling and thinking: Preferences Need No Inferences. *The American Psychologist, 35*(2), 151–175. doi:10.1037/0003-066X.35.2.151

## ADDITIONAL READING

Arbib, M. A., & Fellous, J. M. (2004). Emotions: From brain to robot. *Trends in Cognitive Sciences, 8*(12), 554–561. doi:10.1016/j.tics.2004.10.004 PMID:15556025

Bertalanffy, L. (1950). The Theory of Open Systems in Physics and Biology. *Science, 111*(2872), 23–29. doi:10.1126cience.111.2872.23 PMID:15398815

Bonarini, A. (2016). Can my robotic home cleaner be happy? Issues about emotional expression in non-bio-inspired robots. *Adaptive Behavior*, *24*(5), 335–349. doi:10.1177/1059712316664187

Breazeal, C. (2003). Emotion and sociable humanoid robots. *International Journal of Human-Computer Studies*, *59*(1–2), 119–155. doi:10.1016/S1071-5819(03)00018-1

Dupré, J. (2015). Pluralism and Processes in Understanding Human Nature. *Rivista di Filosofia Neo-Scolastica*, *1-2*, 15–28.

Vitiello, G. (2019). The World Opacity and Knowledge. In L. Urbani Ulivi (Ed.), *The Systemic Turn in Human and Natural Sciences. A Rock in The Pond* (pp. 41–51). Springer. doi:10.1007/978-3-030-00725-6_2

## KEY TERM AND DEFINITIONS

**Conduct:** In philosophy conduct is a key term within the morality domain as well as ethics. It refers to the capacity for the human subject to be a moral agent. Morality deals properly with normative claims and sets of rules; ethics is more deeply related to the human agency. Thus, conduct could be also said an inclination to act freely in the direction of a final end.

**Enlarges Sensitivity:** In the Onlife perspective, this term refers to an augmented capacity of sensing within the hyperconnected world.

**Moral Enabler:** An object (a digital device, a Pc) or an agent (a person) who addresses someone to act. It/he/her facilitates the making of an action.

**Onlife:** The term, coined by Luciano Floridi (2014, 2015) refers to the melted environment due to the interactions between offline and online.

**Reason:** The principle that regulates and order reality and knowledge. It allows the humans «to be distinguished from the environment in which it is immersed, while the order is mainly the result of an organization of objects (both concrete, theoretical or even mental) between which relationships are established. It follows rules, laws, prescriptions, constraints. It results from negentropy, from symmetry breaking, from self-organization. Reason has many aspects and shows different faces depending on the focus of each investigation: it is, and can be, subjective and objective, conscious and unconscious, explicit and implicit, pragmatic and theoretical, argumentative and apprehensive, and much more» (Urbani Ulivi and Fisogni, 2021: 204).

**Sensing:** In the metaphysical discourse of Thomas Aquinas is the act of grasping some essential traits of reality. This very idea has been relaunched by phenomenology: it grounds upon the idea that things/data are directly given to consciousness.

**System Thinking:** An interdisciplinary approach aimed at investigating phenomena in terms of processes. Each phenomenon can be interpreted as «an ordered of interrelated parts whose characteristics depend both on the characteristics of the parts and on the web of their interconnections» (Agazzi, 2019, p. x). Each system, then, can be seen as a simple and a complex unit that interacts with the whole.

M

# Machine Learning Enables Decision–Making Processes for an Enterprise

**N. Raghavendra Rao**
*FINAIT Consultancy Services, India*

## INTRODUCTION

The terms such as "Problem Solving", "Decision Making", and 'Business Strategy" are used in business enterprises. These terms are used interchangeably. Any action taken by an executive or a team of executives in an enterprise in the context of the above terms depends on the skill, professional experience, and business knowledge of the executives. Sometimes action is also taken by the executives based on their intuitions. Business Strategy and addressing business issues are made based on choosing among the alternatives available to decision-makers.

Generally, the established business management models are made use of by the executives in enterprises. These models are such as statistical tools for forecasting, deciding the inventory level, and determining the resources allocation. Financial models such as "Make or Buy Decision", "Equipment Replacement" are based on the quantitative method. When the problems and business issues are complex, the qualitative, standard models cannot solve or such a decision. Rich experience and in-depth knowledge of the business are needed. The interdisciplinary approach is also required to address business issues or handle complex and complicated business situations. Mainly the factors affecting decision-making are 1-global market scenario, 2- political stability in a country, 3-consumerism, and 4-government intervention, and 5- new competitors in the markets. Many new concepts are emerging in the discipline of information and communication technology. These concepts along with the concepts in business management are facilitating in developing business models for an effective decision-making approach.

## BACKGROUND

The advent of computer systems and the integration of information and communication technology provided scope for designing and developing business tools and business models. Some of them are management information systems, executive information systems, and business analytics, business intelligence, case tools, expert systems, and customer resource management. The above list is not exhaustive. In the present business scenario, the concepts such as cloud computing, artificial intelligence, and machine learning are facilitating in developing business models for the qualitative decision process or improving the existing decision process. Ultimately the decision-making process of choosing among the alternative course of action to attain a goal or achieve a set objective.

DOI: 10.4018/978-1-7998-9220-5.ch056

## Focus in the Chapter

Designing a business model in the machine learning environment needs special efforts. The reason being computer system is required to be trained to think like an intelligent human being. Collective intelligence of domain experts, functional specialists besides making the computer system familiar with the business processes and procedures of a particular business operation. On the basis of the requirements of a particular business application algorithms need to be developed. Collaborative concepts in the discipline of information and communication technology are required to be identified for designing an effective business model under the machine learning environment. This chapter mainly explains how the approach mentioned above will facilitate in designing a business model with the concept of machine learning.

## Literature Review

The author (Iqbal H Sarkar,2021) rightly observes in the article titled "Machine Learning Algorithms, Real-world Applications and Research Direction" in the current age of Industry 4.0 the digital world has a wealth of data such as IOT data, business data, social media data and other related sources. One should have the knowledge of artificial intelligence particularly machine learning is the key. The author talks about the decision makers in the various real world situations and application arrears. The author highlights the challenges and potential research directions in machine learning environment.

The authors (Raffaele Cioffi, Marta Travaglioni, Giuseppina Piscitelli and Fabio Defelice, 2020) in their article titled "Artificial Intelligence and Machine Learning Applications in Smart Production: Progress, Trends, and Directions" stress the adaption and innovation are extremely important in manufacturing industry. Further they say that this development should lead to sustainable manufacturing using new technologies. To promote sustainability, smart production requires global perspective of smart production application technology. In this regard they indicate the intense research efforts in the field of artificial intelligence, a number of artificial intelligence based technique such as machine learning have already been established in the industry to achieve sustainable manufacturing.

The author (Weijin, 2020) in the paper titled "Research on Machine Learning and Its Algorithms and Development" analyses the basic classifications machine learning includes supervised learning, unsupervised learning, and reinforcement learning. It combines analysis on common algorithms in machine learning such as decision tree algorithm, random forest algorithm, and artificial neural network algorithm.

## The Approach Followed in This Chapter

The concepts of artificial intelligence, machine learning, and cloud computing are selected for designing a business model for a textile mill in India. This chapter consists of three sections. Section 1 provides an overview of the concepts mentioned above. Section 2 gives an overview of collaborative concepts. Section 3 discusses a case illustration in the context of the above concepts and Section 4 talks about future trends and conclusions.

## SECTION-1 OVERVIEW OF THE CONCEPTS MENTIONED IN THIS CHAPTER

### Artificial Intelligence and Machine Learning

Machine learning is a form of artificial intelligence that facilitates a system to learn from the data rather than through explicit programming. Artificial intelligence and machine learning algorithms are not new. The concept of artificial intelligence dates back to the year 1950s. Arthur Lee Samuel, an IBM researcher-developed one of the earlier machine learning programs. A self-learning program for playing checkers. The term machine learning and his approach to machine learning were explained in a paper published in the IBM journal of research and development in the year 1959.

Over the decades artificial intelligence techniques have been widely used as a method of improving the performance of underlying the code (Kristian Hammond, 2015, Russell,2015)). In the last few years with the focus on distributed computing models and cheaper computers and storage, there has been a surge of interest in artificial intelligence and machine learning (Mitchell T). This has led to a huge amount of money being invested in startup software companies. Consequent to this many major advancements and commercial solutions have taken place. Six key factors have facilitated these concepts to become effective for applications in almost all disciplines under the sun.

1- Present-day processors have become increasingly powerful and also dense. Density to performance rating has improved dramatically.
2- The cost of storage and managing a large volume of data has become affordable.
3- Distributed computer processing across the clusters of computer systems has also improved in analysing complex data in a recorded time.
4- There are more commercial data sets available to support analytics including weather data, social media data, and medical data sets. Many of these are available in the cloud computing environment. Many well-defined application programs are available with the interface in the cloud computing environment
5- Machine learning algorithms are available through open source communities with larger user bases. It means that there are more resources, frameworks, and libraries that make development easier.
6- One need not be a data scientist to interpret results. Machine learning facilitates the users in interpreting results.

### Machine Learning Methods

Machine learning has mainly three categories. They have supervised learning, unsupervised learning, and reinforcement learning. Supervised learning is a process of inducing knowledge from a set of observations whose outcomes are known. Unsupervised learning is used to discover knowledge from a set of data whose outcomes are unknown. Reinforcement learning is a behavioural learning model. In this case, the system is not trained with the sample data set. The system learns through a trial and error process (Ethem Alpayidan, 2004).

## MACHINE LEARNING CYCLE

The machine learning cycle is a continuous process. The steps in the machine learning cycle are given below.

### 1-Identification of Data

Identifying the relevant data sources is the major step in the cycle. Business decisions need to be made based on constantly changing data from a variety of sources. The data is from internal and external sources. The internal data mainly relates to customers, products, and finances. The external data relates to news, social media, and other related sources. In addition, many data structures are critical for analysis. It is because the information is in structured and unstructured form (Christopher M Bishop, 2006).

### 2-Preparation of Data

Data should be clean, secured, and governed.

### 3-Selection of Algorithm

There are many machine learning algorithms are available in the market. One has to evaluate carefully these algorithms from the perspective of data sets and business challenges. It would be better to develop an algorithm depending on the enterprise's data and business needs.

### 4-Training Process

An enterprise needs to train the algorithm for creating a model. Depending on the type of data and algorithm, the training process may be supervised, unsupervised, and reinforcement learning (Andrew Kellher & Adam Kellher, 2019).

### Training Machine Learning System

Training a machine learning algorithm for creating an accurate model can be broken into three steps.

### Representation

The algorithm creates a model to transform the input data into the desired results. As the learning algorithm is exposed to more data, it will begin to learn the relationship between the raw data. Then data points are strong predictors for the desired outcome (Judith Hurwitz and Daniel Kirsch, 2018).

### Evaluation

As the algorithm creates multiple models. It needs the efforts of the human being or the algorithm to evaluate the model. These efforts will facilitate understanding the predications

## Optimization

After the algorithm creates multiple models, it needs to be selected the best performing algorithm.

## Team Members for the Machine Learning Process

Machine learning is not a solitary endeavour. It is a team process that requires data scientists, business analysts, functional and domain experts. Information and communication technology experts play an important role in designing models in the machine learning environment.

## Importance of the Following Terms

The following terms need the attention of the team members who are involved in the development machine learning process for any application.

## Case-Based Reasoning

A methodology in which knowledge and/ or inference are derived from the historical data.

## Cognitive Style

This is a subjective process through which individuals organize and change information during the decision-making process.

## Heuristics

Informal, judgmental knowledge of an application area that constitutes the "rules of good judgment in the field. Heuristics also encompasses the knowledge of how to solve problems efficiently and effectively.

## Inductive Learning

This is a machine learning approach in which rules are inferred from the facts or data.

## Inductive Reasoning

This is a logical approach. Reasoning depends from general to specific. It can be conditional or antecedent reasoning.

## Intellectual Asset

This is a specific part of the know-how of an organization. Intellectual assets often include the knowledge that employees possess.

## Business Intelligence

It is the use of analytical methods either manually or automatically to derive the relationships from the data (Ahmed Sherif, 2016),

## SECTION-2 OVERVIEW OF THE COLLABORATIVE CONCEPTS

## Cloud Computing Environment

Cloud computing provides four types of environments to end-users. An enterprise can choose any of the following environments for its requirements (Thomas ERL, 2014).

## Private Cloud

This type of infrastructure is owned or leased by a single enterprise and is operated solely for that enterprise.

## Community Cloud

This type of cloud infrastructure is shared by several enterprises and supports a specific community.

## Public Cloud

This type of cloud infrastructure is owned by an enterprise providing cloud services to the general public or a large industrial or business group.

## Hybrid Cloud

This type of cloud infrastructure is a composition of two or more cloud environments such as internal community or public that remains unique entities. They are bound together by standardized or proprietary technology that enables data and application portability.

## Data Warehouse

The data warehouse concept facilitates enterprises to store a huge volume of data for analysis and research. The Data warehouse is a central store of data that is extracted either from the operational database or from a historical database. The data in data warehouses are subject-oriented, non-volatile, and of a historical nature. So data warehouse tends to contain extremely large data sets. It can be inferred that the purpose of a data warehouse is 1) To slice and dice through data 2) To ensure that past data is stored accurately 3) To provide one version of data 4) To operate for analytical process and 5) To support the decision process (Joe Krayank, 2017)

## Data Science

The role of a data scientist is to apply statistical models, evaluation metrics, predictive analysis, and data visualization. The results of these methods will be useful in interpreting business decisions (Joel Grus, 2019).

## SECTION -3 CASE ILLUSTRATION

Coimbatore is a textile town in South India. This town is known as Manchester of South India. There are many textile units in this town producing yarn, cloth, and dress materials. The first generation of people in this town has either started their units after getting a formal training or inherited the textile units. Most of them have basic education only. They have started their units with small capital. Most of the units were established in the middle of the last century. It was because of the favourable market conditions; many units made profits and expanded their business activities. Most of the units have created a brand image for their textile products. The people who start a textile unit is known as mill owner. Even though many of them have more than one textile unit, still they are known as mill owners. Generally, they are never referred to as industrialists.

3 G textile mill was started in the mid-1950s by a textile mill owner. He has rich experience and good knowledge about the textile business. He has basic schooling only. His interest and passion for the textile business have helped him to create a name for his textile products. He has trained a group of employees for his business. They are loyal to him. They take pride in being associated with him for a long period. Most of them have either formal or no basic education. The mill owner alone thinks of business strategies. He never involves the group trained by him for designing business strategies. He expects them to carry out his instructions only.

## MILL OWNER'S METHOD OF WORKING:

Cotton is a very important raw material for manufacturing yarn. Cloth material is manufactured based on the quality of yarn used. The selection of cotton mix is an important element for the production of yarn. He updates himself with the latest information about technical aspects and markets for his textile business. He is confident of himself because of his rich experience in the technical process of manufacturing yarn and cloth material.

The mill owner has identified a large room in his mill's premises for selecting cotton for the production of yarn. Samples of cotton are brought by the different cotton merchants and kept on a big table in the room. Brief details of sample cotton are kept along with it. The details mostly cover the information about the year of production name of the country type of cotton has been grown along with the rate of cotton per bale. The mill owner makes use of his both hands for testing the strength of the cotton. He can select the cotton from his manual method. He does not believe in using any equipment for testing and selecting the cotton for the production of yarn. Further, he decides the mix of cotton from his experience. His decision is based on the percentage of imported cotton to be mixed with the cotton produced in India. While mentally he thinks of the mixture of the cotton par alley he visualizes the color of dyes to be used. He also works out mentally the cost of yarn per spindle. He also decides the price at which the yarn is to be sold. While deciding the type of cloth is to be produced, he keeps in mind the prospective customer's tastes and trends in the market. He also interacts with the suppliers and makes inquiries about the welfare of their families. He feels that this interaction with them is required for maintaining a good relationship with the suppliers. Later he gives instructions to his supporting staff for placing the orders. He has been following the above procedure from the day he started his business activities.

The next generation from his family is not interested in the management of the mills. They prefer to pursue their professional interests. He has not forced his sons to take over the management of the mills. He has realized that he did not make effects to create interest among his sons for the textile business. Further, he felt bad that he did not give the opportunities to his loyal staff for involving the decision process. He did not encourage them to express their views and strategic planning for the business. He shared his concern with Ahalya who is his granddaughter. She has a master's degree in computer science. She is working as a software project manager in a software company. She has considerable experience in designing and developing business application software in the manufacturing sector.

She felt it would be advisable to help her grandfather in the business. She resigned from her job at the software company. She started going along with her grandfather to their textile mill daily. She observed that her grandfather is involved in every activity in the mills. He is also committed. Everyone takes instructions from him.

## Ahalya's Role of Involvement in the Business

She has studied the existing information systems in the organization. Most of the data and information are available in the different standalone systems. They are not integrated. She has recruited software professionals who have professional experience in the areas of machine learning and artificial intelligence. A team has been formed to create a database and transfer the data from the standalone systems to the database. The team has decided to create a data warehouse under the private cloud environment. The team has identified the required data in the database and followed the machine learning cycle process. After following the process, the data has been stored in the data warehouse. The team has decided to develop and write the required algorithms. A quality department has been created for testing the samples of the cotton. Reports given by the department are also stored in the data warehouse.

Ahalya has analysed and concluded, her grandfather has business intelligence, cognitive style of using the information related to business. In some situations, he is applying the heuristic concept in judging a business situation. His rich knowledge can be considered an intellectual asset. She has related all the above aspects are part of artificial intelligence and machine learning approaches.

## Designing of the Textile Model

Ahalya explained the significance and importance the machine learning and artificial intelligence concepts to her grandfather. Services of data scientists will be made use of analysing the data and information. A core team has been formed in designing a business model with the concept of machine learning (Krishna Chandran V N, 2018). Her grandfather has taken interest in the design of the textile database. He has also started updating himself on the concepts applied in designing a database.

A textile database has been created with the data and information about the following. The entire data is stored in a data warehouse under the private cloud computing environment.

1- Varieties of the cotton
2- Origin of the country of the cotton

3-   Indigenous details of the variety of cotton grown in India
4-   Purchase price of the cotton related to imported and indigenous
5-   Test reports of the various cotton from the quality testing department
6-   Various colors of the dyes purchased
7-   Tastes and culture of the people across the globe
8-   Traditional and the current trends of the design of cloth and garments
9-   Texture of the proposed design of the cloth
10-  Business Processes
11-  Components of costs
12-  Inference from the earlier case studies
13-  Climatic conditions of the various regions across the globe
14-  Sales details relating the textile products to monthly and region wise

## Decision Making Process

The following machine learning methods are adopted in training the computer system for facilitating the core team to take decision.

## Supervised Learning Method

The following parameters are considered for writing algorithms under this method. Mixing of cotton related to foreign with Indian on the basic quality details provided by the quality department along with other details such as the color of dyes along with the tastes of the customers and culture are considered for the production of cloth and garments.

## Unsupervised Learning Method

Ahalya's grandfather has provided the details when his textile products were not received well in the market. He explained how to handle difficult situations. Ahalya has written case studies based on the information provided by her grandfather. Inferences of the earlier decision processes and case studies are the main parameters along with the parameters mentioned under supervised learning for writing algorithms under this method.

## Reinforcement Learning Method

This method is applied by the team members for designing textile products of their imagination.

## Three Steps Are Followed Under this Method

First step is that the data stored in the data warehouse related to test reports of the various cotton from the quality testing department along with the texture of the proposed design of the cloth are made use as a part of decision making process.

Under the second step the core team has taken into account the mix of colors of the dyes keeping in mind the tastes and culture of the people across the globe.

79

The final step talks about the costing of the proposed design of textile products. After analysing the competitors' price at the global level and the price that will be acceptable to the prospective customers will be deciding factor in fixing the market price for their textile products.

## Data Scientist

The data scientist has applied the statistical tool, evaluating the metrics, and predictive analysis on the sales of the organization. Reports are generated and given to the management for business decisions and framing business strategies.

## Open Innovation Initiative Approach for Making Decision

The core team has requested the marketing executives to invite some high profile customers for ascertaining their views on their proposed textile products. They have invited some selected priority customers to their office during office hours to view the design on the computer screen at their office (Vyas, 2014). Some of the customers have expressed their views and gave suggestions to the design shown to them. The marketing executives have taken note of their views and suggestions. These inputs are discussed with the core team. After analyzing the inputs they have decided to carry out the changes wherever is feasible. These interactions helped them to know the latest tastes of the group of customers. This helped them to redesign their products (Goel, 2016). The sale of their products is likely to increase. Open innovation initiative with the machine learning methodologies approach followed by the team members has widened their knowledge in designing textile products (Wadhwa & Harper, 2015).

## Observation

It may be noted that the textile mill owner in the case illustration though he did not have a formal education, he depended on his own approach from his business experience. His analysis related to business can be considered as "Business Intelligence". His application of the knowledge related to the textile business may be related to the term "Heuristics". While making use of the data in the data warehouse Ahlaya trained the computer system to follow the "Inductive Learning" approach. Ahalya has identified the certain traits in her grandfather are equal to "Intellectual Assets". Essence of the "Intellectual Assets" is stored under "Inference from the earlier case studies" in the data warehouse. The data warehouse in the private cloud computing environment will also be useful to data scientists for analysis and expressing their views in framing business strategies. A novel approach is followed under open innovative method to know the prospective customers opinion for their proposed new textile products range.

## SECTION 4 FUTURE TRENDS AND CONCLUSIONS

## Future Trends

In the present business world there is no dearth of data and information for designing a business model for an enterprise. The sources of data in the present digital world are available in the sources such as IOT data, Social Media data, business and industry data. Decision making models can be developed for various real world situations and business application from the above sources. So there is wide scope for making use of the machine learning concept in designing and developing an effective business model for an enterprise in any discipline.

**M**

## Conclusion

The complex thinking process is a common characteristic of deep expertise. It explains why an expert finds it difficult to share the process of thinking in his/her field of specialization. Once the thinking process is converted to an explicit approach then it becomes a practical learning aid. Conscious engagement in the learning and updating process will facilitate enterprises taking decisions. Now machine learning concept is playing an important role in the creation of a business model that will be useful for business enterprises. The case illustration discussed in this chapter clearly explains the complex thinking process of human being can be captured by applying the concept of machine learning for achieving a business goals.

## REFERENCES

Alpayidan. (2004). *Introduction to Machine Learning*. MIT Press.

Bishop. (2006). Pattern Recognition & Machine Learning. Springer.

Goel. (2016). *Product Innovation through Knowledge Management and Social Media Strategies*. IGI Global.

Grus. (2019). *Data Science from Scratch*. O'Reilly.

Hammond. (2015). *Practical Artificial Intelligence for Dummies*. John Wiley & Sons Inc.

Hurwitz & Kirsch. (2018). *Machine Learning for Dummies. John Wiley & Sons.*

Kellher & Kellher. (2019). *Machine Learning in Production: Developing and Optimizing Data Science Work Flows & Applications*. Addison-Wesley.

Krayank. (2017). *Cloud Data Warehousing Dummies*. John Willey & Sons.

Krishna Chandran, V. N. (2018). *Lecture Notes in Machine Learning*. Vidya Academy of Science & Technology.

Sarker. (2021). Machine Learning Algorithms, Real world Applications and Research Directions: SN. *Computer Science*.

Mitchell, T. (2020). *Artificial Intelligence and Machine Learning Applications in Smart Production: Progress, Trends and Directions*. MDPI.

Russell. (2015). *Artificial Intelligence*. Pearson.

Sherif, A. (2016). *Practical Business Intelligence*. Puckt Publishing Ltd.

Thomas, E. R. L. (2014). *Cloud Computing Concepts, Technology and Architecture*. Pearson.

Vyas. (2014). *Business Process Transformation*. Real Publishers.

Wadhwa & Harper. (2015). *Technology Innovation and Enterprise Transformation*. IGI Global.

Weijin. (2020). *Research on Machine Learning and Its Algorithms and Development*. ICSP.

## ADDITIONAL READING

Consoli, S., Recupero, D. R., & Saisana, M. (2021). *Data Science for Economics and Finance, Methodologies and Application*. Springer. doi:10.1007/978-3-030-66891-4

Geron, A. (2020). *Hands on Machine Learning with Scikit-Learn Keras & Tensor Flow, Concepts, and Tools &Techniques to build intelligent systems*. O'Reilly.

Kuhn, M., & Johnson, K. (2020). *Applied Predictive Models*. Springer.

Kumbat, M. (2021). *An Introduction to Machine Learning* (3rd ed.). Springer. doi:10.1007/978-3-030-81935-4

Lovelyn Rose, S., Ashok Kumar, L., & Karthika Renuka, A. (2019). *Deep Learning using Python*. Wiley.

## KEY TERMS AND DEFINITIONS

**Artificial Intelligence:** This is the subfield of computer science concerned with symbolic reasoning and problem solving.

**Business Intelligence:** This is related to using analytical methods either manually or automatically for deriving relationships from the data.

**Cloud Computing:** This is a computing model that makes information technology resources such as servers, middleware, and application available over the internet as services to business organizations in self-service manner.

**Data Warehouse:** This is a large data store containing the organization's historical data which is used primarily for data analysis and data miming.

**Heuristics:** This is an informal and judgemental knowledge of an application area that constitutes the "Rules of Good Judgment" in the field. Heuristics also encompasses the knowledge of solving problems efficiently and effectively. It also facilitates to improve performance a particular activity in an organization.

**Inductive Learning:** This is a machine learning approach in which rules are inferred from facts or data.

**Intellectual Assets:** This is referred to a specific part of know-how of an organization. This is also referred as intellectual capital. Intellectual capital often includes the knowledge that employees possess.

**Machine Learning:** The process by which a computer system learns from experience. Algorithms are developed to make the computer system learn from the historical cases.

S

# Sentiment Analysis Using LSTM

**Anweshan Mukherjee**
*St. Xavier's College (Autonomous), India*

**Rajarshi Saha**
*St. Xavier's College (Autonomous), India*

**Ashwin Gupta**
*St. Xavier's College (Autonomous), India*

**Debabrata Datta**
*St. Xavier's College (Autonomous), India*

**Anal Acharya**
*St. Xavier's College (Autonomous), India*

## INTRODUCTION

Sentiment Analysis is a field of study in Natural Language Processing (NLP) domain that focuses on determining the sentiment of data given as input; mostly, classified into three classes – negative, neutral and positive. It focuses on identification and classification of opinions or sentiments conveyed in the source text (Neethu, M. S., & Rajasree, R, 2013). Sentiment analysis can be defined as a process that automates mining of attitudes, opinions, views and emotions from text, speech, tweets, and database sources through NLP. It is also referred to as subjectivity analysis, opinion mining, and appraisal extraction. Analysis of user generated data to extract the sentiment or opinion of the crowd is of prime importance in the real world (Kharde, V., & Sonawane, P, 2016).

There are three basic methodologies of Sentiment Analysis:

1. Symbolic techniques or Rule-based approach
2. Machine learning techniques or Automatic approach
3. Hybrid techniques

Rule-based techniques require an outsized database of predefined emotions and sentiments and an efficient knowledge representation for classifying sentiments properly (Neethu, M. S., & Rajasree, R, 2013). In rule-based approach, we use a set of human-crafted rules or guidelines to help determine the subjectivity, polarity, or the subject of an opinion. Rule-based systems are very naive since they do not consider how words are combined in a sequence. Although more advanced processing techniques can be used, and new rules added to support new expressions and vocabulary. However, adding new rules may affect the previous results, and eventually the whole system may get very complex. Since rule-based systems often need fine-tuning and maintenance, they also need regular investment.

DOI: 10.4018/978-1-7998-9220-5.ch057

Machine learning approach in sentiment analysis involves using a training set to train and develop a sentiment classifier model that categorizes or classifies sentiments. It is simpler than rule-based approach since such a large database of predefined emotions or sentiments is not required (Neethu, M. S., & Rajasree, R, 2013). Machine learning techniques for sentiment classification are useful because they are able to capture the context accurately by modelling many features efficiently. They are capable of adapting to changing input and can calculate as a part of the process the degree of uncertainty of classification, making them a suitable technique for many applications (Boiy, E., & Moens, M. F, 2008). Machine learning techniques or Automatic approaches rely on different machine algorithms to classify opinions. In this technique, a sentiment analysis task is modelled as a classification problem, where a classifier is loaded with a text and returns a category, e.g., positive, negative, or neutral. This approach involves a training and a prediction process. In the training process the model learns to associate a particular input i.e., a text to the corresponding output or tag, based on the test samples used for training. The feature extractor then transfers the text input into a feature vector. Pairs of feature vectors and tags (positive, negative, or neutral) are input into the machine learning algorithm to generate a model. In the prediction process, the feature extractor is used to transform unknown text inputs into feature vectors. These feature vectors are then input into the model, which then generates the predicted tags (positive, negative, or neutral). For classifying the text, various statistical models may be used such as Naïve Bayes (NB), Support Vector Machines (SVM), Linear Regression, and Deep Learning.

Finally, hybrid approaches combine the desirable elements of rule-based and Machine Learning techniques into one system. The main advantage of this approach is that the results are often more accurate.

The research work highlighted in this paper uses a machine learning based approach for classifying texts into three classes – negative, positive and neutral. The methodology proposed here was also deployed into a web application so that anyone can use it, and if developed further, can be used in several critical applications such as in the field of psychology or, detecting the overall opinion from the reviews obtained for any product or, predicting the sentiment of a suspected criminal during interrogation.

## Background

Pang et al. (2002) tried to tackle the problem of classifying a document based on its overall sentiment, instead of classifying it by topic. The document contained a review, and the aim was to determine whether the review is positive or negative. They used movie reviews as their data and found out that machine learning techniques outperformed human-produced rules and guidelines. However, it was also observed that the three Machine Learning methods that were employed, namely Naïve Bayes (NB), Maximum Entropy Classification (ME) and Support Vector Machines (SVM) do not perform as well on sentiment classification as they do on traditional topic-based categorization. On researching the effects of the three machine learning techniques (NB, ME and SVM) in the specific domain of movie reviews, they were able to achieve an accuracy of 82.9% using SVM and an unigram model. The results produced by machine learning techniques were better in comparison to the human generated guidelines. In terms of relative performance, Naive Bayes performed the worst and SVMs performed the best, although the differences are not very large. Despite trying out several different types of features, they were unable to achieve accuracies on the sentiment classification problem comparable to those reported for standard topic-based categorization.

In another research work, Turney (2002) introduced a simple unsupervised algorithm for rating a review as positive (thumbs up) or negative (thumbs down). The classification of a review was predicted by the average semantic orientation of the words and phrases in the reviews that contained adjectives and adverbs. In their research, the semantic orientation of a phrase was determined by the mutual information between the given phrase and the word "excellent" minus the mutual information between the given phrase and the word "poor". A review was classified as "positive" if the average orientation of its phrases in positive. The algorithm used followed Pointwise Mutual Information (PMI) and Information Retrieval (IR) to measure the similarity between pairs of words or phrases.

Pang and Lee (2004) worked on document-level polarity classification. They found that the polarity classification can be improved by removing objective sentences in the document and working with only the subjective sentences. Hence, they first used a subjectivity detector that determined whether a sentence is subjective or not. Then they discarded the objective sentences and created an extract. This extract better represented the polarity of the content. They examined the relation between subjectivity detection and polarity classification and found out that subjectivity detection compresses review into much shorter extracts, which still retain the polarity comparable to that of a full review. For polarity classification, they used Support Vector Machines (SVM) and Naïve Bayes (NB).

Barbosa and Feng (2010) designed a 2-step automatic sentiment analysis method for classifying tweets, which first classified tweets as subjective and objective ones and then further classified the subjective tweets as positive or negative, discarding the objective ones. They used a noisy training set to reduce the labelling load in developing classifiers. The target of this approach was to automatically detect sentiments of tweets. This approach also explored certain characteristics of how tweets are written and the metainformation about the words that compose the tweets. The noisy training set reduced the labelling effort in developing classifiers. Using this approach, they were able to capture a more abstract representation of tweets. This solution was more effective than the previous ones and also more robust regarding biased and noisy data, which is the kind of data usually found on Twitter.

Pak and Paroubek (2010) studied how microblogging can be used for sentiment analysis purposes. In their study, they used a dataset that was formed by collecting messages from Twitter. Using this dataset, they built a sentiment classifier based on the multinomial Naive Bayes classifier that used N-gram and POS-tags as features. The sentiment classifier was trained using this collected corpus. This sentiment classifier was able to determine positive, negative, and neutral sentiments for a document. In their method, there was a chance of error since emotions of tweets in training set were labelled solely based on the polarity of emoticons. The training set was also less efficient since it contains only tweets having emoticons.

Peddinti and Chintalapoodi (2011) utilized the information from other publicly available databases like IMDB and Blippr after proper modifications to aid twitter sentiment analysis in movie domain. They focused on the technique of performing sentiment analysis of tweets by adapting data from other sources, known as 'domain adaptation'. Domain adaptation proved to be useful in predicting sentiments. They used Expectation Maximization (EM) and Rocchio SVM iterative algorithms to filter noisy data during adaptation and train only on valid data. To maintain accuracy, they used a combination of two feature reduction techniques called 'thresholding' and Relative Information Index (RII).

Neethu and Rajasree (2013) researched different Symbolic and Machine Learning techniques to identify sentiments from text. They analyzed tweets about electronic products like mobiles, laptops, etc. and found out that machine learning techniques are simpler and more efficient than symbolic techniques and these techniques can be applied for twitter sentiment analysis. During their research, they noted certain issues that arise while dealing with identifying emotional keywords from tweets having multiple keywords. Another issue was that it was difficult to handle misspellings and slang words. To deal with these issues, after preprocessing, an efficient feature vector was created by performing feature extraction. Here the twitter specific features were extracted and added to the feature vector. After that, these features were removed from tweets and again feature extraction was done as if it is done on normal text. These features were also added to the feature vector. Classification accuracy of the feature vector was tested using different classifiers like Naive Bayes, Support Vector Machines, Maximum Entropy and Ensemble classifiers. All these classifiers had almost similar accuracy for the new feature vector.

Wang and Castanon (2015) showed that emoticons are widely used by Twitter users and in particular, emoticons expressing positive sentiment, such as:) and ;), were the dominant majority on Twitter. Moreover, they noted that a group of emoticons expressing negative sentiment was commonly used too, while many others were used relatively infrequently. They conducted a survey to understand the perception of sentiment polarity of the emoticons by humans, which revealed that some emoticons are strong and reliable signals of sentiment polarity while many others were complex and ambiguous indicators of emoticon. They carried out three analyses using one of day of the Twitter data and investigated the relationship between emoticons and sentiment expression on the platform to conclude that emoticons are indeed strong indicators of human sentiment in tweets.

Monicka and Krishnaveni (2019) used tweets to analyze the prevalence of Myocardial Infarction (MI) among the users. They proposed an MI detection and tweet classification approach based on the concept of deep learning. They developed a method to gauge the measure of concern expressed by Twitter users for public health specialists and government decision makers. They developed a two-step sentiment classification approach which was different from the traditional Twitter sentiment classification problem which classified tweets into positive and negative, or positive, negative, and neutral categories. Those approaches classified the tweets without distinguishing personal tweets from non-personal ones. Although some news tweets may also express concerns about a certain disease, they usually do not reflect a direct emotional impact of the disease from the personal point of view of an individual. Hence such news tweets were discarded. The overall process aimed at tuning a model and then predicting the class for whether the patient is suffering from any heart related problem or not.

## PROPOSED METHODOLOGY

The proposed methodology has been divided into few distinct yet interrelated steps. These are described below:

### Data Preparation

### Data Cleaning

Data cleaning is the process of getting rid of irrelevant or corrupt data from the dataset. These unwanted data are either completely removed from the dataset or replaced with their correct (relevant) forms after modifying them.

Removing contractions from the phrases in the dataset is an important step for data cleaning. In English Language, contractions are words formed by shortening some other word. Some letters of a word are omitted to get contracted words. Generally, not always, a contracted word can be identified by the presence of an apostrophe in it. For example, *don't* is the contracted form of *do not*; *won't* is the contracted form of *will not*.

The next step was to remove commas, periods and '@'. Finally, as a part of data cleaning, apostrophe was removed.

Algorithm for replacing contracted words with their original forms:

```
for each row in the dataset
        replace the text data with contractions(text)
```

Algorithm for removing commas, periods and '@':

```
for each row in the dataset {
        create a temporary null string variable temp
        for each character c in the text in that line {
                if c is not a comma, full stop or '@'
                        add c to temp
                else {
                        if the comma is in a number, ignore it
                        else if the period is in a number, add it to temp
                        else add " " to temp
                }
        }
        replace current row in the dataset with temp
}
```

Algorithm for removing apostrophe:

```
for each row in the dataset {
        create a temporary null string variable temp
        loop - go through each character c in the current line {
                if c is an apostrophe {
if c is not the last character in the line AND the character next to c is 's',
go to the next character
                }
                else if c is not an apostrophe, add c to temp
                go to next character
        }
        replace current row in dataset with temp
}
```

## Tokenization

Tokenization is the process of breaking up a text into smaller units, called tokens. In the research work proposed in this paper, individual words (separated by spaces) are considered to be tokens.

The algorithm followed tokenizes a string given as input and splits off punctuation marks too other than periods.

Algorithm for tokenization:

```
for each row in the dataset
        replace text data with word_tokenize(text)
```

## Filtering – Removing Stop Words

Stop words are those words which are generally of little or no importance to the overall meaning of the sentence. They can be referred to as 'noise' in the text. Meaning of the sentence can be obtained without their involvement too. Example of stop words in the English Language are 'a', 'an', 'and', 'the'.

For generating a list of stop words, the strategy would be to sort the words by their respective frequencies in a particular collection of documents, select the most frequent ones from them (sometimes hand-filtered according to the semantic content with respect to the domain of the documents indexed), and removing them (filtering them out) during indexing. Removing stop words enables to store less data and prevents overfitting of data on those words which do not help in classifying the text according to their sentiments.

Algorithm for removing stop words:

```
download a set of English stop words
for each row in the dataset {
tokenized_words = tokenized words in the current line of the dataframe
create a temporary list filtered_sentence (currently blank list)
loop - go through each word w in tokenized_words {
        if w is not present in the downloaded set of stop words
                add w to filtered_sentence
        }
replace tokenized_words in the current row of the dataset with filtered_sen-
tence
}
```

## Stemming

In English Language, there are several words that are derived from some other words. This is called Inflectional Language and is used for various speech changes. A stem (root) is the base word to which inflectional affixes such as -ed, -ize, -s, -de, -ing are concatenated to create new words. Stemming is a type of lexicon normalization where the ends of the words are chopped off to get the root word. These root words are called stems (Datta, D., Majumdar, S., Sen, O., & Sen. 2019). Since stems are created by removing the suffixes or prefixes from a word, it not always gives meaningful results. For example, stemmed word for 'hatred' is 'hatr' and that of 'forgive' is 'forgiv'. The major role of stemming is to make a common word for all linguistically similar words but it does not check whether that root word that is converging to is meaningful to or not.

There are two common stemming algorithms: Porter Stemmer and Lancaster Stemmer

In the methodology proposed in this research work, Porter Stemmer algorithm has been used which involves trimming suffixes to produce the stems. It is the most common algorithm for stemming English words and empirically, it has been proved to be effective. It consists of 5 phases of sequential reductions. At each phase, there are various rules. These rules are used to decide whether the suffix in a word is to be trimmed or not.

Algorithm for stemming:

```
for each row in dataset {
        create a temporary list stemmed_words (currently blank)
        for each word w in the current line {
                stemmed = PorterStemmer.stem(w)
                add stemmed to stemmed_words
        }
        replace the current row in dataset with stemmed_words
}
```

## Lemmatization

Lemmatization refers to removing inflectional additions to a word using a proper vocabulary of that language so that the base words are linguistically correct, that is the root word also belongs to that language (Datta, D., Majumdar, S., Sen, O., & Sen. 2019). Thus, lemmatization is more sophisticated than stemming.

In the research work highlighted in this paper, the stemmed words were lemmatized because there are some words which stemming does not reduce to its root form. Using lemmatizing only, also brings some problems such as the root word for 'walking' is ambiguous when trying to reduce by lemmatization since here it is unknown whether the word is an adjective or a verb. If it is a verb, 'walking' should be reduced to 'walk'; if it is an adjective, it is already in its base form.

Algorithm for lemmatization:

```
for each row in dataset {
        create a temporary list lemmatized_words (currently blank)
        for each word w in the current line {
                lemmatized = WordNetLemmatizer.lemmatize(w)
                add lemmatized to lemmatized_words
        }
        replace the current row in dataset with lemmatized_words
}
```

## Separating Phrases (reviews) and Sentiment Labels into Two Lists

The phrases were kept in a list named 'reviews'. The sentiment labels were kept in another list named 'labels'. That means, for each row of the dataset, the phrases were extracted and stored in the list 'reviews' and the sentiment label (negative, neutral or positive) corresponding to that review was kept in the list 'labels'. So, the element at the $i^{th}$ position of the list 'labels' contain the sentiment corresponding to the phrase stored in the $i^{th}$ position of the list 'reviews'.

In the list 'labels', instead of storing the whole terms 'negative', 'neutral' or 'positive', they were stored using the following convention:

- Negative = 0
- Neutral = 1
- Positive = 2

Algorithm for separating phrases and labels into two lists:

```
create two empty lists - reviews and lists
for each row in the dataset {
        add the review words in the current line to the list reviews
        if the label in current line negative
                add 0 to labels
        else if the label in current line is neutral
                add 1 to labels
        else
                add 2 to labels
}
```

At the end of this step, the list 'reviews' is a list of several lists. Each sub-list contains cleaned words.

## Converting Data into Useful Form

### Creating an Internal Vocabulary of The Words Used

A dictionary was formed and, in that dictionary, each unique word was indexed with some integer. In the research work highlighted in this paper, the first 10,000 unique words were chosen to form the vocabulary.

### Converting Text in Reviews into Corresponding Index Values

The list 'reviews' contain the phrases in the dataset. Each word of each phrase was replaced by the index number of that word in the vocabulary formed in the previous step. If any word exists which do not belong to the vocabulary, that word is replaced by the number 0. Thus, at the end of this step, the list 'reviews' contain no words; it only contains numerical data, that is, 'reviews' is a list of several lists where each sub-list contains the index values.

Algorithm for converting index to sequences:

```
create an empty list - sequences
for each review in reviews {
temp1 = tokenizer.texts_to_sequences(reviews[i]) /*Gives a list of list*/
        temp2 = []
        for each list in temp1 {
if length of list is not 0, extract the only element in list and add it to
```

```
temp2
        }
        add temp2 to sequences
}
```

## Padding Each Sequence with Zeroes

After the reviews have been converted into index values, the problem is that the sequences would be of various lengths. To overcome this problem, each sequence was padded with zeroes so that all sequences were of the same length.

It was assumed that the texts were of 100 words or lesser. If any text is present with more than 100 words, only the first 100 words were considered for final classification and padding was not done in that case.

## Converting the Labels to One-Hot Encoding

The classification was ultimately done based on the probabilities of each class. For that reason, the labels were converted to their corresponding probability values. In the proposed methodology, the method of One-Hot Encoding has been used to carry out this conversion.

For example, if a text is positive, the probabilities are:

P(negative | text) = 0
P(neutral | text) = 0
P(positive | text) = 1

This positive label is represented by the sequence [0 0 1]. This is known as One-Hot Encoding.

Note that for getting the One-Hot Encoding of a label, only two of the three labels are needed to be checked. For example, if both negative and neutral is 0, the positive has to be 1. For this, Dummy Variable Encoding technique was used because checking all three sentiment labels increases redundancy.

After the padding was done, there was a padded sequence of data and one-hot encoded labels. These one-hot encoded labels are the ideal situations that are to be aimed for, but they cannot be used to compare similarities between two words.

For example, consider the words 'MOTEL' and 'HOTEL' and their one-hot encodings are:

MOTEL: [0 0 0 0 1 0 0 0]
HOTEL: [0 1 0 0 0 0 0 0]

These one-hot encodings alone are not sufficient enough to know how these two words are related to each other. One-hot encodings do not take into account the semantics of the words. So, the words like MOTEL and HOTEL or, AIRPLANE and AIRCRAFT are considered to be two completely different words in spite of their meanings being very similar. Moreover, when applying one-hot encoding to words, few sparse (one containing many zeroes) vectors of high dimensionality could be obtained, which could cause performance issues on large data sets. So, one-hot encodings could be applied only to the labels and not to the reviews.

## Splitting The Data into Training And Validation Sets

The data was divided into two sets:

1. <u>Training set</u>: The training set was used as input to the model for training the parameters. In the training process, the proposed model learns to associate a particular input (text) to the corresponding output label based on the samples for training.
2. <u>Validation set</u>: In the validation process, the validation set was used as the 'unseen data' to calculate the accuracy at the end of each epoch.

The training and validation sets were split in the ratio = 80:20

## Word Embedding and Model Building

### Incorporating GloVe Word Embeddings

Word embeddings are dense vectors having much less dimensionality than the ones obtained had reviews been represented by one-hot vectors (Almeida, F., & Xexéo, G. 2019). A major advantage of using word embeddings is that the semantic relationships between the words are reflected in the distance and direction of the vectors.

Each word is projected to a multi-dimensional space. The number of dimensions could be chosen based on the number of factors determining the classification process. Each word is represented by a distribution across all these dimensions. A word's vector values represent its position in the embedding space. Synonyms are placed close to each other while antonyms have a large distance between them. Each element in the vector contributes to the definition of many words – making the job of meaningful comparisons easier. Hence, the representation of words is spread out across all dimensions (elements of the vector) instead of having an one-to-one mapping from an element to a word.

For example, consider the following hypothetical word vectors with labeled dimensions (there are no such pre-assigned labels actually, though) given in Table 1.

The features 'Royalty', 'Masculinity', 'Feminity' and 'Age' represent the meaning of each word in some abstract way. A 4-dimensional word embedding for the word 'King' from the above representation is:

Vector['King'] = [0.99, 0.99, 0.05, 0.7]

This representation captures the semantic relations effectively.

*Table 1. To explain the concept of word embeddings*

| Words vs Features | King | Queen | Woman | Princess |
|---|---|---|---|---|
| **Royalty** | 0.99 | 0.99 | 0.02 | 0.98 |
| **Masculinity** | 0.99 | 0.05 | 0.01 | 0.02 |
| **Femininity** | 0.05 | 0.93 | 0.999 | 0.94 |
| **Age** | 0.7 | 0.6 | 0.5 | 0.1 |

GloVe, coined from the term 'Global Vectors' is a model for distributed word representation. GloVe is an unsupervised learning algorithm used for obtaining vector representations for words (Pennington, J., Socher, R., & Manning, C. D. 2014, October). The parameters are trained based on co-occurrence statistics aggregated from a global corpus.

In the research work highlighted in this paper, the length of each review was considered to be 100 and hence the vectors for word embeddings were of dimension 100, that is, d = 100.

## Model Structure

The proposed model has the structure given in Figure 1.

*Figure 1. Model structure*

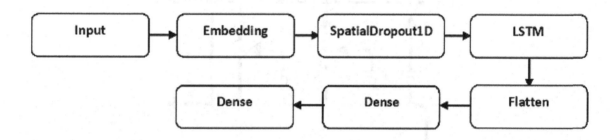

### Layer 1 – Input

This layer provides input to the model. It takes the size of sequences of training as input parameter.

### Layer 2 – Embedding

This layer takes in the parameters: input dimension, output dimension and input length. The input dimension is the size of vocabulary, i.e. 10000. The output dimension is the size of the embedding vectors, i.e. 100. Input length is the size of the sequences that are given as input for the training data. This layer provides the embeddings of the words, denoted by numbers in the sequence. This layer is responsible for holding the parameters to be trained. Since the proposed methodology in this paper focuses on having word vectors as input, the parameter matrix at this layer is the most important set of parameters to be tuned for getting optimum accuracy on unseen data. The parameters at this layer were set as the embedding matrix generated from GloVe Word Embeddings so that the model could be trained in lesser number of epochs using the already trained word vectors.

### Layer 3 – SpatialDropout1D

SpatialDropout1D performs variational dropout in NLP models. It is a type of regularization which is done to prevent overfitting. In SpatialDropout1D, several columns are dropped at random from the output generated by the previous layer. This prevents overfitting. Since, columns are dropped at random, a new type of data is generated every time. For this reason, the local minima are ignored in the gradient descent, and a point with least loss on most occasions could be reached.

In the proposed model, 20% of the columns (rate = 0.2) were chosen at random and they were dropped.

*Layer 4 – LSTM*

LSTM stands for 'Long Short Term Memory'. It is a type of recurrent neural network, capable of learning long range term dependencies of words in a large text. LSTMs can selectively remember patterns for long duration of time (Hochreiter, S., & Schmidhuber, J. 1997). Figure 2 shows the schematic representation of one cell of a LSTM.

*Figure 2. One cell of a LSTM*
*[https://colah.github.io/posts/2015-08-Understanding-LSTMs/, 09.05.2021, 22:01 hours]*

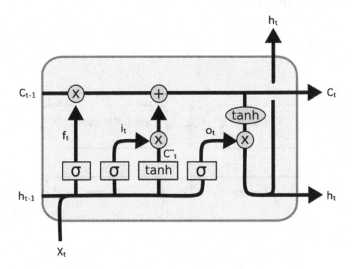

A LSTM comprises of several memory blocks called cells. The working of LSTMs is divided into a series of steps. At step $t$, there is a hidden state $h^{(t)}$ and cell state $c^{(t)}$. Both $h^{(t)}$ and $c^{(t)}$ are vectors of length $n$. The LSTM can erase, read and write information from the cell to preserve long-term information (Hochreiter, S., & Schmidhuber, J. 1997).

The selection of which information is to be erased/written/read is controlled by three corresponding gates – Forget gate, Input gate and Output gate. The gates are also vectors of length $n$. At each timestep, each element of the gates can be open (1), close (0) or somewhere in between. The gates are dynamic in nature that is, their value is computed based on the current context. Gates are modelled by sigmoid function:

$$\sigma(h) = \frac{1}{1 + e^{-h}} \in [0,1] \tag{1}$$

If the value of a gate is close to 0, then it is closed, else opened. The value of gate at the current timestep is computed using the previous hidden state $h^{(t-1)}$ and the input to the LSTM at the current state $x^{(t)}$.

Computation of gates:

Given a sequence of inputs $x^{(t)}$, a sequence of hidden states $h^{(t)}$ and cell state $c^{(t)}$ needs to be computed. At timestep $t$, the gates are computed as:

<u>Forget gate</u>: Controls what is kept and what is forgotten from cell state.

$$f^{(t)} = \sigma \left( W_f h^{(t-1)} + U_f x^{(t)} + b_f \right) \tag{2}$$

<u>Input gate</u>: Controls what parts of the new cell content are written to the cell.

$$i^{(t)} = \sigma \left( W_i h^{(t-1)} + U_i x^{(t)} + b_i \right) \tag{3}$$

<u>Output gate</u>: Controls what parts of the cell are output to hidden state.

$$o^{(t)} = \sigma \left( W_o h^{(t-1)} + U_o x^{(t)} + b_o \right) \tag{4}$$

Where, $W_f$, $W_i$, $W_o$ are the weights with respect to the inputs
And,, $U_f$, $U_i$, $U_o$ are the weights with respect to the hidden states
And, $b_f$, $b_i$, $b_o$ are the biases.

<u>New cell content</u>: This is the new cell content to be written to the cell.

$$c^{\sim(t)} = \tan h \left( W_c h^{(t-1)} + U_c x^{(t)} + b_c \right) \tag{5}$$

<u>Cell state</u>: To erase ('forget') some content from last cell state and write ('input') some new cell content.

$$c^{(t)} = f^{(t)} . c^{(t-1)} + i^{(t)} . c^{\sim(t)} \tag{6}$$

<u>Hidden state</u>: To read ('output') some content from the cell.

$$h^{(t)} = o^{(t)} . \tan h(c^{(t)}) \tag{7}$$

Where, $W_c$, $U_c$ are the weights and, $b_c$ is the bias.

The main advantage of using LSTM over other types of neural networks is that it can remember long-range dependencies. For example, in a sentence, "At first, it seemed like we were going to lose the match but eventually we won." Here, if any other type of networks had been used which could only learn from short-range dependencies, then the phrase "we were going to lose the match" would evaluate to negative sentiment and the phrase "we won" would evaluate to positive sentiment. Considering both of these, the overall sentiment would evaluate to be neutral. But, if a LSTM is used, it could learn long-range dependencies and evaluate the sentiment of the whole sentence to be positive.

In the proposed model, 10 neurons were used in the hidden state, a dropout of 0.2 were used at the current time step and a recurrent dropout of 0.2 was used for dropout from the previous state.

## Layer 5 – Flatten

In this layer, all the parameters were transformed into a 1D vector so that it could be passed through dense neural networks for classification.

## Layer 6 – Dense

Dense layers map each neuron at the current layer to every neuron in the next layer. Dense layers when used with a proper non-linearity outputs values between 0 and 1 which could be used as probabilities of each class. This helps in final classification. There are a large number of parameters in dense neural networks and hence, the backpropagation can be computationally expensive, but these parameters help in obtaining better accuracy on unseen data.

A dense layer with 100 neurons having batch normalization integrated was used to let the network train faster. This layer was used with ReLU activation.

The ReLU activation is given by the function:

$$\operatorname{Re}Lu(x) = \begin{cases} x, & x \geq 0 \\ 0, & x < 0 \end{cases} \tag{8}$$

## Layer 7 – Dense

The final layer of the model, a dense layer with 3 neurons (because there are 3 classes – negative, neutral and positive) was used for classification. Softmax activation was used in this layer, given by:

$$soft\max(h_i) = \frac{e^{h_i}}{\sum_{k=1}^{c} e^{h_k}} \tag{9}$$

The values returned by the softmax activation represent the probabilities of each class. These probability values were used to calculate the loss at each epoch.

Equation followed by the gradient descent algorithm for updating weights:

$$w_{new} \leftarrow w_{old} - \eta \left. \frac{\partial L}{\partial w} \right|_{w=w_{old}} \tag{10}$$

Where, $w$ are the parameters; $\eta$ is the learning rate and L is the loss function.

Thus, the activation function/non-linearity needs to differentiable, which both softmax and ReLU are. ReLU also helped in solving the problem of vanishing gradients. Softmax outputs a vector containing only elements belonging to the interval [0, 1], and the sum of these elements equal to 1. Thus, these values (elements of the vector) could be interpreted as the probability values – how probable each of the three classes were. This helped in performing soft classification.

Optimizer used: Adam with initial learning rate of 0.001
Callback used: ReduceLROnPlateau with factor of 0.2, patience of 3 and minimum learning rate of $10^{-7}$
  was made to monitor the validation loss. This was used to facilitate faster training when the model did not show any more improvement.

Loss function used: Categorical Cross-entropy

$$Total\ Loss\ L = -\frac{1}{N}\sum_{S=1}^{N}\left(\sum_{i=1}^{c} y_{d,i}\ \log(y_i)\right) \tag{11}$$

Where, $y_i$ is the output of softmax

Evaluation metrics used: Accuracy

## Model Tuning

## Hyperparameter Tuning

Hyperparameters are the parameters which enable to optimize the parameters. For example, learning rate, number of neurons, etc. are hyperparameters (Yang, L., & Shami, A. 2020).

For tuning the hyperparameters, various set of hyperparameter values were chosen (different from the model already proposed) and it was checked whether they perform better than the proposed model. If any model for a particular set of hyperparameters works better than the proposed model, that model is saved and the best among them were to be considered for further computations. Hyperparameters were tried to be tuned using the following set of values:

spatial_dropout_rate = {min_value = 0.1, max_value = 0.4, step = 0.05, default = 0.2}
lstm_units = {min_value = 80, max_value = 120, step = 10, default = 100}
lstm_dropout = {min_value = 0.1, max_value = 0.4, step = 0.05, default = 0.2}
lstm_recurrent_dropout = {min_value = 0.1, max_value = 0.4, step = 0.05, default = 0.2}
dense_units = {min_value = 80, max_value = 120, step = 10, default = 100}
adam_learning_rate = One of {1e-2, 1e-3, 1e-4}

5 trial runs were made each of 6 epochs and the model having the best validation accuracy was chosen.

## Fine Tuning Dense Layers

The proposed model was tried to be fine-tuned by freezing the training for all layers except the last dense layer once; and the last two dense layers once.

## RESULTS AND ANALYSIS

## Dataset Used

The dataset used for training the model contains tab-separated phrases (movie reviews) from Rotten Tomatoes dataset. There are 156060 phrases with each phrase being labeled as one of:

Negative – 0
Somewhat negative – 1
Neutral – 2
Somewhat positive – 3
Positive – 4

The proposed methodology converts (negative, somewhat negative) to negative and (positive, somewhat positive) to positive as part of data preparation step so that the labels are classified into 3 classes – negative, neutral and positive. From the dataset, only the data falling under the labels of 'Phrases' and 'Sentiments' were extracted and read as a pandas DataFrame, to enable easier operations on the same.

Training set: Validation set = 80: 20

## Methods and Functions Used

The methods and functions used for the research work are listed in Table 2.

*Table 2. Methods and functions used*

| Job | Method/Function | Library/Package used |
|---|---|---|
| Tokenization | word_tokenize() | nltk.tokenize |
| Filtering | words('english') | nltk.corpus.stopwords |
| Stemming | stem() | nltk.stem.PorterStemmer |
| Lemmatization | lemmatize() | nltk.stem.wordnet.WordNetLemmatizer |
| Creating vocabulary | fit_on_texts() | keras.preprocessing.text.Tokenizer |
| Converting text to index values | texts_to_sequences() | keras.preprocessing.text.Tokenizer |
| Padding with zeroes | pad_sequences() | keras.preprocessing.sequence |
| One-hot encoding | get_dummies() | Pandas |
| Splitting data into training and validation sets | train_test_split() | sklearn.model_selection |
| Model building | Input()<br>Embedding()<br>SpatialDropout1D()<br>LSTM()<br>Flatten()<br>Dense()<br>BatchNormalization()<br>Activation()<br>Model()[1] | keras.models [For 1 only]<br>keras.layers [For the rest] |
| Hyperparameter tuning | RandomSearch() | kerastuner.tuners |

NLTK stands for Natural Language Toolkit. All the methods/functions and libraries/packages mentioned in Table 2 are supported and used in Python programming language.

## Results

## Training the Original Model

The model was trained for 10 epochs with a batch size of 128 (the dataset been shuffled before providing as input). The training was stopped since it started overfitting after the 8th epoch. ReduceLROnPlateau callback reduced the learning rate from 0.001 to 0.0002 so that the validation loss could be decreased, but it did not prove to be beneficial and the training had to be stopped at the 10th epoch. The model showed the results as given in Table 3 and the performance plots are given in Figure 3.

*Table 3. Results after training the original model*

| Loss and Accuracy vs Epochs | Training | | Validation | |
|---|---|---|---|---|
| | Loss | Accuracy | Loss | Accuracy |
| Epoch 1 | 0.9038 | 0.5890 | 0.7003 | 0.7039 |
| Epoch 2 | 0.6722 | 0.7171 | 0.6608 | 0.7292 |
| Epoch 3 | 0.6170 | 0.7424 | 0.6502 | 0.7347 |
| Epoch 4 | 0.5801 | 0.7567 | 0.6450 | 0.7346 |
| Epoch 5 | 0.5502 | 0.7700 | 0.6406 | 0.7390 |
| Epoch 6 | 0.5302 | 0.7771 | 0.6467 | 0.7428 |
| Epoch 7 | 0.5094 | 0.7846 | 0.6542 | 0.7428 |
| Epoch 8 | 0.4932 | 0.7925 | 0.6661 | 0.7428 |
| Epoch 9 | 0.4618 | 0.8054 | 0.6813 | 0.7405 |
| Epoch 10 | 0.4532 | 0.8077 | 0.6917 | 0.7411 |

*Figure 3. Performance plots after training the original model*

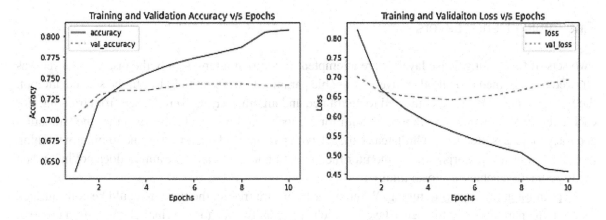

## Hyperparameter Tuning

The following parameters were tried to be tuned so that the best validation accuracy could be obtained:

spatial_dropout_rate = {min_value = 0.1, max_value = 0.4, step = 0.05, default = 0.2}
lstm_units = {min_value = 80, max_value = 120, step = 10, default = 100}
lstm_dropout = {min_value = 0.1, max_value = 0.4, step = 0.05, default = 0.2}
lstm_recurrent_dropout = {min_value = 0.1, max_value = 0.4, step = 0.05, default = 0.2}
dense_units = {min_value = 80, max_value = 120, step = 10, default = 100}
adam_learning_rate = One of {1e-2, 1e-3, 1e-4}

5 different sets of hyperparameters were chosen using the Keras Tuner library and the model giving the best validation accuracy score of them (after running for 6 epochs) was chosen as the best model. The different sets of hyperparameters and their training are described in Table 4.

*Table 4. Hyperparameter tuning*

| Trial number | spatial_ dropout_rate | lstm_ units | lstm_ dropout | lstm_recurrent_ dropout | dense_ units | adam_learning_ rate | Validation accuracy |
|---|---|---|---|---|---|---|---|
| Trial 1 | 0.15 | 80 | 0.40 | 0.40 | 110 | 0.01 | 0.7371 |
| Trial 2 | 0.25 | 110 | 0.15 | 0.20 | 90 | 0.01 | 0.7370 |
| Trial 3 | 0.30 | 110 | 0.35 | 0.30 | 100 | 0.01 | 0.7345 |
| Trial 4 | 0.25 | 90 | 0.25 | 0.40 | 90 | 0.001 | 0.5379 |
| Trial 5 | 0.30 | 100 | 0.15 | 0.15 | 100 | 0.01 | 0.5336 |

Thus, none of the new sets of hyperparameters were able to obtain a higher validation accuracy than the original model. So, the original model was used for further computation.

## Fine-Tuning Dense Layers

Two sets of fine-tuning dense layers were attempted. In the first attempt, only the last dense layer was allowed to be trained and all other layers' trainable parameters were set to False. In the second attempt, the last two dense layers were allowed to be trained and all other layers were frozen from training. For each attempt, the model was allowed to train for 5 epochs, and it was checked whether the validation accuracy increases. ReduceLROnPlateau callback with patience = 3, factor = 0.2 and minimum learning rate = $10^{-7}$ was also incorporated to monitor the validation loss so that the training does not halt when the loss function achieves a local minima.

Reason for attempting fine-tuning: When other layers are frozen, the training could be concentrated more on the parameters of the dense layers, which are actually used for the final classification process.

Tables 5 and 6 show the results after fine-tuning one dense layer and two dense layers respectively.

Fine-tuning did not prove to be beneficial on the validation set. So, the original model was used for building the web application and letting end users get results on unseen data.

*Table 5. Results of fine-tuning the last dense layer only*

| Loss and Accuracy vs Epochs | Training | | Validation | |
|---|---|---|---|---|
| | Loss | Accuracy | Loss | Accuracy |
| Epoch 1 | 0.4505 | 0.8100 | 0.6990 | 0.7409 |
| Epoch 2 | 0.4467 | 0.8107 | 0.7083 | 0.7404 |
| Epoch 3 | 0.4435 | 0.8139 | 0.7131 | 0.7405 |
| Epoch 4 | 0.4395 | 0.8136 | 0.7143 | 0.7389 |
| Epoch 5 | 0.4300 | 0.8178 | 0.7207 | 0.7408 |

*Table 6. Results of fine-tuning last two dense layers*

| Loss and Accuracy vs Epochs | Training | | Validation | |
|---|---|---|---|---|
| | Loss | Accuracy | Loss | Accuracy |
| Epoch 1 | 0.4273 | 0.8188 | 0.7263 | 0.7401 |
| Epoch 2 | 0.4277 | 0.8180 | 0.7272 | 0.7404 |
| Epoch 3 | 0.4266 | 0.8188 | 0.7302 | 0.7397 |
| Epoch 4 | 0.4255 | 0.8198 | 0.7306 | 0.7396 |
| Epoch 5 | 0.4238 | 0.8194 | 0.7314 | 0.7399 |

## Analysis of Obtained Results

The original model achieved a validation accuracy of 0.7411, that is 74.11%. This works quite well in normal circumstances. Since the model is trained on a movie review dataset, most of the errors are based on such inputs in which the words are generally absent in a typical movie review. Some of the results on test (unseen) data are listed in Table 7.

The final model deals with most of the unseen data very well. It also recognizes oxymorons and predicts the sentiment accurately most of the times. Some phrases such as 'eagerly waiting' could be used in both positive and negative sentiment sentences – it is where the model makes the errors.

The training process could not be halted at the epoch having the best validation accuracy because:

1. It was unknown at the present moment whether that validation accuracy was the best.
2. Forcible interruption of the program would result in KeyboardInterruptError which could result in losing the data acquired from the previous epochs.
3. Keras offers a ModelCheckpoint callback which saves the best model and its parameters at run-time, but it does not save the current optimizer state, which could result in starting the whole process again if more number of epochs were required for the model to be trained.

Using GloVe word embeddings helped in obtaining better accuracy in lesser number of epochs, thus saving both time and power. Thus, the web application associated with this model, if improved further, could be used in the field of psychology for detecting sentiments.

*Table 7. Results on test (unseen) data*

| No. | Text | P(Negative Sentiment) | P(Neutral Sentiment) | P(Positive Sentiment) | Predicted Sentiment | Results/ Remarks |
|---|---|---|---|---|---|---|
| 1 | How are you? | 0.2760 | 0.7178 | 0.0062 | Neutral | √ |
| 2 | I will punch you. | 0.0474 | 0.7519 | 0.2007 | Neutral | X |
| 3 | You look good in this dress. | 0.0352 | 0.6159 | 0.3489 | Neutral | X |
| 4 | This painting is so realistic! | 0.1137 | 0.1176 | 0.7687 | Positive | √ |
| 5 | The weather is gloomy today. | 0.7316 | 0.2490 | 0.0194 | Negative | √ |
| 6 | This is the best chocolate I ever had! | 0.0007 | 0.0294 | 0.9685 | Positive | √ |
| 7 | The anger welled inside me with nowhere to go. | 0.5825 | 0.3815 | 0.0359 | Negative | √ (Probability of Negative Sentiment could be higher) |
| 8 | Life's better when we are happy, healthy and successful. | 0.1228 | 0.1516 | 0.7256 | Positive | √ |
| 9 | Dhoni finishes off in style. A magnificent strike into the crowd! India lift the World Cup after 28 years! | 6.64e-05 | 0.0029 | 0.9970 | Positive | √ |
| 10 | This was not the 1st time delta IOS app lost my login info. Annoying. | 0.9431 | 0.5559 | 0.0009 | Negative | √ |
| 11 | I do love my iPhone 6 plus but I am definitely not a fan of the fact that I just accidentally sat on it and it is now of another shape. | 0.0046 | 0.0693 | 0.9261 | Positive | X |
| 12 | My 9th Grade Art Teacher had her phone stolen from the classroom; someone took the SIM card out so she couldn't track it. | 0.1011 | 0.8933 | 0.0055 | Neutral | X |
| 13 | First day back at work after a terrible week off and I've forgotten my ID card at home! | 0.8360 | 0.1620 | 0.0019 | Negative | √ |
| 14 | I am eagerly waiting for Arijit Singh's latest song to release! | 0.7195 | 0.2644 | 0.0160 | Negative | X |
| 15 | The Sun rises in the east and sets in the west. | 0.0018 | 0.7292 | 0.2690 | Neutral | √ |
| 16 | The new kittens enjoyed being alone together. | 0.0806 | 0.3277 | 0.5917 | Positive | √ (Probability of Positive Sentiment could be higher) |

## Comparative STUDY

There have been many research works done in the field of 'Sentiment Analysis', each of them having several advantages and disadvantages. A comparative study of some of them with the research work mentioned in this paper has been explained in Table 8.

*Table 8. Comparative study of some of the research works done on 'Sentiment Analysis'*

| Work | Target | General methodology | Remarks | Drawbacks |
|---|---|---|---|---|
| Pang et al. (2002) | To classify document by its overall sentiment. | Machine learning methods namely Naïve Bayes (NB), Maximum Entropy Classification (ME) and Support Vector Machines (SVM) were used. | Machine learning techniques outperformed methods that used human-produced baselines. Naïve Bayes performed the worst and SVMs performed the best. Achieved accuracy of 82.9% using SVM and a unigram model. | Were unable to achieve satisfactory accuracies on the sentiment classification problem comparable to those reported for standard topic-based categorization. |
| Turney (2002) | To classify reviews as recommended (thumbs up) or not recommended (thumbs down). | A review was classified by calculating the average sentiment orientation of the phrases in the review using Pointwise Mutual Information (PMI) and Information Retrieval (IR). | This approach can be considered as a bag-of-words approach for sentiment analysis, since here the relationships between the individual words are not considered and the document is represented as a mere collection of words. Achieved an average accuracy of 74%. | The time required for processing the queries was high considering the hardware limitations at that time. For some applications, the level of accuracy achieved was not adequate. |
| Pang and Lee (2004) | To perform polarity classification for a document containing multiple sentences. | Followed a 2-step process: 1. Label the sentences in the document as either subjective or objective and discard the objective ones. 2. Apply a standard machine-learning classifiers, Support Vector Machines (SVMs) and Naïve Bayes (NB), to obtain the classifications. | As compared to the earlier research done by Pang and Lee, the accuracy increased to 86.4% from 82.9%. | Not reported |
| Barbosa and Feng (2010) | To design an automatic sentiment analysis method for classifying tweets. | Followed a 2-step approach: 1. Distinguish subjective tweets from non-subjective tweets. 2. Classify the subjective tweets into positive and negative, i.e., the polarity detection. The classification prediction used an abstract representation of the sentences as features. | This approach used biased and noisy labels as input to build its models. Hence it created a more abstract representation of the messages, instead of using a raw word representation. | The accuracy was low in cases of sentences that contained antagonistic sentiments. |
| Pak and Paroubek (2010) | To analyse the sentiments of texts from microblogging sites like Twitter. | A sentiment classifier was built, based on the multinomial Naïve Bayes classifier that used N-gram and POS-tags as features. | A twitter corpus was created by automatically collecting tweets using a Twitter API, and automatically annotating those using emoticons. Using this corpus, the sentiment classifier was built. | There was a chance of error since emotions of tweets in training set were labelled solely based on the polarity of emoticons. The training set was less efficient since it contained only tweets having emoticons. |
| Peddinti and Chintalapoodi (2011) | To perform sentiment analysis of tweets by adapting data from other sources, i.e., 'domain adaptation'. | Expectation Maximization (EM) and Rocchio SVM iterative algorithms were used to filter noisy data during adaptation and train only on valid data. To maintain accuracy, a combination of two feature reduction techniques called 'Thresholding' and Relative Information Index (RII) were used. For classification, Naïve Bayes and SVMs were used. | It was found that domain adaptation is a useful technique to aid Sentiment analysis of tweets and it also gave a high F-score of 0.9 using SVM. | Not reported. |
| Neethu and Rajasree (2013) | To analyze twitter posts about electronic products like mobiles, laptops etc. using a Machine Learning approach. | A new feature vector was used for classifying the tweets, and to extract peoples' opinion about products. After creating the feature vector, classification was done using Naïve Bayes, Support Vector Machine, Maximum Entropy and Ensemble classifier. | Naïve Bayes showed better precision compared to the other three classifiers but showed a slightly lower accuracy and recall. SVM, Maximum Entropy Classifier and Ensemble classifiers showed similar accuracy, precision, and recall. They obtained an accuracy of 90% whereas Naïve Bayes had 89.5%. | There were issues while dealing with identifying emotional keywords from tweets having multiple keywords. It was also difficult to handle misspellings and slang words. |
| Wang and Castanon (2015) | To demonstrate the prevalence of emoticons on social media, and to examine the relationship between emoticons and sentiment polarity, as well as the contexts in which emoticons are used. | A version of word2vec, an algorithm based on deep neural networks, was used to define the representation of the words, including emoticons in the data set. The k-means algorithm was used to cluster the words to understand the exact meaning of the emoticons through the words that appeared in the same cluster. The sentiment of a tweet before and after emoticons were removed from the text were compared. This comparison revealed how much emoticons were relied on to express a sentiment in a tweet. | The results from the analyses confirmed that a few emoticons are strong and reliable signals of sentiment polarity. In about a half of the cases, emoticons were the only signal of sentiment and in the other half of the cases emoticons were facilitating the expression of sentiment. When the emoticons were removed, the sentiment of those tweets became neutral or unclear. | A large group of the emoticons convey complicated sentiments and hence they should be treated with extreme caution. |
| Research work in this paper | To classify a movie review dataset into three sentiments – negative, neutral and positive. | The dataset was cleaned, tokenized, filtered, stemmed and lemmatized. An internal vocabulary of words was maintained. Sentiment labels were converted to one-hot encoded vectors and text data was converted to GloVe word embeddings. A combination of embedding, dropout (20%), LSTM and dense neural networks were used as the model for classification. | LSTMs and GloVe word embeddings made the model perform well on unseen data. Validation accuracy achieved = 74.11% | Relatively poor performance on sarcasms and on text which are almost never present in movie reviews. |

## FUTURE RESEARCH DIRECTIONS

In future, this model should be trained on different types of datasets with a larger vocabulary so that the model learns newer words and performs better on unseen data. The sentiments can also be further classified into various emotions such as satisfied, joyful, excited or cheerful for positive sentiment; and, stressed, depressed, angry or shocked for negative sentiment. Doing so, and deploying it into an application, would be of huge help in the field of psychology. Further, the model currently learns to understand only English text, which could be improved by making the model learn and understand emojis and texts in other languages.

## CONCLUSION

Most of the research work described in this paper was done using Keras library of Python. The final model, with a validation accuracy of 74.11% performs quite well on most circumstances.

Using the proposed model has a number of advantages. The movie review dataset has 156060 phrases and 80% of these were used for training (after shuffling the dataset). This means that it covers large varieties of samples for the model to train on. The model was trained on a movie review dataset with already pre-trained GloVe vectors. These GloVe word vectors enable the model to predict the sentiment efficiently. Using LSTM helps in getting the word co-occurrences and eventually getting the correct overall sentiment most of the times (even in long sentences).

Disadvantages of using the model: The model performs poorly on data which are generally not present in movie reviews. The model also fails to understand the phrases which could be present in both positive and negative sentences, such as sarcasms. Also, the internal vocabulary formed considers 10000 words, which is much less compared to the volumes of words used in day-to-day life. Although the model has achieved a validation accuracy of 74.11%, it still cannot be used in medical purposes because in such fields, almost 100% accuracy is required.

Hybrid models, combining the advantages of rule-based and machine learning techniques might give us an even better result but it was not tested, because of the fact that already established models provide results almost similar to the approach followed in this research work.

## REFERENCES

Almeida, F., & Xexéo, G. (2019). *Word embeddings: A survey.* arXiv preprint arXiv:1901.09069.

Barbosa, L., & Feng, J. (2010, August). Robust sentiment detection on twitter from biased and noisy data. In *Coling 2010* (pp. 36–44). Posters.

Boiy, E., & Moens, M. F. (2009). A machine learning approach to sentiment analysis in multilingual Web texts. *Information Retrieval, 12*(5), 526–558. doi:10.100710791-008-9070-z

Datta, D., Majumdar, S., Sen, O., & Sen, A. (2019). *Mood and Vulnerability Prediction through Natural Language Processing.* Academic Press.

Hochreiter, S., & Schmidhuber, J. (1997). Long short-term memory. *Neural Computation, 9*(8), 1735–1780. doi:10.1162/neco.1997.9.8.1735 PMID:9377276

S

Kharde, V., & Sonawane, P. (2016). *Sentiment analysis of twitter data: a survey of techniques.* arXiv preprint arXiv:1601.06971.

Monicka, M. B., & Krishnaveni, A. (2019). *Sentiment Analysis on Myocardial Infarction Using Tweets Data.* https://www.trp.org.in/

Neethu, M. S., & Rajasree, R. (2013, July). Sentiment analysis in twitter using machine learning techniques. In *2013 Fourth International Conference on Computing, Communications and Networking Technologies (ICCCNT)* (pp. 1-5). IEEE. 10.1109/ICCCNT.2013.6726818

Pak, A., & Paroubek, P. (2010, May). Twitter as a corpus for sentiment analysis and opinion mining. In LREc (Vol. 10, No. 2010, pp. 1320-1326). Academic Press.

Pang, B., & Lee, L. (2004). *A sentimental education: Sentiment analysis using subjectivity summarization based on minimum cuts.* arXiv preprint cs/0409058.

Pang, B., Lee, L., & Vaithyanathan, S. (2002). *Thumbs up? Sentiment classification using machine learning techniques.* arXiv preprint cs/0205070.

Peddinti, V. M. K., & Chintalapoodi, P. (2011, August). Domain adaptation in sentiment analysis of twitter. *Workshops at the Twenty-Fifth AAAI Conference on Artificial Intelligence.*

Pennington, J., Socher, R., & Manning, C. D. (2014, October). Glove: Global vectors for word representation. In *Proceedings of the 2014 conference on empirical methods in natural language processing (EMNLP)* (pp. 1532-1543). 10.3115/v1/D14-1162

Turney, P. D. (2002). *Thumbs up or thumbs down? Semantic orientation applied to unsupervised classification of reviews.* arXiv preprint cs/0212032.

Wang, H., & Castanon, J. A. (2015, October). *Sentiment expression via emoticons on social media.* In *2015 IEEE international conference on big data (big data).* IEEE.

Yang, L., & Shami, A. (2020). On hyperparameter optimization of machine learning algorithms: Theory and practice. *Neurocomputing, 415,* 295–316. doi:10.1016/j.neucom.2020.07.061

## ADDITIONAL READING

Agarwal, A., Xie, B., Vovsha, I., Rambow, O., & Passonneau, R. J. (2011, June). Sentiment analysis of twitter data. In *Proceedings of the workshop on language in social media (LSM 2011)* (pp. 30-38). Academic Press.

Ahuja, S., & Dubey, G. (2017, August). Clustering and sentiment analysis on Twitter data. In *2017 2nd International Conference on Telecommunication and Networks (TEL-NET)* (pp. 1-5). IEEE. 10.1109/TEL-NET.2017.8343568

Bakshi, R. K., Kaur, N., Kaur, R., & Kaur, G. (2016, March). Opinion mining and sentiment analysis. In *2016 3rd international conference on computing for sustainable global development (INDIACom)* (pp. 452-455). IEEE.

Blackwell, R. T., Galassi, J. P., Galassi, M. D., & Watson, T. E. (1985). Are cognitive assessment methods equal? A comparison of think aloud and thought listing. *Cognitive Therapy and Research*, 9(4), 399–413. doi:10.1007/BF01173089

Hosmer, D. W. Jr, Lemeshow, S., & Sturdivant, R. X. (2013). *Applied logistic regression* (Vol. 398). John Wiley & Sons. doi:10.1002/9781118548387

Kibriya, A. M., Frank, E., Pfahringer, B., & Holmes, G. (2004, December). Multinomial naive bayes for text categorization revisited. In *Australasian Joint Conference on Artificial Intelligence* (pp. 488-499). Springer. 10.1007/978-3-540-30549-1_43

Liu, B. (2012). Sentiment analysis and opinion mining. *Synthesis lectures on human language technologies, 5*(1), 1-167.

Park, C. W., & Seo, D. R. (2018, April). Sentiment analysis of Twitter corpus related to artificial intelligence assistants. In *2018 5th International Conference on Industrial Engineering and Applications (ICIEA)* (pp. 495-498). IEEE. 10.1109/IEA.2018.8387151

Suykens, J. A., & Vandewalle, J. (1999). Least squares support vector machine classifiers. *Neural Processing Letters*, 9(3), 293–300. doi:10.1023/A:1018628609742

## KEY TERMS AND DEFINITIONS

**Artificial Neural Network:** A subset of machine learning whose structure is inspired by the human brain and they mimic the way biological neurons signal each other.

**Fine-Tuning:** Process of adjusting the concerned parameters precisely to get optimum results.

**Long Short-Term Memory:** A type of Recurrent Neural Network which can process long sequence of data and remember values over arbitrary time intervals.

**Recurrent Neural Network:** A type of Artificial Neural Network which can use its internal memory to process an input sequence.

**Sentiment Analysis:** A field of study in Natural Language Processing (NLP) domain that focuses on determining the sentiment of data given as input.

**Stemming:** The process of transforming an inflected word to its root form.

**Tokenization:** The process of separating sections of an input string based on a delimiter.

# Understanding Machine Learning Concepts

**Javier M. Aguiar-Pérez**
*University of Valladolid, Spain*

**María A. Pérez-Juárez**
*University of Valladolid, Spain*

**Miguel Alonso-Felipe**
https://orcid.org/0000-0001-7721-8460
*University of Valladolid, Spain*

**Javier Del-Pozo-Velázquez**
*University of Valladolid, Spain*

**Saúl Rozada-Raneros**
*University of Valladolid, Spain*

**Mikel Barrio-Conde**
*University of Valladolid, Spain*

## INTRODUCTION

The intelligence of machines, i.e., their ability to learn in a way similar to how humans do, is increasingly important in many domains. Within the so-called Artificial Intelligence (AI), Machine Learning (ML) stands out, which is the branch of Artificial Intelligence that allows machines to learn without being expressly programmed for it.

Machine Learning is present in many ways in our daily lives, even though we are not aware of it. The recommendations of popular applications such as Netflix or Spotify, or Alexa speech are just some quick examples that Machine Learning is already fully present in our society, and not only in the field of engineering and technology, but in the everyday life of the ordinary citizen.

In this chapter, the authors want to explain what Machine Learning is, as well as to clearly establish the differences and relation of Machine Learning with other important related concepts such as Artificial Intelligence or Deep Learning. Moreover, some possible practical use cases and applications will be named in order to give the reader a clear idea of what the potential of Machine Learning is.

To fulfil this objective the rest of the chapter is organized in several sections that provide brief and clear descriptions of the main concepts regarding 1) Artificial Intelligence, 2) Machine Learning (covering Supervised, Unsupervised, Semisupervised and Reinforcement Learning) and 3) Deep Learning. Finally, future research directions are suggested, and the main conclusions are presented.

DOI: 10.4018/978-1-7998-9220-5.ch058

## BACKGROUND

Defining Artificial Intelligence is not a simple task (Wang, 2019). Artificial Intelligence can be seen as the intelligence exhibited by machines, that is, the study of the intelligent agents of any device that are capable of perceiving their environment and taking actions that allow a certain objective to be successfully carried out. Therefore, it is possible to speak of Artificial Intelligence if a machine imitates the cognitive functions of the human being to learn and solve problems. Artificial Intelligence has undergone great development in recent years. Today, there are many areas where it is being used successfully. Some examples are speech recognition, high-level competition in strategy games such as chess, autonomous vehicles, smart roads, smart buildings, intelligent routing in energy distribution networks, etc.

A good part of the success of Artificial Intelligence is due to the limited human ability to face certain types of problems, which solution would require to invest an enormous amount of time and resources, and also without guarantees of success. An example is the limited human ability to find relevant patterns, objects, or variables within a large mass of data. The problem becomes more complex and beyond the reach of human capabilities as the amount of data to be examined increases. Also, patterns, objects, or variables may sometimes not be easy for the human eye to detect. However, machines can learn to distinguish the patterns and make a reasonably good prediction (Ongsulee, 2017).

In order for the massive data analysis to be effective, computers that offer significant computational capacity, which is not diminished with the passage of time and / or exhaustion, should be used. Moreover, for the analysis of the data to be effective, a specific process is required, so that the computer executes a series of sentences in a precise order to achieve the objective set.

For an Artificial Intelligence system to be able to take decisions based on the data available, different type of learning methods, such as Machine Learning need to be applied.

## MACHINE LEARNING

Machine Learning is a learning technique that gives machines the ability to learn without being explicitly programmed. It addresses the study and creation of algorithms that are capable of learning from data and making predictions about it. It is also important to notice that Machine Learning is seen as a subset of Artificial Intelligence, and not the other way around.

According to Raz, Llinas, Mittu and Lawless (2020), the basic idea behind Machine Learning methods is that a computer algorithm is trained to learn the behavior presented as part of previous experience and/ or dataset to the extent that an outcome can be produced by the computer algorithm when it is presented with a never-before-seen dataset or situation.

Cohen (2021) explains that Machine Learning refers to a class of computer algorithms that learn from examples rather than being explicitly programmed to perform a task. It learns to formulate a general rule from a set of concrete examples. Thus, like human learning, the computer becomes capable of improving its performance from acquired knowledge. The difference is that, at the current state of our knowledge, the computer needs many more learning examples than humans do.

One of the main driving factors of the Machine Learning hype is related to the fact that it offers a unified framework for introducing intelligent decision-making into many domains (Bonetto & Latzko, 2020). This type of learning is used in many areas where good performance is necessary, and where the development of algorithms to achieve the desired objectives would be complex.

U

Machine Learning is therefore one of the main tools of Artificial Intelligence. It seeks to develop algorithms capable of analyzing large amounts of data to find patterns or coincidences. Depending on what is being searched for in the data, an algorithm or a set of them must be applied. Very often these algorithms are developed in the Python programming language, which in recent years has experienced significant growth (Subasi, 2020). Machine Learning algorithms can be divided into different categories including: Supervised Learning (SL), Semisupervised Learning, Unsupervised Learning (UL), and Reinforcement Learning (RL). These different categories of algorithms are explained in the following sections.

## Supervised Learning

The main characteristic of Supervised Learning is that it uses labeled data. These Machine Learning algorithms are able to map an input to an output taking as a base example input-output pairs. The algorithms infer a function from a set of labeled training data examples. As a consequence, Machine Learning algorithms are able to predict label values when input has unlabeled data.

Choi, Coyner, Kalpathy-Cramer, Chiang and Campbell (2020) explain that in a supervised approach the model infers an algorithm from feature-target pairs and is informed, by the target, whether it has predicted correctly. That is, features (x), are mapped to the target (y), by learning the mapping function (f), so that predictions can be approximated using the algorithm $y = f(x)$. The performance of the algorithm is evaluated on the test dataset, data that the algorithm has never seen before. According to these authors, the basic steps of Supervised Machine Learning are (1) acquire a dataset and split it into separate training, validation, and test datasets; (2) use the training and validation datasets to inform a model of the relationship between features and target; and (3) evaluate the model via the test dataset to determine how well it predicts for unseen instances. It is also important to remark that in each iteration, the performance of the algorithm on the training data is compared with the performance on the validation dataset, which means that the algorithm is tuned by the validation set.

Delua (2021) explains that Supervised Learning can be separated into two types of problems when data mining. These types of problems are classification and regression.

Classification problems use an algorithm to accurately assign test data into specific categories. In classification, a class label is predicted for a given example. Mathematically, classification maps a function (f) from input variables (x) to output variables (y) as target, label or categories.

Sarker (2021) summarizes the most common classification problems:

- Binary classification: This classification approach refers to classification tasks that have two class labels ("true and false", "yes and no"). An example can be the detection of cancer ("cancer detected" or "cancer not detected"), or the detection of spam ("spam" and "not spam").
- Multiclass classification: This classification approach refers to classification tasks that have more than two class labels. An example can be the classification of various types of network attacks.
- Multi-label classification: This classification approach refers to classification tasks where an example is associated with several classes or labels, unlike traditional classification tasks where class labels are mutually exclusive. An example is multi-level text classification. For instance, Google news can be presented under different categories: "technology", or "latest news", etc.

On the other side, regression uses an algorithm to understand the relationship between dependent and independent variables. Regression methods allow to predict a continuous (y) result variable based on the value of one or more (x) predictor variables.

Methods used for Supervised Learning include Naive Bayes (NB), Linear Discriminant Analysis (LDA), Logistic Regression (LR), K-nearest Neighbors (KNN), Support Vector Machine (SVM), Decision Tree (DT), Random Forest (RF), Adaptive Boosting (AdaBoost), Extreme Gradient Boosting (XGBoost), Stochastic Gradient Descent (SGD), Rule-based Classification (for classification); and linear/non-linear regression, local regression, and ordinary least squares regression (for regression) (Choi et al., 2018; Sarker, 2021).

In which regards to the methods used for Supervised Learning, Alloghani, Al-Jumeily, Mustafina, Hussain and Aljaaf (2020) conducted a systematic review to analyze scholarly articles addressing or implementing supervised and unsupervised Machine Learning techniques in different problem-solving paradigms. These authors found that Decision Tree, Support Vector Machine, and Naïve Bayes algorithms appeared to be the most cited, discussed, and implemented supervised learners.

Supervised Learning algorithms can be used in many ways. For example, a piece of equipment may have points labeled as failures, the algorithm receives a set of input examples along with the corresponding correct outputs, and it learns, comparing its current outputs with the correct outputs, if it is a failure or not.

Another interesting practical applications and use cases of Supervised Machine Learning include text classification such as classifying spam in a separate folder from your inbox, or predicting the sentiment of a text, like a tweet or other social media, or a product review. Sentiment analysis is important for businesses and brands to understand the social sentiment of their brand, product, or service. Other practical applications include predicting the cost of an accident (useful for insurance companies), bank fraud detection, identity fraud detection, image classification, diagnostics, weather forecasting, estimating life expectancy, population growth prediction, advertising popularity prediction, financial forecasting, cost estimation, trend analysis, time series estimation or drug response modelling.

Satinet and Fouss (2022) used Supervised Learning to easily and quickly assess clothing products' environmental sustainability throughout their life cycle.

On the other hand, this type of learning is also increasingly used in mental health research, and has the potential to advance our understanding of how to characterize, predict, and treat mental disorders and associated adverse health outcomes (e.g., suicidal behavior) (Jiang, Gradus, & Rosellini, 2020).

Finally, another field of application are Internet of Things (IoT) applications, for example, traffic or parking availability prediction in smart cities, or estimating the usage of energy in peak hours.

## Unsupervised Learning

Unsupervised Learning, for its part, is an approach to Machine Learning used with unlabeled data. This means that the system is not told the answer, but it is given data so that the model can work on its own to discover patterns and information that was previously undetected. In this type of learning, the system does not predict the correct output, but instead, it explores the data and can draw inferences from datasets to describe hidden structures from unlabeled data.

Choi et al. (2020) remark that in unsupervised algorithms the patterns that may or may not exist in a dataset are not informed by a target, and are left to be determined by the algorithm.

In Unsupervised Learning, machines do not identify patterns in tagged databases, but instead look for similarities. In this case, the algorithms are not programmed to detect a specific type of data, as would be the case with images containing a certain object, but instead look for examples that look alike and can be grouped.

Unlike Supervised Learning, Unsupervised Learning methods cannot be directly applied to a regression or a classification problem as possible values for the output are not known (El Bouchefry & de Souza, 2020).

Delua (2021) explains that Unsupervised Learning models are used for three main tasks that are clustering, association and dimensionality reduction.

Clustering is a data mining technique for grouping unlabeled data based on their similarities or differences (El Bouchefry & de Souza, 2020; Uddamari & Ubbana, 2021). Sarker (2021) summarizes the most common clustering methods:

- Partitioning methods: This clustering approach categorizes the data into multiple groups or clusters, basing on the features and similarities found in the data.
- Density-based methods: To identify distinct groups or clusters, this clustering approach bases on the concept that a cluster in the data space is a contiguous region of high point density isolated from other clusters by contiguous regions of low point density. Points that are not part of a cluster are considered as noise. This clustering methods typically struggle with clusters of similar density and high dimensionality data.
- Hierarchical-based methods: This clustering approach typically seeks to construct a hierarchy of clusters, i.e., a tree structure. There are two possibilities: (1) agglomerative hierarchical clustering, that works by sequentially merging similar clusters - "bottom-up" approach -, and (2) divisive hierarchical clustering, that works initially grouping all the observations into one cluster, and then successively splitting these clusters - "top-down" approach -.
- Grid-based methods: These algorithms partition the data space into a finite number of cells to form a grid structure, and then form clusters from the cells in the grid structure. This clustering approach is especially suitable to deal with massive datasets.
- Model-based methods: These algorithms can be of two main types, depending on if they use statistical learning, or if they are based on a method of neural network learning.
- Constraint-based methods: A clustering approach that uses application or user-oriented constraints to incorporate domain knowledge.

On the other side, association is a learning technique that uses different rules to identify new and relevant insights between different objects in a set, or frequent pattern in transactional data or any type of relational database.

And finally, dimension reduction is a learning technique used when the number of features (or dimensions) in a given dataset is too high. The objective in this case is to reduce the number of data inputs to a manageable size while also preserving the data integrity. Sarker (2021) remarks that high-dimensional data processing is a challenging task for both researchers and application developers, and dimensionality reduction decreases a model's complexity by eliminating the irrelevant or less important features and allows for faster training of Machine Learning algorithms. This is important because it leads to better human interpretations, lower computational costs, and minimizes overfitting and increases the model's accuracy. Dimensionality reduction can be done through a process of feature selection that keeps a subset of the original features, or through a process of feature extraction that creates brand new features.

Most popular clustering algorithm is probably K-means clustering that assign similar data points into groups, where the *k* value represents the size of the grouping and granularity (Choi et al., 2018; Khanum, Mahboob, Imtiaz, Ghafoor, & Sehar, 2015; Saker, 2021). Other clustering algorithms include Mean-shift clustering, Density-based spatial clustering of applications with noise (DBSCAN) or Gaussian Mixture

Models (GMMs). Association algorithms include Apriori, Equivalence Class Transformation (Eclat) and Frequent Pattern (F-P) Growth algorithms. Regarding dimension reduction, Chi-squared test, Analysis of Variance (ANOVA) test, Pearson's correlation coefficient, Recursive Feature Elimination (RFE), are some techniques commonly used for feature selection; and Principal Components Analysis (PCA) is often used for feature extraction.

The systematic review conducted by Alloghani et al. (2020) to analyze scholarly articles addressing or implementing supervised and unsupervised Machine Learning techniques in different problem-solving paradigms, revealed that, in the case of unsupervised learners, K-means, hierarchical clustering, and Principal Component Analysis emerged as the most commonly used techniques.

As in the case of Supervised Learning, Unsupervised Learning algorithms can have many practical applications. For example, a set of customer data with different attributes can be offered to the system. Then, taking these data into account, the system groups customers with similar attributes to later treat them in a similar way in marketing campaigns.

Another good example is facial recognition. In this case, the algorithm does not look for specific features, but rather a series of common patterns that indicate that it is the same face. The objective in this case is not to detect a specific type of data, as would be the case with images containing a certain object, but instead look for examples that look alike and can be grouped.

Other possible use cases and applications in which Unsupervised Machine Learning can be used are customer classification in a bank, patient classification in a hospital, market basket analysis (which items are bought together), customer clustering in retail (which stores people tend to visit together), content recommendations according to the user's consumption in streaming video or music platforms, or product recommendations according to users' profile in online shopping platforms.

Another interesting application of Unsupervised Learning algorithms is detecting cyber-attacks or intrusions. This is quite interesting, as with the increase in network connectivity in modern society, there is an escalation in cyber-crime activity, which prompts organizations to address network security issues by attempting to detect malicious activity using Machine Learning algorithms (Avinash, William, & Ryan, 2020).

This type of Machine Learning algorithms can also be useful to do data analysis in the astronomical field, such as, capturing new stars, new extraterrestrial planets, and even dark matter. As Unsupervised Learning is capable to find some potential quality that humans cannot, these can be useful when researchers observe some galaxies that have never been seen before, and there is no knowledge of them (Chen, Kong, & Kong, 2020).

In fact, Unsupervised Learning is a data-driven process widely used for extracting generative features, identifying meaningful trends and structures, groupings in results, and exploratory purposes (Sarker, 2021).

Finally, Figure 1 shows a comparison of Supervised and Unsupervised learning, highlighting the type of input data used in each case (labeled vs unlabeled data), and the main tasks both types of learning are mainly used for (classification, and regression vs clustering, association, and dimensionality reduction).

## Semisupervised Learning

Another possibility is Semisupervised Learning that combines labeled and unlabeled data during training. Semisupervised Learning can be defined as a hybrid of the above-described Supervised and Unsupervised Learning techniques, as it operates on both labeled and unlabeled data. Conceptually situated between learning with and without supervision (Supervised and Unsupervised learning), it permits harnessing the large amounts of unlabeled data available in many use cases in combination with typically smaller

*Figure 1. Supervised Learning vs Unsupervised Learning*

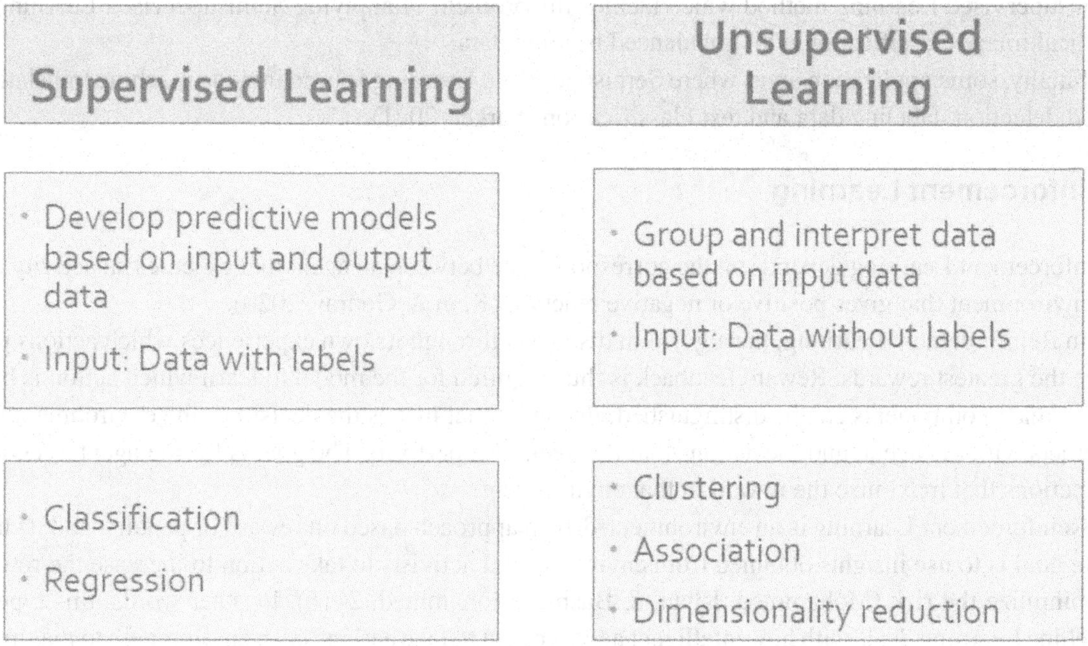

sets of labeled data (van Engelen & Hoos, 2020). The possibilities opened by Semisupervised learning are quite interesting as, in the real world, labeled data could be rare in several contexts, while unlabeled data are more frequent, and a Semisupervised Learning model can provide a better outcome for prediction than that produced using the labeled data alone from the model (Sarker, 2021).

ZhongKaizhu and Huang (2018) remark that Semisupervised Learning is an important area of Machine Learning that deals with problems that involve a lot of unlabeled data, and very scarce labeled data.

Consequently, candidate applications and use cases for Semisupervised Learning are those in which it is available only a small set of hard-to-obtain labeled examples, and a lot of easy-to-acquire unlabeled ones. This means that it would be possible to take any common Supervised task, such as a classification or a regression one, and transform it into a Semisupervised one.

Some authors like Dickson (2021) also explains that one way to do Semisupervised Learning is to combine clustering and classification algorithms. Clustering algorithms are Unsupervised Machine Learning techniques that group data together based on their similarities. The clustering model will help to find the most relevant samples in the data set. Then, it is possible to label those, and use them to train the Supervised Machine Learning model for the classification task.

This type of learning comes in handy when the labeling effort is too high to do throughout training. For example, Semisupervised Learning is ideal for medical images, where a small amount of training data can lead to a significant improvement in accuracy. In this case, a radiologist can label a small subset of computed tomography scans for tumors or diseases so the machine can more accurately predict which patients might require more medical attention (Delua, 2021).

In fact, medical image classification is often challenging for two reasons: (1) a lack of labeled examples due to expensive and time-consuming annotation protocols, and (2) imbalanced class labels due to the relative scarcity of disease-positive individuals in the wider population. Huynh, Nibali and He (2022) highlight that Semisupervised Learning methods deal with a lack of labels, but they generally do not address the problem of class imbalance. For this reason, these authors have purposed a perturbation-based Semisupervised Learning method which tackles the problem of applying Semisupervised Learning to medical image classification with imbalanced training data.

Finally, some application areas where Semisupervised Learning is used include machine translation, fraud detection, labeling data and text classification (Sarker, 2021).

## Reinforcement Learning

Reinforcement Learning depends on the correspondence between an agent that executes an activity and its environment that gives positive or negative reaction (Kaur & Gourav, 2020).

In Reinforcement Learning, the algorithm discovers through its own experiences which actions produce the greatest rewards. Reward feedback is thus required for the model to learn which action is best. Three main components can be distinguished: the agent that makes the decisions, the environment that interacts with the agent, and the actions that the agent can perform. The goal is for the agent to choose the actions that maximize the reward in that environment.

Reinforcement Learning is an environment-driven approach based on reward or penalty, and its ultimate goal is to use insights obtained from environmental activists to take action to increase the reward or minimize the risk (Mohammed, Khan, & Bashier Mohammed, 2016). In other words, this type of Machine Learning deals with how intelligent agents ought to take actions in an environment to maximize the cumulative reward.

Most popular Reinforcement Learning algorithms include Monte Carlo methods, Q-learning and Deep Q-learning (Sarker, 2021).

Reinforcement Learning is typically used in games, as for example, strategy games like chess. This type of learning is also a powerful tool for training Artificial Intelligence models that can help increase automation or optimize the operational efficiency of sophisticated systems such as autonomous driving tasks, manufacturing and supply chain logistics, however, this type of learning is not a good option for solving the basic or straightforward problems (Sarker, 2021).

Tanveer, Haider, Ali and Kim (2022) have conducted a 5G mobility management survey in Ultra-Dense Small Cells (UDSC) networks using Reinforcement Learning techniques. These authors discuss how this type of Machine Learning algorithms can help in different Handover scenarios. According to these authors, Machine Learning techniques are well capable to support 5G latest technologies that are expected to deliver high data rate to upcoming use cases and services such as Massive Machine Type Communications (mMTC), Enhanced Mobile Broadband (eMBB), and Ultra-Reliable Low Latency Communications (uRLLC).

Also, decision support systems based on Reinforcement Learning have been implemented to facilitate the delivery of personalized care (Liu et al., 2020). Other domains of application include operation research, robotics, economics, information theory, control theory, simulation based optimization, statistics and genetic algorithms (Kaur & Gourav, 2020).

## DEEP LEARNING

Machine Learning can be subdivided into shallow and Deep Learning, depending upon the structure and complexity of the algorithm (Cohen, 2021). For this reason, Deep Learning can be seen as subset of Machine Learning.

**U**

One question that arises is when it is appropriate to use Machine Learning algorithms and when it is more convenient to use Deep Learning algorithms. In relation to this question, Nichols, Herbert Chan and Baker (2019) explains that the choice of a particular Machine Learning algorithm for a given problem is determined by the characteristics of the data as well as the type of desired outcome. A primary consideration is the number of unique data points. Large data sets, of the order of $10^6$ unique data points, mean more sophisticated Deep Learning algorithms may be suitable. Fewer data points indicate that robust classical techniques like linear regression, or decision-tree methods which segment data sets into regions according to fixed rules, are likely to perform better. Care must be also taken to tailor the approach to the characteristics of the data, whether it is a collection of images, a time-series signal or general descriptive data.

Deep Learning tries to model high-level abstractions of data using multiple layers of neurons consisting of complex structures or non-linear transformations (Hao, Zhang, & Ma, 2016). Deep Learning uses Artificial Neural Networks (ANNs) with more than one hidden layer. These authors explain that with the increase of the amount of data and the power of computation, neural networks with more complex structures have attracted widespread attention and are being applied to various fields.

These deep networks cascade many layers of processing units for the extraction and transformation of features that occur among the observed data. The algorithms employed can be supervised or unsupervised. In Deep Learning, the scalability of neural networks is important as results get better with more data and larger models that in turn require more computation to train. Another benefit of Deep Learning models is their ability to perform automatic feature extraction from raw data (or feature learning). This means that algorithms must have the ability to exploit the unknown structure in the input distribution in order to discover good representations, often at multiple levels, with higher-level learned features defined in terms of lower-level features (Bengio, 2012).

As previously mentioned, currently, Deep Learning is considered a part of Machine Learning because Artificial Neural Networks solve the same type of problems as algorithms in this field. However, this area of work is growing rapidly and generating new expectations, which is why there are researchers who consider itself a branch within Artificial Intelligence.

Deep Learning domains of application include automatic speech recognition, natural language processing, audio recognition, or image and video reconstruction.

## Artificial Neural Networks

Artificial Neural Networks is a modelling technique inspired by the human nervous system that allows learning by example from representative data that describes a physical phenomenon or a decision process (Sadiq, Rodriguez, & Mian, 2019). This type of network consists of a layer of input nodes and a layer of output nodes, connected by one or more layers of hidden nodes. Input layer nodes pass information to hidden layer nodes by firing activation functions, and hidden layer nodes fire or remain dormant depending on the evidence presented. The hidden layers apply weighting functions to the evidence, and when the value of a particular node or set of nodes in the hidden layer reaches some threshold, a value is passed to one or more nodes in the output layer. These neural networks follow different types of architectures, the most widely used being the Multilayer Perceptron (MLP), the Convolutional Neural Network (CNN or ConvNet), the Generative Adversarial Network (GAN), and the Long Short-Term Memory Recurrent Neural Network (LSTM-RNN).

The Multilayer Perceptron is the base architecture of Deep Learning, i.e., a fully connected network consisting of an input layer, one or more hidden layers, and an output layer as described above. This architecture is sensitive to scaling features and allows a variety of hyperparameters to be tuned, such as the number of hidden layers, neurons, and iterations, which can result in a computationally costly model (Sarker, 2021).

The Convolutional Neural Networks are biologically inspired networks specifically designed to process pixel data. ConvNet are very similar to the regular neural networks as they are also made up of neurons with learnable weights. But, in contrast to MLPs, this type of network makes the explicit assumption that inputs have specific structure like images (Teuwen & Moriakov, 2020). ConvNet are widely used in various domains including image classification, object detection, face detection, facial expression recognition, or vehicle recognition (Indolia, Goswami, Mishra, & Asopa, 2018).

For its part, inspired by two-player zero-sum game, Generative Adversarial Networks comprise a generator and a discriminator, both trained under the adversarial learning idea (Wang et al., 2017). The generator is responsible for generating an object as realistic as possible by interacting with the discriminator. For example, the generator can generate an image, and the discriminator will determine if it is real (with a one) or false (with a zero). The discriminator behaves like an image classifier and the generator uses the feedback from this block together with a noise vector at its input to generate images that are as close to the original as possible. When the behavior of both blocks (generator and discriminator) is represented, it can be seen that, as time passes, the lines of the generator and the discriminator are closer and closer until, finally, they are one. This occurs at the moment when the training of the network converges and the discriminator can no longer distinguish between the real objects and the false ones generated. These types of networks have become a fundamental part in the use of Artificial Intelligence for creative activities such as image generation, art and music creation or realistic generation of faces that do not exist.

Finally, Long Short-term Memory networks are a special kind of Recurrent Neural Networks (RNN). Unlike standard feedforward neural networks, these networks have feedback connections, and can process not only single data points (such as images), but also entire sequences of data (such as speech or video). These networks are well-suited for analyzing and learning sequential data, such as classifying, processing, and predicting data based on time series data, which differentiates it from other conventional networks (Sarker, 2021). These networks have been used for dynamic system modelling in diverse application areas such as image processing, speech recognition, manufacturing, autonomous systems, communication or energy consumption (Lindemann, Müller, Vietz, Jazdi, & Weyrich, 2021); to classify network attacks (Muhuri, Chatterjee, Yuan, Roy, & Esterline, 2020); to predict nonlinear structural seismic response (Xu, Chen, Shen, & Xiang, 2022); or to detect violence in automated video surveillance (Roshan, Srivathsan, Deepak, & Chandrakala, 2021).

## FUTURE RESEARCH DIRECTIONS

Barro and Davenport (2019) highlight that the adoption of intelligent technologies will be essential for the survival of many companies. But simply implementing the newest technologies and automation tools won't be enough. Success will depend on whether organizations use them to innovate in their operations, and in their products and services, and whether they acquire and develop the human capital to do so.

The decision to use one or another type of Machine Learning, that is, Supervised, Unsupervised, Semisupervised or Reinforcement Learning will depend on the specific circumstances of each use case.

For example, it is important to take into account that in Supervised Learning human intervention is needed to label, classify, and enter the data in the algorithm, while in Unsupervised Learning input data is entered without labeling, and there is no need of human intervention. Also, in Unsupervised Learning, the system does not predict the correct output, as it happens in Supervised Learning, but instead, it explores the data and can draw inferences from datasets to describe hidden structures from unlabeled data. And, for its part, Semisupervised Learning is best to deal with problems that involve a lot of unlabeled data and very scarce labeled data. Finally, Reinforcement Learning enables an agent to learn in an interactive environment by trial and error using feedback from its own actions and experiences.

For its part, Deep Learning as a concept is very similar to Machine Learning, however it uses different algorithms. While Machine Learning works with regression algorithms or decision trees, Deep Learning uses Artificial Neural Networks that work in a very similar way to the biological neuronal connections of our brain. Machine Learning algorithms are mathematical algorithms that allow machines to learn by mimicking the way humans learn. On the other side, in the case of Deep Learning, algorithms try to imitate human perception inspired by the human brain and the connection between neurons. For this reason, it can be said that Deep Learning is the technique that is closest to the way humans learn.

Most Deep Learning methods use Neural Networks architecture. It is for this reason that Deep Neural Networks is often spoken of, instead of Deep Learning. As previously explained, the term deep is used to describe Artificial Neural Networks, and refers to the fact that these Neural Networks have a significant number of layers.

The success of an Artificial Intelligence model depends on both the data and the performance of the learning algorithms.

Having quality and reliable data is essential to ensure the effective operation of any type of Artificial Intelligence learning model. Without reliable and quality data, neither Machine Learning nor Deep Learning will be effective. The learning algorithms need to be trained through real-world data before the system can assist intelligent decision-making. However, to collect, clean and preprocess the data in a certain domain, such as agriculture or healthcare, is a challenging task. Counting with poor quality data can make learning models useless, or will produce lower accuracy. For this reason, the development of new data preparation techniques is a promising area for future research. On the other side, selecting an adequate learning algorithm for a target domain and application is a decision that must be carefully taken, as choosing a wrong learning algorithm would never produce a good result.

## CONCLUSION

Machine Learning is currently very prominent in our society. Nowadays, almost every common domain is powered by Machine Learning applications which are necessary to achieve target results efficiently, and this trend is expected to increase in the incoming years. Actually, many key areas including healthcare, education or digital marketing are major beneficiaries of Machine Learning.

One of the main strengths of Machine Learning is the possibility of causing profound transformations in very diverse areas. Things as different as a marketing campaign or a Learning Management System (LMS) can be totally transformed thanks to the use of Machine Learning. For this reason, the future of Machine Learning is exceptionally promising.

This chapter provides brief and clear descriptions of the main concepts related to Machine Learning (including Supervised Learning, Semisupervised Learning, Unsupervised Learning, and Reinforcement Learning), and explains the reader the relationship between Machine Learning and Artificial Intelligence and Deep Learning.

# REFERENCES

Alloghani, M., Al-Jumeily, D., Mustafina, J., Hussain, A., & Aljaaf, A. J. (2020). A systematic review on supervised and unsupervised machine learning algorithms for data science. In M. Berry, A. Mohamed, & B. Yap (Eds.), *Supervised and Unsupervised Learning for Data Science* (pp. 3–21). Springer. doi:10.1007/978-3-030-22475-2_1

Avinash, K., William, G., & Ryan, B. (2020). Network attack detection using an unsupervised machine learning algorithm. *Proceedings of Hawaii International Conference on System Sciences*. http://hdl.handle.net/10125/64537 doi:10.24251/HICSS.2020.795

Barro, S., & Davenport, T. H. (2019). People and machines: Partners in innovation. *MIT Sloan Management Review*, *60*(4), 22–28.

Bengio, J. (2012). Deep learning of representations for unsupervised and transfer learning. In *Proceedings of ICML Workshop on Unsupervised and Transfer Learning* (*vol. 27*, pp. 17–36). Academic Press.

Bonetto, R., & Latzko, V. (2020). Machine learning. In F. H. P. Fitzek, F. Granelli, & P. Seeling (Eds.), *Computing in Communication Networks, From Theory to Practice* (pp. 135–167). Academic Press. doi:10.1016/B978-0-12-820488-7.00021-9

Chen, Y., Kong, R., & Kong, L. (2020). Applications of artificial intelligence in astronomical big data. In L. Kong, T. Huang, Y. Zhu, & S. Yu (Eds.), *Big Data in Astronomy* (pp. 347–375). Elsevier. doi:10.1016/B978-0-12-819084-5.00006-7

Choi, R. Y., Coyner, A. S., Kalpathy-Cramer, J., Chiang, M. F., & Campbell, J. P. (2020). Introduction to machine learning, neural networks, and deep learning. *Translational Vision Science & Technology*, *9*(2), 14. doi:10.1167/tvst.9.2.14 PMID:32704420

Choy, G., Khalilzadeh, O., Michalski, M., Do, S., Samir, A. E., Pianykh, O. S., Raymond Geis, J., Pandharipande, P. V., Brink, J. A., & Dreyer, K. J. (2018). Current applications and future impact of machine learning in radiology. *Radiology*, *288*(2), 318–328. doi:10.1148/radiol.2018171820 PMID:29944078

Cohen, S. (2021). The basics of machine learning: strategies and techniques. In Artificial Intelligence and Deep Learning in Pathology. Elsevier. doi:10.1016/B978-0-323-67538-3.00002-6

Delua, J. (2021). *Supervised vs. unsupervised learning: What's the difference?* Retrieved 04/20/22 from https://www.ibm.com/cloud/blog/supervised-vs-unsupervised-learning

Dickson, B. (2021). *What is semi-supervised machine learning?* Retrieved 04/18/22 from https://bdtech-talks.com/2021/01/04/semi-supervised-machine-learning/

El Bouchefry, K., & de Souza, R. S. (2020). Learning in big data: Introduction to machine learning. In P. Škoda & F. Adam (Eds.), *Knowledge Discovery in Big Data from Astronomy and Earth Observation* (pp. 225–249). Elsevier. doi:10.1016/B978-0-12-819154-5.00023-0

Hao, X., Zhang, G., & Ma, S. (2016). Deep learning. *International Journal of Semantic Computing*, *10*(3), 417–439. doi:10.1142/S1793351X16500045 PMID:28113886

Huynh, T., Nibali, A., & He, Z. (2022). Semisupervised learning for medical image classification using imbalanced training data. *Computer Methods and Programs in Biomedicine, 216*, 106628. www.sciencedirect.com/science/article/pii/S016926072200013X doi:10.1016/j.cmpb.2022.106628

Indolia, S., Goswami, A. K., Mishra, S. P., & Asopa, P. (2018). Conceptual understanding of convolutional neural network - a deep learning approach. *Procedia Computer Science, 132*, 679–688. doi:10.1016/j.procs.2018.05.069

Jiang, T., Gradus, J. L., & Rosellini, A. J. (2020). Supervised machine learning: A brief primer. *Behavior Therapy, 51*(5), 675–687. https://www.sciencedirect.com/science/article/pii/S0005789420300678 doi:10.1016/j.beth.2020.05.002

Kaur, A., & Gourav, K. (2020). A study of reinforcement learning applications & its algorithms. *International Journal of Scientific & Technology Research, 9*(3), 4223–4228.

Khanum, M., Mahboob, T., Imtiaz, W., Ghafoor, H., & Sehar, R. (2015). A survey on unsupervised machine learning algorithms for automation, classification and maintenance. *International Journal of Computers and Applications, 119*(13), 34–39. doi:10.5120/21131-4058

Lindemann, B., Müller, T., Vietz, H., Jazdi, N., & Weyrich, M. (2021). A survey on long short-term memory networks for time series prediction. *Procedia CIRP, 99*, 650–655. https://www.sciencedirect.com/science/article/pii/S2212827121003796 doi:10.1016/j.procir.2021.03.088

Liu, S., See, K. C., Ngiam, K. Y., Celi, L. A., Sun, X., & Feng, M. (2020). Reinforcement learning for clinical decision support in critical care: Comprehensive review. *Journal of Medical Internet Research, 22*(7), e18477. doi:10.2196/18477

Mohammed, M., Khan, M. B., & Bashier Mohammed, B. E. (2016). *Machine Learning: Algorithms and Applications*. CRC Press. doi:10.1201/9781315371658

Muhuri, P. S., Chatterjee, P., Yuan, X., Roy, K., & Esterline, A. (2020). Using a long short-term memory recurrent neural network (LSTM-RNN) to classify network attacks. *Information (Basel), 11*(5), 243. doi:10.3390/info11050243

Nichols, J. A., Herbert Chan, H. W., & Baker, M. (2019). Machine learning: Applications of artificial intelligence to imaging and diagnosis. *Biophysical Reviews, 11*(1), 111–118. doi:10.100712551-018-0449-9 PMID:30182201

Ongsulee, P. (2017). Artificial intelligence, machine learning and deep learning. In *Proceedings of 15th International Conference on ICT and Knowledge Engineering (ICT&KE)* (pp. 1–6). 10.1109/ICTKE.2017.8259629

Raz, A. R., Llinas, J., Mittu, R., & Lawless, W. F. (2020). Engineering for emergence in information fusion systems: A review of some challenges. In W. F. Lawless, R. Mittu, & D. A. Sofge (Eds.), *Human-Machine Shared Contexts* (pp. 241–255). Academic Press. doi:10.1016/B978-0-12-820543-3.00012-2

Roshan, S., Srivathsan, G., Deepak, K., & Chandrakala, S. (2020). Violence detection in automated video surveillance: Recent trends and comparative studies. In D. Peter, A. H. Alavi, B. Javadi, & S. L. Fernandes (Eds.), *Intelligent Data-Centric Systems, The Cognitive Approach in Cloud Computing and Internet of Things Technologies for Surveillance Tracking Systems* (pp. 157–171). Academic Press. doi:10.1016/B978-0-12-816385-6.00011-8

Sadiq, R., Rodriguez, M. J., & Mian, H. R. (2019). Empirical models to predict disinfection by-products (DBPs) in drinking water: An updated review. In J. Nriagu (Ed.), *Encyclopedia of Environmental Health* (2nd ed., pp. 324–338). Elsevier. doi:10.1016/B978-0-12-409548-9.11193-5

Sarker, I. H. (2021). Machine learning: Algorithms, real-world applications and research directions. *SN Computer Science*, 2(3), 160. doi:10.100742979-021-00592-x PMID:33778771

Satinet, C., & Fouss, F. (2022). A supervised machine learning classification framework for clothing products' sustainability. *Sustainability*, 14(3), 1334. doi:10.3390u14031334

Subasi, A. (2020). Machine learning techniques. In A. Subasi (Ed.), *Practical Machine Learning for Data Analysis Using Python* (pp. 91–202). doi:10.1016/B978-0-12-821379-7.00003-5

Tanveer, J., Haider, A., Ali, R., & Kim, A. (2022). An overview of reinforcement learning algorithms for handover management in 5G ultra-dense small cell networks. *Applied Sciences (Basel, Switzerland)*, 12(1), 426. doi:10.3390/app12010426

Teuwen, J., & Moriakov, N. (2020). Convolutional neural networks. In S. K. Zhou, D. Rueckert, & G. Fichtinger (Eds.), *Handbook of Medical Image Computing and Computer Assisted Intervention* (pp. 481–501). Elsevier and MICCAI Society Book Series. doi:10.1016/B978-0-12-816176-0.00025-9

Uddamari, N., & Ubbana, J. (2021). A study on unsupervised learning algorithms analysis in machine learning. *Turkish Journal of Computer and Mathematics Education*, 12(14).

van Engelen, J. E., & Hoos, H. H. (2020). A survey on semi-supervised learning. *Machine Learning*, 109(2), 373–440. doi:10.100710994-019-05855-6

Wang, K., Gou, C., Duan, Y., Lin, Y., Zheng, X., & Wang, F. Y. (2017). Generative adversarial networks: introduction and outlook. *IEEE/CAA Journal of Automatica Sinica, 4*(4), 588–598. doi:10.1109/JAS.2017.7510583

Wang, P. (2019). On defining artificial intelligence. *Journal of Artificial General Intelligence*, 10(2), 1–37. doi:10.2478/jagi-2019-0002

Xu, Z., Chen, J., Shen, J., & Xiang, M. (2022). Recursive long short-term memory network for predicting nonlinear structural seismic response. *Engineering Structures, 250*, 113406. https://www.sciencedirect.com/science/article/pii/S0141029621015133 doi:10.1016/j.engstruct.2021.113406

ZhongKaizhu, G., & Huang, H. (2018). Semisupervised learning: Background, applications and future directions. Nova Science Publishers.

# ADDITIONAL READING

Alloghani, M., Al-Jumeily, D., Mustafina, J., Hussain, A., & Aljaaf, A. J. (2020). A systematic review on supervised and unsupervised machine learning algorithms for data science. In M. Berry, A. Mohamed, & B. Yap (Eds.), *Supervised and Unsupervised Learning for Data Science* (pp. 3–21). Springer. doi:10.1007/978-3-030-22475-2_1

Bonetto, R., & Latzko, V. (2020). Machine learning. In F. H. P. Fitzek, F. Granelli, & P. Seeling (Eds.), *Computing in Communication Networks, From Theory to Practice* (pp. 135–167). Academic Press. doi:10.1016/B978-0-12-820488-7.00021-9

Choi, R. Y., Coyner, A. S., Kalpathy-Cramer, J., Chiang, M. F., & Campbell, J. P. (2020). Introduction to machine learning, neural networks, and deep learning. *Translational Vision Science & Technology*, *9*(2), 14. doi:10.1167/tvst.9.2.14 PMID:32704420

Kaur, A., & Gourav, K. (2020). A study of reinforcement learning applications & its algorithms. *International Journal of Scientific & Technology Research*, *9*(3), 4223–4228.

Khanum, M., Mahboob, T., Imtiaz, W., Ghafoor, H., & Sehar, R. (2015). A survey on unsupervised machine learning algorithms for automation, classification and maintenance. *International Journal of Computers and Applications*, *119*(13), 34–39. doi:10.5120/21131-4058

Sarker, I. H. (2021). Machine learning: Algorithms, real-world applications and research directions. *SN Computer Science*, *2*(3), 160. doi:10.100742979-021-00592-x PMID:33778771

Subasi, A. (2020). Machine learning techniques. In A. Subasi (Ed.), *Practical Machine Learning for Data Analysis Using Python* (pp. 91–202). doi:10.1016/B978-0-12-821379-7.00003-5

van Engelen, J. E., & Hoos, H. H. (2020). A survey on semi-supervised learning. *Machine Learning*, *109*(2), 373–440. doi:10.100710994-019-05855-6

# KEY TERMS AND DEFINITIONS

**Artificial Neural Network:** A computing system inspired by the biological neural networks that constitute a human brain.

**Convolutional Neural Network:** A type of deep neural network designed for processing structured arrays of data and most commonly applied to analyze visual imagery because its ability to identify patterns in the input image, such as lines, gradients, circles, or even eyes and faces.

**Deep Learning:** It refers to Artificial Neural Networks and related Machine Learning algorithms that uses multiple layers of neurons. It is seen as a subset of Machine Learning in Artificial Intelligence.

**Generative Adversarial Network:** A type of deep neural network framework made of two neural networks (generator and discriminator) which compete against each other, and use a cooperative zero-sum game to learn. The generator is trained to produce fake data, and the discriminator tries to differentiate the generator's fake data from real examples.

**Long Short-Term Memory:** A type of deep neural network with a Recurrent Neural Network (RNN) architecture that, unlike standard feedforward neural networks, has feedback connections, and can process not only single data points (such as images), but also entire sequences of data (such as speech or video).

**Machine Learning:** It refers to a learning technique that gives machines the ability to learn without being explicitly programmed. It is seen as a subset of Artificial Intelligence.

**Reinforcement Learning:** It is a type of Machine Learning. The algorithm discovers through its own experiences which actions produce the greatest rewards.

**Semisupervised Learning:** It is a type of Machine Learning. A hybrid of Supervised and Unsupervised learning techniques that combines labeled and unlabeled data during training.

**Supervised Learning:** It is a type of Machine Learning. It is characterized by the use of labeled datasets to train algorithms that classify data or predict results accurately.

**Unsupervised Learning:** It is a type of Machine Learning. It uses learning algorithms to analyze and cluster unlabeled datasets. These algorithms focus on discovering hidden patterns or data groupings without the need for human intervention.

# Section 13
# Computational Statistics

# Effect of Large–Scale Performed Vedic Homa Therapy on AQI

**Rohit Rastogi**

https://orcid.org/0000-0002-6402-7638

*Dayalbagh Educational Institute, India & ABES Engineering College, India*

**Devendra Kumar Chaturvedi**

https://orcid.org/0000-0002-4837-2570

*Dayalbagh Educational Institute, India*

**Mamta Saxena**

*Independent Researcher, India*

**Sheelu Sagar**

*Amity University, Noida, India*

**Neeti Tandon**

*Vikram Unversity, Ujjain, India*

**T. Rajeshwari**

*Gayatri Chetna Kendra, Kolkata, India*

## INTRODUCTION

### Scientific Experiments and Analysis of Yajna Therapy

#### Air Purification

Dr. Mamta Saxena, Dir. Gen. in ministry of Statistics and Program Implementation conducted her experiments in joint collaboration with CPCB (Central Pollution Control Board, Delhi, India) The Study was done to check the effect of Yajna on pollutant gases like SO2 and NO2. (Pl. refer Fig. 1); (Rastogi, et al., 2021).

There are many other benefits are also there. When we give oblations (ahutis) with havishyanna (rice); it creates the cloud formation for pure rain that helps in harvest to get more crops. Fragrant medicinal herbs used for oblations helps in cleansing the thought patterns. Sweetened things used as oblations helps us to enhance our health, keeps us free from ailments. So we have to understand the purpose of Yagya and offer oblations accordingly. The cow ghee (clarified butter) is considered the best as it increases the level of Oxygen in the environment and helps to keep all beings healthy (Rastogi, et al., 2020a; Rastogi, et al., 2020b).

DOI: 10.4018/978-1-7998-9220-5.ch059

*Figure 1. Critical face of Air Pollution at Delhi, India*

National Botanical Research Institute at Lucknow has found through research that when Aahuti (oblations) are given by medicinal herbs; as prescribed in the scriptures found that along with firewood of mango tree, (1 kg. of firewood with half kg Hawan Samagri) reduces the bacteria up to 94% in the hall where Yajna activity has been done. The site maintained the atmospheric environment even after 24 hours. On doing Yajna, research was established repeatedly that the area was maintained with pollution free environment. This report was published in Ethno Pharmacology Research paper in December, 2007.

It was also mentioned that not only human beings, but Yajna and Mantra also work as anti- bacterial in all crops and vegetation, reducing the chemicalised fertilizers in larger extent. In all the above conditions, it is observed that our ancient procedure of Yajna is based on scientific background and also useful for the whole society. By doing daily Yajna at home one can prevent many pandemic infections. With less cost, and a maximum time of 10 minutes one can do this and by uplifting oneself with the society for an optimal health and environment.

Instructions for Yajna-Therapy are as below;

- As per the state of disease, mix 10% Clarified butter of Cow and give 21, 51 or 108 oblations of Gayatri Mantra, daily at dawn and dusk along with Cow-dung stick and Peepal Samidha.
- Keep open the doors and windows while doing Yajna.
- After Yajna, on peaceful and cool fire, as per the nature of disease, one forth Guggal and Clarified butter along with specified herbal mixture is placed and lightly burnt on fire and subject has to perform the selected Asan and Pranayam in the vaporized atmosphere as per state n symptoms of diseases.
- It is always well said in Indian Scriptures that "if one wants to get rid of all diseases, one should go for Yajna Therapy every day" as it's a preventive medicinal treatment to purify the environment and make the environment bacteria free.

- The vaporized medicinal herbal bath, Consuming Yajna Bhasma (ashes) and rubbing on external body organs is also useful in skin diseases.

## BACKGROUND

The Mantra works on subtle and casual bodies of the patient which is not possible in other modern pathies. They are simply working on that anatomy which can be seen in microscope i.e. on gross body merely. Neuro-Scientists, equipped with advanced brain-imaging tools, are beginning to quantify and confirm some of the health benefits of this ancient practice. There are specific mantra for specific problems and diseases. Without mantra the flame of Yajna is just like a flame of a furnace (Saxena, et al., 2018; Sharma, 2010).

One more part of the Yagyopathy is related to the micro part of organic and medicinal Havan Samgri which directly reaches in blood and works immediately on the problem area. All know that only it is the heat that can turn an element into it's smallest part but not only heat does so, it also enhances the power of element. One can know that when an element is in it's smallest form, it would be most powerful. Atom bomb is a simple example to understand the power of Atomic part of any element (Sanders, 2017; Rastogi, et al., 2020c).

Yajna and its effects on environment reveal that the ancient Indian traditions have shown many ways to keep society healthy, strong and successful. One of it as main and important way was doing Yagya because it not only cleanses the atmosphere, environment but also keeps pandemic creating viruses at bay by destroying them. In the celestial sphere by rotation and revolution of earth and Sun the seasons changes and different atmospheric conditions occurs (Rastogi, et al., 2020j; Rastogi, et al., 2020k).

Cold, hot, humid, dense air, light air, dust and smoke creates effects on atmosphere and its impact creates different kinds of viruses, their growth and their end keep going on as cycle, so the atmosphere sometimes becomes polluted and sometimes clear (McCorron, et al., 2018).

The virus enters the human body from this atmosphere. To keep these different viruses away and to have a pollution free environment our ancient sages and seers presented us with procedure of Yagya an amazing and matchless way for healthy society. The medicinal herbs and certain medicinal mixtures in the form of powder were used to attain the pollution free environment (Gupta, et al., 2012; Limaye, et al., 2019).

Formic Aldehyde gas is emitted whenever we use Samidha (firewoods) of the Mango tree and destroys all, life threatening, prevailing bacteria's, and Viruses from the atmosphere and makes the environment pollution free. When we offer Jaggery into oblations, it too provides the same effect. All plants that have medicinal properties are not necessarily can be used as Samidha; because those properties are converted into gaseous form, having chemical changes, that may be harmful (Nautiyal, et al., 2007).

Timru if not mistaken is what we call Chiraunji seeds used in the deserts, kheer (Sweet milk content) etc. It has oil. There are some plants used by Tantriks, when burnt, the inhaled fumigations can make a person insane. As per diet, a seed that increases omega, serotonin in your brain; will make you energetic, but too much serotonin will make you drowsy; (Golden eggs duck story) will be the outcome. Too much of anything is bad. That's why Timru Samidha may prove harmful. There are Ayurveda Acharyas in India, who can throw more light on this (Oprea, et al., 2011).

## EXPERIMENTAL SETUP AND METHDOLOGY

E

*Figure 2. The Air Veda Device installed at Different Centers for Measuring the AQI*

Yagya or Havan, the rituals in our culture has a vast meaning in it. Before getting into science let's understand the philosophy of yagya. During discussions on yagya and treatment of environment, human through yagya in a center, after explaining when the team started doing yagya so that all can participate, a few students were sulking back, on speaking to them got to know they are afraid of death? It was asked what's the connection between Yagya and Death (Rastogi, et al., 2020h; Rastogi, et al., 2020i).

Out came an astonishing reply, they were taught by someone " always remember Yagya reminds us this how we end, after death we will be cremated, burnt to ashes. The flame warns us to be on the righteous path and so on. It was explained to them the philosophy of Yagya (Ghorani, et al., 2016; Ghosh, et al., 2015; Karatzas, et al., 2010).

Air Veda Device was used and mounted at 23 pre decided stations to measure the pollutions and AQI. (Pl. refer Fig. 2 and Fig. 3).

Under Gruhe-Gruhe Gayatri Yagya Movement where more than 25 Thousands house hold entities performed Yajna at the same day and same time and Dr. Mamta Saxena, authors' team member, and Director General in Ministry of Statistics and Program implementation (MoS-PI) and her team analyzed the data (Rastogi, et al., 2020d).

*Figure 3. School going Students performing Yajna for Environmental Purification*

## RESULTS AND DISCUSSIONS

## Ujjain City - Live Monitoring Station Data of Mahkaleshwar

The Data was centrally collected at CPCB (Central Pollution Control Board), New Delhi, India.

The whole Experiment was conducted at Ujjain city Mahakaleshwar temple, M.P. India. They found the drastic change and reduction in the environmental pollution. Readings are as following (Pl. refer Table 1).

*Table 1. Comparative Analysis of AQI parameters on different days between mahakaleshwar and Motibagh colony, Ujjain, India*

| | Mahakaleshwar | | | MotiBagh Colony | | |
|---|---|---|---|---|---|---|
| From Date | PM2.5 | PM10 | AQI | PM2.5 | PM10 | AQI |
| 23-05-21 | 26.11 | 83.33 | 92.17 | 26.50 | 83.00 | 83.00 |
| 24-05-21 | 27.18 | 92.89 | 106.83 | 27.50 | 91.50 | 93.50 |
| 25-05-21 | 37.09 | 144.15 | 112.38 | 40.00 | 128.50 | 133.50 |
| 26-05-21 | 28.90 | 111.77 | 125.96 | 33.00 | 108.50 | 101.50 |
| 27-05-21 | 26.14 | 94.22 | 97.21 | 26.00 | 91.00 | 89.00 |

## Graphical Visualizations and Analysis

(Pl. refer Fig. 4) The Gruhe Gruhe Gayatri Yajna Activity was conducted in the mass level and sensors were placed at different locations. At Mahakaleshwar temple, Ujjain, the pollution control board has placed the AQI measurement devices which measured the PM 2.5 and PM10 level of Air quality between 23-27 May 2021.

Graphical Analysis shows that before one day on 25 may 2021, of the main event at Buddha poornima at 26 May 2021, The PM2.5 level was at its peak at the record of 144.15, which was much curtailed after the Mass Yajna event on 26 May and came down at 111.77 and till evening, on 27th may, it came down to 94.22 when all the activities were completed by the Gayatri Parivaar volunteers, and around 33% reduction consecutively was recorded after this mass event. It shows the high reduction in PM 2.5 which is much dangerous for human health and AQI was significantly improved.

*Figure 4. PM 2.5 and PM 10 level of AQI at MahaKaleshwar Temple, Ujjain, MP India after Grahe Grahe Gayatri Yajna Event on 23 to 27 May, 2021*

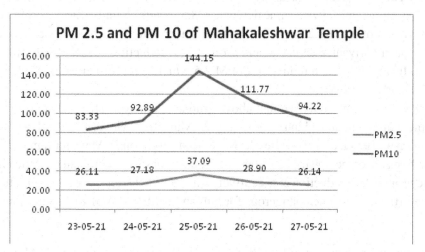

Regarding PM10, we can easily see that above graphical Analysis shows that before one day on 25 may 2021, of the main event at Buddha Poornima at 26 May 2021, The PM 10 level was at its peak at the record of 37.09, which was much curtailed after the Mass Yajna event on 26 May and came down at 28.9 and till evening, on 27th may, it came down to 26.14 when all the activities were completed by the Gayatri Parivaar volunteers, and around 43% reduction consecutively was recorded after this mass event. It shows the high reduction in PM 10 which is much dangerous for human health and AQI was significantly improved.

(Pl. refer Fig. 5) The Gruhe Gruhe Gayatri Yajna Activity was conducted in the mass level and sensors were placed at different locations. At Motibagh colony, Ujjain, the pollution control board has placed the AQI measurement devices which measured the PM 2.5 and PM10 level of Air quality between 23-27 May 2021.

*Figure 5. PM 2.5 and PM 10 level of AQI at Motibagh Colony, Ujjain, MP India after Grahe Grahe Gayatri Yajna Event on 23 to 27 May, 2021*

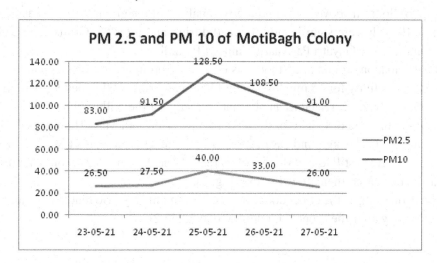

Graphical Analysis shows that before one day on 25 may 2021, of the main event at Buddha poornima at 26 May 2021, The PM 10 level was at its peak at the record of 128.5, which was much curtailed after the Mass Yajna event on 26 May and came down at 108.5 means around 20% reduction and till evening, on 27th may, it came down to 91.22 again 22% consecutive reduction when all the activities were completed by the Gayatri Parivaar volunteers, and around 23% reduction consecutively was recorded after this mass event. It shows the high reduction in PM 2.5 which is much dangerous for human health and AQI was significantly improved.

Regarding PM10, we can easily see that above graphical Analysis shows that before one day on 25 may 2021, of the main event at Buddha Poornima at 26 May 2021, The PM 10 level was at its peak at the record of40, which was much curtailed after the Mass Yajna event on 26 May and came down at 33 and till evening, on 27th may, it came down to 26 when all the activities were completed by the Gayatri Parivaar volunteers, and around 48% reduction consecutively was recorded after this mass event. It shows the high reduction in PM 10 which is much dangerous for human health and AQI was significantly improved.

*Figure 6. Comparative Analysis of AQI by PM 2.5 and PM 10 etc. parameters at Mahakaleshwar and Motibagh Colony, Ujjain, MP India after Grahe Grahe Gayatri Yajna Event on 23 to 27 May, 2021*

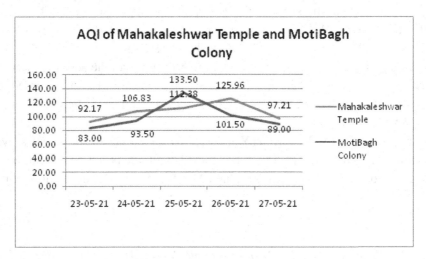

(Pl. refer Fig. 6) So from above both comparative analysis of the graphs, we can easily conclude that PM 2.5 and PM 10 both were significantly reduced during and after the Gruhe Gruhe Gayatri Yajna Activity was conducted by Gayatri Parivaar Ujjain, M.P., India.

The Mass participation around in 25 thousnds household brought significant changes in the AQI of the city. Daily Yajna activity for 15 min. to half and hour can bring AQI at better position significantly and Agnihotra therapy can be treated as an alternate remedy for the pollution control.

Here one can see the data of Ujjain for the next 10 days after 26th May. There is decrease in PM 2.5 and PM 10 as compared to background day of 25.5.21 until 4.6.21 after which PM 10 has risen to almost the same level bu PM 2.5 is still less. PM 2.5 had increased one day on 1.6.21 more than the background day figure but has decreased thereafter (Pl. refer Fig. 7).

So, it can be deduced that, the effect does not last for so many days. So that is why authors' team has shown for just one day after the event (Pl. refer the data table 2).

*Figure 7. PM 2.5 and PM 10 etc. parameters at Mahakaleshwar before and after the main event, a 10 days study at Ujjain, MP India after Grahe Grahe Gayatri Yajna Event on 26 May, 2021*

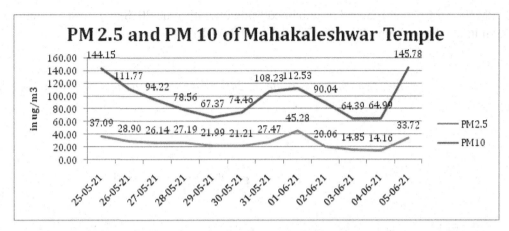

*Table 2. PM 2.5 and PM 10 etc. parameters at Mahakaleshwar before and after the main event, a 10 days study at Ujjain, MP India after Grahe Grahe Gayatri Yajna Event on 26 May, 2021*

|  | Mahakaleshwar Temple, Ujjain | |
|---|---|---|
| From Date | PM2.5 | PM10 |
| 25-05-21 | 37.09 | 144.15 |
| 26-05-21 | 28.90 | 111.77 |
| 27-05-21 | 26.14 | 94.22 |
| 28-05-21 | 27.19 | 78.56 |
| 29-05-21 | 21.99 | 67.37 |
| 30-05-21 | 21.21 | 74.46 |
| 31-05-21 | 27.47 | 108.23 |
| 01-06-21 | 45.28 | 112.53 |
| 02-06-21 | 20.06 | 90.04 |
| 03-06-21 | 14.85 | 64.39 |
| 04-06-21 | 14.16 | 64.99 |
| 05-06-21 | 33.72 | 145.78 |

## Gruhe Gruhe Yajna: External Experiments at Mass Level

24 June 2018 and 2 June 2019, Delhi NCR region conducted a mass experiment where 5 to 6 thousands households conducted Yajna process at their homes and the different pollutant component quantity were recorded in the atmosphere.

The daily based 24 hours annals were collected from 23 monitoring stations, equipped at different places of NCR and their average data was compiled.

## Experiment of 24 June, 2018

PM 2.5, PM10 and CO was reduced or remained same on 24th June 2018 in almost 16 stations out of 23 in Delhi in the day of Yajna (Pl. refer Fig. 8, Fig. 9, Fig. 10).

*Figure 8. PM 2.5 was reduced or remained same on 24th june 2018 in almost 16 stations out of 23 in Delhi in the day of Yajna*

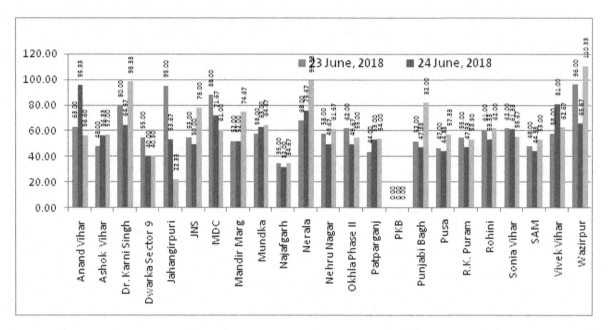

*Figure 9. PM 10 was reduced or remained same on 24th june 2018 in almost 21 stations out of 23 in Delhi in the day of Yajna*

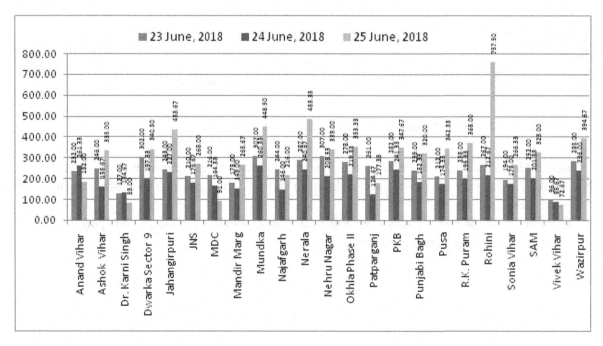

*Figure 10. CO was reduced or remained same on 24th june 2018 in almost 20 stations out of 23 in Delhi in the day of Yajna*

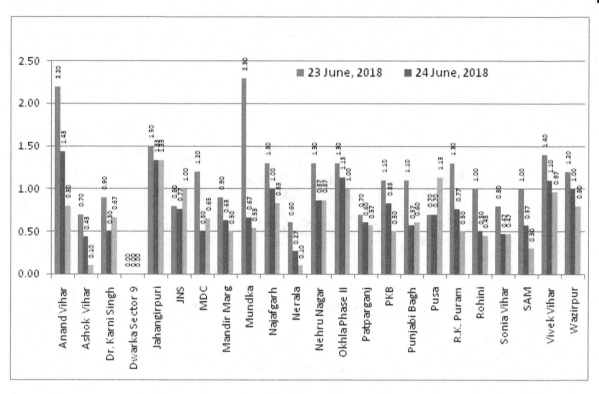

## Experiment of 2 June, 2019

Pl. refer Fig. 11, Fig. 12, Fig. 13 and Fig. 14 to check the effect on PM2.5, PM10, CO and NO2.

*Figure 11. PM10 was reduced or remained same on 2nd June, 2019 in almost 19 stations out of 16 in Delhi in the day of Yajna*

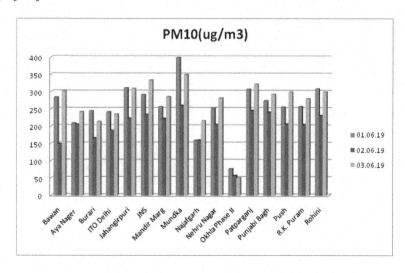

*Figure 12. PM2.5 was reduced or remained same on 2ⁿᵈ June, 2019 in almost 16 stations out of 19 in Delhi in the day of Yajna*

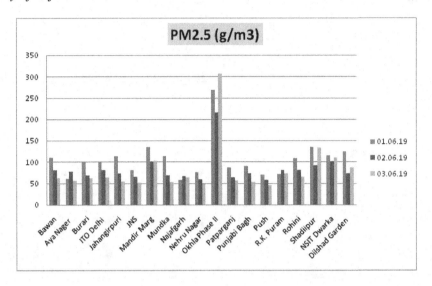

*Figure 13. CO was reduced or remained same on 2ⁿᵈ June, 2019 in almost 18 stations out of 19 in Delhi in the day of Yajna*

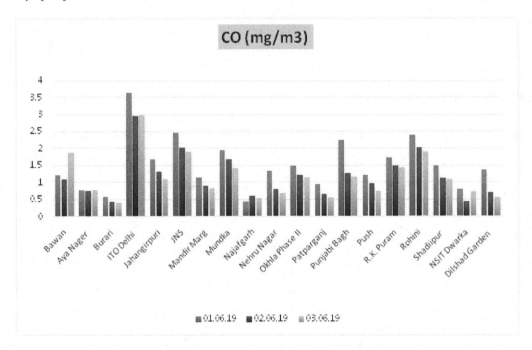

*Figure 14. NO2 was reduced or remained same on 2<sup>nd</sup> June, 2019 in almost 19 stations out of 19 in Delhi in the day of Yajna*

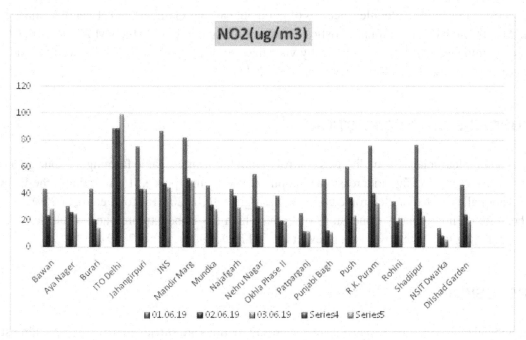

## Discussion

### Analysis of Results

The derivations from all the experiments were as below

Control on Pollution by Cow-dung based Samidha over mango wood was comparatively higher especially on PM2.5 and PM10.

Cow dung Samidha was used with quantity 30 gm. To conduct whole Yajna activity but the mango wood quantity should be 130 to 150 grams.

Clove of cow was used up to 20-30 grams and around 30-40 gm. Havan samagri of herbs was used. The amount of CO and other pollutant gaseous elements was at minimum level before taking Yajak (person doing Yajna) one's position. It was found to keep the water vessel (Kalash) at heights of 2 feet in Yagyashala that the level of $CO_2$ was continuously decreasing.

## RECOMMENDATIONS

The above graphs are valid to prove that Yajna reduces the air pollution at significant level. Yagya acts in a multiple dimension and clove used in this condense the air and the chemiacal reactions change the pollutant gaseous elements in to acceptable particles (MM Zaman, et al., 2015); (Apte, et al. 2016); (Rastogi, et al., 2020e).

## NOVELTY

This is a first of its kind the detailed analysis of pollutant gaseous elements and effect of Yajna to reduce them. Also through compurational statistics, the effect of Agnihotra over the PM 2.5, PM 10, CO2 and SO2 etc. Components have been graphically visualized to display the effect of this Vedic ritual on the environment (Cortes, et al., 2000; Chauhan, et al., 2015).

## FUTURE RESEARCH DIRECTIONS

Yajna is a complete sciencefrom diseases control to rain fall, from organic farming to cloud generation. Negative ions created y Yajna increase the happiness and mental peace. It also reduces the EMR flux and radiational pollution of electronic gadgets (Rastogi, et al., 2020f; Rastogi, et al., 2020g).

There are definitely many dimensions of Yajna which has to be explored and whole science community is getting fascinate towards it. (Dev, et al., 2017; Devender, et al., 2019).

## CONCLUSION

The graphical interpretations explained above in result sections are sufficient to display that almost in all the centers which were measuring the effect of Yajna over environmental conditions reported benefits and difefernt pollutant components were reduced even at the time of Yajna, after one day, four fays and seven days of the process.

Significant drop was recorded on PM 2.5, PM 10, SO2, NO2, CO and Benzene etc. when oblations were done with Vedic mantras. Hence we can conclude that Yajna is much significant and beneficial for mankinf in perspective of increasing global warming, pollution and pandemic based threats in 21st century. It ahs been an inevitable activity to be followed by all individual irresepective of any caste, creed, sect or culture and its scientific benefits will save the mankind from unforeseen and unprecedented threats.

## ACKNOWLEDGMENT

The Team of authors would love to pay our deep sense of gratitude to the ABES Engineering College, Ghaziabad & Amity International Business School, Amity University, and Noida for arranging us all the facilities, the direct-indirect supporters for their timely help and valuable suggestions and the almighty for blessing us throughout. We would also like to extend the vote of thanks to IIT Delhi, IIT Roorkee, Dev Sanskriti Vishwavidyalaya, Haridwar, Patanjali Foundation and Ayurveda Institute, Dehradun for their support and guidance in accomplishing our research paper.

## REFERENCES

ApteK.SalviS. (2016). Household air pollution and its effects on health. *F1000 Research, 5,* F1000 Faculty Rev-2593. doi:10.12688/f1000research.7552.1

Chauhan, P. (2015). An overview of air pollution in India at present scenario, *International Journal of Research Graant Halayah, 3*(1).

Cortés, U., Sànchez-Marrè, M., & Ceccaroni, L. (2000). Artificial Intelligence and Environmental Decision Support Systems. *Applied Intelligence, 13*(1). link.springer.com

Dev, M. (2017). Indian culture and lifestyle for environment conservation: A path towards Sustainable development. *International Journal on Emerging Technologies, 4*(1), 256-260.

Devender, K. (2019). Air pollution mitigation through yajna: Vedic and modern views. *Environment Conservation Journal, 20*(3), 57–60. doi:10.36953/ECJ.2019.20308

Ghorani-Azam, A., Riahi-Zanjani, B., & Balali-Mood, M. (2016). Effects of air pollution on human health and practical measures for prevention in Iran. *J Res Med Sci.* http://www.jmsjournal.net/text.asp?2016/21/1/65/189646 doi:10.4103/1735-1995.189646

Ghosh, D., & Parida, P. (2015). Air Pollution and India: Current Scenario. *International Journal of Current Research, 7*(11), 22194–22196.

Gupta, S. (2012). *Hawan for cleansing the Environment.* https://www.speakingtree.in>blog

Karatzas, K. (2010). Artificial Intelligence Applications in the Atmospheric Environment: Status and Future Trends. *Environmental Engineering and Management Journal, 9,* 171-180. doi:10.30638/eemj.2010.026

Limaye, V.G. (2019). Agnihotra (The Everyday Homa) and production of Brassinosteroids: A scientific validation. *International Journal of Modern Engineering Research, 8*(2), 41-51.

McCarron, G. (2018). Air Pollution and Human Health Hazards: a compilation of air toxins acknowledged by the gas industry in Queensland's Darling Downs. *International Journal of Environmental Studies, 75*(1), 171-185.

Nautiyal, C. S., Chauhan, P. S., & Nene, Y. L. (2007, December 3). Medicine smoke reduces air born bacteria. *Journal of Ethnopharmacology, 114*(3), 446–451. doi:10.1016/j.jep.2007.08.038 PMID:17913417

Oprea, M., & Iliadis, L. (2011). An Artificial Intelligence-Based Environment Quality Analysis System. In L. Iliadis & C. Jayne (Eds.), *Engineering Applications of Neural Networks. EANN 2011, AIAI 2011. IFIP Advances in Information and Communication Technology* (Vol. 363). Springer. doi:10.1007/978-3-642-23957-1_55

Rastogi, Chaturvedi, Gupta, & Singhal. (2020f). Intelligent Mental Health Analyzer by Biofeedback: App and Analysis. In *Handbook of Research on Optimizing Healthcare Management Techniques.* IGI Global. doi:10.4018/978-1-7998-1371-2.ch009

Rastogi, Chaturvedi, & Gupta, (2020i). Exhibiting App and Analysis for Biofeedback Based Mental Health Analyzer. In *Handbook of Research on Advancements of Artificial Intelligence inHealthcareEngineering.* . doi:10.4018/978-1-7998-2120-5

Rastogi, Chaturvedi, & Gupta. (2020j). Computational Approach for Personality Detection on Attributes: An IoT-MMBD Enabled Environment. In *Handbook of Research on Advancements of Artificial Intelligence in Healthcare Engineering.* Doi: doi:10.4018/978-1-7998-2120-5

Rastogi, Chaturvedi, & Gupta (2020k). Tension Type Headache: IOT and FOG Applications in Health-care Using Different Biofeedback. *Handbook of Research on Advancements of Artificial Intelligence in Healthcare Engineering.* Doi: . doi:10.4018/978-1-7998-2120-5

Rastogi, R., & Chaturvedi, D. K. (2020d). Intelligent Personality Analysis on Indicators in IoT-MMBD Enabled Environment. In Multimedia Big Data Computing for IoT Applications: Concepts, Paradigms, and Solutions. Springer Nature. doi:10.1007/978-981-13-8759-3_7

Rastogi, R., & Chaturvedi, D. K. (2020g). Surveillance of Type –I & II Diabetic Subjects on Physical Characteristics: IoT and Big Data Perspective in Healthcare @NCR, India. doi:10.1007/978-3-030-37468-6_23

Rastogi, R., Chaturvedi, D. K., Gupta, M., Sirohi, H., Gulati, M., & Pratyusha. (2020h). Analytical Observations Between Subjects' Medications Movement and Medication Scores Correlation Based on Their Gender and Age Using GSR Biofeedback. In *Pattern Recognition Applications in Engineering* (pp. 229-257). IGI Global. . doi:10.4018/978-1-7998-1839-7.ch010

Rastogi, R., Chaturvedi, D. K., Satya, S., Arora, N., Gupta, M., Verma, H., & Saini, H. (2020c). An Optimized Biofeedback EMG and GSR Biofeedback Therapy for Chronic TTH on SF-36 Scores of Different MMBD Modes on Various Medical Symptoms. In Studies Comp. Intelligence, Vol. 841: Hybrid Machine Intelligence for Medical Image Analysis. doi:10.1007/978-981-13-8930-6_8

Rastogi, R., Chaturvedi, D. K., Satya, S., Arora, N., Trivedi, P. M., Gupta, M., Singhal, P., & Gulati, M. (2020e). MM Big Data Applications: Statistical Resultant Analysis of Psychosomatic Survey on Various Human Personality Indicators. Proceedings of Second International Conference on Computational Intelligence 2018. 10.1007/978-981-13-8222-2_25

Rastogi, R., Chaturvedi, D. K., Verma, H., Mishra, Y., & Gupta, M. (2020a). Identifying Better? Analytical Trends to Check Subjects' Medications Using Biofeedback Therapies. *International Journal of Applied Research on Public Health Management, 5*(1). doi:10.4018/IJARPHM.2020010102

Rastogi, R., Gupta, M., & Chaturvedi, D.K. (2020b). Efficacy of Study for Correlation of TTH vs Age and Gender Factors using EMG Biofeedback Technique. *International Journal of Applied Research on Public Health Management, 5*(1), 49-66. . doi:10.4018/IJARPHM.2020010104

Rastogi, R., Saxena, M., Gupta, M., Rastogi, A. R., Kumar, P., Jain, M., & Srivatava, P. (2021). Happiness Index and Gadget Radiation Analysis on Yajna and Mantra Chanting Therapy in South Asian Continent: COVID-19 vs. Ancient Rich Culture from Vedic Science. *International Journal of International Commission on Radiological Protection (ICRP) Health Systems and Translational Medicine, 1*(1), 1–46. doi:10.4018/IJHSTM.2021010101

Sanders, C. L. (2017). *Radiobiology and Radiation Hormesis.* Springer. doi:10.1007/978-3-319-56372-5

Saxena, M., Sharma, M., Sain, M. K., Bohra, G., & Sinha, R. (2018). Yagya reduced level of indoor Electro-Magnetic Radiations (EMR). *Interdisciplinary Journal of Yagya Research, 1*(2), 22–30. doi:10.36018/ijyr.v1i2.12

Sharma, S. (2010). *Super Science of Gayatri. Revised Edition. Mathura-India: Yug Nirman Yojana Vistar Trust, Gayatri Tapobhumi.* http://literature.awgp.org/book/Super_Science_of_Gayatri/v1

Zaman Tanim. (2015). *Electromagnetic Radiation and Human Health.* Technical Report.

## ADDITIONAL READING

Mills, A. (2009, June 29). Kirlian Photography. *History of Photography*, *33*(3), 278–287. doi:10.1080/03087290802582988

Sia, P. D. (2016). *Mindfulness: Consciousness and Quantum Physics*. University of Padova.

Smith, J. A., Suttie, J., Jazaieri, H., & Newman, K. M. (2018). *Things We Know About the Science of Meditation*. Mindfulness Research.

Sui, C. K. (2012). *Pranic Energy: Feel Divinity All Around You*. IJITEE.

## KEY TERMS AND DEFINITIONS

**Ayurveda:** Ayurveda system of medicine with historical roots in the Indian subcontinent. Globalized and modernized practices derived from Ayurveda traditions are a type of alternative medicine. In countries beyond India, Aurvedic therapies and practices have been integrated in general wellness applications and in some cases in medical use. The main classical Ayurveda texts begin with accounts of the transmission of medical knowledge from the Gods to sages, and then to human physicians. In SushrutaSamhita (Sushruta's Compendium), Sushruta wrote that Dhanvantari, Hindu god of Ayurveda.

**Emission of Gases:** A greenhouse gas (sometimes abbreviated GHG) is a gas that absorbs and emits radiant energy within the thermal infrared range. Greenhouse gases cause the greenhouse effect on planets. The primary greenhouse gases in Earth's atmosphere are water vapor ($H_2O$), carbon dioxide ($CO_2$), methane ($CH_4$), nitrous oxide ($N_2O$), and ozone ($O_3$). Without greenhouse gases, the average temperature of Earth's surface would be about $-18$ °C (0 °F), rather than the present average of 15 °C (59 °F). The atmospheres of Venus, Mars and Titan also contain greenhouse gases.

**Energy Measurements:** There are various kind of units used to measure the quantity of energy sources. The Standard unit of Energy is known to be Joule (J). Also, other mostly used energy unit is kilowatt /hour (kWh) which is basically used in electricity bills. Large measurements may also go up to terawatt/hour (TWh) or also said as billion kW/h. Other units used for measuring heat include BTU (British thermal unit), kilogram calorie (kg-cal) and most commonly Tonne of Oil Equivalent. Actually it represents the quantity of heat which can be obtained from a tonne of oil. Energy is also measured in some other units such as British Thermal Unit(BTU), calorie, therm, etc which varies generally according to their area of use.

**Jap:** Jap is the meditative repetition of a mantra or a divine name. It is a practice found in Hinduism, Jainism, Sikhism, Buddhism, and Shintoism. The mantra or name may be spoken softly, enough for the practitioner to hear it, or it may be spoken within the reciter's mind. Jap may be performed while sitting in a meditation posture, while performing other activities, or as part of formal worship in group settings.

**Machine Learning:** Machine learning (ML) is the study of computer algorithms that improve automatically through experience. It is seen as a subset of artificial intelligence. Machine learning algorithms build a mathematical model based on sample data, known as "training data", in order to make predictions or decisions without being explicitly programmed to do so. Machine learning algorithms are used in a wide variety of applications, such as email filtering and computer vision, where it is difficult or infeasible to develop conventional algorithms to perform the needed tasks.

**Mantra:** A mantra is a sacred utterance, a numinous sound, a syllable, word or phonemes, or group of words in Sanskrit believed by practitioners to have psychological and/or spiritual powers. Some mantras have a syntactic structure and literal meaning, while others do not.

**PM Level:** Particulates – also known as atmospheric aerosol particles, atmospheric particulate matter, particulate matter (PM), or suspended particulate matter (SPM) – are microscopic particles of solid or liquid matter suspended in the air. The term aerosol commonly refers to the particulate/air mixture, as opposed to the particulate matter alone. Sources of particulate matter can be natural or anthropogenic. They have impacts on climate and precipitation that adversely affect human health, in ways additional to direct inhalation. Types of atmospheric particles include suspended particulate matter, thoracic and respirable particles, inhalable coarse particles, designated PM10, which are coarse particles with a diameter of 10 micrometers (µm) or less, fine particles, designated PM2.5, with a diameter of 2.5 µm or less, ultrafine particles, and soot.

**Pollution:** Pollution is the introduction of contaminants into the natural environment that cause adverse change. Pollution can take the form of chemical substances or energy, such as noise, heat or light. Pollutants, the components of pollution, can be either foreign substances/energies or naturally occurring contaminants. Pollution is often classed as point source or nonpoint source pollution. In 2015, pollution killed 9 million people in the world. The major kinds of pollution, usually classified by environment, are air pollution, water pollution, and land pollution. Modern society is also concerned about specific types of pollutants, such as noise pollution, light pollution, and plastic pollution. Pollution of all kinds can have negative effects on the environment and wildlife and often impacts human health and well-being.

**Sanskrit:** Sanskrit is an Indo-Aryan language of the ancient Indian subcontinent with a 3,500-year history. It is the primary liturgical language of Hinduism and the predominant language of most works of Hindu philosophy as well as some of the principal texts of Buddhism and Jainism. Sanskrit, in its variants and numerous dialects, was the lingua franca of ancient and medieval India. In the early 1st millennium AD, along with Buddhism and Hinduism, Sanskrit migrated to Southeast Asia, parts of East Asia and Central Asia, emerging as a language of high culture and of local ruling elites in these regions.

**Sensor and IoT:** The internet of things (IoT) is a system of interrelated computing devices, mechanical and digital machines provided with unique identifiers (UIDs) and the ability to transfer data over a network without requiring human-to-human or human-to-computer interaction. Sensorsare devices that detect and respond to changes in an environment. Inputs can come from a variety of sources such as light, temperature, motion, and pressure. Sensors output valuable information and if they are connected to a network, they can share data with other connected devices and management systems. They are an integral part of the Internet of Things (IoT). There are many types of IoT sensors and an even greater number of applications and use cases.

**Vedic:** The Vedic period or Vedic age (c. 1500 – c. 500 BCE), is the period in the history of the northern Indian subcontinent between the end of the urban Indus Valley Civilization and a second urbanization which began in the central Indo-Gangetic Plain c. 600 BCE. It gets its name from the Vedas, which are liturgical texts containing details of life during this period that have been interpreted to be historical and constitute the primary sources for understanding the period. These documents, alongside the corresponding archaeological record, allow for the evolution of the Vedic culture to be traced and inferred.

**Yajna:** Yajna literally means "sacrifice, devotion, worship, offering", and refers in Hinduism to any ritual done in front of a sacred fire, often with mantras. Yajna has been a Vedic tradition, described in a layer of Vedic literature called Brahmanas, as well as Yajurveda. The tradition has evolved from offering oblations and libations into sacred fire to symbolic offerings in the presence of sacred fire (Agni).

# Imputation–Based Modeling for Outcomes With Ceiling and Floor Effect

**Selen Yilmaz Isikhan**

 https://orcid.org/0000-0002-3725-2987
*Hacettepe University, Turkey*

**Gozde Erturk Zararsiz**
*Erciyes University, Turkey*

## INTRODUCTION

Data with ceiling or floor effects frequently occur in psychology and educational researches, and even in the evaluation of treatment effect, well-being, and responses from scales such as health-related quality of life in clinical studies. According to the definitions in some studies (Reissmann et al., 2022), ceiling or floor effects occur when the questionnare is relatively easy or difficult, so that a significant proportion of individuals will achieve maximum or minimum scores (Liu & Wang, 2021). The ceiling effect occurs at the top of a scale range, while the floor effect occurs at the lower end of the scale range. When floor or ceiling effects occur, actual differences between individuals with the lowest (or largest) possible score are indistinguishable.

Limited information is available about the scores of those who actually scored at the bottom or the ceiling. Scores on the floor and ceiling are said to be censored because only the lower and upper limit of the score is known (McBee, 2010). The highest (or lowest) possible value of a measurement tool is called the censoring point (Gustavsen et al., 2022). For instance, scenarios such as the following can be considered to define floor and ceiling effective scores in clinical studies. When patients are tested for pain degrees after surgery, patients report pain degrees between 0-10. In this case, depending on the time passed after surgery, many patients may have a score of "0" or many patients may report the pain they feel distinctly as "10." Another example is that, in the audiology department, a 5-point Likert scale questionnaire can be applied to patients who have a unilateral implant or bilateral implants to measure the success in hearing after a while. In this case, the actual hearing success (development) of those who answer the question as "5" may differ from each other. Therefore, the hearing achievement test has a very low ceiling for distinguishing the true hearing level of patients who score their hearing achievement as "5."

The main purpose of this chapter is to compare the performances of a few commonly used estimation methods in the solution of ceiling and floor effect observations (i.e., excluding ceiling and floor effective observations, Tobit regression, and zero-inflated regression) and the regression-based imputation method that considers these observations as missing data in the missing not at random (MNAR) structure (Loos et al., 2022).

DOI: 10.4018/978-1-7998-9220-5.ch060

## BACKGROUND

Ignoring the observations with ceiling or floor effect and analyzing this type of data with classical statistical analysis methods causes problems such as biased, artificial, and nonlinear solutions or the regression coefficients being insignificant (Yenilmez et al., 2018).

As a first method, (Liu & Wang, 2021) applied t-test and ANOVA by ignoring the ceiling observations (i.e., assuming the real value). As a second method, they suggested removing ceiling effective observations. As a third method, they showed censored regression, that is, Tobit regression. As a final method, they proposed an adjusted mean and variance estimation based on the truncated distribution. However, their second approach may not yield good results when the number of observations is insufficient. For this reason, estimating ceiling effective observations as if they were missing data by regression-based imputing according to the MNAR approach, instead of removing problematic observations, formed the basis of this study.

Very few studies have examined and compared the regression-based methods used to estimate the outcome variable with ceiling and floor effect. In some identified studies, methods such as ordinary least square (OLS) regression, ridge regression, Tobit regression, and beta regression were examined (Ogundimu & Collins, 2018; Sayers et al., 2020; Taku et al., 2018).

## METHODS

In the following subsections, the authors explain Tobit regression, zero-inflated Poisson regression, which are the main estimation methods the authors considered in the study, and the regression-based imputation method proposed for ceiling and floor effective observations, respectively.

### Tobit Regression

The Tobit model, also known as the censored regression model, was developed to predict linear relationships between variables when there is left or right censoring in the dependent variable. The Tobit model is defined as a latent variable model. The Tobit regression model basically improved as a left-censored model as follows:

$$y_i^* = x_i'\beta + u_i \, , \, u_i \sim N(0, \sigma^2) \tag{1}$$

$a$ defines the censoring point:

$$y_i = y_i^* \, y_i^* > a \tag{2}$$

$$y_i = a \, y_i^* \le a \tag{3}$$

Here, $y_i$ is an observed value that is equal to $y_i^*$ when $y_i^* > a$, and $y_i = a$ when $y_i^* \le a$. On the other hand, the right-censored Tobit model can be defined as follows:

$$y_i^* = x_i'\beta + u_i \, , \, u_i \sim N(0, \sigma^2) \tag{4}$$

$b$ is the censoring point:

$$y_i = y_i^* \quad y_i^* < b \tag{5}$$

$$y_i = b \quad y_i^* \geq b \tag{6}$$

In this case, $y_i$ is an observed value that is equal to $y_i^*$ when $y_i^* < b$, and $y_i = b$ when $y_i^* \geq b$. The latent variable $y_i^*$ satisfies the classical linear model assumption.

Substituting the Tobit regression model in Equation (1), the following equation is obtained:

$$y_i = x_i'\beta + u_i, \, y_i^* > a \tag{7}$$

$$y_i = a, \, y_i^* \leq a \tag{8}$$

The Tobit regression model is solved with the maximum likelihood estimator with the help of the probability equation, which is a combination of the probability density functions of the censored and uncensored observations (Yenilmez et al., 2018).

## Zero-Inflated Poisson Regression

In the Poisson regression, the dependent variable $y$ is modeled as follows:

$$P\left(y_i\right) = \frac{e^{\lambda_i}\lambda_i^{y_i}}{y_i!} \tag{9}$$

Here, the conditional variance is equal to the conditional mean:

$$E(y_i\backslash x_i) = V(y_i\backslash x_i) = \lambda_i = exp(x_i^T\beta) \tag{10}$$

Log-likelihood function of Poisson regression is:

$$l(\beta) = \sum_{i=1}^{n}\left[y_i x_i^T \beta - \exp\left(x_i^T\beta\right) - \ln\left(y_i!\right)\right] \tag{11}$$

The $\beta$ regression coefficients can be estimated using the maximum likelihood method. The derivative of the log-likelihood function with respect to $\beta$ is set to zero:

$$\frac{dl\left(\beta\right)}{d\beta} = \sum_{i=1}^{y}\left(y_i - e^{x_i^T\beta}\right)x_i = 0 \tag{12}$$

The zero-inflated Poisson distribution is a modification of the known poisson distribution with an excessive amount of zeros in the data (Weisburd et al., 2022). The basic idea is that the data come from two different states. In the first case the result is always counted as zero, while in the second case the counts follow a standard poissonian process:

$$Pr[y_i \in D_1] = w_i \; ; \; Pr[y_i \in D_1] = (1-w_i) \tag{13}$$

Then, the probability function is:

$$P(y_i) = w_i + (1 - w_i)e^{-\lambda_i} \qquad y_i = 0 \tag{14}$$

$$(1 - w_i)\frac{\lambda_i^{y_i} e^{-\lambda_i}}{y_i!} \qquad\qquad y_i > 0 \tag{15}$$

As with the Poisson distribution, covariates enter the model via the conditional mean of the Poisson distribution:

$$\lambda_i = \exp(x_i^T \beta) \tag{16}$$

Here, $x_i'$ is the (1*k) dimensional matrix of the i'th observation over the covariants, and $\beta$ is the (k*1) coefficients vector. Expected value and variance are as follows:

$$E[y_i \backslash x_i] = (1 - w_i)\lambda i \text{ and } Var\left[y_i \backslash x_i\right] = (1 - w_i)(\lambda_i + w_i\lambda_i^2) \tag{17}$$

According to Lambert (1992), it is common and convenient to model $w_i$ using a good logit model (Lambert, 1992):

$$w_i = \left[exp(z_i'\gamma)\right] / \left[1 + exp(z_i'\gamma)\right] \tag{18}$$

$z_i$ is the vector (1*p) of the i-th observation on some covariant, and $\gamma$ is the vector of the additional parameters (p*1). When n independent samples occur, the log-likelihood function is as follows:

$$Log L(\beta, \gamma) = \sum_{y_i=0} log\left[\exp(z_i'\gamma) + \exp(-\exp(x_i'\beta))\right]$$
$$+ \sum_{y_i \neq 0}\left[y_i x_i'\beta - \exp(x_i'\beta) - \log(y_i!)\right] - \sum_{i=1}^{n}\log\left[1 + \exp(z_i'\gamma)\right] \tag{19}$$

The first line and the last term are the log likelihood for $w_i$, and the intermediate term is the log likelihood of the standard poisson distribution.

In this study, the regression-based imputation method, whose performance the authors want to examine in addition to the classical methods, is explained in detail in the next section. The main purpose of trying this method is that the repetitive (problematic) observations of the scale question can be brought closer to the scores in the range of the scale questions, and the difficulty level of the questions can be adjusted better. In other words, the goal is to bring these problematic observations closer to their actual scores. At this stage, first of all, the randomness of the missing data should be examined with the help of independent variables, assuming that the dependent variable values with ceiling or floor effect are missing data. Following this, not available (NA) value assignment is made to the largest and smallest values with ceiling or floor effects by treating them as missing data. Then, a linear regression model is created for the part of the data that is not missing. This model is tested over the independent variables in the entire data set, and predictions of the values, assigned to NA, are obtained. These estimation values can be obtained sometimes higher than the upper limit "b" for the values with ceiling effect and smaller than the lower limit "a" for the floor effect values.

## Estimation with Regression-Based Imputation Method in Ceiling and Floor Effects

### Missing Data Identification for Ceiling Effect

The randomness of the missing data was investigated by assuming observations with a score of 100 in the outcome variable as "missing data." Values equal to 100 in the HEAR-QL-26 were encoded as 1, and values below 100 as 0. Whether these two groups were homogeneously distributed among variables that were previously found significant was examined using the Pearson Chi-Square test (Table 1). The missing data rates, namely the observation rates with ceiling, were found to be statistically significantly different among the hearing groups (p <0.001). While the rate of missing data is 49.2% in those with normal hearing, there are almost no patients with missing data in the other two groups. On the other hand, as a result of the analysis made according to the mother's education level and health insurance variables, there was no difference in the distribution of missing data between the groups (p ≥ 0.05). For this reason, in this case, the missing data (repetitive 100s) are a type of MNAR structure, so the best possible solution is to use one of the special modeling methods for missing observations (KA et al., 2022). Since the variable with missing data is the dependent variable, estimation values were assigned via regression-based imputation method, instead of the values of 100 in this variable. As explained above; basic steps such as testing the randomness of the ceiling observations, assigning values to ceiling effected observations with MNAR structure based on regression and creating a final model are visualized in Figure 1.

*Table 1. Examination of missing data type for HEAR-QL score*

| Variable | | Not Missing | Missing = 100 | p-Value |
|---|---|---|---|---|
| **Degree of hearing loss** | Hearing is normal | 61 (50.8) | 59 (49.2) | <0.001 |
| | Moderate hearing loss | 14 (100) | 0 (0) | |
| | Severe hearing loss | 114 (99.1) | 1 (0.9) | |
| **Maternal education** | Primary school | 55(83.3) | 11(16.7) | 0.380 |
| | Middle school | 27(79.4) | 7(20.6) | |
| | High school | 40(72.7) | 15(27.3) | |
| | University | 56(70) | 24(30) | |
| | MSc/PhD | 11(78.6) | 3(21.4) | |
| **Health insurance** | Social security institution | 131 (72.8) | 49 (27.2) | 0.151 |
| | Pension fund | 42 (82.4) | 9 (17.6) | |
| | Green card | 16 (88.9) | 2 (11.1) | |

*Figure 1. Assignment and modeling steps for ceiling observations*

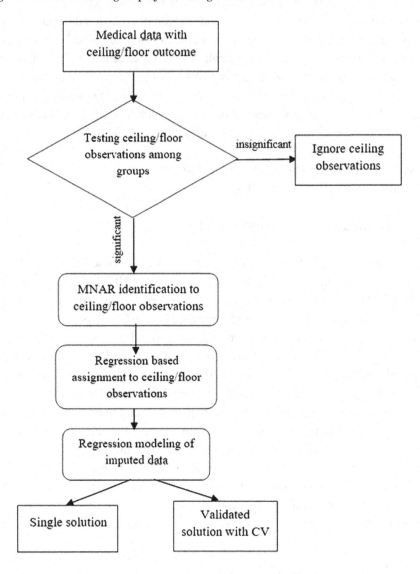

## Material

### Data Sets

In application, the performances were evaluated on two data sets, one was real clinical data and the other was synthetic data related to the health sector. The first data set was used from a master's thesis in Hacettepe University Health Sciences Institute Audiology program, with the approval of thesis advisor Assoc. Dr. Merve Batuk. The research group for the child version of the HEAR-QL-26 (The Effect of Listening Environments and Reflections on Quality of Life Scale) consists of 249 child participants, 119 of whom have normal hearing and 130 of whom have hearing loss. The degree of hearing loss (none, moderate, and high), maternal education (primary school, middle school, high school, undergraduate, and M.bachelor/PhD), and health insurance (social security institution, pension fund, and green card) were used as explanatory variables, whereas HEAR-QL total score was used as a dependent variable. The ceiling effect rate on the HEAR-QL-26 outcome variable was 24%.

As a second data set, The United States National Medical Expenditure Survey (NMES) data for the years 1987-1988 were used in comparison of the methods (Kleiber & Zeileis, 2008). The data set was taken from the "AER" package of the R statistical software (Kleiber et al., 2020). The response variable "yi: the number of doctor's office visits" was modeled with the help of 4 covariates. These are: "x1: number of chronic diseases," "x2: health insurance," "x3: years of education," and "x4: gender." In the latter data, "the number of doctor's office visits," which is the outcome variable, has 16% floor effective observations. Table 2 provides summary statistics of the datasets.

*Table 2. Descriptive statistics of data sets*

| Data Set 1 | | | | |
|---|---|---|---|---|
| | $\bar{x} \pm sd$ | Min-Max | Median | Ceiling Effect (%) |
| **HEAR-QL total score** | 80.46±21.46 | 5.16-100 | 89.25 | 60/249 = 24% |
| | **Frequency** | **Percent (%)** | | |
| **Degree of hearing loss** | | | | |
| None | 120 | 48.2 | | |
| Moderate | 14 | 5.6 | | |
| High | 115 | 46.2 | | |
| **Maternal education** | | | | |
| Primary school | 66 | 26.5 | | |
| Middle education | 34 | 13.7 | | |
| High school | 55 | 22.1 | | |
| University | 80 | 32.1 | | |
| M. Bachelor/PhD | 14 | 5.6 | | |
| **Health insurance** | | | | |
| Social security institution | 180 | 72.3 | | |
| Pension fund | 51 | 20.5 | | |
| Green card | 18 | 7.2 | | |
| Data Set 2 | | | | |
| | $\bar{x} \pm sd$ | Min-Max | Median | Floor Effect (%) |
| **Number of visits** | 5.77±6.75 | 0-89 | 4.00 | 683/4406=16% |
| **Number of chronic diseases** | 1.54±1.34 | 0-8.00 | 1.00 | |
| **Health insurance (Yes/No)** | 3421/985 | | | |
| **Year of education** | 10.29±3.73 | 0-18.00 | 11.00 | |
| **Gender (Frequency)(F/M)** | 2628/1778 | | | |

The solution of both data sets with the estimation methods was firstly obtained on the whole data set individually. In addition, the performances of the considered estimation methods on the data sets were verified with 500 repetitive cross-validation (CV) by dividing the data sets into 70% training set and 30% testing set. In the performance comparison of the methods, the regression coefficients ($\hat{\beta}$), standard errors and p-values for the variables in the model, as well as the root mean square error (RMSE) and mean absolute deviation (MAD) criteria were taken into account. The VGAM package of R (Yee et al.,

2021) was used for Tobit regression and pscl package (Jackman, 2017) was used for zero-inflated Poisson regression. Regression-based imputation and related predictions were also carried out by R codes.

## SOLUTIONS AND RECOMMENDATIONS

The HEAR -QL total score was significantly skewed to the left, with 24% of the participants scoring the highest (100) (Figure 2). Some subdimensions of HEAR -QL also have the highest score (100) ranging from 20% to 60%. The distributions of the original total HEAR-QL score and its regression-based imputed version by accepting ceiling observations as missing data are depicted in Figure A-D, respectively. After the regression-based imputation, the authors applied to the observations with ceiling effect, the HEAR-QL variance decreased slightly, and at the same time the left skewness decreased.

*Figure 2. Distribution of total HEAR-QL score A) and B) original values, C) and D) ceiling observations accepted as missing data and distribution after regression based imputation*

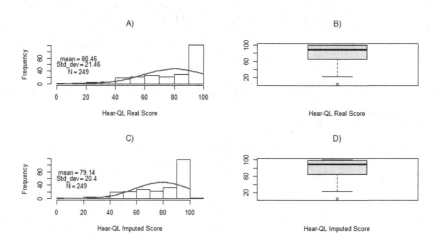

Considering Table 3 for the first data set, based on the standard errors of the regression coefficients, their p-values, and the RMSE estimates, the regression-based assignment method provided the best performance thanks to the significant decrease in the RMSE estimates, the reasonable standard errors of the coefficients, and the significant p-values. However, the negative aspect of this solution is that the $R^2$ measure shows inconsistent results, as some observation values are replaced with estimates.

When the estimation performances of physician office visits having floor effect were examined, the regression-based imputation method provided the best decrease in terms of RMSE and MAD criteria. However, the regression-based imputation method gave weak results in terms of both the $R^2$ criterion and the significance of the coefficients (p-value). When zero-inflated Poisson regression and Tobit regression were evaluated, all explanatory variables in the model were found to be significant (p < 0.001), and $R^2$, RMSE, and MAD criteria were obtained very close to the findings of the OLS method.

Table 5 and Table 6 provide the validated solutions of the datasets by CV with 500 repetitions (70% train and 30% training set). Single solutions of the methods were more overfit than solutions with 500 replicates of validation. In particular, the standard errors of the regression coefficients and the RMSE

*Table 3. Estimation results of the total score on hearing quality with ceiling effect*

| Parameter/Method | OLS Ignoring Ceiling | OLS Omitting Observations with Ceiling | Regression-Based Imputation | Tobit Regression (Ceiling Point 100) |
|---|---|---|---|---|
| Estimation ( $\hat{^2}$ ) | | | | |
| Constant | 96.193 | 93.189 | 93.189 | 103.416<br>2.736 |
| Degree of hearing loss | -11.150 | -10.363 | -10.363 | -13.441 |
| Maternal education | 1.723 | 1.988 | 1.988 | 2.080 |
| Health insurance | -2.780 | -2.986 | -2.986 | -3.812 |
| **Standard error** | | | | |
| Degree of hearing loss | 0.583 | 0.566 | 0.566 | 0.731 |
| Maternal education | 0.652 | 0.635 | 0.635 | 0.808 |
| Health insurance | 1.387 | 1.350 | 1.350 | 1.678 |
| **p-value** | | | | |
| Degree of hearing loss | <0.001 | <0.001 | <0.001 | <0.001 |
| Maternal education | 0.009 | 0.019 | 0.002 | 0.010 |
| Health insurance | 0.040 | 0.097 | 0.028 | 0.023 |
| $R^2$ | 0.621 | 0.508 | 0.605 | 0.621 |
| RMSE | 13.29 | 14.95 | 12.94 | 14.07 |
| MAD | 10.25 | 10.76 | 9.85 | 10.52 |

values in Table 3 were lower than those in Table 5. In Table 5, maternal education and health insurance variables were not found to be statistically significant in the first two methods for the first data set (known OLS and OLS by subtracting ceiling-effected observations) ($p \geq 0.05$). The regression-based imputation method provided the best performance, both with a significant decrease in the standard errors of the regression coefficients compared to other methods and with the smallest RMSE (Table 5). These findings are consistent with the single solution performances in Table 3.

Similarly, in Table 6, the estimates of standard errors and RMSE measure increased slightly compared to the single solutions of the floor effect data set. However, the smallest RMSE and standard error estimates for the floor effected data set were obtained by the regression-based imputation method. When both the significance of the coefficients and the RMSE criteria were evaluated, the performance of the zero-inflated poisson regression was found to be quite close to the performance of the linear model, which is found by ignoring the floor effected values. Although Tobit regression found all variables in the model statistically significant in floor-effect data, it was determined that the RMSE value and the standard errors of the coefficients increased.

## FUTURE RESEARCH DIRECTIONS

In this study, the performances of different estimation methods were evaluated on two different data sets with both ceiling effect and floor effect. The findings were then confirmed by CV performances of 500 replicates generated in R. In the study, regression-based imputation technique in the estimation of

*Table 4. Estimation results of the number of visits to the physician's office with floor effect*

| Parameter/Method | OLS Ignoring Ceiling | Regression-Based Imputation | Zero-Inflated Poisson Model | | Tobit Regression (Floor Point: 0) |
|---|---|---|---|---|---|
| Estimation ( $\hat{}^2$ ) | | | Count Model | Zero-Inflation Model | |
| Constant | 2.016 | 3.832 | 1.466 | -0.081 | 0.022 1.990 |
| Number of chronic patients | 1.343 | 1.139 | 0.154 | -0.569 | 1.657 |
| Health insurance | 0.999 | 0.444 | 0.070 | -0.744 | 1.588 |
| Year of education | 0.112 | 0.086 | 0.013 | -0.055 | 0.154 |
| Gender | -0.610 | -0.356 | -0.056 | 0.405 | -0.908 |
| **Standard error** | | | | | |
| Number of chronic patients | 0.072 | 0.068 | 0.004 | 0.043 | 0.084 |
| Health insurance | 0.248 | 0.235 | 0.017 | 0.101 | 0.293 |
| Year of education | 0.027 | 0.026 | 0.001 | 0.012 | 0.032 |
| Gender | 0.199 | 0.188 | 0.013 | 0.088 | 0.233 |
| **p-value** | | | | | |
| Number of chronic patients | <0.001 | <0.001 | <0.001 | <0.001 | <0.001 |
| Health insurance | <0.001 | 0.058 | <0.001 | <0.001 | <0.001 |
| Year of education | <0.001 | <0.001 | <0.001 | <0.001 | <0.001 |
| Gender | 0.002 | 0.058 | <0.001 | <0.001 | <0.001 |
| R² | 0.080 | 0.082 | 0.079 | | 0.079 |
| RMSE | 6.485 | 6.122 | 6.491 | | 6.545 |
| MAD | 4.202 | 3.653 | 4.211 | | 4.061 |

ceiling and floor-effect dependent variable with regression provided lower regression error estimation (RMSE) for both data types compared to other methods. However, the validation results found with 500 CV, especially for the floor effect data set, made some regression coefficients meaningless, although the regression-based imputation method provided the smallest estimations in RMSE and standard error.

In (Liu & Wang, 2021), among the 1-3 methods, method 2 (i.e., extracting data with ceilings) gave the highest type 1 error rate, followed by method 1 (i.e., treating ceiling data as real data), followed by method 3 (i.e., censored regression). As the ceiling proportion increased, the confidence interval coverage ratios were also lower than 95%. As a result, they stated that they obtained the lowest accuracy in their iterative simulations in the case of method 2 (i.e., removing the ceiling observations). In the authors' validation results for the floor effective data set, the p-value of the two variables was not found to be significant with the regression-based imputation method. Apart from this, p < 0.05 was provided in all of the other three methods. (Altun, 2018), who proposed zero-inflated Poisson-Lindley regression, again found it to be more successful than Poisson regression and its zero-inflated versions in estimating the number of floor-effective physician office visits. Standard errors and p-values of the coefficients were obtained close to each other in all methods, and these findings are also in line with the authors' results.

Ghassemi et al. (2020) obtained the best model from multiple linear regression in the case where the response variable was normally distributed and there was no censoring (ceiling and floor effect). On the other hand, in a high censoring (28.89% of the ceiling effect) data set and a response variable with

*Table 5. Prediction performances of regression methods on ceiling-effected HEAR-QL total score (cross-validation with 500 repetitions)*

| Method | OLS Ignoring Ceiling | | | OLS Omitting Observations with Ceiling | | |
|---|---|---|---|---|---|---|
| Parameter | $\hat{\beta}^2$ ±SE | p-Value | RMSE | $\hat{\beta}^2$ ±SE | p-Value | RMSE |
| Constant | 96.29±3.45 | <0.001 | | 93.81±4.56 | <0.001 | |
| Degree of hearing loss | -11.17±0.69 | <0.001 | 13.26 | -10.58±0.95 | <0.001 | 14.93 |
| Maternal education | 1.65±0.78 | 0.064 | | 1.86±0.99 | 0.100 | |
| Health Insurance | -2.77±1.67 | 0.159 | | -2.81±2.05 | 0.238 | |
| **Method** | **Regression-Based Imputation** | | | **Tobit Regression (Ceiling Point 100)** | | |
| Parameter | $\hat{\beta}^2$ ±SE | p-Value | RMSE | $\hat{\beta}^2$ ±SE | p-Value | RMSE |
| Constant | 93.83±3.37 | <0.001 | | 103.38±4.29 | <0.001 | |
| Degree of hearing loss | -10.58±0.68 | <0.001 | 12.95 | -13.48±0.87 | <0.001 | 14.34 |
| Maternal education | 1.87±0.76 | 0.033 | | 2.05±0.97 | 0.055 | |
| Health insurance | -2.83±1.63 | 0.142 | | -3.72±2.01 | 0.100 | |

almost normally distributed (p-value of skewness < 0.05), the appropriate model according to the AIC criteria was detected by Tobit regression (Qasemi et al., 2020). Qasemi et al. (2020) found that RMSE standard scale for the classic Tobit model was 28.74, which is much higher than the standard scale for the multiple linear regression model (14.23). They reported that the best model for the high censoring was CLAD. Examining the deep learning approach with mean imputation of missing data, (Jang et al., 2020) found that zero-inflated denoising convolutional autoencoder method exhibited the smallest RMSE of standard deviation for their two datasets. McBee (2010) compared the known OLS regression method with the Tobit regression model with a summary simulation study on the ceiling effective data set (McBee, 2010). As a result, Tobit regression showed findings closer to OLS solutions of uncensored data compared to OLS on the censored sample (500 repetitions). More recently, Pellekooren et al. (2022) used OLS and Tobit regression models to estimate patients' EQ-5D-3L utility scores from the Oswestry Disability index and compared the findings (Pellekooren et al., 2022). They found that OLS and Tobit models had a more or less similar $R^2$ (range 45-52%) and RMSE (range 0.21-0.22) in all models.

## CONCLUSION

The literature review highlighted few publications considered observations with ceiling and floor effects as missing data and the analysis obtained by regression-based imputation comparing with the performance of other methods. In this study, regression-based imputation method provided the best performance on the data with ceiling effect according to both single and 500 repetition CV validation results, while the weakest performance was obtained by OLS via removing observations with ceiling effect.

*Table 6. Floor effect estimation performance of regression methods for number of physician office visits (500 repeated CV)*

| Method | OLS Ignoring Ceiling | | | Regression-Based Imputation | | |
|---|---|---|---|---|---|---|
| Parameter | $\hat{\beta} \pm$ SE | p-Value | RMSE | $\hat{\beta} \pm$ SE | p-Value | RMSE |
| Constant | 2.01±0.40 | <0.001 | | 3.82±0.38 | <0.001 | |
| Number of chronic patients | 1.34±0.08 | <0.001 | | 1.14±0.08 | <0.001 | |
| Health insurance | 1.00±0.29 | <0.001 | 6.49 | 0.44±0.28 | 0.148 | 6.132 |
| Year of education | 0.11±0.03 | 0.003 | | 0.08±0.03 | 0.015 | |
| Gender | -0.61±0.23 | 0.022 | | -0.36±0.22 | 0.160 | |
| **ZIP (Count Model)** | | | | **Tobit Regression** | | |
| Parameter | $\hat{\beta} \pm$ SE | p-Value | RMSE | $\hat{\beta} \pm$ SE | p-Value | RMSE |
| Constant | 1.46±0.02 | <0.001 | | 0.02±0.48 | 0.663 | |
| Number of chronic patients | 0.15±0.00 | <0.001 | | 1.65±0.10 | <0.001 | |
| Health insurance | 0.07±0.02 | 0.025 | 6.50 | 1.59±0.35 | <0.001 | 6.55 |
| Year of education | 0.01±0.00 | 0.002 | | 0.15±0.03 | 0.001 | |
| Gender | -0.05±0.01 | 0.030 | | -0.92±0.27 | 0.003 | |
| **Zero-Inflation Model** | | | | | | |
| Parameter | $\hat{\beta} \pm$ SE | p-Value | | | | |
| Constant | -0.09±0.16 | 0.560 | | | | |
| Number of chronic patients | -0.56±0.05 | <0.001 | | | | |
| Health insurance | -0.74±0.12 | <0.001 | | | | |
| Year of education | -0.05±0.01 | 0.001 | | | | |
| Gender | 0.41±0.10 | 0.001 | | | | |

On the other hand, for floor effect data set, again according to the performances of both single and CV validations, while Tobit regression showed the weakest performance, the regression-based imputation method showed the best performance. However, the regression-based imputation method in the floor-effect data set distorted the significance of some regression coefficients. Especially in the estimation of the ceiling effective outcome variable by regression-based imputation, although there was instability in $R^2$ performance, significant decreases were obtained in the RMSE or regression error estimation. The main reason for the inconsistency in $R^2$ values is that Tobit regression gives the result of pseudo-$R^2$ instead of the known $R^2$ measure reported in linear regression (Boulton & Williford, 2018; Oliveira et al., 2022). The findings in this chapter are a preliminary evaluation and the authors aim to examine the method performances with further simulation trials depending on the changing parameter adjustments.

# REFERENCES

Altun, E. (2018). A new zero-inflated regression model with application. *İstatistikçiler Dergisi: İstatistik ve Aktüerya, 11*(2), 73-80.

Boulton, A. J., & Williford, A. (2018). Analyzing skewed continuous outcomes with many zeros: A tutorial for social work and youth prevention science researchers. *Journal of the Society for Social Work and Research, 9*(4), 721–740. doi:10.1086/701235

Gustavsen, G. W., Berglann, H. B., Jenssen, E., Kårstad, S., & Rodriguez, D. G. P. (2022). The Value of Urban Farming in Oslo, Norway: Community Gardens, Aquaponics and Vertical Farming. *International Journal on Food System Dynamics, 13*(1), 17–29.

Jackman, S. (2017). pscl: Classes and methods for R developed in the political science computational laboratory. United States Studies Centre, University of Sydney. Sydney. New South Wales, Australia. R package version, 1(2).

Jang, J.-H., Choi, J., Roh, H. W., Son, S. J., Hong, C. H., Kim, E. Y., Kim, T. Y., & Yoon, D. (2020). Deep Learning Approach for Imputation of Missing Values in Actigraphy Data: Algorithm Development Study. *JMIR mHealth and uHealth, 8*(7), e16113. doi:10.2196/16113 PMID:32445459

KA, N. D., Tahir, N. M., Abd Latiff, Z. I., Jusoh, M. H., & Akimasa, Y. (2022). Missing data imputation of MAGDAS-9's ground electromagnetism with supervised machine learning and conventional statistical analysis models. *Alexandria Engineering Journal, 61*(1), 937–947. doi:10.1016/j.aej.2021.04.096

Kleiber, C., & Zeileis, A. (2008). *Applied econometrics with R*. Springer Science & Business Media. doi:10.1007/978-0-387-77318-6

Kleiber, C., Zeileis, A., & Zeileis, M. A. (2020). Package 'aer'. *R package version 1.2, 4*.

Lambert, D. (1992). Zero-inflated Poisson regression, with an application to defects in manufacturing. *Technometrics, 34*(1), 1–14. doi:10.2307/1269547

Liu, Q., & Wang, L. (2021). t-Test and ANOVA for data with ceiling and/or floor effects. *Behavior Research Methods, 53*(1), 264–277. doi:10.375813428-020-01407-2 PMID:32671580

Loos, N. L., Hoogendam, L., Souer, J. S., Slijper, H. P., Andrinopoulou, E.-R., Coppieters, M. W., ... van der Avoort, D.-J. J. (2022). Machine Learning Can be Used to Predict Function but Not Pain After Surgery for Thumb Carpometacarpal Osteoarthritis. *Clinical Orthopaedics and Related Research, 10*, 1097.

McBee, M. (2010). Modeling outcomes with floor or ceiling effects: An introduction to the Tobit model. *Gifted Child Quarterly, 54*(4), 314–320. doi:10.1177/0016986210379095

Ogundimu, E. O., & Collins, G. S. (2018). Predictive performance of penalized beta regression model for continuous bounded outcomes. *Journal of Applied Statistics, 45*(6), 1030–1040. doi:10.1080/0266 4763.2017.1339024

Oliveira, J. S., Ifie, K., Sykora, M., Tsougkou, E., Castro, V., & Elayan, S. (2022). The effect of emotional positivity of brand-generated social media messages on consumer attention and information sharing. *Journal of Business Research, 140*, 49–61. doi:10.1016/j.jbusres.2021.11.063

Pellekooren, S., Ben, Â. J., Bosmans, J. E., Ostelo, R. W., van Tulder, M. W., Maas, E. T., ... van Hooff, M. L. (2022). Can EQ-5D-3L utility values of low back pain patients be validly predicted by the Oswestry Disability Index for use in cost-effectiveness analyses? *Quality of Life Research: An International Journal of Quality of Life Aspects of Treatment, Care and Rehabilitation, 31*(7), 1–13. doi:10.100711136-022-03082-6 PMID:35040002

Qasemi, Z., Yaseri, M., & Hosseini, M. (2020). Selection of appropriate model for quality of life data of strabismus patients despite censorship. *Journal of Biostatistics and Epidemiology, 6*(3), 221–233.

Reissmann, D. R., Aarabi, G., Härter, M., Heydecke, G., & Kriston, L. (2022). Measuring oral health: the Physical Oral Health Index: Physical Oral Health Index (PhOX). *Journal of Dentistry, 118*, 103946. doi:10.1016/j.jdent.2022.103946 PMID:35017019

Sayers, A., Whitehouse, M. R., Judge, A., MacGregor, A. J., Blom, A. W., & Ben-Shlomo, Y. (2020). Analysis of change in patient-reported outcome measures with floor and ceiling effects using the multilevel Tobit model: A simulation study and an example from a National Joint Register using body mass index and the Oxford Hip Score. *BMJ Open, 10*(8), e033646. doi:10.1136/bmjopen-2019-033646 PMID:32859657

Taku, K., Iimura, S., & McDiarmid, L. (2018). Ceiling effects and floor effects of the posttraumatic growth inventory. *Journal of Child and Family Studies, 27*(2), 387–397. doi:10.100710826-017-0915-1

Weisburd, D., Wilson, D. B., Wooditch, A., & Britt, C. (2022). Count-Based Regression Models. In *Advanced Statistics in Criminology and Criminal Justice* (pp. 233–271). Springer. doi:10.1007/978-3-030-67738-1_6

Yee, T. W., Yee, M. T., & VGAMdata, S. (2021). *Package 'VGAM'*. Academic Press.

Yenilmez, İ., Kantar, Y. M., & Acitas, S. (2018). Estimation of censored regression model in the case of non-normal error. *Sigma Journal of Engineering and Natural Sciences, 36*, 513–521.

## ADDITIONAL READING

Ali, E. (2022). A simulation-based study of ZIP regression with various zero-inflated submodels. *Communications in Statistics. Simulation and Computation*, 1–16. doi:10.1080/03610918.2022.2025840

Crambes, C., & Henchiri, Y. (2019). Regression imputation in the functional linear model with missing values in the response. *Journal of Statistical Planning and Inference, 201*, 103–119. doi:10.1016/j.jspi.2018.12.004

Isikhan, S. Y., Karabulut, E., Samadi, A., & Kılıçkap, S. (2019). Adaptation of Error Adjusted Bagging Method for Prediction. *International Journal of Data Warehousing and Mining, 15*(3), 28–45. doi:10.4018/IJDWM.2019070102

Resch, A., & Isenberg, E. (2018). How do test scores at the ceiling affect value-added estimates? *Statistics and Public Policy (Philadelphia, Pa.), 5*(1), 1–6. doi:10.1080/2330443X.2018.1460226

Šimkovic, M., & Träuble, B. (2019). Robustness of statistical methods when measure is affected by ceiling and/or floor effect. *PLoS One, 14*(8), e0220889. doi:10.1371/journal.pone.0220889 PMID:31425561

Simon, C. M., Wang, K., Shinkunas, L. A., Stein, D. T., Meissner, P., Smith, M., Pentz, R., & Klein, D. W. (2022). Communicating with diverse patients about participating in a biobank: A randomized multisite study comparing electronic and face-to-face informed consent processes. *Journal of Empirical Research on Human Research Ethics; JERHRE*, *17*(1-2), 144–166. doi:10.1177/15562646211038819 PMID:34410195

Twisk, J., Spriensma, A., Eekhout, I., de Boer, M., Luime, J., de Jong, P., ... Heymans, M. (2018). Analysing outcome variables with floor effects due to censoring: A simulation study with longitudinal trial data. *Epidemiology, Biostatistics, and Public Health*, *15*(2).

## KEY TERMS AND DEFINITIONS

**Ceiling Effect:** The ceiling effect occurs when a high proportion of observations in a study have a maximum score on the observed variable.

**Censored Outcome:** Intensity of the dependent variable at the lower limit or the upper limit.

**Floor Effect:** The floor effect occurs when a high proportion of observations in a study have a minimum score on the observed variable.

**Imputation-Based Regression Model:** A regression model is estimated to predict observed values of a variable based on other variables, and this model is then used to impute values in cases where the value of that variable is missing.

**Tobit Regression:** Tobit regression is a latent variable model in which the dependent variable is concentrated at the smallest or the largest value.

**Zero-Inflated Distribution:** Zero-inflated distribution is used to model count data with excess zeros.

**Zero-Inflated Poisson Regression:** Zero-inflated Poisson regression is used to model count data with an excessive amount of zeros.

# Section 14
# Computer Vision

# Validating Machine Vision Competency Against Human Vision

**Vani Ashok Hiremani**
*Presidency University, Bangalore, India*

**Kishore Kumar Senapati**
*Birla Institute of Technology, Mesra, India*

## INTRODUCTION

This chapter presents an empirical analysis of human intelligence as how human perceive an image and based upon which prominent facial features he/she is deciding upon the class of image before training the machine for classification. At present image classification accuracy is not high enough because of large number of redundant information as well as features. The visual capacity of humans has par excellence in object identification and recognition under critical impediments which evolves to much competent with age so primary focus should be given on how human intelligence works on image classification rather than training the machine for the image classification. Human brain processes visual statistics in semantic space by extracting the semantically imperative features such as contour information, line segments, edges which are hardly detected by computers. On the other hand machines require high end resolution images and rigorous processing of images to fit for training. Machines have to process visual statistics in data space obtained by the strongly detectable but less informative features like texture patterns and chromatic information (Zhang, 2010). Hence the primary motto of underlying chapter involves human interaction and response analysis to validate the competency of machine intelligence under face classification. Understanding the way human extracts features can enable a variety of AI applications with human-like performance. Over the years humans have showcased clever proficiency in judging age, gender, behavior, state of mind and race by face even under many obstacles (Chellappa, 2010; Jain et al., 2011; Sinha et al., 2006; Sinha et al., 2007). This chapter elucidates the intra class classification problem like classifying Indian face vs Indian Face (Kattia & Aruna, 2018). The racial classification problem in a highly populated and most diversified country like India is more apprehensive where every region epitomizes different culture and traditions. This leads to fabricate the labeled face structure. Racial classification of Caucasian, Black and Asian abrasive races along with gender (Brooks & Gwinn, 2010; Fu et al., 2014) has been performed precisely using computer vision (Tariq et al., 2016). Knowledge of races is an important initial step in discrimination. Geographical regional faces have stereotyped structure which incorporates many discriminative features. Both human and machine process them in a systematic way applying experience and computational logic respectively. Classification problem becomes handy with subtle feature variations i.e. finer grained race such as Chinese/Japanese/Korean (Duan et al., 2010), Chinese sub-ethnicities (Tin & Sein, 2010) and Myanmar (Bruce, 1986) but these studies have not characterized the human performance in systematic way. Eventually, what features does human consider for classification is mystery. To address this concern an Automated Human Intelligence System (AHIS) is designed involving randomly selected untrained identifiers in a fine-grained race classification problem to evaluate the potential of human vision. The interrogation of identifiers based on given regional face

DOI: 10.4018/978-1-7998-9220-5.ch061

images emphasized on local conventional facial features like skin tone, face shape, shape of eyes, eyebrows, shape of nose, orientation of mouth and non-conventional features like style of applying vermillion, its color, style of dressing, draping sari as per regional tradition, physic, moustache, accessories like jewelry and regional amulet thread. This rich feature set will be prospected as a reference input set to train neural models for solving computer vision problems. The insight of non-conventional features can be seen sufficing the absence of conventional features. Augmentation of these symmetric features can bring tangible gain in classification. The experimental results of human vision analysis have shown accuracy of 88% when both identifiers and person in image are from different regions. 96% accuracy is achieved when both are from same region. This familiarity of faces reinforced improved performance in classification. The proficiency of humans in underlying classification problem is systematically measured and the derived discriminative features are characterized using computer vision algorithms using novel face database. This work emphasizes on CNNs since they have achieved commendable success in image classification on large scale datasets for a long time. The success of the AlexNet has influenced researchers to carry out advances in classification precision by either sinking filter size or escalating the network deepness and the efficient pre-trained model like GoogLeNet containing trained weights for the network reduced the number of steps required for the output to converge. CNN model training is global optimization problem. The authors have described different variations to improve traditional CNN model to find the best fitting set of parameters by incorporating three aspects: Inception module, spectral pooling and leaky ReLu activation function. Using canny edge detection approximation method face contour information is obtained and characterized through CNN model. This leads to explore the perceptual annotation of individual features influence in overall face. To this end the authors have developed a novel Indian regional face database (IRFD) consisting of large set of distinctive face images of north, east, west and south regions of India to mitigate the scarcity of regional and labeled face images for future supervised classification process. The face images are collected from different universities and acquired through both online and offline mode. IRFD is made public for further research work in addition to relatively available few datasets of Indian faces. Meanwhile, as a result of study apart from facial features dressing style, physic, moustache, style of applying vermillion, regional amulet thread are few other non-facial factors which have influenced human intelligence decision. The experimental results have yielded accuracy of 96% with the assumption that the identifier (human) belongs to the same state. The experimental outcome evidences the effectiveness and viability of the study on human intelligence. The findings of the experiments will be prospected and act as a booster for machine intelligence in feature selection.

## Database Preparation and Processing

Though many face databases are available in market but many were not labeled with geographical region to fit in for underlying supervised classification process so to satiate underlying requirement a face database consists of color face images of four regions of India is developed. Face images are captured real in nature (unprocessed) which human get to see daily so that he can authenticate accurately the person in image, hence a primary focus is given on creating own database by collecting face images of different age group in real form from all regions of India. To collect face images belonging to different regions of India, University students are asked provide their family members photos and basic information of their native region in a form through online portal. The population consists of 69 students belonging to north, east, west and south region states like Uttar Pradesh, Delhi, Bihar, Jharkhand, West Bengal, Odisha, Chhattisgarh, Madhya Pradesh, Maharashtra, Andhra Pradesh, Telangana and Tamil Nadu have filled the form with their family photos and information. The received raw photos of family members from each individual consist of face images of father, mother and siblings. This provided a way to have different age group face database. Aging is a challenging factor in face recognition (Tariq et al., 2016) since identifying adult is easy than child, hence varying age group face image collection is thought to record human intellect as solution to this problem. An automated face acquisition model is developed to capture real time face images under the consent of candidates. To capture images, we have used Lenovo Easy Camera of 2mp with aspect ratio 1.33 and resolution of size 640x480. The candidate is positioned in front of Lenovo easy camera, the undecorated room wall being at background. The region of interest (ROI) is detected through Viola jones algorithm and captured to the size 250x350.

In offline mode the scanned Bio-data forms shown in figure 1 are collected from various universities. These forms consist of minimal information like gender, age and region of person in image. These bio-data forms are segmented into number of images present in it. These segmented images are then browsed through the automated face acquisition model where the unnecessary background and labeled information are removed and only ROI is captured to the size of 250x350 selected as illustrated in Figure 2. Around 2010 images acquired from both these modes are stored with primary key as Region_Number (e.g. EAST_01). Hence only cropping is carried under pre-processing after image acquisition to keep the original image intact.

To experience the real time trials in surveillance system where prepossessed images are not available for identification and to see how well human sight is susceptible to this problem, no rigorous pre-processing is carried out in this work. Hence the trained dataset obliging to realize the existing challenges in face identification like pose variation, illumination, low resolution, non-uniform background and non-frontal image, old photos, cropped images from group photo and photocopy of photos.

## Human Intelligence Analyzing

Man vs Machine, has always been a matter of debate. The proposed work carried an empirical research by gaining knowledge direct from humans to analyse their intelligence to understand how well his brain has established automated system towards recognizing people surrounding him based on his experience and observation. Human vision has evolved with experience and has effective recognition ability under many challenging condition where machine fails, as illustrated in Figure 3, one can easily recognize who is in image.

Let's Consider S, an Automated Human Intelligence (AHIS) system is a set of input image, questionnaire, answer, features and class as given below,

$AHFR(S) = \{ x_i \mid x_i \in X, Q, A, F, M \}$

Where $x_i$ is an input image selected from X (facet database) and i = 1, 2,......N

$X = \{ x_1, x_2 \ldots x_N \}$

Let F be a feature vector

$F = \{ f_1, f_2 \ldots \ldots f_L \}$

In more general case L features fi, i=1, 2, 3.......L are extracted.

*Figure 1. Bio-data forms with face images describing basic information like age, gender and state of participant*

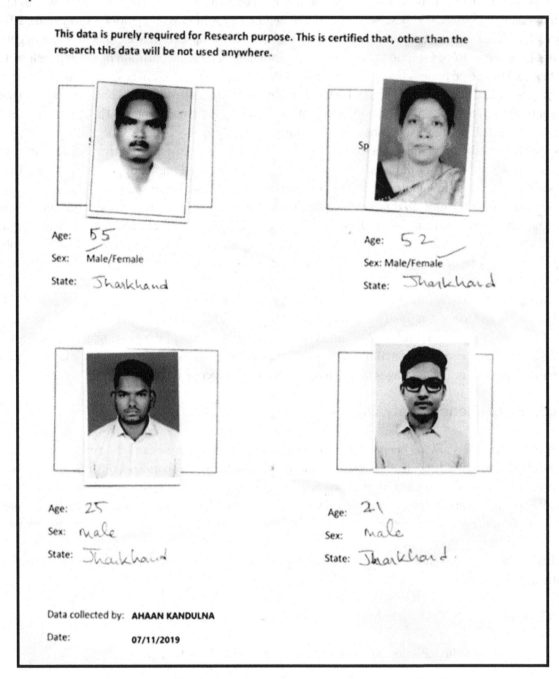

Let Q be the questionnaire set

Q = {q₁......... q₅} and A be the subset of features in terms of answers.

A ⊆ F

*Figure 2. Region of Interest (ROI) acquisition*

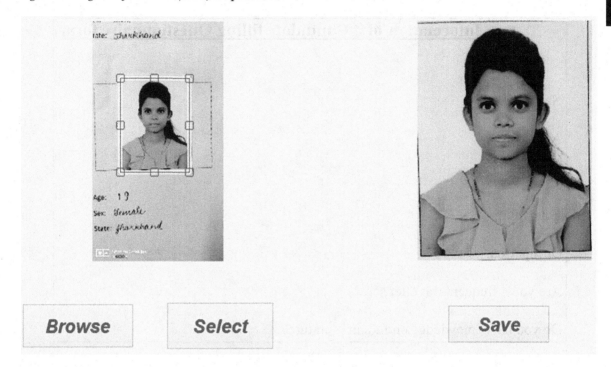

Given, classification task of M classes $w_1, w_2, ...., w_M$ and unknown pattern, which is represented by a feature vector F, we form the M conditional probability

$P(w_i | F)$ where i = 1, 2..... M

In other words each of them represents the probability that the unknown pattern belongs to the respective class $w_i$, given that the corresponding feature vector takes the value F.

Let $w_1$, $w_2$ be the two classes in which expected pattern belongs. The priori probability $P(w_1)$ and $P(w_2)$ are estimated from the available training feature vectors. Indeed if N is total available training pattern and $N_1$, $N_2$ of them belong to $w_1$ and $w_2$ respectively, then

$P(w_1) \approx N_1/N$ & $P(w_2) \approx N_2/N$

*Figure 3. Human can identify familiar faces with sever pose variation and occlusion*

*Figure 4. Identifier Information form*

---

### **Information of a Candidate filling Questionnaire form**

Name:

Age:

State:

Education:

Occupation:

Are you a frequent traveller?

Do you have knowledge on Indian literature?

---

The classification now can be stated as

If $P(w_1 \mid F) > P(w_2 \mid F)$, F be classified to $w_1$
If $P(w_1 \mid F) < P(w_2 \mid F)$, F be classified to $w_2$

Let $R_1$ be the region of the feature space which we decide in favour of $w_1$ and $R_2$ be the corresponding region for $w_2$, then error is made if $F \in R_1$, although it belongs to $w_2$ or if $F \in R_2$, although it belongs to $w_1$. That is,

$$P_e = P(F \in R_2, w_1) + P(F \in R_1, w_2)$$

Where $P(.,.)$ is the joint probability of two events.

The optimal features from feature set are selected and will be used as input to train the model for further classification.

The above figure 4 shows information form, to know basic information of randomly picked untrained identifiers including factors like their education, age, state, profession, their travelling frequency and knowledge of Indian literature and find how each factor affects identification. Frequency of travelling and hailing from same region are the two factors appeared most effective among others. When human come across people of same and other region on frequent and non-frequent bases respectively a feature set which he has built in his mind helps him differentiate people region wise. It is like training human brain with people faces of different region. Familiarity of faces on repeated view plays influential role in good identifying (Duan et al., 2010).

## Questionnaire Form

In this step identifiers are given collected face image and asked to fill questionnaire form to understand their strength of vision in terms:

- How they find adequacy of image for identifying it?
- If image is not adequate enough then what factor is to improve its appearance?
- Though the image not adequate still can human capable of identifying difference between genders?
- Any regional accessories making them to understand person in image? (Underlying database images are cropped to size of passport so certainly they give hint of region based on appearance),
- What feature they find more prominent in face image?
- Based on their intellect of visualizing face how they deciding the region of person in image?

The Figure.5 shows the digital copy of questionnaire form.

Out of 255 dataset images 220 face images are arranged in 22 sets with 10 images in each set and distributed to 22 untrained individuals belonging to different states and falling into either of two age groups 20-30 and 30-40. It stood as important phase as it provided essential way of gathering more potential information to comprehend how human intelligence worked on given image dataset. Digitally signed filled forms from identifiers are evaluated by keeping in mind the provided face image and its label at back. Response sheet is created to record the answers of identifiers on the details of facial features and non-facial features observed.

## The Demographics of the Identifiers

30 un-trained individuals (identifiers) are randomly chosen from across the country.

Different parameters are observed during primary survey those stimulated the results show in Table 2:

Perhaps the factor of belonging to same region played significant role in correct identification it gives clear sense that human intelligence is more robust with more experience.

## Response Analysis and Summary

The response is gathered from digitally signed filled forms by identifiers. Each form is assessed by keeping in mind the provided face image and its basic information associated with it.

The accumulative percentile of correct response given by all identifiers to every question is shown in following Figure 6 a), b), c) and d).

Subsequently the factors observed from human response are: 1.Human considered both conventional and non-conventional facial feature for recognizing face, 2. Human has responded well to challenges of face recognition, 3. Belonging to same region and Pre trained knowledge has increased accuracy, 4. Education, Frequent travelling and knowledge of Indian literacy are the factors that tremendously influenced the accuracy and 5. Human intellect was not much affected by pose variation and illumination.

## Features Selection Based on Human Intelligence

After analysis of response sheet of all identifiers features set is drawn based on majority of same response i.e., on majority how many observed same features in common pertaining to a region. Interesting

*Figure 5. Questionnaire form*

**Questionnaire regarding how you are identifying person**

1. Is image of a person shown to you is adequate for identification?

a) Yes      b) No      c) Moderate

Answer:

2. What factor would make image more clear/adequate for identification?

a) Image is adequate      b) Pose of image      c) Illumination      d) Uniform background

Answer:

3. What is the gender of a person in image?

a) Female      b) Male

Answer:

4. Is image of person accommodated with any regional accessories or giving any indication?

a) Yes      b) No      c) Moderate

Answer:

5. Which feature do you find more prominent in image?

a) Eyes      b) Nose      c) Mouth      d) Face shapee) if other please specify

Answer:

6. What do you think to which region of India, this person in image belong to?

a) North      b) East      c)West      d) South

Answer:

7. What do you think which state does the person in image belong to?

Answer:

8. What made you to decide a person in image belong to particular state or region?

Answer:

9. Any other observation?

Answer:

Disclaimer: I filled this form truly on my observation of face image provided at time, with no intervention of any.      Sign:

observation was many identifiers have mentioned that non-facial features like dressing style, the way sari draped, vermilion, moustache and regional amulet thread factors have helped them along with facial

*Table 1. Age Profile of identifiers*

| Identifiers Age Profile | Age |
|---|---|
| Group A consist of 15 identifiers | 20-30 |
| Group B consist of 15 identifiers | 30-40 |

*Table 2. Stimuli parameters*

| Parameter | Effect |
|---|---|
| Age | Group A is of age 20-30 comprising students. Compare to Group A Group B turn out to be more reliable and recognised faces more appropriate with accuracy of above 90%. Group B has shown more sensibility and solemnity towards process. The growing age evolves strength of statistical memory of human. |
| Profession | Group A is comprise of students and had seen different region students of same group notable Group B has broad exposure of meeting many people of different age group so this factor stood more effective for Group B. |
| Frequent Travel | Group B has got more number of frequent travellers as compared to Group A so evidently Group B shown effective recognition of people from different regions. |

features like nose, eyes, chick bones, skin tone etc. Based on majority measure the Table.3 shows the most prominent features observed by 30 individuals to classify given face image to particular region.

Perhaps the factor of belonging to same region played significant role in correct identification it gives clear sense that human intelligence is more robust with more experience. They have already seen people from their region many times which acted as trained image and the image given to them acted as testing image which led to accurate result. Frequent travelling and knowledge of Indian literacy are

*Figure 6. Pie chart of accumulative percentile of response*

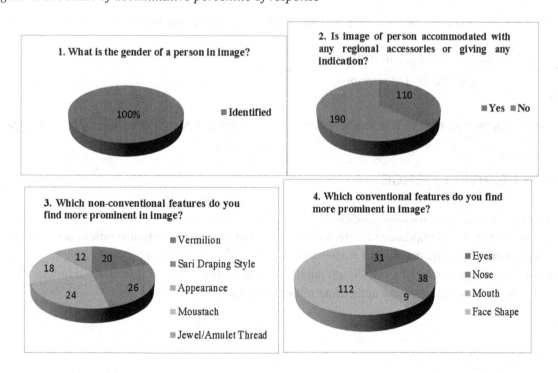

*Table 3. Final features selected by identifiers*

| Region | Facial features | Non facial feature |
|--------|-----------------|--------------------|
| North | Complexion: fair, light brown<br>Nose: straight, sleek<br>Eyes: normal size<br>Face shape: oval, sleek | Make up, hair style, vermillion, saree draping style, appearance |
| East | Complexion: light brown, dark brown<br>Nose: wider, prominent in face, tiny nose, flatten nose bone, Broad forehead<br>Eyes: bigger, puffy, hooded eyelids, tiny eyes, small eyebrows, significant distance between eyebrows,<br>Lips: fuller, small<br>Face shape: round, bulgy, double chin square, smooth skin texture, | Vermillion style and color, head cover with saree, saree draping style, amulet thread color |
| West | Complexion: fair light brown<br>Nose: small<br>Eyes: normal size | Jewellery, vermillion, saree style, studs |
| South | Complexion: fair, light brown, dark brown<br>Eyes: normal size, dark eyebrows<br>Face shape: round, oval | Traditional vermillion and jewellery, flower, hair style, saree style, moustache |

*Note: state wise response fitted into regions

the aspects which definitely favored identifier more towards accuracy. The performance of the proposed model is measured using Genuine Acceptance Rate (GAR) and False Acceptance Rate (FAR). GAR is the ratio of total number of correctly identified face images by identifier to the total number of face images. It is stated as follows:

$$GAR = \frac{Number\ of\ Correctly\ Identified\ faces}{Total\ no.\ of\ face\ images} \times 100\% \tag{1}$$

FAR is the ratio of number of wrongly identified face images to the total number of face images.

$$FAR = \frac{Number\ of\ wrongly\ Identified\ faces}{Total\ no.\ of\ face\ images} \times 100\% \tag{2}$$

GAR of approximate 96% is achieved when both identifier and person in image share same region.

## MACHINE INTELLIGENCE

Here we evaluated computational models like **CLBP** and **CNN**. First the Color Local Binary Patterns (LBP) is evaluated to comprehend the feasibility of underlying classification problem and further we have built two *Convolutional Neural Networks* one comprising more layers trained with 1800 normal face database images referred as **CNN** and another one is trained with 1000 contoured images of face obtained by canny edge detection approximation method referred as **CNN-FC**.

*Figure 7. (a) LBP Operation performed on image and histogram is plotted*

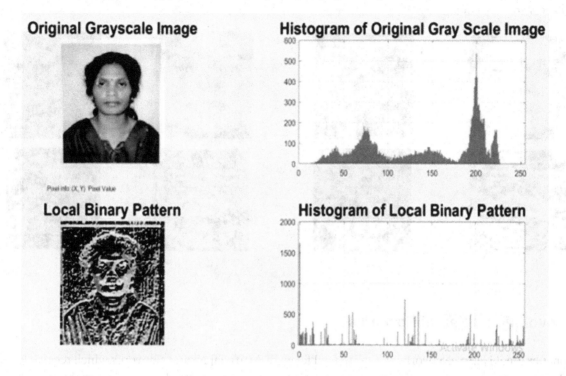

## Extraction of Color Local Texture Features

Features are most crucial in computer vision problems which decide the fate. Local Binary Pattern (LBP) features are most principal features and shown commendable results in recognition problem[24] hence the basic color LBP features are considered for face classification. The CLBP model has shown 67% accuracy in identifying correct region of given input face image. The input color image is divided into 256 cells (16×16 rows and columns respectively) i.e. each cell consists of 8×8 pixels resolutions. The LBP function is applied to each block of the color image. The resulting images after employing the LBP and CLBP function is as shown in figure 8(a) and 8(b) along with histogram. The feature vector is constructed from the 256 intensity values computed from the histogram generated using Y, R, G and B color components of the individual instances of the face images.

Hence, the size of template for 100 users is 10000×256. The LBP texture operator is prevalently used in various applications due to its discriminative power, illumination invariant, and its computational simplicity which makes it possible to analyse images in challenging real-time scenarios.

During the construction of LBP feature vector, the bilinear interpolation method is adopted on LBP grid to estimate the values of neighbors that do not fall exactly on pixels. Since correlation between pixels decreases with distance, much of the texture information in an image can be obtained from local neighborhoods. We have considered 300 face image datasets consisting of 5 different images of 60 people from East and South region. 4 images are trained 1 tested among 5. The CLBP features from trained images are matched against CLBP features of testing image using Manhattan distance-based algorithm.

*Figure 8. Color Space Conversion: (a) Y color component (b) R color component (c) G color component (d) B color component*

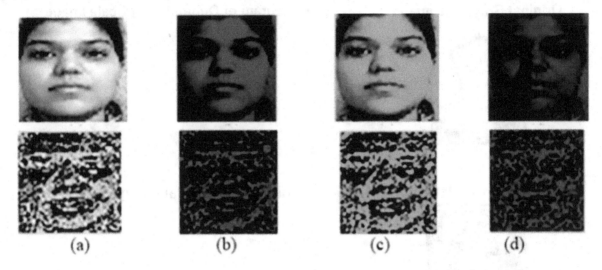

(a)  (b)  (c)  (d)

## Convolutional Neural Networks

Convolutional Neural Network is a type of feed forward Artificial Neural Networks which receive external signals and keep propagating these through further layers to obtain the end result without feedback connection to previous layers as represented in figure 9. The output of such neural network for any given input pattern $z_p$ is calculated with a single forward pass through network. For each output $O_{k,}$ we have (assuming few hidden layers in between input layer and output layer).

$$O_{k,p} = f_{ok} (net_{ok, p})$$

$$= f_{ok} (\sum_{j=1}^{J+1} w_{kj} f_{yj} (net_{yj, p}))$$

$$= f_{ok} (\sum_{j=1}^{J+1} w_{kj} f_{yj} (\sum_{i=1}^{I+1} v_{ji} z_{i, p})) \quad (3)$$

Where $f_{ok}$ and $f_{yj}$ are respectively the active functions for output $O_k$ and hidden layer $y_j$, $w_{kj}$ is the weight between output $O_k$ and $y_j$. $Z_{i, p}$ is the value of input $z_i$, the $(I+1)^{th}$ input unit and the $(J+1)^{th}$ hidden unit are bias units representing the threshold values of neurons in further layer to adjust the weight.

CNN's are made up of neurons that have learnable weights and biases. They compare the image patch by patch. Each neuron receives some inputs, performs a convolution operation between 3x3 patch of image and 3x3 filters. The strength of CNN lies in its learning local patterns of images as compared to densely connected layers which learn global patterns. The key characteristics of CNN are 1. The patterns are translation invariant and 2. They learn spatial hierarchies of patterns this allows convnets to efficiently learn increasingly from abstract to complex features layer by layer. In CNN the neuron in a layer is only connected to small portion of layer ahead of it this reduces the number of computing

*Table 4. Summary of splitting of dataset into training and testing sets*

| Dataset | South | East | Total |
|---------|-------|------|-------|
| Train_Set | 900 | 900 | 1800 |
| Test_Set | 105 | 105 | 210 |
| Total | 1005 | 1005 | 2010 |

parameters. CNN compares images piece by piece i.e., features. The two key parameters of CNN are 1) Size of patches extracted from input image typically 3x3 or 5x5 matrices and 2) Depth of the output feature map i.e., the number of filters computed by convolution.

## Data Pre-Processing

Images are undergone pre-processing instead of direct feeding to CNN. A one hot encoded vector is generated from categorical name of images. The dependant variables i.e., labels are encoded for machine understanding as the dataset is consisting of categorical names (i.e., SOUTH_01 and EAST_01). The dataset is consisting of varying size images so the different resolution images are reduced to the size 50*50 pixels and converted into grayscale images to curtail processing speed. The following Table 4 shows the summary of dataset split.

Both the Train_Set and Test_Set images are reshaped to size (-1, 50, 50, 1) to fit in TensorFlow.

## ARCHETECTURE OVERVIEW

The following figure 9 represents the CNN architecture used in underlying work. The CNN architecture has 5 layers: Convolutional Layers, ReLU Layers, Pooling Layers, Fully connected layers and Dropout layer.

## Convolution Layers

These layers are basic building blocks of CNN model. To handle dataset around 2010 face images comprising similar features we applied trial and error method while encompassing number of convolutional layers. Initially we have selected 3 convolutional layers which generated moderate performance ($\pm70\%$) then we switched to 5 convolutional layers which suited our system requirements with adequate performance. Our CNN model consists of 5 layers, the first convolutional layer 32x32 filters, second layer is of 64x64 filters, third layer is of 128x128 filters, fourth layer if of filter size 64x64 and fifth layer is of 32x32 filters having kernel size 5x5 each as the input image size is greater than 128x128 to quickly reducing spatial dimension.

## Steps Involved in Convolutional Layers:

**Step.1.** The 3x3 or 5x5 filters and the patches of images are lined up (the image size is taken of 9 pixels).
**Step.2.** Perform the dot operation between each image pixel and the corresponding filter pixel.
**Step.3.** Slide the filter throughout the image by stride 1 or 2.
**Step.4.** Add them up and divide by the total number of pixels in the filter.

*Figure 9. ConvNet architecture used for geographical region wise face classification*

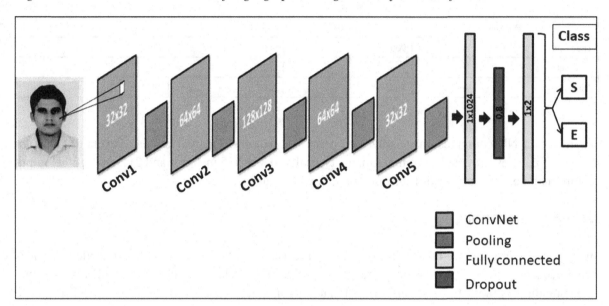

The filters are moved to every other position of the image to get the output of convolutional layer.

## ReLu Layers (Rectified Linear Unit) Layers

Rectified Linear Unit is a transform function f(x) which activates the nodes if the input (x) is above threshold value, while the input is below zero, the output is zero represented. It shows linear relationship with the dependent variable once the input rises above a certain threshold value as represented in eq. (4).

$$f(x) = \begin{cases} o \; if \; x < 0 \\ x \; if \; x \geq 0 \end{cases} \tag{4}$$

To avoid the values of filtered image received from convolutional layer from summing up to zero, this layer removes every –ve values from the filtered image and replaces –ve values with 0's. The ReLu activation function is favorable choice in CNNs because of its non-saturation of gradient quality.

## Pooling Layers

In this layer we shrink the images obtained from ReLu layer into smaller size. This is the best part of CNN where the size of the feature maps is halved after every Max Pooling layer without compromising the information. This technique confine from having more parameters i.e. more neurons, weights and eventually avoiding overfitting. We have used 5 max pooling layers with 5x5 windows.

The steps involved in pooling are:

**Step.1.** Pick a window of 2x2 or 3x3 or 5x5.
**Step.2.** Pick a stride of 2.
**Step.3.** Run the window throughout the filtered image.

*Figure 10. (a) Contour information attained from original image (b) Contour information of ROI is procured from whole image to feed CNN-FC.*

**Step.4.** From each window, consider the maximum value.

## Fully Connected Layers

These are the final layers where the actual classification takes place. Here the filtered and shrunken images are put in single list. We have use two fully connected layers one is of 1024 neurons and others one is of 2 neurons.

## Dropout Layer

This is regularization technique used for avoiding overfitting by preventing co-adaptations on *Train_Set*. A single dropout layer is added with 0.8 (p=0.8) key probability followed by a dual-node decision layer.

Finally, to reduce cross entropy loss the *Adam* optimizer is used with learning rate α=0.001. The 1024 feature vector for each face is obtained from this CNN model.

## CNN-FC

The summary of analysis of human response articulates majority of people relied on face silhouette of given face images to classify them to region. To probe this we have built a separate model considering 1000 images to deal with face contour part where the ROI is extracted using Viola and Jones algorithm, where-in a system object is created to detect the face by combining skin region and rejecting non skin regions with additional property like bounding box and centroid to detect face. Further the canny edge detection method is applied to ROI of face images to retrieve contour information with respect to the centroid using $C_x = M_{10}/M_{00}$ and $C_y = M_{01}/M_{00}$ as shown in figure 10. The contour approximation method ensured that all the points of image are stored keeping original image intact. These images then fed to CNN model referred as CNN-FC to see impact on output.

The performance of the model CNN-FC did recede the CNN model yet showed significant effect on accuracy of classification of faces to the correct race which opened many prospects in future to have other face features in consideration. This pandemic situation restricted us from acquiring dynamic high-resolution images which in turn affected our database collection process and made us to compromise with static images with moderate resolution collected by students through online mode. The CNN model tested with good quality images yielded comparatively significant accuracy as of moderate resolution images. The canny edge images of elderly people showed a greater number of contours as compared to young face image this would be another success in age prediction problem.

*Figure 11. The graph exhibits the accuracy of each of the computational model taken in consideration and the human intelligence accuracy. An experimental result shows the proficiency of human intelligence is dominating the machine intelligence.*

Note*: non state is the condition where human identifier is not sharing region with person in face image and same state indicates both identifier and person in face are from same region/ state.

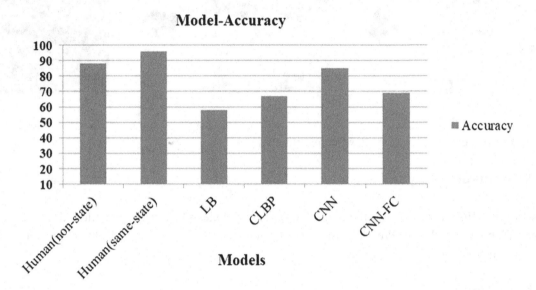

## EXPERIMENTATIONS AND RESULTS

### Development Environment

Our system is implemented based on Microsoft windows 10, using Anaconda to create Jupyter Notebook and the environment method of Python 3 to build the CNN model. The model ran on a machine equipped with a 2 GHz CPU and 4 GB of RAM.

### Experimental Results

The following figure 11 shows the comparative description of all models used towards underlying work.

## CONCLUSION

In this work we investigated the human intelligence performance and machine intelligence in race classification incorporating a sample of 120 human identifiers and computational models like CNN, CNN-FC and CLBP. This work precisely emphasized on creating novel Indian color face image database consisting of 2010 face images of east and south region to satiate the underlying requirement. The experimental outcome showed the high proficiency of human compared to machine algorithms. The findings of this paper will be prospected and act as a booster for machine intelligence in feature selection, in future results will be modeled for machine learning algorithm, which will be applicable in surveillance system, criminal identification, missing person trace, human trafficking and more.

*Figure 12. Visualization of feature mapping of training set images to testing image set using Tensorboard graphs (a) Accuracy of model drawn from training the training set images with respect to image batch (b) Validation of model with respect to testing image set and (c) Loss by cross entropy.*

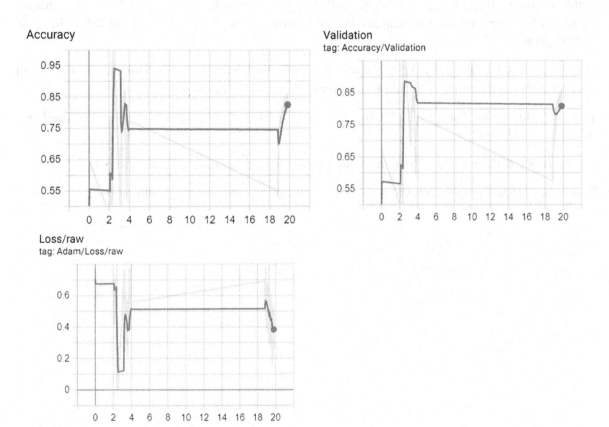

## REFERENCES

Brooks, K., & Gwinn, O. (2010). No role for lightness in the perception of black and white? Simultaneous contrast affects perceived skin tone, but not perceived race. *Perception*, *39*(8), 1142–1145. doi:10.1068/p6703 PMID:20942364

Bruce. (1986). *Influences of Familiarity on the Processing of Faces*. Academic Press.

Chellappa, R. (2010). *Face recognition by computers and humans*. IEEE Computer Society.

Duan, X., Wang, C., Liu, X-D., Li, Z., Wu, J., & Zhang, H. (2010). Ethnic features extraction and recognition of human faces. *2nd IEEE ICACC*.

Fu, S., He, H., & Hou, Z. G. (2014). Learning race from face: A survey. *IEEE Transactions on Pattern Analysis and Machine Intelligence*, *36*(12), 2483–2509. doi:10.1109/TPAMI.2014.2321570 PMID:26353153

Jain, A. K., Klare, B., & Park, U. (2011). Face Recognition: Some Challenges in Forensics. *IEEE International Conference*.

Kattia & Aruna. (2018). *Are you from North or South India? A hard race classification task reveals systematic representational differences between humans and machines.* arXiv: 1703.07595v2.

Sinha, P., Balas, B., Ostrovsky, Y., & Russell, R. (2006). Face Recognition by Humans: Nineteen Results All Computer Vision Researchers Should Know About. *Proceedings of the IEEE.* 10.1109/JPROC.2006.884093

Sinha, P., Balas, B., Ostrovsky, Y., & Russell, R. (2007). Face Recognition by Humans: 20 Results all Computer Vision Researchers Should Know About. *Proceedings of the IEEE.*

Tariq, U., Hu, Y., & Huang, T. S. (2016). *Gender and ethnicity identification from silhouetted face profiles. 16th IEEE ICIP.*

Tin, H. H. K., & Sein, M. M. (2010). *Race identification for face images.* IEEE Transaction.

Zhang, B. (2010). Computer Vision vs. Human Vision. *IEEE International Conference.*

# Section 15
# Customer Analytics

# Customer Analytics Using Sentiment Analysis and Net Promoter Score

**Thanh Ho**

*University of Economics and Law, Ho Chi Minh City, Vietnam & Vietnam National University, Ho Chi Minh City, Vietnam*

**Van-Ho Nguyen**

*University of Economics and Law, Ho Chi Minh City, Vietnam & Vietnam National University, Ho Chi Minh City, Vietnam*

## INTRODUCTION

Providing the best experience for customers through products and services provided by businesses is a crucial and critical task during each company's operation. This means that the products and services that companies offer satisfy and meet customers' needs: the right products and services, at the right place, and at the right time. The first step is listening to customers through the information conveyed in customer feedback on the business's sales channels and finding ways to improve and overcome the extraordinary things necessary steps of firms in the digital age. Today, with the strong development of technology and the intense application of interactive technologies on e-commerce sites, a large amount of data is collected from customer comments and feedback. The presence of technologies built on artificial intelligence and machine learning methods, and data analysis tools make it possible to analyze and extract meaningful data from textual data like comments or customer feedback is more accessible and more practical. This approach can be considered as the cutomer analytics method that is to gain customer insight necessary as well as customer satisfaction that are anticipated, timely, and relevant.

Besides, the digital transformation has helped businesses monitor their processes, including branding, promotion, advertising, production, channel distribution, based on collected data and interaction. Business managers analyze customer experience and can make more accurate and data-driven decisions (Marda, 2018; Ludbrook, 2019). In the transition and adaptation to the digital economy, it is necessary to have a new approach to analyzing user experience and emotions to predict and take advantage of disruptive technologies effectively. Advances in information technology have changed how communication makes it easier for customers to access information and exchange ideas about products and services on a large scale in real-time (Ghani et al., 2019). The advent of social networks and online review websites allows customers to give their opinions through reviews of products and services. From an e-commerce point of view, detecting the right user sentiment will help us display better advertising content. (Sarkar & Palit, 2020).

Customer analytics is critical for extracting insights from massive data in order to improve service innovation, product development, personalisation, and management decision-making (Hossain et al., 2022). Businesses utilize this data in particular for very direct marketing, location selection, and customer relationship management in a subtle way. There are many different definitions of customer satisfaction, and much debate is about this definition. Many researchers believe that satisfaction is between customer expectations and feeling practically received. According to Philip Kotler, customer satisfaction is the

DOI: 10.4018/978-1-7998-9220-5.ch062

level of sensory status of a person derived from comparing the results obtained from the consumption of products or services with their expectations. The level of satisfaction depends on the difference between the results received and the expectation. If the actual results are lower than the expectation, the customer is not satisfied; if the actual results are commensurate with the expectation will be satisfied; if the actual results are higher than expectations, customers are delighted. Customer expectations are formed from the shopping experience, friends, colleagues, and the information of sellers and competitors. In order to improve customer satisfaction, businesses need additional investments and at least invest in more marketing programs.

This research aims to review the opinion mining research and propose a method exploiting customers' reviews in natural languages based on the machine learning method. This research applies the knowledge mining method from data collected by automatic programs, including reviews from customers on online ordering services, and eating places review channels. Then, data preprocessing will be conducted and machine learning methods will be applied to find the best model and predict sentiment scores for the rest of the corpus (Mishra & Tiruwa, 2017; Rao & Kakkar, 2017). In addition, the study is also going to calculate and analyze the Net Promoter Score (NPS) (Reichheld, 2003; Mandal, 2014) from customer rating scores and used data visualization tech NPS on an overview dashboard.

## BACKGROUND

This section concentrates on exploring related research in the field of customer opinion mining, sentiment analysis, especially in the online service sector. The machine learning and lexicon-oriented approaches are also utilized to form the basis of this research. The method of NPS will be surveyed to measure customer satisfaction in the food service industry.

### Customer Analytics: Customer Satisfaction, Customer Opinion and Sentiment Analytics

Currently, satisfied customers have many different definitions as well as many controversies about this definition. According to Philip Kotler (2017), satisfaction is a person's feeling of satisfaction or disappointment due to comparing the actual received product (or outcome) concerning their expectations. It can be understood that satisfaction is the customer base on his understanding of a product or service (Singh & Verma, 2020). Satisfaction is a psychological state of feeling after a customer's needs and expectations are satisfied. Customer satisfaction is formed based on experience, especially when purchasing and using products or services (Ahmed et al., 2021). After trying to buy and use, customers will have a comparison between reality and expectations.

The study by El-Adly (2019) uses structural equation modeling (SEM) to study the relationship between aspects of customer perceived value, customer satisfaction, and customer loyalty in the hotel context. Research results show that four aspects of hotel perceived value (hedonistic, price, quality, transactional) indirectly influence customer loyalty through satisfaction as intermediaries. Finally, customer satisfaction was found to have a direct positive influence on customer loyalty.

Customer experience is one of the critical concerns for the airline industry. To understand the customer experience, Kumar and Zymbler (2019) proposed a machine learning-based approach to analyze customer tweets on social network Twitter to gain insights and improve their experience. The author used the Glove dictionary approach and the n-gram approach in this study. SVM (support vector machine) and several ANN (artificial neural network) architectures are considered to develop a classification model that maps tweets into positive and negative categories.

Emotions and feelings are issues of interest and research by many scientists (Shelke & Deshpande, 2018; Mostafa, 2019; Salunkhe & Chavan, 2020). So there are different views on the number of types of emotions. A context-based text mining and analysis function to identify and extract customer information in the database system, helping businesses measure and evaluate user feedback from character responses. It is widely used in campaigns to measure brand health based on fluctuations in information from social media streams (such as Facebook applications, Linkedin, Google, Newspaper). Written sentiment analysis helps businesses know: (1) Aspects and problems of the brand's products/services that customers are interested in, (2) Intentions and feelings of users about the issue.

Sentiment analysis provides insight into the business performance and customer service of the business. Help businesses know the actual status of the community/customers is thinking about them. These are the pros and cons of business processes, products, and services. In this way, businesses can improve the efficiency of their business operations.

## Customers Sentiment Analytics Based on Machine Learning and Lexicon Approaches

The importance of sentiment analysis increases with the growth of social media such as review sites, discussion forums, and social networks. Primarily, in the era of digital development, in recent years, with the explosion of the internet, many studies are focusing on social networking domains such as Facebook, Twitter. Because some language features on social networks, such as character limitations or emotions, depend highly on what users read and listen to, classifying user emotions in social networks is challenging. Machine learning methods have been applied and succeeded in emotion analysis (Neethu & Rajasree, 2013; Kansal et al., 2020). Vocabulary-based emotion analysis methods depend on emotional lexical sources (Aung and Myo, 2017). A dynamic lexicon, often understood as a dictionary, is a collection of inspirational words, with each word being evaluated for polarity by an actual number (Feldman, 2013). These dictionaries can be manually or semi-manufactured. The advantage of this approach is that no training is required, hence no need for labeled data. This method is often used for sentiment analysis on common text types: blog or forum posts, movie or product reviews, or forums. Some other studies build their dictionaries based on different sources. Research of Taboada (2011) confirms that building a dictionary helps create a solid foundation for this approach. Eachempati et al. (2022) performed study that found that customer sentiment is a primary driver of investor sentiment, which in turn has a significant influence on the stock market and business value.

## NPS in Customer Satisfaction Analytics

NPS is an indicator that has a substantial impact on the growth and development of an enterprise (Reichheld, 2003). NPS will ensure the best customer experience, thereby helping to build customer relationships and loyalty to the business. Businesses can adjust products and services through the NPS score to help improve customer satisfaction and awareness.

Customer experience analytics collects and processes customer data to gain insight into a customer's views, weaknesses, and experience with a product or service (Jain & Kumar, 2017). Quality customer experience analytics provides valuable insights that enable brands to make intelligent data-driven decisions that can potentially improve the customer's shopping experience, support, and service. Additionally, the information collected can help create optimized marketing campaigns. An improved customer experience often leads to better customer sentiment, sales, and earnings (Schneider et al., 2008; Situmorang et al., 2017). Emotion when buying is one of the most critical factors that help attract new customers and increase the loyalty of old customers. The study of Gallagher (2019) on text mining supports psychoanalysis to understand what customers are saying about products, services, and interactions with businesses. This is commonly known as the voice of the customer (VoC) data, which is the key to unlocking customer sentiment. Gao et al. (2021) grouped according to their ease-of-use rating and their NPS identifier (promoter/passive/detractor) to show a positive correlation between ease-of-use score and a user's NPS cloud computing products, primarily when their user experience is centered on the operating console.

## Machine Learning Algorithms

### Support Vector Machine (SVM)

SVM (Cortes & Vapnik, 1995) is a supervised machine learning method that may solve classification and regression problems. It is, however, mainly employed to solve classification issues. Each data item is plotted as a point in n-dimensional space (where n is the number of features you have), with the value of each element being the value of a particular coordinate in the SVM algorithm. Then we classify by locating the hyper-plane that clearly distinguishes the two classes. Simply put, support vectors are the coordinates of each unique observation. The SVM classifier is a method that effectively separates the two classes (hyper-plane/line).

### Logistics Regression (LR)

Logistic regression (Pregibon, 1981) is a statistical model that utilizes a logistic function to describe a binary dependent variable in its most basic form; however, there are many more complicated variants. Logistic regression estimates the parameters of a logistic model in regression analysis (a form of binary regression). A binary logistic model mathematically has a dependent variable with two potential values, true/false, represented by an indicator variable, with the two values labeled 0 and 1. The dependent variable is a binary logistic regression model with two (categorical) levels. Multinomial logistic regression is used to model outputs with more than two values. In contrast, ordinal logistic regression is used if the many categories are ordered (for example, the proportional odds ordinal logistic model).

### Random Forest (RF)

Random forests, also known as random decision forests, are an ensemble learning approach for classification, regression, and other problems that work by training many decision trees. Random decision forests address the problem of decision trees overfitting their training set. Random forests outperform decision trees in most cases, but they are less accurate than gradient-enhanced trees. On the other hand, data features might have an impact on their performance. Ho (1995) invented the first random decision forest algorithm using the random subspace method, which, in Ho's definition, is a technique to apply Eugene Kleinberg's stochastic discrimination approach to classification (Ho, 1998).

## Challenges in Customers Sentiment Analytics

Language is complex, and the process of quantifying and grading language based on sentiment is equally complex. It can be much easier for humans to judge the other person's feelings subjectively in communication; the person talking to you is happy, sad, satisfied, or angry. Nevertheless, it is different; communication characteristics must be converted into objective, quantifiable scores for each person in different communication states. The opinion mining method is not new; however, each method has its advantages and disadvantages, no method is considered accurate. In particular, applying the lexical method in opinion mining of Vietnamese is a big challenge for researchers because of the complexity of the language structure. Currently, there are not many sets of emotional vocabulary. Contacts and good processing tools in Vietnamese language. Small companies are starting to understand the importance of social media to accomplish their business goals. Therefore, it is necessary to apply the machine learning method and evaluate its accuracy to choose the most suitable method in the field of research through the collected data set

## RESEARCH METHOD AND PROPOSED MODEL

### Research Method and Overview Proposed Model

This section describes the research's general model (Figure 1). For the research purposes, the research data, containing 48,471 raw data records, was collected from the customers' reviews of the Foody.vn website. After collecting raw data from the foody.vn and diddiemanuong.com websites, the research team preprocesses the data. Here we will use two libraries for opinion analysis in this study. The first is the pandas' library, an open source library that provides easy-to-use data structures and analytic functions in Python. The second library will be used is a powerful Python library called nltk (Natural Language Toolkit), a popular natural language processing library with lots of corpora, models, and algorithms. The sampling data were divided into training, validation, and test data. The training dataset is used during the learning process to fit the parameters; the validation dataset is a dataset of examples used to tune the hyperparameters of a classifier. Test datasets are used only once as the final step to reporting estimated error rates for future predictions. In the experimental machine learning-based phase, a model will be applied to choose the best algorithms within Logistic Regression, Support Vector Machine, and Random Forest. In the study of the NPS model, the chapter uses datasets collected and, after preprocessing, removes duplicate, blank, and malformed data. Then, NPS will be calculated based on rating scores of customers and applied to help business managers classify customers into three groups: Detractors, Passives, and Promoters.

### Data Scraping

Python libraries are used to collect data on websites. If a website has a stable structure, it will be easier for us to get data than a website with a different format because it is mainly based on "elements" to get data. Then from the data stored as JSON, we will convert and store it into the database easily. This data set will be included in the labeling, preprocessing, and cleaning steps to provide input for the following stages of the model.

*Figure 1. Overview of Proposed Model*
*Source: Authors*

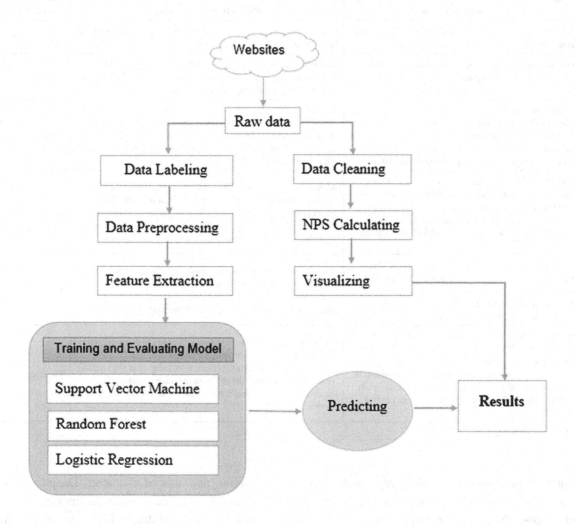

## Data Labeling

In this study, opinion analysis is approached by the supervised machine learning method. This means that a labeled dataset already contains the correct answers. This study assigned data labels based on customer ratings through online comments. Comments with rating scores of less than 7.0 have a negative meaning (Negative), and conversely, comments with rating scores greater than 7.0 have positive meaning (Nguyen et al., 2014). Table 1 is an illustration of the labeled data results.

## Data Preprocessing

The collected data will be in raw form because it has not been processed, the data may be empty, the data is misspelled, too short, too long, or contains icon characters. This will affect the analysis results, so the data are needed to clean.

Remove icon and special characters: Otherwise, special characters will create interference during analysis because they have no categorization significance. Convert everything to lowercase: a binary

*Table 1. Data labeling results*

| Example data in Vietnamese | Example data in English | Label |
|---|---|---|
| Đặt 3 ly nhưng lại giao có 2 ly cho mình. Không hiểu làm việc kiểu gì @@ Thực sự không hài lòng | Ordered 3 cups but delivered 2 cups for me. I don't understand how it works @@ Really not satisfied | Negative |
| Đặt Now mua hai ly sữa tươi trân châu đường đen bánh flan mà một ly có con gì trong đó. Quán buôn bán ẩu thả, ko coi trong vấn đề vệ sinh. | Order Now to buy two cups of fresh milk with pearls, black sugar, flan, one of which has something in it. The shop trades sloppily, not considering the issue of hygiene. | Negative |
| Ý thức nhân viên rất kém dù nước ngon cũng rất bức xúc về thái độ làm việc của nhân viên. Anh nhân viên mập mập chắc là quản lý ở đây mặt nhăn nhó khó chịu kiểu không muốn mình mua vậy. Đã vậy còn k hỏi mình về mức đường đá uống ngọt quá trời luôn | The staff's awareness is very poor even though the water is delicious, they are also very upset about the working attitude of the staff. The fat employee must be the manager here with an annoyed face like he doesn't want me to buy it. Also, don't ask me about how sweet the iced sugar is | Negative |
| Sau 1 ngày làm việc , ghé qua Ryucha , vẫn là món nước cũ . Trà sữa olong cho tỉnh táo , uống rất thơm mùi trà, mình thích nhất topping trân châu cacao với củ năng . Sự kết hợp độc đáo đó đã tạo nên 1 ly trà sữa excellent . Không gian quán khá ok mình rất ưng ý . | After a working day, stop by Ryucha, still the same old dish. Oolong milk tea for alertness, very fragrant tea, I like topping cocoa pearls with tapioca root. That unique combination has created an excellent cup of milk tea. The restaurant space is quite ok, I am very satisfied. | Positive |
| Quán hầu như món nào cũng ngon các bác ạ, không gian quán sạch sẽ, nhạc hay, phù hợp cho tất cả đối tượng lớn nhỏ. Còn hay có chương trình giảm giá nữa í, phục vụ dễ thương và tận tình nữa nè. Các bác nên đến thử nhé! Highly recommend! | Almost every dish is delicious, guys, the space is clean, the music is good, suitable for all audiences, big and small. There is also a discount program, cute and dedicated service. You guys should come try it! Highly recommend! | Positive |
| Mình ít khi bình luận quán nào lắm nhưng nay phải ghi vì Ryucha PXL thật sự rất dễ thương. Mình hay đặt qua Now Trà Olong Macchiato. Mà không hiểu sao nay mấy bạn giao một ly chua lè, mình gọi anh tài xế nhắn cho quán biết. Và quán gọi và đền cho mình một ly mới. Mình thật sự thích dịch vụ của các bạn. Nên 10/10 ạ. | I rarely comment on shops but now I have to because Ryucha PXL is really cute. I often order through Now Tea Olong Macchiato. But I don't understand why today, you guys deliver a cup of sour, I called the driver to message the shop. And the shop called and bought me a new drink. I really like your service. So 10/10. | Positive |

(Source: Authors)

sequence in computer memory represents each number, letter, and special character. Despite being semantically equivalent, uppercase letters have a distinct Unicode code than lowercase letters. On the other hand, the computer will be unable to discriminate between the input data, which may impact the prediction results. As a result, changing all letters to lowercase for the analysis and prediction system is appropriate.

Word normalization: evident word transformation is necessary for the data preprocessing step. Vietnamese users make comments on websites, so abbreviations or misspellings are inevitable. This will have much impact on analysis results.

Remove invalid data: the collected data set will have a lot of blank data; empty data has no meaning in the analysis process, consuming storage memory.

## Feature Extraction

TF-IDF technique (Term Frequency/Inverse Document Frequency) is a method for calculating the number of words in a collection of documents. We usually assign each word a score to indicate its relevance in the document and corpus. This approach is frequently used in text mining and information retrieval. As input for the classification algorithm, this step will pick the usual characteristics (keywords) indicative of the data set. In this chapter, keywords are chosen using the TF-IDF technique. The TF-IDF value of a keyword is a statistical approach from statistics indicating the phrase's relevance in one review. The following formula (1) is used to compute the TF-IDF of the keyword wi in comment d:

$$TF-IDF_{id} = F_{id} x \log \frac{N}{n_i} \qquad (1)$$

With,

Fid: Frequency of occurrence of keyword wi in comment d,

N: Total of comments

ni: The number of comments where the keyword wi appears

## Training and Evaluating Model

After training and evaluating the results, a model was obtained to classify emotions in new, unlabeled hotel reviews. After performing sequentially and fully following the above data preprocessing procedure, a clean dataset will be input for the next model phase. Then, using the Hold-Out method, divide the data in the ratio 80:20 to get the training data and the evaluation set. This rate is the same for each label. It is necessary to apply many machine learning algorithms to choose the most suitable model for each data set. The problem arises, how to evaluate and select models. In addition to the machine learning algorithm, the performance of the model may depend on other factors such as the distribution of classes, the cost of misclassification, the size of the training and test sets, the performance measure. In this chapter, we will evaluate the performance focusing on the predictive accuracy of the model rather than the speed of classification or model building, scalability. Usually, the effectiveness of the opinion classification model is evaluated based on the indicators, including Accuracy, Precision, Recall, and F1_Score.

## Net Promoter Score (NPS)

In this Chapter, NPS (Reichheld, 2003) was calculated based on the customer's rating on the feedback pages. Detractors (0-6 points) are unhappy customers. They have a terrible view of the business's brand and affect the brand by sharing with friends. Passives (7 – 8 points) are people who do not care much. A customer that can easily buy a competitor's product if the business does not take care of customers. Promoters (9-10 points) are loyal, brand-friendly customers. The customer can bring a great source of revenue to the business and help the company have more new potential customers. Formula (2) is the calculation of NPS:

NPS Score = %(Promoters) - %(Detractors) $\qquad (2)$

## EXPERIMENTAL RESULTS

The data collection, preprocessing, training, and model evaluation are presented in this section. The results are visualized and discussions related to the research topic.

*Table 2. Results of data crawling*

| Sources | Number of comments |
|---|---|
| foody.vn | 40,397 |
| diadiemanuong.com | 8,074 |
| Total | 48,471 |

(Source: Authors)

## Results of Data Scraping

The collected data set has 48,471 feedback from customers (Table 2), including store name, address, comment customer name, comment time, comment content, and customer rating score for that store. The number of comments collected from foody.vn is 40,397; for diadiemanuong.com is 8,074.

Figure 2 is the data collection results presented by year, from 2016 to 2020.

## Results of Sentiment Analysis Model

This study conducted training using three algorithms, including Support Vector Machines (SVM), Logistic Regression (LR), Random Forest (RF). The training results are shown in Table 3 and Figure 3. The training results show that the SVM and RF models have high accuracy.

These models are suitable for the training datasets. Therefore, subsequent applications can use these two models as a tool to classify comments for unclassified comment data or newly generated comment data without retraining. The results of this study have helped to determine the appropriate method and tool to classify opinions. This is considered the essential step of the opinion mining process as the foundation for applying opinion mining in many fields.

*Figure 2. Collected corpus by year*
*Source: Authors*

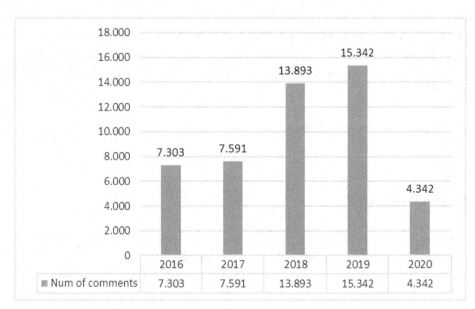

*Table 3. Experimental Results*

| Datasets | Metrics | RF | LR | SVM |
|----------|---------|-----|-----|-----|
| **Dataset of foody.vn** | Precision | 78% | 77% | 81% |
| | Recall | 76% | 75% | 77% |
| | F_score | 77% | 75% | 78% |
| | Accuracy | 78% | 76% | **80%** |
| **Dataset of diadiemanuong. com** | Precision | 78% | 78% | 97% |
| | Recall | 75% | 73% | 77% |
| | F_score | 76% | 75% | 84% |
| | Accuracy | 66% | 78% | **94%** |

(Source: Authors)

Figure 4 is Dashboard of Sentiment Analytics, and there are three charts in this view. The pie chart shows an overview of sentiment. The area chart shows sentiment over time (by year). The stacked column chart shows customer sentiment by store. These charts help managers monitor customer sentiment intuitively and accurately promptly.

## Results of NPS model

The experimental results of the NPS Score are shown through the Dashboard of Net Promoter Score (NPS) – Figure 5. Visualized results are convenient for users to view and analyze, especially for managers.

The NPS has a shallow score. This means that many people are not satisfied with companies' products or services. However, this is also an opportunity to collect feedback from customers objectively so that businesses can come up with the closest and most realistic strategies. Therefore, when conducting an NPS analysis, customers should be asked to leave specific comments on why they gave that score. This way, we can evaluate with a qualitative approach, which will help businesses pinpoint where to improve

*Figure 3. Experimental Results by charts*
Source: Authors

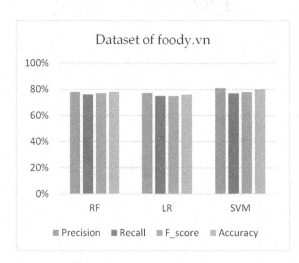

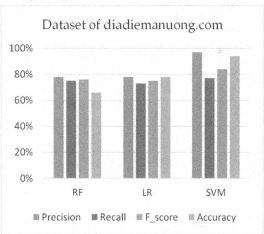

*Figure 4. Dashboard of Sentiment Analytics*
*Source: Authors*

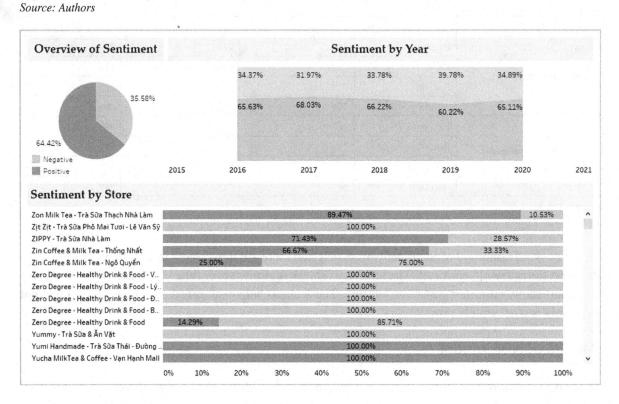

*Figure 5. Dashboard of Net Promoter Score*
*Source: Authors*

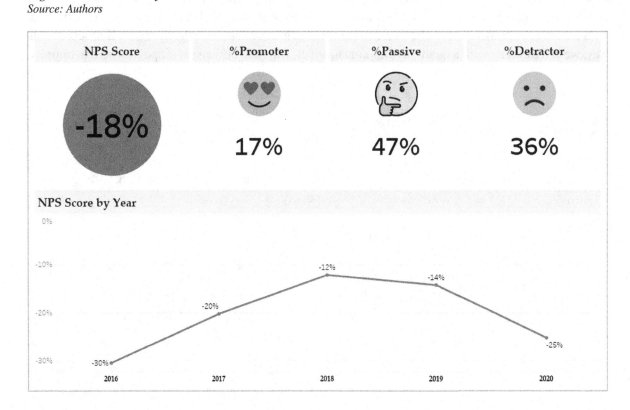

rather than just relying on statistics from the NPS score. For sure, not all feedback from customers is help-ful, and there will be superficial reviews. Therefore, businesses need to consider all feedback carefully.

## DISCUSSIONS

In this chapter, the research will compare and select suitable machine learning methods to analyze and classify sentiment based on customers' opinions in Vietnamese natural language. The applications of the opinion categorization depend on the field, the analysis model, and the source of the collected data. The research results can enable enterprise managers and service providers to know customers' satisfaction with their products or services and deeply understand their feelings so that there is a degree of adjustment that has corrected business decisions. It also helps food e-commerce managers in better e-commerce service design and delivery. It is difficult for businesses to foresee all the customers' issues with their products and services. Therefore, let customers be the ones who speak their opinions; this is customer-centricity. Furthermore, businesses can apply NPS in their work:

- Controlling the rate of Detractors to avoid losing customers: following up with Detractors can help businesses realize that the majority of customer complaints about your company are due to too long waiting times for quotes. With this finding, you can improve the level of happiness for your clients by changing your workflow reducing waiting times for them.
- Enabling Promoters to introduce more customers: The value of customers introduced by acquain-tances is higher than that of ordinary customers. Visitors who come to the business from the refer-ral channel have a higher rate of returning to use products or services, but the rate of leaving travel is lower than that of ordinary customers. Visitors coming from the referral channel bring higher profits for businesses than ordinary customers.
- Improving product and service quality: Enterprises can also use NPS as a tool to develop their products. A survey can be sent to customers to gain their opinion. From the survey, filter out com-ments related to products and services. Then compare the NPS score of each product or service feature to the customer's complaint issues to find out where the product needs perfection.

## FUTURE RESEARCH DIRECTIONS

Artificial intelligence or machine learning will not replace existing digital marketing jobs. Instead, it will help expand the capabilities of the modern manager, providing a basis for doing and getting better at analyzing user experience. In future studies, we will grow by setting the system to update data auto-matically. The data will automatically be extracted from the website and removed before saving it to the database. Collect more data from multiple sources, and develop research towards big data analytics. The application deploys user opinion analysis reports on the website, especially on mobile devices, making it more convenient for businesses to view information and make better decisions. Leverage the power of artificial intelligence and machine learning to empower the business, identify current problems, fix existing weaknesses, and start making a future impact.

## CONCLUSION

In this chapter, the research has tested, compared, and selected appropriate machine learning methods to analyze and classify emotions based on customer opinions. The applications of opinion classification will depend on the domain, the analytical model, and the source of the data collected. This study proposes an application solution in natural language analysis, specifically analyzing customer emotions based on comments posted on the e-commerce website. The solution is tested on many machine learning methods to compare the model's advantages and disadvantages and choose the best model through the F1-Score measure. With a seemingly endless pool of online content and data quirks, businesses are slowly transforming a digital marketer's job from a business storyteller to a technology manager. To streamline processes and increase productivity, digital marketers – both current and future – must start using machine learning tools to automate processes and use data effectively. If managers' goal is to increase engagement and brand awareness with potential customers, they need to understand their customers, especially their emotional perspective. The research results have some significant contributions as follows:

- Firstly, collecting the data set of online reviews of customers on the online food ordering service.
- Secondly, proposing an applied supervised machine learning model in analyzing online customer behavior, the research results show that the model has high accuracy and is suitable for the practical requirements of today's businesses.
- Thirdly, analyzing and illustrating NPS results through visual and analytical reports combined with information dimensions serves the decision-making needs of enterprises.
- Finally, the chapter contributes an interdisciplinary study that combines data collection and analysis methods and user perception analysis in customer experience management.

## REFERENCES

Ahmed, H. M., Javed Awan, M., Khan, N. S., Yasin, A., & Faisal Shehzad, H. M. (2021). Sentiment Analysis of Online Food Reviews using Big Data Analytics. *Elementary Education Online*, *20*(2), 827–836.

Aung, K. Z., & Myo, N. N. (2017, May). Sentiment analysis of students' comment using lexicon based approach. In *2017 IEEE/ACIS 16th international conference on computer and information science (ICIS)* (pp. 149-154). IEEE.

Cortes, C., & Vapnik, V. (1995). Support-vector networks. *Machine Learning*, *20*(3), 273–297.

Eachempati, P., Srivastava, P. R., Kumar, A., de Prat, J. M., & Delen, D. (2022). Can customer sentiment impact firm value? An integrated text mining approach. *Technological Forecasting and Social Change*, *174*, 121265.

El-Adly, M. I. (2019). Modelling the relationship between hotel perceived value, customer satisfaction, and customer loyalty. *Journal of Retailing and Consumer Services*, *50*, 322–332.

Feldman, R. (2013). Techniques and applications for sentiment analysis. *Communications of the ACM*, *56*(4), 82–89.

Gallagher, C., Furey, E., & Curran, K. (2019). The application of sentiment analysis and text analytics to customer experience reviews to understand what customers are really saying. *International Journal of Data Warehousing and Mining, 15*(4), 21–47.

Gao, X., Zhi, S., & Wang, X. (2021). Investigating the Relationship Among Ease-of-Use, NPS, and Customers' Sequent Spending of Cloud Computing Products. In HCI International 2021 - Posters. HCII 2021. Communications in Computer and Information Science, vol 1421. Springer.

Ghani, N. A., Hamid, S., Hashem, I. A. T., & Ahmed, E. (2019). Social media big data analytics: A survey. *Computers in Human Behavior, 101*, 417–428.

Ho, T. K. (1995, August). Random decision forests. In *Proceedings of 3rd international conference on document analysis and recognition* (Vol. 1, pp. 278-282). IEEE.

Hossain, M. A., Akter, S., & Yanamandram, V. (2022). Customer Analytics Capabilities in the Big Data Spectrum: A Systematic Approach to Achieve Sustainable Firm Performance. In I. Management Association (Ed.), Research Anthology on Big Data Analytics, Architectures, and Applications (pp. 888-901). IGI Global.

Kansal, N., Goel, L., & Gupta, S. (2020). A literature review on cross domain sentiment analysis using machine learning. *International Journal of Artificial Intelligence and Machine Learning, 10*(2), 43–56.

Kotler, P. (2017). Philip Kotler: Some of my adventures in marketing. *Journal of Historical Research in Marketing, 9*(2), 203–208.

Kumar, S., & Zymbler, M. (2019). A machine learning approach to analyze customer satisfaction from airline tweets. *Journal of Big Data, 6*(1), 1–16.

Ludbrook, F., Michalikova, K. F., Musova, Z., & Suler, P. (2019). Business models for sustainable innovation in industry 4.0: Smart manufacturing processes, digitalization of production systems, and data-driven decision making. *Journal of Self-Governance and Management Economics, 7*(3), 21–26.

Mandal, P. C. (2014). Net promoter score: A conceptual analysis. *International Journal of Management Concepts and Philosophy, 8*(4), 209–219.

Marda, V. (2018). Artificial intelligence policy in India: A framework for engaging the limits of data-driven decision-making. *Philosophical Transactions - Royal Society. Mathematical, Physical, and Engineering Sciences, 376*(2133), 20180087.

Mishra, V. K., & Tiruwa, H. (2017). Aspect-Based Sentiment Analysis of Online Product Reviews. In S. Trivedi, S. Dey, A. Kumar, & T. Panda (Eds.), *Handbook of Research on Advanced Data Mining Techniques and Applications for Business Intelligence* (pp. 175–191). IGI Global.

Mishra, V. K., & Tiruwa, H. (2017). Aspect-Based Sentiment Analysis of Online Product Reviews. In S. Trivedi, S. Dey, A. Kumar, & T. Panda (Eds.), *Handbook of Research on Advanced Data Mining Techniques and Applications for Business Intelligence* (pp. 175–191). IGI Global.

Mostafa, M. M. (2019). Clustering halal food consumers: A Twitter sentiment analysis. *International Journal of Market Research, 61*(3), 320–337.

Neethu, M. S., & Rajasree, R. (2013). Sentiment analysis in twitter using machine learning techniques. In *2013 Fourth International Conference on Computing, Communications and Networking Technologies (ICCCNT)* (pp. 1-5). IEEE.

Nguyen, D. Q., Nguyen, D. Q., Vu, T., & Pham, S. B. (2014). Sentiment classification on polarity reviews: an empirical study using rating-based features. *Proceedings of the 5th Workshop on Computational Approaches to Subjectivity, Sentiment and Social Media Analysis*, 128–135.

Pregibon, D. (1981). Logistic regression diagnostics. *Annals of Statistics*, *9*(4), 705–724.

Rao, S., & Kakkar, M. (2017, January). A rating approach based on sentiment analysis. In *2017 7th International Conference on Cloud Computing, Data Science & Engineering-Confluence* (pp. 557-562). IEEE.

Reichheld, F. F. (2003). The one number you need to grow. *Harvard Business Review*, *81*(12), 46–55.

Sarkar, S., & Palit, S. (2020). Sentiment Analysis of Product Reviews of Ecommerce Websites. In *International Conference on Artificial Intelligence: Advances and Applications 2019* (pp. 55-63). Singapore: Springer.

Schneider, D., Berent, M., Thomas, R., & Krosnick, J. (2008). *Measuring customer satisfaction and loyalty: Improving the 'Net-Promoter' score.* Poster presented at the Annual Meeting of the American Association for Public Opinion Research, New Orleans, LA.

Shelke, N. M., & Deshpande, S. P. (2018). Exploiting Chi Square Method for Sentiment Analysis of Product Reviews. *International Journal of Synthetic Emotions*, *9*(2), 76–93.

Singh, R. K., & Verma, H. K. (2020). Influence of Social Media Analytics on Online Food Delivery Systems. *International Journal of Information System Modeling and Design*, *11*(3), 1–21.

Situmorang, S. H., Rini, E. S., & Muda, I. (2017). Customer experience, net emotional value and net promoter score on muslim middle class women in medan. *International Journal of Economic Research*, *14*(20), 269–283.

Taboada, M., Brooke, J., Tofiloski, M., Voll, K., & Stede, M. (2011). Lexicon-based methods for sentiment analysis. *Computational Linguistics*, *37*(2), 267–307.

## ADDITIONAL READING

Albrecht, M., & Schlüter, T. (2022). Customer Journey Analytics. In M. Halfmann & K. Schüller (Eds.), *Marketing Analytics*. Springer Gabler.

Baehre, S., O'Dwyer, M., O'Malley, L., & Lee, N. (2022). The use of Net Promoter Score (NPS) to predict sales growth: Insights from an empirical investigation. *Journal of the Academy of Marketing Science*, *50*(1), 67–84.

Barsky, J. D., & Labagh, R. (1992). A strategy for customer satisfaction. *The Cornell Hotel and Restaurant Administration Quarterly*, *33*(5), 32–40.

Fisher, N. I., & Kordupleski, R. E. (2019). Good and bad market research: A critical review of Net Promoter Score. *Applied Stochastic Models in Business and Industry*, *35*(1), 138–151.

Li, H., Chen, Q., Zhong, Z., Gong, R., & Han, G. (2022). E-word of mouth sentiment analysis for user behavior studies. *Information Processing & Management, 59*(1), 102784.

Rahman, M. M., & Islam, M. N. (2022). Exploring the Performance of Ensemble Machine Learning Classifiers for Sentiment Analysis of COVID-19 Tweets. In S. Shakya, V. E. Balas, S. Kamolphiwong, & K. L. Du (Eds.), *Sentimental Analysis and Deep Learning. Advances in Intelligent Systems and Computing* (Vol. 1408). Springer.

Theodoridis, P. K., & Gkikas, D. C. (2019). How Artificial Intelligence Affects Digital Marketing. In A. Kavoura, E. Kefallonitis, & A. Giovanis (Eds.), *Strategic Innovative Marketing and Tourism*. Springer.

Trivedi, S. K., & Singh, A. (2021). Twitter sentiment analysis of app based online food delivery companies. Global Knowledge. *Memory and Communication, 70*(8/9), 891–910.

## KEY TERMS AND DEFINITIONS

**Customer Analytics:** Is a process by which data from customer behavior is used to help make key business decisions via market segmentation and predictive analytics.

**Customer Behavior:** The study of individuals, groups, or organizations and all the activities associated with the purchase, use and disposal of goods and services.

**Customer Satisfaction:** A measurement that determines how happy customers are with a company's products, services, and capabilities.

**Latent Dirichlet Allocation:** A three-level hierarchical Bayesian model, in which each item of a collection is modeled as a finite mixture over an underlying set of topics.

**Machine Learning:** The study of computer algorithms that can improve automatically through experience and by the use of data. It is seen as a part of artificial intelligence.

**Net Promoter Score:** A widely used market research metric that typically takes the form of a single survey question asking respondents to rate the likelihood that they would recommend a company, product, or a service to a friend or colleague.

**Sentiment Analysis:** The use of natural language processing, text analysis, computational linguistics, and biometrics to systematically identify, extract, quantify, and study affective states and subjective information.

**Text Mining:** Also referred to as text data mining, similar to text analytics, derives high-quality information from text.

# Customer Analytics:
## Deep Dive Into Customer Data

**Shivinder Nijjer**

https://orcid.org/0000-0002-0245-4263
*Chitkara University, India*

**Devesh Bathla**

https://orcid.org/0000-0003-3990-5934
*Chitkara University, India*

**Sandhir Sharma**

https://orcid.org/0000-0002-3940-8236
*Chitkara University, India*

**Sahil Raj**
*Punjabi University, India*

## INTRODUCTION

Customer analytics is defined as "the use of data to understand the composition, needs and satisfaction of the customer. Also, the enabling technology used to segment buyers into groupings based on behavior, to determine general trends, or to develop targeted marketing and sales activities" (Gartner, 2021). The leading analytics firm across the globe, SAS, defines customer analytics as "the processes and technologies that give organizations the customer insight necessary to deliver offers that are anticipated, relevant and timely" (Gray, 2021). As per the figures of a report by Mordor Intelligence (January, 2021), the customer analytics market, currently valued at USD 3.74 billion, is expected to grow three times in a period of five years (by 2026), to a value of approximately USD 10.2 billion. The compounded annual growth rate will amount to 18.2% over the forecast period 2021 – 2026, as per this report. Proliferation and advancement of cloud-based tools will enable integration of customer related intelligence such as data storage, analytical models, applications, in addition to added computing power. This integration will in turn enable generation of better and unprecedented insights about customers, and that too in real time.

The report also says that currently the leading provider of customer analytics solutions is North America; while the leading players in the field are giants like Adobe Systems Inc., IBM Corporation, Oracle Corporation, and so on, who have made substantial investments in R&D and expanded their innovative capacities through mergers and acquisitions. It is interesting to note that Asia Pacific market is the region identified with fastest growth rate. The scope of customer analytics is huge as it has diverse applications in all industries irrespective of their sizes, or region of geographical operation. The firms which leverage on Big data and customer data are seen to grow massively and sustain their business (Palmatier and Martin, 2019). Further, the companies that have developed business models centralized on customer data have been one of the most successful and promising firms.

DOI: 10.4018/978-1-7998-9220-5.ch063

Loyalty of customers is highly questionable, and firms are debating globally whether there is a need to purse this aspect anymore (Deloitte, 2020). Irrespective of the industry of operation, dwindling customer loyalty is hurting profits of the companies. Primarily, globalization, more information accessibility, higher interactions among consumers, global reach are a few factors which leave a daunting impact on consumer's mind and ultimately make them fickle and less loyal. The only alternative available to the firms is to develop ways to understand their customers intimately, evolve their needs, and through this understanding help them grow thereby retaining them for company's growth. The basic point of emphasis is that for this intimate understanding, companies need to tap into all probable sources of customer data by leveraging on customer analytics.

It is also important to understand that there are many channels and sources generating data about customers which firms can tap into to gain insights about customer's mindset through the application of analytics. For example (Zaki, 2019), Zara uses big data to detect current fashion trends and dynamically adapt its supply chain to stay in tune with changing customer's fashion preferences. Similarly, the leading newspaper 'The Times' offered free content to its readers through its website. The Times tapped into the weblogs and clickstream data generated by online readers to develop unique reader profiles through application of descriptive analytics. This enabled them to better target advertisement and premium content based on preferences suggested by the digital profile. There are many such examples where analytics applied on unconventional customer data sources has provided competitive advantage to the firms. Every interaction with customers leaves a trail of data. Customer analytics drills into this trail to draw a wider and clearer picture of customer interaction enlisting everything from their product choices, preferences, reasons for purchase and need for interaction with the firm. They can be understood by analyzing and interviewing customer-facing employees. Social networks, weblogs, transactional data, journals, feedback and reviews, purchase history, demographic details, sensor data such as tracking eye movement, customer pathways, needs and preferences, channel preferences, payment preferences, and so on. All of these are diverse data sources from which information about a customer can be extracted. Advances in machine learning enables embedding analytics using multiple data points garnered throughout the consumer journey (Zaki, 2019), which provides a real time picture of consumer experience, compared with traditional methods like Net Promoter score or satisfaction surveys.

Customer analytics also comes in handy by catering to real time information needs of the customer (Mordor Intelligence, 2021). For example, recommendations generated by online shopping websites and tailored offers being displayed dynamically during product searches build loyalty of the customer. The emerging technological trends like Artificial Intelligence and Machine learning, Marketing 5.0 and digital transformation are also significantly changing the way of interaction and understanding a customer. Use of machine learning enables the firms to build a holistic picture of the customer. Cloud technologies enable integration of customer data, models and simulations at one platform, and thereby, reforming the reach to customers.

## BACKGROUND

### Definition, Concept of Customer data

When customers interact with the companies, they generate different data in varying quantities (Ahmed, 2020). For example, their interests, behavior, demographics, social media profiles are all tapped by the companies. Firms can leverage on these data to generate lots of customer insights and gain competitive edge. The nature of data collected generates different value for the companies. All these data hold different values for the firms as they contribute differently to enhancing the customer experience (Krie and Micheaux,2006). Consumer attitudes play the most important role in gaining customer insights and thereby delivering best customer experience. For example, understanding how customers behave and their patterns of purchase enable firms to apply segmentation and devise a customized sales strategy (Lam et al, 2021). Internet, digitalization, Artificial Intelligence and cloud computing has led to unconventional and diverse customer data sources. These can be broadly categorized into structured and unstructured data sources. Structured implies that they have a specific standard format and therefore can be easily written to data stores and extracted for analysis. For example, account details of a customer are structured data as it has a fixed number of fields like Name, date of birth, email ID, address, gender and so on, which require data entry in fixed format and length. This data holds lot of potential for providing descriptive insights about customers, such as frequent purchasing age groups or regions. Unstructured data possess heterogeneity in structure, such as a Facebook post may contain images, audio, text, emoticons and so on. This makes it difficult to store and analyze, however, many advanced analytical techniques are available these days to generate insights from such data. For example, unstructured call log data generated from call centers can be used for prediction of customer churn (Vo et al, 2021).

Although no precise topology of customer data is available, lots of previous research have attempted to develop the same (Crie and Micheaux, 2006; Fabijan et al, 2016; Kiely, 1998; Morey et al, 2015; Zahay et al, 2012). They have come up with different terms such as qualitative and quantitative data, psychographic data, historical data, relational data, socio-demographic data and so on. Using the categories provided by Keener et al (2020), this work has attempted to summarize different types of customer data encountered in previous research works in Table 1. Keener and others (2020) summarize that there are four basic categories of customer data – Basic data, Interaction data, Behavioral data and Attitudinal data. Basic data refers to standard personal details like Name, age, gender, income and so on which can be used by firms to understand common attributes shared by customers of a firm. Interaction or engagement data refers to different customer touchpoints such as emails, Facebook ads, webpage views, and so on. This is useful to understand how consumers respond to interaction efforts of firm such as effectiveness of a campaign. Behavioral data refers to the insights about customer experience such as account deactivation, feature uses, purchase patterns and so on. Attitudinal data enables understanding what customers think about a brand and its offerings and includes reviews posted online, feedback, satisfaction surveys and so on.

Platforms such as Facebook, Twitter, and Amazon have enabled visibility to quantitative data such as likes, shares, star ratings, as well as qualitative data such as consumer comments, replies, and reviews. Reviews, comments, posts, likes, and shares can provide important information to the retailer on where it stands with regards to competitors and how products are performing among different consumer segments (Krafft et al, 2021). This data can improve consumer-firm interactions by informing product ranking systems (Ghose et al. 2012), personalizing product webpages using click stream data (Hauser et al. 2009), and developing actionable brand sentiment metrics (Schweidel and Moe 2014).

Journal data which captures audio, video, or Webtracking records of customer behavior, use of CCTV footage inside store to analyze customer pathways and design store layouts (Watson, 2015). Pictures, events, 'likes,' and networks of a customer extracted from social media data may provide additional insights into purchase motivation and consumption patterns. These may prove useful for tailored customer recommendations.

Demographics, account history and customer interaction data from call centre phone logs can be used to predict the risk of client churns and develop customer segments based on their interaction and use behavior (Vo et al, 2021). Using purchase behavior data, customers with similar consumption re-

*Table 1. Summary of Customer Data types*

| S.No. | Data Types | Examples | |
|---|---|---|---|
| | | **Structured** | **Unstructured** |
| 1 | **Basic Data** | Demographics like name, address, phone type, nationality, weight and body size, marital status, household size, political affiliation, monthly income<br>Favourite shoe brand, Account registration details and account balance, location, number of search requests, duration of search, Business transactions, Billing details, Shipping details, IP address | Mobile location<br>Facebook profile<br>Shipping instructions<br>Cooking instructions |
| 2 | **Interaction Data** | Webpage clicks<br>ATM transactions<br>Sensors<br>Number of website visits and number of exposures, Incident requests, customer touchpoints like POS | Call records, website reviews, social media reviews, Customer voice, Images posted, Moves in a game, Referrals, GPS data, mobile signal data, Impressions and clicks on Digital Ad banner, Email clicks, Customer interviews |
| 3 | **Attitudinal Data** | Satisfaction surveys, Sensors | Feedback, Facebook likes and engagement, Conversion rate |
| 4 | **Behavioural Data** | Timings and duration of logging to a website, Number of social media followers, Credit card information, friend list, Personality traits | Web surfing history, Web browsing history, Purchase history, social media posts, Customer orders, Products added in cart, Products wishlishted, Internet banking, Followers data, facial movements, CCTV footage inside stores |

cords can be clustered into similar groups for effective group targeting and recommendations, identify abnormal behavior like infrequent purchases or high-volume purchase contradicting past pattern which will benefit both firm and customer (Huang, 2021). Social media posts of customers can be used to infer how consumers respond to marketing activities of firms such as use of AI enabled chatbots (Kushwaha et al, 2021), or how effective reviews can aid in consumer decision making (Lee et al, 2021). Similarly, customer mobile location, purchase feedback, purchase pattern can be used for location based advertising and dynamic pricing (Alrumiah and Hadwan, 2021). Previous transactions can be used to make next best offer to consumers, gamification can be used to enhance customer experience and predict next clicks and make recommendations, sentiments of customers can be analyzed to predict sales and referral management (Shakya and Smys, 2021). It is worth mentioning here that when any of these customer data possesses the features of 7V viz. Volume, Velocity, Veracity, Variety, Variability, Visualization and Value, it is described as Big Data (Mach-Krol and Hadasik, 2021). For example, customer complaints data such as from call logs, opinions and sentiments expressed in social media posts or website reviews, form Big Data and are useful for analyzing customer needs and better serve them.

## FOCUS OF THE ARTICLE

Experts have reported numerous benefits of using customer analytics, prominent among which are increased sales to new and existing customers, lower customer acquisition and retention costs, reduction in customer churn and increased loyalty, improved channel mix, increased sales force effectiveness, and delivery of higher returns on marketing and promotions investments (Deloitte, 2020). Therefore, considering the novelty and significance of customer analytics, this book chapter attempts to explore this area by focusing on answering three questions primarily:

1. How customer analytics and machine learning models transform the consumer journey?
2. Which major machine learning solutions are used for customer analytics?
3. How does customer analytics reap benefit for both the firm and the customer?

## How Customer Analytics and Machine Learning Models Transform the Consumer Journey?

The current competitive landscape has made customer retention and acquisition an urgent priority among retailers. As reported by a Mordor Intelligence (2021) report, customers are prone to switching between brands, implicating the brands to invest substantially to enhance their understanding about the customers. Technology is evolving that understanding by leaps and bounds. In the year 2012, when Gothe Nyman, a professor of psychology, proposed that firms should engage in the idea of Internet of Behaviors (IoB) – gathering Internet of Things (IoT) data regarding a customer (Javaid et al, 2021), it led the firms to not only gain insights about customer choice, but also led to supply chain restructuring. This is because IoB enables to develop a single comprehensive view of customers by tracking their interactions starting right from visit alert to post purchase use. When analytics is embedded into this comprehensive integration, several transformations are possible such as deeper understanding of consumer behavior, promoting and motivating consumer loyalty, forecast response to shopping advertisements, generation and sharing of prompts to change consumer behavior, in addition to tracking food, sleep habits, heart rate, and blood sugar levels to detect problems with the user's health and recommend behavioral changes. Using IoB, physical and online movements of individuals can be tracked providing details at lowest level of granularity about desires, dislikes, lifestyles, preferences, favorite restaurants, clothes shops, travel plans and locations and travel times of customers.

Embedding analytics into customer data has brought about changes in the way customers are managed by the firms. The journey of a consumer with a firm starting from acquisition to engagement, post purchase behaviour and churn analysis, is now being managed dynamically or real time using analytics. The journey can be represented by different touchpoints or points serving as medium of interaction between consumer and the firm, and each of them leaves a positive, negative or neutral effect on the consumer mindset (Buhalis and Volchek, 2021).

Analytics is also enhancing pre and post purchase behavioural understanding and management for consumers. Through different touchpoints, customer interaction is dynamically handled which leads to better customer engagement, satisfaction, and experience. Customers are experiencing lesser wait time and reduction in time to service due to analytics. For example, Dominos AI (artificial intelligence) enabled chatbot handles customer support requests during peak hours and aid customers to navigate the product offerings without putting them in a waiting queue (Kushawa et al, 2021). Amazon also uses big data analytics to provide an automated customer service (Alrumiah and Hadwan, 2021). Segmentation of consumers is another dominant application of customer analytics which provides personalized delivery of products and services to consumers through better understanding of their behaviour. Pandora, which is a music streaming company, applied segmentation to categorize millions of songs based on 450 attributes based on its rich database of consumer preferences, delivering almost individually tailored radio stations to its consumers (Hagiu and Wright, 2020). Besides this, consumers now experience real-time effect on their purchase intention, attitude towards brand and decision making through communication strate-

*Figure 1. Impact of customer analytics on customers*

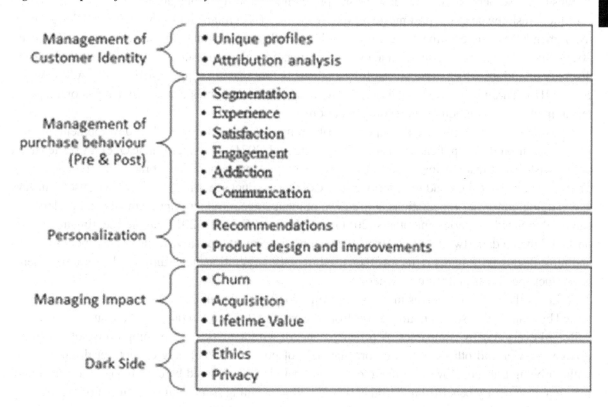

gies implemented by the marketers through different touchpoints. These touchpoints can be webpages, emails, social media, surveys, word of mouth and so on. For example, consumer is walking through a store and receives a discount offer through his mobile message, or while browsing Facebook, user ends up signing a course whose advertisement flashed on his webpage. Therefore, touchpoints are important for generating awareness of products and services, considering them for consumption, purchase decisions, repeat purchases, and advocating to others. With companies inventing new ways to gauge customer satisfaction such as gamification (Shakya and Smys, 2021), consumers are more willing to respond and reaping benefit in terms of product or service improvement. For example, a Finnish startup Happy or Not (HON) uses a terminal with four push buttons containing smiley faces and has been able to yield 600 million responses from customers so far (Thomke, 2019). Further, companies are using newer means to effect purchase decision of consumers through analytics. Alrumiah and Hadwan (2021) demonstrate that factors like image quality, reviews quality, past purchase patterns have an impact on purchase decision making and their presentation to the consumer makes a significant effect on their final decision. Lam and others (2021) also demonstrate that a customised sales strategy can be developed for different segments of consumers based on their behaviour and past purchase patterns. Similarly, Lee and others (2021) suggest how helpfulness of reviews can be enhanced to aid the consumers in both writing and searching for effective reviews.

Recommendation engines or recommendation systems are one of the prominent uses of analytics in customer domain. These allow dynamic real-time display of tailored offers during product searches and aid in building loyalty of the customer (Mordor Intelligence, 2021). Many companies have implemented these systems like Amazon used which gained 35% of the sales for the company, Netflix which suggests movies to consumers based on their taste and preferences, Spotify which automatically tailor playlists and finds fresh music as per past music played by the user (Alrumiah and Hadwan, 2021). Google even recommends news in real time using this technology while also personalizing search content (Kim et al, 2021). Such systems reduce search and evaluation time, introduce new items to consumers, and present diversity of options which user can carefully evaluate before making a purchase decision (Adomavicius et al, 2018). Through post use feedback, the recommendation engines can improvise personalization, reaching closer to individualized recommendations.

Consumers are now playing an important role in market research for product development and improvement through the application of analytics (Tsang et al, 2021). The smartphone OnePlus started as an online wish-list of features for a smartphone and developed into a formidable brand (Krafft et al, 2021). Through analysis of short and long-term trends, existing product specifications, personas, user journeys and gauging consumer expectations at pre-development stage, product improvements and preferences can be elucidated. Banerjee and others (2021) and Mars and Gouider (2017) applied sentiment analysis on social media data (tweets) to understand consumer sentiments (positive or negative) about products and most discussed features. This was then used to make suggestions regarding product improvements to product specialists and feature owners.

With all the positive changes made in consumer journey by analytics, there is also a dark side presented by many articles. This mainly arises from the amount, type and frequency of consumer data being collected every day by companies. A primary concern with analytics is the compromise of consumer privacy. Auxier and others (2019) report that 62% of consumers feel they cannot get through a day without being tracked. However, now the personal data is being shared by consumers consciously not merely for monetary benefits but for other benefits like obtaining some value addition. For example, by sharing additional personal details, what additional service would they receive is the trade-off consumers are willing to invest in. The dark side of customer analytics in retailing is mainly related to security and privacy, incentives, risks, data sharing management, and data vulnerabilities that ultimately erode customer confidence and satisfaction level (Goi, 2021). There is a risk that the consumer data maybe misused or shared with third party for monetary benefits. In addition to the privacy concerns, there is a rising concern of shopping addiction arising out of enhancing stickiness feature of customer analytics (Alrumiah and Hadwan, 2021). They demonstrate that understanding peak time of shopping and then enticing consumers through flash messages, discount offers, and real-time advertising has caused shopping addiction among consumers. Another notable concern is the manipulation of preferences of consumers caused by recommendation engines (Adomavicius et al, 2018). Faulty recommendation engines that inaccurately estimate consumers' true preferences stand to pull down willingness to pay for some items and increase it for others, regardless of the likelihood of actual fit. This may also promote unethicality as some firms may inflate such recommendations artificially to attract users. Surprisingly, recommendation systems alter how much consumers are willing to pay for a product that they just listened to. Consumers don't just prefer what they have experienced and know they enjoy; they prefer what the system said they would like. Although recommendation systems generate a wide variety of options for the consumers, they need to spend considerable time and energy in careful evaluation of these alternatives for purchase or consumption which is not recoverable.

## Which Major Machine Learning Solutions Are Used for Customer Analytics?

The application of machine learning tools for customer analytics can be broadly classified into three major areas – predictive, prescriptive and descriptive analytics. Another term which has emerged due

*Figure 2. Customer analytics solutions*

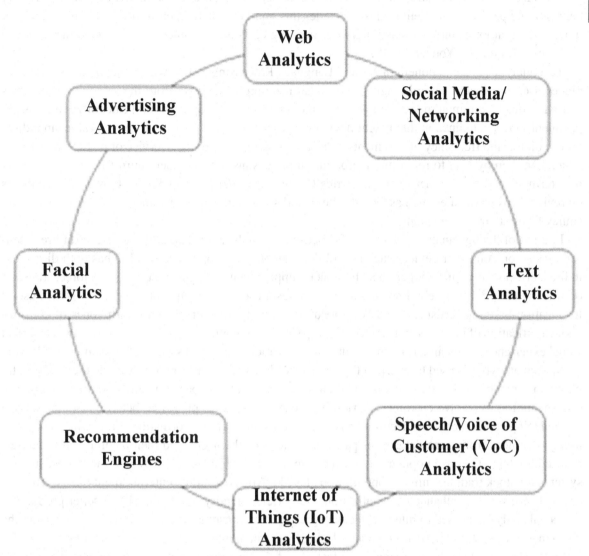

to volume, veracity and velocity of customer data is Big Data Analytics. Predictive analytics is used to predict consumer behavior such as next purchase, prescriptive analytics is used to make recommendations while descriptive analytics is used to profile the customers. This has vase number of applications for the firms such as attribution analysis (which interaction touchpoint generated the maximum consumer engagement), spot influencers, segment consumers, predict customer churn, target products and services, pragmatic advertising and so on. The solutions of customer analytics are classified based on the source of customer data, as shown in Figure 2.

Web analytics involves collection of customer data from all sources of Internet such as weblog data, click stream data, browsing data, user search queries, and so on; and aids in understanding consumer behavior on website and optimize website performance for attracting and converting maximum number of users. This can be useful to enhance user stickiness, optimize search results, and so on. Social media analytics involves interpret data collected from social media sites such as Facebook, Twitter, and so on. It is useful to segment the consumers by different demographics like age, gender, and identify influencers (who fetch maximum likes and followers) among each segment. It is also useful to understand consumer behavior and perform sentiment analysis. Besides this, market structure, customer preferences, areas of improvement among employees and building shopping carts for customers, can be aided through web analytics (Miloud and Youcef, 2020).

Text analytics is a component of Natural Language Processing (NLP) which encompass set of techniques used to process natural languages to glean meaningful insights from the same. Text analytics is used to detect common themes in the text, mine sentiments and opinions and categorize texts as per prevalent topics contained in them. Sentiment analysis can be used to generate "buzz" value, an indicator of volume and frequency of comments of customers around a product, service or marketing activity, which can thereby lead to real time interpretation of reasons for customer churn (Stoddler, 2012). A new term Voice of Customer (VoC) analytics (Grinvald, 2019) involves application of text analytics on reviews posted on sites such as Google, Yelp, and so on and gauge customer feedback devices with smiley faces at airport terminals.

Internet of Things analytics is primarily focused on analysis of data collected from different sensors placed on consumer devices such as mobiles, cameras, microphones etc.) IoT has both direct and indirect effect on consumer experience. It impacts supply chain through better planning, forecasting and optimizing the prices, thereby lowering the service response time for end consumers. IoT is also useful for location-based advertising (identifying location through GPS sensors on smartphones of consumers), gamification of products and services (laptop signals indicating how colors, temperature, etc, effect visual experience of consumers), time spent in a store (tracking hotspot signals of consumer), and so on.

Speech analytics is used to interpret the voice recordings of consumers, for example their call centre phone logs can be analysed to understand their sentiments, rate of speech, identify solutions from past documentation to resolve customer queries. This can be useful in providing better consumer service and reducing customer churn. Recommendation systems are sort of information filters which can mine user preferences from huge datasets of past transactions of the users, and then recommend them new relevant content. They are popularly used to enhance consumer experience by news websites, support systems for stock trading, online shopping websites like Amazon, online entertainment like Netflix and so on. These systems enhance personalization, club offers, identify trending and best seller products.

Facial analytics is used to interpret facial expressions of consumers, maybe in real time or using the consumer images stored in firm's database. Using facial recognition, firms are devising newer ways for faster checkout at stores by scanning facial features of the customers. Similarly facial analytics is used by stores to fetch real time offers for consumers based on their past purchase patterns. Firms can also devise tailored promotions by tracking real time expressions of consumers such as excited, depressed, and so on. Another important area is to develop effective advertising campaigns using customer data. Click stream data, eye movements, time spent on webpage, basic account details, images posted by customers, reviews and feedback provided can be used to determine how consumers respond to different advertisements. Real time bidding or auctions is also an application of advertising analytics (Camilleri, 2020). Application of facial analytics and image recognition techniques on selfies data can be used to identify influencers while in stores, they can assist in speeding up customer purchase decision and intelligent shelf display (Kietzmann et al, 2018). Feedback about products can also be generated by gauging and interpreting customer reactions while in store. Natural language processing-based AI speaking agents can write advertisements and tailor to different customer segments. Advertising analytics can be used for content creation for chatbots, reducing complaint resolution time and return queries quickly.

## REAL LIFE USE CASE OF FACIAL ANALYTICS

This small caselet presents a real-life use case of facial analytics in retailing (NTech Lab, 2021). A retail store deployed a facial recognition software which tracks new and repeat faces of visitors in store each day. This data is saved in customer's CRM account also containing past purchase history of a customer. When the software recognizes a repeat customer at Point of Sale (PoS) system in the store, it activates a personal discount, even if the customer does not have a discount card. Besides this, the client profile is also fetched from social media based on image matching, and personalized offers are made to the clients. This is useful for enhancing customer loyalty.

## IMPLICATIONS AND FUTURE RESEARCH DIRECTIONS

With plethora of tools available for application of analytics on hugely diverse customer, data, it is time companies take stock of their data and apply to leverage benefits for both the growth of the firm and fulfilment of the customer. One prominent implication for the firms is that more the firms pay attention to customer needs and preferences and translates it into creation of a better experience, it ultimately leads to more number of customers adopting the product, since customers understand that they are being cared for by the firms (Haigu and Wright, 2020). The point here is that firms need to leverage on the network effects created by this implication. The ultimate goal of analytics is individual customization and while inferring network effects through application of analytics initially will aid the firms to understand what people with similar preferences (belonging to a group) want, drilling down to individual customer data will allow for customization at individual (most granular) level. Although this will create switching cost for the firms, improvement in the products and services through this method has a possibility of causing network effects, that is wider acceptability and therefore, larger customer base. At the same time, former technique will allow for enhancing customer loyalty, also in turn raising the barrier to entry. A classic example as illustrated by Haigu and Wright (2021) is that of Pandora which is music streaming application. It initially was the only big player in digital music streaming owing to its huge customer database and analytics. This gave Pandora the power to interpret the customer's taste for music at individual level through their voting mechanism for each song. However, since the user base and therefore customer data majorly belonged to United States, it could not be a hit globally losing its market space to Spotify and Apple. As the authors put it, Spotify leveraged on network effects by offering sharing and discovery features on its application like users can listen to other's playlists and stations. This was Spotify fetched more customers and has become a global player.

Another prominent implication for the firms is to adopt techniques to manage huge variety and volume of customer data. Through adoption of customer master data management (MDM) strategies and systems, the firms are able to offer a 360 degree view of customer data to all levels of management irrespective of time and place (Stoddler, 2012). As is seen in Section 1 of this text, customer data resides in many different systems and applications, and MDM enables integrated uniform view and storage of this data. Many firms have reported that the most challenging issue that they face for implementation of customer analytics is integration of data to offer a unified comprehensive view. In addition to unification of records, another significant concern which MDM eradicates is the availability and storage of real time data. Dynamic applications like CRM which deploy real time data analytics have only one main requirement which is speed of access. Competitive advantage in the present scenario can be gained by responding to market demand and understanding customer cues faster than the competitors. Again, MDM allows for storing such data in a different manner which is well suited for real time access and enables faster application of real time analytics. One example is that of implementing columnar databases instead of transaction-oriented databases for storage of real time data.

Another implication is the impact it has on marketing and sales and finance functions of the firm. For example, using customer analytics, marketing executives can generate insights to create better awareness about their brands and corporate image. Analytics can enable a better view of the impact of analytics on finances of the firm. For example, return on investment (ROI) of the analytics-based campaigns can be gauged through availability of data and application of analytics. A report by McKinsey DataMatics (2016) suggests that the firms which use customer analytics are likely to take decisions which will make them ahead in terms of profit, sales and sales growth from their competitors by at least 126 percent. Analytics ensures that profit margins are enhanced for the firms. For example, customer analytics flags the customers who frequently return their items imposing high costs to the company and companies can use this information to ban such customers as Amazon does (Kollmeyer, 2016). Similarly, customer segments created through application of analytics allow the companies to impose varied fee structure depending on the level of profitability for the firm.

The wider the variety of available data, the better will be the outcome of the application of analytics. For example, Griva and colleagues (2021) applied segmentation to customers visiting retail stores. In this, they added lots of data like visits to the store, categories of products, basket value, volume of transactions, and so on and noticed that with each addition the outcome of segmentation was enriched. They further played with four Ps of marketing, by adding other features of product to the data, transactions related to promotions, pricing of products, and different channels of offering the products. Although each 'P' affected the segments differently, but again consistency was seen in the fact that more the variables, better is the quality of results, given that variables influence the outcomes.

Most of the firms are plagued with the inferring the starting point of implementation of customer analytics. The basic premise of any successful adoption of customer analytics is the culture of the firm. It is advised that solely focusing on IT solutions would not enable success in analytics, rather it has to adopted holistically. Merely focusing on hiring skilled employees and investing in IT infrastructure would not deliver value until the leadership is enthusiastic to base their decisions on these outcomes and turn them into actions. It is therefore, implied for the firms that to derive value from customer analytics, management of the firm has to set up a system which empowers all leadership to take fact based decisions, value the inputs from analytics solutions, generate actionable insights and develop action based plans, hire and believe in in-house expertise of the firm, enable quality data management and development of holistic, unified and integrated IT systems. Specifically, it is advised that companies benchmark their processes and services, in order to highlight performance gaps which can be better understood and acted upon through application of analytics. A successful customer analytics strategy therefore needs to be developed which focuses on customer MDM systems, building a culture supportive of analytics, development of benchmarks and identification of metrics for the application of analytics, and measurement of ROI from the same.

## REFERENCES

Adomavicius, G., Bockstedt, J., Curley, S. P., Zhang, J., & Ransbotham, S. (2018, November 13). The Hidden Side Effects of Recommendation Systems. *MIT Sloan Management Review*. Accessed at: https://sloanreview.mit.edu/article/the-hidden-side-effects-of-recommendation-systems/

Ahmed, S. (2020). *A Beginner's Guide to Customer Data: Definition, Types, Collection, and Management.* Smart Karrot. Accessed at: https://www.smartkarrot.com/resources/blog/customer-data/

Alrumiah, S. S., & Hadwan, M. (2021). Implementing big data analytics in e-commerce: Vendor and customer view. *IEEE Access: Practical Innovations, Open Solutions, 9*, 37281–37286. doi:10.1109/ACCESS.2021.3063615

Auxier, B., Rainie, L., Anderson, M., Perrin, A., Kumar, M., & Turner, E. (2019, November 15). *Americans and Privacy: Concerned, Confused and Feeling Lack of Control Over Their Personal Information.* Pew Research Center. Accessed from https://www.pewresearch.org/internet/2019/11/15/americans-and-privacy-concerned-confused-and-feeling-lack-of-control-over-their-personal-information/]

Banerjee, S., Singh, J. P., Dwivedi, Y. K., & Rana, N. P. (2021). Social media analytics for end-users' expectation management in information systems development projects. *Information Technology & People, 34*(6), 1600–1614. doi:10.1108/ITP-10-2020-0706

Buhalis, D., & Volchek, K. (2021). Bridging marketing theory and big data analytics: The taxonomy of marketing attribution. *International Journal of Information Management, 56*, 102253. doi:10.1016/j.ijinfomgt.2020.102253

Camilleri, M. A. (2020). The use of data-driven technologies for customer-centric marketing. *International Journal of Big Data Management, 1*(1), 50–63. doi:10.1504/IJBDM.2020.106876

Crie, D., & Micheaux, A. (2006). From customer data to value: What is lacking in the information chain? *Database Marketing & Customer Strategy Management, 13*(4), 282–299. doi:10.1057/palgrave.dbm.3240306

Deloitte. (2020). *Customer Analytics. The Three-minute guide.* Accessed at: https://www2.deloitte.com/content/dam/Deloitte/global/Documents/Deloitte-Analytics/dttl-analytics-us-da-customeranalytics3minguide.pdf

Foss, B., Henderson, I., Johnson, P., Murray, D., & Stone, M. (2002). Managing the quality and completeness of customer data. *Journal of Database Marketing & Customer Strategy Management, 10*(2), 139–158. doi:10.1057/palgrave.jdm.3240105

Gartner. (2021). *Customer Analytics.* Information Technology Glossary, Gartner Glossary. Accessed at: https://www.gartner.com/en/information-technology/glossary/customer-analytics

Germann, F., Lilien, G. L., Fiedler, L., & Kraus, M. (2014). Do retailers benefit from deploying customer analytics? *Journal of Retailing, 90*(4), 587–593. doi:10.1016/j.jretai.2014.08.002

Gray, C. (2021). *Customer Analytics: What it is and why it matters.* SAS. Accessed at: https://www.sas.com/en_us/insights/marketing/customer-analytics.html

Grinvald, B. (2019). *5 Ways Big Data Customer Analytics Can Impact Business Results.* Accessed at: https://revuze.it/blog/5-ways-big-data-customer-analytics-can-impact-business-results/

Hagiu, A., & Wright, J. (2020). When Data created Competitive Advantage and when it doesn't? *Harvard Business Review*, 94–101.

He, W., Tian, X., & Wang, F. K. (2019). Innovating the customer loyalty program with social media: A case study of best practices using analytics tools. *Journal of Enterprise Information Management, 32*(5), 807–823. doi:10.1108/JEIM-10-2018-0224

Helm, Y. Y., Khedr, A. E., Kolief, S., & Haggag, E. (2019). An enhanced business intelligence approach for increasing customer satisfaction using mining techniques. *International Journal of Computer Science and Information Security, 17*(4), 159–175.

Huang, X. (2021, August). Design of Rural E-commerce Customer Data Mining System. *Journal of Physics: Conference Series, 1992*(3), 032087. doi:10.1088/1742-6596/1992/3/032087

Javaid, M., Haleem, A., Singh, R. P., Rab, S., & Suman, R. (2021). Internet of Behaviours (IoB) and its role in customer services. *Sensors International, 2*, 100122. doi:10.1016/j.sintl.2021.100122

Jayaram, D., Manrai, A. K., & Manrai, L. A. (2015). Effective use of marketing technology in Eastern Europe: Web analytics, social media, customer analytics, digital campaigns and mobile applications. *Journal of Economics, Finance and Administrative Science, 20*(39), 118–132. doi:10.1016/j.jefas.2015.07.001

Keener, M. (2020). *What are different types of customer data?* Insightly. https://www.insightly.com/blog/2020/04/customer-data-types

Kiely, D. A. (1998). Synchronizing supply chain operations with consumer demand using customer data. *The Journal of Business Forecasting, 17*(4), 3.

Kietzmann, J., Paschen, J., & Treen, E. (2018). Artificial intelligence in advertising: How marketers can leverage artificial intelligence along the consumer journey. *Journal of Advertising Research, 58*(3), 263–267. doi:10.2501/JAR-2018-035

Kim, J., Choi, I., & Li, Q. (2021). Customer satisfaction of recommender system: Examining accuracy and diversity in several types of recommendation approaches. *Sustainability, 13*(11), 6165. doi:10.3390u13116165

Kollmeyer, B. (2016). *Want to get banned from shopping at Amazon? Do this.* Accessed at: https://www.marketwatch.com/story/if-youre-returning-a-lot-of-amazon-purchases-heres-your-cautionary-tale-2016-03-21?__hstc=23243621.f3cafb6a7a19981d21f7583ea432d bd3.1468105118941.1471110620348.1471118976204.144&__hssc=23243621.1.1471118976204&__ hsfp=1551434154

Kushwaha, A. K., Kumar, P., & Kar, A. K. (2021). What impacts customer experience for B2B enterprises on using AI-enabled chatbots? Insights from Big data analytics. *Industrial Marketing Management, 98*, 207–221. doi:10.1016/j.indmarman.2021.08.011

Lam, H. Y., Tsang, Y. P., Wu, C. H., & Tang, V. (2021). Data analytics and the P2P cloud: An integrated model for strategy formulation based on customer behaviour. *Peer-to-Peer Networking and Applications, 14*(5), 2600–2617. doi:10.100712083-020-00960-z

Lee, M., Kwon, W., & Back, K. J. (2021). Artificial intelligence for hospitality big data analytics: Developing a prediction model of restaurant review helpfulness for customer decision-making. *International Journal of Contemporary Hospitality Management, 33*(6), 2117–2136. doi:10.1108/IJCHM-06-2020-0587

Lin, W.-C., Ke, S.-W., & Tsai, C.-F. (2017). Top 10 data mining techniques in business applications: A brief survey. *Kybernetes*, *46*(7), 1158–1170. doi:10.1108/K-10-2016-0302

Liu, X., Shin, H., & Burns, A. C. (2021). Examining the impact of luxury brand's social media marketing on customer engagement: Using big data analytics and natural language processing. *Journal of Business Research*, *125*, 815–826. doi:10.1016/j.jbusres.2019.04.042

Liu, Y., Soroka, A., Han, L., Jian, J., & Tang, M. (2020). Cloud-based big data analytics for customer insight-driven design innovation in SMEs. *International Journal of Information Management*, *51*, 102034. doi:10.1016/j.ijinfomgt.2019.11.002

Mach-Król, M., & Hadasik, B. (2021). On a Certain Research Gap in Big Data Mining for Customer Insights. *Applied Sciences (Basel, Switzerland)*, *11*(15), 6993. doi:10.3390/app11156993

Mars, A., & Gouider, M. S. (2017). Big data analysis to Features Opinions Extraction of customer. In *International Conference on Knowledge Based and Intelligent Information and Engineering Systems*. Elsevier. 10.1016/j.procs.2017.08.114

McKinsey DataMatics. (2016). *Why Customer Analytics Matter?* Accessed at: https://www.google.com/url?sa=t&rct=j&q=&esrc=s&source=web&cd=&ved=2ahUKEwjw3ur2ndPzAhU4zzgGHcmRBpYQFnoECAwQAQ&url=https%3A%2F%2Fwww.mckinsey.com%2F~%2Fmedia%2FMcKinsey%2FBusiness%2520Functions%2FMarketing%2520and%2520Sales%2FOur%2520Insights%2FWhy%2520customer%2520analytics%2520matter%2FWhy_customer_analytics_matter_final.ashx&usg=AOvVaw3YQ547oWfs0sG-8LFP9t6u

Mordor Intelligence. (2021). *Customer Analytics Market - Growth, Trends, COVID-19 Impact, and Forecasts (2021 - 2026).* Research and Markets. Accessed at: https://www.researchandmarkets.com/reports/4622302/customer-analytics-market-growth-trends-covid

Morey, T., Forbath, T. T., & Schoop, A. (2015). Customer Data: Designing for Transparency and Trust. *Harvard Business Review*, 1–15.

Nauck, D. D., Ruta, D., Spott, M., & Azvine, B. (2006). A Tool for Intelligent Customer Analytics. *2006 3rd International IEEE Conference Intelligent Systems*, 518-521. 10.1109/IS.2006.348473

NTech Lab. (2021). *Facial Recognition Module for the Bitrix24 CRM.* NTech Lab Success Stories. Accessed at: https://ntechlab.com/success-stories/bitrix/

Palmatier, R. W., & Martin, K. D. (2019). Understanding and Valuing Customer Data. In *The Intelligent Marketer's Guide to Data Privacy*. Palgrave Macmillan. doi:10.1007/978-3-030-03724-6_7

Plangger, K., & Watson, R. T. (2015). Balancing customer privacy, secrets, and surveillance: Insights and management. *Business Horizons*, *1241*(6), 1–9. doi:10.1016/j.bushor.2015.06.006

Sabbeh, S. F. (2018). Machine-learning techniques for customer retention: A comparative study. *International Journal of Advanced Computer Science and Applications*, *9*(2), 273–281.

Seiferling, I. (2021). Adaviv Raises $2.3M in Upsized and Oversubscribed Seed Round Led by Delta Emerald Ventures to Scale their AI-Driven Plant Intelligence Platform for Indoor Farming. *Yahoo! Finance*. Accessed at: https://finance.yahoo.com/news/adaviv-raises-2-3m-upsized-124900792.html

Shakya, S., & Smys, S. (2021). Big Data Analytics for Improved Risk Management and Customer Segregation in Banking Applications. *Journal of ISMAC, 3*(03), 235–249. doi:10.36548/jismac.2021.3.005

Stodder, D. (2012). Customer analytics in the age of social media. *The Data Warehousing Institute Research*, 1-41.

Terragni, A., & Hassani, M. (2018, August). Analyzing customer journey with process mining: From discovery to recommendations. In *2018 IEEE 6th International Conference on Future Internet of Things and Cloud (FiCloud)* (pp. 224-229). IEEE.

Tsang, Y. P., Wu, C. H., Lin, K. Y., Tse, Y. K., Ho, G. T. S., & Lee, C. K. M. (2021). Unlocking the power of big data analytics in new product development: An intelligent product design framework in the furniture industry. *Journal of Manufacturing Systems*.

Vo, N. N., Liu, S., Li, X., & Xu, G. (2021). Leveraging unstructured call log data for customer churn prediction. *Knowledge-Based Systems, 212*, 106586. doi:10.1016/j.knosys.2020.106586

Wassouf, W. N., Alkhatib, R., Salloum, K., & Balloul, S. (2020). Predictive analytics using big data for increased customer loyalty: Syriatel Telecom Company case study. *Journal of Big Data, 7*(1), 1–24. doi:10.118640537-020-00290-0

Zahay, D., Peltier, J., & Krishen, A. (2012). Building the foundation for customer data quality in CRM systems for financial services firms. *Journal of Database Marketing & Customer Strategy Management, 19*(1), 5–16. doi:10.1057/dbm.2012.6

Zamil, A. M. A., Al Adwan, A., & Vasista, T. G. (2020). Enhancing customer loyalty with market basket analysis using innovative methods: A python implementation approach. International Journal of Innovation. *Creativity and Change, 14*(2), 1351–1368.

## KEY TERMS AND DEFINITIONS

**Customer Analytics:** Customer analytics drills into the trail of data generated from every interaction with customer to draw a wider and clearer picture of this interaction, enlisting everything from their product choices, preferences, reasons for purchase and need for interaction with the firm.

**Customer Data:** Each point of interaction with the customer generates some knowledgeable insight about the customer enhancing the chances of delivering greater customer value and enhancing their experience. These can be generated through Internet, social media, Artificial Intelligence and so on. This may be structured or unstructured.

**Facial Analytics:** A stream of analytics used to interpret facial expressions of consumers, maybe in real time or using the consumer images stored in firm's database.

**Internet of Things Analytics:** A stream of analytics primarily focusing on analysis of data collected from different sensors placed on consumer devices such as mobiles, cameras, microphones, etc. useful to explain consumer experience.

**Recommendation Engines:** Refers to a dominant application of customer analytics which allows dynamic real-time display of tailored offers during product searches. These are sort of information filters which can mine user preferences from huge datasets of past transactions of the users, and then recommend them new relevant content.

**C**

**Sentiment Analysis:** A subset of NLP techniques which refers to the use of analytics to detect the common sentiment prevalent in each text or speech. This is useful to generate "buzz" value, an indicator of volume and frequency of comments of customers around a product, service or marketing activity; helpful to explain real time customer churn.

**Social Media Analytics:** A stream of analytics involved in interpreting data collected from social media sites such as Facebook, Twitter, and so on. It is useful to segment the consumers by different demographics, identify influencers (who fetch maximum likes and followers) among each segment, understand consumer behavior and perform sentiment analysis.

**Speech Analytics:** A stream of analytics used to interpret the voice recordings of consumers, for example their call centre phone logs and can be analysed to understand their sentiments, rate of speech, identify solutions from past documentation to resolve customer queries.

**Text Analytics:** A component of Natural Language Processing (NLP) which encompass set of techniques used to process natural languages to glean meaningful insights from the same such as detect common themes in the text, mine sentiments and categorize texts.

**Voice of Customer (VoC) Analytics:** This analytics stream refers to application of text analytics on reviews posted on sites such as Google, Yelp, and so on and gauge customer feedback devices with smiley faces at airport terminals.

# Dynamics of User–Generated Content in Industry 4.0

**Anshu Rani**

https://orcid.org/0000-0001-9459-5604

*REVA University, India*

**Ruchika Sharma**

https://orcid.org/0000-0002-4284-125X

*REVA University, India*

**Pavithra S.**

https://orcid.org/0000-0001-6106-3214

*Dayananda Sagar University, India*

**Raghvendra Kumar Singh**

*Entrepreneurship Development Institute of India, Ahmedabad, India*

## INTRODUCTION

The world is constantly changing, developing and advancing to create an interrelated effect on business, Industry, people and society. The widespread Fourth Industrial Revolution or Industry 4.0 has been one such development that worked as a disruptive force for business advances (Bulent, 2020). Automation, machine learning, big data, interconnection, and digitization of processes are all key components of Industry 4.0, which aims to move enterprises toward becoming intelligent (Dubedi, 2019) Modern technology can communicate between human and interactive devices & programs to create a seamless integration between the digital and physical world. This explains the connection between e-commerce & Industry 4.0 practices and current management trends(Restart-project.eu, 2018). The rapid growth of digital technology is changing the way business practices work so far and is also responsible for the emergence of marketing 4.0.

In a computer-mediated world, the field of marketing is actively developing profitable business models. Consumers build, share, and choose the information they want in Internet-based marketing models, which are highly personalized, appropriate, and efficient (Rani & Shivprasad, 2018). Ever since Chris Anderson coined the term "Long Tail Business Model" in 2004 in Wired magazine, 'consumer participation in information creation online' has been a demand-side attribute to move demand from niches to successes. Online customers expect that users will discuss the positive aspects of a product and the negative aspects that increase the credibility of such information (Thoumrungroje, 2014). This is focused on using user-generated content (UGC) to help buyers make better decisions and sellers perform better.

UGC has grown in popularity with the advent of social media. Reviews, ratings, questions and answers, social media posts, and photographs and videos are all examples of user-generated content. Product reviews and ratings on various web-based platforms account for more than 70% of all UGC, making it electronic word of mouth (eWOM) (Collins, 2019). According to the survey conducted by

DOI: 10.4018/978-1-7998-9220-5.ch064

Statista (2021), most consumers use UGC since it increases perceived confidence in the purchase, is more interesting than brands generated promotion, creates a more authentic shopping experience, and encourages customer engagement (statista.com, 2021). Besides, 35% of Consumers have reported that they are less likely to buy a product or hold purchase decisions if there is no UGC available on any website/social media. This data represents the significance of UGC on consumer behaviour in the era of Industry 4.0. Therefore, measuring UGC in the form of eWOM communication will allow stakeholders to evaluate their effectiveness on the Internet and will amplify the digital process needed to perform modern marketing (Duan et al. 2009).

## Objective and Methodology

Potential customers feel that user-generated content (UGC) teaches them about companies and items since they believe the users have no commercial purpose (Mir & Rehman, 2013). However, the research field still lacks a comprehensive understanding of the UGC phenomenon and a conceptual framework to describe the measures. The main aim of this chapter would be to examine the determinants of UGC on digital platforms which influence consumer decisions making and the overall effectiveness of marketing programs for modern business firms. The study will essentially cover the motivation towards UGC formation and how this information is used to bring the desired outcome for the entire stakeholder. A detailed literature review will be conducted to combine the fragmented pieces of information to understand the comprehensive conceptual framework of UGC. Several research papers will be categorized into seven categories, elaborating the concepts of UGC, eWOM, UGC/eWOM effect, Factors of source credibility, factors of Content credibility, Receiver's Behaviour and Platform Credibility to conceptualize the concept under consideration. The purpose is to link ideas found in literature and present a wholesome picture of UGC by focusing on a research perspective.

Another goal is to provide best practices for managing the UGC system and benefit from eWOM techniques incorporated into their business models. As a result, successful organizations gain the power of UGC/eWOM more abundantly, and the organically produced customer feedback benefits mainly from the modern business models in Industry 4.0. At this point, real-world examples will be explored, and best practices should be revealed in order to incorporate marketing analytics strategies. The case study approach should be more appropriate to link the real-life background with the available evidence.

## BACKGROUND

The rise of technology and globalization directly impacts both the business and marketing fields, therefore initiating the genesis of new waves called Industry 4.0. Nevertheless, Industry and marketing have differences in how they adapt to technological advances and the shifting global climate (Guven, 2020). A new wave of digital technology, Industry 4.0, was ushered in by the incorporation of the Internet into value chain activities. Technology and marketing have evolved in tandem. Hence, the number of Marketing 4.0-based studies has been rising daily (Guven, 2020). To ensure long-term success and remain relevant in a rapidly changing marketplace, firms should follow the changing marketing landscape and constantly update themselves. Organizations must improve their marketing in order to succeed in the face of competition (Akkaya & Tabak, 2017; Guven, 2020).

## Digital Technology and E-commerce

Digital technology's internet-based software and applications make it possible to connect to other networks effortlessly. This reduces the impact of typical marketing strategies and activities. In the age of internet technology, many consumers have found most of their demands being met virtually (Guven, 2020). Technological advances in internet usage and the presence of internet users in virtual environments have created the necessary conditions for electronic commerce to come into being. These days, most people buy things on the Internet (Akkaya & Tabak, 2017). People will buy more of what they need online in the future, while manufacturers will see more sales over the Internet than they did before. As the result of the growth of information and communication technology, together with globalization, the impact of electronic commerce on the economy is significant. E-commerce has shown to be both convenient and helpful to all types of economic activities because of its extensive reach (Akkaya & Tabak, 2017; Guven, 2020). Because of the rise of online commerce, customers may obtain goods and services at their fingertips. Due to its capabilities, e-commerce is widely used in economic life.

## UGC AND eWOM

Electronic Word of Mouth (eWOM) and User Generated Content (UGC) is not new research fields as many studies were undertaken respectively from the 1960s and the beginning of 2000. UGC is an online user activity that involves the expression of individual thoughts, ideas and feedback about what it has experienced with a product or brand (Guven, 2020). The content is usually posted on social media since it believes that shared information would help others to decide on their purchases. Many previous studies focus mostly on users seeking knowledge to support their purchasing decisions and post opinions on other YouTube videos, but rarely on social networking outlets. In the current economic situation, the input of others will undoubtedly impact an individual's purchase decision, with countless numbers of online vendors. However, one of the most important questions is how marketers take advantage of these developments.

### Introduction to User-Generated Content

UGC has been considered the most influential source of information for purchasing products since the emergence of Industry 4.0. It is a revolutionary way of developing and organizing online information services(Yuxiang & Zhe, 2012). User-generated content is a term that refers to any media content which is created or developed by members of the general public/users rather than paid professionals and is mainly circulated via Internet-related technologies. Despite the fact that content creation and sharing have existed for hundreds of years, Web 2.0 technologies have only lately made it possible for the average user to interact with and influence a huge audience (Timoshenko & Hauser, 2019) Web 2.0-based Web sites like YouTube, MySpace, Facebook, Wikipedia, Flickr, Blogger, LinkedIn, and personal Web pages encourage the creation and consumption of User Generated Content (UGC) (Daugherty, 2008). Online reviews, photos, and videos about related products are all made possible by the e-commerce platform. More than 69 million people utilise user-generated content (UGC), which generates over $450 million in advertising revenue annually, thanks to the explosion of Web 2.0 technologies (Filieri et al., 2014). This is shifting the paradigm of the online information industry from a media-centric model to a user-centric one. Various scholars have investigated and evidenced that UGC strongly influences purchase, purchase intention, cross-buying, Consumer Attitude, Brand-building, Brand value and customer engagement (Colicev & Kumar, 2018). Nevertheless, what influences a consumer to participate in the creation of UGC is an active research area even today.

## Motivation Behind UGC on Internet

UGC includes many unpaid individuals cooperating in the creation of material (Crowston & Fagnot, 2018). One of the active fields of research is regarding the motivation for UGC contributions. UGC sharing uses a rising variety of portal sites and network technologies to target unidentified persons. Personal and social motivation are both important factors in UGC sharing. (Timoshenko & Hauser, 2019; Park, & Lee, 2021). UGC has remained a vital component of the Internet because of the increased availability of broadband innovation and electronic devices. One of the studies by Crowston & Fagnot (2018) has described various key motives of UGC creation in the online domain. The study examined nine motives at three stages of content creation by integrating multiple theoretical views, containing theories of stages, work satisfaction, and social movements. The study suggests that the primary motivation behind participating in UGC are Perceived need for contribution, source expertise, agreement with content philosophy, curiosity, opportunity to learn, feeling of enjoyment, positive feedback from other participants and negative feedback from the content creator. The other motives are listed below:

### Self Actualization

Self-actualization, which may be described as "working on one's own identity and reflecting on one's personality," is a notion related to self-expression. It may be a powerful motivation for achieving specific objectives, such as seeking recognition and a desire for celebrity. As a result, self-actualization is crucial for UGC production. (Wang & Li, 2014).

### Attitude

Media consumption is a conscious, active process in which viewers seek content based on their internal motives. These internal motives serve as the foundation for attitude development, eventually affecting behaviour and fulfilling specific customer demands. (Daugherty et al., 2008).

### Social Obligation

A mix of sentiments of societal obligation and/or responsibility, as well as a self-perceived competence to respond, must motivate an individual to act. The volunteer's capacity to respond is determined by his or her resources, skills, and expertise that are relevant to the volunteer job. (Wilson, 2000).

### Attention

To begin, an individual must see a need for assistance in others. This state, known as attentiveness, focuses on identifying situational signs that indicate the need for assistance. The importance and intensity of these situational signals vary (Crowston & Fagnot, 2018).

The question of how to motivate Web users to continually and permanently produce Web content in the Web community has become a focal point. However, some researchers have looked at ways to motivate users to create UGC through a process known as self-enhancement (SE), which is internalized from the standpoint of the user's personal qualities and then used to improve UGC intention.

## Forms of UGC

On the Cloud, web-based businesses are rapidly forming their own virtual brand communities. UGC is created by ordinary people who voluntarily contribute data, information, or material, which is then made available to others helpfully or amusingly, generally on the Internet—for example, restaurant reviews, wikis, and videos. Several researchers have looked at the implications of using users as a source of persuasive messaging. Nevertheless, the likeability, trustworthiness, and perceived quality of user-generated advertising were at the heart of their research (Mayrhofer et al., 2020; Timoshenko & Hauser, 2019).UGC is frequently employed in marketing strategies, and the result is intentional. Content is the essential element of a successful marketing campaign, and they are various types of excellent content creation platforms and marketing strategy (Creately Blog, 2016). The various types and forms of UGC to be created by source are as follows:

### Blogs

A blog is a compilation of the writer's ideas, opinions, and experiences that can be written as a diary/journal or as a collection of product or service evaluations. Personal blogs that represent an online journal are increasingly often utilized as blogs. Blogs are primarily text-based, although they frequently incorporate digital images and connections to other websites or blogs. (Chu & Kim, 2011).

### Vlogs

Vlogging is becoming increasingly popular as a tool for destination marketing on social media. Vlogging is a variation on text blogging in that it incorporates not just words and photos but also videos taken with technology such as a smartphone or digital camera. (Peralta,2019). Vlogs are a type of blog shortening of online video weblogs; much as eWOM is an extension of WOM, vlogs are an extension of blogs. Vlogs are video-based blogs, whereas blogs are text-based. Vlogs, like blogs, can cover a wide range of topics and are frequently self-filmed by the information source rather than by a film crew, as is the case with traditional video media. (Lockie, 2019: Müller & Christandl, 2019).

### Social Media Content

Social media has become essential for branding because of the brand's capacity to engage with customers in a more dynamic and personalized manner. As a result, brands are becoming increasingly interested in social media-based brand communities for the purpose of cultivating relationships with customers through community-building activities. Although there are still diverse opinions on how to achieve it, brand experts agree that community development via social media leads to increased brand loyalty and trust (Müller & Christandl, 2019).

## eWOM in the Form of Online Reviews

All informal communications addressed at customers using Internet-based technology linked to the usage or features of certain goods and services, or their sellers" is what electronic word-of-mouth (eWOM) is. (Rani & Shivapasad, 2019; Rani & Shivapasad, 2022). E-commerce relies heavily on electronic word-of-mouth marketing. With the exponential rise of internet users and their acceptance of eWOM for product information, it is more necessary than ever to investigate the elements that influence eWOM's efficacy. (Rani & Shivaprasad, 2018).

## Virtual Communities

Virtual communities (VCs) for peer-to-peer sharing continue to be one of the most popular online destinations, and they have a significant impact on consumer decisions (Müller & Christandl, 2019). Individuals are increasingly accessing such social networking sites to engage with people and solve problems that they have, as mobile device ownership has reached an all-time high and is continuing to increase.

Over the past few decades, the tremendous amount of power held by marketers has been moved to millions of people worldwide who are just curious about getting their voices heard, putting up new ideas, and sharing their knowledge. Traditionally, ideas that consider production and promotion are being displaced by a new understanding that places customers, now participants rather than passive recipients of innovation and promotion, at the center of industry activity (Bulent, 2020). UGC is highly related to different knowledge flows, intentions, and ramifications, yet each type offers the potential to affect future marketing on a worldwide scale greatly. One of the significant parts of UGC is eWOM in the online context (Rani et al., 2021), and therefore next, the chapter will highlight the content of eWOM.

## Introduction to eWOM

A definition of eWOM is a web-based interpersonal connection between virtual persons with the goal of disseminating knowledge about items and organisations without the intent of making a financial profit (Litvin et al., 2008; Cheng & Zhou, 2010, Wu Mei-hsin, 2013). A number of studies have been conducted in an attempt to discover the essence of eWOM, according to Breazeale (2009). eWOM refers to the dissemination of consumer product experience information where online opinion leaders play an important role in disseminating material (Menkveld, 2013). The contact is connected to the network via the Internet and is addressed to many people. Without time or location restrictions, eWOM has spread and grown over the years. Since 2015 eWOM has experienced unprecedented growth of more than 278% over various platforms. 84% of people rate product reviews as equal to the recommendation given by friends. Furthermore, 72% of people can only make the purchase decision after reading all of the reviews and UGC on the product (York, 2020). Incorporating UGC allows other customers to read about other user's online experiences and participate in those. Literature has used UGC and CGM (consumer-generated media) interchangeably (Ukpabi & Karjaluoto, 2018). The major source of the UGC is eWOM, and therefore, the study will further take up eWOM to discuss the factor influencing UGC in the form of eWOM. Additionally, the prepositions are provided to help future studies on UGC. The next segment will take UGC and eWOM communication and discuss source, message, medium, and outcome.

## Source Related Determinant

Consumers can readily say about their thoughts, experiences, or ideas about the products & services that they would be interested in using a. blogs, b. product reviews, c. retail websites,d. social media sites. We can find many research issues related to stabilizing source credibility for receivers especially to trust in eWOM (Lee & Lee, 2009; Forman et al., 2008; Shivaprasad & Rani, 2019). There are study concerns about stabilizing source credibility for receivers to trust more on eWOM since the authenticity of such material, which is present in big numbers, may have contradicting perspectives and is difficult to be evaluated for trustworthiness. (Lee & Lee, 2009; Forman et al., 2008). The perceived utility of eWOM communication is determined by source credibility. Source credibility is defined as the degree to which a communicator is viewed as a trustworthy source of information. (Hussain et al., 2017). Another technique to assess source credibility is to assess the level of trust in the source's willingness to share and communicate.

The credible source of eWOM communication is determined by how convincing, knowledgeable, and trustworthy a communicator is perceived (Ukpabi&Karjaluoto, 2018). As a result, the source's credibility indicates that the receiver will perceive the message receiver will look at the message as more believable trustworthy and informed (Ukpabi&Karjaluoto, 2018). According to current literature, source credibility is determined by assessing the trust with the source, the knowledge of the source being shown, the link between source and receiver how strong it is, and the source homophily. Below table 1 shows the factors influencing Source credibility.

*Table 1. Source related factors*

| Authors | Factors | Definition |
|---|---|---|
| Lee & Lee, 2009; Ukpabi&Karjaluoto, 2018; Rani &Shivprasad, 2019 | Source Credibility | source credibility as to how a consumer perceives and trusts the source of the eWOM recommendations |
| Hussain et al., 2017; Lee & Lee, 2009 | Expertise | It can be defined as prior experience with the eWOM suggestion. |
| Ukpabi&Karjaluoto, 2018; Rani &Shivprasad, 2018; Rani et al 2021 | Trustworthiness | It talks about the authenticity of the source being genuine |
| Lee & Lee, 2009; Rani &Shivprasad, 2018; Rani et al 2021 | Homophily | The likeness between the source of eWOM recommendation and the receiver. |

Source Credibility

One of the variables that go into determining source credibility is source trustability. According to the literature so far, consumer behaviour toward e WOM is influenced by perceived confidence in the source. The level of trust that a receiver has in an eWOM message coming from a source is referred to as trustability (Lee & Lee, 2009). The aspect of trust is based on source identity cues. It is widely assumed that giving the source's "actual name" rather than a pseudonym, "real profile photo" rather than no profile photo, and other details such as email address, purchase location, and other details will increase the recipient's trust in the source (Hussain et al., 2017; Lee & Lee, 2009). Various research on source credibility has indicated that the level of trust between the source and the receivers influences the efficiency of eWOM communication. As a result, source trustability influences the overall effectiveness of eWOM by regulating source credibility (Hussain, 2017; Rani & Shivaprasad, 2019).

## Expertise of Sources

The capacity of the source to demonstrate their competence in evaluating the product is another essential factor in determining source trustworthiness. Prior use of knowledge and expertise are typically seen as evidence that a source considers a "knowledgeable source." In other words, a source's capacity to demonstrate prior knowledge of actual product applications is crucial in determining source credibility throughout the adoption of an eWOM message. (Cheung et al., 2012; Lee & Lee, 2009). When a source is seen to have a high level of competence, eWOM communication is more effective. The receiver believes that the receiver can judge the source's actual product usage and knowledge display based on the eWOM communication they put out. According to the cognitive fit theory, the effectiveness of eWOM for recipients is determined by the message provider's level of skill. (Hussain et al., 2017). A consumer who tries a product and subsequently expresses an opinion about its performance and usage is frequently referred to as an eWOM source. As a result of the source knowledge and expertise, the receiver perceives that the viewpoint is based on personal experience (Lee & Lee, 2009). The degree to which eWOM recipients regard the information source as correct and genuine is described by knowledge and expertise (Ukpabi&Karjaluoto, 2018). When a source uses technical terminology to describe a product and gives an example of how to utilise it, the receiver gets the impression that the source knows what they're talking about, making them more credible than others.

## Trustworthiness and Homophily

The receiver's 'Source homophily' and 'Tie strength' with the source are other crucial criteria in determining the source's credibility. (Ukpabi&Karjaluoto, 2018; Rani &Shivprasad, 2018; Rani et al. 2021). Tie strength is a metric that measures the level of social intensity and intimacy in a source-receiver interaction. (Cheung & Thadani, 2012; Rani et al., 2022). WOM communication involves meeting real people and sharing their experiences, as well as product and service ideas. Because of the trustworthiness of known sources, this activity is more credible and believable for the customer in making decisions.

Electronic proximity might be viewed as 'experiential similarity' rather than 'social structural similarity in the case of eWOM (Rani &Shivprasad, 2018; Rani et al., 2021). The experimental similarity takes into account the sender and receiver's shared experience. If a customer sees similarities in perception and identity, they are more likely to absorb eWOM content. The closer the creator of eWOM is to the recipient of eWOM, the more credible the source becomes and the more successful eWOM communication becomes (Ukpabi&Karjaluoto, 2018). However, in the case of eWOM, the relationship can serve as a foundation for similarity in experience. Individuals who are similar to them are more appealing to others, according to studies, which boosts their interpersonal appeal and persuasion abilities (Rani &Shivapasad, 2019). In terms of age, gender, education, and social standing, source homophily relates to how similar people are (Cheung & Thadani, 2012). Homophily is a concept that describes how similar people are in terms of age, geographic region, and gender (Ukpabi&Karjaluoto, 2018; Rani et al., 2021). Source homophily affects the receiver's likeability, persuasion, and believability of eWOM.Overall, the success of eWOM communication is determined by the reliability of the source, which determines the author's credibility in eWOM communication.

## Message-Related Determinant

Adoption is influenced not only by the source of UGC but also by the content. The uniqueness of the content of the message is prominent among these factors (Menkveld, 2013). The eWOM communication is done through written messages that are viral and ageless, transcending geographical limits. The messages in eWOM differ from those in traditional WOM communication because of these qualities. As a result, message qualities are another factor that influences the efficiency of eWOM. In addition, the credibility of both the author and the message is considered when evaluating eWOM communication. Many previous researchers have used text analysis to investigate message features and their impact on the adoption of eWOM (Rani & Shivaprasad, 2022; Menkveld, 2013).

Additionally, the valence of UGC (positive or negative) has an effect on whether or not it is adopted. UGC is typically used to share good or negative thoughts about a product or service experience. Burcher (2012) study indicated that reading positive evaluations about a hotel before making a reservation increased both booking intention and trust. Mislove et al. 2007, further asserted that good online comments enhance booking intentions and significantly raise consumers' expectations. Therefore, managers of hotels have a constant improvement process in place so that their services fulfill the expectations of their customers. In the case of eWOM messaging, there is enough evidence in the literature to show that message valence (positive, negative, or neutral) and message volume have an impact on message believability. Other decisive factors, on the other hand, have received less attention (Cheung & Thadani, 2012). Taking the entire element of message characteristics and their effect to know the likely effects of eWOM communication would be considerable, however, when compared to traditional WOM literature. The factor connected to the content of UGC in the form of eWOM is described in table 2 below.

*Table 2. Message related factors*

| Authors | Factors | Definition |
|---|---|---|
| Chiou et al., 2013 | Novelty | eWOM message the quality and strength of the argument. |
| Cheung & Thadani, 2012; Rani &Shivaprasad, 2019; Rani et al., 2022 | Valence | An eWOM message's valence shows whether it is positive or negative. 2021 (Cheung & Thadani) |
| Chiou et al., 2013; Xie et. al. 2022 | Aesthetics | The characteristics of appeal in eWOM message which is appreciated. |
| Cheung & Thadani 2012; Rani et al., 2021; Yin et. al 2014 | Argument Quality | eWOM message talks about the quality and strength of the argument which is important. |
| Ukpabi&Karjaluoto, 2018; Lee & Lee, 2009 | Information Quality | This talks about the overall ratings given by the consumer for eWOM Recommendations. |

## eWOM Novelty, Valence and Aesthetics

The valence of an eWOM message is critical in deciding how effective it is (Cheung & Thadani, 2012; Rani &Shivaprasad, 2019). eWOM communications are required to include both positive and negative information that is readily available in huge quantities. The investigation of the pleasant valance and negative valence of eWOM messaging produced mixed results. Park and Lee (2009) looked into the effect of message valence on purchasing decisions and found that negative eWOM had a stronger influence than positive eWOM. The investigation, on the other hand, discovered the opposite. Negatively framed eWOM is more influential than positively framed eWOM, notwithstanding disputes in the field of eWOM research (Cheung & Thadani, 2012; Rani et al., 2022). On the other hand, negative eWOM is more expressive, original, valuable, and attention-getting than positive eWOM (Rani &Shivaprasad, 2021; Rani &Shivaprasad, 2022). Because there is a paucity of empirical research in this sector, it would be fascinating to learn the difference between one-sided and two-sided communication. The volume of eWOM is highly linked to product sales, according to current studies (Cheung & Thadani, 2012; Chiou et al., 2013). Consumers interpret the lack of a rating or review for a product as a lack of interest in purchasing the product or service.

The aesthetics and appeal of user-generated material in the form of eWOM have an impact on its usage. Using colors, font type, music, or animation to portray a message's emotional appeal or aesthetics can pique people's attention in the message (Chiou et al., 2013). Blogs and video material play a significant role in information searches because they allow the presenter to be creative while also adding fun and enjoyment to the presentation. When the volume of an eWOM message is large, this practice distinguishes the message's worth.

## eWOM Argument and Information Quality

The persuasive strength of the argument inherent in the eWOM message can be defined as the information quality. The recipient of the communication perceives the worth of information to be relatively high (Ukpabi & Karjaluoto, 2018; Lee & Lee, 2009). The quality of an eWOM message determines its argument power, and it plays a critical part in information influence, which affects the receiver's eWOM adoption, attitude alteration, and purchase intention (Yin et al., 2015; Rani et al., 2021). When a valid argument is seen in an eWOM message, the recipient develops a good attitude toward it in both face-to-face and computer-mediated communication (Ukpabi&Karjaluoto, 2018). The quality of the message determines the persuasive power of information (Lee & Lee, 2009: Rani & Shivaparasd, 2022). The effectiveness of eWOM is influenced by the reader's credibility assessments of the message and author, which are related to the quality of the eWOM message. Each of these factors should be included in studies as a predictor of eWOM message trustworthiness.

## Receiver's Related Determinant

The receiver's characteristics like age, income, gender and education level would constitute the consumer's profile. Young People and middle-aged receivers are the ones who are more into social media (Filieri& McLeay 2014). This inquisitive age group uses a variety of social media platforms to meet new people and stay up to date on current events in politics, the economy, entertainment, and sports. Income is also a significant driver of participation in various activities. The availability of disposable cash has a significant impact on a consumer's ability to obtain things such as computer gadgets that allow them to browse social media sites (Bulent, 2020). The relationship between an individual's educational level and his or her income has been discovered, impacting his or her use of computer devices and allowing the examination of social media with such devices to become an important factor.

There is a lot of literature on engagement in the fields of sociology, psychology, and consumer behaviour (Leung & Bai, 2013). Consumer involvement has been found to have a significant impact on their decision-making process. "A person's perceived importance of the object based on underlying needs, values, and interests," according to the definition (Charo&Pershant Sharma, 2015).

*Table 3. Receiver related factors*

| Authors | Factors | Definition |
|---------|---------|------------|
| Filieri& McLeay, 2013 | Consumer Profile | Includes variables such as a. age, b. gender, c. income, and d. literacy level. |
| Leung & Bai, 2013; Rani &Shivapasad, 2019 | Involvement | The relevance of the information search to the receivers' perceptions |
| Colicev & Kumar, 2018; Cheung & Lai, 2005 | Enjoyment | To the extent that the receiver thinks it is amusing and entertaining |
| Pietro & Pantano, 2013 | Experience | This refers to the receiver's knowledge/skills that would aid in their search. |
| Chung et al., 2015; Perea et al., 2016 | Benefit | To the extent that the receiver gains something from the search. |

Perceived enjoyment is another intrinsic drive that has garnered many studies that have incorporated subjective satisfaction into the TAM model and have yielded varying outcomes depending on the circumstance. In the utilitarian context, Venkatesh (2002) performed tests in which employees were introduced to an online help desk system, multimedia system, and PC environment (Windows 95) for a payroll system. The study revealed that enjoyment was a weaker predictor of wanting to use the new information system and actually using it. Perceived enjoyment is a crucial motivator of attitude and intention for information search, according to Pietro &Pantano, 2013.

Consumers are looking for a variety of advantages. These advantages could be functional, social, psychological, or hedonic in nature (Parra-Lopez et al., 2011). Finding low prices and efficient services, for example, are both functional benefits. In terms of social benefits, social media provides a platform for customers to connect and share information about topics that are important to them. Some of the social benefits acquired via such platforms include bonding, engagement, emotional support, companionship, and encouragement (Chung et al., 2015). Several studies have found that consumers' interest in and willingness to use social media derives from the satisfaction, pleasure, and playfulness they have while doing so (Rani et al., 2022).

## Outcome of UGC

Consumers' intent to use eWOM and determine the benefit sought. Consumers use UGC for a variety of reasons. Parra-Lopez et al. (2011) state that these users can be functional, social, psychological, or hedonistic. Finding the most extraordinary content, affordable charges, and efficient services are some of the functional advantages. As a result, customers looking for these advantages think about using UGC to gather relevant data. Social media offers users a way to connect and share information about shared interests. These platforms have social advantages such as bonding, engagement, emotional support, friendship, and encouragement that are acquired from their usage (Chung et al., 2015; Timoshenko & Hauser, 2019). According to several academics, the fun, pleasure, enjoyment, and playfulness consumers get from using social media determines their interest in and intention to use it(Park & Lee, 2009).

## INTEGRATIVE FRAMEWORK OF UGC FOR AI ENABLED DECISION-MAKING

There are two people involved in every WOM event: the sender and the receiver (Cheung & Thadani, 2012). UGC adoption is based on three factors: source-based characteristics, user-basis characteristics, and content-basis characteristics, as shown in Figure 1. The study's framework is built on categories found in the reviewed literature (Timoshenko & Hauser, 2019). Characteristics associated with the sender are called source-based, while those associated with the receiver are called user-based. Content-based characteristics are those that pertain to the message itself. These are the variables that aid machine learning-assisted decision-making in Industry 4.0. The framework can be used by artificial intelligence (AI) systems to access further the power of UGC for the brands.

*Figure 1. Integrative Framework*

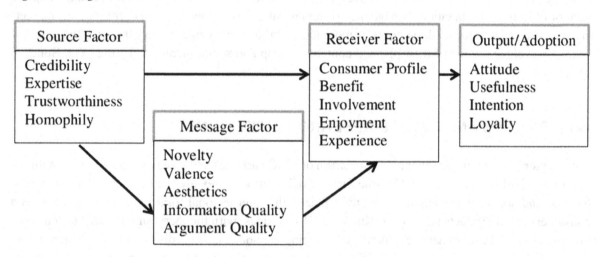

The Source, message, and receiver-related factors produce a certain response from the adopter and are therefore named as an outcome of UGC. The integrative framework is the output of the systematic literature review carried out in this research study.

## STRATEGIES TO MANAGE UGC

### Source Related

Source profiling can be done with the help of in-built software to create more credibility in UGC. In addition, in-house marketing material can be reduced by using UGC software to help establish a community and generate income from interesting, real-life use cases (Mislove, 2007). It can also aid in gaining the right to disseminate information and compensate users whose contributions have the greatest social impact to prevent any legal issues.

## Content Related

UGC platforms look for relevant message content on one or more popular social networking sites. This has been accomplished along with other things like the use of hashtags, keywords, and geolocation. Therefore markets can create software and business analytics systems to make popular novel messages/content and suggest the keywords, and hashtags to get better receiving from users (Chaffey, 2010).

## Receiver/user Relater

Static or live streaming of user-generated material can be created using these platforms and other applications, such as digital signs, e-commerce platforms, and content management systems for websites (Shenglin, 2017). UGC solutions can be capable of pulling content across video hosting services as well as social networks. In addition to influencer marketing software, certain UGC networks may integrate with or offer digital reputation management or review site software features. In current times, marketers are expected to allocate three hours or more to reputation management every day over the next few years, on average, on top of their planned content creation and social media marketing (Yin, Bond, & Zhang, 2014).

## IMPLICATIONS AND FUTURE RESEARCH DIRECTIONS

The chapter has brought together a vast spectrum of UGC variables and research perspectives. With the rapid growth of the Internet, UGC in the form of online product reviews and ratings on online blogs, forums, and social media has increasingly replaced the interpersonal, oral communication between consumers about products (Colicev & Kumar, 2018). Besides, with the increasing internet penetration, the influence of UGC remains essential for emerging economies. According to the World Economic Forum (2014), every 10% increase in internet penetration in emerging economies results in a 1.2 percent increase in per capita GDP (Shenglin, 2017). Therefore, modern business has been looking for newer marketing strategies to overcome competition in Industry 4.0.

To begin, UGC in the form of eWOM is influenced by three distinct features: the qualities of the source, the characteristics of the receiver, and the characteristics of the message. The earlier study found that trust had the largest impact on attitude(Yuxiang & Zhe, 2012). A second finding from previous research found multiple alternative theories, frameworks, and models, with the Technology acceptance model (TAM) and Elaboration Likelihood Model (ELM) being the most widely (Wu & Wang, 2011). The next lead of this study is that it provides an excellent theoretical foundation for future research (Saremi, 2014; Park & Lee, 2021) by identifying antecedents from various studies; as a result, scholars who wish to conduct research can conduct an empirical study to support the theoretical framework of this chapter.

## Practical Implications

There are several implications for the study based on our systematic review. A better approach is to engage your customers as co-creators rather than as consumers who passively receive marketing messages. Two pillars support customer evaluation of satisfaction: core services and relationship elements. UGC in the form of eWOM can impact both(Yuxiang & Zhe, 2012). As a result, managers must keep improving their services to keep up with the rising demands of their customers and retain them by managing relationships positively. Finally, marketers can make extensive use of social media to express thoughts, questions, and responses.

Besides, the chapter has contributed to knowing how to manage the effectiveness of big data in the form of UGC in Industry 4.0. To be precise, readers will gain a basic understanding of UGC and its current state of knowledge. Marketers should identify when and how to focus their efforts to generate UGC/eWOM organically and reap meaningful benefits from it(Stephen, 2012; Rani & Shivapasad, 2018; Rani et al., 2022). Firms that can continue to grow their customer base through UGC can achieve higher long-term profitability and will be allowed to spend less on customer retention. Finally, this chapter will contribute significantly to the strategies of market analytics activities for the digital economy.

## CONCLUSION

The chapter has tried to bring together a diverse set of variables and research perspectives related to UGC. In present times, the comprehensive process of businesses embedded in artificial intelligence and machine learning requires insights for better decision-making. The organization will need unique capability and business intelligence to make better customer experiences and meaningful relationships than ever before (Dubedi, 2019). The chapter provides access to valuable data on UGC, which will become the future of marketing in the coming decades. A comprehensive understanding of the UGC and eWOM has made firms strategize their resource and effort. In a true sense, this chapter has suggested the synergy between humans (customers) and the parameter for analysis of their content (Data science and machine learning).

## REFERENCES

Akkaya, B., & Tabak, A. (2017). The impact of dynamic capabilities on firm perceived marketing performance of small and medium-sized enterprises. *Transnational Marketing Journal, 5*(2), 121–125. doi:10.33182/tmj.v5i2.383

Breazeale, M. (2009). Word of mouse-An assessment of electronic word-of-mouth research. *International Journal of Market Research, 51*(3), 1–19. doi:10.1177/147078530905100307

Bulent, A. (2020). Industry 4.0 and Marketing 4.0: In Perspective of Digitalization and E-Commerce. In Agile Business Leadership Methods for Industry 4.0 (pp. 25–46). Academic Press.

Chaffey, D. (2010). Applying Organizational Capability Models to Assess the maturity of Digital-Marketing Goverance. *Journal of Marketing Management, 26*(3-4), 187–196. doi:10.1080/02672571003612192

Cheng, X., & Zhou, M. (2010, August). Study on effect of eWOM: A literature review and suggestions for future research. In *2010 International conference on management and service science* (pp. 1-4). 10.1109/ICMSS.2010.5576663

Chiou, J. S., Hsiao, C. C., & Chiu, T. Y. (2018). The credibility and attribution of online reviews: Differences between high and low product knowledge consumers. *Online Information Review, 17*(5), 34–45. doi:10.1108/OIR-06-2017-0197

Chu, S. C., & Kim, Y. (2011). Determinants of consumer engagement in electronic word-of-mouth (eWOM) in social networking sites. *International Journal of Advertising, 30*(1), 47–75. doi:10.2501/IJA-30-1-047-075

Colicev, A., & Kumar, A. (2018). Modeling the relationship between firm and user generated content and the stages of the marketing funnel. *International Journal of Research in Marketing*, 17–28.

Collins, K. (2019, May 15). *how user-generated content ugc can increase online sales by 15%.* Retrieved May 15, 2019, from https://www.clickz.com/photoslurp-how-user-generated-content-ugc-can-increase-online-sales-by-15%25/234729/

Creately Blog. (2016, Feb 2). *How To Boost Your Marketing Efforts With User Generated Content.* Retrieved July 2021, 22, from Creately Blog: https://creately.com/blog/marketing/marketing-user-generated-content/

Crowston, K., & Fagnot, I. (2018). Stages of motivation for contributing user-generated content: A theory and empirical test. *International Journal of Human-Computer Studies, 109*, 89–101. doi:10.1016/j.ijhcs.2017.08.005

Daugherty, T., Eastin, M. S., & Bright, L. (2008). Exploring consumer motivations for creating user-generated content. *Journal of Interactive Advertising, 8*(2), 16–25. doi:10.1080/15252019.2008.10722139

Duan, W., Gu, B., & Whinston, A. (2009). Do online reviews matter?—an empirical investigation of Panel data. Decision Support System, 45(4), 1007-1016.

Dubedi, A. (2019, July 27). *All About Fourth Industrial Revolution-How Industry 4.0 Can Transform Your Business?* Retrieved May 14, 2021, from https://www.sfuptech.com: https://www.sfuptech.com/all-about-fourth-industrial-revolution-how-industry-4-0-can-transform-your-business/

Filieri, R., Acikgoz, F., Ndou, V., & Dwivedi, Y. (2020). Is TripAdvisor still relevant? The influence of review credibility, review usefulness, and ease of use on consumers' continuance intention. *International Journal of Contemporary Hospitality Management.*

Forman, C., Ghose, A., & Wiesenfeld, B. (2008). Examining the relationship between reviews and sales: The role of reviewer identity disclosure in electronic markets. *Information Systems Research, 19*(3), 291–313. doi:10.1287/isre.1080.0193

Guven, H. (2020). Industry 4.0 and Marketing 4.0. In *Perspective of Digitalization and E-Commerce. In Agile Business Leadership Methods for Industry 4.0.* Emerald Publishing Limited. doi:10.1108/978-1-80043-380-920201003

Hussain, S., Ahmed, W., Jafar, R. M. S., Rabnawaz, A., & Jianzhou, Y. (2017). eWOM source credibility, perceived risk and food product customer's information adoption. *Computers in Human Behavior, 66*, 96–102. doi:10.1016/j.chb.2016.09.034

Lee, K.-T., & Koo, D.-M. (2012). Effects of attribute and valence of eWOM on message adoption: Moderating roles of subjective knowledge and regulatory focus. *Computer in Human Behavior, 28*, 1974–1984.

Leung, X. Y., & Bai, B. (2013). How motivation, opportunity, and ability impact Travelers' social media involvement and revisit intention. *Journal of Travel & Tourism Marketing, 30*(1-2), 58–77. doi:10.1080/10548408.2013.751211

D

Litvin, S. W., Goldsmith, R. E., & Pan, B. (2008). Electronic word-of-mouth in hospitality and tourism management. *Tourism Management, 29*(3), 458–468. doi:10.1016/j.tourman.2007.05.011

Lockie, M. A. (2019). *In Vlogs We Trust: Consumer Trust in Blog and Vlog Content* (Doctoral dissertation). Auckland University of Technology.

Mayrhofer, M., Matthes, J., Einwiller, S., & Naderer, B. (2020). User generated content presenting brands on social media increases young adults' purchase intention. *International Journal of Advertising, 39*(1), 166–186. doi:10.1080/02650487.2019.1596447

Menkveld, B. (2013). *Exploring credibility in electronic word of mouth* [Master Thesis]. University of Twente.

Mir, I. A., & Ur Rehman, K. (2013). Factors affecting consumer attitudes and intentions toward user-generated product content on YouTube. *Management & Marketing, 8*(4).

Mislove, A., Marcon, M., Gummadi, K. P., Druschel, P., & Bhattacharjee, B. (2007, October). Measurement and analysis of online social networks. In *Proceedings of the 7th ACM SIGCOMM conference on Internet measurement* (pp. 29-42). 10.1145/1298306.1298311

Müller, J., & Christandl, F. (2019). Content is king–But who is the king of kings? The effect of content marketing, sponsored content & user-generated content on brand responses. *Computers in Human Behavior, 96*, 46–55. doi:10.1016/j.chb.2019.02.006

Park, C., & Lee, T. M. (2009). ParkInformation direction, website reputation and eWOM effect: A moderating role of product type. *Journal of Business Research, 62*(1), 61–67. doi:10.1016/j.jbusres.2007.11.017

Park, D. H., & Lee, S. (2021). UGC Sharing Motives and Their Effects on UGC Sharing Intention from Quantitative and Qualitative Perspectives: Focusing on Content Creators in South Korea. *Sustainability, 13*(17), 9644. doi:10.3390u13179644

Parra-López, E., Bulchand-Gidumal, J., Gutiérrez-Taño, D., & Díaz-Armas, R. (2011). Intentions to use social media in organizing and taking vacation trips. *Computers in Human Behavior, 27*(2), 640–654. doi:10.1016/j.chb.2010.05.022

Peralta, R. L. (2019). How vlogging promotes a destination image: A narrative analysis of popular travel vlogs about the Philippines. *Place Branding and Public Diplomacy, 15*(4), 244–256. doi:10.105741254-019-00134-6

Pietro, L. D., & Pantano, E. (2013). Social network influences on young tourists: An exploratory analysis of determinants of the purchasing intention. *Journal of Direct, Data and Digital Marketing Practice, 15*(1), 4–19. doi:10.1057/dddmp.2013.33

Rani, A., Itam, U., & Shivaprasad, H. N. (2021). Determinants of Customer Engagement in Electronic Word of Mouth (eWOM) communication. In Insights, Innovation, and Analytics for Optimal Customer Engagement (pp. 196-225). IGI Global.

Rani, A., Roy, A., Boaler, M., & Jagadeeswari, I. U. (2022). Determinants of Influencer Credibility and Platform Credibility to Understand the Effectiveness of Indian Fashion Influencers. *International Journal of Online Marketing, 12*(1), 1–16. doi:10.4018/IJOM.299399

Rani, A., & Shivaprasad, H. N. (2018). Determinants of Electronic Word of Mouth Persuasiveness: A Conceptual Model and Research Propositions. *Journal of Contemporary Management Research, 12*(2).

Rani, A., & Shivaprasad, H. N. (2019), Where the electronic word of mouth stands in consumer information search: An empirical evidence from India. *UNNAYAN: International Bulletin of Management and Economics, 10*(1), 36-46.

Rani, A., & Shivaprasad, H. N. (2019). Electronic Word of Mouth (eWOM) Strategies to Manage Innovation and Digital Business Model. In *Managing Diversity, Innovation, and Infrastructure in Digital Business* (pp. 41–63). IGI Global. doi:10.4018/978-1-5225-5993-1.ch003

Rani, A., & Shivaprasad, H. N. (2021). Revisiting the antecedent of electronic word-of-mouth (eWOM) during COVID-19 Pandemic. *Decision (Washington, D.C.), 48*(4), 419–432.

Rani, A., & Shivaprasad, H. N. (2022). An Empirical Analysis of Receiver's Psychological Characteristics in eWOM Engagement. *International Journal of Cyber Behavior, Psychology and Learning, 12*(1), 1–19. doi:10.4018/IJCBPL.298686

Rani, A., Toni, M., & Shivaprasad, H. N. (2022). Examining the effect of electronic word of mouth (eWOM) communication on purchase intention: A quantitative approach. *Journal of Content, Community & Communication, 15*(1), 130-146.

Restart-project.eu. (2018, Aug 1). *Industry 4.0 and its effect on e-Commerce*. Retrieved May 1, 2021, from https://restart-project.eu: https://restart-project.eu/industry-4-0-effect-e-commerce/

Saremi, H. Q. (2014). *Effectiveness of electronic word of mouth recommendations* [Ph.D thesis]. McMaster University.

Shenglin, B. (2017). Digital infrastructure: Overcoming Digital Divide in Emerging Economies. Zhejiang University Center for Internet and Financial Innovation: G20 Insight.

Shivaprasad, H. N., & Rani, A. (2020). Building web-analytics system to measure perceived source credibility in electronic word of mouth communication. *International Journal of Information Systems and Social Change, 11*(2), 1–13. doi:10.4018/IJISSC.2020040101

statista.com. (2021, Jan.). *ugc-content-submission-type-shopper*. Retrieved May 16, 2021, from https://www.statista.com/statistics/731710/ugc-content-submission-type-shopper-usa/

Thoumrungroje, A. (2014). The influence of social media intensity and EWOM on conspicuous consumption. *Procedia: Social and Behavioral Sciences, 148*, 7–15. doi:10.1016/j.sbspro.2014.07.009

Timoshenko, A., & Hauser, J. R. (2019). Identifying customer needs from user-generated content. *Marketing Science, 38*(1), 1–20. doi:10.1287/mksc.2018.1123

Ukpabi, D. C., & Karjaluoto, H. (2018). What drives travelers' adoption of user-generated content? A literature review. *Tourism Management Perspectives, 28*, 251–273. doi:10.1016/j.tmp.2018.03.006

Venkatesh, V., Speier, C., & Morris, M. G. (2002). User acceptance enablers in individual decision making about technology: Toward an integrated model. *Decision Sciences, 33*(2), 297–316. doi:10.1111/j.1540-5915.2002.tb01646.x

Wang, X., & Li, Y. (2014). Trust, psychological need, and motivation to produce user-generated content: A self-determination perspective. *Journal of Electronic Commerce Research, 15*(3), 241–253.

Wu, M. H. (2013). *Relationships among source credibility of electronic word of mouth, perceived risk, and consumer behavior on consumer generated media.* Academic Press.

Yin, D., Bond, S., & Zhang, H. (2014). Anxious or Angry? Effects of discrete emotions on the Perceived Helpfulness of Online Reviews. *Management Information Systems Quarterly, 38*(2), 539–560. doi:10.25300/MISQ/2014/38.2.10

York, J. a. (2020, June 4). *How Do Online Reviews Bring Your Business Value?* Retrieved May 17, 2021, from https://www.textrequest.com/blog/online-reviews-value/

Yuxiang, Z., & Zhe, F. &. (2012). Conceptualization and Research Progress on User-Generated Content. *Journal of Library Science in China, 5.*

## ADDITIONAL READING

Assaker, G. (2020). Age and gender differences in online travel reviews and user-generated-content (UGC) adoption: Extending the technology acceptance model (TAM) with credibility theory. *Journal of Hospitality Marketing & Management, 29*(4), 428–449. doi:10.1080/19368623.2019.1653807

Charo, N., Sharma, P., Shaikh, S., Haseeb, A., & Sufya, M. Z. (2015). Determining the impact of ewom on brand image and purchase intention through adoption of online opinions. *International Journal of Humanities and Management Sciences, 3*(1), 41–46.

Filieri, R., & McLeay, F. (2014). E-WOM and accommodation: An analysis of the factors that influence travelers' adoption of information from online reviews. *Journal of Travel Research, 53*(1), 44–57. doi:10.1177/0047287513481274

Kim, J. (2012). The institutionalization of YouTube: From user-generated content to professionally generated content. *Media Culture & Society, 34*(1), 53–67. doi:10.1177/0163443711427199

Xie, C., Zhang, J., Huang, Q., Chen, Y., & Morrison, A. M. (2022). An analysis of user-generated crisis frames: Online public responses to a tourism crisis. *Tourism Management Perspectives, 41*, 100931. doi:10.1016/j.tmp.2021.100931

## KEY TERMS AND DEFINITIONS

**Aesthetics:** The characteristics of appeal in eWOM message which is appreciated.

**Argument Quality:** eWOM message talks about the quality and strength of the argument which is important.

**Benefit:** To the extent that the receiver gains something from the search.

**Electronic Word of Mouth (eWOM):** eWOM is refered to any content which is created or developed by members of the general public/users rather than paid professionals and is mainly circulated via Internet-related technologies.

**Enjoyment:** To the extent that the receiver thinks it is amusing and entertaining.

**Experience:** This refers to the receiver's knowledge/skills that would aid in their search.

**Expertise:** It can be defined as prior experience about the eWOM suggestion.

**Homophily:** The likeness between the source of eWOM recommendation and the receiver.

**Industry 4.0:** New Digital orientation of Business sector.

**Information Quality:** This talks about the overall ratings given by the consumer for eWOM Recommendations.

**Involvement:** The relevance of the information search to the receivers' perceptions.

**Novelty:** eWOM messages the quality and strength of the argument.

**Source Credibility:** Source credibility is how a consumer perceives and trusts the source of the eWOM recommendations.

**Trustworthiness:** It talks about the authenticity of the source is genuine.

**User-Generated Content (UGC):** UGC is an online user activity that involves the expression of individual thoughts, ideas and feedback about what it has experienced with a product or brand.

**Valence:** An eWOM message's valence shows whether it is positive or negative.

# Factors Shaping the Patterns of Online Shopping Behavior

**Fahima Khanam**
*BSMR Aviation and Aerospace University, Bangladesh*

**Mahmud Ullah**
https://orcid.org/0000-0001-7472-2477
*Department of Marketing, University of Dhaka, Bangladesh*

**Muhammad Omar Al-Zadid**
*Carson College of Business, Washington State University, USA*

## INTRODUCTION

As globalization has taken the world by storm, it has given a substantial momentum to the idea of online business. The growth of online business is intertwined with the increasing popularity of online shopping.

Online shopping is still a kind of new practice for the shoppers in developing countries like Bangladesh. Shoppers in these countries are not as habituated in online shopping as their counterparts in the developed countries. Online shopping behavior is yet to take a definable and sustainable pattern in these countries. So, the behavioral patterns of the online shoppers among the different countries in the world would certainly differ. These differences will not be there because of the nuance of the phenomenon only. There are many other social, cultural, technological, technical, economic, political, legal, educational, religious, etc. factors as well.

Hence, it is important for the business professionals to understand the root causes of the patterns of shopping behavior of the online shoppers in each of the countries / markets they operate or plan to operate. In this context, the authors felt that an exploratory research in this area will be a good help to the business professionals with some basic data on the shoppers' behavioral pattern to help them make their decisions based on DSS (Data Support System) by using some authentic data.

Bangladesh has taken massive programs to digitalize all the government, nongovernment, and business operations in the country. People are responding very eagerly to, and adjusting quite quickly with these programs. They are truly adopting the digitalization process very rapidly. As a result, online shopping has increased manifold in Bangladesh in the last couple of years or so.

The research findings described in the respective sections of this chapter will certainly help the academicians, researchers, students, business organizations, marketers, and other stakeholders get a detailed understanding of the various aspects of online business within a frame of statistical inferences. This chapter adds mainly a few aspects of knowledge to the existing knowledge of online shopping intention of consumers and its various dimensions in relation to multiple underlying factors in the forms of the summarized scenario of the current situation of e-commerce in Bangladesh, future prospect of e-commerce, transmission of shoppers' behavior from brick & mortar shoppers to online shoppers, classification of the significantly influencing factors determining online shoppers' shopping behavior into some specific categories, etc.

DOI: 10.4018/978-1-7998-9220-5.ch065

## BACKGROUND

The power of internet is very much evident in this world now which leads customers to choose things sitting at their homes rather than going to a store physically. The online shopping is a crazy thing to do now for people of all ages that is creating crowd for the online entrepreneurs. But this shopping behavior of customers can be affected or influenced by many factors. Some aspects of online purchasing are liked by customers while others are not. It is evident that neither all the aspects of online shopping are liked by the customers, nor any single aspect influences all the customers similarly.

A decent number of studies have been conducted to find out the different factors of online shopping which are proactive and prominent, as well as to measure what factors influence the intention, attitude and behavior of online shoppers, and how do those factors play the respective influential roles in shaping the behavioral pattern of the online shoppers. It is the crying demand of time to understand the shopping behavior and the factors which affect the purchase decision of the online shoppers. A small scale study done by the authors in this area, is reasonably a more comprehensive one to explore the behavioral patterns of these newly generated online shoppers in Bangladesh.

In order to explore consumers' motivation behind shopping online, evolution of the e-commerce environment, and evaluation of factors influencing consumers to get involved in e-commerce are important. The study aims to determine the factors that originally influence consumers' online shopping behavior in the city of Dhaka, Bangladesh. For this reason, the study assumes that there might be an association between these underlying factors and the patterns of consumers' online shopping habits to form their sustainable online shopping behavior. The possible factors have been extracted from the analysis of some related literature. Furthermore, the study also attempts to focus on the existing problems and provide some recommendations to resolve those problems.

### Stimulants of Outgrowth of E-commerce

The growth of e-commerce market is the result of expansion of technology and development of other demographic and social issues. Because of the economic growth, people's purchasing and consumption power is increasing. People are spending more money in buying luxury and foreign products. Availability of smartphones and internet are other reasons to expand the e-commerce market to a great extent.

### Excrescence of Internet

The rise of internet is now at a reasonably recognized level. Bangladesh has witnessed a tremendous growth in the number of mobile internet subscribers over the last decade. The number of internet users in Bangladesh expanded by 3.3 core between 2010 and 2019 which indicates that 20 per cent of the population are using internet. According to the Bangladesh Telecommunication Regulatory Commission, the number of internet users in Bangladesh reached 11.11 core in September 2020 which is a 13 per cent increase compared to the same period in 2019. By 2025, Bangladesh will have six per cent of all mobile connections under 5G. BTRC has already taken preparation to launch 5G services as soon as possible. If the growth of internet usage is continued at this pace, Bangladesh will become a highly potential e-commerce market in near future from its low potential operations at present (Hasan, 2020).

F

## Affordability and Availability of Smartphones

The most affordable tech product in developing countries like Bangladesh is smartphones now-a-days. People are using internet and social media sites by using smartphones without having a laptop or personal computer. Consequently, they are doing their shopping activities just by clicking the buttons / links on their mobile screens.

## Fatal Traffic Conditions

The traffic condition of Bangladesh, especially in Dhaka city, is deteriorating day by day. Every year, five million work hours lost due to traffic congestion as well as Tk 37,000 crore is wasted due to traffic condition. For avoiding traffic jam and saving valuable time, the city dwellers prefer to buy from online shops or platforms. As population are increasing day by day which is a prime cause of traffic jam in the cities, online shopping is becoming proportionately popular based on this ground. While stuck-up on the way to home or office in traffic jam, people utilize the time browsing different sites for searching products to order them.

## Younger Generation

Among all the buyers of online platforms, young people are the main contributors. This vibrant sector of buyers loves to purchase the essential products as well as funky and fashion items. Young generations are playing significant role behind the popularity of online shopping. (IDLC Finance Limited, 2018).

## Transmuted Consumer Behavior

As online shopping has become a rapidly growing phenomenon almost in each of the countries in our world, particularly during the unprecedented Corona pandemic all around the globe including Bangladesh – putting the whole world into an absolute confinement and almost stand still over the last one and a half year, it has become obvious for the academicians and marketing professionals to have up to date research based knowledge of behavioral pattern of online shoppers to make data based marketing decisions to operate their businesses more effectively, profitably and sustainably.

Because of the technologies, consumer behavior has changed a lot, especially in recent times. By simply browsing internet, it is possible to buy and consume products which is very much popular among consumers. The number of online buyers are increasing which indicates a growing trend of using internet among people. The traditional local shoppers in the recent years are now preferring online purchasing. As a result, e-commerce is booming around the globe which increases the online transactions rapidly.

Bangladesh is not far behind in this rapidly growing fast-paced trend. Online sales have increased compared to the previous years. Consequently, businesses are expanding dramatically and creating job opportunities for thousands to millions of people. According to the German-based research institute Statista, the e-commerce market of Bangladesh has already exceeded one and a half billion US dollars which is undoubtedly a great achievement, and it is expected to reach two billion dollars this year and three billion dollars by 2023. ("eCommerce - Bangladesh | Statista Market Forecast", 2022).

This drastic rise of e-commerce span is not only creating job opportunities but also helping people to become entrepreneurs. Most importantly, women are the core beneficiaries of this new era. Though about four lakh women entrepreneurs are operating business in online platform which indicates a tremendous growth, the demographic profile and buying pattern of consumers brought out some noteworthy dimensions also. One noticeable thing is consumers mostly prefer to buy more essential products which helps to rise (300 per cent growth in the last one year) some segments, especially commodities and food business. Other thing is compared to lower class to lower-middle class families, middle class and upper-middle class people are more likely to shop from /on the online shops / platforms. Mainly city dwellers are the buyers of e-commerce. Dhaka, Gazipur and Chottogram covered 80% of the online buyers. At the same time majority of the buyers are young people, aging 18 to 34. At present, more than 160,000 deliveries are being made every day (Chowdhury et al., 2022).

## FOCUS OF THE STUDY

The prime focus of this paper is to identify the factors responsible for different patterns of behavior demonstrated by the online shoppers around the world. Online platforms create global citizens & actors to perform in their stages operating worldwide, by providing scopes for demonstrating country and culture specific customized behavior by each online shopper within the general rules set by each platform. Identifying the behind the scenes causes of the prominent patterns of online shopping behavior is the theme of this paper to help the business run their online operations more efficiently and effectively.

## Significant Factors of Online Shopping

People are very much interested in online shopping for various reasons obviously. Consumers prefer to become digitalized now-a-days because of changing lifestyle. Before go for online purchasing, consumers think of some crucial issues, and take those in their hearts or minds to consider as their comfort factors. Many researchers and academicians did lots of studies and researches to find out the underlying factors of popularity of online shopping and the considerable factors from the consumers' perspectives.

In a study based in Iran on analysis of factors affecting online shopping behavior, Javadi et al. (2012) categorized some risk factors under "perceived risks" that influence consumers' online shopping behavior. These risks are financial risk, product risk, convenience risk and non-delivery risk. Among these, according to the study, the effects of product and convenience risks are not significant on attitude toward online shopping. Results furthermore indicated that infrastructural variables (after sales service, cyber laws and shipping fees) and return policy were not significant either. However, the results showed significant influence of domain specific innovativeness and opinion of friends and peers on online shopping behavior.

Strong relationship between opinion of friends and peers and purchase intention was also supported by another study covering the mediating role of online purchase intention (Lim et. al., 2016). This study also supported the low significance of product risks. It found out that usefulness of products had weak relationship with online purchase intention. Another study (Forsythe and Shi, 2003) provides a completely opposite result in case of product risks and convenience risks. According to this study, these two risks are very significant on consumers' frequency of purchasing online. This study also examines another risk called psychological risk, the effect of which is not significant on consumers.

A study on online shopping behavior of consumers (Uzun and Poturak, 2014) concluded that price is the most important factor for consumers to purchase online. The study concluded that consumers' future buying is not affected by web design and delivery time rather by last experience. This study also declared the convenience of products as one of the most influencing factors to satisfy consumers. An interesting insight was found in a study on e-commerce factors influencing consumers' buying decision

(Baubonienė and Gulevičiūtė, 2015). According to this study lower price is more valued by women, whereas time and convenience are more important to men. The study also concluded that 25–34-year-old people more often chose online shops because of lower prices and greater variety of products.

Another study covering the same area (Akbar and James, 2014) categorized the factors of online shopping under three stages, information search stage, alternative evaluation stage and purchase decision stage. The result indicated that price, brand and convenience under the alternative evaluation stage strongly influence online purchase behavior. Under the purchase decision stage, security and refund had a moderate effect and promotion had a weak effect on online purchasing.

A Kolkata based study on the same area (Sen, 2014) concluded that cost factor was the most significant factor to influence online purchase decision. It suggested that price reduction, offer, discount and sales promotional techniques positively influence online purchase decision. After cost, it put importance on convenience factors such as time, secure payment, cash on delivery and product information. It declared the seller related factors as the least significant factors to influence online purchase decision.

A different perspective was examined by a study (Topaloglu, 2012) covering consumer motivation and concern factors for online shopping in Turkey. It identified two broad factors, namely, motivation factors and concern factors, to examine whether they influence online search and purchase intention. Motivation factors included utilitarian value and hedonic value. On the other hand, concern factors included privacy and security.

Based on the research done before, five types of variables have been identified as significant.

## Convenience Factors

To avoid gatherings in shopping malls or restaurants, people prefer to buy from home. Because of busy lifestyles and long working hours, consumers shopping from home is a convenient and time-saving solution over the traditional shopping along with reduced traveling time & cost, and easy payment system.

## Psychological Factors

Online orders can be done through websites or by social media sites. Design and features of websites and Facebook pages play crucial role in encouraging shoppers to shop from a particular site. Online retailers have started giving plenty of offers that have increased the online traffic to a great extent.

Furthermore, from the detailed information and plenty of available retailers and suppliers, customers can purchase by comparing the quality and price. Besides, in case of online shopping, it is possible to get insights about product quality and offerings from the friends and peers, as in recent times people are giving reviews and sharing their opinions about a particular brand or product with respect to their most recent or the latest purchases.

## Promotional Factors

Online ads and social media exposure are very much influential factors. When customers encounter Facebook ads or Google ads, they can get to know about a new offering or a completely new product. Online giants like Amazon, Flipkart, AliExpress, etc. are advertising huge discounts and offering a large variety of offerings which is a good source of information for people. These kinds of promotional ads are enticing the customers to purchase.

## Technical Factors

Customers want to get user-friendly websites to purchase from as not all of the people are too much skilled at browsing complicated sites. Another thing is, while purchasing online, customers should get the pros and cons of a product which will overcome the barriers of getting a product without being physically observed.

## Motivational Factors

Consumers' perceived value motivates them to decide on which they are going to consume which is associated with senses, pleasures, feeling and emotions. Motivational factors behind online shopping is of two types. One is Utilitarian Value that is the value that a customer receives based on a task-related and rational consumption behavior (Bell et al. 2020). On the other hand, Hedonic Value is defined as that value which a customer receives based on the subject experience of fun and playfulness. The degree to which a product/service arouses emotions and creates pleasant experiences.

## Conceptual Framework

Based on the above-mentioned studies conducted previously, five types of very important factors shaping the patterns of shopping behavior of the online shoppers can be identified. These factors are convenience factors, psychological factors, promotional factors, technical factors, and motivational factors.

Each factor has some distinct variables. Convenience factors include less time, home delivery, and ease of transaction. Psychological factors include domain specific innovativeness, and opinion of friends and peers. Promotional factors include online ads, and social media exposure. Technical factors include user-friendliness of websites, and display of product details. Motivational factors include utilitarian and hedonic values. How these variables influence consumers' online shopping intention are the main issues covered in this study.

So, these factors containing the above-mentioned variables act as independent variables and consumers' online shopping intention act as dependent variable. On the basis of this frame, the conceptual framework was developed (Figure 1). Using this model, the hypotheses can be developed as below:

$H_0$: Factors of online shopping do not significantly influence consumers' online shopping behavior and purchase intention.

$H_1$: Factors of online shopping significantly influence consumers' online shopping behavior and purchase intention.

## Objectives

This study measures the strength of the relevant factors that influence the consumers' intention and decision to purchase online. While this can be taken as the broad objective, this study aims to achieve a few more specific objectives as follows too.

- Determining the level of impact of the factors influencing purchase intention of the online shoppers to categorize those on the basis of their significance.

*Figure 1. Conceptual Framework*

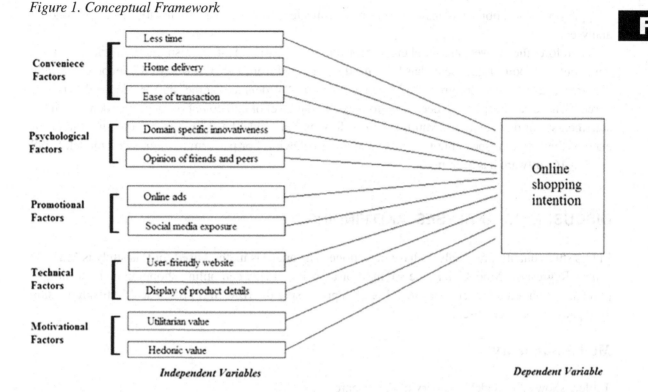

- Examining the applicability of these particular factors in the context of the online shopping environment existing for the online shoppers in Bangladesh.
- Obtaining online retailers' insights about the expectations of Bangladeshi consumers, and online shoppers' suggestions for possible modifications in the shopping system to make it more convenient and customer friendly.

## RESEARCH DESIGN

This is a descriptive study since it tries to find out the influence of factors on consumers to purchase online. Both primary and secondary data have been used to conduct this study. Secondary data have been collected from other studies related to online shopping. Primary data have been collected from the uncountable number of online shoppers, the target population of this study, by using a survey method.

Since this kind of test-marketing studies use 150-200 respondents, the sample size for this study has been determined as 150. Convenience non-Probability sampling technique has been used to select the samples. The reasons for selecting non-probability sampling technique are 1) the variability in the population is low, 2) population size in undefined, 3) time and cost issues are available.

In this study, the sample unit is an active Internet user who purchased online more than once. The sampling frame is the Facebook friends of the researcher because these users have the greatest possibility of purchasing online. However, it was ensured that each respondent purchased online at least once.

A statement based structured questionnaire representing independent and dependent variables with multiple choice of answers has been used as the instrument to conduct the survey for collecting primary data. Since the study is supposed to find out the influence of the factors in shaping the pattern of online shopping behavior, objective answers have been collected from the respondents for the corresponding analyses.

Therefore, the answers are numbered according to a measurement scale so that numerical findings come out. A 5-point Likert scale has been used that ranged from 1 to 5 in which "1" denotes "strongly disagree", "2" denotes "disagree", "3" denotes "neutral", "4" denotes "agree" and "5" denoted "strongly agree". These categories have been used to measure the level of agreement of the respondents with the statements. For data analyses, Multiple Linear Regression Model has been used to measure the influence of the factors responsible for online shopping behavior. For performing regression model, SPSS version 16 software has been used.

## DISCUSSIONS, ANALYSES, AND FINDINGS

In this study quantitative analyses have been done. The analysis method used for this study is Multiple Linear Regression Model. Here the strength of association between online shopping and consumers' purchase intention has been measured. For data processing the IBM SPSS Statistical Software version 16.0 package has been used.

### Model Summary

Table 1 shows the model summary of the research.

*Table 1. Model summary*

| Model | R | R Square | Adjusted R Square | Std. Error of the Estimate |
|---|---|---|---|---|
| 1 | .556[a] | .310 | .239 | .920 |

Here, by stating the model summary of the research, an attempt was made to identify the association between factors shaping online shopping behavior, and purchase intention created in consumers. R is called the correlation coefficient that represents the strength of association between dependent variable and independent variables. Its value ranges between -1 and +1. When the value of R is positive, it suggests a positive association between dependent variable and independent variables (Malhotra and Dash, 2012-2013). From the above table, the value of R is .556 which indicates that there is a positive association between online marketing and shopping behavioral pattern of the online shoppers in Bangladesh.

From the aforementioned figure, it can be observed that the value of R square is .310 which means that dependent variable is weekly associated with independent variables, i.e., 31.0% of variation in dependent variable is explained by independent variables. "The strength of association is measured by the coefficient of determination, $R^2$. It varies between 0 and 1 and signifies the proportion of the total variation in Y that is accounted for by the variation in X" (Malhotra, 2015).

Here, the value of the adjusted R square is .239. As moderate difference between R square and adjusted R square can be noticed, there are opportunities to add more variables. "$R^2$ is adjusted for the number of independent variables and the sample size to account for diminishing returns. After the first few variables, the additional independent variables do not make much contribution" (Malhotra, 2015).

## ANOVA Model

Table 2 shows the ANOVA model.

*Table 2. ANOVA*

| ANOVA | | | | | | |
|---|---|---|---|---|---|---|
| | Model | Sum of Squares | df | Mean Square | F | Sig. |
| 1 | Regression | 40.974 | 11 | 3.725 | 4.402 | .000[a] |
| | Residual | 91.392 | 108 | .846 | | |
| | Total | 132.367 | 119 | | | |

The significance level in the model was 0.00 which is less than 5% level of significance used in the model. It therefore follows that the model is statistically significant in predicting how the independent variables affect consumers' online purchase intention. On the other hand, F critical at 5% significance level is 3.17 while the F-calculated is 4.402. It therefore follows that the overall model is significant since the F-calculated is greater than the F-critical.

## Data Analysis

Data in Table 3 have been used for the following analyses.

*Table 3. Coefficient chart*

| Model | | Unstandardized Coefficients | | Standardized Coefficients | t | Sig. |
|---|---|---|---|---|---|---|
| | | B | Std. Error | Beta | | |
| 1 | (Constant) | .997 | .478 | | 2.085 | .039 |
| | Less time | -.031 | .131 | -.030 | -.237 | .813 |
| | Home delivery | .473 | .115 | .482 | 4.129 | .000 |
| | Ease of transaction | -.179 | .127 | -.204 | -1.405 | .163 |
| | Domain specific innovative ness | -.335 | .121 | -.358 | -2.764 | .007 |
| | Opinions of friends and peers | .206 | .118 | .237 | 1.747 | .083 |
| | Online ads | .059 | .134 | .068 | .441 | .660 |
| | Social media exposure. | .100 | .113 | .108 | .887 | .377 |
| | User-friendly website | -.029 | .088 | -.038 | -.329 | .743 |
| | Display of product details. | .116 | .102 | .148 | 1.137 | .258 |
| | Utilitarian value. | .323 | .100 | .334 | 3.238 | .002 |
| | Hedonic value | .045 | .084 | .054 | .544 | .588 |

Dependent Variable: I would like to purchase things from online stores next time

## Coefficient Analysis

Using the values shown in Table 3, the regression model becomes the following: Consumers' purchase intention = .997 (Constant) - .030 (less time) + 0.482 (home delivery) - 0.204 (ease of transaction) - 0.358 (domain specific innovativeness) + 0.237 (opinions of friends and peers) + 0.068 (online ads) + 0.108 (social media exposure) – 0.038 (user-friendly website) + 0.148 (display of product details) + 0.334 (utilitarian value) + 0.054 (hedonic value) + $e_i$ (error term).

Standardized coefficients calculated for each predictor variables, showing the percentage of variation in the dependent variable caused by the individual independent variables. It can be revealed that only the variable *'home delivery'* and *'utilitarian value'* are significant at 5% level. The Standardized beta coefficient of home delivery is *0.482*(the highest) which means it is also the most important variable that influences final step / outcome of the shopping behavior of the online shoppers i.e., purchase intention. The second most important variable is *'utilitarian value'* having a standardized coefficient of *0.334*. The third most important variable is *'opinions of friends and peers'*. Its standardized coefficient is *0.237*. The next important variable is *'display of product details'* having a standardized coefficient of *0.148*. Less time, ease of transaction, domain specific innovativeness and user-friendly website– these variables have negative standardized beta coefficient.

## Correlation Matrix Analysis

In the correlation matrix, maximum values are less than 0.5. If the maximum values of correlation matrix exceed 0.5, the research result is said to be suffering from multi-collinearity problem. "Multicollinearity arises when the inter-correlations among the predictors are very high" (Malhotra, 2015). So, it can be concluded that the research result is not suffering from the multi-collinearity problem.

## Hypotheses Testing

$H_0$: Factors of online shopping do not significantly influence consumers' online shopping behavior and purchase intention.

$H_1$: Factors of online shopping significantly influence consumers' online shopping behavior and purchase intention.

From the coefficient table, the significance values for the two independent variables are 0.000 and 0.004. So, the null hypothesis (There is no significant impact of the factors of online shopping on consumers' online shopping behavior and purchase intention) can be rejected. So, it can be concluded that factors of online shopping have significant impact on consumers' online shopping behavior and purchase intention.

## RECOMMENDATIONS

According to the result of the study, though customers prefer online shopping due to convenience in terms of less time consuming and hassle-free shopping, in some cases they didn't find that the online shopping is saving their time, i.e. less time-consuming. They face difficulties in browsing the websites, or searching the desired products, which kill their valuable time. Marketers should improve their websites,

Facebook pages or other sites and develop in such a way which will reduce the overall time needed to process the order and deliver the product so that time is saved on their part.

To attract more customers, word-of-mouth can be a good strategy. Positive reviews form others, especially from the friends and known persons can boost a brand by creating positive image. Recently, posting in different groups for product reviews or recommendations from others who used that product before is an effective strategy for customers to know about a brand or a particular product. Customers are now intelligent and knowledgeable enough to do research about a brand before purchasing. Besides, they become motivated by the opinion of friends and peers in case of choosing products from numerous options. Marketers should focus on spreading positive words through various mediums.

In case of online shopping in Bangladesh, social media exposure is a vital medium to serve customers. Many brick and mortar businesses do branding using social media through Facebook. Moreover, businesses are, now, operating their activities by both stores. A good image in social media can create a customer base for a particular brand. Prompt service, attractive page design, updated and detailed information, quick response in social media are considered as wise to build up a vivid reputation.

There are lots of advantages to shop from online. Though customers prefer availability of products, low prices, scopes of comparison, variety to choose from, user friendliness while deciding to purchase from e-commerce sites, trustworthiness is becoming their main concern for first or repeated purchase(s). Some customers feel risky to transact through online as the product quality of all sites are not up to the mark, even in some cases some businesses sell fake products, or something duplicate which are very harmful to use.

It is a common phenomenon that trust brings loyalty which is being reflected in the behavior of consumers through repeated purchase. In case of online shopping, there is no face-to face interaction between sellers and customers, which makes it challenging for customers to build up the trust. Marketers should put focus on creating trust in the mind of customers which is crucial to convert potential customers to actual and loyal customers. Besides, it is the responsibility of the online sellers to reduce the level of risk of the digital platform by providing quality product and service, and secured form of payment.

## FUTURE RESEARCH DIRECTIONS

In recent time, E-commerce has been passing its highest level of popularity in Bangladesh because of the Coronavirus pandemic situation. Physical markets are becoming less popular because of excessive crowd in online. Undoubtedly, this trend will be going on based on the demand of customers. The future of e-commerce in Bangladesh is glorious and bright.

Some issues are noteworthy to focus which are mostly responsible behind the growth of e-commerce in Bangladesh. First of all, due to the Covid-19 pandemic, the necessity of e-commerce has been revealed to the people and they do the best possible use of it. This trend has made it possible to move Bangladesh 5 years ahead, as well as created huge opportunities and facilitated the market condition for both entrepreneurs and customers. The rise of online platform has made the strategy makers understand the necessity of making the pathway and for enabling the infrastructure to be technologically and digitally strong for expanding the sector to a new extent.

Bangladeshi e-commerce market is big enough for transactions and there are still huge rooms to explore and create more (Tsiakis, 2012). Particularly, a potential number of people are now considering this sector seriously for building their career, especially women are the proactive starter in this case which will be the best option for them to become independent.

Gradually, the nation will be benefitted by getting a self-dependent women sector as well as the people will be benefitted by getting numerous products from both country and abroad (Daroch, Nagrath and Gupta, 2021). Currently, in the market there are a quite good line of products and services are existing such as, clothing lines, shoes, bags, imported food items, books, organic products, jewelry, diamonds, cars, medicines etc. (IDLC Finance Limited, 2018). Apart from these retail stores, services are coming up, for example, banks are providing online services which is termed as internet banking. Buses, railways, airlines are selling online tickets through booking.com or other related sites. Electronics, cars, building materials haven't a large portion yet but people are showing their interest to these sectors too. These sectors will be great areas of businesses for future entrepreneurs. That is why it is necessary to find out the line of products and services which can be the future potential prospect for growing the e-commerce sector (Forsythe et al., 2006).

The drastic movement of internet usage because of the improvement of telecommunication infrastructure in the country is connected with the privately owned transactional businesses. M-commerce and F-commerce are very popular in the country as these are preferred by people. A variety of technologies are being used in this sector for example, electronic data interchange (EDI), electronic mail (e-mail) and electronic fund transfer (EFT) (Financial Express, 2020).

Online transactions are increasing day by day. Despite the popularity of the cash-on delivery system, customers want some other payment methods for their convenience. Many merchants of online are now giving facilities to pay through, bkash, nagad, rocket which are mainly Mobile financial services (MFS).

Maximum banks and other financial organizations have introduced MFS because of this ongoing demand and popularity among people of all classes. MFS is very fruitful and feasible mode of transactions for students and young customers who don't have any bank account. Besides, paying through debit cards, visa cards, credit cards are also becoming popular. Customers prefer to pay using MFS rather than cash on delivery (Jadhav and Khanna, 2016).

Because of the growth rate and technological advancement of the current situation of e-commerce market, few big investors are expressing their interest to invest in the Bangladeshi e-commerce market. International Finance Corporation (IFC) has already started to monitor, research, collect information in order to consider it seriously. Moreover, many global investors are announcing to operate their businesses to India which can be shifted to Bangladesh in future.

Population and its size are a great concern while studying the online shopping behavior of customers. Social class, living standard, purchase power, income level are the factors affecting how the customers will behave. Recent statistics revealed that in the next 25 years, the total population of 168 million in Bangladesh will be under the age of 35 which indicates an emergence of young era. People aged between 20-35 years are more prone to shopping online.

As young people are the prime customers of online, it will be a golden opportunity to capture a vast potential market for Bangladesh by providing a business-friendly environment which will change the economic profile and business standard of the country (Aziz and Wahid, 2018). More and more studies need to be done to know the perspectives of this young sector and their experiences of online shopping. The result will enable the marketers to think differently and to revise their business policy. Not only the age but also the family structure and their profession are needed to be considered to study.

There is a relationship between family structure and likeliness to prefer online shopping. People from nuclear families or families where both of the parents are employed prefer online shopping most than the joint families. So, these issues should be studied a lot by businesses to find out more accurate target customer group.

## CONCLUSION

As consumers' online shopping tendency is rising with time, a steep competition is being visible between online and offline shopping intention of the consumers. Such a competition is mostly underpinned by the comparative analysis of the benefits and drawbacks of both types of shopping by the consumers. Although there are myriad issues concerned with online shopping, the potential of paradigm shifts in consumers' perspectives regarding being inclined toward online shopping is fairly high provided that the businesses can identify such problems and take measures to condescend them.

However, not necessarily online shopping is always taking away customers from the stores, rather it is often creating new customers for various brands as well. As many studies suggest, the wide use of social media has made a solid foundation for online shopping and intrigued consumers to purchase online more than ever before. Hence, social media sites are being used by the marketers more wisely today by targeting customers through online marketing tools such as SEOs and Artificial Intelligence.

On the other hand, some negative factors regarding offline shopping are contributing to the tendency of consumers toward online shopping. Several factors such as traffic congestion, less varieties in product lines and increasing busy schedules of consumers are also making offline shopping less attractive to people. To be more specific, recent surge of infectious diseases all around the globe has made it evident that consumers will continue to prefer safe and contactless shopping as well as transactions more than ever before.

Like other countries, consumers in Bangladesh are also creating an online shopping habit that will create more research opportunities in this field. With the emergence of online shopping trends, new problems will arise as well, and new inventions will appear alongside. All these things are more likely to form a momentum in obtaining new knowledge in the field.

Therefore, the online shopping behavior of the consumers would certainly be the center of many studies in the future. This chapter devoted its principal focus on the factors shaping the behavioral pattern of online shopping and purchase intention of the online shoppers / customers and tried to take into considerations the impact of those factors independently and collectively. There are more to add to this field as it will be the field in which future business visionaries are more likely to invest their money and conduct research projects in the coming days.

Under such circumstances, new factors might appear and more studies concerning the online shopping behavior and purchase intention of consumers will be conducted. Most importantly, behavior pattern of consumers may be changed in future which will generate new areas for more in depth studies. To conclude, the main focus of this chapter might be the source of future studies in this field.

## REFERENCES

Akbar, S., & James, P. T. J. (2014). Consumers' attitude towards online shopping: Factors influencing employees of crazy domains to shop online. *Journal of Management and Marketing Research*, *14*(1), 1–11.

Aziz, N., & Wahid, N. (2018). Factors influencing online purchase intention among university students. *International Journal of Academic Research in Business & Social Sciences*, *8*(7), 702–717. doi:10.6007/IJARBSS/v8-i7/4413

Baubonienė, Z., & Gulevičiūtė, G. (2015). Commerce factors influencing consumers' online shopping decision. *Social Technologies*, *5*(1), 78–80.

Bell, L., McCloy, R., Butler, L., & Vogt, J. (2020). Motivational and affective factors underlying consumer dropout and transactional success in ecommerce: An overview. *Frontiers in Psychology*, *11*, 1546. doi:10.3389/fpsyg.2020.01546 PMID:32714258

Chowdhury, M. S. A., Bappi, M. A. U., Imtiaz, M. N., Hoque, S., Islam, S., & Haque, M. S. (2022). The Transition of E-Commerce Industry in Bangladesh: Added Concerns & Ways of Recovery. *International Journal of Economics and Finance*, *14*(7), 1–18. doi:10.5539/ijef.v14n7p18

Daroch, B., Nagrath, G., & Gupta, A. (2021). A study on factors limiting online shopping behaviour of consumers. *Rajagiri Management Journal*, *15*(1), 39–52. doi:10.1108/RAMJ-07-2020-0038

*eCommerce - Bangladesh | Statista Market Forecast*. (2022). Retrieved 25 August 2022, from https://www.statista.com/outlook/dmo/ecommerce/bangladesh

Forsythe, S., Liu, C., Shannon, D., & Gardner, L. (2006). Development of a scale to measure the perceived benefits and risks of online shopping. *Journal of Interactive Marketing*, *20*(2), 55–75.

Forsythe, S. M., & Shi, B. (2003). Consumer patronage and risk perceptions in internet shopping. *Journal of Business Research*, *56*(11), 867–875.

Hasan, M. (2020, November 9). Bangladesh adds 3.3 cr internet users in a decade. *The Daily Star*. https://www.thedailystar.net/business/news/bangladesh-adds-33cr-internet-users-decade-1991761

IDLC Finance Limited. (2018, Aug.). E-commerce of Bangladesh: Shaping the future of shopping. *IDLC Monthly Business Review*, 6-19.

Jadhav, V., & Khanna, M. (2016). Factors influencing online buying behavior of college students: A qualitative analysis. *Qualitative Report*, *21*(1), 1–15.

Javadi, M. H. M., Dolatabadi, H. R., Nourbakhsh, M., Poursaeedi, A., & Asadollahi, A. R. (2012). An analysis of factors affecting on online shopping behavior of consumers. *International Journal of Marketing Studies*, *4*(5), 81–98.

Lim, Y. J., Osman, A., Salahuddin, S. N., Romle, A. R., & Abdullah, S. (2016). Factors influencing online shopping behavior: The mediating role of purchase intention. *Procedia Economics and Finance*, *35*, 401–410.

Malhotra, N. K. (2015). *Marketing research: An applied orientation* (7th ed.). Pearson, Inc.

Sen, R. A. (2014). Online shopping: A study of the factors influencing online purchase of products in Kolkata. *International Journal of Management and Commerce Innovations*, *2*(1), 44–52.

Topaloglu, C. (2012). Consumer motivation and concern factors for online shopping in Turkey. *Asian Academy of Management Journal*, *17*(2), 1–19.

Tsiakis, T. (2012). Consumers' issues and concerns of perceived risk of information security in online framework. *The Marketing Strategies Procedia - Social and Behavioral Sciences, 62*(2), 1265-1270.

Uzun, H., & Poturak, M. (2014). Factors affecting online shopping behavior of consumers. *European Journal of Social and Human Sciences*, *3*(3), 163–170.

## ADDITIONAL READING

F

Akhter, S., Rahman, N., & Rahman, M. N. (2014). Competitive strategies in the computer industry. *International Journal of Technology Diffusion*, *5*(1), 73–88. doi:10.4018/ijtd.2014010106

Arief, M. (2021). Marketing analysis: security and public trust online Shopping at shopee.co.id. *Enrichment: Journal of Management, 11*(2), 345-352.

Baeshen, Y. (2021). Factors influencing consumer purchase intention while buying online. *International Journal of Research -Granthaalayah, 9*(2), 99-107. . doi:10.29121/granthaalayah.v9.i2.2021.3293

Chaturvedi, D., Gupta, D., & Singh Hada, D. (2016). Perceived risk, trust and information seeking behavior as antecedents of online apparel buying behavior in india: An exploratory study in context of Rajasthan. SSRN *Electronic Journal, 6*(4), 935-943. doi:10.2139/ssrn.3204971

Chusminah, S. M., Haryati, R. A., & Lestari, R. (2020). Factors influencing online buying behaviour of millennial generation. *LPPM UPN Veteran Yogyakarta Conference Series Proceeding on Economic and Business Series, 1*(1), 165–171.

Garg, A., Agarwal, P., & Singh, S. (2019). A study of different aspects of consumer behavior for online buying in Delhi NCR for FMCD products. *Pranjana: The Journal of Management Awareness*, *22*(2), 76–87. doi:10.5958/0974-0945.2019.00007.4

Khan, S. S. (2020, January 15). E-commerce in Bangladesh: Where are we headed? *The Financial Express*.

Kiew, C., Abu Hasan, Z., & Abu Hasan, N. (2021). Factors influencing consumers in using shopee for online purchase intention in East Coast Malaysia. *Universiti Malaysia Terengganu Journal of Undergraduate Research*, *3*(1), 45–56. doi:10.46754/umtjur.2021.01.006

Lixăndroiu, R., Cazan, A., & Maican, C. (2021). An analysis of the impact of personality traits towards augmented reality in online shopping. *Symmetry*, *13*(3), 416. doi:10.3390ym13030416

Muljono, W., Pertiwi, S.P., Kusuma, D.P.S. (2021). Online shopping: Factors affecting consumer's continuance intention to purchase. *St. Petersburg State Polytechnical University Journal - Economics: π-Economy, 14*(1), 7–20. . doi:10.18721/JE.14101

Rahman, N., Rutz, D., Akhter, S., & Aldhaban, F. (2014). Emerging technologies in business intelligence and advanced analytics. *ULAB Journal of Science and Engineering*, *5*(1), 7–17.

Schlesinger, P. A., & Rahman, N. (2015). Self-service business intelligence resulting in disruptive technology. *Journal of Computer Information Systems*, *56*(1), 11–21. doi:10.1080/08874417.2015.11645796

Shah, J. (2014, December 29). Online shopping increases. *Prothom Alo, Dhaka, Bangladesh*. https://en.prothomalo.com/bangladesh/Online-shopping-increases

Singh, P., & Kashyap, P. (2015). Assessing attitude of male and female shoppers towards online shopping. *International Journal of Scientific Research*, *4*(4), 591–593.

Svatosova, V. (2020). The importance of online shopping behavior in the strategic management of e-commerce competitiveness. *Journal of Competitiveness*, *12*(4), 143–160. doi:10.7441/joc.2020.04.09

## KEY TERMS AND DEFINITIONS

**Behavior:** Generally, any sorts of responses made by any living organism complying with the driving forces generated from within that organism due to the influence of and interaction with the other stimulus or forces received by the receptor organs of that organism from the surrounding environment at a particular point in or over a period of time.

**Digital Divide:** A differential condition existing in the countries around the world in terms of the diffusion and usage of the ever developing and most booming information technology, which includes internet infrastructure, data speed, usage of internet, availability & adoption of smart phone, regulatory policies and restriction ranges on different global websites, attitude of the people of any specific country towards technology, etc.

**Online Shoppers:** Anyone who would like to spend some time to search and browse the websites of the business and/or service organizations with the purpose of just passing time, seeing the product / service assortments, comparing prices with those at the brick and mortar stores, intending to purchase or finalize a transaction right away or sometime in future, referring any important information to friends, families, and peers, doing mere research to learn something new, planning to do similar business in future etc.

**Pattern:** A specific form of any activity or anything which is built, cherished, consumed, demonstrated, done, organized, picked, referred, seen, etc. repeatedly in the same or a similar manner within the limits of the reasonable range of variations.

**Shaping:** Giving something a form up to a desired level by reinforcing the related factors as the required catalysts or nutrients. Shaping any behavior requires sufficient amount of practice within an acceptable time limit so that the early memories of the behavior are not lost before it gets reinforced with the repetition of the same or similar behavior.

# Semantic Features Revealed in Consumer–Review Studies

**Jing Yang**

https://orcid.org/0000-0002-9173-3888

*SUNY Oneonta, USA*

**Tao Wu**

*SUNY Oneonta, USA*

**Jeffrey Yi-Lin Forrest**

https://orcid.org/0000-0002-5124-9012

*Slippery Rock University, USA*

## INTRODUCTION

Consumer reviews are an invaluable resource for assisting online shoppers in determining the quality of a product or service. To date, much research has been conducted in this field. Prior empirical research on consumer reviews has tended to focus on observable aspects of either the reviews themselves (such as review ratings, review volume, and review length) or the reviewers who submit them online (such as reviewer reputation, expertise, social network, and so on). Numerous studies have found that these elements have a significant impact on online buyers' purchase decisions by influencing their purchase intention, perceived usefulness of a review, and, ultimately, product sales. For example, review rating is regarded as a critical factor in determining the perceived usefulness of a review (Hong et al., 2017). A review's star rating indicates how extreme it is (the more stars a review received, the more positive the review is) (Hong et al., 2017). The majority of review sites allow users to rate their interactions with a product or service using a single signal that reflects overall satisfaction. These studies have aided in establishing a link between review ratings, review usefulness, and purchase intent.

However, as some researchers have suggested, condensing a lengthy analysis into a single number may be problematic (Schindler & Bickart, 2012). A single number, such as review rating, may not provide readers with all of the information they needed to make a purchasing decision. As a result, review length has emerged as an important factor to consider in consumer review studies. Review length literally refers to the number of words in a review (Wang et al., 2018). Because reviews are typically written and delivered in text form, the number of words becomes a natural way to quantify the amount of information transmitted in the review. According to Yin et al., review length has a greater impact on a review's perceived helpfulness than other variables (Yin et al., 2014). Short reviews are thought to be shallow and lack a comprehensive evaluation of product features; longer reviews, on the other hand, contain relatively more information, allowing consumers to obtain indirect consumption experiences (Wang et al., 2018). Understanding the textual characteristics of a review will undoubtedly reveal more information to us at this point. As a result, we intend to discuss textual characteristics embedded in consumer reviews in this study.

DOI: 10.4018/978-1-7998-9220-5.ch066

## BACKGROUND

Textual characteristics in a consumer review can be understood from three perspectives: basic, content, and stylish features (Schindler & Bickart, 2012). Basic features are the previously mentioned observable characteristics, which refer to those review readers can directly observe from reviews, such as review rating (positive or negative), review age (posting date), and review extremity (the average discrepancy between this review's opinion and other reviews), and so on (Cao et al., 2011). Content features refer to the information provided in reviews, whereas stylish features refer to the words used by reviewers to express this information in those reviews (Schindler & Bickart, 2012). Semantic analysis studies typically concentrate on the wording of reviews (content and stylish features) rather than their source (basic features) (Schindler & Bickart, 2012).

Researchers use semantic analysis (also known as opinion mining) to uncover linguistic patterns in consumer reviews. This methodology was used by many researchers to create a concept taxonomy with the goal of capturing product attributes mentioned in consumer reviews as well as the structural relationship between these attributes. Typically, researchers in this field are interested in two variables: sentiment and polarity. In this context, polarity and sentiment are two concepts that are closely related but not interchangeable. Sentiment literally refers to the total amount of sentiment expressed in a text (either positive or negative), whereas polarity refers to the direction of the sentiment expressed in the text, which could be positive, negative, or neural (Salehan & Kim, 2016). Sentiment analysis on consumer reviews is used to extract semantic cues (the substance of a review, which is the precise meaning of text in this review) from a large volume of online reviews (Sun et al., 2019).

Technically, there are two approaches to consider when conducting a semantic analysis: statistical and lexicon-based approaches (Wimmer & Yoon, 2017). The statistical (or machine learning) approach is a supervised approach that creates classifiers from labeled instances of texts or sentences. This type of approaches perform well as a supervised method when large, labeled instances are available for training and validating classifiers, while the lexicon-based approach identifies a document's orientation based on the semantic orientation of the document's words or phrases (Wimmer & Yoon, 2017). However, when working with dynamic content, such as online consumer reviews, the lexicon-based approach is thought to be more appropriate than the statistical approach, because the time required to update the training set and retrain the classifiers could be significant (Wimmer & Yoon, 2017). As a result, when a training data set is insufficiently large to accumulate the necessary feature frequency information, lexicon-based approaches outperform statistical or machine learning approaches.

The content and style of reviews, according to the most recent research on text-based communication, are important decision inputs that help determine the relative diagnosticity and accessibility of these reviews (Ludwig et al., 2013; Yi & Oh, 2022). It is widely acknowledged that the arguments in a review provide varying levels of information to future consumers depending on the topic of discussion. Product evaluative statements, for example, are more influential than descriptive statements that do not provide product evaluative information because they contain evaluative words on products that can be either positive or negative in valence (Schindler & Bickart, 2012). Furthermore, style words, which are frequently used interchangeably with function words, shape the content of a communication (Ludwig et al., 2013). Pronouns, prepositions, articles, conjunctions, auxiliary verbs, and a few other esoteric categories are examples of style or function words. These categories differentiate not only what people say (sentential meaning), but also how they write (sentential style), and both have diagnostic value that influences decisions (Ludwig et al., 2013).

Given the significance of textual features embedded in consumer reviews, we reviewed related literature published in the previous decade and attempted to create a conceptual map of content and stylish features in consumer reviews and their relationship in the hope of providing insights to future researchers. We provide more articulation on the major findings on both content and stylish features in the remainder of the paper. The paper concludes with a discussion of the study's contribution.

## CONTENT FEATURES

The content of consumer reviews, more specifically the narratives provided by reviewers, influences consumer behavior. According to the findings of extensive content analyses, review narratives can range from simple recommendations accompanied by strong positive or negative assertions to sophisticated product evaluations supported by substantial reasoning. The product feature discussion is limited to the specifics of the product attributes under consideration. They are usually descriptions of aspects of a product or features of a product. For instance, "This tablet is slim and light," or "this tablet has expandable memory via TF card." Many studies on opinion mining concentrate on the extraction of product features.

To comprehend the information contained in review content, researchers are attempting to build a method for identifying connected linguistic cues. In recent years, techniques based on linguistic patterns have been extensively studied for the extraction of explicit aspects. The majority of studies examined relationships between aspects and opinions using dependency parser-based techniques (Rana & Cheah, 2017). These dependency parsers place a high emphasis on adhering to grammatical rules and linguistic limitations. However, because review sites often do not require users to adhere to these criteria, users frequently write in a casual manner and occasionally break such rules. It is not uncommon to find aspects mixed in with opinion words.

Kang and Zhou suggest that depending on how opinions regarding product attributes are presented in a review, the expressions can be classed as subjective or objective (Kang & Zhou, 2017) . They believe that if an expression about a feature is related with subjective judgments expressed in a review, it is subjective; but, if an expression is not associated with any opinions expressed in a review, it is objective. In this context, the term "feature" refers to the attributes, components, and associated concepts of both the object as a whole and its constituents (Kang & Zhou, 2017). Subjective features are frequently used to convey an opinion on the quality of the object being discussed. For instance, "My daughter loves her new tablet!" or "The display and color are beautiful!" Typically, subjective feature research is concerned with the extraction of opinion words. Kang and Zhou believe that when compared to objective features, subjective reviews mislead consumers' purchasing decisions. (Kang & Zhou, 2017).

More generally, researchers examine the effects of aspects from explicit versus implicit views (Poria et al., 2014; Rana & Cheah, 2017). They believe that certain aspects discussed in reviews are stated explicitly, while others are implicit. For example, a review that states, "The screen is small." In this statement, the fact is "screen," and the sentence demonstrates an implicit aspect, as "small" is an adjective indicating the size of the screen, despite the fact that the word "size" is not explicitly mentioned in the sentence. The majority of researchers concentrated on explicit aspects, while analyzing implicit aspects is more difficult (Rana & Cheah, 2017). The next section adheres to this classification.

## Explicit Aspects

Aspect-based opinion mining is used to extract aspects (or product attributes) from opinionated texts and derive polarity values for these messages. When extracting aspects, users frequently break words into product features and then assign polarity values to each of these features individually (Poria et al., 2014). The extraction process in practice consists of three steps: identifying product features on which consumers have expressed their thoughts; identifying review sentences that provide positive or negative judgments for each feature; and providing a summary based on the acquired information (M. Hu & Liu, 2004). There are two types of methods used to investigate product features: statistical methods and rule-based methods (Kang & Zhou, 2017). These two types of methods are further subdivided into supervised and unsupervised methods based on whether training data labeled with product features is required. Both types of methods are widely used in the extraction of product features.

The statistical methods are primarily used to generate meaningful patterns for extracting product features from online reviews (Kang & Zhou, 2017). Lee and Bradlow (2011), for example, proposed an automated method for analyzing online product reviews. They assert that key features mentioned in reviews can help with product marketing and design. They believe that the must-have features mentioned in the reviews define the basic product requirements. Customers criticize products for failing to deliver on must-have features; they do not praise products for delivering on must-have features because these features are expected. These comments reveal a brand's position in relation to its competitors, highlight key product features, and uncover hidden segments (Lee & Bradlow, 2011).

The rule-based methods employ rules derived from textual patterns. For example, Rana and Cheah proposed a two-fold rule-based model that accomplishes the task in three steps: (1) extracting explicit aspects associated with regular opinions via sequential pattern-based rules; (2) increasing aspect extraction accuracy via a frequency-based approach combined with normalized Google distance; and (3) extracting implicit aspects associated with regular opinions via a frequency-based approach combined with normalized Google distance in the second fold (Rana & Cheah, 2017). Statistical methods, in comparison to rule-based methods, often require huge corpora to address the data scarcity issue when estimating probability (Kang & Zhou, 2017).

## Implicit Aspects

In comparison to the extraction of explicit aspects, less progress has been made in the extraction of implicit aspects. This task is difficult since the occurrence of implicit features is more common in consumer reviews (Poria et al., 2014). For example, while evaluating the performance of a cell phone, reviewers may use phrases like light-weighted, sleek, or user-friendly to refer to features like weight, appearance, or interface, even though these words do not occur directly in the review sentences. As a result, the method of extracting implicit aspects normally consists of two steps: first, find implicit aspect clues (such as light-weighted, sleek, or user-friendly in the preceding example); and second, map these clues to the relevant aspects (such as weight, appearance, or interface) (Poria et al., 2014).

According to Hu and Liu, using natural language processing algorithms to analyze opinion words can determine the opinion orientation of each sentence (whether the opinion expressed in the sentence is positive or negative) (M. Hu & Liu, 2004). Opinion words are frequently a collection of adjective words used to express opinions). Researchers can determine the semantic orientation of each opinion word, such as positive or negative, and thus the opinion orientation of each phrase. The aspect extraction process used in semantic analysis of consumer reviews is depicted in Figure 1.

*Figure 1. The Aspect Extraction Process in Semantic Analysis of Consumer Reviews*

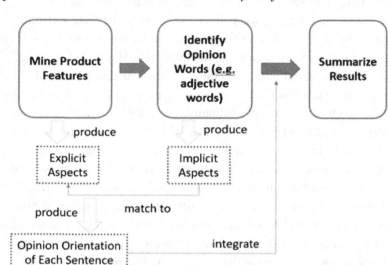

## STYLISH FEATURES

Stylish features refer to key features representing reviewers' wording choices that cannot be easily discerned by skimming a review, such as the number of words, sentences, average characters per word, average word per sentence, number of words in pros and cons, and so on (Cao et al., 2011). These choices are likely to have a strong effect on the impressions created by a review. Schindler and Bickart (2012) asserted that some wording characteristics, such as misspellings, poor grammar, and the use of inexpressive slang, will give readers of these reviews a negative impression of the reviewers' credibility as well as the value of these reviews. Other wording characteristics, on the other hand, such as the use of expressive slang and humor, first-person pronouns, the presence of personal information worded in a self-effacing manner, and so on, would give a review a sense of authenticity in the minds of readers and lead them to feel more confident about the information in the review (Schindler & Bickart, 2012).

The discussions on stylish features are primarily focused on two aspects: consumer emotions and writing styles. Consumer emotions reflect sentiment and polarity expressed in reviews, and reviewers' writing styles are the ways in which they write their reviews. To some extent, consumer emotions motivate people to write reviews and tell others about their experiences, and the writing style they use aids in the transmission of such emotions. This understanding will serve as the foundation for the rest of our discussion in this section.

### Consumer Emotions

Emotions are a primary reason for writing online reviews. Empirical evidence suggests that emotions expressed in reviews can be treated as information. Emotions are usually associated with two or more main appraisal dimensions, such as valence (either pleasant or unpleasant) and any other. Pleasant emotions include happiness, pride, challenge, surprise, interest, and hope, according to Ahmad and Laroche (2016), while unpleasant emotions include shame, guilt, disgust, fear, anger, contempt, frustration, boredom, and sadness. They believe that when a person is feeling proud, he or she considers the situation to be pleasant and accepts responsibility for it (since the person has done something good). If, on the other hand, a person is surprised, he or she perceives the situation as pleasant and is also associated with other responsibilities (since surprise is evoked when some other entity has done something). Furthermore, if a person feels ashamed, he or she perceives the situation to be unpleasant and self-responsible (since shame is evoked when the person has done something wrong) (Ahmad & Laroche, 2016).

As Ludwig et al. (2013) point out, affective content words can and are more likely to be considered by people who have low motivation and limited processing resources (e.g., due to distraction and/or time constraints), as well as when other bases of evaluation are unclear or unrevealed. These circumstances are common in the online purchasing process, under which text-based affective content words could provide more quickly accessible and diagnostic signals about targets (Ludwig et al., 2013). They contend that affective content, as a whole, will influence consumer conversion rates. Affective cues embedded in review words are more accessible than factual or descriptive information. Furthermore, affective cues provide decision inputs only if they are received as sufficiently diagnostic in terms of two dimensions: representativeness (the extent to which consumers believe that affective content reflects the target and whether the sender's representation indicates qualifications to express his or her opinions) and validity (whether affective cues appear consistent with other cues and across multiple sources).

## Dimensions of Emotions

Dimensional theories and cognitive appraisal theories of emotion are two popular approaches to understanding the impact of consumer emotions (Yin et al., 2014). Dimensional theories hold that all emotions can be demonstrated to vary along multiple dimensions. Valence (pleasant versus unpleasant, reflecting evaluation), arousal (activated versus deactivated, reflecting activity), and power (or potency, reflecting dominance) are among the commonly acknowledged dimensions (Yin et al., 2014). Among these dimensions, valence is almost universally accepted, as evidenced by numerous consumer review studies. However, the dimensional view of emotions is increasingly being called into question. One frequently cited limitation of this approach is that global dimensions such as valence and arousal are less useful for capturing emotions that differ little across these fundamental dimensions (Yin et al., 2014). For example, whereas anxiety and rage share a similar valence and arousal (both are unpleasant and active), they have a separate phenomenology and likely to produce distinct responses (Yin et al., 2014). Other differences are likely to have a significant impact on the development and resolution of emotional experiences due to their diversity and complexities.

Cognitive appraisal theories of emotion are concerned with the nuanced cognitive bases that underpin various emotional states. This approach argues that emotions are determined not by events, but by how an individual interprets and evaluates those events (Ismagilova et al., 2020). According to this theory, the interpretation of an emotion is dependent on how an individual evaluates the environment along a number of cognitive dimensions. Among the commonly recognized cognitive dimensions are (Ismagilova et al., 2020): 1) pleasantness (valence): positive or negative outcome of the situation on the evaluator; 2) attention: the need to allocate attention to the situation; 3) control: whether the situation is controlled by the person, another person or impersonal circumstances; 4) certainty: whether the outcome of the event is certain or not; 5) perceived obstacle: presence of a goal or obstacle to the goal; 6) fairness (legitimacy): whether the outcome of the situation is fair or not; 7) agency-responsibility: responsibility for the situation (other-agency, self-agency); 8) anticipated effort: whether the situation needs a high or low level of effort.

Research has documented a link between appraisal patterns and consumption/post-consumption emotions. Ismagilova et al., for example, believed that applying cognitive appraisal theory of emotions could improve understanding of consumers' information processing, particularly the current understanding of the role of emotions in an information-seeking situation (Ismagilova et al., 2020). According to Ahmad and Laroche (2016), certainty appraisal of emotions has a positive and significant impact on online product reviews. They discovered that reviews with certainty-related emotions have a positive effect on perceived review helpfulness, whereas reviews with uncertainty-related emotions have a negative effect (Ahmad & Laroche, 2016).

Numerous attempts have been made to identify a constricted set of appraisal dimensions. To uncover the logical relationship of these findings, we discuss them further based on the impact they have on consumer cognition.

## The Influence of Emotions on Purchasing Behavior

In practice, most online shopping websites allow customers to assess the potential usefulness (or helpfulness) of each review. Reviews are thought to be useful to readers because of their perceived diagnostic qualities. According to research, the sentiment expressed in reviews may influence how useful a review is perceived by consumers. According to Ahmad and Laroche, discrete emotional content (such as happiness, hopefulness, disgust, and anxiety) in a review has a significant impact on potential customers, as evidenced by helpfulness votes (Ahmad & Laroche, 2016). According to their findings, happiness expressed in a review has a greater impact on people's perceptions of helpfulness than hope. Anxiety, on the other hand, reduces perceived helpfulness, whereas disgust increases it. Kim and Gupta's research looked at the impact of positive and negative emotions on the usefulness of online reviews (Kim & Gupta, 2012). The study discovered that convergent negative emotions in multiple reviews increase perceived informative value; similarly, positive emotions increased perceived informative value.

Ismagilova et al. discovered that negative discrete emotions such as regret and frustration, as well as positive discrete emotions, influence perceptions of the helpfulness of online reviews (Ismagilova et al., 2020). While regret and frustration are both negative emotions, they discovered that regret is associated with perceived fairness and frustration with perceived unfairness. They believe that by expressing fairness emotions in an online review, a reader will find it more useful, and the reviewer will thoroughly evaluate their experience. Reviews that express feelings of injustice, on the other hand, will be less helpful. As a result, it is hypothesized that if a consumer is dissatisfied with a product's performance and expresses their dissatisfaction in a review, the review will be perceived as less helpful than if the reviewer regrets purchasing the product.

Moreover, emotions may influence consumers' other related perceptions, such as rationality. People's reasoning processes and logical rationality have been found to be influenced by their emotional states (Ismagilova et al., 2020). When customers express their emotions in online reviews, eWOM recipients can interpret them as a sign of rationality. Kim and Gupta (2012), for example, used attribution theory to investigate the impact of negative emotions on perceived reviewer rationality in the context of US consumers using online reviews of laptops (Kim & Gupta, 2012). When a reviewer expresses negative emotions, they are perceived as irrational, whereas when they express positive emotions, they are perceived as rational. Other studies found similar results with negative emotions (Ismagilova et al., 2020). It is obvious that the emotions elicited by review narratives influence consumer purchasing decisions.

*Figure 2. The Cognitive Process Explaining How Emotions Influence Consumer Perceptions*

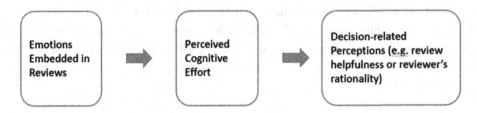

## Writing Styles

A lot of text mining research is based on writing styles. According to the psychology literature, reviews have three linguistic characteristics: adjectives, state verbs, and action verbs (Krishnamoorthy, 2015). Because adjective features are commonly used to describe consumer emotions, they are frequently addressed in the literature on consumer review opinion mining. State verbs are those that describe a person's emotional, affective, or mental state as well as a specific behavior or scenario. "Am" is a state verb in a review sentence like "I use this computer on a regular basis," and "use" is an action verb because the sentence describes a specific action. A state verb, in general, is more abstract and describes a broad category of behaviors that stretches beyond a specific situation, whereas an action verb is more specific, objective, and describes a specific scenario and observable activity (Krishnamoorthy, 2015).

These categories were manually coded in traditional psychology studies, often by multiple coders or annotators. Coding reliability is evaluated using standard statistical measures such as Cohen's kappa coefficients (Krishnamoorthy, 2015). This method can be used if the experiment is small, controlled, and the nature of the messages is known ahead of time (Krishnamoorthy, 2015). However, for a large-scale review helpfulness assessment problem, the preparation of a training corpus and manual annotation of linguistic features is a time-consuming and tedious process that does not add much value to people's understanding. As a result, it is more common in text mining studies for researchers to develop models, rules, or algorithms in the hope of summarizing and forecasting the effects of these linguistic features on consumer behavior, such as purchase intention or perceived helpfulness of reviews. The remainder of the discussion focuses on the factors discovered in relation to the writing style of reviews on an aggregate level.

### Objectivity/Subjectivity

The studies on the arguments in reviews can be understood from two perspectives: objective or subjective arguments. Review subjectivity refers to the total number of subjective words (positive and negative opinion words) normalized by review length (Krishnamoorthy, 2015). The subjectivity of words and phrases may depend on their context and an objective document may contain subjective sentences (e.g., a news article quoting people's opinions) (Krishnamoorthy, 2015).

This classification of objective versus subjective arguments is derived from an understanding of how customers' purchase intentions are formed. Purchase intent is thought to be determined by a person's estimated value of a product (Lee & Lee, 2009). Some people have general standards for evaluating specific attributes of that product that they consider important when estimating the value of that product, while others do not (Lee & Lee, 2009). When a consumer evaluates a product, he or she may consider factors such as weight, capacity, and design, and etc. If the prices were the same, a product with better performance on those attributes would be perceived more favorably. However, in terms of other attributes such as color and texture, consumers may have varying opinions based on their own experience.

The main contrast between these two types of attributes is whether or not they are evaluated using a ranking system (Lee & Lee, 2009). The evaluation process is less prone to misinterpretation or bias if all attributes are objectively measurable. The product's style, color, and shape may provoke varying tastes, and a significant degree of subjectivity is assumed. These two product features establish an objectivity/subjectivity dichotomy (Lee & Lee, 2009).

The effect of objectivity/subjectivity in review content varies depending on context. Lee and Koo, for example, discover that negative and negative objective online reviews are more credible than positive and subjective online reviews (Lee & Koo, 2012). Their research confirms that the negativity effect is more valid than the positivity effect, expanding our understanding that the effect produced by objective online reviews is more important than the effect produced by subjective online reviews, and introducing the moderating effect of subjective knowledge, which explains the inconsistent results found in the relationship between review characteristics and review credibility. Furthermore, Jeong and Koo (2015) assert that the tone of online reviews influences perceived helpfulness. In terms of message helpfulness, their findings show that objective negative reviews and subjective negative reviews posted on consumer-generated websites are more helpful than reviews posted on marketer-generated websites (Jeong & Koo, 2015). As a result, other factors such as review valence or platform types, as mentioned in the examples, should be included in the explanation for the effect of objectivity/subjectivity in review content.

## Argument Density/Diversity

Much empirical research in communication science reveal that message argument density (the proportion of arguments) is connected to message compliance (Willemsen et al., 2011). Stating the arguments behind an opinion invites evaluation of the supported viewpoint. In computer-mediated communication, when online discussants can only rate information based on the rigor of arguments, the mere presence of arguments increases a communicator's confidence and persuasiveness. They won't believe a review unless it provides sufficient information on the arguments used to make assertions about or evaluate a product or service. Reviews are thought to be more valuable if they include more evidence to support their arguments (Willemsen et al., 2011).

Aside from argumentation density, argumentation diversity plays an important role in what buyers gain knowledge from reviews. Texts that present both sides of an argument are thought to be more persuasive than other texts (Willemsen et al., 2011). Contrary to one-sided augmentation, two-sided argumentation that includes both the advantages and disadvantages of a stance is more likely to align people's attitudes, brand, and product preferences with the message's content. Furthermore, the presentation of negative facts with positive facts can validate a consumer's first-hand experience, rather than a commercial endorser's. Many customers are concerned that the anonymity of internet reviews encourages commercial endorsers to post product reviews under phony customer identities in order to promote products and brands. Consumers who believe a source is not telling the truth will dismiss it. As a result, reviews that include a variety of positive and negative reasons are deemed more valuable (Willemsen et al., 2011).

## Readability Features

The extent to which an individual needs to comprehend the information can present the level of readability (Krishnamoorthy, 2015). The readability of a review is another important factor that can influence the usefulness of a review. Reader readability, which reflects the cognitive efforts required to read and comprehend reviews, is regarded as a sophisticated measure of review depth (Wang et al., 2018). A well-written review is more likely to be read and voted on by a larger number of people (Krishnamoorthy, 2015). A review is more useful if it is easier to understand.

Readability, it is widely believed, is a numerical value that can be calculated using a readability formula and is derived from a mathematical model that evaluated the readability of various pieces of text by a variety of subjects. The following metrics can be used to assess review readability: the Automated Readability Index (ARI), the SMOG, the Flesch–Kincaid Grade Level, the Gunning Fog Index, and the Coleman–Liau Index (Wang et al., 2018). The readability test evaluates a piece of text's understandability based on its syntactical elements and underlying style.

Hu et al., for instance, used ARI to assess the readability of reviews in their study (N. Hu et al., 2012). They chose ARI over other metrics because they believe that ARI is determined by the number of characters in each word, not the number of syllables in each word. They believe that determining the number of characters in a word is more straightforward and accurate than determining the number of syllables in a word. They calculated ARI using the following formula in the study:

$$ARI=4.71*(\text{Total number of characters}/\text{Total number of words})+0.5*(\text{Total number of words}/\text{Total number of sentences})-21.43 \tag{1}$$

The API value approximated the grade level of education required to comprehend a passage of text. For instance, an ARI score of 8.3 indicated that a piece of text could be understood by an average eighth-grade student in the United States. They proposed that the readability of a genuine customer review should be random due to the wide range of educational backgrounds, clarity of expression, and ability to communicate their thoughts appropriately among customers, whereas manipulated reviews should be consistent in terms of readability.

## FUTURE RESEARCH DIRECTIONS

Numerous studies on consumer reviews have been conducted. These findings not only help individual consumers compare products and businesses, but they also help business owners develop business strategies. There is, however, a lack of a systematic understanding of these findings that can assist prospective researchers in understanding what has been done and what needs to be done in the future. We reviewed the literature on consumer reviews that focuses on textual features in the reviews in this study. We are particularly interested in identifying the key factors outlined in semantic analysis studies. We reveal linguistic features that make an online review more appealing to consumers using the theoretical framework discussed in the literature.

The literature suggests three types of major features: basic, content, and stylish features. Basic features such as review quantity, valence, quantity, and so on were the most commonly discussed of these three types of features. A systematic understanding of the internal relationships of these basic consumer review features has gradually been accumulated. There is, however, a lack of comprehensive understanding of how content features and writing features are related. There are two technical reasons for this. First and foremost, this field is still in its infancy. The type of analysis is heavily reliant on technical developments in data mining, particularly text mining, which can be a technical barrier for more researchers to continue their studies in this field. We reviewed the major findings in semantic analysis studies in this study. We purposefully ignored basic features because our goal is to create a conceptual map that describes the relationship between the factors pertaining to textual features of consumer reviews. As a result, commonly discussed factors such as reviewer information disclosure, reviewer expertise, reviewer follow numbers, and so on are not covered.

In a literal sense, content features and stylish features are two distinct categories. The term "content features" refers to aspects affecting the content of reviews, more specifically what reviewers say about items and their features. The term "stylish features" refers to the writing styles employed by reviewers. However, when these two notions are examined more closely, they become interconnected. As mentioned previously, content features can be seen via two lenses: implicit and explicit aspects. In comparison to explicit aspects, an implicit aspect review incorporates some evaluative remarks. To a certain extent, such judgmental remarks are accompanied by stylish features. Implicit characteristics are associated with writing styles at this point. Subjectivity and argument density, which influence the consumer emotions portrayed in those reviews and their readability, were used to determine the extent of implicitness.

It is worth noting that all of the discussions in this study are limited to the semantic features embedded in consumer reviews. We did not cover other content features such as product feature discussions, reviewer expertise, seller credibility, and so on. This is not to say that these characteristics are unimportant. It's only because they're unrelated to the main point we're attempting to make here. They are undeniably worthy of investigation.

## CONCLUSION

This study makes two contributions. To begin, we conducted a review of the literature regarding the findings of textual features in consumer reviews. Among the several frameworks provided in earlier study, we choose the most plausible one to aid future researchers in comprehending the relationships between elements discovered in numerous semantic analysis/opinion mining investigations that employed quantitative models or text mining approaches. Second, we summarized and classified the significant findings in the existing literature. Current research on the textual features of consumer reviews is disorganized. Because semantic analysis heavily relies on the content of reviews, results may vary according to context, particularly when it comes to product features. By reading various papers, one might gain a variety of perspectives. After examining a considerable amount of paper, we summarized and organized the important findings, which will aid future scholars in improving these findings and providing insight for future research.

## REFERENCES

Ahmad, S. N., & Laroche, M. (2016). How do expressed emotions affect the helpfulness of a product review? Evidence from reviews using latent semantic analysis. *International Journal of Electronic Commerce*, 20(1), 76–111. doi:10.1080/10864415.2016.1061471

Cao, Q., Duan, W., & Gan, Q. (2011). Exploring determinants of voting for the "helpfulness" of online user reviews: A text mining approach. *Decision Support Systems*, 50(2), 511–521. doi:10.1016/j.dss.2010.11.009

Hong, H., Xu, D., Wang, G. A., & Fan, W. (2017). Understanding the determinants of online review helpfulness: A meta-analytic investigation. *Decision Support Systems, 102*, 1–11. doi:10.1016/j.dss.2017.06.007

Hu, M., & Liu, B. (2004). Mining and summarizing customer reviews. *KDD-2004 - Proceedings of the Tenth ACM SIGKDD International Conference on Knowledge Discovery and Data Mining*, 168–177.

Hu, N., Bose, I., Koh, N. S., & Liu, L. (2012). Manipulation of online reviews: An analysis of ratings, readability, and sentiments. *Decision Support Systems, 52*(3), 674–684. doi:10.1016/j.dss.2011.11.002

Ismagilova, E., Dwivedi, Y. K., & Slade, E. (2020). Perceived helpfulness of eWOM: Emotions, fairness and rationality. *Journal of Retailing and Consumer Services, 53*, 101748. doi:10.1016/j.jretconser.2019.02.002

Jeong, H. J., & Koo, D. M. (2015). Combined effects of valence and attributes of e-WOM on consumer judgement for message and product The moderating effect of brand community type. *Internet Research, 25*(1), 2–29. doi:10.1108/IntR-09-2013-0199

Kang, Y., & Zhou, L. (2017). RubE: Rule-based methods for extracting product features from online consumer reviews. *Information & Management, 54*(2), 166–176. doi:10.1016/j.im.2016.05.007

Kim, J., & Gupta, P. (2012). Emotional expressions in online user reviews: How they influence consumers' product evaluations. *Journal of Business Research, 65*(7), 985–992. doi:10.1016/j.jbusres.2011.04.013

Krishnamoorthy, S. (2015). Linguistic features for review helpfulness prediction. *Expert Systems with Applications, 42*(7), 3751–3759. doi:10.1016/j.eswa.2014.12.044

Lee, J., & Lee, J. N. (2009). Understanding the product information inference process in electronic word-of-mouth: An objectivity-subjectivity dichotomy perspective. *Information & Management, 46*(5), 302–311. doi:10.1016/j.im.2009.05.004

Lee, K. T., & Koo, D. M. (2012). Effects of attribute and valence of e-WOM on message adoption: Moderating roles of subjective knowledge and regulatory focus. *Computers in Human Behavior, 28*(5), 1974–1984. doi:10.1016/j.chb.2012.05.018

Ludwig, S., De Ruyter, K., Friedman, M., Brüggen, E. C., Wetzels, M., & Pfann, G. (2013). More than words: The influence of affective content and linguistic style matches in online reviews on conversion rates. *Journal of Marketing, 77*(1), 87–103. doi:10.1509/jm.11.0560

Poria, S., Cambria, E., Ku, L.-W., Gui, C., & Gelbukh, A. (2014). A Rule-Based Approach to Aspect Extraction from Product Reviews. *Proceedings of the Second Workshop on Natural Language Processing for Social Media (SocialNLP)*, 28–37. 10.3115/v1/W14-5905

Rana, T. A., & Cheah, Y. N. (2017). A two-fold rule-based model for aspect extraction. *Expert Systems with Applications, 89*, 273–285. doi:10.1016/j.eswa.2017.07.047

Salehan, M., & Kim, D. J. (2016). Predicting the performance of online consumer reviews: A sentiment mining approach to big data analytics. *Decision Support Systems, 81*, 30–40. doi:10.1016/j.dss.2015.10.006

Schindler, R. M., & Bickart, B. (2012). Perceived helpfulness of online consumer reviews: The role of message content and style. *Journal of Consumer Behaviour, 11*(3), 234–243. doi:10.1002/cb.1372

Sun, Q., Niu, J., Yao, Z., & Yan, H. (2019). Exploring eWOM in online customer reviews: Sentiment analysis at a fine-grained level. *Engineering Applications of Artificial Intelligence, 81*, 68–78. doi:10.1016/j.engappai.2019.02.004

Wang, Y., Wang, J., & Yao, T. (2018). What makes a helpful online review? A meta-analysis of review characteristics. *Electronic Commerce Research, 19*(2), 257–284. doi:10.100710660-018-9310-2

Willemsen, L. M., Neijens, P. C., Bronner, F., & de Ridder, J. A. (2011). "Highly Recommended!" The Content Characteristics and Perceived Usefulness of Online Consumer Reviews. *Journal of Computer-Mediated Communication, 17*(1), 19–38. doi:10.1111/j.1083-6101.2011.01551.x

Wimmer, H., & Yoon, V. Y. (2017). Counterfeit product detection: Bridging the gap between design science and behavioral science in information systems research. *Decision Support Systems, 104*, 1–12. doi:10.1016/j.dss.2017.09.005

Yi, J., & Oh, Y. K. (2022). The informational value of multi-attribute online consumer reviews: A text mining approach. *Journal of Retailing and Consumer Services, 65*, 102519. doi:10.1016/j.jretconser.2021.102519

Yin, D., Bond, S. D., & Zhang, H. (2014). Anxious or Angry? Effects of Discrete Emotions on the Perceived Helpfulness of Online Reviews. *Management Information Systems Quarterly, 38*(2), 539–560. doi:10.25300/MISQ/2014/38.2.10

## ADDITIONAL READING

Acheampong, F. A., Wenyu, C., & Nunoo-Mensah, H. (2020). Text-based emotion detection: Advances, challenges, and opportunities. *Engineering Reports, 2*(7), e12189. doi:10.1002/eng2.12189

Hong, H., Xu, D., Wang, G. A., & Fan, W. (2017). Understanding the determinants of online review helpfulness: A meta-analytic investigation. *Decision Support Systems, 102*, 1–11. doi:10.1016/j.dss.2017.06.007

Jeong, H. J., & Koo, D. M. (2015). Combined effects of valence and attributes of e-WOM on consumer judgement for message and product: The moderating effect of brand community type. *Internet Research, 25*(1), 2–29. doi:10.1108/IntR-09-2013-0199

Kang, D., & Park, Y. (2014). Review-based measurement of customer satisfaction in mobile service: Sentiment analysis and VIKOR approach. *Expert Systems with Applications, 41*(4), 1041–1050. doi:10.1016/j.eswa.2013.07.101

Lee, A. J. T., Yang, F. C., Chen, C. H., Wang, C. S., & Sun, C. Y. (2016). Mining perceptual maps from consumer reviews. *Decision Support Systems, 82*, 12–25. doi:10.1016/j.dss.2015.11.002

Lu, Y., Lu, Y., & Wang, B. (2012). Effects of dissatisfaction on customer repurchase decisions in e-commerce-an emotion-based perspective. *Journal of Electronic Commerce Research, 13*(3), 224–237.

Moore, S. G. (2020). How online word-of-mouth impacts receivers. *Counselling Psychology Review, 3*, 34–59.

## KEY TERMS AND DEFINITIONS

**Content Feature:** A aspect affecting the content of reviews, more specifically what reviewers say about items and their features.

**Explicit Aspect:** One aspect that is explicitly stated in a review's sentence.

**Implicit Aspect:** One aspect that appears in a sentence of reviews as a noun or noun phrase.

**Stylish Feature:** A key feature representing reviewers' wording choices that cannot be easily discerned by skimming a review, such as the number of words, sentences, average characters per word, average word per sentence, number of words in pros and cons, and so on.

# Section 16
# Data Processing, Data Pipeline, and Data Engineering

# Beyond Technology:
## An Integrative Process Model for Data Analytics

**Chaojie Wang**

https://orcid.org/0000-0001-8521-9420

*The MITRE Corporation, USA*

## INTRODUCTION

Over the years, many different terms have been used to describe the process and activities that extract information and discover knowledge from data to enable evidence-based decision making and problem solving. For example, data mining, knowledge discovery in databases, business intelligence, business analytics, data analytics, big data analytics, and data science are among the most popular ones. For simplicity and consistency, in this chapter we use data analytics as a generic umbrella term to cover a myriad of activities that use statistical models, machine learning algorithms, and software platforms and tools to uncover patterns, discover knowledge, and inform decision making through systematic acquisition, preparation, analysis, and presentation of data and information.

It is well understood that software engineering efforts require the adoption of a development process model, such as the Waterfall, the Agile, or a hybrid of both. Since the core of data analytics is software, it can greatly benefit from the adoption of a process model to improve its efficiency and effectiveness and achieve meaningful and impactful outcomes. A process model serves as a shared mental model for a team and improves the communication and collaboration and increases the chances for success. However, according to surveys conducted by KDNuggets.com about 40% of data scientists and business analysts don't use any process model even though many are available (Piatetsky-Shapiro, 2014). This low adoption rate can be attributed to two main limitations in the existing models. Firstly, they were derived mainly from practical experiences and lack strong theoretical basis. Secondly, they were developed by and for technical professionals and do not incorporate sufficient consideration for human factors and organizational contexts.

This chapter introduces an integrative data analytics process model grounded on human-centered design principles and industry best practices, the A2E Process Model for Data Analytics. It was created and evaluated using design science methodology as part of a doctoral dissertation project (Wang, 2019). The author reviewed the three leading process models for data analytics along with various efforts by prior researchers and practitioners to improve and extend them (Wang, 2019, p. 25 - 37). "One common issue with the existing process models is the lack of consideration for human-factors and user experience. These models target technical professionals and generally don't pay attention to simplicity and style which are the key elements of human-centered design" (Wang, 2019, p. 52). Recognizing this gap, the author applied the human-centered design principles in the development of the A2E Model, A2E is an acronym for A, B, C, D, and E, representing five steps in data analytics process: Assess Needs, Blend Data, Create Analytics, Discover Insights, and Explore Ideas. This model was evaluated through a real-world case study in a healthcare quality improvement data analytics effort to demonstrate its utility and efficacy (Wang, 2019, p. 83 – 131). In addition, the model was reviewed by subject matter experts for

DOI: 10.4018/978-1-7998-9220-5.ch067

relevancy and quality (Wang, 2019, p.136 – 140). Both the case study and the expert review confirmed that the model is effective in helping data scientists and domain experts communicate and collaborate to achieve higher quality and deliver greater impacts for their data analytics efforts.

This chapter provides detailed description of the A2E Model including its theoretical foundation and step-by-step descriptions and guidelines. The goal of this chapter is to provide a concise, easy to follow guidance for data scientists and domain experts to apply this novel process model in their day-to-day analytics effort.

## BACKGROUND

Data analytics is a key to unlock the untapped power of knowledge hidden in the trenches of big data in the age of information and intelligence. However, not all analytics efforts can achieve the desired outcomes and impacts. A successfully executed data analytics project relies on the application of an effective process model that facilitates multidisciplinary collaborations and balance technical efficiency with organizational effectiveness. Despite the abundance of existing analytics process models, many analytics professionals and project teams choose to use their own, or not to use any at all (Piatetsky-Shapiro, 2014). This low adoption rate of process models and the lack of a universal model inhibit the maturity and growth of the analytics profession in satisfying the increasing demand for data analytics.

The abundance and rapid growth of digital data and the increasing demand for analytics bring forth opportunities as well as challenges. To ensure consistency, repeatability, quality, and maturity of data analytics, to reduce the risk of project failure, and to improve the outcomes and impacts, the data analytics community has used a variety of process models and best practices over the years. Leading among them are the Cross Industry Standard Process for Data Mining (CRISP-DM), the Knowledge Discovery in Databases (KDD), and the Sample-Explore-Modify-Model-Assess (SEMMA). **Table 1** summarizes these three leading data analytics process models.

*Table 1. The three leading data analytics process models*

| Name | Year Created | Creator |
|---|---|---|
| Cross-Industry Standard Process for Data Mining (CRISP-DM) | 1999 | The consortium of SPSS (now part of IBM), Teradata, Daimler AG, NCR, and OHRA funded by European Commission (Wirth & Hipp, 2000). IBM's data mining software SPSS Modeler provides built-in support for the model (IBM, 2017). |
| Sample-Explore-Modify-Model-Assess (SEMMA) | 1997 | SAS Institute. SAS's data mining software SAS Enterprise Miner provides built-in support for this model (SAS Institute Inc., 2017). |
| Knowledge Discovery in Databases (KDD) | 1996 | Developed by academia (Fayyad, Piatetsky-Shapiro, & Smyth, 1996). |

According to surveys conducted in 2007 and 2014 by KDNuggets.com, a leading online community for data analytics professionals, about 60% of professionals surveyed used one of the above three methodologies and the remaining 40% used either a proprietary process model or did not use any model at all. There had been little change in the adoption rate over the seven-year span between 2007 and 2014 (Piatetsky-Shapiro, 2014).

Existing process models, including the three leading ones, are technology-driven and have been developed for technical professionals, with more emphasis on models, algorithms, tools, and techniques than on people and organizational aspects. In addition, there is a lack of consideration for human factors and user experience. Existing models target technical professionals and tend to lack simplicity and style, which are the key elements of human-centered design.

These limitations lead to the low and stagnant rate of adoption and prompt a call for an improved model to fill in the gap. The A2E Model is the answer to that call. It is designed to unify the existing process models by leveraging their strengths while addressing their limitations. Professionals will find this model easy to understand, remember, and use.

The A2E Model has the potential to close the gap and hence increase the maturity level of the professional data analytics community. It strives to strike a balance between business and technology perspectives and serve as a bridge between business and technical professionals, between humans and machines, and between human intelligence and artificial intelligence. It is for anyone interested in data analytics, whether as a practitioner or as a stakeholder. Data analytics is an interdisciplinary field that requires the collaboration of people from both business and technology. Whether one is an executive or a manager, a business analyst or a data analyst, a software engineer or a data scientist, this model can help you gain a deep and thorough understanding of the many perspectives of the data analytics process and help guide you through the challenging but rewarding process of gaining insights from data for better decision making and problem solving.

## THEORETICAL FOUNDATION

The A2E Model is designed based on four theories: Wisdom Pyramid, Semiotic Ladder, and Communication Theory.

### Wisdom Pyramid

The wisdom pyramid is a commonly used construct representing the ascending nature of human understanding – data, information, knowledge, and wisdom. It has many synonyms, such as DIKW hierarchy, information hierarchy, and knowledge hierarchy. Rowley (2007) provided an extensive literature review of the structure and meaning of this construct. Wang (2018) compared three different perspectives to shed light on the relevance of DIKW model in data analytics as summarized in **Table 2**.

*Table 2. The three perspectives of data, information, knowledge, and wisdom (Wang, 2018)*

| Wisdom Pyramid | Ackoff (1989) - Information process perspective | Davenport and Prusak (1998) – Knowledge management perspective | Zeleny (2006) |
|---|---|---|---|
| Data | Symbols | A set of discrete, objective facts about events | Know nothing |
| Information | Data that are processed to be useful; provides answers to who, what, where and when questions. | Data that makes a difference | Know what |
| Knowledge | Application of data and information | Derives from minds at work | Know how |
| Wisdom | Evaluated understanding | Higher-order concept lumped into knowledge for practical purpose | Know why |

## Semiotic Ladder

Semiotics is the study of signs, symbols, and their meanings. In his seminal work, Stamper (1993) created the semiotic ladder as part of the research on management and information systems in the purview of organizational semiotics. The semiotic ladder is like the wisdom pyramid but provides more granular and ascending six steps: physical world, Empirics, Syntactics, Semantics, Pragmatics, and the social world. The physical world includes sensors, devices, and systems that generate data for the analytics to consume. The social world is where people and organizations apply intuition, judgement, value, and beliefs to the information and knowledge discovered from the data to make sound decisions and solve real-world problems.

## Communication Theory

Communication is at the heart of our personal life and social discourse. It is both a technical and a social matter. At the technical level, it concerns the efficiency and accuracy of data transmission. At the social level, it concerns the effectiveness of messages and understanding of meanings. There are many models of communication, the most notable one being the Shannon-Weaver Model, which lays the foundation for modern information theory and information science. Scholars extend the Shannon-Weaver Model when applying it to various domains. Notably among them is the Schramm Model, which has been widely used in social and political science.

Shannon and Weaver (1949) introduced a model representing the technical aspect of data transmission. This model has seven components: the sender, the encoder, the channel, the decoder, the Receiver, the noise, and the feedback. The Shannon-Weaver Model aims to minimize the impact of the noise along the communication channel and maximizes the efficiency of the data exchange through encoding and decoding.

Schramm (1954) introduced the concept of *"field of experience"* to highlight the differences and complexity in human experiences and the need to achieve mutual understanding through constant and continuous feedback loops. Field of experience includes a person's cultural background, knowledge, and experiences, which can influence their understanding and interpretation of the messages received and further influence their reactions and responses. Due to the influence of the field of experience on communication, it is vital for constant and continuous feedback among all parties involved since each of them possesses unique field of experience.

## Put it Together

**Figure 1** illustrates the relationship between the four theories and the synergy among them. At the center is the wisdom pyramid, which provides the theoretical constructs for the A2E Model. To the left is the Semiotic Ladder representing the increasing level of human understanding from the lowest level, our senses of the physical world, to the highest, our deep understanding of the social world. To the right are the two models of communication stacked one on top of the other. At the bottom is the Shannon-Weaver Model, which deals with data and information in the technical realm; on the top is the Schramm Model, which deals with knowledge and wisdom in the social realm.

The complexity increases as we move from physical realm to social realm. At the same time, the need increases to achieve deeper understanding of technology and its role in human activities. The data analytics process is like claiming the pyramid starting from the base with data and reaching the top with wisdom.

*Figure 1. The fusion of four theories*

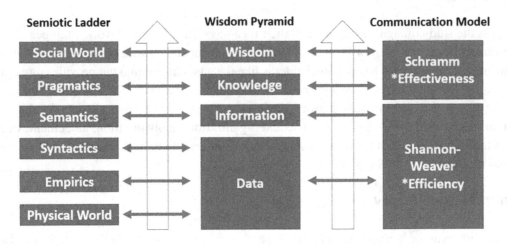

**Table 3** summarizes the four foundational theories, key takeaways, and their relevancy to data analytics. Data analytics activities should not be treated as purely technical tasks performed by only technical professionals using tools and techniques. Data analytics processes must incorporate technology into the overall human experiences, organizational culture, business processes, and social value chain.

*Table 3. Summary of foundational theories for an analytics process*

| Theory | Brief Description | Key Takeaway | Relevance to Data Analytics |
|---|---|---|---|
| Wisdom Pyramid | Data, Information, Knowledge, and Wisdom (DIKW) represents the increasing level of human observation and understanding of the reality. | Moving from senses to higher consciousness. | Data analytics process is to gain broader and deeper understanding of a phenomenon by extracting information from data, gaining insights from information, and applying the discovered knowledge to inform decision-making. |
| Semiotic Ladder | The ladder has six steps. Between physical world at the bottom and social world at the top there exist four escalating steps: empirics, syntactics, semantics, pragmatics like the Wisdom Pyramid. | Seeking meaning from signs and symbols. | Data analytics process starts with observation and data collection at the physical level through sensors and devices and reach the final goal of problem solving through evidence-based decision making and human collaborations. |
| Shannon-Weaver Model of Communication | There are seven components of communication: the sender, the encoder, the channel, the decoder, the receiver, the noise, and the feedback. Efficiency of communication is affected by noise. Accuracy of communication is improved via feedback. | Minimizing noise to achieve communication efficiency. | Shannon-Weaver Model lays the foundation for computer science and information technology which provide the techniques and tools for data analytics. |
| Schramm Model of Communication | Interpretations of messages are influenced by people's field of experience. The message sender and the receiver may have different context to interpret the same message. | Breaking barriers to achieve common understanding and communication effectiveness. | Schramm Model covers human communication and provides the theoretical basis for the social aspect of data analytics. |

## THE A2E PROCESS MODEL

In his popular book, *The Design of Everyday Things,* author Don Norman, an industrial psychologist and leading design expert, wrote eloquently, "Human-centered design (HCD), is an approach that puts human needs, capacities, and behavior first, then designs to accommodate those needs, capacities, and way of behaving" (Norman, 2013, p. 8). HCD enhances "effectiveness and efficiency, improves human well-being, user satisfaction, accessibility and sustainability; and counteracts possible adverse effects of use on human health, safety and performance" (International Organization for Standardization, 2010). One key to putting people first is to keep the design simple and minimal to avoid unnecessary complexity and information overload. According to the psychologist George Miller (1956), the human brain can only effectively deal with seven, plus or minus two, chunks in the working memory. Humans have trouble processing information beyond the maximum of nine chunks. The smaller the number of chunks, the easier it is to process information. Good design strives to reduce the memory load and avoid information overload for people. An effective process model must be value-driven as opposed to technology-driven, and human-centric as opposed to machine-centric.

The A2E Model has only five steps, which is at the lower limit of the seven plus or minus nine rule and uses mnemonics to help people easily remember the steps. The A2E model is simple, minimal, and flexible. It can be used by one person on a very small project, or many people on a large project. It provides the basis for establishing a shared mental model for the team and helps facilitate effective communication, coordination, and collaboration.

The following five steps represent the major stages or phases in a data analytics process: **A** for Assess Needs, **B** for Blend Data, **C** for Create Analytics, **D** for Discover Insights, **E** for Explore Ideas. The A, B, C, D, E mnemonics are easy to remember. The name of each step is phrased using the simple but impactful construct of Verb + Object.

**Table 4** provides a brief description and typical activities for each step. The activities are not exhaustive but serve as examples. Each data analytics project is unique. This mode provides conceptual framework and guidelines but leave the implementation specifics to individual projects.

This process model can be illustrated with two figures. **Figure 2** represents the essence of the A2E Model. This diagram follows two lines of reasoning. On the vertical line, the y-axis represents the wisdom hierarchy. Moving from data to information, from information to knowledge, and from knowledge to wisdom, represents the increasing level of understanding of the problem or situation at hand. On the horizontal line, the x-axis represents the nature of the activities as we move from transactional to analytical, from analytical to intellectual, and from intellectual to transformational. The first step, "Assess Needs", is outside of the normal range since it is at the front and center of the process and must incorporate all aspects, from data to wisdom and from transactional to transformative.

Even though the process appears to be sequential and "waterfall" like, data analytics effort is an iterative and incremental process which requires constant validation at every step and continuous feedback between all steps. The needs and requirements may not be crystal clear at the outset and will become more granular and apparent along the various steps. They tend to change as more information and knowledge are discovered. In practice, we must instill agility into the analytics process and emphasize continuous improvement that is necessary for a successful data analytics project. To that end, **Figure 3** provides a more agile and sophisticated view of the process.

*Table 4. The five steps of the A2E model*

| Step | Description | Activities |
|------|-------------|------------|
| **Assess Needs** | Perform systemic assessment of organizational needs and business requirements. Start with the end in mind. This is also equivalent to project planning. | Assess business needs<br>Assess data needs<br>Assess technology and tools needs<br>Assess financial resource needs<br>Assess knowledge and skill needs |
| **Blend Data** | Data from various sources are acquired, cleansed, filtered, and merged to form coherent datasets. Data quality is inspected and ensured. Data privacy is evaluated and ethical concerns, if any, are addressed. Data schema, semantic definitions are documented in the data dictionary. Descriptive data analysis is performed to help gain preliminary understanding of the data. | Obtain data from internal & external sources<br>Validate data quality & privacy compliance<br>Cleanse & consolidate data from sources |
| **Create Analytics** | Use data visualization tools, statistical models, and machine learning algorithms to create analytics to support knowledge discovery. This is the most technical aspect of data analytics. | Perform feature engineering<br>Evaluate & select algorithms & models<br>Create exploratory data analysis<br>Perform descriptive, predictive, and prescriptive analytics using ML models<br>Create reports, visualizations, & dashboard |
| **Discover Insights** | Discover insights and create knowledge that can be used to inform decision making. Business expertise and existing body of knowledge are utilized to interpret and validate the analytics. | Discover Patterns<br>Discover Trends<br>Apply Intuition<br>Apply existing knowledge & experience |
| **Explore Ideas** | Engage with all stakeholders and subject matter experts to share the insights and knowledge, leverage their experience and expertise, accommodate their needs and interests, collaborate on ideas and recommendations, explore potential interventions, and execute on the plan to solve the business problem or improve social conditions. | Consider organizational contexts<br>Consider values & beliefs<br>Consider costs & benefits<br>Consider unintended consequences<br>Cross-check with business needs |

*Figure 2. The two dimensions of the A2E Model*

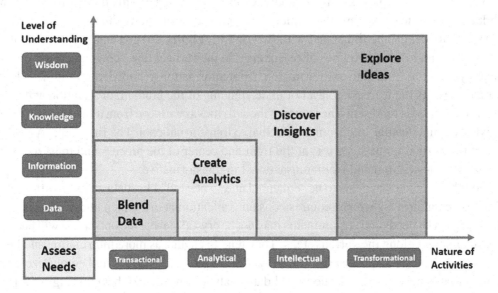

*Figure 3. The three loops of the A2E Model*

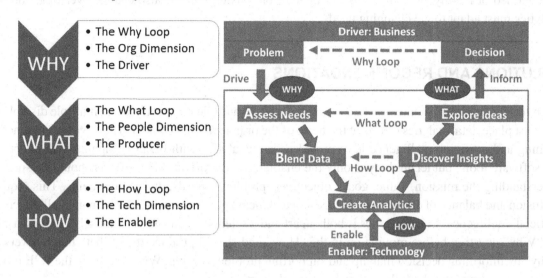

In his 2011 book, *Start with Why: How Great Leaders Inspire Everyone to Take Action,* author Simon Sinek created the Golden Circle of Why, How, and What (Sinek, 2011). The Golden Circle provides a simple yet powerful compass to guide any human endeavor, including data analytics effort. **Figure 3** contains three loops that map to the golden circle. The three loops represent three level of data analytics maturity. The How loop represents the low level of maturity, the What loop represents the medium level of maturity, and the Why loop represents the high level of maturity.

The How loop is at the bottom. It travels from step B (Blend data) to step C (Create analytics) to step D (Discover insights) and back to step B for feedback and validation. This loop focuses more on the application of technology, including data visualization, feature engineering, algorithm selection and validation, hyperparameter tuning, and deployment. The How loop represents a low maturity level of data analytics when much effort is focused on the technical aspect and less on the understanding of the problem situation and idea generation to inform and support decision making.

The What loop travels from A->B->C->D->E and back to A for feedback and validation. This is the typical scope of data analytics. It starts out by assessing the business needs and ends with the ideas that are evaluated and validated against the needs. Organizations performing at this loop have a medium maturity level and should strive to move up to the highest level by performing at the Why loop.

The Why loop starts from the problem that drives the whole data analytics process which produces the knowledge, insights, and ideas to inform decision making. The decision leads to actions that aim to solve problems. This loop aligns data analytics with organizational decision making and problem solving. Organizations that regularly perform at this loop have a high maturity level of data analytics.

While each of the five steps is equally important, the first step, "Assess Needs", has a special place in the process. We all know that technology is only a means to an end; it is not an end by and of itself. Technology must serve human needs. The mission of data analytics is to support evidence-based decision making to solve social problems and improve human conditions. We must place the first step, "Assess Needs", at the center. At every step along the way, activities must be constantly and continuously validated against the needs. This is particularly critical when dealing with complex and ill-defined problems. The business needs may not be clear upfront, and the data needed to support the business needs may not be well-defined or readily available early on. In addition, business needs also change over time and data analytics must adapt to the changing needs.

## SOLUTIONS AND RECOMMENDATIONS

Analytics process encapsulates the fusion and synergy of multiple perspectives and multiple disciplines. We must place data analytics efforts at the heart of the organizational context. The advances in machine learning and artificial intelligence have provided data analytics with better computational algorithms and software tools, but technology is only the enabler, not the driver. More efforts should be spent on understanding the mission, value, goals, objectives, problems, needs, and requirements. This requires the fusion and balance of domain knowledge and technical knowledge as well as human intelligence and artificial intelligence. Data analytics is both an art and a science. Data analytics must begin with asking the "Why" question before moving on to the "How" and should produce the "What" that answers the "Why" by informing decision making and supporting problem solving. When applying the A2E model, we need to be aware of the following two essential points.

### Keep the Balance of Technology and Humanity

Data analytics is a collaborative effort involving multiple disciplines from science, technology, engineering, and math (STEM) to management, sociology, psychology, and art. It encompasses multiple perspectives, including technical, people and organizational perspectives. There are two types of intelligence involved in data analytics efforts. One is human intelligence; the other is artificial intelligence (AI). The AI is defined loosely here to represent the capability a computer system and its many hardware components and software applications provides. The former is the driver and the latter the enabler as depicted in **Figure 3**.

In many ways, human intelligence and artificial intelligence are complementary. On one hand, AI powered by computer processors, storages, and algorithms has the capability to process large volumes of data much faster than human beings. On the other hand, in more complex situations where social and cultural context and value judgement are required to make decisions, AI in its current stage will not be able to replace human beings. The human-machine symbiosis is about taking advantage of the best of both worlds.

The human-machine symbiosis is not the only type of symbiosis. There is also a need for machine-machine symbiosis, where multiple algorithms and multiple tools are utilized to corroborate, cooperate, and complement each other to minimize machine biases and maximize accuracy. Collaboration between diverse individuals and groups will help reduce cognitive biases and bring out innovative ideas. We shall call this human-human symbiosis or simply teamwork.

To extend this concept, we also recognize the symbiosis of the business professionals and technology professionals as well as the symbiosis of the domain knowledge and technical knowledge. Striking the right balance between human intelligence and artificial intelligence and between business and technology is a critical success factor for data analytics and is the subtle message the A2E Model tries to deliver.

## Be Mindful of Bias and Ethics

B

Biases exist in data, algorithms, and human minds. Data analytics is inherently biased since it relies on data as inputs, algorithms as the enabler, and humans as the driver. Great care should be given to the accuracy, applicability, limitations, and consequences (intended or unintended; desired or undesired) of data analytics.

Reality is complex and unknowable, as famously stated by Laozi in the 2500-year-old Taoist text *Tao Te Ching*, "The Tao that can be told is not the eternal Tao. The name that can be named is not the eternal Name. The unnamable is the eternally real." (Laozi, 1989). Echoing Laozi, statistician George Box (1976) was famously quoted "all models are wrong" because models are only approximations of the true reality. Statistical and computational models that underlie data analytics are no exceptions. They come naturally with their designers' cognitive biases (intentional or unintentional).

It is also worth pointing out that data, whether collected through human observations or sensory devices, are also approximate measures of the actual properties of the observed entities. Even correct or accurate data collected cannot escape from the bias of those who define the measurement, who measure and collect data or design the data collection instruments. In addition, incomplete, inaccurate, and missing data are typical in data analytics and can distort the outcome of the analytics - "garbage in, garbage out".

King, Keohane, and Verba (1994) defined scientific research as "an ideal to which any actual quantitative or qualitative research, even the most careful, is only an approximation". The authors further presented four characteristics of scientific research, one of which is "The conclusions are uncertain". They stated that:

*By definition, inference is an imperfect process. Its goal is to use quantitative or qualitative data to learn about the world that produced them. Reaching perfectly certain conclusions from uncertain data is obviously impossible. Indeed, uncertainty is a central aspect of all research and all knowledge about the world. Without a reasonable estimate of uncertainty, a description of the real world or an inference about a causal effect in the real world is uninterpretable. (King et al., 1994)*

We should also recognize that both men and machines have limitations. Even though the partnership between the two helps overcome the limitations to some extent, it will not eliminate them. This leads to the realization that data analytics empowered by human intelligence and enabled by artificial intelligence are not panacea to all problems. Not all complex problems have clear-cut solutions. One quality that is important for all professionals, whether business or technical, is humility. To be humble is to know:

- the complexity, uncertainty, and unknowability of reality
- the limitation of the human mind and machine power
- what to believe and what to doubt
- when to act and when not to act
- the why before performing the how and producing the what
- to anticipate the unintended consequences of actions
- to understand the unforeseen benefits of inactions
- to recognize an individual's limitation and the need for collaboration and teamwork the limitation of technology and the wisdom of humanity

## FUTURE RESEARCH DIRECTIONS

Design an artifact is only half the story in design science. Evaluation of an artifact for its utility and efficacy is the other half and is equally important. The A2E Model has been evaluated using the method of Illustrative Scenario (Wang, 2019, pp. 83 – 131) and Expert Review (Wang, 2019, pp. 136 – 140). The Illustrative Scenario used a real-world healthcare analytics project to illustrate how the five steps of the A2E Model were followed and the activities and outcomes of each step. The scenario demonstrated the importance of human collaboration and human-machine symbiosis. In the Expert Review, the A2E Model received positive feedback of experts from both industry and academia, and their comments and recommendations have been incorporated in the improvement of the model. However, these two evaluations are considered small sample validations and should not be taken as large-scale validations. Additional evaluations covering different application settings and project scales should be performed. In addition, additional evaluation methods such as Case Study and Action Research should be used as outlined by Peffers et al (2012). Readers are encouraged to apply the A2E Model in their data analytics effort and provide evaluations with critics and recommendations for future improvement.

## CONCLUSION

A process model helps guide the planning and execution of any human endeavor. Much like a software development process model guiding the effort of developing a software system to meet its quality standards, schedule, and budgetary constraints, a data analytics process model aims to guide the effort of data analytics to ensure that it delivers quality outcomes and achieves valuable impacts within schedule and budget.

Design Science calls for both relevance and rigor. To address the aspect of relevance, the A2E model was motivated by the problem of low adoption rate of existing data analytics process models due to their limitations and the poor outcome and low impact achieved from data analytics efforts in the industry. As the volume, velocity, and variety of data increase exponentially due to the proliferation of emerging technologies including Internet of Things, mobile and cloud computing, and social media networks, the demand for extracting actionable insights from data to inform decision making is increasing exponentially as well. A better process model is much needed to help improve the efficiency and effectiveness of data analytics effort. To address the aspect of rigor, the researcher surveyed the landscape of existing data analytics process models from both industry and academia with focus on the three leading ones and their extensions. In addition, A2E Model was designed based on strong theoretical foundation including the wisdom pyramid, the semiotic ladder, the information and communication theory, the systems engineering model, and the human-centered design principles.

The contributions of this A2E Model are three-fold. First, it provides a theoretical framework to the understanding and knowledge of the data analytics process. In contrast to the existing process models which are technology-oriented and lack the emphasis on organizational context and human factors, it integrates organization, people, and technology in a holistic and balanced view. Secondly, it provides a shared mental model to guide both technical and business professionals and their diverse stakeholders in the data analytics effort. Thirdly, it provides a pedagogical framework to guide the curriculum design of balanced multidisciplinary data analytics programs.

To summarize, the A2E Model provides methodological and practical guidance to data analytics efforts with the following distinctive features:

**B**

- It is designed with strong theoretical foundation, including the wisdom pyramid, organizational semiotics and communication theories.

- It is value-driven as opposed to technology-driven. This model starts with business needs arising from social and organizational needs and ends with ideas and recommendations which inform decision and problem solving. As machine learning and data science become more mature and automated, technology becomes less of a barrier and organizational drivers become more critical for the success of data analytics.

- It integrates perspectives from technological, people, and organizational standpoints; It integrates and aligns business and technology; It integrates and aligns human intelligence and artificial intelligence; It integrates multiple disciplines including knowledge management, organizational learning, human-centered design, and human-computer symbiosis.

- It follows the agile principles. Data analytics is an exploratory and learning process. It takes multiple iterations over time to gain insights from data. It also takes multiple feedback loops in the applications of insights to decision making and problem solving.

- It is designed with simplicity and elegance in mind for usability and user experience. The model uses the A, B, C, D, E mnemonics to help people easily remember the five essential steps. The model does not inundate the practitioners with complicated steps, tasks, and activities that are incoherent and hard to follow in practice.

- It is universal and is technology and industry agnostic. It can be used by one person on a small effort, or by many people on a large project. It is especially powerful and beneficial when a team of multidisciplinary professionals collaborate in a large data analytics project. For example, in a healthcare data analytics project, the team may include data engineers, data scientists, business analysts, physicians, nurses, and healthcare quality and policy experts. This model provides the basis for establishing a shared mental model for a team and helps facilitate effective communication, coordination, cooperation, and collaboration.

# REFERENCES

Ackoff, R. L. (1989). From data to wisdom. *Journal of Applied Systems Analysis, 16*(1), 3–9.

Box, G. E. (1976). Science and statistics. *Journal of the American Statistical Association, 71*(356), 791–799. doi:10.1080/01621459.1976.10480949

Davenport, T. H., & Prusak, L. (1998). *Working knowledge: How organizations manage what they know.* Harvard Business Press.

Fayyad, U., Piatetsky-Shapiro, G., & Smyth, P. (1996). The KDD process for extracting useful knowledge from volumes of data. *Communications of the ACM, 39*(11), 27–34. doi:10.1145/240455.240464

IBM. (2017). *IBM SPSS Modeler CRISP-DM Guide.* Retrieved from ftp://public.dhe.ibm.com/software/analytics/spss/documentation/modeler/18.1/en/ModelerCRISPDM.pdf

International Organization for Standardization. (2010). *Ergonomics of human system interaction Part 210: Human-centered design for interactive systems.* Author.

King, G., Keohane, R. O., & Verba, S. (1994). *Designing social inquiry: Scientific inference in qualitative research*. Princeton university press. doi:10.1515/9781400821211

Laozi. (1989). *Tao Te Ching* (S. Mitchell, Trans.). Harper Perennial.

Miller, G. A. (1956). The magical number seven, plus or minus two: Some limits on our capacity for processing information. *Psychological Review*, *63*(2), 81–97. doi:10.1037/h0043158 PMID:13310704

Norman, D. A. (2013). *The design of everyday things: Revised and expanded edition*. Basic Books.

Peffers, K., Rothenberger, M., Tuunanen, T., & Vaezi, R. (2012). Design science research evaluation. *The Seventh International Conference on Design Science Research in Information Systems and Technology*.

Piatetsky-Shapiro, G. (2014). *CRISP-DM, still the top methodology for analytics, data mining, or data science projects*. Retrieved from https://www.kdnuggets.com/2014/10/crisp-dm-top-methodology-analytics-data-mining-data-science-projects.html

Rowley, J. (2007). The wisdom hierarchy: Representations of the DIKW hierarchy. *Journal of Information Science*, *33*(2), 163–180. doi:10.1177/0165551506070706

SAS Institute Inc. (2017). *Getting started with SAS®Enterprise Miner™ 14.3*. Retrieved from http://documentation.sas.com/api/docsets/emgsj/14.3/content/emgsj.pdf?locale=en#nameddest=n0gurzayfolktun1e8vl6n7qsi88

Schramm, W. (1954). How communication works. *The process and effects of mass communication*, 3-26.

Shannon, C., & Weaver, W. (1949). *The mathematical theory of communication*. University of Illinois Press.

Sinek, S. (2011). *Start with why: How great leaders inspire everyone to take action*. Penguin Group.

Stamper, R. (1993). *A semiotic theory of information and information systems*. Academic Press.

Wang, C. (2018). Integrating data analytics and knowledge management: A conceptual model. *Issues in Information Systems*, *19*(2).

Wang, C. (2019). *Beyond technology: Design a value-driven integrative process model for data analytics* (Order No. 27665947). Available from Dissertations & Theses @ Robert Morris University; ProQuest Dissertations & Theses Global. (2551201774). Retrieved from https://reddog.rmu.edu/login?url=https://www-proquest-com.reddog.rmu.edu/dissertations-theses/beyond-technology-design-value-driven-integrative/docview/2551201774/se-2?accountid=28365

Wirth, R., & Hipp, J. (2000). CRISP-DM: Towards a standard process model for data mining. *The 4th International Conference on the Practical Applications of Knowledge Discovery and Data Mining*.

Zeleny, M. (2006). From knowledge to wisdom: On being informed and knowledgeable, becoming wise and ethical. *International Journal of Information Technology & Decision Making*, *5*(04), 751–762. doi:10.1142/S0219622006002222

## ADDITIONAL READING

Graaf, R. (2019). *Managing your data science projects: Learn salesmanship, presentation, and maintenance of completed models.* Apress. doi:10.1007/978-1-4842-4907-9

Martins, S., Pesado, P. M., & García-Martínez, R. (2016). Information mining projects management process. *28th International Conference on Software Engineering and Knowledge Engineering, SEKE 2016.* 10.18293/SEKE2016-009

Nonaka, I., & Takeuchi, H. (1995). *The knowledge-creating company: How Japanese companies create the dynamics of innovation.* Oxford University Press.

O'Neil, C. (2016). *Weapons of math destruction: how big data increases inequality and threatens democracy.* Brown Publishers.

Provost, F., & Fawcett, T. (2013). *Data science for business: What you need to know about data mining and data-analytic thinking.* O'Reilly Media, Inc.

Shafique, U., & Qaiser, H. (2014). A comparative study of data mining process models (KDD, CRISP-DM and SEMMA). *International Journal of Innovation and Scientific Research, 12*(1), 217–222.

Sharda, R., Delen, D., & Turban, E. (2016). *Business intelligence, analytics, and data science: A managerial perspective.* Pearson.

Thomasonm, J. (2020). *Building analytics teams: Harnessing analytics and artificial intelligence for business improvement.* Packt Publishing.

## KEY TERMS AND DEFINITIONS

**Business Intelligence (BI):** A conceptual framework or a software application for managerial decision support. It combines technical architecture, databases, data warehouses data marts, analytical tools, data visualizations.

**Cross-Industry Standard Process for Data Mining (CRISP-DM):** A data analytics process model developed by a consortium of software vendors and users including IBM and Daimler Chrysler and funded by European Commission. It consists of a sequence of six steps that starts with a good understanding of the business and the need for the data mining project (i.e., the application domain) and ends with the deployment of the solution that satisfied the specific business need.

**Decision Support Systems (DSS):** A software system or application that supports managerial decision making, usually by modelling problems and employing quantitative models for solution analysis.

**Design Science:** A emerging research methodology focusing on the creation of artifacts (methods, techniques, and tools) and the evaluation of their performance in the physical, social, and cultural environment. Like a software application, a process model can be considered as an artifact and created and evaluated by following design science methodology.

**Knowledge Discovery in Databases (KDD):** A term coined by Piatetsky-Shapiro in 1989 and later was adopted as a data analytics process for discovering useful knowledge from a collection of data proposed by Fayyad, Piatetsky-Shapiro, and Smyth in 1996.

**Process Model:** A standardized practice pattern or framework such as steps, associated tasks and activities, principles, and guidelines for planning, organizing, and executing a human endeavor. In modern society, human endeavors typically involve the use of technologies and the collaboration of people.

**Sample-Explore-Modify-Model-Assess (SEMMA):** A data analytics process model developed by the SAS Institute and is incorporated in its SAS Enterprise Miner software product. SEMMA represents six steps in data mining.

# Bias in Data-Informed Decision Making

**B**

**Harini Dissanayake**
*DOT loves data, New Zealand*

**Paul J. Bracewell**
*DOT loves data, New Zealand*

## INTRODUCTION

With vast amounts of data becoming available in a machine-readable format, decision makers in almost every sector are focused on exploiting data and machine learning to drive the phenomena of automated decision making, whilst rapidly dissolving the human oversight in the process. The description of bias in decision making arising from machine learning outlined in this chapter sets to demonstrate the scale of the issue and the value of transparency in decision making that affects the daily life of ordinary humans.

As a practical example, in New Zealand, the extent of algorithm use has already extended to use cases such as a New Zealand Police tool that assesses family violence risk, and a Ministry of Social Development classification tool for identifying school leavers that require the greatest education and employment support. The concern raised by many of the government bodies that adopt operational algorithms is the potential bias in such modelling, with identifying and improving these potential biases a priority in the future (Statistics New Zealand, 2018). This chapter identifies such biases in both government and non-government decision making data, with a special focus in identifying discriminatory bias of operational algorithms and sample selection bias inherent in decision making data.

Behavioral research finds that human decision making is clouded by 'human errors'. In various contexts, the literature documents that human problem solving tends to systematically differ from the predictions of rational choice models. From the past 50 years of work in behavioral research and decision making, it is well established that human decision making is often not as rational as one might expect. The development of 'data science' allows decision makers to detect present day human errors impacting specific decisions in real time. One of the objectives of this chapter is to reveal the extent of human biases found in the decision-making information in present day New Zealand.

Machine learning systems are becoming increasingly prominent in automated decision making in New Zealand. Using systems that are sensitive to the type of bias that results in discrimination, must be undertaken with caution. Given the scale and impact of the bodies that have already adopted machine learning, it is crucial that measures are taken to prevent unfair discrimination through legal as well as technical means. There has been significant effort to avoid and correct discriminatory bias in algorithms while also making them more transparent. In New Zealand, the government recently claimed world first in setting standards for how public agencies should use the algorithms that increasingly drive decision making by officials about every aspect of public life. New Zealand has produced a set of standards; "Algorithm charter for Aotearoa New Zealand", designed to guide government use of algorithms and to improve data transparency and accountability. It outlines several measures including:

1. how decisions are informed by algorithms:
2. making sure data is fit for purpose by identifying and managing bias

DOI: 10.4018/978-1-7998-9220-5.ch068

3. ensuring that privacy, ethics, and human rights are safeguarded by regularly peer-reviewing algorithms
4. explaining the role of humans in decisions informed by algorithms, and
5. providing a channel for citizens to appeal against decisions informed by algorithms.

New Zealand hopes to set a standard for other nations by leading the way with responsible algorithm oversight and by demonstrating the value of transparency of algorithms that affect daily life. "Many government agencies are already harnessing the power of data to deliver improved public services for New Zealanders – coming up with innovative solutions to complex problems…but as these techniques grow in scale and sophistication, it's critical that New Zealanders can be confident their data is being handled appropriately, and that proper safeguards are being applied" Minister for Statistics James Shaw said (Shaw, 2019). Dokyun Lee (Business Professor at Tepper School of Business), advises that the art of human interpretation and reasoning cannot be replaced by artificial intelligence - machine learning works best only as a tool (Carnegie Mellon University, 2019). Lee describes "machine learning, if sufficiently transparent, is great for helping humans discern patterns and understand the nuance of complex big data…but inherently, making connections about how the world works and creating hypotheses to find answers that stand the test of time — we (humans) are the only ones who can do that, at least for now." As deep learning thrived under machine learning, many recognized the potential power of harnessing big data sets, beginning to employ these systems that appeared as a revolutionary panacea. The algorithms on which these systems are based learn by example, rather than rules or data features engineered by humans. The algorithm identifies patterns in the data and arrives at a decision using those patterns. As the machine's decision-making process occurs outside of human control, the method the machine is learning for drawing its inferences is not readily understood by algorithm users. Consequently, human oversight is critical to evaluate any machine's decision that could be wrong.

This chapter, which describes bias in decision making, is motivated by the need for approaching any analysis with caution. Fully automated solutions without appropriate governance can be problematic due to the replication of human biases which can be captured and imposed upon the training process of a machine learning models. Bias is omnipresent in machine learning. Decision makers alike must be aware of limitations within the data and proceed with caution. As such, transparency in how data is used to make decisions is vital. Despite the ever-increasing reliance on algorithms in decision making, human oversight is critical (Statistics New Zealand, 2018). This chapter serves to raise awareness of this aspect of machine learning.

## DECISION MAKING AS A QUEST FOR RATIONALITY

Behavioral research finds that human decision making is clouded by 'human errors.' In various contexts, the literature documents that human problem solving tends to systematically differ from the predictions of rational choice models. For instance, humans tend to focus on irrelevant information (Kahneman, 2013), fall victim to variables that are contextual and situational (Danziger et al., 2011) and go as far as to rationalize the bad decisions made (Harmon-Jones & Mills, 1999).

With vast amounts of data becoming available, decision makers in almost every sector are focused on exploiting data for decision making. However, the volume and variety of data generated exceeds the ability of manual analysis. Data, power of computers and algorithms have accelerated, together powering broader and deeper analyses than previously imagined (Provost & Fawcett, 2013). The convergence of these has given rise to the increasingly widespread application of data science in almost all sectors for decision making. To empower rational decision making, computing pioneer Licklider had envisioned man-computer interaction as a means of improving quality and efficiency of human problem solving (Licklider, 2001). Data science involves principles, processes, and techniques for understanding phenomena through the automated analysis of data.

Some decision science researchers have turned to fuzzy logic, neural networks, and probabilistic reasoning to challenge "the ability of the human mind to effectively employ modes of reasoning that are approximate rather than exact. . . the cognitive processes humans employ so effectively in the performance of daily tasks" (Zeleznikow & Nolan, 2001).

## Data Science for Detecting Biases in Human Decision Making

From the past 50 years of work in behavioral research and decision making, it is well established that human decision making is often not as rational as one might expect. In fact, the development of 'data science' allows decision makers to detect present day human errors impacting specific decisions in real time.

## Selective Sample Data in New Zealand

### Family Violence Data

Family violence is largely under-reported in New Zealand (and there are more deaths that are not counted in the total number of family violence deaths (Health Quality & Safety Commission New Zealand et al., 2017). The Family Violence Death Review Committee discusses that there are many reasons for the undercounting, including: neonaticide deaths that difficult to identify as homicide deaths; intimate partner violence deaths where it was not identified an intimate relationship existed between offender and victim (e.g., same-sex relationships); homicides that have been classified as suicides or accidents; missing persons; and unsolved homicides. The 2013 New Zealand Crime and Safety Survey which investigated the nature of underreporting of crime found that the incidents most likely to be unreported to Police in 2013 were those where the offender was an intimate partner; 76% under-reported (New Zealand Ministry of Justice, 2015). The officially reported incidences are consequently a selective sample drawn from the sub-population of incidences, such that the distribution of the reported incidences is different from the distribution of the non-reported incidences. In such a case, statistical inference for non-reported incidences directly from the reported sub-population is unreliable as the sample would not represent the target population.

### 2018 New Zealand Census Data

There has been widespread concern about the incompleteness of census information, information that is used to prioritize government services. Statistics New Zealand describes the hard-to-reach populations as:

- 15–29-year-olds: response down from 88.5% to 75% in 2018 census
- deprived communities who cannot access online to complete census
- disabled Communities
- elderly
- rural communities

- Māori: response down from 88.5% to 68.2%

Government funding for social and other services is targeted to the groups in most need, and planners use census information to identify these population cohorts. It is described that many of these groups in need of government services are in fact the groups hardest to reach by online methods (Dashfield, 2018a).

"We're working alongside our community outreach centers in Rotorua to target our whanau who are not digitally connected. The reality for us is that only 24% of households completed the Census in 2013 which equals how we've been funded by the Government since then" (Dashfield, 2018b).

## Access to Internet Data

A priority of the government is closing the Digital Divide, to allow all New Zealanders access to the benefits of being online. However, to assess the magnitude, location and cause of the divide accurate research data is vital for informing the Government on how to best prioritize support and measure its interventions. Dashfield describes that non-internet users have been disproportionately missed by the recent World Internet Project (WIP) NZ 2017 survey which undercounted and misreported New Zealanders offline. Dashfield explains that the non-user sample is biased towards older people and would be inaccurate to make inferences from this misrepresentative sample to the whole of New Zealand.

## Traffic Crash Data

The New Zealand's Transport Agency (NZTA) Crash Analysis System (CAS) records all traffic crashes as reported to NZTA by the New Zealand Police. However not all crashes are reported to the Police (New Zealand Transport Agency, 2020). NZTA describe how the level of reporting increases with the severity of the crash and due to the nature of non-fatal crashes it is believed that these are under-reported. Traffic crash data is used by policymakers, engineers, and road safety practitioners to design and ensure safer New Zealand communities and due to underreporting of non-fatal crashes, road safety statistics are underestimated at a community level and necessary action to improve community wellbeing is not taken.

## COVID-19 Testing and Infection Data

During the early stages of the COVID-19 pandemic in New Zealand, preferential testing was conducted by focusing on infected individuals belonging to a cluster and those individuals who have been near those individuals. Preferential testing means that the individuals in New Zealand tested during the early stages of the pandemic are systematically different from the wider population of interest which the statistics reports on. The selection bias arises because these individuals preferentially tested do not represent all of New Zealand.

## Political Opinion in Digital Media

Political articles and the response to those articles in the digital media provide a rich source of public opinion in real-time. It provides an opportunity to generate the very stance of New Zealanders towards the political parties and controversial political agendas as they unfold in media coverage. However, it is critical to ensure that any analysis properly reflects the New Zealand population as not all New Zealanders currently access digital platforms. It is vital to understand the demographic of digital platform users and consequently whose opinion is missing in the raw data.

## Reject Inference Methods for Remedying Sample Selection Bias

A particular data issue this research will consequently focus on remedying is sample selection bias through the application of reject inference methods. Reject inference methods (RIM) were developed to treat the sample selection issue in credit scoring. Credit scoring models are commonly developed using a sample that is limited to accepted known good/bad applications, as credit lenders only hold information on the performance of those applicants accepted in the past. Consequently, the credit scoring model is not indicative of the entire through-the-door population which consists of individuals who will be rejected alongside applicants accepted.

Reject inference methods are designed to address the sample selection bias by assigning an inferred good/bad status to rejected applications - imputing the missing information with inference. In the credit scoring application, the literature notes eight main reject inference methods, briefly introduced below:

### All Rejects Default (ARD)

Suited mostly in situations of high-risk lending where the default rate is high, or when number of rejected applicants is low, the all rejects default method, ARD is the crudest RIM that classifies all rejects as defaults (Siddiqi, 2006) Thomas et. al. (2002) justifies such an arbitrary approach "on the grounds that there must have been bad information about them for them to have been rejected previously".

### Augmentation (AUG)

Augmentation is a RIM which takes a LOG model on the accepted applicants weighted by the probability of rejection. Marginally accepted applicants and rejected applicants both have a high likelihood of rejection (Ash & Meester, 2002) and in the AUG method these "marginal accepts" are taken to be similar to the "marginal rejects." To specialize the model for new applicants straddling the cut off for default risk, marginally accepted applicants are upweighted when records by weighting records by probability of rejection. Finlay describes that in the marginal risk regions that influence lending decisions this LOG model performance has less sampling bias (Finlay, 2012). To produce a predicted probability of rejection for each accepted applicant, all applicants are used to directly model rejection as a response variable using LOG (p.243). Another option Finlay proposes is to cluster all applicants and within each cluster set the probability of rejection as the rejection rate (p.249). Boundary Cluster Reclassification (BCR) This method reclassifies rejected applicants in low and high clusters using unsupervised clustering. K-means is used by Chen et al. to identify and reclassify records based on default risk (Chen et al., 2012).

### Extrapolation (EXT)

Across the literature, the method of extrapolation is described differently. This may be due to whether to compensate for sampling bias the predicted probabilities are adjusted.

- Finlay describes EXT as FUZ parceling with adjusted probabilities, using only accepts applicant records (Finlay, 2012)

- Anderson describes it as any parceling technique, and discusses adjustment separately as 'Bivariate Inference' (Anderson, 2007)
- Hand & Henley describes EXT as "extrapolating a model built on the accepted applicants into the reject region" (Hand & Henley, 1993)

This earlier approach described by Hand & Henley is settling as the predicted default probability in regions of high-rejection would be underestimated in an unadjusted accepted applicant model. For rejects, the probability of default must be adjusted to offset sampling bias to extend accepted applicant trends into the high rejection region. Uniform shift adjusts the probability of default for rejects by a set amount. Adding 0.1 to the predicted probability of default of all rejects is recommended by Finlay.

To deal with statistical problems involving unobservable variables, 'Tobit' regression models were introduced (Tobin, 1958). Reject inference research in the earliest days focused on joint distribution models, including:

- 'bivariate probit with sample selection' (Meng & Schmidt, 1985)
- 'bivariate censored probit' (Boyes et al., 1989)
- and Heckman's Two-Step Method (Heckman, 1976; Heckman, 1979)

Analogous to LOG model on accepted applicant records only, the performance of bivariate probit models is described as only having minor accuracy improvements (Kim & Sohn, 2007) or no change in accuracy (Banasik & Crook, 2007). Even under optimal assumptions, Wu and Hand conclude that the Heckman Two-step model does not produce significant accuracy improvement (Wu & Hand, 2007). Consequently, more and more cited textbooks focus on direct adjustment of probabilities rather than separate bivariate probit models such that when the probability of rejection is used, the adjustment is typically called 'Bivariate Inference' or Heckman's Bias Correction (Ash & Meester, 2002).

Thus, in the Bivariate Inference approach, the estimated probability of not default (determined by a LOG on the accepted applicant data) is multiplied by the estimated probability of acceptance (determined by a rejection LOG on the rejected applicant data). To the extent of the sampling bias, this succeeds to inflate the probability of default in proportion to the probability of rejection.

## Iterative Reclassification (ITR)

Using an iteratively applied application scoring LOG, this method originating from Joanes implements "fractional allocation of the rejects" (Joanes, 1993). A parceled (PRP/FUZ/NID) model on accepted applicants produces a final prediction LOG. This is used to reclassify previously classified rejects. On the updated combined data set, the LOG is re-trained. The process is repeated until the convergence of LOG parameters to one solution is achieved - Finlay (p.248) states that the parameters should converge within ten iterations.

## Random Supplementation

To 'buy' future reductions in sampling bias, the random supplementation method involves 'buying' data that would otherwise have been rejected with the main disadvantage being the cost of these applicants defaulting. In practice, only 'accepted rejects' below an upper limit of default risk are sampled. Finlay establishes that "accepted rejects only need to be taken from the region where the good:bad odds are greater than one quarter of the cut-off odds" (Finlay, 2012). The cited hypothetical limit is a good:bad odds cut-off of 8:1 to 2:1. Thus, in Random Supplementation, True Random Supplementation (TRS) is when the whole population of rejected applicants is included and Marginal Random Supplementation (MRS) is when default risk is capped by a set threshold.

## Three-Group Approach (TGA)

In the TGA approach the response variable is restructured such that the applicants are divided "into three groups: goods, bads, and rejects" (Thomas et al., 2002) and uses a multinomial logistic model (Reichert et al., 1983). Explanation for applying TGA is limited in the literature. Expressing concern as to how lenders deal with having scorecards that predict both default and rejection, Thomas et al. (2002) present TGA as a branch alternative to LOG. However, the unique advantage of TGA is that the predicted probability of applicant rejection is already provided by using multinomial modelling, thus avoiding the need for a separate LOG to predict rejection status.

## Data Surrogacy

'Data Surrogacy' can be found in the literature named as 'In-House' (Finlay, 2012, pp. 240-243) or 'Bureau Data Based Method', (Siddiqi, 2006, p.104-105) or 'Cohort Performance' (Anderson, 2007, pp. 413-414). The Data Surrogacy method assumes customers defaulting in other credit products (e.g., loan repayments) will default on the inferred product (e.g., credit cards) allowing rejected applicant performance in other accounts to 'surrogate' for real outcomes.

### Extending Reject Inference Methods

Currently, reject inference methods have not been applied to improving human guided decision-making analysis. However, the potential to reduce sampling bias in any application with censored or biased data (Verstraeten & Poel, 2005) reject inference methods have been discussed with praise frequently. It yields a competitive advantage, given that the pre-existing depth of model sophistication remains unchanged while sampling bias is corrected. The performance of the RIM used, and the initial extent of the bias, determines the potential for model improvement (Banasik & Crook, 2010).

A particular application RIM founders advocate its use in is polling. An objective of this research is to investigate the application of RIMs in polling insights, as a first in applying RIMs for improved decision insights.

## DATA AND ALGORITHM ISSUES IN USING DATA SCIENCE

Fundamentally, performance in machine learning is achieved by maximizing an optimization problem, whilst minimizing a cost function. Algorithms learn a model for the output data by approximating a function that takes features as input and approximates the output. It decides the best parameters for this function based on which ones minimize the difference between the function outputs and the actual results. Selecting a model and therefore the search space along with the possible values of the minimum introduces what is known as productive bias into the system. Productive bias can further occur dependent on the availability of appropriate training and test data, the context and purpose of the problem, and the optimization method used along with the trade-offs between speed, accuracy, overfitting and overgeneralizing where each choice has a corresponding opportunity cost (Sandhu, 2019).

## Discriminatory Bias

Compared to human decision making, algorithmic systems are objective. However, this does not necessarily result in fair outcomes. In other words, algorithmic systems are potentially objectively discriminatory. The algorithm optimizes a cost function to generate the best approximation of the true predictive function that is generating the output.

In some cases, if the best approximated function is to classify all members of a disadvantaged group as reoffending or unable to pay a loan, the algorithm will select this, wrongfully imposing a relative disadvantage on individuals based on their membership in the salient social group, for example race or gender.

The increasing application of algorithms by governments around the world – particularly when they are used to profile or generate decisions about citizens by law enforcement, immigration, welfare, and health agencies – has proved controversial in recent years (Graham-McLay, 2020). There are fears that algorithms will only further entrench and propagate human biases. In health care: that algorithms will mirror human biases in medical decision making (Char et al., 2018), contribute to socioeconomic disparities in healthcare (Gianfrancesco 2018) and automate moral hazard (Mullainathan & Obermeyer, 2017). In banking: financial decision-making algorithms may import unconscious biases and the algorithms may disadvantage lower-income families (Johnson et al., 2019). In the criminal justice system: that machine learning may exacerbate unwarranted and unjust disparities that are already far too common in the existing system (Yapo & Weiss, 2018).

In more recent times, a Dutch court ruled in February that an automated surveillance system to detect welfare fraud was unlawful. This decision provoked debate about the need for greater scrutiny in other nations (Henley & Booth, 2020). Another example is Robodebt, an automated debt recovery service in Australia which put debt collectors on to innocent people to chase unlawful debts as it wrongly clawed back historic debts through a flawed algorithm (Murphy, 2019).

## Operational Algorithms in New Zealand Government Decision Making

New Zealand is no exception. The New Zealand Statistics Minister describes the use of algorithms in the public sector as containing "huge variability as to the extent of the use and how they were being used." He said algorithms determined matters from the seemingly innocuous: such as when the traffic lights changed on a central Wellington street; to the more serious, including police decision-making for frontline officers.

Statistics New Zealand published the "Algorithm Assessment Report" in 2018 which focused on "operational algorithms that result in or materially inform decisions which impact significantly on individuals or groups." It analyzed algorithms in fourteen agencies over June and July of this year. Table 1 summarize these below (Statistics New Zealand, 2018).

A potential ethical minefield of using algorithms for decision-making outlined in the report describes the algorithm deployed by Work and Income's Youth Service "to help identify those school leavers who may be at greater risk of long-term unemployment, and proactively offers them support in terms of qualifications and training opportunities." For the algorithm to produce "risk indicator ratings" for school leavers, personal data such as "whether a young person's parents were on a benefit" and "whether

*Table 1. Role of operational algorithms in New Zealand Government agencies*

| Agency | Role of Operational Algorithms |
|---|---|
| ACC | To proactively identify cases of fraud, waste and abuse that need further investigation |
| Department of Corrections | To generate scores that express the probability that an offender will be reconvicted and re-imprisoned for new offending within the following five-year period |
| Department of Internal Affairs | All Passport applications are automatically assessed against identified risk factors. To establish the identity of an applicant all passport photos undergo automated facial recognition testing. |
| Inland Revenue | To administer the tax system the 'law' and associated calculations have been turned into an 'automated decision algorithm'. To identify irregularities in payments schedules, returns, amounts, circumstances. To identify fraudulent or criminal relationships networks. To identify an opportunity to support the customer process by offering additional information as part of the overall customer experience. |
| Ministry of Business, Innovation and Employment | To support Immigration New Zealand's operational processes across the customer journey. |
| Ministry of Education | To help make resource allocation decisions, determine eligibility for various types of funding and support, and to help monitor student achievement and engagement. |
| Ministry of Health | To assess the physical and social support needs of older people. To rank individual patients based on clinically developed criteria with appropriately weighted points attached to each case. Elective surgery prioritization. |
| Ministry of Justice | To support frontline staff to make decisions about the collection of fines and reparation. |
| Ministry of Social Development | To identify clients that may benefit from more active case management. To identify school leavers that may require additional support to get into education, employment, or training. |
| New Zealand Customs Service | To determine and identify risk and the subsequent facilitation of that traffic of passengers and goods which is low risk. |
| New Zealand Police | To support the cumulative assessment frontline staff make at initial scene attendance and for follow-up safety actions. For example: 'Youth Offending Risk Screening Tool' and 'Family violence risk assessment tools'. |

a young person has ever been the subject of a notification to Oranga Tamariki" is collected and processed. Dr Emily Keddell, a Senior Lecturer in Otago University's Social Work program, raises concerns about these rules set to determine whether a young person is deserving of help and describes that an algorithm is "essentially a very complex classification tool that sorts people into categories, based on a set of programming rules" drawing attention to "the assumptions built into those rules that inevitably contain implicit ideas about who is deserving and undeserving, or those who are deemed easier as opposed to harder to help." (MacManus, 2018).

Overall, the Statistics NZ report about algorithms clarifies the influence computer technology has had in New Zealand decision-making. Given that algorithms are used by all facets of government, providing insight into how those algorithms truly work will help hold the Government accountable to keeping them equitable.

Sandhu (2019) conveys: "Ultimately, algorithmic systems will be a reflection of the society that they attempt to model and approximate, and it will take active efforts from government as well as the private sector to make sure that it works not just to entrench and further exacerbate the inequalities inherent in decision making structures but correct them by putting strict measures and constraints that penalize it. This allows us to envision a society in which decision making can be potentially rid of the subjectivity of human bias by replacing it with objective algorithmic decisions, that is aware of its biases if not entirely free of them."

## FUTURE RESEARCH DIRECTIONS

There exist tested techniques for making decisions, particularly in credit risk. This chapter has described various approaches that are used in reject inference, to account for systematic bias with the intent of improving the quality of the decision. As reject inference methods were developed to treat the sample selection issue in credit scoring. Credit scoring models are commonly developed using a sample that is limited to accepted known good/bad applications, as credit lenders only hold information on the performance of those applicants accepted in the past. Consequently, the credit scoring model is not indicative of the entire through-the-door population which consists of individuals who will be rejected alongside applicants accepted. Future research will involve quantitative assessment of the eight approaches described to demonstrate the wider applicability of these approaches to quantitatively identify and resolve latent bias in automated decision making.

## CONCLUSION

Human oversight is critical in automated decision making. With machine learning systems becoming increasingly prominent in automated decision making in New Zealand, using these systems that are sensitive to the type of bias that results in discrimination, notably discrimination on illegal grounds, must be proceeded with caution. Given the scale and impact of the bodies that have already adopted machine learning, it is crucial that measures are taken to prevent unfair discrimination in them through legal as well as technical means.

There has been significant effort to avoid and correct discriminatory bias in algorithms while also making them more transparent and in New Zealand, the government recently claimed world first in setting standards for how public agencies should use the algorithms that increasingly drive decision-making by officials about every aspect of public life. New Zealand has produced a set of standards, "Algorithm charter for Aotearoa New Zealand", designed to guide government use of algorithms and to improve data transparency and accountability. It outlines several measures including:

- explaining how decisions are informed by algorithms
- making sure data is fit for purpose by identifying and managing bias
- ensuring that privacy, ethics, and human rights are safeguarded by regularly peer-reviewing algorithms
- explaining the role of humans in decisions informed by algorithms, and
- providing a channel for citizens to appeal against decisions informed by algorithms.

By leading the way with responsible algorithm oversight, New Zealand hopes to set a model for other countries by demonstrating the value of transparency of algorithms affect daily life. "We live in a data rich world where algorithms play a crucial role in helping us to make connections and identify relationships and patterns across vast quantities of information," minister for statistics James Shaw said (Hunt, 2020). "This helps to improve decision-making and leads to benefits such as the faster delivery of targeted public services." Within this revolutionary change powered by vast data, artificial intelligence, predictive algorithms, risk modeling and biometrics, the human element of decision making is gradually becoming obsolete. In the public sector context, instead of talking to a caseworker who personally assesses the person's needs, individuals are channeled online where predictive analytics will assign a future risk score and an algorithm ultimately decides the fate.

This chapter "Data informed decision bias", is motivated by the need for approaching any analysis with caution - that going fully automated solutions is problematic. Bias is omnipresent in machine learning. Decision makers alike must proceed with caution where transparency is critical. Despite the ever-increasing reliance on algorithms in decision making, human oversight is critical (Statistics New Zealand, 2018).

# REFERENCES

Anderson, R. (2007). The Credit Scoring Toolkit: Theory and Practice for Retail Credit Risk Management and Decision Automation (Illustrated edition). Oxford University Press.

Ash, D., & Meester, S. (2002). *Best Practices in Reject Inferencing*. Credit Risk Modeling and Decisioning.

Banasik, J., & Crook, J. (2007). Reject inference, augmentation, and sample selection. *European Journal of Operational Research*, *183*(3), 1582–1594. doi:10.1016/j.ejor.2006.06.072

Banasik, J., & Crook, J. (2010). Reject inference in survival analysis by augmentation. *The Journal of the Operational Research Society*, *61*(3), 473–485. doi:10.1057/jors.2008.180

Boyes, W. J., Hoffman, D., & Low, S. A. (1989). An econometric analysis of the bank credit scoring problem. *Journal of Econometrics*, *40*(1), 3–14. doi:10.1016/0304-4076(89)90026-2

Carnegie Mellon University. (2019). *The Human Element: Machine Learning Cannot Replace Critical Thought*. Tepper School of Business - Carnegie Mellon University. https://www.cmu.edu/tepper/news/stories/2019/august/dokyun-lee-machine-learning.html

Char, D. S., Shah, N. H., & Magnus, D. (2018). Implementing Machine Learning in Health Care—Addressing Ethical Challenges. *The New England Journal of Medicine*, *378*(11), 981–983. Advance online publication. doi:10.1056/NEJMp1714229 PMID:29539284

Chen, W., Xiang, G., Liu, Y., & Wang, K. (2012). Credit risk Evaluation by hybrid data mining technique. *Systems Engineering Procedia*, *3*, 194–200. doi:10.1016/j.sepro.2011.10.029

Danziger, S., Levav, J., & Avnaim-Pesso, L. (2011). Extraneous factors in judicial decisions. *Proceedings of the National Academy of Sciences of the United States of America*, *108*(17), 6889–6892. doi:10.1073/pnas.1018033108 PMID:21482790

Dashfield, B. (2018a, June 22). *Digital Divide worse than appears in latest report*. 20/20 Trust. https://2020.org.nz/blog/2018/06/22/digital-divide-worse-than-seems-in-latest-report/

Dashfield, B. (2018b, July 12). *Digital First Census 2018—What went wrong?* 20/20 Trust. https://2020.org.nz/blog/2018/07/12/census-2018-what-went-wrong/

Finlay, S. (2012). Credit Scoring, Response Modeling, and Insurance Rating: A Practical Guide to Forecasting Consumer Behavior (2nd ed.). Palgrave Macmillan UK. doi:10.1057/9781137031693

Gianfrancesco, M. A., Tamang, S., Yazdany, J., & Schmajuk, G. (2018). Potential Biases in Machine Learning Algorithms Using Electronic Health Record Data. *JAMA Internal Medicine*, *178*(11), 1544. Advance online publication. doi:10.1001/jamainternmed.2018.3763 PMID:30128552

Graham-McLay, C. (2020, July 27). New Zealand claims world first in setting standards for government use of algorithms. *The Guardian*. https://www.theguardian.com/world/2020/jul/28/new-zealand-claims-world-first-in-setting-standards-for-government-use-of-algorithms

Hand, D., & Henley, W. (1993). Can reject inference ever work? *IMA Journal of Management Mathematics*, *5*(1), 45–55. doi:10.1093/imaman/5.1.45

Harmon-Jones, E., & Mills, J. (1999). *Cognitive Dissonance: Progress on a Pivotal Theory in Social Psychology*. American Psychological Association. https://www.apa.org/pubs/books/4318830

Health Quality & Safety Commission New Zealand, Family Violence Death Review Committee, & Health Quality & Safety Commission New Zealand. (2017). *Fifth report data: January 2009 to December 2015*. http://natlib-primo.hosted.exlibrisgroup.com/NLNZ:NLNZ:NLNZ_ALMA21290842300002836

Heckman, J. J. (1976). The Common Structure of Statistical Models of Truncation, Sample Selection and Limited Dependent Variables and a Simple Estimator for Such Models. *Annals of Economic and Social Measurement*, *5*(4), 475–492. https://www.nber.org/books-and-chapters/annals-economic-and-social-measurement-volume-5-number-4/common-structure-statistical-models-truncation-sample-selection-and-limited-dependent-variables-and

Heckman, J. J. (1979). Sample Selection Bias as a Specification Error. *Econometrica*, *47*(1), 153. doi:10.2307/1912352

Henley, J., & Booth, R. (2020, February 5). Welfare surveillance system violates human rights, Dutch court rules. *The Guardian*. https://www.theguardian.com/technology/2020/feb/05/welfare-surveillance-system-violates-human-rights-dutch-court-rules

Hunt, M. (2020). *New Zealand launches government algorithm standards – Global Government Forum*. https://www.globalgovernmentforum.com/new-zealand-launches-government-algorithm-standards/

Joanes, D. N. (1993). Reject inference applied to logistic regression for credit scoring. *IMA Journal of Management Mathematics*, *5*(1), 35–43. doi:10.1093/imaman/5.1.35

Johnson, K., Pasquale, F., & Chapman, J. (2019). Artificial Intelligence, Machine Learning, and Bias in Finance: Toward Responsible Innovation. *Fordham Law Review*, *88*(2), 499.

Kahneman, D. (2013). *Thinking, Fast and Slow* (1st ed.). Farrar, Straus and Giroux.

Kim, Y., & Sohn, S. Y. (2007). Technology scoring model considering rejected applicants and effect of reject inference. *The Journal of the Operational Research Society*, *58*(10), 1341–1347. doi:10.1057/palgrave.jors.2602306

Licklider, J. (2001). Man-Computer Symbiosis. In *IRE Transactions on Human Factors in Electronics: Vol. HFE-1* (pp. 4–11). https://groups.csail.mit.edu/medg/people/psz/Licklider.html

MacManus, R. (2018). *How Government algorithms are judging you*. https://www.newsroom.co.nz/how-government-algorithms-are-judging-you

Meng, C.-L., & Schmidt, P. (1985). On the Cost of Partial Observability in the Bivariate Probit Model. *International Economic Review*, *26*(1), 71–85. doi:10.2307/2526528

Mullainathan, S., & Obermeyer, Z. (2017). Does Machine Learning Automate Moral Hazard and Error? *The American Economic Review*, *107*(5), 476–480. doi:10.1257/aer.p20171084 PMID:28781376

Murphy, K. (2019, September 17). Robodebt class action: Shorten unveils 'David and Goliath' legal battle into Centrelink scheme. *The Guardian*. https://www.theguardian.com/australia-news/2019/sep/17/robodebt-class-action-shorten-unveils-david-and-goliath-legal-battle-into-centrelink-scheme

New Zealand Transport Agency. (2020). *Crash Analysis System (CAS)*. https://www.nzta.govt.nz/safety/partners/crash-analysis-system

Provost, F., & Fawcett, T. (2013). Data Science and its Relationship to Big Data and Data-Driven Decision Making. *Big Data*, *1*(1), 51–59. doi:10.1089/big.2013.1508 PMID:27447038

Reichert, A. K., Cho, C.-C., & Wagner, G. M. (1983). An Examination of the Conceptual Issues Involved in Developing Credit-Scoring Models. *Journal of Business & Economic Statistics*, *1*(2), 101–114. doi:10.1080/07350015.1983.10509329

Sandhu, J. (2019). *Understanding and Reducing Bias in Machine Learning*. Medium. https://towardsdatascience.com/understanding-and-reducing-bias-in-machine-learning-6565e23900ac

Shaw, J. (2019). *Driving transparency, ethics and accountability in government use of algorithms*. The Beehive. http://www.beehive.govt.nz/release/driving-transparency-ethics-and-accountability-government-use-algorithms

Siddiqi, N. (2006). *Credit Risk Scorecards: Developing and Implementing Intelligent Credit Scoring* (1st ed.). Wiley.

Statistics New Zealand. (2018). *Algorithm Assessment Agency Submissions: June-July 2018*. Statistics New Zealand. https://www.data.govt.nz/assets/Uploads/Algorithm-Assessment-Report-Oct-2018.pdf

Thomas, L. C., Crook, J. N., Edelman, D. B., & Society for Industrial and Applied Mathematics. (2002). *Credit scoring and its applications*. Society for Industrial and Applied Mathematics. https://www.books24x7.com/marc.asp?bookid=9434

Tobin, J. (1958). Estimation of Relationships for Limited Dependent Variables. *Econometrica*, *26*(1), 24–36. doi:10.2307/1907382

Verstraeten, G., & den Poel, D. V. (2005). The Impact of Sample Bias on Consumer Credit Scoring Performance and Profitability. *The Journal of the Operational Research Society*, *56*(8), 981–992. doi:10.1057/palgrave.jors.2601920

Wu, I.-D., & Hand, D. J. (2007). Handling selection bias when choosing actions in retail credit applications. *European Journal of Operational Research*, *183*(3), 1560–1568. doi:10.1016/j.ejor.2006.10.063

Yapo, A., & Weiss, J. (2018). *Ethical Implications of Bias in Machine Learning*. http://128.171.57.22/bitstream/10125/50557/paper0670.pdf

Zeleznikow, J., & Nolan, J. (2001). Using soft computing to build real world intelligent decision support systems in uncertain domains. *Decision Support Systems*, *31*(2), 263–285. doi:10.1016/S0167-9236(00)00135-4

## ADDITIONAL READING

Ash, D., & Meester, S. (2002). *Best Practices in Reject Inferencing*. Credit Risk Modeling and Decisioning.

Banasik, J., & Crook, J. (2007). Reject inference, augmentation, and sample selection. *European Journal of Operational Research, 183*(3), 1582–1594. doi:10.1016/j.ejor.2006.06.072

Dissanayake, H., & Bracewell, P. (2021). Family violence in the news: An analysis of media reporting of family violence in Aotearoa New Zealand. *Kotuitui, 0*(0), 1–18. doi:10.1080/1177083X.2021.1976224

Fuchs, D. (2018). The Dangers of Human-Like Bias in Machine-Learning Algorithms. *Missouri S&T's Peer to Peer, 2*(1). https://scholarsmine.mst.edu/peer2peer/vol2/iss1/1

Galimard, J.-E., Chevret, S., Protopopescu, C., & Resche-Rigon, M. (2016). A multiple imputation approach for MNAR mechanisms compatible with Heckman's model. *Statistics in Medicine, 35*(17), 2907–2920. doi:10.1002im.6902 PMID:26893215

Heckman, J. J. (1979). Sample Selection Bias as a Specification Error. *Econometrica, 47*(1), 153. doi:10.2307/1912352

Statistics New Zealand. (2018). *Algorithm Assessment Agency Submissions: June-July 2018.* Statistics New Zealand. https://www.data.govt.nz/assets/Uploads/Algorithm-Assessment-Report-Oct-2018.pdf

Williams, B. A., Brooks, C. F., & Shmargad, Y. (2018). How Algorithms Discriminate Based on Data They Lack: Challenges, Solutions, and Policy Implications. *Journal of Information Policy, 8*, 78–115. doi:10.5325/jinfopoli.8.2018.0078

## KEY TERMS AND DEFINITIONS

**Automated:** Is where a system minimizes human intervention for operations to be employed automatically.

**Decision Making:** A process involving gathering information and assessing alternative solutions to arrive at the optimal choice.

**Discriminatory Bias:** A result where, based on patterns in the training data, an algorithm learns to employ prejudicial treatment.

**Human Error:** Is an individual's mistake due to limitations of human ability, rather than an external failure such as a machine.

**Missing Not at Random:** Is when the values of a variable are related to the tendency for the value to be missing.

**Operational Algorithm:** Algorithms that are in use and have an impact on some aspect of everyday life.

**Sample Selection Bias:** Is when the sample does not represent the target population due to the sample not being randomly selected.

# Data Science in the Database:
## Using SQL for Data Preparation

**Antonio Badia**
*University of Louisville, USA*

## INTRODUCTION

The analysis of data requires several steps that are usually denoted as the data life cycle. Typically, these steps include data discovery and upload, data exploration, data cleaning and wrangling, data analysis proper, and dissemination of results/further analysis (Badia, 2019). While much research focuses on the analysis itself, in the form of algorithms for Data Mining (DM) or Machine Learning (ML), popular accounts indicate that data scientists spend up to 80% of their time preparing the data for analysis, that is, in the exploration, cleaning and wrangling stages (Dasu & Johnson, 2003; Wickham, 2014). Hence, this part of the process requires proper attention and analysts need the proper tools to deal with the problems that arise at these stages.

Much data resides in databases; however, it is common to transfer such data to other environments like R (Wickham and Grolemund, 2017) or text files to be processed by programs in languages like Python (VanderPlas, 2016), since database usually do not provide tools for in-depth data analysis. In some cases, it can be beneficial to deal with data exploration and cleaning in the database itself. The objective of this article is to describe how data exploration, cleaning and preparation can be carried out in typical relational databases using the already existing capabilities of most SQL systems (Badia, 2019; Linoff, 2008; Trueblood, 2001). We show how to carry out basic data analysis and cleaning by providing examples of SQL commands over a simple table. We assume that the reader has basic knowledge about SQL, but not necessarily in-depth expertise. The references provided are excellent resources for the reader interested in learning more SQL.

## BACKGROUND

Data must be prepared for analysis. Most DM) and ML algorithms make assumptions about the format and other properties of data (Dasu & Johnson, 2003). However, 'data in the wild' rarely conforms to such expectations. Discovering any problems or issues that could render data not ready for analysis and solving them is the goal of the data preparation process.

The process starts with Exploratory Data Analysis (EDA), where data is examined with simple, descriptive statistics in order to determine whether data problems exist. Most datasets often come with *dirty data* (Wickham, 2014); typical problems found at this stage include missing data, outliers, formatting problems and structure problems. Missing data refers to values that are absent. This can be a serious issue when the number of missing values is high (as a percent of all values) or when the values are not *missing at random* (that is, certain values are more likely than others to be missing), since this may introduce bias in the analysis. An outlier is a data point that is quite different from other data points and therefore could potentially be the result of an error in data gathering or storage. Some DM and ML algorithms can

DOI: 10.4018/978-1-7998-9220-5.ch069

be greatly affected by the presence of outliers; for instance, linear regression is particularly sensitive to this issue (Dasu & Johnson, 2003). Formatting problems refer to data values that are not encoded in the expected shape or arrangement. This includes issues like numbers that are not written out as numbers ("42"), dates that cannot be recognized as dates by the system ("Feb ten 2020"), and similar. This type of error is not infrequent, since computers expect values to be represented in certain ways, and any deviations may result in values being ignored or misinterpreted. Finally, structure problems arise because data is not structured in the way required by the data analysis algorithm to be used. In a typical dataset, there is a set of attributes that describe the data, and data elements are represented by a tuple or row of values, one for each attribute. However, some datasets do not come with this 'table-like' structure, while most DM and ML algorithms assume it (Wickham, 2014). All these are issues that must be detected and solved before analysis can proceed (Berthold et al., 2010).

## FOCUS OF THE ARTICLE

In this section, we describe the typical activities that are carried out in data preparation; for each, we provide a short description, an example, and describe how it could be handled in a relational database using SQL. The first step is to load data into the database; the second one is to carry out some Exploratory Data Analysis (EDA) in order to discover characteristics of the dataset and any issues the data may have. At that point, *Data Cleaning* is attempted, in order to solve the issues and get data ready for analysis. Issues that are especially important are missing data, outliers, structural problems and duplication. We describe each step in a separate subsection.

### Getting Data In and Out of the Database

Relational databases store data in units called *tables*. In fact, a database can be considered a collection of tables.

To create a table, the SQL language has a command, called (not surprisingly) CREATE TABLE. A very simple example of this command is

```
CREATE TABLE Employees (
  name char(64),
  age int,
  date-of-birth date,
  salary float)
```

Here, 'Employees' is the name of the table, and 'name', 'age', date-of-birth' and 'salary' are the names of the 4 attributes (typically called 'variables' in statistics and 'features' in Data Mining and Machine Learning) that make up the *schema* or structure of the table. Each attribute is given a data type: 'char(64)' means a string of up to 64 characters; 'int' denotes an integer, 'date' a data and 'float' a real-valued number. All database systems provide several data types to represent collections of values, including different types of numbers, strings, and temporal types (dates, times and timestamps).

If data is already in a file, it is possible to load the data into the database in one swoop. All database systems have some command which takes a file name and a table name and brings in the data from the file into the table -as far as the data in the file is compatible with the schema of the table. This command assumes that the data in the file can be broken down into lines, each line corresponding to a row/tuple for the table (Linoff, 2008; Trueblood, 2001).

The *load* command is system dependent, although the basic outline is the same for most systems. Generally, one specifies the location of the file in the computer, the table to load into, and provides a description of how the lines in the file are to be broken down into the values that make up a row/tuple by indicating how values are separated from each other and a few other characteristics. For instance, the typical csv files use the comma as a separator; other typical separators are the semicolon character or the tab.

However, the fact that most datasets often come with dirty data often creates a problem when trying to load the data in the database. Some of the most common issues found, and typical solutions, include:

- **Missing values:** Lack of values can be manifested in a file in two ways: by an empty field (that is, two consecutive appearances of the delimiter), or by some marker (markers like 'N' or 'NA', for 'Not Available', are particularly common). Dealing with empty fields is relatively straightforward. Some systems will automatically set the corresponding attribute in the table to a *default value*: the empty string, for string types; zero, for numeric types; and the date or time 'zero' for dates and times. Other systems will create a NULL in the database. However, dealing with markers may create several issues. The first problem is that different datasets may use different conventions to mark missing values; the dataset may need to be explored before it can be loaded in the database to identify such markers (command line tools are the appropriate tools for this task (Janssens, 2008)). A second problem is that null markers may confuse the loader about the type of data it is reading. In numerical attributes, the system expects strings that can be transformed into numbers (essentially, strings made up of digits, and optionally a hyphen (-) or a period (.). Even numbers with commas can create problems). When a string like 'NA' is found, the system is unable to transform it into a number or recognize it as a missing value marker. The same problem happens with temporal information, where the system expects a string in a certain format that it can parse and recognize as a date or time. Even in string-based values, the system may likewise confuse a string like 'NA' with a valid value, not a missing value marker. The best way to avoid errors is system dependent: in some systems, it's better to delete unrecognized markers and leave empty fields; in others, it may be necessary to create a special value of the right type (for instance, using -1 for a numeric field that contains only positive values).

- **String representation:** Strings are represented differently in different datasets. In some cases, strings are stored by surrounding them with single quotes ('), sometimes with double quotes (``); sometimes they are stored without any quotes. This can cause confusion in the loader, especially when strings include characters other than letters or numbers. For instance, the string ``Spring, Summer, Fall, Winter ... and Spring'' is the title of a movie, but it includes 3 commas and 3 dots, and may confuse a loader when stored in a CSV file. Again, solutions depend on the system: some systems are smart enough to leave everything in quotes alone (in which case, making sure that all strings are surrounded by quotes is the way to go); others may require that those extra commas go away.

- **Dates and times:** Dates and times are typically recognized by most database systems if they follow a certain format. When the data in the file does not conform to the format, the system tends to read it as a string. Hence, date and time values may need reformatting before they can be properly loaded.

As a result of these issues, loading a dataset into a database may require some upfront work, but once the loading is accomplished, we have the advantage that each attribute is assigned a type, which makes the next steps much simpler, as we will see. Also, databases can handle very large datasets, unlike other approaches that are limited by computer memory.

## EDA: The Univariate Case

Once data is in the table, Exploratory Data Analysis (EDA) can begin. EDA can be roughly broken down into two steps: analysis of single attributes in isolation (the 'univariate' part) and analysis of several attributes together (the 'multivariate' part). Analysis of single attributes depends on the nature of the data; for EDA purposes (and much analysis, too), attributes can be divided into *categorical* or *nominal*, *ordinal*, or *numerical*. The first type refers to sets of labels or names, typically with no relation or order among the elements. A typical example would be the name of a person, as in the first attribute of our table Employee. This kind of attribute is typically expressed by a string type, and the most common analysis is to build a histogram showing the frequency of different values in the dataset (i.e., whether values are all unique, or some repeat and, if so, how the number of repetitions is distributed). In SQL, this can be achieved with a query like

```
SELECT name, count(*) as frequency
FROM Employee
GROUP BY name;
```

The query will return the frequency (number of appearances) of each name in Employee; this will tell us whether names are unique (all frequencies are 1), otherwise it will indicate how common names are (adding an 'ORDER BY frequency desc' will show the most common names first).

In many cases, we would like to have a probability distribution of the values of an attribute. This can be obtained by relativizing the histogram to express the number of repetitions of a value as a percentage of all values:

```
SELECT name, sum(1.0/total) as percent
 FROM Employee,
      (SELECT count(*) AS total FROM Employee) AS Temp
 GROUP BY name;
```

Instead of associating the frequency (as an absolute number) with each name, this query will associate a number between 0 and 1 that expresses the frequency as a fraction of the total number of values in the dataset (here, the subquery in the FROM clause computes the total number of values in the table as 'total'); for instance, a percent of 0.15 means a 15% of all names.

Histograms are really one example of a more general technique, *binning* (also called *bucketing*). In binning, the values of a variable are divided into disjoint intervals (called bins or buckets), and all the values that fall within a given interval are replaced by some representative value. This makes the technique applicable to continuous (numerical) variables too. For categorical values, it is customary that each value is its own interval (resulting in a histogram), but this does not necessarily have to be the case.

Binning also generalizes histograms in that the representative value for an interval is not limited to the frequency; it can be another statistic too. We can do binning in SQL, and some systems have built-in facilities to calculate percentages (which divide the domain into 100 intervals, so that each one has 1% of the data); quartiles (which divide which divide the domain into 4 intervals, corresponding to 25, 50, 75 and 100% of the data); deciles (which divide which divide the domain into 10 intervals, corresponding to 10, 20, ... and 100% of the data) and so on. Unfortunately, when such facilities are not present, simulating them can be quite tricky -for details, see (Badia, 2019). A simple binning given by pre-determined buckets is simple to compute:

```
SELECT type, count(*)
FROM Employee
GROUP BY (CASE WHEN age > 60 THEN 'senior'
          WHEN age <= 60 and age > 30 THEN 'medium'
          ELSE 'young' END) as type;
```

This will divide all employees into 3 groups (bins or buckets) based on their age, with pre-defined cut points at 30 and 60.

The second type of attribute, ordinal, has (as the name indicates) an order relation defined on the values. A typical example of this is an attribute with temporal information like 'date-of-birth', since the values can be ordered by 'earlier than': for instance, we have that '10-12-2020 < 10-13-2020' (here we use the 'month-day-year' pattern). This type of attributes is typically used to compute some kind of *ranked correlation* (see later).

The third type of attribute, numerical, is usually the result of some measurement and is expressed by a number. Typically, we want to know how the values are distributed by finding out the range of values present in the dataset, their largest and smallest value, and basic statistics like mean, median and average. Such results can be obtained in SQL as follows:

```
SELECT count(age) as number-values,
       count(distinct age) as cardinality,
       min(age) as minimum,  max(age) as maximum,
       max(age) - min(age) as range,
       avg(age) as mean,
       stddev(age) as standard-deviation
FROM Employee;
```

This will provide us with a good description of the values in attribute 'age', which can be compared to expected values in order to ascertain whether the data is correct.

When computing these simple statistics, it is important to realize that they describe the data as given; in other words, if there are problems like missing data or outliers (see below), they will affect the values computed. For instance, it is well known that the mean is greatly affected by outliers, so it may be a good idea (as a precaution) to compute the *trimmed mean*, one where some extreme values are discarded:

```
SELECT avg(salary)
FROM Employee,
     (SELECT max(salary) as Amax FROM Employee) AS T1,
     (SELECT min(salary) as Amin FROM Employee) AS T2
WHERE A < Amax and A > Amin;
```

This query will compute the average of all salaries except the largest one and the smallest one. A slightly more complicated query can discount the *k* top and bottom *k* values instead, for a given *k*.

Another issue is that some statistics, even basic ones, may be hard to compute in SQL. A typical example of this is the *mode. The* mode is the most frequently occurring value in an attribute; in SQL, it can be calculated using a histogram of the attribute:

```
WITH Histogram as
(SELECT age as value, count(*) as freq
FROM Employee
GROUP BY age)
SELECT value
FROM Histogram,
     (SELECT max(freq) as top FROM Histogram) AS T
WHERE freq = top;
```

The median is another example of simple statistic that can be computed in SQL, albeit not in a straightforward manner (for details, see (Badia, 2019)).

## EDA: The Multivariate Case

Besides finding out information about individual attributes, we would like to also establish if the values of different attributes are somehow connected; if an attribute is highly correlated with another, it may not be a good idea to use both attributes in analysis. A basic measure of such correlation is the joint probability and Pointwise Mutual Information (PMI). Both concepts are based on having a probability distribution of the values of the attributes involved, which we saw above how to compute. Given two attributes A and B, we can check whether they are *independent* (no correlation exists) as follows: compute the probability distribution of A, P(A), and the probability distribution of B, P(B), as usual; we also compute the *joint probability* of A and B, P(A,B). Once this is one, we use the following test: if P(A,B) = P(A)P(B), the attributes are independent. Using SQL and attributes 'age' and 'salary' from our example, this would be written as

```
WITH PrAge AS
 (SELECT age, sum(1.0/total) as PrA
  FROM Employee, (SELECT count(*) as total FROM Employee) as T
  GROUP BY age),
    PrSalary AS
 (SELECT salary, sum(1.0/total) as PrB
  FROM Employee, (SELECT count(*) as total FROM Employee) as T
  GROUP BY salary),
    PrAgeSalary AS
 (SELECT age, salary, sum(1.0/total) as PrAB
  FROM Employee, (SELECT count(*) as total FROM Employee) as T
  GROUP BY age, salary)
SELECT sum(PrAgeSalary - (PrAge * PrSalary))
FROM (SELECT age, salary, PrA, PrB, PrAB
```

```
    FROM PrAge, PrSalary, PrAgeSalary
    WHERE PrAge.age = PrAgeSalary.age and PrSalary.salary = PrAgeSalary.sal-
ary)
    AS Probabilities;
```

If attributes 'age' and 'salary' are independent, we would expect the final result of this query to be 0 (note: due to the limitations of real number arithmetic in computers, the result could be a very small, non-zero number). To compute PMI in SQL, we can use

```
SELECT log(sum (PrAgeSalary / (PrAge * PrSalary)))
FROM Probabilities;
```

where Probabilities is the table of joint probabilities computed above (we are using 'log' for the logarithmic function, provided by most database systems).

A simpler way to compare attributes is to check their *covariance*, which is based on comparing their means (averages):

```
SELECT (avg(age*salary) - (avg(age)* avg(salary)))
FROM Employee;
```

In some systems, a built-in function (usually called covar or similar) exists for this purpose. Pearson correlation (essentially, a covariance normalized with the standard deviation) can also be computed in SQL with

```
SELECT (avg(age*salary) - (avg(age)* avg(salary))) / (std(age) * std(salary))
FROM Employee;
```

For ordinal attributes, it is common to use *rank correlation*, a measure of the relationship between the rankings on each variable. The idea here is to compare the rank of the attributes (their position in the order), instead of the attribute values. There are several rank correlation measures; the most popular ones are Kendall's and Spearman's ranks (Berthold et al., 2010). These can also be computed in SQL with some effort (Badia, 2019).

There are many other multivariate analyses possible, but a word of caution is needed. In general, this type of analysis considers not only pairs of attributes, but any set of attributes. However, when a schema has $n$ attributes, there are $2n$ possible sets of attributes to consider, and it is well known that this number grows very fast. Hence, consideration of all subsets of attributes is not practical or feasible in most realistic cases, and multivariate analysis is usually restricted by the analyst to cases where domain knowledge strongly suggests that the attributes under consideration are indeed related.

## Finding and Dealing with Missing Data

Missing data refers to the absence of values in some records for certain attributes; for instance, the salary for some Employees may be unknown, leading to a missing value where the salary should be. Many algorithms for Data Mining and Machine Learning do not deal well with incomplete datasets; hence, it is usually necessary to locate and deal with missing values (Berthold et al., 2010; Dasu & Johnson 2003).

As indicated above, this task starts when data is loaded into the database, since missing values may be explicitly indicated by markers like 'N/A' that confuse the data loader. If all such markers have been identified and eliminated, relational databases will use a special NULL marker to indicate missing values. To find the records with missing values on some attribute in SQL, one must use the IS NULL predicate:

```
SELECT *
FROM Employee
WHERE name IS NULL;
```

This query will find all records where the value of 'name' is not present. If one wants to find the records that have any missing values, it is necessary to search through the schema. For instance, in our Employee table example, one would write:

```
SELECT *
FROM Employee
WHERE name IS NULL or age IS NULL or date-of-birth IS NULL or salary IS NULL;
```

Clearly, the approach is unwieldy for tables with a very large number of attributes, but it's the only available method in SQL.

Once records with nulls are identified, there are two basic strategies to follow: ignore (delete) the missing data, or try to 'recreate' it -that is, guess values for the absent data. In the first approach, there is the option of deleting the attribute where data is missing (useful when all or most missing data is concentrated in one or two attributes) or deleting the records with any data missing (useful when missing data is scattered across attributes but concentrated on a few records). In the second approach, one can try to *impute* the missing data from other values. This in turn can be done using other values in the same attribute, or using values in other attributes of the same record. An example of the first kind of imputation would be to substitute missing values by the average of all present values in the attribute:

```
UPDATE Employee
SET salary = (SELECT avg(salary) FROM Employee)
WHERE salary IS NULL;
```

An example of the second kind would be to substitute missing values by the result of a computation based on other attributes in the incomplete record. Assume, for instance, that we know that we have missing values in Salary, but we know that seniority is the most important factor in determining salaries, so that there is a connection between Age and Salary. We can use the relationship between values of Age and Salary in records where both values are present to impute a value for Salary in a record where only Age is present; the idea is to find records with a similar Age, and use their Salary to guess the missing salary. Assume the age of the incomplete record is 47; then the SQL query

```
SELECT avg(salary)
FROM (SELECT salary from Employee order by abs(age - 47) limit 2) as KNN;
```

This is an example of a general technique called K *Nearest Neighbor(s)*, which is very useful in Data Mining (Dasu & Johnson, 2003). In the above example, we set K = 2.

## Finding and Dealing with Outliers

Finding outliers in an attribute is a complex task due to the fact that there is no formal definition of what qualifies as an outlier. Such values are characterized by being very different from the vast majority ('typical') values for the attribute, but it can be difficult to determine how 'different' the value must be, and what a typical value is.

One easy and approximate attempt is to find out the extremes (minimum and maximum) of an attribute and compare them with expected values. For instance, in the attribute 'age' of Employee, we would expect all values to be between 18 (if we do not employ minors) and 65 (if that is the retirement age); a minimum under 18 or a maximum over 65 may indicate errors on how values for 'age' were gathered. Another approximate method is to compute the mean and the trimmed mean (see above) of an attribute; if these are very different, this could be due to the presence of outliers.

A more general (but more costly) family of methods rely on computing a 'distance' between any two values of an attribute (this can be extended to several attributes, but see the discussion about scaling below). A distance is a function $f(x,y)$ that tells us how 'close' or 'apart' two data points $x$ and $y$ are; it needs to obey some basic properties: $f(x,x) = 0$; $f(x,y) = f(y,x)$; and for any third point $z$, $f(x,y) < f(x,z) + f(z,y)$. In the case of numerical attributes, the distance can simply be the absolute value of their difference ($f(x,y) = |x - y|$, with '||' denoting absolute value). Once a distance is determined, there are several ways to use this information to check for outliers. One of the simplest methods is the *density-based* approach: given a distance $d$, a percentage $p$, a record $x$ is considered an outlier if there are more than $p$ percent records at a distance from $x$ greater than $d$. In SQL, we can first compute the distance with a self-join (a join of a table with itself):

```
CREATE TABLE Distance(salary1, salary2, dist) AS
SELECT E1.salary, E2.salary, abs(E1.salary -  E2.salary)
FROM Employee as E1, Employee as E2;
```

Note that this query can be costly over large tables; it can be (slightly) improved by adding the condition

```
WHERE E1.salary > E2.salary;
```

Once we have this, we implement the above approach as follows:

```
Select salary1, count(*)/total as percent
From Distance, (select count(*) as total from Distance) T
where dist > d
group by salary1
having percent > p;
```

This will, for each record, find out how many there are at a distance greater than $d$; convert this count to a percentage, and filter the results where the percentage is greater than $p$. The result will be the salaries that are considered too 'far apart' from many others and so could be considered as outliers.

## Other Issues: Duplicate Detection and Removal

Sometimes the basic fact or entity may be duplicated (appear more than once) in the dataset. This is usually due to a faulty data collection scheme or to the fact that the dataset is the result of integrating ('unioning') several datasets from different sources -overlap among the sources will result in duplicates. Finding duplicates, like finding outliers, can be extremely complex because we have to determine when two records are duplicates (refer to the same real-life entity or fact). If duplication is determined based on having equal values in certain key attributes, the task is greatly simplified. For instance, assume that any two employees with the same name and age are duplicates; then the query

```
SELECT name, age
FROM Employee
GROUP BY name, age
HAVING count(*) > 1;
```

will retrieve such records (the name and age in them, actually). The issue gets much trickier when simple equality is not enough. For instance, we may want to account for the fact that names may have been misspelled. In such cases, *approximate matching* (in which values do not have to be identical, but similar enough) must be used, but this can be tricky to implement in SQL. In some systems, approximate string matching functions are available for string-based attributes, and the idea of distance seen above can be used for numerical attributes (when the distance between values $x$ and $y$ is smaller than a given threshold, we can consider $x$ and $y$ as 'similar enough' -this accounts for rounding errors, etc.)

Other issues, like *attribute transformation*, can be attacked with database-provided functions. In attribute transformation we want to change the values of an attribute in order to 'normalize' the values, that is, put all value within certain pre-established ranges. For categorical attribute, this usually means putting all values in a certain format -for instance, making sure all names are in uppercase (this facilitates sorting and searching the names). As these attributes are represented by strings, we use string functions (which all databases provide) to accomplish this:

```
UPDATE Employees SET name = Upper(name);
```

Here, 'Upper' is a function that transforms a string by changing all letters to uppercase (and ignoring other characters). For numerical attributes, transformations usually involve having all values on a certain scale -for instance, expressing them as values between 0 and 1. This can be accomplished with numerical functions we have already seen:

```
UPDATE Employee
SET salary = (salary - (SELECT avg(salary) FROM Employee)) /
            ((SELECT max(salary) FROM Employee) -
             (SELECT min(salary) FROM Employee));
```

Unfortunately, this will not work in all SQL databases (for instance, it works in Postgres, but it does not in MySQL), due to the fact that we are, in the same operation (UPDATE) changing values in the table but also computing some statistics (mean, minimum, maximum) on it. The intended meaning, of course, is that such statistics must be obtained from the table before any changes are applied to the table;

however, some systems will not understand this order of evaluation. To work around this problem, the query can be rewritten to isolate the statistics computation and make clear that it should happen before any changes:

```
UPDATE Employee
SET salary = (salary - (SELECT mean
                        FROM (SELECT avg(salary) as mean
                              FROM Employee) as D1))
              (SELECT maxa - mina
               FROM (SELECT max(salary) as maxa,
                            min(salary) as mina
                     FROM Employee) as D2);
```

This type of normalization is very useful (actually, required) by many Data Mining and Machine Learning algorithms, since without them the algorithm could be led stray by absolute values. Imagine, for instance, a dataset describing houses where one attribute, NumBeds, refers to the number of bedrooms in the house (a value usually between 1 and 5), while another attribute, SqFt, gives the size of the house in square feet (a value usually between 500 and 5000). Assume an algorithm that tries to guess the price of the house by combining all information about the house (including NumBeds and SqFt); such an algorithm will usually combine the values from each attribute in some formula (for instance, it could use Linear Regression (Berthold et al., 2010)). In this case, attribute SqFt would be considered about 10 times more important than NumBeds simply because the typical value would be about 10 times larger; normalizing both attributes as shown above, so that both consist of values between 0 and 1, would correct this imbalance.

## SOLUTIONS AND RECOMMENDATIONS

As shown in this article, SQL is capable of expressing many common tasks in data preparation. However, it is also clear that SQL also falls short in certain cases, making the development of solutions cumbersome or even impossible. Hence, it would be desirable that the SQL standard be extended to include some advanced functionality for data preparation. A few desirable capabilities can be inferred from the examples shown above:

- **Loading and data type inference:** currently, loading data in the database is a two-step process, where the first step requires pre-defining a table in SQL (which in turn requires knowledge about the dataset to be loaded). A single step process, whereby the system automatically analyzes and infers data types for the data in the file, would be very useful for the data analyst. Although some facilities towards this end already exist in many relational database systems, such facilities need to be made more robust in order to deal with missing values and other problems.
- **Data changes:** creating a new attribute by applying a function to existing ones is a very common activity that encompasses data cleaning (reformatting a date, trimming a string value, etc.) and data transformation (scaling a numeric value, etc.). This is cumbersome in SQL; it should be possible, at the very least, to have a command that adds the newly created attribute to the schema of a table and computes the values, all in one step.

- **Computation across a schema:** many operations for data analysis apply to each attribute in a table, or each attribute of a certain type. Writing such queries in SQL is very difficult; having the ability to simplify this type of processing would be of considerable help to data analysts using SQL.
- **Representation of graph and matrix data:** while this data can be readily expressed as a table, algorithms over such tables are burdensome to write in SQL. This issue can be attacked by either having specific data types for graphs and matrices or allowing SQL to include constructs to compute graph and matrix computations. To note, there are databases that focus on graph data and offer data types and languages specifically for this kind of data (Robinson et al., 2015).

These suggestions do not exhaust the scope of this topic, but they would constitute a solid first step towards supporting data exploration and cleaning in databases in a more appropriate manner than is currently available.

## FUTURE RESEARCH DIRECTIONS

Several commercial database systems are moving towards support for complex Data Mining and Machine Learning algorithms, so that data can be analyzed inside the database, without a need to move it to other environments. For instance, MS SQL Server provides with several extensions ... However, as pointed out earlier while discussing the data life-cycle., before data can be analyzed it must be examined, its quality (as in: absence of problems like missing data, outliers, badly formatted data and so on) determined, and any issues found solved. Many SQL-based systems fall short in this particular. Hence, future research should focus on incorporating into the SQL language the necessary commands to make EDA and data cleaning easier. The issues pointed out in the previous section provide a beginning, but more research is needed in order to come out with a set of commands that would support the more common data exploration and wrangling tasks. Since databases tend to deal with large amounts of data, this research will have to take into account efficiency concerns; implementations should be able to scale well, and also handle data that does not fit in main memory (a major limitation of other environments like R, although this situation is slowly changing (Wickham and Grolemund, 2017)).

## CONCLUSION

Relational databases provide basic functionality for data exploration and cleaning. Thus, when dealing with data in databases, data scientists should use SQL to their advantage in order to explore, clean and filter data. This would minimize the amount of data to be moved (if some data is considered not suitable for the analysis at hand or can be summarized). However, SQL can make certain data preparation tasks cumbersome to implement, as we have noticed. Thus, it would be desirable for relational systems to provide better support for this kind of work. In the meantime, though, there is quite a bit that a good SQL programmer can accomplish; this chapter has shown some of the basic ideas that can be currently implemented in any relational system.

# REFERENCES

Badia, A. (2019). *SQL for Data Science: Data Cleaning, Wrangling and Analysis with Relational Databases*. Springer.

Berthold, M., Borgelt, C., Hoppner, F., & Klawonn, F. (2010). *Guide To Intelligent Data Analysis*. Springer. doi:10.1007/978-1-84882-260-3

Dasu, T., & Johnson, T. (2003). *Exploratory Data Mining and Data Cleaning*. John Wiley and Sons. doi:10.1002/0471448354

Janssens, J. (2015). *Data Science at the Command Line*. O'Reilly.

Linoff, G. (2008). *Data Analysis Using SQL and Excel*. Wiley.

Robinson, I., Webber, J., & Eifrem, E. (2015). *Graph Databases* (2nd ed.). O'Reilly Media, Inc.

Trueblood, R., & Lovett, J. (2001). *Data Mining and Statistical Analysis Using SQL*. Apress. doi:10.1007/978-1-4302-0855-6

VanderPlas, J. (2016). *Python Data Science Handbook*. O'Reilly.

Wickham, H. (2014). Tidy Data. *Journal of Statistical Software*, *51*(10). Advance online publication. doi:10.18637/jss.v059.i10

Wickham, H., & Grolemund, G. (2017). *R for Data Science*. O'Reilly.

# ADDITIONAL READING

Batini, C., & Scannapieca, M. (2006). *Data Quality: Concepts, methodologies and techniques*. Springer.

Chopra, R., England, A., & Alaudeen, M. (2019). *Doing Data Science with Python*. O'Reilly.

Malik, U., Goldwasser, M., & Johnston, B. (2019). *SQL for Data Analytics: Perform Fast and Efficient Data Analysis with the Power of SQL*. Packt Publishing.

Mohri, M., Rostamizadeh, A., & Talwalkar, A. (2012). *Foundations of Machine Learning*. The MIT Press.

O'Neil, C., & Schutt, R. (2013). *Doing Data Science*. O'Reilly.

Skillcorn, D. (2017). *Understanding Complex Datasets: Data Mining with Matrix Decompositions*. Chapman & Hall.

Tan, P.-N., Steinbach, M., Karpatne, A., & Kumar, V. (2019). *Introduction to Data Mining*. Pearson.

Tanimura, C. (2021). *SQL for Data Analysis: Advanced Techniques for Transforming Data into Insights*. O'Reilly.

Teate, R. M. P. (2021). *SQL for Data Scientists: A Beginners Guide to Building Datasets for Analysis*. Wiley.

## KEY TERMS AND DEFINITIONS

**Data Cleaning:** Set of activities carried out to take 'dirty' data (data with problems like missing data, outliers, etc.) and transform it into 'clean' or 'tidy' data. Its focus is on solving any issues the data may have so as to get the data ready for further analysis.

**Data Preparation:** Set of activities carried out to prepare data for analysis. Most Data Mining and Machine Learning expect data to be 'clean' (to be well formatted, without missing values, outliers, duplicates or other problems) and to be in a certain format (usually some kind of table). Moreover, some attributes may need special treatment (categorical attributes may need to be standardized or even transformed into numerical; numerical attributes may need to be scaled). Data Preparation is a fundamental activity within the Data Life-Cycle.

**Data Wrangling:** Another term for Data Cleaning, sometimes it is used in a wider sense to include activities that are not properly Data Cleaning, like getting the data in the format required by some analysis tool or algorithm, changing the structure of the data (by pivoting or getting the data in a certain pre-defined structure, like a graph or a matrix), creating new attributes from existing ones, etc.

**Exploratory Data Analysis (EDA):** Lightweight analysis of data that uses descriptive statistics, graphics and other tools in order to describe the data and discover whether any problems are present. Data analysts use EDA as a first approach to a dataset in order to gain an understanding of what it means, what kind of values it contains, and what issues the data may have.

**Missing Data:** data values that should be present in a dataset but are not. Most datasets are based on a tabular model, with a collection of homogeneous records (that is, records that contain values for the same, fixed collection of attributes). When a record is incomplete (it does not contain values for all attributes), we say that there is missing data. This situation creates a problem for many analyses and therefore must be addressed during Data Cleaning.

**Outlier:** An outlier is a data value that is very different, in some sense, from most other data values in the same attribute. As such, it lies outside what is considered 'typical' or 'normal' for that attribute. The definition of outlier is context-dependent and often not completely precise. The presence of an outlier may indicate an extreme and exceptional data value faithfully recorded or a regular data value that has not been recorded properly. It may be extremely hard to separate these two cases without domain knowledge.

**SQL:** Structured Query Language is an industry standard that defines the language used to manage data in a Relational Database System (RDBMS). It includes commands to create, store, and access data. It is a declarative language, with the implementation of the commands left to each system. SQL has become ubiquitous to such an extent that Relational databases are sometimes called SQL databases, and systems that do not follow the Relational model are called NoSQL.

# Data Science Methodology

**Matthias Pohl**

https://orcid.org/0000-0002-6241-7675

*Otto von Guericke University, Germany*

**Christian Haertel**

*Otto von Guericke University, Germany*

**Daniel Staegemann**

https://orcid.org/0000-0001-9957-1003

*Otto von Guericke University, Germany*

**Klaus Turowski**

*Otto von Guericke University, Germany*

## INTRODUCTION

Data Science (DS) represents a relatively new, emerging field of science (Cao, 2017; Pohl et al., 2018). In summary, this discipline aims to extract knowledge and value from data using structured methods and techniques (I. Martinez et al., 2021; L. S. Martinez, 2017). The knowledge can be desirable in companies and other organizations to achieve improvements in performance. In order to profit from the promising advantages of DS as an organization, associated projects require successful completion. Therefore, process models for the project management are needed to conduct goal-oriented DS and provide further support in execution (Saltz & Shamshurin, 2015).

Up to 80 percent of data-intensive projects are not completed or do not meet the set goals, which emphasizes the need of a supporting project structure (Kelly & Kaskade, 2013; VentureBeat, 2019). A wide range of process models were developed from different application directions after the appearance of the first approaches (e.g., KDD, CRISP-DM). Handling data requires a high level of attention in such projects and is always a challenge (Chapman et al., 2000; Fayyad et al., 1996b; Saltz et al., 2017). This chapter is intended to provide an overview of DS process models that have emerged and to highlight project-specific features, such as activities, roles, and documents, without addressing specific elements of project management. The so-called process models are widely considered as methodologies and could be led to a reference model in future. The designation as a process model or framework is used equivalently in the presentations at hand. The common structure of the process models can certainly be termed methodology.

Other concepts have been established in the context of DS. In the last decade, Big Data has become a ubiquitous term. In the meantime, it is no longer exclusively mentioned in information technology, but can also be found in other fields such as sociology, medicine, biology, management and economics (de Mauro et al., 2016). Big Data is described as fast-growing data volumes that are too large for classic data processing systems and therefore require new technologies (Provost & Fawcett, 2013). The National Institute of Standard Technology even relates the term directly to DS (NIST Big Data Public Working Group, 2019).

DOI: 10.4018/978-1-7998-9220-5.ch070

In the course of the terminological development of data science, it became clear that there is a conceptual proximity to data mining (Martinez, 2017). It is therefore imperative that this term is addressed here. Fayyad et al. described data mining as a sub-step of the process, in which algorithms of data analysis and discovery are applied to identify certain patterns in data (Fayyad et al., 1996a, 1996b). Shearer took a different view when he presented his data mining process model, which also assigns the phases of business understanding and data preparation to the data mining process (Shearer, 2000).

In the age of digitalization, artificial intelligence (AI) is a widespread term. However, different interpretations make it difficult to break AI down to a common definition. As descriptions are discussed since the 1960s, the scientific field is concerned with teaching computers to do things that humans are currently better at (Rich, 1983). At this point, a definition of AI should not be discussed, only the connection to DS is stated.

Concrete applications can be found in the field of machine learning (ML), which is characterized as a subfield of AI (Ho et al., 2007). ML is concerned with the development of algorithms and techniques to create computer systems that can improve themselves through experience (Ho et al., 2007). These algorithms use large amounts of data for pattern recognition and effective learning to train the machine to be able to make autonomous decisions (Helm et al., 2020).

The representing terms and related models will be integrated at the presentation in the following sections.

## BACKGROUND

For years, the individual experiences of data scientists were held only in inner circles of research institutions or companies. In the 1990s, the first attempts were made to bring together the experiences in DS process frameworks. The Knowledge Discovery in Databases (KDD) and the Cross-Industry Standard Process for Data Mining (CRISP-DM) models have evolved from these aspirations and are already widely used in science and industry. Further developments have been made with new experiences gained from the developed data landscape and led to new approaches. The following overview of data science frameworks (Table 1) is the result of a reproduced literature analysis (Martinez et al., 2021). It is not excluded that further derivatives of these approaches will be developed and applied in companies or research institutions for individual use.

Instead of describing each process model in detail, the similarities and differences should be highlighted. Within projects, the sequential process stages and activities are of primary interest. The corresponding activities require certain skills of the participants, so that a further comparison of the intended roles is made. For the documentation and traceability of the project results, a final view is taken of the artifacts to be produced in the methodological frameworks.

### Stages and Activities

First, an overview of the phases or super-activities of all DS process models included is to be given (see Table 2). Accordingly, only the methods are mentioned that contain such a task structure at all. The Agile Data Science Lifecyle and MIDST frameworks do not integrate such phase models and are excluded from the overview. CRISP-DM and RAMSYS are listed here in one column because they contain the same stages. The methodological phases assigned in the further comparison are already shown in the first columns.

*Table 1. Overview of data science methodologies*

| Abbreviation | Process Methodology | Reference |
|---|---|---|
| ADF | Agile Delivery Framework | (Larson & Chang, 2016) |
| ADSLC | Agile Data Science Lifecycle | (Jurney, 2017) |
| AI Ops | AI Operations | (Thomas, 2019) |
| Analytics Canvas | Analytics Canvas | (Kühn et al., 2018) |
| ASUM-DM | Analytics Solutions Unified Method-Data Mining | (IBM Corporation, 2015) |
| BDIAI | Big Data Ideation, Assessment and Implementation | (Vanauer et al., 2015) |
| BDMC | Big Data Management Canvas | (Kaufmann, 2019) |
| BDMF | Big Data Management Framework | (Dutta & Bose, 2015) |
| CRISP-DM | Cross-Industry Standard Process for Data Mining | (Chapman et al., 2000; Shearer, 2000) |
| DWDS | Development Workflows for Data Scientists | (Byrne, 2017) |
| DASC-PM | Data-Science-Process-Model | (Schulz et al., 2020) |
| Domino DS | Domino Data Science Lifecyle | (Domino Data Lab, 2017) |
| DSE | Data Science Edge | (Grady, 2016; Grady et al., 2017) |
| DSW | Data Science Workflow | (Guo, 2012) |
| EMC DALC | Data Analytics Life Cycle | (Dietrich & EMC, 2016) |
| FMDS | Foundational Methodology for Data Science | (Rollins, 2015) |
| KDD | Knowledge Discovery in Databases | (Fayyad et al., 1996b, 1996a) |
| MIDST | Modular Interactive Data Science Tool | (Crowston et al., 2019) |
| RAMSYS | Rapid Collaborative Data Mining System | (Moyle & Jorge, 2001) |
| SEMMA | Sample, Explore, Modify, Model, Assess | (SAS, 2017) |
| SRBD | Systematic Research on Big Data | (Das et al., 2015) |
| TDME | Toward data mining engineering | (Marbán et al., 2009) |
| TDSP | Team Data Science Process | (Microsoft, 2020) |

Most process models start data science projects by illuminating the business background, setting goals and designing the project framework. Only SEMMA, the Big Data Management Canvas and the Data Science Workflow do not include such a phase. In the other process models, this initial constitution phase is pronounced. KDD includes it under "Learn application domain", while CRISP-DM, RAMSYS, TDSP and the Foundational Methodology for Data Science refer to "Business Understanding". FMDS is unique in that case because the business context is considered in additional steps "Analytical Approach" and "Data Requirements". In the Domino DS Lifecycle and BDIAI, on the other hand, this section is called "Ideation", and in the DASC the term "Project Order" is used. In the Development Workflows for Data Scientists there are two phases: "Ask interesting question" and "Examine previous work". The same applies to the Toward Data Mining Engineering model, where the activities outlined to clarify the technical background fall under "Organizational processes" and "Project management processes". "Strategic groundwork" for the Big Data Managing Framework, "Analyze" for ASUM-DM, "Scope" for the Agile Delivery Framework and for AI Ops, "Plan" for Data Science Edge, "Understanding the Domain" for the Analytics Canvas are the names in the other process models. Systematic Research on Big Data is a special case where the generation of research objectives/hypotheses is not done at the beginning of the project, but rather after the data has been processed.

*Table 2. Overview of process stages (1/3)*

| | | KDD | CRISP-DM / RAMSYS | SEMMA | ASUM-DM | TDSP | Domino DS | DASC-PM |
|---|---|---|---|---|---|---|---|---|
| I | Learn application domain | Business Understanding | | Analyze | Business Understanding | Ideation | Project Order |
| II | Create target datasets | Data Understanding | Sample | Design | Data acquisition and understanding | Data Acquisition and Exploration | Data Provision |
| II | Data cleaning and preprocessing | Data Preparation | Explore | | | | |
| II | Data reduction and projection | | Modify | | | | |
| III | Choose DM function | Modeling | Model | Configure & Build | Modeling | Research & Development | Analysis |
| III | Choose DM algorithm | Evaluation | Assess | | | Validation | |
| III | Data Mining | | | | | | |
| III | Interpretation | | | | | | |
| IV | Use discovered knowledge | Deployment | | Deploy | Deployment | Delivery | Deployment |
| IV | | | | Operate & Optimize | Customer Acceptance | Monitoring | Utilization |

*Table 3. Overview of process stages (2/3)*

| | | DWDS | BDMF | BDIAI | BDMC | SRBD | ADF | DSE |
|---|---|---|---|---|---|---|---|---|
| I | Ask interesting questions | Strategic groundwork | Ideation | | | Scope | Plan |
| I | Examine previous work | | | | | | |
| II | Get data | Data Analytics | Implement-ation | Data Preparation | Information Extraction & Cleaning | Data acquisition | Collect |
| II | Explore the data | Implementation | | | Preliminary Data Analysis | | Curate |
| I | | | | | Research Goal / Hypothesis Generation | | |
| III | Model the data | | | Data analytics | Research Data Design | Analysis | Analyze |
| III | Test | | | | Model and Feature Selection | Model development | |
| III | Document the code | | | | Output Evaluation | Validation | |
| IV | Deploy to production | | | Data interaction | Visualization | Deployment | Act |
| IV | Communicate results | | | Data effectuation | | | |
| | | | | | Data intelligence | | | |

*Table 4. Overview of process stages (3/3)*

| | FMDS | AI Ops | DSW | EMC DALC | TDME | Analytics Canvas |
|---|---|---|---|---|---|---|
| I | Business Understanding | Scope | | | Organizational process | Understanding the Domain |
| I | Analytic approach | | | | Project management processes | |
| I | Data requirements | | | | | |
| II | Data collection | Understand | Data preparation | Data discovery | | Understanding the Data |
| II | Data understanding | | | Data preparation | | Data Acquisition, storage and Preparation |
| II | Data preparation | | | | | |
| III | Modeling | Build (Dev) | Analysis | Model planning | Development processes | Analysis and Implementation |
| III | Evaluation | | Reflection | Model building | | |
| IV | Deployment | Deploy and run (QA) | Dissemination of results | Communication of the results | | |
| IV | Feedback | Deploy, run and manage (Prod) | | Operationalization | Integral processes | |

With the exception of BDIAI, all the process models consider a specific phase for data operations. Basically, activities of data collection, data discovery, and data preparation/processing are depicted. While some process models such as TDSP combine these activities under a single stage ("Data acquisition and understanding"), others divide these tasks into several process steps (e.g. KDD with "Create target dataset", "Data Cleaning and preprocessing", and "Data reduction and projection"). SEMMA lists "Sample", "Explore", and "Modify" for this purpose. ADF assigns the data operations to the phases "Data acquisition" and "Analysis", while DSE does this with "Collect" and "Curate". FMDS describes data acquisition as "Data Collection" and exploration as "Data Understanding", just like CRISP-DM and RAMSYS. Similar to CRISP-DM, RAMSYS, BDMC, and DSW, FMDS declare a separate activity for wrangling the data as "Data preparation". DWDS integrates a simple "Get data" followed by "Explore the data". SRBD uses "Preliminary Data analysis", "Information extraction & Cleaning" and "Research Data Design" while the Analytics Canvas attaches "Understanding the Data" and "Data Acquisition, Storage and Preparation". Domino DS with "Data acquisition and exploration", AI Ops with "Understand", EMC DALC with "Data discovery", ASUM-DM with "Design", and DASC-PM with "Data Provision" each combine the above data-related activities under one phase. Exceptions are the BDMF, where these activities are part of the major step "Data analytics", and TDME, where the described tasks belong to the "Development Processes".

Subsequently, with the exception of BDIAI, the process models provide for the implementation of analysis procedures or the creation of models as well as a corresponding evaluation of the achieved results. KDD does this with "Choosing DM function", "Choosing DM algorithm", "Data Mining" and "Interpretation" for evaluation. CRISP-DM, RAMSYS, TDSP, and FMDS summarize the process steps as "Modeling". While TDSP also considers the evaluation underneath, CRISP-DM, RAMSYS, and FMDS use an extra step ("Evaluation"). SEMMA uses "Model" and "Assess", Domino DS "Research & Development" and "Validation", ADF "Model development" and "Validation", DSW "Analysis" and

"Reflection", DWDS "Model the data", "Test" and "Document the Code", SRBD "Model and Feature Selection" followed by "Output Evaluation", EMC DALC "Model planning" and "Model building", whereas in TDME the model activities fall under "Development Processes". In the remaining process models, these activities each come together under a single rough phase: ASUM-DM ("Configure & Build"), DASC-PM ("Analysis"), BDMC, DSE ("Analyze"), and AI Ops ("Build (dev)") are among them. In BDMF with "Data Analytics" and in the Analytics Canvas with "Analysis and Implementation", these analysis activities are each part of a coarser phase.

With the exception of SEMMA, all the process models considered include phases that deal with the provision of the analysis results. However, the way the provision is done varies between the models. While some prescribe the communication or use of the results in some form, e.g. KDD with "Use discovered knowledge", SRBD with "Visualization", DSE with "Act", and DSW with "Dissemination of results", some process models pronounce specific activities to integrate the product of the analysis procedures into the business operations in the most meaningful and effective way (including through training of the users). These concern CRISP-DM, RAMSYS, and the ADF with "Deploy", the DWDS with "Deploy to production" and "Communicate results", BDMF and BDIAI with "Implementation", BDMC with "Data interaction", "Data effectuation", and "Data intelligence", EMC DALC with "Communication of results" and "Operationalization" as well as the Analytics Canvas with "Analysis & Implementation". In TDME, these activities are located under "Integral processes". Some process models even go one step further and, in addition to commissioning, deal with specifications for support and monitoring in order to ensure the creation of value through the analysis artefact during operation. This applies to ASUM-DM with "Deploy, Operate & Optimize", TDSP with "Deployment" and "Customer Acceptance", Domino DS with "Delivery" and "Monitoring", DASC-PM with "Deployment" and "Utilization", FMDS with "Deployment" and "Feedback" as well as for AI Ops with "Deploy and run" (QA) and "Deploy, run, manage" (Prod).

## Functional Roles

Several of the frameworks presented state functional personnel roles. Role definitions should clarify the task contents and responsibilities in the respective process model to meet the requirement of team's cooperation. The roles are categorized thematically to understand what type of personnel appear relevant in a Data Science project.

For the area of the project management, the assignment in the procedure models is obvious. ASUM-DM, TDSP, DASC-PM, and EMC DALC provide for a "Project Manager", whereas TDSP additionally mentions a "Group Manager" and "Project Lead". The latter is responsible for coordinating daily tasks in TDSP. In Domino DS, the project management tasks are taken over by the so-called "Data Product Manager", whereby this role also exists in a similar form in the Agile Data Science Lifecycle ("Product Manager"). In RAMSYS, these activities are the responsibility of the "Management Committee", while the Analytics Canvas uses the "Analytics Architect". DASC-PM is the only reference model that still provides a separate position for "Compliance Support".

Data science projects require the involvement of the respective application domain and management. Depending on the process model, the degree of differentiation varies. The users are considered in the form of roles such as "Key System Users" (ASUM-DM), "Custodians" (ADSLC), "Business Units" (BDMF) or "Business Users" (AI Ops and EMC DALC). In some cases, "Subject Matter Experts" (ASUM-DM), "Operations Personnel" (BDIAI) or "Domain Experts" (DASC-PM and Analytics Canvas) are also included, who provide decisive domain-specific input for the solution to be developed. "Business

Stakeholders" (Domino DS) or "Business Decision Makers" (BDMF) can occupy a similar position. Certain process models also consider slightly more strategic roles such as "Business Development" (ADSLC), "Sales" (BDIAI), "Marketers" for the promotion of the solution (ADSLC) or "Strategists" (BDIAI). The management area is considered by ASUM-DM with "Business Sponsor", EMC DALC with "Project Sponsor", by Analytics Canvas with "Management", and by BDIAI even with "Senior Management" and "First/mid-level Management". Overall, the boundaries between management and domain within the roles in the process models are not very clear. As a conclusion, however, it can be said that representatives of the application domains should be included in the project team to contribute their technical expertise, as well as participants from management.

In the area of data, the DS process models contain a relatively broad field of personnel roles. ASUM-DM and EMC DALC are the only ones to provide for a "Database Admin". In RAMSYS, this responsibility is partly assigned to the "Data Master", who also takes care of data transformations. AI Ops has a similar role in the form of the "Data Steward", as this position deals with guidelines and access to the data. AI Ops integrates the "Data Provider" for data exploration and cataloguing and the "Data Consumer", among other things to ensure data understanding. In addition, DASC- PM, DWDS, EMC DALC, and AI Ops plan to have a "Data Engineer" who is responsible for designing the tools and infrastructure that the "Data Scientist", which is introduced later, and the operation of the analysis artifacts need. In the Domino DS Lifecycle, this role is called, slightly modified, "Data Infrastructure Engineer". BDMF summarizes the activities of the data operations under "Data Modelers", while ASUM-DM and BDIAI also provide for a "Data Analyst", who is responsible for the qualitative preparation of the data.

For model creation and evaluation, all considered process models provide for the role of the "Data Miner" or "Data Scientist", except RAMSYS ("Modelers"), which covers the analysis of data, but the complete data science process. A detailed definition could be derived from the National Institute of Standards and Technology (NIST Big Data Public Working Group, 2019). Other roles mentioned are "ML Engineer" (DWDS), who takes care of performance and scaling of the models, "Data Storyteller" (Domino DS), who creates visually appealing narratives for the analytical solutions, "AI Operations" from AI Ops, the "BI Analyst" from the EMC DALC, and the "Researchers" from the ADSLC, who assist the "Data Scientists" with more sophisticated problems (e.g., introducing new methods of statistics or machine learning). The BDMF plans to have experts in the field of cognitive science or customer behavior who can interpret trends in the data and derive insights and knowledge.

Finally, there are the roles of the technical or IT department. Although these are relatively heterogeneous between the DS process models, one can conclude from the literature review that their importance is particularly evident in the deployment and subsequent operation of the solution. ASUM-DM provides for a wide range of administrative positions: "Application Administrator", "Network Admin", "Security Administrator", "Support Manager", and "Tool Admin". DASC-PM has a separate role for support ("Technical Support"). Many of the roles relate specifically to the commissioning of the analysis artifacts, since, unlike in the early DS project phases, the classic IT area is more involved. Consequently, positions such as "Enterprise Architect" (ASUM-DM and BDIAI), "Solution Architect" (TDSP), and "Software Engineer"(AI Ops) show increased engineering characteristics, as the project approaches more closely an IT development project during deployment. ADSLC makes the broadest role distinction at this point: "Web Developers", "Engineers", "Platform Engineers", "DevOps Engineers", "User Experience Designers", and "Interaction Designers". The BDMF and Analytics Canvas only name "IT experts".

TDSP ("Individual Contributors") and BDIAI ("Relevant Innovators") still contain roles that cannot be clearly classified along the selected thematic categories or could occur in each of these areas.

## Artefacts and Documents

An expected output of individual phases or activities, for example in the form of a document or artefact, are only clarified in some process models. Especially in project monitoring, the documents allow a concrete overview and assessment of the project progress and success. Furthermore, the result could be typified in advance. The following illustrates which of the process models contain such templates and what they are used for. Overall, it must be noted that only a minority of the examined DS process models explicitly identify such documents, which can help with traceability, collaboration, and coordination (Crowston et al., 2019).

In summary, CRISP-DM, ASUM-DM, and Microsoft TDSP have the broadest portfolio of such templates. The business background is the most strongly represented. Domino DS requires the creation of a pre-flight "Project Checklist", CRISP-DM expects the description of the business context in the "Background", and ASUM-DM requires the creation of a "Project Success Plan", which contains various elements of project management. TDSP establishes the so-called "Charter Document", a dynamic template that centrally contains, among other things, new findings and the changing requirements to promote transparency and communication (I. Martinez et al., 2021). The "Information Vault" from RAMSYS reflects it in a similar direction. CRISP-DM and ASUM-DM recommend a document called "Business Objectives and Success Criteria" for recording business objectives and corresponding explanations, BDIAI calls this "Objectives Decision" and "Challenges Identification". CRISP-DM ("Data Mining Goals" and "Success Criteria") and ASUM-DM ("Data Mining Goals") provide a similar concept for the technical goals. For the preparation of the DS project, there is a situation assessment integrated in which, according to CRISP-DM and ASUM-DM, existing resources and requirements are to be catalogued in the "Inventory of resources" and under "Requirements, assumptions, and constraints" (BDIAI: "Key Resources Identification"). CRISP-DM promotes the documentation of risks ("Risks and Contingencies") and the creation of a glossary ("Terminology", ASUM-DM: "Glossary of Terminology"). Furthermore, the comparison of costs and benefits is required as an artefact: CRISP-DM with "Costs and Benefits", ASUM-DM with "Project Financial Plan", and ASUM-DM as well as BDIAI with "Cost/Benefits Analysis". The project, milestone and task planning for CRISP-DM and ASUM-DM is recorded in the so-called "Project Plan", while the BDMF introduces the "Project Roadmap" for this purpose. Finally, ASUM-DM summarizes all findings from the analysis of the business background in the "Business Understanding Report", while CRISP-DM already provides for the creation of an "Initial Assessment of Tools and Techniques" based on the project goals.

CRISP-DM is the most broadly based in the area of data. An initial "Data Collection Report", "Data Description Report", "Data Exploration Report", "Data Quality Report", and a "Dataset Description Report" are to be prepared along the acquisition, exploration, and preparation stages. ASUM-DM summarizes the documentation activities related to these tasks in the "Data Understanding Report" and the "Data Preparation Report". TDSP provides templates for the documentation of data sources, data dictionaries and for the data quality report. The "Solution Architecture" is used to describe the data pipeline that is used to perform evaluations or predictions for new data after a model has been created.

In preparation for model creation, CRISP-DM recommends writing down modelling assumptions, while ASUM-DM leads to document the process of algorithm selection in "Modeling Techniques Selection". Furthermore, a "Test Design" (ASUM-DM and CRISP-DM) must be specified beforehand, which provides information about the process of model evaluation. RAMSYS includes a so-called "Hypothesis Investment Account", which makes it possible to establish and document theses that can be investigated within the analysis procedures. To meet the ideas of traceability and reproducibility in the modelling experiments, the following documents are intended in the reference models: "Model Description" (CRISP-DM), "Model Build" (ASUM-DM), and "Technical Documentation" as well as "Model Documentation" (DASC-PM). For the technical quality evaluation of the models, CRISP-DM and ASUM-DM install a document called "Model Assessment". Another evaluation step in this context is the assessment in relation to the business objectives. In CRISP-DM this artefact is called "Assessment of data mining results with respect to business success criteria", ASUM-DM uses the name "Model Evaluation", and DASC-PM assesses the usefulness of the analysis artefact in the "Evaluation Report". Before proceeding with deployment in CRISP-DM, a critical "Review of Process" and a "List of Possible Actions" must be prepared. If, at this point in the application of the TDSP, the review point decision has been made in favor of continuing, a final "Modelling Report" must be prepared.

The process models also specify several documents for provision and use. CRISP-DM pronounce the "Deployment Plan", ASUM-DM the "Roll-out Plan", TDSP the "Final Solution Architecture" document, which represents a revision of the "Solution Architecture", and BDIAI contains an impact assessment in the form of a "Transformation Assessment" and the "Implementation Roadmap". In order to ensure smooth deployment and safe operation, CRISP-DM provides for a "Monitoring and Maintenance Plan". For this intention, ASUM-DM denotes "Test Plans" and a "Launch Communication Plan", which is addressed to end users, supporters, and other relevant parties. DASC-PM specifies that "Bug reports" are created for errors that arise during use. A final report usually forms the end of the project, summarizing all the work done (CRISP-DM and ASUM-DM: "Final Report", TDSP: "Exit Report").

Comprehensive documentation is prejudged as a burden, whereas it supports team coordination (Crowston et al., 2019) and contributes to problems being tardily identified (Domino Data Lab, 2017). Consequently, Domino DS recommends the creation and establishment of templates for project deliverables (Domino Data Lab, 2017). For this reason, such templates form a crucial part of the DS. DASC-PM only provides a few documentation templates but refers to a detailed checklist of activities to be completed for each important task in the DS process.

## COMMON DATA SCIENCE METHODOLOGY

Following the analysis, it can be stated that there are typical phases of conduct, typical functional roles, and typical documentation artifacts in data science frameworks. The claim to develop a new model from those mentioned here should not be given, insofar as there are no concrete gaps. The common features are clearly evident, both in the approaches of the individual process models and in the artifacts. Most of the frameworks start with an **ideation phase** (I) in which the goals of the project are established from a domain perspective. In a subsequent **data phase** (II), data related to the task are collected, explored, prepared and pre-analysed. This preliminary assessment of the data is necessary so that the best possible modelling and analysis can be conducted in the **analysis phase** (III). The appropriate use and provision of the results are to be determined in a **deployment phase** (IV). Nevertheless, it is considered to jump back between phases to adjust objectives, data and models to improve the results. This classification is intended to provide additional orientation. A concrete selection of a framework for the implementation of a DS project is not mandatory. Instead, a prior consideration of the overall processes represented as well as the supporting artifacts is recommended (see Figure 1).

*Figure 1. An overview of the data science phases*

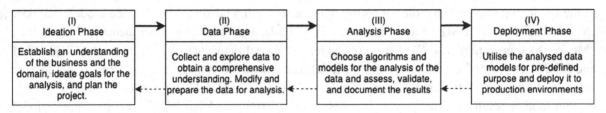

In order to further explain the common data science methodology, a simple exemplary application in an artificial DS project should be outlined. Assuming a financial company is facing fraudulent transactions. The manual tracking of potential suspicious cases is time-consuming and inefficient. Undetected frauds cause severe damage for affected customers and in turn, negatively influence the firm's image, churn and revenue. Accordingly, the company aims to develop an automated fraud detection system using artificial intelligence. The ideation phase (I) of the DS project would be concerned with defining high-level project goals such as reducing customer churn and claims for compensation as a result of a fraudulent transaction. From this point, a further project structure can be set. The data phase (II) involves the collection and exploration of the transaction data to gain an understanding for potential features that are relevant for identifying fraudulent operations. Afterwards, the data would be prepared for the next stage (e. g. through enhancing data quality). In the analysis phase (III), different analysis procedures such as decision tree or logistic regression are experimented to achieve the targeted accuracy in correctly classifying a transaction (fraud or non-fraud) on the test data. If successful, the transition to the deployment phase (IV) is undertaken to provision the fraud detection system into production. This will require preparational activities such as software tests or training of the users.

## FUTURE RESEARCH DIRECTIONS

A major challenge in the field of data science is the growing demand for human resources for the implementation of data science projects. Since it is highly improbable that the demand can be met by appropriately skilled and trained professionals, a more profound description of activities and processes is required (Saltz, 2015; Saltz et al., 2018; Saltz & Hotz, 2018). Thus, qualification offers can be created for the further training of non-specialized users in the application domains. In the literature, the term "Citizen Data Scientist" has already been established, which describes users without prior knowledge of statistics or information technology who have been trained in data science through supporting application software (Martinez, 2017).

The detailed process description of data science further enables the development of automation of data science activities. However, this is accompanied by additional challenges, such as the selection of technologies for processing large amounts of data (e.g., big data) or the consideration of legal-regulatory conditions (e.g., data privacy, ethical decision making).

This chapter showed that there are many reasons for a data science team to employ a process model. Nevertheless, most teams seem to use ad hoc techniques to manage their DS projects instead (Saltz et al., 2018). It might due to the fact that the explorative nature of DS and therefore, its teams contradict the idea of possibly being restricted by a methodology that guides the entire process (Saltz & Hotz, 2021). Moreover, another literature analysis of DS process models outlined that most of them cannot be regarded as "complete" or "integral" (Martinez et al., 2021). Thus, these methodologies display several weaknesses in the areas of project management, team management as well as data and information management, likely preventing practitioners from adopting such models. Accordingly, further research endeavors are necessary to mitigate these weak points by either overhauling the existing process models or developing new ones. Ultimately, the trend of more remote work and complex undertakings with a larger team inevitable demand the application of a DS methodology to aid the DS project process (Saltz & Hotz, 2021).

The implementation of, if necessary, automated data science processes requires an exact, formalized specification of the problem or objective of a project. This challenge is a prerequisite for organizational knowledge management and automated decision making.

## CONCLUSION

An overview of common process models for the implementation of DS is presented in this chapter. Since the development of KDD and CRISP-DM, the central ideas have been examined from broader perspectives and further frameworks have been created. In addition to the core activities that are conducted in the individual process phases, typical roles and project-supporting artifacts are outlined. In summary, a distinction can be made between four process phases that relate to ideation, data, analysis, and deployment. These phases are considered as a holistic methodology of Data Science. The overview is an orientation for data scientists and project managers in the preparation and realization of DS projects. However, many challenges need to be overcome to further specify and specialize the processes, which may also lead to new approaches to DS methodology in the future.

## REFERENCES

Byrne, C. (2017). *Development workflows for data scientists*. O'Reilly Media.

Cao, L. (2017). Data science: Challenges and directions. *Communications of the ACM, 60*(8), 59–68. Advance online publication. doi:10.1145/3015456

Chapman, P., Clinton, J., Kerber, R., Khabaza, T., Reinartz, T., Shearer, C., & Wirth, R. (2000). *CRISP-DM 1.0: Step-by-step data mining guide*. SPSS.

Corporation, I. B. M. (2015). *Analytics solutions unified method*. ftp://ftp.software.ibm.com/software/data/sw-library/services/ASUM.pdf

Crowston, K., Saltz, J., Rezgui, A., Hedge, Y., & You, S. (2019). Socio-technical affordances for stigmergic coordination implemented in MIDST. *Proceedings of the ACM on Human-Computer Interaction, 3*(CSCW), 1–25. doi:10.1145/3359219

Das, M., Cui, R., Campbell, D. R., Agrawal, G., & Ramnath, R. (2015). Towards methods for systematic research on big data. *2015 IEEE International Conference on Big Data*, 2072–2081. 10.1109/BigData.2015.7363989

de Mauro, A., Greco, M., & Grimaldi, M. (2016). A formal definition of big data based on its essential features. *Library Review, 65*(3), 122–135. doi:10.1108/LR-06-2015-0061

Dietrich, D. & EMC. (2016). *Data analytics lifecycle processes* (Patent No. 9,262,493). EMC.

Domino Data Lab. (2017). *Managing data science projects.* https://www.dominodatalab.com/resources/field-guide/managing-data-science-projects/

Dutta, D., & Bose, I. (2015). Managing a big data project: The case of Ramco Cements Limited. *International Journal of Production Economics, 165,* 293–306. doi:10.1016/j.ijpe.2014.12.032

Fayyad, U., Piatetsky-Shapiro, G., & Smyth, P. (1996a). Knowledge discovery and data mining: Towards a unifying framework. *KDD-96 Proceedings,* 82–88.

Fayyad, U., Piatetsky-Shapiro, G., & Smyth, P. (1996b). The KDD process for extracting useful knowledge from volumes of data. *Communications of the ACM, 39*(11), 27–34. doi:10.1145/240455.240464

Grady, N. W. (2016). KDD meets big data. *2016 IEEE International Conference on Big Data (Big Data),* 1603–1608. 10.1109/BigData.2016.7840770

Grady, N. W., Payne, J. A., & Parker, H. (2017). Agile big data analytics: AnalyticsOps for data science. *2017 IEEE International Conference on Big Data (Big Data),* 2331–2339. 10.1109/BigData.2017.8258187

Guo, P. J. (2012). *Software tools to facilitate research programming.* ProQuest Dissertations Publishing.

Helm, J. M., Swiergosz, A. M., Haeberle, H. S., Karnuta, J. M., Schaffer, J. L., Krebs, V. E., Spitzer, A. I., & Ramkumar, P. N. (2020). Machine learning and artificial intelligence: Definitions, applications, and future directions. *Current Reviews in Musculoskeletal Medicine, 13*(1), 69–76. doi:10.100712178-020-09600-8 PMID:31983042

Ho, T. B., Kawasaki, S., & Granat, J. (2007). Knowledge acquisition by machine learning and aata mining. In A. Wierzbicki & Y. Nakamori (Eds.), *Creative Environments* (pp. 69–91). Springer., doi:10.1007/978-3-540-71562-7_4

Jurney, R. (2017). *Agile data science 2.0: Building full-stack data analytics applications with Spark.* O'Reilly Media.

Kaufmann, M. (2019). Big data management canvas: A reference model for value creation from data. *Big Data Cogn. Comput., 3*(1), 19. Advance online publication. doi:10.3390/bdcc3010019

Kelly, J., & Kaskade, J. (2013). CIOs & big data: What your IT team wants you to know. *Infochimps, 3.*

Kühn, A., Joppen, R., Reinhart, F., Röltgen, D., von Enzberg, S., & Dumitrescu, R. (2018). Analytics canvas – A framework for the design and specification of data analytics projects. *Procedia CIRP, 70,* 162–167. doi:10.1016/j.procir.2018.02.031

Larson, D., & Chang, V. (2016). A review and future direction of agile, business intelligence, analytics and data science. *International Journal of Information Management, 36*(5), 700–710. doi:10.1016/j.ijinfomgt.2016.04.013

Marbán, O., Segovia, J., Menasalvas, E., & Fernández-Baizán, C. (2009). Toward data mining engineering: A software engineering approach. *Information Systems, 34*(1), 87–107. doi:10.1016/j.is.2008.04.003

Martinez, I., Viles, E., & Olaizola, I. G. (2021). Data science methodologies: Current challenges and future approaches. *Big Data Research, 24.* Advance online publication. doi:10.1016/j.bdr.2020.100183

Martinez, L. S. (2017). Data science. In *Encyclopedia of Big Data* (pp. 60–61). Springer., doi:10.1007/978-3-319-32001-4_60-1

Microsoft. (2020). *What is the team data science process?* https://docs.microsoft.com/en-us/azure/machine-learning/team-data-science-process/overview

Moyle, S., & Jorge, A. (2001). RAMSYS - A methodology for supporting rapid remote collaborative data mining projects. *ECML/PKDD01 Workshop: Integrating Aspects of Data Mining, Decision Support and Meta-Learning (IDDM-2001), 64.*

NIST Big Data Public Working Group. (2019). *NIST big data interoperability framework* (Vol. 1). Definitions., doi:10.6028/NIST.SP.1500-1r2

Pohl, M., Bosse, S., & Turowski, K. (2018). A data-science-as-a-service-model. In *Proceedings of the 8th International Conference on Cloud Computing and Services Science*. CLOSER. 10.5220/0006703104320439

Provost, F., & Fawcett, T. (2013). Data science and its relationship to big data and data-driven decision making. *Big Data, 1*(1), 51–59. doi:10.1089/big.2013.1508 PMID:27447038

Rich, E. (1983). *Artificial Intelligence*. McGraw-Hill.

Rollins, J. (2015). *Foundational methodology for data science*. https://tdwi.org/~/media/64511A895D86457E964174EDC5C4C7B1.PDF

Saltz, J. (2015). The need for new processes, methodologies and tools to support big data teams and improve big data project effectiveness. *IEEE International Conference on Big Data 2015*, 2066–2071. 10.1109/BigData.2015.7363988

Saltz, J., & Hotz, N. (2018). *Shortcomings of ad hoc—Data science project management*. https://www.datascience-pm.com/ad-hoc/

Saltz, J., & Hotz, N. (2021). Factors that influence the selection of a data science process management methodology: An exploratory study. *Proceedings of the 54th Hawaii International Conference on System Sciences*, 949–959. 10.24251/HICSS.2021.116

Saltz, J., Hotz, N., Wild, D., & Stirling, K. (2018). Exploring project management methodologies used within data science teams. *Americas Conference on Information Systems 2018: Digital Disruption, AMCIS 2018*.

Saltz, J., & Shamshurin, I. (2015). Exploring the process of doing data science via an ethnographic study of a media advertising company. *2015 IEEE International Conference on Big Data (Big Data)*. 10.1109/BigData.2015.7363992

Saltz, J., Shamshurin, I., & Crowston, K. (2017). Comparing data science project management methodologies via a controlled experiment. *Proceedings of the 50th Hawaii International Conference on System Sciences*. 10.24251/HICSS.2017.120

SAS. (2017). *Introduction to SEMMA*. SAS. https://documentation.sas.com/?docsetId=emref&docsetTarget=n061bzurmej4j3n1jnj8bbjjm1a2.htm&docsetVersion=14.3&locale=en

Schulz, M., Neuhaus, U., Kaufmann, J., Badura, D., Kuehnel, S., Badewitz, W., Dann, D., Kloker, S., Alekozai, E. M., & Lanquillon, C. (2020). Introducing DASC-PM: A data science process model. *Australasian Conference on Information Systems 2020*.

Shearer, C. (2000). The CRISP-DM model: The new blueprint for data mining. *Journal of Data Warehousing, 5*(4), 13–22.

Thomas, J. (2019). *Operationalizing AI - Managing the end-to-end lifecycle of AI*. Insige Machine Learning. https://medium.com/inside-machine-learning/ai-ops-managing-the-end-to-end-lifecycle-of-ai-3606a59591b0

Vanauer, M., Böhle, C., & Hellingrath, B. (2015). Guiding the introduction of big data in organizations: A methodology with business- and data-driven ideation and enterprise architecture management-based implementation. *48th Hawaii International Conference on System Sciences*, 908–917. 10.1109/HICSS.2015.113

VentureBeat. (2019). *Why do 87% of data science projects never make it into production?* https://venturebeat.com/2019/07/19/why-do-87-of-data-science-projects-never-make-it-into-production/

## KEY TERMS AND DEFINITIONS

**Artificial Intelligence:** Machines are to be empowered by various algorithms to be able to take over activities that recently only humans have been able to perform accurately, and thus advance to an artificial intelligence.

**Big Data:** The challenge of Big Data was initially posed by the aspects of increasing data volumes, data that needs to be rapidly handled and the increasing complexity of data structures in data processing.

**Data Mining:** Data mining is the key process step of analyzing the data to gain insights that can then be used to achieve the defined goals. The application of algorithms and statistical models is part of data mining.

**Data Science:** Data science is the higher-level process of developing an analytical objective, providing, and preparing data, conducting the analysis and utilization, or disseminating the results.

**Data Science Methodology:** The methodical approach in which data science processes should be carried out in order to achieve a defined goal in a structured way are called Data Science Methodology.

**Data Scientist:** The personnel role that carries out the functional tasks of a Data Science process is generally also called Data Scientist. Furthermore, core competencies in statistics, computer science and the application domain should be covered by the role.

**Machine Learning:** One of the concepts for obtaining artificial intelligence is machine learning. A machine should be enabled to independently gain and process knowledge through algorithms and statistical models.

# Machine Learning Experiment Management With MLFlow

M

**Caner Erden**

ⓘ https://orcid.org/0000-0002-7311-862X

*Department of International Trade and Finance, Faculty of Applied Science, AI Research and Application Center, Sakarya University of Applied Sciences, Turkey*

## INTRODUCTION

Machine learning applications are a branch of science that has proven itself and its value both academically and in the business world. These areas include customer relationship management (Mizgier et al., 2018), credit card fraud detection (Maniraj et al., 2019; Thennakoon et al., 2019), insurance and banking (Doss, 2020; Paul et al., 2021), earthquake forecasting applications (Beroza et al., 2021; Johnson et al., 2021; Jordan & Jones, 2010), logistics and supply chain management (Hazen et al., 2014; Treiblmaier & Mair, 2021; Waller & Fawcett, 2013) or to model, forecast the trend of the pandemics (Alamo et al., 2020; Ray et al., 2020). Thanks to deep learning methods, high-level machine learning applications such as image & video processing and speech recognition have become possible. In deep learning applications, more parameters such as the number of neural network layers, regularization method, training parameters are used compared to classical machine learning applications. Models with different parameter values will have different performance metrics such as classification (accuracy, precision, recall, F1-score) and regression (mean squared error, mean absolute error). ML researcher's experience is essential for tuning the parameters, as well as many trial-and-error processes. Most of the time, the automatically adjusted parameters will work worse than the parameters tuned by machine learning experts. Again, the very first machine learning trial is tried with the default parameters. This stage is just the beginning phase and does not make sense in terms of performance metrics. A better option is needed by trying different parameter combinations instead of the default parameters. In other words, the processes of training a data set and establishing a model can be seen from a general point of view of machine learning studies. In short, the data enters the model, and the result of classification or clustering is revealed by the model. So, the process can be shown in a simple way as in Figure 1. As a result of a detailed examination of the ML, the complex structures of machine learning applications will be revealed.

One of the most important goals of machine learning studies is to optimize specified performance metrics. Performance metrics vary depending on whether the problem is a classification, clustering, or regression problem. Some metrics can be given as; confusion matrix, precision, ROC-AUC curves, accuracy score for classification, mean squared error (MSE), mean absolute error (MAE), $R^2$ score for regression analysis. Machine learning engineers work for the model to achieve the best learning (best performance metric). After the pre-preprocessing phase, the available data are divided into training and test sets. In the pre-processing data stage, statistical analyzes are made about the data, dirty data is cleaned, and feature selection is made. Learning is performed on the training set, and the test set shows how generalizable the learning can be. One of the challenges encountered at this stage is underfitting or overfitting. For learning to be accepted, such difficulties must be overcome by cross-validation, adding more relevant data, working with more feasible features, and regularization. These types of situations

DOI: 10.4018/978-1-7998-9220-5.ch071

are complex parts of machine learning. The complexity in learning is explained in terms of bias and variance. Bias shows how well the algorithm fits the data. On the other hand, variance measures the consistency in the algorithm's performance in different data sets. The relevance between overfitting and underfitting and bias and variance is shown in Figure 2.

*Figure 1. Machine Learning as a Black Box*

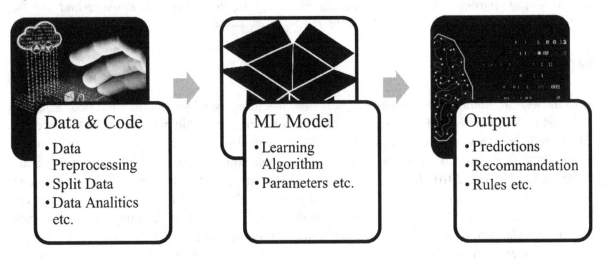

*Figure 2. Overfitting and underfitting with low and high biases*

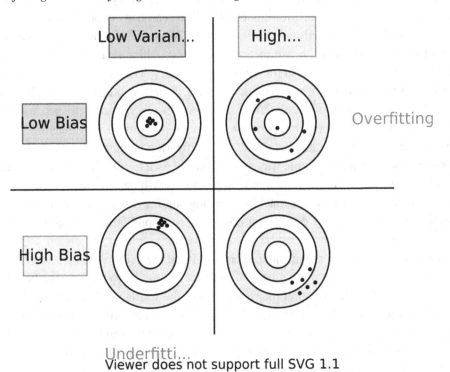

There are different parameters for all machine learning algorithms developed in the literature. The performance will change with the change of algorithm parameters. In machine learning, hyperparameters express parameters that directly affect the algorithm's performance. For example, hyperparameters are used for maximum depth, the minimum number of sample leaves, or branching criteria used in decision trees. Alternatively, the number of layers and activation functions in artificial neural networks are examples of hyperparameters. Deep learning and big data studies work with more parameters than traditional machine learning studies. Big data can be defined as over one terabyte with volume, variety, and velocity (3v) capability (De Mauro et al., 2016).

For this reason, studies of choosing between parameters and determining the best combination of parameters have led to hyperparameter optimization (HPO) studies. The performance evaluation process in machine learning can be given as in Figure 3. The HPO study aims to achieve the best combination of hyper-parameters. Therefore, algorithms in the literature that give precise or approximate results can also be used for HPO. Grid search and random search can be given as examples of successful optimization techniques in HPO (Bergstra & Bengio, 2012). In the case of a high number of hyperparameters, approximation solution algorithms should be used. Among the algorithms that give approximate results, such as genetic and ant colony algorithms, particle swarm optimization algorithms can be used in this sense.

*Figure 3. Hyperparameter optimization and model training*

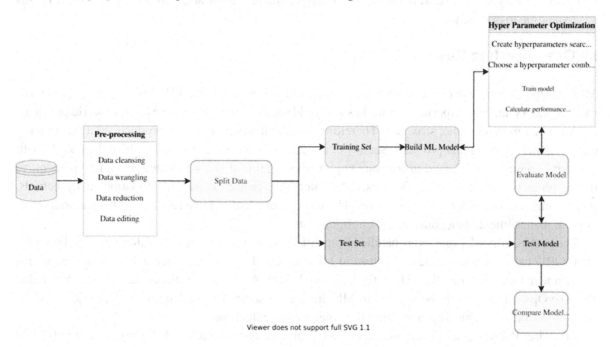

The mentioned topics are among the current topics of machine learning. New perspectives are needed to solve complex ML processes such as version control systems, tuning parameters, model development, and reproducibility. DevOps (develop + operations) strategies, a method used in software development, can be applied to solve it. DevOps studies unify the development, testing, and operations stages. DevOps' principles include providing automation at these stages, making continuous improvements, and running feedback mechanisms. Considering all these explanations, we can say that in the future, the topics mentioned in the field of machine learning can come to the fore much more. In this section, data workflow, automated data management, ML pipelines, hyperparameter optimization tools, which are the most important and complex tasks of machine learning applications, will be discussed. At the same time, the most preferred ML tools will be examined, and comparative analysis will be presented in the section. We can summarize the topics to be mentioned in other sections as follows: Second section will give more detailed information about DevOps and the MLOps concepts. The third section will explain how to save the models developed with the MLFlow application and compare the models. A data set will be trained with different parameters in the application, and then the results will be shown comparably.

## BACKGROUND

Machine learning applications consist of numerous trials and mistakes called "experiments." Each experiment may have different parameters, metrics, or outputs. Saving and comparing inputs and outputs in experiments are evaluated in MLOps(machine learning operations), i.e., machine learning processes. MLOps consists mainly of 3 stages such as (i) continuous integration, (ii) continuous delivery, and (iii) continuous training for ML models(*MLOps*, 2021). Automated machine learning (AutoML) methods can eliminate the complexities contained in the details. Thus, the necessary attention and care for performance comparisons can be demonstrated thanks to AutoML. If MLOps studies are not automated, an Excel file may be created to track the experiments, and all inputs and outputs can be saved. In this case, the time losses are too much.

### MLOps Literature Review

MLOps studies can be divided into scientific and production. Scientific MLOps studies focus on ML models' theory and how experimental studies will yield successful results. However, real-world problems have a much more complex structure. Therefore, ML applications may not produce solutions quickly and accurately. Noting this problem, Sculley et al. (2015) explained these problems in their study with the term "technical debt" used in software engineering. In this study, it is stated that a tiny percentage of ML projects consist of codes. Besides, data collection, feature extraction, validation, analysis tools, monitoring, and tracking take much longer. Therefore, these costs can be seen as hidden and long-term costs in management, data consistency, configuration.

The problems in ML projects are handled from different perspectives. In one of these studies, Polyzotis et al. (2017) also mentioned the difficulties in ML projects. This study collected data-related problems under understanding, validation, cleaning, and enrichment. As a result of these studies, it is concluded that DevOps stages need to be applied in ML projects to solve the challenges in ML projects. Thus, easy-to-follow, verifiable, reproducible ML projects can be deployed.

Likewise, Paleyes et al. (2021) mentioned the problems encountered in ML projects and published a survey on this subject. In the study, publications where ML projects were developed, and compilation studies were included. As a result of the study, "Cross-cutting aspects" were included in the section that drew particular attention. These are examined under the headings of ethical, end users' trust, and security. A similar study was conducted by Schelter et al., (2018) in which it is stated that problems in maintenance, deployment, monitoring, organization, and documentation of ML projects will cause poor performance. On the other hand, Bradley, (2019) has mentioned chiefly the capabilities that data scientists need to have to solve problems in ML projects.

When the literature review related to MLOps is carried out, it will be seen that there are many book studies. Table 1 summarizes the book studies in the MLOps field.

*Table 1. Book studies on MLOps*

| Reference | Note |
|---|---|
| **(Alla, 2020)** | The book explains how to improve ML projects using the MLFlow library. There is also a focus on practices with AWS Sage Maker, Google Cloud, and Microsoft Azure. |
| **(Anoshin et al., 2020)** | Key concepts related to the Snowflake tool are explained. Cloud technologies have been mentioned to establish bridges between business intelligence (BI) and data. |
| **(Burkov, 2020)** | Machine learning engineering concepts are introduced to solve complex problems in the real world. Moreover, the book is enriched with applications. |
| **(Dubovikov et al., 2019)** | Problem solutions are shown in a hands-on way in data science. It has been demonstrated how ML projects can be improved with DevOps. |
| **(Grant et al., 2020)** | MLOps operations using Kubeflow are shown in a hands-on way. |
| **(Hutter et al., 2019)** | There is a focus on the concept of automated machine learning (AutoML). How to provide complete automation in ML Projects is explained. |
| **(Kakarla et al., 2021)** | One of the essential questions in data science studies is complex and messy data. At the same time, the answer to how data science can be applied in a scalable and parallel processing way is given. The answers to these questions are presented with the practice of PySpark. |
| **(Zheng & Safari, 2015)** | The difficulties encountered for the evaluation of ML models were noted. Evaluation metrics, hyperparameter optimization, A/B testing are focused. |

## MLOps Tools

After ML, MLOps, and DevOps definitions are given, the tools used for those technologies can be listed. ML researchers create their working environments and often try not to change their work environment. Because the standard order is always accessible, innovation or change can be considered time-consuming. ML researchers generally try to improve the model after installing traditional machine learning models. For this purpose, researchers develop different Python libraries such as Scikit-Learn for conventional machine learning methods (Pedregosa et al., 2011), or mlr3(Lang et al., 2019, p. 3), a library in R programming language, or models with a packaged program such as MATLAB, WEKA. Alternatively, they choose between Tensorflow(TensorFlow Developers, 2021), PyTorch(Paszke et al., 2019) for deep learning applications. Although the tools offer critical automation, developing applications only requires many manual interventions. The process of installing the model, determining the parameters, and driving the model into production using the product can be automated. Some big companies also develop their MLOps-related tools such as Spotify's Luigi (*Spotify/Luigi*, 2012/2021), Microsoft's AutoML-azure (*Microsoft Azure*, 2021), Uber's Michelangelo (*Meet Michelangelo*, 2021), Facebook's FBLearner ('Introducing FBLearner Flow', 2016), Amazon's AutoGluon (Erickson et al., 2020). Some of the other tools for MLOps can be given as follows: Kuberfllow(*Kubeflow/Kubeflow*, 2017/2021), Weights and Biases (Biewald, 2020), Sacred (Greff et al., 2017), Neptune (neptune.ai, 2020), Comet (*Comet*, 2021), Sage Maker(Liberty et al., 2020), lazypredict (Pandala, 2019/2021), auto-Scikit-Learn (Feurer et al., 2015) and MLFlow (*MLflow*, 2018/2021) which has been chosen for the practices.

A detailed review is given at https://ploomber.io/posts/survey/ in which MLOps tools are compared. In this review, the tools are examined in terms of "Ease of use, Development experience, Debugging,

Testing, Deployment, Programming languages, Maintainability, Jupyter notebooks support." According to the specified criteria, all alternatives are given scores(1-Supported with some limitation, 2- Good, 3- Excellent, NA-Unsupported)—the average scores and performance feature points are shown in Table 2-Table 4.

*Table 2. Tools for MLOps and their average points*

| Tool Reference | Basic Usage | Points |
|---|---|---|
| *(Ploomber/Ploomber, 2020/2021)* | A tool for building data pipelines. | 2.625 |
| *(PrefectHQ/Prefect, 2018/2021)* | Data workflow and management system | 1.625 |
| *(Metaflow, 2019/2021)* | ML deployment tool | 1.375 |
| *(Apache Airflow, 2015/2021)* | Execute ML tasks on cloud platforms: Google Cloud Platform, Amazon Web Services, Microsoft Azure and many other | 1.25 |
| *(Dagster, 2018/2021)* | Data Science Productivity Tool | 1.25 |
| *(Elyra, 2019/2021)* | Data Workflow Extension for a JupyterLab Notebook | 1.25 |
| *(Quantumblacklabs/Kedro, 2019/2021)* | Data, analytics, and design tool | 1.25 |
| *(Spotify/Luigi, 2012/2021)* | Building complex pipelines | 1.25 |
| *(Iterative/Dvc, 2017/2021)* | Data Version Control | 1.125 |
| *(Kubeflow-Kale/Kale, 2019/2021)* | Automated pipelines Engine for Data Scientists | 1 |
| **(TFX)** *(TFX, 2019/2021)* | Google-production-scale machine learning platform | 1 |
| *(Flyte, 2019/2021)* | Automation for data and ML processes at scale | 0.75 |
| *(Kubeflow/Kubeflow, 2017/2021)* | Easy, portable, and scalable ML Toolkit | 0.5 |

*Table 3. General repository information of tools*

| Repository | Date Created | Days Since Created | Primary Language | Last Push at (ago) | Watchers |
|---|---|---|---|---|---|
| kedro-org/kedro | Apr 18 2019 | 875 | Python | 2 hours | 98 |
| kubeflow/kubeflow | 30 Nov 2017 | 1379 | Jsonnet | 8 hours | 384 |
| spotify/luigi | 20 Sep 2012 | 3276 | Python | 14 hours | 495 |
| Netflix/metaflow | 17 Sep 2019 | 723 | Python | 10 minutes | 223 |
| ploomber/ploomber | 20 Jan 2020 | 598 | Python | 17 hours | 12 |
| PrefectHQ/prefect | 30 Jun 2018 | 1167 | Python | 3 hours | 141 |
| tensorflow/tfx | 04 Feb 2019 | 938 | Python | 37 minutes | 96 |
| elyra-ai/elyra | 23 Oct 2019 | 688 | Python | 12 minutes | 39 |
| flyteorg/flyte | 21 Oct 2019 | 689 | Python | 2 hours | 274 |
| kubeflow-kale/kale | 24 Jan 2019 | 959 | Python | 2 days | 16 |
| apache/airflow | 13 Apr 2015 | 2341 | Python | 11 minutes | 742 |
| dagster-io/dagster | 30 Apr 2018 | 1228 | Python | a minute | 73 |
| iterative/dvc | 04 Marc 2017 | 1650 | Python | 3 hours | 125 |
| mlflow/mlflow | 05 Jun 2018 | 1192 | Python | 26 minutes | 264 |

*Table 4. Number of forks and stars of tools by 9 September 2021*

| Repository | Number of Forks | Number of Stars |
|---|---|---|
| apache/airflow | 8837 | 23040 |
| spotify/luigi | 2205 | 14947 |
| mlflow/mlflow | 2171 | 12500 |
| kubeflow/kubeflow | 1688 | 10687 |
| iterative/dvc | 802 | 10200 |
| PrefectHQ/prefect | 641 | 6830 |
| Netflix/metaflow | 282 | 4635 |
| elyra-ai/elyra | 262 | 1056 |
| flyteorg/flyte | 244 | 1630 |
| kedro-org/kedro | 690 | 4316 |

## About MLFlow

One of the tools used for the MLOps features described in the previous section is MLFlow, an open-source project. It can work with Scikit-learn, Tensorflow, and PyTorch. In this section, the features of the MLFlow library will be mentioned. With the MLFlow library, ML models can be put into production by writing several lines of code. A simple code example is shared in the MLFlow quick start tutorial documentation as follows (*Quickstart — MLflow 1.20.2 Documentation*, 2021):

```
import os
from random import random, randint
from mlflow import log_metric, log_param, log_artifacts

if __name__ == "__main__":
    # Log a parameter (key-value pair)
    log_param("param1", randint(0, 100))

    # Log a metric; metrics can be updated throughout the run
    log_metric("foo", random())
    log_metric("foo", random() + 1)
    log_metric("foo", random() + 2)

    # Log an artifact (output file)
    if not os.path.exists("outputs"):
        os.makedirs("outputs")
    with open("outputs/test.txt", "w") as f:
        f.write("hello world!")
    log_artifacts("outputs")
```

Features of MLFlow can be summarized as follows.

- Tracking, collection, and recording of experiments
- Reproduce, rerunning the same models. As known, other developers may be asked to run the same model.
- Deploy can be used to produce machine learning applications. For example, the MLFlow API can be used when a mobile or web application is developed.

MLFlow is also used in academic studies. Publications published with models developed with ML-Flow are available in the literature, such as (Ackermann et al., 2018; Amblard et al., 2021; Domenech & Guillén, 2020; Raghavendra, 2020; Zaharia et al., 2018; Zumar et al., 2019).

## HOW TO USE MLFLOW FOR A ML PROJECT

In this section, experiment tracking processes will be shown using MLFlow. Anaconda program for installing Jupyter notebooks and other fundamental data science libraries, which are the environment to be used in the application, can be installed by downloading free of charge from the following link https://www.anaconda.com/ with Python version 3.7. Figure 4 provides information about the used Anaconda program.

*Figure 4. About Anaconda Version*

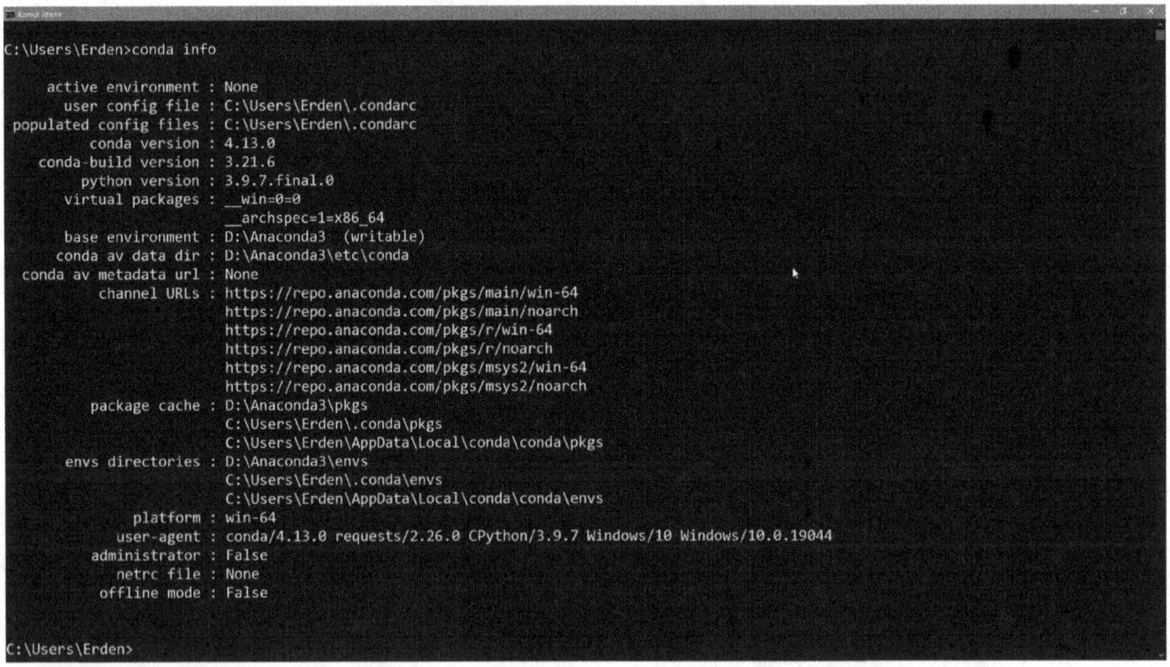

The all imports are given as follows:

```
import mlflow
from matplotlib.pyplot import savefig
from mlflow import log_artifact, log_metric, log_param
from sklearn.datasets import load_breast_cancer
from sklearn.metrics import accuracy_score, plot_confusion_matrix
from sklearn.model_selection import train_test_split
from sklearn.tree import DecisionTreeClassifier
```

In this tutorial, ML models working with different parameters will be given. Thanks to the MLFlow library, experimentation, storing the parameters of experiments, and comparing various experiments can be done quickly. First, the installation of the package can be performed with the following code.

```
conda install -c conda-forge mlflow
```

If the MLFlow installation was done correctly, it should print out as follows:

```
!mlflow
Usage: mlflow [OPTIONS] COMMAND [ARGS]...
Options:
  --version  Show the version and exit.
  --help     Show this message and exit.
Commands:
  artifacts    Upload, list, and download artifacts from an MLflow artifact...
  azureml      Serve models on Azure ML.
  db           Commands for managing an MLflow tracking database.
  deployments  Deploy MLflow models to custom targets.
  experiments  Manage experiments.
  gc           Permanently delete runs in the `deleted` lifecycle stage.
  models       Deploy MLflow models locally.
  run          Run an MLflow project from the given URI.
  runs         Manage runs.
  sagemaker    Serve models on SageMaker.
  server       Run the MLflow tracking server.
  ui           Launch the MLflow tracking UI for local viewing of run...
```

After MLFlow installation, the data can be loaded. In this example, Breast Cancer Wisconsin (diagnostic) dataset from Scikit-Learn toy data sets will be studied (Wolberg, 1995). The diagnostic study is carried out with "radius, texture, perimeter, area, smoothness, compactness, concavity, concave points, symmetry, fractal dimension" as a multivariate classification study.

The data set is divided into training and testing:

```
# Load the data
X, y = load_breast_cancer(return_X_y=True)
X_train, X_test, y_train, y_test = train_test_split(X, y, random_state=123)
```

Then, the MLFlow environment is prepared. A tracking URL is assigned to run the environment in localhost:

```
mlflow.set_tracking_uri("http://localhost:5000")
```

MLFlow interface is accessed by typing mlflow ui to the command line(cmd) (Figure 5):

*Figure 5. Accessing the MLFlow Interface*

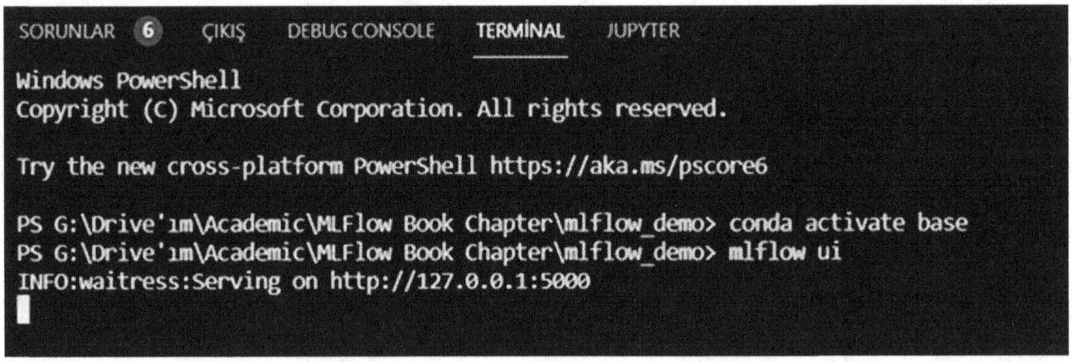

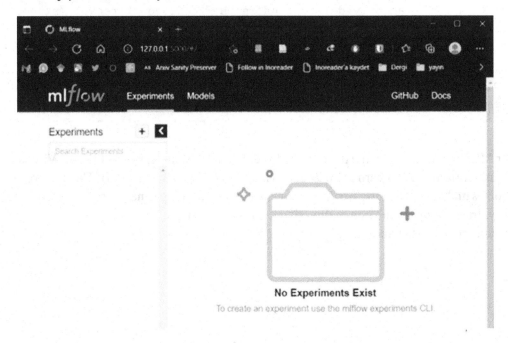

The MLFlow interface is accessed when the serving on the link is clicked. MLFlow dashboard will initially come as a blank page, as shown in Figure 6.

*Figure 6. An Empty MLFlow Interface*

M

After the environment is created, a new experiment considered a new model trial with a learning algorithm and parameter values can be created with the following codes. If the experiment has not been created before, it is created automatically.

```
mlflow.set_experiment("Decision Tree 1")
```

The experiment can be seen when the MLFlow interface is reloaded. As shown in Figure 7, the "Decision Tree 1" experiment has not yet been experimented. This step also opens a working folder called "test id." The necessary experiment comparisons can also be made in the folder.

*Figure 7. Decision Tree 1 Experiment Creation*

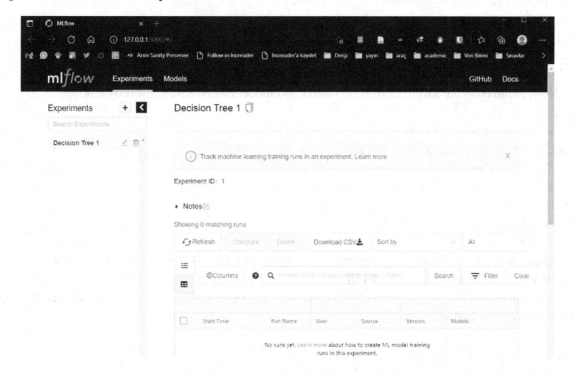

Now this tutorial is carried out with the default parameters by creating the model:

```
# model with default parameters
dt = DecisionTreeClassifier(criterion='entropy')
# fit the model
dt.fit(X_train,y_train)
# predict y_test
y_pred = dt.predict(X_test)
# calculate the accuracy
acc = accuracy_score(y_test, y_pred)
```

The essential log functions in the MLFlow library and what to use them for are summarized below (*Mlflow — MLflow 1.2.0 Documentation*, 2021).

- mlflow.log_param(key, value): Log only one parameter with "key" name. (Parameter: key-value inputs)
- mlflow.log_params(params): Log multiple parameters
- mlflow.log_metric(key, value, step=None): Log only one metric with "key" name (Metrics are stored as numeric values)
- mlflow.log_metrics(metrics, step=None): Log multiple metrics
- mlflow.log_artifacts(local_dir, artifact_path=None): Log all the contents of a local directory as artifacts (Artifacts can be files, data, and models)

```
# log parameters
for k in dt.get_params().keys():
    print(k, dt.get_params()[k], "logged")
    mlflow.log_param(k, dt.get_params()[k])
# log metrics
mlflow.log_metric("accuracy", acc)
```

Now, parameters are saved. Confusion matrix and model can be saved if it is as follows:

```
# save confusion matrix
plot_confusion_matrix(dt, X_test, y_test)
savefig("confusion_matrix.png")
mlflow.log_artifact("confusion_matrix.png")
# save the model
mlflow.sklearn.log_model(dt, "model")
```

After this is done, the model's parameters, metrics, and visuals can be shown on the interface in Figure 8. At the same time, the model file is saved as a ".pkl" file.

Let us give another sample run to make a comparison. Instead of repeating the same lines of code, a function can be written:

```
def train_dt(classifier, parameters):
  with mlflow.start_run(nested=True):
    dt = classifier(**parameters)
    dt.fit(X_train, y_train)
    y_pred = dt.predict(X_test)
    acc = accuracy_score(y_test, y_pred)
    # log parameters
    for k in dt.get_params().keys():
        print(k, dt.get_params()[k], "logged")
        mlflow.log_param(k, dt.get_params()[k])

    # log metrics
    mlflow.log_metric("accuracy", acc)
    # save confusion matrix
    plot_confusion_matrix(dt, X_test, y_test)
```

```
savefig("confusion_matrix.png")
mlflow.log_artifact("confusion_matrix.png")

# save the model
mlflow.sklearn.log_model(dt, "model")
```

*Figure 8. Results of the First Experiment in the MLFlow Interface*

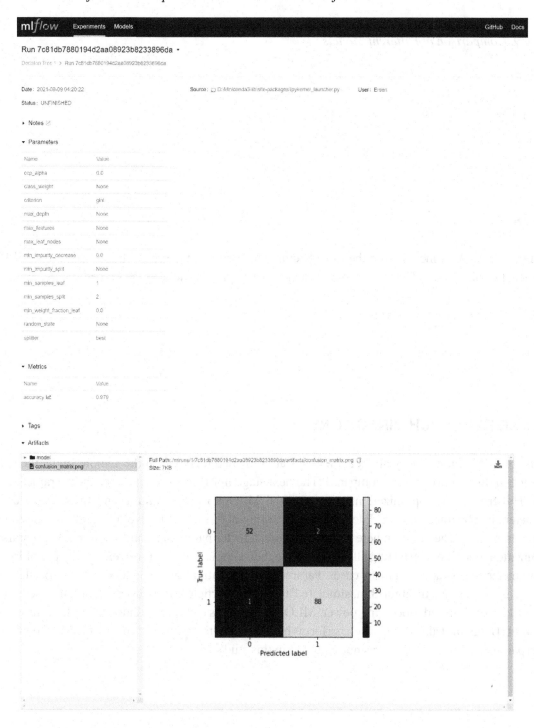

A new model is created and registered with MLFlow:

```
params = {'criterion': 'entropy'}
train_dt(DecisionTreeClassifier, params)
```

Finally, two different runs have been generated to make comparisons. Runs are selected first and then "Compare," as shown in Figure 9 and Figure 10 for the comparison of these models.

*Figure 9. Comparison of Different Models*

Choosing the best model from the models compared can be made from the menus in the MLFlow interface. Or the model selection process is carried out with the functions developed for MLFlow:

```
experiments = mlflow.search_runs()
# find the best
exp_id = experiments.loc[experiments['metrics.accuracy'].idxmax()]['run_id']
model = mlflow.sklearn.load_model("mlruns\\1\\" + exp_id)
```

## FUTURE RESEARCH DIRECTIONS

In this study, MLFlow library application codes are provided together. In the sample study, the results of only two different runs were compared. The next stage in ML projects is how other parameters will work. Hyperparameter optimization is an essential MLOps issue. Training any model with default parameters is a beginner's work. Each machine learning algorithm will give different results with different parameters. The question here is how to obtain a better parameter combination. Hyperparameter optimization is achieved by testing all parameters in their simplest form. However, it is not possible to try all parameter combinations in many cases. Parameter optimization can be done with heuristic algorithm techniques such as genetic algorithm, simulated annealing, particle swarm optimization in case of many trials or lack of time and processing power. MLOps operations can be continued using libraries such as Hyperopt (Bergstra et al., 2013), which performs hyper-parameter optimization with the MLFlow library. Hyperparameters optimization was not included in this study.

*Figure 10. Comparison Screen*

## CONCLUSION

The MLFlow library provides the researcher with a more straightforward MLOps operation. This section mentions MLFlow and keeping track of parameters, metrics, and model files (artifacts) with each run. The MLFlow is an open-source library that can work with popular libraries such as Scikit-Learn, PyTorch, PySpark. For these reasons, it has significant advantages. MLFlow work can then be produced through Amazon Sage Maker, Google Cloud, and Microsoft Azure.

# REFERENCES

Ackermann, K., Walsh, J., De Unánue, A., Naveed, H., Navarrete Rivera, A., Lee, S.-J., Bennett, J., Defoe, M., Cody, C., & Haynes, L. (2018). Deploying machine learning models for public policy: A framework. *Proceedings of the 24th ACM SIGKDD International Conference on Knowledge Discovery & Data Mining*, 15–22. 10.1145/3219819.3219911

Alamo, T., Reina, D. G., & Millán, P. (2020). *Data-driven methods to monitor, model, forecast and control covid-19 pandemic: Leveraging data science, epidemiology and control theory.* ArXiv Preprint ArXiv:2006.01731.

Alla, S. (2020). *Beginning MLOps with MLFlow: Deploy Models in AWS SageMaker.* Google Cloud, and Microsoft Azure.

Amblard, A., Youlton, S., & Coupe, W. J. (2021). Real-Time Unimpeded Taxi Out Machine Learning Service. *AIAA Aviation 2021 Forum*, 2401.

Anoshin, D., Shirokov, D., & Strok, D. (2020). *Jumpstart Snowflake: A Step-by-Step Guide to Modern Cloud Analytics.* Academic Press.

*Apache Airflow.* (2021). The Apache Software Foundation. https://github.com/apache/airflow

Bergstra, J., & Bengio, Y. (2012). Random search for hyper-parameter optimization. *Journal of Machine Learning Research*, *13*(2).

Bergstra, J., Yamins, D., & Cox, D. (2013). Making a science of model search: Hyperparameter optimization in hundreds of dimensions for vision architectures. *International Conference on Machine Learning*, 115–123.

Beroza, G. C., Segou, M., & Mostafa Mousavi, S. (2021). Machine learning and earthquake forecasting—Next steps. *Nature Communications*, *12*(1), 1–3. doi:10.103841467-021-24952-6 PMID:34362887

Biewald, L. (2020). *Experiment Tracking with Weights and Biases.* https://www.wandb.com/

Bradley, J. (2019). Addressing Challenges in Data Science: Scale, Skill Sets and Complexity. *Proceedings of the 25th ACM SIGKDD International Conference on Knowledge Discovery & Data Mining*, 3163–3163. 10.1145/3292500.3340407

Burkov, A. (2020). *Machine Learning Engineering.* True Positive Incorporated.

*Comet.* (2021). https://www.comet.ml/site

*Dagster.* (2021). https://github.com/dagster-io/dagster

De Mauro, A., Greco, M., & Grimaldi, M. (2016). A formal definition of Big Data based on its essential features. *Library Review*, *65*(3), 122–135. doi:10.1108/LR-06-2015-0061

Domenech, A. M., & Guillén, A. (2020). Ml-experiment: A Python framework for reproducible data science. *Journal of Physics: Conference Series*, *1603*(1), 012025. doi:10.1088/1742-6596/1603/1/012025

Doss, S. (2020). Digital Disruption Through Data Science: Embracing Digital Innovation In Insurance Business. *Bimaquest, 20*(3).

Dubovikov, K. (2019). *Managing Data Science.* https://ezproxy.torontopubliclibrary.ca/login?url=https://learning.oreilly.com/library/view/-/9781838826321/?ar

*Elyra.* (2021). https://github.com/elyra-ai/elyra

Erickson, N., Mueller, J., Shirkov, A., Zhang, H., Larroy, P., Li, M., & Smola, A. (2020). *AutoGluon-Tabular: Robust and Accurate AutoML for Structured Data.* ArXiv Preprint ArXiv:2003.06505.

Feurer, M., Klein, A., Eggensperger, K., Springenberg, J., Blum, M., & Hutter, F. (2015). Efficient and Robust Automated Machine Learning. In C. Cortes, N. D. Lawrence, D. D. Lee, M. Sugiyama, & R. Garnett (Eds.), Advances in Neural Information Processing Systems (Vol. 28, pp. 2962–2970). Curran Associates, Inc. https://papers.nips.cc/paper/5872-efficient-and-robust-automated-machine-learning.pdf

*Flyte.* (2021). https://github.com/flyteorg/flyte

Grant, T., Karau, H., Lublinsky, B., Liu, R., & Filonenko, I. (2020). *Kubeflow for Machine Learning: From Lab to Production* (1st ed.). O'Reilly Media.

Greff, K., Klein, A., Chovanec, M., Hutter, F., & Schmidhuber, J. (2017). The Sacred Infrastructure for Computational Research. *Proceedings of the 16th Python in Science Conference*, 49–56. 10.25080hinma-7f4c6e7-008

Hazen, B. T., Boone, C. A., Ezell, J. D., & Jones-Farmer, L. A. (2014). Data quality for data science, predictive analytics, and big data in supply chain management: An introduction to the problem and suggestions for research and applications. *International Journal of Production Economics*, *154*, 72–80. doi:10.1016/j.ijpe.2014.04.018

Hutter, F., Kotthoff, L., & Vanschoren, J. (2019). *Automated machine learning: Methods, systems, challenges.* Springer Nature. doi:10.1007/978-3-030-05318-5

Introducing FBLearner Flow. Facebook's AI backbone. (2016, May 9). *Facebook Engineering.* https://engineering.fb.com/2016/05/09/core-data/introducing-fblearner-flow-facebook-s-ai-backbone/

*Iterative/dvc.* (2021). https://github.com/iterative/dvc

Johnson, P. A., Rouet-Leduc, B., Pyrak-Nolte, L. J., Beroza, G. C., Marone, C. J., Hulbert, C., Howard, A., Singer, P., Gordeev, D., Karaflos, D., Levinson, C. J., Pfeiffer, P., Puk, K. M., & Reade, W. (2021). Laboratory earthquake forecasting: A machine learning competition. *Proceedings of the National Academy of Sciences of the United States of America*, *118*(5), e2011362118. doi:10.1073/pnas.2011362118 PMID:33495346

Jordan, T. H., & Jones, L. M. (2010). Operational earthquake forecasting: Some thoughts on why and how. *Seismological Research Letters*, *81*(4), 571–574. doi:10.1785/gssrl.81.4.571

Kakarla, R., Krishnan, S., & Alla, S. (2021). *Applied Data Science Using PySpark: Learn the End-to-End Predictive Model-Building Cycle.* Academic Press.

*Kubeflow-kale/kale.* (2021). https://github.com/kubeflow-kale/kale

*Kubeflow/kubeflow.* (2021). https://github.com/kubeflow/kubeflow

Lang, M., Binder, M., Richter, J., Schratz, P., Pfisterer, F., Coors, S., Au, Q., Casalicchio, G., Kotthoff, L., & Bischl, B. (2019). mlr3: A modern object-oriented machine learning framework in R. *Journal of Open Source Software*, *4*(44), 1903. doi:10.21105/joss.01903

Liberty, E., Karnin, Z., Xiang, B., Rouesnel, L., Coskun, B., Nallapati, R., Delgado, J., Sadoughi, A., Astashonok, Y., Das, P., Balioglu, C., Chakravarty, S., Jha, M., Gautier, P., Arpin, D., Januschowski, T., Flunkert, V., Wang, Y., Gasthaus, J., ... Smola, A. (2020). Elastic Machine Learning Algorithms in Amazon SageMaker. *Proceedings of the 2020 ACM SIGMOD International Conference on Management of Data*, 731–737. 10.1145/3318464.3386126

Maniraj, S. P., Saini, A., Ahmed, S., & Sarkar, S. (2019). Credit card fraud detection using machine learning and data science. *International Journal of Engine Research*, *8*(09).

*Meet Michelangelo*. (2021). https://eng.uber.com/michelangelo-machine-learning-platform/

*Metaflow*. (2021). Netflix, Inc. https://github.com/Netflix/metaflow

*Microsoft Azure*. (2021). https://azure.microsoft.com/en-us/services/machine-learning/automatedml/

Mizgier, K. J., Kocsis, O., & Wagner, S. M. (2018). Zurich Insurance uses data analytics to leverage the BI insurance proposition. *Interfaces*, *48*(2), 94–107. doi:10.1287/inte.2017.0928

MLflow. (2021). *A Machine Learning Lifecycle Platform*. https://github.com/mlflow/mlflow

*mlflow—MLflow 1.2.0 documentation*. (2021). https://mlflow.org/docs/1.2.0/python_api/mlflow.html

*MLOps: Continuous delivery and automation pipelines in machine learning*. (2021). Google Cloud. https://cloud.google.com/architecture/mlops-continuous-delivery-and-automation-pipelines-in-machine-learning?hl=tr

neptune.ai. (2020). *Neptune: Experiment management and collaboration tool*. https://neptune.ai

Paleyes, A., Urma, R.-G., & Lawrence, N. D. (2021). *Challenges in Deploying Machine Learning: A Survey of Case Studies*. https://arxiv.org/abs/2011.09926

Pandala, S. R. (2021). *Shankarpandala/lazypredict*. https://github.com/shankarpandala/lazypredict

Paszke, A., Gross, S., Massa, F., Lerer, A., Bradbury, J., Chanan, G., Killeen, T., Lin, Z., Gimelshein, N., Antiga, L., Desmaison, A., Kopf, A., Yang, E., DeVito, Z., Raison, M., Tejani, A., Chilamkurthy, S., Steiner, B., Fang, L., ... Chintala, S. (2019). PyTorch: An Imperative Style, High-Performance Deep Learning Library. In H. Wallach, H. Larochelle, A. Beygelzimer, F. d'Alché-Buc, E. Fox, & R. Garnett (Eds.), Advances in Neural Information Processing Systems 32 (pp. 8024–8035). Curran Associates, Inc.

Paul, L. R., Sadath, L., & Madana, A. (2021). Artificial Intelligence in Predictive Analysis of Insurance and Banking. In *Artificial Intelligence* (pp. 31–54). CRC Press.

Pedregosa, F., Varoquaux, G., Gramfort, A., Michel, V., Thirion, B., Grisel, O., Blondel, M., Prettenhofer, P., Weiss, R., & Dubourg, V. (2011). Scikit-learn: Machine learning in Python. *Journal of Machine Learning Research*, *12*, 2825–2830.

*Ploomber/ploomber*. (2021). https://github.com/ploomber/ploomber

Polyzotis, N., Roy, S., Whang, S. E., & Zinkevich, M. (2017). Data management challenges in production machine learning. *Proceedings of the 2017 ACM International Conference on Management of Data*, 1723–1726.

*PrefectHQ/prefect*. (2021). https://github.com/PrefectHQ/prefect

*Quantumblacklabs/kedro*. (2021). QuantumBlack Labs. https://github.com/quantumblacklabs/kedro

*Quickstart—MLflow 1.20.2 documentation*. (2021). https://www.mlflow.org/docs/latest/quickstart.html#installing-mlflow

Raghavendra, S. K. J. R. B. (2020). Big data Performance Evaluation using Machine Learning. *Solid State Technology*, *63*(6), 13702–13707.

Ray, D., Salvatore, M., Bhattacharyya, R., Wang, L., Du, J., Mohammed, S., Purkayastha, S., Halder, A., Rix, A., & Barker, D. (2020). Predictions, role of interventions and effects of a historic national lockdown in India's response to the COVID-19 pandemic: Data science call to arms. *Harvard Data Science Review, 2020*(Suppl 1).

Schelter, S., Biessmann, F., Januschowski, T., Salinas, D., Seufert, S., & Szarvas, G. (2018). *On challenges in machine learning model management*. Academic Press.

Sculley, D., Holt, G., Golovin, D., Davydov, E., Phillips, T., Ebner, D., Chaudhary, V., Young, M., Crespo, J.-F., & Dennison, D. (2015). Hidden technical debt in Machine learning systems. *Proceedings of the 28th International Conference on Neural Information Processing Systems*, *2*, 2503–2511.

*Spotify/luigi*. (2021). Spotify. https://github.com/spotify/luigi

TensorFlow Developers. (2021). *TensorFlow* (v2.4.3) [Computer software]. Zenodo. doi:10.5281/ZENODO.4724125

*TFX*. (2021). tensorflow. https://github.com/tensorflow/tfx

Thennakoon, A., Bhagyani, C., Premadasa, S., Mihiranga, S., & Kuruwitaarachchi, N. (2019). Real-time credit card fraud detection using machine learning. *2019 9th International Conference on Cloud Computing, Data Science & Engineering (Confluence)*, 488–493.

Treiblmaier, H., & Mair, P. (2021). Textual Data Science for Logistics and Supply Chain Management. *Logistics*, *5*(3), 56.

Waller, M. A., & Fawcett, S. E. (2013). *Data science, predictive analytics, and big data: A revolution that will transform supply chain design and management*. Wiley Online Library.

Wolberg, O., Street, W., & Mangasarian, W. (1995). *Breast Cancer Wisconsin (Diagnostic)*. Academic Press.

Zaharia, M., Chen, A., Davidson, A., Ghodsi, A., Hong, S. A., Konwinski, A., Murching, S., Nykodym, T., Ogilvie, P., & Parkhe, M. (2018). Accelerating the machine learning lifecycle with MLflow. *IEEE Data Eng. Bull.*, *41*(4), 39–45.

Zheng, A. (2015). *Evaluating Machine Learning Models*. https://www.safaribooksonline.com/library/view//9781492048756/?ar

Zumar, C., Chen, A., Davidson, A., Ghodsi, A., Hong, S. A., Konwinski, A., Murching, S., Nykodym, T., Ogilvie, P., & Parkhe, M. (2019). *Demonstration of MLflow: A System to Accelerate the Machine Learning Lifecycle*. Academic Press.

## ADDITIONAL READING

Asanka, D. (2020). *Introduction to Azure Machine Learning using Azure ML Studio*. Retrieved May 03, 2022, from https://www.sqlshack.com/introduction-to-azure-machine-learning-using-azure-ml-studio/

Callaert, Y. (2020). *Getting started with MlFlow*. Retrieved May 03, 2022, from https://towardsdatascience.com/getting-started-with-mlflow-52eff8c09c61

Jenkner, P. (2021). *15 best tools for tracking machine learning experiments*. Retrieved May 03, 2022, from https://medium.com/neptune-ai/15-best-tools-for-tracking-machine-learning-experiments-64c6eff16808

Microsoft Azure. (2016). *Reprint, Microsoft Docs*. Retrieved May 03, 2022, from https://github.com/MicrosoftDocs

Schmitt, M. (2020). *Airflow vs. Luigi vs. Argo vs. MLFlow vs. KubeFlow*. Retrieved May 03, 2022, from https://towardsdatascience.com/airflow-vs-luigi-vs-argo-vs-mlflow-vs-kubeflow-b3785dd1ed0c

Synopsys. (2020). *What is DevOps and how does it work?* Retrieved May 03, 2022, from https://www.synopsys.com/glossary/what-is-devops.html

Vázquez, F. (2019). *Manage your machine learning lifecycle with MLflow*. Retrieved May 03, 2022, from https://towardsdatascience.com/manage-your-machine-learning-lifecycle-with-mlflow-part-1-a7252c859f72

Visengeriyeva, L. (2021). *Awesome MLOps*. Retrieved May 03, 2022, from https://github.com/visenger/awesome-mlops

## KEY TERMS AND DEFINITIONS

**Artifacts:** Files, data, and models in MLFlow.

**DevOps (Development and Operations):** demonstrates the operations that organizations need to follow to deliver their applications more quickly and reliably.

**Experiment:** Multiple runs on MLFlow.

**Metrics:** Performance criteria.

**ML (Machine Learning):** Inference statistic studies, classification, and clustering from the data sets.

**MLOps (Machine Learning Operations):** Combining machine learning and DevOps studies.

**Parameters:** Inputs of the learning algorithms.

**Run:** Runs on MLFlow.

R

# Research Data Management

**Tibor Koltay**

*Eszterházy Károly Catholic University, Hungary*

## INTRODUCTION

Desk research, followed by critical analysis was conducted. The interdisciplinary literature, identified Research Data Management (RDM) as a widely published subject, portrayed by a considerable number of papers that reflect on a wide variety of issues. RDM is related to varied subjects, described in this encyclopedia, as there is scholarly interest for RDM in the natural sciences, social sciences, as well as in the business sphere. The supposedly most data-intensive branch of the human sciences is digital humanities.

This chapter stresses the centrality of data sharing, whereby the ideas of the FAIR Principles are characterized as main drivers of data reuse. The importance of data management plans (DMPs) is emphasized. Other RDM processes, such as adding metadata, citing, retrieving, and curating datasets are also presented. The need for cooperating between disciplinary researchers and different data professionals is highlighted. Furthermore, it is underlined that a number of educational programs to data science also give attention to data management.

## BACKGROUND

The consistent management of research data is especially crucial for the success of any long-term and large-scale collaborative research. RDM is also "the basis for efficiency, continuity, and quality of the research, as well as for maximum impact and outreach, including the long-term publication of data and their accessibility" (Finkel et al., 2020, p. 1).

As emphasized by several researchers, as well as by funding agencies and publishers, organizing and sharing research data is a fundamental part of the research process, thus comprehensive RDM is indispensable not only for ensuring reproducible and open scientific research, but increases citation rates for publications, and fosters research reproducibility (Borycz, 2021).

The main drivers of RDM are Open Science and Open Data. These initiatives gained momentum with the adoption of the Fair Access to Science and Technology Research Act in 2013 (US Congress, 2013), but this culture change is strongly supported also by the European Commission through the European Open Science Cloud (EOSC, n.d.).

RDM is often viewed as a set of mechanical, managerial, and technical handling processes (Ojanen et al., 2020). However, by encouraging the collaboration between researchers, and fostering better science, it can lead to better decision-making (USGS, n.d.).

RDM falls mainly into the domain and responsibility of researchers and data professionals. The latter group includes (data) librarians, data curators, and data stewards. It is unimaginable without services, offered by research offices, academic libraries, and computing (information technology) service units. Beside of these professionals, data scientists must be knowledgeable of RDM because it is one of the main services that provide them with the data that they are working with. Contrarily, RDM is also a

DOI: 10.4018/978-1-7998-9220-5.ch072

data science issue, which should not be restricted to machine learning or statistics, thus data scientists need to face the challenges of organizing and storing data. As declared by Davenport and Patil (2012, p. 73), data scientist's job is "bringing structure to large quantities of formless data and making analysis possible." In the light of this, we need to acknowledge that their job goes beyond formal data analysis, among others by including RDM.

Strongly related to the broad and varied aspects of RDM and data science are the activities of the Research Data Alliance, which is a "community-driven organization dedicated to the development and use of technical, social, and community infrastructure promoting data sharing and data-driven exploration. This organization is particularly important for "the global academic community where research infrastructure is often ad hoc, may have a short shelf-life, and hard to fund (Berman & Crosas, 2020).

Data stewardship also deserves attention because these professionals take care of data assets that do not belong to the stewards themselves. Data stewards' aim is ensuring that data-related work is performed in accordance with policies and practices. Together with preservation of data, their activities also fall into the domain of data science.

Data stewards should be involved in all phases of the research lifecycle, e.g. when designing and planning data-intensive experiments, co-supervising data capture, then running the data processing and curation. To be able to do all this, data stewards should have good knowledge of available methods and tools for data modelling and interpretation (Mons, 2018).

Among the key objectives of Open Science is the provision of Open Access to research results and Open Data. Both imply free use, reuse, and redistribution of data by anyone, who complies with the requirements, set by data licenses. These objectives can be achieved only if RDM and data stewardship meet criteria with respect to the collection, annotation, long-term preservation and archiving of data.

The efficient and consistent management of research data is crucial for the success of individual researchers and research teams (Finkel et al., 2020). As affirmed by Kanza and Knight (2022, p. 4) in their wittily titled and thought-provoking paper "Behind every great research project is great data management." They also underline that pursuing good research data management includes the following steps:

- Starting data management strategy early and covering it from data collection to publishing and sharing the results,
- Using sensible folder/file structures,
- Deciding early on the version control systems,
- Considering short- and long-term data storage by implementing the rule of keeping three copies of the data, within two types of media, with one stored at a separate site.

## FOUNDATIONAL SKILLS, PRACTICES, AND PROCESSES

The most important facts about data sharing and reuse, the requirement for responsible conduct and research integrity will be presented here. We will also discuss general RDM skills and the importance of data management plans. The role of metadata and data citation will be touched on, as well.

## Data Sharing and Reuse

Good data management is not a goal in itself, but leads to "knowledge discovery and innovation, and to subsequent data and knowledge integration, and reuse by the community after the data publication process" (Wilkinson et al., 2016, p. 1).

When speaking about data sharing and reuse, it should be accentuated that both demand the provision of high quality, curated data resources (Neylon et al., 2019). This requirement is in harmony with the idea that managing quality and providing data governance is on its way to become a crucial aspect of RDM, because without proper quality management, the old phenomenon of 1980s, described in the saying "garbage in, garbage out," will reappear in the big data age (Wang, 2018).

Data governance itself refers to the "exercise of authority and control over the management of data, with the purpose of increasing the value of data and minimize data-related cost and risk" (Abraham, Schneider & Vom Brocke, 2019, p. 424).

Several stakeholders, representing academia, industry, funding agencies, and scholarly publishers try to steer researchers into the direction of embracing a concise and measurable set of principles that is usually referred to as the FAIR Data Principles, referring to data (or any digital object), metadata, and infrastructure, and covering Findability, Accessibility, Interoperability, and Reuse.

Finding data calls for the presence of metadata and findability also asks for data that is uniquely identifiable e.g., by having a unique identifier such as a Digital Object Identifier (DOI), or a persistent URL (PURL). Once the users have found the required data, they need to know, how to access it, possibly including authentication and authorization. The FAIR Principles also emphasize the ability of machines to automatically find and use the data (Wilkinson et al., 2016).

Datasets usually need to be integrated with other data and be interoperable with applications or workflows for analysis, storage, and processing. The ultimate goal is then to optimize the reuse of data (GOFAIR, n.d.; Hart et al., 2016). Beside reuse, defined as using the data more than once for the same purpose, there is repurposing, which means the use of data for a completely different purpose, differing from the original goal (Yoon & Lee, 2019).

Despite the above, often successful initiatives, many researchers create new primary data rather than reusing existing data, especially if their do not have knowledge about such data, or do not have access to it (Bugaje & Chowdhury, 2018, p. 340). Moreover, many scientists, especially early-career researchers may be insecure about early sharing, because it may lead to losing their competitive edge. They must also decide whether it is worth spending valuable research time for curating and sharing datasets (Popkin, 2019). Notwithstanding, a scientometric analysis of varied researchers worldwide shows that the major incentive for data sharing is the desire for recognition or receiving credit (Dorta-González et al., 2021).

Due to the existence of datasets that need to be protected for some reason, data sharing faces further challenges. Other areas of continual concern, such as protecting the professional interests of data generators also should be taken into account when wanting to make data widely available. These activities may include not only focusing on academic research activities, but also applying data to wider societal and citizenship-related issues (Majumder & McGuire, 2020, pp. 168–169).

Openly sharing data allows the verification of research results by peers. This also helps avoiding the duplication of data, and – on the long run – increases the visibility of research and reputation of the given researcher. Furthermore, it can lead to new collaborations and partnerships (Pratt, 2021). Today, a number of scholarly journals promote reuse by requiring articles to be accompanied by the underlying research data. Such policies lead to the benefit of reducing transaction costs, increasing the rigor of research, and decreasing redundant activities (Gold et al., 2019). Beside of these, there are data journals that publish citable and cross-linked data papers that provide access to research data. These data papers contain information on the acquisition, methods, and processing of the datasets (Hrynaszkiewicz, 2019).

## Responsible Conduct of Research and Research Integrity

Good research data requires answering methodological and ethical questions about permissions for collecting, recoding, measuring, or compiling data. Digitizing, transcribing, translating data also raise questions (Beckers et al., 2020). In this context, the notion of responsible conduct of research (RCR) refers to conforming to published rules or guidelines. Accordingly, RDM can be interpreted as one of the dimensions of RCR (Jensen et al., 2020).

Planning, proposing, performing, reporting, and reviewing research in accordance with objectivity, honesty, openness, accountability, and fairness are the constituent elements of research integrity that complements RCR (Bukusi et al., 2019). It focuses on ensuring reliability, respect, and responsibility for all activities and results, associated with the research process. Another aspect of integrity is complying with codes and regulations, relevant to the discipline of the given researcher (ALLEA, 2017). This compels researchers to be accountable for the research process in its entirety by focusing on ensuring and improving the quality of scientific work, and meeting the requirements that have been set before engaging in research. The completeness of reporting also must be monitored (WCRIF, 2019).

Proper storage, mentioned above, is a prerequisite for sharing data, because data may undergo decay or become less accessible through time that reminds us not to lose the importance of reproducibility out of sight. Failing to guarantee this is a very serious problem on the one hand. On the other hand, it does not mean cheating intentionally, but results from failing to live up to standards in good faith (Jensen et al., 2020).

## General RDM Skills and Practices

RDM would not be complete without the following activities:

- Identifying and locating datasets,
- Defining roles and responsibilities,
- Keeping sufficient documentation,
- Writing data management plans,
- Organizing files and naming them consistently,
- Applying version control (versioning),
- Providing data backup,
- Identifying, preparing, and collocating key research files to determine provenance (history), and improve future retrieval.

Creating a research workflow is often shaped by the available tools or the technical requirements, enabling the proper use of these tools. As the type of data also can shape the workflow, proper decisions about which tool to use are indispensable.

For research involving data that can be made publicly available, it is still important to provide adequate security, but comprehensive integrity of research data is also a concern in any research activity. Cooperating service partners may include data scientists, research coordinators, data curators, digital preservation librarians, repository managers, subject librarians, legal advisors, research ethics advisors, and data access managers (Briney et al., 2020).

A part of the data may be put into a repository either by the researchers' own decision or by following the mandate of a funding body. A data repository (data archive) has a database infrastructure that is set up to manage, share, access, and archive researchers' datasets (Chigwada et al., 2019).

Academic libraries see a potential role in curating data, produced by researchers in their universities or other organizations, but may not wish to compete with repositories. On the other hand, they can provide help by identifying repositories, where data can be deposited. Usually, they are also willing to apply their expertise in information organization (Borgman, 2016). Universities are interested in recording and displaying the scholarly output of their researchers and students. This can be done among others by maintaining data repositories that care for the long-term ability of data resources. Data repositories are also run by non-profit consortia, and there is commercial interest in hosting data and providing access to it, as well. However, the activities of commercial repositories are often limited to hosting data, without readiness for curating it. Discipline-specific repositories may have the largest outreach and impact in a given field, but generalist, institutional, or national repositories also can be suitable for ingesting and appraising data (Beckers et al., 2020).

The essence of versioning is in saving new copies of files when there were changes in them, while retaining the older ones. This allows going back and retrieving specific versions of the files later and may enable rescuing or fixing a portion of deleted material without the need of recreating it.

A different approach to RDM is offered by data literacy as it enables data producers and users "to access, interpret, critically assess, manage, handle, and ethically use data" (Calzada Prado & Marzal, 2013). If we accept that managing comprises preservation and curation, data literacy can be seen as an important constituent of RDM. By relying on self-management, innovative thinking, and problem-solving abilities (Lee, 2013), this set of skills "empowers individuals to transform data into information and into actionable knowledge by enabling them to access, interpret, critically assess, manage, and ethically use data" (Koltay, 2017, p. 10).

## The Role and Importance of Data Management Plans

An important step towards Open Science and efficient work with data is that a growing number of funding bodies require researchers to write DMPs. In 2001, the US National Science Foundation (NSF) took this important step towards the openness of data. Moreover, DMPs are also an important pillar of the European Open Science Cloud (EOSC Pillar, n.d.).

DMPs provide researchers "with a mechanism for stating how they will manage data associated with at least part of a research project's data lifecycle." A DMP is also a piece of documentation that describes directions and data management practices, related to data of a particular research project. Data management planning is an active process, concerning the researchers as DMPs must be designed for both the research team and the funding body (Smale et al., 2020, pp. 2-3).

Data management plans should be set up at the beginning of project life cycle but may improve throughout its entire lifetime (Kanza & Knight, 2022). These documents briefly describe how the researchers are planning to manage the data gathered in the course of their project. A DMP should address questions about the type(s) of data that they will collect and how will they describe it. It must indicate how the data will be stored and kept secure. Researchers should declare, who will be allowed to give access to the data after the completion of the project, and determine under what conditions and for how long can this happen (Writing a Data Management Plan, n.d.)

As described by Ojanen (2020), when setting up a DMP, the following question must be answered:

- How and when to make agreements,
- How to meet data privacy and security requirements,
- How to keep and share datasets securely,
- How to decide what data can be destroyed and what is valuable, thus needs to be preserved,
- How to prepare data for archiving and publishing.

The evaluation and comparative analysis of openly available DMP tools, using 45 selected parameters revealed among others that the earlier released DMP tools did not properly support FAIR principles. This indicates that researchers could enhance the planning of their DMPs by involving stakeholders, such as collaborators, librarians, and administrators into planning (Gajbe et al., 2021).

Looking at the characteristics of research teams is more than useful. Using outcome-focused approaches to align DMP's use with specific goals by defining their explicit purpose also may prove beneficial. This is especially true if these documents are written by reflecting on the well-specified concerns of an individual researcher, a specific funding agency, or institution instead of addressing the requirements of multiple stakeholders. The level of openness in the different disciplines and in the teams, as well as the willingness to advocate good data management practices influence the content of a DMP. Team heterogeneity is also an influencing factor, while the rules regarding protecting human subjects involved into research are compulsory.

The potential professional, institutional, and economic benefits of DMPs are clear. However, there is no apparent evidence that researchers can gain professional benefits through the act of completing these documents. DMPs may in fact be ineffective, because in some cases they do not describe RDM processes to any acceptable level of detail and quality, among others because many researchers do not want, or are not able to execute what was described in their own plans (Smale et al., 2020). Nonetheless, when devising DMPs, attention should be directed towards changes in the global scholarly communication ecosystem.

## Metadata and Data Citation

Metadata (added manually or created in a machine-readable form) describes physical material and digital data. By adding context to data, metadata enables the identification and understanding of data both in the short and in the longer term, facilitating thereby further analysis, replication, and other follow-up work. Metadata can be embedded in the data or dataset itself or separated from it.

Descriptive metadata supports discovery and general assessment by describing the content and context of a dataset or document for discovery and identification, including title, creator/author, subject, keywords, and description and/or abstract. Structural metadata enables linking the components of a resource, indicating the internal structure of a dataset, while administrative metadata provides information, such as the date of creation, file type, copyright permissions, software required to manage the data, provenance, and information on who can access the data. It also supports technical and other operational aspects, affiliated with preservation and rights (Beckers et al., 2020; Leipzig et al., 2021).

The goal of citing data is to provide evidence by identifying cited items unambiguously and improving access to them. To make citations interpretable, data must be combined with contextual information, because otherwise they are not interpretable. Data citations should facilitate access not only to the data itself, but also to associated metadata, and any material, necessary for making informed use by both humans and machines (Borgman, 2106).

Data citation is much more complex than providing citations to research publications. It enables identifying, accessing, and retrieving datasets. By involving crediting the researchers, who created and curated the given dataset, citations help giving credit to researchers and institutions, fostering thereby the willingness of scientists to share their data. It also can serve as means for connecting scholarly papers with the underlying data, on which they are based (Silvello, 2018).

## Data Retrieval

Data retrieval is a less obvious task than retrieving research papers that are available in a predominantly textual form, among others because the average file size of retrieved datasets is several times larger than that of retrieved research papers, although these sizes vary from one discipline to another.

In contrast to research publications that contain only the publication itself, datasets are usually accompanied by separate documentation files. Furthermore, data files and single dataset item records may constitute several composite files, comprising fragments or versions of the dataset.

Due to the characteristics of research data and to the user interactions that data requires, adapting standard text retrieval to data is impractical. As the retrieved datasets may contain different file types and/or file formats, it may be necessary to download them in order to be readable or used (Bugaje & Chowdhury 2017).

## Data Curation

Research data is often collected beyond research projects in order to become subject of curation and preservation (Robinson, 2016). Accordingly, RDM should be complemented by data curation that consists of a set of general activities, such as organizing, collecting, describing, and storing data for communication among scholars. It also includes planning, acquiring, preparing, analyzing, preserving, and discovering the data to be curated (Pouchard, 2016).

Data curation aims at preventing data loss and adding value to trusted data assets for current and future use. Its main goals overlap with the ones of digital curation, requiring a long-term engagement of which technology is only one of the components, because – due to the heterogeneity of data-related roles – the involvement of humans is a necessity (Poole, 2016). Preservation for reusability should stand in data curation's center, especially if we accept that the value of data is exclusively in its extrinsic properties, i.e., their fitness for use (Sposito, 2017).

Data curation is a costly activity, as it requires advanced practices, training, specific technical competencies, and relevant subject expertise (Johnston et al., 2018).

## FUTURE RESEARCH DIRECTIONS

RDM is often tied to intellectual effort. However, data retrieval, metadata and data citation have the potential to be automated. What is more, in the future data curation may fall into this category, as well.

Despite their widespread traditional use, data management plans also seem to be a possible topic for further research, because instead of the free-form texts, there is already research to produce them in a machine-actionable form. Progress has already been made toward achieving this goal, and a set of principles is already available (Miksa et al., 2020). Making use of semi-automated workflows, machine actionable DMPs promise automated integration of information and updates, as well as enabling interoperability with existing systems (Miksa et al., 2021). Nonetheless, to make such systems operational, there seems to be a number of issues to be solved.

Intelligible AI methods and effective research data management can transparently document research findings. This is illustrated by the case of an AI-driven system that "acts on an explicability and open science maxim in order to foster collaborative actions in respect to sustainability objectives" (Hermann & Hermann, 2021, p. 2). This shows that there is considerable potential in for development in this direction.

## CONCLUSION

The spread of RDM has been uneven in different countries, institutions, professions, and among varied professionals. Notwithstanding, the complexity and unquestionable usefulness of RDM may predestine it to become in the future important part of information- and data-related tasks for a wider range of institutions and disciplines. Many of these may be performed then by data scientists. In this regard, we must agree with Song and Zhu (2017), who argue that data science education must face the emergence of new data management topics (especially the ones, related to Big Data), and include them into the curricula of institutions, involved in it. There is apparently much room to carry out research in this area in future.

## REFERENCES

Abraham, R., Schneider, J., & Vom Brocke, J. (2019). Data governance: A conceptual framework, structured review, and research agenda. *International Journal of Information Management*, *49*, 424–438. doi:10.1016/j.ijinfomgt.2019.07.008

ALLEA. (2017). *The European code of conduct for research integrity*. European Science Foundation. Retrieved from https://www.allea.org/wp-content/uploads/2017/05/ALLEA-European-Code-of-Conduct-for-Research-Integrity-2017.pdf

Beckers, S. D. B., Hüser, F., Wildgaard, L. E., Rasmussen, L. H., Drachen, T. M., Larsen, A. V., & Sandøe, P. (2020). Research Data Management. In K. K. Jensen, M. M. Andersen, L. Whiteley, & P. Sandøe (Eds.), *RCR – A Danish textbook for courses in responsible conduct of research* (pp. 55–74). University of Copenhagen.

Berman, F., & Crosas, M. (2020). The research data alliance: Benefits and challenges of building a community organization. *Harvard Data Science Review*, *2*(1). Advance online publication. doi:10.1162/99608f92.5e126552

Borgman, Ch. L. (2016). Data citation as a bibliometric oxymoron. In C.R. Sugimoto (Ed.), Theories of Informetrics and Scholarly Communication (pp. 93-115). de Gruyter.

Borycz, J. (2021). Implementing data management workflows in research groups through integrated library consultancy. *Data Science Journal*, *20*(9), 1–9. doi:10.5334/dsj-2021-009

Briney, K. A., Coates, H. L., & Goben, A. (2020). Foundational practices of research data management. *Research Ideas and Outcomes*, *6*, e56508. doi:10.3897/rio.6.e56508

Bugaje, M., & Chowdhury, G. (2018). Identifying design requirements of a user-centered research data management system. In M. Dobreva, A. Hinze, & M. Žumer (Eds.), *Maturity and Innovation in Digital Libraries* (pp. 335–347). Springer. doi:10.1007/978-3-030-04257-8_35

Bukusi, E. A., Manabe, Y. C., & Zunt, J. R. (2019). Mentorship and ethics in global health: Fostering scientific integrity and responsible conduct of research. *The American Journal of Tropical Medicine and Hygiene*, *100*(1), 42–47. doi:10.4269/ajtmh.18-0562 PMID:30430980

Calzada Prado, J. C., & Marzal, M. Á. (2013). Incorporating data literacy into information literacy programs: Core competencies and contents. *Libri*, *63*(2), 123–134. doi:10.1515/libri-2013-0010

Chigwada, J. P., Hwalima, T., & Kwangwa, N. (2019). A proposed framework for research data management services in research institutions in Zimbabwe. In R. K. Bhardwaj & P. Banks (Eds.), *Research Data Access and Management in Modern Libraries* (pp. 29–53). IGI Global. doi:10.4018/978-1-5225-8437-7.ch002

Davenport, T., & Patil, D. (2012). Data scientist: The sexiest job of the 21st century. *Harvard Business Review*, *90*(5), 70–76. PMID:23074866

Dorta-González, P., González-Betancor, S. M., & Dorta-González, M. I. (2021). To what extent is researchers' data-sharing motivated by formal mechanisms of recognition and credit? *Scientometrics*, *126*(3), 2209–2225. doi:10.100711192-021-03869-3

EOSC. (n.d.) *European Open Science Cloud*. Retrieved from https://eosc-portal.eu/about/eosc

EOSC Pillar. (n.d.) *D1.2: Data Management Plan*. Retrieved from https://www.eosc-pillar.eu/d12-data-management-plan

Finkel, M., Baur, A., Weber, T. K., Osenbrück, K., Rügner, H., Leven, C., Schwientek, M., Schlögl, J., Hahn, U., Streck, T., Cirpka, O. A., Walter, T., & Grathwohl, P. (2020). Managing collaborative research data for integrated, interdisciplinary environmental research. *Earth Science Informatics*, *13*(3), 1–14. doi:10.100712145-020-00441-0

Gajbe, S. B., Tiwari, A., & Singh, R. K. (2021). Evaluation and analysis of data management plan tools: A parametric approach. *Information Processing & Management*, *58*(3), 102480. doi:10.1016/j.ipm.2020.102480

GOFAIR. (n.d.). *FAIR principles*. GO FAIR International Support & Coordination Office. Retrieved from https://www.go-fair.org/fair-principles/

Gold, E. R., Ali-Khan, S. E., Allen, L., Ballell, L., Barral-Netto, M., Carr, D., & Cook-Deegan, R. (2019). An open toolkit for tracking open science partnership implementation and impact. *Gates Open Research*, *3*(1442), 1442. Advance online publication. doi:10.12688/gatesopenres.12958.2 PMID:31850398

Hart, E. M., Barmby, P., LeBauer, D., Michonneau, F., Mount, S., Mulrooney, P., & Hollister, J. W. (2016). Ten simple rules for digital data storage. *PLoS Computational Biology*, *12*(10), e1005097. doi:10.1371/journal.pcbi.1005097 PMID:27764088

Hermann, E., & Hermann, G. (2021). Artificial intelligence in research and development for sustainability: The centrality of explicability and research data management. *AI and Ethics*, *505*, 1–5. doi:10.100743681-021-00114-8

Hrynaszkiewicz, I. (2019). Publishers' responsibilities in promoting data quality and reproducibility. In A. Bespalov, M. C. Michel, & T. Steckler (Eds.), *Good research practice in non-clinical pharmacology and biomedicine* (pp. 319–348). Springer. doi:10.1007/164_2019_290

Jensen, K. K., Andersen, M. M., Whiteley, L., & Sandøe, P. (2020). *RCR - A Danish textbook for courses in responsible conduct of research* (4th ed.). University of Copenhagen.

Johnston, L. R., Carlson, J., Hudson-Vitale, C., Imker, H., Kozlowski, W., Olendorf, R., & Hull, E. (2018). Data curation network: A cross-institutional staffing model for curating research data. International *Journal of Digital Curation, 13*(1), 125-140. doi:10.2218/ijdc.v13i1.616

Kanza, S., & Knight, N. J. (2022). Behind every great research project is great data management. *BMC Research Notes, 15*(1), 1–5. doi:10.118613104-022-05908-5 PMID:35063017

Koltay, T. (2017). Data literacy for researchers and data librarians. *Journal of Librarianship and Information Science, 49*(1), 3–4. doi:10.1177/0961000615616450

Lee, A. Y. (2013). Literacy and competencies required to participate in knowledge societies. In A. Y. Lee, J. Lau, T. Carbo, & N. Gendina (Eds.), *Conceptual relationship of information literacy and media literacy in knowledge societies* (pp. 3–75). UNESCO.

Leipzig, J., Nüst, D., Hoyt, C. T., Ram, K., & Greenberg, J. (2021). The role of metadata in reproducible computational research. *Patterns, 2*(9), 100322. doi:10.1016/j.patter.2021.100322 PMID:34553169

Majumder, M. A., & McGuire, A. L. (2020). Data sharing in the context of health-related citizen science. *The Journal of Law, Medicine & Ethics, 48*(1), 167–177. doi:10.1177/1073110520917044 PMID:32342743

Miksa, T., Oblasser, S., & Rauber, A. (2021). Automating research data management using machine-actionable data management plans. *ACM Transactions on Management Information Systems, 13*(2), 1–22. doi:10.1145/3490396

Miksa, T., Simms, S., Mietchen, D., & Jones, S. (2019). Ten principles for machine-actionable data management plans. *PLoS Computational Biology, 15*(3), e1006750. doi:10.1371/journal.pcbi.1006750 PMID:30921316

Mons, B. (2018). *Data stewardship for open science: Implementing FAIR principles.* CRC Press. doi:10.1201/9781315380711

Neylon, C., Belsø, R., Bijsterbosch, M., Cordewener, B., Foncel, J., & Laakso, M. (2019). *Open Scholarship and the need for collective action.* Knowlede Exchange.

Ojanen, M. (2020). *Effective research data management? – DMP to the rescue!* Retrieved from https://blogs.helsinki.fi/thinkopen/know-your-data-rdm-series-5/

Ojanen, M., Lindholm, T., & Siipilehto, L. (2020). *What is Research Data Management (RDM)?* Retrieved from https://blogs.helsinki.fi/thinkopen/know- -data-rdm-series-1/

Poole, A. H. (2016). The conceptual landscape of digital curation. *The Journal of Documentation, 72*(5), 961–986. doi:10.1108/JD-10-2015-0123

Popkin, G. (2019). Data sharing and how it can benefit your scientific career. *Nature, 569*(7756), 445–447. doi:10.1038/d41586-019-01506-x PMID:31081499

Pouchard, L. (2016). Revisiting the Data Lifecycle with Big Data curation. *International Journal of Digital Curation, 10*(2), 176–192. doi:10.2218/ijdc.v10i2.342

Pratt, I. (2021) *Essentials of open data sharing*. Retrieved from https://scds.github.io/intro-rdm/sharing.html

Robinson, L. (2016). Between the deluge and the dark age: Perspectives on data curation. *Alexandria (Aldershot), 26*(2), 73–76. doi:10.1177/0955749016661067

Silvello, G. (2018). Theory and practice of data citation. *Journal of the Association for Information Science and Technology, 69*(1), 6–20. doi:10.1002/asi.23917

Smale, N. A., Unsworth, K., Denyer, G., Magatova, E., & Barr, D. (2020). A review of the history, advocacy and efficacy of Data Management Plans. *International Journal of Digital Curation, 15*(1), 30. Advance online publication. doi:10.2218/ijdc.v15i1.525

Song, I. Y., & Zhu, Y. (2017). Big data and data science: Opportunities and challenges of iSchools. *Journal of Data and Information Science, 2*(3), 1–18. doi:10.1515/jdis-2017-0011

Sposito, F. A. (2017). *What do data curators care about? Data quality, user trust, and the data reuse plan*. Paper presented at IFLA WLIC 2017. Retrieved from http://library.ifla.org/1797/

US Congress. (2013). *S.350 - Fair Access to Science and Technology Research Act of 2013*. Retrieved from https://www.congress.gov/bill/113th-congress/senate-bill/350

USGS. (n.d.) *Data Management. Why you share your data*. Retrieved from https://www.usgs.gov/products/data-and-tools/data-management/why-share-your-data

Wang, L. (2018). Twinning data science with information science in schools of library and information science. *The Journal of Documentation, 74*(6), 1243–1257. doi:10.1108/JD-02-2018-0036

WCRIF. (2019). *Hong Kong Principles*. World Conference on Research Integrity Foundation. Retrieved from https://wcrif.org/guidance/hong-kong-principles

Wilkinson, M. D., Dumontier, M., Aalbersberg, I. J., Appleton, G., Axton, M., Baak, A., & Mons, B. (2016). The FAIR guiding principles for scientific data management and stewardship. *Scientific Data, 3*(1), 1–9. doi:10.1038data.2016.18 PMID:26978244

Writing a Data Management Plan. (n.d.). Retrieved from https://www.ucl.ac.uk/library/research-support/research-data-management/policies/writing-data-management-plan

Yoon, A., & Lee, Y. Y. (2019). Factors of trust in data reuse. *Online Information Review, 43*(7), 1245–1262. doi:10.1108/OIR-01-2019-0014

## ADDITIONAL READING

Cardoso, J., Proença, D., & Borbinha, J. (2020). Machine-actionable data management plans: A knowledge retrieval approach to automate the assessment of funders' requirements. *Advances in Information Retrieval: 42nd European Conference on IR Research (ECIR 2020),* 118–125. 10.1007/978-3-030-45442-5_15

CODATA. (n.d.). *About CODATA*. Retrieved from https://codata.org/about-codata/

Dominik, M., Nzweundji, J. G., Ahmed, N., Carnicelli, S., Mat Jalaluddin, N. S., Fernandez Rivas, D., Narita, V., Enany, S., & Rios Rojas, C. (2022). Open Science – For Whom? *Data Science Journal*, *21*(1), 1–8. doi:10.5334/dsj-2022-001

Ramezani, S., Aalto, T., Gruenpeter, M., Herterich, P., Hooft, R., & Koers, H. (2021). *Framework for assessing FAIR Services*. Digital Curation Centre. Retrieved from https://dcc.ac.uk/biblio/d27-framework-assessing-fair-services

UK Data Service. (n.d.) *10 top tips for citing data. Find it, use it, cite it*. Retrieved from https://www.ukdataservice.ac.uk/media/622247/toptentips.pdf

Virkus, S., & Garoufallou, E. (2020). Data science and its relationship to library and information science: A content analysis. *Data Technologies and Applications*, *54*(5), 643–663. doi:10.1108/DTA-07-2020-0167

## KEY TERMS AND DEFINITIONS

**Data Curation:** A complex activity for the active and ongoing management of data through its lifecycle in order to preserve, share, and discover it.

**Data Management Plan:** A formal document that states what researchers intend to do with the data in the course and after their research project.

**Data Retrieval:** A process of identifying and extracting data by queries, made in a database.

**Data Reuse:** A set of activities for enabling the availability of data in order to eliminating, or reducing repeated accesses to the same data, and bringing in varied benefits for scientific research.

**Data Sharing:** A complex activity for making data available to other investigators in order to allow its use and reuse for scholarly research.

**Research Data Management:** An integral part of the research process, helping to ensure that datasets, pertaining to a project are properly organized, described, preserved, and shared. By involving the care and maintenance of the data, RDM is exercised in the course of the given research cycle.

# About the Contributors

**John Wang** is a professor in the Department of Information Management and Business Analytics at Montclair State University, USA. Having received a scholarship award, he came to the USA and completed his Ph.D. in operations research at Temple University. Due to his extraordinary contributions beyond a tenured full professor, Dr. Wang has been honored with two special range adjustments in 2006 and 2009, respectively. He has published over 100 refereed papers and seventeen books. He has also developed several computer software programs based on his research findings.

\* \* \*

**Nassir Abba-Aji**, PhD, is a Senior Lecturer at the Department of Mass Communication, University of Maiduguri, Borno State, Nigeria, and the Sub-Dean, Faculty of Social Sciences of the university. He is a one-time Chairman, Jere Local Government Area, Borno State, as well as Commissioner for Religious Affairs during the Senator Ali Modu Sheriff Administration in Borno State. Dr Nassir has published several articles and book chapters, and has presented papers at several conferences.

**Peter Abraldes** completed his BA in political science at the University of Pittsburgh. He completed graduate work in statistics and earned his masters in data analytics at the Pennsylvania State University. Peter also spent time studying development economics in Argentina and Brazil, especially how international trade impacts developing countries. His studies include labor economics, trade export policies, and national industrial development policies. He is a maritime trade analyst for the Philadelphia Regional Port Authority, focused on optimizing the organization's cargo development strategy. The strategy includes understanding how the port can differentiate itself and make it more resilient to supply chain disruptions and international policy changes. He has been the scholarship chair for the World Trade Association of Philadelphia since 2018.

**Anal Acharya** is currently Assistant Professor in Computer Science department in St. Xavier's College, Kolkata. His current research interest is Educational Data Mining.

**Prageet Aeron** is presently an Assistant Professor at the department of Information Management at MDI Gurgaon. He is a Fellow (FPM) of Computers and Information Systems Group from the Indian Institute of Management Ahmedabad, and a B.Tech from the Indian Institute of Technology-BHU, Varanasi. He has over 10 years of teaching experience across various B-schools in NCR and is actively engaged in teaching and research in the areas of Entrepreneurship, Strategic Information Systems, e-Commerce and Big Data Applications in Management. His research work has been regularly accepted in reputed International Journals and Conferences.

**Javier M. Aguiar Pérez** is Associate Professor at University of Valladolid, and Head of the Data Engineering Research Unit. His research is focused on Big Data, Artificial Intelligence, and Internet of Things. He has managed international research projects and he has contributed in the standardisation field as expert at the European Telecommunications Standards Institute. He serves as editor, guest editor and reviewer, and author in several international journals, books and conferences. Furthermore, he has been involved as reviewer and rapporteur in several international research initiatives.

**Gilbert Ahamer** is inclined to analyse fundamentals of philosophy for the target of designing new paradigms driven by foresight when it comes to develop policies for mastering globalisation. As a physicist, environmentalist, economist, technologist, and geographer, he suggests that radically new concepts might beneficially contribute to solving the pressing problems of global change. He co-founded the 'Global Studies' curriculum at Graz University, Austria, studied and established global long-term scenarios when affiliated to the International Institute for Applied Systems Analysis IIASA, and is active in institutionalised dialogue-building for the Environment Agency Austria in Central Asia, Ukraine, and Georgia since his earlier affiliation to the Austrian Academy of Sciences.

**Md. Omar Al-Zadid** is currently working as a Senior Officer in Bank Asia Limited, Dhaka, Bangladesh. He began his career as a corporate professional in The Daily 'Prothom Alo', one of the top ranking newspapers in Bangladesh. His primary responsibilities in Prothom Alo included key account management and customer relationship management in advertisement department. He achieved 2nd Category Ptak Prize Award in recognition of global supply chain understanding and leadership in the young supply chain community organized by International Supply Chain Education Alliance (ISCEA) in 2013. He obtained Certificate of Achievement for completion of ITES Foundation Skills Training on Digital Marketing under NASSCOM IT-ITES sector Skill Council Certification in 2015. He holds an MBA in Marketing from the University of Dhaka, Bangladesh. His principal research interests include marketing analytics, innovation adoption, digital marketing, online banking, consumer behavior and psychology, Blue Ocean marketing strategy etc.

**İnci Albayrak** is an Professor in the Department of Mathematical Engineering at Yildiz Technical University (YTU),Turkey, where she has been a faculty member since 1992. She received her BS in 1990, MS in 1993 and PhD in 1997 in Mathematical Engineering from Yildiz Technical University. She had studied spectral theory and operator theory. She has lots of papers in these areas. In recent years, she has collaborated actively with researchers and focused on fuzzy mathematics. She has ongoing research projects about fuzzy linear equation systems and fuzzy linear programming problem.

**Dima Alberg** is a Researcher in SCE – Shamoon College of Engineering. His areas of specialty are financial data mining, scientific programming, and simulation methods. His current and future research plans focus on developing new models and tools that allow researchers and practitioners to analyze and solve practical problems in data science research areas.

**Miguel Alonso Felipe** received his M.S. degrees in telecommunication engineering from the University of Valladolid, Spain. In addition, he is PhD Candidate at University of Valladolid and Researcher of the Data Engineering Research Unit. His research is mainly focused on Big Data, Artificial Intelligence, and Internet of Things. Besides, he is co-author of some publications in journals, dealing with topics related to his lines of research.

**Yas Alsultanny** is the scientist of machine learning, data mining, and quantitative analysis, he is a computer engineering and data analysis PhD holder. He was spent his past 30 years of his life dedicated to the advancement of technological convergence and knowledge transfer to students. He was developed a high standard of research methods for graduate students and MBA through his supervising 100 MSc and PhD theses, and consulting 140 MBA projects, moreover he supervised 40 higher diploma projects and 100 BSc projects. Professor Alsultanny served for a reputed university in Bahrain: Arabian Gulf University (AGU), French Arabian Business School, and University of Bahrain. In Jordan: Applied Science University (ASU), Amman Arab University, Al-Balqa Applied University, and the Arab Academy for Banking and Financial Sciences. In Iraq: University of Baghdad, University of Technology, Al-Mustansiriya University, and Institute of Technology. In Germany: Arab German Academy for Science and Technology (online). Besides these, he was held position director of the AGU University Consultations, Community Services, Training, and Continuous Teaching Centre in Bahrain. And the position of head of the Computer Information Systems department and vice dean College of Information Technology in ASU University in Jordan. Alsultanny was worked a chair of statistical and KPIs committees in AGU University, chair of quality assurance and accreditation committee in Amman Arab University, member of quality assurance and accreditation committee in ASU and AGU Universities, member of establishing PhD Innovation Management programme in AGU University, member of establishing the college of Information Technology, ASU University, member of establishing Graduate College of Computing Studies, Amman Arab University, member of developing MSc Technology Management programme, member council of College of Graduate Studies, AGU University, and member council of College of Information Technology, ASU University. He is a trainer and a consultant for several public and private organizations, he led more than 100 workshops, and main speaker in many symposiums and conferences. He is a main writer of the UN Environment report, as well as member of writing AGU university strategic plans. In addition, he is reviewer and editor for various international journals.

**Gerardo Amador Soto** is a PhD student in Energy Systems from the National University of Colombia, Researcher in Energy Efficiency for Complex Systems.

**Billie Anderson** is an Assistant Professor of Applied Statistics at UMKC's Henry W. Bloch School of Management. Billie earned her Ph.D. in Applied Statistics from the University of Alabama, Masters of Mathematics and Statistics from the University of South Alabama, and her Bachelor of Mathematics from Spring Hill College. Before entering academia, Billie was a Research Statistician for SAS. SAS is a statistical software company headquartered in North Carolina. Billie wrote data mining algorithms for the banking and insurance industries. Billie maintained a consultancy relationship with SAS as an analytical trainer from 2012-2020. In this role, she taught analytical-based classes to professionals in organizations to help promote best statistical practices. And, she has consulted with different companies like Ann Taylor, Dunn & Bradstreet, Blue Cross Blue Shield of Michigan, Lowes Home Improvement Store, and Starbucks. She assisted these organizations in applying analytics to solve their business problems. Billie's research focus is in the statistical modeling of credit scoring with a particular interest in reject inference.

**Issa Annamoradnejad** is a Ph.D. candidate at the Sharif University of Technology, Tehran, Iran.

**Rahimberdi Annamoradnejad** wrote a chapter on the current and potential application of machine learning for predicting housing prices. He is an Iranian urban planner and an associate professor of geography and urban planning at the University of Mazandaran.

**Joel Antúnez-García** was born in Ensenada B. C., México, in 1975. He received the B. Sc. degree in Physics from Universidad Autónoma de Baja California (UABC), México, in 1999. The M. Sc. from Centro de Investigación Científica y de Educación Superior de Ensenada (CICESE), México, in 2004. The Ph. D. in Physical-Industrial Engineering from Universidad Autónoma de Nuevo Léon (UANL), Méxio, in 2010. From 2012 to 2013, he did a postdoctoral stay at Centro de Nanociencias y Nanotecnología at UNAM, working on DFT calculations to obtain different zeolites' electronic properties. From 2013-2015 he worked as a professor at Centro de Enseñanza Técnica y Superior (CETYS university). From 2016 to date, he has been involved in the theoretical study of bi-and tri-metallic catalysts based on MoS2 compounds and zeolites.

**Dounia Arezki** (), after obtaining an MSc in Artificial Intelligence, pursued her Ph.D. program in information technology at the Computer Science faculty of Science and Technology university of Oran (USTO) from 2017 to 2021. January 2022, she started an MSc program in international business. Presently her research interests are focused on spatial data processing, clustering algorithms, data analysis, risk, and project management.

**Heba Atteya** is the Senior Director of Business Intelligence and Data Analytics unit at The American University in Cairo (AUC). She led the founding team who built AUC's enterprise data-warehouse and business intelligence (BI) platform. In her current role, she manages the full-spectrum of the BI process including: setting AUC's BI roadmap, leading the data architecture and modeling functions, as well as the automated data extraction from the different source systems. Heba completed her MSc in Computer Science at AUC in Spring 2017 in the topic of visualizing large datasets. She earned her bachelor of science in Information Systems with honors in 2010 and joined AUC as a full-time staff member since 2011. She had a successful track record of achievements which qualified her for the position of BI and Data Analytics Director in 2017. Ever since then, she has successfully expanded the BI platform to extract data from the main ERP of the University, the main student information system, and the university CRM, as well as several other source systems providing a 360-degree view of student, faculty, staff and alumni of the University. Recently, she has led the efforts of the AUC's first big data project, analyzing Wi-Fi big data streams to support COVID-19 contact tracing process, as well as AUC's first AI-powered Chat-bot supporting the IT Help Desk function. She has always found inspiration in working with data and finding its underlying hidden patterns. She believes that informed decision-making is what every institution needs to compete in this highly competitive market.

**Antonio Badia** is an Associate Professor in the Computer Science and Engineering department at the Speed School of Engineering, University of Louisville. His research focuses on database systems and data science; his previous projects have been funded by the National Science Foundation and US Navy. He's the author of over 50 publications and 2 books.

**Youakim Badr** is an Associate Professor of Data Analytics in the Great Valley campus of the Pennsylvania State University, USA. He earned his Ph.D. in computer science from the National Institute of Applied Sciences (INSA-Lyon), where he worked as an associate professor in the computer science and engineering department. Over the course of his research, Dr. Badr has worked extensively in the area of service computing (distributed systems) and information security. His current research strategy aims at developing a new software engineering approach for designing and deploying "smart connected devices" and building "smart service systems" for the Internet of Things.

**Surajit Bag** is an Associate Professor at the Institute of Management and Technology, Ghaziabad, India (AACSB accredited). He is also working as a Visiting Associate Professor in the Department of Transport and Supply Chain Management, University of Johannesburg, South Africa. He has 11 years of industry experience. He has teaching experince from India, Morocco, South Africa and U.K. Educationally, Dr. Surajit earned his second Ph.D. in Information Management from the Postgraduate School of Engineering Management, University of Johannesburg, South Africa, and holds his first Ph.D. in Supply Chain Management from the School of Business, University of Petroleum and Energy Studies, India. Prior to getting a Ph.D., he obtained an MBA in Marketing Management (major) from MAKAUT (formerly the West Bengal University of Technology), India. His substantive areas of interest include Industry 4.0, big data, artificial intelligence applications in marketing and supply chain, sustainability. His expertise lies in the areas of Multivariate Data Analysis Techniques, Mediation Analysis, Moderation Analysis, and Structural Equation Modeling. He is familiar with data analysis software such as WarpPLS, PLS-SEM, SPSS, and Python. Surajit has published some of the most cited papers in the Industrial Marketing Management, International Journal of Production Economics, International Journal of Production Research, Technological Forecasting & Social Change, Production, Planning & Control, IEEE Transactions on Engineering Management, Journal of Cleaner Production, Annals of Operations Research, Information Systems Frontiers, Journal of Business Research, and Supply Chain Management: An International Journal. He is the proud recipient of the "AIMS-IRMA Young Management Researcher Award 2016" for his significant contribution to management research. He is the proud recipient of best "Doctoral Research Award 2020" from the Postgraduate School of Engineering Management, University of Johannesburg in recognition of the outstanding academic excellence. Dr. Surajit was listed in World's Top 2% Scientists which was released by Stanford University. He is a professional member of the Association of International Business, (AIB), Chartered Institute of Procurement and Supply (CIPS); Association for Supply Chain Management (ASCM); Institute of Electrical and Electronics Engineers (IEEE); Indian Rubber Institute; Association of Indian Management Scholars (AIMS International); and Operational Research Society of India (ORSI).

**Sikha Bagui** is Professor and Askew Fellow in the Department of Computer Science, at The University West Florida, Pensacola, Florida. Dr. Bagui is active in publishing peer reviewed journal articles in the areas of database design, data mining, Big Data analytics, machine learning and AI. Dr. Bagui has worked on funded as well unfunded research projects and has 85+ peer reviewed publications, some in highly selected journals and conferences. She has also co-authored several books on database and SQL. Bagui also serves as Associate Editor and is on the editorial board of several journals.

**Samir Bandyopadhyay** is presently a distinguished professor of The Bhawanipur Education Society College.

**Soumya Banerjee** is the Chief Technical Advisor & Board member of Must with specialised on ML & Security.

**Sarang Bang** is currently Studying at Vellore Institute of Technology, Vellore (India) pursuing Btech in Computer Science with Specialization in Data Science. He completed his schooling from Bhavan's Bhagwandas Purohit Vidya Mandir, Nagpur wherein he secured 10 cgpa in 10th grade and few other merit awards . He has been District Level Volleyball player during his schooling year. After choosing PCM and completing his 12th grade with 86.7 percentage he developed a lot of interest in coding and hence chose Computer Science as his career. In VIT, he is core committee member at VIT Mathematical Association Student chapter and also member at Lions Club International Leo Club Victory, Nagpur. He is passionate about Web Development and has worked on many projects as well as contributed to Hackathons as a front end developer. He also has interest in flutter development, machine learning. He wants to focus on a career in research and is currently exploring Machine learning and Artificial Intelligence.

**Bazila Banu** is a Professor and Head in the Department of Artificial Intelligence and Machine Learning at Bannari Amman Institute of Technology, India. She received her PhD degree in Information and Communication Engineering at Anna University, India in 2015 and guiding PhD Scholars. She holds 16 years of professional experience including academic and software Industry. She published 15 articles in National and International journals . She is an active reviewer and Guest Editor for International journals and technical committee member for International conferences. Her research interest includes Big Data and Data Analytics. She has filed three National level Patents and received grants from AICTE for Margdarshan scheme (19 Lakhs) and National Commission for women.

**Isak Barbopoulos**, PhD, has worked as a research psychologist studying the situational activation of consumer motives. He is currently working as a data scientist at Insert Coin, where he is developing and implementing a system for adaptive gamification.

**Mikel Barrio Conde** is a PhD candidate at University of Valladolid, who received his M.S. degrees in telecommunication engineering from the University of Valladolid, Spain. He is researcher of the Data Engineering Research Unit and his research is focused on Artificial Intelligence, and Internet of Things. Also, he is co-author of some publications in journals, dealing with topics related to his lines of his research.

**Sotiris Batsakis** is a Laboratory Teaching member of the Technical University of Crete, Greece and he has worked as Affiliated Senior Researcher and Senior Lecturer at the University of Huddersfield, UK. He received a diploma in Computer Engineering and Informatics from the University of Patras, Greece with highest distinction, and a Master's degree and a Ph.D. in Electronic and Computer Engineering from the Technical University of Crete Greece. He is an experienced researcher having participated on various research projects and with over 50 research publications in the areas of Knowledge Representation, Artificial Intelligence and Information Retrieval.

**Andrew Behrens** is an Instructor of business analytics courses at Dakota State University and is pursuing a Ph.D. in Information Systems at Dakota State University. He has worked with Cherie Noteboom for three years and has published in IS Conferences (MWAIS, IACIS, and AMCIS).

**Santiago Belda** https://orcid.org/0000-0003-3739-6056 (ORCID ID) From 2011 to 2015, he engaged in a PhD in Mathematical Methods and Modeling in Science and Engineering at Universidad de Alicante. He worked in various projects and is currently affiliated to Universidad de Alicante as a Distinguished postdoc researcher Presently his research interests are Astronomy, VLBI, Earth Orientation Parameters, Terrestrial and Celestial Reference Frames. Santiago Belda was partially supported by Generalitat Valenciana SEJIGENT program (SEJIGENT/2021/001), European Union – NextGenerationEU (ZAMBRANO 21-04) and European Research Council (ERC) under the ERC-2017-STG SENTIFLEX project grant number 755617.

**Zakaria Bendaoud** is an associate professor at the University of Saida. His research focuses on information retrieval, supply chain and transportation.

**Mustapha Benramdane** is a Ph.D. student in Computer Science at CNAM. His main research domains are matchmaking and Intent-based Contextual Orchestration inside Digital Business Ecosystems and Platforms.

**Níssia Bergiante** is a Doctor in Transportation Engineering (COPPE UFRJ– Federal University of Rio de Janeiro - Brazil). Production Engineer with a Master in Production Engineering (UFF-Brazil). Background in Production Engineering, focusing on Operational Management and Operational Research, acting on the following subjects: Decision Analysis and Soft Operation Research (Problem Structuring Methods); Operation Management and Process improvement.

**Aditi A. Bhoir** is a final year undergraduate student, currently pursuing Bachelor of Technology (B. Tech.) in Mechanical Engineering, at Sardar Patel College of Engineering, Mumbai, India. She will be doing Master of Science (MS) in abroad from fall 2022. Her focus research interest is design and robotics.

**Trevor J. Bihl** is a Senior Research Engineer with the Air Force Research Laboratory, Sensors Directorate where he leads a diverse portfolio in artificial intelligence (AI) and autonomy. Dr. Bihl earned his doctorate in Electrical Engineering from the Air Force Institute of Technology, Wright Patterson AFB, OH, and he also received a bachelor's and master's degree in Electrical Engineering at Ohio University, Athens, OH. Dr. Bihl is a Senior Member of IEEE and he has served as a board member as Vice President of Chapters/Fora for INFORMS (The Institute of Operations Research and the Management Sciences). His research interests include artificial intelligence, autonomous systems, machine learning, and operations research.

**Sanjay Krishno Biswas** is a faculty of Anthropology at Shahjalal University of Science and Technology, Bangladesh. He is currently pursuing his Ph.D. His academic interest includes Anthropological Theory, Mobility, and Migration, Diaspora and Transnationality, Ethnicity and Marginality, and Ecology and Climate Change. Mr. Biswas has a number of articles in reputed journals and book chapters from reputed publishers including Routledge.

**Karim Bouamrane** received the PhD Degree in computer science from the Oran University in 2006. He is full Professor of computer Science at the same university. He is member of computer science laboratory (LIO). He is the head of the team decision and piloting system. His current research interests deal with decision support system, transportation system, risk management, Health system, bio-inspired approach. He participates in several scientific committees' international/national conferences in Algeria and others countries in the same domain and collaborate in Algerian-French scientific projects. He is co-author of more than 60 scientific publications and communications.

**Samia Bouzefrane** is Professor at the Conservatoire National des Arts et Métiers (Cnam) of Paris. She received her PhD in Computer Science from the University of Poitiers (France) in 1998. After four years at the University of Le Havre (France), she joined in 2002 the CEDRIC Lab of Cnam. She is the co-author of many books (Operating Systems, Smart Cards, and Identity Management Systems). She is a lead expert in the French ministry. She is involved in many scientific workshops and conferences. Her current research areas cover Security and AI Internet of Thing.

**Paul Bracewell** is Co-Founder of New Zealand-based data science firm, DOT loves data and Adjunct Research Fellow at Victoria University of Wellington. He received his PhD in Statistics from Massey University and has contributed to more than 50 peer reviewed publications.

**James Braman** is an Associate Professor in the Computer Science/Information Technology Department at the Community College of Baltimore County for the School of Business, Technology and Law. He earned a B.S. and M.S. in Computer Science and D.Sc. in Information Technology from Towson University. He is currently pursuing a M.S. in Thanatology from Marian University. From 2009 to 2017 he was a joint editor-in-chief for the European Alliance for Innovation (EAI) endorsed Transactions on E-Learning with Dr. Giovanni Vincenti. Dr. Braman's research interests include thanatechnology, virtual and augmented reality, e-Learning, affective computing, agent-based technologies, and information retrieval.

**Alexis D. Brown** is an Assistant Professor in the Computer Science & Information Technology Department at the Community College of Baltimore County. They hold a master's degree in Management Information Systems from the University of Maryland Baltimore County. Their main research interests focus on education and instructional technology but includes varied technology-related topics.

**Joseph Budu** is an award-winning research scholar within the information systems discipline. He received the University of Ghana Vice Chancellor award for the outstanding doctoral dissertation for the humanities for the 2019/2020 academic year. Prior to this feat, he has undertaken several academic research and consultancies. Dr. Budu has written one mini-book, and one research workbook to guide students in conducting academic research. See https://bit.ly/BuduContentfolio for various contents Joseph has produced (e.g. manuals, blog posts, lead magnets, and presentations).

**Rachel Cardarelli** graduated from Bryant University with a degree in Actuarial Mathematics and concentration in Applied Statistics. Since graduating, she has been working as an Actuarial Analyst.

**Ferhan Çebi** is a Professor in Istanbul Technical University Faculty of Management, Management Engineering Department. She holds a B.S. in Chemical Engineering from ITU, a M.S. and a Ph.D. in Management Engineering from ITU. She gives the lectures on Operations Research and Operations Management at the undergraduate level and graduate level. Her main research areas are application of Operations Research techniques to the manufacturing and service problems, production planning and control, fuzziness and mathematical modelling, decision analysis, decision support systems, information technology for competitiveness. She is acting scientific committee member and organization committee member for a number of national & international conferences. Ferhan Cebi is member of editorial boards of International Journal of Information Systems in the Service Sector, International Journal of Information & Decision Sciences, and International Journal of Data Sciences. Her works have been published in several international and national conference proceedings and journals such as Computers and Industrial Engineering, Information Sciences, Information Systems Frontiers, Journal of Enterprise Information Management, Logistics Information Management, International Journal of Information and Decision Sciences.

**Shuvro Chakrobartty** has made significant contributions to identifying, conceptualizing, and formulating the research objective and methodology, the proposed framework, and the analysis of the findings. With a prior educational background in Computer Science and Business, currently, he is a Ph.D. student of Information Systems at Dakota State University. His research interests lie in responsible AI and data analytics. He has work experience in multiple industries within the software, cloud, and data engineering domain. He is a member of the Association for Information Systems (AIS) professional organizations and serves as a peer-reviewer for multiple conferences, books, and journal publications.

**Hannah H. Chang** is Associate Professor of Marketing at Lee Kong Chian School of Business, Singapore Management University. She received a PhD in Marketing from Graduate School of Business, Columbia University.

**Hsin-Lu Chang** is a professor in the Department of Management Information Systems, National Chengchi University. She received a Ph.D. in information systems at the School of Commerce, the University of Illinois at Urbana-Champaign. Her research areas are in E-Commerce, IT value, and technology adoption. She has published in Decision Support Systems, Information Systems Journal, International Journal of Electronic Commerce, Journal of Organizational Computing and Electronic Commerce, and Information Systems and e-Business Management.

**D. K. Chaturvedi** is Professor in Electrical Engineering at DEI, Agra, India.

**Akhilesh Chauhan** is a fourth-year Ph.D. (IS) student in the College of Business and Information Systems at the Dakota State University (Madison, S.D., USA). He is received a master's degree in Analytics from Dakota State University. He is currently working as a graduate research assistant at DSU. His current research interest includes association rule mining, machine learning, healthcare informatics, transfer learning, text mining, and data mining.

**Tanvi Chawla** completed her B.Tech in Information Technology (IT) from MDU, Rohtak in 2012 and received her M.Tech in Software Engineering (SE) from ITM University, Gurgaon in 2014. She has completed her Ph.D. in Computer Science and Engineering (CSE) from Malaviya National Institute of Technology (MNIT), Jaipur in 2022. During her Ph.D. she published articles in premier journals and conferences. Her research interests are Semantic Web, Big Data, Distributed Data Storage, and Processing.

**Xi Chen** is a lecturer in the College of Humanities at Beijing University of Civil Engineering and Architecture. She is also a research assistant in the Beijing Research Base for Architectural Culture. Her current research interests include English academic writing, settlement evolution, and urbanization in China and the U.S., etc.

**Xiaoyan Cheng** is a professor at University of Nebraska at Omaha. Dr. Cheng's research has been published in Auditing: A Journal of Practice & Theory, Advances in Accounting, Review of Quantitative Finance and Accounting, Research in Accounting Regulation, Global Finance Journal, Asian Review of Accounting, and Review of Pacific Basin Financial Markets and Policies.

**Xusen Cheng** is a Professor of Information Systems in the School of Information at Renmin University of China in Beijing. He obtained his PhD degree from the University of Manchester, UK. His research is in the areas of information systems and management particularly focusing on online collaboration, global teams, the sharing economy, e-commerce, and e-learning.

**Paula Chimenti** is an Associate Professor of Strategy and Innovation at COPPEAD graduate school of business, Federal University of Rio de Janeiro, Brazil. She holds a PhD in Administration from Coppead. She is the coordinator of the Center of Studies in Strategy and Innovation, where she develops research about the impact of disruptive innovations on business ecosystems. She has several works published in journals in Brazil and abroad, such as JGIM and JCR. Her article on Business Ecosystems received the first prize in one of the most important academic conferences in Brazil. She teaches Management Networked Businesses, Digital Marketing and Research Methodology in the Executive MBA, Master's and Doctorate programs at COPPEAD / UFRJ. She coordinated the Master program and Executive MBA programs at COPPEAD. Paula is the cases for teaching Editor for RAC - Revista de Administração Contemporânea, one of the top journals in Brasil.

**Jahid Siraz Chowdhuy** is a Fellow Ph.D. the program, Department of Social Administration and Justice, Faculty of Arts and Social Sciences, University of Malaya, 50603, Kuala Lumpur, Malaysia and Ex-faculty of Anthropology, Shahjalal University of Science and Technology, Bangladesh.

**Parvathi Chundi** is a professor of computer science at University of Nebraska at Omaha. Her primary research interests are in the fields of data mining, big data, and computer vision. She is currently focused on developing algorithms for automatic labeling of data for semantic and instance segmentation of biofilm images.

**William Chung** is an associate professor of Management Sciences at the City University of Hong Kong. He earned his Ph.D. in Management Sciences at the University of Waterloo, Canada. His personal research interests mainly focus on developing mathematical methodologies for energy-environmental policy problems, like large-scale equilibrium models, benchmarking methods for the energy consumption performance of buildings, and decomposition analysis of energy intensity. His papers can be found in the following journals: Operations Research, European Journal of Operational Research (EJOR), Computational Economics, Energy Economics, Energy Policy, Energy, Applied Energy, and Energy and Buildings. In addition, he is the director and founder of the Energy and Environmental Policy Research

Unit at the City University of Hong Kong. He was a visiting professor of the Center for International Energy and Environment Strategy Studies, Renmin University of China.

**Mateus Coimbra** holds a PhD in Administration from COPPEAD school of business in Federal University of Rio de Janeiro, Brazil.

**Mirko Čubrilo** is BSc in Mathematics, MSc in Mathematics, PhD in Computer Science (all from Zagreb University, Croatia). Full professor with tenure (Zagreb University, Croatia). Currently engaged at the University of the North (Varaždin, Croatia). Scientific interest includes mathematical logic, theory of algorithms, logic programming, artificial intelligence in a broad context, including neural nets and deep learning. Author of two books on the topics of mathematical logic and programming and more than fifty papers, published in journals and conference proceedings around the world (Germany, Japan, UK, USA, Egypt, Slovakia, Greece, Italy).

**Marcin Czajkowski** received his Master's degree (2007) and his PhD with honours (2015) in Computer Science from the Bialystok University of Technology, Poland. His research activity mainly concerns bioinformatics, machine learning and data mining, in particular, decision trees, evolutionary algorithms and relative expression analysis.

**Jeya Mala D.** has a Ph.D. in Software Engineering with Specialization on Software Testing and is currently working as 'Associate Professor Senior' in Vellore Institute of Technology, Chennai, India. She had been in the industry for about 4 years. She has a profound teaching and research experience of more than 24 years. She has published a book on "Object Oriented Analysis and Design using UML" for Tata McGraw Hill Publishers, also she has published 2 edited books for IGI Global, USA. She has published more than 70 papers about her research works at leading international journals and conferences such as IET, ACM, Springer, World Scientific, Computing and Informatics etc. As a researcher, Dr. Jeya Mala had investigated practical aspects of software engineering and object oriented paradigms for effective software development. Her work on Software Testing has fetched grants from UGC under Major Research Project scheme. Her dissertation has been listed as one of the best Ph.D. thesis in the CSIR – Indian Science Abstracts. She has successfully guided numerous Software Development based projects for the IBM- The Great Mind Challenge (TGMC) contest. The project she has mentored during 2007, has received national level Best Top 10 Project Award – 2007, from IBM. Currently she is guiding Ph.D. and M.Phil research scholars under the areas of Software Engineering and optimization techniques. She is a life member of Computer Society of India and an invited member of ACEEE. She forms the reviewer board in Journals like IEEE Transactions on Software Engineering, Elsevier – Information Sciences, Springer, World Scientific, International Journal of Metaheuristics etc. She has organized several sponsored national level conferences and workshops, notably she is one of the organizers of "Research Ideas in Software Engineering and Security (RISES'13) – A run-up event of ICSE 2014 sponsored by Computer Society of India". She has been listed in Marquis Who's Who list in 2011. She has completed certification on Software Testing Fundamentals, Brain bench certification on Java 1.1 programming, IBM certification as Associate Developer Websphere Application Studio. She is a proud recipient of several laurels from industries like Honeywell, IBM and Microsoft for her remarkable contributions in the field of Software Development and Object Orientation.

**Karim Dabbabi** is currently working as an assistant professor at the Faculty of Sciences of Tunis (FST). He held the postdoctoral position for a year and a half at the same faculty. He obtained his doctorate degree in electronics in July 2019 from the FST in addition to that of a research master's degree in automatic and signal processing from the National School of Engineers of Tunis in 2014. He has worked on various research projects in Automatic Speech Recognition (ASR), speaker diarization, automatic indexing of audio documents, audio segmentation and natural language processing (NLP) in general. In addition, he has worked on the identification of different neurological diseases, including Parkinson's and Alzheimer's using different voice features.

**Indraneel Dabhade** completed his M.S. in Engineering at Clemson University. He is a CISSP and has studied Cybersecurity from the Massachusetts Institute of Technology Center for Professional Education. He is currently pursuing an advanced certification in information security at the Stanford Center for Professional Development. Indraneel is a published author in Data Science, Human Factors, and Intellectual Property Rights. He has over 7 years of industry experience. Currently, Indraneel heads an automation firm (O Automation) in India.

**Debabrata Datta** is currently an Assistant Professor In Computer Science at St. Xavier's College (Autonomous), Kolkata. His research interest is Data Analytics and Natural Language Processing.

**Magdalene Delighta Angeline D.** is currently in the Department of Computer Science and Engineering as Assistant Professor, Joginpally B.R Engineering College, Hyderabad, India. Her research area includes data mining, computer networks. She has a good number of research publications.

**Boryana Deliyska** is professor retired in Department of Computer Systems and Informatics of University of Forestry, Sofia, Bulgaria. She obtained a PHD Degree in Computer Science from Technical University of Sofia, BG. She has long-standing research and practical experience in Semantic Web technologies, e-learning, computer lexicography, ontology engineering, web design and programming, geographical information systems (GIS), databases and information systems. She teaches information technologies, programming, CAD, computer graphics and computer networks. She is an author of 4 monographies, 7 Elsevier's dictionaries, 18 textbooks, more of 130 journal articles and conference papers.

**Javier Del-Pozo-Velázquez** received his M.S. degrees in telecommunication engineering from the University of Valladolid, Spain. In addition, he is PhD Candidate at University of Valladolid and Researcher of the Data Engineering Research Unit. His research is mainly focused on Big Data, Artificial Intelligence and Internet of Things. Besides, he is co-author of some publications in journals, dealing with topics related to his lines of research.

**Chitra A. Dhawale** (Ph.D in Computer Science) is currently working as a Professor Department of Computer Engineering P.R. Pote College of Engineering and Management, Amravati (MS), India. Earlier She worked as a Professor at Symbiosis International University, Pune (MS). To her credit, 06 research scholars have been awarded PhD. so far under her guidance, by S.G.B. Amravati and R.T.M. Nagpur University. Her research interests include Image and Video Processing, Machine Learning, Deep Learning, Multi-Biometric, Big Data Analytics. She has developed many projects for Machine Learning, Deep Learning, Natural Language Processing Algorithms using python. She also has hands on experience in

R-Programming, Hadoop-MapReduce, Apache Spark, Tableau. She has published 02 books, 08 Book Chapters, 26 Research papers in Journals (02- SCI-Indexed,15-Scopus Indexed, 06-UGC Journals and 03 in other research journals) and presented 35 papers in International Conferences (Abroad Conference-08, IEEE-18, ACM-02, Elsevier-01,Springer-04, Others-02) and 19 papers in National Conferences. She has reviewed 09 books for various publishers.

**Kritika Dhawale** is working as Deep Learning Engineer at SkyLark Drones, Bangalore. She has published 2 book chapters on Deep Learning. Her Research interest is Deep Learning and Cloud Computing.

**Harini Dissanayake** is a research student at Victoria University of Wellington, New Zealand working on her project 'Data informed decision bias.' The project focuses on identifying discriminatory bias in operational algorithms and remedying sample selection bias in datasets used for informing both commercial and government decisions.

**Emmanuel Djaba** is an early-stage academic with an avid interest in data science and machine learning. With extensive experience in industry, he is interested in doing innovative research that can be readily applied to interesting problems. He is currently a PhD student at the University of Ghana where he is pursuing a PhD in information systems.

**Matt Drake** has been a researcher in supply chain management for twenty years, focusing mainly on the areas of supply chain education and ethics. He has published over 30 articles and book chapters during this time. His chapter discusses the use of IoT technology to improve supply chain management. As firms look to improve their supply chain resilience in response to the COVID-19 pandemic and other disruptions, IoT data increases visibility, traceability, and can help firms to mitigate risks through added agility and responsiveness. The improved decision making made possible from IoT data creates a competitive advantage in the market.

**Dorin Drignei** received his PhD in Statistics from Iowa State University in 2004. Following his graduation, he was a postdoctoral researcher at the National Center for Atmospheric Research for two years. In 2006 he joined Oakland University where he is currently a Professor of Statistics. His current research interests include statistical modeling of big time series data.

**Yuehua Duan** is a PhD student in Computer Science Department at the University of North Carolina, Charlotte. Her research interests include recommender systems, business analytics, data mining, natural language processing, and machine learning.

**Dishit Duggar** is currently Studying at Vellore Institute of Technology, Vellore (India) pursuing Btech in Computer Science with Specialization in Information Security. He completed his schooling from Delhi Public School, Jaipur wherein he secured 10 cgpa in 10th grade and was a gold medal recipient for being a scholar for 6 consecutive years. After choosing PCM and completing his 12th grade with 93.8 percentage, He developed a lot of interest in coding and hence chose Computer Science as his career. In VIT, he is the App Lead of VinnovateIT which is a lab setup by Cognizant and also a member at Student Technical Community which is backed by Microsoft. He is passionate about Apps, Blockchain and Machine Learning and has worked on many projects as well as contributed and lead teams in multiple Hackathons. He wants to focus on a career in research and is currently exploring Cyber Security and Artificial Intelligence.

**Ankur Dumka** is working as Associate Professor and head of department in Women Institute of Technology, Dehradun. He is having more than 10 years of academic and industrial experience. He is having more than 60 research papers in reputed journals and conferences of repute. He contributed 4 books and 12 book chapters with reputed publisher. He is also associated with many reputed journals in the capacity of editorial board members and editor.

**Abhishek Dutta** has completed BS in Computer Science from Calcutta University and MS in Data Science and Analytics from Maulana Abul Kalam Azad University of Technology, Kolkata, India in 2020. He has authored seven conference papers which are published in IEEE Xplore and Springer Link. His research areas include Machine Learning, Deep Learning and AI applications in Finance.

**Santosha Kumar Dwivedy** received the Ph.D. in Mechanical Engineering from Indian Institute of Technology Kharagpur (IIT Kharagpur), India in 2000. He is currently Professor in Department of Mechanical Engineering at Indian Institute of Technology Guwahati (IIT Guwahati). He was also a Visiting Professor at Institute of Engineering and Computational Mechanics, University of Stuttgart, Germany under DAAD-IIT faculty exchange scheme. He has over 180 journal and conference publications with a focus on integrating robotics and dynamics in various fields. His research interests include both industrial and medical robotics, biomechanics, nonlinear vibration, and control along with the applications.

**Brent M. Egan**, MD, is Vice-President, Cardiovascular Disease Prevention in the Improving Health Outcomes group of the American Medical Association. He also serves as Professor of Medicine at the University of South Carolina School of Medicine, Greenville and as Past-President of the South Carolina Upstate affiliate of the American Heart Association. He received his medical degree and training in medicine and hypertension at the University of Michigan. He also served on the Board of Directors and President of the International Society of Hypertension in Blacks for many years. His professional interests center on hypertension, metabolic syndrome and vascular disease, which led to some 350 original papers and reviews. Dr. Egan remains committed to working with colleagues to translate the evidence-base into better cardiovascular health, especially for medically underserved populations.

**Amal El Arid** has earned a Masters' degree in Electrical and Computer Engineering from the American University of Beirut. She has been an instructor in the Department of Computer Science and Information Technology at the Lebanese International University since 2012. In addition, she specializes in programming and networking fields, earning a trainer certificate from the CISCO organization as a CCNA instructor since 2016. She is now working in the artificial intelligence and machine learning research field.

**Houda El Bouhissi** graduated with an engineering degree in computer science from Sidi-Bel-Abbes University - Algeria, in 1995. She received her M. Sc. and Ph. D. in computer science from the University of Sidi-Bel-Abbes, Algeria, in 2008 and 2015, respectively. Also, she received an M. Sc. in eLearning from the University of sciences and technologies, Lille1, France. Currently, she is an Assistant Professor at the University of Bejaia, Algeria. Her research interests include recommender systems, sentiments analysis, information systems interoperability, ontology engineering, and machine learning.

**Mohamed El Touhamy** is a Senior Data Engineer at The American University in Cairo (AUC). He completed his undergraduate studies at the Faculty of Computers and Information, Cairo University, earning a bachelor's degree in Computer Science. Mohamed started his journey in data science in 2017, participating in and leading many mega projects. He has excellent experience in big data engineering, data extraction using different technologies, data quality checks automation, and data warehouse enterprise solution management. He is also a graduate student at The American University in Cairo, seeking his master's degree in Computer Science.

**Caner Erden**, currently working as Assistant Professor in the Faculty of Applied Sciences, Sakarya University of Applied Sciences, Sakarya, Turkey. He worked as resarch assistant of Industrial Engineering at Sakarya University and researcher at Sakarya University Artificial Intelligence Systems Application and Research between 2012-2020. He holds a PhD degree in Industrial Engineering from Natural Science Institue Industrial Engineering Department, Sakarya University, Turkey with thesis titled "Dynamic Integrated Process Planning, Scheduling and Due Date Assignment". His research interests include scheduling, discrete event simulation, meta-heuristic algorithms, modelling and optimization, decision-making under uncertainty, machine learning and deep learning.

**Omar El-Gayar** has made a significant contribution to the conceptualization and formulation of the research objective and methodology, the proposed framework, and the interpretation of the findings. He is a Professor of Information Systems at Dakota State University. His research interests include analytics, business intelligence, and decision support. His numerous publications appear in various information technology-related venues. Dr. El-Gayar serves as a peer and program evaluator for accrediting agencies such as the Higher Learning Commission and ABET and as a peer reviewer for numerous journals and conferences. He is a member of the association for Information Systems (AIS).

**Gozde Erturk Zararsiz** is a faculty member in Biostatistics Department of Erciyes University. Her research mostly focuses on statistical modeling, method comparison, survival analysis and machine learning. Zararsiz completed her M.Sc. from Cukurova University, Institute of Health Sciences, Department of Biostatistics with the thesis entitled as "Evolution of Competing Risks Based on Both Dependent-Independent Real and Simulated Data by Using Self-Developed R Program". In 2015, Zararsiz has started her Ph.D. in Department of Biostatistics of Eskisehir Osmangazi University. During her Ph.D. in 2016, Zararsiz worked as a visiting researcher under the supervision of Prof. Dr. Christoph Klein at the laboratory of the Dr von Hauner Children's Hospital, LMU in Munich. During her research period, Zararsiz has published international papers and received awards. Zararsiz completed her PhD with the thesis entitled as "Bootstrap-Based Regression Approaches in Comparing Laboratory Methods".

**Tasnia Fatin** is a PhD Candidate in Management at Putra Business School, UPM, Malaysia. She has been a Lecturer of Marketing at Northern University Bangladesh (BBA, MBA) where she has taught Brand Management, Strategic Marketing, Principles of Marketing and Marketing Management. She had also been a Lecturer at Independent University Bangladesh. She takes keen interest in Entrepreneurship and has been running her own Business Solutions Agency and a Skill Training Institute. She holds an

MBA in Marketing from the University of Dhaka. She has also worked as a Strategic Marketing Manager for Prasaad Group of Companies to develop real estate projects home and abroad. She has also separately worked on projects in Urban Waste Management and Sustainable Agriculture that has been presented at George Washington University (USA), MIT (USA), Queens University (Canada) and at KLCC (Malaysia). Her research interests include digital marketing, disruptive innovations and the way they shape the world, IoT (Internet of Things), and sustainable business practices. She participated in several national level, Government level, and International level Youth Conferences and Forums home and abroad mentored by Industry leaders, experts, and professors from Harvard, Oxford, and many other prestigious institutions.

**Arafat Febriandirza** is a junior researcher at the Research Center for Informatics, The Indonesia Institute of Sciences (LIPI), Indonesia since 2020. He obtained his bachelor degree in Electrical Engineering from University of General Achmad Yani, Indonesia in 2008. He earned a Master's degree in Information Technology from the University of Indonesia in 2011 and a Doctorate in Communication and Transportation Engineering from Wuhan university of Technology in 2018. Arafat Febriandirza's research interests include issues in the field of Machine Learning, Modeling, Simulation, and Social Informatics.

**Egi Arvian Firmansyah** is a permanent lecturer at the Faculty of Economics and Business Universitas Padjadjaran, Indonesia. He has been published numerous journal articles and conferences proceedings. He is also a finance and managing editor at Jurnal Bisnis dan Manajemen, which is an accredited and reputable journal in Indonesia. Currently, he is a Ph.D student in finance at Universiti Brunei Darussalam.

**Robert Leslie Fisher** was educated in New York City. He attended Stuyvesant High School, a special science high school, has a bachelors degree (cum laude) in sociology from City College of New York, and a graduate degree in sociology from Columbia University. He is the author of several books including "Invisible Student Scientists (2013)" and the forthcoming Educating Public Interest Professionals and the Student Loan Debt Crisis." He has previously contributed chapters to encyclopedias and handbooks published by IGI Global including John Wang International Handbook of Business Analytics and Optimization as well as the International Encyclopedia of Information Sciences and Technology, and the International Encyclopedia of Modern Educational Technologies, Applications, and Management (both edited by Mehdi Khosrow-Pour). Mr. Fisher resides in the USA. He is an independent contractor.

**Wendy Flores-Fuentes** received the bachelor's degree in electronic engineering from the Autonomous University of Baja California in 2001, the master's degree in engineering from Technological Institute of Mexicali in 2006, and the Ph.D. degree in science, applied physics, with emphasis on Optoelectronic Scanning Systems for SHM, from Autonomous University of Baja California in June 2014. By now she is the author of 36 journal articles in Elsevier, IEEE, Emerald and Springer, 18 book chapters and 8 books in Springer, Intech, IGI global Lambert Academic and Springer, 46 proceedings articles in IEEE ISIE 2014-2021, IECON 2014, 2018, 2019, the World Congress on Engineering and Computer Science (IAENG 2013), IEEE Section Mexico IEEE ROCC2011, and the VII International Conference on Industrial Engineering ARGOS 2014. Recently, she has organized and participated as Chair of Special Session on ''Machine Vision, Control and Navigation'' at IEEE ISIE 2015-2021 and IECON 2018, 2019. She has participated has Guest Editor at Journal of Sensors with Hindawi, The International Journal of Advanced

Robotic Systems with SAGE, IEEE Sensors, and Elsevier Measurement. She holds 1 patent of Mexico and 1 patent of Ukraine. She has been a reviewer of several articles in Taylor and Francis, IEEE, Elsevier, and EEMJ. Currently, she is a full-time professor at Universidad Autónoma de Baja California, at the Faculty of Engineering. She has been incorporated into CONACYT National Research System in 2015. She did receive the award of "Best session presentation" in WSECS2013 in San-Francisco, USA. She did receive as coauthor the award of "Outstanding Paper in the 2017 Emerald Literati Network Awards for Excellence". Her's interests include optoelectronics, robotics, artificial intelligence, measurement systems, and machine vision systems.

**Jeffrey Yi-Lin Forrest** is a professor of mathematics and the research coach for the School of Business at Slippery Rock University of Pennsylvania. His research interest covers a wide range of topics, including, but not limited to, economics, finance, mathematics, management, marketing and systems science. As of the end of 2020, he has published over 600 research works, 24 monographs and 27 special topic edited volumes.

**Raksh Gangwar** is working as Professor and Director in Women Institute of Technology, Dehradun. He is having more than 35 years of experience. He has guided many Ph.D and M.Tech scholars. He is also member of many committee of national/international repute. He has contributed many research papers. He has also contributed many patents under his name.

**Ge Gao** is a Professor at Zhuhai College of Science and Technology and Management School at Jilin University. Her research focuses on Blockchain application, Supply Chain Management, Big Data application, user interface management in mobile commerce, and Social electronic commerce.

**Araceli Gárate-García** is a full-time professor at the Universidad Politécnica de Baja California (UPBC) since 2017. She received her PhD in electronics and telecommunications in conjoint between the CICESE research center, Mexico and the IRCCyN research center of the ECN university, France in 2011, the M.Sc. degree in electronics and telecommunications from CICESE research center in 2006 and her bachelor degree in Electronic Engineering in 2003 from the ITM university. Her main research interests are the analysis and control of nonlinear systems with and without time delays and the symbolic computation.

**María J. García G.** is Bachelor in Chemistry and has a master in Operations Research (OR). Together others authors had increase their investigations, already two hundred and forty, mainly in the areas of Evaluation and Management of Projects, Knowledge Management, Managerial and Social Decision making and OR, especially in multi-criteria decision. They have been presented or published in different countries, having publications and offering their reports, chats or conferences in: Azerbaijan, Finland, Poland, Croatia, Switzerland, Greece, Germany, Italy, Czech Republic, Iceland, Lithuania, Spain, France, Portugal, United States, Panama, Uruguay, Brazil, Mexico, Argentina and Chile besides attending as guest speaker, in lectures to relevant events in Colombia, Peru, Spain and Venezuela. Among other works she is coauthor of: "Inventories control, the Inventory manager and Matrixes Of Weighing with multiplicative factors (MOWwMf)"; "A Methodology of the Decision Support Systems Applied to Other Projects of Investigation"; "Matrixes Of Weighing and catastrophes"; "Multiattribute Model with Multiplicative Factors and Matrixes Of Weighing and the Problem of the Potable Water"

**Nuno Geada** has a Master's degree in Systems Information Management by Polytechnic Institute of Setúbal - School of Business Sciences and Management -Setúbal, Degree in Industrial Management and Technology by Polytechnic Institute of Setúbal - School of Technology of Setubal. He has written chapters, and papers to journals about topics regarding information technology management and strategic change management. He is from the Editorial Board - Associate Editor from International Journal of Business Strategy and Automation (IJBSA). He is the Editor of the book Reviving Businesses with New Organizational Change Management Strategies. His main research interests in information systems management, strategy, knowledge management, change management, and information technology management adoption in business contexts throw models and frameworks. He works as a Professor and a Researcher.

**Natheer K. Gharaibeh** is currently Associate Professor at College of Computer Science & Engineering at Yanbu - Taibah University from June 2016. He has more than 17 years of experience: He worked as Assistant Professor at College of Computer Science & Engineering at Yanbu – Taibah University from September. 2013 till June 2016. Before that he worked as an Assistant Professor at Balqa Applied University. He also worked as part-time Lecturer at Jordan University of Science and Technology (JUST) and other Jordanian universities. He published many papers in International Journals and participated in several International Conferences. His current research interests are: Business Intelligence, NLP, IR, Software Engineering, and Knowledge Societies. He got a grant for a joint project from the DFG with Rostock Technical University - Germany. He is editorial board Member, reviewer, and Keynote speaker in many International Journals and Conferences, he also has membership in many International and Technical Societies.

**Abichal Ghosh** is a final year B.E. student pursuing his degree in Computer Science from BITS Pilani K.K. Birla Goa campus. His field of interest lies in the research areas of Artificial Intelligence, Machine Learning, Deep Learning, Image Processing, Computer Vision and their application in various fields such as Desalination by Membrane technology, Ozonation, and more. Recently, he has been working for the prediction of the optimal conditions of Thin Film Nanocomposite Membranes for efficient desalination. For the topics related to Computer Vision, he has previously worked in the topic of Segmentation and is also currently working on the topic of Learned Image Compression.

**Christoph Glauser** was born in Berne in 1964. After studying History, Political Science and Media Science in Berne and Law in Geneva, he obtained a doctorate at the University of Berne in 1994. Christoph Glauser then participated in the national research programme, NFP27 at the University of Geneva. As a lecturer in Journalism and Online Research, he worked at various universities. He lectured in the subject, „Organisational Learning" in Social Psychology at the University of Zurich and for six years, he was the leading researcher and lecturer at ETH Zurich. In 1997-1998 he was a Visiting Lecturer at the University of Washington in Seattle, for which he continued to lecture their graduate students in Rome until 2006. During that time, he was Visiting Lecturer for online research at various universities both in Switzerland and abroad. Since 1998, Christoph Glauser has developed a successful career as online expert, CEO and delegate of governing boards, in particular (delete 'of') MMS – Media Monitoring Switzerland AG - and in diverse IT companies. Since 1994, he has been running the Institute for Fundamental Studies in Computer-assisted Content Analyses IFAA in Berne. In 2001, Glauser founded the URL study factory for competition analyses, ArgYou (Arguments for You), in order to study content of websites on the internet and compare these via search engines with the searched-for content (online effect research). In 2006, this company evolved into ArgYou AG in Baar (Switzerland), where he has remained as Chair of the governing board up to the present. For some years, Glauser has been serving on several European committees as an expert in e-governance. Subsequently, in 2007, he was one of the sixteen members of the jury for the European Union e-Government award, which honours the best European e-government projects on behalf of the European Commission. Since 2014 he has been operating the IFAAR find-engine set up directly for purposes of digital evaluation.

**Rajesh Godasu** is pursuing a Ph.D. in information systems at Dakota State University, his research interest is Deep learning in medical images. He has worked with Dr. Zeng for the past three years on different Machine Learning, Data Science, and Predictive Analytics topics. Conducted research on the Topic "Transfer Learning in Medical Image Classification" and published two papers in Information systems conferences, MWAIS and AMCIS.

**Jorge Gomes** is a researcher at ADVANCE, ISEG, School of Economics & Management of the Universidade de Lisboa. He holds a PhD in Management from ISEG and a Masters in Management Sciences from ISCTE-IUL, He also have a post-graduation in Project Management from INDEG/ISCTE, and a degree in Geographic Engineering from the Faculty of Sciences of the Universidade de Lisboa. During the past 30 years, he has worked as an engineer, project manager, quality auditor and consultant. Teaches Management at ULHT, Lisboa. His research interests include Benefits Management, Project Management, Project Success, Maturity Models, IS/IT Investments, IS/IT in Healthcare, and IS/IT Management.

**Hale Gonce Kocken** is an Associate Professor in the Department of Mathematical Engineering at the Yildiz Technical University (YTU), Istanbul, Turkey. She has been a faculty member of YTU since 2004. She completed her Ph.D. entitled "Fuzzy approaches to network analysis" in Applied Mathematics (2011) from the same department. Her current area of research is mathematical programming, supply chain management, and some related Operational Research subjects in multi-criteria and fuzzy environments.

**Rick Gorvett** is Professor and Chair of the Mathematics Department at Bryant University. He is a Fellow of the Casualty Actuarial Society.

**M. Govindarajan** is currently an Associate Professor in the Department of Computer Science and Engineering, Annamalai University, Tamil Nadu, India. He received the B.E, M.E and Ph.D Degree in Computer Science and Engineering from Annamalai University, Tamil Nadu, India in 2001, 2005 and 2010 respectively. He did his post-doctoral research in the Department of Computing, Faculty of Engineering and Physical Sciences, University of Surrey, Guildford, Surrey, United Kingdom in 2011 and at CSIR Centre for Mathematical Modelling and Computer Simulation, Bangalore in 2013. He has visited countries like Czech Republic, Austria, Thailand, United Kingdom (twice), Malaysia, U.S.A (twice), and Singapore. He has presented and published more than 140 papers at Conferences and Journals and also received best paper awards. He has delivered invited talks at various national and international conferences. His current research interests include Data Mining and its applications, Web Mining, Text Mining, and Sentiment Mining. He has completed two major projects as principal investigator and has produced four Ph.Ds. He was the recipient of the Achievement Award for the field in the Conference in Bio-Engineering, Computer Science, Knowledge Mining (2006), Prague, Czech Republic. He received

Career Award for Young Teachers (2006), All India Council for Technical Education, New Delhi, India and Young Scientist International Travel Award (2012), Department of Science and Technology, Government of India, New Delhi. He is a Young Scientists awardee under Fast Track Scheme (2013), Department of Science and Technology, Government of India, New Delhi and also granted Young Scientist Fellowship (2013), Tamil Nadu State Council for Science and Technology, Government of Tamil Nadu, Chennai. He also received the Senior Scientist International Travel Award (2016), Department of Science and Technology, Government of India. He has published ten book chapters and also applied patent in the area of data mining. He is an active Member of various professional bodies and Editorial Board Member of various conferences and journals.

**Ashwin Gupta** has currently completed his BSc with Major in Computer Science from St. Xavier's College, Kolkata. His current research interest is Data Analytics and Machine Learning.

**Neha Gupta** is currently working as an Professor, Faculty of Computer Applications at Manav Rachna International Institute of Research and Studies, Faridabad campus. She has completed her PhD from Manav Rachna International University and has done R&D Project in CDAC-Noida. She has total of 12+ year of experience in teaching and research. She is a Life Member of ACM CSTA, Tech Republic and Professional Member of IEEE. She has authored and coauthored 30 research papers in SCI/SCOPUS/Peer Reviewed Journals (Scopus indexed) and IEEE/IET Conference proceedings in areas of Web Content Mining, Mobile Computing, and Web Content Adaptation. She is a technical programme committee (TPC) member in various conferences across globe. She is an active reviewer for International Journal of Computer and Information Technology and in various IEEE Conferences around the world. She is one of the Editorial and review board members in International Journal of Research in Engineering and Technology.

**Jafar Habibi** is an associate professor at the Computer Engineering Department, Sharif University of Technology, Iran. He has been the head of the Computer Society of Iran and the Department of Computer Engineering. His main research interests are Internet of Things, Simulation, System Analysis and Design, and Social Network Analysis.

**Christian Haertel** studied business informatics at Otto von Guericke University Magdeburg. He joined the VLBA research team in 2021 and accompanies research projects with external partners (e.g., Google Cloud, Accenture Digital). The modelling and development of concepts in the areas of data science and cloud computing are his main areas of research.

**J. Michael Hardin** is the Provost and Vice President and Professor of Quantitative Analysis at Samford University. Dr. Hardin came to Samford University in July 2015 from the University of Alabama at Tuscaloosa, where he served as the Culverhouse College of Commerce and Business Administration dean. Dr. Hardin had previously served as Culverhouse's senior associate dean, associate dean for research, director of the University of Alabama's NIH Alabama EPSCoR Agency and director of Culverhouse's Institute of Business Intelligence. Dr. Hardin's service as a Culverhouse professor of quantitative analysis, business and statistics was widely credited for establishing the University of Alabama as an internationally-known resource in the field of data analytics. His Culverhouse career followed his numerous administrative and faculty appointments at the University of Alabama in Birmingham in biostatistics, biomathematics, health informatics and computer science. Dr. Hardin holds a Ph.D. in Applied Statistics from the University of Alabama, M.A. in Mathematics from the University of Alabama, M.S. in Research Design and Statistics from Florida State University's College of Education, B.A. in Mathematics from the University of West Florida, B.A. in Philosophy from the University of West Florida and M.Div. from New Orleans Baptist Theological Seminary. He is an ordained Southern Baptist minister. Dr. Hardin has authored or co-authored more than 150 papers in various journals, edited numerous professional journals, authored multiple book chapters, presented more than 250 abstracts at national meetings and given more than 150 invited lectures or talks. For 25 years he served as a National Institutes of Health (NIH) grant reviewer and participated as Investigator or co-Investigator on more than 100 U.S. Department of Health and Human Services/NIH-funded projects. He has served as a consultant for other national healthcare and financial organizations and was among the inventors receiving a U.S. patent licensed to MedMined, a Birmingham-based firm dedicated to controlling hospital infection rates and improving patient care.

**Shanmugasundaram Hariharan** received his B.E degree specialized in Computer Science and Engineering from Madurai Kammaraj University, Madurai, India in 2002, M.E degree specialized in the field of Computer Science and Engineering from Anna University, Chennai, India in 2004. He holds his Ph.D degree in the area of Information Retrieval from Anna University, Chennai, India. He is a member of IAENG, IACSIT, ISTE, CSTA and has 17 years of experience in teaching. Currently he is working as Professor in Department of Computer Science and Engineering, Vardhaman College of Engineering, India. His research interests include Information Retrieval, Data mining, Opinion Mining, Web mining. He has to his credit several papers in referred journals and conferences. He also serves as editorial board member and as program committee member for several international journals and conferences.

**Budi Harsanto** is a lecturer at Universitas Padjadjaran, Bandung, Indonesia. His research interests are in sustainability innovation, and operations and supply chain management.

**Md Salleh Salleh Hassan**, Prof., PhD, is a retired Professor at the Department of Communication, Faculty of Modern Languages and Communication, Universiti Putra Malaysia. He has graduated many PhD, master's and undergraduate students. He was once the Deputy Dean of the Faculty, and has published many research papers, attended many conferences both local and international.

**Miralem Helmefalk**, PhD, is an assistant senior lecturer at the Department of Marketing in School of Business and Economics at Linnaeus University in Sweden. Miralem's research interests lie in concepts within consumer psychology, digitalization, gamification as well as sensory marketing. He believes that machine learning represents the perfect storm for his research interests.

**Gilberto J. Hernández** is a Bachelor in Chemistry and have a master in Technology of foods. Together others authors had increase their investigations, mainly in the areas of Food technologies, Playful, in particular in the fantastic sports leagues, Knowledge Management, Managerial and Social Decision making, Logistics, Risk Management and Operations research, especially in multi-criteria decision and making decision under uncertainty and risk. They have been presented or published in different countries, having publications and offering their reports, chats or conferences in: Finland, Poland, Croatia, Switzerland, Greece, Czech Republic, Spain, Portugal and United States besides attending as guest speaker, in lectures to relevant events in Costa Rica and Venezuela. Among other works he is coauthor of: "Enterprise Logistics, Indicators and Physical Distribution Manager"; "Multiattribute Models with Multiplicative factors in the Fantasy Sports"; "The Industrial design manager of LoMoBaP and Knowledge Management"; "Dynamic knowledge: Diagnosis and Customer Service".

**José Hernández Ramírez** is a Chemical Engineer and have a master in Operations Research. Together others authors had increase their investigations, already above two hundred and forty, mainly in the areas of Knowledge Management, Managerial and Social Decision making, Logistics, Risk Management and Operations research, especially in multi-criteria decision. They have been presented or published in different countries, having publications and offering their reports, chats or conferences in: Azerbaijan, Finland, Croatia, Switzerland, Greece, Germany, Italy, Czech Republic, Iceland, Lithuania, Spain, France, Portugal, United States, Panama, Paraguay, Uruguay, Brazil, Cuba, Mexico, Argentina and Chile besides attending as guest speaker, in reiterated occasions, in lectures to relevant events in Colombia, Peru, Costa Rica, Brazil, Spain and Venezuela. Among other works he is coauthor of: "Teaching Enterprise Logistics through Indicators: Dispatch Manager"; "Enterprise diagnosis and the Environmental manager of LoMoBaP"; "Logistics, Marketing and Knowledge Management in the Community of Consumer".

**Thanh Ho** received M.S. degree in Computer Science from University of Information Technology, VNU-HCM, Vietnam in 2009 and PhD degree in Computer Science from University of Information Technology, VNU-HCM, Vietnam. He is currently lecturer in Faculty of Information Systems, University of Economics and Law, VNU-HCM, Vietnam in 2018. His research interests are Data mining, Data Analytics, Business Intelligence, Social Network Analysis, and Big Data.

**Victoria Hodge** is a Research Fellow and Software Developer in the Department of Computer Science at University of York. Her research interests include AI, outlier detection, and data mining. She is currently researching the safety assurance of machine learning for autonomous systems. A focus of this research is assuring robot navigation including localisation. She is on the editorial board of two journals and has authored over 60 refereed publications. She has worked in industry as a software architect for a medical diagnostics company; and as a software developer on condition monitoring in industrial environments, and deep learning for robot navigation.

**Essam H. Houssein** received his PhD degree in Computer Science in 2012. He is an associate professor at the Faculty of Computers and Information, Minia University, Egypt. He is the founder and chair of the Computing & Artificial Intelligence Research Group (CAIRG) in Egypt. He has more than 100 scientific research papers published in prestigious international journals in the topics for instance meta-heuristics optimization, artificial intelligence, image processing, IoT and its applications. Essam H. Houssein serves as a reviewer of more than 40 journals (Elsevier, Springer, IEEE, etc.). His research interests include WSNs, IoT, AI, Bioinformatics and Biomedical, Image processing, Data mining, and Meta-heuristics Optimization techniques.

**Adamkolo Mohammed Ibrahim** is a Lecturer at the Department of Mass Communication, University of Maiduguri, Nigeria and a PhD Research Scholar at Bayero University, Kano (BUK), Nigeria. He received his master's degree in Development Communication at Universiti Putra Malaysia (UPM) in 2017. In 2007, he had his first degree (BA Mass Communication) at the Department of Mass Communication, University of Maiduguri, Nigeria. Currently, he teaches mass communication at the University of Maiduguri. He conducts research and writes in ICT adoption for development, social media, cyberbullying, cyber terrorism/conflict, gender and ICT, gender and conflict and online shopping. He has published several journal articles, book chapters and a few books. His most recent work explores the impacts of fake news and hate speech in Nigerian democracy and proposes a theoretical model as a fact-checking tool. More details on his most recent works and all his other publications can be accessed on his website: https://unimaid.academia.edu/AdamkoloMohammedIbrahim. Malam Adamkolo is currently serving as an Editorial Board Member of Jurnal Komunikasi Ikatan Sarjana Komunikasi Indonesia (the Communication Journal of the Indonesian Association of Communication Scholars) and a co-researcher in a research project by The Kukah Centre, Abuja, Nigeria. The proposed title of the research is: "Engaging Local Communities for Peacebuilding, Social Cohesion, Preventing and Countering Violent Extremism in Nigeria's northeast". Adamkolo has received Publons Top Reviewer Award in 2018 (for being among the top 1% global peer reviewers in Psychiatry/Psychology). In 2017, Elsevier had awarded him a certificate of outstanding peer review with one of Elsevier's prestigious journals, Computers in Human Behaviour (CHB) which he reviews for; he also reviews for Emerald's Journal of Systems and Information Technology (JSIT) and several other journals. Much earlier, from 2000 to 2010, he worked as a broadcast journalist in Yobe Broadcasting Corporation (YBC) Damaturu, and from 2008 to 2010 was deployed to Sahel FM (formerly Pride FM, a subsidiary of YBC Damaturu as DJ-cum-producer/presenter/journalist). From 2008 to 2010, he worked as YBC's focal person on UNICEF and Partnership for the Revival of Routine Immunisation in Northern Nigeria-Maternal, newborn and Child Health (PRRINN-MNCH). From September to October 2018, he served as a consultant to ManienDanniels (West Africa Ltd.) and MNCH2 programme.

**Funda Ipekten**'s research focused on a statistical analysis of high-throughput metabolomics data, multi-omics data integration, feature selection for multi-omics.

**Adelina Ivanova** is Assisted Professor Dr. in Department of Computer Systems and Informatics of University of Forestry, Sofia, Bulgaria. Her research interests are in the areas of ontology engineering, sustainable development, databases, and office information systems.

**Sajan T. John** is an Associate Professor of Industrial Engineering in the Department of Mechanical Engineering at Viswajyothi College of Engineering and Technology, Vazhakulam, Kerala. He received PhD from the National Institute of Technology Calicut in 2015. His research interests are in the areas of operations research, mathematical modelling, supply chain management and reverse logistics. He has published papers in international journals and proceedings of international and national conferences.

**Rachid Kaleche** is a PhD student of computer science since 2018. He is member of computer science laboratory (LIO) of Oran 1 university in Algeria. His current research interests deal with artificial intelligence, transportation system, logistic systems, machine learning, and bio-inspired approach. He is co-author of many publications and communications.

**Reddi Kamesh** received B.Tech in Chemical engineering from Acharya Nagarjuna University, Guntur, India, in 2011, and M.Tech and Ph.D. from Academy of and Innovative Research (AcSIR), CSIR-Indian Institute of Chemical Technology (IICT), Campus, Hyderabad, India, in 2014 and 2019 respectively. Dr. Kamesh has extensive experience in the field of Process Systems Engineering (PSE), Artificial Intelligence (AI) and Machine Learning methods, Integrated Multi-Scale Modelling methods, and Process Intensification. He is working as a scientist in CSIR-IICT since 2016. He has actively engaged in basic research as well as applied research. He has developed process model-based as well as AI-based methodologies to simulate, design, control, and optimize processes, for accelerated product and process design, and to achieve performance improvements to existing processes in terms of improving productivity and selectivity while maintaining their safety and environmental constraints. Dr. Kamesh was a recipient of the Ambuja Young Researchers Award in 2014 from Indian Institute of Chemical Engineers (IIChE).

**Shri Kant** has received his Ph. D. in applied mathematics from applied mathematics departments of institute of technology, Banaras Hindu University (BHU), Varanasi in 1981. He is working as a Professor and head of "Center of Cyber Security and cryptology", Department of Computer Science and Engineering of Sharda University, India and involved actively in teaching and research mainly in the area of cyber security and Machine learning. His areas of interest are Special Functions, Cryptology, Pattern Recognition, Cluster Analysis, Soft Computing Model, Machine Learning and Data Mining.

**Nurdan Kara** is an Assistant Prof. in the Department of Mathematics at National Defence University (MSU), Istanbul, Turkey. She has been a faculty member of Ankara University since 1998. She completed her Ph.D. entitled "Fuzzy approaches to multiobjective fractional transportation problem" in Applied Mathematics (2008) from Yildiz Technical University. Her current area of research is mathematical Programming, fractional programming, supply chain management and some related Operational Research subjects in multi criteria and fuzzy environments.

**Prasanna Karhade** is Associate Professor of IT Management, Shidler College Faculty Fellow and a Faculty Fellow at the Pacific Asian Center for Entrepreneurship [PACE] at the University of Hawai'i at Mānoa. His research interests include digital innovation and digital platforms in growing, rural, eastern, aspirational and transitional [GREAT] economies.

**Bouamrane Karim** received the PhD Degree in computer science from the Oran University in 2006. He is Professor of computer Science at Oran1 University. He is the head of "Decision and piloting system" team. His current research interests deal with decision support system and logistics in maritime transportation, urban transportation system, production system, health systems and application of bio-inspired based optimization metaheuristic. He participates in several scientific committees' international/national conferences in Algeria and others countries in the same domain and collaborated in Algerian-French scientific projects. He is co-author of more than 40 scientific publications.

**Joseph Kasten** is an Assistant Professor of Information Science and Technology at the Pennsylvania State University in York, PA. He earned a PhD in Information Science at Long Island University in Brookville, NY, an MBA at Dowling College in Oakdale, NY, and a BS in engineering at Florida Institute of Technology in Melbourne, FL. Before joining academia, Joe was a senior engineer with the Northrop-Grumman Corp. where he worked on various military and commercial projects such as the X-29 and the Boeing 777. His research interests center on the implementation of data analytics within the organization as well as the application of blockchain technology to emerging organizational requirements. Professor Kasten's recent research appears in the International Journal of Business Intelligence Research and International Journal of Healthcare Information Systems and Informatics.

**Tolga Kaya** is a full-time researcher and lecturer at the department of Management Engineering in Istanbul Technical University. His research areas are consumer modeling, statistical decision making, input-output modeling, multicriteria decision making, machine learning and fuzzy applications in business and management. He has published several papers and presented his research at a number of international conferences in these areas.

**Wei Ke**, Ph.D., is the Adjunct Associate Professor of Quantitative Revenue and Pricing Analytics at Columbia Business School. Previously, he was Managing Partner and the head of financial services practice in North America at Simon-Kucher & Partners. Wei received a Ph.D. in Decision, Risk, and Operations from Columbia Business School, and a BSc in Electrical Engineering & Applied Mathematics, summa cum laude, from Columbia University.

**Vanessa Keppeler** is a Senior Associate with PwC Germany's Financial Services Consulting practice. She specializes on the design and implementation of Data and AI Governance. Her research and studies focus on the practical enablement of Explainable AI in Financial Institutions. Vanessa holds a master's degree in Management (Finance).

**Mehrnaz Khalaj Hedayati** is an Assistant Professor of Management at Georgia College & State University, J. Whitney Bunting College of Business. Mehrnaz received her Ph.D. from the University of Rhode Island in 2020. Mehrnaz has published several academic journal articles. She is a Lean Six Sigma Certified from the URI College of Business. She has taught undergraduate and master's level courses in Business Quantitative Analysis, Business Statistics, and Operations Management. She has also served as ad-hoc reviewer for several academic journals.

**Fahima Khanam** is a Lecturer in the department of Aviation Operation Management at Bangabandhu Sheikh Mujibur Rahman Aviation and Aerospace University. Prior to joining the BSMRAAU, she served as Lecturer in the Department of Business Administration at Sheikh Burhanuddin Post Graduate College, European University, Victoria University and German University, Bangladesh where she taught Principles of Marketing, Marketing Management, Operations Management, International Business, and Business Communication. She also worked as a corporate professional in The Daily 'Prothom Alo', one of the top daily newspapers in Bangladesh. She holds an MBA in Marketing from University of Dhaka, Bangladesh. Her most recent publication appeared in the International Journal of Big Data and Analytics in Healthcare (IJBDAH). Her principal research interests include e-commerce, online shopping, social media marketing and branding strategy, marketing strategy and technology adoption.

**Shardul Khandekar** has his BE completed in E&TC and his research area includes machine learning and deep learning.

**Mubina Khondkar** serves as a Professor in the Department of Marketing at the University of Dhaka. She has interdisciplinary knowledge in the areas of marketing and development economics. She has both industry and research experiences with organizations including ANZ Grindlays Bank, Care Bangladesh, USAID, DFID, Concern, IFPRI, World Bank, SEDF, IFC, JICA, CIDA, UNICEF, BIDS, the University of Manchester, and the University of Cambridge. Her research interests include value chain analysis, marketing, poverty, microfinance, development economics, gender, and women's empowerment. Further details can be found here: https://www.researchgate.net/profile/Mubina-Khondkar.

**Soumya Khurana** has his BE completed in E&TC and his research area includes machine learning and deep learning.

**Necla Koçhan** is currently working as a postdoctoral researcher at Izmir Biomedicine and Genome Center, IBG. Her research interests are computational biology, statistical data analysis, fuzzy theory, classification, and biostatistics.

**Koharudin** is a master student in IPB University, Indonesia. In 2014 he joined the Bureau of Organization and Human Resource, Indonesian Institute of Sciences (LIPI), as IT Engineering. In 2020 He moved to Center for Scientific Data and Documentation, Indonesian Institute of Sciences (LIPI). His current roles include building and maintaining web applications, designing database architecture, integrating data and providing data through service point. He obtained his bachelor degree in Computer Science from the Sepuluh Nopember Institute of Technology in 2011. He has developed some applications such as Human Resources Information System, Mobile applications and API Gateway. His research interests include Bioinformatics, High Performance Computing and Machine Learning.

**Tibor Koltay** is Professor retired from the Institute of Learning Technologies at Eszterházy Károly Catholic University, in Hungary. He graduated from Eötvös Loránd University (Budapest, Hungary) in 1984 with an MA in Russian. He obtained there his PhD in 2002. In 1992 he was awarded the Certificate of Advanced Studies in Library and Information Science at Kent State University, Kent. OH.

**Xiangfen Kong** is an Associate Professor from the Civil Aviation University of China. Her research interests include smart airports, system reliability, operational research, and big data.

**Elena Kornyshova** is an Associate Professor at CNAM, Ph.D. in Economics and Management Sciences and Ph.D. in Computer Science. Her main research domains are method and process engineering, decision-making, enterprise architecture, and digitalization. She is/was involved in organization of multiple international conferences and workshops. She has significant experience in industry and consultancy sector mainly in the fields of IS engineering and enterprise architecture.

**Maximiliano E. Korstanje** is editor in chief of International Journal of Safety and Security in Tourism (UP Argentina) and Editor in Chief Emeritus of International Journal of Cyber Warfare and Terrorism (IGI-Global US). Korstanje is Senior Researchers in the Department of Economics at University of Palermo, Argentina. In 2015 he was awarded as Visiting Research Fellow at School of Sociology and Social Policy, University of Leeds, UK and the University of La Habana Cuba. In 2017 is elected as Foreign Faculty Member of AMIT, Mexican Academy in the study of Tourism, which is the most prominent institutions dedicated to tourism research in Mexico. He had a vast experience in editorial projects working as advisory member of Elsevier, Routledge, Springer, IGI global and Cambridge Scholar publishing. Korstanje had visited and given seminars in many important universities worldwide. He has also recently been selected to take part of the 2018 Albert Nelson Marquis Lifetime Achievement Award. a great distinction given by Marquis Who´s Who in the world.

**Mika Kosonen** is a graduate student in University of Lapland. He has bachelor's degree in social sciences and is currently finishing his master's degree. His bachelor's thesis was concerning artificial intelligence and ethics, and master's thesis contributes to morality in human-technology interaction, both with excellent grades. With strong interest in technology and human experience he is always wondering the world where technology mediates the reality, whether in suburbans or the wilderness found in northernmost parts of Europe.

**Anjani Kumar** is a Ph.D. student of computer science at the University of Nebraska at Omaha. He is working as a Data Scientist at Data Axle Inc. His primary research interests are in the fields of Big Data, Deep Learning, and Machine Learning.

**Sameer Kumar** is an Associate Professor at Universiti Malaya, Malaysia.

**Madhusree Kundu** is presently Professor, Department of Chemical Engineering, National Institute of Technology Rourkela, Orissa, India. Currently, HOD, Central Instrument Facility (CIF), NIT Rourkela. Experience: Worked as Process Engineer in Simon Carves India Limited (A Design Consultancy). First Academic Appointment: Assistant Professor, Birla Institute of Technology and Science (BITS) Pilani, Rajasthan, India. PhD: Indian Institute of Technology Kharagpur Research Interest: Fluid Phase equilibrium and its application, Modeling, & Simulation and Control, Chemommetrics/Machine Learning applications, Process Identification monitoring and Control, Biomimetic device development and Digitized Sustainable Agriculture.

**Mascha Kurpicz-Briki** obtained her PhD in the area of energy-efficient cloud computing at the University of Neuchâtel. After her PhD, she worked a few years in industry, in the area of open-source engineering, cloud computing and analytics. She is now professor for data engineering at the Bern University of Applied Sciences, investigating how to apply digital methods and in particular natural language processing to social and community challenges.

**Kevin Kwak** is an Information Systems and Accounting student at the University of Nebraska at Omaha. He received a Master's in Accounting and as of this writing is pursuing a Master's in Information Systems. His current interests of study are accounting, data security, and data mining. Currently, he has had five articles published in various journals.

**Wikil Kwak** is a Professor of Accounting at the University of Nebraska at Omaha. He received Ph.D. in Accounting from the University of Nebraska in Lincoln. Dr. Kwak's research interests include the areas of mathematical programming approaches in bankruptcy prediction, capital budgeting, transfer pricing, performance evaluation and Japanese capital market studies. He has published more than 57 articles in the Engineering Economist, Abacus, Contemporary Accounting Research, Review of Quantitative Finance and Accounting, Management Accountant, Journal of Petroleum Accounting and Financial Management, Business Intelligence and Data Mining, Review of Pacific Basin Financial Markets and Policies, and Multinational Business Review.

**Georgios Lampropoulos** received his BSc degree with the title of Information Technology Engineer specialized as a Software Engineer from the Department of Information Technology at Alexander

Technological Educational Institute of Thessaloniki (currently named International Hellenic University) in 2017 and he received his MSc in Web Intelligence from the same department in 2019. Currently, he is a PhD candidate and Visiting Lecturer in the Department of Information and Electronic Engineering at International Hellenic University and a MEd student in Education Sciences at Hellenic Open University. He has published his work in several peer reviewed journals and conferences, he has taken part in international research programs and he has also served as a reviewer and a member of the organizing and scientific committees of international conferences and international journals.

**Torben Larsen** is an MSc Econ from University of Aarhus and an international Degree in Strategic Management from University of Maryland-Tietgenskolen Dk. He has broad experience in regional planning of healthcare with Academic Awards from 1) Association of Hospital Managers in Norway, Lundbeck Fonden Dk and MIE96. He is a former Chief Research Consultant at University of Southern Denmark which included leadership of an EU-sponsored research project in Integrated Homecare. He has been involved with various courses and conferences and has written research papers in Health Economics, Neuroeconomics, Meditation and Biofeedback. 2017 he published "Homo Neuroeconomicus" (IJUDH(1)). 2020 he published "Neuroeconomic Pcyshology. 3 Modules for End-users . . . .", IJPCH Actually, he is giving guest lectures in cybernetic economics.

**Matthias Lederer** is Full Professor of Information Systems at the Technical University of Applied Sciences Amberg-Weiden. Prior to this, he was a professor at the ISM International School of Management Munich and at the same time Chief Process Officer at the IT Service Center of the Bavarian justice system. His previous positions include research assistant at the University of Erlangen-Nuremberg and strategy consultant at the German industrial company REHAU. His research and studies focus on business process management and IT management. Prof. Lederer holds a doctorate as well as a master's degree in international information systems and is the author of over 70 scientific publications in this field.

**Eva Lee** applies combinatorial optimization, math programming, game theory, and parallel computation to biological, medical, health systems, and logistics analyses. Her clinical decision-support systems (DSS) assist in disease diagnosis/prediction, treatment design, drug delivery, treatment and healthcare outcome analysis/prediction, and healthcare operations logistics. In logistics, she tackles operations planning and resource allocation, and her DSS addresses inventory control, vehicle dispatching, scheduling, transportation, telecom, portfolio investment, public health emergency treatment response, and facility location/planning. Dr. Lee is Director of the Center for Operations Research in Medicine and HealthCare, a center established through funds from the National Science Foundation and the Whitaker Foundation. The center focuses on biomedicine, public health and defense, translational medical research, medical delivery and preparedness, and the protection of critical infrastructures. She is a subject matter expert in medical systems and public health informatics, logistics and networks, and large-scale connected systems. She previously served as the Senior Health Systems Engineer and Professor for the U.S. Department of Veterans Affairs and was Co-Director for the Center for Health Organization Transformation. Dr. Lee has received numerous practice excellence awards, including the INFORMS Edelman Award on novel cancer therapeutics, the Wagner prize on vaccine immunity prediction, and the Pierskalla award on bioterrorism, emergency response, and mass casualty mitigation She is a fellow at INFORMS and AIMBE. Lee has served on NAE/NAS/IOM, NRC, NBSB, DTRA panel committees related to CBRN and WMD incidents, public health and medical preparedness, and healthcare systems innovation. She holds ten patents on medical systems and devices. Her work has been featured in the New York Times, London Times, disaster documentaries, and in other venues.

**Jinha Lee** is an Assistant Professor in the Department of Public and Allied Health at Bowling Green State University. His research interests include healthcare operations, data analytics, economic decision analysis, and system modeling in healthcare service. His work has examined practice variance and systems analysis for quality and process improvement and new clinical guidelines establishment. Also, his research has focused on economic analysis on industry networks, resource allocations, and the R&D process in healthcare services. His research primarily utilizes large datasets and clinical observations derived from various healthcare databases and field studies in clinical facilities. He has collaborated actively with hospitals, healthcare research institutes, and healthcare delivery organizations both in the U.S. and in foreign countries.

**Ulli Leucht** is a Manager in PwC Germany's Financial Services Technology Consulting team. He is an expert in AI and its use in Financial Institutions - which includes how AI use cases are identified, perceived, implemented, operated and surrounding governance, compliance, and legal requirements. Prior to joining PwC Germany, he worked with some of the most innovative FinTechs in the United Kingdom and the United States in the context of AI. Ulli's research and studies focus is the usage of AI in Financial Institutions. He holds a master's degree in Sensors and Cognitive Psychology.

**Carson Leung** is currently a Professor at the University of Manitoba, Canada. He has contributed more than 300 refereed publications on the topics of big data, computational intelligence, cognitive computing, data analytics, data mining, data science, fuzzy systems, machine learning, social network analysis, and visual analytics. These include eight chapters in IGI Global's books/encyclopedia (e.g., Encyclopedia of Organizational Knowledge, Administration, and Technology (2021)). He has also served on the Organizing Committee of the ACM CIKM, ACM SIGMOD, IEEE DSAA, IEEE ICDM, and other conferences.

**Siyao Li** is a student at the City University of Macau. She studies in the International Business program.

**Gilson B. A. Lima** is a Professor in the Industrial Engineering Department at Federal Fluminense University (UFF), Brazil. He received his PhD in the Rio de Janeiro Federal University, Brazil. His current research interests include industrial safety, risk management, industrial maintenance and industrial environmental management.

**Yu-Wei Lin** is an assistant professor in the Leavey School of Business, Santa Clara University. He received a Ph.D. in information systems at Gies College of Business, the University of Illinois at Urbana-Champaign. His research interests are in User-Generated Content, Healthcare Analytics, Online Review Analysis, Machine Learning, Decision Making, and Decision Support Systems.

**Fangyao Liu** is an assistant professor in the College of Electronic and Information at the Southwest Minzu University, China. He received Ph.D. in Information Technology from the University of Nebraska at Omaha, USA. Dr. Liu's research interests include the areas of data mining, artificial intelligence, and statistics. He has published more than 20 articles in the International journal of Computers Communications & Control, Journal of Urban Planning and Development, Journal of software, Journal of Asian Development, Journal of Contemporary Management, Procedia Computer Science, and several IEEE conferences.

**Haoyu Liu** is an assistant professor at the Faculty of Business, City University of Macau. He received an MPhil and a PhD in Operations Management from HKUST Business School in 2017 and 2020, respectively. He serves as a reviewer for Manufacturing & Service Operations Management (MSOM), Naval Research Logistics (NRL), International Journal of Applied Management Science (IJAMS), International Journal of Retail & Distribution Management (IJRDM), International Journal of E-Business Research (IJEBR), International Conference on Information Systems (ICIS), and INFORMS Conference on Service Science (ICSS). He has broad interests in issues related to healthcare, emerging technologies, charitable organizations, and marketing. In solving problems, he employs various techniques, ranging from game-theoretical and stochastic models to typical tools in empirical and experimental studies.

**Ran Liu** is an Assistant Professor in the Marketing department at Central Connecticut State University. His research focuses on online relationships, user-generated content (UGC), data modeling, and International businesses. He serves as Associate Editor (Asia) for Journal of Eastern European and Central Asian Research (JEECAR) and Faculty Advisor for American Marketing Association Collegiate Chapter.

**Cèlia Llurba** is currently a PhD student in Educational Technology in the Department of Pedagogy at the URV. Graduate in East Asian Studies from the UOC and a graduate in Mining Engineering from the UPC. She is currently a teacher of Technology in a high school in Cambrils (state employee) and also teaches in the subjects of Vocational Guidance and Citizenship, and Educational Processes and Contexts, within the Master's Degree in Teacher Training at the URV. Her main lines of research are: intellectual learning environments, data analytics and artificial intelligence in intellectual areas.

**Manuel Lozano Rodriguez** is American University of Sovereign Nations (AUSN) Visiting Prof. in his own discipline that takes bioethics off the medical hegemony to land it on social sciences, futurism, politics and pop culture through metaphysics of displacement. Born in Barcelona in 1978, Ph.D. in Bioethics, Sustainability and Global Public Health, AUSN; Master of Science in Sustainability, Peace and Development, AUSN; Graduate in Fundamentals of Sustainability Organizational, Harvard.

**Lorenzo Magnani**, philosopher, epistemologist, and cognitive scientist, is a professor of Philosophy of Science at the University of Pavia, Italy, and the director of its Computational Philosophy Laboratory. His previous positions have included: visiting researcher (Carnegie Mellon University, 1992; McGill University, 1992–93; University of Waterloo, 1993; and Georgia Institute of Technology, 1998–99) and visiting professor (visiting professor of Philosophy of Science and Theories of Ethics at Georgia Institute of Technology, 1999–2003; Weissman Distinguished Visiting Professor of Special Studies in Philosophy: Philosophy of Science at Baruch College, City University of New York, 2003). Visiting professor at the Sun Yat-sen University, Canton (Guangzhou), China from 2006 to 2012, in the event of the 50th anniversary of the re-building of the Philosophy Department of Sun Yat-sen University in 2010, an award was given to him to acknowledge his contributions to the areas of philosophy, philosophy of science, logic, and cognitive science. A Doctor Honoris Causa degree was awarded to Lorenzo Magnani by the Senate of the Ştefan cel Mare University, Suceava, Romania. In 2015 Lorenzo Magnani has been appointed member of the International Academy for the Philosophy of the Sciences (AIPS). He currently directs international research programs in the EU, USA, and China. His book Abduction, Reason, and Science (New York, 2001) has become a well-respected work in the field of human cognition. The book Morality in a Technological World (Cambridge, 2007) develops a philosophical and cognitive theory of the relationships between ethics and technology in a naturalistic perspective. The book Abductive Cognition. The Epistemological and Eco-Cognitive Dimensions of Hypothetical Reasoning and the last monograph Understanding Violence. The Intertwining of Morality, Religion, and Violence: A Philosophical Stance have been more recently published by Springer, in 2009 and 2011. A new monograph has been published by Springer in 2017, The Abductive Structure of Scientific Creativity. An Essay on the Ecology of Cognition, together with the Springer Handbook of Model-Based Science (edited with Tommaso Bertolotti). The last book Eco-Cognitive Computationalism. Cognitive Domestication of Ignorant Entities, published by Springer, offers an entirely new dynamic perspective on the nature of computation. He edited books in Chinese, 16 special issues of international academic journals, and 17 collective books, some of them deriving from international conferences. Since 1998, initially in collaboration with Nancy J. Nersessian and Paul Thagard, he created and promoted the MBR Conferences on Model-Based Reasoning. Since 2011 he is the editor of the Book Series Studies in Applied Philosophy, Epistemology and Rational Ethics (SAPERE), Springer, Heidelberg/Berlin.

**Mazlina Abdul Majid** is an Associate Professor in the Faculty of Computing at University Malaysia Pahang (UMP), Malaysia. She received her PHD in Computer Science from the University of Nottingham, UK. She held various managerial responsibilities as a Deputy Dean of Research and Graduate Studies and currently acts as the head of the Software Engineering Research Group in her Faculty. She also taught courses on the undergraduate and master's levels. She has published 130 research in local and international books, journals and conference proceedings. She is also a member of various committees of international conferences. Her research interests include simulation, software agent, software usability and testing.

**Jasna D. Marković-Petrović** received her B.Sc. (1992) and M.Sc. (2011) degrees in electrical engineering and her Ph.D. degree (2018) in technical sciences, all from the University of Belgrade, Serbia. She is with the Public Enterprise "Electric Power Industry of Serbia" for more than 25 years. Her activities involve implementation of the technical information system, participation in projects concerning upgrading the remote control system of the hydropower plant, and implementation of the SCADA security system. She is a member of the Serbian National CIGRÉ Study Committee D2. As author or coauthor, she published a number of book chapters, journal articles and conference papers in her field. Her main research interests involve smart grids, SCADA and industrial control systems security, and cyber risk management.

**Roberto Marmo** received the Laurea (cum laude) in Computer Science from Salerno University (Italy) and Ph.D. in Electronic and Computer Engineering obtained from the University of Pavia (Italy). He is presently contract teacher of computer science at Faculty of Engineering of Pavia University, Italy. His most recent work is concerned with mathematical models and software for social network analysis. He is author of "Social Media Mining", a textbook in Italian language on extraction of information from social media, website http://www.socialmediamining.it.

**Nikolaos Matsatsinis** is a full Professor of Information and Decision Support Systems in the School of Production Engineering and Management of the Technical University of Crete, Greece. He is President of the Hellenic Operational Research Society (HELORS). He is Director of DSS Lab and Postgraduate Programs. He has contributed as scientific or project coordinator on over of fifty national and international projects. He is chief editor of the Operational Research: An International Journal (Impact Factor 2020: 2.410) and International Journal of Decision Support Systems. He is the author or co-author/editor of 25 books and over of 120 articles in international scientific journals and books. He has organized and participated in the organization of over of ninety scientific conferences, including EURO 2021, and he has over of one hundred and ninety presentations in international and national scientific conferences. His research interests fall into the areas of Intelligent DSS, Multi-Agent Systems, Recommendation Systems, Multicriteria Decision Analysis, Group Decision Making, Operational Research, e-Marketing, Consumer Behaviour Analysis, Data Analysis, Business Intelligence & Business Analytics.

**Hubert Maupas** is graduated from Ecole Centrale de Lyon (France) and holds a PhD in Integrated Electronics, obtained with several patents and publications. He has spent most of his career in medical device industry and is currently working as COO of MUST, a all-in-one B2B Metaverse platform to manage DBE (Digital Business Ecosystem) embedding advanced matchmaking algorithms.

**Iman Megahed** is the AVP for Digital Transformation, Chief Strategy and Knowledge Officer at the American University in Cairo (AUC). She is currently responsible for all Information Technology, Information Security, Business Intelligence and institutional effectiveness functions. She co-founded the business intelligence and data governance functions to support informed based decision making. She also founded the office of Online Student Services which applied web services and portal technology to enhance student services. With a successful track record in technology and effectiveness administrative positions in Higher Education since 1992, Iman has accumulated extensive technical expertise, unique project management skills coupled with results-oriented leadership style and passion for informed based decision making. Iman earned her PhD in Organizational Behavior from Cairo University, MBA and BS in Computer Science from The American University in Cairo.

**Natarajan Meghanathan** is a tenured Full Professor of Computer Science at Jackson State University, Jackson, MS. He graduated with a Ph.D. in Computer Science from The University of Texas at Dallas in May 2005. Dr. Meghanathan has published more than 175 peer-reviewed articles (more than half of them being journal publications). He has also received federal education and research grants from the U. S. National Science Foundation, Army Research Lab and Air Force Research Lab. Dr. Meghanathan has been serving in the editorial board of several international journals and in the Technical Program Committees and Organization Committees of several international conferences. His research interests are Wireless Ad hoc Networks and Sensor Networks, Graph Theory and Network Science, Cyber Security, Machine Learning, Bioinformatics and Computational Biology. For more information, visit https://www.jsums.edu/nmeghanathan.

**Abelardo Mercado Herrera** has a PhD from the National Institute of Astrophysics, Optics and Electronics (INAOE), specializing in Astrophysics, Postdoctorate in Astrophysics from the Institute of Astronomy from the National Autonomous University of Mexico (UNAM), Electronics Engineer from the Autonomous University of Baja California (UABC). He is a specialist in the mathematical-statistical description of stochastic processes and/or deterministic systems, nonlinear systems, complex systems, chaos theory, among others, as well as its application to physical phenomena such as astronomy, medicine, economics, finance, telecommunications, social sciences etc., in order to determine the dynamics underlying in such processes, and given the case, its connection with real physical variables and possible prediction. He has worked on the development of interfaces and programs to carry out electrical tests in industry, as well as in scientific instrumentation, applied to telemetry, infrared polarimetry, optics and spectroscopy. He has also specialized in image analysis, measurement techniques and noise reduction.

**Shivlal Mewada** is presently working as an Assistant Professor (contact) in the Dept. of CS, Govt. Holkar (Autonomous, Model) Science College, Indore, India. He shared the responsibility of research activities and coordinator of M.Phil.(CS) at Govt. Holkar Sci. Collage, Indore. He has also received JRF in 2010-11 for M.Phil. Programme under UGC Fellow scheme, New Delhi. He is a member of IEEE since 2013 and editorial member of the ISROSET since 2013. He is a technical committee and editorial member of various reputed journals including Taylor & Francis, Inderscience. He chaired 5 national and international conferences and seminars. He organized 2 special for international conferences. He also contributed to the organization of 2 national and 4 virtual international conferences. Mr. Mewada has published 3 book chapters and over 18 research articles in reputed journals like SCI, Scopus including IEEE conferences. His areas of interest include; cryptography, information security and computational intelligence.

**Tanish Ambrishkumar Mishra** is an undergraduate student at Sardar Patel College of Engineering, Mumbai, India. Currently pursuing his Bachelor of Technology (B.Tech) in Department of Mechanical Engineering. His research areas of interest are mobile robotics, biomimetic robot design, robotic prosthetic limb design, control systems and AI/ML.

**Mayank Modashiya** is a Data Scientist 1 at Kenco Group, Chattanooga, TN, USA. He earned is Bachelor's in Engineering in Mechanical Engineering, India. He earned his Masters in Industrial Engineering from the University of Texas at Arlington. Mayank has passion for applying machine learning (ML) and artificial Intelligence (AI) to solve complex supply chain problems. Mayank has more than 2 years' experience in developing and implementing AI/ML for problem solving. His research interest includes supply chain networks, logistics and manufacturing. He is member of INFORMS and IISE.

**Jordi Mogas** holds a PhD in Educational Technology and a Bachelor's in Information and Documentation with mention in information systems management. Currently, he is a postdoc researcher at GEPS research center (Globalisation, Education and Social Policies), at the Universitat Autònoma de Barcelona, and belongs to ARGET (Applied Research Group in Education and Technology). Dr. Mogas teaches at both the Department of Pedagogy at the Universitat Rovira i Virgili (professor associate) and at the Department of Education at the Universitat Oberta de Catalunya (professor collaborador). His main research lines are: Smart Learning Environments, Virtual Learning Environments and Self-Regulated Learning.

**Siddhartha Moulik** is working as a Scientist in CSIR-IICT. His field of specialization deals with wastewater treatment, cavitation based advanced oxidation processes, sonochemistry as well as in membrane separation technology along with experiences in practical field applications.

**Adam Moyer** is an Assistant Professor in the Department of Analytics and Information Systems at Ohio University's College of Business. Moyer received a BBA from Ohio University and has had experience managing information systems for non-profit organizations, has worked as a systems engineer, and has consulted for various companies. While earning an MS in Industrial & Systems Engineering at Ohio University, Adam developed and taught courses related to information systems, programming, system design and deployment, business intelligence, analytics, and cybersecurity at Ohio University. After gaining additional professional experience in the counterintelligence community, Moyer returned to Ohio University and earned a Ph.D. in Mechanical and Systems Engineering.

**Anirban Mukherjee** is faculty in marketing. He received a PhD in Marketing from The Samuel Curtis Johnson Graduate School of Management, Cornell University.

**Anweshan Mukherjee** has completed his BSc with Major in Computer Science from St. Xavier's College, Kolkata and is currently pursuing MSc in Computer Science from the same college. His current research interest is Data Analytics and Machine Learning.

**Partha Mukherjee**, assistant professor of data analytics, received his bachelor's degree in mechanical engineering in 1995 from Jadavpur University in India. He received his Master of Technology in Computer Science from Indian Statistical Institute in 2001. He earned his second graduate degree in computer Science from the University of Tulsa in 2008. He completed his Ph.D. from Penn State in information and technology with a minor in applied statistics in 2016.

**Fabian N. Murrieta-Rico** received B.Eng. and M.Eng. degrees from Instituto Tecnológico de Mexicali (ITM) in 2004 and 2013 respectively. In 2017, he received his PhD in Materials Physics at Centro de Investigación Científica y Educación Superior de Ensenada (CICESE). He has worked as an automation engineer, systems designer, as a university professor, and as postdoctoral researcher at Facultad de Ingeniería, Arquitectura y Diseño from Universidad Autónoma de Baja California (UABC) and at the Centro de Nanociencias y Nanotecnología from Universidad Nacional Autónoma de México (CNyN-UNAM), currently he works as professor at the Universidad Politécnica de Baja California. His research has been published in different journals and presented at international conferences since 2009. He has served as reviewer for different journals, some of them include IEEE Transactions on Industrial Electronics, IEEE Transactions on Instrumentation, Measurement and Sensor Review. His research interests are focused on the field of time and frequency metrology, the design of wireless sensor networks, automated systems, and highly sensitive chemical detectors.

**Balsam A. J. Mustafa** holds an MS.c in Information Systems from the UK and earned her Ph.D. in Computer Science (Software Engineering) from Malaysia. Her research interests are in the areas of empirical software engineering, intelligent health care systems, and data mining & analytics. Dr. Balsam has served on more than 25 international conference program committees and journal editorial boards, and has been a keynote and invited speaker at several international conferences. She is a member of IEEE and a professional member of the Association of Computing Machinery (ACM). Dr. Balsam has published 30 technical papers in various refereed journals and conference proceedings.

**Ambika N.** is an MCA, MPhil, Ph.D. in computer science. She completed her Ph.D. from Bharathiar university in the year 2015. She has 16 years of teaching experience and presently working for St.Francis College, Bangalore. She has guided BCA, MCA and M.Tech students in their projects. Her expertise includes wireless sensor network, Internet of things, cybersecurity. She gives guest lectures in her expertise. She is a reviewer of books, conferences (national/international), encyclopaedia and journals. She is advisory committee member of some conferences. She has many publications in National & international conferences, international books, national and international journals and encyclopaedias. She has some patent publications (National) in computer science division.

**Jyotindra Narayan** is a regular doctoral fellow at the Department of Mechanical Engineering, Indian Institute of Technology Guwahati, currently practicing and working on "Design, Development and Control Architecture of a Low-cost Lower-Limb Exoskeleton for Mobility Assistance and Gait Rehabilitation". Moreover, he employs the intelligent and soft computing algorithms in his research. He has a substantial experience in kinematics, dynamics and control of robotic devices for medical applications. He has published several journals, book chapters and conference papers on the broad topic of medical and rehabilitation devices.

**Ghalia Nasserddine** is a Ph.D in information technology and systems. She has been an assistant professor at Lebanese International University since 2010. In addition, she is active research in machine learning, belief function theory, renewable energy and High voltage transmission.

**Son Nguyen** earned his master's degree in applied mathematics and doctoral degree in mathematics, statistics emphasis, both at Ohio University. He is currently an assistant professor at the department of mathematics at Bryant University. His primary research interests lie in dimensionality reduction, imbalanced learning, and machine learning classification. In addition to the theoretical aspects, he is also interested in applying statistics to other areas such as finance and healthcare.

**Van-Ho Nguyen** received B.A. degree in Management Information System from Faculty of Information Systems, University of Economics and Law (VNU–HCM), Vietnam in 2015, and Master degree in MIS from School of Business Information Technology from University of Economics Ho Chi Minh City, Vietnam in 2020, respectively. His current research interests include Business Intelligence, Data Analytics, and Machine Learning.

**Shivinder Nijjer**, currently serving as Assistant Professor in Chitkara University, Punjab, has a doctorate in Business Analytics and Human Resource Management. She has authored books and book chapters in the field of Business Analytics, Information Systems and Strategy for eminent publication groups like Taylor and Francis, Emerald, Pearson and IGI Global. She is currently guiding two PhD candidates and is on reviewer panel of three Scopus indexed journals.

**Roberto Nogueira** is Grupo Globo Full Professor of Strategy at COPPEAD Graduate School of Business, The Federal University of Rio de Janeiro, where he is also executive director of the Strategy and Innovation Research Center. He joined COPPEAD in 1984 and since that teaches at the MSc, PhD and Executive Education courses. He was visiting professor at the University of San Diego (USA), San Jose State University (USA), Alma Business School (Italy), Audencia (France) and Stellenbosch (South

Africa). He is co-founder and board member of the Executive MBA Consortium for Global Business Innovation, encompassing Business Schools from five continents - Alma Business School (Italy), Cranfield (UK), Coppead (Brazil), ESAN (Peru), FIU (USA), Keio Business School (Japan), Kozminski (Poland), MIR (Russia), Munich Business School (Germany), San Jose State (Silicon Valley - USA) and Stellenbosch (South Africa) promoting the exchange of Executive MBA students. Nogueira wrote two books and has published dozens of scholarly articles on such topics as Corporate Strategy, Business Ecosystems, Innovation and Emerging Technologies and Business Reconfiguration, analyzing sectors such as Health, Energy, Education, Media and Entertainment and Space.

**Cherie Noteboom** is a Professor of Information Systems in the College of Business and Information Systems, Coordinator of the PhD in Information Systems and Co-Director of the Center of Excellence in Information Systems at Dakota State University. She holds a Ph.D. in Information Technology from the University of Nebraska-Omaha. In addition, she has earned an Education Doctorate in Adult & Higher Education & Administration & MBA from the University of South Dakota. She has a BS degree in computer science from South Dakota State University. She researches in the areas of Information Systems, Healthcare, and Project Management. Her industry experience runs the continuum from technical computer science endeavors to project management and formal management & leadership positions. She has significant experience working with Management Information Systems, Staff Development, Project Management, Application Development, Education, Healthcare, Mentoring, and Leadership.

**Zinga Novais** is a project manager. She holds a Master's in Project Management from ISEG, School of Economics & Management of the University of Lisbon. She also holds a post-graduation in Project Management and a postgraduation in Management & Business Consulting, both from ISEG - University of Lisbon; and a degree in Public Administration from ISCSP, School of Social and Political Sciences of the University of Lisbon.

**Poonam Oberoi** is an Associate Professor of Marketing at Excelia Business School. She joined Excelia Group in 2014 after successfully defending her thesis at Grenoble Ecole de Management the same year. On the research front, Dr. Oberoi's primary focus is in the area of innovation and technology management. Her work examines the technology and innovation sourcing decisions that firms make, and the consequences of these decisions. Since her appointment at Excelia Business School, she has published research papers on these topics in well-regarded, peer reviewed, international journals such as M@n@gement and Journal of Business Research. Furthermore, she has published many book chapters and case studies on related topics. For more information, please visit: https://www.excelia-group.com/faculty-research/faculty/oberoi.

**Ibrahim Oguntola** is a Research Assistant, Industrial Engineering, Dalhousie University, Canada.

**Kamalendu Pal** is with the Department of Computer Science, School of Science and Technology, City, University of London. Kamalendu received his BSc (Hons) degree in Physics from Calcutta University, India, Postgraduate Diploma in Computer Science from Pune, India, MSc degree in Software Systems Technology from the University of Sheffield, Postgraduate Diploma in Artificial Intelligence from the Kingston University, MPhil degree in Computer Science from the University College London, and MBA degree from the University of Hull, United Kingdom. He has published over seventy-five international research articles (including book chapters) widely in the scientific community with research papers in the ACM SIGMIS Database, Expert Systems with Applications, Decision Support Systems, and conferences. His research interests include knowledge-based systems, decision support systems, blockchain technology, software engineering, service-oriented computing, and ubiquitous computing. He is on the editorial board of an international computer science journal and is a member of the British Computer Society, the Institution of Engineering and Technology, and the IEEE Computer Society.

**Ramon Palau** is a researcher and lecturer in the Pedagogy Department of the Rovira and Virgili University. As a researcher he did internships in UNESCO París and Leipzig University. His current work as a researcher is in ARGET (Applied Research Group of Education Technology) focused in e-learning, digital technologies, digital competences and educational application of digital technologies. In this group he has participated in several research projects. Currently his research is centered in smart learning environments publishing the first fundings. He has worked as a content developer for several institutions as Universitat Oberta de Catalunya, Fundació URV, Fundació Paco Puerto, Editorial Barcanova and Universitat de Lleida. Previously of the works in academia, he has worked as a primary and secondary teacher as a civil servant. From 2003 until 2007 he had been a principal in a public school. Concerning teaching, in higher education level, he has taught in Master of Educational Technology in Universitat Rovira i Virgili and Universitat Oberta de Catalunya and the Master of Teaching in Secondary School where is the director of the program.

**Adam Palmquist** is an industrial PhDc at the department of Applied IT at Gothenburg University and works as Chief Scientific Officer (CSO) at the Swedish Gamification company Insert Coin. Palmquist has a background in learning and game design. He is the author of several books addressing the intersection of design, technology, and learning. Adam has worked as a gamification and learning advisor for several international companies in the technology and production industries. His PhD-project is a collaboration between Gothenburg University and Insert Coin concerning Gamified the World Engine (GWEN), a unique system-agnostic API constructed to make gamification designs scalable. The interdisciplinary project transpires at the intersection of Human-Computer Interaction, Design Science in Information Systems and Learning Analytics.

**Chung-Yeung Pang** received his Ph.D. from Cambridge University, England. He has over 30 years of software development experience in a variety of areas from device drivers, web, and mobile apps to large enterprise IT systems. He has experience in many programming languages, including low-level languages like Assembler and C, high-level languages like COBOL, Java and Ada, AI languages like LISP and Prolog, and mobile app languages like Javascript and Dart. For the past 20 years he has worked as a consultant in various corporate software projects. He worked in the fields of architecture design, development, coaching and management of IT projects. At one time he was a lead architect on a project with a budget of over $ 1 billion. In recent years, despite limited resources and high pressure in some projects, he has led many projects to complete on time and on budget.

**Severin Pang** completed a combined degree in mathematics, statistics, and economics at the University of Bern. He also received the Swiss federal state diploma for computer engineers. He has more than 10 years of experience in computing engineering in companies such as Swiss Re, Zurich Insurance and IBM. At IBM he implemented AI functionalities for a hovering robot to support ISS astronauts. Severin Pang is currently working as a data scientist at Cognitive Solutions & Innovation AG in Switzerland, where he formulates mathematical models for predictive maintenance of machines, develops an intelligent sensor to detect anomalies in the frequency spectrum, and verifies the effectiveness of fuel-saving measures for Airbus aircraft and optimizes the energy consumption of more than 6000 hotels around the world. He has contributed to a number of publications in the fields of data science, AI, and software engineering.

**Renan Payer** holds a PhD and a Master's degree in Production Engineering from Fluminense Federal University (Brazil). Graduated in Chemical Engineering (University of the State of Rio de Janeiro UERJ) in Industrial Chemistry (Fluminense Federal University - UFF). He has an MBA in Production and Quality Management. It carries out academic research in the area of sustainability, circular economy and digital transformation.

**Jean-Eric Pelet** holds a PhD in Marketing, an MBA in Information Systems and a BA (Hns) in Advertising. As an assistant professor in management, he works on problems concerning consumer behaviour when using a website or other information system (e-learning, knowledge management, e-commerce platforms), and how the interface can change that behavior. His main interest lies in the variables that enhance navigation in order to help people to be more efficient with these systems. He works as a visiting professor both in France and abroad (England, Switzerland) teaching e-marketing, ergonomics, usability, and consumer behaviour at Design Schools (Nantes), Business Schools (Paris, Reims), and Universities (Paris Dauphine – Nantes). Dr. Pelet has also actively participated in a number of European Community and National research projects. His current research interests focus on, social networks, interface design, and usability.

**María A. Pérez** received her M.S. and Ph.D. degrees in telecommunication engineering from the University of Valladolid, Spain, in 1996 and 1999, respectively. She is presently Associate Professor at University of Valladolid, and member of the Data Engineering Research Unit. Her research is focused on Big Data, Artificial Intelligence, Internet of Things, and the application of technology to the learning process. She has managed or participated in numerous international research projects. She is author or co-author of many publications in journals, books, and conferences. In addition, she has been involved as reviewer in several international research initiatives.

**Vitalii Petranovskii** received the Ph.D. degree in physical chemistry from the Moscow Institute of Crystallography in 1988. From 1993 to 1994, he worked as a Visiting Fellow at the National Institute of Materials Science and Chemical Research, Japan. Since 1995, he has been working with the Center for Nanotechnology and Nanotechnology, National University of Mexico, as the Head of the Department of Nanocatalysis, from 2006 to 2014. He is a member of the Mexican Academy of Sciences, the International Association of Zeolites, and the Russian Chemical Society. He has published over 160 articles in peer-reviewed journals and five invited book chapters. He is also a coauthor of the monograph Clusters and Matrix Isolated Clustered Superstructures (St. Petersburg, 1995). His research interests include the synthesis and properties of nanoparticles deposited on zeolite matrices, and the modification of the zeolite matrices themselves for their high-tech use.

**Frederick E. Petry** received BS and MS degrees in physics and a PhD in computer and information science from The Ohio State University. He is currently a computer scientist in the Naval Research Laboratory at the Stennis Space Center Mississippi. He has been on the faculty of the University of Alabama in Huntsville, the Ohio State University and Tulane University where he is an Emeritus Professor. His recent research interests include representation of imprecision via soft computing in databases, spatial and environmental and information systems and machine learning. Dr. Petry has over 350 scientific publications including 150 journal articles/book chapters and 9 books written or edited. For his research on the use of fuzzy sets for modeling imprecision in databases and information systems he was elected an IEEE Life Fellow, AAAS Fellow, IFSA Fellow and an ACM Distinguished Scientist. In 2016 he received the IEEE Computational Intelligence Society Pioneer Award.

**Birgit Pilch** studied Biology and then Technical Protection of Environment at Graz University and Graz University of Technology.

**Matthias Pohl** is a research associate in the Very Large Business Application Lab at the Otto von Guericke University Magdeburg since 2016. His main research and work interests are data science, statistical modeling and the efficient design of innovative IT solutions. Matthias Pohl studied Mathematics and Informatics and holds a Diplom degree in Mathematics from Otto von Guericke University Magdeburg.

**Peter Poschmann**, M.Sc., works as a research associate at the Chair of Logistics, Institute of Technology and Management, at the Technical University of Berlin. Within the scope of several research projects, he focuses on the technical application of Machine Learning to logistic problems, in particular the prediction of transport processes. Previously, he worked as a research associate at a Fraunhofer Institute with a focus on Data Science. He graduated in industrial engineering with a specialization in mechanical engineering at the Technical University of Darmstadt.

**Brajkishore Prajapati** is an associate Data Scientist at Azilen Technologies Pvt. Ltd. He is living in Gwalior, Madhya Pradesh. He is very passionate and loyal to his work and finishes his work on time. His dream is to become one of the great researchers in the field of Artificial Intelligence. He is a very big fan of cricket and reading.

**Sabyasachi Pramanik** is a Professional IEEE member. He obtained a PhD in Computer Science and Engineering from the Sri Satya Sai University of Technology and Medical Sciences, Bhopal, India. Presently, he is an Assistant Professor, Department of Computer Science and Engineering, Haldia Institute of Technology, India. He has many publications in various reputed international conferences, journals, and online book chapter contributions (Indexed by SCIE, Scopus, ESCI, etc.). He is doing research in the field of Artificial Intelligence, Data Privacy, Cybersecurity, Network Security, and Machine Learning. He is also serving as the editorial board member of many international journals. He is a reviewer of journal articles from IEEE, Springer, Elsevier, Inderscience, IET, and IGI Global. He has reviewed many conference papers, has been a keynote speaker, session chair and has been a technical program committee member in many international conferences. He has authored a book on Wireless Sensor Network. Currently, he is editing 6 books from IGI Global, CRC Press EAI/Springer and Scrivener-Wiley Publications.

**Abdurrakhman Prasetyadi** is a junior researcher at the Research Center for Data and Information Science, The Indonesia Institute of Sciences (LIPI), Indonesia since 2019. He was a researcher at the Center for Information Technology (UPT BIT LIPI) for 6 years. He obtained his bachelor's degree in

Library and Information Sciences from the University of Padjadjaran, Indonesia in 2008. He earned a Master's degree in Information Technology for Libraries from the IPB University in 2017. Abdur-rakhman Prasetyadi's research interests include issues in the field of Library and Information Science, Social Informatics, and Informetrics.

**Bitan Pratihar** obtained his Bachelor of Technology degree in Chemical Engineering from National Institute of Technology Durgapur, India, in 2017. He completed his Master of Technology degree in Chemical Engineering department of National Institute of Technology Rourkela, India, in 2019. His research interests were the application of Fuzzy Logic in data mining, controller design, and soft sensor design for several chemical engineering applications and others. Currently, he is a doctoral student in Membrane Separation Laboratory of Chemical Engineering Department, Indian Institute of Technology Kharagpur, India.

**Alessandro Puzzanghera** is a PhD student at the University for foreigners "Dante Alighieri" in Reggio Calabria. He worked many years as legal assistant at the FIDLAW LLP a law firm in London. He successfully completed her studies in the Master of Studies (MSt) postgraduate level degree program of the European Law and Governance School at the European Public Law Organization in Athens. His fields of research include: Artificial Intelligence, Administrative law, Personal Data in particular about GDPR. He published papers for Hart publishing (Oxford), EPLO publication (Athens) and various italian scientific journals.

**John Quinn** is a Professor of Mathematics at Bryant University and has been teaching there since 1991. Prior to teaching, he was an engineer at the Naval Underwater Systems Center (now the Naval Undersea Warfare Center). He received his Sc.B. degree from Brown University in 1978, and his M.S. and Ph.D. degrees from Harvard University in 1987 and 1991, respectively. Professor Quinn has published in multiple areas. He has done previous research in mathematical programming methods and computable general equilibrium models. He currently does research in probability models and in data mining applications, including the prediction of rare events. He is also doing research in pension modeling, including the effects of health status on retirement payouts.

**Parvathi R.** is a Professor of School of Computing Science and Engineering at VIT University, Chennai since 2011. She received the Doctoral degree in the field of spatial data mining in the same year. Her teaching experience in the area of computer science includes more than two decades and her research interests include data mining, big data and computational biology.

**Sreemathy R.** is working as Associate Professor in Pune Institute of Computer Technology, Savitribai Phule Pune University, India. She has her Master's degree in Electronics Engineering from college of Engineering, Pune. Savitribai Phule Pune University and Doctoral degree in Electronics Engineering from Shivaji University, India. Her research areas include signal processing, image processing, Artificial Intelligence, Machine Learning and Deep Learning.

**Kornelije Rabuzin** is currently a Full Professor at the Faculty of organization and informatics, University of Zagreb, Croatia. He holds Bachelor, Master, and PhD degrees - all in Information Science. He performs research in the area of databases, particularly graph databases, as well as in the field of data warehousing and business intelligence. He has published four books and more than eighty scientific and professional papers.

**Kaleche Rachid** is a PhD student of computer science since 2018. He is member of computer science laboratory (LIO) of Oran1 university in Algeria. His current research interests deal with artificial intelligence, transportation system, logistic systems, machine learning, bio-inspired approach. He is co-author of many publications and communications.

**Rulina Rachmawati** earned a bachelor degree in Chemistry from the Sepuluh Nopember Institute of Technology, Indonesia, in 2009. She started her career as a technical librarian at the Library and Archive Agency of the Regional Government of Surabaya city, Indonesia. Her passion for librarianship brought her to pursue a Master of Information Management from RMIT University, Australia, in 2019. Presently, she is a librarian at the Center for Scientific Data and Documentation, the Indonesian Institute of Sciences. Her current roles include providing library services, providing content for the Indonesian Scientific Journal Database (ISJD), and researching data, documentation and information. Her research interests include bibliometrics, library services, information retrieval, and research data management.

**Nayem Rahman** is an Information Technology (IT) Professional. He has implemented several large projects using data warehousing and big data technologies. He holds a Ph.D. from the Department of Engineering and Technology Management at Portland State University, USA, an M.S. in Systems Science (Modeling & Simulation) from Portland State University, Oregon, USA, and an MBA in Management Information Systems (MIS), Project Management, and Marketing from Wright State University, Ohio, USA. He has authored 40 articles published in various conference proceedings and scholarly journals. He serves on the Editorial Review Board of the International Journal of End-User Computing and Development (IJEUCD). His principal research interests include Big Data Analytics, Big Data Technology Acceptance, Data Mining for Business Intelligence, and Simulation-based Decision Support System (DSS).

**Vishnu Rajan** is an Assistant Professor in the Production & Operations Management Division at XIME Kochi, Kerala, India. His current research interests include supply chain risk management, operations research, reliability engineering, manufacturing systems management, quantitative techniques and statistics. He has published research articles in reputed peer-reviewed international journals of Taylor & Francis, Emerald, Inderscience, Elsevier, IEEE and IIIE publications. He also has a scientific book chapter to his credit. Besides this, Vishnu serves as an editorial board member of the International Journal of Risk and Contingency Management (IJRCM) of IGI Global.

**T. Rajeshwari** is freelancer and Yagyopathy researcher. She usually writes up article in science forums related to Hindu Mythology and their scientific proofs. She belongs to Kolkata and travels across globe for social work and spreading the science of Hindu rituals.

**P. N. Ram Kumar** is Professor in the QM & OM area at the Indian Institute of Management Kozhikode. Prior to this appointment, he had worked as a Post-Doctoral Research Fellow in the School of Mechanical and Aerospace Engineering at the Nanyang Technological University, Singapore. He obtained his Bachelor in Mechanical Engineering from the JNTU Hyderabad in 2003, Master in Industrial Engineering from the PSG College of Technology, Coimbatore in 2005 and PhD from the IIT Madras in 2009.

His primary areas of research include, but not limited to, transportation network optimisation, military logistics, reliability engineering and supply chain management. He has authored several international journal papers and his work has been published in reputed journals such as Journal of the Operational Research Society, Defense and Security Analysis, Strategic Analysis, and Journal of Defense Modeling & Simulation, to name a few.

**Perumal Ramasubramanian** holds BE, ME from Computer Science and Engineering from Madurai Kamaraj University and PH.D Computer Science from Madurai Kamaraj University in the year 1989, 1996 and 2012. He has 31 years teaching experience in academia. He was published 55 papers in various international journal and conferences. He has authored 14 books and has 135 citations with h-index 5 and i10 index 4. He is also actively involved in various professional societies like Institution of Engineers(I), Computer Science Teachers Association, ISTE, ISRD, etc.

**Célia M. Q. Ramos** graduated in Computer Engineering from the University of Coimbra, obtained her Master in Electrical and Computers Engineering from the Higher Technical Institute, Lisbon University, and the PhD in Econometrics in the University of the Algarve (UALG), Faculty of Economics, Portugal. She is Associate Professor at School for Management, Hospitality and Tourism, also in the UALG, where she lectures computer science. Areas of research and special interest include the conception and development of business intelligence, information systems, tourism information systems, big data, tourism, machine learning, social media marketing, econometric modelling and panel-data models. Célia Ramos has published in the fields of information systems and tourism, namely, she has authored a book, several book chapters, conference papers and journal articles. At the level of applied research, she has participated in several funded projects.

**Anshu Rani** has more than 12 years of experience in teaching and learning at various reputed institutes. She is a researcher associated with the online consumer behaviour area.

**Bindu Rani** is a Ph.D. scholar from Department of Computer Science and Engineering, Sharda University, Greater Noida, India and works as assistant professor in Information Technology Department, Inderprastha Engineering College, Ghaziabad, Dr. A.P.J Abdul Kalam Technical University, India. She received Master in Computer Science and Application degree from Aligarh Muslim University (AMU), India. Her research interests are Data Mining, Big Data and Machine learning techniques.

**N. Raghavendra Rao** is an Advisor to FINAIT Consultancy Services India. He has a doctorate in the area of Finance. He has a rare distinction of having experience in the combined areas of Information Technology and Finance.

**Zbigniew W. Ras** is a Professor of Computer Science Department and the Director of the KDD Laboratory at the University of North Carolina, Charlotte. He also holds professorship position in the Institute of Computer Science at the Polish-Japanese Academy of Information Technology in Warsaw, Poland. His areas of specialization include knowledge discovery and data mining, recommender systems, health informatics, business analytics, flexible query answering, music information retrieval, and art.

**Rohit Rastogi** received his B.E. degree in Computer Science and Engineering from C.C.S.Univ. Meerut in 2003, the M.E. degree in Computer Science from NITTTR-Chandigarh (National Institute of Technical Teachers Training and Research-affiliated to MHRD, Govt. of India), Punjab Univ. Chandigarh in 2010. Currently he is pursuing his Ph.D. In computer science from Dayalbagh Educational Institute, Agra under renowned professor of Electrical Engineering Dr. D.K. Chaturvedi in area of spiritual consciousness. Dr. Santosh Satya of IIT-Delhi and dr. Navneet Arora of IIT-Roorkee have happily consented him to co supervise. He is also working presently with Dr. Piyush Trivedi of DSVV Hardwar, India in center of Scientific spirituality. He is a Associate Professor of CSE Dept. in ABES Engineering. College, Ghaziabad (U.P.-India), affiliated to Dr. A.P. J. Abdul Kalam Technical Univ. Lucknow (earlier Uttar Pradesh Tech. University). Also, he is preparing some interesting algorithms on Swarm Intelligence approaches like PSO, ACO and BCO etc.Rohit Rastogi is involved actively with Vichaar Krnati Abhiyaan and strongly believe that transformation starts within self.

**Mark Rauch** is a database administrator and a graduate student in the program for Database Management at the University of West Florida. Mark Rauch is actively working in the healthcare industry and has experience working with several Oracle database platforms as well as SQL Server. His experience extends across Oracle 11g, 12c, and 19c. He has also supported several aspects of Oracle Middleware including Oracle Data Integrator, Oracle Enterprise Manager, Web Logic, and Business Publisher.

**Yuan Ren** is an instructor in Shanghai Dianji University. He was born in 1984. He got his bachelor's degree in mathematics from Jilin University in 2007, and doctor's degree in computer software from Fudan University in 2013. His multidisciplinary research interests include image understanding, artificial intelligence, and data science.

**M. Yudhi Rezaldi** is a researcher at the Research Center for Informatics, National Research and Innovation Agency (BRIN). His academic qualifications were obtained from Pasundan Universiti Bandung for his bachelor degree, and Mater degree in Magister of Design from Institut Teknologi Bandung (ITB). He completed his PhD in 2020 at Computer Science from Universiti Kebangsaan Malaysia (UKM). And he is also an active member of Himpunan Peneliti Indonesia (Himpenindo). His research interests include visualization, modeling, computer graphics animation, multimedia design, Information Science, particularly disaster. He received an award The best researcher in the 2011 researcher and engineer incentive program in Indonesian Institute of Science (LIPI). and once received the Karya Satya award 10 years in 2018 from the Indonesian government for his services to the country.

**Moisés Rivas López** was born in June 1, 1960. He received the B.S. and M.S. degrees in Autonomous University of Baja California, México, in 1985, 1991, respectively. He received PhD degree in the same University, on specialty "Optical Scanning for Structural Health Monitoring", in 2010. He has written 5 book chapters and 148 Journal and Proceedings Conference papers. Since 1992 till the present time he has presented different works in several International Congresses of IEEE, ICROS, SICE, AMMAC in USA, England, Japan, turkey and Mexico. Dr. Rivas was Dean of Engineering Institute of Autonomous University Baja California, Since1997 to 2005; also was Rector of Polytechnic University of Baja California, Since2006 to 2010. Since 2012 to 208 was the head of physic engineering department, of Engineering Institute, Autonomous University of Baja California, Mexico. Since 2013 till the present time member of National Researcher System and now is Professor in the Polytechnic University of Baja California.

**Julio C. Rodríguez-Quiñonez** received the B.S. degree in CETYS, Mexico in 2007. He received the Ph.D. degree from Baja California Autonomous University, México, in 2013. He is currently Full Time Researcher-Professor in the Engineering Faculty of the Autonomous University of Baja California, and member of the National Research System Level 1. Since 2016 is Senior Member of IEEE. He is involved in the development of optical scanning prototype in the Applied Physics Department and research leader in the development of a new stereo vision system prototype. He has been thesis director of 3 Doctor's Degree students and 4 Master's degree students. He holds two patents referred to dynamic triangulation method, has been editor of 4 books, Guest Editor of Measurement, IEEE Sensors Journal, International Journal of Advanced Robotic Systems and Journal of Sensors, written over 70 papers, 8 book chapters and has been a reviewer for IEEE Sensors Journal, Optics and Lasers in Engineering, IEEE Transaction on Mechatronics and Neural Computing and Applications of Springer; he participated as a reviewer and Session Chair of IEEE ISIE conferences in 2014 (Turkey), 2015 (Brazil), 2016 (USA), 2017 (UK), 2019 (Canada), IECON 2018 (USA), IECON 2019 (Portugal), ISIE 2020 (Netherlands), ISIE 2021 (Japan). His current research interests include automated metrology, stereo vision systems, control systems, robot navigation and 3D laser scanners.

**Mário José Batista Romão** is an Associate Professor of Information Systems, with Aggregation, at ISEG – University of Lisbon. He is Director of the Masters program in Computer Science and Management. He holds a PhD in Management Sciences by ISCTE-IUL and by Computer Integrated Manufacturing at Cranfiel University (UK). He also holds a MsC in Telecommunications and Computer Science, at IST - Instituto Superior Técnico, University of Lisbon. He is Pos-Graduated in Project Management and holds the international certification Project Management Professional (PMP), by PMI – Project Management International. He has a degree in Electrotecnic Engineer by IST.

**James Rotella** did his BS in physics at Pennsylvania State University and MS in physics at the University of Pittsburgh. While at the University of Pittsburgh he focused on doing epigenetic research in the biophysics department. He went on to work for 4 years as a failure analysis engineer at a Dynamics Inc. working on improving their lines of flexible microelectronics. He focused on improving yield internally in the factory, and designing and carrying out accelerated life and field tests to improve field performance. After working at Dynamics, he moved on to begin work programming at K&L Gates where he maintains analytics pipelines, models, and databases. While at K&L Gates, he completed an Masters in Data Analytics at Pennsylvania State University.

**Anirban Roy** is the founder of Water-Energy Nexus Laboratory in BITS Pilani Goa Campus Founder and Promoter and CEO of Epione Swajal Solutions India LLP, focussing on Membrane Manufacturing. Experience in membrane synthesis, manufacturing, handling, devices, and prototypes.

**Parimal Roy** studied in Anthropology. Later he obtained papers on MBA, Project management, and Criminology (paper is better than a certificate) to enhance his knowledge. He is currently working in a state own institution in the field of Training & Development. Decolonizing, Marginal community, subaltern voice, Project management - all are interest arena in academic world. His written book is

Extra-marital love in folk songs. Co-author of Captive minded intellectual; Quantitative Ethnography in Indigenous Research Methodology; and so many book chapters and journals.

**Saúl Rozada Raneros** is a PhD candidate at University of Valladolid, who received his M.S. degrees in telecommunication engineering from the University of Valladolid, Spain. He is researcher of the Data Engineering Research Unit and his research is focused on Internet of Things, and Virtual Reality. Also, he is co-author of some publications in journals, dealing with topics related to his lines of his research.

**Rauno Rusko** is University lecturer at the University of Lapland. His research activities focus on cooperation, coopetition, strategic management, supply chain management and entrepreneurship mainly in the branches of information communication technology, forest industry and tourism. His articles appeared in the European Management Journal, Forest Policy and Economics, International Journal of Business Environment, Industrial Marketing Management, International Journal of Innovation in the Digital Economy and International Journal of Tourism Research among others.

**Rashid bin Mohd Saad** is an educationist and serving as an Assistant professor at the Department of Education at Universiti Malaya. At present, he is working in the Drug Discoveries of Indigenous communities in Bangladesh.

**Sheelu Sagar** is a research scholar pursuing her PhD in Management from Amity University (AUUP). She graduated with a Bachelor Degree of Science from Delhi University. She received her Post Graduate Degree in Master of Business Administration with distinction from Amity University Uttar Pradesh India in 2019. She is working at a post of Asst. Controller of Examinations, Amity University, Uttar Pradesh. She is associated with various NGOs - in India. She is an Active Member of Gayatri Teerth, ShantiKunj, Haridwar, Trustee - ChaturdhamVed Bhawan Nyas (having various centers all over India), Member Executive Body -Shree JeeGauSadan, Noida. She is a social worker and has been performing Yagya since last 35 years and working for revival of Indian Cultural Heritage through yagna (Hawan), meditation through Gayatri Mantra and pranayama. She is doing her research on Gayatri Mantra.

**Rajarshi Saha** has currently completed his BSc with Major in Computer Science from St. Xavier's College, Kolkata. His current research interest is Data Analytics and Machine Learning.

**Sudipta Sahana** is an Associate Professor at a renowned University in West Bengal. For more than 11 years he has worked in this region. He has passed his M.tech degree in Software Engineering and B.Tech Degree in Information Technology from West Bengal University of Technology with a great CGPA/DGPA in 2010 and 2012 respectively. He completed his Ph.D. from the University of Kalyani in 2020. He has published more than 60 papers in referred journals and conferences indexed by Scopus, DBLP, and Google Scholar and working as an editorial team member of many reputed journals. He is a life member of the Computer Society of India (CSI), Computer Science Teachers Association (CSTA), and also a member of the International Association of Computer Science and Information Technology (IACSIT).

**Pavithra Salanke** has more than a decade of experience in Teaching and she is an active member in the research area of HR using social media.

**Hajara U. Sanda**, PhD, is an Associate Professor at the Department of Mass Communication, Bayero University, Kano, Kano State, Nigeria. She is also a former Dean, Student Affairs of the university, and has published many research articles, presented many conference papers, and published a couple of books.

**Enes Şanlıtürk** holds B.S. in Industrial Engineering in Istanbul Technical University and M.S. in Management Engineering in Istanbul Technical University. Also, his Ph.D. education continues in Industrial Engineering in Istanbul Technical University. He has study in Machine Learning. His main contributions is enhancing defect prediction performance in machine learning on production systems. In addition, he works in private sector as an Analyst.

**Loris Schmid** was born in 1992 in Visp, Switzerland. Studying at the University of Berne he attained a Master of Science in Economics. During the UMUSE2 (User Monitoring of the US Election) project, Loris Schmid was employed by the University of Neuchâtel from August 2020 until February 2021 performing data analysis and processing. He works as an Analyst and Research Assistant at IFAAR since 2019.

**Dara Schniederjans** is an Associate Professor of Supply Chain Management at the University of Rhode Island, College of Business Administration. Dara received her Ph.D. from Texas Tech University in 2012. Dara has co-authored five books and published over thirty academic journal articles as well as numerous book chapters. Dara has served as a guest co-editor for a special issue on "Business ethics in Social Sciences" in the International Journal of Society Systems Science. She has also served as a website coordinator and new faculty development consortium co-coordinator for Decisions Sciences Institute.

**Jaydip Sen** obtained his Bachelor of Engineering (B.E) in Electrical Engineering with honors from Jadavpur University, Kolkata, India in 1988, and Master of Technology (M.Tech) in Computer Science with honors from Indian Statistical Institute, Kolkata in 2001. Currently, he is pursuing his PhD on "Security and Privacy in Internet of Things" in Jadavpur University, which is expected to be completed by December 2018. His research areas include security in wired and wireless networks, intrusion detection systems, secure routing protocols in wireless ad hoc and sensor networks, secure multicast and broadcast communication in next generation broadband wireless networks, trust and reputation based systems, sensor networks, and privacy issues in ubiquitous and pervasive communication. He has more than 100 publications in reputed international journals and referred conference proceedings (IEEE Xplore, ACM Digital Library, Springer LNCS etc.), and 6 book chapters in books published by internationally renowned publishing houses e.g. Springer, CRC press, IGI-Global etc. He is a Senior Member of ACM, USA a Member IEEE, USA.

**Kishore Kumar Senapati**'s experiences at BIT, Mesra complement both teaching and research, which brought innovation culture at academia and Industry. He has significant Industry driven research and teaching experience in the leading organizations of the country working nearly two decades, including ≈ 16 years at current place as an Assistant Professor in the Department of Computer Science and Engineering at Birla Institute of Technology, MESRA, Ranchi, INDIA. He has obtained PhD in Engineering from Birla Institute of Technology, MESRA. He has Master of Technology in Computer Science from UTKAL University, ODISHA. He has more than 18 years of teaching and research experience. He has guided more than 41 students of ME & M. Tech and four PhD scholars are currently working under his supervision in Computer Science field. He has capabilities in the area of algorithm design, Image processing, Cyber Security and Machine learning. He has published more than 40 peer reviewed papers on various national and international journals of repute including conference presentations. He has delivered invited talks at various national and international seminars including conferences, symposium, and workshop. He is also professional member of national and international societies. He was also active members in various program committees of international conference and chaired the sessions. He serves as editor of International and National Journal of high repute. He has successfully conducted several workshops in his organization on various topics. He is an honorary computer science expert and serves the nation in multiple areas.

**Oleg Yu. Sergiyenko** was born in February, 9, 1969. He received the B.S., and M.S., degrees in Kharkiv National University of Automobiles and Highways, Kharkiv, Ukraine, in 1991, 1993, respectively. He received the Ph.D. degree in Kharkiv National Polytechnic University on specialty "Tools and methods of non-destructive control" in 1997. He received the DSc degree in Kharkiv National University of Radio electronics in 2018. He has been an editor of 7 books, written 24 book chapters, 160 papers indexed in Scopus and holds 2 patents of Ukraine and 1 in Mexico. Since 1994 till the present time he was represented by his research works in several International Congresses of IEEE, ICROS, SICE, IMEKO in USA, England, Japan, Canada, Italy, Brazil, Austria, Ukraine, and Mexico. Dr.Sergiyenko in December 2004 was invited by Engineering Institute of Baja California Autonomous University for researcher position. He is currently Head of Applied Physics Department of Engineering Institute of Baja California Autonomous University, Mexico, director of several Masters and Doctorate thesis. He was a member of Program Committees of various international and local conferences. He is member of Academy (Academician) of Applied Radio electronics of Bielorussia, Ukraine and Russia.

**Martina Šestak** received her Master's degree in Information and Software Engineering from the Faculty of Organization and Informatics, University of Zagreb in 2016. She is currently a Ph.D. student in Computer Science at Faculty of Electrical Engineering and Computer Science in Maribor. She is currently a Teaching Assistant and a member of Laboratory for Information Systems at the Faculty of Electrical Engineering and Computer Science, University of Maribor. Her main research interests include graph databases, data analytics and knowledge graphs.

**Rohan Shah** is a Director in the Financial Services practice at Simon-Kucher & Partners. Rohan holds a Master's degree in Operations Research, specializing in Financial and Managerial Applications from Columbia University in the City of New York.

**Aakanksha Sharaff** has completed her graduation in Computer Science and Engineering in 2010 from Government Engineering College, Bilaspur (C.G.). She has completed her post graduation Master of Technology in 2012 in Computer Science & Engineering (Specialization- Software Engineering) from National Institute of Technology, Rourkela and completed Ph.D. degree in Computer Science & Engineering in 2017 from National Institute of Technology Raipur, India. Her area of interest is Software Engineering, Data Mining, Text Mining, and Information Retrieval. She is currently working as an Assistant Professor at NIT Raipur India.

**Michael J. Shaw** joined the faculty of University of Illinois at Urbana-Champaign in 1984. He has been affiliated with the Gies College of Business, National Center for Supercomputing Applications, and the Information Trust Institute. His research interests include machine learning, digital transformation, and healthcare applications.

**Yong Shi** is a Professor of University of Nebraska at Omaha. He also serves as the Director, Chinese Academy of Sciences Research Center on Fictitious Economy & Data Science and the Director of the Key Lab of Big Data Mining and Knowledge Management, Chinese Academy of Sciences. He is the counselor of the State Council of PRC (2016), the elected member of the International Eurasian Academy of Science (2017), and elected fellow of the World Academy of Sciences for Advancement of Science in Developing Countries (2015). His research interests include business intelligence, data mining, and multiple criteria decision making. He has published more than 32 books, over 350 papers in various journals and numerous conferences/proceedings papers. He is the Editor-in-Chief of International Journal of Information Technology and Decision Making (SCI), Editor-in-Chief of Annals of Data Science (Springer) and a member of Editorial Board for several academic journals.

**Dharmpal Singh** received his Bachelor of Computer Science and Engineering and Master of Computer Science and Engineering from West Bengal University of Technology. He has about eight years of experience in teaching and research. At present, he is with JIS College of Engineering, Kalyani, and West Bengal, India as an Associate Professor. Currently, he had done his Ph. D from University of Kalyani. He has about 26 publications in national and international journals and conference proceedings. He is also the editorial board members of many reputed/ referred journal.

**Aarushi Siri Agarwal** is pursuing an undergraduate degree in Computer Science Engineering at Vellore Institute of Technology Chennai. Her interest is in using Machine Learning algorithms for data analysis, mainly in areas such as Cyber Security and Social Network Analysis.

**R. Sridharan** is a Professor of Industrial Engineering in the Department of Mechanical Engineering at National Institute of Technology Calicut, India. He received his PhD in 1995 from the Department of Mechanical Engineering at Indian Institute of Technology, Bombay, India. His research interests include modelling and analysis of decision problems in supply chain management, job shop production systems and flexible manufacturing systems. He has published papers in reputed journals such as IJPE, IJPR, JMTM, IJLM, IJAMT, etc. For the outstanding contribution to the field of industrial engineering and the institution, he has been conferred with the Fellowship award by the National Council of the Indian Institution of Industrial Engineering in 2017.

**Karthik Srinivasan** is an assistant professor of business analytics in the School of Business at University of Kansas (KU). He completed his PhD in Management Information Systems from University of Arizona and his master's in management from Indian Institute of Science. He has also worked as a software developer and a data scientist prior to joining academia. His research focuses on addressing novel and important analytics challenges using statistical machine learning, network science, and natural language processing. His research has been presented in top tier business and healthcare analytics conferences and journals. Karthik teaches database management, data warehousing, big data courses for undergraduates and masters students at KU.

**Gautam Srivastava** is working as an Assistant Professor with GL Bajaj Institute of Management and Research. He has 15+ years of academic experience. He has completed his Ph.D. from the University of Petroleum and Energy Studies, India. His area of specialization is Marketing. He has published and presented many research papers in national and international journals.

**Daniel Staegemann** studied computer science at Technical University Berlin (TUB). He received the master's degree in 2017. He is currently pursuing the Ph.D. degree with the Otto von Guericke University Magdeburg. Since 2018, he has been employed as a research associate with OVGU where he has authored numerous papers that have been published in prestigious journals and conferences, for which he is also an active reviewer. His research interest is primarily focused on big data, especially the testing.

**Mirjana D. Stojanović** received her B.Sc. (1985) and M.Sc. (1993) degrees in electrical engineering and her Ph.D. degree (2005) in technical sciences, all from the University of Belgrade, Serbia. She is currently full professor in Information and Communication Technologies at the Faculty of Transport and Traffic Engineering, University of Belgrade. Previously, she held research position at the Mihailo Pupin Institute, University of Belgrade, and was involved in developing telecommunication equipment and systems for regional power utilities and major Serbian corporate systems. Prof. Stojanović participated in a number of national and international R&D projects, including technical projects of the International Council on Large Electric Systems, CIGRÉ. As author or co-author she published more than 170 book chapters, journal articles, and conference papers in her field. She was lead editor of the book on ICS cyber security in the Future Internet environment. Mirjana Stojanović also published a monograph on teletraffic engineering and two university textbooks (in Serbian). Her research interests include communication protocols, cyber security, service and network management, and Future Internet technologies.

**Frank Straube** studied Industrial Engineering, received his doctorate in 1987 from the Department of Logistics at the Technical University of Berlin under Prof. Dr.-Ing. H. Baumgarten and subsequently worked in a scientifically oriented practice, including more than 10 years as head of a company with more than 100 employees planning logistics systems. After his habilitation (2004) at the University of St. Gallen, Prof. Straube followed the call to the TU Berlin and since then has been head of the logistics department at the Institute for Technology and Management. He is a member of the editorial boards of international logistics journals. Prof. Straube founded the "International Transfer Center for Logistics (ITCL)" in 2005 to realize innovative planning and training activities for companies. He is a member of different boards at companies and associations to bridge between science and practice.

**Hamed Taherdoost** is an award-winning leader and R&D professional. He is the founder of Hamta Group and sessional faculty member of University Canada West. He has over 20 years of experience in both industry and academia sectors. Dr. Hamed was lecturer at IAU and PNU universities, a scientific researcher and R&D and Academic Manager at IAU, Research Club, MDTH, NAAS, Pinmo, Tablokar, Requiti, and Hamta Academy. Hamed has authored over 120 scientific articles in peer-reviewed international journals and conference proceedings (h-index = 24; i10-index = 50; February 2021), as well as eight book chapters and seven books in the field of technology and research methodology. He is the author of the Research Skills book and his current papers have been published in Behaviour & Information Technology, Information and Computer Security, Electronics, Annual Data Science, Cogent Business & Management, Procedia Manufacturing, and International Journal of Intelligent Engineering Informatics. He is a Senior Member of the IEEE, IAEEEE, IASED & IEDRC, Working group member of IFIP TC and Member of CSIAC, ACT-IAC, and many other professional bodies. Currently, he is involved in several multidisciplinary research projects among which includes studying innovation in information technology & web development, people's behavior, and technology acceptance.

**Toshifumi Takada**, Professor of National Chung Cheng University, Taiwan, 2018 to present, and Professor Emeritus of Tohoku University Accounting School, served as a CPA examination commissioner from 2001 to 2003. He has held many important posts, including the special commissioner of the Business Accounting Council of the Financial Service Agency, councilor of the Japan Accounting Association, President of the Japan Audit Association, and Director of the Japan Internal Control Association. Professional Career: 1979-1997 Lecturer, Associate Professor, Professor of Fukushima University, Japan 1997-2018 Professor of Tohoku University, Japan 2018-present Professor of National Chung Cheng University, Taiwan.

**Neeti Tandon** is Yagypathy researcher, scholar of fundamental physics in Vikram University Ujjain. She is active Volunteer of Gayatri Parivaar and highly involved in philanthropic activities.

**Ahmet Tezcan Tekin** holds B.S. in Computer Science in Istanbul Technical University and Binghamton University, a M.S. and Ph.D. in Management Engineering in Istanbul Technical University. He has studies in Machine Learning, Fuzzy Clustering etc. He gives lectures on Database Management and Big Data Management in different programs. His main contributions in this research area is improving prediction performance in machine learning with the merging Ensemble Learning approach and fuzzy clustering approach.

**Gizem Temelcan** obtained her Ph.D. entitled "Optimization of the System Optimum Fuzzy Traffic Assignment Problem" in Mathematical Engineering from Yildiz Technical University in 2020. She is an Assistant Professor in the Department of Computer Engineering at Beykoz University, Istanbul, Turkey. Her research interests are operational research, optimization of linear and nonlinear programming problems in the fuzzy environment.

**Ronak Tiwari** is a graduate student of Industrial Engineering and Management in the Department of Mechanical Engineering at National Institute of Technology Calicut, India. He worked in the industry for two years after receiving his bachelor's degree. He received his bachelor's degree in Industrial Engineering, in 2018, from Pandit Deendayal Petroleum University, Gujarat, India. He also received a silver medal for his academic performance during his undergraduate studies. He received a Government of India Scholarship under INSPIRE scheme to pursue basic sciences. He is an active researcher, and his research interests are mainly in supply chain risk, supply chain resilience, location theory problems, and humanitarian logistics. He has also acted as a reviewer of some internationally reputed journals.

**Carlos Torres** is CEO of Power-MI, a cloud platform to manage Predictive Maintenance. Born in San Salvador, 1975. Mechanical Engineer, Universidad Centroamericana "José Simeon Cañas", El Salvador. Master in Science Mechatronics, Universität Siegen, Germany. INSEAD Certificate in Global Management, France. Harvard Business School graduated in Global Management Program, USA.

**Cahyo Trianggoro** is Junior Researcher at Research Center for Informatics, Indonesia Institute of Science (LIPI). Cahyo is completed study from University of Padjadjaran, where he received a Bachelor degree in Information and Library Science and currently pursue for master degree in graduate school University of Padjadjaran. Cahyo having research interest study in data governance, digital preservation, and social informatics.

**B. K. Tripathy** is now working as a Professor in SITE, school, VIT, Vellore, India. He has received research/academic fellowships from UGC, DST, SERC and DOE of Govt. of India. Dr. Tripathy has published more than 700 technical papers in international journals, proceedings of international conferences and edited research volumes. He has produced 30 PhDs, 13 MPhils and 5 M.S (By research) under his supervision. Dr. Tripathy has 10 edited volumes, published two text books on Soft Computing and Computer Graphics. He has served as the member of Advisory board or Technical Programme Committee member of more than 125 international conferences inside India and abroad. Also, he has edited 6 research volumes for different publications including IGI and CRC. He is a Fellow of IETE and life/senior member of IEEE, ACM, IRSS, CSI, ACEEE, OMS and IMS. Dr. Tripathy is an editorial board member/reviewer of more than 100 international journals of repute.

**Gyananjaya Tripathy** has completed his graduation in Information Technology in 2012 from Biju Patnaik University of Technology, Odisha. He has completed his post graduation Master of Technology in 2016 in Computer Science & Engineering (Specialization- Wireless Sensor Network) from Veer Surendra Sai University of Technology, Burla (Odisha) and pursuing his Ph.D. degree in Computer Science & Engineering from National Institute of Technology Raipur, India. His area of interest is Wireless Sensor Network and Sentiment Analysis.

**Klaus Turowski** (born 1966) studied Business and Engineering at the University of Karlsruhe, achieved his doctorate at the Institute for Business Informatics at the University of Münster and habilitated in Business Informatics at the Faculty of Computer Science at the Otto von Guericke University Magdeburg. In 2000, he deputized the Chair of Business Informatics at the University of the Federal Armed Forces München and, from 2001, he headed the Chair of Business Informatics and Systems Engineering at the University of Augsburg. Since 2011, he is heading the Chair of Business Informatics (AG WI) at the Otto von Guericke University Magdeburg, the Very Large Business Applications Lab (VLBA Lab) and the world's largest SAP University Competence Center (SAP UCC Magdeburg). Additionally, Klaus Turowski worked as a guest lecturer at several universities around the world and was a lecturer at the Universities of Darmstadt and Konstanz. He was a (co-) organizer of a multiplicity of national and international scientific congresses and workshops and acted as a member of several programme commitees, and expert Groups. In the context of his university activities as well as an independent consultant he gained practical experience in industry.

**Mousami Turuk** is working as Assistant Professor in Pune Institute of Computer Technology, Savitribai Phule Pune University, India. She has her Master's degree in Electronics Engineering from Walchand College of Engineering, Sangli, Shivaji University Kolhapur. She has Doctoral degree in Electronics Engineering from Sant Gadge Baba, Amaravati University India. Her research areas include computer vision, Machine Learning and Deep Learning.

**M. Ali Ülkü**, Ph.D., M.Sc., is a Full Professor and the Director of the Centre for Research in Sustainable Supply Chain Analytics (CRSSCA), in the Rowe School of Business at Dalhousie University, Canada. Dr. Ülkü's research is on sustainable and circular supply chain and logistics management, and analytical decision models.

**Mahmud Ullah** is an Associate Professor of Marketing at the Faculty of Business Studies, University of Dhaka, Bangladesh. He teaches Behavioral and Quantitative courses in Business, e.g., Psychology, Organizational Behavior, Consumer Behavior, Business Mathematics, Business Statistics, Quantitative Analyses in Business etc., in addition to the Basic and Specialized Marketing courses like Marketing Management, Non-Profit Marketing, E-Marketing etc. He also taught Basic & Advanced English, and IELTS in a couple of English language Schools in New Zealand during his stay over there between 2002 and 2006. He has conducted a number of research projects sponsored by different international and national organizations like the World Bank (RMB), UNICEF, UNFPA, USAID, JAICA, AUSAID, IPPF, PPD, Die Licht Brucke, Andheri Hilfe, BNSB, FPAB etc. He did most of his research in the field of Health, Education, and Environment. His research interests include ethical aspects of human behavior in all these relevant fields, specifically in the continuously evolving and changing field of Digital Business and Marketing.

**Nivedita V. S.** is an Assistant Professor in the Department of Computer Science and Technology at Bannari Amman Institute of Technology, India. She is pursuing her doctoral degree in Information and Communication Engineering at Anna University, India. She holds 6 years of professional experience in academic institutions affiliated under Anna University. Her research interests include information filtering and retrieval, explainable intelligence, big data, etc.

**Satish Vadlamani** is a Director of Data Science and BI at Kenco Group, Chattanooga, TN, USA. He earned B.Tech. in Electronics and Communications Engineering, India. A Masters and Ph.D. in Industrial and Systems Engineering from Mississippi State University, USA. Before joining Kenco, Dr. Vadlamani worked at other global supply chain companies like APLL and XPO. Dr. Vadlamani has passion for applying operations research, machine learning (ML) and artificial (AI) intelligence to solve complex supply chain problems. Dr. Vadlamani has seven years of experience applying ML and AI for problem solving. Dr. Vadlamani has published at multiple journals and conferences and teaches data science and analytics to people around the globe. His research interests include networks, wireless sensor networks, wireless ad-hoc networks, supply chain networks, network interdiction, location problems, transportation, and meta-heuristics. Dr. Vadlamani has been an invited speaker at various colleges, universities, and other professional organizations across the globe. He is a member of IEOM, INFORMS and IISE.

**Phuong Vi** was born in Thai Nguyen, Vietnam. She is a lecturer at the Faculty of Journalism - Communications, Thai Nguyen University of Science, Vietnam. Her current research focuses on the following: Media culture; Social Media; Journalism History; Online newspaper; Journalism and public opinion; Public Relations. Her research is articles about journalism - modern media; books and book chapters have been published in prestigious international journals. "I am a journalist, researcher, author, writer, and university lecturer that never tires of learning and learning and teaches others for posterity, and for social development."

**Takis Vidalis** completed his basic legal studies at the University of Athens. In 1995, he received his Ph.D. in law. In 2001 he was elected a senior researcher and legal advisor of the Hellenic National Bioethics Commission (now, Commission for Bioethics and Technoethics). He is the author (or co-author) of 7 books and more than 50 academic papers in topics related to ethics and law of advanced technologies, constitutional law, philosophy of law, and sociology of law. Currently, he teaches "Artificial Intelligence: Ethics and Law", at the Law School of the Univ. of Athens, and "Biolaw and Bioethics," at the International Hellenic University. He is the president of the Research Ethics Committee of the National Centre for Scientific Research "Democritos" (the largest multidisciplinary research centre of Greece), and a member of the European Group on Ethics in Science and New Technologies (European Commission).

**Fabio Vitor** is an Assistant Professor of operations research in the Department of Mathematical and Statistical Sciences at the University of Nebraska at Omaha. He received a Ph.D. in Industrial Engineering and M.S. in Operations Research from Kansas State University, and a B.S. in Industrial Engineering from Maua Institute of Technology, Brazil. Dr. Vitor has nearly 10 years of industry experience, working for companies such as Monsanto, Kalmar, and Volkswagen. Dr. Vitor's research includes both theoretical and applied topics in operations research. His theoretical research creates algorithms to more quickly solve continuous and discrete optimization problems while some of his applied research has involved the application of optimization models and other operations research tools to reduce inventory costs, improve delivery routings, optimize nursery planting allocation, improve airport operations, and create strategies to overcome human trafficking.

**Rogan Vleming** is the Head of Data Science & Engineering at Simon-Kucher & Partners. Rogan received an M.B.A. in Finance specializing in financial engineering from McMaster University's De-Groote School of Business, and a B.Sc. in Mechanical Engineering from McMaster University.

**Haris Abd Wahab**, PhD, is an Associate Professor in the Department of Social Administration and Justice, Faculty of Arts and Social Sciences, University of Malaya, Malaysia. He graduated in the field of human development and community development. He has conducted studies on community work, community development, volunteerism, and disability. He has extensive experience working as a medical social worker at the Ministry of Health, Malaysia.

**Chaojie Wang** works for The MITRE Corporation, an international thinktank and operator of Federally Funded Research and Development Centers (FFRDC). In his capacity as a principal systems engineer, Dr. Wang advises the federal government on IT Acquisition & Modernization, Data Analytics & Knowledge Management, Health IT and Informatics, and Emerging Technology Evaluation & Adoption. Dr. Wang currently serves as the Editor-in-Chief for the International Journal of Patient-Centered Healthcare (IJPCH) by IGI Global and is on the Editorial Review Board of the Issues in Information System (IIS) by the International Association for Computer Information Systems (IACIS). Dr. Wang teaches Data Science graduate courses at University of Maryland Baltimore County (UMBC) and Healthcare Informatics graduate courses at Harrisburg University of Science and Technology. Dr. Wang holds a Bachelor of Engineering in MIS from Tsinghua University, a Master of Art in Economics and a Master of Science in Statistics both from the University of Toledo, an MBA in Finance from Loyola University Maryland, and a Doctor of Science in Information Systems and Communications from Robert Morris University.

**Di Wang** received his B.S. and M.S. degree in electrical engineering from Fuzhou University, China and Tianjin University, China. He is currently pursuing his Ph.D. degree in the Industrial Engineering Department, University of Illinois at Chicago, USA. His current research interests include multi-agent systems, distributed control, and energy schedule in the smart city.

**Yue Wang** is a doctoral candidate at the Computer Network Information Center, Chinese Academy of Sciences. Her research interests cover data mining, machine learning, user behavior analysis, etc. She has been working at the intersection of machine learning and information management for several years. Recently, she is working on NEW ARP technical research. In this paper, she handles the research on the technologies of the NEW ARP.

**Manuel Weinke** works as a research associate at the Chair of Logistics, Institute of Technology and Management, at the Technical University of Berlin. Within the scope of several research projects, he focuses on the utilization of Machine Learning in logistics management. Previously, he worked as a senior consultant in a management consultancy. He graduated in industrial engineering with a major in logistics, project, and quality management at the Technical University of Berlin.

**Thomas A. Woolman** is a doctoral student at Indiana State University's Technology Management program, with a concentration in digital communication systems. Mr. Woolman also holds an MBA with a concentration in data analytics from Saint Joseph's University, a Master's degree in Data Analytics from Saint Joseph's University and a Master's degree in Physical Science from Emporia State University. He is the president of On Target Technologies, Inc., a data science and research analytics consulting firm based in Virginia, USA.

**Brian G. Wu** received his Bachelor of Arts in Mathematics & Piano Music from Albion College in 2014. He pursued his graduate education at Oakland University, where he received his MS in Applied Statistics in 2016 and his PhD in Applied Mathematical Sciences, Applied Statistics Specialization, in 2020. His PhD thesis addressed computational and modeling aspects of big time series data. He will continue his career as a Visiting Assistant Professor at Southwestern University in the 2021-22 academic year.

**Tao Wu** is an assistant professor of Computer Science at SUNY Oneonta. He has extensive research experience in the fields of data science, information science, wireless communications, wireless networks, and statistical signal processing. He is also an expert in computer hardware and programming.

**Mengying Xia**'s research interests focus on molecular epidemiology and women's health. Her current research involves molecular predictors of ovarian cancer severity, recurrence, and prognosis.

**Hang Xiao** is a project manager in SSGM at State Street Corporation. He earned a M.S. in Information System from Northeastern University in 2012. His research interests include IoT, AI, Big Data, and Operational Research.

**Khadidja Yachba** (born in Oran, Algeria) is a Teacher (Assistant Professor) in Computer sciences department of University Centre Relizane and a research assistant at LIO Laboratory, Oran, Algeria. She received her Ph. D. in transport maritime and optimization at University of Oran 1, Ahmed Benbella in 2017. Her research interests are in Decision Support Systems (urban, road, maritime transportation, and health), Optimization, Simulation, Cooperative and Distributed System, Knowledge bases and Multi Criteria Decision Making. Khadidja Yachba has published in journals such as transport and telecommunication, International Journal of Decision Sciences, Risk and Management.

**Ronald R. Yager** has worked in the area of machine intelligence for over twenty-five years. He has published over 500 papers and more then thirty books in areas related to artificial intelligence, fuzzy sets, decision-making under uncertainty and the fusion of information. He is among the world's top 1% most highly cited researchers with over 85,000 citations. He was the recipient of the IEEE Computational Intelligence Society's highly prestigious Frank Rosenblatt Award in 2016. He was the recipient of the IEEE Systems, Man and Cybernetics Society 2018 Lotfi Zadeh Pioneer Award. He was also the recipient of the IEEE Computational Intelligence Society Pioneer award in Fuzzy Systems. He received honorary doctorates from the Azerbaijan Technical University, the State University of Information Technologies, Sofia Bulgaria and the Rostov on the Don University, Russia. Dr. Yager is a fellow of the IEEE and the Fuzzy Systems Association. He was given a lifetime achievement award by the Polish Academy of Sciences for his contributions. He served at the National Science Foundation as program director in the Information Sciences program. He was a NASA/Stanford visiting fellow and a research associate at the University of California, Berkeley. He has been a lecturer at NATO Advanced Study Institutes. He is a Distinguished Adjunct Professor at King Abdulaziz University, Jeddah, Saudi Arabia. He was a distinguished honorary professor at the Aalborg University Denmark. He was distinguished visiting scientist at King Saud University, Riyadh, Saudi Arabia. He received his undergraduate degree from the City College of New York and his Ph. D. from the Polytechnic University of New York. He was editor and chief of the International Journal of Intelligent Systems. He serves on the editorial board of numerous technology journals. Currently he is an Emeritus Professor at Iona College and is director of the Machine Intelligence.

**Jing Yang** is an associate professor of management information systems at the State University of New York at Oneonta. She has authored multiple research papers on consumer reviews that have been published in a variety of high-quality peer-reviewed journals, including Decision Support Systems, Nakai Business Review International, Wireless Personal Communications, and the International Journal of Operations Research and Information Systems.

**Lanting Yang** is a student at the City University of Macau. She studies in the International Business program.

**Pi-Ying Yen** is an assistant professor at the School of Business, Macau University of Science and Technology. She received her PhD in Industrial Engineering and Decision Analytics from HKUST in 2020. She serves as a reviewer for Manufacturing & Service Operations Management (MSOM) and Naval Research Logistics (NRL). Her research interests include socially responsible operations, supply chain management, and consumer behavior.

**Iris Yeung** received her B.Soc.Sc. Degree from the University of Hong Kong, M.Sc. degree from Imperial College, University of London, and a Ph.D. degree from University of Kent at Canterbury, UK. Her major research and teaching areas are time series analysis and multivariate data analysis. She has published articles in the Journal of Statistical Computation and Simulations, Statistica Sinica, Journal of Royal Statistical Society: Series C, Journal of Applied Statistical Science, Environmental Monitoring and Assessment, Environmental Science and Pollution Research, Waste Management, Marine Pollution Bulletin, Energy Policy, Applied Energy, Energy and Buildings, and Energy for Sustainable Development. She has participated in a number of consulting projects, including the British Council, Mass Transit Railway Corporation, Hong Kong Ferry (Holdings) Co. Ltd., Greenpeace East Asia, and Environmental Protection Department, The Government of the Hong Kong Special Administrative Region.

**Selen Yılmaz Işıkhan** carried out an integrated master and doctorate education in biostatistics department of Hacettepe University Faculty of Medicine. She has been working as a lecturer at the same university since 2010. Some examples of her research interests are machine learning, data mining, multivariate statistical analyses, regression analysis, meta analysis, and gut microbiota analysis.

**Ambar Yoganingrum** is a senior researcher at the Research Center for Informatics, National Research and Innovation Agency (BRIN), Indonesia, since 2019. She was a researcher in Center for Scientific Documentation and Information, Indonesian Institute of Sciences (PDII LIPI) for 18 years. She obtained her bachelor degree in Pharmaceutical Sciences from University of Padjadjaran, Indonesia in 1990. She earned a Master's degree in Health Informatics from the University of Indonesia in 2003 and a Doctorate in Information Systems from the same university in 2015. Ambar Yoganingrum's research interests include issues in the field of Library and Information Sciences, Information processing, Applied Informatics for Social Sciences purposes, and Multimedia.

**M. Yossi** is an Associate Professor and the Head of the Department of Industrial Engineering and Management at SCE – Shamoon College of Engineering. His areas of specialty are work-study, DEA, and ranking methods. He has published several papers and six books in these areas. He received his BSc, MSc, and Ph.D. (Summa Cum Laude) in Industrial Engineering from the Ben-Gurion University of the Negev, Israel.

**William A. Young II** is the Director of the Online Masters of Business Administration (OMBA) program, the Director of the Online Masters of Business Analytics (OMBAn), and a Charles G. O'Bleness Associate Professor of Business Analytics in the Department of Analytics and Information Systems. As an Associate Professor, Young received Ohio University's University Professor Award in 2020. Young earned his doctorate in Mechanical and Systems Engineering from Ohio University's Russ College of Engineering and Technology in 2010. William also received a bachelor's and master's degree in Electrical Engineering at Ohio University in 2002 and 2005, respectively. William has collaborated with multidisciplinary teams of faculty, students, and professionals on projects and programs that have been funded by General Electric Aviation, the National Science Foundation, Sogeti Netherlands, and Ohio's Department of Labor. Young's primary research and teaching interests relate to business analytics and operations management.

**Jianjun Yu** is currently the researcher, doctoral supervisor at the Computer Network Information Center, Chinese Academy of Sciences. His research interests cover big data analysis, collaborative filtering recommendations, and cloud computing. Recently, he is working on New ARP technical research.

**Gokmen Zararsiz** is a PhD researcher working in Dept. of Biostatistics, Faculty of Medicine, Erciyes University, Turkey.

**Alex Zarifis** is passionate about researching, teaching and practicing management in its many facets. He has taught in higher education for over ten years at universities including the University of Cambridge, University of Manchester and the University of Mannheim. His research is in the areas of information systems and management. Dr Alex first degree is a BSc in Management with Information Systems from the University of Leeds. His second an MSc in Business Information Technology and a PhD in Business Administration are both from the University of Manchester. The University of Manchester PhD in Business Administration is ranked 1st in the world according to the Financial Times.

**David Zeng** is a faculty member in College of Business and Information Systems at Dakota State University. David received his PhD at University of California, Irvine specializing in Information Systems. David's Teaching Interests include Predictive Analytics for Decision-making, Programming for Data Analytics (Python), Business Intelligence & Visualization, Deep Learning, AI Applications, Applied AI & applications, and Strategy & Application of AI in Organizations. David's research has been published at top-tier, peer-reviewed journals including MIS Quarterly, and has been funded by both internal and external grants. David received the Merrill D. Hunter Award of Excellence in Research in 2020. David is the Director of Center for Business Analytics Research (CBAR) at DSU.

**Jin Zhang** is a full professor at the School of Information Studies, University of Wisconsin-Milwaukee, U.S.A. He has published papers in journals such as Journal of the American Society for Information Science and Technology, Information Processing & Management, Journal of Documentation, Journal of Intelligent Information Systems, Online Information Review, etc. His book "Visualization for Information Retrieval" was published in the Information Retrieval Series by Springer in 2008. His research interests include visualization for information retrieval, information retrieval algorithm, metadata, search engine evaluation, consumer health informatics, social media, transaction log analysis, digital libraries, data mining, knowledge system evaluation, and human computer interface design.

**Peng Zhao** is a data science professional with experience in industry, teaching, and research. He has a broad range of practical data science experience in different industries, including finance, mobile device, consumer intelligence, big data technology, insurance, and biomedical industries. He is a leading machine learning expertise in a Big Data & AI company in New Jersey. He also manages a data scientist team providing a variety of data consulting services to individuals, businesses, and non-profit organizations.

**Yuehua Zhao** is a research assistant professor at the School of Information Management, Nanjing University, China. Her research interests include consumer health informatics, social network analysis, and social media research.

# Index

# D

# G

# H

# I

# T

# U

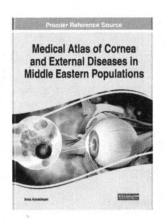
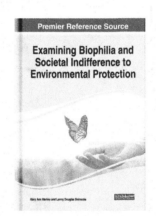

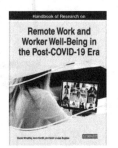

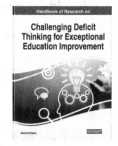

# Have Your Work Published and Freely Accessible
# Open Access Publishing

With the industry shifting from the more traditional publication models to an open access (OA) publication model, publishers are finding that OA publishing has many benefits that are awarded to authors and editors of published work.

**Freely Share Your Research**

**Higher Discoverability & Citation Impact**

**Rigorous & Expedited Publishing Process**

**Increased Advancement & Collaboration**

## Acquire & Open

When your library acquires an IGI Global e-Book and/or e-Journal Collection, your faculty's published work will be considered for immediate conversion to Open Access *(CC BY License)*, at no additional cost to the library or its faculty *(cost only applies to the e-Collection content being acquired)*, through our popular **Transformative Open Access (Read & Publish) Initiative**.

Provide Up To
**100%**
OA APC or
CPC Funding

Funding to
Convert or
Start a Journal to
**Platinum
OA**

Support for
Funding an
**OA
Reference
Book**

IGI Global publications are found in a number of prestigious indices, including Web of Science™, Scopus®, Compendex, and PsycINFO®. The selection criteria is very strict and to ensure that journals and books are accepted into the major indexes, IGI Global closely monitors publications against the criteria that the indexes provide to publishers.

**Learn More Here:**

For Questions, Contact IGI Global's Open Access Team at openaccessadmin@igi-global.com

www.igi-global.com

Printed in the United States
by Baker & Taylor Publisher Services